קונטרס העבודה

LOVE LIKE FIRE AND WATER
A Guide to Jewish Meditation

Essay on the Service of the Heart
by the Rebbe Rashab נ"ע

With translation and commentary
by Rabbi David Sterne

Jerusalem Connection Publishing
New York/ Jerusalem

Love like Fire and Water
Kuntres Ha'avoda

©
All rights reserved
Copyrighted by the author, Sept. 2005
Second Edition 2011

Library of Congress LCCN 2007557273

Third Edition 2020

POB 28186
Jerusalem, Israel

jerconn1@gmail.com

Printed in U.S.A.

Dedicated to all the beautiful souls,
students, new immigrants and others who pass
through the Old City of Jerusalem, looking
for knowledge and inspiration
May this book help you find your way!

Credits

To Rabbi Elek Friedman
for checking the initial draft for accuracy

To Rabbi Imanuel Schochet
for making invaluable scholarly suggestions

To Rabbi Nissim Mangel and Rabbi Simon Jacobson
for offering encouragement

To Ms. Uriela Sagiv for editing

To Ms. Barbara Sopkin
for editing and proofreading

To Rabbi Yosi ben Shachar and Rabbi Moshe Kaplan
for typesetting

To my parents
for inspiring within me commitment to Torah and Judaism

TABLE OF CONTENTS

Table of Contents composed by the Lubavitcher Rebbe, ztz'l	vi
Foreword by Rabbi Dr. J. Immanuel Schochet	ix
Author's Note	xiii
Introduction	xv
Chapter 1 - Soul Levels	3
Chapter 2 - Guarding our Senses	38
Chapter 3 - Meditating to attain fear of G-d	62
Chapter 4 - Meditating to attain love of G-d	86
Chapter 5 - Advanced meditative techniques	123
Chapter 6 - Detailed Meditation	157
Chapter 7 - Things to be avoided	203
Endnotes	221
Appendix I - Letter from the Previous Rebbe	233
Appendix II - Notes of the Lubavitcher Rebbe	249
Appendix III - Lessons on K'Avoda from R' Chaim Shalom Deitsch שיח', Rosh Collel and Mashpia, *Tzemach Tzedek,* Old City of Jerusalem	303

TABLE OF CONTENTS

(COMPOSED BY THE LUBAVITCHER REBBE,
R' MENACHEM MENDEL SCHNEERSON, ztz'l
in the original printed edition of Kuntres Ha'avoda)

Kuntres Ha'avoda

Chapter 1
Prayer is about uniting the G-dly soul with G-d, as well as purifying the animal soul. Both take place through [the medium of] love of G-d. Service of [the various levels of the soul] *nefesh*, *ruach*, *neshama* and *chaya*. The inclusion of *nefesh* in *ruach*, and both of them in *neshama*, and all of them in the essence of the soul. Acknowledgment of G-d, within the *avoda* of the emotions and of the intellect. *Kavana* (intention) and speech within prayer.

Chapter 2
Eyesight and [the necessity of] guarding it. Guarding the senses. Acceptance of the yoke of G-d, fear of transgression, fear of G-d. The reasons for foreign (un-spiritual) thoughts. The nature of weakness of the G-dly soul, and advice for dealing with it.

Chapter 3
Factors that bring about fear of G-d. Love of G-d does not occur naturally from birth, but fear does. Love is associated with revealed spirituality, fear with the essence of G-dliness. Dimensions of fear - fear that is inferior to the service of prayer, and fear that surpasses prayer.

Chapter 4
Love like water, love like flames of fire, and their various aspects. The meditation associated with each of them. Their effect upon the animal soul, whether weakness or nullification. Love versus *tshuva* (return to G-d). Meaning of offering the "fat and blood" in service of G-d.

Chapter 5

The will of the [soul level of] *yechida*. And of *chaya*. Love that is dependent upon something, and two kinds of love that are not dependent on anything. The effect of the *chaya* and *yechida* upon the animal soul. Whether or not *mesirat nefesh* (self-sacrifice) is associated with the natural soul. The spiritual arousal of the ten days of *tshuva*, and one's service during the course of the year.

Chapter 6

General meditation, its effects and its drawbacks. "Engraving" from the outside, "engraving" from the inside. The reasons for indifference that may occur after initial meditative excitement. Everyone has their particular character trait(s) to rectify.

Chapter 7

Service that surpasses one's true spiritual level. Spiritual excitement detached from the animal soul, and how it comes about. Step-by-step *avoda*. The generation of Jews that wandered in the desert, and those that entered the land of Israel, and what we have to learn from them.

FOREWORD

When R. Shneur Zalman of Liadi, founder of Chabad Chassidism and known as the "Alter Rebbe," turned eighteen, he was already a renowned scholar with vast knowledge in all subjects of the Torah. Nonetheless, he felt a need for a special mentor. Considering several options, he decided on R. Dov Ber, known as the Maggid of Mezhirech, the major disciple of the Baal Shem Tov and his successor as leader of the Chassidic movement. At a number of occasions the Alter Rebbe explained this choice in slightly varying ways:

Proficiency in Torah-knowledge and methodology in the study of Talmud and Halachah study he had mastered already, but "as for *tefilah* I hardly knew anything."[1] At another time he expressed it in terms of "I was not aware how to serve G-d (*avodah*)."[2] And at a third occasion he said that elsewhere one learns how to master the Torah; in Mezhirech one learns how to let the Torah master you, i.e., "how the Torah teaches man to become a Torah himself."[3]

Torah-study is the comprehensive core of Jewish life: *"Talmud Torah keneged kulam* – Torah-study is equivalent to them all."[4] On the one hand it is a *mitzvah* on its own, thus a meritorious end by itself. On the other hand it is also a means towards another end: the practice of the Divine precepts and the spiritual perfection of man, which are impossible without prior study and knowledge of Torah - as Hillel taught: "A boor cannot be fearful of sin, nor can an unlearned person be a *chasid* (a person of scrupulous piety)."[5] Torah-study, in spite of its unique and superior quality on its own,[6] may never be divorced from its application on the practical level. He who claims to have nothing but Torah – he has not even Torah, for one must be occupied with Torah and the performance of *chassadim*[7] (lit. acts of kindness, which include not only kindness to fellow-beings but also, as it were, to G-d, i.e., the performance of *mitzvot* and the worship of G-d[8]). The Torah is but the gateway to *yirat Shamayim* (the fear of, or reverence for, G-d).[9] The superiority of Torah, therefore, lies in the fact that "Torah-study leads to practical observance."[10]

Thus Torah must lead to *avodah*. It will do so when studied *lishmah*. *Lishmah* means (a) for its own sake, as opposed to ulterior motives of personal benefits (which include the objective of becoming a renowned scholar), as derived from the verse "to love G-d and to obey His voice and to cleave unto Him" (Deuteronomy 30:20).[11] (b) *Lishmah* also means literally "for its name's sake." The "name" Torah is an idiom of *hora'ah* - teaching, instruction, guidance.[12] This "name," then, implies that the Torah instructs, guides and counsels man to be wholehearted with his Maker and Master who, by means of revealing the Torah, "seeks to benefit man in this world and in the world-to-come."[13] In this sense, therefore, learning Torah *lishmah* means to absorb and internalize this guidance and counsel, to generate *ahavah veyirah*, love and fear (reverence) of G-d[14] - "oneself to become a Torah."

Man was created to serve his Maker by means of Torah and *mitzvoth*.[15] His mission on earth is to manifest to himself and others the concealed G-dliness that pervades all of creation - "I fill the heavens and the earth" (Jeremiah 23:24) and there is no place devoid of His Presence even in the physical realm.[16] Thus one must breach the barriers of mundane illusions and bring about a full consciousness of the reality of Divine Presence.[17] This *avodah*, service of G-d, cannot be perfunctory "as a commandment of men learned by rote" (Isaiah 29:13). Without *kavanah*, encompassing intent and concentration, the heart and the mind, it is lifeless, a "body without soul." Torah, *mitzvot* and *tefilah* that lack *ahavah veyirah* will not achieve their goal of ascending.[18] True *avodah* means the consciousness of "Now, Israel, what does G-d, your G-d, ask of you but to fear G-d, your G-d, to go in all His ways and to love Him, and to serve G-d, your G-d, with all your heart and with all your soul!" (Deuteronomy 10:12)

This fundamental principle is the major focus of Chassidism. It applies universally, equally to scholar and layman, to each according to his or her capacities. The Alter Rebbe once said: "I received from the Maggid of Mezhirech, and he had received that teaching from the Baal Shem Tov: the *mitzvah* of *ve'ahavta* (you shall love [G-d]) means to 'thrust' one's thought and mind (in Yiddish he said *men zol zich arajn tohn* - to immerse oneself) in those subject-matters that will stir that love,[19] while the resulting effects are not of the basic precept."[20]

Much has been taught by the Chassidic masters throughout the generations to emphasize this principle and to motivate its application. In this context, the fifth Rebbe of Chabad, R. Sholom Dov Ber of Lubavitch, known by the acronym "the Reshab," composed a special treatise *Kuntres Ha'avodah*, as a primer for those seeking guidance in *avodah* to explain "the principle of *avodah shebalev* (service of the heart), i.e., prayer, to draw near and cause one's soul to cleave unto G-dliness..."

This treatise touches upon many basic ideas of Chassidism, but its inspiration is not lessened by its profound scholarship. A proper study of its contents will most assuredly affect the student with new insights, a proper understanding of the issues, and above all result in the true and enhanced *avodah* it sets out to achieve.

Rabbi David Sterne deserves much credit for undertaking the arduous task of translating *Kuntres Ha'avodah*, thus making this treasure available and accessible to the English-speaking public. Moreover, he added numerous explanations for complex concepts as well as most helpful diagrams to ease the student's journey. His work is most certainly a tremendous achievement. Unfortunately, the restraints on my time did not allow me to review the translation. The few passages I did manage to scan, however, were sufficient to impress and to evoke admiration for the great effort Rabbi Sterne must have put into this labor of love, of which it may be said with confidence that he has the zechut that his work will cause many to attain merit. Hopefully he will use his blessed talents for further contributions.

Toronto, Tishrei 5766
J. Immanuel Schochet

1. Likkutei Diburim, III:p. 966
2. Ibid., IV:p. 1324
3. Ibid., II:II:p. 492
4. Pe'ah I:1
5. Avot II:5
6. See Tanya, ch. 5-6
7. Yevamot 109b, and see there 105a. Note the Rebbe's glossary comment in Sefer
   Hama'amarim 5708, p. 266, note 7. Cf. Zohar III:119a, and the references cited there in Nitzutzei Zohar. Tanya, Igeret Hakodesh, sect. 5.
8. Zohar III:281a. See also Zohar II:214b and III:222b; Tikunei Zohar 1b.
9. Shabbat 31b; Yoma 72b and Rashi ad loc.
10. Kidushin 40b
11. Sifre, Eikev, end of sect. 48. Nedarim 62a
12. Zohar III:53b. Redak on Psalms 19:8. Maharal, Gur Aryeh on Genesis 1:1; Netivot Olam, Netiv Hatorah, ch. 1, and Netiv Ha'emunah, ch. 2.
13. Zohar II:82b. See also ibid. I:11a, II:96b. Cf. Avodah Zara 17b; Sifre, Ha'azinu, end of sect. 322. Rambam, Hilchot Shechitah 14:16, and Hilchot Temurah 4:13.
14. Maggid of Mezhirech, Or Torah, sect. 317. See there also sect. 453.
15. Kidushin 82a
16. Tikunei Zohar 57:91b; ibid. 70:122b. Shemot Rabba 2:9. See Tanya, Igeret Hakodesh, sect. 25. Note also Tanya, ch. 41.
17. See Tanya, ch. 32
18. Zohar I:24a. Tikunei Zohar 10:25b. See also Zohar II:121a.
19. See Rambam, Hilchot Yessodei Hatorah 2:2 and 4:12; Hilchot Teshuvah 10:6.
20. Keter Shem Tov, Hossafot, sect. 38. See the Rebbe's glossary comments on Sefer Hama'amarim 5701, p. 116.

Author's Note to the Second Edition of
LOVE LIKE FIRE AND WATER
(*Kuntres Ha'Avoda*)

Five years have passed since the publication of the first edition of LOVE LIKE FIRE AND WATER, translation of the *Kuntres Ha'Avoda* ("Tractate on Divine Service") in 2005. In the ensuing years, the original edition has passed the "test of time." It has found acceptance among wide swaths of readership, among people who are thirsty to learn and practice the meditative path of spiritual connection inherent in Judaism. This path is implicit within Chasidic literature, and finds its most explicit expression in the Chasidut of Chabad and especially in the *Kuntres Ha'Avoda* of the Rebbe Rashab (1860-1920). It is perhaps for this reason that the English translation has found its way into so many houses and libraries. For some time, there has been an unfulfilled demand for a second printing, and that is the purpose of this new edition of the work.

However, it would be inappropriate to produce a new edition of the translation without adding something to its content and depth. Just as a live person grows continuously, striving for new horizons, so his/her breadth and depth of knowledge must expand as well.

Anyone who takes the trouble to examine the footnotes of the Lubavitcher Rebbe (R' Menachem Mendel Schneerson) that appear in the Hebrew edition of *Kuntres Ha'Avoda* will see that they "open up worlds." The notes that the Rebbe appended to *Kuntres Ha'Avoda* illuminate many of the roots and antecedents from which the Rebbe Rashab drew his teachings and system. Thus, they shed more light on how to climb the ladder of spirituality and cling to the One Above. But, they do far more than that. Sometimes, by simply quoting another text, the Rebbe points us in a new direction, showing how a particular principle of meditation may equally apply to another aspect of connecting on high, for example, through the process of *tshuva*, or "return" to the One Above. At other times, the Rebbe's notes elucidate an otherwise obscure spiritual process, letting us know that it is equivalent or similar to something that we have read or learned elsewhere. In these and all other cases, the Rebbe's notes allow us to take the teaching of the Rebbe Rashab and apply them to new contexts and situations in service of the One Above.

For this reason, we are happy to present this new, expanded edition of LOVE LIKE FIRE AND WATER, which includes translations of the reference notes of the Lubavitcher Rebbe, appended by him to the original Hebrew edition of *Kuntres Ha'avoda*. In this way, we hope that the reader will not only strive to adopt the meditative approach to Jewish prayer that is found in *Kuntres Ha'Avoda*, but will also discover how it is an integral part of *avodat Hashem* and of Judaism in general.

> Rabbi David Sterne
> Jerusalem Connection in the Old City of Jerusalem
> *Chodesh Shvat, 5771* – January, 2011

INTRODUCTION TO
"LOVE LIKE FIRE AND WATER" - *KUNTRES HA'AVODA*

Some twenty-six years ago, I was present when the Lubavitcher Rebbe *ztz'l* spoke of the necessity of responding to the hunger for meditation techniques that would be compatible with Jewish sources. As a beginning yeshiva student at the time, I thought to myself that it should be easy to search Jewish sources and find out exactly what Jewish meditation is, or should be. However, it would take me years of learning and practice before I could integrate it and explain it to others. As a rabbi, I have had the opportunity, thank G-d, to gain the experience necessary in order to begin passing on some of that information to others. Through the Old City of Jerusalem, where I live, pass many of the most spiritually inclined Jews of this generation (and in truth, all Jews are spiritually inclined). It is my privilege to have contact with them, and it is to them that this translation and commentary is dedicated.

One of the distinguishing characteristics of our generation is the search for spirituality. Jews are especially active in this regard – we seem to be in the vanguard of almost every spiritual movement that exists. Yet, when we look for the spiritual well-springs of our own heritage, they're not necessarily easy to find. While *Shulchan Aruch,* the Code of Jewish Law, provides the essential framework within which a Jew is supposed to live his life, in order to find the spiritual connection with the One Above and strive to be more G-dly, our generation needs the inner dimensions of Torah – explained in Chassidic and Kabballistic literature. It is here that we find the intellectual meaning of G-dliness and spirituality, as well as the emotional excitement leading to love and fear of the One Above. But, that only comes about when we embark upon a path of learning combined with meditation. And the latter is an essential which most Jews don't even know exists.

In the 12th century, long before the advent of the Chassidic movement, Maimonides, the first codifier of the Jewish law, wrote that the way to achieve love and fear of G-d is through meditation on the creation and the amazing wisdom that goes into it. First, he said, one will be overcome with love. Then, upon further contemplation, he will be overwhelmed with fear and awe. He then proceeded to describe succinctly the nature of the spiritual and physical realms of the universe (*Hilchot Yesodei HaTorah,* Chapter 2, Halacha 2 and onwards). It is clear that he intended meditation to cover the abstract and spiritual as well as the physical creation. Following Maimonides, in the 16th century, Rabbi Yoseph Karo authored the *Shulchan Aruch* which is universally accepted by all Jews today (with amendments for the Ashkenazi community); he wrote, "...the early pietists and men of action would go off on their own and work on their spiritual intentions to the point of abstraction from the physical world and devotion to the spiritual on a level which was close to prophecy." To which the *Ramah* (Rabbi Moshe Isserles) added, "and one should think of the greatness of G-d and the lowliness of man" (*Shulchan Aruch Orach Chaim* 98:1). Clearly, Jewish meditation is no latter day augmentation of Judaism. It is a vital and integral element of Judaism that no Jew should be without.

In our own generation, since the 18th century, it is the Chassidic movement that has developed Jewish meditation into a technique. In Hebrew, it's called *hitbonenut*. The etymological source of the word is *boneh*, meaning "build." To practice Jewish meditation, you "build" a spiritual structure inside of yourself. Also implicit in the word *hitbonenut* is the word *bina*, "understanding" or intellectual analysis. The structure that you build consists of G-dly concepts and ideas that you must understand thoroughly and deeply. They become the framework and girders of your inner "building." When you properly understand a series of G-dly concepts and put them together in your mind, you are building your own inner spiritual structure. When you actively dwell in this inner structure for a certain period of time each day (usually before morning prayers), exploring its nooks and crannies and reinforcing its girders while building it ever higher, you are practicing Jewish meditation, or *hitbonenut*. The sages of the Talmud (mentioned above) used to do this three times a day, for an hour before each set of prayers. Additionally, they would spend an hour "coming down" after each set of prayers. In our own generation, by studying and meditating upon the infinite concepts and G-dly ideas contained in contemporary Chassidic literature, we gain the proper understanding that allows us to build a spiritual edifice inside of ourselves, climb all the way to the top of it, and cling to the One Above.

***

The purpose of this free translation and commentary is to serve as a handbook, an instruction booklet, if you will, of Jewish meditation for the serious person who knows next to nothing about Judaism, but wants to be convinced that there is something seriously spiritual in his or her heritage. Such a book could have been written as a simple, direct set of instructions. However, it makes much more sense to show how a true spiritual master, a Chassidic Rebbe, whose very life was dedicated to G-d and other Jews, explained the subject. From him, we can glean the basics of the technique and hopefully pass it on and explain it to others in terms that they understand.

***

The years 1909-1910 (when *Kuntres Ha'avoda* was written) were tumultuous years in Russia. These were the twilight years of the czarist regime, and the forces of Communism and Bolshevism were on the rise. As always when there is strife, the Jews were the scapegoats. The pogroms and physical suffering were great, and yet somehow the spiritual lives of Russian Jewry not only continued, but in some cases thrived. Such was the case with the Jews of Lubavitch. Under the leadership of the fifth Lubavitcher Rebbe, Rebbe Shalom Dov Ber Schneerson, they managed (in 1896) to establish a yeshiva dedicated not only to the study of Jewish law, but to the inner dimensions of Torah, as well. Under the leadership of the Rebbe Rashab, as he was called, the yeshiva (called Tomchei Tmimim), grew and developed. Its goal was to cultivate not only rabbis who knew the legal texts of the Jewish tradition-the Talmud and code of Jewish law-but also to develop *ovdei HaShem*, true "servants of God," pious and learned Jews who knew how to meditate and pray, using the wellsprings of Chassidic literature.

The *Zohar* predicted that the opening of the "wellsprings" of the inner dimensions of Torah would be accompanied by a corresponding development in the secular disciplines. The period indicated by the *Zohar*, the sixth millenium (from 5500 to 5600, or roughly 1740 to 1840) saw not only the revelation of the Chassidic movement, but the beginning of the scientific, and soon after, the industrial revolution. But, the prediction wasn't restricted to the scientific disciplines. As the Rebbe Rashab was writing his longest Chassidic dissertations (discourses of the years 5666 -5608, or 1906-1908, and also 5612- 5616, or 1912-1916, but written earlier), Russian novelists (such as Leo Tolstoy, *lehavdil*, died 1910) were penning their long novels. It was a period that was well-suited to long, detailed, and nuanced literature, and since this was expressed first of all in the G-dly discipline of the Rebbe's Chassidus, it was expressed in secular literature as well.

In addition, the Rebbe penned four *kuntresim*, or shorter tractates for the specific purpose of guiding the students of Yeshivat Tomchei Tmimim in *avodat HaShem*, "service of G-d." One of them – *Kuntres Ha'avoda* – deals with the subject of meditation. The *ovdim*, the pious students of Lubavitch were guided in their service by the Rebbe's Chassidic discourses and his instructions on how to lose their *yeshut* (ego), while praying and getting closer to G-d. However, the vicissitudes of the time, including the Bolshevik revolution and with it the uprooting of the yeshiva, nearly caused this meditative approach to disappear from the world. The Rebbe Rashab's son, Harav Yoseph Yitzhak Schneerson *ztz'l*, continued to teach his father's tradition and *avoda*, first in Russia, then in Poland, and ultimately in New York during the awful years of World War II. However, the Holocaust decimated the ranks of the Chassidim, and the *ovdim* of yesteryear are no longer to be found among us. Nevertheless, by reading and studying the *Kuntres Ha'avoda*, and focusing on the study of other Chassidic texts, we can try to reconstruct the *avoda* of the Chassidim who lived roughly one hundred years ago.

It was the previous Rebbe, HaRav Yoseph Yitzhak Schneerson (son of the Rebbe Rashab and director of Tomchei Tmimim) who foretold the necessity of this reconstruction. He wrote in his introduction to his father's work:

"The days will come and a young generation will arrive with a claim from the depths of their souls against all of their leaders, and in particular toward the directors of the yeshivas and their heads, saying:

WHY DIDN'T YOU REBUKE US FOR OUR CONDUCT?

WHY DIDN'T YOU TELL US THE TRUTH, THE TRUTH OF THE LIVING TORAH OF G-D, IN ITS COMPLETENESS?

WHY DIDN'T YOU INSTRUCT US IN THE PATH OF LIFE AS IT IS LIVED IN DAILY LIFE, TELLING US:

HOW WE SHOULD PRAY EVERY DAY BEFORE OUR FATHER ABOVE, THE KING OF KINGS, THE HOLY ONE BLESSED BE HE...

HOW WE SHOULD LEARN HIS TORAH, AS COMMANDED "IN FEAR AND AWE, TREMBLING AND SWEAT"...

HOW WE SHOULD FULFILL HIS COMMANDMENTS, AS COMMANDED "IN HAPPINESS AND A GOOD HEART," -WHICH ITSELF IS A TREMENDOUS SERVICE OF THE ONE ABOVE...

And what will we say and how will we justify ourselves on that day?

It is incumbent upon all of us, and especially upon the administrations of the yeshivot to organize our service and to make the schedule and conduct of the yeshiva such that it doesn't only teach the 'sterile' professions of becoming a scholar, rabbi, rosh yeshiva, and the like, but imparts the guidance necessary for the student to become a complete Jew in his body (mitzvot), in his soul (prayer) and in his Torah [learning]. Anyone looking at the student should recognize that in him are combined the three levels of "Israel, Torah, and G-d [are one], all three of them both hidden and revealed..."

That day is upon us, but it is certainly not only the students of the yeshivot who are asking the questions. Every Jew with a G-dly soul in his or her body is asking, "how can I serve G-d?" Sometimes the question is concealed deep inside, and sometimes (especially among those who make their way to Jerusalem, and to the Old City), the question is obvious and on the tips of their tongues. It is also for them that the Rebbe Rashab wrote the *Kuntres Ha'avoda,* and I hope that I have succeeded in bringing his words to them in a way they can understand and internalize.

Rabbi David Sterne
Chodesh Tammuz and Av, 5765/August 2005
Old City of Jerusalem, Israel

Kuntres Ha'Avodah - **Essay on the Service of the Heart**

An explanation of the service of the heart - prayer - with which
we approach and attach our soul to G-d, while also purifying
and refining our natural (animal) soul. About this subject, it is written,
"And you should know today and take it to heart ... "
leading to love (*ve'ahavta*) with all our heart,
including both our divine and natural inclinations ...

Essay on Service of the Heart - Love Like Fire and Water

CHAPTER 1 / פרק א

The *avoda* (service/worship) of the heart in prayer is a labor leading to love of G-d. As such, it serves two purposes. The first is to cleave to G-d, in order to unite our [divine] soul with G-dliness [and the second is to purify and refine our animal soul].

הִנֵּה כָּל הָעֲבוֹדָה וְהַיְגִיעָה שֶׁל עוֹבְדֵי ה' בִּתְפִלָּה הוּא לָבוֹא לְמִדַּת הָאַהֲבָה. כִּי הַתְּפִלָּה כְּלָלוּת עִנְיָנָהּ הוּא ב' דְּבָרִים, הָא' לְקַשֵּׁר וּלְדַבֵּק נַפְשׁוֹ בֶּאֱלֹקוּת,

Prayer is a labor of love that unites our soul with its infinite source.

> All Jews are endowed with two souls or spiritual dimensions: a G-dly soul that imparts spirituality, and a natural soul that enlivens the physical body.

In the [first] case, we understand prayer — *tefila* in Hebrew — to mean "joining," as in *tofel*, "joining pieces of ceramic." This definition of prayer refers to joining our divine soul with the One Above. In this case, prayer

וְזֶהוּ מַה שֶּׁתְּפִלָּה הוּא לְשׁוֹן הִתְחַבְּרוּת וּכְמוֹ הַתּוֹפֵל כְּלִי חֶרֶס דְּהַיְנוּ הִתְקַשְּׁרוּת וְהִתְחַבְּרוּת נַפְשׁוֹ בֶּאֱלֹקוּת, וְעַל שֵׁם זֶה נִקְרֵאת הַתְּפִלָּה סֻלָּם וּכְמוֹ שֶׁכָּתוּב סֻלָּם

COMMENTARY

In Chassidic meditation *(hitbonenut)* — whose purpose is to unite the intellect with the heart — there is no such thing as going "up" without going "in." When the Chassidic masters took the secrets of Kabbalah from the plane of spiritual space and revealed how they can be understood via the psychological dimension — that is, the dimension in which the soul operates in this world— they also established the concept that we must delve inward in order to go upward, spiritually. Going inward means stripping away layers of perceived reality in order to expose the true kernel of G-dliness inside ourselves and in creation.

Chassidic literature defines five different levels of inner consciousness *(p'nimiyut)* within the soul, corresponding to five levels of spiritual reality in the outer world, the macrocosm. There are infinite nuances within each of the five, and the divisions among them are only general rather than clear-cut.

For purposes of clarity, we will give English names to each of the five levels which correspond very roughly to the experience of each level, as described in Chassidic literature.

מִצָּב אַרְצָה וְרֹאשׁוֹ מַגִּיעַ הַשָּׁמַיְמָה וְאִיתָא בַּזֹּהַר סֻלָּם דָּא צְלוֹתָא שֶׁעַל יְדֵי הַסֻּלָּם דִּתְפִלָּה מִתְעַלִּים נֶפֶשׁ רוּחַ וּנְשָׁמָה שֶׁבְּנַפְשׁוֹ עַד שֶׁרֹאשׁוֹ מַגִּיעַ הַשָּׁמַיְמָה,

is also called a "ladder," as in the verse [in Genesis 28:12] which describes a "ladder placed on the earth, with its head reaching into the heavens." The *Zohar* says that "the ladder represents prayer," since by way of prayer, we elevate [our lower soul-levels], our *nefesh*, *ruach*, and *neshama*, [which are en-clothed in the body] until our head reaches into the heavens.

The divine soul has five levels; the lower three (1, 2, and 3) are en-clothed in the body, while the higher two (4 and 5) connect the essence of the soul with its source in the infinite light of G-d, as follows:		
1.	*Nefesh*	"Enlivening soul"	Action Consciousness
2.	*Ruach*	"Spirit"	Emotion consciousness
3.	*Neshama*	"Intellectual Soul"	Intellect consciousness
4.	*Chaya* or *Nishmata d'Nishmata*	"Living one"	Transcendent consciousness
5.	*Yechida*	"Single one"	Unity consciousness

הַיְנוּ הִתְקַשְּׁרוּת עַצְמוּת הַנְּשָׁמָה בְּחִינַת נִשְׁמְתָא לְנִשְׁמְתָא בִּמְקוֹר חוּצָבָהּ בְּעַצְמוּת אוֹר אֵין סוֹף בָּרוּךְ הוּא בִּתְפִלַּת שְׁמוֹנֶה עֶשְׂרֵה, שֶׁגַּם הַנֶּפֶשׁ רוּחַ וּנְשָׁמָה עוֹלִים וְנִכְלָלִים בְּהִתְקַשְּׁרוּת זֹאת לֶאֱלֹקוּת

This means that we unite the essence of our soul — the *nishmata d'nishmata*[1] [equivalent to the *chaya*] — with its source in the infinite light of the essence of the Holy One. We achieve this in the course of praying the *Amida* [which is the pinnacle of prayer], when the *nefesh*, *ruach*, and *neshama* ascend and are included in this supernal unity.

(וַעֲלִיַּת וְהִתְקַשְּׁרוּת הַנְּשָׁמָה הוּא עַל יְדֵי הָעֲבוֹדָה בְּכָל מַדְרֵגָה שֶׁבָּהּ בִּפְרָט. תְּחִלַּת הָעֲבוֹדָה דִּבְחִינַת נֶפֶשׁ בִּבְחִינַת הַהוֹדָאָה וּכְמוֹ שֶׁכָּתוּב בְּמָקוֹם אַחַר עִנְיַן הַבִּטּוּל דְּהוֹדָאָה. וְכֵן קִיּוּם הַתּוֹרָה וְהַמִּצְוֹת בְּפֹעַל

The elevation and unity of the soul require effort on all its levels.[i] It begins with the *avoda* on the level of *nefesh*, when we acknowledge the existence and presence of G-d.[ii] On this level emphasis is placed on adherence to the commandments — both the

---

i) See footnote of the Rebbe on page 249

The elevation of the soul starts with acknowledgment of G-d.

ii) See footnote of the Rebbe on page 258

Essay on Service of the Heart - Love Like Fire and Water

positive and the negative *mitzvot*. This constitutes *avoda* of the One Above in the World of *Asiya* [the World of Action, the lowest of the four worlds].

מַמָּשׁ בְּסוּר מֵרָע וַעֲשֵׂה טוֹב, שֶׁזֶּהוּ הָעֲבוֹדָה דִּבְחִינַת עֲשִׂיָּה כַּנּוֹדָע.

G-d created existence by means of a number of worlds. In this discussion we are concerned with the following four (from lowest to highest):		
1. *Asiya*	"World of Action"	Particular existence; individual creatures
2. *Yetzira*	"World of Formation"	General existence; archetypes, species
3. *Bria*	"World of Creation"	Potential existence; formless substance
4. *Atzilut*	"World of Emanation"	Awareness of God only; no self-awareness

With this *avoda*, we rise to [the next world], the World of *Yetzira* [the World of Formation], where we serve the One Above on the

וְעַל יְדֵי זֶה עוֹלֶה לִבְחִינַת הַיְצִירָה הַיְנוּ שֶׁיַּעֲלֶה וְיַגִּיעַ לְהָעֲבוֹדָה דִּבְחִינַת רוּחַ בְּחִינַת הִתְפַּעֲלוּת הַמִּדּוֹת, וְגַם בְּחִינַת נֶפֶשׁ מִתְעַלָּה

The elevation proceeds to a more emotional level of acknowledgment.

--- **COMMENTARY** ---

The English names bear little or no relationship to the corresponding Hebrew names of the levels of the soul, but will help us to understand what is meant by each level. These levels are:

#	Soul level	Experience	World	Morning Prayer
1.	*Nefesh* "Enlivening soul"	Action consciousness	World of *Asiya* "World of Action"	*Modeh Ani* until *Baruch Sh'amar*
2.	*Ruach* "Wind/spirit"	Emotion consciousness	World of *Yetzira* "World of Formation"	*Baruch Sh'amar* until *Barchu*
3.	*Neshama* "Soul/breath"	Intellect Consciousness	World of *Bria* "World of "Creation"	*Barchu* through the *Shema*
4.	*Chaya* "Living one"	Transcendent consciousness	World of *Atzilut* "World of Emanations"	*Shmoneh Esreh* or *Amida*
5.	*Yechida* "Single one"	Unity consciousness	Beyond worlds	Beyond prayer, Level of Prophecy

בָּזֶה וּכְעִנְיַן הַתְכַּלְלוּת הָעֲשִׂיָּה בִּיצִירָה, וְהַיְנוּ דְּהַהוֹדָאָה הִיא בְּמַדְרֵגָה עֶלְיוֹנָה יוֹתֵר וּבִידִיעָה בְּיוֹתֵר אֵיךְ שֶׁצָּרִיךְ לְהוֹדוֹת. וְהַיְדִיעָה בְּהַמַּדְרֵגָה שֶׁמּוֹדֶה בָּזֶה וּבִבְחִינַת הֶרְגֵּשׁ פְּנִימִי יוֹתֵר –

soul-level of *ruach*, the level of emotional excitement. Our *nefesh* also rises in the process, just as the World of *Asiya* rises to the World of *Yetzira*. This means that our acknowledgment of the One Above takes place on a higher soul-level, that is, on a higher plane of consciousness. Here, we have a better understanding of how we must acknowledge G-d's Presence, and we have a deeper understanding of the divinity we are acknowledging. In addition, our understanding is imbued with more feeling.

The worlds, together with *Keter*, the infinite light transcending the World of *Atzilut*, correspond to the five levels of the soul:			
1. *Asiya*	Particular creations	Action consciousness	*Nefesh*
2. *Yetzira*	General creations, templates	Emotion consciousness	*Ruach*
3. *Bria*	Possibility of creation	Intellect consciousness	*Neshama*
4. *Atzilut*	*Sephirot*, emanations	Transcendent consciousness	*Chaya*
5. *Keter*	Infinite light	Unity consciousness	*Yechida*

We differentiate between general and specific acknowledgment of G-d's presence.

(גַּם יֵשׁ לוֹמַר דְּיֵשׁ הוֹדָאָה כְּלָלִית וּכְמוֹ מוֹדֶה אֲנִי לְפָנֶיךָ כוּ' שֶׁהוֹדָאָה זוֹ אֵינָהּ בְּמַדְרֵגָה פְּרָטִית בֶּאֱלוֹקוּת כִּי אִם הוֹדָאָה כְּלָלִית לֶאֱלוֹקוּת וְכֵן הַבִּטּוּל וּנְתִינַת עַצְמוּתוֹ בְּהוֹדָאָה זוֹ אֵין בָּזֶה אֵיזֶה עִנְיָן פְּרָטִי כִּי אִם מַה שֶׁבִּכְלָלוּת מְצִיאוּתוֹ הוּא נוֹתֵן אֶת

(There is a difference between *general* acknowledgement, as when we rise in the morning and say *Modeh Ani* — "I am thankful," that is, "I acknowledge the One Above" — [and *specific* acknowledgment of G-d's Presence on a particular spiritual level]. General acknowledgment en-

--- **COMMENTARY** ---

1. *NEFESH*

First of all — and lowest of all — is the level of "action consciousness." On this level, one acknowledges that G-d exists, while experiencing little or no emotional or intellectual awareness of Him. It is on this level as well, that emphasis is placed on fulfilling the commandments (*mitzvot*) which connect us to Him. When performing an action, it is not necessary to feel or understand (although it is often beneficial). The main thing is the action itself, and that is why this level of G-d awareness is called "action consciousness." In Hebrew, its name *nefesh* means

Essay on Service of the Heart - Love Like Fire and Water

tails no recognition of any specific levels of spirituality. Rather, it is an overall affirmation of G-d's existence and also general nullification of our ego, a giving over of ourselves to Him in totality. There is no reference to any specific soul-level of self-nullification in this acknowledgment; we simply deliver ourselves into G-d's hands.)

עַצְמוֹ לֶאֱלוֹקוּת בְּהוֹדָאָה זוֹ

> "Acknowledgment of G-d" — *hoda'ah* in Hebrew — means consciously affirming G-d's existence and living with an awareness of Him. *Generally*, this entails thanking G-d at every step for the gifts He constantly bestows on us, especially the gift of life, and giving over this life to the *avoda* of the One Above. *Specifically*, this means acknowledging G-d while meditating on particular spiritual levels.

(The advantage of this general/overall acknowledgment is that it is usually more sincere than an affirmation of His presence on any specific level. [Understanding] particular levels of spirituality may be beyond us, but the ability to give ourselves over completely to G-d is well within the capability of every Jew. There's another advantage to this general acknowledgement, and that is that we give ourselves over in totality and in all our essence. Therefore, general acknowledgment is a foundation and cornerstone of serving the One Above all day long, as explained elsewhere.)

(וְיֵשׁ בָּזֶה יִתְרוֹן מַעֲלָה בְּעֶצֶם נְתִינַת עַצְמוּתוֹ שֶׁהִיא אֲמִתִּית יוֹתֵר מֵהַנְּתִינָה בְּאֵיזֶה עִנְיָן פְּרָטִי, וְהוּא לְפִי שֶׁהָעִנְיָן הַפְּרָטִי הוּא לְמַעְלָה מִמַּדְרֵגָתוֹ מַה שֶׁאֵין כֵּן הַנְּתִינָה לֶאֱלוֹקוּת בִּכְלָל (שֶׁלְּמַעְלָה מִמַּדְרֵגָה פְּרָטִית) זֶה קָרוֹב מְאֹד לְכָל אֶחָד מִיִּשְׂרָאֵל. וְגַם יֵשׁ בָּזֶה יִתְרוֹן מַה שֶּׁהַנְּתִינָה הִיא בְּכָל מַהוּתוֹ, וְלָכֵן בֶּאֱמֶת הוֹדָאָה זוֹ הִיא יְסוֹד הָעֲבוֹדָה דְּכָל הַיּוֹם וּכְמוֹ שֶׁכָּתוּב בְּמָקוֹם אַחֵר)

General acknowledgment is the foundation of daily avoda.

COMMENTARY

"enlivening soul" and refers to that aspect of the soul which enlivens the physical body. "Action consciousness" corresponds to the World of *Asiya*, the "World of Action." It is the lowest of the worlds, but it is "where the action is," where G-d wants spiritual revelation and revolution to take place. It is the world that most conceals anything spiritual and G-dly, but which G-d nevertheless seeks to transform into a world permeated with spirituality.

וְזֶהוּ הָעֲבוֹדָה דַּעֲשִׂיָּה בִּבְחִינַת נֶפֶשׁ שֶׁהִיא בְּחִינַת הוֹדָאָה כְּלָלִית לְבַד (וּבִפְרָטִיּוּת בַּתְּפִלָּה הוּא עַד בָּרוּךְ שֶׁאָמַר).

This [overall affirmation], then, is the spiritual *avoda* of the World of *Asiya*, on the soul-level of *nefesh*. It constitutes a general acknowledgement of G-d's Presence alone. (In the [morning] prayers, this level extends from the beginning of *Hodu* until *Baruch She'amar*.)

Specific acknowledgment extends to the highest levels of G-dliness.

אָמְנָם יֵשׁ הוֹדָאָה פְּרָטִית הַיְנוּ בְּמַדְרֵגוֹת פְּרָטִיּוֹת כְּמוֹ בְּעִנְיָן יִחוּדָא עִילָּאָה אֵיךְ שֶׁכֹּלָּא קַמֵּי כְּלָא חֲשִׁיבֵי, דַּאֲמִתִּית הַשָּׂגָה זֹאת הִיא רַק בִּנְשָׁמוֹת גְּבוֹהוֹת אֲשֶׁר עֲבוֹדָתָם הִיא בִּבְחִינַת הַבִּטּוּל דְּיִחוּדָא עִילָּאָה,

It is true that acknowledgment of the One Above may also occur on specific levels of spiritual awareness, such as the level known as *yichuda ila'ah* [2] [supernal unity]. On this level, we become aware of the ephemeral nature of creation in light of His true Presence. However, [this is such an elevated level that] real understanding is only achieved by lofty souls who reach [total] self-nullification, corresponding to *yichuda ila'ah*.

> *Yichuda ila'ah* (literally "higher unity") is a state of mind in which our primary awareness is of G-d and G-dliness, while the creation and universe are in the background. It takes place when we have achieved total nullification of our self — known as *bitul b'metziut*.

אַךְ בְּכָל אֶחָד מִיִּשְׂרָאֵל צָרִיךְ לִהְיוֹת בָּטוּל זֶה וּכְמוֹ שֶׁכָּתוּב בְּקוּנְטְרֵס עֵץ הַחַיִּים פ"ז, רַק שֶׁבְּדֶרֶךְ כְּלָל הוּא בִּבְחִינַת הוֹדָאָה לְבַד וּמִכָּל מָקוֹם בְּהוֹדָאָה זוֹ יֵשׁ בְּחִינַת יְדִיעָה וְהַשָּׂגָה וּבְחִינַת הֶרְגֵּשׁ פְּנִימִי כוּ' וּכְמוֹ שֶׁכָּתוּב שָׁם פְּזוּ"ח. וְעִם הֱיוֹת שֶׁהַיְדִיעָה הַזֹּאת אֵינָהּ אֲמִתִּית כִּי אֲמִתִּית הַיְדִיעָה

Of course, it is true that all Jewish people should strive to achieve this level of total self-nullification, as is written in *Kuntres Eitz Chaim*, chapter 7. While generally speaking, *yichuda ila'ah* implies only acknowledgement of G-d's existence, it also includes dimensions of knowledge and intellect as well as deep feeling, as written in *Kuntres Eitz Chaim*,

─── **COMMENTARY** ───

In prayer, the time for experiencing "action consciousness" is from the time we wake up, saying *Modeh Ani* — "I am thankful" or "I acknowledge the One Above" — until *Baruch she'amar* ("Blessed is He who spoke"), the beginning words of *P'sukei D'Zimra* ("Verses of Praise"). During that time, we dress, say chapters 7-8. The knowledge associated with *yichuda ila'ah* isn't full and true [spiritual] awareness. [True awareness] arrives only via *hitamtut* [confirmation of one's spiritual level from Above], which involves seeing G-dliness in the mind's eye. Or at the very least, it [comes cloaked] as the profound knowledge of *p'nimiyut bina*[4] [the inner abstract understanding that remains after we have stripped away our "outer garments" of perception and reasoning]. That is why *bina* is sometimes called the "Supernal Bride"[5] (*kalah*) — the one who "consumes" the [external] physical realm.[iii] If our comprehension is only superficial, utilizing the "outer garments of understanding," we do not gain true knowledge of the subject. Nevertheless, [even our shallow understanding] contains elements of inner knowledge and deep feeling.

דִּבְחִינַת יְחוּדָא עִילָאָה הִיא שֶׁבָּאָה בִּבְחִינַת הִתְאַמְּתוּת דַּוְקָא שֶׁזֶּהוּ עִנְיַן רְאִיַּת עֵין הַשֵֹכֶל כַּנּוֹדָע, וְעַל כָּל פָּנִים בִּבְחִינַת הַשָּׂגָה פְּנִימִית דִּבְחִינַת פְּנִימִיּוּת בִּינָה (דְּעַל שֵׁם זֶה נִקְרֵאת בִּינָה כַּלָּה עִילָאָה בְּחִינַת אִישְׁתֵּיצֵי גוּשְׁמָא כו' וּכְמוֹ שֶׁכָּתוּב בְּמָקוֹם אַחֵר) אֲבָל מַה שֶּׁיּוֹדֵעַ וּמַשִּׂיג הָעִנְיָן בִּבְחִינַת חִיצוֹנִיּוּת הַהַשָּׂגָה אֵין זֶה הַשָּׂגָה אֲמִיתִּית בָּעִנְיָן הַזֶּה, מִכָּל מָקוֹם הֲרֵי זֶה בָּא בִּבְחִינַת יְדִיעָה וְהֶרְגֵּשׁ פְּנִימִי

iii) See footnote of the Rebbe on page 261 ←

(Therein lies the advantage of specific acknowledgment over the general acknowledgment described above. Specific acknowledgment [implying inner understanding and feeling] is a stage of progress in serving the One Above, while general acknowledgment is not a stage but a foundation and beginning.)

(שֶׁבָּזֶה יֵשׁ יִתְרוֹן בְּהוֹדָאָה זוֹ לְגַבֵּי הַהוֹדָאָה כְּלָלִית הַנַּ"ל. וְהִיא דַרְגָּא בַּעֲבוֹדָה מַה שֶּׁאֵין כֵּן הוֹדָאָה כְּלָלִית הַנַּ"ל אֵינָהּ בְּחִינַת דַּרְגָּא עֲדַיִן כִּי אִם הִיא יְסוֹד הָעֲבוֹדָה וְרֵאשִׁיתָהּ כוּ׳)

Specific acknowledgment is a stage of progress in avoda, not the foundation.

Specific acknowledgment may be described as an elevation of the level of *nefesh* and its inclusion in the level of *ruach*, or even higher.

וּבְחִינַת הַהוֹדָאָה זוֹ יֵשׁ לוֹמַר שֶׁזֶּהוּ עֲלִיַּת מַדְרֵגַת נֶפֶשׁ וְהִתְכַּלְלוּתָהּ בְּמַדְרֵגַת הָרוּחַ אוֹ גַּם לְמַעְלָה מִזֶּה).

COMMENTARY
---

morning blessings and also recite the details of the services in the Temple, all of which are physical and action-oriented. [Other things corresponding to "action consciousness" include the final *hey* of four-letter Name of G-d (the Tetragrammaton), the tenth and final *sephira* — *malchut* ("sovereignty") — and the mineral world within creation.]

1. *Nefesh*	World of *Asiya*	General Acknowledgement
2. *Ruach* (*nefesh* within *ruach*)	World of *Yetzira*	Specific Acknowledgement
3. *Neshama*	World of *Bria*	Intellect

וְעַל יְדֵי אֲמִתִּית הָעֲבוֹדָה בִּבְחִינַת רוּחַ הֲרֵי הוּא עוֹלֶה אַחַר כָּךְ לְעוֹלָם הַבְּרִיאָה, וְהַיְנוּ שֶׁיַּעֲלֶה וְיַגִּיעַ לְמַדְרֵגַת נְשָׁמָה שֶׁהִיא הָעֲבוֹדָה דִּבְחִינַת הַמֹּחִין וְגַם בְּחִינַת רוּחַ עוֹלֶה וְנִכְלָל בָּזֶה כְּהִתְכַּלְלוּת הַיְצִירָה בְּעוֹלָם הַבְּרִיאָה כו'.

וְהָעִנְיָן הוּא דְהִנֵּה בְּסֵפֶר שֶׁל בֵּינוֹנִים פל"ח ול"ט מְבֹאָר דְּהָעֲבוֹדָה בִּבְחִינַת דְּחִילוּ וּרְחִימוּ טִבְעִיִּים עוֹלֶה בְּעוֹלָם הַיְצִירָה וּדְחִילוּ וּרְחִימוּ שִׂכְלִיִּים הֵם בִּבְרִיאָה, וְלִכְאוֹרָה נִרְאֶה דְהַיְנוּ הָאַהֲבָה וְיִרְאָה שֶׁבְּהִתְגַּלּוּת הַלֵּב הַבָּאָה עַל יְדֵי הִתְבּוֹנְנוּת כו', אַךְ בֶּאֱמֶת נִרְאֶה הַכַּוָּנָה שָׁם דִּדְחִילוּ וּרְחִימוּ שִׂכְלִיִּים הֵמָּה נַעֲלִים הַרְבֵּה יוֹתֵר מֵאַהֲבָה וְיִרְאָה הנ"ל, וְהֵמָּה מַה שֶּׁבָּאִים בְּדֶרֶךְ מִמֵילָא מֵהַהִתְבּוֹנְנוּת בִּגְדֻלַּת אוֹר אֵין סוֹף בָּרוּךְ הוּא כו', וּמִמַּה שֶּׁכָּתוּב שָׁם בפל"ט "אַךְ הַיְנוּ דַּוְקָא נְשָׁמוֹת מַמָּשׁ שֶׁהֵן בְּחִינַת מֹחִין דְּגַדְלוּת אֵין סוֹף בָּרוּךְ הוּא אֲבָל בְּחִינַת הָרוּחַ שֶׁל הַצַּדִּיקִים וְכֵן שְׁאָר כָּל נִשְׁמוֹת יִשְׂרָאֵל שֶׁעָבְדוּ אֶת ה' בִּדְחִילוּ וּרְחִימוּ הַמֻּסְתֶּרֶת בְּלֵב כְּלָלוּת יִשְׂרָאֵל כו'",

Intellectual love and fear of G-d are on a higher level than natural fear and love in the heart.

Through true *avoda* on the level of *ruach*, we rise to the World of *Bria* [the World of Creation], ascending to the soul-level called *neshama* and *avoda* of the intellect. Our soul-level of *ruach* also rises and is included on this level, just as the World of *Yetzira* is included in the World of *Bria*.

To make things clearer, let us refer to *Tanya*, chapters 38-39. There, it is explained that *avoda* that is motivated by "natural fear and love" of the One Above [the innate fear and love of G-d in our hearts] is associated with the World of *Yetzira*, while [the *avoda* motivated by] "intellectual fear and love" is associated with the higher World of *Bria*. At first glance, it would seem that "intellectual fear and love" become revealed in the heart by meditation [on G-d as He fills creation]. [Upon further investigation], it becomes clear that the "intellectual fear and love" referred to here are far superior to this level of emotion in the heart. True intellectual fear and love flow spontaneously from the mind as a result of meditation on the infinite light of G-d [as He transcends the universe]. *Tanya* states in chapter 39:

Essay on Service of the Heart - Love Like Fire and Water

"This [intellectual love and fear] is only among souls that are blessed with **"mature mindfulness"** capable of meditating upon the Infinite One, may He be blessed, but the **ruach** of *tzadikim* and also the **rest of the Jews** who serve G-d with **love hidden** in the collective hearts of the Jewish people…"

This statement defines *neshama* as "mature mindfulness" and differentiates between the levels of *ruach* of *tzadikim* and the *avoda* of hidden love and fear — synonymous with "natural love and fear" — of the rest of the Jews. Thus, there are three levels, corresponding to the three soul-levels of *nefesh*, *ruach*, and *neshama*. The hidden love — about which it says in *Tanya*, chapter 16, that it is the love that G-d "deserves" — is on the level of *nefesh* alone. It doesn't involve true desire [for Him], but rather "acquiescence" [so that we should worship Him with love]. (Even the intellectual comprehension which causes this acquiescence is not true comprehension.) This acquiescence is not the same as the "agreement" that remains after we experience love of G-d during prayer. After prayer, this agreement only leaves an impression that enables us to conduct ourselves properly all day long. The acquiescence to love G-d, though, because He deserves it, includes more spiritual energy and feeling, though it remains only acquiescence and not true desire.

הִנֵּה מִמַּה שֶּׁאָמַרְנוּ גַּבֵּי נְשָׁמָה שֶׁהִיא בְּחִינַת מֹחִין דְּגַדְלוּת וּמִמַּה שֶׁכּוֹתֵב בכ׳ חֲלוּקוֹת בְּחִינַת הָרוּחַ שֶׁל הַצַּדִּיקִים וְהָעֲבוֹדָה דִּשְׁאָר כָּל נִשְׁמוֹת יִשְׂרָאֵל בִּדְחִילוּ וּרְחִימוּ הַמְסֻתֶּרֶת דְּהַיְנוּ דְּחִילוּ וּרְחִימוּ טִבְעִיִּים, נִרְאֶה בִּפְרָטִיּוּת הַמַּדְרֵגוֹת דְּנֶפֶשׁ רוּחַ וּנְשָׁמָה, דְּהָאַהֲבָה הַמְסֻתֶּרֶת אֲשֶׁר כָּךְ יָאֲתָה לָהֶן כו׳ הַמְבֹאָר בְּסֵפֶר שֶׁל בֵּינוֹנִים פט״ז הִיא בְּחִינַת נֶפֶשׁ לְבַד לִהְיוֹת שֶׁהָאַהֲבָה אֵינָהּ מַה שֶּׁחָפֵץ בֶּאֱמֶת כִּי אִם בִּבְחִינַת הֶסְכֵּם לְבַד (וְגַם הַהַשָּׂגָה הַמְּבִיאָה לָזֶה אֵינָהּ הַשָּׂגָה גְּמוּרָה) (וְהֶסְכֵּם זֶה אֵינוֹ כְּמוֹ הַהֶסְכֵּם הַנִּשְׁאָר אַחַר הָאַהֲבָה בַּתְּפִלָּה שֶׁהוּא בִּבְחִינַת רֹשֶׁם לְבַד הַשַּׁיָּךְ לְקִיּוּם בְּפֹעַל כָּל הַיּוֹם, מַה שֶׁאֵין כֵּן הַהֶסְכֵּם דְּכָךְ יָאֲתָה לוֹ הוּא בִּבְחִינַת חַיּוּת וְהֶרְגֵּשׁ יוֹתֵר וּמִכָּל מָקוֹם הֲרֵי זֶה רַק בִּבְחִינַת הֶסְכֵּם לֹא שֶׁחָפֵץ בֶּאֱמֶת כו׳).

"rest of the Jews…with love hidden"	Acquiescence	*Nefesh*
"*ruach* of *tzadikim*"	Natural love and fear	*Ruach*
"mature mindfulness"	Intellectual love and fear	*Neshama*

As for what is stated there [in Ch. 16 of *Tanya*] — "and also his *nefesh* and his *ruach* that are within him..." — this would seem to indicate inter-inclusion of the two lower levels of *nefesh* and *ruach*. But this inter-inclusion is not similar to the one mentioned above, in which the level of *nefesh* rises to that of *ruach*. Here, it refers to the combination of the two different levels [as opposed to one rising to the level of the other].

וּמִמַּה שֶׁכָּתוּב שָׁם וְגַם נַפְשׁוֹ וְרוּחוֹ אֲשֶׁר בְּקִרְבּוֹ כו' נִרְאֶה שֶׁזֶּהוּ הִתְכַּלְלוּת מִבְּחִינַת נֶפֶשׁ וְרוּחַ (וְלֹא בְּעִנְיַן הִתְכַּלְלוּת הַנַּ"ל דְּהַיְינוּ שֶׁהַנֶּפֶשׁ נִכְלָל בִּבְחִינַת רוּחַ וְכָאן הוּא הִתְכַּלְלוּת מַדְרֵגָתָן,

During the inter-inclusion described earlier, the level of *nefesh* remains associated with acknowledgment. Since the person is operating on the level of *ruach*, or even higher, the acknowledgment also takes place on a higher level. Here, however, the inter-inclusion of *nefesh* and *ruach* means they become one level. That is, they become a higher level within *nefesh* itself, similar to [but not on the true level of] *ruach*, and this constitutes their inter-inclusion. Although we are speaking of *nefesh* [as it rises to *ruach*], it nevertheless remains *nefesh*. However, [it attains] the level of *nehy* [acronym for *netzach-hod-yesod*, the lower three instinctual *sephirot*].[6]

רְצוֹנוֹ לוֹמַר דְּבַהִתְכַּלְלוּת הַנַּ"ל הַנֶּפֶשׁ הוּא בְּחִינַת הוֹדָאָה, רַק לִהְיוֹתוֹ עוֹמֵד בַּעֲבוֹדָתוֹ בְּמַדְרֵגַת רוּחַ, אוֹ גַּם לְמַעְלָה מִזֶּה, לָכֵן הַהוֹדָאָה הִיא בְּמַדְרֵגָה נַעֲלֵית כַּנַּ"ל, וְכָאן הַהִתְכַּלְלוּת הוּא שֶׁהַנֶּפֶשׁ וְהָרוּחַ הֵן בְּמַדְרֵגָה אַחַת, וְהַיְינוּ שֶׁזֶּה מַדְרֵגָה גָּבוֹהַּ יוֹתֵר בְּמַדְרֵגוֹת הַנֶּפֶשׁ שֶׁהוּא כְּמוֹ בְּחִינַת רוּחַ (אֲבָל אֵין זֶה (אֲמִתִּית בְּחִינַת הָרוּחַ) וְזֶהוּ הִתְכַּלְלוּת מַדְרֵגָתָן, וּמִכָּל מָקוֹם הוּא בְּחִינַת נֶפֶשׁ, רַק שֶׁזֶּהוּ בְּחִינַת נֶצַח הוֹד יְסוֹד

> The process of "inter-inclusion" allows different *sephirot* and soul-levels to interact. Every *sephira* and soul-level incorporates within it something of all the others. In this way, creation reflects its underlying "holographic" unity, demonstrating that it is the handiwork of one G-d. This can only take place when the *sephirot* or soul-levels are sufficiently nullified to accept and interact with one another.

(*Nehy* is also called *nefesh* and is considered one of the three "governors" — the mind, the heart,

(שֶׁנִּקְרָא גַּם כֵּן נֶפֶשׁ כַּנּוֹדָע בְּעִנְיַן תְּלַת שַׁלִּיטִין אִינוּן מוֹחָא לִבָּא וְכַבְדָּא שֶׁהֵן חָכְמָה בִּינָה וְדַעַת חֶסֶד

Essay on Service of the Heart - Love Like Fire and Water

and the liver, which correspond to *chabad*, *chagat*, and *nehy*. [In the structure of the *sephirot*,] *nehy* is situated just above the [lowest] level of *malchut*, which itself corresponds to the level of acknowledgment.)

גְּבוּרָה וְתִפְאֶרֶת נֶצַח הוֹד יְסוֹד) שֶׁלְּמַעְלָה מִבְּחִינַת הַמַּלְכוּת (שֶׁזֶּהוּ בְּחִינַת הוֹדָאָה).

The structure of the *Sephirot* (emanations)		
	Keter "crown"	
3. Intellectual *sephirot* CHABAD	Bina "understanding" Da'at "knowledge"	Chochma "wisdom"
2. Emotional *sephirot* CHAGAT	Gevura "strength/restraint" Tiferet "beauty"	Chesed "loving-kindness"
1. Instinctual *sephirot* NEHY	Hod "acknowledgment/thanksgiving" Yesod "foundation"	Netzach "victory"
	Malchut "kingdom"	

The love and fear — which become revealed in the heart as a result of meditation on the greatness of G-d, and which cause us to truly cleave to Him with heartfelt desire — are called *ruach*. The meditation that brings us to this level focuses on G-dliness that can be grasped intellectually [even

וְהָאַהֲבָה וְיִרְאָה שֶׁבְּהִתְגַּלּוּת הַלֵּב שֶׁבָּאָה מֵהַהִתְבּוֹנְנוּת בִּגְדֻלַּת ה' שֶׁאוֹהֵב אֶת ה' וְחָפֵץ בֶּאֱמֶת לְדָבְקָה בּוֹ בִּתְשׁוּקָה מַרְגֶּשֶׁת בַּלֵּב זֶהוּ בְּחִינַת רוּחַ, וְהַהִתְבּוֹנְנוּת בַּזֶּה הוּא בְּמַדְרֵגָה בֶּאֱלוֹקוּת שֶׁשַּׁיָּךְ בָּהֶם הַשָּׂגָה וְהוּא בְּאוֹר וְחִיּוּת אֱלוֹקִי הַבָּא בִּבְחִינַת

Ruach meditation relates to the G-dly illumination within the universe.

COMMENTARY
---

2. RUACH

Going in and up the spiritual ladder, we come to the level known as "emotion consciousness." Here, we discover our own natural love and fear of the One Above through meditation on the "garments of G-d" — that is, creation itself. Just as we get to know a person by the effect he has upon the world, so we begin to get to know G-d by considering the variation,

הִתְלַבְּשׁוּת בָּעוֹלָם לִהְיוֹת וּלְהַחֲיוֹת אֶת הָעוֹלָמוֹת וּבְדֶרֶךְ כְּלָל בִּבְחִינַת מְמַלֵּא כָּל עָלְמִין שֶׁבְּכָל זֶה שַׁיָּךְ בְּחִינַת הַשָּׂגָה גְּמוּרָה כְּמוֹ שֶׁכָּתוּב בְּלִקּוּטֵי תּוֹרָה דִּבּוּר הַמַּתְחִיל וְיָדַעְתָּ דְּרוּשׁ הָרִאשׁוֹן,

though *ruach* is associated with the emotions]. That is, this meditation focuses on the G-dly light and energy that is en-clothed in the universe in order to create and maintain it. In general, it is called *ohr memalle* ("immanent light"), which is well understood by the human intellect (as related in *Likutei Torah*, *Vayadata*, in the first discourse).

Ohr memalle ("inner/immanent light") is the spiritual energy within the creation. *Ohr makif* ("transcendent light") is the spiritual energy beyond creation (and the source of *ohr memalle*).

Ruach meditation demands "labor of the soul and labor of the flesh."

וְהָעֲבוֹדָה בָּזֶה הוּא לִיגַע אֶת עַצְמוֹ בִּיגִיעַת נֶפֶשׁ וִיגִיעַת בָּשָׂר בְּהַשָּׂגָה וְהִתְבּוֹנְנוּת זוֹ לֵידַע וּלְהַשִּׂיג הָעִנְיָנִים הֵיטֵב לֹא בִּידִיעָה כְּלָלִית לְבַד כִּי אִם בִּידִיעָה פְּרָטִית וַעֲמֻקָּה בְּעֹמֶק וַאֲמִתַּת הָעִנְיָנִים הָאֵלּוּ וְיִתְקַע וִיקַשֵּׁר דַּעְתּוֹ בְּחֹזֶק בָּזֶה לִהְיוֹת הָעִנְיָן נִרְגָּשׁ הֵיטֵב בְּמוֹחוֹ וְלִבּוֹ וְעַל יְדֵי זֶה יִתְעוֹרֵר בְּאַהֲבָה אֲמִתִּית לַה' יִתְבָּרַךְ וּבִתְשׁוּקָה מֻרְגֶּשֶׁת בְּהִתְגַּלּוּת לִבּוֹ לְדָבְקָה בּוֹ יִת'.

The *avoda* on this level requires "labor of the soul and the labor of the flesh." It necessitates intellectual acumen in order to properly grasp and internalize G-dly concepts through meditation. We must not be satisfied with a general, superficial knowledge alone, but must develop a deep and detailed comprehension of these topics. [In order to do so], we must focus our concentration on the subject, so that it becomes clear in our minds, and it is felt in our hearts. By doing so, we will arouse true love of G-d within ourselves, and [then] a strong desire will be revealed in our heart to cling to the One Above.

וְהִנֵּה עִם הֱיוֹת דַּעֲבוֹדָה זוֹ הִיא בִּבְחִינַת הַמֹּחִין בִּבְחִינַת הַשָּׂגָה וְהִתְבּוֹנְנוּת טוֹבָה כנ"ל מִכָּל מָקוֹם

Even though this requires intellectual acumen and as such is an "*avoda* of the mind," it still takes place

--- **COMMENTARY** ---

complication, and sheer beauty of His creation. Humanity is a mere speck in the scheme of things, and when we recognize this, the natural result is fear of the One who created the whole thing, together with love of Him over the wonder of it all. This meditation reveals the natural love and fear in the heart of the meditator. It was there all along, but it takes an outside on the level of *ruach* ["emotion consciousness"]. This is because the main objective is to arouse the [G-dly] emotions of the heart, and this intellectual meditation does indeed lead to the arousal of [G-dly] feelings. Although deep concentration is involved here, all of the intellectual activity is still "external." The meditation engages the intellect as it is associated with the emotions [as opposed to pure intellect, which is devoid of emotions]. (See what is written in the *Siddur* of the *Alter Rebbe* regarding the verse, "The heavens tell of His honor..." and in the book of Chassidic discourses of the year 5670, *Parshat Trumah*.⁷) The nullification associated with this level involves letting go of our [natural, unG-dly] emotions. It is called *ego*-nullification. The higher level, associated with pure intellect, is called *self*-nullification.

הֲרֵי זֶה בְּחִינַת רוּחַ לִהְיוֹת שֶׁהָעִקָּר כָּאן הוּא הִתְעוֹרְרוּת הַמִּדּוֹת שֶׁבַּלֵּב, וְהַהִתְבּוֹנְנוּת הִיא לְעוֹרֵר אֶת הַמִּדּוֹת. וְהָגַם שֶׁהוּא בְּהַשָּׂגָה גְמוּרָה וּבְהַעֲמָקַת הַדַּעַת מִכָּל מָקוֹם כָּל זֶה הוּא בְּחִינַת חִיצוֹנִיּוּת הַמּוֹחִין כְּמוֹ שֶׁהֵן בִּלְבוּשֵׁי הַשָּׂגָה שֶׁזֶּהוּ בְּחִינַת הַמּוֹחִין הַשַּׁיָּכִים אֶל הַמִּדּוֹת. וְעַיֵּן מַה שֶּׁכָּתוּב בַּסִּדּוּר בְּשַׁבָּת בְּבִרְכוֹת * בְּפָסוּק הַשָּׁמַיִם מְסַפְּרִים וְעַיֵּן מַה שֶׁכָּתוּב בְּדְרוּשׁ תִּקְעוּ עֵת"ר דִּבּוּר הַמַּתְחִיל וְזֹאת הַתְּרוּמָה. וְהַבִּטּוּל בַּזֶּה הוּא הַבִּטּוּל שֶׁמִּבְּחִינַת הַמִּדּוֹת דְהַיְנוּ בִּטּוּל הַיֵּשׁ לֹא הַבִּטּוּל דְמוֹחִין שֶׁלְּמַעְלָה מִבְּחִינַת בִּטּוּל הַיֵּשׁ לְבַד כוּ'

The objective of ruach meditation is to arouse the emotions of the heart.

Nullification" — *bitul* in Hebrew — refers to getting our self-centered concerns out of the way of our encounter with G-d. Different levels of *bitul* lead to different levels of *da'at*, consciousness of G-d's presence in the universe. Here we are concerned with two: ego-nullification and self-nullification.

1. Ego nullification (*Bitul hayesh*) ⇓	2. Self nullification (*Bitul b'metziut*) ⇓
Nullification of one's pride and ego (effecting emotions but not intellect)	Nullification of one's whole self (effecting intellect as well as emotions)
Associated with: ⇓	**Associated with:** ⇓
Da'at tachton or *Yichuda tat'ah* "lower awareness"	*Da'at elyon* or *Yichuda ila'ah* "elevated awareness"
Our primary awareness is of creation, with G-d in the background	Our primary awareness is of G-d, with the creation in the background

(וְזוֹ הִיא עֲבוֹדָה שֶׁבַּלֵּב שֶׁעַל זֶה נֶאֱמַר וְיָדַעְתָּ הַיּוֹם וַהֲשֵׁבֹתָ אֶל לְבָבֶךָ דַּוְקָא, דְּאַהֲבָה וְיִרְאָה שֶׁבְּהִתְגַּלּוּת הַלֵּב הֵן מִצְוֹת אַהֲבָה וְיִרְאָה שֶׁנִּצְטַוִּינוּ עֲלֵיהֶם. וְהֵן הַשַּׁיָּכִים לְקִיּוּם הַתּוֹרָה וּמִצְוֹת רְמַ"ח מִצְוֹת עֲשֵׂה וְשַׁסַ"ה לֹא תַעֲשֶׂה כְּמוֹ שֶׁכָּתוּב בְּסֵפֶר שֶׁל בֵּינוֹנִים פ"ד וּפ"מ וּבְכַמָּה דּוּכְתֵּי, וּבָהֶם וְעַל יָדָם דַּוְקָא הוּא בֵּרוּר וְזִכּוּךְ הַנֶּפֶשׁ הַבַּהֲמִית, וְהוּא מִדַּת כָּל אָדָם אֲשֶׁר כָּל אֶחָד מְחֻיָּב לֵידַע אֶת ה' לִיגַע אֶת עַצְמוֹ בְּהַשְׂגָּה וְהִתְבּוֹנְנוּת כְּדַבְעֵי לְמַהוֹי וּלְהַעֲמִיק דַּעְתּוֹ בְּחֹזֶק וּלְהִתְעוֹרֵר בְּאַהֲבָה וַחֲפִיצָה וּתְשׁוּקָה מַרְגֶּשֶׁת בַּלֵּב לִהְיוֹת לִבּוֹ חָפֵץ בֶּאֱמֶת בֶּאֱלֹקוּת (וְעַל יְדֵי זֶה הוּא בֵּרוּר וְזִכּוּךְ הַנֶּפֶשׁ הַבַּהֲמִית כוּ') וּלְדָבְקָה בּוֹ עַל יְדֵי קִיּוּם הַתּוֹרָה וְהַמִּצְוֹת כוּ').

All that has been discussed here is the "service of the heart" about which the verse states, "And you should know today and put it in your heart..." in your heart specifically, since the love and fear of G-d, which become revealed in our heart, are the fulfillment of the Biblical commands to love and fear G-d. These are the emotions associated with fulfilling the commandments of the Torah, the 248 positive and 365 negative *mitzvot*, as discussed in *Tanya*, chapters 4 and 40, and in other places. It is precisely through these emotions of love and fear that the animal soul becomes purified and refined. Therefore, we all must know G-d and appropriately labor at meditation, while focusing our concentration with determination, in order to arouse love and desire to the extent that it becomes felt in the heart. Then, our heart will truly yearn for G-dliness, and this yearning will bring about the purification and refinement of the animal soul, so that we will desire to cleave to G-d through fulfillment of the Torah's commandments.

COMMENTARY

inspiration — "impression from the outside," meaning meditation on the garments of the Creator — to bring it into revelation. "Emotion consciousness" is called *ruach* in Hebrew. *Ruach* means "wind/spirit" and corresponds to the World of *Yetzira* ("World of Formation") in the macrocosm. The World of *Yetzira* is the world of general archetypes and templates of creation, also known as angels. Here in the World of *Yetzira*, there are only spiritual creatures (angels), each one corresponding to and including details of many specific creations of the lower World of *Asiya*.

The level known as *neshama* corresponds to *mochin*[8] ("spiritual intellect"), as it is written (Job 32:8), "The breath [*nishmat*] of G-d gives understanding." At this level, through meditation, we can grasp the essential G-dliness that is the "soul" of the concept, stripped of its outer garments. What is left is essential G-dliness, and it becomes revealed in our mind. It shines with a tremendous light, riveting our attention and causing us to cleave mightily to this illumination in our mind. (The sign of this occurring is that we completely lose awareness of anything physical because of our intense connection to the G-dly light revealed in our mind.) This level of intellectual understanding is beyond anything emotional.[9]

אָמְנָם בְּחִינַת נְשָׁמָה הִיא בְּחִינַת הַמֹּחִין וּכְמוֹ שֶׁכָּתוּב נִשְׁמַת שַׁדַּי תְּבִינֵם, וְהוּא הַהַשָּׂגָה וְהַהִתְבּוֹנְנוּת בִּבְחִינַת פְּנִימִיּוּת הַמֹּחִין דְּהַיְינוּ בִּבְחִינַת הַפְּשָׁטָה מִלְּבוּשֵׁי הַהַשָּׂגָה כִּי אִם בְּעֶצֶם הָעִנְיָן הָאֱלֹקִי כְּמוֹ שֶׁהוּא שֶׁמֵּאִיר הָעִנְיָן הָאֱלֹקִי בְּגִלּוּי בְּמוֹחוֹ בִּבְחִינַת גִּלּוּי אוֹר רַב וּמִתְקַשֵּׁר וְנִדְבַּק מְאֹד בְּמוֹחוֹ בְּהָאוֹר הָאֱלֹקִי (וְהָאוֹת עַל זֶה הוּא שֶׁמִּתְבַּטְּלִים אֶצְלוֹ כָּל חוּשֵׁי הַהֶרְגֵּשׁ הַטִּבְעִיִּים מֵחֲמַת הַדְּבֵקוּת בְּאוֹר הָאֱלֹקִי הַמֵּאִיר בְּגִלּוּי בְּמוֹחוֹ כוּ') וְהַשָּׂגָה זוֹ הִיא לְמַעֲלָה מִבְּחִינַת הַמִּדּוֹת

Neshama meditation penetrates to the 'soul' of G-dliness in the world, and rivets our attention.

---- **COMMENTARY** ----

In prayer, the stage in which we experience "emotion consciousness" begins from *Baruch sh'amar* and continues until we say *Barchu* ("Bless Him") which begins the introduction to the *Shema*. This gives us sufficient time during recitation of *Pesukei D'zimra* to meditate upon the creation *ex nihilo* ("from nothing") and to produce wonder and amazement in our souls. [Other things corresponding to the soul-level of "emotion consciousness" include the *vav* of the four-letter Name of G-d, the lower six *sephirot* which are active in creation (*Chesed* through *Yesod*) and the vegetable world in creation (plants grow, as do emotions).]

3. NESHAMA

Finally, we reach the highest of the three soul-levels that are en-clothed in the body (two higher levels are not en-clothed in the body). It is called "intellect consciousness," or *neshama*. In Hebrew, *neshama* means "soul," and it is on this level that the meditator penetrates to the "soul" of creation and finds there the spiritual essence and enlivening power that brings creation

Kuntres Ha'Avoda - קונטרס העבודה

(וְהִיא הָעֲבוֹדָה בִּבְחִינַת הַמֹּחִין בִּבְחִינַת הַתְאַחֲדוּת וּבִבְחִינַת דְּבֵקוּת בְּהָאוֹר הָאֱלֹקִי, וְהַבִּטּוּל בָּזֶה יֵשׁ בּוֹ חִלּוּקֵי מַדְרֵגוֹת כְּמוֹ שִׁית' בְּסָמוּךְ. מִכָּל מָקוֹם הֲרֵי זֶה לְמַעְלָה מִבְּחִינַת בִּטּוּל הַיֵּשׁ לִהְיוֹתוֹ בְּחִינַת פְּנִימִיּוּת הַמֹּחִין כו'),

רַק שֶׁהָאוֹר מִתְפַּשֵּׁט וּמֵאִיר גַּם בַּלֵּב (דְּכַאֲשֶׁר הָאוֹר הָאֱלֹקִי מֵאִיר בְּגִלּוּי אֵינוֹ בִּבְחִינַת הַגְבָּלָה לִהְיוֹת דַּוְקָא בַּמֹּחִין וְלֹא בַּלֵּב וְאֵינוֹ מִתְעַלֵּם בְּמֵצַר הַגָּרוֹן לָכֵן מֵאִיר גַּם בַּלֵּב כו' כְּמוֹ שֶׁכָּתוּב בְּמָקוֹם אַחֵר) וְגַם הַלֵּב מִתְפַּעֵל בָּזֶה בְּדֶרֶךְ מִמֵּילָא שֶׁאֵין צָרִיךְ לַעֲשׂוֹת הַהִתְפַּעֲלוּת וְהָאַהֲבָה בַּלֵּב כָּל אֶחָד בָּא מִמֵּילָא מֵהִגָּלוּי אוֹר, וְהִיא גַּם כֵּן בִּבְחִינַת דְּבֵקוּת לֹא בִּבְחִינַת הִתְפַּעֲלוּת כָּל כָּךְ. וְהוּא בִּבְחִינַת גַּדְלוּת הַמֹּחִין וְגַדְלוּת הַמִּדּוֹת כו'

Neshama emotions respond spontaneously to the G-dly light; the meditator cleaves automatically to G-dliness.

iv) See footnote of the Rebbe on page 262

(This *avoda* [of the *neshama*] leads to unity with the G-dly light. There are differences in the levels of self-nullification associated with this spiritual level, as will be explained shortly. In any case, the level of nullification here is beyond ego-nullification alone, since it involves pure intellect.)

The illumination spreads from the mind and illuminates the heart as well. (Since when the G-dly light shines, it shines without limitations, and is not confined to the mind; it does not become trapped in the "narrow straits of the throat" — that is, in the inability of the mind to express itself in emotions — and, therefore, it is able to illuminate the heart as well.) The heart responds spontaneously.[iv] There is no need for us to bring ourselves to feel the excitement of the heart through meditation, since the G-dly light is revealed spontaneously in the heart. It is a state of cleaving [to the One Above], rather than excitement [about Him]. This state is called [in the Kabbalistic literature], a spiritually "mature intellect/mind" and "mature heart."

COMMENTARY

constantly into existence. Creation didn't just happen during the six days and then remained in existence. Constant input of spiritual energy from the Creator is required in order to sustain it. This spiritual energy, conveyed by the letters of the Hebrew alphabet, is embedded in each and every aspect of creation, according to its individual needs and nature.

When we penetrate the "outer garments" described above and discover the "soul" of creation — the spiritual energy that keeps it going — we arrive at the level of *neshama*, or "intellect

Essay on Service of the Heart - Love Like Fire and Water

In general, what is being described here is the complete structure — that is, the ten *sephirot* — of the spiritual intellect. In this condition of full intellectual and spiritual maturity, the emotions are similar to the intellect. The emotions are neither felt nor expressed as excitement, but rather as unity with the One Above. In chapter 39 of *Tanya*, this love of G-d is called *reuta d'liba* ("will of the heart").[10] To put it simply, it is the state in which our heart truly desires G-d [and so ignites] a love which is then revealed in the heart. (See *Likutei Torah* on "Song of Songs," regarding the verse, "Behold, you are the most beautiful..." about *rayayoti*.[11]) However, it is possible to explain *reuta d'liba* as the spontaneous will of the heart, rather than as the love which is ignited in the heart as a result of meditation. In the latter case [of meditation], the meditation takes place in the outer garments of the intellect, and it produces love which is commensurate with that level of intellect (as is written in *Torah Ohr, Parshat Tezave*, beginning with *Zachor*....)

(וּבִכְלָלוּת זֶהוּ צִיּוּר קוֹמָה דִּבְחִינַת מֹחִין לִהְיוֹת שֶׁגַּם הַמִּדּוֹת הֵן כְּמוֹ הַמֹּחִין דְּהַיְנוּ לֹא בִּבְחִינַת מֶרְגָּשׁ וּבִבְחִינַת הִתְפַּעֲלוּת כִּי אִם בִּבְחִינַת אַחֲדוּת וּדְבֵקוּת כו') (וּבְסֵפֶר שֶׁל בֵּינוֹנִים פֵּל"ט כ' שֶׁאַהֲבָה זוֹ נִקְרֵאת רְעוּתָא דְלִבָּא. וְעַל פִּי פְּשָׁט הוּא מַה שֶּׁלִּבּוֹ חָפֵץ בֶּאֱמֶת כו' וְהִיא הָאַהֲבָה בְּהִתְגַּלּוּת הַלֵּב כו' וְעַיֵּן מַה שֶּׁכָּתוּב בְּלִקּוּטֵי תּוֹרָה שה"ש בְּדִבּוּר הַמַּתְחִיל הִנָּךְ יָפָה בְּעִנְיַן רַעֲיָתִי. אָמְנָם יֵשׁ לוֹמַר דִּפֵּי רְעוּתָא דְלִבָּא הוּא מַה שֶּׁהַלֵּב חָפֵץ מִמֵּילָא וְלֹא הָאַהֲבָה הָעֲשׂוּיָה בַּלֵּב עַל יְדֵי הַהִתְבּוֹנְנוּת בִּבְחִינַת חִיצוֹנִיּוּת הַמֹּחִין שֶׁזֶּהוּ הָאַהֲבָה שֶׁעַל פִּי טַעַם וָדַעַת כו' וּכְמוֹ שֶׁכָּתוּב בְּדִבּוּר הַמַּתְחִיל זְכֹר בְּתוֹרָה אוֹר פ' תְּצַוֶּה).

In neshama meditation, the emotions cleave to the mind. They are not felt as excitement, but as rapture and awe.

--- **COMMENTARY** ---

consciousness." Why "intellect consciousness?" Because at this point, the intellect is dominant. Although emotions are aroused as a result of "intellect consciousness," they are not the same as the natural love and fear that were present in the heart at the lower level of *ruach*. Here, the spiritual experience is so powerful that the resulting emotions are lifted up to the level of the intellect itself. In fact, we don't even feel the emotions, as they are nullified and "caught up" within the intellectual experience. We know this is happening in our meditation when we lose contact with the physical world. We are so enraptured with the spiritual essence of our experience that we don't know what is going on around us.

Sometimes we need meditation on the outer "garments" in order to reach the inner soul.

וְהִנֵּה נִת' דְהָעֲבוֹדָה בִּבְחִינַת פְּנִימִיּוּת הַמֹּחִין דְהַיְינוּ הַהִתְבּוֹנְנוּת בְּעֶצֶם הָעִנְיָן הָאֱלֹקִי הִיא בְּחִינַת נְשָׁמָה. אָמְנָם יֵשׁ בָּזֶה חִלּוּקֵי מַדְרֵגוֹת, דְּכַאֲשֶׁר הַהַשָּׂגָה בְּעֶצֶם הָעִנְיָן הָאֱלֹקִי בָּא לְאַחַר הַהַשָּׂגָה תְּחִלָּה בִּלְבוּשֵׁי הַשָּׂגָה, דְהַיְינוּ שֶׁאֵין בִּיכָלְתּוֹ לִתְפֹּס וּלְהַשִּׂיג אֵיזֶה עִנְיָן אֱלֹקִי כְּמוֹ שֶׁהוּא בְּעֶצֶם, כִּי אִם כַּאֲשֶׁר מִתְלַבֵּשׁ תְּחִלָּה בִּלְבוּשֵׁי הַשָּׂגָה דְהַיְינוּ שֶׁבָּא הָעִנְיָן אֱלֹקִי בְּעִנְיָנִים הַמְצַיְּרִים אוֹתוֹ בִּדְבָרִים הַמֻּשָּׂגִים (כְּמוֹ בְּחִינַת זְעֵיר אַנְפִּין בְּעִנְיָן הַמִּדּוֹת וּבְחִינַת חָכְמָה וּבִינָה בְּעִנְיָן יְדִיעָה וְהַשָּׂגָה וּבְחִינַת מְמַלֵּא כָּל עָלְמִין כְּמוֹ הַנְּשָׁמָה שֶׁמְמַלְאָה אֶת הַגּוּף וְסוֹבֵב כָּל עָלְמִין בִּבְחִינַת רָצוֹן וִידִיעָה כְּלָלִית כו' וּכְהַאי גַּוְנָא) וּבְעִנְיָנִים הַמְבָאֲרִים אֶת הַדָּבָר הַמֻּשָּׂג (כְּמוֹ מְצִיאוּת עִנְיַן הַמִּדּוֹת וְעִנְיַן הַיְדִיעָה וְכוּ')

We have explained that the *avoda* of "pure intellect" (*pni'miyut hamochin*), involving meditation on the spiritual essence of G-d, constitutes the level of *neshama*. Within this level, several approaches exist. One may arrive at the "soul" (*neshama*) of the concept only after a lengthy meditation on its outer garments. This approach can be used when it is beyond our ability to directly grasp the inherent G-dliness of the concept, without first en-clothing it in outer garments. We are capable of grasping the inner spiritual "kernel" only when it comes "packaged" in images and examples that we understand. (For example, when we want to understand the Kabbalistic concept of *zeir anpin*,[12] we associate it with emotions that we feel, and we describe *chochma* and *bina*[13] as "intellect" and "understanding." [To explain] *memalle kol olamim*,[14] or "immanent G-dliness," we use the simile: "as the soul permeates the body." [To explain] *sovav kol olamim*,[15] or "transcendent G-dliness," we use the example of will, or general knowledge, and so forth...)

COMMENTARY

In prayer, we experience "intellect consciousness" from *Barchu* through the reading of *Shema*. This section of prayer speaks of higher spiritual creations which we can only comprehend through our intellects. The effort to appreciate that there are higher levels of creation makes an "impression from the inside" on us. If these very high spiritual creations are nullified before the One Above and would not do anything without His consent, all the more so that we, with our limited minds and intellects, must be nullified before Him.

Essay on Service of the Heart - Love Like Fire and Water

The "packaging" enables us to understand the G-dly concept with all its details. For, it is impossible to grasp the concept without its details. This understanding comes as a result of the explanations and analogies, through which the concept becomes clear. Afterward [upon achieving intellectual understanding], we must negate, abstract and strip away all of the packaging, through which we initially understood the concept, in order to penetrate to the spiritual essence. In this way, we arrive at the essence of the G-dly concept to whatever extent we are able to grasp it, using the "tools" mentioned above. We remove the concept from its physical shrouds (the image which enabled us to comprehend it). We then come to understand that this is a G-dly concept, whose essence cannot be depicted by the image that we had formerly evoked. After we realize that, in general, G-dliness is beyond anything that we can grasp, we can come to understand the concept in G-dly terms.

שֶׁבָּהֶם מֵבִין וּמַשִּׂיג אֶת הָעִנְיָן הָאֱלֹקִי אֵיךְ וּמַה הוּא, וּבִפְרָטֵי הָעִנְיָנִים שֶׁבּוֹ, דְּאִי אֶפְשָׁר לִהְיוֹת הַשָּׂגַת דָּבָר מִבְּלִי שֶׁיְּפָרֵט אוֹתוֹ לִפְרָטִים שֶׁהֵמָּה מְבָאֲרִים אֶת הָעִנְיָן, וְכָל זֶה בָּא בְּהֶסְבֵּרִים וְגַם בִּמְשָׁלִים שֶׁבָּהֶם וְעַל יָדָם מֵבִין וּמַשִּׂיג אֶת הָעִנְיָן הֵיטֵב, וְאַחַר כָּךְ שׁוֹלֵל וּמַפְשִׁיט וּמֵנִיחַ אֶת הָעִנְיָנִים שֶׁבָּהֶם הוּא מַשִּׂיג אֶת הָעִנְיָן וּבָא אֶל עֶצֶם הַדָּבָר הַמְּשָׁג אֵיךְ שֶׁהוּא מֵבִין אוֹתוֹ מִכָּל הָעִנְיָנִים הַנַּ"ל, וְהַיְנוּ שֶׁבָּא אֶל עֶצֶם הָעִנְיָן הַמֻּשָּׂג אֵיךְ וּמַה הוּא וּמַפְשִׁיט אוֹתוֹ מִגַּשְׁמִיּוּתוֹ (הַיְנוּ מֵהַצִּיּוּר הַמֻּשָּׂג) שֶׁהֲרֵי זֶהוּ עִנְיַן אֱלֹקִי שֶׁאֵינוֹ כְּלָל בְּאֹפֶן וְצִיּוּר כָּזֶה בְּעֶצֶם הַמַּהוּת, וְאַחֲרֵי הַיְדִיעָה אֵיךְ שֶׁבִּכְלָל הָאֱלֹקוּת מֻשְׁלָל מֵעִנְיָנִים הַמֻּשָּׂגִים לָנוּ, יְצַיֵּר הָעִנְיָן הַמֻּשָּׂג אֵיךְ שֶׁהוּא בֶּאֱלֹקוּת.

Afterward, we must negate, abstract and strip away the "garments," in order to penetrate to the spiritual essence of the concept.

COMMENTARY

The soul-level of "intellect consciousness" corresponds to the World of *Bria* ("World of Creation"). This world was the first to be created in which there is awareness of the "self," as opposed to the higher worlds in which there is only awareness of the One Above. The subjective experience of the World of *Bria* is not one of direct contact with the One Above; rather, we feel that we have some existence, or at least possibility of existence as an entity separate from the One Above. But, *Bria* is still close enough to the One Above that we cannot feel ourselves to be entirely independent. We are very much aware of the One Above,

We must always remember that we're involved in a G-dly process, not an intellectual exercise.

(וְגַם בָּעֲבוֹדָה בִּבְחִינַת חִיצוֹנִיּוּת הַמֹּחִין צָרִיךְ לִהְיוֹת הֶרְגֵּשׁ זֶה שֶׁהַהִתְעַסְּקוּת שֶׁלּוֹ הוּא בְּעִנְיָן אֱלֹקִי הַיְנוּ שֶׁמֵּבִין וּמַשִּׂיג עִנְיָן אֱלֹקִי, וְלֹא כְּמוֹ בְּלִמּוּד שֶׁהוּא טָרוּד בְּהַשְׂכִּיל רַק לְהָבִין אֶת הָעִנְיָן וּלְהַשִּׂיגוֹ. וּבְהִתְבּוֹנְנוּת הִנֵּה עִם הִשְׁתַּדְּלוּתוֹ לְהָבִין אֶת הָעִנְיָן הֵיטֵב שֶׁיּוּנָח בְּמוֹחוֹ בְּהַנָּחָה טוֹבָה יְהִי' אֶצְלוֹ הַרְגָּשָׁה זוֹ תָּמִיד (הַרְגָּשָׁה קְרוֹבָה בְּמוֹחוֹ) שֶׁהִתְעַסְּקוּתוֹ הוּא בְּעִנְיָן אֱלֹקִי, וּמִכָּל מָקוֹם אֵין לוֹ מֻשָּׂג עֲדַיִן כְּלָל בְּעֶצֶם עִנְיָן הָאֱלֹקִי אֵיךְ שֶׁהוּא רַק כְּמוֹ שֶׁהוּא בִּלְבוּשֵׁי הַשָּׂגָה שֶׁזֹּאת הִיא הַשָּׂגָתוֹ וַעֲבוֹדָתוֹ וּכְמוֹ שֶׁנִּתְבָּאֵר לְעֵיל שֶׁזּוֹ הִיא עֲבוֹדָה שֶׁבַּלֵּב וְשֶׁהִיא מִדַּת כָּל אָדָם כו', וּמַה שֶּׁנִּת' כָּאן הוּא שֶׁמִּתּוֹךְ הַהַשָּׂגָה הִנֵּה עַל יְדֵי הַהַפְשָׁטָה וְהַשְּׁלִילָה בָּא אֶל הַמֻּשָּׂג בְּעֶצֶם הָעִנְיָן הָאֱלֹקִי אֵיךְ וּמַה הוּא. וְזֶה מוּבָן שֶׁאֵין הַכַּוָּנָה כָּאן עַל עִנְיָן יְדִיעַת הַשְּׁלִילָה הַמְבֹאָר בְּמָקוֹם אַחֵר).

When the approach of the outer garments is used, there must be a feeling that, as we are meditating, we are involved in a G-dly process. That is, we are delving into a G-dly matter, [which cannot be compared with] something that we seek to learn intellectually. Even as we strive to grasp the concept with our minds in such a way that we understand it well and are able to internalize it, we must never lose the feeling (in our consciousness) that the concept is a G-dly one, and that we have no real understanding of the essential G-dliness, except through the intellectual garments that correspond to our own *avoda* of the One Above.

This, as we mentioned before, constitutes the "service of the heart," and it is demanded of every Jew. What is being established here is that intellect — through a process of negation and abstraction — leads us to comprehend the G-dliness at the very core of the concept. We gain an awareness of just what it is and how it exists. (It is understood that this is not referring [to the *avoda* of G-d that is called] *yediat hashlila* [circumscribed knowledge couched in negative terms, since positive terms are inapplicable when describing G-d, as explained by the Rambam].)[16]

———— **COMMENTARY** ————

and therefore the Chassidic masters described *Bria* as the world of "possibility of existence." [Other things corresponding to "intellect consciousness" include the first *hey* of the four-letter Name of G-d, the *sephira* of *bina* ("understanding"), and the animal kingdom within creation (animals move, and the intellect also moves us from one plane of comprehension to the next).]

Essay on Service of the Heart - Love Like Fire and Water

After all this — wherein by way of intellect we strip away the garments and arrive at the essential G-dlliness of the concept at the level known as *neshama* — the essence of the G-dly light still doesn't shine in a fully revealed manner. Since we came to the G-dly "kernel" of the concept only by way of the outer garments of the intellect, even when we have succeeded in stripping them away, they are never completely gone. We find the concept still clad in a thin, refined intellectual garment. Even after we have negated the image with which we grasped the concept, our understanding remains tainted with a residue of our own imagination. (In truth, it is not within human power to hold onto a G-dly concept without some kind of garment.) For this reason, even though our intellectual grasp is of the inner essence of the concept (*p'nimiyut hamochin*), nevertheless, it has a connection to the emotions [as opposed to pure intellect, which has no connection whatsoever to the emotions]. (That is, our meditation is still "tainted" by some sense of emotional excitement, even if only a little. It is not to the same extent as when we were meditating on the outer garments of the intellect, but nonetheless, we still have not left the realm of excitement and feeling behind.)

The same is true of the emotions. Although they arise spontaneously, this is not because the G-dly light illuminates the heart as it does the mind, but because the heart feels the light and revelation that is in the mind

וְאַחַר כָּל זֹאת מֵאַחַר שֶׁעַל יְדֵי הַהַשָּׂגָה בִּבְחִינַת הִתְלַבְּשׁוּת בָּא אֶל עֶצֶם עִנְיָן הָאֱלֹקִי הִנֵּה עִם הֱיוֹת שֶׁזֶּהוּ בְּדַרְגּוֹת דְּמַדְרֵגַת נְשָׁמָה, מִכָּל מָקוֹם אֵינוֹ מֵאִיר בָּזֶה עֶצֶם הָאוֹר בְּגִלּוּי מַמָּשׁ, דְּלְפִי שֶׁבָּא לָזֶה עַל יְדֵי לְבוּשֵׁי הַהַשָּׂגָה הִנֵּה גַם כְּשֶׁמַּפְשִׁיט אוֹתוֹ מִפְשַׁט לְגַמְרֵי וְהוּא מְלֻבָּשׁ עֲדַיִן בִּלְבוּשׁ דַּק מִלְּבוּשֵׁי הַשָּׂגָה. וְהַיְנוּ שֶׁגַּם לְאַחַר הַהַפְשָׁטָה וְהַשְּׁלִילָה מֵהַצִּיּוּר הַמֻּשָּׂג הוּא מִכָּל מָקוֹם מַשִּׂיג וּמַרְגִּישׁ אֶת הָעִנְיָן בַּאֲחִיזָה קְצָת בַּהַצִּיּוּר הַמֻּשָּׂג (כִּי בֶּאֱמֶת אֵין בִּיכָלְתּוֹ לִתְפֹּס וּלְהַשִּׂיג עִנְיָן אֱלֹקִי בְּלִי שׁוּם לְבוּשׁ) וְעַל כֵּן גַּם הַשָּׂגָה זוֹ הֲגַם שֶׁהִיא בְּמַדְרֵגַת פְּנִימִיּוּת הַמּוֹחִין יֵשׁ לָהּ שַׁיָּכוּת אֶל הַמִּדּוֹת (הַיְנוּ אֶל חוּשׁ הַמִּדּוֹת בִּבְחִינַת הִתְפַּעֲלוּת וּמַרְגָּשׁ קְצָת, וְלֹא כָּל כָּךְ כְּמוֹ בִּבְחִינַת חִיצוֹנִיּוּת הַמּוֹחִין אֲבָל מִכָּל מָקוֹם אֵינוֹ יוֹצֵא עֲדַיִן מִבְּחִינַת הִתְפַּעֲלוּת וּמַרְגָּשׁ).

With the approach of the "garments," the essence of the G-dly light still does not illuminate fully.

וְכֵן בְּעִנְיָן הַמִּדּוֹת עִם הֱיוֹת דְּהִתְפַּעֲלוּת הַמִּדּוֹת בָּאִים בִּבְחִינַת מִמֵּילָא מִכָּל מָקוֹם אֵין זֶה שֶׁהָאוֹר מֵאִיר בַּלֵּב כְּמוֹ בַּמֹּחַ כִּי אִם מַה שֶׁהַלֵּב מַרְגִּישׁ אֶת הָאוֹר וְהַגִּלּוּי שֶׁבַּמֹּחַ וְנִמְשָׁךְ אַחַר הַמֹּחַ כו',

וּמִמֵּילָא הַמִּדּוֹת אֵינָם בִּבְחִינַת גַּדְלוּת מַמָּשׁ לִהְיוֹת בִּבְחִינַת דְּבֵקוּת מַמָּשׁ אַחַר שֶׁאֵינוֹ מֵאִיר בָּהֶם הָאוֹר מַמָּשׁ רַק מַה שֶּׁנִּרְגָּשׁ כוּ' הֲרֵי הוּא בִּבְחִינַת הִתְפַּעֲלוּת קְצָת וְרַק שֶׁמִּשְׁתַּוִּים קְצָת אֶל בְּחִינַת הַמֹּחִין כוּ' (רְצוֹנוֹ לוֹמַר אֶל אֲמִתִּית בְּחִינַת הַמֹּחִין שֶׁיִּתְבָּאֵר בְּסָמוּךְ). וְיֵשׁ לוֹמַר שֶׁזֶּהוּ מַדְרֵגַת רוּחַ הָעוֹלָה וְנִכְלָל בְּמַדְרֵגַת נְשָׁמָה הַיְנוּ שֶׁמַּדְרֵגַת הָרוּחַ מִשְׁתַּוָּה קְצָת אֶל מַדְרֵגַת הַנְּשָׁמָה כוּ'.

and is drawn to it. As a result, the emotions are not truly "mature" in a spiritual sense and don't cleave strictly to the One Above, since the G-dly light isn't shining directly into them from above. It is only that the emotions respond to the G-dly light [as something separate that they are drawn toward] and become excited. [As this happens], the emotions rise to the level of the intellect (that is, to the true dimension of intellect, which will be explained shortly). It is possible that this is the level described as *ruach*, as it ascends to and is included in the level of the *neshama*, in which case the *ruach* becomes equal, in a way, to the *neshama*.

On the true level of neshama, we sense G-dliness. We grasp a G-dly concept in its essence, without need of intellectual garments.

אָמְנָם מִי שֶׁהוּא בְּמַדְרֵגַת נְשָׁמָה הוּא יֵשׁ לוֹ בְּעֶצֶם חוּשׁ בֶּאֱלֹקוּת וְתוֹפֵס וּמַשִּׂיג עִנְיָן אֱלֹקִי כְּמוֹ שֶׁהוּא בְּעֶצֶם לֹא עַל יְדֵי לְבוּשֵׁי הַשָּׂגָה

However, when we are [truly] on the level of *neshama*, we are able to sense G-dliness. We grasp a G-dly concept in its essence, without need of intellectual garments [to clothe and describe it].

(וּבְחִינָה זוֹ הִיא גַּם כֵּן כְּמוֹ שֶׁהָאוֹר הָאֱלֹקִי יָרַד לְהָאִיר בִּבְחִינַת צִמְצוּם כְּדֵי שֶׁיּוּכְלוּ שְׂכָלִים נִבְרָאִים לְקַבֵּל מֵהֶם חָכְמָה בִּינָה וָדַעַת לֵידַע אֶת ה' וּלְהָבִין וּלְהַשִּׂיג כוּ' כְּמוֹ שֶׁכָּתוּב בְּסֵפֶר שֶׁל בֵּינוֹנִים פְּל"ט, וּמִכָּל מָקוֹם הִיא הַיְדִיעָה וְהַהַשָּׂגָה בְּעֶצֶם הָעִנְיָן כוּ')

(This level is also associated with the G-dly light that descends to illuminate creation after contracting, in order to allow mortal minds to receive it — with their wisdom, understanding, and knowledge [*chochma, bina,* and *da'at*, i.e., *chabad*]. They are enabled to know and understand G-dliness, as is written in Tanya, chapter 39, and their knowledge and understanding is of the essence of the G-dly concept.)

וּמֵאִיר אֶצְלוֹ הָאוֹר הָאֱלֹקִי בְּגִלּוּי מַמָּשׁ בְּמוֹחוֹ בְּאֹפֶן שֶׁהוּא לְמַעְלָה מִבְּחִינַת הַמִּדּוֹת מִצַּד הָאוֹר וְהַגִּלּוּי שֶׁבַּוָּה כוּ', וְהָאוֹר מֵאִיר בַּלֵּב גַּם כֵּן

[When we are able to grasp G-dliness without garments], the G-dly light is completely revealed in our mind in a way that is above and

Essay on Service of the Heart - Love Like Fire and Water

beyond emotions, due to the spiritual illumination within us. The G-dly light shines into and permeates our hearts as well, and arouses in them a powerful love and desire. This is not a love and desire of excitement and feeling. It is a mighty attraction to the One Above. It is an expression of spiritually "mature emotions" that rise to equivalence with [and are possibly transformed into] the intellect. Even though, in general, the nullification associated with the Worlds of *Asiya*, *Yetzira*, and *Bria* is ego-nullification alone, the type of nullification associated with the soul-level of *neshama* is one that results in total unity, rather than emotional excitement.

וּמִתְעוֹרֵר גַּם בְּלִבּוֹ בְּאַהֲבָה וּתְשׁוּקָה נִפְלָאָה אֲבָל אֵין זֶה בִּבְחִינַת הִתְפַּעֲלוּת וּבְמֻרְגָּשׁ כִּי אִם מַה שֶּׁנִּמְשָׁךְ וְנִדְבַּק מְאֹד בֶּאֱלֹקוּת כוּ' וְהוּא בְּחִינַת גַּדְלוּת הַמִּדּוֹת שֶׁמִּשְׁתַּנִּים אֶל הַמֹּחִין. וְהַבִּטּוּל בָּזֶה עִם הֱיוֹת דִּכְלָלוּת הַבִּטּוּל דִּבְרִיאָה יְצִירָה עֲשִׂיָּה הוּא בְּחִינַת בִּטּוּל הַיֵּשׁ לְבַד מִכָּל מָקוֹם הַבִּטּוּל דִּבְחִינַת נְשָׁמָה הוּא בְּחִינַת דְּבֵקוּת וּבִבְחִינַת יִחוּד יוֹתֵר לֹא בִּבְחִינַת הִתְפַּעֲלוּת וּמֻרְגָּשׁ,

This is not the case at the soul-level of *ruach*. Even on the high level mentioned above, *ruach* produces some feeling in the heart, but nothing like the strong excitement associated with meditation on the outer garments of the intellect. It is possible that just as the World of *Bria* does not imply existence but only the possibility of creation,[v] (meaning that it only "makes room" for existence, while the next world down, *Yetzira*, implies actual existence [but not yet physical which comes into being in the World of *Asiya*], as written elsewhere), so also is there a corresponding difference in their levels of nullification. The nullification of the soul-level of *neshama* [corresponding to the World of *Bria*] is not noticeable and conscious. It allows room for the self to be experienced. It isn't total self-nullification. Total abnegation is

מַה שֶּׁאֵין כֵּן בְּחִינַת רוּחַ גַּם בַּמַּדְרֵגָה הָעֶלְיוֹנָה הַנַּ"ל הוּא בִּבְחִינַת מֻרְגָּשׁ קְצָת, וְגַם זֶה לֹא כְּמוֹ בְּהָעֲבוֹדָה בִּבְחִינַת חִיצוֹנִיּוּת הַמֹּחִין שֶׁהוּא בִּבְחִינַת רַעַשׁ וּמֻרְגָּשׁ מַמָּשׁ כוּ', וְיֵשׁ לוֹמַר דִּכְמוֹ שֶׁעוֹלָם הַבְּרִיאָה אֵינוֹ בִּבְחִינַת יֵשׁ עֲדַיִן כִּי אִם בְּחִינַת אֶפְשָׁרֵי הַמְצִיאוּת דְּהַיְנוּ רַק מַה שֶּׁנּוֹתֵן מָקוֹם לַיֵּשׁ אֲבָל יְצִירָה הוּא בְּחִינַת יֵשׁ כוּ' וּכְמוֹ שֶׁכָּתוּב בְּמָקוֹם אַחֵר, כְּמוֹ כֵן הוּא הַהֶפְרֵשׁ בְּהַבִּטּוּל שֶׁלָּהֶם דְּהַבִּטּוּל דִּנְשָׁמָה הוּא לֹא בִּבְחִינַת יֵשׁ וּמֻרְגָּשׁ רַק שֶׁנּוֹתֵן מָקוֹם לַיֵּשׁ בָּזֶה שֶׁאֵינוֹ בִּבְחִינַת בָּטוּל בִּמְצִיאוּת מַמָּשׁ כְּמוֹ בִּבְחִינַת יִחוּדָא עִילָּאָה, וְהַבִּטּוּל דִּבְחִינַת רוּחַ הוּא בִּבְחִינַת יֵשׁ וּמֻרְגָּשׁ (וְזֶהוּ עִנְיַן בִּטּוּל הַיֵּשׁ דְּיֵשׁ הַמִּתְבַּטֵּל הוּא בְּרַעַשׁ וְהִתְפַּעֲלוּת

This is not the case with ruach. Even on the high level, ruach produces some feeling in the heart.

v) See footnote of the Rebbe on page 263 ←

וּכְמוֹ עֵצִים הַנִּשְׂרָפִין שֶׁהֵן בְּרַעַשׁ, וְגַם בְּהַבִּטּוּל שֶׁלּוֹ הוּא בִּבְחִינַת יֵשׁ שֶׁזֶּהוּ עִנְיַן הַמַּרְגָּשׁ כו', וְהַכֹּל עִנְיָן א').

associated with "supernal/ higher unity" (*yichuda ila'ah*), [when we realize that there is none other than G-d, and therefore all experience of self is lost]. However, the nullification associated with the soul-level of *ruach* involves consciousness of our self and our emotions; this is nullification of the ego [not the self]. When the ego becomes nullified, it is with noise and excitement, as when wood burns, making noise. Even during the process of its own nullification, it experiences itself [becoming nullified], which is the same as feeling oneself.

The purpose of ruach meditation is to arouse the emotions of the heart, but this does not contradict the use of intellect.

(בְּמָקוֹם אַחֵר מְבֹאָר דִּפְסוּקֵי דְזִמְרָה הוּא הַהִלּוּלִים וְתִשְׁבָּחוֹת מֵעִנְיָנִים שֶׁהֵן לְמַעְלָה מֵהַשָּׂגָה וּכְמוֹ הַמְהַלֵּל וּמְשַׁבֵּחַ אֶת הַמֶּלֶךְ בְּעֶצֶם גְּדֻלָּתוֹ שֶׁאֵין לוֹ שׁוּם הַשָּׂגָה בִּגְדֻלַּת וְרוֹמְמוּת הַמֶּלֶךְ כו' וְהוּא הָעוֹשֶׂה בְּחִינַת הַחֲקִיקָה מִבַּחוּץ שֶׁמִּתְרוֹמֵם נַפְשׁוֹ בְּמַדְרֵגָה גְּבוֹהָ וְעֶלְיוֹנָה יוֹתֵר כו', וְאֵין זֶה סוֹתֵר לְמַה שֶּׁנִּתְבָּאֵר לְעֵיל דְּרוּחַ הוּא בְּחִינַת הָאַהֲבָה שֶׁעַל פִּי טַעַם וָדַעַת שֶׁבְּהִתְגַּלּוּת הַלֵּב, כִּי יֵשׁ כַּמָּה מַדְרֵגוֹת בִּבְחִינַת רוּחַ, וְגַם בָּעִנְיָן הַנַּ"ל אֵין הַכַּוָּנָה שֶׁזֶּהוּ בְּלִי הַשָּׂגָה וְהִתְבּוֹנְנוּת כְּלָל, כִּי אִם שֶׁהָעִנְיָנִים הַמְבֹאָרִים בִּפְסוּקֵי דְזִמְרָה דִּכְלָלוּת עִנְיָנָם הוּא עִנְיַן בְּרִיאָה יֵשׁ מֵאַיִן דְּעֶצֶם וְגוּף הָעִנְיָן הַזֶּה הוּא לְמַעְלָה מֵהַשָּׂגַת הַנִּבְרָאִים גַּם לֹא בִּבְחִינַת יְדִיעַת הַמְּצִיאוּת כו', אֲבָל מִכָּל מָקוֹם הֲרֵי יֵשׁ בָּזֶה כַּמָּה הַשָּׂגוֹת וּבִפְרָט בְּהָאוֹר וְחַיּוּת אֱלֹקִי שֶׁבָּא בִּבְחִינַת הִתְלַבְּשׁוּת לְהַחֲיוֹת הָעוֹלָמוֹת דְּבָזֶה הוּא הָעֲבוֹדָה

(Elsewhere, it is explained that the *P'sukei D'zimra*,[17] "Verses of Praise" [appearing in prayer after *Baruch She'amar* and corresponding to the second soul-level, *ruach*], consist of exaltations of matters beyond intellect. This is like the person who praises a king in his majesty, even though this person has no grasp of the king's true greatness. Nevertheless, the sheer act of praying on this level creates an "impression from outside" on the person praying which uplifts and elevates his soul to a higher level. This does not contradict what was explained earlier that *ruach* corresponds to a love of the One Above based upon intellectual meditation revealed in the heart. There are several approaches to the soul-level of *ruach*, and even the approach described above [that *ruach* is based upon meditation on subjects beyond intellect] doesn't imply that the meditation of the *P'sukei D'zimra* is completely beyond intellectual activity. Rather, the general topic of meditation associated with *P'sukei D'zimra* is creation

Essay on Service of the Heart - Love Like Fire and Water

ex-nihilo (something "from nothing"), a concept that in essence is beyond the ability of mortal men to grasp.

דְּלְאַהֲבָה אֶת ה' אֱלֹקֶיךָ כִּי הוּא חַיֶּיךָ כו').

Even awareness of the existence of this process is beyond us. Nonetheless, within the process are to be found several ideas, in particular those concerning the G-dly light and energy that en-clothe themselves in creation in order to enliven it. This is the *avoda* of "coming to love the Lord your G-d because He is your life..."[18]

The soul-level of *neshama* is the intermediary level, leading to the *avoda* of the One Above from the essence of the soul, beyond intellect. [This refers to the G-dly core of the soul-level of *neshama*, as is written, "And put in our hearts *bina* to understand." [*Bina* means "understanding," so the implication of the verse is that one must be involved in a process of greater and greater understanding. That is, we request from

וְהִנֵּה בְּחִינַת נְשָׁמָה הוּא מְמֻצָּע לָבוֹא לַעֲבוֹדַת עֶצֶם הַנְּשָׁמָה שֶׁלְמַעְ' מִטַּעַם וְדַעַת שֶׁזֶּהוּ בְּחִינַת הָאֱלוֹקוּת דִּנְשָׁמָה וּכְמוֹ שֶׁאָנוּ אוֹמְרִים וְתֵן בְּלִבֵּנוּ בִּינָה לְהָבִין דְּהַיְנוּ לְהָבִין דָּבָר מִתּוֹךְ דָּבָר, דְּתוֹךְ דָּבָר הוּא בְּחִינַת מְמַלֵּא כָּל עָלְמִין וְדָבָר הוּא בְּחִינַת סוֹבֵב כָּל עָלְמִין.

The soul-level of neshama leads to the essence of the soul, beyond intellect.

the One Above to enable us to undergo a process of understanding one concept from within another. In Hebrew, this is called *lehavin davar, mitoch davar* — "to understand the concept within the concept" — and refers to how we come to understand one idea after having delved deeply into another idea]. The word *mitoch* ("from within") alludes to immanent G-dliness [how He permeates the universe and enlivens it on various spiritual levels], while *davar* — that is, the idea under consideration — alludes to transcendent G-dliness [how He transcends the universe and is essentially beyond it; in other words, when delving deeply into and meditating upon immanent spirituality, we request that the One Above enable us to grasp transcendent G-dliness].

--- **COMMENTARY** ---

4. CHAYA

We have thus far examined the soul levels en-clothed in the body, those associated with our actions, emotions, and intellect. We will now take up the levels of the soul which are beyond the body, and beyond the normal perception of the human being. The first of these we'll call "transcendent consciousness," because

Neshama meditation ultimately leads to yediat hashlila and to meditation upon transcendent G-dliness.

וְעַל יְדֵי הַהַשָּׂגָה וְהַהִתְבּוֹנְנוּת דִּבְחִינַת נְשָׁמָה בִּבְחִינַת מְמַלֵּא כָּל עָלְמִין עַל יְדֵי זֶה בָּא לִבְחִינַת סוֹבֵב כָּל עָלְמִין דְּהַיְנוּ הַיְדִיעָה וְהַהַשָּׂגָה בִּבְחִינַת הַפְלָאַת וְרוֹמְמוּת אֵין סוֹף בָּרוּךְ הוּא, אֵיךְ שֶׁהוּא מֻפְלָא וּמְרוֹמָם מֵהָעוֹלָמוֹת, וּבִידִיעַת עֶצֶם הָאוֹר אֵין סוֹף הַמֻּפְלָא, וְהוּא עִנְיַן יְדִיעַת הַשְּׁלִילָה וְהַכָּרַת הַהַפְלָאָה וּבְחִינַת הַהִתְאַמְּתוּת דִּרְאִיַּת עֵין הַשֵּׂכֶל

Meditating on the level of *neshama*, or immanent G-dliness, we ultimately arrive at the level of transcendent G-dliness. This entails understanding of the grandeur of the Infinite One as He transcends creation and knowledge of the essence of His infinite transcendent light. It involves the process of circumscription [literally, negation of knowledge – *yediat hashlila* – in which whatever understanding we gain of G-dliness, we circumscribe and describe G-d as necessarily beyond it]; it also involves recognition of His amazing splendor [*hakarat hahafla*],19 and confirmation of His existence by way of seeing Him in the mind's eye [*hit'amtut d'reiyat eyn hasechel*].20

COMMENTARY

it accesses realms of transcendent spirituality that are beyond the scope of the soul as it is en-clothed in the body.

After we have achieved the third soul-level of "intellect consciousness," in which we have penetrated to the very core of G-dly energy that enlivens the creation, we must continue our intellectual pursuit. Because, the truth is that the G-dly energy enlivening the creation has its own spiritual source beyond the creation. Thus if we achieve "intellect consciousness," we have accessed the spiritual energy within the creation, known in the Chassidic texts as *ohr memalle*, or inner, immanent light.

However, even if we have succeeded in doing this, we still have not arrived at the *source of ohr memalle* — this source is the transcendent light of G-dliness called *ohr makif* which exists beyond the universe, beyond the creation. To get to this point is to realize the soul level of "transcendent consciousness" called in Hebrew *chaya* ("living one"). This demands a special technique within Jewish meditation, called by the Rambam (Maimonides) "circumscription [literally, negation] of knowledge," and by the Chassidim "understanding one thing from within another."

Essay on Service of the Heart - Love Like Fire and Water

(This knowledge is beyond intellectual grasp. Its true character is only understood by lofty souls of the World of *Atzilut* [the World of Emanation] and *Chabad* of *Atzilut*, which is far beyond the intellect of any created being, as stated in *Tanya*. Within each individual soul, it is the essence of the soul, the G-dliness within it, which is beyond the grasp of the intellect.)

(וִידִיעָה זֹאת הִיא לְמַעְלָה מִבְּחִינַת שֵׂכֶל הַמַּשִּׂיג. וַאֲמִתַּת הַיְדִיעָה הַזֹּאת הִיא רַק בִּנְשָׁמוֹת דַּאֲצִילוּת וְהֵן בְּחִינַת חָכְמָה בִּינָה וְדַעַת דַּאֲצִילוּת שֶׁלְּמַעְלָה מִשֵּׂכֶל הַנִּבְרָאִים וּכְמוֹ שֶׁכָּתוּב בְּסֵפֶר שֶׁל בֵּינוֹנִים שָׁם. וּבְכָל נְשָׁמָה הוּא בְּעֶצֶם הַנְּשָׁמָה שֶׁהוּא בְּחִינַת הָאֱלֹקוּת שֶׁבַּנְּשָׁמָה שֶׁלְּמַעְלָה מִבְּחִינַת שֵׂכֶל מַשִּׂיג כו')

This knowledge is only grasped by lofty souls of the world of Atzilut.

COMMENTARY

Whatever we know about G-d is necessarily deficient. Whatever we can say about Him, and however we understand Him, we cannot know Him as He truly is. Therefore, even the deep awareness and understanding associated with "intellect consciousness" gives us no clue as to how He exists beyond creation. For that, we need to use our understanding of Him (as He is manifest in creation) as a "springboard" to a different realm. We need to circumscribe our knowledge of Him as we know Him from within creation and attempt to reach Him as He exists beyond creation. We do this by negating the spiritual light shining in our minds as a result of *ohr memalle*. This has the effect of giving us a "lift" to the higher level of illumination associated with *ohr makif*, or G-dliness as it transcends creation. It is understood that we don't reject the reality of the initial revelation of immanent light; it is just that we admit it cannot be the whole truth of His existence, and that we, therefore, demand some perception of G-d, as He exists on a transcendent level.

The awareness of "transcendent consciousness" does not come as a clear and precise revelation, as does "intellect consciousness." We are accessing levels that are beyond the senses. Whatever is revealed is amazing and beyond ordinary expression. Nevertheless, some awareness and understanding of transcendent spirituality beyond creation is part of the perception of G-dliness associated with "transcendent consciousness." Such levels are beyond the grasp of most people aside from the most advanced

וּבְכָל זֶה נַעֲשָׂה בְּחִינַת יִחוּד וּדְבֵקוּת נַפְשׁוֹ בְּעַצְמוּת אוֹר אֵין סוֹף בָּרוּךְ הוּא בִּבְחִינַת בִּטוּל בִּמְצִיאוּת מַמָּשׁ, וְהוּא עִנְיָן וְרֹאשׁוֹ מַגִּיעַ הַשָּׁמַיְמָה בְּהִשְׁתַּחֲוָאוֹת דִּשְׁמוֹנֶה

This nullification — which amounts to total abnegation of our very being — brings about a unity of the soul with the essence of the infinite light of G-d (may He be blessed). This then is what is meant by "...and

―――――― *COMMENTARY* ――――――

"servants of G-d" (*ovdei HaShem*) — the most accomplished meditators and devotees of the pursuit of truth. However, every Jew can become a "servant of G-d."

"Transcendent consciousness" during prayer is associated with the *Amida*, also known as the *Shmoneh Esreh* ("Eighteen Benedictions"), a prayer which is the pinnacle of the morning service. During the *Amida*, we are totally still and quiet, uttering the blessings under our breath, and asking the One Above to open our mouths since we ourselves are so nullified before Him that we don't have the power even to speak. We take three steps back and then three steps forward, facing the direction of the Temple in Jerusalem, feeling ourselves to be in His Presence as we pray. We bow four times during the *Amida*, and it is then that we are likely, according to the Chassidic literature, to experience "transcendent consciousness" and even unity consciousness (of course, this only occurs if we have meditated through the lower soul levels in prayer).

"Transcendent consciousness" is associated with the World of *Atzilut* ("World of Emanations"). On this level, there is no awareness of self, but only of the Holy One Above. Spiritual awareness of G-d on this level is like a ray coming from the sun; the ray is always connected with its source and ceases to exist the moment the source chooses. ["Transcendent consciousness" is also associated with the first letter, the *yud* of G-d's Name, and with the first of the ten *sephirot* — *chochma* ("wisdom") and with the human species within creation.]

5. *YECHIDA*

Finally, we come to the highest soul level — *yechida* ("single one") — which we'll describe as "unity consciousness." A few souls come into this world on such a high level that they are constantly in touch with the transcendent light of G-d even its head reached into the heavens" [regarding the ladder in Jacob's dream, mentioned above]. It occurs when we are [absorbed in the most intense moments of prayer, while] bowing during the *Amida* and is accompanied by a state of total nullification of our existence. At such times, our lower three soul-levels (*nefesh*, *ruach*, and *neshama*) are elevated to

עֶשְׂרֵה בִּבְחִינַת בִּטּוּל בַּמְצִיאוּת מַמָּשׁ כוּ' וְאָז גַּם כְּלָלוּת נֶפֶשׁ רוּחַ וּנְשָׁמָה שֶׁלּוֹ מִתְעַלֶּה שֶׁהֵן בְּמַדְרֵגוֹת נַעֲלוֹת וּמֻפְלָאוֹת בְּיוֹתֵר, כְּמוֹ הַהַשָּׂגָה שֶׁלּוֹ הִיא בְּעִנְיָנִים מֻפְלָאִים יוֹתֵר וְעֶצֶם הַהַשָּׂגָה הִיא עֲמֻקָּה יוֹתֵר וּבְאֹפֶן אַחֵר לְגַמְרֵי (עַר נֶעמט גאָר אַנדערש אַ עִנְיָן אֱלֹקִי)

This is what is meant by "our head reaches the heavens..."

tremendously exalted heights. Our intellect is empowered to grasp astonishing matters, and we are able to penetrate to the very depths and essence of the concept, in a completely different way than before.

(This is similar to what happens to us when, while operating on the level of *neshama*, we immediately grasp the essence of G-dliness without need of the outer garments which "package" it. It is understood that our grasp of the outer garments is also different than at such a time when we need them in order to grasp the concept. Since we immediately know the

(וּכְמוֹ בְּמַדְרֵגַת הַנְּשָׁמָה הַנַּ"ל כְּשֶׁתּוֹפֵס וּמַשִּׂיג אֶת עֶצֶם הָעִנְיָן הָאֱלֹקִי שֶׁלֹּא עַל יְדֵי לְבוּשֵׁי הַשָּׂגָה מִתְּחִלָּה הֲרֵי מוּבָן שֶׁעַל יְדֵי זֶה גַּם הַשָּׂגָתוֹ בִּבְחִינַת חִיצוֹנִיּוּת הָעִנְיָן הוּא בְּאֹפֶן אַחֵר מִזֶּה שֶׁמַּתְחִיל לִתְפֹּס הָעִנְיָן בְּחִיצוֹנִיּוּתוֹ, דִּמֵאַחַר שֶׁיּוֹדֵעַ אֶת עֶצֶם הָעִנְיָן מִמֵּילָא הַשָּׂגָתוֹ בְּהָעִנְיָן הִיא גְּדוֹלָה וַעֲמֻקָּה בְּיוֹתֵר,

---
COMMENTARY
---

when they are born in a physical body. They are called *tzaddikim*. They have no "evil inclination" hiding or concealing spirituality from them. Therefore, they need not meditate on the greatness of the Creator in order to recognize, feel, and understand His presence at all times.

All Jews possess this aspect in their soul, but very few of us realize it at more than the rarest of moments. It is that part of the soul that is always united with the One Above, which is always receiving "messages" from the One Above (but it depends upon our level of refinement and our commitment to the Torah and its *mitzvot* as to whether we consciously receive these messages). This aspect of the soul comes into full expression if and when it is demanded of us that we give up our life in honor of the One Above. For example, if it were to be demanded

כֵּן וְיוֹתֵר מִכֵּן לְאֵין קֵץ בִּידִיעַת אוֹר אֵין סוֹף בָּרוּךְ הוּא הַמֻּפְלָא וּמְרוֹמָם כו', שֶׁגַּם הַהַשָּׂגָה הִיא נַעֲלֵית וְנִפְלָאָה בְּיוֹתֵר כו')

essence of the concept, automatically our overall grasp of the topic is deeper and stronger. If this is true [regarding the level of *neshama*, where we meditate on the immanent light of G-d permeating the creation], then it certainly applies to meditation on the infinite light of G-d as it transcends the creation; whatever intellectual grasp is associated with it is very high and astounding.)

וְכֵן הַמִּדּוֹת הַכֹּל הוּא בְּמַדְרֵגָה גְבוֹהָה וְנַעֲלֵית לְאֵין קֵץ כו'. וְכָל זֹאת הִיא הָעֲבוֹדָה דִתְפִלָּה בִּבְחִינַת הִתְקַשְּׁרוּת וּדְבֵקוּת נַפְשׁוֹ בֵּאלֹקוּת בִּבְחִינַת נֶפֶשׁ רוּחַ וּנְשָׁמָה שֶׁבְּנַפְשׁוֹ וּבִבְחִינַת נִשְׁמָה לִנְשָׁמָה כו').

The above is also true of the emotions. Everything is on an extremely high spiritual level. This is the *avoda* of prayer, which is the uniting of our divine soul (*nefesh*, *ruach*, *neshama*, and *nishmeta d'nishmeta*) with G-dliness.

This is what is meant by "pouring out the soul," meaning an elevation and desire for the infinite light above.

וְזֶהוּ גַּם כֵּן מַה שֶׁהַתְּפִלָּה נִקְרֵאת שְׁפִיכַת הַנֶּפֶשׁ וּכְמוֹ שֶׁכָּתוּב וָאֶשְׁפֹּךְ אֶת נַפְשִׁי לִפְנֵי ה' שֶׁהוּא בְּחִינַת הָעֲלִי' וְהָרָצוֹא לְאוֹר אֵין סוֹף בָּרוּךְ הוּא וּכְמוֹ אֵלֶיךָ ה' נַפְשִׁי אֶשָּׂא (וּלְמַעְלָה הוּא מַה שֶׁהַמַּלְכוּת נִקְרֵאת תְּפִלָּה וּכְמוֹ שֶׁכָּתוּב וַאֲנִי תְפִלָּה וְהוּא בְּחִינַת הָרָצוֹא דְמַלְכוּת דִּלְמַעַן יְזַמֶּרְךָ כָבוֹד כו' נְהוֹרָא תַתָּאָה קָארֵי תָּדִיר לִנְהוֹרָא

This is, as well, what is meant by the description of prayer as "pouring out of the soul," as the verse says [1 Samuel 1:15], "And I'll pour out my soul before G-d..." which indicates an ascent and desire for the infinite light of the One Above. This is also what is indicated by the verse [Psalms 25:1], "To you I will lift up my soul..." (In the abstract, this is why the supernal *sephira* of *malchut* is called "prayer,"

COMMENTARY

that we either bow down before an idol (thereby committing the cardinal sin of idolatry) or be executed, the soul level of "unity consciousness" would dictate that we choose death rather than transgress. That is, our *yechida* would compel us to give up our own life rather than risk spiritual disconnection from the One Above.

However, the subjective experience of "unity consciousness" cannot be achieved by any meditation. That is, unlike the previous soul levels, which we can reach by working on ourselves, the experience of "unity consciousness" is strictly at

Essay on Service of the Heart - Love Like Fire and Water

as it is said [in Psalms 109:4], "I am prayer..." This indicates the longing of *malchut*, the level of "to sing to Your honor..." [The *Zohar* explains that the singing is that of] the "lower illumination" [the soul] crying out to the "higher illumination" [the One Above].) It is also what is referred to as the "fiery flames of desire" and thirst to be included in the essence of the infinite light of the One Above.[21]

עִילָאָה כו') וְהוּא בְּחִינַת רִשְׁפֵּי אֵשׁ הַתְּשׁוּקָה וְהַצִּמָּאוֹן לְהִכָּלֵל בְּעַצְמוּת אוֹר אֵין סוֹף בָּרוּךְ הוּא.

The second aspect of prayer is the purification and refinement of the animal soul. It is in this sense that prayer is offered in lieu of the sacrifices, as is written [Leviticus 1:2], "Man, when offering *from you* a sacrifice," indicating that the sacrifice is that of the animal soul within us.[22] It is possible that this is what is meant by "intention" in prayer, as opposed to the "speech" of prayer. Sometimes it is explained that the most important aspect of prayer is the intention within our heart, while the voice (that is, the speech of prayer) is [only] for the sake of arousing us to greater intention during prayer. On the other hand, it is understood from the say-

וְהָעִנְיָן הַב' בַּתְּפִלָּה הוּא בֵּרוּר וְזִכּוּךְ הַנֶּפֶשׁ הַבַּהֲמִית, שֶׁזֶּהוּ מַה שֶּׁהַתְּפִלָּה הִיא בִּמְקוֹם קָרְבָּן וּכְמוֹ שֶׁכָּתוּב אָדָם כִּי יַקְרִיב מִכֶּם קָרְבָּן כו' דְּהַיְינוּ הַקְרָבַת הַנֶּפֶשׁ הַבַּהֲמִית כַּנּוֹדָע. וְיֵשׁ לוֹמַר שֶׁזֶּהוּ עִנְיַן כַּוָּנַת הַתְּפִלָּה וְהַדִּבּוּר דִּתְפִלָּה, דְּלִפְעָמִים מְבֹאָר דְּעִקַּר הַתְּפִלָּה הוּא כַּוָּנַת הַלֵּב וְהַקּוֹל (וְהוּא הַדִּבּוּר דִּתְפִלָּה) הוּא לְעוֹרֵר אֶת הַכַּוָּנָה וּכְמוֹ שֶׁאָמְרוּ רַבּוֹתֵינוּ זִכְרוֹנָם לִבְרָכָה סַנְדַּ"ל קוֹשֵׁר כְּתָרִים לְקוֹנוֹ מִתְּפִלּוֹתֵיהֶן שֶׁל יִשְׂרָאֵל וּמְבֹאָר בְּמָקוֹם אַחֵר שֶׁזֶּהוּ מֵהָאוֹתִיּוֹת דִּתְפִלָּה, מַשְׁמַע מִזֶּה דְּהָעִקָּר הוּא הַדִּבּוּר דִּתְפִלָּה. וְיֵשׁ לוֹמַר עַל פִּי

The second aspect of prayer is the purification and refinement of the animal soul.

COMMENTARY

the discretion of the One Above. We can refine ourselves, meditating, learning Torah, and fulfilling its *mitzvot*; and if the One Above decides that we are ready, then He may grant us the gift of "unity consciousness."

Yechida is too high to be associated with any world. The Hebrew word for "world" — *olam* — implies hiddenness and concealment. Any world, spiritual or physical, conceals G-dliness to a greater or lesser degree. But, the soul level of "unity consciousness" breaches no hiddenness, and therefore transcends the worlds. Likewise, it is beyond prayer, associated

ing of the Sages that the angel *Sandal*[23] makes crowns for the Creator from the prayers of the Jewish people, that it is the letters and speech of the prayers which are important (as explained elsewhere).[vi] The conclusion is that our intention is the important aspect of prayer, when considering the G-dly soul and its elevation. But when considering the animal soul within us, which needs refining and purification, it is the speech of prayer which is more important.

הנ"ל שֶׁהֵן ב' הָעִנְיָנִים הַנ"ל דְּכַוָּנַת הַתְּפִלָּה הַיְנוּ הָעֲבוֹדָה שֶׁמִּצַּד הַנֶּפֶשׁ הָאֱלֹקִית בְּחִינַת עֲלִיַּת וְהִתְקַשְּׁרוּת נַפְשׁוֹ כו', וְהַדִּבּוּר דִּתְפִלָּה זֶהוּ מֵהַבֵּרוּר דְּנֶפֶשׁ הַבַּהֲמִית שֶׁבַּתְּפִלָּה.

vi) See footnote of the Rebbe on page 264

Now, it is known that there is a difference between the letters of Torah and the letters of prayer. The letters of Torah are the letters of *Ma"h*,[24] [from the already purified World of *Atzilut*], while the letters of prayer are of *Ba"n* [from the lower three worlds which need rectification and elevation].

דְּהִנֵּה יָדוּעַ הַהֶפְרֵשׁ בֵּין אוֹתִיּוֹת הַתּוֹרָה וְאוֹתִיּוֹת הַתְּפִלָּה דְּאוֹתִיּוֹת הַתּוֹרָה הֵן אוֹתִיּוֹת דְמ"ה וְאוֹתִיּוֹת הַתְּפִלָּה הֵן אוֹתִיּוֹת דב"ן

Ma"h and *Ba"n* are numerical values of the name of G-d. Both are forms of the Tetragrammaton, the four-letter essential name, spelled out to its fullest.	
Ma"h (45)	*Ba"n* (52)
Equals *adam* or "man"	equals *behama*, or "animal"
represents the rectified World of *Tikun* (i.e. *Atzilut*),	corresponds to the not yet rectified realm of *Tohu* (i.e. *Bria, Yetzira, Asiya*)
Yud: Yud-vav-dalet	**Yud**: Yud-vav-dalet
Hai: Hai-alef	**Hai**: Hai-hai
Vav: Vav-alef-vav	**Vav**: Vav-vav
Hai: Hai-alef	**Hai**: Hai-hai

COMMENTARY
---

with the level of prophecy in the scheme of creation. ["Unity consciousness" is associated with the infinite light of G-d, called *keter*, meaning "crown" (referring to the transcendent light, just as the crown transcends the head), which is above even the spiritual World of *Atzilut* ("Emanations"). It manifests itself as a gift from Above for those who have worked hard on

Essay on Service of the Heart - Love Like Fire and Water

וְהוּא עִנְיַן בְּחִינַת אֶבֶן וּלְבֵנָה, דְּאֶבֶן הוּא בְּרִיאָה בִּידֵי שָׁמַיִם וְהֵן אוֹתִיּוֹת הַבָּאוֹת מִלְמַעְלָה שֶׁהַתּוֹרָה נִתְּנָה בְּאוֹתִיּוֹת אֵלּוּ דַּוְקָא שֶׁהֵן כֵּלִים לְגִלּוּי בְּחִינַת חָכְמָה עִילָּאָה וּבָהֶם וְעַל יָדָם קוֹרְאִים וּמַמְשִׁיכִים גִּלּוּי אוֹר אֵין סוֹף בָּרוּךְ הוּא דִּלָכֵן צָרִיךְ לִהְיוֹת עֵסֶק הַתּוֹרָה בְּדִבּוּר דַּוְקָא וּכְמוֹ שֶׁכָּתוּב בַּתּוֹרָה אוֹר דִּבּוּר הַמַּתְחִיל וַיִּרְאוּ אֵת אֱלֹקֵי יִשְׂרָאֵל, וּלְבֵנִים הֵם הַנַּעֲשִׂים בִּידֵי אָדָם וְהֵן אוֹתִיּוֹת הַתְּפִלָּה שֶׁזֶּהוּ דִּבּוּר הָאָדָם, וְהַיְנוּ שֶׁאֵין זֶה אוֹתִיּוֹת הַבָּאִים מִלְמַעְלָה כִּי אִם אוֹתִיּוֹת הַבָּאִים מִלְמַטָּה לְמַעְלָה מֵהָאָדָם הַמִּתְפַּלֵּל (דְּגַם בִּשְׁמוֹנֶה עֶשְׂרֵה שֶׁנֶּאֱמַר עַל זֶה אֵין מִילִין בִּלְשׁוֹנִי רַק אֲדֹנָי שְׂפָתַי תִּפְתָּח, הֵן מִכָּל מָקוֹם דִּבּוּר הָאָדָם רַק שֶׁהוּא דִּבּוּר הַבָּא מִמֵּילָא לֹא בְּכַוָּנָה וּבְסֵדֶר עַל פִּי הַשֵּׂכֶל לְפִי שֶׁהַבִּטּוּל דִּתְפִלָּה הוּא לְמַעְלָה מִטַּעַם וָדַעַת הַמֻּשָּׂג כוּ' וּכְמוֹ שֶׁכָּתוּב בְּמָקוֹם אַחֵר) וְהֵן אוֹתִיּוֹת הַבָּאִים מִקֶּרֶב וְלֵב עָמֹק מֵהַקֵּרוּב שֶׁאַחַר הָרִחוּק, וְהַיְנוּ בְּעָסְקוֹ כָּל הַיּוֹם בַּהַכָּחוֹת הַטִּבְעִיִּים שֶׁלּוֹ וּמִתְקָרֵב אַחַר כָּךְ בַּתְּפִלָּה גַּם בַּהַכָּחוֹת הַטִּבְעִיִּים שֶׁלּוֹ דִּלְבִי וּבְשָׂרִי יְרַנְּנוּ כוּ', הִנֵּה אוֹתִיּוֹת אֵלּוּ נַעֲשִׂים כֶּתֶר לְקוֹנוֹ וּכְמוֹ הָעֲטָרָה

The concept here is equivalent to the distinction [mentioned in *Torah Ohr, parshat Mishpatim*] between *avanim* ("stones") and *levanim* ("bricks"). Stones are a creation of G-d, and therefore symbolize the letters that come from above, the letters with which the Torah was given. These letters are appropriate vessels to contain the spirituality of the highest *sephira* — that of *chochma*. Through these letters, the infinite light of G-d is transmitted [and brought into the creation]. Therefore, one who learns Torah must pronounce the words out loud. *Levanim* are man-made, and they symbolize the letters of prayer, which is the speech of man. That is, these are not letters that come from above, but letters that come from below. (Even in the *Amida*[vii] about which it says "there are no words on my tongue," and "Lord, please open my lips," the words are nonetheless words of man. It is just that these are words that flow spontaneously, without any effort on our part when praying. They also emerge without any apparent logical design, since the self-nullification of the prayer is beyond reason, as explained elsewhere.)[viii] The letters of prayer come from the inner recesses and depths of our heart when

vii) See footnote of the Rebbe on page 264

viii) See footnote of the Rebbe on page 266

--- COMMENTARY ---

themselves, but it cannot be expected or predicted. It is associated with the upper tip of the *yud* of G-d's Name and with the *sephira* of *keter* ("crown").]

שֶׁנַּעֲשֵׂית מֵאֲבָנִים טוֹבוֹת וּמְאִירוֹת (וּכְמוֹ שֶׁכָּתוּב בְּמָקוֹם אַחֵר שֶׁבָּאֲבָנִים טוֹבוֹת יֵשׁ שֶׁמְּאִירוֹת בְּעַצְמָם וְיֵשׁ שֶׁמְּאִירוֹת עַל יְדֵי שֶׁמִּזְדַּכְּכוֹת בִּפְעֻלַּת הַכּוֹכָבִים וְכַנּוֹדָע מֵעִנְיָן שֹׁהַם וְיָשְׁפֵה).

praying, as we have been far away from the One Above and now we come near. We have been working all day with our natural [physical and mental] abilities, and now we come close to the One Above in prayer, with our natural abilities as well — [as it says in Psalms 84:3] "my heart and my flesh sing." Then, the letters of our prayers become "crowns" for the Creator, like a crown that is made of precious shining stones. (Elsewhere, it is written that there are gems which shine of their own accord, and other gems which shine only on account of the polishing they receive from the light of the stars above, as is known regarding the two stones, *shoham* and *yashpe*.)

כָּךְ מֵאוֹתִיּוֹת הַתְּפִלָּה שֶׁהֵן אוֹתִיּוֹת שֶׁנִּתְבָּרְרוּ וְנִזְדַּכְּכוּ (וּבִפְרָטִיּוּת הֵן הַדִּבּוּרִים דְּכָל הַיּוֹם וּבִכְלָלוּת הֵן הַכֹּחוֹת הַטִּבְעִיִּים שֶׁמִּשְׁתַּמֵּשׁ בָּהֶם כָּל הַיּוֹם בְּעִנְיָנָיו הַגּוּפָנִיִּים) וְנַעֲשִׂים טוֹבִים וּמְאִירִים וְנַעֲשִׂים בְּחִינַת כֶּתֶר לְקוֹנוֹ כוּ' (וְהוּא עִנְיָן יְהִי רָצוֹן כוּ' וּכְמוֹ שֶׁכָּתוּב בְּמָקוֹם אַחֵר). וּב' הָעִנְיָנִים הַנַּ"ל שֶׁבַּתְּפִלָּה הֵם עַל יְדֵי הִתְעוֹרְרוּת מִדַּת הָאַהֲבָה וּכְמוֹ שֶׁיִּתְבָּאֵר אִי"ה וְלָכֵן כָּל הָעֲבוֹדָה דִתְפִלָּה הוּא לָבוֹא לִבְחִינַת אַהֲבָה:

ix) See footnote of the Rebbe on page 267

The letters of prayer are letters that have become purified and refined. (In particular, the letters of prayer represent the words of speech in which we engage all day long. In general, they are our natural abilities that we utilized all day long, for physical purposes.) They become precious and luminescent and thus become crowns for the Creator (which is the topic of the prayer *Yehi Ratzon*,[ix] as explained elsewhere.) Both aspects of prayer mentioned above come about through arousal of our feeling of love, as will be explained, G-d willing. Therefore, the entire *avoda* of prayer is in order to attain love [of the One Above].

קִצּוּר. כָּל הַיְגִיעָה דִתְפִלָּה הִיא לָבוֹא לְמִדַּת הָאַהֲבָה כִּי בַּתְּפִלָּה יֵשׁ ב' עִנְיָנִים, הָא' הִתְקַשְּׁרוּת וּדְבֵקוּת נַפְשׁוֹ בֶּאֱלֹקוּת וּלְהַעֲלוֹתָהּ בִּבְחִינַת רָצוֹא כוּ' וְהַב' לְבָרֵר וּלְזַכֵּךְ אֶת הַנֶּפֶשׁ הַבַּהֲמִית, וּשְׁנֵיהֶם

SYNOPSIS:

All of the labor of prayer is in order to come to love the One Above. As such, prayer includes two aspects: The first is the unity with and the cleaving of our soul to G-dliness, which involves the elevation of our soul by means of strong will and

Essay on Service of the Heart - Love Like Fire and Water

desire. The second is purification and refinement of our animal soul. Both goals are served and motivated by love of G-d. This is the *avoda* of the lower three soul levels — *nefesh*, *ruach* and *neshama* — and their inter-inclusion within their respective higher levels.

נַעֲשִׂים עַל יְדֵי מִדַּת הָאַהֲבָה (וְנִתְ׳ עִנְיַן הָעֲבוֹדָה בִּבְחִינַת נֶפֶשׁ רוּחַ וּנְשָׁמָה וּנְשָׁמָה לִנְשָׁמָה וְהִתְכַּלְלוּת כָּל אַחַת מֵהֶם בְּמַדְרֵגָה שֶׁלְּמַעְלָה הֵימֶנָּה):

CHAPTER 2 / פרק ב

Fear is a necessary ingredient, but not of the avoda of prayer.

וְהִנֵּה זֹאת וַדַּאי אֲשֶׁר צָרִיךְ לִהְיוֹת גַּם יִרְאָה וְאַדְּרַבָּה הַיִּרְאָה הִיא מֻכְרַחַת לִהְיוֹת בְּכָל אֶחָד וְאֶחָד מַמָּשׁ שֶׁאִי אֶפְשָׁר לִהְיוֹת בִּלְעָדֶיהָ וְהִיא גַּם הַתְחָלַת הָעֲבוֹדָה וִיסוֹדָהּ אָמְנָם לֹא זוֹ הִיא הָעֲבוֹדָה וִיגִיעָה דִתְפִלָּה.

We must certainly develop the characteristic of fear [of G-d]. In fact, fear is a necessary ingredient of our *avoda* of G-d. It is impossible to serve G-d without fearing Him; indeed, fear [of G-d] is the beginning and foundation [of *avoda*]. However, it is *not* part of the labor of prayer ["the service of the heart"].

The essential fear is "yirat chait" — fear of transgression. For this, we must guard our senses.

דְּהִנֵּה הַיִּרְאָה הַמֻּכְרַחַת לִהְיוֹת בְּכָל אֶחָד וְאֶחָד הוּא עִנְיַן יִרְאַת חֵטְא וְהוּא שֶׁיְּרֵא לַעֲשׂוֹת כָּל דָּבָר שֶׁהוּא נֶגֶד הֲוָיָ' וּרְצוֹנוֹ יִתְבָּרֵךְ וְלָאו דַּוְקָא בִּדְבַר חֵטְא וְעָוֹן בְּפֹעַל מַמָּשׁ כִּי אִם הַהַגְדָּרָה בְּהַחוּשִׁים שֶׁלּוֹ לִהְיוֹת עוֹצֵם עֵינָיו מִלִּרְאוֹת בְּרָע וְאוֹטֵם אָזְנוֹ מִשְּׁמֹעַ דָּבָר רַע וְהָיְנוּ שֶׁחוּשׁ הָרְאִיָּ' שֶׁלּוֹ אֵינוֹ פָּתוּחַ לִרְאוֹת כָּל מַה שֶּׁלְּפָנָיו וְכָל שֶׁכֵּן בִּרְאִיָּ' וְהִסְתַּכְּלוּת הָאֲמוּרָה

(אֲשֶׁר בֶּאֱמֶת הָרְאִיָּ' וְכָל שֶׁכֵּן הַהִסְתַּכְּלוּת הִיא הַסִּבָּה הַגּוֹרֶמֶת לְכָל דְּבַר רַע וְהִיא הַמְּבִיאָה לְרַע

The fear that is essential for everyone to attain is *yirat chait*, [fear of sin, or fear of transgressing His will]. That is, we are afraid to do anything that is against the will of G-d. Fear of sin relates not only to wrongful deeds or transgressions, but also to guarding the senses. We must constantly guard our eyes to prevent them from seeing and block our ears from hearing anything evil. We shouldn't expose our eyesight to all that is in front of us, and of course we shouldn't stare.

The truth is that seeing — and even more, staring — is the cause of all bad things and can bring us to absolute

---
COMMENTARY

CHAPTER 2: THE FOUNDATION OF MEDITATION

Chapter 1 of *Kuntres Ha'Avoda* is an overview of soul levels that are attainable by steady and concentrated meditation (*hitbonenut*) on G-dly concepts over a period of time. Chapter 2 brings us down to earth. Here, the Rebbe doesn't speak about states of consciousness nor about getting closer to the One Above, but rather about seemingly mundane things like guarding our senses, thought, speech, and action. People who are looking for an immediate "high" in their spiritual work may have a hard time evil, G-d forbid. As is stated [in *Midrash Tanchuma* ch.15], "the eye and the heart are two intermediaries of sin; the eye sees, and the heart desires, and whoever looks ... in the end will transgress." It is known that the main enjoyment which we experience is through eyesight, and the blind person has no enjoyment in anything,[x] as is written elsewhere regarding [the verse in Psalms 90:15] "Make us glad as many days as You have afflicted us." Thus, our sight arouses enjoyment in the soul, and that's why we see that even [seasoned and experienced] "servants of G-d," who are very far from anything bad, are also slightly affected by what they see (aside from those who through their *avoda* have — temporarily at least — removed themselves from anything physical so that at that moment they are not affected by anything). But since they are "servants of G-d," what they see has no permanent effect on them, G-d forbid, but only leaves a fleeting impression which passes away, and immediately they re-connect themselves to what they are [anyway] connected to, and the matter is dismissed from their hearts. However,

גְּמוּר רַחֲמָנָא לִיצְלָן וּכְמַאֲמָר עֵינָא וְלִבָּא תְּרֵין סַרְסוּרִין דַּעֲבֵרָה הָעַיִן רוֹאָה וְהַלֵּב חוֹמֵד וְכָל הַמִּסְתַּכֵּל כו׳ סוֹף בָּא לִידֵי עֲבֵרָה, וְכַנּוֹדָע דְּעִקָּר הַתַּעֲנוּג הוּא בְּחוּשׁ הָרְאִיָּ׳ וְהַסּוּמָא אֵין לוֹ תַּעֲנוּג בְּשׁוּם דָּבָר וּכְמוֹ שֶׁכָּתוּב בְּמָקוֹם אַחֵר בְּעִנְיַן שַׂמְּחֵנוּ כִּימוֹת עִנִּיתָנוּ, וְעַל כֵּן הָרְאִיָּ׳ מְעוֹרֵר הַתַּעֲנוּג שֶׁבַּנֶּפֶשׁ, וְלָכֵן אָנוּ רוֹאִים שֶׁגַּם בְּעוֹבְדֵי ה׳ הָרְחוֹקִים לְגַמְרֵי מִכָּל דָּבָר רַע הִנֵּה עַל יְדֵי הָרְאִיָּ׳ מִתְעוֹרְרִים וּמִתְפַּעֲלִים קְצָת (לְבַד בְּאוֹתָן שֶׁהָעֲבוֹדָה פּוֹעֵל בָּהֶם שֶׁלְּפִי שָׁעָה עַל כָּל פָּנִים הֵמָה מְפֻשָּׁטִים מִן הַגֶּשֶׁם שֶׁבְּעֵת הַהִיא אֵינָם מִתְפַּעֲלִים מִשּׁוּם דָּבָר) רַק לִהְיוֹתָם עוֹבְדֵי ה׳ אֵין זֶה עוֹשֶׂה בָּהֶם אֵיזֶה חֲקִיקָה חַס וְחָלִילָה כִּי אִם הוּא בְּהַעֲבָרָה בְּעָלְמָא וּמִיָּד יְקַשֵּׁר אֶת עַצְמוֹ אֶל מַה שֶּׁהוּא מְקֻשָּׁר וְנִשְׁכָּח הַדָּבָר מִלִּבּוֹ. אֲבָל אוֹתָם שֶׁאֵינָם

Eyesight can be the cause of much negative sensory input.

x) See footnote of the Rebbe on page 267

COMMENTARY

accepting what the Rebbe says in this chapter, and may wonder what this has to do with coming closer to the One Above.

The truth is that we cannot get close to G-d without first establishing a foundation on which to build our spiritual edifice. We cannot create a spiritual environment in our mind unless we have first fulfilled certain conditions of purity and refinement. This involves guarding ourselves from certain sensory inputs and expressions that damage the soul and raise barriers between us and the One Above. Chapter 2 tells us what these inputs

עוֹבְדֵי ה' כִּדְבָעֵי הֲרֵי הוּא נִלְכָּדִים בַּפַּח הַזֶּה וְהוּא הַמְבִיאָם לְכָל דָּבָר רַע רַחֲמָנָא לִיצְלָן וּמוֹרִיד אוֹתָם לִשְׁאוֹל תַּחְתִּית ה' יִשְׁמְרֵנוּ וְיַצִּילֵנוּ.

those who are not in the category of "servants of G-d" in the real sense, are caught in this trap [of following their eyes and heart]. This leads them to all kinds of base things, G-d forbid, and pulls them down to the lowest depths. May G-d guard and rescue them.

Guarding eyesight is vital; if we don't, then all of our avoda is invalid.

וְכָל מִי שֶׁחָשׁ לְנַפְשׁוֹ שֶׁלֹּא לַהֲבִיאָהּ לִידֵי טֻמְאָה רַחֲמָנָא לִיצְלָן יַגְדִּיר אֶת עַצְמוֹ בְּחוּשׁ הָרְאִי'. וְאִם הַדָּבָר קָשֶׁה לוֹ יִתְגַּבֵּר עַל עַצְמוֹ בְּכָל תֹּקֶף וְעוֹז וְיֵדַע אֲשֶׁר מַמָּשׁ בְּנַפְשׁוֹ הוּא וְאִם לֹא יַגְדִּיר אֶת עַצְמוֹ בָּזֶה כָּל עֲבוֹדָתוֹ כְּאַיִן וּכְאֶפֶס נֶחְשָׁב וְלֹא יִפְעַל דָּבָר בִּיגִיעָתוֹ וַעֲבוֹדָתוֹ וְאַדְּרַבָּא יֵרֵד רַחֲמָנָא לִיצְלָן מַטָּה מַטָּה, וְעַל כֵּן יִתְגַּבֵּר כַּאֲרִי לְהַגְדִּיר אֶת עַצְמוֹ בְּכָל תֹּקֶף וְעוֹז וְגַם אִם יְהִי' נִכָּר אַל יָחוּשׁ לְשִׂיחוֹת בנ"א, וַהֲלֹא בְּדָבָר הַנּוֹגֵעַ לְחַיֵּי הַנֶּפֶשׁ בְּגַשְׁמִיּוּת אֵינָם מַבִּיטִים עַל שׁוּם דָּבָר וְכָל שֶׁכֵּן בְּהַנּוֹגֵעַ לְחַיֵּי הַנֶּפֶשׁ הָרוּחָנִי, וְהַכְּבֵדוּת בָּזֶה הִיא רַק בְּעֵת הָרִאשׁוֹנָה שֶׁצָּרִיךְ לְהַכְבִּיד עַל עַצְמוֹ וּלְהִתְגַּבֵּר עַל טִבְעוֹ וּרְצוֹנוֹ וּבְמֶשֶׁךְ הַזְּמַן יִתְרַגֵּל כָּךְ. וּבְהַגְדָּרָה זֹאת יִמְצָא מָנוֹחַ לְנַפְשׁוֹ מִכַּמָּה

Those of us who are concerned about our soul, and who don't wish to bring it to a state of impurity, G-d forbid, should guard our sense of eyesight. And if this is difficult for us, we must overcome our weakness with all of our power. We must know that this matter is vital to our soul, and that if we don't guard ourselves in this regard, then all of our *avoda* of the One Above is invalid. All of our effort will have no effect, and quite the opposite, we will sink lower and lower. Therefore, we should strengthen ourselves and guard ourselves with all of our power, and even if it becomes noticeable [to others], we should pay no attention to what people say. When it comes to matters of physical life and death, no one is concerned about what another person thinks, all the more so with regard to a matter of spiritual life and

─────── **COMMENTARY** ───────

and expressions are and how to fend them off.

Chapter 1, detailing many of the higher levels of spiritual consciousness, was a "gift" — it was meant to whet our appetites and let us know what is in store for us if we decide to pursue *hitbonenut*. (And, as it says in Chapter 6 of *Kuntres Ha'Avoda*, "if you're not practicing *hitbonenut*, then what are you doing here?")

Essay on Service of the Heart - Love Like Fire and Water

death. The difficulty in this [exercise in restraint] is only in the beginning, when we have to concentrate in order to overcome our own nature and will.

רָעוֹת וּבִלְבּוּלִים וְאָז יוּכַל לַעֲבֹד עֲבוֹדָתוֹ. וּבִיגִיעָתוֹ יִפְעַל יְשׁוּעוֹת בְּנַפְשׁוֹ בְּעֶזְרָתוֹ יִתְ׳.

The difficulty in guarding our eyesight is only in the beginning.

However, with time, we will become accustomed to doing this, and by guarding ourselves, we will find an escape from much evil and confusion, and then we will be able to serve G-d [in prayer with serenity]. And through our effort we will bring salvation to our soul, with the help of the One Above.

Now, there are people who are far from actually committing any kind of transgression, G-d forbid, but their hearts pull them [nevertheless] to look and to stare. They do so with coldness and detachment, and they feel no excitement at the time they look. But, in truth the underlying reason for their attraction is that the soul is deriving essential enjoyment from bonding with what they are looking at.

וְהִנֵּה יֶשְׁנָם בְּנֵי אָדָם אֲשֶׁר רְחוֹקִים הֵמָּה מֵאֵיזֶה דָּבָר רַע בְּפֹעַל חַס וְחָלִילָה, אֲבָל לִבָּם מוֹשֵׁךְ אוֹתָם לִרְאוֹת וּלְהַבִּיט וְהַהַבָּטָה הִיא כְּמוֹ בְּקֹר רוּחַ וְאֵינוֹ מַרְגִּישׁ בְּעַצְמוֹ בְּעֵת מַעֲשֶׂה אֵיזֶה הִתְפַּעֲלוּת, וּבֶאֱמֶת סִבַּת הַמְּשִׁיכָה הוּא מִפְּנֵי שֶׁתַּעֲנוּג נַפְשׁוֹ בְּעֶצֶם הוּא מְקֻשָּׁר בָּזֶה

(This is similar to what is written elsewhere,[xi] regarding [the statement of one of the Sages], "I don't know in which direction I am being led..." [This was said by R'Yohanan ben Zakkai, just before he passed away.

(וְעַל דֶּרֶךְ הַמְבֹאָר בְּעִנְיַן אֵינִי יוֹדֵעַ בְּאֵיזֶה דֶּרֶךְ כו׳, שֶׁיָּכוֹל לִהְיוֹת דְּבַכֹּחוֹת הַגְּלוּיִים הוּא בְּעֵסֶק הַתּוֹרָה וַעֲבוֹדָה וְעֶצֶם נַפְשׁוֹ הִיא בְּתוֹךְ הַקְּלִפָּה וְהַסִּטְרָא אַחֲרָא כו׳

xi) See footnote of the Rebbe on page 268 ←

He was a righteous person and could presume that his soul was about to be taken to heaven and not the opposite. Nevertheless, he worried] that it is possible to serve G-d and learn Torah with the conscious faculties, while the essence of the soul is given over to forces opposed to holiness.

COMMENTARY

Here's how it might be possible to relate to Chapter 2 in a personal way. When we realize that there is a path and lifestyle leading to connection with the One Above, we naturally want to "leave behind" everything familiar, in order to cling to the new lifestyle. Some of us do so slowly, making changes step by step, gradually taking on more *mitzvot* of the Torah, while others insist upon "burning all their bridges" in order to get closer to

Even if we observe with detachment, it can bring negative results from the unconscious essence of our animal soul.

כֵּן הוּא בַּדָּבָר הַזֶּה שֶׁגַּם שֶׁהוּא רָחוֹק מֵרַע בְּפֹעַל מַמָּשׁ וְאַדְּרַבָּא הוּא עוֹשֶׂה טוֹב בִּכֹחוֹתָיו הַגְּלוּיִּים. מִכָּל מָקוֹם עֶצֶם תַּעֲנוּג נַפְשׁוֹ הוּא מֻשְׁקָע וּמְקֻשָּׁר בְּעִנְיָן רַע רַחֲמָנָא לִיצְלָן וְזֹאת הִיא סִבַּת הַמְשִׁיכָה אֶל הַהַבָּטָה וְהַהִסְתַּכְּלוּת) וְהַהַבָּטָה עִם הֱיוֹתָהּ בְּקֹר רוּחַ לִכְאוֹרָה הִנֵּה הִיא עוֹשָׂה רֹשֶׁם וַחֲקִיקָה גְדוֹלָה בַּנֶּפֶשׁ וְלֹא תַעֲבֹר בְּלִי הִתְעוֹרְרוּת רַע בְּהִתְגַּלּוּת רַחֲמָנָא לִיצְלָן

xii) See footnote of the Rebbe on page 269 →

(וְעִנְיַן הַקְּרִירוּת בָּזֶה בֶּאֱמֶת הוּא מֵחֲמַת עֹצֶם טִרְדָּתוֹ בַּהַבָּטָה וְהוּא כֹּחַ הַתַּעֲנוּג הַנֶּעְלָם שֶׁבְּנַפְשׁוֹ שֶׁבָּא בְּהֶרְאִי׳ וְהַהַבָּטָה וְהִיא כְּמוֹ נְקוּדָה וּמְקוֹר הָרַע רַחֲמָנָא לִיצְלָן. וְכַנּוֹדָע שֶׁבַּנְּקוּדָה הַמְּקוֹרִית אֵין בָּזֶה הִתְפַּעֲלוּת בְּהִתְגַּלּוּת) וְהִיא מִתְפַּשֶּׁטֶת וּמוֹצִיאָה לְהִתְגַּלּוּת עֹמֶק הָרַע רַחֲמָנָא לִיצְלָן וְהַשֵּׁם יִתְבָּרֵךְ יִשְׁמְרֵנוּ מִכָּל רַע.

So too here. When we look [even with detachment], we may indeed be far from actually committing a sin, and moreover may actually be doing good. Nevertheless, our deepest, subconscious enjoyment is connected to a corrupt matter, G-d forbid, and that's the [real] reason for the temptation to stare. Our staring, even though seemingly performed with detachment, nevertheless makes a strong impression on our soul, [and this impression] will not dissipate[xii] without arousing us to some kind of evil, G-d forbid.

(The truth is that the detachment [with which we stare] is due to an intense [though subconscious] absorption in the matter. It comes from a hidden need in our soul, which is expressed in looking and staring. This [intense absorption] is like the core and origin of bad — G-d save us — where there is no conscious awareness of excitement.) It then expands and brings the depths of evil to the surface, may the One Above save us from all bad things.

COMMENTARY
---

the One Above as quickly as possible. But, whether slow or quick, we agree that to the extent our previous lifestyle prevented us from connecting to the One Above, it needs to be left behind. There's a precedent for this in the Torah, in the story of the father of the Jewish people, none other than Abraham himself. After he "found G-d" in Mesopotamia (probably present day Iraq), he was told [Genesis 12:1], "Go on your way, from your land, from your birthplace, and from the house of your father." That is, "leave everything behind." The Chassidic commentaries

Essay on Service of the Heart - Love Like Fire and Water

We are drawn in the direction of what we observe; therefore, we must control our eyesight and this will bring rest and salvation to the soul.

The Sages tell us [in *Esther Rabbah* 7,10]: "What the righteous see, raises them to greatness." This is what is referred to as "looking at the Glory of the King." This takes place with [great] cleaving of the soul to the infinite light of G-d, may He be blessed, and with the deepest and most sublime enjoyment. The opposite is true in regard to the corrupt forces that are opposed to holiness [*Esther Rabbah* continues: "And what the wicked see, lowers them to *gehinom*."]

וְרַבּוֹתֵינוּ זִכְרוֹנָם לִבְרָכָה אָמְרוּ מַרְאוֹת עֵינֵיהֶם שֶׁל הַצַּדִּיקִים מַעֲלִים אוֹתָם לִגְדֻלָּה וְהוּא עִנְיָן לְאִסְתַּכְּלָא בִּיקָרָא דְּמַלְכָּא בִּבְחִינַת דְּבֵקוּת נַפְשׁוֹ בְּעֶצֶם הַתַּעֲנוּג שֶׁבּוֹ בִּבְחִינַת עַצְמוּת אוֹר אֵין סוֹף בָּרוּךְ הוּא וְהַהֶפֶךְ הוּא בִּלְעֻמַּת זֶה כו'.

There is an obligation upon all of us to control ourselves and guard our sense of sight. In so doing we will save our soul from evil, and then our *avoda* of the One Above will be accepted, and we will bring salvation to our soul, and will rise higher and higher...

וְהַחוֹבָה הִיא עַל כָּל אָדָם לְהִתְגַּבֵּר עַל עַצְמוֹ וּלְהַגְדִּיר אֶת עַצְמוֹ בְּחוּשׁ הָרְאִיָּ׳ וּבָזֶה יַצִּיל אֶת נַפְשׁוֹ מִן הָרַע וְאָז תִּהְיֶ׳ עֲבוֹדָתוֹ רְצוּיָ׳ וְיִפְעַל יְשׁוּעוֹת בְּנַפְשׁוֹ וְיַעֲלֶה מַעְלָה כו'.

The same holds true for the sense of hearing; we must block our ears from hearing forbidden words, such as boasting and scoffing, and anything that isn't appropriate to hear. As the Sages said [in *Ketubot* 5] commenting on the verse [in Deuteron-

וְכֵן בְּחוּשׁ הַשְּׁמִיעָה אוֹטֵם אָזְנוֹ מִשְּׁמֹעַ דִּבּוּרִים הָאֲמוּרִים כְּמוֹ דִּבְרֵי הוֹלְלוּת וְלֵיצָנוּת וְכָל דָּבָר שֶׁאֵינוֹ הָגוּן וּכְמוֹ שֶׁאָמְרוּ רַבּוֹתֵינוּ זִכְרוֹנָם לִבְרָכָה בִּכְתֻבּוֹת דַּ"ה סֵ"א עַ"פ וְיָתֵד תִּהְיֶה לְךָ עַל אֲזֵנֶךָ, וְכֵן גַּם

COMMENTARY

explain that the three things that Abraham was told to leave ("land, birthplace, and house of your father") refer to all that is ingrained and habitual in our behavior. "Land" stands for our physical habits and desires; "birthplace" stands for our inborn genetic personality, and the "house of your father" stands for all that we've learned from our family and environment. So, we needn't be embarrassed or feel a need to explain our desire to run away from a spiritually negative past to a future that is filled with connection to the One Above. (We may want, however, to regulate and modify how we go about it in consultation with our personal rabbi or one who knows us well.) As we are

דְּבָרִים בְּטֵלִים שֶׁגַּם הֵמָּה פּוֹעֲלִים פְּעֻלָּה רָעָה בַּנֶּפֶשׁ וּכְמוֹ שֶׁאָמְרוּ רַבּוֹתֵינוּ זִכְרוֹנָם לִבְרָכָה שָׁם אַל יַשְׁמִיעַ אָדָם לְאָזְנָיו דְּבָרִים בְּטֵלִים מִפְּנֵי שֶׁהֵן נִכְוֹות תְּחִלָּה לָאֵבָרִים, הֲרֵי שֶׁגַּם הֵמָּה כו' לַנֶּפֶשׁ כו'.

omy 23:14], "Make for yourselves a peg on your weapon/ear." [That is, we must be able to plug our ears when we hear something we don't need to hear.] This is true as well of idle talk since it also has a negative effect on the soul, as the Sages said there, "One should not let his ears hear idle talk, because his ears are the first of all the limbs to be 'burned' [that is, they are the most sensitive]." Thus, we see that idle talk can also "burn" the soul.

We must guard our hearing and all forms of speech, as well.

וְכֵן הַהַגְדָּרָה בְּדִבּוּר שֶׁלֹּא יְדַבֵּר דִּבּוּרִים הָאֲסוּרִים כְּמוֹ דִּבּוּרִים הנ״ל וְלָשׁוֹן הָרַע וּרְכִילוּת וּכְהַאי גַוְונָא וְלֹא דְּבָרִים בְּטֵלִים וְלֹא יַרְחִיב פִּיו וּלְשׁוֹנוֹ בְּשׁוּם דָּבָר. וּבְדֶרֶךְ כְּלָל הוּא מְגֻדָּר בְּכָל הַחוּשִׁים וְהַכֹּחוֹת שֶׁלּוֹ מִפְּנֵי פַּחַד אֱלֹקִים שֶׁעָלָיו. וְהוּא עִנְיַן קַבָּלַת עוֹל מַלְכוּת שָׁמַיִם, כִּי הַהִפּוּךְ מִזֶּה

In addition, we must be careful with our speech and refrain from speaking that which is forbidden, such as the kinds of speech mentioned above, and *lashon hara* [negative expressions regarding others] and *rechilut* [gossip], and so forth. Included in this category is "idle talk" and speaking unnecessarily at length. In general, we must be circumspect

―――――― **COMMENTARY** ――――――

doing so, we should be aware that we are either consciously or sub-consciously laying the foundation of all of our future connection with the One Above.

In Torah literature, there are instructions for those who want to attain the "way of Torah." One [Avot 6:4] states: "...eat bread with salt, drink water, and sleep on the ground..." In other words, throw away all that is extraneous, do only that which is necessary to maintain your physical well being, and throw yourself into learning Torah until you have reached your goal. It sounds ascetic, but for the one who is fleeing a spiritually empty past and seeking a direct connection with the One Above, there is no greater comfort. At the same time, though, the Torah prescribes such behavior only until we have formed our personal connection and foundation in service of G-d. The way of Torah is not a way of escape from the physical world. We don't detach ourselves entirely from the world. We have to deal with other people, if only to meet our minimal physical needs. More commonly, after in how we use our senses and abilities and be mindful to fear G-d. This is the result of "accepting the yoke of heaven," which is the opposite of "throwing off the yoke of heaven." The latter is evidenced by the person who [willfully] follows the whims of his heart in order to satisfy his lust; he may not succeed, but even the lapse that allows him to speak whatever arises in his mind (even if forbidden), or to hear and see everything, constitutes a breach which will lead him [down the road] to complete evil. G-d save him. What leads to such openness

הוּא פְּרִיקַת עוֹל. וְהוּא הַהוֹלֵךְ בִּשְׁרִירוּת לִבּוֹ לְמַלֵא תַּאֲוָתוֹ לְכָל אֲשֶׁר יִרְצֶה. וְלָאו דַוְקָא בְּדָבָר תַּאֲוָה בְּפֹעַל כִּי אִם גַּם הַפְּתִיחָה בַּחוּשִׁים שֶׁלוֹ לְדַבֵּר כָּל מַה שֶׁעוֹלֶה עַל רוּחוֹ גַּם דִבּוּר הָאָסוּר וְכֵן לִשְׁמֹעַ וְלִרְאוֹת הַכֹּל שֶׁהֵן הַשְׁעָרִים וְהַמְקָרִים הַמְבִיאִים לִידֵי תַּאֲוָה וְלִידֵי רַע גָּמוּר רַחֲמָנָא לִיצְלָן כנ״ל. וְסִבַּת הַפְּתִיחָה הַזֹּאת הוּא מִפְּנֵי פְּרִיקַת עוֹל מַלְכוּת שָׁמַיִם שֶׁהוּא כְּמוֹ חָפְשִׁי לְעַצְמוֹ (בִּלְשׁוֹן אַשְׁכְּנַז זייער פריי ביי זיך, ער פילט קיין

Even the lapse that allows us to speak or to hear and see everything is a breach that leads to evil.

COMMENTARY
---

having passed the stage of "acquiring Torah," we have to return to function in a world that is neither supportive nor expressive of Torah values. How must we act then? That is the subject of Chapter 2. Because only when you know how to maintain your inner environment and equilibrium can you start building your spiritual edifice through *hitbonenut*.

In general, while Chapter 1 discusses love of G-d, Chapter 2 discusses fear of G-d. Without a certain level of respect which comes from fear, there is no love. If we don't respect G-d, we won't come to love Him either.

Fear of the One Above starts with three different but related mind-states:

#	*Mind-state*	**Sephira**	*Experience*
1.	Kabbalat ol shamayim "Accepting the yoke of heaven"	Malchut "Sovereignty"	Unconscious attitude of subjugation to the will of G-d
2.	Yirat chait "Fear of sin"	Netzach *"Victory"* Hod *"Thanksgiving"* Yesod *"Foundation"*	Avoidance of occasions of sin out of concern not to transgress the will of G-d
3.	Yirat Elokim "Fear of G-d"	Gevura "Strictness/constriction"	Emotion-based fear of G-d

Kuntres Ha'Avoda - קונטרס העבודה

עוֹל אוֹיף זִיךְ) וּמִשּׁוּם זֶה יַעֲשֶׂה מַה שֶּׁלִּבּוֹ חָפֵץ.

is the [state of] throwing off the "yoke of heaven," whereupon he feels free to do whatever he [that is, his animal soul] wants, and therefore he does whatever his heart desires.

וּכְמוֹ בְּטֶבַע בְּנֵי אָדָם הֲרֵי אֵינוֹ דּוֹמֶה הָאָדָם כְּמוֹ שֶׁהוּא בְּבֵיתוֹ בִּפְנֵי עַצְמוֹ וּכְמוֹ שֶׁיּוֹשֵׁב עִם אֲחֵרִים וְכָל שֶׁכֵּן עִם גְּדוֹלִים וְטוֹבִים מִמֶּנּוּ שֶׁעוֹצֵר אֶת עַצְמוֹ בְּכָל הַכֹּחוֹת שֶׁלּוֹ וְעַל כֻּלָּם בְּחֶשְׁבּוֹן יָבוֹא אֵיךְ לַעֲמֹד וְלֵישֵׁב וְאֵיךְ לְדַבֵּר אֲבָל בְּבֵיתוֹ כְּשֶׁהוּא לְעַצְמוֹ לֹא יִתְחַשֵּׁב כְּלָל וְיִטֶּה עַל צִדּוֹ אוֹ יִשְׁכַּב וִידַבֵּר כְּכָל הָעוֹלֶה עַל רוּחוֹ.

We're different in our own houses than we are with others, especially when they are more important than we are.

We know that our nature is different when we are in our own house alone, than when we are with others. This is all the more true when those with whom we keep company are more important than we are. Under such circumstances, we restrain ourselves in all respects, thinking carefully about how to use each and every faculty: how to stand, how to sit, and how to speak. But, in our own house alone, we don't give these details any consideration and doesn't hesitate to lounge around and talk about whatever we want.

וְכֵן הוּא בְּרוּחָנִיּוּת הַפְּתִיחָה בַּהַחוּשִׁים שֶׁאֵין מַעֲצוֹר לְרוּחוֹ לִרְאוֹת וּלְהַבִּיט וְכוּ' הוּא מִפְּנֵי שֶׁאֵין עָלָיו עוֹל מַלְכוּת שָׁמַיִם כְּלָל שֶׁאֵינוֹ נִרְגָּשׁ בּוֹ כְּלָל (גַּם לֹא בְּהֶעְלֵם) עוֹל הָאָדוֹן אֲדוֹן כָּל הָאָרֶץ בָּרוּךְ הוּא אֲשֶׁר מְיַחֵד מַלְכוּתוֹ

This applies as well to *ruchniyut* [spiritual mattters]. When our senses are unguarded and totally open, nothing stops us from looking and staring, and this is because we haven't accepted the "yoke of heaven" upon ourselves. We fail to experience (even in a subconscious way) the yoke of

---
COMMENTARY

1. KABBALAT OL SHAMAYIM

The first is called "accepting the yoke of heaven" (*kaballat ol shamayim*). This is the state of mind that says, "whatever He says to do, that's what I'll take upon myself to do." This is not a conscious attitude. It's not as if we constantly repeat to ourselves that we are under the command of the One Above. Rather, it is an unconscious attitude to life, and it determines our approach to fulfilling the will of the One Above. If we feel that we are subjects of the King, we will at all times want to do what He wants of us and we will constantly worry that we may be doing

Essay on Service of the Heart - Love Like Fire and Water

the Master of the Universe, Who uniquely bestows His kingship on us, and therefore we do whatever we please. Because of this, we absolutely neglect to fear G-d. That is, we are not upset nor at all concerned that this is against the will of G-d, and that this blemishes our soul, destroying it completely. May He save us.

But, when we have accepted the "yoke of heaven" upon ourselves, we are careful in how we use our senses, like a servant[xiii] who is always discreet because the yoke of his master is upon him. He is neither free nor open because he perpetually feels the yoke of the master. Even when he is physically distant from him [the master], he does not escape from this yoke; he feels it always. He gets accustomed to this yoke, and it isn't burdensome to him at all. He doesn't know any other way of being, as written elsewhere.

So it is, as well, with us when we have accepted the "yoke of heaven."

יִתְבָּרֵךְ עָלֵינוּ בִּפְרָט לָכֵן יַעֲשֶׂה כָּל מַה שֶׁיַּחְפֹּץ וּמִשּׁוּם זֶה לֹא יָשִׂים פַּחַד אֱלֹקִים נֶגֶד עֵינָיו כְּלָל וּכְלָל, וְהַיְנוּ שֶׁלֹּא יִפֹּל לִבּוֹ וְלֹא יָחוּשׁ כְּלָל עַל שֶׁזֶּהוּ נֶגֶד רְצוֹן ה' וַאֲשֶׁר פּוֹגֵם בְּנִשְׁמָתוֹ לְשַׁחֲתָהּ לְגַמְרֵי רַחֲמָנָא לִיצְּלָן.

אֲבָל כְּשֶׁיֵּשׁ עָלָיו עוֹל מַלְכוּת שָׁמַיִם הֲרֵי הוּא מְגֻדָּר וּמְכֻוָּץ בְּכָל הַחוּשִׁים שֶׁלּוֹ וּכְמוֹ הָעֶבֶד שֶׁהוּא מְכֻוָּץ תָּמִיד מִפְּנֵי עוֹל הָאָדוֹן שֶׁעָלָיו וְאֵין לוֹ שׁוּם חָפְשִׁיּוּת וּפְתִיחָה בְּעַצְמוֹ (ער אִיז נִיט פְרַיי אוּן נִיט אָפֶען בַּיי זִיךְ נָאר שְׁטֶענְדִיג פַארְקְוֶועטְשְׁט אוּן וִוי פָארְצַאמְט) מִפְּנֵי שֶׁנִּרְגָּשׁ בּוֹ תָּמִיד עוֹל הָאָדוֹן, וְגַם כְּשֶׁהוּא מֵרָחוֹק מִן הָאָדוֹן אֵינוֹ יוֹצֵא מִן הָעֹל הַזֶּה הַנִּרְגָּשׁ בּוֹ תָּמִיד וְהוּא מֻרְגָּל בָּעֹל הַזֶּה שֶׁאֵינוֹ כָּבֵד עָלָיו כְּלָל וְאֵינוֹ יוֹדֵעַ אַחֶרֶת כְּלָל וּכְמוֹ שֶׁכָּתוּב בְּמָקוֹם אַחֵר,

וּכְמוֹ כֵן הוּא בְּעוֹל מַלְכוּת שָׁמַיִם שֶׁנִּרְגָּשׁ בּוֹ תָּמִיד שֶׁיֵּשׁ לוֹ אָדוֹן

When we accept the "yoke of heaven," we are careful with our senses, and yet we don't find it burdensome.

xiii) See footnote of the Rebbe on page 269

COMMENTARY

that which the King is opposed to. We won't make a move unless we know that this is what the King wants. It sounds clumsy and difficult, but once we become accustomed to this attitude, we don't find it onerous. Quite the opposite, it lends direction and structure to a life that would be otherwise dominated by ego and lust.

Although not explicitly stated by the text, the unconscious mind-state of accepting the "yoke of heaven" corresponds to the lowest of the ten *sephirot*, or G-dly emanations—*malchut*

We're not conscious of the "yoke of heaven" upon us, but it permeates and influences all of our behavior.

עָלָיו, וְהֶרְגֵּשׁ זֶה אֵינוֹ בְּהִתְגַּלּוּת בְּהַכֹּחוֹת כִּי אִם הֶרְגֵּשׁ נֶעֱלָם שֶׁיֵּשׁ עָלָיו עוֹל הַמְכַוֵּץ אוֹתוֹ וּמַגְדִּיר אוֹתוֹ בְּהַחוּשִׁים שֶׁלּוֹ לִבְלִי לְהִתְפַּשֵּׁט בָּהֶם נֶגֶד רְצוֹן ה׳ חַס וְחָלִילָה,

וּכְמוֹ כֵן יְהִי׳ פַּחַד אֱלֹקִים תָּמִיד לְנֶגֶד עֵינָיו שֶׁיִּרָא לִמְרֹד בְּמֶלֶךְ מַלְכֵי הַמְּלָכִים הַקָּדוֹשׁ בָּרוּךְ הוּא כוּ׳ (דְּעוֹל מַלְכוּת שָׁמַיִם וְיִרְאַת חֵטְא וְיִרְאַת אֱלֹקִים הַכֹּל א׳ רַק דְּעוֹל מַלְכוּת שָׁמַיִם הוּא בְּהֶעְלֵם וְיִרְאַת חֵטְא וְיִרְאַת אֱלֹקִים הוּא בְּהִתְגַּלּוּת דְּהַיְנוּ הִתְעוֹרְרוּת נִגְלֵית בְּהַכֹּחוֹת,

We feel at all times that we have a Master. The feeling isn't conscious but is rather a subconscious awareness of a yoke that inhibits us and guards our senses to prevent us from acting freely in a manner that is opposed to the will of the One Above.

Similarly, the fear of G-d must be with us at all times, so that we are afraid to rebel against the King of Kings, the Holy One Blessed be He. (The "yoke of heaven," "fear of sin," and "fear of G-d" are all one [in their inception]. It's just that the "yoke of heaven" is a subconscious trait, while "fear of sin" and "fear of G-d" are conscious traits. That is, they imply a conscious arousal of the soul-powers [so that we become aware of them].

1.	*Kabbalat ol shamayim* "Accepting the yoke of heaven"	Unconscious attitude of subjugation to the will of G-d
2.	*Yirat chait* "Fear of sin"	Avoidance of occasions of sin out of conscious concern not to transgress the will of G-d
3.	*Yirat Elokim* "Fear of G-d"	Conscious emotion-based fear of G-d

---
COMMENTARY

("sovereignty") — which is characterized by awareness of the reign and kingship of the One Above. When we are in this mind-state, we feel that we have nothing of our own, that our ego is nullified, and that all that is important is that which we receive from the levels of holiness that are beyond ourselves. Therefore, we willingly subjugate ourselves to whatever directions we receive that enable us to connect with the One Above, with the King Himself. This attitude is not conscious, but

Essay on Service of the Heart - Love Like Fire and Water

The "yoke of heaven" acts automatically, as when we become instinctively careful in the use of our senses, as if we don't see and don't hear, and likewise don't experience lust or get angry, all of which results from the "yoke of heaven" which is upon us. And fear [of G-d] is [also] necessary when we need reinforcement in order to guard ourselves. That is, [we are able] to control ourselves by power of the fear and awe of G-d before our eyes. Fear of G-d is more outwardly evident than is fear of sin. That is, it [fear of G-d] implies more G-dly awareness, since it is a result of contemplation of G-dliness as will be explained regarding [the verse in Psalms 33:8] "Let all the earth fear G-d."

Just as we must guard our senses, so must we guard our thoughts. We must not think strange thoughts nor negative thoughts, mindful that we fear G-d. At first, we might assume that strange thoughts and negative reflections are the result of the vulgar earthiness of our natural personality

וְלָכֵן עוֹל מַלְכוּת שָׁמַיִם הוּא מַה שֶׁפּוֹעֵל בְּדֶרֶךְ מִמֵּילָא, הַיְנוּ שֶׁהוּא מְגַדֵּר מִמֵּילָא בְּהַכֹּחוֹת וְהַחוּשִׁים כְּמוֹ שֶׁאֵינוֹ רוֹאֶה וְאֵינוֹ שׁוֹמֵעַ וכו' וּכְמוֹ כֵן אֵינוֹ מִתְאַוֶּה אוֹ אֵינוֹ כּוֹעֵס מִפְּנֵי עוֹל מַלְכוּת שָׁמַיִם שֶׁעָלָיו. וְהַיִּרְאָה הִיא בְּמָקוֹם שֶׁצָּרִיךְ הִתְגַּבְּרוּת לִגְדֹּר אֶת עַצְמוֹ וְהַיְנוּ שֶׁמַּגְדִּיר אֶת עַצְמוֹ מִפְּנֵי הַיִּרְאָה וּפַחַד אֱלֹקִים שֶׁנֶּגֶד עֵינָיו, וְיִרְאַת אֱלֹקִים הִיא בְּהִתְגַּלּוּת יוֹתֵר מִיִּרְאַת חֵטְא, וְהַיְנוּ שֶׁיֵּשׁ בָּזֶה יוֹתֵר הֶרְגֵּשׁ אֱלֹקִי הַבָּא עַל יְדֵי אֵיזֶה הִתְבּוֹנְנוּת בֶּאֱלֹקוּת וּכְמוֹ שֶׁיִּתְבָּאֵר בְּעִנְיַן יִרְאוּ מֵה' כָּל הָאָרֶץ כו').

וּכְמוֹ הַהַגְדָּרָה בַּחוּשִׁים הנ"ל כֵּן הוּא הַהַגְדָּרָה בְּחוּשׁ הַמַּחֲשָׁבָה שֶׁלֹּא לַחֲשֹׁב מַחֲשָׁבוֹת זָרוֹת וְלֹא יָבִיא אֶת עַצְמוֹ לִידֵי הִרְהוּר מִפְּנֵי פַּחַד אֱלֹקִים כו'. וְהִנֵּה לִכְאוֹרָה סִבַּת הַמַּחֲשָׁבוֹת זָרוֹת וְהַהִרְהוּרִים רָעִים הוּא מֵחֲמָרִיּוּת הַמִּדּוֹת טִבְעִיִּים

The yoke of heaven is instinctive and unconscious, but we also need to develop conscious fear of G-d in order to successfully control ourselves.

COMMENTARY

rather the result of a decision to live a lifestyle under the spiritual umbrella of the One Above.

2. YIRAT CHAIT

The second mind-state mentioned in Chapter 2 is called "fear of sin" (*yirat chait*), which is an action-oriented fear. When we are in this mind-state, we take care not to make the wrong move and transgress the will of the King. There is little or no emotion involved with fear of sin. Rather, we are simply aware of the

It is also necessary to control our thoughts, which we do in part by refining our physical desires.

דְּמִפְּנֵי שֶׁמִּתְאַוֶּה בְּלִבּוֹ דְּבַר תַּאֲוָה וְחֶמְדָּה הֲרֵי זֶה עוֹלֶה מִן הַלֵּב אֶל הַמֹּחַ לַחְשֹׁב וּלְהַרְהֵר בָּזֶה וְכַאֲשֶׁר פּוֹעֵל זִכּוּךְ הַמִּדּוֹת הַטִּבְעִיִּים שֶׁלּוֹ שֶׁאֵינוֹ מִתְאַוֶּה לִדְבָרִים חָמְרִיִּים מִמֵּילָא אֵינָם נוֹפְלִים לוֹ מַחְשָׁבוֹת וְהִרְהוּרִים כו'. וּכְמוֹ שֶׁאָנוּ רוֹאִים בְּחוּשׁ דְּכַאֲשֶׁר פּוֹעֲלִים בַּעֲבוֹדָה הַכְנָעַת הַמִּדּוֹת הַטִּבְעִיִּים יַעֲבֹר מֶשֶׁךְ זְמַן שֶׁלֹּא יִפְּלוּ לוֹ מַחְשָׁבוֹת זָרוֹת כְּלָל, וְכַאֲשֶׁר מִתְרַפִּים בַּעֲבוֹדָה וּמִתְגַּבְּרִים הַמִּדּוֹת בְּחָמְרִיּוּת בָּאִים הַמַּחְשָׁבוֹת הַמְבַלְבְּלִים כו'

(וְהִנֵּה בְּחָמְרִיּוּת הַמִּדּוֹת וְתַאֲוָתָם יֵשׁ כַּמָּה פְּרָטִים וְכָל אֶחָד וְאֶחָד יוֹדֵעַ בְּנַפְשׁוֹ אֵיזֶה עִנְיַן פְּרָטִי מַגִּיעַ לְחֶלְקוֹ לְבָרֵר וּלְזַכֵּךְ, אַךְ בְּדֶרֶךְ כְּלָל הַכֹּל תָּלוּי בְּתַאֲוַת אֲכִילָה וּכְמַאֲמָר' אֵין אֲרִי נוֹהֵם מִתּוֹךְ קֻפָּה שֶׁל תֶּבֶן אֶלָּא מִתּוֹךְ קֻפָּה שֶׁל בָּשָׂר וּכְמַאֲמָר' מָלֵי' כְּרֵיסֵי' זִינָא בִּישָׁא וּכְמוֹ שֶׁכָּתוּב וַיִּשְׁמַן יְשֻׁרוּן כו', וְהִיא

Kuntres Ha'Avoda - קונטרס העבודה

traits. The lusts of our heart for objects of physical desire arise from the heart to the mind and cause us to think about them. But when we refine our natural character, we will no longer lust for gross physical things, and then automatically, strange thoughts will not come to mind either. We will see clearly that when, through [self-improvement] work, we subjugate our natural character, for some time no foreign thoughts will arise to disturb us. But, when we weaken in our efforts and our natural characteristics have an opportunity to regroup, negative ruminations come back to plague us.

(There are several details involved in the coarse physical nature and lusts of our character traits, and we all know in our soul which particular trait we must purify and refine. But, in general, all lusts stem from the lust to eat [gluttony], as the sages said [*Berachot* 32,1], "The lion doesn't roar from a trough of straw, but from a trough of meat," and "A full stomach

——————— ***COMMENTARY*** ———————

negative ramifications of violating the will of the One Above, and we therefore try our best to guard ourselves from any thought, speech, or action that would lead to a transgression. This causes us to guard our eyesight, to guard our hearing, and to curtail our speech in order to avoid any kind of situation that would lead to sin. The world we live in is so full of sensory stimulation that by simply walking in a public thoroughfare, we may become overwhelmed by negative images and sensations. The problem here is not only that many of these stimuli are

Essay on Service of the Heart - Love Like Fire and Water

is a form of sin" [Also there]. Also, "Yeshurun became fat and kicked..." [Deuteronomy 32:15] The lust for eating is the source of all negative character traits. Regarding Esau, the Torah says [in Genesis 25:34], "And he ate and drank, and got up and left," and the Sages commented that what he left was his "world" [that is, "his world-to-come," which was promised by the birthright he sold to Jacob in return for food]. It is said as well regarding the rebellious son of the Torah that he is judged according to his end [including all the negative character traits he developed after gluttonous eating and drinking]. The refinement of this negative trait promotes the refinement of all character traits, because its weakening — by refraining from eating in response to this lust — weakens all of the negative character traits.)

הַסִבָּה הַגּוֹרֶמֶת לְכָל הַמִדּוֹת רָעוֹת וּכְמוֹ שֶׁכָּתוּב וַיֹּאכַל וַיֵּשְׁתְּ וַיָּקָם וַיֵּלֶךְ שֶׁיָּצָא מֵעוֹלָמוֹ כו', וּכְמוֹ בֵּן סוֹרֵר וּמוֹרֶה שֶׁנִדוֹן עַל שֵׁם סוֹפוֹ כו' (וְלָאו דַּוְקָא בְּלִיסְטוּת אֶלָּא בְּכָל הַמִדּוֹת רָעוֹת). וְזִכּוּךְ הַמִדָּה הָרָעָה הַזֹּאת הוּא הַמְסַיֵּעַ וְהַמֵּקֵל זִכּוּךְ כָּל הַמִדּוֹת כִּי בְּחַלִישׁוּת הַמִדָּה הַזֹּאת הֵינוּ שֶׁאֵינוֹ לְמַלֵּא תַּאֲווֹת נַפְשׁוֹ נֶחְלָשִׁים כָּל הַמִדּוֹת.

The lust for food is the source of all desires.

But the truth is that [negative] thoughts rise spontaneously from the heart to the mind. They are an extension of the emotions, but by effort to purify our emotions, the negative thoughts automatically cease coming to mind, as mentioned above.

אַךְ הָעִנְיָן הוּא דְּמַחְשָׁבוֹת אֵלּוּ הֵן הַבָּאִים מִמֵּילָא מִן הַלֵּב אֶל הַמֹּחַ לְהַרְהֵר שֶׁהֵן הִתְפַּשְׁטוּת הַמִדוֹת וְעַל יְדֵי הָעֲבוֹדָה וְהַיְגִיעָה שֶׁמְזַכֵּךְ אֶת הַמִדּוֹת מִמֵּילָא אֵינָם נוֹפְלִים הַמַחְשָׁבוֹת כו' כנ"ל.

The *beinoni* [defined in *Tanya*] is one who hasn't transformed the essence of the powers of his animal

וְלִהְיוֹת שֶׁהַבֵּינוֹנִי הוּא שֶׁאֵינוֹ הוֹפֵךְ מַהוּת הַכֹּחוֹת דְּנֶפֶשׁ הַבַּהֲמִית רַק הַהִתְפַּשְׁטוּת שֶׁלוֹ וּבִשְׁעַת הַתְּפִלָּה

COMMENTARY

not acceptable by any spiritual standard, but that the sheer quantity of stimuli overwhelms our senses. Aside from the obvious spiritual benefits that accrue from circumscribing our sensory input, we simply derive a tremendous peace of mind by censoring most of them and focusing on our own spiritual welfare. This is what the Rebbe means in Chapter 2 when he says that if we will focus our attention on our own "four cubits" (our own sensory locale), we will see salvation.

By refining and purifying our emotions, we minimize our lusts, but even if they recur, the "beinoni" pushes them away with both hands.

הֲרֵי הַנֶּפֶשׁ הַבַּהֲמִית הוּא כְּיָשֵׁן שֶׁהוּא כָּפוּף וּבָטֵל וְאֵינוֹ מִתְאַוֶּה תַּאֲוָה כו', וְכַאֲשֶׁר הָעֲבוֹדָה הִיא כִּדְבָעֵי הֲרֵי זֶה נִמְשָׁךְ זְמַן רַב גַּם אַחַר הַתְּפִלָּה שֶׁהַנֶּפֶשׁ הַבַּהֲמִית נִכְנַע וּבָטֵל כו', וּבִפְרָט בִּשְׁקִידַת הַתְּפִלָּה יוֹם יוֹם יִדְרְשׁוּן כו', אֲבָל לִהְיוֹת שֶׁלֹּא נֶהְפַּךְ לְגַמְרֵי הֲרֵי הוּא חוֹזֵר וְנֵעוֹר וְנוֹפְלִים לוֹ מַחֲשָׁבוֹת זָרוֹת וְהִרְהוּרִים כו', רַק שֶׁאֵינוֹ מְקַבֵּל אֶת הַהִרְהוּר הָרַע בְּרָצוֹן חַס וְחָלִילָה וְדוֹחֵהוּ בִּשְׁתֵּי יָדַיִם וּמֵסִיחַ דַּעְתּוֹ מִיָּד שֶׁנִּזְכָּר שֶׁהוּא הִרְהוּר רַע כו', וּכְמוֹ שֶׁכָּתוּב בְּסֵפֶר שֶׁל בֵּינוֹנִים פי"ב ופכ"ז וכ"ח. אֲבָל כְּשֶׁמְּהַרְהֵר בְּרָצוֹן דְּהַיְנוּ גַּם כְּשֶׁנִּזְכָּר שֶׁהוּא הִרְהוּר רַע הֲרֵי הוּא מְהַרְהֵר בּוֹ בְּרָצוֹן שֶׁזֶּהוּ מִפְּנֵי שֶׁאֵין יִרְאַת אֱלֹקִים בְּלִבּוֹ. וְכֵן כַּאֲשֶׁר מַמְשִׁיךְ עָלָיו הַהִרְהוּרִים רָעִים מִצַּד הַפְּרִיקַת עוֹל בְּהִתְפַּשְּׁטוּת הַחוּשִׁים בִּשְׁמִיעַת דִּבְרֵי הוֹלְלוּת וְלֵיצָנוּת וְכָל שֶׁכֵּן בִּרְאִיָּ' וְהַבָּטָה וּמַחֲשָׁב וּמְהַרְהֵר בָּזֶה וּמְטַמֵּא אֶת נַפְשׁוֹ רַחֲמָנָא לִיצְלָן בְּהִרְהוּרִים רָעִים בִּשְׁאָט נֶפֶשׁ (וּמִמֵּילָא בָּא לִידֵי טֻמְאָה בְּפֹעַל

soul, but only the manifestations thereof [thought, speech and action]. During prayer, his animal soul — which is subjugated and nullified — is as if "sleeping," having no desires [of its own]. When his prayer is as it should be, this condition lasts for a considerable amount of time afterward, since his animal soul remains subdued and nullified, as "day after day they seek Me" [Isaiah 58:2]. However, since his animal soul hasn't been transformed completely, it regroups and revives once more, and the *beinoni* again is subject to strange thoughts and negative reflections. [But] the *beinoni* refuses to willingly give in and pushes these thoughts away with "both hands." He takes his mind off them completely as soon as he recognizes them for what they are — corrupt thoughts — as described in *Tanya*, chapters 12, 27, and 28. But, if he willingly entertains these thoughts [in which he case he is no longer considered a *beinoni*, but a *rasha*] — meaning that even after he recognizes them for what they are, he continues to indulge in them — it is because the fear of G-d has left his

——————— **COMMENTARY** ———————

If accepting the "yoke of heaven" is associated with the lowest *sephira (malchut*, or "sovereignty"*)*, fear of sin is associated with the somewhat higher (but still low in the hierarchy) *sephirot* of *netzach* ("victory"), *hod* ("thanksgiving") and *yesod* ("foundation"). These are the *sephirot* which guide our actions and instincts, though they do not impart conscious emotion or understanding. However, fear of sin is more than an unconscious

Essay on Service of the Heart - Love Like Fire and Water   53

heart. And if he purposely draws down upon himself such negative thoughts, it is because he has thrown off the "yoke of heaven." He lets himself hear words of frivolity and mockery and even worse, allows himself to see and stare, think and ponder, and in so doing recklessly contaminate his soul, G-d forbid, with impure thoughts (and then automatically he comes to a state of actual uncleanliness, G-d forbid). This [downslide] cannot be attributed to the gross physicality of his character traits alone, but also to his throwing off the

רַחֲמָנָא לִיצְלָן) אֵין זֶה מִצַּד חָמְרִיּוּת הַמִּדּוֹת לְבַד כִּי אִם מִצַּד פְּרִיקַת עוֹל וְהֶעְדֵּר יִרְאַת אֱלֹקִים. וּבָזֶה עוֹד גּוֹרֵם רַע לְנַפְשׁוֹ שֶׁנּוֹפְלִים לוֹ אַחַר כָּךְ מַחֲשָׁבוֹת וְהִרְהוּרִים רָעִים גַּם כְּשֶׁאֵינוֹ חָפֵץ בָּהֶם וְהַרְבֵּה יוֹתֵר מִכְּפִי הַמִּדָּה עַד שֶׁתִּגְעַל נַפְשׁוֹ בָּהֶם וְאֵינוֹ יָכוֹל לַהֲסִירָם בְּשׁוּם אֹפֶן וְהוּא עִנְיַן מֶמְשֶׁלֶת זֵדִים דְּהַחַיָּבָא מְבַלְבְּלִים לוֹ וּמְטַמְּאִים אוֹתוֹ רַחֲמָנָא לִיצְלָן וּכְמוֹ שֶׁכָּתוּב בַּאֲרִיכוּת בְּדֶרֶךְ חַיִּים בְּעִנְיַן גַּם מִזֵּדִים חֲשֹׂךְ עַבְדֶּךָ כו'.

If we entertain or encourage such thoughts, it is because we have thrown off the yoke of heaven.

"yoke of heaven," and his lack of fear of G-d. Furthermore, [this decline] causes his soul more harm in that afterward he has unclean thoughts even when he doesn't want them, and to a much greater degree than would be expected. He becomes disgusted with himself, but he is unable to free himself from this situation which is known as "the rule of the wicked," where the wicked plague and contaminate him. This is described at length in *Derech Chaim*[xiv] [a tractate from the second Lubavitcher Rebbe], regarding the verse [Psalms 19:14] "also from the wicked may your servants be shaded."

xiv) See footnote of the Rebbe on page 270 ←

And [it is on account of this phenomenon that we seek to develop] cautiousness of thought based upon accepting the "yoke of heaven." We become very careful regarding anything that would bring us to lowly and impure thoughts, and we develop an intense dislike for such impure reflections. Even when such a reflec-

וּבָזֶה הִיא הַהַגְדָּרָה בַּמַּחֲשָׁבָה מִצַּד קַבָּלַת עוֹל מַלְכוּת שָׁמַיִם שֶׁנִּזְהָר מְאֹד לְנַפְשׁוֹ מִכָּל דָּבָר הַמֵּבִיא לִידֵי הִרְהוּר רַע וְאֵינוֹ חָפֵץ מְאֹד בְּהִרְהוּרִים רָעִים, וְגַם כְּשֶׁנּוֹפֵל לוֹ אֵיזֶה הִרְהוּר הִנֵּה מִיָּד שֶׁנִּזְכָּר שֶׁזֶּה הִרְהוּר רַע דּוֹחֵהוּ בִּשְׁתֵּי יָדַיִם וּמֵסִיחַ דַּעְתּוֹ מִזֶּה לְגַמְרֵי מִצַּד יִרְאַת

─────── **COMMENTARY** ───────

attitude — it is an awareness-based approach to serving the One Above. It is a result of our taking upon ourselves the "yoke of heaven," and therefore it is informed by our concern not to transgress G-d's will.

Accepting the yoke of G-d and cultivating fear of sin free us completely from negative thoughts.

אֱלֹקִים שֶׁבְּלִבּוֹ. וְעַל יְדֵי הַקַּבָּלַת עוֹל מַלְכוּת שָׁמַיִם הוּא נִצּוֹל מֵהַרְהוּרִים רָעִים שֶׁאֵינָם נוֹפְלִים לוֹ כְּלָל וּכְמוֹ שֶׁכָּתוּב בְּדֶרֶךְ חַיִּים שָׁם פ"ז שֶׁמִּפְּנֵי הֶאָרַת מַלְכוּת שָׁמַיִם הָאֱלֹקִית בּוֹרְחִים הַקְּלִפּוֹת וּכְמוֹ שֶׁכָּתוּב כְּהִמֵּס דּוֹנַג כו' יֹאבְדוּ רְשָׁעִים מִפְּנֵי הָאֱלֹקִים.

tion occurs to us [spontaneously], as soon as we recognize it for what it is, we push it away with "both hands," and take our mind off it completely. All of this is as a result of fear of sin in our heart. And once we accept upon ourselves the "yoke of heaven," we are freed from negative thoughts completely; it is written in *Derech Chaim*, chapter 7, that as a result of the light of heavenly kingship, the forces opposed to holiness "run away." As it says [Psalms 68:3], "...like wax melts before fire, the wicked are destroyed in front of G-d."

וְעַל כֵּן יִרְאָה זוֹ דְּבִכְלָלָהּ הוּא עִנְיַן קַבָּלַת עוֹל מַלְכוּת שָׁמַיִם הִיא מֻכְרַחַת לִהְיוֹת בְּכָל אֶחָד וְאֶחָד וְאִי אֶפְשָׁר בִּלְעָדֶיהָ כְּלָל כִּי בְּהֶעְדֵּר זֶה הֲרֵי הוּא פּוֹרֵק עוֹל וַהֲרֵי הוּא עָלוּל לְכָל מִינֵי רַע רַחֲמָנָא לִיצְּלָן כַּנַּ"ל. וְלָזֹאת עִנְיַן קַבָּלַת עוֹל מַלְכוּת שָׁמַיִם וְיִרְאַת אֱלֹקִים הֲרֵי זֶה מֻכְרָח לִהְיוֹת בְּכָל אֶחָד וְאֶחָד מַמָּשׁ וְעַל יְדֵי זֶה הוּא סָר מֵרַע, וְנִכְלָל בָּזֶה גַּם כֵּן עִנְיַן וַעֲשֵׂה טוֹב, הַיְנוּ לַעֲשׂוֹת כָּל

Therefore, fear of G-d — which in general is a result of accepting upon ourselves the "yoke of heaven" — must exist in each and every one of us. It is perfectly impossible to serve G-d without it, since in its absence, we throw off the "yoke of heaven," and then we are likely to encounter all kinds of negative circumstances, as mentioned above, G-d forbid. And therefore, acceptance of the "yoke of heaven" and fear of G-d are absolutely necessary prerequisites for every one of us in order to avoid anything bad. Included in this is also "doing good," meaning that we are likewise committed to fulfilling everything commanded

---

COMMENTARY

3. *YIRAT ELOKIM*

The third and final mind-state mentioned in Chapter 2 is *yirat Elokim* ("fear of G-d"). It is a step higher in the hierarchy than *yirat chait* ("fear of sin"). Whereas fear of sin involves no emotional feeling, but caution regarding how to act and curtail the senses, fear of G-d involves fear of the One Above. It is an emotional form of fear. Thus, it corresponds to the higher emotional *sephira* of *gevura* ("strictness/constriction.")

Essay on Service of the Heart - Love Like Fire and Water

[by G-d]. This is what is meant by [the verse in Ecclesiastes 12:13] "in the end... fear G-d and fulfill His commandments, since this is the entire duty of a person."

מַה שֶׁנִּצְטַוָּה וְזֶה שֶׁכָּתוּב סוֹף דָּבָר כו' אֶת הָאֱלֹקִים יְרָא וְאֶת מִצְוֹתָיו שְׁמוֹר כִּי זֶה כָּל הָאָדָם,

Thus, the crux of the matter is [cultivating] fear [of G-d], since only by means of it can we fulfill the positive and negative *mitzvot* in practice. Love of G-d is developed by servants of G-d [those who serve Him in prayer and meditation]. But, even if we do not fall into this category, it need not affect our fulfillment of the *mitzvot*, neither the positive nor the negative *mitzvot*. However, we will lack closeness to the One Above (meaning that we have not fulfilled the *mitzvah* of "you shall love [G-d]"). In such a situation, [it can be assumed that] the coarse nature of our animal soul will come to the fore, and even though we keep the Torah and its *mitzvot*, we will be earthy, vulgar, and crude as a result of [involvement in] gross matters of permitted pleasures. So also, we will totally lack interest in anything G-dly, such as learning Torah or fulfilling *mitzvot*.

שֶׁהָעִקָּר הוּא בְּחִינַת הַיִּרְאָה שֶׁעַל יְדֵי זֶה דַּוְקָא הוּא סוּר מֵרַע וַעֲשֵׂה טוֹב בְּפֹעַל מַמָּשׁ כו' (דְּאַהֲבָה הוּא בְּעוֹבְדֵי ה', וְגַם אִם אֵינוֹ עוֹבֵד ה' אֵין זֶה שַׁיָּךְ מִכָּל מָקוֹם לְקִיּוּם הַמִּצְווֹת לָסוּר מֵרַע וַעֲשֵׂה טוֹב בְּפֹעַל רַק שֶׁאֵין לוֹ קֵרוּב וּדְבֵקוּת בֶּאֱלֹקוּת (וְהַיְנוּ שֶׁלֹּא קִיֵּם מִצְוַת וְאָהַבְתָּ) וּמִמֵּילָא מִתְגַּבֵּר בּוֹ הַחָמְרִיּוּת וְגַסּוּת הַנֶּפֶשׁ הַבַּהֲמִית וְעִם הֱיוֹתוֹ מְקַיֵּם תּוֹרָה וּמִצְווֹת הֲרֵי הוּא חָמְרִי וְגַס וְנִתְעָב בִּדְבָרִים מְתֹעָבִים בְּתַאֲווֹת הֶתֵּר כו', וּכְמוֹ כֵן אֵין לוֹ שׁוּם חַיּוּת אֱלֹקִי בְּעֵסֶק הַתּוֹרָה וְקִיּוּם הַמִּצְווֹת

The crux of the matter is fear of G-d since only by this means can we fulfill the mitzvoth properly.

(It is possible that this is what is meant in *Tanya*, Part 1, chapter 4, "and without it [love of G-d] they [the positive *mitzvot*] are not truly fulfilled, because the one who truly fulfills them... [is one who loves G-d]." The meaning here is that [without love of G-d], the *mitzvot* are without life, like a body without a soul. And furthermore, attention to the fine details of the *mitzvot* certainly comes only from *avoda* [that is, working on ourselves to develop attachment to the One Above], as will be explained in chapter 7. Embellishment

(וְיֵשׁ לוֹמַר דְּזֶהוּ מַה שֶׁכָּתוּב בְּסֵפֶר שֶׁל בֵּינוֹנִים ח"א פ"ד וּבִלְעָדֶיהָ אֵין לָהֶן קִיּוּם אֲמִתִּי כִּי הַמְקַיְּמָן בֶּאֱמֶת כו', הַיְנוּ שֶׁאֵין לָהֶם חַיּוּת וַהֲרֵי הֵן כְּגוּף בְּלֹא נְשָׁמָה, וְדִקְדּוּקֵי מִצְווֹת הֵן וַדַּאי עַל יְדֵי הָעֲבוֹדָה דַּוְקָא

וכמשית"ל פ"ז, וכן הדור מצוה הוא על ידי החיות שבמצוה והיקר שבה)

אבל מכל מקום אינו ברע גמור חס וחלילה ולא יעבור חס וחלילה על שום דבר, אבל בהעדר היראה הנ"ל הרי נפשו ברע הוא רחמנא ליצלן וכנ"ל, ועל כן היראה היא מוכרחת ואי אפשר להיות בלעדיה וזהו הנקרא יראת שמים שהוא ענין קבלת עול מלכות שמים ויראת אלקים) והיא התחלת העבודה ויסודה

We must first go through a stage known as "forget your nation and the house of your father," and this enables us to accept the yoke of heaven and the commandments.

וכנודע דקבלת עול מלכות שמים קודמת לכל המצוות וכמא' קבלו מלכותי ואחר כך קבלו גזרותי, ובפרט בעבודה הרי קדם כל דבר צריך להיות שכחי עמך ובית אביך שהיא היציאה מעניניו שהוא מרגל בהם, דהנה עיר פרא אדם יולד בכחותיו וחושיו הטבעיים שמהנפש הבהמית דאקדמי טעניתא המושך אותו לכל ענינים הגופניים והוא מתרגל בענינים אלו ונשרש בהם והינו שהטבעית עוד מתגברת במשך הזמן.

of the *mitzvot*, as well, takes place among those who fulfill the *mitzvot* with energy and care.)

Nevertheless, [though crude] we haven't fallen into completely bad ways, G-d forbid, and we won't transgress anything. But if we lack fear [of G-d], we lower our soul into evil, G-d forbid, as described above. Therefore, fear is a necessary ingredient, and it's impossible to be without it. This is called "fear of heaven," which [includes] acceptance of the "yoke of heaven," and "fear of G-d." It is the beginning of the *avoda* of G-d and its foundation.

It is known that accepting the "yoke of heaven" precedes all of the *mitzvot*, as the Sages said [in Mechilta on Exodus 20:3]: "Accept my sovereignty, and afterward accept my decrees..." Certainly, when we begin the *avoda* of G-d [by establishing a relationship with the One Above], we must go through an initial stage called "forget your nation and the house of your father," which means leaving behind all that we have become habituated to. The truth is that "a person is born like a wild donkey" [as is stated in Job 11:12]. When it comes to our natural senses and the abilities of our animal soul, these have a prior claim on us and draw us toward all kinds of bodily attractions. We become accustomed to them and steeped in them, which means that our natural [animal] souls become even stronger with the passage of time.

וכל זה מעלים ומסתיר על הכחות דנפש האלקית שהוא ענין חלישות

All of this serves to conceal the powers of our divine souls, and this

Essay on Service of the Heart - Love Like Fire and Water

concealment [in turn] leads to the weakening of the divine soul, as is stated [Psalms 31:11] "my strength has left me because of my misdeeds." It is known that the word *avon* ["misdeed"] does not imply an actual transgression, but a crookedness and distortion, as evidenced by the person who bends his path and walks in a circuitous fashion. Such is the path of our animal souls, and it causes a weakening and stumbling of the divine soul, as it is written [in Jeremiah 17: 9], "The heart is crooked, it is Enosh," meaning: "It is weak." [Enosh represents the lowest form of humanity, a form that is weak in serving G-d]. The weakness expresses itself in different ways; there may be no revelation of the powers of the divine soul whatsoever.

(And within this there are distinctions. We may be totally unaware of any divine matter or feeling in our souls, meaning that our spiritual powers have become so hidden that we know nothing but the physical world and everything in it. Or, we may feel that the ultimate purpose of man in this world is not to be like a "horse or mule," but rather to strive for a higher purpose. However, the strong pull of the physical doesn't permit us to forsake our physical concerns and draw close to that higher purpose. Sometimes, we [respond to the call of G-dliness], approaching and working hard on it, but we are still unable to receive it — meaning to grasp and experience it — because our [spiritual] faculties are so hidden that the G-dly

הַנֶּפֶשׁ הָאֱלֹקִית וּכְמוֹ שֶׁכָּתוּב כָּשַׁל בַּעֲוֹנִי כֹחִי. וְיָדוּעַ דְּעָוֹן אֵין פֵּרוּשׁוֹ חֵטְא וְעָוֹן בְּפֹעַל מַמָּשׁ כִּי אִם לְשׁוֹן עִוּוּת וְעִקּוּם וְהַיְנוּ שֶׁמְּעַקֵּם דַּרְכּוֹ וְהוֹלֵךְ בְּדֶרֶךְ עֲקַלָּתוֹן שֶׁהוּא דַּרְכּוֹ שֶׁל הַנֶּפֶשׁ הַבַּהֲמִית עַל יְדֵי זֶה נִכְשַׁל וְנֶחֱלָשׁ כֹּחוֹ *) הָאֱלֹקִית, וּכְמוֹ שֶׁכָּתוּב עָקֹב הַלֵּב מִכֹּל וְאָנוּשׁ הוּא פֵּי' חַלָּשׁ הוּא כוּ', וְהַחֲלִישׁוּת הוּא בְּכַמָּה אוֹפַנִּים אִם שֶׁלֹּא יֵשׁ הִתְגַּלּוּת הַכֹּחוֹת דְּנֶפֶשׁ הָאֱלֹקִית כְּלָל

(וּבָזֶה גּוּפָא יֵשׁ חִלּוּקִים אִם שֶׁהוּא בְּהֶסַּח הַדַּעַת לְגַמְרֵי מֵאֵיזֶה עִנְיָן וְהַרְגֵּשׁ אֱלֹקִי בְּנַפְשׁוֹ, וְהַיְנוּ שֶׁכָּל כָּךְ נִתְעַלְּמוּ כֹחוֹתָיו הָאֱלֹקִיּוֹת עַד שֶׁאֵינוֹ יוֹדֵעַ דָּבָר אַחֵר בְּעוֹלָמוֹ כִּי אִם הָעוֹלָם הַזֶּה וּמְלוֹאוֹ. אוֹ שֶׁמַּרְגִּישׁ שֶׁאֵין זֶה כָּל הָאָדָם לִחְיוֹת בְּעִנְיְנֵי הָעוֹלָם הַזֶּה כְּסוּס וּכְפֶרֶד כוּ', רַק תַּכְלִיתוֹ הוּא אֵיזֶה עִנְיָן נַעֲלֶה, אֲבָל הִתְגַּבְּרוּת הַטִּבְעִית אֵינוֹ מֵנִיחַ אוֹתוֹ לַעֲזֹב עִנְיָנָיו הַטִּבְעִיִּים וּלְהִתְקָרֵב אֶל הָעִנְיָן הַנַּעֲלֶה, וְיֵשׁ שֶׁמְּקָרֵב אֶת עַצְמוֹ לְאֵיזֶה עִנְיַן אֱלֹקִי וּמַגִּיעַ אֶת עַצְמוֹ בָּזֶה אֲבָל לֹא יוּכַל לְקַבֵּל הַיְנוּ לְהַשִּׂיג וּלְהַרְגִּישׁ הָעִנְיָן מִפְּנֵי הִתְעַלְּמוּת כֹּחוֹתָיו שֶׁאֵינוֹ מֵאִיר בָּהֶם הָאוֹר. דְּהַנֶּפֶשׁ הָאֱלֹקִית הוּא

Otherwise, our animal soul dominates, hiding and concealing the divine soul inside of us.

light does not penetrate to them. The divine soul is like a polished object, which receives light and reflects it. Therefore, everything G-dly is absorbed by the divine soul, and it shines as a result. However, when there is a thick covering that conceals and hides the divine soul, the G-dly light isn't received. This is what is meant by [the verse in Isaiah 59:2] "but your transgressions [came] between yourselves and your G-d." The deviousness of the animal soul conceals the divine soul and acts as a divider between G-dliness and the [divine] soul, which then fails to become illuminated with G-dly light, as written elsewhere.) Or, there may be a minimal revelation of the soul powers of the divine soul, which is [nonetheless] insufficient to overcome the animal soul and its coarseness.

כִּדְבָר מְלֻטָּשׁ הַמְקַבֵּל בְּתוֹכוֹ אוֹר וּמִתְנוֹצֵץ עַל יְדֵי זֶה, וְעַל כֵּן כָּל עִנְיָן אֱלֹקִי הוּא מִתְקַבֵּל בַּנֶּפֶשׁ הָאֱלֹקִית וְהַנֶּפֶשׁ מְאִירָה עַל יָדוֹ, אֲבָל כַּאֲשֶׁר יֵשׁ מִכְסֶה עָב הַמְכַסֶּה וּמַעֲלִים עַל הַנֶּפֶשׁ הָאֱלֹקִית אֵינוֹ מִתְקַבֵּל בְּתוֹכוֹ הָאוֹר הָאֱלֹקִי, וְזֶה שֶׁכָּתוּב כִּי אִם עֲוֹנוֹתֵיכֶם כוּ' בֵּינֵיכֶם וּבֵין אֱלֹקֵיכֶם כוּ' דְּהָעַוְתוּת שֶׁמֵהַנֶּפֶשׁ הַבַּהֲמִית מַעֲלִים וּמַסְתִּיר עַל הַנֶּפֶשׁ הָאֱלֹקִית וּמַפְסִיק בֵּין הַנְּשָׁמָה וְהָאֱלֹקוּת שֶׁאֵינוֹ מֵאִיר בָּהּ אוֹר אֱלֹקִי כוּ' וּכְמוֹ שֶׁכָּתוּב בְּמָקוֹם אַחֵר) אוֹ שֶׁגַּם בְּהִתְגַּלּוּת קְצָת דְּהַכֹּחוֹת דְּנֶפֶשׁ הָאֱלֹקִית אֵין בִּיכָלְתּוֹ לְהִתְגַּבֵּר עַל הַנֶּפֶשׁ הַבַּהֲמִית וְחָמְרִיּוּתוֹ.

If we desire the "life of the soul," we cannot begin with intellect and meditation; we must first lay the spiritual foundation by accepting the yoke of heaven and leaving behind our coarse physical behavior.

Thus, if we desire the life of the soul and want to illuminate our divine soul with the light of the "life of the living" through the service of the heart [which is prayer], and if we wish to master our natural [physical] traits and purify and refine them, we cannot start with *avoda* [meditation] based on logic and intellect. We are not a "vessel" for such G-dly understanding and arousal of the heart, because the faculties of our divine soul are so concealed and our animal soul is so strong, as explained above. Therefore, the first thing we must do is accept upon ourselves the "yoke of heaven,"

וְעַל כֵּן הֶחָפֵץ בְּחַיֵּי נַפְשׁוֹ לְהָאִיר נַפְשׁוֹ הָאֱלֹקִית בְּאוֹר חַיֵּי הַחַיִּים בַּעֲבוֹדָה שֶׁבַּלֵּב וּלְהִתְגַּבֵּר עַל כֹּחוֹתָיו הַטִּבְעִיִּים לְבָרְרָם וּלְזַכְּכָם, אִי אֶפְשָׁר לוֹ לְהַתְחִיל בַּעֲבוֹדָה שֶׁעַל פִּי טַעַם וָדַעַת, הַיְנוּ בְּהַשָּׂגוֹת אֱלֹקוּת וּבְהִתְעוֹרְרוּת בַּלֵּב כוּ' מֵאַחַר שֶׁאֵינוֹ כְּלִי לָזֶה מִפְּנֵי הִתְעַלְּמוּת הַכֹּחוֹת דְּנֶפֶשׁ הָאֱלֹקִית וְהִתְגַּבְּרוּת הַכֹּחוֹת דְּנֶפֶשׁ הַבַּהֲמִית כַּנַּ"ל. וְעַל כֵּן רֵאשִׁית כָּל דָּבָר הוּא לְקַבֵּל עָלָיו עוֹל מַלְכוּת שָׁמַיִם לַעֲזוֹב עִנְיָנָיו שֶׁמֻּרְגָּל בָּהֶם מִצַּד הַטִּבְעִית וְלִתֵּן אֶת עַצְמוֹ לֶאֱלֹקוּת,

Essay on Service of the Heart - Love Like Fire and Water

leave behind all that we have become accustomed to as a result of our natural, [physical] nature, and give ourselves over to G-dliness. We must serve the One Above just as a [simple] servant [serves his master].

לַעֲבֹד אוֹתוֹ יִתְבָּרֵךְ בְּכָל מִינֵי עֲבוֹדַת עֶבֶד

(At first glance, we might think that this "leaving behind" could take place by our controlling ourselves, without accepting the "yoke of heaven." However, in truth, the "leaving behind" must be motivated by the fact that we are forsaking behavior that is opposed to the will of G-d. This will last much longer when it is accompanied by a certain light shining into our hearts, as in the story I once told regarding one of the great [early] Chassidim.[xv] After this Chasid had his first personal audience with the Alter Rebbe [first Lubavitcher Rebbe, the Ba'al HaTanya], he succeeded in reaching a state wherein whatever desires arose from his natural, animal soul, he simply wouldn't do. At a minimum, this ["leaving behind"] should be motivated by a subconscious feeling of accepting the "yoke of heaven.")

(וְלִכְאוֹרָה הֲרֵי הָעֲזִיבָה יְכוֹלָה לִהְיוֹת עַל יְדֵי הִתְגַבְּרוּת עַל עַצְמוֹ גַם בְּלִי קַבָּלַת עוֹל. אַךְ בֶּאֱמֶת צָרִיךְ לִהְיוֹת הָעֲזִיבָה מִצַּד שֶׁזֶּה נֶגֶד רְצוֹן ה'. וְתִתְקַיֵּם בְּיוֹתֵר כַּאֲשֶׁר הִיא מִצַּד הֶרְגֵּשׁ אֵיזֶה אוֹר בְּנַפְשׁוֹ, וְכַאֲשֶׁר כְּבָר סִפַּרְתִּי מֵאֶחָד מֵהַחֲסִידִים הַגְּדוֹלִים אֲשֶׁר בַּכְּנִיסָה הָרִאשׁוֹנָה לכ"ק אדמו"ר זצוקללה"ה נ"ע זי"ע פָּעַל בְּעַצְמוֹ שֶׁכָּל מַה שֶּׁרוֹצֶה מִצַּד הַטִּבְעִי לֹא יַעֲשֶׂה (אַז וואס ער וויל זאל ער ניט טאָן). וּלְכָל הַפָּחוֹת יְהִי' זֶה מֵהֶרְגֵּשׁ הַנֶּעְלָם דְּקַבָּלַת עוֹל מַלְכוּת שָׁמַיִם)

The "leaving behind" will be more effective if accompanied by a sense of spiritual illumination shining in our heart.

xv) See footnote of the Rebbe on page 270 ←

By "leaving behind" [our former habits], we remove the coarseness of the animal soul, such that it no longer conceals the divine soul so much. And by the act of giving ourselves over to G-dliness, we prepare ourselves for the service of the heart with meditation upon G-dly concepts. [Then] the G-dly concepts will be retained and well-integrated in our soul. The light of our divine soul will shine and enable us to master our coarse natural tendencies. It has been explained

וּבַעֲזִיבָה זוֹ נָטַל הַחֲמָרִיּוּת דְּנֶפֶשׁ הַבַּהֲמִית שֶׁאֵינוֹ מַעֲלִים וּמַסְתִּיר כָּל כָּךְ עַל הַנֶּפֶשׁ הָאֱלֹקִית, וְהַנְּתִינָה שֶׁנּוֹתֵן עַצְמוֹ לֶאֱלֹקוּת הִיא הַמַּכְשִׁירָתוֹ אֶל הָעֲבוֹדָה שֶׁבַּלֵּב בְּהַשָּׂגָה וְהִתְבּוֹנְנוּת שֶׁיַּשִּׂיג עִנְיָן אֱלֹקִי וְיִתְקַבֵּל בְּנַפְשׁוֹ הֵיטֵב שֶׁיָּאִיר אוֹר נַפְשׁוֹ הָאֱלֹקִית וְתִתְגַּבֵּר עַל הַחֲמָרִיּוּת כו' וּכְמוֹ שֶׁכָּתוּב בְּמָקוֹם אַחֵר וְנִזְכָּר גַּם כֵּן לְעֵיל דְּהוֹדָאָה הָרִאשׁוֹנָה בְּאָמְרוֹ מוֹדֶה אֲנִי לְפָנֶיךָ

כו' הִיא יְסוֹד הָעֲבוֹדָה דְּכָל הַיּוֹם כֵּן וְיוֹתֵר מִכֵּן הוּא בְּקַבָּלַת עוֹל מַלְכוּת שָׁמַיִם שֶׁזֶּהוּ יְסוֹד כָּל הָעֲבוֹדָה, כִּי הַבִּטּוּל וְהַהַנָּחָה הַזֹּאת מַכְשִׁירָתוֹ לִהְיוֹת מֻכְשָׁר וּמְסֻגָּל לְכָל עֲבוֹדָה הַיְנוּ לַעֲבוֹדָה בְּמֹחַ וְלֵב וְגַם זֶה יְסוֹד מוּסָד לַעֲבוֹדָה בְּמַדְרֵגוֹת הַיּוֹתֵר נַעֲלוֹת כו'

elsewhere and was also mentioned previously, that the initial *hoda'ah* ["acknowledgment"] when we [rise in the morning and] say *Modeh Ani* ["I acknowledge the One Above"] is the foundation of *avoda* for the entire day. If so, it is certainly true that accepting the "yoke of heaven," is a foundation of all worship of the One Above, since the self-nullification [associated with this acceptance] prepares us for, and renders us capable of, any type of *avoda* of the One Above, including of the mind and of the heart. It is also a suitable foundation for the highest levels [of *avoda* of the One Above].

וְזֶה שֶׁכָּתוּב זֶה הַשַּׁעַר לַה' דְּקַבָּלַת עוֹל מַלְכוּת שָׁמַיִם וְהוּא עִנְיַן הַיִּרְאָה הִיא הַשַּׁעַר וְהַפֶּתַח לַעֲלוֹת אֶל ה' כו' וּכְמוֹ שֶׁכָּתוּב בְּזֹאת יָבוֹא אַהֲרֹן אֶל הַקֹּדֶשׁ, בְּזֹאת דַּוְקָא בְּחִינַת יִרְאָה תַּתָּאָה דָּא תַּרְעָא לְעֵילָאָה לָבוֹא אֶל הַקֹּדֶשׁ פְּנִימָה בְּעִלּוּי אַחַר עִלּוּי כו':

xvi) See footnote of the Rebbe on page 271

xvii) See footnote of the Rebbe on page 271

This is what is meant by [the verse in Psalms 118:20] "This is the gate to G-d." Acceptance of the "yoke of heaven," which is fear of G-d, is the gateway and opening to [spiritual] elevation toward G-d, as it says (Leviticus 16:3), "With *this* will Aaron come to the *Kodesh* ["Holy of Holies"].[xvi] *This* refers to the lower level of fear, which is the gate by which we enter and ascend into the inner sanctums of holiness, with one elevation after another.[xvii]

There are two basic levels of fear and two of love:		
1.	*Yirah Tatah* "Lower fear"	Acceptance of the yoke of heaven; fear of sin; fear of G-d
2.	*Ahavat Olam* "Wordly love"	Love focused on G-d as the life-force of the world
3.	*Ahava Rabba* "Great love"	Love focused on the infinite light of G-d
4.	*Yirah Ila'ah* "Higher fear"	Awe

Essay on Service of the Heart - Love Like Fire and Water

SYNOPSIS:

There certainly must be fear of G-d as well [as the love mentioned in the first chapter], and [though] quite the opposite [of love], fear is vital. The *avoda* of G-d is impossible without it. [By this] we are referring to the "lower level of fear of G-d" and the acceptance of the "yoke of heaven." As a part of taking on the "yoke of heaven" and of developing "fear of G-d," we must guard all of our senses. This applies to our sight and hearing and speech (and it is explained exactly how crucial it is that we guard our eyesight, and that each and every person is obligated to do so) as well as to our thoughts. We shouldn't willingly and recklessly reflect on impure, negative subjects, in deference to the fear of G-d within us (and by so doing, impure reflections will not occur to us). This level of fear is the beginning and foundation of *avoda* of the One Above (as written in *Tanya*, chapter 41, that it is the start of *avoda* and its core and root). It implies that we must leave behind all that we became accustomed to and submit ourselves entirely to G-dliness...

קִצוּר.

זֹאת וַדַּאי שֶׁצָּרִיךְ לִהְיוֹת גַּם יִרְאָה, וְאַדְּרַבָּא הִיא מְכְרַחַת וְאִי אֶפְשָׁר לִהְיוֹת בִּלְעָדֶיהָ וְהַיְנוּ בְּחִינַת יִרְאָה תַּתָּאָה וְקַבָּלַת עוֹל מַלְכוּת שָׁמַיִם לְהַגְדִּיר עַצְמוֹ בְּכָל הַחוּשִׁים שֶׁלּוֹ מִצַּד קַבָּלַת עוֹל מַלְכוּת שָׁמַיִם וְיִרְאַת אֱלֹקִים שֶׁבּוֹ, וְהַיְנוּ בְּהַחוּשִׁים דִּרְאִיָּ' וּשְׁמִיעָה וְדִבּוּר (וְנִתְבָּ' אֵיךְ שֶׁהַהַגְדָּרָה בִּרְאִיָּ' נוֹגֵעַ מְאֹד וְכָל אֶחָד וְאֶחָד מְחֻיָּב בָּזֶה) וְכֵן הַהַגְדָּרָה בַּמַּחֲשָׁבוֹת שֶׁלֹּא יְהַרְהֵר הִרְהוּר רַע בִּרְצוֹן וִישַׂאַט נֶפֶשׁ מִצַּד יִרְאַת אֱלֹקִים שֶׁבּוֹ (וְעַל יְדֵי זֶה מִמֵּילָא לֹא יִפְּלוּ לוֹ הִרְהוּרִים רָעִים) וְיִרְאָה זוֹ הִיא הַתְחָלַת הָעֲבוֹדָה וִיסוֹדָהּ (וּכְמוֹ שֶׁכָּתוּב בְּסֵפֶר שֶׁל בֵּינוֹנִים פמ"א שֶׁהִיא רֵאשִׁית הָעֲבוֹדָה וְעִקָּרָהּ וְשָׁרְשָׁהּ) וְהוּא לַעֲזֹב הָרְגִילוּת שֶׁלּוֹ וְלִתֵּן עַצְמוֹ לֶאֱלֹקוּת כוּ':

CHAPTER 3

The lower form of fear of G-d is not part of the avoda of prayer.

פרק ג

אָמְנָם כֵּן הוּא אֲשֶׁר הַיִּרְאָה הִיא מֻכְרַחַת לִהְיוֹת בְּכָל אֶחָד וְאֶחָד מַמָּשׁ מַה שֶׁאִי אֶפְשָׁר לִהְיוֹת כְּלָל בִּלְעֲדֵי זֹאת. אַךְ לֹא זוֹ הִיא הָעֲבוֹדָה דִּתְפִלָּה, דְּהִנֵּה בִּכְדֵי לָבוֹא לִבְחִינַת יִרְאָה זוֹ אֵין זֶה עַל יְדֵי הִתְבּוֹנְנוּת בִּתְפִלָּה כִּי אִם יֵשׁ לָזֶה עֵצוֹת מְיֻחָדוֹת לְהַמְשִׁיךְ עָלָיו הַיִּרְאָה, וְהֵן בְּכָל הַיּוֹם תָּמִיד

Although we must all possess [the lower level of] fear since nobody can function without it, it is not the *avoda* of prayer. The way we should try to achieve this [lower level of] fear is not through meditation in prayer, but with specific reminders throughout the day that are intended to draw fear down upon us.

There are two basic levels of fear and two of love:			
1.	*Yirah Tata'ah* "Lower fear"	Fear of G-d as a consequence of sin	Acceptance of the yoke; fear of sin; fear of G-d
2.	*Ahavat Olam* "Wordly love"	Love of G-d as a consequence of His benevolence	Meditation focused on G-d as the life-force of the world
3.	*Ahava Rabba* "Great love"	Love of G-d based on His transcendent greatness	Meditation focused on the infinite light of the G-d transcending the creation
4.	*Yirah Ila'ah* "Higher fear"	Loss of awareness of self before G-d	Awe

(וְכַנּוֹדָע דְּהִתְבּוֹנְנוּת אִי אֶפְשָׁר לִהְיוֹת בִּתְמִידִיּוּת רַק בְּשָׁעָה דִתְפִלָּה שֶׁצְּרִיכִים לְהַאֲרִיךְ

(It is known that meditation cannot be constant. Rather, it should take place during prayer, since it is then

---
COMMENTARY

CHAPTER 3: FEAR AND LOVE

After we've accepted that without control over the stimuli reaching our mind, we don't have the minimum basis for getting closer to the One Above, it's time to start putting things into practice. That means working on the basic, "entry-level" meditations that lead to fear of G-d (described in detail in this chapter) to be followed by the more time-specific meditations before and during prayer that lead to love of G-d (described in Chapters 4 and 5).

Essay on Service of the Heart - Love Like Fire and Water

that we can meditate at length, each one of us according to our own level and strength. After prayer, the intellectual grasp and [understanding of G-d achieved through] meditation dissipate. Likewise, the love that was born [and revealed] in our heart as a result of the meditation during prayer goes away. Only an impression is left, as is stated in *Tanya*, section 1, chapter 12 and 13. But the [lower] fear described earlier, together with its accompanying stimuli, must be present at all times; it is not connected to the meditative process, but [consists of] concepts that must remain constantly [pervasive] in our memory.)

בְּהִתְבּוֹנְנוּת כָּל חַד וְחַד לְפוּם שִׁיעוּרָא דִילֵיהּ. וְאַחַר הַתְּפִלָּה מִסְתַּלֶּקֶת הַהַשָּׂגָה וְהַהִתְבּוֹנְנוּת, וְכֵן הָאַהֲבָה הַנּוֹלֶדֶת מֵהִתְבּוֹנְנוּת בְּהִתְגַּלּוּת בְּלִבּוֹ הִיא רַק בִּשְׁעַת הַתְּפִלָּה וְאַחַר כָּךְ הִיא חוֹלֶפֶת וְעוֹבֶרֶת וְנִשְׁאָר רַק רְשִׁימוּ לְבַד וּכְמוֹ שֶׁכָּתוּב בְּסֵפֶר שֶׁל בֵּינוֹנִים ח״א פי״ב וי״ג, אֲבָל הַיִּרְאָה הנ״ל וְהָעִנְיָנִים הַמְבִיאִים לְזֶה צְרִיכִים לִהְיוֹת תָּמִיד, לְפִי שֶׁאֵין זֶה עִנְיְנֵי הִתְבּוֹנְנוּת כִּי אִם עִנְיָנִים שֶׁצְּרִיכִים לִהְיוֹת תָּמִיד בְּזִכְרוֹן הָאָדָם)

Lower fear is cultivated by constant reminders of G-d's presence and omniscience.

It is stated in *Tanya*, chapter 42:
And moreover, one should remember...[that] the main thing is regularity, as one must get used to focusing his thought constantly, such that it becomes [etched] permanently in his heart and mind as well, that all that he sees with his eyes [are] the heavens and the earth [that is, the outer garments of G-d]...and in this way he will constantly recall their inner core and life-force...and [xviii]

וּכְמוֹ שֶׁכָּתוּב בְּסֵפֶר שֶׁל בֵּינוֹנִים פמ״ב וְעוֹד זֹאת יִזְכֹּר כו׳ אֶלָּא הָעִיקָר הוּא הַהֶרְגֵּל לְהַרְגִּיל דַּעְתּוֹ וּמַחֲשַׁבְתּוֹ תָּמִיד לִהְיוֹת קָבוּעַ בְּלִבּוֹ וּמוֹחוֹ תָּמִיד אֲשֶׁר כָּל מַה שֶּׁרוֹאֶה

xviii) See footnote of the Rebbe on page 272 ←

─────── **COMMENTARY** ───────

There are two levels of fear, and two levels of love. Each divides into various sub-categories and nuances, but all are subsumed by these four basic levels, as follows:

1.	*Yirah Tata'ah* "Lower fear"	Acceptance of the yoke of heaven; fear of sin; fear of G-d	World of *Asiya* "World of Action"
2.	*Ahavat Olam* "Wordly love"	Love focused on G-d as the life-force of the world	World of *Yetzirah* "World of Formation"
3.	*Ahava Rabba* "Great love"	Love focused on the infinite light of G-d	World of *Bria* "World of Creation"
4.	*Yirah Ila'ah* "Higher fear"	Awe	World of *Atzilut* "World of Emanation"

also he must remember at all times the saying of the Sages regarding accepting the "yoke of heaven" ... he also must remember constantly how at all times the King of Kings stands over him and observes his actions and examines his "kidneys and heart," and all of his steps are counted... and in so doing he will come to accept upon himself the "yoke of heaven," and there will be "fear of G-d" in his heart.

This indicates that by remembering the One Above through everything that we see, and by recalling that He uniquely bestows His sovereignty upon us, we will accept upon ourselves the "yoke of heaven." And by remembering that G-d observes everything we do, we will draw down upon ourselves fear of G-d. This is a constant awareness which must be ongoing during all of our days, including [our nights, as well].

In addition, this [lower level of] fear is only that which is required to prevent us from rebelling against the King of Kings, G-d forbid, and to insure that we actually fulfill the *mitzvot*, both positive and negative. Although it is the foundation underlying everything, fear nonetheless is not in the category of *avoda*.

As explained in Chapter 2, actual fulfillment of the *mitzvot* is not dependent upon inner, [meditative] *avoda* whose objective is to unite our

Lower fear of G-d underlies the fulfillment of the commandments.

בְּעֵינָיו הַשָּׁמַיִם וְהָאָרֶץ כו' וְעַל יְדֵי זֶה יִזְכֹּר תָּמִיד פְּנִימִיּוּתָם וְחִיּוּתָם כו' וְגַם לִהְיוֹת לְזִכָּרוֹן תָּמִיד לְשׁוֹן חֲזַ"ל קַבָּלַת עוֹל מַלְכוּת שָׁמַיִם כו' וּכְמוֹ כֵן יִזְכֹּר תָּמִיד אֵיךְ שֶׁמֶּלֶךְ מַלְכֵי הַמְּלָכִים הַקָּדוֹשׁ בָּרוּךְ הוּא עוֹמֵד עָלָיו וְרוֹאֶה בְּמַעֲשָׂיו וּבוֹחֵן כִּלְיוֹתָיו וְלִבּוֹ כו' וְכָל צְעָדָיו יִסְפֹּר כו' וְעַל יְדֵי כָּל זֹאת יָבוֹא לִידֵי קַבָּלַת עוֹל מַלְכוּת שָׁמַיִם עָלָיו וְיִהְיֶ' יִרְאַת אֱלֹקִים בְּלִבּוֹ.

וְהַיְנוּ שֶׁעַל יְדֵי הַזִּכָּרוֹן בְּמֶלֶךְ הַקָּדוֹשׁ בָּרוּךְ הוּא עַל יְדֵי כָּל מַה שֶּׁרוֹאֶה בְּעֵינָיו כו' וְעַל יְדֵי הַזִּכָּרוֹן תָּמִיד שֶׁמְּיַחֵד מַלְכוּתוֹ עָלֵינוּ כו' יַמְשִׁיךְ עָלָיו קַבָּלַת עוֹל מַלְכוּת שָׁמַיִם, וּבַזִּכָּרוֹן שֶׁרוֹאֶה וּמַבִּיט בְּכָל מַעֲשָׂיו כו' יַמְשִׁיךְ עָלָיו יִרְאַת אֱלֹקִים כו' וְהוּא עִנְיָן תְּמִידִי שֶׁצָּרִיךְ לִהְיוֹת כָּל הַיָּמִים לְרַבּוֹת כו'.

וְעוֹד זֹאת שֶׁהֲרֵי יִרְאָה זֹאת הִיא רַק שֶׁלֹּא לִמְרֹד חַס וְחָלִילָה בְּמֶלֶךְ מַלְכֵי הַמְּלָכִים הַקָּדוֹשׁ בָּרוּךְ הוּא לִהְיוֹת סוּר מֵרַע וַעֲשֵׂה טוֹב בְּפֹעַל. וְעִם הֱיוֹת שֶׁזֶּהוּ עִקַּר וִיסוֹד הַכֹּל, מִכָּל מָקוֹם אֵין זֶה עֲדַיִן עִנְיַן הָעֲבוֹדָה.

(וּכְמוֹ שֶׁנִּתְבָּאֵר לְעֵיל פ"ב דְּקִיּוּם הַמִּצְווֹת בְּפֹעַל מַמָּשׁ יָכוֹל לִהְיוֹת גַּם בְּלִי עֲבוֹדָה פְּנִימִית דְּעִנְיָנָהּ הוּא לְקַשֵּׁר וּלְדַבֵּק נַפְשׁוֹ בֶּאֱלֹקוּת

Essay on Service of the Heart - Love Like Fire and Water

[divine] souls with G-dliness and to refine the physicality and natural coarseness of our animal souls. That objective is associated with prayer, "the service of the heart," as explained in Chapter 1. It is achieved through effort, application of intellect, meditation, and through other means (depending upon whether we are dealing with *ruach* or *neshama*, as explained earlier), all of which constitute the process of prayer.

A clear proof is that we see people who are born such that the "yoke of heaven" and "fear of G-d" are "[written] on their faces." They are careful in how they use all of their senses and are unable to do anything against the will of G-d, since "how is it possible to see or look upon something forbidden, and how can one hear, etc., since this is forbidden." They need not work upon themselves at all to become cautious; rather, they instinctively guard themselves because of the "yoke of heaven" which is upon them. They constantly feel the "yoke of the Master, the One Above," and they are always like a "servant before his master."

This is not the case though regarding love [of G-d]. We don't find that love [of G-d] is in our nature from birth. The reason for this is that love of G-d [comes with] proximity and cleaving to G-dliness. It is the outcome of thorough knowledge

וּלְבָרֵר וּלְזַכֵּךְ אֶת חָמְרִיּוּת וְטִבְעִיּוּת דְּנֶפֶשׁ הַבַּהֲמִית. שֶׁזֶּהוּ עִנְיַן הַתְּפִלָּה וַעֲבוֹדָה שֶׁבַּלֵּב וּכְמוֹ שֶׁנִּתְבָּאֵר לְעֵיל פ"א, לִהְיוֹת שֶׁכָּל זֶה בָּא עַל יְדֵי עֲבוֹדָה וִיגִיעָה בְּהַשָּׂגָה וְהִתְבּוֹנְנוּת וּבְכַמָּה אוֹפַנִּים שׁוֹנִים (כְּפִי הַמַּדְרֵגוֹת דְּרוּחַ וּנְשָׁמָה שֶׁנִּתְבָּאֵר לְעֵיל) שֶׁהִיא הִיא הָעֲבוֹדָה דִּתְפִלָּה.

וּרְאַיּ' מוּחֶשֶׁת לָזֶה שֶׁהֲרֵי אָנוּ רוֹאִין שֶׁיֵּשׁ בְּנֵי אָדָם שֶׁבְּטִבְעָם בְּתוֹלַדְתָּם יֵשׁ בָּהֶם קַבָּלַת עוֹל מַלְכוּת שָׁמַיִם וְיִרְאַת אֱלֹקִים עַל פְּנֵיהֶם שֶׁמִּגְדָּרִים הֵמָּה בְּכָל הַחוּשִׁים שֶׁלָּהֶם וְאֵינָם יְכוֹלִים לַעֲשׂוֹת חַס וְחָלִילָה נֶגֶד רְצוֹן ה', כִּי אֵיךְ יִרְאֶה וְיַבִּיט בְּדָבָר הָאָסוּר וְאֵיךְ יִשְׁמַע כו' וּכְהַאי גַּוְונָא הֲלֹא זֶה אָסוּר (מֶען טָאר דָאךְ נִיט) וְאֵין צָרִיךְ עַל זֶה שׁוּם יְגִיעָה כְּלָל לְהַגְדִּיר אֶת עַצְמוֹ כִּי אִם הוּא מֻגְדָּר מִמֵּילָא מִפְּנֵי קַבָּלַת עוֹל מַלְכוּת שָׁמַיִם שֶׁעָלָיו שֶׁנִּרְגָּשׁ בּוֹ תָּמִיד עוֹל הָאָדוֹן ה' צְבָאוֹת וְהוּא תָּמִיד כְּעַבְדָּא קַמֵּי' מָארֵי' כו',

מַה שֶׁאֵין כֵּן בְּאַהֲבָה לֹא מָצִינוּ שֶׁיְּהֵא אוֹהֵב ה' בְּטִבְעוֹ וְתוֹלַדְתּוֹ. וְהוּא לִהְיוֹת כִּי הָאַהֲבָה הִיא הַקֵּרוּב וְהַדְּבֵקוּת בֶּאֱלֹקוּת הַבָּאָה עַל יְדֵי יְדִיעָה פְּרָטִית בְּעִנְיְנֵי אֱלֹקוּת בְּהַשָּׂגָה וְהִתְבּוֹנְנוּת טוֹבָה

We find people who are born with innate "fear of heaven," but not with inborn love of G-d.

וּבְהַעֲמָקַת הַדַּעַת וּכְמוֹ שֶׁכָּתוּב וְיָדַעְתָּ הַיּוֹם וַהֲשֵׁבֹתָ אֶל לְבָבֶךָ כוּ' וְאֵינוֹ שֶׁיִּהְיֶה כֵּן מִתּוֹלַדְתּוֹ כִּי אִם תָּלוּי בַּיְגִיעָה לֵידַע אֶת ה' וּלְהִתְבּוֹנֵן כוּ', וְעַל יְדֵי הַהִתְעַסְּקוּת וְהַשְּׁקִידָה בָּזֶה הֲרֵי הוּא הוֹלֵךְ מִמַּדְרֵגָה לְמַדְרֵגָה כוּ'

[and understanding] of specific concepts associated with G-dliness. It demands intellectual acumen and incisive meditation, together with deep insight, as is written [in Deuteronomy 4:39], "And you shall know today and put it in your heart..." Clearly, we are not born this way. [Love of G-d] is dependent upon effort to [get to] know G-d and upon meditation, upon involvement [in spiritual pursuit] and upon persistence; by doing so, we progress from one level to the next.

We may be born with a natural inclination for the avoda of prayer, but not with natural love of G-d.

רַק זֹאת יָכוֹל לִהְיוֹת שֶׁמִּתּוֹלַדְתּוֹ הוּא מְסֻגָּל לַעֲבוֹדָה שֶׁבַּלֵּב דְּהַיְנוּ מִצַּד מַעֲלַת נִשְׁמָתוֹ שֶׁיֵּשׁ לוֹ חוּשִׁים טוֹבִים בְּעִנְיְנֵי אֱלֹקוּת וּמְקַבֵּל אֶת הָאוֹר כִּי טוֹב וְגַם הַנֶּפֶשׁ הַבַּהֲמִית אֵינוֹ מַחְשִׁיךְ וּמַסְתִּיר עָלָיו. וְעַל כֵּן אֵין צָרִיךְ יְגִיעָה כָּל כָּךְ וַעֲבוֹדָתוֹ הִיא אֲמִתִּית בִּבְחִינַת גִּלּוּי אוֹר מַמָּשׁ בְּנַפְשׁוֹ. וְזֶהוּ רַק שֶׁמְּסֻגָּל לַעֲבוֹדָה, אֲבָל צָרִיךְ עֲבוֹדָה וִיגִיעָה לֵידַע וּלְהַשְׂכִּיל וּלְהָבִין כוּ'

It is possible, however, that we may be more inclined from birth to the "service of the heart." That is, [we may be blessed with a higher soul-level], granting us a certain talent for thinking about G-dliness and receiving illumination from above. At the same time, our animal soul doesn't darken and obscure [as much]. Therefore, we don't need to invest as much effort [in our *avoda*], yet our *avoda* is honest, with actual revelation of [G-dly] light in our soul. This indicates only that we have superb potential for *avoda*. Nevertheless, we still require labor and effort in order to know, to grasp, and to understand.

אֲבָל לֹא יֻלַּד בְּאַהֲבָה בְּטִבְעוֹ בְּתוֹלַדְתּוֹ, מַה שֶּׁאֵין כֵּן עִנְיַן קַבָּלַת עֹל מַלְכוּת שָׁמַיִם וְיִרְאַת אֱלֹקִים יוּכַל לִהְיוֹת בְּטִבְעוֹ מִתּוֹלַדְתּוֹ כנ"ל, וְהַיְנוּ מִפְּנֵי שֶׁאֵין זֶה תָּלוּי בְּאֵיזֶה יְדִיעָה פְּרָטִית וּבְהַשָּׂגָה וְהִתְבּוֹנְנוּת כִּי אִם בְּהֶרְגֵּשׁ אֱלֹקִי, שֶׁהָאֱלֹקוּת בִּכְלָל נִרְגָּשׁ בְּנַפְשׁוֹ תָּמִיד שֶׁאֵינוֹ נִשְׁכָּח מִמֶּנּוּ אֲפִלּוּ רֶגַע אֶחָד

In any case, we are not born with a natural love. Acceptance of the "yoke of heaven," and fear of G-d on the other hand, may very well be part of our natural birthright, as mentioned earlier, since they are not dependent upon any detailed knowledge, understanding, or on meditation. They are based solely upon a [pervasive] awareness of G-dliness. In general, G-dliness is constantly felt in our soul, such that it is not forgotten for even a minute.

Essay on Service of the Heart - Love Like Fire and Water

And this, in truth, is an experience of the essence of the infinite light of the One Above, beyond any particular [spiritual] level. But it is hidden, [that is, subconscious]. The truth regarding all levels of love and fear of G-d is that fear is [ultimately] spiritually higher than love. While love is [concerned with] illumination and revelation of G-d's infinite light above (and this is so even on the highest levels of love, as explained elsewhere), fear — even the [lowest] level of *yirah tata'ah* — is concerned with the very "essence" of G-d's infinite light. (However, the higher level of fear, [more properly described as "awe"], corresponds to His essence as it is revealed, while the lower fear corresponds to His essence as it is hidden. And within this distinction, there are sub-categories differentiating between "acceptance of the yoke of heaven" [a subconscious process], as opposed to "fear of sin," and "fear of G-d," which are more conscious, meaning that they entail more [awareness and] G-dly feeling, as explained in Chapter 2. And this is what is meant in *Tanya*, chapter 42, that "in order that it [the "fear of sin"] comes to [a state where it influences actual behavior], one must reveal it ...") Therefore, fear is associated with self-nullification and is on a higher spiritual level than is love.

It is thus understood that those of us who don't feel the "yoke of heaven" upon ourselves, nor the fear of G-d in our soul, from birth — on account of the low level of our

(וְהוּא בֶּאֱמֶת הֶרְגֵּשׁ בְּחִינַת עַצְמוּת אוֹר אֵין סוֹף בָּרוּךְ הוּא שֶׁלְּמַעְלָה מִמַּדְרֵגוֹת פְּרָטִיּוֹת. רַק שֶׁהוּא בְּהֶעְלֵם כוּ'. דְּבֶאֱמֶת בָּאַהֲבָה וְיִרְאָה הִנֵּה בְּכָל הַמַּדְרֵגוֹת שֶׁבָּהֶם הַיִּרְאָה הִיא לְמַעְלָה מֵהָאַהֲבָה, דְּאַהֲבָה הִיא בִּבְחִינַת אוֹרוֹת וְגִלּוּיִם דְּאוֹר אֵין סוֹף בָּרוּךְ הוּא. שֶׁכֵּן הוּא גַם בַּמַּדְרֵגוֹת הַיּוֹתֵר גְּבֹהוֹת וְנַעֲלוֹת שֶׁבָּאַהֲבָה וּכְמוֹ שֶׁכָּתוּב בְּמָקוֹם אַחֵר וְהַיִּרְאָה גַם בְּחִינַת יִרְאָה תַּתָּאָה הִיא בִּבְחִינַת עַצְמוּת אוֹר אֵין סוֹף בָּרוּךְ הוּא (רַק שֶׁיִּרְאָה עִילָאָה הִיא בִּבְחִינַת גִּלּוּי הָעַצְמוּת וְיִרְאָה תַּתָּאָה בִּבְחִינַת הֶעְלֵם כוּ'. וְיֵשׁ בָּזֶה גּוּפָא הֶפְרֵשׁ בֵּין קַבָּלַת עוֹל מַלְכוּת שָׁמַיִם לְיִרְאַת חֵטְא וְיִרְאַת אֱלֹקִים שֶׁהֵן בְּהִתְגַּלּוּת יוֹתֵר הֵינוּ יוֹתֵר בִּבְחִינַת הֶרְגֵּשׁ הָאֱלֹקִי וּכְמוֹ שֶׁנִּתְבָּאֵר לְעֵיל פ"ב. וְזֶה שֶׁכָּתוּב בְּסֵפֶר שֶׁל בֵּינוֹנִים פמ"ב שֶׁכְּדֵי שֶׁתָּבוֹא כוּ' צָרִיךְ לְגַלּוֹתָהּ כוּ') וְלָכֵן הַיִּרְאָה בִּכְלָל הִיא בְּחִינַת בִּטּוּל וּלְמַעְלָה מִבְּחִינַת אַהֲבָה כוּ')

וּמִמֵּילָא מוּבָן דְּמִי שֶׁאֵין בּוֹ קַבָּלַת עוֹל מַלְכוּת שָׁמַיִם וְיִרְאַת אֱלֹקִים מִתּוֹלַדְתּוֹ מִצַּד פְּחִיתוּת נַפְשׁוֹ וּבִפְרָט מִצַּד חֲמָרִיּוּת הַנֶּפֶשׁ הַבַּהֲמִית שֶׁמַּחְשִׁיךְ וּמַסְתִּיר וְצָרִיךְ

On all levels, fear of G-d is higher than love of G-d. We fear G-d Himself, while we what we love is spiritual revelation of His light.

[divine] soul, and in particular because of the coarseness of our animal soul that conceals — need [a lot of] work and advice. However, this [work] is not the "service of the heart" of prayer.

עַל זֶה יַגִּיעַ וְעֵצוֹת בְּנַפְשׁוֹ כנ״ל אֵין זֶה עֲבוֹדָה שֶׁבַּלֵּב דִּתְפִלָּה.

We must cultivate the awareness that nothing is hidden or concealed from G-d.

In *Tanya*, chapter 42, the meditation that leads to fear of G-d is explained at length. It says there that we must labor in thought and delve deeply...for a good hour. It [also] says that there is a type of soul, pure in nature, that "as soon as he meditates..." [he achieves "fear of G-d"]. Certainly, we must understand [intellectually] that nothing can hide or conceal anything from G-d, and that no place is devoid of His Presence, and that the universe is full of His honor. G-d stands over us and observes our deeds, for should not the Creator of the eye Himself be able to see, so to speak? Everything is known and revealed before Him.

וְהִנֵּה בְּסֵפֶר שֶׁל בֵּינוֹנִים פמ״ב מְבֹאָר בַּאֲרִיכוּת הַהִתְבּוֹנְנוּת הַמְּבִיאָה לִידֵי יִרְאָה וְכ׳ שָׁם לִיגַע מַחֲשַׁבְתּוֹ לְהַעֲמִיק כו׳ שָׁעָה גְּדוֹלָה כו׳, הֲרֵי כ׳ שָׁם יֵשׁ נֶפֶשׁ זַכָּה בְּטִבְעָהּ שֶׁמִּיָּד שֶׁמִּתְבּוֹנֶנֶת כו׳, וּבְוַדַּאי שֶׁצָּרִיךְ לִהְיוֹת הַשָּׂגַת הָעִנְיָן אֵיךְ שֶׁאֵין שׁוּם דָּבָר מַעֲלִים וּמַסְתִּיר לְפָנָיו יִתְבָּרֵךְ וְלֵית אֲתַר פָּנוּי מִינֵּיהּ וּמְלֹא כָל הָאָרֶץ כְּבוֹדוֹ שֶׁעוֹמֵד עָלָיו וְרוֹאֶה בְּמַעֲשָׂיו דְּהַיּוֹצֵר עַיִן הֲלֹא יַבִּיט בְּעַצְמוֹ כִּבְיָכוֹל וְהַכֹּל גָּלוּי

COMMENTARY

1. YIRAH TATA'AH

The first and lowest level is that of *yirah tata'ah* ("lower fear"). It includes the three sub-levels discussed in Chapter 2—*kabalat ol shamayim* ("acceptance of the yoke of heaven"), *yirat chait* ("fear of sin"), and *yirat Elokim* ("fear of G-d"). It is chiefly brought about by reminders that the One Above is watching us and aware of our every thought, speech, and action. (There are also other levels of *yirah tata'ah* that don't involve awareness of His attention upon us at all times, as we will see.) *Yirah tata'ah* corresponds to the lowest World of *Asiyah* [as well as the final *hey* of the essential four-letter Name of G-d, and to the *sephira* of *malchut*.]

We already learned in Chapter 2 that the lower level of fear includes *kabbalat ol shamayim* ("accepting the yoke of heaven"), as well *yirat chait* ("fear of sin") and *yirat Elokim* ("fear of G-d"). Acceptance of the "yoke of heaven" is an unconscious attitude that permeates our activities, thoughts, and speech, infusing

Essay on Service of the Heart - Love Like Fire and Water

All of the above [constitutes] a profound intellectual concept, requiring us to meditate at length and concentrate intensely, until fear [of G-d] penetrates our heart.

This means that even the naturally pure soul must occasionally meditate at length in order to establish "fear of G-d" in a revealed state in the heart. This is especially true of those of us who have a lowly soul by nature and birth, and even more so if we have become contaminated by the "sins of our youth." Then the natural fear of G-d is absent. And even when we recall the greatness of the One Above, and how His honor permeates the

וְיָדוּעַ לְפָנָיו יִתְבָּרֵךְ דְּכָל זֹאת הִיא הַשָּׂגָה גְּדוֹלָה וְצָרִיךְ לְהַאֲרִיךְ בָּזֶה וּלְהַעֲמִיק דַּעְתּוֹ בְּחֹזֶק עַד שֶׁתִּקָּבַע הַיִּרְאָה בְּלִבּוֹ

(וְהַיְנוּ שֶׁגַּם נֶפֶשׁ זַכָּה בְּטִבְעָהּ צָרִיךְ לְעִתִּים לְהִתְבּוֹנֵן בָּזֶה בַּאֲרִיכוּת הַהִתְבּוֹנְנוּת בִּכְדֵי שֶׁתִּהְיֶה הַיִּרְאָה בְּהִתְגַּלּוּת בְּלִבּוֹ, וּבִפְרָט מִי שֶׁהוּא נֶפֶשׁ שְׁפָלָה בְּטִבְעָהּ וְתוֹלַדְתָּהּ וּבִפְרָט כְּשֶׁנִּטְמְאָה בְּחַטֹּאת נְעוּרִים כו' שֶׁאֵין בּוֹ בְּחִינַת הַיִּרְאָה בְּטִבְעוֹ. וְגַם כְּשֶׁנִּזְכָּר עַל גְּדֻלַּת ה' וְאֵיךְ שֶׁמָּלֵא כָל הָאָרֶץ כְּבוֹדוֹ (שֶׁזֶּהוּ מַה שֶּׁכָּתוּב שֶׁמִּיד שֶׁמִּתְבּוֹנֶנֶת כו' כְּשֶׁיִּתְבּוֹנֵן הָאָדָם כו') אֵינוֹ נוֹפֵל

Even the naturally pure soul must occasionally meditate in order to instill fear of G-d into the heart.

COMMENTARY
---

them with obedience to a Higher Authority. Fear of sin, on the other hand, is a conscious attitude, in which we develop fear of the One Above based on the fact that He is aware of our every move. It differs from the next level up, fear of G-d, in emphasis. The former (fear of sin) places the emphasis on the fear itself and on avoiding occasions of sin, while the latter (fear of G-d) places the emphasis upon its emotional and spiritual dimension. There is more G-dly awareness in fear of G-d than there is in fear of sin, in which we are more aware of our fear of G-d than of G-d Himself. Both lead to proper fulfillment of the commandments of the Torah. But, while fear of sin leads to enhanced adherence to the negative commandments (those things that the Torah forbids) because of fear of transgression, fear of G-d leads to enhanced fulfillment of all the *mitzvot*, both negative and positive, because they are the commandments of the One Above.

Chapter 3 tells us that there are two sub-categories within fear of G-d that lead to more substantial fear of the One Above (though both are still within the category of *yirah tata'ah* "lower fear"): appreciation of and reverence for His power.

entire universe (which is what is meant by the statement there [in *Tanya* chapter 42] "as soon as he meditates," and "when one meditates..."), no fear of G-d will come over us. Then we must work on our inner self. This includes the "labor of the body," and the "labor of the soul," as described there [in chapter 42]. And we must work hard at this, in proportion to the lowly nature of our soul, until fear of G-d penetrates our heart.

עָלָיו הַיִּרְאָה צָרִיךְ לִיגַּע אֶת עַצְמוֹ בִּיגִיעַת בָּשָׂר וִיגִיעַת נֶפֶשׁ הַמְבֹאָר שָׁם וּלְפִי אֹפֶן פְּחִיתוּתוֹ וְשִׁפְלוּתוֹ כָּךְ צָרִיךְ לִיגַּע עַצְמוֹ בִּיגִיעָה הנ"ל בְּיוֹתֵר עַד שֶׁתִּקָּבַע בְּלִבּוֹ הַיִּרְאָה (כו׳)

After fear of G-d has penetrated the heart, only a minimal amount of meditation is necessary to maintain it.

עַד שֶׁיַּסְפִּיק לוֹ אַחַר כָּךְ גַּם מְעַט הַהִתְבּוֹנְנוּת הַיְנוּ מַה שֶׁנִּזְכַּר כו׳ (וְגַם בְּקַבָּלַת עוֹל מַלְכוּת שָׁמַיִם צָרִיךְ לִהְיוֹת הַהִתְבּוֹנְנוּת בִּגְדֻלַּת אוֹר אֵין סוֹף בָּרוּךְ הוּא דְּאִיהוּ מְמַלֵּא כָּל עָלְמִין וְסוֹבֵב כָּל עָלְמִין כו׳ וְהַנִּיחַ הָעֶלְיוֹנִים וְהַתַּחְתּוֹנִים וּמְיַחֵד

After fear of G-d has penetrated our heart, only a minimal amount of meditation is necessary as a reminder. (Acceptance of the "yoke of heaven" also requires meditation. We must consider the greatness of the infinite light of the One Above — that He permeates and transcends all worlds

---

COMMENTARY

After practicing the contemplation leading to fear of sin because He is "standing over us" and watching our every move, we must also meditate upon the wondrous nature of His creation. When we consider G-d's creation and come to the conclusion that He is omnipotent and almighty, our fear is then no longer of punishment alone. It includes another element — appreciation of His power. If we continue to meditate, going into detail about the wondrous and amazing physical nature of creation, we will deepen our fear even more. That is, when we meditate upon the sheer number of creations, how they differ from one another and yet complement each other, and the variety of shapes and sizes, we will arrive at a tremendous reverence and fear of the One Above and His ability to create. This is the kind of appreciation that a scientist, based upon his research and knowledge of the world, might come to even without knowledge of religion; his broad understanding of creation may bring him to a deep belief and reverence for the One Above that transcends mere fear of G-d's ability to reward and punish. However, even this fear is derived from contemplation of the physical

Essay on Service of the Heart - Love Like Fire and Water

[and the entire universe] and, that nevertheless, He "left behind" [so to speak] both the higher and lower [worlds] in order to bestow His sovereignty upon the Jewish people in general and upon each person in particular, as is written in *Tanya*, chapter 41.)

מַלְכוּתוֹ עַל עַמּוֹ יִשְׂרָאֵל בִּכְלָל וְעָלָיו בִּפְרָט כו' כְּמוֹ שֶׁכָּתוּב שָׁם פמ״א).

It is understood that the most propitious time for this meditation, which brings us to fear G-d, is at the time of [morning] prayer, which is a time of *mochin d'gadlut*, [mature intellectual and spiritual mindfulness]. This is a time that is generally appropriate for intellectual grasp of, and meditation upon, G-dly topics. However, this [meditation leading to fear of G-d] can take place at other times as well. For the meditation upon, and grasp of, how G-d truly permeates the upper and lower worlds and how

וּמוּבָן דְּהַזְּמַן הַמְסֻגָּל בְּיוֹתֵר לְהִתְבּוֹנְנוּת הַנַּ״ל הַמְּבִיאָה לִידֵי יִרְאָה הִיא בְּעֵת הַתְּפִלָּה שֶׁהוּא הַזְּמַן דְּמוֹחִין דְּגַדְלוּת וּמֻכְשָׁר בִּכְלָל לְהַשָּׂגָה וְהִתְבּוֹנְנוּת אֱלֹקִי, אֲבָל מִכָּל מָקוֹם הִיא יְכוֹלָה לִהְיוֹת גַּם שֶׁלֹּא בִּזְמַן הַתְּפִלָּה. דְּהִנֵּה הַשָּׂגָה זוֹ אֵיךְ שֶׁהַקָּדוֹשׁ בָּרוּךְ הוּא מָלֵא מַמָּשׁ אֶת הָעֶלְיוֹנִים וְהַתַּחְתּוֹנִים וּמִמֵּילָא הַכֹּל גָּלוּי וְיָדוּעַ לְפָנָיו יִתְבָּרֵךְ זֶה יָכוֹל לִהְיוֹת בְּכָל עֵת וּבְכָל זְמָן. אָמְנָם מַה שֶּׁנּוֹגֵעַ אֶל

The best time to meditate to achieve fear of G-d is before the morning prayers, but it can take place at other times as well.

--- **COMMENTARY** ---

creation (G-d's "garments") and not from the spiritual energy enlivening the creation. It is a more mature and developed form of fear of G-d (the more minor form being appreciation of His power), but nevertheless, it remains in the category of *yirah tata'ah*.

In summary:

	Sub-level of *Yirah*	Focus of Meditation	
Yirah Tata'ah "Lower fear"	Acceptance of the yoke of heaven *(Kaballat Ohl Malchut Shamayim)*	Consideration of the infinite light permeating and transcending creation, but that He "gave it all up" in order to be with the Jews	1.
	Fear of sin *(Yirat chait)*	Awareness of G-d's attention upon us at every moment	2.
	Fear of G-d *(Yirat Elokim)*	Appreciation of G-d's power and omnipotence	3.
		Reverence for G-d's ability to create	4.

What is important is to become aware that G-d sees and understands all of our deeds.

הַיִּרְאָה בִּפְרָט הוּא לִהְיוֹת נִרְגָּשׁ בַּנֶּפֶשׁ אֵיךְ שֶׁצּוֹפֶה וּמַבִּיט כו' וּמֵבִין כָּל מַעֲשֵׂהוּ כו' הִנֵּה הֶרְגֵּשׁ זֶה הוּא בְּנָקֵל לְהַרְגִּישׁ בַּנֶּפֶשׁ גַּם לֹא בִּזְמַן הַמֻּכְשָׁר דִּתְפִלָּה דַּוְקָא, מִשּׁוּם דְּהֶרְגֵּשׁ זֶה קָרוֹב מְאֹד בְּכָל אֶחָד וְאֶחָד מִיִּשְׂרָאֵל אֵיךְ דְּלֵית אֲתַר פָּנוּי מִינֵי' וְצוֹפֶה וּמַבִּיט וּמַאֲזִין וּמַקְשִׁיב וּמֵבִין כו'

everything is therefore [automatically] revealed and known to Him, can take place at any time. But what is particularly necessary, as far as fear is concerned, is that we be conscious that G-d sees and understands all of our deeds. This feeling is easy to generate in the soul, even at times that are not appropriate for prayer, because it is well within the grasp of each and every Jewish person to become aware that no place is devoid of G-d, and that He is looking, listening, paying attention, and understanding...

(וּמִכָּל מָקוֹם בִּכְדֵי שֶׁיְהֵי' בְּקִיּוּם בְּנַפְשׁוֹ זֶהוּ כַּאֲשֶׁר כְּבָר הָיָ' לוֹ אֵיזֶה פְּעָמִים הִתְעוֹרְרוּת זוֹ בִּתְפִלָּה עַל יְדֵי הִתְבּוֹנְנוּת וְהֶרְגֵּשׁ הַנַּ"ל שֶׁעַל יְדֵי זֶה נַעֲשָׂה מֻכְשָׁר בִּכְלָל לְהִתְעוֹרְרוּת יִרְאָה. וְיוּכַל

(However, we will not permanently acquire [fear of G-d] in our soul, until we experience this arousal several times during prayer after meditating and [experiencing] the above feeling. By so doing, we become well-prepared overall for the arousal

---
COMMENTARY

Techniques of meditation leading to fear of G-d differ from those leading to love of G-d. Since lower fear — and especially acceptance of the "yoke of heaven" that is a part of it — forms the foundation of all subsequent connection with G-d, it must be with us at all times. We can't get close to the One Above if we forget to fear and respect Him. If we treated someone we claimed to love with disrespect, we could expect that person to distance himself or herself from us. The same is true of G-d. Although in essence, He is close to all of His creations, nevertheless we wouldn't expect Him to make His love felt where He isn't respected.

Understanding the important of maintaining this lower fear, we might well ask: how do we attain it? The Chassidic literature tells us that it's a little like drilling for oil. All the time that the oil is under the earth's surface, it isn't accessible. But, by drilling (i.e. meditating), we open up the oil field and can thereafter return and access it at any time that we want to or need to. The

Essay on Service of the Heart - Love Like Fire and Water

of fear [of G-d]. And then afterward, we may arouse this feeling at any time. It is also possible that constant practice will lead to the same result, as written in *Tanya* there, "when one will meditate on this for a long hour every day...).

The general point here is that we may consciously experience "fear of G-d" even without meditation, just by recalling the topics which lead to fear, especially if we have a "pure soul." And even those of us who require meditation (and it's good for

לְהִתְעוֹרֵר אַחַר כָּךְ בְּכָל עֵת כו' וְאֶפְשָׁר יוּכַל לִהְיוֹת כֵּן גַּם כֵּן עַל יְדֵי הַשְּׁקִידָה וּכְמוֹ שֶׁכָּתוּב בְּסֵפֶר שֶׁל בֵּינוֹנִים שָׁם כְּשֶׁיִּתְבּוֹנֵן בָּזֶה שָׁעָה גְדוֹלָה בְּכָל יוֹם כו').

(וּכְלָלוּת הָעִנְיָן בָּזֶה דְּיִרְאַת אֱלֹקִים יְכוֹלָה לִהְיוֹת בְּהִתְגַּלּוּת גַּם בְּלֹא הִתְבּוֹנְנוּת רַק עַל יְדֵי שֶׁיִּזְכֹּר הָעִנְיָנִים הַמְּבִיאִים לִידֵי יִרְאָה וּבִפְרָט בְּנֶפֶשׁ זַכָּה. וְגַם מִי שֶׁצָּרִיךְ לָזֶה הִתְבּוֹנְנוּת (וְכֵן בְּכָל אֶחָד וְאֶחָד

COMMENTARY

same applies to true of fear of G-d. There is a reservoir of respect and fear of G-d in every Jewish person. It may be covered over — especially in times of transgression and sin, which conceal and obscure the natural fear of G-d that is deep within us. Even so, by constant and applied meditation, it is possible to pierce the layer of obfuscation surrounding this store of natural fear and reveal it. There are those for whom the natural fear is not so hidden and who therefore don't require a lot of meditation to uncover it. But, there are those for whom the reservoir of natural fear requires a lot of work to reveal. That is why the *Tanya* says that if we do not succeed in revealing it immediately, we must continue working at it until we succeed.

Once we have accessed and revealed our hidden store of fear of G-d, we need no longer establish fixed times for meditating upon it. It becomes an integral part of our life and is readily accessible. We need only remind ourselves of it from time to time in order to achieve this lower fear. After we have done so, fear of G-d becomes an integral part of our approach to life, even if we aren't aware of it.

In this respect, fear of G-d differs from love of G-d, which demands constant and regular meditation. Fear differs from love in that it is not associated with a particular level of G-dliness,

Love of G-d cannot possibly develop without meditation, and this takes place only at the time of prayer.

טוֹב לִהְיוֹת לְעִתִּים הַהִתְבּוֹנְנוּת בְּעִנְיָנִים הַמְבִיאִים לִידֵי יִרְאָה) יְכוֹלָה לִהְיוֹת הַהִתְבּוֹנְנוּת וְהַהֶרְגֵּשׁ פְּנִימִי בְּזֶה שֶׁלֹּא בִּשְׁעַת הַתְּפִלָּה (וּבְוַדַּאי בִּתְפִלָּה הַזְּמַן מֻכְשָׁר יוֹתֵר) אֲבָל הָאַהֲבָה אִי אֶפְשָׁר שֶׁתִּהְיֶה בְּלִי הִתְבּוֹנְנוּת, וְהַהִתְבּוֹנְנוּת הַמְבִיאָה לִידֵי אַהֲבָה בִּכְדֵי שֶׁיִּנְחוּ וְיִקָּלְטוּ הָעִנְיָנִים בְּמוֹחוֹ וְיֻרְגַּשׁ בְּמוֹחוֹ וְלִבּוֹ לְהִתְפַּעֵל בָּהֶם בְּאַהֲבָה הוּא בִּזְמַן הַמֻּכְשָׁר דִּתְפִלָּה דַּוְקָא

everyone to occasionally contemplate the topics which lead to fear) can meditate and gain an inner experience of fear outside of the regular time of prayer. (But, certainly the time of prayer is more ideally suited). However, love of G-d cannot possibly develop without meditation. The meditation that brings it about — such that the topics [of meditation] become integrated and absorbed in our intellect, as well as felt in our mind and heart, bringing us to an arousal of love [of G-d] — is only [possible] at the appropriate time of prayer.

--- **COMMENTARY** ---

but rather with G-d Himself. If we fear G-d, we fear G-d Himself, in essence, not as He reveals Himself on some spiritual level. Therefore, once we have revealed the hidden store of fear of G-d within ourselves, we need only remind ourselves from time to time that it exists, and "tap into it," rather than make special efforts every day to meditate upon it.

All this does not apply to love of G-d. The meditation techniques that bring us to love the One Above require daily effort. The best time to meditate on the topics that bring us to the love of G-d is at the beginning of the day before morning prayers. The Chabad technique calls for the meditator to first study a Chassidic text and fully understand it, then meditate upon the concepts found within it, and finally to pray. It helps as well to immerse in the *mikveh* ("ritual pool") and to give some *tzedakah* ("charity") before prayers.

This meditation has as its goal to achieve intellectual grasp of particular spiritual levels, which in turn give birth to a thirst for G-d and a desire to draw closer to Him. The actual drawing closer takes place during prayer. But, because we must train our mind to understand very refined and subtle spiritual concepts — of which only an impression remains for the rest of the day — the meditation must take place and be repeated on a daily

Essay on Service of the Heart - Love Like Fire and Water   75

All of this is because fear is associated with the essential infinite light of the One Above. And also the meditation [leading to fear] focuses on high and elevated levels of infinite G-dly illumination, as well as upon how G-d Himself sees and observes, so to speak. Love of G-d, on the other hand, is associated with divine

(וְכָל זֶה הוּא מִפְּנֵי שֶׁהַיִּרְאָה הִיא בִּבְחִינַת עַצְמוּת אוֹר אֵין סוֹף בָּרוּךְ הוּא וְגַם הַהִתְבּוֹנְנוּת הִיא בְּמַדְרֵגוֹת גְּבֹהוֹת וְנַעֲלוֹת בָּאוֹר אֵין סוֹף בָּרוּךְ הוּא וְאֵיךְ שֶׁהוּא רוֹאֶה וּמַבִּיט בְּעַצְמוֹ כִּבְיָכוֹל, וְאַהֲבָה הִיא בִּבְחִינַת אוֹרוֹת וְגִלּוּיִים כוּ') וְעוֹד זֹאת שֶׁאַהֲבָה אֵינָהּ בְּהִתְגַּלּוּת כָּל

——————— *COMMENTARY* ———————

basis. It's a little like physical exercise — the more you do it, the easier it gets, and the better you become at it. But if you leave it alone, it leaves you.

2. AHAVAT OLAM

Beyond *yirah tata'ah* is the lower level of love of G-d: *ahavat olam* ("wordly love"). It is the level on which we begin to feel closeness to G-dliness. It also is produced by meditation on the outer "garments" of the Creator — that is, on nature and the universe. But, unlike the lower level of fear (in its more mature manifestation of *yirat Elokim*), love of G-d derives from meditation upon the G-dly energy and life-force enlivening each and every aspect of creation. In this respect, the word *olam* in *ahavat olam* means both "world" and "eternal." Although this love of G-d is derived from the world, it is an eternal and integral part of the Jewish soul, inherited from the world's first lover of G-d, our forefather Abraham. It is activated by meditation on creation, but in essence it is present within us from birth. In its natural form, "worldly love," before it has been fanned into flames of fiery love, is associated with the World of *Yetzira* [and with the *vav* of G-d's Name, and with the six emotional *sephirot* (from *chesed* to *yesod*)].

3. AHAVA RABBA

Higher than *ahavat olam* is *ahava rabba* ("great love"). It is derived from meditation on the source of creative energy — the transcendent light and spiritual illumination from Above. That is, while "wordly love" is derived from focusing upon the life-force that enlivens the world, "great love" comes from

הַיּוֹם רַק רְשִׁימוֹ בִּלְבַד וְהַנִּשְׁאָר מֵהַגַּדְלוּת דִּתְפִלָּה, וְיִרְאָה צְרִיכָה לִהְיוֹת בְּהִתְגַּלּוּת כָּל הַיּוֹם (דְּהַיְנוּ הַהִתְגַּלּוּת דְּיִרְאָה הַמֻּסְתֶּרֶת כוּ') עַל יְדֵי שֶׁיִּתְבּוֹנֵן בְּהִתְבּוֹנְנוּת קַלָּה כוּ' שֶׁהוּא עִנְיַן הַזִּכָּרוֹן כוּ' כנ"ל וְהָא בְּהָא תַּלְיָא וּכְמוֹ שֶׁנִּתְבָּאֵר לְעֵיל.

illumination and revelation [not with divine essence]. Furthermore, love of G-d is not part of our daily consciousness. During the day, only an impression of the spiritual heights of love — the remnant of our [morning] prayers — remains in our consciousness. Fear of G-d, though, must permeate our consciousness at all times (meaning that the latent fear within us must be revealed). This is brought about by cursory meditation, which constitutes the "recalling" [of His Presence] mentioned above. These two factors are dependent upon one another, as explained earlier. [That is, since fear is associated with His essential infinite light, it is always present and pervasive. It doesn't require a lengthy meditation, but just a reminder. But love of G-d flows from awareness of specific levels of spiritual light and illumination, and thus demands lengthy meditation on those levels at specific times.]

וּבְזֹהַ"ק בַּהַקְדָּמָה אִיתָא יִרְאָה דְּאִיהוּ עִיקָּרָא לְמִדְחַל ב"נ לְמָארֵי' בְּגִין דְּאִיהוּ רַב וְשַׁלִּיט עִיקָּרָא וְשָׁרְשָׁא דְּכֹלָּא עָלְמִין וְכֹלָּא קַמֵּי' כְּלָא חֲשִׁיב,

In the *Zohar*, part 1, in the introduction, it is stated:

Fear is crucial. [What is fear?] That man should venerate his Master; since He is great and governs, He is the foundation and root of all worlds, and everything before Him is as if it doesn't exist.

וְהַיְנוּ הַיִּרְאָה מֵעֶצֶם גְּדֻלָּתוֹ יִתְבָּרֵךְ (בְּלִי יְצָרֵף לָזֶה אֵיךְ שֶׁעוֹמֵד עָלָיו

The *Zohar* is speaking here of veneration of G-d's essential great-

---

COMMENTARY

meditation upon the transcendent source of that energy, the infinite light of the One Above. If we are able to access this level of love and energy, we totally transform our being into one of G-dliness, in the process destroying our animal nature. *Ahava rabba* is associated with the World of *Bria* [and the first *hey* of G-d's Name, and the *sephira* of *bina*.]

4. YIRAH ILA'AH

Highest of all is *yirah ila'ah* ("higher fear") — awe. After a certain amount of meditation and contemplation on the infinite

Essay on Service of the Heart - Love Like Fire and Water

ness (leaving out the additional element of G-d standing over us and observing our deeds). Such an experience of His greatness can take place only at the appropriate time of prayer, as "servants of G-d" can testify.

It would seem then that this is a [higher level of] fear of G-d, more aptly described as "awe," which is an inner feeling of self-abashment in front of Him, as explained in *Tanya*, part 1, chapter 4, and in *Reishit Chochmah, Sha'ar Hayirah*, chapter 1. It is the "higher fear" (*yirah ila'ah*) described in *Tanya*, chapter 43, where it says: "but the 'higher fear' — awe — is an inner fear which comes from [wonder at] the deep level of G-dliness which is within the worlds..." And in chapter 41: "and *yirah ila'ah* is fear that is akin to abashment...which is a state of total self-nullification, *ma'h* [nothingness] of the *sephira* of *chochmah*; [this self-nullification is the feeling that] 'everything stands before Him as if it were nothing,' like

וְרוֹאֶה בְּמַעֲשָׂיו כִּי אִם מֵעֹצֶם הַגְּדֻלָּה לְבַד) וְהַרְגֵּשׁ גְּדֻלָּתוֹ יִתְבָּרֵךְ זֶה יָכוֹל לִהְיוֹת בַּזְּמַן הַמֻּכְשָׁר דִּתְפִלָּה דַּוְקָא כַּנִּרְגָּשׁ לְעוֹבְדֵי ה'.

וְנִרְאֶה דְּיִרְאָה זוֹ הִיא בְּחִינַת יִרְאָה פְּנִימִית שֶׁמִּתְבּוֹשֵׁשׁ מִגְּדֻלָּתוֹ יִתְבָּרֵךְ הַמְבֹאֶרֶת בְּסֵפֶר שֶׁל בֵּינוֹנִים ח״א פ״ד וּכְמוֹ כֵן בְּרֵאשִׁית חָכְמָה שַׁעַר הַיִּרְאָה פ״א, וְהַיְנוּ בְּחִינַת יִרְאָה עִילָאָה וּכְמוֹ שֶׁכָּתוּב בְּסֵפֶר שֶׁל בֵּינוֹנִים פמ״ג אַךְ הַיִּרְאָה עִילָאָה יָרֵא בּשֶׁת וְיִרְאָה פְּנִימִית שֶׁהִיא נִמְשֶׁכֶת מִפְּנִימִיּוּת הָאֱלֹקוּת שֶׁבְּתוֹךְ הָעוֹלָמוֹת כו' וּבפמ״א כְּ' וְיִרְאָה עִילָאָה הוּא יָרֵא בּשֶׁת כו' שֶׁהוּא בְּחִינַת בִּטּוּל מַמָּשׁ בְּחִינַת מַה דְּחָכְמָה דְּכֹלָּא קַמֵּי' כְּלָא חֲשִׁיבֵי כְּבִטּוּל זִיו הַשֶּׁמֶשׁ בַּשֶּׁמֶשׁ כו' וּכְמוֹ שֶׁכָּתוּב שָׁם בפמ״ג, וּמַדְרֵגָה זוֹ הִיא לְמַעְלָה מֵעִנְיַן הַתְּפִלָּה שֶׁנִּתְבָּאֵר לְעֵיל לִקְשֹׁר וּלְדַבֵּק נַפְשׁוֹ כו'. וְהוּא בִּשְׁמוֹנֶה

Higher fear, or awe, only takes place at the time of prayer, specifically during the "amida."

COMMENTARY

light of the One Above, we reach a state of *devekut* ("cleaving") where we totally forget ourselves. We realize that in essence there is no one other than G-d. We are in awe of Him, unable even to open our own lips without "permission" from Above. Although technically, *yirah ila'ah* is a form of fear, it is not the lower fear of G-d who has the ability to reward or punish us, or fear of G-d's incredible might and wisdom. Neither is it love of Him, that causes us to be attracted to and transfixed by elevated spiritual levels. It is rather the stunning realization that, without Him, nothing exists. That's why it's called awe.

עֲשָׂרָה שֶׁהוּא עִנְיָן בִּטּוּל בִּמְצִיאוּת מַמָּשׁ וּכְמוֹ שֶׁכָּתוּב בפל״ט בְּעִנְיָן הִשְׁתַּחֲוָאוֹת דִּשְׁמוֹנֶה עֶשְׂרֵה כוּ׳.

the nullification of the rays of the sun within the sun." The spiritual level of this experience is beyond that of prayer, which has as its goal the "uniting of the soul with G-dliness," as explained already. It is associated with the *Shmoneh Esreh* [within prayer] during which the person is "nullified in existence" [totally lacking awareness of self], as written in chapter 39 of *Tanya* regarding bowing down during *Shmoneh Esreh*.[25]

There is an inner dimension to "lower fear" of G-d, and that is the reverence that we may develop for G-d's creation and creative power.

וּמַה שֶּׁכָּתוּב יִרְאוּ מֵה׳ כָּל הָאָרֶץ כוּ׳ כִּי הוּא אָמַר וַיֶּהִי כוּ׳ הִנֵּה עַל פִּי פְּשׁוּטוֹ הִיא הַיִּרְאָה מִבְּחִינַת יְכָלְתּוֹ יִתְבָּרֵךְ שֶׁהוּא בּוֹרֵא הָעוֹלָם וּמְחַיֵּה אוֹתוֹ וּבִיכָלְתּוֹ יִתְבָּרֵךְ לַעֲשׂוֹת הַכֹּל אַיִן וָאֶפֶס חַס וְחָלִילָה וּבִפְרָט שֶׁמָּא יִגְרוֹם הַחֵטְא כוּ׳ וּכְעִנְיָן שֶׁכָּתוּב בְּרֵאשִׁית חָכְמָה שַׁעַר הַנַּ״ל פ״נ בִּבְחִינַת ב׳ וְג׳. אָמְנָם פְּנִימִיּוּת הָעִנְיָן בָּזֶה הוּא הַיִּרְאָה מִגְּדֻלַּת ה׳ בִּבְרִיאַת וְהִתְהַוּוּת הָעוֹלָמוֹת, דְּהִתְהַוּוּת יֵשׁ מֵאַיִן הוּא עִנְיָן נִפְלָא מְאֹד וּכְמוֹ שֶׁכָּתוּב בְּמָקוֹם אַחֵר וּמוֹרָא עַל עֹצֶם גְּדֻלָּתוֹ יִתְ׳, וּמִכָּל מָקוֹם יִרְאָה זוֹ הִיא בְּחִינַת יִרְאָה חִיצוֹנִיּ׳ שֶׁהֲרֵי אוֹמֵר עַל זֶה יִרְאוּ

And as for the fear mentioned in the verse [from Psalms 33:8-9] — "Let them fear G-d, all the earth...because He spoke and it came to be..." — the simple meaning is that it refers to fear of G-d's omnipotence. Since He created the universe and enlivens it and has within His power to return it to nothingness — and especially because our sins could bring this about, G-d forbid, as is written in *Reishit Chochma, Sha'ar Hayirah*, chapter 3, regarding the second and third levels — [we should fear Him]. However, the inner dimension of this [type of] fear is reverence of His ability to create the universe and worlds. Creation *ex nihilo* (something "from

---
COMMENTARY

Chapter 3 touches briefly on the subject of *yirah ila'ah*, telling us that this level of fear is predicated on the very elevated state of self-nullification known as *bitul b'metziut* ("nullification of existence.") While the lower level of *yirah tata'ah* necessitate only nullification of the ego, but not total negation of self, the higher level of *yirah ila'ah* which leads to awe necessitates that we totally forget our own being. While the lower level lays the foundation and basis for G-dliness as experienced in prayer, the higher level is beyond prayer. It is associated with the *Amida* in which we ask G-d to "open our mouths" because we don't have the ability

Essay on Service of the Heart - Love Like Fire and Water

nothing") is an amazing and wondrous process,[xix] as written elsewhere, and is one indication of the mighty power of the One Above. Nevertheless, this reverence is only external, which is why the literal translation of the [above] verse reads, "let them fear *from* G-d" [in Hebrew, *yiru mei HaShem*]. This is referring to the lower level of fear, as is known[xx] regarding the difference between "fear G-d" [*yiru mei HaShem*] and "fear G-d Himself [*yiru et HaShem*]."[26]

"Fear of [lit. from] G-d" is considered superficial because it only concerns that which is known and experienced of His greatness in creating the worlds. This is the knowledge that comes about by [meditation upon] His "outer garments," so to speak. Included in this category is meditation on the greatness of G-d in creating such a multitude of creatures in the physical world — that is, the mineral, vegetable, animal, and human kingdoms. [It includes also contemplation on how] He created separate species without limit and measure, and how each one of them draws

מַה' שֶׁזֶּהוּ יִרְאָה תַּתָּאָה, וְכַנּוֹדָע הַהֶפְרֵשׁ בֵּין יִרְאוּ מה' לְיִרְאוּ אֶת ה' כו',

וְהַיְנוּ לְפִי שֶׁזֶּהוּ מַה שֶׁנּוֹדָע וְנִרְגָּשׁ גְּדֻלָּתוֹ יִתְבָּרֵךְ מֵהִתְהַוּוּת הָעוֹלָמוֹת דְּהַיְנוּ הַיְדִיעָה עַל יְדֵי לְבוּשִׁים כו'. וּבִכְלָל זֶה גַּם כֵּן הַהִתְבּוֹנְנוּת בִּגְדֻלָּתוֹ יִתְבָּרֵךְ בְּרִבּוּי הַהִתְהַוּוּת לְמַטָּה בְּדוֹמֵם צוֹמֵחַ חַי וּמְדַבֵּר מִינִים מִמִּינִים שׁוֹנִים עַד אֵין קֵץ וְשִׁעוּר וּלְכֻלָּם נִמְשָׁךְ חַיּוּת מְיֻחָד וּפְרָטִי לְפִי מִזְגּוֹ וּתְכוּנָתוֹ, וְכֵן בְּצָבָא מַעְלָה בְּרִבּוּי יוֹתֵר עַד אֵין שִׁעוּר כו' וּבְגַדְלוּת הַנִּבְרָאִים כו' וּבְרִבּוּי הַהִשְׁתַּלְשְׁלוּת וּבְרִבּוּי עוֹלָמוֹת עַד אֵין מִסְפָּר כו' וְהוּא עִנְיָן מָה רַבּוּ מַעֲשֶׂיךָ וּמָה גָּדְלוּ מַעֲשֶׂיךָ כו'

upon a specific spiritual energy that enlivens it, each according to its nature. The same is true concerning the heavenly hosts, of which there are a tremendous variety and number, [literally] "without number." There is also the huge size and mass of the creations. Then there are also the multiple levels of spiritual devolution and innumerable worlds that He created. All of this is implied by the verses [in Psalms 104:24 and Psalms 92:6], "how many are Your works... how great are Your works..."[xxi] ["many' referring to variety, and "great" referring to size]. In general, all of this is [also]

---------- **COMMENTARY** ----------

to speak of our own volition. However, it is not part of the meditative process that is associated with prayer. Rather, it is the result of all of the effort that we invested in prayer, but it is not part of the process itself.

---

xix) See footnote of the Rebbe on page 272

xx) See footnote of the Rebbe on page 274

Reverence is developed by contemplation of the variety, size and number of creatures.

xxi) See footnote of the Rebbe on page 276

Reverence is still in the category of "lower fear" because it comes from contemplation of the "garments" of creation. It leads to greater fulfillment of the mitzvoth.

implied in the verse [in Psalms 48:2, 96:4, 145:3], "Great is G-d and very praiseworthy," as written elsewhere.

While the reverence derived from this meditation is higher (in our conscious awareness) than the fear derived from meditation on how G-d stands over us and observes all our deeds, it is, nevertheless, also in the category of fear leading merely to the fulfillment of the *mitzvot*. This is the fear that is explained in the beginning of chapter 43 of *Tanya*, and it is a more mature and developed dimension of [lower] fear of G-d. In general, fear is a conscious attitude that aids in our overall fulfillment of the *mitzvot*. Fear of sin aids specifically with *sur mei'rah* ["refraining from evil"], as is written in the introduction to *Derech Chaim* and as explained in chapter 42 of *Tanya*: "fear of sin helps one refrain from evil." But fear of G-d leads to overall fulfillment of the *mitzvot*, that is, fulfillment of [all of] His commandments due to fear of G-d, as is written [in Ecclesiastes 12:13]: "Fear G-d and keep His commandments" meaning both negative and positive commandments alike. In truth, failure to fulfill a positive *mitzvah* is also a transgression, and so fulfillment of the positive *mitzvot* is also motivated by fear of sin. The difference is that fulfillment of the

וּכְלָלוּת הָעִנְיָן הוּא מַה שֶּׁכָּתוּב גָּדוֹל ה' וּמְהֻלָּל מְאֹד כו' וּכְמוֹ שֶׁכָּתוּב בְּמָקוֹם אַחֵר,

וְהַיִּרְאָה הַבָּאָה מִזֶּה עִם הֱיוֹת שֶׁהִיא לְמַעְלָה (בְּעִנְיַן הַהִתְגַּלּוּת) מֵהַיִּרְאָה הַבָּאָה מֵהַהִתְבּוֹנְנוּת דְּהַקָּדוֹשׁ בָּרוּךְ הוּא עוֹמֵד עָלָיו וְרוֹאֶה בְּמַעֲשָׂיו כו' מִכָּל מָקוֹם הִיא גַּם כֵּן בִּכְלַל יִרְאַת אֱלֹקִים הַנּוֹגֵעַ לַמַּעֲשֶׂה לְבַד, וְהִיא הַיִּרְאָה הַמְבֹאֶרֶת בְּסֵפֶר שֶׁל בֵּינוֹנִים רפמ"ג. וְהִיא בְּחִינַת הַגַּדְלוּת דְּיִרְאַת אֱלֹקִים כו', דְּבְדֶרֶךְ כְּלָל עִנְיַן יִרְאַת אֱלֹקִים הוּא שֶׁהַיִּרְאָה הִיא בְּהִתְגַּלּוּת וְלָכֵן יִרְאַת אֱלֹקִים הִיא לְקִיּוּם הַמִּצְווֹת בִּכְלָל, דְּיִרְאַת חֵטְא עִקָּרָהּ הוּא לָסוּר מֵרָע וּכְמוֹ שֶׁכָּתוּב בְּהַקְדָּמַת דֶּרֶךְ חַיִּים וּכְמוֹ שֶׁכָּתוּב בְּסֵפֶר שֶׁל בֵּינוֹנִים תּוֹךְ פמ"ב בִּבְחִינַת יִרְאַת חֵטְא לִהְיוֹת סוּר מֵרָע כו' וְיִרְאַת אֱלֹקִים הִיא לְקִיּוּם הַמִּצְווֹת בִּכְלָל הַיְנוּ לִשְׁמוֹר מִצְוֹתָיו יִתְבָּרֵךְ מִצַּד יִרְאַת אֱלֹקִים וּכְמוֹ שֶׁכָּתוּב אֶת הָאֱלֹקִים יְרָא וְאֶת מִצְוֹתָיו שְׁמוֹר הֵן בְּסוּר מֵרָע וְהֵן בְּוַעֲשֵׂה טוֹב. וּבֶאֱמֶת הֲרֵי הַהֶעְדֵּר דְּוַעֲשֵׂה טוֹב חַס וְחָלִילָה הוּא גַּם כֵּן חֵטְא וְעָוֹן וְאִם כֵּן הֲרֵי זֶה נִכְלָל גַּם כֵּן בִּכְלַל יִרְאַת חֵטְא (וְהַיְנוּ דְּיִרְאַת חֵטְא מֵאַנְט אוֹיף גַּם כֵּן קִיּוּם הַמִּצְווֹת בְּוַעֲשֵׂה

COMMENTARY

Yirah ila'ah is associated with the World of *Atzilut* [and with the *yud* of G-d's Name, and with the *sephira* of *chochma*].

Essay on Service of the Heart - Love Like Fire and Water

mitzvot because of fear of sin is equivalent to motivation derived from the fear of transgression alone, and we don't feel so much of the G-dliness of the *mitzvot* — that they are G-d's commandments. But fear of G-d motivates us to fulfill the *mitzvot* because of our own [inner] fear. That is, our fear of G-d induces in us a greater sense of G-dliness, as well as awareness that these are G-d's commandments, and therefore we [are motivated to] fulfill them on account of our fear of G-d. Thus fear of G-d is a more conscious experience than fear of sin, since it implies fear [not only of transgression, but] of the One Above.

(Nonetheless, even fear of sin is a more conscious experience than accepting the "yoke of heaven," which is a subconscious event and also an aid in keeping *all* of the *mitzvot* [like fear of G-d, as explained above]. Furthermore, it causes us to become careful and guarded in all of our movements. This is the wariness of the senses described earlier that comes about spontaneously, albeit through hidden activity in the soul. There is a conscious experience of fear in fear of sin, and yet it is not the same

טוב) רַק הַהֶפְרֵשׁ בָּזֶה דְּיִרְאַת חֵטְא הוּא שֶׁקִּיּוּם הַמִּצְוֹת הוּא מִצַּד יִרְאַת הַחֵטְא וְאֵינוֹ נִרְגָּשׁ בָּזֶה כָּל כָּךְ הָאֱלֹקוּת וְשֶׁהֵן מִצְוֹתָיו ית׳, וְיִרְאַת אֱלֹקִים הוּא שֶׁקִּיּוּם הַמִּצְוֹת הוּא מִצַּד הַיִּרְאָה שֶׁבּוֹ הַיְנוּ מִצַּד יִרְאַת הָאֱלֹקִי׳ שֶׁבּוֹ שֶׁנִּרְגָּשׁ בּוֹ יוֹתֵר הָאֱלֹקוּת וְשֶׁהֵן מִצְוֹתָיו יִתְבָּרֵךְ וְעַל כֵּן הוּא שׁוֹמֵר כָּל מִצְוֹתָיו מִצַּד הַיִּרְאָה הָאֱלֹקִית שֶׁבּוֹ. וְזֶהוּ דִּירָא אֱלֹקִים הוּא שֶׁהַיִּרְאָה הִיא בְּהִתְגַּלּוּת יוֹתֵר מִבְּיִרְאַת חֵטְא לִהְיוֹת שֶׁהִיא יִרְאָה אֱלֹקִית.

(וּמִכָּל מָקוֹם גַּם יִרְאַת חֵטְא הִיא בִּבְחִינַת הִתְגַּלּוּת לְגַבֵּי קַבָּלַת עוֹל מַלְכוּת שָׁמַיִם שֶׁהוּא בְּהֶעְלֵם (וְהִיא, רְצוֹנוֹ לוֹמַר קַבָּלַת עוֹל מַלְכוּת שָׁמַיִם, הִיא גַּם כֵּן לְקִיּוּם הַמִּצְוֹת בִּכְלָל, וְעוֹד זֹאת יִתְרָה שֶׁפּוֹעֵל עָלָיו בְּכָל תְּנוּעוֹתָיו בִּפְרָט וְהוּא עִנְיַן הַהַגְדָּרָה הַנַּ"ל הַבָּאָה בְּדֶרֶךְ מִמֵּילָא, רַק שֶׁהִיא פְּעֻלָּה נֶעֱלֶמֶת בַּנֶּפֶשׁ) וּבְיִרְאַת חֵטְא הֲרֵי יֵשׁ כָּאן יִרְאָה בְּהִתְגַּלּוּת וּמִכָּל מָקוֹם אֵינוֹ דוֹמֶה לְהִתְגַּלּוּת שֶׁבְּיִרְאַת

COMMENTARY

In summary:

Yirah Tata'ah "Lower fear"	Acceptance of the yoke of heaven; fear of sin; fear of G-d	Nullification of ego; foundation for prayer
Yirah Ila'ah "Higher fear"	Awe	Total negation of self; result of effort invested in prayer

as the conscious revelation of fear of G-d. In fear of sin only the fear is felt, while in fear of G-d, there is revelation and experience of G-dliness [perhaps more aptly described as "spiritual reverence"], wherein the fear itself is G-dly.)

The spiritual element in our fear of G-d itself breaks down into two [different] levels: a minor and a mature level. The minor level is the result of constant reminders of G-d's immanence in meditation upon His outer "garments," as described in the end of chapter 42. (The fear coming from awareness that He observes our deeds is more associated with fear of sin.) The mature level of fear of G-d is the product of contemplation of the greatness of G-d as He permeates all the worlds, as explained in *Tanya*, beginning of chapter 43. All of this [meaning, acceptance of the "yoke of heaven," fear of sin, and the two levels of fear of G-d] falls into the category of *yirah tata'ah* ["lower fear"] associated with actual fulfillment of the *mitzvot*. This is the fear implied in the verse [from Psalms cited earlier], "Let them fear [lit: from] G-d," since "He is the One who spoke, and it came about..."

אֱלֹקִים, דְּיִרְאַת חֵטְא הוּא רַק הִתְגַּלּוּת הַיִּרְאָה וִירֵא אֱלֹקִים הוּא שֶׁיֵּשׁ כָּאן הִתְגַּלּוּת אֱלֹקִי שֶׁנִּרְגָּשׁ הָאֱלֹקוּת וְהַיִּרְאָה הִיא יִרְאָה אֱלֹקִית).

וּבָזֶה גּוּפָא יֵשׁ קַטְנוּת וְגַדְלוּת. וְהַקַּטְנוּת הִיא כְּשֶׁבָּאָה מִזֶּה שֶׁנִּזְכָּר תָּמִיד הַפְּנִימִיּוּת עַל יְדֵי הַלְּבוּשִׁים הַחִיצוֹנִים כו' הַמְבֹאָר בִּסְפמ"ב (וְעִנְיַן מַה שֶׁהַקָּדוֹשׁ בָּרוּךְ הוּא רוֹאֶה בְּמַעֲשָׂיו כו' שַׁיָּךְ יוֹתֵר לְעִנְיַן יִרְאַת חֵטְא) וְהַגַּדְלוּת הִיא כְּשֶׁבָּאָה הַיִּרְאָה מֵהִתְבּוֹנְנוּת בִּגְדֻלַּת ה' דְּאִיהוּ מְמַלֵּא כָּל עָלְמִין הַמְבֹאָר בְּרֵפמ"ג. וְהַכֹּל בְּחִינַת יִרְאָה תַּתָּאָה הַשַּׁיָּךְ לְקִיּוּם הַמִּצְוֹת בְּפֹעַל מַמָּשׁ וְהוּא עִנְיַן יְרָאוּ מֵה' כו' כִּי הוּא אָמַר וַיֶּהִי כו'.

Yirah ila'ah ["higher fear" of G-d] is associated with a great measure of self-nullification, known as "nullification of existence" [in which we lose awareness of our very self, as opposed to "nullification of ego," in which our ego is deflated, but our sense of self remains intact]. It flows from experience of the very essence of G-dliness, the awareness that He is great and

Higher fear (awe) of G-d flows from experience of His essence.

וְיִרְאָה עִילָּאָה הִיא עֶצֶם בְּחִינַת הַבִּטּוּל בִּבְחִינַת בָּטֵל בִּמְצִיאוּת הַנִּמְשֶׁכֶת מֵעֶצֶם הָאֱלֹקוּת דְּאִיהוּ רַב וְשַׁלִּיט כו' וְכוֹלָּא קַמֵּיהּ כְּלָא חָשִׁיב כו', וְכֵן מַה שֶׁכָּתוּב בְּמָקוֹם אַחֵר בְּהִתְבּוֹנְנוּת שֶׁהָאוֹר אֵין סוֹף נִמְצָא לְמַטָּה כְּמוֹ לְמַעְלָה שֶׁהַיִּרְאָה הַנִּמְשֶׁכֶת מִזֶּה (הַיְנוּ מֵעֶצֶם הָאוֹר אֵין סוֹף בָּרוּךְ הוּא, לֹא מַה שֶׁעוֹמֵד

governs everything, and that everything is as if "non-existent" before Him. It results as well from meditation on how He is present below [in this world] as well as above, as written elsewhere. The fear derived from this awareness (of the essential infinite light of the One Above, not how He is standing over him, watching and observing, but how G-d in His essence is found revealed in the physical world no less than He is in the spiritual worlds above, as written elsewhere) is a very inward awe, equivalent to "nullification of existence."

עָלָיו וְרוֹאֶה וּמַבִּיט כו' כִּי אִם מַה שֶׁהָאוֹר אֵין סוֹף כְּמוֹ שֶׁהוּא בְּעֶצֶם הֲרֵי הוּא נִמְצָא לְמַטָּה בִּבְחִינַת גִּלּוּי מַמָּשׁ כְּמוֹ שֶׁהוּא כו' וּכְמוֹ שֶׁכָּתוּב בְּמָקוֹם אַחֵר) הִיא בְּחִינַת יִרְאָה פְּנִימִית בִּבְחִינַת בִּטּוּל בִּמְצִיאוּת מַמָּשׁ,

Higher fear (awe) is awareness that all of creation is as "naught" before G-d. It requires a very high level of self-nullification.

Forms of Fear of the One Above		
Yirah Tata'ah (lower fear) *Yiru mei HaShem*	*Kaballat Ohl Malchut Shamayim* acceptance of the "yoke of heaven"	Unconsciousness fear of the One Above
	Yirat Chait fear of sin	Conscious fear of transgression
	Yirat Elokim fear of G-d	Conscious fear of G-d (minor form of *Yirat Elokim* based on reminders of Him)
		Reverence of G-d (mature form of *Yirat Elokim* based upon His almighty power in creation)
Yirah Ila'ah (higher fear) *Yiru et HaShem*)	awareness that all is as if "non-existent" before G-d	Awe predicated upon nullification of one's self before G-d

Fear, in general, is associated with nullification, and correspondingly, it has the effect of nullifying the animal soul (rather than purifying and refining it). [That is,] fear, in general, corresponds to "putting oneself aside." The lesser level of fear (*yirah*

וּבְדֶרֶךְ כְּלָל הַיִּרְאָה הוּא עִנְיַן הַבִּטּוּל וּכְמוֹ כֵן מַה שֶּׁפּוֹעֵל בַּנֶּפֶשׁ הַבַּהֲמִית הוּא גַם כֵּן עִנְיַן הַבִּטּוּל שֶׁלּוֹ (לֹא עִנְיַן הַזִּכּוּךְ וְהַבֵּרוּר) וּבְדֶרֶךְ כְּלָל הוּא עִנְיַן הֲנָחַת עַצְמוּתוֹ כו', רַק דְּיִרְאָה תַּתָּאָה

Kuntres Ha'Avoda - קונטרס העבודה

Lower fear precedes prayer, but higher fear surpasses prayer. Neither involve cleaving to G-d or purifying the animal soul, which take place in love and prayer.

דְּהַיְנוּ קַבָּלַת עוֹל מַלְכוּת שָׁמַיִם וְיִרְאַת חֵטְא וְיִרְאַת אֱלֹקִים הוּא לְמַטָּה בְּמַדְרֵגָה (בְּעִנְיַן הַהִתְגַּלּוּת) מֵעִנְיַן הָעֲבוֹדָה דִּתְפִלָּה שֶׁהִיא לְקַשֵּׁר וּלְדַבֵּק נַפְשׁוֹ כוּ', וְיִרְאָה עִילָאָה הִיא לְמַעְלָה הַרְבֵּה מֵהָעֲבוֹדָה דִתְפִלָּה הַנַ"ל. וְהִתְקַשְּׁרוּת וּדְבֵקוּת נַפְשׁוֹ בֶּאֱלֹקוּת וְכֵן הַבֵּרוּר וְהַזִּכּוּךְ דְּנֶפֶשׁ הַבַּהֲמִית הוּא עַל יְדֵי מִדַּת הָאַהֲבָה דַּוְקָא. וְלִהְיוֹת שֶׁעִנְיַן הַתְּפִלָּה וַעֲבוֹדָה שֶׁבַּלֵּב הִיא ב' עִנְיָנִים הַנַ"ל כְּמוֹ שֶׁנִּתְבָּאֵר לְעֵיל פ"א, לָזֹאת כָּל הָעֲבוֹדָה וְהַיְגִיעָה דִתְפִלָּה הִיא לָבוֹא לְמִדַּת הָאַהֲבָה:

קִצּוּר.

וְהִנֵּה וַדַּאי כֵּן הוּא שֶׁהַיִּרְאָה מֻכְרַחַת לִהְיוֹת בְּכָל אֶחָד וְאֶחָד. אָמְנָם לֹא זוֹ הִיא עִנְיַן עֲבוֹדָה שֶׁבַּלֵּב דִּתְפִלָּה, דְּהַיִּרְאָה צָרִיךְ לִהְיוֹת בִּתְמִידוּת וּבָאָה רַק עַל יְדֵי הַזִּכָּרוֹן שֶׁיִּזְכֹּר תָּמִיד בְּמֶלֶךְ מַלְכֵי הַמְּלָכִים הַקָּדוֹשׁ בָּרוּךְ הוּא וְאֵיךְ שֶׁהוּא רוֹאֶה בְּמַעֲשָׂיו וּכְלָלוּת עִנְיָנָהּ הוּא לִהְיוֹת סוּר מֵרַע וַעֲשֵׂה טוֹב בְּפֹעַל מַמָּשׁ, וְיֵשׁ בָּזֶה גַּם כֵּן הִתְבּוֹנְנוּת וְהַעֲמָקַת הַדַּעַת אֲבָל הֵן בְּעִנְיָנִים כְּאִלּוּ שֶׁיְּכוֹלִים לִהְיוֹת וְלִפְעֹל גַּם שֶׁלֹּא בִּשְׁעַת הַתְּפִלָּה. וְהָעִקָּר בָּזֶה הוּא הַשְּׁקִידָה (וּמִכָּל מָקוֹם מֻכְשָׁר יוֹתֵר הַזְּמַן דִּתְפִלָּה) וְקִצּוּר הַהִתְבּוֹנְנוּת (וְהוּא עִנְיַן הַזִּכָּרוֹן הַנַ"ל) צָרִיךְ לִהְיוֹת תָּמִיד. וְנִתְ' עִנְיַן יִרְאָה

tata'ah) — which includes acceptance of the "yoke of heaven," fear of sin, and fear of G-d — is lower (on the scale of revelation) than the *avoda* of prayer, whose purpose it is to unite our soul [to the One Above]. But, the higher level of fear ("awe" or *yirah ila'ah*) is much higher than the *avoda* of prayer. The cleaving of the soul to G-d and also the purification and refinement of the animal soul are a function of love of G-d alone. And since the object of prayer and of the "service of the heart" are precisely these two goals, as mentioned in Chapter 1, the entire effort and labor of prayer is directed toward love of G-d.

SYNOPSIS:

It is certainly true that everyone must develop fear of G-d. However, this is not the content of the "service of the heart" of prayer. Fear must be constant, based upon our memory reminding us at all times of the King of Kings, the One Above, and how He observes all of our deeds. In general, this fear leads us to turning away from bad and doing good, [meaning toward actual fulfillment of the negative and positive *mitzvot*]. Meditation and deep thought are involved in this process, but their focus is on matters that can also be contemplated and effective [at other times, not just] during prayer. The key is regular (with the best time being during prayer) and concise meditation

Essay on Service of the Heart - Love Like Fire and Water   85

(consisting of the reminders mentioned above) at all times. [In this chapter] were explained the two levels of fear (*yirah tata'ah*, or "lower fear," and *yirah ila'ah*, or "higher fear") as well as the difference between fear of sin (*yirat cheit*) and fear of G-d (*yirat Elokim*), and also the minor and mature levels within fear of G-d. The "service of the heart" of prayer — which involves uniting our soul with G-d as well as purifying and refining our animal soul, and which is described as "and you should know today and put it in your heart..." — is specifically associated with the attribute of love of G-d. And therefore, the entire labor and effort of prayer is aimed at achieving this attribute of love of G-d.

עִילָאָה וְיִרְאָה תַּתָּאָה, וְהַהֶפְרֵשׁ בֵּין יִרְאַת חֵטְא לְיִרְאַת אֱלֹקִים, וְאֵיךְ שֶׁבְּיִרְאַת אֱלֹקִים יֵשׁ בְּחִינַת קַטְנוּת וְגַדְלוּת. וַעֲבוֹדָה שֶׁבַּלֵּב דִּתְפִלָּה שֶׁהוּא עִנְיַן הִתְקַשְּׁרוּת וּדְבֵקוּת נַפְשׁוֹ בֵּאלֹקוּת וּבֵרוּר וְזִכּוּךְ הַנֶּפֶשׁ הַבַּהֲמִית שֶׁהוּא מַה שֶּׁכָּתוּב וְיָדַעְתָּ הַיּוֹם וַהֲשֵׁבֹתָ אֶל לְבָבֶךָ כו' זֶהוּ בְּמִדַּת הָאַהֲבָה דַּוְקָא. וְעַל כֵּן כָּל הָעֲבוֹדָה וְהַיְגִיעָה דִּתְפִלָּה הִיא לָבוֹא לְמִדַּת הָאַהֲבָה:

CHAPTER 4 / פרק ד

Two kinds of love; like water, and like fire

וְהִנֵּה בָּאַהֲבָה יֵשׁ ב' מַדְרֵגוֹת כְּלָלִיּוֹת הָא' בְּחִינַת אַהֲבָה כַּמַּיִם וּכְמוֹ שֶׁכָּתוּב זְכוֹר אָב נִמְשַׁךְ אַחֲרֶיךָ כַּמַּיִם וְהַב' אַהֲבָה בְּרִשְׁפֵּי אֵשׁ וְצִמָּאוֹן (וְהֵן בְּחִינַת חֶסֶד וּגְבוּרָה שֶׁבַּחֶסֶד)ˣˣⁱⁱⁱ

When it comes to love of the One Above, there are two general levels.[xxii] One is "love as water," from the verse [in the prayer for rain recited during *musaf* of *Shmini Atzeret*], "Remember the Father, who was drawn after You like water…" The other is described as "love like flames of fire and thirst." (These two levels represent *chesed sheb'chesed* [love within "loving-kindness"] and *gevura sheb'chesed* [strength within loving-kindness").[27]

[xxii] See footnote of the Rebbe on page 277

[xxiii] See footnote of the Rebbe on page 278

דְּהָאַהֲבָה כַּמַּיִם הִיא בִּבְחִינַת קָרוֹב וּדְבֵקוּת בֶּאֱלֹקוּת, וְהוּא עַל יְדֵי הַהִתְבּוֹנְנוּת בְּהָאוֹר וְחַיּוּת הָאֱלֹקִי הַמִּתְלַבֵּשׁ בָּעוֹלָמוֹת וּכְמוֹ שֶׁכָּתוּב וְאַתָּה מְחַיֶּה אֶת כֻּלָּם שֶׁבְּכָל אֶחָד וְאֶחָד הַיְנוּ בְּכָל נִבְרָא וְנִבְרָא בִּפְרָט יֵשׁ אוֹר וְחַיּוּת אֱלֹקִי הַמְחַיֶּה אוֹתוֹ וּמִבְּשָׂרִי אֶחֱזֶה אֱלֹקָהּ שֶׁכָּל אָדָם מַרְגִּישׁ בְּעַצְמוֹ שֶׁיֵּשׁ בּוֹ חַיּוּת הַמְחַיֶּה אוֹתוֹ וּכְמוֹ כֵן הוּא בָּעוֹלָם שֶׁנִּקְרָא גּוּף גָּדוֹל כַּנּוֹדָע. שֶׁעַל יְדֵי טִיב הַהַשָּׂגָה וְהַהִתְבּוֹנְנוּת בָּזֶה בְּהַעֲמָקַת הַדַּעַת נִרְגָּשׁ וְנִרְאֶה אֶצְלוֹ אֵיךְ שֶׁהָעוֹלָם חַי מְאוֹר הָאֱלֹקִי. וּכְשֶׁמְּקַשֵּׁר וּמַעֲמִיק דַּעְתּוֹ בְּהָאוֹר

"Love like water" is associated with closeness to G-dliness. It results from meditation on the G-dly light and energy en-clothed in the worlds, as is written [in Nechemiah 9:6], "And You enliven them all…" Within each and every specific aspect of creation is to be found a G-dly light and energy which enlivens it. [As it says in Job 19:26,] "From my flesh, I will see G-d"; we all feel within ourselves a life-force enlivening us. And so it is also in the world at large, which is called a macrocosm, as is known. By meditating properly with intellectual understanding, while concentrating deeply, we feel and perceive

---
COMMENTARY

CHAPTER 4: LOVE LIKE WATER AND FIRE

Chapter 4 is the heart of *Kuntres Ha'Avoda*. More than any other chapter, it describes the "nuts and bolts" of Jewish meditation.

The previous chapters established the difference between love and fear of G-d. Love of G-d demands attention and meditation at fixed times and intervals (usually before and during

Essay on Service of the Heart - Love Like Fire and Water

within ourselves how the world gets its life from a G-dly light. When we concentrate and focus our attention on this G-dly light enlivening the universe, we begin to experience the preciousness and spiritual elevation of G-dliness (that is, that G-dliness in itself is very desirable and uplifting). This brings us to unite our soul with G-dliness, such that our entire will and desire is focused on G-d and nothing else. This love grows stronger when we meditate on the fact that G-dliness constitutes the life-force of the universe in general and of our own soul in particular.

(It would seem that here, we are talking about one level of G-dliness—the divine ray of light that is en-clothed in the universe. But, within this level, the first part of the meditation [on the "G-dly light enlivening the world"] focuses on experiencing the G-dliness in the world, while the second part of the meditation [on "our own soul in particular"] results in a feeling and awareness of how divinity is the life-force of the universe in general, and of ourselves in particular.) As it is written [in Isaiah 26:9], "'My soul desires You....,' which is to say, "since You, G-d,

הָאֱלֹקִי שָׂמְחֵי אֶת הָעוֹלָם נִרְגָּשׁ אֶצְלוֹ הַיְקָר וְהָעִלּוּי דֶּאֱלֹקוּת (הַיְנוּ מַה שֶּׁאֱלֹקוּת בְּעֶצֶם הוּא עִנְיָן יָקָר וְנַעֲלֶה מְאֹד) וְעַל יְדֵי זֶה מִתְקַשֵּׁר נַפְשׁוֹ וְנִדְבָּק בֶּאֱלֹקוּת אֲשֶׁר כָּל חֶפְצוֹ וּרְצוֹנוֹ הוּא אֱלֹקוּת וְאֵינוֹ חָפֵץ בְּשׁוּם דָּבָר אַחֵר. וְתִגְדַּל הָאַהֲבָה יוֹתֵר כַּאֲשֶׁר מִתְבּוֹנֵן אֵיךְ שֶׁאֱלֹקוּת הוּא חַיֵּי הָעוֹלָם בִּכְלָל וְחַיֵּי נַפְשׁוֹ בִּפְרָט

(וְנִרְאָה שֶׁהַכֹּל הוּא בְּמַדְרֵגָה אַחַת בֶּאֱלֹקוּת הַיְנוּ בְּהֶאָרַת הָאֱלֹקִי הַמִּתְלַבֵּשׁ בָּעוֹלָם, רַק דִּבְהִתְבּוֹנְנוּת הַנַּ"ל הוּא שֶׁמִּתְבּוֹנֵן וּמַרְגִּישׁ אֶת הָאֱלֹקוּת שֶׁבָּעוֹלָם וְהִתְבּוֹנְנוּת זוֹ הִיא שֶׁהַהִתְבּוֹנְנוּת וְהַהֶרְגֵּשׁ הוּא אֵיךְ שֶׁאֱלֹקוּת הוּא חַיּוּת הָעוֹלָם בִּכְלָל וְחַיּוּתוֹ בִּפְרָט) וּכְמוֹ שֶׁכָּתוּב נַפְשִׁי אִוִּיתִיךָ כְּלוֹמַר מִפְּנֵי שֶׁאַתָּה ה' נַפְשִׁי וְחַיֵּי הָאֲמִתִּיִּים לָכֵן אִוִּיתִיךָ פֵּי' שֶׁאֲנִי מִתְאַוֶּה וְתָאֵב לְךָ כְּאָדָם הַמִּתְאַוֶּה לְחַיֵּי נַפְשׁוֹ כו' וְכֵן כְּשֶׁהוּא הוֹלֵךְ כו' כָּךְ אֲנִי מִתְאַוֶּה וְתָאֵב לָאוֹר אֵין סוֹף בָּרוּךְ הוּא חַיֵּי הַחַיִּים

Love like water is an experience of the preciousness of G-dliness, such that we want to be one with it.

COMMENTARY

the morning prayers). Fear, once it has been attained, needs only reminders from time to time. Chapters 2 and 3 explained the details of fear of G-d. Chapter 4 begins to tell us the details of love of G-d.

Just as there are different kinds of love and relationships between people, so it is with the One Above. Most of us have

There is love like water because He is the life-force of the universe, and love like water because He is the life-source of our own soul.

הָאֲמִתִּיִּים לְהַמְשִׁיכוֹ בְּקִרְבִּי עַל יְדֵי עֵסֶק הַתּוֹרָה כו׳ וּכְמוֹ שֶׁכָּתוּב בְּסֵפֶר שֶׁל בֵּינוֹנִים פמ״ד.

are my soul, and my true life, I desire You; I desire and long for You like one who longs for the life of his own soul..." And so it is when we is go to sleep: "I desire and long for the infinite light, which is true life, to draw it down within myself by learning Torah..." (*Tanya*, chapter 44, from *Zohar*, part. 3, 67a).

There are two "modes" or "rays" of G-dliness in the world. One, the more external, enlivens and maintains the physical creation. It is constant and unchanging. Chassidic literature compares it to speech, since the Torah tells us that G-d created the world with ten utterances. The other mode is the ray of G-dliness that enlivens our souls. It is more personal, intimate, and dependent upon our avoda, or worship of the One Above. Chassidic literature compares it to thought.

We might have assumed that the two meditations mentioned above correspond to the two levels of speech and thought, but the parenthetical note above forewarns us that the two meditations are two dimensions, an inner and an outer, of the same ray of G-dliness enlivening the world, comparable to G-d's speech. The following parantheses indicate that perhaps after all, they correspond to the two different modes of speech and thought.

(וְהַיִּתְרוֹן בְּאַהֲבָה זוֹ שֶׁהִיא בִּבְחִינַת פְּנִימִיּוּת יוֹתֵר, וְהִיא הַמְּבִיאָה אוֹתוֹ לְעֵסֶק הַתּוֹרָה לְהַמְשִׁיךְ אוֹר אֵין סוֹף בָּרוּךְ הוּא בִּפְנִימִיּוּת נַפְשׁוֹ כו׳ (וְנִרְאֶה דְּהַהַמְשָׁכָה הִיא בְּמַדְרֵגָה גְּבוֹהָה יוֹתֵר הַרְבֵּה מִן הָאַהֲבָה שֶׁנִּתְבָּאֵר לְעֵיל דְּהָאַהֲבָה דְּנַפְשִׁי

(The advantage of this level of love is that it is more internal, and it brings us to learn Torah in order to draw down upon ourselves the infinite light of the One Above into the inner recesses of our soul. And it would seem that this influx [from learning Torah] is on a much higher level than

---

COMMENTARY

---

experienced love between siblings, such as between brothers and sisters, or love between parents and children. This kind of love is always present, but not always felt. Such, as well, is one kind of love that we feel for the Creator. In the *Song of Songs*, G-d expresses His relationship with the Jewish people as *achoti* ("my sister"), among other appellations. This is a love that is unconscious, but always present. A brother and sister, or parent and child, do not spend a lot of time pining for each other. It

Essay on Service of the Heart - Love Like Fire and Water

that of the love mentioned earlier. While the love of "You are my soul, I desire You" is brought about by meditation on the ray of G-dliness which enlivens the worlds, the G-dliness brought down by learning the Torah comes from the infinite light of G-d which transcends the worlds, as described in *Tanya*, chapter 23. It is possible that the love of "You are my soul, I desire You" is also above the ray of G-dliness mentioned above [which enlivens creation], as is written elsewhere regarding the injunction [in Deuteronomy 30:20] "to love the Lord your G-d...because He is your life," meaning that He is the life-force of all souls. [If so, then it] is an expression of the four-letter Name of G-d [translated as "Lord" and denoting G-d as He transcends nature] clad in *Elokim* [the name of G-d as He manifests Himself in nature]. It is also transcendent G-dliness enmeshed in immanent spirituality. It is as well the exalted level of the *sephira* of *malchut* [His kingship], as discussed in the Chassidic discourse *Tiku* from the year 5670, starting with the words: *Achat Sha'alti*.[28]

אֲוִיתִיךָ הִיא גַם כֵּן בַּהֶאָרָה הָאֱלֹקִית שֶׁבָּעוֹלָמוֹת, וְהַהַמְשָׁכָה שֶׁעַל יְדֵי הַתּוֹרָה הֲרֵי הִיא בִּבְחִינַת אוֹר אֵין סוֹף שֶׁלְמַעֲלָה מֵהָעוֹלָמוֹת וּכְמוֹ שֶׁכָּתוּב בְּסֵפֶר שֶׁל בֵּינוֹנִים פכ״ג. וְאֶפְשָׁר דְּהָאַהֲבָה דְנַפְשִׁי אֲוִיתִיךָ הִיא גַם כֵּן לְמַעֲלָה מֵהַהֶאָרָה הנ״ל וּכְמוֹ שֶׁכָּתוּב בְּמָקוֹם אַחֵר בְּעִנְיָן לְאַהֲבָה אֶת ה׳ אֱלֹקֶיךָ כִּי הוּא חַיֶּיךָ דְּהַיְנוּ חַיֵּי הַנְּשָׁמוֹת שֶׁזֶּהוּ מִבְּחִינַת הוי׳ שֶׁבֶּאֱלֹקִים בְּחִינַת סוֹבֵב שֶׁבִּמְמַלֵּא וְהוּא בְּחִינַת הָרוֹמְמוּת שֶׁבַּמַּלְכוּת כו׳ וּכְמוֹ שֶׁכָּתוּב מִזֶּה בִּדְרוּשׁ תִּקְעוּ עת״ר בְּדִבּוּר הַמַּתְחִיל אַחַת שָׁאַלְתִּי.

Love like water because He is our own soul's life-source leads us to learn more Torah.

COMMENTARY

is sufficient that they renew the connection from time to time, and their love for each other immediately surfaces. There is no burning desire to be with each other all the time, since in an unconscious sense they are always part of one another. This kind of love of G-d is in our genes; it has been handed down through the generations from the first great lover of G-d, Abraham. It influences our thoughts and permeates our activities, but only subconsciously, without awareness on our part. Nevertheless — just as with the love between siblings or between parents and children — we can raise this love to consciousness and express it. By thinking of His creation and how He maintains it, we can come to conscious awareness and expression of love for the One Above.

A third kind of love like water – because G-d is our "father."

וְהָאַהֲבָה כְּבְרָא דְּאִשְׁתַּדֵּל כו' הַמְבֹאֶרֶת שָׁם בפמ"ד הוּא מֵהַהִתְבּוֹנְנוּת שֶׁאַתָּה אָבִינוּ מַמָּשׁ שֶׁזֶּהוּ לְמַעְלָה מַעְלָה מִמַּה שֶּׁאַתָּה ה' נַפְשִׁי כו' וְהַהֶרְגֵּשׁ בָּזֶה הוּא בְּאֹפֶן אַחֵר לְגַמְרֵי וְהוּא בְּחִינַת אַהֲבָה פְּנִימִית וְעַצְמִית כו'. וְיֵשׁ לוֹמַר שֶׁזֶּהוּ בְּעֶצֶם הוי' שֶׁלְּמַעְלָה מִשֵּׁ' אֱלֹקִים שֶׁהוּא מְקוֹר חַיֵּינוּ (וּכְמוֹ שֶׁכָּתוּב בְּמָקוֹם אַחֵר בְּעִנְיַן הוי' אֱלֹקֵינוּ) וְאָבִינוּ הָאֲמִתִּי בָּרוּךְ הוּא).

Then there is the love of the "son who exerts himself for his father," as explained in *Tanya*, chapter 44, which results from meditation on the concept, "You are our Father" and which, in reality is far beyond the level of "You, G-d, are my soul." The emotion associated with this meditation is completely different—it is an inner and essential love. It might be said that it is associated with the essential [four-letter] Name of G-d, which is above the name *Elokim* and is the source of our lives—as written elsewhere regarding [the verse from Deuteronomy 6:4] *HaShem Elokeinu*, "The Lord is our G-d"—and our true Father, may He be blessed.)

The essential four-letter Name of G-d (which we are forbidden to pronounce and which is known as the Tetragrammaton) corresponds to the various soul-levels and worlds which are the subject of our meditation:			
#	Name of G-d	Soul level	Experience	World
5.	Tip of *yud*	*Yechida* "Single one"	Unity consciousness	Infnite light Beyond worlds
4.	*Yud*	*Chaya* "Living one"	Transcendent consciousness	World of *Atzilut* "World of Emanations"
3.	*Hey*	*Neshama* "Soul/breath"	Intellect Consciousness	World of *Bria* "World of "Creation"
2.	*Vav*	*Ruach* "Wind/spirit"	Emotion consciousness	World of *Yetzira* "World of Formation"
1.	*Hey*	*Nefesh* "Enlivening soul"	Action consciousness	World of *Asiya* "World of Action"

COMMENTARY

In Chassidic literature, and especially in the *Kuntres Ha'Avoda*, this kind love is known as "love like water." Deep under the surface of the earth are aquifers that we never see, and deep in the Jewish psyche are currents of love of G-d that are part of the collective Jewish consciousness. We don't feel them, but

A fourth category of love like water – "as in water, face responds to face."

There is, though a certain advantage to meditation on G-dliness as found in the world. In such meditation, our attachment is to the G-dliness within physical things and not to the physical as such. However, although this meditation satisfies our thirst for closeness to G-d, it does not quite bring us to learn Torah. And therein lies the advantage of the love of "You are my soul, I desire You"—it does bring us closer to learning Torah, as mentioned earlier. And since the ultimate purpose of love of G-d is to serve Him with love (as written in *Tanya*, end of chapter 40)—meaning to cleave to Him by fulfilling the *mitzvot* of the Torah—therefore we must develop the above-mentioned love of "You are my soul, I desire You." [There must be] as well the love discussed in chapter 46 of *Tanya*, "as in water, face answers to face" [in which we becomes acutely aware of G-d's love for us, and this arouses, in turn, a tremendous love in our heart for G-d]. So, we must also practice and become constant in the love of the "son who exerts himself for his father," since all of these techniques bring us closer to fulfilling the *mitzvot* of the Torah with love.

וְיֵשׁ יִתְרוֹן גַּם כֵּן בְּהִתְבּוֹנְנוּת הַנַּ"ל בֶּאֱלֹקוּת שֶׁבָּעוֹלָם שֶׁעַל יְדֵי זֶה גַּם בַּדְּבָרִים הַגַּשְׁמִיִּים תַּכְלִית רְצוֹנוֹ הוּא בָּאֱלֹקוּת שֶׁבָּהֶם לֹא בַּגַּשְׁמִי מִצַּד עַצְמוֹ, רַק דְּבְהִתְבּוֹנְנוּת זוֹ הֲרֵי הוּא מַרְוֶה נַפְשׁוֹ בַּקֵּרוּב לֶאֱלֹקוּת וְאֵינוֹ מֵבִיא כָּל כָּךְ לְעֵסֶק הַתּוֹרָה. וּבָזֶה יִתְרוֹן הָאַהֲבָה דְּנַפְשִׁי אִוִּיתִיךָ הַמְּבִיאָה יוֹתֵר לְעֵסֶק הַתּוֹרָה כַּנַּ"ל. וְלִהְיוֹת דְּתַכְלִית הָאַהֲבָה הִיא הָעֲבוֹדָה מֵאַהֲבָה כְּמוֹ שֶׁכָּתוּב בְּסֵפֶר שֶׁל בֵּינוֹנִים ספ"מ וְהַיְנוּ לִדְבֹּק בּוֹ עַל יְדֵי תּוֹרָה וּמִצְוֹת, לָזֹאת בֶּאֱמֶת צָרִיךְ לִהְיוֹת הָאַהֲבָה הַנַּ"ל דְּנַפְשִׁי אִוִּיתִיךָ גַּם הָאַהֲבָה דְּכַמַּיִם הַפָּנִים אֶל הַפָּנִים שבפמ"ו בְּסֵפֶר שֶׁל בֵּינוֹנִים. וְכֵן לְהַרְגִּיל עַצְמוֹ בְּהָאַהֲבָה כִּבְרָא דְּאִשְׁתַּדַּל כוּ', שֶׁכֻּלָּן הֵן הַמְּבִיאִים לְעֵסֶק הַתּוֹרָה וּמִצְוֹת מֵאַהֲבָה.

--- **COMMENTARY** ---

they influence us. The deep waters of the inner earth might never emerge to the surface, nor even become wells, but because they are there, the earth is fruitful and moist. We may not be aware of our love for the Creator, but it colors and influences our approach to life nonetheless. And if we dig and look for it, it comes to the surface.

Completely different from this is the love between a man and a woman, between husband and wife. In the *Song of Songs*, G-d also refers to the Jewish people as *ra'yati* ("my spouse").

Type of love like water	Aspect of G-dliness	Level of difficulty	Result
"G-dly light enlivening the world"	*Elokim* G-dliness invested in and enlivening the creation (worlds of *Bria, Yetzira, Asiya*)	Easiest meditation, upon ray of G-dliness enlivening creation	Leads to closeness to G-liness in the physical world, weakening of the animal soul
"because He is the life of my soul…" (*Tanya*, ch. 44)	Inner aspect of *Elokim* or perhaps essential four-letter name of G-d illuminating *Elokim* (*malchut* of *Atzilut*)	Intermediate meditation, based on G-dliness in creation or on transcendent G-dliness illuminating creation	Leads to learning Torah and fulfillment of *mitzvot*
"like a son exerting himself for his father" (*Tanya*, ch. 44)	Essential G-dliness, the essential four-letter name of G-d as Creator (*chochma* of *Atzilut*)	More difficult meditation, based upon transcendent G-dliness	Learning Torah and fulfillment of *mitzvot*
"As in water, face answers face…" (*Tanya*, ch. 46)	Essential four-letter name of G-d beyond any connection to creation (above *Atzilut*, *Keter*)	Most difficult meditation, rarely achieved.	Learning Torah and fulfillment of *mitzvot*

רַק שֶׁהִתְבּוֹנְנוּת וְקֵרוּב הַנַּ"ל בָּהָאֱלֹקוּת שֶׁבָּעוֹלָמוֹת הוּא בְּקֵרוּב יוֹתֵר אֶל הַנֶּפֶשׁ וּבְנָקֵל יוֹתֵר לָבוֹא

The meditation and closeness based upon the ray of G-dliness invested in the worlds, as described

——————— COMMENTARY ———————

Needless to say, when husband and wife are separated, within a short time, their longing turns into a visceral need and fiery desire to reunite. This is not a simple matter of keeping a memory

Essay on Service of the Heart - Love Like Fire and Water

earlier, is closer to our [divine] soul and easier to achieve. It also has more effect on our animal soul, weakening it and inducing it to love G-dliness, as will be explained soon. Therefore, the *avoda* of the One Above begins with this love and closeness [based upon meditation on the G-dly ray invested in the world], which brings us as well to involvement in Torah and fulfillment of its *mitzvot*, since in general we desire G-dly matters. And in particular, we want to learn Torah and fulfill its *mitzvot*, because they are precious to us, and we derive energy from them, since they are G-dly. As it says in the *Midrash Tanhuma*, "Honor the *mitzvot* since they are My emissaries," and "the emissary of someone is like that very person himself." We then have to continue to strive for the various levels of love of G-d mentioned earlier. By drawing our [divine] soul closer to G-dliness and by weakening our animal soul—due to the love and closeness to the One Above—we prepare ourselves for arrival to the higher levels of love of G-d mentioned earlier.)

לָזֶה, וְגַם זֶה פּוֹעֵל יוֹתֵר עַל הַנֶּפֶשׁ הַבַּהֲמִית לְהַחֲלִישׁוֹ וְשֶׁיִּהְיֶה לוֹ גַּם כֵּן אַהֲבָה לֶאֱלֹקוּת שֶׁיִּתְ' לְקַמָּן בְּסָמוּךְ, וְעַל כֵּן תְּחִלַּת הָעֲבוֹדָה הִיא בְּאַהֲבָה וְקֵרוּב זֶה וְהִיא מְבִיאָה אוֹתוֹ גַּם כֵּן לַעֲסֹק הַתּוֹרָה וְקִיּוּם הַמִּצְוֹת, מִפְּנֵי שֶׁבְּדֶרֶךְ כְּלָל הוּא חָפֵץ בְּעִנְיְנֵי אֱלֹקוּת וּבִפְרָט בְּעֵסֶק הַתּוֹרָה וְקִיּוּם הַמִּצְוֹת מִפְּנֵי הַיֹּקֶר וְהַחַיּוּת שֶׁיֵּשׁ לוֹ בָּהֶן שֶׁהֵן אֱלֹקוּת, וּבַמדר"ת אִי' כַּבְּדוּ אֶת הַמִּצְוֹת שֶׁהֵן שְׁלוּחַי וּשְׁלוּחוֹ שֶׁל אָדָם כְּמוֹתוֹ כו'. וְאַחַר כָּךְ צָרִיךְ לִהְיוֹת אַהֲבוֹת הַנַּ"ל, אֲשֶׁר בֶּאֱמֶת עַל יְדֵי קֵרוּב נַפְשׁוֹ לֶאֱלֹקוּת וְעַל יְדֵי הַחֲלִישׁוּת דְּנֶפֶשׁ הַבַּהֲמִית הַנַּעֲשָׂה עַל יְדֵי הָאַהֲבָה וְהַקֵּרוּב הַנַּ"ל הֲרֵי הוּא מֻכְשָׁר לָבוֹא לְמַדְרֵגוֹת אַהֲבוֹת הַנַּ"ל).

The first level of love like water is the easiest to attain and has more effect upon our animal soul.

COMMENTARY

alive and re-connecting from time to time. Here, the memory forces itself into their consciousness and won't leave them alone. It is true that separation for a short time can renew and strengthen the bond between them, but within a relatively short period of time the couple feels a burning need to reunite. This kind of love between G-d and man is called "love like fire." It is not a love of familiarity as is "love like water," it is a love of consuming desire and tendency to "lose" oneself out of love for the other. This love is also likened to gold, as opposed to love like water, which is compared to silver.

Afterward, we shift our attention to the spiritual illumination of the higher worlds.

וּבִפְרָט כְּשֶׁמִּתְבּוֹנֵן בַּמַּדְרֵגָה בֶּאֱלֹקוּת שֶׁלְּמַעְלָה מֵהֶהָאָרָה הַמִּתְלַבֶּשֶׁת בָּעוֹלָם הַתַּחְתּוֹן וְהַיְנוּ בָּהָאוֹר הָאֱלֹקִי הַמִּתְלַבֵּשׁ וּמֵאִיר בָּעוֹלָמוֹת הָעֶלְיוֹנִים. וְכַנּוֹדָע דְּבָהָאוֹר דִּמְמַלֵּא כָּל עָלְמִין יֵשׁ בָּזֶה חִלּוּקֵי מַדְרֵגוֹת מַעְלָה וּמַטָּה דִּבְעוֹלָמוֹת עֶלְיוֹנִים מֵאִיר אוֹר עֶלְיוֹן יוֹתֵר וְהַיְנוּ שֶׁהָאוֹר הוּא שָׁם בִּבְחִינַת גִּלּוּי יוֹתֵר בְּלִי צִמְצוּם כָּל כָּךְ וּכְמוֹ שֶׁכָּתוּב בְּסֵפֶר שֶׁל בֵּינוֹנִים פ"מ (כְּמוֹ שֶׁבַּשֵּׂכֶל יֵשׁ כַּמָּה מִינֵי שְׂכָלִים דְּבַשֵּׂכֶל גָּבוֹהַּ וְנַעֲלֶה יוֹתֵר הֲרֵי יֵשׁ בּוֹ גִּלּוּי אוֹר שֵׂכֶל יוֹתֵר, וּבְשֵׂכֶל עָמֹק הַבָּא בִּבְחִינַת הַפְשָׁטָה הָאוֹר וְהַגִּלּוּי בּוֹ בְּיוֹתֵר כו', וְעַל דֶּרֶךְ זֶה בְּכָל עוֹלָם שֶׁהוּא עֶלְיוֹן בְּמַדְרֵגָה מִתְלַבֵּשׁ בּוֹ אוֹר נִגְלֶה יוֹתֵר שֶׁאֵינוֹ מְצַמְצֵם כָּל כָּךְ שֶׁזֶּהוּ בְּחִינַת הַמַּעְלָה שֶׁבְּהָאוֹר וְכָל שֶׁכֵּן בְּעֶשֶׂר הַסְּפִירוֹת שֶׁבָּעוֹלָם הַהוּא שֶׁמֵּאִיר

This is especially true when we meditate on levels of G-dliness above those invested in the lower world, [raising our attention to] the G-dly light illuminating the upper worlds. As is known, the immanent light that permeates the universe comes on many different levels, higher and lower. In the upper worlds, there shines a "higher" illumination, meaning the light is more revealed there, illuminating with less contraction, as is written in *Tanya*, chapter 40. (The intellect operates on many levels, and on the higher levels there is more revealed intellectual illumination. A deep concept, accompanied by abstraction, contains more light and revelation. So we find in every world, that the higher it is, the more revealed light is shining there, and the less spiritual contraction occurs. This is the special quality of the [G-dly] illumination, and even more of the

---

COMMENTARY

The goal of meditation, as described in the Chassidic texts, is to move from "love like water" to "love like fire." "Love like fire" has an advantage over "love like water," in the same way as gold has an advantage over silver. (See chapter 50 of the *Tanya*.) "Love like fire" consumes our animal soul, such that we are left with no other desire or interest than G-dliness.

In summary:

"Love like water"	"Love like fire"
Love between siblings, or between children and parents	Love between husband and wife
Familiar connection	Fiery consuming desire
Compared to silver	Compared to gold

Essay on Service of the Heart - Love Like Fire and Water

ten *sephirot* of that particular world, that the G-dly light is shining into them with more revelation.)

There are, as well, variations in each particular level, such as [stated in *Tikunei Zohar* 6, p. 23]: "The supernal mother nests in the throne and the six *sephirot* in *Yetzira*." [This refers to the emphasis on the *sephira* of *bina* in the World of *Bria* and the emphasis on the lower six *sephirot* in the World of *Yetzira*.] The same is true regarding the soul-levels of *nefesh-ruach-neshama*; we all know the advantage of our *ruach* over our *nefesh* and the advantage of our *neshama* over our *ruach*, which is like the advantage of intellect over emotion. So it is with the *nefesh-ruach-neshama* of the Worlds of *Bria-Yetzira-Asiya*. (And, in truth, there is also a distinction as to how the light and G-dly revelation shines. It can be an illumination of an essential inward dimension, or it can shine from an external dimension. The intellect [corresponding to *neshama*] is [generally] the illumination of an inner dimension; the emotions [corresponding to *ruach*] are expressions of a less essential and more external facet; and *nefesh* is the "external of the external" [*nefesh* is an extension of the emotions and is therefore a superficial expression], as written elsewhere.)

בָּהֶם הָאוֹר וְהַגִּלּוּי יוֹתֵר כו')

וְגַם יֵשׁ בָּזֶה חִלּוּקִים בְּמַדְרֵגוֹת פְּרָטִיּוֹת וּכְמוֹ אִמָּא עִילָאָה מְקַנְּנָא בְּכוּרְסֵי' וְשִׁית סְפִירָן בִּיצִירָה כו', וּכְמוֹ בְּנֶפֶשׁ רוּחַ וּנְשָׁמָה שֶׁבַּנֶּפֶשׁ שֶׁהָאָדָם יוֹדֵעַ בְּעַצְמוֹ מַעֲלַת הָרוּחַ עַל הַנֶּפֶשׁ וּמַעֲלַת הַנְּשָׁמָה עַל הָרוּחַ כְּמַעֲלַת הַשֵּׂכֶל עַל הַמִּדּוֹת כו' וְכֵן הוּא בְּנֶפֶשׁ רוּחַ וּנְשָׁמָה דִּבְרִיאָה יְצִירָה עֲשִׂיָּה כו' (וּבֶאֱמֶת הַהֶפְרֵשׁ בָּזֶה הוּא גַּם כֵּן בְּאֹפֶן הָאוֹר וְהַגִּלּוּי אִם שֶׁמֵּאִיר בְּחִינַת פְּנִימִיּוּת הָאוֹר אוֹ חִיצוֹנִיּוּת הָאוֹר, דְּמוֹחִין הֵן בְּחִינַת פְּנִימִיּוּת וּמִדּוֹת הֵן חִיצוֹנִיּוּת וְנֶפֶשׁ בְּחִינַת חִיצוֹנִיּוּת דְּחִיצוֹנִיּוּת כו' וּכְמוֹ שֶׁכָּתוּב בְּמָקוֹם אַחֵר)

There are variations in the levels of spiritual illumination of the higher worlds.

COMMENTARY

LOVE LIKE WATER

"Love like water" is the more basic of the two, requiring "entry level" meditation on how the G-dly energy enlivens the universe in general and ourselves in particular. Water possesses the trait of clinging to an object and "bathing" it, and so with the proper meditation we cling to G-dliness and bask in it, developing "love like water." This meditation is a calm, cultivated attempt to develop our positive connection with the One Above using the intellect. It starts with the realization that He

The above paragraph says that the differences in spiritual levels are two-fold: One, they can be in either the macrocosm (here meaning the three worlds of *Bria, Yetzira,* and *Asiya*), or they can be in the microcosm (the soul *neshama, ruach,* and *nefesh*). And within the two, the G-dly light may illuminate either internally (as in the soul-level of *neshama*), or externally (as in the soul-levels of *ruach* and *nefesh*):

World	Sephira emphasis	Kabbalistic description	Soul level	Spiritual "distance"
1. *Asiya*	*Malchut* (submission, acceptance)	"has no qualities it can call its own…"	*Nefesh*	"like through a tiny hole"
2. *Yetzira*	Six *sephirot* from *chesed* to *yesod* (emotions)	*zeir anpin* "six *sephirot* nest in *Yetzira*"	*Ruach*	"like through a window"
3. *Bria*	*Bina* (intellect)	"supernal mother nests in the throne (*Bria*)"	*Neshama*	"far-away"
4. *Atzilut*	*Chochma* (spiritual insight)	"supernal father nests in *Atzilut*"	*Neshama d'neshama,* or *chaya*	"close-by"

וּכְשֶׁמִּתְבּוֹנֵן בְּכָל זֶה בִּבְחִינַת הָאֱלֹקוּת הַמֵּאִיר בְּכָל מַדְרֵגָה וּמַדְרֵגָה וּבְהַעֲמָקַת הַדַּעַת שֶׁיִּקָּלֵט הָעִנְיָן הֵיטֵב בְּמוֹחוֹ וְיָאִיר בְּנַפְשׁוֹ וְנִרְגָּשׁ בּוֹ הָעִלּוּי דֶּאֱלֹקוּת (וּבְכָל

When we meditate on all of this, on the different kinds of G-dliness that illuminate every level and delve into the subject deeply, it becomes well embedded in our consciousness. It illuminates our soul, and we feel

---

COMMENTARY

creates and enlivens everything in the world, and that everything in the universe is permeated with His G-dly energy. Within this meditation, Chapter 4 of *Kuntres Ha'Avoda* alludes to three steps, as implied in this statement from near the end of Chapter 4:

"This may be a meditation on the lower world, on the G-dly light and energy infusing each and every aspect of creation and every specific detail. This meditation in itself is enough to bring our soul to an experience of G-dliness and the good and the preciousness associated with it. Or, we may also throw ourselves into this meditation with more

Essay on Service of the Heart - Love Like Fire and Water

the elevation of G-dliness (and at every higher level of illumination, we feel greater elevation). Our soul then gets much closer to G-d and cleaves to G-dliness. This, then, is love of G-d since the nature of water is to cause two things to cling to each other... (So it is on all levels of love of G-d, like that of "You are my soul, I desire You," and the "son who exerts himself for his father." The love is a strong desire to have the infinite light of G-d illuminate our soul and to cleave to Him by fulfilling the *mitzvot* of the Torah. And so it is regarding the love of "as in water, face answers to face," as written in *Tanya*, chapter 49, "to cleave to Him, may He be blessed, with desire..." So it is, as well, regarding the "love like flames of fire," [which causes us to long for G-d], as is written at the end of chapter 38 of *Tanya* regarding love which comes from meditation on His greatness; see what is written in chapter 43 and at the end of chapter 44: "to cleave to Him by fulfilling the *mitzvot* of the Torah"—this is a level of thirst...[as opposed to the level of "love like water"].)

אוֹר עֶלְיוֹן יוֹתֵר נִרְגָּשׁ הָעִלּוּי בְּיוֹתֵר) הֲרֵי מִתְקָרֵב נַפְשׁוֹ מְאֹד בִּבְחִינַת דְּבֵקוּת בֶּאֱלֹקוּת כוּ' וְזֶהוּ בְּחִינַת אַהֲבָה שֶׁהוּא הַקֵּרוּב וְהַדְּבֵקוּת בֶּאֱלֹקוּת וּכְטֶבַע הַמַּיִם לִדְבֹּק כוּ' (וְכֵן הוּא בְּכָל מַדְרֵגוֹת אַהֲבָה כְּמוֹ בְּאַהֲבָה דְּנַפְשִׁי אִוִּיתִיךָ וְכִבְרָא דְאִשְׁתַּדַּל כוּ' שֶׁזֶּהוּ מַה שֶׁחָפֵץ מְאֹד שֶׁיָּאִיר אוֹר אֵין סוֹף בְּנַפְשׁוֹ וּלְדָבְקָה בּוֹ עַל יְדֵי הַתּוֹרָה וּמִצְווֹת כוּ'. וְכֵן בְּאַהֲבָה דְּכַמַּיִם הַפָּנִים וּכְמוֹ שֶׁכָּתוּב בְּסֵפֶר שֶׁל בֵּינוֹנִים פמ"ט לִדְבְקָה בּוֹ יִתְבָּרֵךְ בִּדְבִיקָה חֲשִׁיקָה כוּ'. וְגַם בְּאַהֲבָה כְּרִשְׁפֵּי אֵשׁ הוּא שֶׁחָפֵץ לְדָבְקָה בּוֹ יִתְבָּרֵךְ וּכְמוֹ שֶׁכָּתוּב בספל"ח בְּעִנְיַן הָאַהֲבָה הַבָּאָה מֵהִתְבּוֹנְנוּת בִּגְדֻלָּתוֹ יִתְבָּרֵךְ (וְעַיֵּין מַה שֶׁכָּתוּב בפמ"ג וספמ"ד) לְדָבְקָה בּוֹ עַל יְדֵי קִיּוּם הַתּוֹרָה וְהַמִּצְוָה כוּ' רַק שֶׁהִיא בִּבְחִינַת צִמָּאוֹן כוּ').

The nature of water is to cause two things to cling together; so love like water "bathes" the soul in G-dliness.

COMMENTARY

energy and focus on how the main point is G-dliness, as in the verse, 'See, I have put before you life and good...' Or, we may focus on how the G-dly light is en-clothed and revealed in the higher worlds, each one of us according to our own level of intellect and level of *avoda*."

Thus we see that the first step in meditation leading to love of the One Above is to focus on the "G-dly light and energy infusing each and every aspect of creation..." This means that we must consider individual creations — whether mineral, vegetable, animal, or human—and think about the G-dly life-force animating

The more that we approach G-dliness, the more we distance ourselves from anything coarse and physical.

וְעַל יְדֵי הַקֵּרוּב וְהַדְּבֵקוּת בֶּאֱלֹקוּת הֲרֵי הוּא מִתְרַחֵק מֵהָעִנְיָנִים הַחָמְרִיִּים הַטִּבְעִיִּים דְּאַהֲבָה הִיא הַעְתָּקָה מִמָּקוֹם לְמָקוֹם וּכְמוֹ שֶׁכָּתוּב הָלוֹךְ וְנָסוֹעַ וּכְמוֹ הַהוֹלֵךְ מִמָּקוֹם לְמָקוֹם כָּל מַה שֶּׁמִּתְקָרֵב אֶל הַמָּקוֹם שֶׁהוֹלֵךְ הֲרֵי הוּא מִתְרַחֵק מֵהַמָּקוֹם שֶׁהָלַךְ מִשָּׁם, וְכָךְ הוּא בְּאַהֲבָה דְּכָל מַה שֶּׁמִּתְקָרֵב יוֹתֵר אֶל אֱלֹקוּת הֲרֵי הוּא מִתְרַחֵק מֵהָעִנְיָנִים הַחָמְרִיִּים וְהוּא עִנְיַן חֲלִישׁוּת הַנֶּפֶשׁ הַבַּהֲמִית שֶׁנֶּחֱלָשׁ טִבְעוֹ הַחָמְרִי עַל יְדֵי הִתְגַּבְּרוּת הָאַהֲבָה, לֶאֱלֹקוּת.

By approaching G-d and cleaving to G-dliness, we [simultaneously] distance ourselves from the coarse physicality of the natural world. Love [of G-d] involves moving from one spiritual "place" to another, as indicated in the verse [from Genesis 12:9 about Abraham, a man of kindness and love, who was] "walking and progressing." When we go from one place to another, we simultaneously approach our goal and distance ourselves from our place of origin. So it is with love of G-d; the more that we approach G-dliness, the more we [simultaneously] distance ourselves from anything coarse and physical. This is what is meant by the "weakening of the animal soul"—that is, its physical nature is weakened in proportion to our increased level of love of G-d.

(וּכְמוֹ שֶׁנִּרְגָּשׁ לְכָל עוֹבֵד ה' דְּעַל יְדֵי הַתְּפִלָּה בַּעֲבוֹדָה טוֹבָה בְּהִתְעוֹרְרוּת אַהֲבָה וְקֵרוּב לֶאֱלֹקוּת הִנֵּה גַּם כַּמָּה שָׁעוֹת אַחַר הַתְּפִלָּה הוּא אָדָם אַחֵר (ער אִיז גָאר אַ אַנְדֶערֶער) אוֹ גַּם יוֹם שָׁלֵם, וּמוּבָן דִּבְכְדֵי שֶׁתִּהְיֶה הַחֲלִישׁוּת

(When we serve G-d through proper prayer, we experience an arousal of love and desire for closeness to G-dliness, so that we become a different person for several hours thereafter or even for an entire day. Of course, it is understood that in order for this weakening of the ani-

---
COMMENTARY
---

each one. As will be explained in Chapter 6, the meditation must be particular — that is, it must focus not only on the overall concept of creation, but upon specific objects and creations, and the G-dly force enlivening them.

Then, we may "focus on how the main point is G-dliness," meaning not only that there is a force enlivening every aspect of creation, but that it — rather than the physical manifestation of the object — is the true reality of creation. We must be sensitive to the G-dly dimension in our understanding of creation, giving it special attention in our meditation. We must

Essay on Service of the Heart - Love Like Fire and Water

mal soul to be real, we must meditate not just once or twice but with constant effort every day. The weakened animal soul then becomes, generally speaking, unable to express itself via the limbs of the body [or] through our thought, speech, and action, as written in *Tanya*, chapter 12 and 13.)

It is also true that, through lack of use, our natural physical powers become weaker, as written in *Sha'arei Tshuva* of Rabeinu Yona, *z"l*, regarding the curbing of lusts—that this happens as a result of actually refraining from the lustful deed. In the course of time, this abstinence brings about a great weakening of physical lusts. In addition, [involvement in spirituality and] getting closer to the One Above awakens us to the vulgarity and grossness of physical things. At the time that we are attracted to them [our physical lusts], we do not

בֶּאֱמֶת הֲרֵי זֶה לֹא בְּפַעַם אַחַת וּשְׁתַּיִם כִּי אִם בִּשְׁקִידַת הָעֲבוֹדָה יוֹם יוֹם וּבְדֶרֶךְ כְּלָל הַחֲלִישׁוּת הִיא שֶׁאֵינוֹ מִתְפַּשֵּׁט לְהִתְלַבֵּשׁ בְּאֵבְרֵי הַגּוּף בְּמַעֲשֶׂה דִּבּוּר וּמַחֲשָׁבָה וּכְמוֹ שֶׁכָּתוּב בְּסֵפֶר שֶׁל בֵּינוֹנִים פי"ב וי"ג)

וְגַם עַל יְדֵי הֶעְדֵּר הַשִּׁמּוּשׁ בַּהַכֹּחוֹת הַטִבְעִיִּים הֲרֵי הֵם מִתְחַלְּשִׁים וּכְמוֹ שֶׁכָּתוּב בְּשַׁעֲ"ת לר"י ז"ל בְּעִנְיַן שְׁבִירַת הַתַּאֲוָה שֶׁזֶּהוּ עַל יְדֵי הֶעְדֵּר הָעֲשִׂיָּה בְּפֹעַל וּבְמֶשֶׁךְ זְמַן בְּהֶעְדֵּר הַהִשְׁתַּמְּשׁוּת בָּהֶם הֲרֵי הֵם נֶחְלָשִׁים הַרְבֵּה. וְעוֹד זֹאת שֶׁעַל יְדֵי הַקֵּרוּב לֶאֱלֹקוּת נִרְגָּשׁ אֶצְלוֹ הַחֻמְרִיּוּת וְהָעֲבִיּוּת שֶׁל הָעִנְיָנִים הַגַּשְׁמִיִּים (די גראבקייט פון דעם) דְּבְעֵת שֶׁהוּא נִמְשָׁךְ אַחֲרֵיהֶם אֵינוֹ מַרְגִּישׁ כְּלָל הָעֲבִיּוּת שֶׁבָּהֶם אֲבָל כַּאֲשֶׁר מִתְקָרֵב לֶאֱלֹקוּת הֲרֵי הוּא מַרְגִּישׁ

We must meditate not just once or twice, but with constant effort, every day.

COMMENTARY

cultivate our awareness of the spiritual dimension that underlies and transcends the physical world.

And, finally, there is the option of including in this meditation a recognition of higher spiritual worlds, as the Rebbe writes: "He may focus on how the G-dly light is clad and revealed in the higher worlds." The G-dly light that we begin to perceive as the true underlying reality manifests itself on higher levels as well. If it gives life to physical creations in the World of *Asiya*, it surely enlivens spiritual creations, such as angels, in the higher Worlds of *Yetzira* and *Bria*. We must develop and cultivate our sense of the spiritual worlds in order to gain some kind of recognition of the "exalted spiritual intellects" (*sichlim nivdalim*) as the Rambam calls them in *Hilchot Yesodei HaTorah*.

There is illumination from the divine soul during prayer, and the powers of the animal soul recede into concealment.

הֵיטֵב אֶת הָעֲבִיּוּת וְהַבַּהֲמִיּוּת אֲשֶׁר בָּהֶם וְאֵינוֹ חָפֵץ בְּשׁוּם אֹפֶן לִהְיוֹת כִּבְהֵמָה

(וְזֶהוּ הַטַּעַם שֶׁבִּכְדֵי לִפְעֹל בְּנַפְשׁוֹ הַכְּפִי' בְּעִנְיָנִים פְּרָטִיִּים הוּא בְּעֵת הַתְּפִלָּה דַּוְקָא מִפְּנֵי שֶׁאָז מֵאִיר בּוֹ הַנֶּפֶשׁ הָאֱלֹקִית וְהַכֹּחוֹת דְּנֶפֶשׁ הַבַּהֲמִית הֵן בְּהֶעְלֵם אָז דְּהוּא עִנְיַן הַחֲלִישׁוּת דְּנֶפֶשׁ הַבַּהֲמִית עַל כֵּן בְּנָקֵל לוֹ אָז לִפְעֹל יוֹתֵר. וְעוֹד מִפְּנֵי שֶׁאָז הוּא רוֹאֶה וּמַרְגִּישׁ הֵיטֵב אֶת הָעֲבִיּוּת בְּזֶה וּבְנָקֵל יִפְעַל בְּעַצְמוֹ לִכְפּוֹת אֶת עַצְמוֹ כוּ')

think of them as vulgar. But as we become more spiritual, we clearly experience their crudeness and bestiality, and we do not want at all to be like an animal.

(In order to achieve the maximum effect of re-training and restraining our personal tendencies, the best time [for us to meditate] is precisely during prayer. There is illumination emanating from our divine soul at the time of prayer, and the powers of our animal soul recede into concealment—this is what is meant by weakness of the animal soul. Therefore, it is easier to accomplish something at that time. Furthermore, because we are at the time of prayer, and we see and feel the coarseness of physical temptations, it becomes easier for us [to work on ourselves in order] to restrain and re-train [our personal tendencies].)

וּבִפְרָט כְּשֶׁמִּתְבּוֹנֵן בְּעִנְיַן רְאֵה נָתַתִּי לְפָנֶיךָ אֶת הַחַיִּים וְאֶת הַטּוֹב וְאֶת הַמָּוֶת וְאֶת הָרָע דְּהַגַּשְׁמִי מִצַּד עַצְמוֹ הוּא דְּבַר מָוֶת וּכְמוֹ גּוּף הַמֵּת

In particular, when we meditate on the concept [revealed in the verse in Deuteronomy 30:15], "See, I have placed before you life and good,

---

COMMENTARY

It is possible that these three levels of meditation correspond to the lower Worlds of *Asiya*, *Yetzira*, and *Bria*. *Asiya* is the world of individual physical creations, each separate and distinct from the others, each with its own distinct G-dly energy. *Yetzira* is the world of spiritual archetypes (angels), each a general template for many of the specific creations of the world of *Asiya*, about which it would be appropriate to say that the "main point is G-dliness," rather than physicality. And finally, intellect is characteristic of *Bria*, which is so spiritually refined that it allows for only the possibility of created existence. Thus, it is appropriate to allude to *Bria* by saying "each person according to his own level in intellect..."

Essay on Service of the Heart - Love Like Fire and Water

death and evil," [we realize that] the physical by itself is an object of death. Just as a corpse is loathsome, totally devoid of life, decaying and despicable, so anything that is solely physical, bereft of any G-dly intention, offering only physical attraction and lust, is disgusting and loathsome. Meditation at length on this subject will bring us to detest, at least in part, all that is physical and bestial as written in the discourse *Tiku* (5670) mentioned earlier.

Another effect of weakening the animal soul is that it prepares us to receive the [G-dly] light. We then come to understand G-dly matters with our natural intellect and also that the main point of existence is G-dliness, while the physical is completely secondary. It doesn't even deserve a name for itself. G-dliness is

הֲרֵי הוּא מָאוּס בְּלִי חַיּוּת וְנִפְסָד וְנִשְׁקָץ בְּיוֹתֵר. כְּמוֹ כֵן כָּל הַדְּבָרִים הַגַּשְׁמִיִּים מִצַּד עַצְמָם בְּלִי הַכַּוָּנָה הָאֱלֹקִית כִּי אִם הַתַּאֲוָה שֶׁבָּהֶם הֲרֵי זֶה דָּבָר מָאוּס וְשֶׁקֶץ, דְּבַאֲרִיכוּת הַהִתְבּוֹנְנוּת בָּזֶה נִמְאָסִים בְּעֵינָיו בְּמִקְצָת עַל כָּל פָּנִים הָעִנְיָנֵי הַגַּשְׁמִיִּים הַחָמְרִיִּים וּכְמוֹ שֶׁכָּתוּב מִזֶּה בַּדְרוּשׁ תִּקְעוּ הנ"ל בַּמַּאֲמָר הנ"ל.

וְגַם עַל יְדֵי הַחֲלִישׁוּת דְּנֶפֶשׁ הַבַּהֲמִית נַעֲשָׂה מֻכְשָׁר לְקַבֵּל אֶת הָאוֹר וְהִיא שֶׁגַּם הַשֵּׂכֶל הַטִּבְעִי יָבִין אֶת הָעִנְיָן הָאֱלֹקִי וְאֵיךְ שֶׁהָעִקָּר הוּא הָאֱלֹקוּת וְהַגַּשְׁמִי הוּא דָּבָר טָפֵל לְגַמְרֵי וְאֵינוֹ עוֹלֶה בְּשֵׁם דָּבָר כְּלָל לְעַצְמוֹ וְאֵיךְ שֶׁאֱלֹקוּת הוּא תַּכְלִית הַטּוֹב מַה שֶּׁאֵין כֵּן הַגַּשְׁמִי

Weakening the animal soul prepares us to receive G-dly light.

--- **COMMENTARY** ---

In summary:

	Meditation of "love like water"		
1.	Focus on: "G-dly light and energy infusing each and every aspect of creation…"	Meditation on how the G-dly life-force enlivens individual creations	World of *Asiya* "World of Action"
2.	Focus on: "how the main point is G-dliness"	Meditation on how G-d's life force is the true reality of creation, in order to cultivate awareness of the spiritual dimension	World of *Yetzira* "World of Formation"
3.	Focus on: "how the G-dly light is en-clothed and revealed in the higher worlds."	Meditation on the various spiritual worlds, in order to gain understanding of the spiritual creations	World of *Bria* "World of Creation"

A major principle is to meditate on the level of the natural everyday intellect, so that it can come to terms with G-dly concepts.

וְהַחָמְרִי אֵינוֹ טוֹב כְּלָל וְאַדְרַבָּא הוּא רַע וְדָבָר מָאוּס בְּעַצְמָם, וְלִבָּבוֹ יָבִין אֵיךְ שֶׁצָּרִיךְ לִרְצוֹת רַק בֶּאֱלֹקוּת וּמִתְעוֹרֵר בֶּאֱמֶת גַּם הוּא בְּרָצוֹן לֶאֱלֹקוּת לְהַנִּיחַ וְלַעֲזֹב כָּל הָעִנְיָנִים הַחָמְרִיִּים וְהַגַּשְׁמִיִּים וְשֶׁיִּהְיֶ' כָּל עִסְקוֹ בְּרָצוֹן וְחֵפֶץ בְּעִנְיְנֵי אֱלֹקוּת בְּעֵסֶק הַתּוֹרָה וְקִיּוּם הַמִצְוֹת, וְיִתְ' לְקַמָּן שֶׁזֶּה עִקָּר גָּדוֹל בָּעֲבוֹדָה לְהָבִיא הַהִתְבּוֹנְנוּת לִידֵי הֲבָנַת הַשֵּׂכֶל הַטִּבְעִי שֶׁגַּם הוּא יָבִין הָעִנְיָן הָאֱלֹקִי וְיִתְעוֹרֵר גַּם כֵּן כוּ'

the ultimate good, as opposed to that which is physical and corporeal, which isn't good at all. Quite the opposite, it is totally evil, and absolutely loathsome. Our heart also understands that we should want only G-dliness, and we become truly aroused with a will for spirituality. [This leads us] to leave and forsake all our physical and corporal matters and involve ourselves only with the will and desire for G-dliness, for learning Torah and fulfilling its *mitzvot*. It will be explained later that a major principle of *avoda* is to meditate on the level of the natural intellect [so that] it can come to understand G-dly concepts and get excited about them.

COMMENTARY

BRIDGES

Chapter 4 of *Kuntres Ha'Avoda* describes other meditations leading to love of G-d, based upon the *Zohar* and the *Tanya*. These meditations may be thought of as bridges between "love like water" and "love like fire."

The next progressive step in meditation occurs when we realize that G-d not only enlivens the entire world, but that He also enlivens our very own soul. This, of course, is a much more personal meditation. (In one of the longest Chabad Chassidic discourses, *Be'shaah Sh'hikdimu* 5672, vol. 3, p. 1310, love of G-d "because He is the life of my soul" is described as a realization that we are "the ultimate intention" and that within us is "a higher and more inner light and G-dly energy...") Suddenly, instead of looking outside at the universe to understand G-d, we are looking within, realizing that we are dependent upon, and a "piece of," G-dliness. We realize that in essence, there is no separation between ourselves and G-d (except the barriers that we erect with our transgressions). We then long for G-d almost like a wife pining for her husband. In the words of the *Zohar*: "One should love the Holy One...with a love of the soul and

Essay on Service of the Heart - Love Like Fire and Water

(At first, this starts out as a simple agreement: the animal soul agrees not to prevent the love of G-d or the desire of the divine soul. It doesn't confuse or distract us with its bestial matters. Matters of the divine soul, such as keeping Torah and its *mitzvot*, are not onerous, and the divine soul does not encounter resistance stemming from physicality. By constant

(וּתְחִלָּה הוּא בְּדֶרֶךְ הֶסְכֵּם שֶׁאֵינוֹ מוֹנֵעַ לְהָאַהֲבָה וּלְהָרָצוֹן בְּפֹעַל דְּנֶפֶשׁ הָאֱלֹקִית, וְהַיְנוּ שֶׁאֵינוֹ מְבַלְבְּלוֹ וְאֵינוֹ מַטְרִידוֹ כָּל כָּךְ בְּעִנְיָנָיו הַחָמְרִיִּים וְאֵין לְנֶפֶשׁ הָאֱלֹקִית כֹּבֶד בְּעִנְיָנָיו הָאֱלֹקִיִּים בַּתּוֹרָה וּמִצְוֹת וּכְהַאי גַּוְונָא וְאֵינוֹ פּוֹגֵשׁ הִתְנַגְּדוּת לָזֶה מִצַּד הַחָמְרִי, וְעַל יְדֵי שְׁקִידַת הָעֲבוֹדָה נַעֲשֶׂה

At first, the animal soul just stays out of the way of the divine soul.

COMMENTARY
---

the spirit, as these are attached to the body, and the body loves them..." We realize that G-d is, in essence, part of our being (which causes us to love Him all the more) and yet we also realize that He doesn't seem to be with us all the time (which causes us anguish). This seeming contradiction motivates us to try to bring G-d into our life more than ever, by learning Torah and fulfilling its *mitzvot*. Therefore, Chapter 4 of *Kuntres Ha'Avoda* tells us that the advantage of this meditation (called "You are the life of my soul") is that it brings us to learn Torah.

Chapter 4 also tells us that there is another, more intense and personal meditation in which we realize not only that G-d is the enlivening force and the life of our souls, but that G-d is our "Father." The natural reaction to Him as the life-force of our souls is to respond as a servant to a master. This love of a servant for a master motivates Torah study and the fulfillment of its *mitzvot*. We want to fulfill the will of our Master so we study His word with great care and attempt to follow His instructions to the most minute detail. However, when we integrate the details of our Master's instructions, we come to realize that He is our "Father." We now want to understand the purpose behind His will for us. In that way, we hope to go beyond the letter of the law and fulfill its spirit. This is described in the *Zohar* as love "like a son who strives for the sake of his father and mother, whom he loves even more than his own body, soul and spirit..." For his father, the son is willing to do anything.

The transformation of the animal soul takes place with love like fire.

הָרָצוֹן גַּם בְּנֶפֶשׁ הַבַּהֲמִית כנ"ל שֶׁגַּם הוּא רוֹצָה בֶּאֱלֹקוּת וּבְעִנְיְנֵי אֱלֹקוּת וְלֹא זוֹ בִּלְבַד שֶׁאֵין לוֹ כֹּבֶד וְהִתְנַגְּדוּת כִּי אִם שֶׁגַּם מִצַּד הַחָמְרִי הוּא חַי בְּעִנְיְנֵי אֱלֹקוּת וְעוֹשֶׂה כָּל דָּבָר בְּרָצוֹן וְחֵשֶׁק וּבְחַיּוּת גָּדוֹל.)

avoda [that is, by constantly attempting to get close to the One Above], the animal soul also comes to desire G-dliness and matters of the spirit. Not only does it not present resistance and opposition, but the corporeal side itself "lives" with G-dly matters and does everything with desire and great enthusiasm.)

אָמְנָם עִקַּר כִּלָּיוֹן וּבִטּוּל הַיֵּשׁוּת דְּנֶפֶשׁ הַבַּהֲמִית הוּא בְּאַהֲבָה דְּכְרִשְׁפֵּי אֵשׁ דְּנֶפֶשׁ הָאֱלֹקִית לִהְיוֹת כִּי הַנֶּפֶשׁ הַבַּהֲמִית בְּהַד' מַדְרֵגוֹת דְּדוֹמֵם צוֹמֵחַ חַי וּמְדַבֵּר הוּא בְּמַדְרֵגַת הַחַי שֶׁזֶּהוּ בְּחִינַת יְסוֹד הָאֵשׁ בְּחִינַת חֲמִימוּת הַתַּאֲוָה,

However, the nullification of the ego of the animal soul is mainly brought about by "love like flames of fire" of the divine soul. This is because the animal soul, on the four levels of "mineral, vegetable, animal, and human," corresponds to the level of "animal," which in turn corresponds to the element of fire, giving rise to the heat of lust [in the soul]. The onslaught of fire in the divine soul, giving rise to flames of desire and thirst for G-dliness, is like "fire which consumes fire." It devours and destroys the power of lust and the fire that [burns in] the animal soul for human pleasures, as written in *Likutei Torah*, in the discourse *Ki Teitzei*, in the first discourse [paragraph 2],29 and in *L'vaer Inyan Yom HaKippurim*, end of second part.30 Now, the true "love like flames of fire" (coming

---
COMMENTARY

The two above-mentioned levels of love of G-d, ("You are the life of my soul," and "like a son striving for his father") correspond to the World of *Yetzira* or to *Bria*, according to the *Tanya*, chapter 44, at different stages. They correspond to *Yetzira* when in a latent state in the person's heart, and to *Bria* when brought to full expression by intellectual meditation. In either case, they are examples of "love like water," as well as *ahavat olam* ("worldly love"), although the *Tanya* goes on to state these two meditations have a component that transcends *ahavat olam*: "...these two distinctions of love...contain a quality of love which is greater and more sublime than the intelligent fear and love, the love termed as *ahavat olam*."

Later, the *Tanya* goes on to describe this greater and more sublime quality as a "blaze of fiery love." So, it would seem that while these

Essay on Service of the Heart - Love Like Fire and Water

True love like fire arises from deep understanding of the heart and recognition of the greatness of G-d

from below, from the divine soul) arises from deep understanding of the heart and recognition of the greatness of G-d, the Infinite One—which permeates and transcends all the worlds—that everything is as nothing before Him. (See the *Biur HaZohar, Parshat Tazriah*, explaining the words of the *Zohar*, p. 49, first side, on the verse, *Hazei aleihem mei chatat*.)

וְהִתְגַּבְּרוּת יְסוֹד הָאֵשׁ דְּנֶפֶשׁ הָאֱלֹקִית בְּרִשְׁפֵּי אֵשׁ הַתְּשׁוּקָה וְהַצִּמָּאוֹן לֶאֱלֹקוּת הוּא בְּחִינַת אֵשׁ אוֹכְלָה אֵשׁ לְכַלּוֹת וְלִשְׂרֹף הַכֹּחַ הַמִּתְאַוֶּה וְהָאֵשׁ דְּנֶפֶשׁ הַבַּהֲמִית בְּתַעֲנוּגוֹת בְּנֵי אָדָם כוּ' וּכְמוֹ שֶׁכָּתוּב בְּלִקּוּטֵי תּוֹרָה בְּדִבּוּר הַמַּתְחִיל כִּי תֵצֵא דְּרוּשׁ הָרִאשׁוֹן וּבְדִבּוּר הַמַּתְחִיל לְבָאֵר עִנְיַן יוֹם הַכִּפּוּרִים סְפ"ב. וְהִנֵּה אֲמִתִּית הָאַהֲבָה בְּרִשְׁפֵּי אֵשׁ (בְּחִינַת אֵשׁ שֶׁלְּמַטָּה דְּנֶפֶשׁ הָאֱלֹקִית) הִיא הַבָּאָה מֵהִתְבּוֹנְנָה וְהַדַּעַת בִּגְדֻלַּת ה' אֵין סוֹף בָּרוּךְ הוּא (וְעַיֵּן מַה שֶּׁכָּתוּב בְּבֵאוּרֵי הַזֹּהַר פ' תַּזְרִיעַ בְּבֵאוּר מַאֲמַ"ז דמ"ט ע"א ע"פ הֲזֵי הַזֶּה עֲלֵיהֶם מֵי חַטָּאת) הַמְמַלֵּא כָּל עָלְמִין וְסוֹבֵב כָּל עָלְמִין וְכוּלָּא קָמֵיהּ כְּלָא חֲשִׁיב כוּ',

By way of this meditation, the love in our soul will burst out of its "garments," meaning that it will no longer be garbed by any object of physical pleasure. Nor will it be clad in any spiritual pleasure [even the most refined]. We will not love or desire anything whatsoever aside from G-d Himself, the Source of all life, and

אֲשֶׁר עַל יְדֵי הִתְבּוֹנְנוּת זוֹ מִמֵּילָא תִּתְפַּשֵּׁט מִדַּת הָאַהֲבָה שֶׁבַּנֶּפֶשׁ מִלְּבוּשֶׁי' דְּהַיְנוּ שֶׁלֹּא תִתְלַבֵּשׁ בְּשׁוּם דָּבָר הֲנָאָה וְתַעֲנוּג גַּשְׁמִי אוֹ רוּחָנִי לְאַהֲבָה וְלֹא לַחְפֹּץ כְּלָל שׁוּם דָּבָר בָּעוֹלָם בִּלְתִּי ה' לְבַדּוֹ מְקוֹר הַחַיִּים שֶׁל הַתַּעֲנוּגִים כוּ' כְּמוֹ שֶׁכָּתוּב בְּסֵפֶר שֶׁל בֵּינוֹנִים פמ"ג

--- **COMMENTARY** ---

two levels of love may initially be described as "love like water," they eventually (through proper meditation) become "love like fire." That is, when our meditation brings us to a complete grasp of the subject, then our love becomes "love like fire."

LOVE LIKE FIRE

In *Be'shaah Sh'hikdimu* 5672, vol. 2, p. 820, it states: "In grasping the subject, one comes to excitement over its inherent G-dliness with flames of fire and desire, but only through complete comprehension..." Thus, an important factor in "love like fire" is complete and total grasp of the subject. Then, the text of Chapter 4 of *Kuntres Ha'Avoda* says in part, "As our meditation

The lust of the animal soul must be transformed into a fiery desire for G-d, corresponding to the sacrifices burning on the altar.

וספמ״ד וּבְלִקּוּטֵי תּוֹרָה פּ׳ שְׁלַח בְּדִבּוּר הַמַּתְחִיל בְּפ׳ נְסָכִים כְּתִיב. וְזֶהוּ עִנְיַן שֶׁהַתְּפִלָּה בִּמְקוֹם קָרְבָּן לְהַקְרִיב אֶת הַנֶּפֶשׁ הַבַּהֲמִית וּלְהַעֲלוֹתוֹ שֶׁיִּתְהַפֵּךְ מִן הַהֵפֶךְ אֶל הַהֵפֶךְ לִהְיוֹת כֹּחַ הַמִּתְאַוֶּה. בְּרִשְׁפֵּי אֵשׁ שַׁלְהֶבֶת לְדָבְקָה בֵּאלֹקִים חַיִּים כו׳ כְּמוֹ שֶׁכָּתוּב בְּדִבּוּר הַמַּתְחִיל כִּי תֵצֵא הנ״ל וּבְדִבּוּר הַמַּתְחִיל בְּפ׳ נְסָכִים הנ״ל

of all pleasures..." (as is written in *Tanya*, chapter 43 and end of chapter 44, and in *Likutei Torah, Parshat Shlach*, discourse *B'Parshat nesachim ketiv...*). This is what is meant by [the words of the Sages in Talmud *Berachot* 26] "Prayer is in lieu of the sacrifices." We must offer up our animal soul and elevate it so that it turns from one extreme to the other. The [animal soul, which is] "something that lusts" must be transformed into a fiery desire to cleave to the living G-d, as written in the discourse *Ki Teitzei* and in the discourse beginning *B'parshat Nesachim*, as mentioned earlier.

(וּמַה שֶּׁכָּתוּב בְּדִבּוּר הַמַּתְחִיל כִּי תֵצֵא הַכַּוָּנָה בַּהִתְבּוֹנְנוּת דְּבִרְכוֹת קְרִיאַת שְׁמַע בְּבִטּוּל הַמַּלְאָכִים שֶׁזֶּהוּ בְּחִינַת אֵשׁ שֶׁלְּמַעְלָה דְּנֶפֶשׁ הַבַּהֲמִית כו׳ וּכְמוֹ שֶׁכָּתוּב מִזֶּה בְּדִרוּשׁ יוֹם טוֹב שֶׁל רֹאשׁ הַשָּׁנָה רס״ו. וּמַה שֶּׁכָּתוּב בְּדִבּוּר הַמַּתְחִיל בְּפ׳ נְסָכִים זֶהוּ בְּחִינַת הָאֵשׁ דְּנֶפֶשׁ הָאֱלֹקִית וְכֵן הוּא בְּדִבּוּר הַמַּתְחִיל וְנִקְדַּשְׁתִּי פ״ה, וּבְנֶפֶשׁ הָאֱלֹקִית

xxiv) See footnote of the Rebbe on page 278 ➡

(That which is written in *Ki Teitzei* refers to meditation during the blessings preceding the reciting of *Shema*, regarding the state of nullification of the angels. It is the "fire from above" of the animal soul, as written in the discourse *Yom Tov shel Rosh Hashana*,[xxiv] 5666.[31] And that which is written in *B'parshat Nesachim*[32] refers to the fire of the divine soul, and so it is in the discourse, *Venikdashti*, part 5. [33] Within the divine soul, the reference

─────── COMMENTARY ───────

comes to the subject of 'You, G-d, are my very soul,' we will become even more inflamed as we considers our distance..." Consideration of our spiritual distance from the One Above, leading to bitterness, combines with the total grasp mentioned above, to bring about "love like fire." Finally, the *Kuntres Ha'avoda* quotes from *Likutei Torah* regarding "love like fire," saying that it comes about through contemplation of the constant renewal of creation, resulting in fiery love over the "newness" of creation at every instant. This occurs only among those who are able to meditate on a high level on the greatness of G-d. For is to "fire from below." The "fire from above" of the divine soul is called *ahava rabbah* — "great love" — which transcends all intellect and logic and comes from the attribute of *chochma* within the soul, as taught in the discourse *L'vaer Inyan Yom Hakippurim*, part 2. It corresponds to the fire of the menorah [in the Holy Temple], which is [spiritually] higher than the fire of the altar. [Kabbalistically speaking,] the fire of the altar is associated with *gevura d'imma*, or "power of analytic thinking,"

(וּבְחִינַת) הוּא בְּחִינַת אֵשׁ שֶׁלְּמַטָּה אֵשׁ שֶׁלְּמַעְלָה דְּנֶפֶשׁ הָאֱלֹקִית הוּא בְּחִינַת אַהֲבָה רַבָּה שֶׁלְּמַעְלָה מִטַּעַם וָדַעַת וְהִיא מִבְּחִינַת הַחָכְמָה שֶׁבַּנֶּפֶשׁ כְּמוֹ שֶׁכָּתוּב בְּדִבּוּר הַמַּתְחִיל לְבָאֵר עִנְיַן יוֹם הַכִּפּוּרִים פ״ב, וְהוּא עִנְיַן אֵשׁ הַמְּנוֹרָה שֶׁלְּמַעְלָה מֵאֵשׁ הַמִּזְבֵּחַ, דְּאֵשׁ הַמִּזְבֵּחַ הוּא גְּבוּרוֹת דְּאִימָּא וְאֵשׁ הַמְּנוֹרָה בְּחִינַת גְּבוּרוֹת דְּאַבָּא וְזֶה הָיְ' עֲבוֹדַת אַהֲרֹן בְּהַעֲלָאַת הַנֵּרוֹת וּכְמוֹ שֶׁכָּתוּב מִזֶּה בְּאֹרֶךְ בַּדְּרוּשׁ הנ״ל)

The fire from above of the divine soul corresponds to the light of the Menorah in the Temple.

while the fire of the menorah is associated with *gevura d'abba*, or the "power of intuitive grasp." The latter was the service of Aaron, [the high priest], when he lit the lights of the menorah, as written there at length in the discourse mentioned earlier. [These Kabbalistic levels refer to two opposite dynamics. *Gevura* in general is strength/restraint, which is required to lift and elevate, but also to draw down levels of spiritual influx. When it is associated with *imma* or *bina* (analytic understanding), it refers to the strength to uplift sparks of holiness from below to above, which is what takes place when sacrifices are burnt on the altar. When it is associated with *abba* (intuitive grasp), it refers to the power to bring down holiness from above to below, which is what Aaron the high priest did when lighting the menorah. To bring holiness down from above to below, such that the physical becomes permeated with the spiritual, is a higher service of G-d than the opposite dynamic, from below to above.])34

COMMENTARY
---

the rest of us, complete understanding and bitterness over our distance from the One Above are what bring about "love like fire."

Chapter 4 of *Kuntres Ha'Avoda* refers to the Chassidic series of discourses called *Yom Tov shel Rosh Hashana, 5666* (also from the Rebbe Rashab). There (page 144), "love like fire" is further subdivided into two categories. First, there is love like fire "from below." When we meditate "from below" — contemplating the higher spiritual creations such as angels — we bring what is called

Level of soul	Type of service	Description of service	
Animal soul	Fire from below	Meditation upon the *seraphim* burning with nullification to G-d	1.
	Fire from Above	Revelation of light from Above from the love of G-d of the angels	2.
Divine soul	Fire from below	The sacrifices on the altar, *gevura d'imma*	3.
	Fire from Above	*Ahava Rabba*, Aharon lighting the Menorah, *gevura d'abba*	4.

וְהוּא הַהִתְבּוֹנְנוּת בִּגְדֻלָּתוֹ יִתְבָּרֵךְ בִּפְסוּקֵי דְזִמְרָה וּקְרִיאַת שְׁמַע. וְנִרְאָה דְּבַנֶּפֶשׁ הַבַּהֲמִית פּוֹעֵל רַק בְּחִינַת בִּטּוּל הַיֵּשׁ שֶׁזֶּה שֶׁכָּתוּב בְּסֵפֶר שֶׁל בֵּינוֹנִים שֶׁלֹּא תִּתְלַבֵּשׁ בְּשׁוּם דָּבָר הֲנָאָה כו' וּבְדִבּוּר הַמַּתְחִיל בפ' נְסָכִים כ' גַּם כֵּן לְהָסִיר הַחֲמִימוּת שֶׁבְּלִבּוֹ כו', וּבִכְדֵי לְהַפְּכוֹ זֶהוּ עַל יְדֵי בְּחִינַת אֵשׁ שֶׁלְּמַעְלָה הנ"ל

The "fire from below" of the divine soul takes place during meditation on His greatness in *P'sukei D'zimra*, ("Verses of Praise") and in *Kriat Shema*—the reciting of the *Shema* [during prayer]. It would seem that this meditation has the effect on the animal soul of bringing about only *bitul hayesh* ("nullification of the ego"). This is what is meant by *Tanya* [in chapter 43] when it says "[love] shouldn't en-clothe itself in any article of pleasure..." as well as in *B'parshat Nesachim* mentioned earlier, where it says [in chapter 1] "to remove the heat in his heart" [towards worldly pleasures]. In order to [go a step further and] transform it [this heat], we need the "fire from above," already mentioned.

COMMENTARY
---

fire "from below." The angels are aware of the G-dly source that creates them; they are also aware of how that G-dly energy is constantly renewed in its source. This awareness brings them to a state of great excitement and nullification (reflected in the blessings preceding the reciting of the *Shema*). Through this contemplation, our animal soul, which has its own source in these angels, becomes consumed, nullified, and transformed in fiery love for the One Above. This love is called the "fire of the altar," after the animal sacrifices that were brought in the Temple

(It is also possible for this "transformation" to take place by prefacing the "fire from above" of the animal soul during the blessings preceding the *Shema*, [and then the transformation takes place with the "fire from Above" during the reciting of the *Shema* itself], as noted earlier. According to what is written in *V'nikdashti*, it would seem that this is *it'hafcha*, or transforming one's lusts completely into G-dliness, and it takes place on the level of [the angels] called *seraphim*, or those who burn up completely [in their service of the One Above], as written elsewhere. It is also explained in the commentary *V'nikdashti* there, that this is the level of self-nullification associated with the *Shema*. In any case, the topic is not so relevant to what is discussed here.)

(וְאֶפְשָׁר כְּמוֹ כֵן הוּא גַּם כֵּן עַל יְדֵי הַקְדָּמַת בְּחִינַת אֵשׁ שֶׁלְּמַעְלָה דְּנֶפֶשׁ הַבַּהֲמִית בְּבִרְכַּת קְרִיאַת שְׁמַע כנ"ל) וּמִכָּל מָקוֹם מִמַּה שֶׁכָּתוּב בְּדִבּוּר הַמַּתְחִיל וְנִקְדַּשְׁתִּי נֵר' שֶׁזֶּהוּ בִּבְחִינַת אִתְהַפְּכָא, וְהוּא בְּמַדְרֵגַת הַשְּׂרָפִים שֶׁנִּשְׂרָף כָּל מַהוּתָם וּכְמוֹ שֶׁכָּתוּב בְּמָקוֹם אַחֵר וְגַם מְבֹאָר שָׁם בְּהַבֵּאוּר שֶׁזֶּה מְסִירַת נֶפֶשׁ דִּקְרִיאַת שְׁמַע. וְאֵין הָעִנְיָן נוֹגֵעַ כָּל כָּךְ לְכָאן).

——— **COMMENTARY** ———

in order to draw the person offering the sacrifice closer to the One Above. This is referred to in Kabbalah as the *hey gevurot d' imma* or "five stringencies of analytic thinking" (since *gevura* or "stringency" has the quality of uplifting and elevating).

In response to the fire "from below," wherein our animal soul is consumed, there may be a response from heaven called the fire "from above." If the fire "from below" corresponds to the sacrifices on the altar, then the fire "from above" corresponds to the fire of the menorah, kindled by the Aharon, the high priest. His job was to bring the light of consuming G-dliness down to the Jewish people, to each person according to his own soul-level. This he did by lighting the menorah. The fire "from above" is also described as *ahava rabba* ("great love") by the *Kuntres Ha'Avoda*, since it totally consumes and transfixes the person. In Kabbalah, this is called the *hey gevurot d'abba* (five stringencies of creative thought). In *Yom Tov shel Rosh Hashana, 5666*, the Rebbe mentions that since we don't have the Temple today, we should not be surprised if the "light of the menorah" doesn't shine on us in the form of love like "fire from above." Even so, the Rebbe says, we should do our best to bring the fire "from below," which also consumes the animal soul and draws one to "love like fire."

Kuntres Ha'Avoda - קונטרס העבודה

The love like fire from Above takes place on most elevated levels.

אָמְנָם זֶהוּ בְּמַדְרֵגוֹת גְּבוֹהוֹת וְהַיְנוּ כְּשֶׁיֵּשׁ הִתְגַּלּוּת אוֹר הַנֶּפֶשׁ הָאֱלֹקִית לְהִתְפַּעֵל כָּל כָּךְ בְּהִתְבּוֹנְנוּת גְּדֻלָּתוֹ יִתְבָּרֵךְ לְהַלְהִיב נַפְשׁוֹ כְּרִשְׁפֵּי אֵשׁ וְשַׁלְהֶבֶת עַזָּה וְלַהַב הָעוֹלֶה הַשָּׁמַיְמָה וּלְהִפָּרֵד מִן הַפְּתִילָה כו'. וּבְלִקּוּטֵי תּוֹרָה דִּבּוּר הַמַּתְחִיל לְבָאֵר עִנְיַן יוֹם הַכִּפּוּרִים מְבֹאָר דְּהַהִתְלַהֲבוּת בְּרִשְׁפֵּי אֵשׁ תִּהְיֶה מֵהַדָּבָר חִדּוּשׁ בְּהִתְחַדְּשׁוּת הַהִתְהַוּוּת חֲדָשִׁים לַבְּקָרִים, דְּכַאֲשֶׁר יִרְאֶה בְּעֵינָיו (דִּבְזֶה שַׁיָּךְ רְאִיַּ' חוּשִׁית

But this "fire from Above" takes place on most elevated levels, when there is revelation of the light of the divine soul such that the soul becomes so aroused with meditation on His greatness, that the revelation inflames it like a torch of fire. It becomes like a flame rising to the heavens, striving to be separated from its wick. In *Likutei Torah*, in the discourse *L'vaer inyan Yom Hakippurim*,[35] it is explained that the excitement of "love like flames of fire" comes from a sense of newness, a sense of renewal in

---

COMMENTARY

In summary:

Dynamic	Factor leading to "love like fire"	Chassidic Description	Kabbalistic Description	Effect on animal soul
From below	Total grasp of concept combined with bitterness over distance from G-d	Compared to sacrifices offered on the altar	"*gevurot d'ima*," or stringencies of analytic thinking	Shatters the animal soul, but doesn't transform it
From Above (also called *ahava rabba*)	Meditation on His greatness, and awareness of renewal of creation at every instant (rare without the Temple)	Compared to Aharon the High Priest lighting the menorah in the Holy Temple	"*gevurot d'abba*," or stringencies of creative thought	Transforms the animal soul and elevates it to be included in G-dly soul

FACE TO FACE

Finally, one more level of love of G-d is described in Chapter 4 of *Kuntres Ha'Avoda*, based upon a verse in Proverbs 27:19 that reads, "As in water, face responds to face, so the heart of man to man." The *Tanya* describes how G-d "abandoned," so to speak, the higher spiritual worlds and associated Himself with

Essay on Service of the Heart - Love Like Fire and Water

creation at every instant, "new every morning." When we "see" with our own "eyes"—(it is appropriate to speak here of the physical sense of vision, as in the verse [in Isaiah 40:26], "See Who created these...")—and our heart understands, it also catches on fire, as it is written [in Eicha 2:18], "their heart cried out..." This involves revelation of the divine soul, as well.

וּכְמוֹ שֶׁכָּתוּב וּרְאוּ מִי בָרָא אֵלֶּה כו') וְלִבּוֹ יָבִין כו' עַל כֵּן יַלְהִיב לִבּוֹ וְיָשִׂים אֵלָיו לִבּוֹ וְנִשְׁמָתוֹ וּכְמוֹ שֶׁכָּתוּב צָעַק לִבָּם כו'. וְגַם זֶה הוּא בְּהִתְגַּלּוּת אוֹר הַנֶּפֶשׁ הָאֱלֹקִית כו'.

But on the average, we who would achieve love "like flames of fire" require meditation on our distance from the One Above. That is, we must think about how far away we are from anything G-dly. We must, first of all, undergo the meditation explained earlier in which we think about the G-dliness inherent in the physical creation, or the nature of the spiritual light and illumination in the upper worlds, and we must feel the preciousness and elevation of G-dliness. We must then combine this with contemplation of our own situation—how far we are from anything G-dly, not only in our soul in general, but even in the garments of our soul: in our thought, speech, and action. This leads us to a state of great bitterness, as a result of which

אַךְ בְּכָל אָדָם בִּכְדֵי שֶׁתִּהְיֶה הָאַהֲבָה בְּרִשְׁפֵּי אֵשׁ הוּא עַל יְדֵי הַהִתְבּוֹנְנוּת בְּרִחוּק שֶׁלּוֹ אֵיךְ שֶׁהוּא מְרֻחָק מֵאֱלֹקוּת, וְהַיְנוּ כַּאֲשֶׁר מִתְבּוֹנֵן בְּהִתְבּוֹנְנוּת הַנַּ"ל בֶּאֱלֹקוּת שֶׁבָּעוֹלָמוֹת הֵן בָּעוֹלָם הַתַּחְתּוֹן אוֹ בְּאֹפֶן הָאוֹר וְהַגִּלּוּי שֶׁבָּעוֹלָמוֹת הָעֶלְיוֹנִים כנ"ל וּמַרְגִּישׁ אֶת הַיֹּקֶר וְאֶת הָעִלּוּי דֶּאֱלֹקוּת, הֲרֵי הוּא מְצָרֵף לָזֶה לְהִתְבּוֹנֵן בְּמַעֲמָדוֹ וּמַצָּבוֹ אֵיךְ שֶׁהוּא מְרֻחָק בְּתַכְלִית מֵאֱלֹקוּת בְּמַחֲשָׁבָה דִּבּוּר וּמַעֲשֶׂה שֶׁלּוֹ וְגַם בִּכְלָלוּת נַפְשׁוֹ הוּא מְרֻחָק לְגַמְרֵי מֵעִנְיַן הָאֱלֹקוּת, הֲרֵי תִתְמַרְמֵר נַפְשׁוֹ מְאֹד עַל זֶה וְתִתְלַהֵב נַפְשׁוֹ בְּרִשְׁפֵּי אֵשׁ שַׁלְהֶבֶת בְּצָמְאוֹן וּתְשׁוּקָה לִהְיוֹת מְקֹרָב לֶאֱלֹקוּת, וְהַיְנוּ לָצֵאת מֵהָעִנְיָנִים

But the average meditator must combine total intellectual grasp with bitterness over his distance from G-d in order to attain "love like fire."

―――――― *COMMENTARY* ――――――

man in this lowest physical world, out of love and devotion to His people. (G-d didn't really "abandon" any part of His creation, but His greatest concern is with His people in this physical universe.) Therefore, we should, in response, cling to Him with the utmost devotion and love. The *Tanya* emphasizes that this clinging gives rise to a "love like fire," though it also contains elements of "love like water."

הַמַּפְרִידִים וְהַמַּרְחִיקִים אוֹתוֹ וְלִהְיוֹת מְקֹרָב לֶאֱלֹקוּת וְאֵלָיו יִתְבָּרֵךְ יְהִי' נָתוּן וּמָסוּר בְּכָל הַכֹּחוֹת שֶׁלּוֹ וּבְמַחְשָׁבָה דִּבּוּר וּמַעֲשֶׂה שֶׁלּוֹ. וְכַאֲשֶׁר הַהִתְבּוֹנְנוּת הִיא אֵיךְ שֶׁאַתָּה ה' נַפְשִׁי כו' עוֹד תִּגְדַּל הַהִתְלַהֲבוּת בְּיוֹתֵר בְּהִתְבּוֹנְנוּת הָרָחוֹק שֶׁלּוֹ כו'

our soul is motivated to catch on fire, flaming like a torch with thirst and desire to be close to the One Above and to abandon all matters which separate and distance it from G-d. We then become close to G-dliness as well as subjugated to Him in all of our soul powers, and in our thought, speech, and action. And when our meditation centers on the subject of "You, G-d, are my very soul," we will become even more enflamed as we consider our distance [from Him].

וְרִשְׁפֵּי אֵשׁ זֶה עוֹשֶׂה כִּלָּיוֹן וּבִטּוּל הַיֵּשׁ דְנֶפֶשׁ הַבַּהֲמִית שֶׁנִּשְׂרָף וְכָלָה מַמָּשׁ (וְלֹא כְּמוֹ בְּאַהֲבָה כַּמַּיִם שֶׁזֶּהוּ בְּחִינַת חֲלִישׁוּת בִּלְבַד לִהְיוֹת שֶׁשָּׁם הַהִתְעַסְּקוּת שֶׁלּוֹ רַק בָּעִנְיָן הָאֱלֹקִי לְבַד, לְהָבִין אֶת הָעִנְיָן הָאֱלֹקִי וּלְהַרְגִּישׁ אֶת הָאֱלֹקוּת וְהַטּוֹב וְהָעִלּוּי בָּזֶה שֶׁעַל יְדֵי זֶה מִתְקָרֵב בֶּאֱמֶת לֶאֱלֹקוּת וְעַל יְדֵי הַקֵּרוּב לֶאֱלֹקוּת מִתְחַלֵּשׁ הַנֶּפֶשׁ הַבַּהֲמִית, אֲבָל הוּא בִּבְחִינַת חֲלִישׁוּת לְבַד לֹא שֶׁמִּתְבַּטֵּל (וּמִכָּל מָקוֹם נִתְבָּאֵר שֶׁנַּעֲשָׂה מֻכְשָׁר לְהָבִין גַּם כֵּן עִנְיָן אֱלֹקִי וּמִתְעוֹרֵר גַּם הוּא בְּרָצוֹן לֶאֱלֹקוּת וְעַיֵּן מַה שֶׁכָּתוּב לְקַמָּן בְּסָמוּךְ) אָמְנָם בְּאַהֲבָה דְכִרְשְׁפֵּי אֵשׁ נִשְׂרָף וְכָלָה וּמִתְבַּטֵּל הַיֵּשׁוּת

The flames of love like fire eradicate and incinerate the animal soul, while love like water only weakens it.

These flames of fire eradicate and nullify the ego of the animal soul, causing it to become totally incinerated and consumed, unlike "love like water" which brings about only a weakening of the animal soul. This is because our involvement [in "love like water"] is only with the G-dly concept, as we strive to understand that G-dly concept and feel G-dliness, and how it is good and elevated. In so doing, we truly come closer to G-d. Through this closeness, our animal soul becomes weakened, but this is only weakening and not nullification. (Nevertheless, it was explained that [through this meditation] we become prepared to understand [and accept] G-dly concepts, and we also become

——————— **COMMENTARY** ———————

This subject is alluded to by the *Kuntres Ha'Avoda* which says that this love contains both *ohr yashar* ("direct light," or illumination from above) and *ohr chozer* ("reflected light," or illumination from below). Two dynamics are described here. One is the love of the One Above for the Jewish people, which induces us to want to cleave to Him, as in "love like water." The other

Essay on Service of the Heart - Love Like Fire and Water

aroused with a desire for G-dliness; see what is explained nearby.) However, when it comes to "love like flames of fire," the ego of the animal soul becomes incinerated, consumed, and nullified. This is because our distress over our distance from G-d brings about the onset of fiery flames and excitement [of love for G-d], which in turn causes the nullification of the animal soul.

דְּנֶפֶשׁ הַבַּהֲמִית, כִּי מִפְּנֵי שֶׁצַּר לוֹ מֵרִחוּקוֹ מֵאֱלֹקוּת וְזֶהוּ הַגּוֹרֵם לוֹ הָרְשָׁפֵי אֵשׁ וְהַהִתְלַהֲבוּת הֲרֵי זֶה גּוֹרֵם הַבִּטּוּל בְּנֶפֶשׁ הַבַּהֲמִית,

So it is in general with "love like flames of fire." Its full expression blossoms out of meditation on G-d's greatness, or at least on the phenomena of constant renewal of creation at all times, as mentioned earlier. Then, the fire of holiness burns and consumes the fire of all that is opposed to holiness. Whenever we amplify the element of G-dly fire [in our soul], we decrease and cool off the natural element of fire [of the "other side," which isn't holy], as written in the discourse of *B'parshat Nesachim*," end of the first chapter). Furthermore, the power of the natural element of fire becomes elevated and included in love of G-d "like flames of fire," as explained there.

וְכֵן הוּא בִּבְחִינַת אַהֲבָה כְּרִשְׁפֵּי אֵשׁ בִּכְלָל דַּאֲמִתִּית עִנְיָנָהּ הוּא כְּשֶׁהִיא מִצַּד הַהִתְבּוֹנְנוּת בִּגְדֻלָּתוֹ יִתְבָּרֵךְ אוֹ עַל כָּל פָּנִים מֵחִדּוּשׁ הַהִתְהַוּוּת כו' כנ"ל הִנֵּה הָאֵשׁ דִּקְדֻשָּׁה שׂוֹרֵף וּמְכַלֶּה הָאֵשׁ דִּלְעֻמַּת זֶה, דְּבְכָל עֵת שֶׁמַּגְבִּיר כֹּחַ יְסוֹד הָאֵשׁ הָאֱלֹקִי מִתְמַעֵט וּמִתְקָרֵר כֹּחַ יְסוֹד הָאֵשׁ הַטִּבְעִי וּכְמוֹ שֶׁכָּתוּב בְּדִבּוּר הַמַּתְחִיל בְּפ' נְסָכִים ספ"א). וְעוֹד זֹאת שֶׁגַּם כֹּחַ יְסוֹד הָאֵשׁ הַטִּבְעִי עוֹלֶה וְנִכְלָל לְאַהֲבָה אֶת ה' בְּהִתְלַהֲבוּת וְרִשְׁפֵי אֵשׁ כו' וּכְמוֹ שֶׁכָּתוּב שָׁם.

COMMENTARY

is our own striving and awareness of Him from afar, which gives rise to "love like fire." We should be ready to forsake and abandon all of the most important aspects of our physical lives in order to cling to G-d with love. This will give rise, according to the *Tanya*, to a love "like a burning fire, in the consciousness of the heart and mind..." This is the highest of the levels of love that are mentioned in Chapter 4 of *Kuntres Ha'Avoda*, beyond even the World of *Atzilut*.

Elsewhere in Chassidic literature — specifically in *B'shaah sh'hikdimu* 5672, vol. 2, pp. 972-4 — is to be found a very deep

Teshuva (tata'ah) shatters the animal soul, but love like fire elevates it.

וְזֶהוּ הַיִּתְרוֹן בְּבִטּוּל הַיֵּשׁוּת דְּנֶפֶשׁ הַבַּהֲמִית בְּאַהֲבָה הַנַּ"ל לְגַבֵּי עִנְיַן הַתְּשׁוּבָה, דִּבְתְשׁוּבָה, (הַיְנוּ בִּתְשׁוּבָה תַּתָּאָה) הֲרֵי כָּל הִתְעַסְּקוּתוֹ הוּא בַּהֲמָרִירוּת עַל הָרִחוּק שֶׁצַּר לוֹ עַל עִנְיָנָיו הַפְּרָטִיִּים וְעַל מַעֲמָדוֹ וּמַצָּבוֹ בִּכְלָל כוּ' (וְהַהֶרְגֵּשׁ הָאֱלֹקִי שֶׁצָּרִיךְ לִהְיוֹת בָּזֶה הוּא בִּכְדֵי שֶׁתִּהְיֶה הַמְּרִירוּת בִּבְחִינַת חַיּוּת אֱלֹקִי וּכְמוֹ שֶׁכָּתוּב בְּמָקוֹם אַחֵר) וְזֶהוּ שֶׁגּוֹרֵם שְׁבִירַת הַיֵּשׁוּת וְהַחָמְרִיּוּת דְּנֶפֶשׁ הַבַּהֲמִית (גַּם כֵּן לֹא רַק חֲלִישׁוּת לְבַד) אֲבָל לֹא שֶׁיִּתְעַלֶּה גַּם הוּא וְיִהְיֶה נִכְלָל בִּקְדֻשָּׁה (לְבַד בִּתְשׁוּבָה אֲמִתִּית שֶׁמִּתְהַפֵּךְ מַהוּת הַנֶּפֶשׁ הַבַּהֲמִית וּבִכְדֵי שֶׁיִּהְיֶה עוֹלֶה וְנִכְלָל כוּ' הוּא דַּוְקָא בִּבְחִינַת תְּשׁוּבָה עִילָּאָה דְּהַיְנוּ בְּהִתְגַּלּוּת אוֹר הַנְּשָׁמָה בִּבְחִינַת רִשְׁפֵּי אֵשׁ בְּיוֹתֵר כַּנּוֹדָע בְּעִנְיַן תֹּקֶף הָרָצוֹא דִּתְשׁוּבָה),

114 Kuntres Ha'Avoda - קונטרס העבודה

This, then, is the advantage of "nullification of existence" of the animal soul out of "love like fire," over the process of *teshuva*, ["return" to the One Above]. In *teshuva*, (the lower form, *teshuva tata'ah*), we are consumed with bitterness over our distance from the One Above. We are distressed over our personal matters [the details of our relationship with the One Above] and over our situation and standing in general. (This bitterness must be accompanied by an awareness of G-dliness, since [only] then will the bitterness be charged with G-dly energy, as written elsewhere.) This causes a shattering of the ego and corporeality of the animal soul (also here, it is not a weakening alone), but not such that the animal soul ascends to be included in holiness. (The exception is a case of true *teshuva* in which the essence of the animal soul is transformed [completely]. In order for it to ascend and to be included in holiness, we must do *teshuva ila'ah*. This is the higher form of *teshuva*, in which the light of the soul becomes revealed in a stupendous rush of fiery flames, as is known regarding the power of the energy of *teshuva*.

COMMENTARY

explanation of this level of love of G-d. There, it is equated with the level attained by Rabbi Akiva when he entered the *pardes* ("orchard" of Torah secrets) and encountered the "slabs of marble." Upon reaching this level — which is clearly a metaphor for an unspeakably high spiritual revelation—Rabbi Akiva proclaimed, "When you reach the marble slabs, don't cry 'water, water.'" The Chassidic discourse explains that Rabbi Akiva wanted to forewarn the meditator who reaches this level

Essay on Service of the Heart - Love Like Fire and Water

[However], in the above-mentioned love ["like flames of fire"], although bitterness also plays a role, the main experience is an excitement and rush for G-dliness. [In this excitement], the element of natural fire [of the animal soul] also ascends to be included in holiness.)

וּבְאַהֲבָה הנ"ל עִם הֱיוֹת שֶׁיֵּשׁ בָּהּ גַּם כֵּן עִנְיַן הַמְּרִירוּת כנ"ל, אֲבָל לִהְיוֹת כִּי הָעִקָּר הוּא הַהִתְלַהֲבוּת וְהָרָצוֹא לֶאֱלֹקוּת עַל כֵּן גַּם הַיְסוֹד הָאֵשׁ הַטִּבְעִי עוֹלֶה וְנִכְלָל בִּקְדֻשָּׁה).

1.	*Teshuva Tata'ah* "Lower repentance"	Distress over our distance from G-d	Shattering of animal soul
2.	"Love like fire"	Excitement over G-dliness, but also remorse over distance from G-d	Transformation of the animal soul and its inclusion in the divine soul
3.	*Teshuva Ila'ah* "Higher repentance"	Revelation of the light of the soul	Transformation of the animal soul

This is the meaning of the *korbanot*, or sacrifices. The fat and blood of the animal correspond to the enjoyment of the animal soul and the hot lust of the blood that are meant to ascend to be included in holiness. (Specifically, the fat offering corresponds to the "love like water," explained earlier. Through it, the animal soul becomes prepared [to accept G-dliness].) When we comprehend a G-dly concept with our natural intellect, and as a result also experience an

וְזֶהוּ עִנְיַן הַקָּרְבָּנוֹת שֶׁהוּא הַקְרָבַת חֵלֶב וְדָם דְּהַיְנוּ בְּחִינַת הַתַּעֲנוּג דְּנֶפֶשׁ הַבַּהֲמִית וּרְתִיחַת הַדָּמִים שֶׁעוֹלֶה וְנִכְלָל בִּקְדֻשָּׁה (וּבִפְרָטִיּוּת הַקְרָבַת הַחֵלֶב הוּא בְּאַהֲבָה הַנִּמְשֶׁכֶת כַּמַּיִם שֶׁנִּתְבָּאֵר לְעֵיל שֶׁעַל יְדֵי זֶה נַעֲשֶׂה הַנֶּפֶשׁ הַבַּהֲמִית מֻכְשָׁר כו', הִנֵּה כַּאֲשֶׁר מֵבִין הַשֵּׂכֶל הַטִּבְעִי הֵיטֵב אֶת הָעִנְיָן הָאֱלֹקִי וּמִתְעוֹרֵר גַּם כֵּן בְּרָצוֹן לֶאֱלֹקוּת נוֹטֵל מִמֶּנּוּ הַתַּעֲנוּג (דֶּער גֶעשְׁמַאק) מֵהָעִנְיָנִים הַחָמְרִיִּים (וּבִפְרָט

COMMENTARY

not to think that what he perceives through meditation is "outside" himself; rather, he must recognize that all that stands between himself and the Creator on this level are the blockages that he himself presents (either his sins and transgressions, or his own inability to integrate G-dly revelation). Therefore, just as

Kuntres Ha'Avoda - קונטרס העבודה

awakening for G-dliness, our enjoyment of physical matters is taken away. (This takes place especially during the meditation of, "See, I placed before you life and good," which was explained earlier.) We, too, begin to enjoy the goodness of G-dliness and of G-dly matters. The sacrifice of hot blood, which is the natural fire [within us], corresponds to "love like flames" from the element of fire within holiness. But, "love like water," in and of itself, has only a weakening effect, as mentioned earlier, and only by working with the natural [animal] soul—such that it also understands and becomes aroused— [do we succeed in nullifying the animal soul].

בְּהִתְבּוֹנְנוּת דִּרְאֵה נָתַתִּי לְפָנֶיךָ אֶת הַחַיִּים וְאֶת הַטּוֹב כוּ' שֶׁנִּתְבָּאֵר לְעֵיל) וּמִתְעַנֵּג גַּם כֵּן בְּהַטּוֹב דֶּאֱלֹקוּת וּבְעִנְיְנֵי אֱלֹקוּת. וְהַקְרָבַת רְתִיחַת הַדָּמִים שֶׁהוּא הָאֵשׁ הַטִּבְעִי הוּא בְּהָאַהֲבָה דְּכִרְשִׁפֵּי אֵשׁ בְּחִינַת יְסוֹד הָאֵשׁ דִּקְדֻשָּׁה. אָמְנָם הָאַהֲבָה כַּמַּיִם הִנֵּה מִצַּד עַצְמָהּ פּוֹעֶלֶת הַחֲלִישׁוּת לְבַד כַּנַּ"ל וְרַק עַל יְדֵי הַהִשְׁתַּדְּלוּת עִם הַנֶּפֶשׁ הַטִּבְעִית שֶׁיָּבִין גַּם הוּא וְיִתְעוֹרֵר גַּם כֵּן

(So should it be among "servants of God."[xxv] They should not be satisfied with intellectual grasp of the divine soul alone and its excitement, but should also strive to have the concept understood by the natural intellect. In general, this is dependent upon the level of the animal soul's closeness to and interest in [the matter]. It is true that all our understanding is en-clothed in the ["external garments" and "packaging" of the] natural intellect. Nevertheless, there is a vast difference. If we use only

(אֲשֶׁר כֵּן צָרִיךְ לִהְיוֹת בְּעוֹבְדֵי ה' שֶׁלֹּא לְהִסְתַּפֵּק בְּהַשָּׂגַת הַנֶּפֶשׁ הָאֱלֹקִית לְבַד וּבְהִתְפַּעֲלוּת שֶׁלּוֹ, כִּי אִם לְהִשְׁתַּדֵּל שֶׁיּוּבַן הָעִנְיָן גַּם בַּשֵּׂכֶל הַטִּבְעִי, שֶׁבְּדֶרֶךְ כְּלָל הוּא תָּלוּי בַּהִתְקָרְבוּת וּנְתִינַת הַנֶּפֶשׁ הַטִּבְעִית לָזֶה (דְּעִם הֱיוֹת שֶׁכָּל הַשָּׂגוֹתָיו הֵן בְּהִתְלַבְּשׁוּת בְּהַשֵּׂכֶל הַטִּבְעִי מִכָּל מָקוֹם יֵשׁ בָּזֶה חִלּוּק גָּדוֹל אִם הַהֲכָנָה בַּנֶּפֶשׁ הִיא רַק לְהָבִין הָעִנְיָן בְּשִׂכְלוֹ הָאֱלֹקִי אֵין לָזֶה שַׁיָּכוּת אֶל הַשֵּׂכֶל הַטִּבְעִי וְאֵינוֹ

xxv) See footnote of the Rebbe on page 279

We should not be satisfied with understanding of the divine soul alone, but should strive for the intellectual grasp of the natural, animal soul as well.

---— **COMMENTARY** ———

when we look into water and see only our own face, so on this level there is nothing between us and G-d except our own ego and the resistance that we present — our own mirrored reflection in the water. (In the discourses of 5666, p. 469, the Rebbe Rashab suggests that the soul is a "garment that clothes the infinite light of G-d, bringing it to en-clothement in the vessels...") If so, this is a meditation associated with the highest levels of perceivable

Essay on Service of the Heart - Love Like Fire and Water

our G-dly intellect to prepare the animal soul to understand the concept, there will be no connection with the natural intellect and little effect on the animal soul (besides the "weakening" mentioned earlier). But if our preparation is such that the concept is understood and accepted by our animal soul as well, then we will also influence and persuade it with our meditation. Then, in truth, the concept will come to be accepted by our natural intellect, and it, too, [the animal soul] will become aroused [with G-dly love]). Sometimes, additional proofs and demonstrations are necessary in order to persuade the natural intellect to accept the concept.)

פּוֹעֵל כָּל כָּךְ עַל הַנֶּפֶשׁ הַטִּבְעִית (כִּי אִם הַחֲלִישׁוּת הַנַּ"ל), אֲבָל כַּאֲשֶׁר הַהֲכָנָה הִיא שֶׁיְהֵי מוּבָן וְיוּנַח הָעִנְיָן גַּם בַּשֵּׂכֶל הַטִּבְעִי הֲרֵי הוּא מְקָרֵב וְנוֹתֵן אֶת הַנֶּפֶשׁ הַטִּבְעִית גַּם כֵּן בַּהִתְבּוֹנְנוּת הַהִיא, דְּאָז בֶּאֱמֶת בָּא הַהַנָּחָה גַּם בַּשֵּׂכֶל הַטִּבְעִי וּמִתְעוֹרֵר גַּם הוּא) וְלִפְעָמִים צְרִיכִים לָזֶה רְאָיוֹת וְהוֹכָחוֹת יוֹתֵר בִּכְדֵי שֶׁיּוּנַח הָעִנְיָן בַּשֵּׂכֶל הַטִּבְעִי),

But, on its own without effort, "love like water" won't produce any arousal in the animal soul, while "love like flames of fire" by itself has an [automatic] effect on the animal soul. An element of G-dly fire burns and consumes the natural fire and elevates it to be included in holiness.

אַךְ מֵעַצְמָהּ לֹא תִפְעַל הָאַהֲבָה כַּמַּיִם עַל הִתְפַּעֲלוּת הַנֶּפֶשׁ הַבַּהֲמִית כִּי אִם עַל יְדֵי הִשְׁתַּדְּלוּת, מַה שֶּׁאֵין כֵּן הָאַהֲבָה דְּכִרְשְׁפֵּי אֵשׁ שֶׁפּוֹעֶלֶת בְּעַצְמָהּ עַל הַנֶּפֶשׁ הַבַּהֲמִית, דִּיסוֹד הָאֵשׁ הָאֱלֹקִי שׂוֹרֵף וּמְכַלֶּה אֶת הָאֵשׁ הַטִּבְעִי וּמַעֲלֶה אוֹתוֹ לִהְיוֹת נִכְלָל בִּקְדֻשָּׁה.

Now, when love is combined with meditation upon our distance from Him, as mentioned above, it becomes apparent how it has an effect on the animal soul. And so it is when the true "love like fire" [of the divine soul consumes the fire of the animal soul], since fire consumes fire. The truth is that also in this love is to be found a hidden tinge of bitterness, [as in

דְּהִנֵּה כַּאֲשֶׁר הָאַהֲבָה בָּאָה בְּצֵרוּף הַהִתְבּוֹנְנוּת בָּרִחוּק כַּנַּ"ל הֲרֵי מוּבָן אֵיךְ שֶׁפּוֹעֵל עַל הַנֶּפֶשׁ הַבַּהֲמִית, אָמְנָם כְּמוֹ כֵן הוּא גַּם בְּאַהֲבָה דְּכִרְשְׁפֵּי הָאֵשׁ הָאֲמִתִּית מִשּׁוּם דְּאֵשׁ אוֹכְלָה אֵשׁ. וּבֶאֱמֶת גַּם בְּאַהֲבָה זֹאת יֵשׁ קְצָת תַּעֲרוֹבוֹת מְרִירוּת בְּהֶעְלֵם אוֹ עַל כָּל פָּנִים שֶׁחוֹשֵׁב אוֹדוֹת הָרִחוּק דְּנֶפֶשׁ

COMMENTARY

spirituality attained by only a select few (Rabbi Akiva's colleagues each perceived this spiritual revelation, but only Rabbi Akiva *teshuva* described earlier]. At the very least, we think about the distance of our animal soul from G-d. This is necessarily so, since the dynamic of this love is to rise like fiery flames, as in a furious charge and ascent upwards. In such a movement we are aware of anything holding us back (each one of us according to our own level) and preventing us from developing [spiritually] and ascending, and as a result of this, we experience distress. The difference is that in the first version of love of G-d, the love is the result of feeling our distance [from G-d] in combination with meditation on G-dliness. But the true version of this love comes as a result of meditation on His greatness, and only afterward do we experience the bitterness of our distance from G-d. (This is because the light of our divine soul comes into revelation, as mentioned earlier, and the physicality which is holding us back is very subtle, and therefore we are able to get excited about the greatness of G-d.) This is written about in the discourse beginning *B'parshat Nesachim*, end of chapter 2:

הַבַּהֲמִית (וּמֻכְרָח הָעִנְיָן לִהְיוֹת כֵּן דְּמֵאַחַר שֶׁהוּא בִּבְחִינַת הִתְלַהֲבוּת רִשְׁפֵּי אֵשׁ שֶׁהוּא בְּחִינַת רָצוֹא וְהַעֲלָאָה נִרְגָּשׁ אֶצְלוֹ הַדָּבָר הָאוֹחֵז אוֹתוֹ (בְּכָל חַד וְחַד לְפִי עֶרְכּוֹ) וְאֵינוֹ מַנִּיחוֹ לְהִתְפַּשֵּׁט וְלַעֲלוֹת וְצַר לוֹ מִזֶּה), רַק הַהֶפְרֵשׁ הוּא שֶׁבְּאוֹפֶן הָא' הֲרֵי בָּאָה הָאַהֲבָה מֵהֶרְגֵּשׁ הָרָחוּק בְּצֵרוּף הַהִתְבּוֹנְנוּת בֶּאֱלֹקוּת וּבַאֲמִתִּית הָאַהֲבָה הַזֹּאת בָּא הֶרְגֵּשׁ הָרָחוּק לְאַחַר שֶׁמִּתְפַּעֵל בְּאַהֲבָה מֵהַהִתְבּוֹנְנוּת בִּגְדֻלָּתוֹ יִתְבָּרֵךְ וּכְהַאי גַּוְונָא (מִפְּנֵי שֶׁאוֹר נַפְשׁוֹ הָאֱלֹקִית הִיא בְּהִתְגַּלּוּת כַּנַּ"ל וְהַחֲמָרִיּוּת הָאוֹחֵז אוֹתוֹ הוּא רַק בְּדַקּוּת וּבִיכָלְתּוֹ לְהִתְפַּעֵל מִגְּדֻלָּתוֹ יִתְבָּרֵךְ) וּכְמוֹ שֶׁכָּתוּב בְּדִבּוּר הַמַּתְחִיל בְּפָ' נְסָכִים סְפָּ"ב

לֶאֱסוֹף וּלְקַבֵּץ כָּל הַכֹּחוֹת כוּ' עַל יְדֵי עֲקִירַת הָרָצוֹן מֵהֶם דְּהַיְנוּ לְהִתְחָרֵט כוּ' וְהַיְנוּ מִפְּנֵי שֶׁהוּא בְּחִינַת יִשְׂרָאֵל שֶׁעָלָה בְּמַחֲ' כוּ').

> And this is what is meant by *Shema Yisrael—shema—*from a word indicating gathering ["come and listen"]...as in gathering and grouping together all of the soul powers and desires of the element of fire within the natural [animal] soul...by removing his will from them, that is, to regret the past and resolve never to return to folly, because he is an aspect of *Yisrael*, who arose in His thought...

Essay on Service of the Heart - Love Like Fire and Water

Thus, the main focus of our effort in the "service of the heart," which is prayer, should be to approach and unite our soul with G-dliness through meditation on the G-dly light en-clothed in the worlds. This may be a meditation on the lower world, on the G-dly light and energy infusing each and every aspect of creation and every specific detail. This meditation in itself is enough to bring our soul to an experience of G-dliness and the good and the preciousness associated with it. Or, we may also throw ourselves into this meditation with more energy and focus on how the main point is G-dliness, as in the verse, "See, I have put before you life and good..." Or, we may focus on how the G-dly light is garbed and revealed in the higher worlds, each one of us according to our own intellectual level and in our level of *avoda*. All of these meditations produce a significant weakening of the animal soul, such that it is not drawn after corporeal matters and doesn't engage our will

וְזֶהוּ עִקַּר הַיְגִיעָה בַּעֲבוֹדָה שֶׁבַּלֵּב זוֹ תְּפִלָּה לְקָרֵב וּלְדַבֵּק נַפְשׁוֹ בֶּאֱלֹקוּת עַל יְדֵי הַהִתְבּוֹנְנוּת בְּהָאוֹר הָאֱלֹקִי הַמִּתְלַבֵּשׁ בָּעוֹלָמוֹת אִם בָּעוֹלָם הַתַּחְתּוֹן מַה שֶּׁיֵּשׁ אוֹר וְחַיּוּת אֱלֹקִי בְּכָל נִבְרָא וְנִבְרָא וּבְכָל דָּבָר בִּפְרָט, דְּעֶצֶם הַהִתְבּוֹנְנוּת הַזֹּאת עַצְמָהּ מַסְפֶּקֶת גַּם כֵּן לְקָרֵב נַפְשׁוֹ בְּהֶרְגֵּשׁ הָאֱלֹקוּת וְהַטּוֹב וְהַיְקָר שֶׁבָּאֱלֹקוּת וְיוֹסִיף אֹמֶץ בְּזֶה בְּהִתְבּוֹנְנוּת זֹאת אֵיךְ שֶׁהָעִקָּר הוּא הָאֱלֹקוּת וּבְעִנְיָן רְאֵה כו' אֶת הַחַיִּים וְאֶת הַטּוֹב כו', אוֹ בְּהִתְבּוֹנְנוּת בְּאֹפֶן הָאוֹר וְהַגִּלּוּי הַמִּתְלַבֵּשׁ וּמֵאִיר בָּעוֹלָמוֹת הָעֶלְיוֹנִים כָּל חַד וְחַד לְפוּם שִׁיעוּרָא דִּילֵיהּ בְּהַשָּׂגָתוֹ וַעֲבוֹדָתוֹ, שֶׁכָּל זֶה עוֹשֶׂה חֲלִישׁוּת גְּדוֹלָה בְּהַנֶּפֶשׁ הַבַּהֲמִית שֶׁאֵינוֹ נִמְשָׁךְ אַחֲרֵי הָעִנְיָנִים הַחָמְרִיִּים וְאֵינוֹ מִתְפַּשֵּׁט רְצוֹנוֹ בָּהֶם וְיִיגַע לְקָרֵב גַּם אֶת הַנֶּפֶשׁ הַבַּהֲמִית שֶׁגַּם הוּא יָבִין אֶת הָעִנְיָן הָאֱלֹקִי וְיִתְעוֹרֵר גַּם הוּא בִּבְחִינַת קֵרוּב לֶאֱלֹקוּת, וּבְכָל זֶה

The main focus of our effort should be to unite our soul with G-dliness through meditation upon the G-dly light enclothed in the worlds.

COMMENTARY

"returned" to everyday life unharmed by it.)

However, even this level of love doesn't bring satisfaction or total fulfillment. We desire only G-d Himself, and no matter what level we achieve in our meditation, we never grasp G-d Himself, and we are overcome with a spiritual "love-sickness." This condition can only be overcome by the advent of *Mashiach* and the re-building of the Temple, at which point everyone will be able to achieve grasp of the true essence of G-dliness, down here in the physical universe.

יִתְחַזֵּק בְּעֵסֶק הַתּוֹרָה וְקִיּוּם הַמִּצְוֹת לִהְיוֹתָן אֱלֹקוּת כנ"ל,

in physicality. We should strive to bring our animal soul as well to an understanding of G-dly matters, such that it will also be aroused by closeness to G-d. Throughout all this, we will become stronger in our Torah learning and fulfillment of the *mitzvot*, since they are G-dly, as mentioned before.

וְהַגְדָּלַת הָאַהֲבָה יוֹתֵר הִיא בִּבְחִינַת נַפְשִׁי אִוִּיתִיךָ כְּשֶׁמִּתְבּוֹנֵן שֶׁאַתָּה ה' נַפְשִׁי כו' (וְיִרְצֶה מְאֹד שֶׁיִּהְיֶ' גִּלּוּי אֱלֹקוּת בְּקִרְבּוֹ עַל יְדֵי הַתּוֹרָה) וְכֵן בְּאַהֲבָה דִכְבְרָא דְּאִשְׁתַּדַּל כו' (וְגַם מִי שֶׁאֵינוֹ בְּדַרְגוֹת אֵלּוּ לִהְיוֹת בּוֹ אֲהָבוֹת הנ"ל בְּהִתְגַּלּוּת יַרְגִּיל עַצְמוֹ בָּזֶה לִהְיוֹת כִּי קָרוֹב הַדָּבָר אֵלָיו כו'). וּבַמַּדְרֵגוֹת גְּבֹהוֹת יוֹתֵר וְגַם בִּפְנִימִיּוּת יוֹתֵר הִיא בְּהִתְבּוֹנְנוּת דְּכַמַּיִם הַפָּנִים אֶל הַפָּנִים כו' וְגַם יְלַהֵב לִבּוֹ בִּבְחִינוֹת הִתְלַהֲבוּת בְּאַהֲבָה כְּרִשְׁפֵּי אֵשׁ (דְּאַהֲבָה זוֹ מִצַּד עַצְמָהּ מֻכְרַחַת לִהְיוֹת מִפְּנֵי שֶׁבָּזֶה דַּוְקָא הִתְגַּלּוּת הָאוֹר דְּנֶפֶשׁ הָאֱלֹקִית יוֹתֵר, וְגַם שֶׁזֶּהוּ עִקַּר בְּחִינַת הָרָצוֹא לֶאֱלֹקוּת) עַל יְדֵי שֶׁמִּתְבּוֹנֵן בְּמַעֲמָדוֹ וּמַצָּבוֹ אֵיךְ שֶׁהוּא מְרֻחָק כו' וַאֲמִתִּית הָאַהֲבָה הַזֹּאת תִּהְיֶה עַל יְדֵי

Even if we are not on a spiritual level to experience these revealed expressions of love of G-d, we should nevertheless get accustomed to thinking about them.

A further development of love [of G-d] is that of "You are my soul, I desire you..." which comes about through meditation on the verse, "You, Lord, are my soul" (and results in a strong yearning, brought about by learning Torah, for revelation of G-dliness within us). Then, there is also the contemplation leading to love like that of "a son who exerts himself for his father." (Even if we are not on a spiritual level to experience these revealed expressions of love of G-d, we should nevertheless get accustomed to thinking about them, since [as it says in Deuteronomy 30:14] the "thing is very close to you [to do]..."). On higher levels, and on more inner levels as well, we come to the meditation of "as in water, face answers to face." And then we can also inflame our heart with "love like fire." (We must of necessity come to this level

---

COMMENTARY

All of the levels of "love like fire" described in *Kuntres Ha'Avoda* would seem to be beyond us. *Kuntres Ha'Avoda* acknowledges this, stating that even if we don't think that we can really attain these levels of love of G-d, we should keep trying, because the "thing is very near to you." That is, love of G-d is latent in the heart of every Jew, and we should keep trying to bring it into a state of revelation. *Kuntres Ha'Avoda* further

Essay on Service of the Heart - Love Like Fire and Water

הַהִתְבּוֹנְנוּת בִּגְדֻלָּתוֹ יִתְבָּרֵךְ כו' וְאֵשׁ זֶה הָאֱלֹקִי שׂוֹרֵף וּמְכַלֶּה אֶת הָאֵשׁ זָר דְּנֶפֶשׁ הַבַּהֲמִית וּמַעֲלֶה אוֹתוֹ לִהְיוֹת נִכְלָל גַּם כֵּן בֶּאֱלֹקוּת בִּבְחִי׳ הִתְלַהֲבוּת וְרִשְׁפֵּי אֵשׁ כו׳ וְעַל זֶה נֶאֱמַר וְיָדַעְתָּ הַיּוֹם וַהֲשֵׁבֹתָ אֶל לְבָבֶךָ לִהְיוֹת הָאַהֲבָה בְּהִתְגַּלּוּת בַּלֵּב, וְעִנְיַן לְבָבְךָ ב׳ לְבָבוֹת הַיְנוּ בְּחִינַת הַקֵּרוּב וְהַדְּבֵקוּת דְּנֶפֶשׁ הָאֱלֹקִית, וְהַזִּכּוּךְ דְּנֶפֶשׁ הַבַּהֲמִית שֶׁגַּם הוּא יִתְבַּטֵּל וְיָבוֹא לִבְחִינַת אַהֲבָה שֶׁזֶּהוּ עִנְיַן וְאָהַבְתָּ כו׳ בְּכָל לְבָבְךָ בִּשְׁנֵי יְצָרֶיךָ כו׳:

since only it strongly reveals the light of the divine soul, and also because it is the main expression of the desire and yearning [of the divine soul] for G-dliness.) This we do by meditating on our own status and situation, and how far away we are [from G-d]. But the truest expression of this love comes about through meditation on His greatness. The G-dly fire burns and consumes the alien fire of the animal soul—and elevates it as well to be included in G-dliness—with excitement and flames of fire. About this, the verse says, "And you should know today and put it in your heart," such that the love is revealed in the heart. The word here for "your heart"—*levavcha*—[seems to be plural and] indicates two hearts, corresponding to the closeness and cleaving of the divine soul [to its Source], and to the refinement of the animal soul, such that it, too, becomes nullified and comes to love G-d, which is what is referred to in *Ve'ahavta*, "You should love...with your whole heart," meaning with both inclinations [the good and the bad].

COMMENTARY

emphasizes that only "love like fire" has the ability to consume and incinerate the physical lusts and temptations of the animal soul. While "love like water" has the ability to weaken the animal soul, it cannot eliminate it. The importance of "love like fire" lies in its ability to devour and do away with our animal soul, turning us into different people altogether.

The goal of our meditation should be to fan the spark of G-dly light within us until it becomes a full-blown flame of love for the One Above. We should always keep trying to attain "love like fire," and in the process, at the very least we will develop our love for G-d to the level of "love like water."

SYNOPSIS:

There are two kinds of love [of G-d]. One is "love like water," which comes about by meditation on the G-dliness within the worlds, and which produces closeness and cleaving of our soul to G-dliness such that we seek only the G-dliness within everything. This love also brings us to learn Torah and keep its *mitzvot* and produces in us a weakening and subjugation of the animal soul. The second is "love like fire," and it comes about when, after meditation on G-dliness, we consider how far we are from G-d in both our soul and in our thought, speech, and action. In so doing, we inflame our heart with a fire of desire and thirst, and this fire burns and consumes the natural fire of the animal soul, causing it to be nullified in its very existence. Then, the fire of the animal soul ascends and is included as well in the excitement and flames of fire of love of G-dliness. And this is [really] the goal of the *avoda* of prayer, to come to these two levels of love of the One Above, such that they produce closeness and cleaving to G-d, and the purification and refinement of the physicality and ego of the animal soul, such that it also ascends. In this chapter are also explained higher levels of both types of love of G-d.

קִצּוּר.

הִנֵּה יֵשׁ ב' בְּחִינוֹת אַהֲבָה, הָא' אַהֲבָה הַנִּמְשֶׁכֶת כַּמַּיִם הַבָּאָה עַל יְדֵי הַהִתְבּוֹנְנוּת בִּבְחִינַת הָאֱלֹקוּת שֶׁבָּעוֹלָמוֹת, שֶׁעַל יְדֵי זֶה נַעֲשֶׂה קֵרוּב וּדְבֵקוּת נַפְשׁוֹ בֶּאֱלֹקוּת וּבְכָל דָּבָר יִרְצֶה רַק הָאֱלֹקוּת שֶׁבּוֹ, וְהִיא הַמְּבִיאָה אוֹתוֹ גַּם כֵּן לְעֵסֶק הַתּוֹרָה וְקִיּוּם הַמִּצְוֹת וּבַנֶּפֶשׁ הַבַּהֲמִית פּוֹעֶלֶת בּוֹ הַחֲלִישׁוּת וְהַכְנָעָה. וְהַב' הָאַהֲבָה כְּרִשְׁפֵּי אֵשׁ וְהוּא שֶׁלְּאַחַר הַהִתְבּוֹנְנוּת טוֹבָה בֶּאֱלֹקוּת יִתְבּוֹנֵן אֵיךְ שֶׁהוּא מְרֻחָק בִּכְלָלוּת נַפְשׁוֹ וּבְמַחְשָׁבָה דִּבּוּר וּמַעֲשֶׂה שֶׁלּוֹ, שֶׁעַל יְדֵי זֶה יִתְלַהֵב לִבּוֹ בְּרִשְׁפֵּי אֵשׁ הַתְּשׁוּקָה וְהַצִּמָּאוֹן וְאֵשׁ זֶה שׂוֹרֵף וּמְכַלֶּה אֶת הָאֵשׁ הַטִּבְעִי דְּנֶפֶשׁ הַבַּהֲמִית לִהְיוֹת בִּבְחִינַת בִּטּוּל מַמָּשׁ, וְעוֹלֶה וְנִכְלַל גַּם הוּא בִּבְחִינַת הִתְלַהֲבוּת וְרִשְׁפֵּי אֵשׁ הָאַהֲבָה לֶאֱלֹקוּת. וְזֶהוּ תַּכְלִית הָעֲבוֹדָה דִּתְפִלָּה לָבוֹא לְב' מַדְרֵגוֹת אַהֲבָה הַנַ"ל שֶׁהֵן בְּחִינַת הַקֵּרוּב וְהַדְּבֵקוּת לֶאֱלֹקוּת. וּבֵרוּר וְזִכּוּךְ הַחֲמָרִיּוּת וְהַיֵּשׁוּת דְּנֶפֶשׁ הַבַּהֲמִית לִהְיוֹת גַּם הוּא עוֹלֶה כו'. וְנִתְ' עוֹד מַדְרֵגוֹת גְּבוֹהוֹת יוֹתֵר בְּב' בְּחִינַת אַהֲבָה הַנַ"ל:

CHAPTER 5

The Hebrew word for "love," *ahava*, comes from the word *ava*, which means "will." The will is the inner dimension of the emotions, and it, as well as the emotions, stems from the intellect. The inner dimension of the emotions rules over and governs them, and it is capable of transforming their very nature. For example, when we detach ourselves from something enjoyable and no longer desire it for some reason, we no longer gain any enjoyment from that experience. The inverse is also true; when we find in front of ourselves a path of pain and suffering, and yet we work on ourselves to accept it, because we know intellectually that it's good for us, we don't feel as much pain and suffering. Quite the opposite, we actually learn to appreciate it. For example, [if we had a bad dream and wish to ameliorate it], we are permitted to fast on the Sabbath day [when fasting is otherwise prohibited], since for us it is beneficial. So, we see that the will can transform the nature of the emotions, since it is [really] the inner dimension of the emotions.

פרק ה

וְהִנֵּה אַהֲבָה הוּא מִלְשׁוֹן אָבָה שֶׁפֵּרוּשׁוֹ רָצוֹן, וְהַיְנוּ הָרָצוֹן שֶׁהוּא פְּנִימִיּוּת הַמִּדּוֹת וְנִמְשָׁךְ גַּם כֵּן מִן הַשֵּׂכֶל. וְהָעִנְיָן דְּמַה שֶׁהוּא פְּנִימִיּוּת הַמִּדּוֹת הַיְנוּ שֶׁמּוֹשֵׁל וְשׁוֹלֵט עַל הַמִּדּוֹת וְיָכוֹל לְשַׁנּוֹת טֶבַע הַמִּדּוֹת, כְּמוֹ כְּשֶׁמְסַלֵּק רְצוֹנוֹ מֵאֵיזֶה דְּבַר תַּעֲנוּג וְאֵינוֹ רוֹצֶה בּוֹ מִצַּד אֵיזֶה טַעַם וְדַעַת אֵינוֹ מְקַבֵּל נַחַת וְתַעֲנוּג מֵהַדָּבָר הַהוּא, וּלְהֶפֶךְ כְּשֶׁיֵּשׁ לְפָנָיו חַס וְחָלִילָה דְּבַר שֶׁל צַעַר וְיִסּוּרִים אִם הוּא עוֹשֶׂה רְצוֹנוֹ לָזֶה עַל פִּי הַשֵּׂכֶל שֶׁמְחֻיָּב שֶׁהַצַּעַר הַזֶּה טוֹב לוֹ אֵינוֹ מַרְגִּישׁ הַצַּעַר וְהַיִּסּוּרִים כָּל כָּךְ וְאַדְרַבָּא יְהִי לוֹ תַּעֲנוּג בַּזֶּה. וְכַנּוֹדָע בְּעִנְיַן תַּעֲנִית חֲלוֹם בְּשַׁבָּת מִפְּנֵי שֶׁהוּא תַּעֲנוּג לוֹ, הֲרֵי שֶׁהָרָצוֹן מְשַׁנֶּה אֶת טֶבַע הַמִּדּוֹת לִהְיוֹתוֹ פְּנִימִיּוּת הַמִּדּוֹת,

In Hebrew, the word for love (ahava) comes from the word for will (ava).

COMMENTARY

CHAPTER 5: KNOWLEDGE AND UNITY

Now that we know something of the kinds of love of G-d that we can experience, it's time to consider how to get there.

Here in Chapter 5, love of G-d derived from reason and logic is described as "love that is dependent upon something." Most relationships that we form are dependent on something (even if they contain an element of true affection as well). One example is the "love" between Amnon and Tamar (as recounted in 2 Samuel, chapter 13). Amnon was physically attracted to Tamar,

Our will is the inner dimension of our emotions, but our will is also influenced by intellect.

וּמִכָּל מָקוֹם גַּם הָרָצוֹן הוּא עַל פִּי הַשֵּׂכֶל דְּהַיְנוּ מַה שֶׁהַשֵּׂכֶל מְחַיֵּב שֶׁצָּרִיךְ לִרְצוֹת כָּךְ לֹא שֶׁהוּא רוֹצֶה כֵּן בְּטִבְעוֹ כִּי אִם מִצַּד חִיּוּב הַשֵּׂכֶל וּכְמוֹ שֶׁכָּתוּב בְּלִקּוּטֵי תּוֹרָה דִּבּוּר הַמַּתְחִיל בְּהַעֲלוֹתְךָ דְּרוּשׁ הָרִאשׁוֹן, וְהוּא בְּחִינַת תִּפְאֶרֶת דְּאִימָּא שֶׁנַּעֲשָׂה כֶּתֶר לִזְעֵיר אַנְפִּין כוּ'. אָמְנָם בִּדְרוּשׁ יָשָׁן מֵרַבֵּינוּ נ"ע אִי' דְּאַהֲבָה הוּא בְּחִינַת רָצוֹן שֶׁלְּמַעְלָה מִטַּעַם וָדַעַת. וְהוּא בְּחִינַת הָרָצוֹן הַטִּבְעִי

Nevertheless, the will is also governed by the intellect. Whatever our intellect dictates as the correct path becomes our will. By nature, we may not desire that path, but because logic dictates it, that path becomes our own as written in the first discourse of *Beha'alotcha* in *Likutei Torah*. [In Kabbalistic terms,] this is the process wherein *tiferet d'imma*, the emotions within intellect, become the crown and motivation of the emotions themselves, *na'aseh keter l'za*. However, there is an old Chassidic discourse by the [Alter] Rebbe, [the founder of the Chabad movement], *Nishmato Eden*, which indicates that *ava* ("will") is beyond the intellect; it is our innate will.

וְהַיְנוּ מַה שֶׁבַּטֶבַע יֵשׁ בַּנְּשָׁמוֹת בְּחִינַת רָצוֹן שֶׁנִּמְשָׁךְ בִּרְצוֹא לְאוֹר אֵין סוֹף בָּרוּךְ הוּא (א צִיא צוּא אוֹר אֵין סוֹף בָּרוּךְ הוּא). וְנוֹדַע דְּרָצוֹן הַטִּבְעִי הוּא בְּחִינַת מַקִּיפִים דְּנְשָׁמָה

By nature, there is an aspect of the soul that is drawn [spontaneously] in a spiritual rush toward the infinite light of the One Above. It is known that our natural will coincides with the transcendent levels of our soul.

COMMENTARY

but once he achieved his desire, he was no longer interested in her. This is love that is "dependent upon something," and it dissipates once the real goal has been achieved.

Love of G-d that results from meditation is dependent upon the intellect. When we think deeply into a spiritual topic and then develop love of G-d based on it, our love dissipates when the meditation ceases. Of course, the amount of time the emotion lasts is dependent on the quality of our meditation and on the depth of the emotion generated by it. But, as long as the love is the product of intellectual activity, it is "dependent upon something" — that is, upon our mental process — and it eventually dissipates.

Essay on Service of the Heart - Love Like Fire and Water

As explained in Chapter 1, the divine soul has five levels, the lower three of which are en-clothed in the body, and the higher two—the transcendent levels—connect the essence of the soul with its source in the infinite light of G-d. The two highest levels are:

4. *Chaya*	"Living one"	Transcendent consciousness
5. *Yechida*	"Single one"	Unity consciousness

There are two levels of transcendence. The first [highest] level is called the *yechida*, and on this level the will needs no reason or stimulation whatsoever in order to come into expression. The soul is drawn spontaneously to its source in the Creator's essential and infinite light, without any meditation whatsoever being necessary. This is because the Jewish soul is "a part of the One Above" [*Tanya*, chapter 2, from Job 31:2]. Like everything that strives to return to its

וְיֵשׁ בָּזֶה ב' מַדְרֵגוֹת הָא' בְּחִינַת מַקִּיף דִּיחִידָה שֶׁהָרָצוֹן הוּא בְּלִי שׁוּם סִבָּה וּבְלִי שׁוּם הִתְעוֹרְרוּת כְּלָל, וְהַיְנוּ שֶׁאֵין צָרִיךְ לְשׁוּם הִתְבּוֹנְנוּת כְּלָל כִּי אִם שֶׁמִּמֵּילָא נִמְשָׁךְ אֶל מְקוֹר חָצְבוֹ בְּחִינַת עַצְמוּת אוֹר אֵין סוֹף בָּרוּךְ הוּא שֶׁהֲרֵי הוּא חֵלֶק אֱלֹקַ' מִמַּעַל וּכְמוֹ טֶבַע כָּל דָּבָר שֶׁנִּמְשָׁךְ לְשָׁרְשׁוֹ וּמְקוֹרוֹ כָּךְ הוּא טֶבַע הַנְּשָׁמָה לִמָּשֵׁךְ וּלְהִכָּלֵל בְּשָׁרְשָׁהּ וּמְקוֹרָהּ בְּחִינַת

Within the will are two transcendent soul-levels; chaya and yechida.

COMMENTARY

Not so, says Chapter 5, when we come to "love that is dependent upon nothing." Two friends, who have true affection for each other, need no reason to help each other, worry about each other, and spend time together. One example is the affection between King David and Jonathan, the son of King Saul (as recounted in 1 Samuel, chatper 18-20). The two were true friends who sought nothing from the bond between them aside from the welfare of one another (this in spite of the fact that King Saul was David's sworn enemy at the time).

In its root, this is the natural love for G-d that is latent within the Jewish soul. It expresses itself on two different levels. First of all, it expresses itself as our desire for real connection with

עַצְמוּת אוֹר אֵין סוֹף בָּרוּךְ הוּא, וְהִיא מְיֻחֶדֶת בֶּאֱמֶת תָּמִיד בִּבְחִינַת עַצְמוּת אוֹר אֵין סוֹף וּכְמַאֲמַר חֲבוּקָה וּדְבוּקָה בָּךְ (וּמַה שֶּׁהוּא בִּבְחִינַת הַמְשָׁכָה וְרָצוֹא, זֶהוּ מִשּׁוּם דְּאֹפֶן מְצִיאוּת הַנְּשָׁמוֹת מִן הָעַצְמוּת הוּא בִּבְחִינַת מָהוּת בִּפְנֵי עַצְמוֹ וּכְמוֹ הַבֵּן מִן הָאָב הֲגַם שֶׁהֵם עֶצֶם א' מִכָּל מָקוֹם הַבֵּן הוּא בִּמְהוּת בִּפְנֵי עַצְמוֹ, שֶׁזֶּהוּ הַהֶפְרֵשׁ בֵּין נְשָׁמוֹת לַתּוֹרָה עִם הֱיוֹת שֶׁשְּׁנֵיהֶם מִבְּחִינַת הָעַצְמוּת כוּ' וּכְמוֹ שֶׁכָּתוּב בְּמָקוֹם אַחֵר)

source of origin, so the way of the soul is to be drawn upward and included in its origin — the essential, infinite light of the One Above. The truth is that this level of the soul, the *yechida*, is at all times united with the essential, infinite light of the One Above, as in the phrase [from the *hoshanot* — supplications for rain recited on the third day of *chol hamoed* Succot—describing the soul and G-d]: "embracing and cleaving to You...". (That the *yechida* is drawn to G-d and has a desire for Him is due to the nature of souls in general. The nature of the soul's emergence into existence from G-d's essence is such that the soul has its own identity, or selfhood. This is analogous to a son in relation to his father; although they are of the same essence, nevertheless the son has his own selfhood and identity. This is, as well, the difference between the soul and the Torah,[xxvi] even though both of them are from His essence, as written elsewhere.)

xxvi) See footnote of the Rebbe on page 280

COMMENTARY

the One Above; this is the level of *chaya*, ("transcendental consciousness") mentioned in Chapter 1. Second, it expresses itself as *yechida* ("unity consciousness"). The *yechida* is the essential point of the soul that is never disconnected from the One Above. It is the spark of G-dliness within us which the *Tanya* calls "an integral part of G-d on high."

| Love of G-d based on logic | Love dependent on something | Amnon and Tamar |
| Love of G-d beyond reason | Love dependent on nothing | David and Jonathan |

LOVE DEPENDENT ON SOMETHING

The process leading to "love that is dependent on something" is based upon intellect (*chabad*). This acronym has largely been made famous by the proactive Chassidic group, but its actual

Essay on Service of the Heart - Love Like Fire and Water

The *yechida* comes into expression as *mesirat nefesh* — "giving up one's life" in honor of the One Above. That we may actually give up our own life is due to the fact that it is absolutely impossible for us to be separated from the One Above, G-d forbid. This "stubbornness" comes from the *yechida* of our soul, which is in [constant and] essential connection with the infinite One Above, and it is impossible for it to be any other way, G-d forbid. (This is also expressed in our sincerity and earnestness in the actual fulfillment of the *mitzvot*, both positive and negative. It is as if the very nature of every Jew is to avoid deliberate sin, G-d forbid, as well as not to disregard any *mitzvah*. This is part of the expression of the *yechida* which is the essential connection of

וְהִיא הַמִּתְגַּלָּה בִּמְסִירַת נֶפֶשׁ עַל קִדּוּשׁ הַשֵּׁם דְּזֶה שֶׁמּוֹסֵר נַפְשׁוֹ בְּפֹעַל מַמָּשׁ הוּא מִפְּנֵי שֶׁאִי אֶפְשָׁר לוֹ בְּשׁוּם אֹפֶן לִהְיוֹת נִפְרָד חַס וְחָלִילָה. וְהַיְנוּ מִבְּחִינַת יְחִידָה שֶׁבַּנֶּפֶשׁ שֶׁהִיא בִּבְחִינַת הַתְקַשְּׁרוּת עַצְמִי בְּעַצְמוּת אֵין סוֹף בָּרוּךְ הוּא וְאִי אֶפְשָׁר לִהְיוֹת כְּלָל בְּאֹפֶן אַחֵר חַס וְחָלִילָה (וְכֵן הוּא בִּתְמִימוּת הַמַּעֲשֶׂה בְּסוּר מֵרַע וַעֲשֵׂה טוֹב בְּפֹעַל מַמָּשׁ, שֶׁזֶּהוּ כְּמוֹ טֶבַע בְּכָל אֶחָד וְאֶחָד מִיִּשְׂרָאֵל שֶׁלֹּא יַעֲבֹר בְּמֵזִיד אֵיזֶה עֲבֵרָה חַס וְחָלִילָה וְשֶׁלֹּא יְבַטֵּל אֵיזֶה מִצְוָה חַס וְחָלִילָה, שֶׁזֶּהוּ מִבְּחִינַת יְחִידָה שֶׁבַּנֶּפֶשׁ שֶׁהִיא עֶצֶם הִתְקַשְּׁרוּתוֹ בֶּאֱלֹקוּת כו' וּכְמוֹ שֶׁכָּתוּב מִזֶּה בְּדֶרֶךְ חַיִּים ספ"ח. וְכֵן הוּא בְּכָל

Yechida is the innate connection of the soul that needs no arousal.

COMMENTARY

meaning is less well known. Chabad stands for three key steps in meditation - *chochma* ("wisdom"); *bina* ("understanding"), and *da'at* ("knowledge"):

We first hear of a concept, or read about it, and we gain an overall grasp of its features. This is called *chochma* (literally "wisdom"), and it corresponds to an initial flash, or inspiration of intellect. Often, this initial inspiration is so ephemeral that — unless we sit down and think about it — it simply dissipates. The process of grasping the concept, analyzing it, and considering all of its details, is called *bina* (intellectual "understanding"). These two processes are so closely related and intertwined that Kabbalah actually refers to the two as "father and mother" and says that they are always together. In this stage of the process, though, the emphasis is on *chochma*, because without the spiritual insight of *chochma*, there can be no analysis on the level of *bina*.

נִסָּיוֹן וְנִסָּיוֹן שֶׁעוֹמֵד עַל נַפְשׁוֹ נֶגֶד הַסָּתוֹת הַיֵּצֶר הָרָע הַגַּשְׁמִית וּמֵדִיחַ רַחֲמָנָא לִצְלָן וַהֲרֵי הוּא מִתְגַּבֵּר עָלָיו בְּכָל תֹּקֶף וְעֹז כו'. שֶׁזֶּהוּ עִנְיַן מַשְׁבִּיעִין אוֹתוֹ שֶׁהוּא לְשׁוֹן שֹׂבַע כַּנּוֹדָע, וְהַיְנוּ שֶׁנּוֹתְנִים לוֹ כֹּחַ וְעֹז מֵעֶצֶם הַנְּשָׁמָה שֶׁקְּשׁוּרָה וּדְבוּקָה בֵּאלֹקִים חַיִּים דְּבְכֹחַ זֶה הוּא עוֹמֵד נֶגֶד כָּל מוֹנֵעַ מִבַּיִת וּמִבַּחוּץ).

the soul with G-dliness, as written in *Derech Chaim*, at the end of chapter 8. And so it is with each and every test that we face. The *yechida* of our soul empowers us to stand firm against the seduction of the evil inclination which attempts to influence us, may G-d protect us. We refuse to be seduced and stand firm with all of our power. This is what is meant [in *Talmud Niddah* 30] by the phrase: "They make him take an oath," [regarding the embryo while still in its mother's womb, that it should take an oath to be a *tzaddik* after it is born]. The Hebrew word for "oath" (*shavuah*) also indicates satisfaction and satiation. This is the condition that results from receiving the power of the essence of the soul, [the *yechida*], which is connected to the living G-d. With this power, we are able to stand up to each and every obstacle, whether originating from within or without ourselves.)

The second transcendent level, chaya, needs arousal to come into expression.

דְּהַמַּדְרֵגָה הַב' הִיא בְּחִינַת מַקִּיף דְחַיָּ' דְּעִם הֱיוֹתָהּ גַּם כֵּן בִּכְלָל בְּחִינַת עַצְמוּת הַנְּשָׁמָה מִכָּל מָקוֹם אֵינָהּ בְּחִינַת עַצְמוּת מַמָּשׁ לִהְיוֹת בִּבְחִינַת הִתְקַשְּׁרוּת עַצְמִית כְּמוֹ בִּבְחִינַת יְחִידָה כִּי אִם שֶׁצְּרִיכִים לְעוֹרֵר הָרָצוֹן וְהַהִתְקַשְּׁרוּת, וְהוּא

The second transcendent level of the soul [below *yechida*] is called *chaya*. While it is true that the *chaya* is also an integral part of the essence of the soul, nevertheless, it is not at one with the essence in the same way as is the *yechida*. While the *yechida* is inherently connected and united, the

---
COMMENTARY

Once we have grasped the concept well, through the faculty of *bina*, we must then focus on it for the purpose of clarity and feeling. The goal of meditation is to feel the G-dliness within the concept while understanding it deeply, so that we are led to greater levels of love and fear of the One Above. We have truly internalized a concept only when in addition to understanding it, we feel it on a visceral level. The focus and concentration necessary to achieve the visceral feeling is called *da'at* ("knowledge").

Essay on Service of the Heart - Love Like Fire and Water

will and desire for connection of the *chaya* requires arousal in order to come into expression. The arousal takes place through meditation upon the essential infinite light of the One Above, with emphasis on its exalted and elevated status, as written elsewhere.[xxvii] Nevertheless, this will [of the *chaya*] is also both essential and innate, even though it has to be aroused. When aroused and expressed, it is as an essential will that is beyond all thought and logic, and therefore beyond limitation as well.

עַל יְדֵי הַהִתְבּוֹנְנוּת בִּבְחִינַת עַצְמוּת אוֹר אֵין סוֹף בִּבְחִינַת הַפְלָאָתוֹ וְרוֹמְמוּתוֹ כו' כְּמוֹ שֶׁכָּתוּב בְּמָקוֹם אַחֵר. וּמִכָּל מָקוֹם גַּם הָרָצוֹן הַזֶּה הוּא בְּחִינַת רָצוֹן עַצְמִי וְטִבְעִי, הֲגַם שֶׁצְּרִיכִים לְעוֹרֵר הָרָצוֹן, מִכָּל מָקוֹם כְּשֶׁמִּתְעוֹרֵר הוּא בִּבְחִינַת רָצוֹן עַצְמִי שֶׁלְּמַעְלָה מִטַּעַם וָדַעַת וְלָכֵן הוּא בִּבְחִינַת בְּלִי גְּבוּל כו',

When it comes into expression, the chaya is beyond all thought and logic, and beyond limitation.

← xxvii) See footnote of the Rebbe on page 281

It is written elsewhere that there is a "love which is dependent upon something," meaning that there is an [external] factor that motivates the love and is the entire reason for its existence. Such a state of love is limited in proportion to the factor that brings the love about. If the factor is eliminated, the love dissipates. Then, there is love that is "not dependent upon anything." It is an essential love,

וּכְמוֹ שֶׁכָּתוּב בְּמָקוֹם אַחֵר שֶׁיֵּשׁ אַהֲבָה הַתְּלוּיָ' בְּדָבָר דְּהַיְנוּ שֶׁכָּל סִבָּתָהּ הוּא הַדָּבָר הַגּוֹרֵם אֶת הָאַהֲבָה וּמִמֵּילָא הִיא מֻגְבֶּלֶת לְפִי אֹפֶן הַדָּבָר הַגּוֹרֵם וּכְשֶׁמִּתְבַּטֵּל הַדָּבָר מִתְבַּטֵּל גַּם כֵּן הָאַהֲבָה וְיֵשׁ אַהֲבָה שֶׁאֵינָהּ תְּלוּיָ' בְּדָבָר כִּי אִם אַהֲבָה עַצְמִית וּכְמוֹ שְׁנֵי אוֹהֲבִים נֶאֱמָנִים שֶׁאֵין אַהֲבָתָם תְּלוּיָ' בְּשׁוּם דָּבָר דְּאַהֲבָה זוֹ אֵינָהּ מֻגְבֶּלֶת

COMMENTARY

Under normal circumstances, our faculty of *da'at* leads us to appreciation of G-dliness embedded in the creation. Our perception of the physical world remains dominant, but we become more and more aware of the immanent G-dliness enlivening the creation. That is, the creation remains in the foreground even as we become more and more aware of the Creator in the background. This consciousness is called *da'at tachton* ("lower awareness"), and the perception associated with it is called *yichuda tata'ah* ("lower unity"). On this level, we appreciate the essential spiritual unity of the universe but remain aware of, and place emphasis on, the physical reality of creation. When this paradigm is mapped upon the structure of the ten *sephirot*, the *sephira* of *da'at* is "located" below *bina* and above

Love that is not dependent on anything never dissipates.

מֵאַחַר שֶׁאֵינָהּ תְּלוּיָה בְּדָבָר שֶׁיַּעֲמֹד אוֹתָהּ וְגַם אֵינָהּ מִתְבַּטֶּלֶת לְעוֹלָם וּמִכָּל מָקוֹם יְכוֹלָה לְהִתְעַלֵּם בְּמֶשֶׁךְ זְמַן כְּשֶׁמִּתְרַחֲקִים זֶה מִזֶּה וּמִתְעוֹרֵר עַל יְדֵי אֵיזֶה דָּבָר כְּמוֹ דְּבַר שִׂמְחָה וּכְהַאי גַּוְונָא. אָמְנָם כְּשֶׁמִּתְעוֹרֵר הָאַהֲבָה אֵינָהּ מֻגְבֶּלֶת לְפִי אֹפֶן הַדָּבָר הַמְעוֹרֵר מִפְּנֵי שֶׁלֹּא הוּא סִבָּתָהּ בֶּאֱמֶת כִּי הָאַהֲבָה הִיא עַצְמִית בְּלִי שׁוּם סִבָּה רַק שֶׁנִּתְעַלְּמָה וּכְשֶׁמִּתְעוֹרֶרֶת הֲרֵי הִיא בְּעַצְמוּתָהּ כְּמוֹ שֶׁהִיא מִצַּד עַצְמָהּ וַהֲרֵי הִיא בִּלְתִּי מֻגְבֶּלֶת. וּלְמַעְלָה מִזֶּה בְּאֵין עֲרוֹךְ אַהֲבָה עַצְמִית מַמָּשׁ כְּמוֹ אַהֲבַת אָב וּבֵן שֶׁאֵינָהּ מִתְעַלֶּמֶת לְעוֹלָם וְאֵין צָרִיךְ

such as that between two loyal friends whose affection for each other is independent of any [external] factors. Their affection is unlimited, since it doesn't depend upon any [outside] factor that limits the love, and so it never completely disappears. It can recede with the passage of time, when the two are geographically far from one another, and then something may cause their love to re-surface — for example, a family *simcha* and the like. But, when their love does re-surface, it is not proportionate to the event that aroused it. The event is not the true reason for their love and affection. Their love for each other is essential, without any reason whatso-

--- **COMMENTARY** ---

the emotional *sephirot* in the structure of the ten *sephirot*. Here, *da'at* functions as the intermediary between the mind and the G-dly emotions, as follows:

Awareness of *Da'at Tachton* and *Yichuda Tata*
Chochma "wisdom"
Bina "understanding"
***Da'at* "knowledge"**
Chesed "loving-kindness"
Gevura "strength"
Tiferet "beauty"

Essay on Service of the Heart - Love Like Fire and Water

ever. It can grow faint, but when re-ignited, it returns to its previous, unlimited state. And far beyond this love is true essential love; for example, the love between a father and son, which never grows faint [or disappears] at all. It needs no factor whatsoever to arouse it, and it is constantly present.

And so it is with the soul. There is a love of G-d in the soul that is "dependent upon something" — such as logic and reason. The entire basis and foundation of this love is comprehension of, and meditation upon, G-dly concepts. Since in this meditation, the essential love of the soul is not shining, and it is only the conscious faculties of the soul that provide G-dly illumination, the love that develops is of the emotions of the heart [alone]. It is the result of meditation, and it is limited in relation to the meditation. It disappears after the meditation is over—this is [generally] after prayer, the time of service of the mind and heart. This is true as well of those emotions that arise spontaneously from the mind — see Chapter

לָשׂוּם דָּבָר הַמְעוֹרֵר וְהִיא בִּתְמִידוּת מַמָּשׁ.

וְכָךְ הוּא בַּנֶּפֶשׁ דְּאַהֲבָה הַתְּלוּיָה בְּדָבָר בַּנֶּפֶשׁ הִיא הָאַהֲבָה שֶׁעַל פִּי טַעַם וְדַעַת שֶׁכָּל סִבָּתָהּ הִיא הַהַשָּׂגָה וְהַהִתְבּוֹנְנוּת בֶּאֱלֹקוּת, לְפִי שֶׁאֵינוֹ מֵאִיר בָּזֶה בְּחִינַת הָאַהֲבָה הָעַצְמִית שֶׁבַּנֶּפֶשׁ רַק בְּחִינַת הַכֹּחוֹת הַגְּלוּיִים לְבַד וְהִיא בְּחִינַת הָאַהֲבָה דְּמִדּוֹת שֶׁבַּלֵּב שֶׁסִּבָּתָהּ הִיא הַהִתְבּוֹנְנוּת וְהִיא מֻגְבֶּלֶת לְפִי אוֹפֶן הַהִתְבּוֹנְנוּת וּמִתְעַלֶּמֶת לְאַחַר הִתְחַלְּקוּת הַהַשָּׂגָה וְהַהִתְבּוֹנְנוּת (הַיְנוּ לְאַחַר הַתְּפִלָּה שֶׁהוּא זְמַן הָעֲבוֹדָה בְּמֹחַ וָלֵב. וְדָבָר זֶה הוּא גַם כֵּן בַּמִּדּוֹת שֶׁבָּאִים בְּדֶרֶךְ מִמֵּילָא מֵהַמֹּחִין, עַל פִּי מַה שֶּׁנִּתְבָּאֵר לְעֵיל בְּפ"א בְּפִי' רְעוּתָא דְלִבָּא (רַק שֶׁבֶּאֱמִתִּית בְּחִינַת פְּנִימִיּוּת הַמֹּחִין שֶׁנִּתְבָּאֵר לְעֵיל

In the soul, there is love dependent upon something – on reason and logic.

COMMENTARY

LOVE DEPENDENT ON NOTHING

However, there are times when we undergo a paradigm shift and experience a different level of consciousness. (Here, we are not referring to prophecy, about which the Rambam says in *Hilchot Yesodei HaTorah* 7:1, "Among the principles that one must know is that G-d visits prophecy upon man and he becomes a different person." Prophecy is an actual experience of G-dly revelation, while here we are speaking only of intellectual grasp of spirituality.). We come to the conclusion that G-d is the true reality and the creation is temporal. G-d creates the physical

אֵינוֹ שַׁיָּךְ בָּזֶה הִתְעַלְּמוּת כָּל כָּךְ כוּ'), דְּעִם הֱיוֹת שֶׁזֶּהוּ בְּחִינַת פְּנִימִיּוּת מִכָּל מָקוֹם הֲרֵי הֵן מִדּוֹת שֶׁעַל פִּי טַעַם וָדַעַת וּכְמוֹ שֶׁכָּתוּב בְּמָקוֹם אַחֵר שֶׁגַּם בַּעֲבוֹדָה שֶׁעַל פִּי טַעַם וָדַעַת יֵשׁ בְּחִינַת פְּנִימִיּוּת הַלֵּב וְחִיצוֹנִיּוּת הַלֵּב (וְהִנֵּה נוֹדָע שֶׁיָּכוֹל לִהְיוֹת הַגְדָּלַת הָאַהֲבָה יוֹתֵר מֵהַמּוֹחִין הַמּוֹלִידָהּ וְזֶהוּ מִבְּחִינַת שֹׁרֶשׁ הַמִּדּוֹת שֶׁלְּמַעְלָה מֵהַמּוֹחִין שֶׁזֶּהוּ עִנְיַן דִּזְעֵיר אַנְפִּין בַּעַתִּיקָא אָחִיד וְתַלְיָא כְּמוֹ שֶׁכָּתוּב בְּמָקוֹם אַחֵר, וְהַגְדָּלָה זוֹ כָּאָמוּר אֵינָהּ מִתְעַלֶּמֶת גַּם לְאַחַר הַתְּפִלָּה כוּ')

132   Kuntres Ha'Avoda - קונטרס העבודה

1, the explanation of *re'uta d'liba*. (But regarding the true "inward mindfulness" described earlier, "disappearance" of the love does not really occur...). Even though the emotions [that rise spontaneously from the mind] are internal [and closer to the essence], they are still emotions based upon reason and logic. And as written elsewhere, even service [of G-d] based upon intellect may give rise to either internal or superficial emotions. It is known that love can grow to surpass even the intellect that gave rise to it. This is because the emotions have a source [of their own] that is beyond the intellect, which is [what the Kabbalists mean when they say], *z'a b'atika achid v'talia*, "the G-dly emotions are united with, and dependent upon, His essence and enjoyment."[xxviii] And in truth, when the emotions achieve the pinnacle of growth, they don't disappear even after the time of prayer.

xxviii) See footnote of the Rebbe on page 282

COMMENTARY
---

universe and He can cease creating it at any instant. Therefore, G-d is real and the creation is questionable.

It is this paradigm shift which gives rise to "love that is dependent upon nothing." This is the awareness that is associated with the level of *chaya*, or transcendent consciousness. It is granted as a gift from Above to those of us who have sufficiently meditated and refined our consciousness. Since it is a gift and not directly dependent on any effort we have invested, we can't predict when it will be bestowed. We can prepare ourselves for it, but there is nothing that we can do to guarantee that it will come. Thus, the love of G-d associated with it (also called *ahava rabba*) is dependent upon nothing.

This consciousness is also brought about through the faculty of *da'at*, but this time *da'at* is on a different level completely. It is called *da'at elyon* (higher knowledge), and the perception associated with it is called *yichuda ila'ah* (higher unity). On this

Essay on Service of the Heart - Love Like Fire and Water

Now, the love in the soul that is "not dependent upon anything" is love of G-d that is [totally] beyond reason and logic. It is an essential love of G-d, within which we find two levels [*chaya* and *yechida*]. The first level is the transcendent level of love and will for connection known as *chaya*, which requires arousal (since it is not the true essence of the soul that is in absolute proximity to the infinite One Above) by meditation on the amazing exaltedness of His infinite light (this, too, is beyond anything that is graspable by human intellect). But once ultimately aroused, this love expresses the very essence of the soul. This is because in truth, it is not the meditation that gives rise to this love [of the One Above]. Rather, within the essence of the soul is a love and intense will for the infinite light of G-d [that is aroused through meditation]. But the *yechida* within the soul does not

וְאַהֲבָה שֶׁאֵינָהּ תְּלוּיָה בְּדָבָר הִיא הָאַהֲבָה שֶׁלְּמַעְלָה מִטַּעַם וְדַעַת דְּהַיְנוּ שֶׁהִיא בְּחִינַת אַהֲבָה עַצְמִית וּבָזֶה יֵשׁ ב' מַדְרֵגוֹת, הָא' בְּחִינַת אַהֲבָה דְּהַיְנוּ הָרָצוֹן דְּמַדְרֵגַת מַקִּיף דְחַי' שֶׁצְּרִיכָה מִכָּל מָקוֹם הִתְעוֹרְרוּת (לְפִי שֶׁאֵינוֹ בְּחִינַת עַצְמוּת הַנְּשָׁמָה מַמָּשׁ שֶׁהִיא בִּבְחִינַת קֵרוּב מַמָּשׁ בְּעַצְמוּת אֵין סוֹף בָּרוּךְ הוּא וְלָזֹאת צְרִיכָה הִתְעוֹרְרוּת) עַל יְדֵי הִתְבּוֹנְנוּת הַהַפְלָאָה דְּאוֹר אֵין סוֹף (שֶׁזֶּהוּ גַּם כֵּן לְמַעְלָה מִבְּחִינַת טַעַם וְדַעַת הַמֻּשָּׂג מַמָּשׁ) אָמְנָם כַּאֲשֶׁר מִתְעוֹרֵר הוּא בִּבְחִינַת רָצוֹן עַצְמִי, כִּי בֶּאֱמֶת לֹא הַהִתְבּוֹנְנוּת הִיא סִבַּת הָאַהֲבָה כִּי אִם מַה שֶּׁבְּעֶצֶם יֵשׁ בַּנְּשָׁמָה בְּחִינַת אַהֲבָה וְרָצוֹא לְאוֹר אֵין סוֹף בָּרוּךְ הוּא. וּבְחִינַת יְחִידָה שֶׁבַּנֶּפֶשׁ אֵין צָרִיךְ לְשׁוּם הִתְעוֹרְרוּת כְּלָל לְפִי שֶׁהוּא בִּבְחִינַת קֵרוּב עִם הָעַצְמוּת וְאֵינוֹ

And there is love dependent upon nothing — beyond reason and logic. It requires meditation on the infinite light of G-d.

---- **COMMENTARY** ----

level, our awareness is of G-d, with creation secondary. G-d is in the foreground, occupying our attention, and His creation is in the background. In this paradigm, the *sephira* of *da'at* is situated above *chochma* and *bina* in the structure of the ten *sephirot*, as opposed to below them. It functions as an intermediary drawing the infinite light of G-d into our mind and emotions together. On this level, *da'at* is the vehicle for bringing down the infinite light of G-d and causing the intellect and the emotions to function as one, in an organic unity. This is the essence of an elevated spiritual experience — we surpass our own ego and are able to view ourselves and the world from a higher, G-dly plane.

Love dependent on nothing is associated with chaya and yechida.

שֶׁיָּךְ בָּזֶה שׁוּם הִתְעַלְּמוּת כְּלָל, וּכְמוֹ אַהֲבַת אָב וּבֵן דְּעִם הֱיוֹת שֶׁאֵינָהּ בְּהִתְגַּלּוּת אֵינָהּ מִתְעַלֶּמֶת לְעוֹלָם וְהִיא בִּבְחִינַת הִתְקַשְּׁרוּת עַצְמִית וּתְמִידִית כו' וּכְמוֹ שֶׁכָּתוּב בְּמָקוֹם אַחֵר.

וְהִנֵּה בְּחִינַת רָצוֹן הַנַּ"ל הֲגַם שֶׁזֶּהוּ מַדְרֵגָה גְּבוֹהָה מְאֹד בַּעֲבוֹדָה מִכָּל מָקוֹם אֵין זֶה פּוֹעֵל כָּל כָּךְ עַל הַחָמְרִיּוּת דְּנֶפֶשׁ הַבַּהֲמִית מִפְּנֵי שֶׁהוּא לְמַעְלָה מִבְּחִינַת הִתְלַבְּשׁוּת

require an arousal at all. It is in such close proximity to the essence [of G-d] that it never [loses its connection nor] becomes hidden at all. It is analogous to the love between father and son—although it is not always expressed, it never disappears. This is an essential, constant bond, as written elsewhere.

Now the will for connection mentioned earlier [the *chaya*], despite being an exceedingly high level of "service of the One Above," nevertheless does not have a noticeable effect on the gross earthiness of the animal

---------- **COMMENTARY** ----------

Also in the paradigm of *da'at elyon*, the ten *sephirot* are arranged differently. Instead of being arranged in a linear fashion, as in *da'at tachton* (lower knowledge) the *sephirot* are arranged in a series of triplets. *Da'at* is located above the intellectual *sephirot* of *chochma* and *bina*, followed by the emotional triplet of *chesed*, *gevura*, and *tiferet*, and finally the action triplet of *netzach*, *hod*, and *yesod*, followed by *malchut*:

Awareness of *Da'at Elyon* and *Yichuda Ila'ah*	
Da'at "knowledge"	
Bina "understanding"	*Chochma* "wisdom"
Gevura "strength"	*Chesed* "loving-indness"
Tiferet "beauty"	
Hod "thanksgiving"	*Netzach* "victory"
Yesod "foundation"	
Malchut "sovereignty"	

Essay on Service of the Heart - Love Like Fire and Water

soul. That is because it is above being clad in the animal soul. (Although love which is beyond logic and reason is generally "love like fire"—aside from *ahava beta'anugim* [love with delight] or cleaving to the One Above, within which there are two levels: *ohr yashar*, ["direct light" from above to below] and *ohr chozer* ["reflected light" from below to above],[xxix] as explained elsewhere—nevertheless since the soul-level that gives rise to this love is above being garbed in the animal soul, it doesn't have much effect upon it.³⁶)

It's true that this level [love from the *chaya*] is also subject to concealment and obfuscation by the animal soul, (as is written in the *Tanya*, chapter 19, and in *Igeret HaKodesh*, chapter 4). Still, [the animal soul may escape], when the arousal of transcendent love of G-d comes from our animal soul itself, from its predicament of exile [where it was consigned] when the inner sanctum of our heart

בְּנֶפֶשׁ הַבַּהֲמִית (עִם הֱיוֹת דְּהָאַהֲבָה שֶׁלְּמַעֲלָה מִטַּעַם וָדַעַת בְּדֶרֶךְ כְּלָל הִיא בִּבְחִינַת אַהֲבָה כְּרִשְׁפֵּי אֵשׁ (לְבַד בְּחִינַת אַהֲבָה בְּתַעֲנוּגִים שֶׁהִיא בִּבְחִינַת דְּבֵקוּת וְגַם בָּזֶה יֵשׁ בְּחִינַת אוֹר יָשָׁר וְאוֹר חוֹזֵר וּכְמוֹ שֶׁכָּתוּב בְּמָקוֹם אַחֵר) וּמִכָּל מָקוֹם לְפִי שֶׁמַּדְרֵגָה זוֹ דִּנְשָׁמָה הִיא לְמַעֲלָה מֵהִתְלַבְּשׁוּת בְּנֶפֶשׁ הַבַּהֲמִית אֵינָהּ פּוֹעֶלֶת כָּל כָּךְ עַל הַנֶּפֶשׁ הַבַּהֲמִית.

הֲגַם שֶׁעַל מַדְרֵגָה זוֹ יֵשׁ גַּם כֵּן הֶעְלֵם וְהֶסְתֵּר הַנֶּפֶשׁ הַבַּהֲמִית וּכְמוֹ שֶׁכָּתוּב בְּסֵפֶר שֶׁל בֵּינוֹנִים פִּי"ט וּבְאִגֶּרֶ"הּ סִי' ד' דִּבּוּר הַמַּתְחִיל אֵין יִשְׂרָאֵל נִגְאָלִין אֶלָּא בִּצְדָקָה, הִנֵּה בֶּאֱמֶת כַּאֲשֶׁר הִתְעוֹרְרוּת הַמַּקִּיף דִּנְשָׁמָה הִיא מִצַּד הַנֶּפֶשׁ הַבַּהֲמִית דְּהַיְינוּ מִן הַמֵּצַר דְּגָלוּת הַנְּשָׁמָה דְּהַיְינוּ מַה שֶּׁהִלְבִּישׁ בְּחִינַת פְּנִימִית נְקֻדַּת לִבָּבוֹ בָּזֶה לְעֻמַּת זֶה כוּ' וְעוֹד

xxix) See footnote of the Rebbe on page 283 ←

Love on the level of chaya has no effect on the animal soul, but sometimes the animal soul breaks out of its own bounds and transforms itself.

COMMENTARY

HITAMTUT

What leads to the paradigm shift described above? The answer is: focus and concentration (see *Yom tov shel Rosh Hashana 5666*, page 151, and *B'sha'ah shehikdimu 5672*, vol. 2, page 1180). Focus and concentration lead us to three more meditative events; *hakara* (recognition), *hitamtut* (validation), and *re'iya b'eyn hasechel* (seeing in the mind's eye).

After delving deeply into a concept, abstracting and removing as much of the "packaging" and "garments" as possible — a process known as *p'nimiyut bina* ("inner dimensions of understanding") — we come to recognize and feel the essence became en-clothed in the "opposing forces" [that is, forces opposed to holiness]. And even more, [the animal soul may find a way out] when we suffer terribly from its coarse physicality with its multiple lusts which even en-clothe the innermost spiritual point of the heart. It is this that produces the [motivation and strength for the soul] to exit all limitations and leave them behind with a rush to G-d, beyond all reason and logic. When this happens, it has an effect on the animal soul, freeing it of all constraints and concealments and even turning them into G-dliness. (There are several levels of ascent to the One Above, depending upon the previous limitations [of the soul].) But, when the arousal comes from the divine soul [alone] (that is, through meditation on the exalted infinite light of G-d), it does not have much of an effect on the physical coarseness of the animal soul. As for that which is written in the *Tanya*, chapter 43, concerning the love of G-d which comes from meditation on His greatness, and which was explained earlier in Chapter 4 [that the love has an effect on the animal soul], this is speaking of the divine soul as en-clothed in the animal soul, as written in *Igeret HaKodesh*, chapter 4, mentioned earlier, where it is stated that this takes place in the outer, external levels of the heart, and so is also stated in the *Tanya*, introduction to part 2, *Chinuch Katan*.

יוֹתֵר מִזֶּה כַּאֲשֶׁר צַר לוֹ מְאֹד מֵחָמְרִיּוּת הַנֶּפֶשׁ הַבַּהֲמִית וְגַסּוּתוֹ בְּרִבּוּי תַּאֲוֹותָיו עַד שֶׁהַלְבִּישׁ גַּם פְּנִימִית נְקֻדַּת לְבָבוֹ בָּזֶה, וּמִזֶּה נַעֲשָׂה הַיְצִיאָה בִּבְחִינַת תֹּקֶף הָרָצוֹא שֶׁלְּמַעְלָה מִטַּעַם וָדַעַת, הֲרֵי זֶה פּוֹעֵל עַל הַנֶּפֶשׁ הַבַּהֲמִית לְהָסִיר הַהֶעְלֵמוֹת וְהַהֶסְתֵּרִים וְגַם לְהָפְכָם לֶאֱלֹקוּת (כִּי יֵשׁ בָּזֶה כַּמָּה מַדְרֵגוֹת בְּאֹפֶן הָרָצוֹא וְתָלוּי בְּהַמֵּיצַר הַקּוֹדֵם כוּ'), אֲבָל כַּאֲשֶׁר הַהִתְעוֹרְרוּת הוּא מִצַּד הַנְּשָׁמָה (דְּהַיְנוּ מֵהִתְבּוֹנְנוּת הַהַפְלָאָה דְּאוֹר אֵין סוֹף בָּרוּךְ הוּא) אֵין זֶה פּוֹעֵל כָּל כָּךְ עַל הַחָמְרִיּוּת דְּנֶפֶשׁ הַבַּהֲמִית. וּמַה שֶּׁכָּתוּב בְּסֵפֶר שֶׁל בֵּינוֹנִים פמ״ג בְּהָאַהֲבָה הַבָּאָה מֵהִתְבּוֹנְנוּת גְּדֻלָּתוֹ יִתְבָּרֵךְ וּכְמוֹ שֶׁנִּתְבָּאֵר לְעֵיל פ״ד, זֶהוּ הַכֹּל בְּמַדְרֵגַת הַנְּשָׁמָה שֶׁמִּתְלַבֶּשֶׁת בַּנֶּפֶשׁ הַבַּהֲמִית וּכְמוֹ שֶׁכָּתוּב בְּאגה״ק סי׳ הַנַ״ל שֶׁזֶּהוּ בְּחִינַת חִיצוֹנִיּוּת הַלֵּב וְכֵן הוּא בְּסֵפֶר שֶׁל בֵּינוֹנִים בְּהַקְדָּמַת ח״ב הַנִּקְרָא חִנּוּךְ קָטָן).

COMMENTARY

of the concept through *da'at*. As noted earlier, we not only understand but internalize it to the point of experiencing the concept on a gut level. This is *hakara* and it is the inner soul experience of *da'at*.

Essay on Service of the Heart - Love Like Fire and Water

But, one cannot say about the *yechida* of the [divine] soul that it has no effect on the coarseness of the animal soul. Certainly, upon revelation of the *yechida*, there is a complete metamorphosis of the animal soul, which is transformed from one extreme to the other. For example, if we were ready to actually die in order to sanctify the Name of G-d, and for whatever reason were saved by Him, there would be no doubt, nor even shadow of a doubt, that our animal soul would be transformed completely, from one extreme to the other. We would become a totally different person. The experience of revelation of the essence of our soul would certainly bring about a change in our animal soul as well, which would become transformed completely. This is not unlike the effect of giving up our life for G-d, [knowing that we must die in order to sanctify the Name of the One Above], when the animal soul wants only to live.

אָמְנָם בִּבְחִינַת יְחִידָה שֶׁבַּנֶּפֶשׁ אִי אֶפְשָׁר לוֹמַר שֶׁאֵינוֹ פּוֹעֵל עַל חָמְרִיּוּת הַנֶּפֶשׁ הַבַּהֲמִית, דְּוַדַּאי בְּהִתְגַּלּוּת בְּחִינַת יְחִידָה שֶׁבַּנֶּפֶשׁ הֲרֵי זֶה פּוֹעֵל בְּהַנֶּפֶשׁ הַבַּהֲמִית לַהֲפֹךְ עֶצֶם מַהוּתוֹ מֵהַהֶפֶךְ אֶל הַהֶפֶךְ, וּכְמוֹ כְּשֶׁבָּא לִידֵי מְסִירַת נֶפֶשׁ בְּפֹעַל מַמָּשׁ עַל קִדּוּשׁ הַשֵּׁם וּמֵאֵיזֶה סִבָּה מֵהַשֵּׁם יִתְבָּרֵךְ נִצַּל מִזֶּה הִנֵּה בְּלִי שׁוּם סָפֵק וּסְפֵק סְפֵיקָא שֶׁנִּשְׁתַּנָּה נַפְשׁוֹ הַטִּבְעִית וְנִתְהַפֵּךְ מִן הַקָּצֶה אֶל הַקָּצֶה שֶׁנַּעֲשֶׂה אָדָם אַחֵר מַמָּשׁ, שֶׁהֲרֵי הֲיִי אֶצְלוֹ הִתְגַּלּוּת עֶצֶם הַנְּשָׁמָה מַמָּשׁ וְזֶה בְּוַדַּאי פּוֹעֵל עַל נַפְשׁוֹ הַבַּהֲמִית הַטִּבְעִית לְשַׁנּוֹתָהּ וּלְהָפְכָהּ לְגַמְרֵי וּכְמוֹ שֶׁפּוֹעֵל בּוֹ עֶצֶם הַמְּסִירוּת נֶפֶשׁ שֶׁיֵּהָרֵג עַל קִדּוּשׁ הַשֵּׁם שֶׁהַנֶּפֶשׁ הַטִּבְעִית מִצַּד עַצְמָהּ רוֹצָה רַק לִחְיוֹת

Upon revelation of the yechida, there is a complete metamorphosis of the animal soul.

COMMENTARY

If we don't stop there but continue to concentrate, we will experience a validation or corroboration of our meditation, called *hitamtut* (from the word for *emet*, meaning truth); this validation is accompanied by seeing the concept in our mind's eye, called *re'iya b'eyn hasechel*. *Hitamtut* is a unifying "moment of truth," an epiphany that confirms our meditation. It is a revelation of the overall picture occuring after we have focused properly on the details of G-dliness in the creation (see ch. 4 of the Mittler Rebbe's *Sha'ar HaYichud*).

In part, *hitamut* is intellectual — after concentrating on the details for a long time, we are suddenly able to synthesize them into a coherent whole. However, there is also a spiritual

(וְצָרִיךְ עִיּוּן אִם יֵשׁ בְּהַנֶּפֶשׁ הַטִּבְעִית גַּם בִּבְחִינַת כֹּחַ נֶעֱלָם לִמְסֹר נַפְשׁוֹ בְּפֹעַל מַמָּשׁ עַל קִדּוּשׁ הַשֵּׁם, שֶׁהֲרֵי הַכֹּחַ דִּמְסִירוּת נֶפֶשׁ הוּא מִצַּד הַהִתְקַשְּׁרוּת עַצְמִית שֶׁאִי אֶפְשָׁר לוֹ לִהְיוֹת נִפְרָד מֵאֱלֹקוּת, וְזֶה שַׁיָּךְ רַק בְּנֶפֶשׁ הָאֱלֹקִית לֹא בַּנֶּפֶשׁ הַטִּבְעִית שֶׁהִיא מִקְּלִפַּת נֹגַהּ, וְהַמְסִירוּת נֶפֶשׁ דְּנֶפֶשׁ הַטִּבְעִית וְכֵן בְּחִינַת תֹּקֶף הָרָצוֹא דְּנֶפֶשׁ הַטִּבְעִית שֶׁהוּא בְּהִתְגַּבְּרוּת יְתֵרָה מֵהָרָצוֹא דְּנֶפֶשׁ הָאֱלֹקִית מִצַּד עַצְמָהּ כַּנּוֹדָע, הַכֹּל מֵהַנֶּפֶשׁ הָאֱלֹקִית שֶׁפּוֹעֵל עַל הַנֶּפֶשׁ הַטִּבְעִית, וְכֵן הַהַעֲלָאָה דְּנֶפֶשׁ הַבַּהֲמִית מִצַּד עַצְמָהּ וְכַנּוֹדָע בְּעִנְיַן הַהַעֲלָאָה מִלְּמַטָּה לְמַעְלָה שֶׁזֶּהוּ מַה שֶּׁהַתַּחְתּוֹנִים מִצַּד עַצְמָם עוֹלִים כוּ' שֶׁזֶּהוּ עִנְיַן מַיִם תַּחְתּוֹנִים בּוֹכִין כוּ' וּכְמוֹ שֶׁכָּתוּב בְּמָקוֹם אַחֵר. כָּל זֶה הוּא מַה שֶּׁהַנֶּפֶשׁ הָאֱלֹקִית פּוֹעֵל

(An investigation is needed in order to ascertain whether there is a hidden power within the animal soul enabling it to surrender and die in sanctification of G-d's Name. This power of giving ourselves up comes from an essential bond that simply does not permit us to become separated from G-dliness. Such a level of commitment is only appropriate to the divine soul, and not to the natural soul which comes from *klipat nogah*, [the level of concealment of G-dliness within which there is mixed good and bad]. The ability of the animal soul to "surrender," as well as the thirst of the animal soul for G-dliness[xxx] — accompanied with extra power beyond the thirst of the divine soul itself, as is known—is all a result of the divine soul having a [positive] effect upon the animal soul. The same is true of

xxx) See footnote of the Rebbe on page 286

COMMENTARY

component in *hitamtut* because the "whole" that emerges from the revelation is greater than the sum of all the details. We are lifted to a new level of G-dly understanding and perception, which transfixes our attention and mesmerizes us. It therefore leads immediately to *re'iya b'eyn hasechel*, or grasping the concept so clearly that it is as if one sees it in his mind's eye (but not with the naked eye).

In prayer, *hitamtut* corresponds to the sentences that we say immediately after the first three paragraphs of the *Shema*. At that point in morning prayers, we recite several phrases beginning with the word *emet*. This is the time during prayer that our divine soul "takes over," so to speak. With the revelation of *hitamtut* from above, it breaks free of the bonds of our animal soul. It then leads us into the highest point of the prayer, the

the ascent and elevation of the animal soul of its own volition, as is known regarding the spiritual elevation of anything in the lower worlds which takes place through the power and incentive of the creations themselves. [This is known in Kabbalah as] "the lower waters cry out [to G-d]..." as written elsewhere. Yet, all of this is [part of] the effect that the divine soul produces within the animal soul. It is true that there is a certain superiority in this [love of the animal soul over the love of the divine soul]. [Its love] transforms the source of the animal soul—which comes from a place of hidden [essential] G-dliness that transcends spiritual revelation, as is known. But, this isn't to say that the animal soul, of its own volition and by its own nature, now desires G-dliness. Nor does this contradict what is written elsewhere in several places that the power of lust and desire isn't bad in of itself, as written in *Likutei Torah*, in the discourse beginning with *Zot chukat HaTorah*. What this does mean is that the animal soul, in and of itself, does not adopt any specific evil form. However, it [certainly] isn't good, and in fact quite the opposite, its nature is to be drawn toward the vulgar and the physical. And if so, the whole matter of surrendering ourselves in order to sanctify His Name is really opposed to the nature of the animal soul.)

בְּנֶפֶשׁ הַבַּהֲמִית וְיֵשׁ בָּזֶה יִתְרוֹן מִצַּד שֹׁרֶשׁ וּמָקוֹר דְּהַהֶעְלָמוֹת וְהַהֶסְתֵּרִים שֶׁלְּמַעְלָה מִבְּחִינַת הַגִּלּוּי כַּנּוֹדָע, אֲבָל לֹא שֶׁהַנֶּפֶשׁ הַבַּהֲמִית בְּעַצְמוֹ בְּטִבְעוֹ יִרְצֶה בֶּאֱלֹקוּת. וְאֵין זֶה סוֹתֵר לְמַה שֶׁכָּתוּב בְּכַמָּה דּוּכְתֵי שֶׁהַכֹּחַ הַמִּתְאַוֶּה בְּעַצְמוֹ אֵינוֹ רַע וּכְמוֹ שֶׁכָּתוּב בְּלִקּוּטֵי תּוֹרָה דִּבּוּר הַמַּתְחִיל זֹאת חֻקַּת הַתּוֹרָה זֶהוּ רַק שֶׁאֵין בּוֹ צִיּוּר רַע בְּעֶצֶם אֲבָל מִכָּל מָקוֹם אֵינוֹ טוֹב וְאַדְּרַבָּא בְּטִבְעוֹ הוּא נִמְשָׁךְ לְעִנְיָנִים חָמְרִיִּים וְאִם כֵּן עִנְיַן הַמְסִירוּת נֶפֶשׁ עַל קִדּוּשׁ הַשֵּׁם הוּא הֵפֶךְ טִבְעוֹ לְגַמְרֵי)

COMMENTARY

Amida, which is recited silently in the presence of the One Above.

It must be noted that *Hitamtut* and *re'iya b'eyn hasechel* do not necessarily lead us to the soul-experience of *chaya* and to *da'at elyon*. This depends on the content of our meditation. If the meditation is focused upon "immanent G-dliness" (*memalle kol olamin*) - concepts of G-dliness en-clothed in the creation, whether in physical creation or in the higher spiritual worlds, -

Revelation of the divine soul transforms the animal soul, as does teshuva.

וְהַנֶּפֶשׁ הָאֱלֹקִית פּוֹעֵל עָלָיו שֶׁאֵין שׁוּם מְנִיעָה מִצִּדּוֹ לִמְסֹר נַפְשׁוֹ וְאַדְרַבָּה גַּם הוּא רוֹצֶה לִמְסֹר נַפְשׁוֹ בְּפֹעַל מַמָּשׁ, מִמֵּילָא מוּבָן שֶׁגַּם עֶצֶם הַחָמְרִיּוּת שֶׁלּוֹ מִתְהַפֵּךְ לְגַמְרֵי מִן הַקָּצֶה אֶל הַקָּצֶה, וּכְמוֹ בִּתְשׁוּבָה אֲמִתִּית בִּיצִיאַת וְהִתְגַּלּוּת עֶצֶם הַנְּשָׁמָה הֲרֵי מִתְהַפֵּךְ מַהוּת עֶצֶם הַנֶּפֶשׁ הַבַּהֲמִית וּבִפְרָט כַּאֲשֶׁר הַצְּעָקָה הִיא גַּם מִן הַנֶּפֶשׁ הַבַּהֲמִית, וְהַיְנוּ כַּאֲשֶׁר הַמֵּצַר הוּא בְּעֹמֶק בְּיוֹתֵר שֶׁאֵין לוֹ שׁוּם מָקוֹם בְּעַצְמוֹ (אַז די ניט גוטסקייט איז זייער טיף אוּן זייער שטארק אז ער האט ניט קיין שום צופרידענקייט און קיין שום נחת בעצמו און האט ביי זיך קיין שום ארט בפועל ממש) שֶׁזֶּהוּ הוֹרָאָה שֶׁהַצַּעַר וְהַמֵּצַר הוּא מֵהַנֶּפֶשׁ הַבַּהֲמִית שֶׁהַנֶּפֶשׁ הַבַּהֲמִית לֹא טוֹב לוֹ וּמִצְטַעֵר עַל רְחוּקוֹ (וְהַיְנוּ מַה שֶּׁהַנֶּפֶשׁ הָאֱלֹקִית פּוֹעֵל עָלָיו כנ״ל)

The divine soul has an effect upon the animal soul, such that it has no objection and presents no obstacle to our surrendering ourselves. Quite the opposite, it as well wants to give itself up for the sake of G-d. We understand that the deep-seated coarseness of the animal soul becomes transformed totally from one extreme to the other. This is similar to true *teshuva*, ("return" to the One Above), in which the expression and revelation of the essence of the soul transforms the basic nature of the animal soul, especially when the [primal] scream [for G-d] is coming from the animal soul itself. When we find ourselves in such dire straits that we lose our [sense of constructive existence], this is an indication that our suffering and feeling of being stifled come from our animal soul. It is the animal soul that feels that things are not good, and it

--- **COMMENTARY** ---

then the corroborating experience of *hitamtut* will be also be of G-dliness en-clothed in and enlivening the world; it will then be on the level of *neshama* rather than *chaya*). We will experience deeper insight into the very essence and G-dly nature of creation (as described in chapters 1 and 4), and we will be granted total grasp and recognition of the essence of G-dliness within creation (see *Yom Tov shel Rosh Hashana*, 5666, page 150). It is when the meditation leading up to *hitamtut* includes concepts of transcendent G-dliness (*sovev kol olamim*), that the resultant revelation includes recognition of the amazing, exalted nature of G-dliness as He surpasses creation. This is the experience of *chaya*, as described below.

Essay on Service of the Heart - Love Like Fire and Water

experiences distress over its distance [from G-d] (as a result of the influence of the divine soul, as mentioned above). The suffering of the animal soul is immense. (This is for two reasons: One, because the animal soul itself has brought about this distance; indeed, it is because of the animal soul that this [distance] is natural; and two, because the animal soul is not an inherently G-dly power.) We understand that there is a sense of G-dliness within this experience of suffering. It comes from the experience of distance, as written elsewhere regarding remorse — that through it, the suffering is magnified. And in the [primal] scream with which we cry out from the bitterness of our soul—with the strength of abandoning our limitations and with a rush to the One Above (as if we were running away from death to

שֶׁהַצַּעַר שֶׁלוֹ הוּא גָּדוֹל בְּיוֹתֵר (וְזֶהוּ מִב' סִבּוֹת א' מִפְּנֵי שֶׁהָרִחוּק הוּא מֵאִתּוֹ וּבְסִבָּתוֹ וְזֶה אֶצְלוֹ עִנְיָן טִבְעִי, וְהַב' מִפְּנֵי שֶׁאֵינוֹ כֹּחַ אֱלֹקִי בְּעַצְמָם) (וּמוּבָן דִּבְהַצַּעַר יֵשׁ בּוֹ הֶרְגֵּשׁ הָאֱלֹקִי מִמַּה שֶׁנִּתְרַחֵק כְּמוֹ שֶׁכָּתוּב בְּמָקוֹם אַחֵר בְּעִנְיַן הַמְּרִירוּת דְּעַל יְדֵי זֶה הַצַּעַר גָּדוֹל בְּיוֹתֵר כו') הִנֵּה בְּהַצְּעָקָה שֶׁצּוֹעֵק בְּמַר נַפְשׁוֹ בִּבְחִינַת תֹּקֶף הַיְצִיאָה וְהָרָצוֹא (כְּבוֹרֵחַ מִן הַמָּוֶת אֶל הַחַיִּים כו') הֲרֵי מִשְׁתַּנֶּה מַהוּתוֹ לְגַמְרֵי מִכֹּל וָכֹל כו'. וּמוּבָן מִכָּל הנ"ל דִּבְחִינַת הִתְגַּלּוּת יְחִידָה שֶׁבַּנֶּפֶשׁ פּוֹעֵל גַּם עַל הַחָמְרִיּוּת וְהוֹפֵךְ מַהוּתוֹ לְגַמְרֵי (וְהַיְנוּ מִפְּנֵי שֶׁבְּחִינַת יְחִידָה שֶׁבַּנֶּפֶשׁ מִפְשֶׁטֶת לְגַמְרֵי וְאֵין לָהּ שׁוּם אֲחִיזָה כְּלָל בְּהַכֹּחוֹת פְּנִימִיִּים הֲרֵי הִיא פּוֹעֶלֶת בְּכָל מָקוֹם מִצַּד הַהַגְדָּרָה שֶׁעֶצֶם

COMMENTARY

ANOTHER WAY

The path to the soul-level of *chaya* requires a new technique. After using our *da'at* to focus on a concept, we bypass *hakara*, *hitamtut* and *re'iya b'eyn hasechel*, and instead we perform what the Rambam calls "circumscription of knowledge" (*yediat hashlila*, already described in the commentary to chapter one). That is, recognizing that G-d is beyond whatever positive description or human comprehension we may apply to Him, we may decide to override our intellectual grasp by describing it in negative terms. Negation here means that we use our understanding as a springboard to arrive at a higher understanding. By circumscribing our understanding, and couching it in negative terms, we actually extend our grasp of G-dliness by a quantum

הַנֶּפֶשׁ מְגֻדֶּרֶת עַל כָּל פָּנִים בְּגוּף כְּמוֹ שֶׁכָּתוּב בְּמָקוֹם אַחֵר, וְהָרְאָיָ׳ שֶׁהֲרֵי בְּחִינַת יְחִידָה נִמְצָא בֶּאֱמֶת בְּכָל הַכֹּחוֹת עַד גַּם בְּסוֹף מַעֲשֶׂה וּכְמוֹ שֶׁכָּתוּב בְּמָקוֹם אַחֵר).

life...)—we completely transform our essence. From all of this, we understand that a revelation of the *yechida* of the soul has an effect on the coarse earthiness [of the animal soul] and transforms it completely. (This is because the *yechida* of the soul is totally abstract and has no connection with any of the inner soul powers. Therefore, it has an overall effect on the totality of the soul, since the essence of the soul is defined as[xxxi] being en-clothed in the body, as written elsewhere. The proof of this is that the *yechida* is found in all of the powers of the soul, including the lowest level of the power of action, as written elsewhere.)

xxxi) See footnote of the Rebbe on page 288

The *yechida*, being totally abstract, is not limited by any of the ten soul powers, which are the inner manifestations of the ten *sephirot* within the soul of a person. However, even though it is not enclothed in the body, the *yechida* is nonetheless associated with it, and may influence any or all of the ten soul powers all of which exist on the five levels of the soul (both the animal and the divine soul).

Sephira	**External Manifestation**	**Soul Power**
Keter: *Atik Yomin*	Unattainable transcendence	Enjoyment
Arich Anpin	Attainable transcendence	Will
10. *Chochma*	Spiritual Insight	Self-nullification
9. *Bina*	Intellectual Analysis	Happiness
8. *Da'at*	Visceral knowledge	Recognition
7. *Chesed*	Kindness	Love of G-d
6. *Gevura*	Strictness/Strength	Fear of G-d
5. *Tiferet*	Beauty	Mercy
4. *Netzach*	Pro-activity	Security
3. *Hod*	Re-activity	Integrity
2. *Yesod*	Perseverance	Truth
1. *Malchut*	Sovereignty	Humility

———— **COMMENTARY** ————

level. We project ourselves to a whole new plane of G-dliness that allows room for both our previous limited grasp and for

Essay on Service of the Heart - Love Like Fire and Water

Even though we crave spirituality, we are tempted by physical attractions.

The hidden love of G-d in each of us as Jews—such that each and every one of us naturally craves G-dliness—is a desire that has no effect on our physical nature. We see clearly that even though each and every Jew truly wants G-dliness, and that this is our nature, nevertheless on a conscious level we are attracted to worldly matters. This is because our "hidden love" is transcendent and unconscious. This is the case as well regarding revelation of the transcendent desire [or soul level] of *chaya*, which comes about through the arousal of meditation, as described earlier. Although it is a very high level, expressing a true reality within our [divine] soul, nevertheless it has no effect on the corporeality of the animal soul. This is because as a

אַךְ בְּחִינַת הָאַהֲבָה מְסֻתֶּרֶת שֶׁבְּכָל אֶחָד וְאֶחָד מִיִּשְׂרָאֵל שֶׁכָּל אֶחָד וְאֶחָד רוֹצֶה בְּטִבְעוֹ בֶּאֱלֹקוּת, הֲרֵי הָרָצוֹן הַזֶּה אֵינוֹ פּוֹעֵל בַּחָמְרִיּוּת, וּכְמוֹ שֶׁאָנוּ רוֹאִין בְּחוּשׁ דְּעִם הֱיוֹת דְּכָל אֶחָד וְאֶחָד מִיִּשְׂרָאֵל רוֹצֶה בֶּאֱמֶת בֶּאֱלֹקוּת שֶׁזֶּהוּ בְּטֶבַע בְּנַפְשׁוֹ, וּמִכָּל מָקוֹם בְּהַכֹּחוֹת הַגְּלוּיִים הֲרֵי הוּא נִמְשָׁךְ אַחֲרֵי עִנְיְנֵי הָעוֹלָם. וְזֶהוּ מִפְּנֵי שֶׁהָאַהֲבָה הִיא בִּבְחִינַת מַקִּיף וּבְהֶעְלֵם הִנֵּה כְּמוֹ כֵן הוּא גַּם בְּהִתְגַּלּוּת בְּחִינַת הָרָצוֹן דִּבְחִינַת מַקִּיף דְּחַיָּ' הַבָּא עַל יְדֵי הִתְעוֹרְרוּת הַהִתְבּוֹנְנוּת הַנַּ"ל, הֲגַם שֶׁהִיא מַדְרֵגָה גְּבוֹהָה מְאֹד וְהִיא אֲמִתִּית בַּנֶּפֶשׁ מִכָּל מָקוֹם אֵין זֶה פּוֹעֵל עַל הַחָמְרִי' דְּנֶפֶשׁ הַבַּהֲמִית מִפְּנֵי שֶׁהָרָצוֹא הוּא בִּבְחִינַת מַקִּיף

COMMENTARY

---

a new spiritual awareness. (For example, while we cannot describe G-d as "merciful" in the same sense as man is merciful, we can say about Him that He is *not* the opposite of merciful. His mercy is not limited by our definitions, but is infinitely greater. Thus, we negate our own understanding of what "merciful" means in order to gain some kind of idea of what G-dly mercy may be.)

This is what the Chassidic teachings mean by "understanding one thing from another." By taking our understanding of G-dliness as en-clothed in the creation and negating it, we arrive at a glimpse of G-dliness as it surpasses and transcends the creation. This technique ultimately brings us to "knowledge of that which is amazing" (*yediat hahafla'ah*), which is also called "gazing upon the glory of the King" (*istaclut b'yikara d'malka*). We now are able to soar to the infinite light of the One Above, an experience which is equivalent to the love of "fire from

The chaya is a transcendent desire for G-dliness that does not affect our physical nature.

דְּנֶפֶשׁ שֶׁאֵינוֹ מַלְבָּשׁ בַּהַכֹּחוֹת פְּנִימִיִּים וּבַכֹּחוֹת הַטִּבְעִיִּים. וַהֲרֵי זֶה כְּמוֹ עִנְיַן הָאֱמוּנָה שֶׁהִיא גַם כֵּן בִּבְחִינַת מַקִּיף (רַק שֶׁזֶּהוּ כְּמוֹ שֶׁבָּא בִּבְחִינַת מַלְכוּת וְהוּא בְּחִינַת כֶּתֶר מַלְכוּת כו') שֶׁאָמְרוּ רַבּוֹתֵינוּ זִכְרוֹנָם לִבְרָכָה עַל זֶה גַּנָּבָא אַפּוּם מַחְתַּרְתָּא רַחֲמָנָא קָרֵי' שֶׁהוּא מַאֲמִין בַּה' וּבְהַשְׁגָּחָתוֹ וִיכָלְתּוֹ יִתְבָּרֵךְ וּמִכָּל מָקוֹם אֵין זֶה פּוֹעֵל עָלָיו שֶׁלֹּא לַעֲבֹר עַל רְצוֹנוֹ ית', דְּעִם הֱיוֹת שֶׁמִּצַּד הַנֶּפֶשׁ הוּא מַאֲמִין בֶּאֱמֶת מִכָּל מָקוֹם מִצַּד הַחָמְרִיּוּת הֲרֵי הוּא עוֹשֶׂה הֵפֶךְ רְצוֹנוֹ יִתְבָּרֵךְ וְהַיְנוּ מִפְּנֵי שֶׁזֶּהוּ בִּבְחִינַת מַקִּיף לְבַד שֶׁאֵינוֹ נִרְגָּשׁ בִּפְנִימִיּוּת, וּכְמוֹ כֵן הוּא בְּחִינַת הָאַהֲבָה שֶׁבִּבְחִינַת מַקִּיף שֶׁבַּנֶּפֶשׁ שֶׁאֵינוֹ פּוֹעֵל כָּל כָּךְ

transcendent desire for G-dliness, it is not en-clothed within the natural inner soul powers. It is like faith, which is also [unconscious and] transcendent (although faith expresses the transcendent powers of the soul as en-clothed in the lowest of the ten *sephirot—malchut—* where it is called *keter malchut*). About this, the Sages said [in *Eyn Yaakov*, tractate *Berachot*, p. 63], "The thief, at the mouth of the tunnel [which he is digging in order to break in] prays to G-d." The thief believes in G-d and in His Divine Providence and His omnipotence, and yet nevertheless, this doesn't impress him enough to refrain from transgressing [and opposing] G-d's will. In his divine soul, he truly believes, but his crass physical nature

――――― **COMMENTARY** ―――――

above" mentioned in Chapter 4 of *Kuntres Ha'Avoda*. It is the illumination of the menorah of Aharon the high priest, and it may be experienced either as "great love" (*ahava rabba*) or "love with deep enjoyment" (*ahava b'tanugim*). Because it is not based on intellect alone, but upon recognizing and seeing (in the mind's eye) the infinite light of the One Above, it is "love that is dependent upon nothing." In this case of meditation upon matters that transcend creation, *hitamatut* leads to *hakarat ha'haflah* (recognition of exalted matters beyond creation) and to experience of *reiah d'chochma* (vision of insight/wisdom).

Whether pursuing meditation upon G-dliness as revealed in creation (on the level of *neshama*), or upon transcendent G-dliness surpassing creation (*chaya*), we must first go through the process of stripping away our perception of reality, in order to become aware of G-dliness within creation. In so doing, we reach what is called "inner dimensions of understanding" (*pnimiyut bina*). As noted above, it is on this level that we can penetrate to the leads him to behave in violation of what G-d wants. This is because his faith is only transcendent and is not felt inside. So it is, as well, regarding the love that is transcendent in his soul. It doesn't affect his physical nature so much. Even though the transcendent aspect of his love of G-d brings him close to G-d, and he truly desires G-dliness, when it comes to his natural inner soul powers, he acts in a deviant manner altogether.

עַל הַחֲמָרִיּוּת, דְּעִם הֱיוֹת שֶׁמִּצַּד הַמַּקִּיף הוּא בִּבְחִינַת קָרוֹב וְרוֹצֶה בֶּאֱמֶת בֶּאֱלֹקוּת הִנֵּה כְּשֶׁבָּא בִּבְחִינַת כֹּחוֹת פְּנִימִיִּים וְכֹחוֹת טִבְעִיִּים הוּא בְּאֹפֶן אַחֵר לְגַמְרֵי.

COMMENTARY

very soul of creation, the G-dliness that is enlivening it (*neshama*). This is the beginning of meditation, in which there is no *bina* without *chochma*.

However, in the latter stages of meditation, the opposite is true. After stripping away perceived layers of reality to arrive at *pnimiyut bina*, we achieve *hakara*. Then, the processes that lead to *hitamtut* and *re'iyah* take us in the "opposite" direction, from below to above. The validation of *hitamtut* and the mental vision of *re'iya* are associated with *chochma*. So, although the initial process (known as *Chabad*) proceeds from *chochma* through *bina* to *da'at*, the subsequent revelation of G-dly understanding brings us in the opposite direction, from *da'at* to *chochma*. Only after experiencing true G-dly reality through *hakara* (deep recognition) of *da'at*, are we able to apprehend truth with the faculty of *chochma*. (See *Yom tov shel Rosh Hashana 5666*, page 150 and also page 373).

The process of circumscription of knowledge (*yediat hashlila*) leads to *yichuda ila'ah* and the soul level of *chaya*. However, the true experience of *yichuda ila'ah* is not based upon meditation. It is an experience of the highest level of the soul - the *yechida* - which is so intimately connected with the One Above that no amount of meditation will reveal it. Even meditation upon matters surpassing creation and based upon *yediat hashlila* will not bring us to the soul level of *yechida*. This is because the *yechida* is the essence of the soul that is connected to G-d. It therefore recognizes and experiences G-dliness without any meditation whatsoever (See *B'sha'ah shehikdimu 5672*, v.2, p.1180).

Many people undergo a spiritual arousal during Rosh Hashana and Yom Kippur, but is has no effect upon them the rest of the year.

(וְדָבָר זֶה נִרְאֶה בְּחוּשׁ בְּכַמָּה בְּנֵי אָדָם בְּרֹאשׁ הַשָּׁנָה וְיוֹם הַכִּפּוּרִים שֶׁמִּתְפָּעֲלִים מְאֹד בְּנַפְשָׁם וְאֵין זֶה פּוֹעֵל לְשַׁנּוֹת בֶּאֱמֶת דַּרְכָּם וְהִלּוּכָם בְּכָל הַשָּׁנָה בִּבְחִינַת וְיַעֲקֹב הָלַךְ לְדַרְכּוֹ כו', וּבָזֶה יֵשׁ כַּמָּה אוֹפַנִּים שֶׁהֲרֵי גַּם הַקַּלִּים וְגַם עוֹבְרֵי עֲבֵרָה רַחֲמָנָא לִיצְלָן מִתְעוֹרְרִים בְּיוֹם כִּפּוּר וּבִפְרָט בְּעִתִּים מְיֻחָדִים כְּמוֹ בִּתְקִיעַת שׁוֹפָר וּבִנְעִילָה דְּיוֹם כִּפּוּר וּמִכָּל מָקוֹם אַחַר כָּךְ הֲרֵי הֵם כְּמוֹ שֶׁהָיוּ מִקֹּדֶם בְּלִי שִׁנּוּי, וְיֵשׁ מֵהֶם אֲשֶׁר בְּרֹאשׁ הַשָּׁנָה וְיוֹם כִּפּוּר בּוֹכִים מֵעֹמֶק לִבָּם עַל מַצָּבָם הַחָמְרִי וּמִתְפַּלְלִים וּמְבַקְּשִׁים עַל הַפַּרְנָסָה וּכְהַאי גַּוְונָא אִישׁ אִישׁ כְּפִי הִצְטָרְכוּתוֹ וְאֵינָם שָׂמִים עַל לִבָּם לְתַקֵּן מַצָּבָם הָרוּחָנִי וְלִהְיוֹת סוּר מֵרָע וַעֲשֵׂה טוֹב בְּפֹעַל מַמָּשׁ עַל כָּל פָּנִים. אָמְנָם גַּם בְּיִרְאֵי אֱלֹקִים וַאֲשֶׁר בִּכְלָל עוֹבְדִים יֵחָשְׁבוּ שֶׁמִּתְעוֹרְרִים בֶּאֱמֶת בְּרֹאשׁ הַשָּׁנָה וְיוֹם כִּפּוּר בְּעַצְּם נַפְשָׁם בִּתְשׁוּבָה וּבְקַבָּלַת עֹל מַלְכוּת שָׁמַיִם,

(It is seen clearly that many people become aroused [to serve G-d] from their very souls on Rosh Hashana and Yom Kippur. Nevertheless, the arousal does nothing to change their courses and paths during the remainder of the year; about this it is written [in Genesis 32:1], "Yaakov went on his way," [indicating the way of Torah and *mitzvot*]. There are various degrees and styles, but even the least observant Jews "wake up" during the High Holidays, and particularly during the special times of blowing the *shofar*, and during *Ne'ila* [the closing prayer of Yom Kippur]. Still, they afterward return to their previous lifestyles, without any variation. Then, there are those who cry from the depths of their hearts over their economic situations during Rosh Hashana and Yom Kippur. They pray and request income for the year, each one according to his needs. It doesn't occur to them to do anything to rectify their spiritual situations, at least to turn away from evil and

---
COMMENTARY

As pointed out in Chapter 4, even *re'iah d'chochma* and *hitamtut* do not ultimately lead to spiritual satisfaction. We will not be satisfied with visions and revelations, but we want G-d Himself. Therefore, even though these phenomena are described as "gazing upon the glory of the King," they only lead to "love-sickeness" (*cholat ahava*). Love-sickness is the result of seeing something desirable that is as yet unattainable — at least not until the advent of the Messianic Age, when we will be able to grasp G-dliness with the naked eye (see *Besha'ah shehikdimu 5672*, vol. 2, page 1200-1203).

turn toward that which is good. There are also those who fear G-d, who are included in the category of "servants [of G-d]," and who are truly stimulated on Rosh Hashana and Yom Kippur from the very essence of their souls, with repentance and acceptance of the "yoke of heaven." And at that particular hour, their distance from the One Above truly bothers them to a great extent, and they cry honestly from bitterness of the soul. At that time, they accept the kingship of the One Above and resolve to be subordinated to G-d during the entire year, to learn Torah, and to keep the commandments. They resolve not to get involved in other matters, but in general to submit themselves only to G-d. With the passage of this auspicious time, however, even these people return to their physicality and nature, each one according to his own traits and character, whether to lusts of the heart, or pride and arrogance, or anger, etc. And it is truly amazing how their natures do not change at all, and how after such an arousal and resolution they can return to their previous spiritual condition. The reason for this is their failure to serve G-d during the entire remainder of the year.

שֶׁבְּאוֹתָהּ שָׁעָה בֶּאֱמֶת צַר לוֹ מְאֹד עַל רְחוּקוֹ מֵה' וּבוֹכֶה עַל זֶה בֶּאֱמֶת בְּמַר נַפְשׁוֹ וּמְקַבֵּל עָלָיו בְּאוֹתָהּ שָׁעָה עוֹל מַלְכוּתוֹ יִתְבָּרֵךְ לִהְיוֹת מָסוּר וְנָתוּן לֶאֱלֹקוּת כָּל הַשָּׁנָה בְּעֵסֶק הַתּוֹרָה וְקִיּוּם הַמִּצְוֹת וְלֹא יִתֵּן נַפְשׁוֹ לְעִנְיָנִים אֲחֵרִים וּבְדֶרֶךְ כְּלָל לִהְיוֹת מְשֻׁעְבָּד לַה' לְבַדּוֹ, וּבַעֲבוֹר הַזְּמַן הנ"ל חוֹזֵר לְחָמְרִיּוּתוֹ וְטִבְעוֹ אִישׁ אִישׁ כְּפִי מִדּוֹתָיו הַטִּבְעִיִּים אִם בְּתַאֲוָה וְחֶמְדַּת הַלֵּב אוֹ בְּהַגְבָּהָה וְהִתְנַשְּׂאוּת אוֹ בְּכַעַס וּכְהַאי גַּוְונָא, וְנִפְלָא הַדָּבָר מַמָּשׁ אֵיךְ שֶׁאֵינוֹ מִשְׁתַּנֶּה הַטֶּבַע כְּלָל וְאֵיךְ לְאַחַר הִתְעוֹרְרוּת וְהֶסְכֵּם כָּזֶה יַחְזוֹר לִהְיוֹת כְּמִקֹּדֶם אַךְ סִבַּת הַדָּבָר הוּא הֶעְדֵּר הָעֲבוֹדָה כָּל הַשָּׁנָה,

It is truly amazing how their nature is not changed after such an arousal.

--- COMMENTARY ---

PITFALLS

Chapter 5, points out a potential pitfall of utilizing the above techniques. If we get so involved with the elevated levels of holiness that we forget the all-important task of purifying and elevating our animal soul, then we are neglecting our duty. If only our divine soul is serving G-d, then we are neglecting our obligation to also refine and elevate our animal soul. This is the

There are those who work on themselves all year long, and they operate on a higher spiritual rung.

דְּמִי שֶׁעוֹבֵד עֲבוֹדָתוֹ כָּל הַשָּׁנָה בְּהַכְנָעַת הַחֹמֶר בִּכְלָלוּת, וְהָעִקָּר בְּהַכְנָעַת הַכֹּחוֹת וְהַמִּדּוֹת פְּרָטִיּוֹת עַל יְדֵי הָעֲבוֹדָה פְּנִימִית בְּמֹחַ וְלֵב אִם בְּאַהֲבָה כְּמַיִם אוֹ בְּהָאַהֲבָה דְּכְרִשְׁפֵּי אֵשׁ וּכְמוֹ שֶׁנִּתְבָּאֵר לְעֵיל פ"ד. וַדַּאי הַהִתְעוֹרְרוּת דְּעֶצֶם הַנְּשָׁמָה דְּרֹאשׁ הַשָּׁנָה וְיוֹם כִּפּוּר פּוֹעֵל הַרְבֵּה עַל הַחָמְרִיּוּת שֶׁלּוֹ, וַעֲבוֹדָתוֹ אַחַר כָּךְ בְּכָל הַשָּׁנָה הִיא בְּמַדְרֵגָה נַעֲלֵית יוֹתֵר הֵן מִצַּד הַנְּשָׁמָה וְהֵן בְּהַזִּכּוּךְ דְּנֶפֶשׁ הַבַּהֲמִית שֶׁהַכֹּל הוּא בְּעִנְיָנִים גְּבוֹהִים וְנַעֲלִים יוֹתֵר כִּי בִּכְלָלוּתוֹ הוּא נַעֲשָׂה בְּדַרְגָּא עֶלְיוֹנָה יוֹתֵר

But there are those who continue to serve the One Above all year long, by subjugating their physical natures in general, but mainly by subduing specific traits through inner service of the mind and heart, whether with "love like water" or "love like fire" (as described in Chapter 4). Certainly [in their case] the arousal of the essence of the soul on Rosh Hashana and Yom Kippur has a powerful effect on their physical nature, and their service of the One Above during the entire rest of the year is on a higher level. [This applies to] both the service of the G-dly soul itself, as well as the refinement of the animal soul. In either case, all of their spiritual efforts are on a more elevated plane, because in general they [are operating] on a higher spiritual rung.

--- **COMMENTARY** ---

danger of "transcendent consciousness" (the level called *chaya*); meditation on this level may lead us to be so involved with the spiritual that we forget that our soul was put down in a physical body in order to refine and uplift it. The way to avoid this pitfall is to begin our meditation on the simple, down-to-earth level of appreciating the G-dliness en-clothed in creation, as in the entry-level meditation leading to "love like water." This is an understanding that the natural, physically-oriented animal soul can also grasp, and therefore it can become involved and transformed through the meditation process. If, at each step along the way we make sure that we understand the concept — not only on a transcendent spiritual level but also in a way that the animal soul understands — we will then continue to transform and elevate the animal soul. If, though, we neglect the lower, simple levels of understanding and go straight to the transcendent levels of "love like fire," we run the risk of leaving our animal soul behind. Only by nurturing the animal soul with

Essay on Service of the Heart - Love Like Fire and Water

(The animal soul also contains various different levels, including the three levels of ox, sheep, and goat, as known.^xxxii For those whose animal soul is not so coarse, there are many things on which they will not have to work, while others may need to expend tremendous energy and labor on them. But through the above-mentioned arousal during the *"avoda"* [of prayer] of the entire year, the animal soul also abandons its coarseness. It rises to new and higher levels, and then the work that they must do to refine their physical nature becomes an entirely different kind of labor.)

(שֶׁהֲרֵי גַּם בְּהַנֶּפֶשׁ הַבַּהֲמִית יֵשׁ כַּמָּה חִלּוּקֵי מַדְרֵגוֹת, וְכַנּוֹדָע מִכְּלָלוּת הַג' מַדְרֵגוֹת דְּשׁוֹר כֶּשֶׂב וָעֵז, וּמִי שֶׁהַנֶּפֶשׁ הַבַּהֲמִית שֶׁלּוֹ אֵינוֹ גַּס כָּל כָּךְ יֵשׁ כַּמָּה דְּבָרִים שֶׁאֵין צָרִיךְ עַל זֶה יְגִיעָה כְּלָל מַה שֶׁזּוּלָתוֹ צָרִיךְ עַל זֶה יְגִיעָה רַבָּה, וְעַל יְדֵי הִתְעוֹרְרוּת הנ"ל אַחֲרֵי הָעֲבוֹדָה דְּכָל הַשָּׁנָה, הִנֵּה גַּם הַנֶּפֶשׁ הַבַּהֲמִית יוֹצֵא מִגַּסּוּתוֹ וְהוּא בְּדַרְגָּא עֶלְיוֹנָה יוֹתֵר וּמִמֵּילָא הָעֲבוֹדָה שֶׁלּוֹ בְּזִכּוּךְ הַחָמְרִיּוּת הוּא בְּאֹפֶן אַחֵר)

By appropriate arousal during prayer all year long, the animal soul becomes refined.

← xxxii) See footnote of the Rebbe on page 288

(It is true that the situation of the animal soul during Rosh Hashana and Yom Kippur is not comparable to its position during the year, and there are times when it is far from G-d—as is written [in Proverbs 24:16]: "A *tzaddik* falls seven times...[and rises each time]" — nevertheless, it is on a higher level.)

(וְאִם כִּי וַדַּאי אֵינוֹ דּוֹמֶה מַעֲמַד וּמַצָּב הַנֶּפֶשׁ הַבַּהֲמִית בְּכָל הַשָּׁנָה לִכְמוֹ שֶׁהוּא בְּרֹאשׁ הַשָּׁנָה וְיוֹם כִּפּוּר וְגַם יֵשׁ רְחוּקִים לְעִתִּים (עַל דֶּרֶךְ שֶׁבַע יִפּוֹל כו') מִכָּל מָקוֹם הוּא בְּדַרְגָּא עֶלְיוֹנָה כו').

--- **COMMENTARY** ---

"love like water" will we later be able to consume and transform it with "love like fire." "Love like water" weakens the animal soul, and then "love like fire" performs the *coup de grace*, finishing it off.

That also is the reason why so many people come to the synagogue on the High Holidays of Rosh Hashana and Yom Kippur and yet do not seem to be affected by their experience during the entire rest of the year. They experience a spiritual high on Rosh Hashana and Yom Kippur, that is honest and real at the time. However, they fail to live up to the decisions and resolutions that they themselves made at that time. The reason that they fail, says the Rebbe Rashab, is because they do not work upon themselves the rest of the year, meditating on

Without work all year long, our physical nature asserts itself and remains strong.

אֲבָל בְּהֶעְדֵּר הָעֲבוֹדָה כָּל הַשָּׁנָה וְהַחָמְרִיּוּת הִיא בְּתָקְפָּהּ וּגְבוּרָתָהּ הִנֵּה הַהִתְעוֹרְרוּת דְּרֹאשׁ הַשָּׁנָה וְיוֹם כִּפּוּר הֲגַם שֶׁמִּתְעוֹרֵר בֶּאֱמֶת כַּנַּ״ל (מִפְּנֵי שֶׁאֵינוֹ בִּבְחִינַת רָחוֹק מַמָּשׁ לִהְיוֹת אֶת פּוֹשְׁעִים נִמְנֶה חַס וְחָלִילָה, וְאַדְּרַבָּא בַּחִיצוֹנִיּוּת הֲרֵי הוּא בְּעֵסֶק הַתּוֹרָה וַעֲבוֹדָה) אֵין זֶה פּוֹעֵל עַל הַחָמְרִיּוּת לְשַׁנּוֹתָהּ בֶּאֱמֶת, וְגַם עֶצֶם הַהִתְעוֹרְרוּת הֲגַם שֶׁהִיא אֲמִתִּית בַּנֶּפֶשׁ הֲרֵי הִיא בִּבְחִינַת מַקִּיף לְבַד שֶׁאֵינָהּ נִרְגֶּשֶׁת בְּהַכֹּחוֹת פְּנִימִיִּים לִהְיוֹת שַׁיָּךְ לִפְעַל מַמָּשׁ, וְהַיְנוּ שֶׁגַּם הַצַּעַר וּמְרִירוּת נַפְשׁוֹ אֵינוֹ בִּבְחִינַת הֶרְגֵּשׁ הַצַּעַר וּמְרִירוּת עֲמֻקָּה מִפְּרָטֵי הָעִנְיָנִים הֲלֹא טוֹבִים שֶׁלּוֹ כִּי אִם מִכְּלָלוּת הֲלֹא טוֹב שֶׁלּוֹ, וְכֵן הַקַּבָּלַת עוֹל שֶׁמְּקַבֵּל עָלָיו עוֹל מַלְכוּתוֹ יִתְבָּרֵךְ בְּרֹאשׁ הַשָּׁנָה לִהְיוֹת מָסוּר וְנָתוּן אֵלָיו יִתְבָּרֵךְ וְכֵן

But, lacking the service [prayer] all year long, our physical nature remains intact, at full strength. Then our spiritual arousal of Rosh Hashana and Yom Kippur — even though honest, as previously mentioned, since we are not really far from G-d in the sense of being a sinner or transgressor, G-d forbid, and outwardly we learn and pray—has no effect on our corporeal nature and does not truly transform it. The arousal itself, even though honest within our soul, is nevertheless transcendent and does not permeate our inner soul powers to become felt and experienced in actual deed. That is, the suffering and bitterness of the soul aren't experienced as deep distress and discomfort over specific negative details that bother us, but rather as a general condition of "I am not the way I should be." The same is true concerning our acceptance of the

--- **COMMENTARY** ---

G-dliness and finding their own inner deficiencies that they need to rectify. Therefore, the spiritual arousal that they experience on Rosh Hashana and Yom Kippur goes to waste. Only when they "plow the ground," so to speak, preparing ourselves for the high revelations of the transcendental levels of the soul, can these revelations have a long-term effect on their animal soul.

Of course, we cannot say of the *yechida*, the highest transcendent level of the soul, that it has no effect upon the animal soul. Even though it is not en-clothed in the body, it nevertheless has an effect upon the animal soul. Since it is the level of the soul that is always united with G-d, it needs no stimulation or arousal to come into expression. It is always

Essay on Service of the Heart - Love Like Fire and Water

בְּהִתְעוֹרְרוּת תְּשׁוּבָה דְּיוֹם כִּפּוּר שֶׁמְּקַבֵּל עָלָיו לִהְיוֹת בְּאֹפֶן אַחֵר מִכְּמוֹ שֶׁהָיָ' אֵין זֶה בָּא בּוֹ בִּבְחִינַת פְּנִימִיּוּת לִהְיוֹת בֶּאֱמֶת בְּהַנְהָגָה אַחֶרֶת לַפֹּעַל וּמִכָּל שֶׁכֵּן שֶׁאֵינוֹ בָא בְּעִנְיָנִים פְּרָטִיִּים הֵן בְּסוּר מֵרַע וְהֵן בְּוַעֲשֵׂה טוֹב

"yoke of heaven" during Rosh Hashana, [when we] submit ourselves to G-d, and concerning our arousal to do *teshuva* on Yom Kippur, [when we] resolve to become a different person altogether than we were before. These commitments don't seep into us and permeate our personality. They don't [change us or] cause us to conduct ourselves differently, and even more, they don't affect our specific behavior in turning away from evil and toward good.

(דְּהַיְנוּ גַּם מַה שֶּׁמְּקַבֵּל עָלָיו לַעֲסֹק בַּתּוֹרָה וּמִצְוֹת וְשֶׁלֹּא יִתֵּן נַפְשׁוֹ לְעִנְיְנֵי הָעוֹלָם אֵין זֶה בִּדְבָרִים פְּרָטִים שֶׁהֵן הֵן אוֹתָם הַדְּבָרִים שֶׁבָּהֶם הוּא הַגֵּרָעוֹן וְהַחִסָּרוֹן שֶׁלּוֹ, כִּי מִתְּחִלָּה אֵינוֹ נוֹתֵן נַפְשׁוֹ לְהַרְגִּישׁ פְּרָטֵי הַחֶסְרוֹנוֹת שֶׁלּוֹ וּלְהִצְטַעֵר עֲלֵיהֶם בֶּאֱמֶת וְכֵן הַקַּבָּלָה וְהַתִּקּוּן הַמְדֻמֶּה אֵינוֹ בִּפְרָטֵי הַדְּבָרִים הָאֵלּוּ. וְזֹאת לָדַעַת שֶׁגַּם אִם הִרְגֵּשׁ

(This means that even our decision to be involved only in Torah and *mitzvot* and not to throw ourselves into worldly matters does not apply to specifics, that is, the very things in which we are lacking and deficient [and which need work]. From the outset, we did not make it our goal to become aware of our specific deficiencies and to honestly regret them. So, our seeming commitment and

---
COMMENTARY

"there," united with G-d, even without meditation on His greatness. At the same time, it is not governed by the limitations of existence; it is at once transcendent and permeating the body.

That is why it is the *yechida* that enables us to give up our life "in honor of G-d," if necessary. If faced with a choice — either to commit one of the three cardinal sins or to give up our life — we, as Jews, will give up our life without thinking, in order to avoid disconnection with the One Above.

This is a function of the *yechida*, that level of the soul that cannot and will not be separated in any way from G-d. Just as it is totally connected with the One Above, it also has complete control over the physical body and its functions. Therefore, when the *yechida* comes into revelation, it overrides and transforms the animal soul.

Without deep inner awareness of our deficiencies, it is impossible to rectify them.

rectification [of our deficiencies] are not geared to specifics. It should be known that even if we experience pain and remorse over the appropriate details, our commitment may not lead to their rectification. It is possible that our resolution may apply only to our general situation. If so, it will not have an effect when it comes to our specific problems. It is also possible that the commitment itself is not coupled with real action, and then, even if we experience the appropriate remorse, our commitment will not necessarily be appropriate [and effective in changing the specifics of our behavior]. So, the correct intention and effort must be devoted to both of these factors, in order that they be appropriate. What is certain is that without deep inner awareness of our own specific deficiencies, it is impos-

הַצַּעַר וְהַמְרִירוּת הִיא עַל הָעִנְיָנִים הַפְּרָטִים, מִכָּל מָקוֹם אֵינוֹ מֻכְרָח שֶׁהַקַּבָּלָה תִּהְיֶה גַּם כֵּן בְּתִקּוּן הַפְּרָטִים דְּיָכוֹל לִהְיוֹת שֶׁהַקַּבָּלָה תְּהֵי' רַק עַל הַכְּלָל, וּמִמֵּילָא לֹא יָבוֹא לִידֵי פֹּעַל כְּשֶׁבָּא לְיָדוֹ הָעִנְיָנִים הַפְּרָטִים וְגַם עֶצֶם הַקַּבָּלָה יָכוֹל לִהְיוֹת בְּאֹפֶן כָּזֶה שֶׁאֵינָהּ שַׁיֶּכֶת לַפֹּעַל מַמָּשׁ, וְנִמְצָא דְּגַם אִם תִּהְיֶה הַמְּרִירוּת כִּדְבָעֵי אֵינוֹ מֻכְרָח עֲדַיִן שֶׁתִּהְיֶה הַקַּבָּלָה כִּדְבָעֵי. וְצָרִיךְ לִהְיוֹת כַּוָּנַת הַמְכֻוָּן וִיגִיעָתוֹ עַל שְׁנֵי הַדְּבָרִים שֶׁיִּהְיוּ רְצוּיִים אָמְנָם זֹאת וַדַּאי שֶׁבִּבְלִי הֶרְגֵּשׁ פְּנִימִי וְעֹמֶק מִפְּרָטֵי הַחֶסְרוֹנוֹת שֶׁלּוֹ אִי אֶפְשָׁר שֶׁתִּהְיֶה הַקַּבָּלָה כִּדְבָעֵי לְמֶהֱוֵי) רַק בִּכְלָלוּת שֶׁלֹּא יְהֵי' רַע וִיהֵי' טוֹב וּמִמֵּילָא זֶה רַק לְפִי שָׁעָה וְיַחֲלֹף וְיַעֲבֹר אַחַר כָּךְ.

sible for us to truly commit ourselves to any rectification.) [Our awareness] will only affect us in general, so that we won't be "bad" and we'll be "good", and therefore [the effect] is only temporary, and it will fade away and disappear afterward.

The reason for this is also a deficiency in our service [of G-d] all year long. When we work on ourselves all year long, rectifying and refining our character traits, we become well aware of exactly what we need to fix, each one of us according to the "portion" of natural attributes entrusted us to fix and refine. We strive with "labor of the soul" and "labor of the flesh" all year long to purify these

דְּסִבַּת הַדָּבָר הוּא גַּם כֵּן בְּהֶעְדֵּר הָעֲבוֹדָה דְּכָל הַשָּׁנָה, דְּכַאֲשֶׁר כָּל הַשָּׁנָה הוּא עוֹבֵד וּמְיַגֵּעַ אֶת עַצְמוֹ בְּתִקּוּן וְזִכּוּךְ מִדּוֹתָיו שֶׁיּוֹדֵעַ הוּא אֶת עִנְיָנָיו מַה שֶׁהוּא צָרִיךְ לְתַקֵּן, אִישׁ אִישׁ כְּפִי מַה שֶּׁנִּתַּן לוֹ לְתַקֵּן וּלְזַכֵּךְ מֵהַמִּדּוֹת הַטִּבְעִיִּים וּמִתְיַגֵּעַ בִּיגִיעַת נֶפֶשׁ וִיגִיעַת בָּשָׂר כָּל הַשָּׁנָה לְבָרֵר וּלְזַכֵּךְ הַמִּדּוֹת הָאֵלּוּ, הִנֵּה בְּרֹאשׁ הַשָּׁנָה וְיוֹם כִּפּוּר שֶׁהוּא עֵת

Essay on Service of the Heart - Love Like Fire and Water

traits. Then, on Rosh Hashana and Yom Kippur, which are a time of favorable will from above, when G-d "unsheathes His holy arm," [the right arm represents revelation and kindness] and "the Source of light draws near to the spark," the essence of our soul becomes aroused and revealed. The general service at that time is one[xxxiii] of inner awareness and [happens at the level of] essence of the soul, as is known. It focuses on those things that we worked on all year long. [During the period of the High Holidays], we are in a state of distress and deep bitterness, touching the very essence of our soul. Our acceptance of the "yoke of heaven" and our commitment to do *teshuva* also come from the essence of our soul, but in such a way that they [the acceptance and the commitment] affect our actions and involve those things on which we have worked. And this is because in essence we are *p'nimi* [dedicated to truly working on ourselves, finding and rectifying our inner deficiencies] in our service all year long. Therefore, during Rosh Hashana and Yom Kippur, when the service comes from the essence of the soul, we perform it with inner feeling and consciousness. We are supported in this service by the revelation from above [that is characteristic of the Ten Days of *Teshuva*] as well as the revelation of the essence of our own soul (which

רָצוֹן לְמַעְלָה וְחָשַׂף ה' אֶת זְרוֹעַ קָדְשׁוֹ בִּבְחִינַת קָרוֹב הַמָּאוֹר אֶל הַנִּיצוֹץ הַמְעוֹרֵר בְּנֶפֶשׁ הָאָדָם הִתְגַּלּוּת עֶצֶם נַפְשׁוֹ, וּכְלָלוּת הָעֲבוֹדָה בַּזְּמַן הַהוּא הִיא בְּחִינַת פְּנִימִיּוּת וְעַצְמוּת הַנֶּפֶשׁ כַּנּוֹדָע, הִנֵּה כָּל זֶה בָּא בְּעִנְיָנִים אֵלּוּ שֶׁעוֹסֵק בָּהֶם כָּל הַשָּׁנָה רַק שֶׁהוּא בִּבְחִינַת מֵצַר וּמְרִירוּת עֲמֻקָּה הַנּוֹגֵעַ לוֹ בְּעַצְמוּת וּפְנִימִיּוּת נַפְשׁוֹ וְכֵן הַקַּבָּלַת עוֹל מַלְכוּת שָׁמַיִם וְקַבָּלַת הַתְּשׁוּבָה הִיא בְּעַצְמִיּוּת נַפְשׁוֹ אֲבָל הוּא בְּאֹפֶן שֶׁיִּהְיֶה נוֹגֵעַ לַפֹּעַל מַמָּשׁ, וּבְאֵלּוּ הָעִנְיָנִים שֶׁעוֹסֵק בָּהֶם. וְהַיְנוּ מִפְּנֵי שֶׁבְּעֶצֶם הוּא פְּנִימִי בַּעֲבוֹדָתוֹ בְּכָל הַשָּׁנָה וּכְמוֹ כֵן הוּא בַּעֲבוֹדָה דְרֹאשׁ הַשָּׁנָה וְיוֹם כִּפּוּר שֶׁהִיא בִּבְחִינַת עֶצֶם הַנֶּפֶשׁ הֲרֵי זֶה בִּבְחִינַת הַרְגֵּשׁ פְּנִימִי, וְגַם מְסַיֵּעַ לוֹ הַגִּלּוּי מִלְמַעְלָה וְהִתְגַּלּוּת עַצְמוּת נַפְשׁוֹ (הַנִּרְגָּשׁ בִּפְנִימִיּוּת) לְהָסִיר מֵאִתּוֹ חֲמָרִיּוּת הַמִּדּוֹת הַטִּבְעִיִּים שֶׁהוּא עוֹסֵק בְּבֵרוּר וְזִכּוּךְ שֶׁלָּהֶם (וּכְמוֹ שֶׁנִּתְבָּאֵר לְעֵיל שֶׁנַּעֲשֶׂה בְּדַרְגָּא עֶלְיוֹנָה יוֹתֵר). אֲבָל בְּהֶעְדֵּר הָעֲבוֹדָה כָּל הַשָּׁנָה, הִנֵּה בְּרֹאשׁ הַשָּׁנָה וְיוֹם כִּפּוּר הֲגַם שֶׁמִּתְעוֹרֵר בְּנַפְשׁוֹ הֲרֵי זֶה רַק כְּמוֹ דָּבָר בְּעִתּוֹ, שֶׁהָעֵת הוּא לְהִתְפַּעֵל וּלְהִתְעוֹרֵר (מִצַּד הַגִּלּוּי מִלְמַעְלָה כנ"ל שֶׁמֵּאִיר עַל כָּל אֶחָד וְאֶחָד מִיִּשְׂרָאֵל (יוֹתֵר מֵהַכְּרוּזִים שֶׁבְּכָל יוֹם שֶׁגַּם הֵם נִרְגָּשִׁים בְּכָל אֶחָד

Without prayer all year long, the high holidays will provide soul stimulation only at the time they occur.

← xxxiii) See footnote of the Rebbe on page 289

we experience with inner feeling and consciousness). This helps us shrug off the physical facade of those natural attributes that we are engaged in refining (and as explained earlier, this takes place [during the High Holidays] on a higher level). However, without the service [of prayer] all year long, Rosh Hashana and Yom Kippur will provide stimulation for our soul only at the time they occur, since it is a time of spiritual excitement and arousal (on account of the aforementioned revelation from above, that illuminates every Jewish person, even more so than the "spiritual messages" which come down everyday and are experienced by everyone,[xxxiv] as is known). This is particularly true of those who are in the category of "servants of G-d," meaning those who are close to the service we're discussing here. But [for the rest], the arousal is only from transcendence, rather than from inner feeling and truth. Therefore, it is not effective in truly changing the person. The arousal may be real on the level of transcendence, but it has no effect on the physicality of the person and will not truly change it.

וְאֶחָד כַּנּוֹדָע), וּבִפְרָט בְּאוֹתָן שֶׁבִּכְלָל עוֹבְדִים יֵחָשְׁבוּ דְּהַיְנוּ הַקְּרוֹבִים לְעִנְיָן הָעֲבוֹדָה שֶׁבַּזֶּה מְדַבְּרִים כָּאן, אֲבָל הוּא בִּבְחִינַת מַקִּיף לְבַד בְּלִי הֶרְגֵּשׁ בִּפְנִימִיּוּת וַאֲמִתּוּת הַנַּ"ל, וְלָכֵן אֵין זֶה שַׁיָּךְ לִפְעַל וְעַל כֵּן הַגַּם שֶׁהִתְעוֹרְרוּת הִיא אֲמִתִּית בִּבְחִינַת הַמַּקִּיף דְּנֶפֶשׁ אֵין זֶה נוֹגֵעַ אֶל הַחָמְרִיּוּת לְשַׁנּוֹתָהּ בֶּאֱמֶת).

xxxiv) See footnote of the Rebbe on page 290

xxxv) See footnote of the Rebbe on page 291

Only the ardent love of ahava rabba, beyond reason, can transform the animal soul.

It is written elsewhere[xxxv] that only *ahava rabbah* ("transcendent love"), which is love beyond reason and logic, is capable of transforming the essence of the animal soul. This occurs only after a previous service of logic and reason within the mind and heart. As is known, the service which corresponds to reason and intellect produces only nullification of the ego (*bitul hayesh*). In order to achieve full nullification of the self (*bitul b'metziut*), we need first to achieve *ahava rabbah* beyond reason and intellect. By way of this love,

וּמַה שֶּׁכָּתוּב בְּמָקוֹם אַחֵר דְּדַוְקָא בְּחִינַת אַהֲבָה רַבָּה שֶׁלְּמַעְלָה מִטַּעַם וָדַעַת מְהַפֵּךְ מַהוּת הַנֶּפֶשׁ הַבַּהֲמִית, זֶהוּ דַּוְקָא לְאַחַר הָעֲבוֹדָה תְּחִלָּה בִּבְחִינַת טַעַם וָדַעַת בְּמֹחַ וָלֵב, וְנוֹדָע דְּהָעֲבוֹדָה שֶׁעַל פִּי טַעַם וָדַעַת הִיא רַק בִּבְחִינַת בִּטּוּל הַיֵּשׁ לְבַד, וּבִכְדֵי שֶׁיִּהְיֶ' הַבִּטּוּל בִּמְצִיאוּת הוּא בְּאַהֲבָה רַבָּה שֶׁלְּמַעְלָה מִטַּעַם וָדַעַת שֶׁעַל יְדֵי זֶה שֶׁתִּתְבַּטֵּל מַהוּת הַנֶּפֶשׁ הַבַּהֲמִית וּמִתְהַפֵּךְ לְטוֹב, וּבָזֶה יֵשׁ גַּם כֵּן מַדְרֵגוֹת וְאֵין כָּאן מְקוֹמוֹ לְבָאֵר

Essay on Service of the Heart - Love Like Fire and Water

the very essence of the animal soul becomes nullified and transformed into a positive entity. There are various levels within this process, and this isn't the place to discuss them. The main point is that all of this can only be achieved if preceded by an inner service [of reason and logic] in the mind and heart, and while purifying and refining the natural attributes. If we engage in the "labors before Shabbat" in the exercise of intellect—which correspond to bending the will of the animal soul (*itkafia*)—we "eat on Shabbat." That is, we succeed in actualizing the desire and "transcendent love" of the soul beyond logic and reason, which corresponds to the complete transformation (*it'hafcha*) of the animal soul. All this is as written in *Torah Ohr*, in the discourses beginning with *Vayakhel*, and *Kechu ma'itchem truma*, and as explained in *Likutei Torah*, in the discourse beginning with *Levaer inyan Yom HaKippurim* regarding the "fire coming down from above" and the "fire from below..."

אֲבָל כָּל זֶה דַּוְקָא בְּהַקְדָּמַת הָעֲבוֹדָה פְּנִימִית בְּמֹחַ וְלֵב לְבָרֵר וּלְזַכֵּךְ אֶת הַמִּדּוֹת טִבְעִיִּים, וּמִי שֶׁטָּרַח בְּעֶרֶב שַׁבָּת בַּעֲבוֹדָה שֶׁעַל פִּי טַעַם וְדַעַת בִּבְחִינַת אִתְכַּפְיָא יֹאכַל בְּשַׁבָּת בִּבְחִינַת הָרָצוֹן וְאַהֲבָה רַבָּה שֶׁלְּמַעְלָה מִטַּעַם וְדַעַת לִהְיוֹת בִּבְחִינַת אִתְהַפְּכָא כו' וּכְמוֹ שֶׁכָּתוּב בְּתוֹרָה אוֹר דִּבּוּר הַמַּתְחִיל וַיַּקְהֵל וְדִבּוּר הַמַּתְחִיל קְחוּ מֵאִתְּכֶם תְּרוּמָה, וּכְמוֹ שֶׁכָּתוּב בְּלִקּוּטֵי תּוֹרָה דִּבּוּר הַמַּתְחִיל לְבָאֵר עִנְיַן יוֹם הַכִּפּוּרִים בְּעִנְיַן אֵשׁ שֶׁל מַעְלָה וְאֵשׁ שֶׁל מַטָּה כו'.

All this can only be achieved if preceded by detailed meditation based on logic and reason.

SYNOPSIS:

Ahava, meaning "love," comes from the Hebrew word *ava*, meaning "will." It is explained elsewhere that this is a will beyond logic and reason, and that it is a [very] high level of serving G-d, although it doesn't affect the physicality of the animal soul. This is because it happens on a transcendent level of the soul which is too high to become en-clothed in the animal soul. Therefore even when it becomes truly aroused with an [abstract] will for connection with the One Above (like in every Jew on Rosh Hashana and Yom Kippur), it is not experienced inside, and doesn't change our nature, unless it is preceded by an inner service of logic and reason in the mind and heart. (But the revelation of the true transcendent level of *yechida* has the effect of transforming and turning over the earthy nature of the animal soul completely.)

קִצּוּר.

הִנֵּה אַהֲבָה לְשׁוֹן אָבָה רָצוֹן. וּמְבֹאָר בְּמָקוֹם אַחֵר שֶׁהוּא בְּחִינַת הָרָצוֹן שֶׁלְּמַעְלָה מִטַּעַם וָדַעַת. וְעִם הֱיוֹת שֶׁזֶּהוּ מַדְרֵגָה גְּבוֹהָה בַּעֲבוֹדָה, אֵין זֶה פּוֹעֵל עַל הַחָמְרִיּוּת דְּנֶפֶשׁ הַבַּהֲמִית מִפְּנֵי שֶׁזֶּהוּ בִּבְחִינַת מַקִּיף דְּנֶפֶשׁ שֶׁלְּמַעְלָה מֵהִתְלַבְּשׁוּת וְעַל כֵּן גַּם שֶׁמִּתְעוֹרֵר בֶּאֱמֶת בִּבְחִינַת הָרָצוֹן הנ״ל (וּכְמוֹ בְּכָל אֶחָד וְאֶחָד בְּרֹאשׁ הַשָּׁנָה וְיוֹם הַכִּפּוּרִים) אֵין זֶה נִרְגָּשׁ בִּפְנִימִיּוּת וְאֵינוֹ מְשַׁנֶּה הַטֶּבַע עַל יְדֵי זֶה וְנִתְבָּאֵר דְּהִתְגַּלּוּת אֲמִתִּית בְּחִינַת הַמַּקִּיף דִּיחִידָה פּוֹעֵל לְשַׁנּוֹת וְלַהֲפֹךְ הַטִּבְעִיּוּת לְגַמְרֵי) כִּי אִם בְּהַקְדִּים תְּחִלָּה הָעֲבוֹדָה פְּנִימִית שֶׁעַל פִּי טַעַם וָדַעַת בְּמֹחַ וְלֵב כו׳:

Essay on Service of the Heart - Love Like Fire and Water

CHAPTER 6

פרק ו

וְהִנֵּה בַּעֲבוֹדָה שֶׁעַל פִּי טַעַם וָדַעַת יֵשׁ גַּם כֵּן שֶׁהָעֲבוֹדָה הִיא בִּבְחִינַת מַקִּיף לְבַד, שֶׁאֵין זֶה עֲבוֹדָה וְאֵינוֹ פּוֹעֵל עַל חָמְרִיּוּת הַנֶּפֶשׁ הַבַּהֲמִית לְהַכְנִיעוֹ וּלְבַטְּלוֹ, וְהוּא כַּאֲשֶׁר הַהִתְבּוֹנְנוּת הִיא בִּבְחִינַת כְּלָלוּת לְבַד, וְהַיְנוּ דִּבְאֵיזֶה עִנְיָן אֱלֹקִי שֶׁמִּתְבּוֹנֵן בּוֹ אֵינוֹ מִשְׁתַּדֵּל לְהִתְבּוֹנֵן בּוֹ בִּבְחִינַת הַשָּׂגָה מַמָּשׁ לֵידַע וּלְהַשִּׂיג אֶת הָעִנְיָן בֶּאֱמֶת כְּמוֹ שֶׁהוּא וּלְהַעֲמִיק דַּעְתּוֹ בָּזֶה, כִּי אִם מִסְתַּפֵּק בַּהִתְבּוֹנְנוּת בִּכְלָלוּת הָעִנְיָן הַהוּא, וּכְמוֹ בִּכְלָלוּת עִנְיַן בְּרִיאָה יֵשׁ מֵאַיִן

(וְנִרְגָּשׁ אֶצְלוֹ גַּם כֵּן כְּלָלוּת עִנְיַן הַהַפְלָאָה שֶׁבָּזֶה מִבְּלִי שֶׁמֵּשִׂים לִבּוֹ לֵידַע אֶת הַכֹּחַ הָאֱלֹקִי הַמְהַוֶּה מֵאַיִן לְיֵשׁ דְּהַיְנוּ אֵיזֶה מַדְרֵגָה פְּרָטִית בֶּאֱלֹקוּת הוּא וְאֵיךְ הוּא אֹפֶן הַהִתְהַוּוּת מֵאַיִן לְיֵשׁ וּפְרָטֵי

Superficial avoda based upon general meditation is not really avoda at all.

Avoda [of prayer] based upon reason and logic may be only superficial and external. In such a case, it is not really *avoda* [at all] and doesn't have any effect on the gross nature of our animal soul, failing to subjugate and nullify it. This [type of *avoda*] results from meditation that is only general; that is, when we meditate on a G-dly concept and fail to do so with true intellectual grasp. We fail to get an accurate understanding of the subject, which would lead to knowledge and true internalization of the concept as it is, nor do we delve into the depths of the subject. Instead, we are satisfied with a meditation on, for example, the overall concept of creation *ex nihilo* (something "from nothing").

(We may also sense the general wonder of the subject, but we don't direct our attention toward becoming aware of the G-dly power that creates something from nothing. That is, we don't think about the specific level of G-dliness that is doing the creating,

---

COMMENTARY

CHAPTER 6: ENGRAVING FROM WITHIN AND WITHOUT

Chapter 6 of *Kuntres Ha'Avoda* is devoted to the difference between proper, detailed meditation, and shallow, superficial meditation.

It starts by telling us what we should avoid. It says, first of all, that shallow and superficial meditation is like someone trying to grasp a complex topic at first glance — there's no depth to our understanding of the subject, and we only get the main points of it, without any true and lasting grasp. This may be good enough to maintain our fear of G-d, which is anyway

Creation from nothing is a truly amazing process.

הַהַפְלָאָה בָּזֶה, וְכַנּוֹדָע דְּעִנְיַן בְּרִיאָה יֵשׁ מֵאַיִן הוּא עִנְיָן נִפְלָא מְאֹד שֶׁאֵינוֹ מֻשָּׂג בֶּאֱמֶת בְּשֵׂכֶל אֱנוֹשִׁי אֵיךְ וּמָה הוּא שֶׁזֶּהוּ עִנְיַן מַה שֶּׁזֶּהוּ רַק בְּחֵיק הַבּוֹרֵא וַאֲמִתִּית כֹּחַ הַהִתְהַוּוּת הוּא מִבְּחִינַת עַצְמוּת אֵין סוֹף בָּרוּךְ הוּא שֶׁהוּא לְבַדּוֹ בְּכֹחוֹ וִיכָלְתּוֹ לִהְיוֹת יֵשׁ מֵאַיִן כוּ' וּכְמוֹ שֶׁכָּתוּב בְּמָקוֹם אַחֵר)

nor do we think about how this creation *ex nihilo* takes place. We don't make ourselves aware of the details and how wondrous this process is. Creation *ex nihilo* is a truly amazing process, the "how and what" of which are not really understood by human intellect, since that is a secret which is only in the possession of the Creator. The real power of creation comes from the essence of the Infinite Light of the One Above, "with Whom alone rests the power and ability to create something from absolute nothing," as written elsewhere [*Tanya, Igeret Hakodesh* 20].) xxxvi

xxxvi) See footnote of the Rebbe on page 292

אוֹ בִּכְלָלוּת עִנְיַן גְּדֻלַּת ה' בְּעִנְיַן הַהִתְהַוּוּת. וְכֵן בְּדֶרֶךְ כְּלָל אֵיךְ דְּאִיהוּ מְמַלֵּא כָּל עָלְמִין וְאִיהוּ סוֹבֵב כָּל עָלְמִין כוּ' וְעִם הֱיוֹת שֶׁמִּתְפַּעֵל בְּנַפְשׁוֹ וּמִתְלַהֵב עַל הָעִנְיָן הָאֱלֹקִי (ער ווערט צעקאַכט אוֹיף אֱלֹקוּת מִיט אַ הִתְפַּעֲלוּת הָרְצוּא כוּ'), הֲרֵי זֶה בִּבְחִינַת מַקִּיף לְבַד וְאֵין זֶה הִתְפַּעֲלוּת אֲמִתִּי כִּי אִם דִּמְיוֹן כּוֹזֵב (וּכְמוֹ שֶׁכָּתוּב בַּאֲרִיכוּת בְּקוּנְטְרֵס הַתְּפִלָּה).

Or, we may briefly contemplate the greatness of G-d in the creation of the universe. In passing, we may consider how "He permeates all the worlds and He transcends all the worlds." But, if we become intrigued and stimulated by this G-dly subject, the excitement is only superficial. It implies no true intensity of interest, but only an illusory facade (as is written about at length in *Kuntres HaTefila*).

COMMENTARY
---

innate in the Jewish soul and needs only gentle reminders in order to surface. But love of G-d requires determined work and attention, and that can only come about through detailed meditation.

Detailed meditation has two stages: "engraving from without" and "engraving from within."

"Engraving from without" is necessary in order to stimulate our heart and produce interest in spiritual matters. This involves detailed meditation on topics such as creation *ex-nihilo* (something "from nothing"). Or we may choose to meditate

Essay on Service of the Heart - Love Like Fire and Water

[Thus we see that] general meditation is somewhat akin to a reminder, by which we recall G-dliness. This is not sufficient to arouse love of G-d, for which we need solid knowledge and intellectual grasp, as this is the only way to achieve real love of G-d.

(Regarding "fear of G-d," simple recall is sufficient. We must remind ourselves of the aspects of G-dliness that bring us to the fear of the One Above, as explained in Chapter 3, where it is also explained that we must first understand the concept [which leads to "fear of G-d"], and afterward a reminder is sufficient.)

But, a reminder alone is not sufficient to arouse love of G-d. Even if we know the topic [well] and have already meditated upon it many times, we must return and actually meditate upon it anew every time that we want to achieve true love of the Creator. Possibly, this is because *bitul* (self-nullification) is in the nature of every Jewish soul, as written elsewhere regarding the verse [in Malachi 3:10] *Ki tihyu atem eretz cheifetz*,[xxxvii]

וְהָעִנְיָן הוּא כִּי הַהִתְבּוֹנְנוּת בְּדֶרֶךְ כְּלָלוּת, הִיא רַק כְּמוֹ זִכָּרוֹן שֶׁנִּזְכָּר עַל אֱלֹקוּת. וְזֶה אֵינוֹ מַסְפִּיק לְעוֹרֵר אֶת הָאַהֲבָה כִּי אִם צָרִיךְ לִהְיוֹת יְדִיעָה וְהַשָּׂגָה מַמָּשׁ, וְעַל יְדֵי זֶה דַּוְקָא מִתְעוֹרֵר הָאַהֲבָה,

(וּבְיִרְאָה מַסְפִּיק הַזִּכָּרוֹן שֶׁזּוֹכֵר אֶת הָעִנְיָנֵי אֱלֹקוּת הַמְּבִיאִים אֶת הַיִּרְאָה וּכְמוֹ שֶׁנִּתְבָּאֵר לְעֵיל פ"ג (וְנִת' שָׁם דְּמִכָּל מָקוֹם צָרִיךְ לִהְיוֹת בִּתְחִלָּה הַשָּׂגַת הָעִנְיָן וְאַחַר כָּךְ מַסְפִּיק הַזִּכָּרוֹן)

מַה שֶּׁאֵין כֵּן בְּאַהֲבָה אֵינוֹ מַסְפִּיק הַזִּכָּרוֹן לְבַד וְגַם שֶׁיּוֹדֵעַ אֶת הָעִנְיָן וּכְבָר הִתְבּוֹנֵן בּוֹ כַּמָּה פְּעָמִים הִנֵּה בְּכָל פַּעַם וּפַעַם בִּכְדֵי שֶׁתִּהְיֶה הָאַהֲבָה אֲמִתִּית צָרִיךְ לִהְיוֹת הִתְבּוֹנְנוּת מַמָּשׁ דַּוְקָא. וְיֵשׁ לוֹמַר מִפְּנֵי שֶׁעִנְיָן הַבִּטּוּל יֵשׁ בְּטֶבַע בְּנִשְׁמוֹת יִשְׂרָאֵל וּכְמוֹ שֶׁכָּתוּב בְּמָקוֹם אַחֵר בְּעִנְיָן כִּי תִּהְיוּ אַתֶּם אֶרֶץ חֵפֶץ דְּנִשְׁמוֹת יִשְׂרָאֵל הֵן

General meditation is like a reminder, sufficient to recall fear of G-d, but not enough to arouse love.

Self-nullification is so ingrained in the Jewish psyche that it is sufficient for us to simply recall G-d.

xxxvii) See footnote of the Rebbe on page 292

--- **COMMENTARY** ---

on the greatness of the Creator based upon the incredible variety, harmony, and number of creations. We may delve deeper and meditate on how each particular aspect of creation receives the G-dly light and energy that is necessary for its own maintenance and growth. Chassidic literature is replete with guided meditations on the above topics, and if we are able to delve into Chassidic discourses on our own, we can extract from them the necessary ingredients to begin meditating alone or with the help of a *mashpiah* ("spiritual guide").

הָאָרֶץ הָרְאוּיָה לִזְרִיעָה עַל יְדֵי תּוֹרָה וּמִצְוֹת מֵחֲמַת כֹּחַ הַבִּטּוּל שֶׁבָּהֶם בְּעֶצֶם וּכְמוֹ שֶׁכָּתוּב כִּי אַתֶּם הַמְעַט מִכָּל הָעַמִּים שֶׁמְּמַעֲטִים אֶת עַצְמָם כוּ', וְהוּא עִנְיָן יִשְׂרָאֵל מוֹנִין לַלְּבָנָה דְּא' קָטָן מוֹנֶה לַקְּטַנָּה יַעֲקֹב בְּנָהּ הַקָּטָן וְכֵן וְדָוִד הוּא הַקָּטָן כוּ', וּמִפְּנֵי שֶׁיֵּשׁ בָּהֶם עִנְיַן הַבִּטּוּל בְּטֶבַע לָכֵן מַסְפִּיק עַל זֶה גַּם הַזִּכָּרוֹן דֶּאֱלֹקוּת שֶׁמִּתְבַּטֵּל עַל יְדֵי זֶה וּמַנִּיחַ אֶת עַצְמוֹ לְגַבֵּי אֱלֹקוּת וּרְצוֹנוֹ יִתְ'. אֲבָל עִנְיַן הָאַהֲבָה הֲגַם שֶׁהִיא גַּם כֵּן בִּירֻשָּׁה לָנוּ מֵאֲבוֹתֵינוּ מִכָּל מָקוֹם אֵין זֶה כְּמוֹ טֶבַע הַבִּטּוּל וְהַנָּחַת עַצְמוּתוֹ שֶׁבְּכָל אֶחָד וְאֶחָד מִיִּשְׂרָאֵל (וַאֲמִתִּית עִנְיַן הָאַהֲבָה מְסֻתֶּרֶת שֶׁבְּכָל אֶחָד וְאֶחָד בִּירֻשָּׁה מֵהָאָבוֹת מְבֹאָר בְּסֵפֶר שֶׁל בֵּינוֹנִים פי"ח שֶׁזֶּהוּ הַכֹּחַ וּמְסִירוּת נֶפֶשׁ שֶׁבְּכָל אֶחָד וְאֶחָד מִיִּשְׂרָאֵל מִשּׁוּם שֶׁאִי אֶפְשָׁר לוֹ לִהְיוֹת נִפְרָד חַס וְחָלִילָה מֵאַחְדוּתוֹ יִתְ'), וּבִפְרָט

meaning that Jewish souls "are like land which is ready for sowing," and the Torah and its *mitzvot* are the seeds; this is due to the *bitul* which is latent in the essence of the Jewish soul. [Also as the verse in Deut. 7:7] states, *Ki atem hame'at mikol ha'amim*, meaning that "you, the Jews, are constantly minimizing yourselves"; this corresponds to the Jewish calendar that follows the moon, because "you," a small people (the Jews) count the smaller luminary (the moon), just as Yaakov was the smaller (younger) son and David as well was the smallest and youngest. The ingredient of self-abnegation is so ingrained in the Jewish psyche that it is sufficient for us to simply recall G-d in order to achieve full subjugation to Him and His will. However, love of G-d is different. Although it also comes to us as an inheritance from our forefathers, nevertheless love is not as natural as *bitul*, which

---
COMMENTARY

For an example of such a Chassidic discourse, see end of commentary to this chapter.

But in order to achieve the kind of spiritual love that transforms our life — rectifying our animal soul and establishing G-dliness as our main concern—we must strive for the "engraving from within" that accompanies meditation on the G-dly energy within creation. Here, our main concern is not with creation per se, but with the G-dly light that energizes all aspects of creation. "Just as the soul fills the body, so G-d fills and permeates the universe"—and this is true regarding both the higher spiritual creations and also the lower, physical

Essay on Service of the Heart - Love Like Fire and Water

Love of G-d is not as natural as fear. Love develops only through deep meditation.

is the ability to nullify and put ourselves aside that is inherent in every Jew. (The true nature of the love hidden in every Jewish soul as an inheritance from our forefathers is explained in the *Tanya*, chapter 18 as the power of *mesirat nefesh*, or "giving up the soul" that is within every Jew. It is impossible for us as Jews to separate ourselves, G-d forbid, from G-d's unity and oneness.) Because love of G-d involves the revelation of something [that is, it requires effort to unveil something inside of ourselves], therefore, it cannot take place without solid intellectual understanding and without meditation.

שֶׁהָאַהֲבָה הִיא הִתְגַּלּוּת דָּבָר עַל כֵּן אִי אֶפְשָׁר לִהְיוֹת כִּי אִם עַל יְדֵי הַשָּׂגָה וְהִתְבּוֹנְנוּת מַמָּשׁ.

As a general rule, light meditation alone brings us bitterness and a worried heart. This is because we feel the core of the concept, on which we are meditating, to be distant. (That is, the concept is not integrated in our mind since we don't grasp all the details with which it is understood. Also, with our overall knowledge, we grasp only the general nature of G-dliness, which is beyond true en-clothement and integration in our mind. This is similar to the difference between the point of *chochma* which is like a lightning flash of insight — called *pele* (wondrous) — and the [down-to-earth analytic] understanding of *bina*, as is known. [*Chochma* is ethereal, beyond understanding, while *bina* brings the fleeting insight of *chochma* into clear

וְעַל פִּי הָרֹב הַהִתְבּוֹנְנוּת בִּבְחִינַת כְּלָלוּת לְבַד הִיא הַמְבִיאָה לִידֵי מְרִירוּת וְלֵב דּוֹאֵג, דִּלְהְיוֹת שֶׁעֶצֶם הָעִנְיָן מֻפְלָא מִמֶּנּוּ (דְּהַיְנוּ שֶׁאֵינוֹ בִּבְחִינַת הִתְיַשְּׁבוּת בְּמוֹחוֹ מֵאַחַר שֶׁאֵינוֹ מַשִּׂיג הַפְּרָטִים שֶׁבָּהֶם נִתְפָּס וּמִתְיַשֵּׁב הָעִנְיָן, וְגַם דְּבִידִיעָה כְּלָלִית הֲרֵי הוּא תּוֹפֵס אֶת הַכְּלָל דֶּאֱלֹקוּת שֶׁהוּא לְמַעְלָה מִבְּחִינַת הִתְלַבְּשׁוּת וְהִתְיַשְּׁבוּת מַמָּשׁ, וְעַל דֶּרֶךְ הַהֶפְרֵשׁ בֵּין נְקֻדַּת הַחָכְמָה. שֶׁבִּבְחִינַת בָּרָק הַמַּבְרִיק וְנִקְרֵאת פֶּלֶא לַהַשָּׂגָה דְּבִינָה כַּנּוֹדָע) הֲרֵי זֶה עוֹשֶׂה הַכִּוּוּץ בְּמוֹחוֹ וּבְנַפְשׁוֹ. וְגַם בִּידִיעָה וְהֶרְגֵּשׁ גַּם בְּמִקְצָת הַהַפְלָאָה דֶּאֱלֹקוּת (הַיְנוּ מַה שֶּׁמֻּפְלָא אֶצְלוֹ מֵחֲמַת הֶעְדֵּר הַהַשָּׂגָה. וְגַם שֶׁתּוֹפֵס הָעִנְיָן כְּבָר

xxxviii) See footnote of the Rebbe on page 293 ←

COMMENTARY

creations. "Therefore," says the *Kuntres Ha'Avoda*, "the beginning of our detailed meditation must be upon the influx of G-dly energy drawn down from [above] in order to enliven the lower, physical creations." This meditation must be undertaken with much labor and concentration, so that we can "come alive with love of G-d."

Light meditation alone brings us to bitterness and worry over our distance from the One Above.

שֶׁהוּא בִּבְחִינַת פֶּלֶא עֲדַיִן כנ״ל) נִרְגָּשׁ פְּחִיתוּת וְשִׁפְלוּת עַצְמוֹ אֵיךְ שֶׁהוּא מְרֻחָק מֵאֱלֹקוּת (וְעַל דֶּרֶךְ שֶׁנִּתְבָּאֵר לְעֵיל פ״ר בְּעִנְיַן הָאַהֲבָה דְּכִרְשַׁפֵּי אֵשׁ שֶׁבְּהָרָצוֹא וְהָעֲלִיָּ' הוּא מַרְגִּישׁ אֶת הַחָמְרִיּוּת שֶׁנֶּאֱחָז בָּהּ כו' וְעַל כֵּן בָּא לוֹ הָעֲבוֹדָה דִּתְפִלָּה בִּמְרִירוּת וּבְלֵב דּוֹאֵג. וּבְיוֹתֵר הוּא בְּמִי שֶׁיֵּשׁ לוֹ חוּשׁ בְּעִנְיָן אֱלֹקִי שֶׁבְּעַצְמָם יֵשׁ לוֹ קֵרוּב לִידִיעָה וְהֶרְגֵּשׁ עִנְיָן אֱלֹקִי, וְכַאֲשֶׁר הַהִתְבּוֹנְנוּת הִיא רַק בִּבְחִינַת כְּלָלוּת וּבִבְחִינַת זִכְרוֹן הָאֱלֹקִי בִּלְבַד, הַתְּפִלָּה שֶׁלּוֹ הִיא בִּמְרִירוּת עֲצוּמָה וּבִבְכִיָּ' וּבְלֵב דּוֹאֵג בְּיוֹתֵר

intellectual focus].) Therefore, a general meditation produces [worry and] contraction in our mind and soul. This is true as well of our awareness and experience (even if only on a minor scale) of the amazing loftiness of G-dliness. (It is lofty to us because of our lack of intellectual understanding, and also because we grasp the concept only as it transcends us, as mentioned earlier.) We become conscious of our own lowliness and inferior standing, insomuch as we are distant from G-dliness. (This is similar to what was explained in Chapter 4 regarding "love like fire" in the rush and ascent to G-dliness, during which we experience our own corporeal nature holding us back.) Therefore, we approach the *avoda* of prayer with bitterness and a worried heart. This is especially true of those of us who have a natural talent for detecting and experiencing anything G-dly. Since in essence we are close to knowledge and perception of G-dly concepts, when our meditation is shallow and based on simple reminders of G-d alone, we will pray with a feeling of tremendous bitterness and [our] crying is accompanied by a very worried heart.

COMMENTARY

Below in this commentary is a translation of a *sicha*, or discussion delivered by the Lubavitcher Rebbe, *ztz'l*, on the subject of meditation. In order to augment the discourse and also to get us started, here is a possible "game plan" for how to do *hitbonenut* according to *Kuntres Ha'avoda*.

1. First of all, the building blocks of creation are the four categories of mineral, vegetable, animal, and human. Take a few examples of each, for which you know the Hebrew names.
2. Contemplate each of the creations that you have chosen, each one individually, in each of the categories of mineral,

Essay on Service of the Heart - Love Like Fire and Water

(It is known that a worried heart is a vessel for receiving the secrets of the Torah and experiencing G-dliness in the inner recesses of our soul, as is written in *Sha'ar HaYichud* [of the Mitteler Rebbe], chapter 6. This experience must take place before prayer, the main time for this being *tikun chatzot*, [the prayers at midnight]. In this way [by praying *tikun chatzot*], we transform ourselves into vessels to receive G-dly awareness during prayer, as is written there. But, if our prayers are preceded by only a general meditation without the benefit of *tikun chatzot*, then we only become empty vessels, devoid of any inner [G-dly] light. There are variations in this phenomenon, and the more *p'nimi* [dedicated to G-dliness] we are, the more our heart is troubled by the immense gulf between ourselves and G-dliness. And those of us who are less *p'nimi* are disturbed by our own perceived distance from the One Above. In any case, in terms of action and behavior, this is not important.)

(וְנוֹדָע שֶׁלֵּב דּוֹאֵג הוּא כְּלִי לְקַבָּלַת רָזִין דְּאוֹרַיְתָא לְהַרְגִּישׁ עִנְיָן אֱלֹקִי בִּפְנִימִיּוּת נַפְשׁוֹ וּכְמוֹ שֶׁכָּתוּב בְּשַׁעַר הַיִּחוּד פ"ו. וְזֶה צָרִיךְ לִהְיוֹת קֹדֶם הַתְּפִלָּה וְהָעִקָּר בְּתִקּוּן חֲצוֹת שֶׁעַל יְדֵי זֶה נַעֲשֶׂה כְּלִי לֶאֱלֹקוּת בִּתְפִלָּה כְּמוֹ שֶׁכָּתוּב שָׁם, וּבְאֹפֶן הנ"ל בִּתְפִלָּה הוּא רַק שֶׁנַּעֲשֶׂה כְּלִי אֲבָל אוֹר פְּנִימִי אֵין בּוֹ) וּבָזֶה יֵשׁ חִלּוּקֵי דְּמִי שֶׁהוּא פְּנִימִי יוֹתֵר הַלֵּב דּוֹאֵג נַעֲשֶׂה בְּיוֹתֵר מֵהַפְלָאָה דֶּאֱלֹקוּת, וּמִי שֶׁאֵינוֹ פְּנִימִי כָּל כָּךְ לִבּוֹ דּוֹאֵג בְּיוֹתֵר עַל רִחוּקוֹ מֵהָאֱלֹקוּת. וּמִכָּל מָקוֹם לַפֹּעַל אֵין זֶה נוֹגֵעַ

Mere general meditation before prayer turns us into vessels without content.

COMMENTARY

vegetable, and animal. (Human is more difficult since there aren't a variety of species that we can name in Hebrew.) Take time to visualize each of them, and then consider its Hebrew name, visualizing the Hebrew letters as well. This is the "engraving from outside" mentioned by the *Kuntres Ha'avoda*.

3. Remember that your goal is to not only visualize the physical creation, but to capture a feeling and understanding of the spiritual life-force enlivening it. That life-force is conveyed by the Hebrew letters that form its name.

4. Go through this process with each of the creations that you choose within the mineral, vegetable and animal realms. Don't worry about the time that this will take — it's laborious at first but becomes easier with practice.

Shallow, general meditation will not bring happiness in learning Torah.

וְאֵינוֹ מְפַקֵּחַ דַּעְתּוֹ גַּם בְּעֵסֶק הַתּוֹרָה. אֲשֶׁר בִּמְרִירוּת אֲמִתִּי יָדוּעַ שֶׁבָּאָה הַשִּׂמְחָה אַחַר כָּךְ בַּתְּפִלָּה וּבְעֵסֶק הַתּוֹרָה עַל יְדֵי הַהִתְבּוֹנְנוּת הַמְבֹאָר בְּסֵפֶר שֶׁל בֵּינוֹנִים פל"א וְעַיֵּן מַה שֶּׁכָּתוּב בפכ"ו. וּבָזֶה אֵין בּוֹ הַשִּׂמְחָה גַּם בְּעֵסֶק הַתּוֹרָה. וְעַל פִּי הָרֹב עֵסֶק הַתּוֹרָה שֶׁלּוֹ הוּא גַּם כֵּן בְּלֵב דּוֹאֵג וְרוּחַ עָצֵב, מַה שֶּׁאֵין כֵּן בְּהִתְבּוֹנְנוּת בְּדֶרֶךְ פְּרָט שֶׁיּוֹדֵעַ וּמַשִּׂיג אֶת הָעִנְיָן אֱלֹקִי שֶׁנִּתְפָּס בְּמוֹחוֹ הֲרֵי הוּא בִּבְחִינַת שִׂמְחַת הַנֶּפֶשׁ וּכְמוֹ שֶׁכָּתוּב אֵם הַבָּנִים שְׂמֵחָה, וְגַם שֶׁעַל יְדֵי זֶה נַעֲשָׂה בִּבְחִינַת קָרוֹב לֶאֱלֹקוּת שֶׁבָּזֶה תִּהְיֶה שִׂמְחַת נַפְשׁוֹ בְּיוֹתֵר (עַד

We are also unable to open up our mind to learning Torah. It is known that true bitterness [over our distance from G-d] leads afterward to happiness in prayer and Torah study as a result of the meditation which is explained in *Tanya*, chapters 31 and 26. If we practice only a shallow, general meditation, we do not find happiness in learning Torah either. In most cases, we will also learn Torah with a worried heart and sad spirit. However, when we engage in a detailed [and honest] meditation, in order to understand a G-dly concept with our minds, we achieve happiness of the soul, as is written [in Psalms 113:9], *aim habanim smaicha*, "the mother of

---
COMMENTARY

5. When you feel that you have internalized that the real creation is the specific spiritual energy that enlivens it, visualize the creation together with its spiritual energy, and prepare to project your impression to a higher plane — a spiritual plane.

6. The next higher spiritual plane is that of the world of *yetzira*, or general templates of creation. Try to abstract the physical qualities of each category of creation described above; and visualize them from a spiritual perspective. Hardness, for example, may mean spiritual impermeability, while color may represent a kind of spiritual mood. Even though the species you have chosen within each category may have different and even opposite characteristics, they should all be included within the spiritual category which you are striving to imagine — that of the world of general templates of creation, or angels in *yetzira*. They are general because they transcend the specific qualities of the physical world of *asiya*. This should produce an inner *bitul* or feeling of nullification, as well as elevation.

Essay on Service of the Heart - Love Like Fire and Water

> Through detailed meditation, we come close to G-dliness, from which we derive great happiness.

the children is happy"—[where there is *aim habonim*, (*bina* or understanding), there is *simcha* (happiness)]. Through detailed meditation, we also come close to G-dliness, from which we derive the greatest amount of happiness in our soul. (This can occur to such an extent that we may need advice on how to maintain a balance between happiness and a sense of *bitul*, "self-nullification." This balance is the concept of "fear of G-d" within "love of G-d," as written in *Torat Chaim*, it seems to me, in the discourse *Vateled Ada*, regarding various types of song, and see there as well the discourse *V'aleh toldot Yitzhak* regarding the wells...)

שֶׁצְּרִיכִים עֵצוֹת לָזֶה שֶׁתִּהְיֶה הַשִּׂמְחָה בִּבְחִינַת בִּטּוּל שֶׁהוּא עִנְיָן הִתְכַּלְלוּת הַיִּרְאָה בָּאַהֲבָה וּכְמוֹ שֶׁכָּתוּב בְּתוֹרַת חַיִּים כִּמְדֻמֶּה בִּדְרוּשׁ וַתֵּלֶד עָדָה בְּעִנְיַן שִׁיר פָּשׁוּט וְכָפוּל כו' וְעַיֵּן מַה שֶׁכָּתוּב שָׁם בְּדִבּוּר הַמַּתְחִיל וְאֵלֶּה תּוֹלְדוֹת יִצְחָק בְּעִנְיָן וְכָל הַבְּאֵרוֹת כו')

About this [detailed meditation], it is written [in Psalms 100:2], "Serve the One Above with happiness..." This is the key to making real changes in our life. [As a result of the detailed meditation,] an impression of the light is left on our soul all day, and all of our focus is on G-dly matters

וְעַל זֶה נֶאֱמַר עִבְדוּ אֶת ה' בְּשִׂמְחָה, וְהִיא דַּוְקָא הַשַּׁיֶּכֶת לַפֹּעַל, וְהַיְנוּ שֶׁנִּשְׁאָר רֹשֶׁם הָאוֹר בְּנַפְשׁוֹ כָּל הַיּוֹם וְכָל עִנְיָנוֹ הוּא בְּעִנְיְנֵי אֱלֹקוּת לְבַד, וְעַל יְדֵי זֶה נַעֲשָׂה חֲלִישׁוּת הַנֶּפֶשׁ הַבַּהֲמִית הַטִּבְעִית כְּמוֹ שֶׁנִּתְבָּאֵר לְעֵיל פ"ה. וּמַה גַּם בִּכְדֵי שֶׁגַּם הַנֶּפֶשׁ

--- **COMMENTARY** ---

7. After considering these spiritual creations and engraving them upon your consciousness, prepare to extrapolate to the next higher level — the world of *bria*. Consider each of the spiritual entities of *yetzira* that we imagined above - the general templates — and contemplate how they would exist as "potentialities." If the general template and archetype for trees, for example, existed only in potential, consider how it would exist. That which is in potential, not yet formed, carries with it far more possibilities than that which is formed already, even if formed spiritually. Considering the creations of the world of *bria* as "possibilities of creation," should give us another spiritual elevation and should produce even more *bitul*, or nullification to the One Above.

Detailed meditation enables the animal soul to understand and absorb G-dly concepts.

הַבַּהֲמִית יָבִין הָעִנְיָן הָאֱלֹקִי כְּמוֹ שֶׁנִּתְבָּאֵר לְעֵיל פ"ה, הֲרֵי בְּהִתְבּוֹנְנוּת בְּדֶרֶךְ כְּלָלוּת אֵין זֶה שַׁיָּךְ כְּלָל לְהַשָּׂגַת הַנֶּפֶשׁ הַבַּהֲמִית, וְרַק כְּשֶׁבָּא הָעִנְיָן בִּבְחִינָה פְּרָטִית בְּהַשָּׂגָה טוֹבָה וִיכוֹלָה לִהְיוֹת הַהַשָּׂגָה גַם בְּהַשָּׂגַת הַנֶּפֶשׁ הַבַּהֲמִית שֶׁגַם הוּא יָבִין כו').

וְעַל כֵּן עִקַּר הָעֲבוֹדָה בַּתְּפִלָּה הִיא בְּהִתְבּוֹנְנוּת בְּדֶרֶךְ פְּרָט דַּוְקָא בְּאֵיזֶה עִנְיָן אֱלֹקִי שֶׁמִּתְבּוֹנֵן אִם בְּעִנְיַן בְּרִיאָה יֵשׁ מֵאַיִן בִּפְרָטִיּוּת הָעִנְיָנִים בְּזֶה כנ"ל, אוֹ בִּגְדֻלַּת ה' בְּעִנְיַן הִתְהַוּוּת בְּרִבּוּי הַנִּבְרָאִים וּגְדוֹלֵי הַנִּבְרָאִים וּלְכָל אֶחָד וְאֶחָד נִמְשָׁךְ חַיּוּת מְיֻחָד לְפִי מִזְגוֹ וְתִכוּנָתוֹ וּכְמוֹ שֶׁכָּתוּב הַמּוֹצִיא בְּמִסְפָּר צְבָאָם כו' מוֹנֶה מִסְפָּר כו' לְכֻלָּם

alone. In this way, we weaken the animal soul, as explained in Chapter 4. This [detailed meditation] helps the animal soul as well to understand the G-dly concept as explained in Chapter 5. While a general meditation has no effect upon the intellectual comprehension of the animal soul, a detailed meditation leading to a solid grasp of the concept, helps bring about the intellectual understanding of the animal soul as well.

Therefore, the main *avoda* of prayer is in detailed meditation, no matter what the subject of the meditation may be. It may be in the details of creation *ex nihilo* (from nothing). Or, it may be a meditation on the greatness of G-d as expressed in the tremendous variety of creations and their size. Or, it may be on how each individual creation receives its own spiritual energy according to its char-

——————— COMMENTARY ———————

8. Finally, we should strive for the "engraving from within" — the spiritual energy imparted by the Hebrew letters alone. Chassidic literature tells us that the letters are associated with *malchut*, or the final *sephira* of the world of *atzilut*.

To reach this level, our meditation must divest itself of all form, even the refined and subtle archetypes of creation (or angels of *yetzira*) and of potential creation (angels of *bria*). Our meditation must be able to access the spiritual energy of the letters of the Hebrew alphabet alone. Thus, we concentrate on the Hebrew letters alone of each creation that we originally chose, divesting them of any form. This is a tall order, but even if we can't achieve it right away, we should at least know what it is and how to strive for it with the above set of preparations.

Essay on Service of the Heart - Love Like Fire and Water

English	Hebrew	Sidenote

acter and nature, as is written [in Isaiah 40:26], "He who takes out by number the heavenly hosts," and as written there also, "He counts each one [star]...and to each He calls its own name." About this it is written there as well, "Great is our Lord, and tremendously powerful..." in the creation and bringing into existence of the creations. Regarding this verse, the Sages said that the "measure of height" of the "creative power is... [236 *parsaot*]."³⁷ This is also the topic of the verse [in Isaiah above], "Raise your eyes to the heights...from immense strength and with great power, no individual is missing..." This refers to the G-dly power inherent in the very act of creation itself. It also indicates that creations were made to endure, both as species [men, animals, plants] and as individuals [the heavenly bodies], as written elsewhere[xxxix] at length, and in this [too] is revealed the infinite power of G-d in the world. We should meditate as well on

שֵׁמוֹת יִקְרָא וְעַל זֶה אָמְרוּ גָּדוֹל אֲדוֹנֵינוּ וְרַב כֹּחַ בִּבְרִיאַת וְהִתְהַוּוּת הַנִּבְרָאִים וּכְמַאֲמָרָם ז"ל ע"פ זֶה שִׁעוּר קוֹמָה שֶׁל יוֹצֵר בְּרֵאשִׁית כוּ', וְזֶהוּ גַּם כֵּן מַה שֶׁכָּתוּב שְׂאוּ מָרוֹם עֵינֵיכֶם כוּ' מֵרֹב אוֹנִים וְאַמִּיץ כֹּחַ אִישׁ לֹא נֶעְדָּר וְהוּא עִנְיָן הַכֹּחַ הָאֱלֹקִי בְּעֶצֶם עִנְיַן הַבְּרִיאָה וְהַהִתְהַוּוּת. וְגַם שֶׁנִּתְהַוּוּ בְּאֹפֶן כָּזֶה שֶׁהֵן קַיָּמִין בְּמִין וּבְאִישׁ כוּ', כְּמוֹ שֶׁכָּתוּב הָעִנְיָן בְּמָקוֹם אַחֵר בְּאֹרֶךְ, וְאֵיךְ שֶׁבָּזֶה נִרְאֶה וְנִגְלֶה כֹּחַ הָאֵין סוֹף שֶׁבָּעוֹלָם כוּ'. וְגַם יִתְבּוֹנֵן אֵיךְ שֶׁכֻּלָּם מְהַלְּלִים וּמְשַׁבְּחִים לְהַקָּדוֹשׁ בָּרוּךְ הוּא (וּכְמוֹ שֶׁכָּתַב הרמב"ם בְּהִלְכוֹת יסה"ת שֶׁיּוֹדְעִים וּמַכִּירִים אֶת עַצְמָם וְאֶת עִלָּתָם וּמַכִּירִים אֶת מִי שֶׁאָמַר וְהָיָה הָעוֹלָם כוּ', וּכְמוֹ שֶׁכָּתוּב מִזֶּה בְּמָקוֹם אַחֵר), וְיֵשׁ בָּזֶה כַּמָּה חִלּוּקֵי מַדְרֵגוֹת בְּאֹפֶן הַהִלּוּל וְהַשֶּׁבַח שֶׁלָּהֶם בַּנִּבְרָאִים הָעֶלְיוֹנִים לְפִי אֹפֶן הַהַשָּׂגָה שֶׁלָּהֶם, עַל יְדֵי הָאוֹר וְהַחַיּוּת הָאֱלֹקִי הַמִּתְלַבֵּשׁ

The main "avoda" of prayer is in detailed meditation. The subject may be creation from nothing, or the variety and number of creations, or the harmony of creation, etc...

xxxix) See footnote of the Rebbe on page 294 ←

COMMENTARY

9. The meditator will want to continue by contemplating all of the ten *sephirot* of the world of *Atzilut*, with their corresponding soul-powers and names of the One Above, and even higher. This is a meditation that transfixes and mesmerizes, as described by the *Kuntres Avoda*, but if we don't undertake it, then **"what are we doing here?"**

Chapter 6 of *Kuntres Ha'Avoda* tells us that many people stumble in thinking that they will receive G-dly illumination as soon as they begin the meditative process. When this doesn't happen, they become disillusioned and end their effort almost

> *This narrative of praise of G-d lifts us to a higher level, and makes an "impression from the outside" upon us.*

בְּתוֹכָם לְהַחֲיוֹתָם וּכְמָה שֶׁכָּתוּב הַלְלוּ אֶת ה' מִן הַשָּׁמַיִם הַלְלוּהוּ בַּמְּרוֹמִים וְכוּ' שֶׁהֵן ד' עוֹלָמוֹת אֲצִילוּת בְּרִיאָה יְצִירָה וַעֲשִׂיָּה כוּ' שֶׁמְּחֻלָּקִים בְּהָאוֹר וְהַגִּלּוּי וּבַהִלּוּל וְהַשֶּׁבַח שֶׁלָּהֶם כוּ', וְכָל זֶה הוּא עִנְיַן סִפּוּר שְׁבָחָיו שֶׁל מָקוֹם שֶׁעַל יְדֵי הִתְבּוֹנְנוּת וְהִתְפַּעֲלוּת נַפְשׁוֹ בְּעִנְיָנִים אֵלוּ נַעֲשָׂה הַחֲקִיקָה מִבַּחוּץ, שֶׁיּוֹצֵא מִמַּעֲמָדוֹ וּמַצָּבוֹ וּמִתְעַלֶּה נַפְשׁוֹ בְּדַרְגָּא עֶלְיוֹנָה יוֹתֵר וּמִתְקָרֵב לֶאֱלֹקוּת כוּ'.

how all the creations praise and extol the One Above (as the Rambam wrote in *Hilchot Yesodei HaTorah* — that they [the higher creations] know and recognize themselves and where they came from, and they recognize "He who 'spoke' and the world came into existence," as written elsewhere on the subject.) Within this meditation are to be found many levels and varieties of praise of the higher creations, each according to its perception and understanding, and each according to the G-dly light and energy invested in it in order to enliven it, as is written [in Psalms 148], "Praise G-d from the heavens, praise Him in the heights," referring to the four worlds[xl] of *Atzilut*, *Bria*, *Yetzira*, and *Asiya*, that differ from each other in levels of illumination and revelation, and in how they praise the One Above. All of this constitutes a narrative of praise of the One Above. By meditation and excitement over these topics, an "impression is made from the outside," causing us to relinquish our previous station in order to come to a higher and more elevated [spiritual] status, approaching the One Above.

xl) See footnote of the Rebbe on page 294

COMMENTARY
---

as soon as it began. Meditation upon G-dliness and spirituality demands persistence and determination. The soul would not have descended from the spiritual worlds above to be en-clothed in a physical body if it was not necessary, and if it was not possible for us to serve G-d in meditation, prayer, and *mitzvot*. Therefore, we should not get discouraged, but rather stay focused on the G-dly energy of the subject of meditation. We should also be consistent, never failing to take a few minutes before prayer for this contemplation. This is the whole purpose of the soul descending to this world, or as the *Kuntres Ha'Avoda* says, "otherwise, what is it doing here in this world?"

Together with the meditation described above, we must also locate and identify which of our character traits are in need of

Essay on Service of the Heart - Love Like Fire and Water

However, [we must strive, in addition, to experience] the "impression from the inside" that actually brings us closer to G-dliness, while also training our animal soul to love G-dliness. This results from the meditation described in Chapter 4, in which we concentrate upon the G-dly light and energy shining into the worlds. Here, we are referring to G-dliness that is en-clothed in creation. This is not the second level that is referred to in *Sha'ar HaYichud*, chapter 5,[38] [in which two levels of G-dly illumination are described]. There, the second [higher] level is meditation upon what is called the *aiyn HaEloki*, or "G-dly nothingness," which is a far higher spiritual level than that which we are referring to here. Of the two levels

אָמְנָם בְּחִינַת הַחֲקִיקָה מִבִּפְנִים לִהְיוֹת בִּבְחִינַת קֵרוּב מַמָּשׁ לֶאֱלֹקוּת וְגַם הַנֶּפֶשׁ הַבַּהֲמִית יְהֵא לוֹ אַהֲבָה לֶאֱלֹקוּת, הוּא עַל יְדֵי הַהִתְבּוֹנְנוּת שֶׁנִּתְבָּאֵר לְעֵיל פ"ד בִּבְחִינַת הָאוֹר וְהַחַיּוּת אֱלוֹקִי שֶׁמֵּאִיר בְּעוֹלָמוֹת (הַיְנוּ מַה שֶּׁבָּא בִּבְחִינַת הִתְלַבְּשׁוּת בָּעוֹלָמוֹת, וְאֵין זֶה מַה שֶּׁכָּתוּב בְּשַׁעַר הַיִּחוּד פ"ד בַּמַּדְרֵגָה הַב' דְּהַיְנוּ הַהִתְבּוֹנְנוּת בְּהָאַיִן הָאֱלֹקִי כו', שֶׁזֶּהוּ מַדְרֵגָה גְבוֹהָה יוֹתֵר בְּאֵין עֲרֹךְ, דְּמַה שֶּׁכָּתוּב שָׁם ב' הָעִנְיָנִים הָא' הִתְהַוּוּת הַנִּבְרָאִים וְהַנֶּאֱצָלִים וְהַב' הָאַיִן הַמְהַוֶּה כו', הַכַּוָּנָה בַּמַּדְרֵגָה הָא' בִּבְחִינַת הָאוֹר וְהַחַיּוּת הַמִּתְלַבֵּשׁ בַּנִּבְרָאִים וְנֶאֱצָלִים, וּכְמוֹ נֶפֶשׁ הַגַּלְגַּלִּים וְכֵן נֶפֶשׁ

But, we must also strive to attain the "impression from the inside" that comes from meditation on the G-dly energy en-clothed in the world.

COMMENTARY
---

rectification. This can take place only through detailed introspection. Last, but not least, we must resolve to create a fixed schedule for this detailed meditative effort, in order that it become a permanent part of our routine. Then we will merit to achieve love of the One Above and succeed in rectifying our own animal soul.

CHASSIDIC DISCOURSE

In order to bring the above advice into perspective and make it accessible to everyone, including those who do not have access to Chassidic literature, included below is a translation of a discourse of the Lubavitcher Rebbe, *z'l* (the *sicha* is printed in Yiddish in *Likutei Sichot*, vol 6, *parshat Yitro*). This discourse may be used as a starting point for meditation. This discourse begins by comparing the giving of the Torah at Mt. Sinai to a wedding. Both, it points out, are accompanied by "five voices," or harmonious components. It continues:

הַמַּלְאָכִים הָעֶלְיוֹנִים שֶׁהוּא בְּחִינַת הָאוֹר וְהַחַיּוּת שֶׁלָּהֶם וְכֵן בַּנֶּאֱצָלִים הָאוֹר הַמִּתְלַבֵּשׁ בְּעֶשֶׂר סְפִירוֹת דַּאֲצִילוּת בְּכָל סְפִירָה וּסְפִירָה בִּפְרָט כוּ׳, וְהַמַּדְרֵגָה הַב׳ הוּא בְּחִינַת עַצְמוּת הָאַיִן הָאֱלֹקִי וְהַיְנוּ בְּחִינַת אוֹר עַצְמוּת הַמַּאֲצִיל שֶׁלְּמַעְלָה מִבְּחִינַת הִתְלַבְּשׁוּת בְּנִבְרָאִים וְנֶאֱצָלִים.

described there [in *Sha'ar HaYichud*], the first is "creation of creatures and emanations [*sephirot*]," while the second is the "[G-dly] nothingness that creates." The first level refers to the [spiritual] light and energy that is invested in the creations and *sephirot*. It includes the "soul" of the planets and of the higher angels, which is their [spiritual] light and energy, and the "soul" of the *sephirot*, which is the [spiritual] light en-clothed in the ten *sephirot* of the World of *Atzilut*, each and every one individually. The second [higher] level is that of the essence of the "divine nothingness" (*aiyn HaEloki*) which is the light of the essence of the Emanator Himself, above and beyond investment in the creations and emanations.

COMMENTARY

A "voice" (*kol*) in Chasidic nomenclature is a drawing down and revelation of something that was previously hidden. This we see exemplified by the human voice, which reveals and expresses one's intellect and emotions. One's voice corresponds to what he wants to express (when one issues a command, for example, he speaks in an imperative voice, while when he explains an intellectural concept he will speak softly and persuasively). So the spiritual voices from above correspond to the various G-dly revelations that they come to express. The five voices that accompanied the giving of the Torah, then, correspond to five different themes, each higher than the previous one. Each theme is brought down and expressed by one of the five "voices."

The exalted spirituality of Torah is expressed in the fact that it is accompanied by five voices, while the creation of the universe is associated with the number "four." There are four spiritual "worlds" leading ultimately to the creation of our physical world, and each (including the spiritual) contains the four categories of creation — mineral, vegetable, animal, and human. "Four" is associated not only with the creation, but with the Creator as well. He performed the act of creation with His four-letter

Essay on Service of the Heart - Love Like Fire and Water

(All of this refers to the "nothingness" which has a connection to "something" [the "something of creation"—*yesh hanivrah*]. There are two levels to this "nothingness"; one is merely a ray that is en-clothed in the "something" [in order to create it], and the second is the essence of the "nothingness" itself, above its investment in creation. This [second level] is referred to there [in *Sha'ar HaYichud*] as *chochma* [which in general lowers itself to become invested in the creation]. However, what is written there refers to *chochma* in the sense of *koach mah*, ["the power of nullification"], which turns the "something" of [creation] into "nothing" [spirituality]. It completely nullifies creation, in a manner of the [absolute] *bitul* of *chochma*—for elaboration turn to *Imrei Bina*, chapter 58,³⁹ on the subject of *yoreh*. This is not as might appear there [in *Sha'ar Hayichud*] at first glance, that the first [lower] level refers to [meditation upon] the creation of existence and substance, while the second [higher] level refers to [meditation upon] G-dly light and energy. Instead, it is as described above. And what is described here [as the subject for meditation] is equivalent to the first [lower] level over there [in *Sha'ar HaYichud*]—the [spiritual] light and energy en-clothed in creation, which is the soul and life-force of the creations and what they are able to grasp intellectually.)

(וְהַכֹּל בִּבְחִינַת הָאַיִן שֶׁל הַיֵּשׁ, שֶׁיֵּשׁ בָּזֶה ב' מַדְרֵגוֹת בְּחִינַת הֶאָרַת הָאַיִן הַמִּתְלַבֵּשׁ בַּיֵּשׁ, וּבְחִינַת עֶצֶם הָאַיִן שֶׁלְּמַעְלָה מֵהִתְלַבְּשׁוּת כו'. וּמַה שֶּׁכָּתוּב שָׁם שֶׁזֶּהוּ בְּחִינַת חָכְמָה, הַיְנוּ כְּמוֹ שֶׁחָכְמָה הִיא בְּחִינַת כ"ח מ"ה שֶׁעוֹשֶׂה לַיֵּשׁ אַיִן (רְצוֹנוֹ לוֹמַר בִּבְחִינַת בִּטּוּל מַמָּשׁ בְּאֹפֶן הַבִּטּוּל דְּחָכְמָה) וְעַיֵּן מַה שֶּׁכָּתוּב בְּאִמְרֵי בִּינָה פנ"ח בְּעִנְיַן בְּחִינַת יוֹרֶה כו') וְלֹא כְּמוֹ שֶׁנִּרְ' שָׁם בִּתְחִלַּת הָעִיּוּן דְּמַדְרֵגָה הָא' הִיא בְּהִתְהַוּוּת הַיֵּשׁ וְהַחֹמֶר וְהַמַּדְרֵגָה הַב' הִיא בִּבְחִינַת הָאוֹר וְהַחַיּוּת הָאֱלֹקִי כו', אֶלָּא הַכַּוָּנָה כנ"ל. וּמַה שֶּׁנִּתְבָּאֵר כָּאן הִיא מַדְרֵגָה הָא' דְּשָׁם דְּהַיְנוּ בְּחִינַת הָאוֹר וְהַחַיּוּת הַמִּתְלַבֵּשׁ שֶׁזֶּהוּ בְּחִינַת נֶפֶשׁ הַנִּבְרָאִים וְהַשָּׂגָתָם כו').

COMMENTARY

essential name (also known as the "Tetragrammaton"). Each of the four letters is the source of one of the four worlds, and within the four worlds, each letter of His name is the source of each of the four categories of creation — mineral, vegetable, animal, and human. Since, as the *Zohar* tells us, G-d "looked into the Torah

	Description	Text Source	Spiritual Level
1. *Yesh ha'nivrah* "created reality"	Force (*Koach*); creative power within creation	Mentioned here, but not subject of meditation	*Malchut* the direct source of creation *ex nihilo*
2. *Ayn shel hayesh ha'nivrah* "the existential nothingness"	Energy (*Chayut*); G-dly light interfacing with creation	The first level in *Sha'ar Hayichud*, mentioned here as **the subject of meditation**	*Chochma* or *koach mah* nullifies "something of creation into spiritual nothing"
3. *Ayn HaEloki* "the divine nothingness"	Light (*Ohr*) the infinite light which illuminates the Essence, above creation	The second level in *Sha'ar Hayichud* of the Mittler Rebbe, chapter 5, not for meditation here	*Keter* creates from "nothing into something"
4. *Yesh Ha'amiti* "true G-dly reality"	Essence Cannot be described even as "light" or as "infinite"	Not mentioned here	Before the *tzimtzum* ("great contraction")

וְהַיְנוּ אֵיךְ דְּאִיהוּ מְמַלֵּא כּוּלְהוּ עָלְמִין דִּכְשֵׁם שֶׁהַנְּשָׁמָה מְמַלֵּא אֶת הַגּוּף כָּךְ הַקָּדוֹשׁ בָּרוּךְ הוּא מְמַלֵּא אֶת הָעוֹלָם, הֵן בָּעוֹלָם הַתַּחְתּוֹן בְּכָל נִבְרָא וְנִבְרָא בִּפְרָט שֶׁיֵּשׁ בּוֹ אוֹר אֱלוֹקִי׳ הַמְחַיֶּי׳ אוֹתוֹ וְהֵן בְּעוֹלָמוֹת עֶלְיוֹנִים בְּאוֹפַנֵּי הָאוֹרוֹת וְהַגִּלּוּיִּים בְּכָל עוֹלָם וְעוֹלָם בְּעֶשֶׂר הַסְּפִירוֹת שֶׁבָּעוֹלָמוֹת וּבַנִּבְרָאִים

[The meditation here in Chapter 6 of *Kuntres Ha'Avoda*], therefore, is on how He permeates all the worlds. Just as the soul fills the body, so G-d permeates the universe. This is true regarding the lower world, in which each and every specific creation contains the G-dly light that enlivens it. It is true as well regarding the upper [spiritual] worlds, each according to

---
COMMENTARY
---

and created the universe," everything found in the creation comes from and is also found in the Torah. Therefore, we must be able to find the four levels of the essential name of G-d within the Torah itself.

Essay on Service of the Heart - Love Like Fire and Water

its own level of illumination and revelation, and each containing its own ten *sephirot* and creations, as explained earlier in Chapter 4. In general, the [G-dly] light and energy [of the creation] emanates from the *sephira* of *malchut* ["sovereignty," the tenth and lowest of the ten *sephirot* of the World of *Atzilut*], which creates and enlivens the [lower three] worlds of *BY'A* (*Bria, Yetzira,* and *Asiya*). About this, the verse [in Nehemia 9:6] says, "And You enliven them all..." [The letters of "You," *aleph-tav*] allude to the letters of the supernal speech of *malchut* of *Atzilut* and to the [G-dly] light en-clothed within these letters. (It is possible that this allusion refers to the vessels of the ten *sephirot* within *malchut* of *Atzilut*, which become the "soul" of

שֶׁבָּהֶם כו' וּכְמוֹ שֶׁנִּתְבָּאֵר לְעֵיל פ"ד, וּכְלָלוּת הָאוֹר וְהַחַיּוּת הוּא מִבְּחִינַת מַלְכוּת דַּאֲצִילוּת הַמְהַוֶּה וּמְחַיֵּי כְּלָלוּת עוֹלָמוֹת בְּרִיאָה יְצִירָה עֲשִׂיָּה, וְעַל זֶה נֶאֱמַר וְאַתָּה מְחַיֶּה אֶת כֻּלָּם שֶׁהֵן אוֹתִיּוֹת דִּבּוּר הָעֶלְיוֹן דִּבְחִינַת מַלְכוּת דַּאֲצִילוּת וּבְחִינַת הָאוֹר הַמִּתְלַבֵּשׁ בָּאוֹתִיּוֹת כו' (וְיֵשׁ לוֹמַר דְּזֶהוּ בְּחִינַת הַכֵּלִים דְּעֶשֶׂר סְפִירוֹת דְּמַלְכוּת דַּאֲצִילוּת שֶׁנַּעֲשִׂים בִּבְחִינַת נְשָׁמָה לְעֶשֶׂר סְפִירוֹת דִּבְרִיאָה יְצִירָה עֲשִׂיָּה וּבְחִינַת הֶאָרַת הַקַּו הַמֵּאִיר בַּכֵּלִים דְּעֶשֶׂר סְפִירוֹת דְּמַלְכוּת שֶׁבָּקַע הַפַּרְסָא עִמָּהֶם כו' כְּמוֹ שֶׁכָּתוּב בְּאגה"ק סִי' כ' דְּבּוּר הַמַּתְחִיל אִיהוּ וְחַיּוֹהִי חַד, וּבִפְרָטִיּוּת בַּנִּבְרָאִים דִּבְרִיאָה יְצִירָה עֲשִׂיָּה יֵשׁ לוֹמַר

There must be detailed meditation on the G-dly light enlivening creation.

COMMENTARY

Now we can begin to grasp the exalted loftiness of the Torah, as expressed in the phrase that it was given "accompanied by 'five voices.'" In addition to the four levels and categories associated with creation and the essential name of G-d, Torah includes a higher level that transcends the Holy Name itself. This is obvious from the first words of the Ten Commandments, with which the Torah was given to us from above to below: "*I* (Whomever I am, beyond grasp or even hint by any letter whatsoever), *the Lord*, (and nevertheless) *your G-d*, (your strength and life-energy)." All five dimensions of Torah, including that which transcends the Name of G-d, were given to us here in the physical world, and this is what is meant by "given with five voices."

We have no way of directly grasping the nature of a spiritual creation. We can only begin to get a handle on it by extrapolating from physical objects in our environment that come from

שֶׁזֶּהוּ ב' מִינֵי חַיּוּת דִּבְחִינַת כֹּחַ וְאוֹר דִּבְחִינַת כֹּחַ זֶהוּ מִבְּחִינַת הַכֵּלִים דִּבְרִיאָה יְצִירָה עֲשִׂיָּה, וּבְחִינַת אוֹר הוּא מִבְּחִינַת אוֹר הַנְּשָׁמָה וְגַם לְמַעְלָה מִזֶּה כו' שֶׁעַל זֶה נֶאֱמַר אֵין קָדוֹשׁ כַּהֲוָיָ' כַּמָּה קַדִּישִׁין אִינוּן וְלֵית קָדוֹשׁ כַּהֲוָיָ' שֶׁהוּא קָדוֹשׁ וּמֻבְדָּל וּמִכָּל מָקוֹם מִתְלַבֵּשׁ כו' וּכְמוֹ שֶׁכָּתוּב בְּמָקוֹם אַחֵר,

the ten *sephirot* of the lower worlds of *Bria, Yetzira,* and *Asiya.*) It could be alluding as well to a reflection of the ray of G-dly light that radiates into the vessels of the ten *sephirot* of *malchut.* In the process of creation, this ray descends with the *sephira* of *malchut* and together they "break through" the "curtain" [separating the World of *Atzilut* from that of creation *BY'A*]. This is written about in *Igeret Hakodesh,* chapter 20, beginning with *ihu...chad.* In greater detail, we can say that there are two kinds of G-dly energy invested in the creations of the lower worlds of *BY'A*: *Koach,* (power) and *Ohr,* (light). *Koach* is the G-dly light that comes from the vessels of *BY'A,* and *ohr* comes from the [spiritual] lights of the soul [of the ten *sephirot* of *BY'A*], and above and beyond this as well. About them, the verse [in 1 Samuel 2:2] states, "There is no holiness like that of *HaShem* (the four-letter essential Name of G-d).[xli]..." [The interpretation of the *Zohar* on this verse is that] "there are many levels of holiness, but none of them are as holy as the four-letter Name of G-d," which is holy and exalted. Nevertheless, He is involved and invested [in creation], as written elsewhere.

xli) See footnote of the Rebbe on page 296

COMMENTARY
---

spiritual sources. By analyzing a physical object, we can estimate and gain some kind of insight into its spiritual source. So, the best way to understand the four letters of His Name (and in this way to gain an appreciation of Torah, which was given with five voices, higher than the essential name of G-d), is by analyzing the four categories of creation (mineral, vegetable, animal, and human) in this physical world. They correspond to the four letters of the Name of G-d, from which they are created and spiritually influenced.

The distinction between the mineral and vegetable worlds is the following: in an inanimate object, one sees only its physical substance and body. One can detect no movement or sign of life, even though the mineral object has an inanimate soul, which is spiritual and brings it into being. An object of the vegetable

Essay on Service of the Heart - Love Like Fire and Water

Malchut, the lowest of the ten *sephirot*, is the direct source of creation. This is because it:
1) Absorbs G-dly influx from the upper nine *sephirot* of *Atzilut*, and
2) Conducts it to the "lower worlds" of *Bria, Yetzira,* and *Asiya*.

This it does by lowering itself through the *parsa* ("curtain") separating *Atzilut* and the lower worlds. The purpose of the *parsa* is to produce apparent distance from G-d in which the creation appears to be separate from Him, much as a physical curtain blocks most, but not all light. What spiritual influx does pass through may take on the following forms:

1. Letters of Hebrew alphabet	Correspond to the *sephira* of *malchut*.	Create the physical world with power (*koach*)
2. Vessels of *malchut*	Contain the light of the upper nine *sephirot* of the World of *Atzilut*	Impart the spiritual element of energy (*chayut*) to the physical world
3. Light of the *kav*, the ray of G-dliness that extends from above *Atzilut*	Conveys the quality of the infinite G-dly light (*ohr*) from above *Atzilut*	Imparts an illumination (*ohr*) that transcends the duality of physical vs. spiritual

Light of holiness in general is brought down into the world via the name of G-d. Just as when we want to attract someone's attention, we call his or her name, so the way to draw holiness down into the creation is to pray and meditate using His divine name. Thus, the *Kuntres Ha'Avoda* tells us that the above paths and techniques bringing down holy light from Above are accessed by using His essential four-letter name, known as the Tetragrammaton.

Therefore, the beginning of our detailed meditation must be upon the influx of G-dly energy drawn down from the spiritual constellations above in order to enliven the physical creations below. This corresponds to

וְעַל כֵּן הַהִתְבּוֹנְנוּת בְּדֶרֶךְ פְּרָט הִיא תְּחִלָּה בְּשֶׁפַע הַחַיּוּת דְּנִבְרָאִים הַתַּחְתּוֹנִים מֵהַמַּזָּלוֹת הָרוּחָנִי׳ וּכְמַאֲמָר אֵין לְךָ עֵשֶׂב מִלְּמַטָּה כו׳ וּכְמוֹ שֶׁכָּתוּב אֲנִי אֶעֱנֶה אֶת הַשָּׁמַיִם וְהֵם יַעֲנוּ כו׳ וְלָכֵן הַגַּשְׁמִי בָּטֵל אֶל

── **COMMENTARY** ──

world, however, contains spiritual energy that may be detected with one's five senses. In this respect, there is a much greater gulf between the mineral and vegetable kingdoms than between the vegetable, animal, and human kingdoms. The latter three worlds all have something in common — the spiritual energy

The beginning of detailed meditation should be on the G-dly energy in creation. Everything in the physical world has a spiritual counterpart above.

הָרוּחָנִי כו' וְהַמַּזָּלוֹת מְקַבְּלִי' מִשְּׁמְרֵי הָאוֹפַנִּים וְהָאוֹפַנִּים מֵהַחַיּוֹת כו' עַד בְּחִינַת הַמַּלְכוּת כו' וּכְמוֹ שֶׁכָּתוּב מִזֶּה בְּדְרוּשׁ תִּקְעוּ עת"ר בַּדִּבּוּר הַמַּתְחִיל אַחַת שָׁאַלְתִּי, וְהוּא בְּחִינַת הַחַיּוּת דִּבְחִינַת כֹּחַ. וְכֵן הוּא בִּבְחִינַת הַחַיּוּת דִּבְחִינַת אוֹר מִמַּדְרֵגָה לְמַדְרֵגָה וּבְאֹפֶן בְּחִינַת הָאוֹר שֶׁבְּכָל מַדְרֵגָה וּמַדְרֵגָה כו').

the saying of the sages [in *Breishit Rabba* 10,6], "There is no blade of grass below...[which doesn't have a spiritual counterpart above that makes it grow]." And [in Hosea 2:23], "I will answer the heavens, and they will answer...[the earth...]" Therefore, the physical creation is nullified to the spiritual. The [spiritual] constellations themselves receive their influx from the "remainders" of the *ofanim* [lower angels of *Asiya*], and the *ofanim* from the *chayot* [angels of *Yetzira*, who are higher on the spiritual hierarchy than *ofanim*], and so forth, all the way up to *malchut* of *Atzilut*. This is written about in the Chassidic discourse *Achat Sha'alti* in the book of discourses of the year 5670. It [the G-dliness invested in the creation] is the *chayut*, or enlivening energy of the level of *koach*, "power." This is also true concerning the *chayut* or enlivening energy of *ohr*, "light," as it descends from one level to the next, each level of light with its own characteristics.

In each of the three lower worlds there exists a class of angels, messengers of G-d whose mission is to manifest His presence and rule over the created entities of the lower worlds:	
1. *Asiya* "World of Action"	*Ofanim* "Wheels of the chariot"
2. *Yetzira* "World of Formation"	*Chayot* "Living creatures"
3. *Bria* "World of Creation"	*Seraphim* "Fiery angels"
4. *Atzilut* "World of Emanation"	Beyond all but the most refined angels

---
COMMENTARY
---

enlivening them may be detected and experienced — and the only difference between them lies in exactly how the energy becomes revealed (as we will see). In the mineral world, however, there is no possibility of finding any spiritual revelation.

Essay on Service of the Heart - Love Like Fire and Water

The nullification of each spiritual level to the level above it continues up to the initial revelation of the ray of the infinite light of the One Above. The ray [which is the first revelation of G-dly light after the great contraction] is the [source of] immanent, permeating light, which illuminates the worlds. The essence of the ray [is the infinite spiritual light that] illuminates the worlds of infinity above the World of *Atzilut*, while a reflection of the ray shines into the World of *Atzilut* and concludes there. Nevertheless, some light of this reflection breaks through the spiritual barrier separating *Atzilut* from the lower worlds of *BY'A* and is then described as "holy," as mentioned earlier.

וּמַגִּיעַ הָעִנְיָן עַד כְּלָלוּת בְּחִינַת גִּלּוּי הַקַּו מָאוֹר אֵין סוֹף בָּרוּךְ הוּא שֶׁהוּא בְּחִינַת הָאוֹר פְּנִימִי שֶׁמֵּאִיר בְּתוֹךְ הָעוֹלָמוֹת כו׳ דִּבְחִינַת עַצְמִיּוּת הַקַּו מֵאִיר בְּעוֹלָמוֹת הָאֵין סוֹף שֶׁלִּפְנֵי הָאֲצִילוּת וְהֶאָרַת הַקַּו מֵאִיר בְּעוֹלָם הָאֲצִילוּת וּמִסְתַּיֵּים שָׁם וּמִכָּל מָקוֹם בָּקַע הַפַּרְסָא עִמָּהֶם כו׳ כנ״ל, וְהוּא בְּחִינַת קָדוֹשׁ כנ״ל (וְהַהִתְבּוֹנְנוּת בִּבְחִינַת גִּלּוּי הַקַּו שֶׁבַּאֲצִילוּת הוּא בְּחִינַת יִחוּדָא עִילָּאָה בִּכְלָל, וְהַהִתְבּוֹנְנוּת בְּמַדְרֵגוֹת דִּבְרִיאָה יְצִירָה עֲשִׂיָּה הוּא בְּחִינַת יִחוּדָא תַּתָּאָה. וּמִכָּל מָקוֹם בְּחִינַת אוֹר הנ״ל יֵשׁ לוֹמַר שֶׁזֶּהוּ לְמַעְלָה מִבְּחִינַת יִחוּדָא תַּתָּאָה כו׳). וְעַיֵּין מַה שֶּׁכָּתוּב בְּשַׁעַר

Every spiritual level is nullified to the level above it.

COMMENTARY

In general, the vegetable kingdom is closer to the mineral than it is to the animal and human realms. So much so, that when one divides the four categories into "soul" and "body," the vegetable world is included with the mineral under the heading of "body" rather than "soul," which includes the animal and human kingdoms. Just as their names suggest, that which falls into the category of vegetation doesn't fit in the category of animal. The gulf between the two categories becomes clearer when we remember that until the great flood in the time of Noah, only vegetation was allowed as food, and only after the flood did it become permissible to eat animals.

The explanation is the following: The quality of spiritual energy invested in the animal kingdom is a "soul" type of energy, which explains why the animal has a will of its own (in which its soul is expressed). The animal's body is directed and guided by the will of the soul, which is so much a part of the animal that the animal's very essence is not physical substance, but

Kuntres Ha'Avoda - קונטרס העבודה

הַיִּחוּד פ"ד (וְשָׁם הַהִתְבּוֹנְנוּת בִּפְרָטִיּוּת בְּכָל סְפִירוֹת פְּרָטִיּוֹת מֵרֵישׁ כָּל דַּרְגִּין עַד סוֹף כָּל דַּרְגִּין שֶׁהוּא יִחוּד פְּרָטִי כְּפִי מַהוּת וּמַדְרֵגַת הַסְּפִירָה הַהִיא כו').

(Meditation on the revelation of the ray within *Atzilut* leads to the state known as *yichuda ila'ah*, [wherein we experience G-d as the true reality while His creation seems ephemeral]. Meditation on the ray within the worlds of *BY'A* leads to the experience of *yichuda tata'ah*, or lower unity, [in which one experiences the creation as reality, while maintaining some awareness of the oneness of the Creator within the creation]. Still, the light mentioned earlier [that breaks through the separation] would seem to be higher than *yichuda tata'ah*. See *Sha'ar HaYichud*, chapter 4,[40] [which describes] meditation in detail of each particular *sephira*, from the highest levels to the lowest, as a particular *yichud*, [deep grasp of the nullification of each level to the level above it] according to the essence and level of each particular *sephira*.)

Detailed meditation demands intense effort.

וּבְכָל הָעִנְיָנִים הָאֵלּוּ תִּהְיֶה הַהִתְבּוֹנְנוּת בִּיגִיעַת נֶפֶשׁ כְּמוֹ שֶׁכָּתוּב בְּסֵפֶר שֶׁל בֵּינוֹנִים פמ"ב שֶׁלֹּא תִּכְבַּד עָלָיו הָעֲבוֹדָה (וְכַאֲשֶׁר יִקְרֶה לְעִתִּים קְרוֹבוֹת שֶׁכָּבֵד עָלָיו עִנְיַן הַהִתְבּוֹנְנוּת וּמִתְרַשֵּׁל בָּזֶה וְאֵין לוֹ שׁוּם חַיּוּת בִּתְפִלָּה וּמִמֵּילָא נַעֲשֶׂה הַכְּבֵדוּת בְּכָל הָעִנְיָנִים

In respect to all of the above-mentioned concepts, the meditation must take place with great effort of the soul, as mentioned in *Tanya*, chapter 42: "the labor should not be onerous to it [the soul]." (It is not uncommon for us not to feel like meditating. We may become negligent, having no energy for

— COMMENTARY —

"soul." This is not true of the vegetable kingdom — not only does the enlivening energy of a plant have no effect upon its physical characteristics, but the energy itself is a "bodily" energy, because its entire purpose is only to grow and enlarge the plant.

The distinction between the vegetable and animal kingdoms is expressed in the following (among other things): The life-energy (growth) of a plant is dependent on its being planted in a specific place (and when we uproot the plant from its place, it loses its ability to grow). An animal, however is not limited to a particular place, although it has other limitations. The reason is the following: a physical object is delimited by "space." Since the life quality of a plant is a "bodily" quality, the plant is limited to a particular place. But since the energy enlivening an animal

Essay on Service of the Heart - Love Like Fire and Water

prayer, and as a result our lethargy extends itself to all of our spiritual matters. We may become like a stone. But if our [spiritual] life is dear to us, we must overcome this lethargy and enter into meditation with *kabalat ohl*, [acceptance of an obligation, even though we may not feel like it]. When we do so, putting ourselves into a meditative state, the energy and enjoyment will come to us. [We should return to the advice of the *Tanya*, chapter 42]: "...to labor within thought" and meditate upon it at great depth, bringing the concept close to ourselves and strongly focusing our attention upon it until the G-dly concept illuminates our soul, and our soul becomes united with G-dliness. Then, our only desire all day long will be for G-dliness, and nothing else will

וְנַעֲשָׂה כְּאֶבֶן מַמָּשׁ (אז עס נעמט זיך ניט צו קיין זער). וְכָל הֶחָפֵץ בְּחַיָּיו צָרִיךְ לְהִתְגַּבֵּר עַל עַצְמוֹ לִכְנֹס אֶל הַהִתְבּוֹנְנוּת בְּדֶרֶךְ קַבָּלַת עֹל, וְכַאֲשֶׁר יִכְנֹס בְּהִתְבּוֹנְנוּת יִתְעוֹרֵר אֶצְלוֹ הַחַיּוּת וְהַתַּעֲנוּג בָּעִנְיָן, (עס ווערט איהם די זאך געשמאק און דער עניו לעבט בײ איהם) לִיגַּע מַחֲשַׁבְתּוֹ וְיִתְבּוֹנֵן בָּזֶה בְּהַעֲמָקָה טוֹבָה וּלְקָרֵב הָעִנְיָן לְעַצְמוֹ וְיִתְקַע דַּעְתּוֹ בָּזֶה בְּחֹזֶק עַד שֶׁהָעִנְיָן הָאֱלֹקִי מֵאִיר בְּנַפְשׁוֹ וְנַפְשׁוֹ מִתְקָרֶבֶת וּמִתְקַשֶּׁרֶת בֶּאֱלֹקוּת, וְכָל רְצוֹנוֹתָיו כָּל הַיּוֹם הוּא רַק בֶּאֱלֹקוּת וְאֵינוֹ שַׁיָּךְ לְשׁוּם עִנְיָן אַחֵר כו' וְיִשְׁתַּדֵּל לְהָבִיא אֶת הָעִנְיָן לִידֵי הַהַשָּׂגָה דְשֵׂכֶל הַטִּבְעִי (כמו שנתבאר לעיל פ״ד) שֶׁגַּם הוּא

By overcoming our lethargy, we'll experience spiritual energy and enjoyment.

COMMENTARY

is spiritual ("soul") energy, it is not so limited in space (it can move).

Although both are of a "bodily" nature, there is a huge gulf between the mineral and vegetable kingdoms (in a certain sense, more so than between the vegetable and animal). The same is true of the "soul" categories of animal and human; there is a tremendous chasm between them. The human world is infinitely removed from the animal kingdom, since man is the "chosen" of creation, for whom the rest of creation was brought into existence. Just as the point that separates the mineral from the vegetable kingdom is that "mineral" existence is expressed in an inanimate body, so it is from the opposite direction. That which separates the human realm from every other category is the ability to speak, which is the ultimate expression of the soul and spirit, as will be explained.

Kuntres Ha'Avoda - קונטרס העבודה

Then, nothing else will matter to us, and the animal soul will also be aroused to love of G-d.

יָבִין אֶת הָעִנְיָן הָאֱלֹקִי וּבְהִתְעוֹרְרוּת הָאַהֲבָה דְּנֶפֶשׁ הָאֱלֹקִית יִתְעוֹרֵר גַּם הוּא בְּאַהֲבָה לֵאלֹקוּת כו'. וְכֵן הַהִתְבּוֹנְנוּת בְּעִנְיַן נַפְשִׁי אִוִּיתִיךָ כו' שֶׁהוּא עִנְיָן לְאַהֲבָה אֶת הוי' אֱלֹקֶיךָ כִּי הוּא חַיֶּיךָ חַיֵּי הַנְּשָׁמוֹת בִּפְרָט כְּמוֹ שֶׁנִּתְבָּאֵר לְעֵיל שָׁם, וְגַם בְּהִתְבּוֹנְנוּת דְּכַמַּיִם הַפָּנִים אֶל הַפָּנִים כו' כְּמוֹ שֶׁכָּתוּב בְּסֵפֶר שֶׁל בֵּינוֹנִים מפמ"ו עַד פ"נ (וּבח"ב בַּהַקְדָּמָה הַנִּקְרֵאת חִנּוּךְ קָטָן כ' הֵן דֶּרֶךְ כְּלָל כִּי הוּא חַיֵּינוּ מַמָּשׁ כו' וְהֵן דֶּרֶךְ פְּרָט שֶׁכְּשֶׁיָּבִין וְיַשְׂכִּיל בִּגְדֻלָּתוֹ כו' וְאַחַר כָּךְ יִתְבּוֹנֵן בְּאַהֲבַת ה' הַגְּדוֹלָה וְהַנִּפְלָאָה כו' אֲזַי כַּמַּיִם הַפָּנִים כו').

be of importance to us. We should [also] strive to make the subject understood in the intellectual framework of our animal soul (as explained in Chapter 4), such that it, too, will comprehend the G-dly concept. When the divine soul is aroused to love, the animal soul will also be stirred to love G-d. This applies as well to the love of "You are my soul, I desire You..." which is "to love G-d, because He is your life," referring to the life of all [G-dly] souls in particular, as explained there. This applies as well to the love of "as in water, face responds to face," as is written in the *Tanya*, chapters 46 through 50. (The introduction to the second section of the *Tanya*, called *Chinuch Katan*, it is written that [meditation arouses love], "both a general meditation on the fact that He is our life absolutely, and also a detailed meditation with which we understand G-d's greatness... and then meditate on G-d's great and wonderful love for us [leading then to love of Him], "as in water, face responds to face...")

COMMENTARY

The true definition of "spirit" is removal from any category or description through which the spiritual entity might otherwise be grasped or defined. This is true even of descriptions and categories that transcend the five senses that apprehend a physical object. For even though a spiritual entity may belong to a category that delimits its existence and distinguishes between it and any other spiritual object, nevertheless its very spirituality bespeaks a refinement and simplicity that transcends description. The simplicity to be found in a spiritual object expresses itself in several ways, among them:

1. A spiritual entity does not contradict the existence of any other object or entity. Just as we see in the most abstract and refined ideas: The more abstract and refined they are,

Essay on Service of the Heart - Love Like Fire and Water

Even when we meditate in a peremptory manner, our soul becomes excited. (For this no effort is necessary, neither for the meditation itself—since it is only superficial, akin to a reminder with which we recall G-dliness—nor for the excitement [of the meditation], which comes about spontaneously. For in a transcendent way everyone gets excited over G-dliness, and yet the excitement has no bearing on anything practical. It does not bring about any closeness to G-dliness or the fulfillment of His will. Even the bitterness described above [resulting from a haphazard contemplation of G-dliness] is very easily achieved by considering the lofty level of G-dliness from which we are distant. This is particularly true of those of us who have a talent for meditating on G-dly matters, as explained earlier.) And when afterward we begin to meditate on a concept in a [serious and] detailed way, our previous [condition of] excitement will "cool off" completely. (This will be the case as well when we begin to pray with a certain amount of energy after we have learned Chassidut before prayers. When we then start to pray with some detailed meditation, we will become [indifferent and] cold.)

וְהִנֵּה כַּאֲשֶׁר מִתְבּוֹנֵן בִּבְחִינַת כְּלָלוּת בִּלְבַד וּמִתְפַּעֵל בְּנַפְשׁוֹ (דְעַל זֶה אֵין צָרִיךְ יְגִיעָה הֵן בְּהִתְבּוֹנְנוּת מֵאַחַר שֶׁהִיא בִּבְחִינַת כְּלָלוּת לְבַד וַהֲרֵי הוּא רַק כְּמוֹ זִכָּרוֹן שֶׁנִּזְכָּר עַל אֱלֹקוּת כנ"ל, וְהֵן הַהִתְפַּעֲלוּת בָּאָה בְּלִי שׁוּם יְגִיעָה כְּלָל, כִּי בִּבְחִינַת מַקִּיף כָּל אֶחָד מִתְפַּעֵל עַל אֱלֹקוּת, וְאֵין זֶה *) לְשׁוּם פֹּעַל כְּלָל, הַיְנוּ שֶׁאֵין בָּזֶה שׁוּם קֵרוּב לֶאֱלֹקוּת וְאֵינָהּ מְבִיאָה לִידֵי קִיּוּם רְצוֹנוֹ יִתְ', וְגַם הַמְּרִירוּת שֶׁנִּתְבָּאֵר לְעֵיל הִיא בְּנָקֵל מְאֹד עַל יְדֵי הַהַפְלָאָה דֶאֱלֹקוּת כנ"ל וּבִפְרָט בְּמִי שֶׁיֵּשׁ לוֹ חוּשׁ בְּעִנְיָן אֱלֹקִי כוּ' וּכְמוֹ שֶׁנִּתְבָּאֵר לְעֵיל) וּכְשֶׁמַּתְחִיל אַחַר כָּךְ לְהִתְבּוֹנֵן בְּאֵיזֶה עִנְיָן בְּדֶרֶךְ פְּרָט יִתְקָרֵר לְגַמְרֵי מֵהַהִתְפַּעֲלוּת הַקּוֹדֶמֶת (וְכֵן הוּא כַּאֲשֶׁר מַתְחִיל לְהִתְפַּלֵּל בְּאֵיזֶה חַיּוּת עַל יְדֵי עֵסֶק הַדִּבּוּרֵי אֱלֹקִים חַיִּים שֶׁקֹּדֶם הַתְּפִלָּה כְּשֶׁמַּתְחִיל אַחַר כָּךְ בַּתְּפִלָּה בְּאֵיזֶה הִתְבּוֹנְנוּת פְּרָטִית מִתְקָרֵר כוּ'),

Casual meditation may cause a state of superficial excitement over G-dliness, from which we may quickly cool off.

COMMENTARY

the more room they leave for other ideas and concepts.

2. Because of its spiritual nature, a non-corporeal object tends toward that which is above and beyond it (as is found even in "spirituality within physicality," such as fire, which is the most refined of the physical elements. Because of its spiritual nature, it strives "upwards"). This is because the true nature

The previous excitement did not imply any real closeness to G-dliness.

הִנֵּה עַל קֵרוּר הַהִתְפַּעֲלוּת הַקּוֹדֶמֶת אַל יָחוּשׁ וְאַל יִדְאַג כְּלָל, כִּי אֵינָהּ הִתְפַּעֲלוּת אֲמִתִּי, וְאֵינָהּ עִנְיָן וּדְבַר מָה הֵן מִצַּד עַצְמָהּ כִּי אֵין בְּזֶה קֵרוּב לֶאֱלֹקוּת (וְגַם הַחַיּוּת הַנַּעֲשֶׂה עַל יְדֵי לִמּוּד דִּבְרֵי אֱלֹקִים חַיִּים קֹדֶם הַתְּפִלָּה הִיא רַק הַקְדָּמָה וּכְמוֹ כְּלִי לְקֵרוּב לֶאֱלֹקוּת כַּאֲשֶׁר יַעֲבֹד עֲבוֹדָתוֹ בִּתְפִלָּה כִּדְבָעֵי לְמֶהֱוֵי) וְהֵן מִצַּד שֶׁאֵינָהּ שַׁיֶּכֶת לִפְעֹל בְּעֵסֶק הַתּוֹרָה וְקִיּוּם הַמִּצְוֹת בְּסוּר מֵרָע וַעֲשֵׂה טוֹב וּבְזִכּוּךְ הַמִּדּוֹת טִבְעִיּוֹת וְהַיְנוּ דְּבִשְׁעַת מַעֲשֶׂה הוּא רַק הִתְפַּעֲלוּת דִּמְיוֹנִי, וְלֹא נִשְׁאַר מִזֶּה

Now, regarding the "cooling off" of the excitement, we should not worry at all. The previous excitement was not real; nor was it something to be concerned about, for two reasons. One: It contained no feeling of closeness to G-dliness. (Also, the energy generated by learning Chassidut before prayers [in the morning] is merely a prelude [to proper prayer], like a vehicle enabling us to come close to G-d through proper *avoda* during prayer.) Two: It had no practical effect on our learning of Torah nor on our fulfillment of *mitzvot*, neither by doing good (positive

---
COMMENTARY

of a spiritual object is not to remain within the limits of its own existence, but to strive to leave its own existence and be included in its source above.

This is why the human realm contains the true essence of spiritual "soul." The distinction between man and the animal world lies in the intellect that the human possesses, which gives rise to the two benefits listed above:

1. Intellect is not limited or categorized by the world of emotions. Since man has intellect, he needn't remain under the sway of the emotions to which he has a natural tendency from birth. (Other creations are limited by the nature of their natural emotions.) He has free choice to choose the nature of his own emotions. That's the reason that man includes within himself all the categories of existence found in the creation (which is why he's called a "small world") — he's not limited by categories.

2. The striving and inclination of the intellect is to leave its own existence and be included in a higher level. In this as well is to be found the major distinction between man (who is characterized by intellect), and animals (characterized by emotions). As the Torah says, "The spirit of man is to be

Essay on Service of the Heart - Love Like Fire and Water

mitzvot) nor by turning away from bad (negative *mitzvot*). The previous excitement also did nothing to help us refine our natural characteristics. [Clearly] the excitement was only imaginary and therefore left no impression on us for the rest of the day. If so, we never really became [indifferent and] cold, because in truth we were never really excited with a true inner arousal, which only results from meditation and solid grasp of G-dly concepts. The superficial excitement that we did felt would have faded anyway after a short time, without leaving any impression.

שׁוּם רֹשֶׁם עַל כָּל הַיּוֹם, וְאִם כֵּן אֵין זֶה שֶׁנִּתְקָרֵר כִּי לֹא נִתְחַמֵּם וְלֹא נִתְפַּעֵל עֲדַיִן בִּבְחִינַת הִתְפַּעֲלוּת פְּנִימִי וַאֲמִתִּי, הַבָּאָה דַּוְקָא עַל יְדֵי הִתְבּוֹנְנוּת וְהַשָּׂגָה טוֹבָה בֶּאֱלֹקוּת, וְהִתְפַּעֲלוּת הַנַּ"ל מִמֵּילָא יַחֲלֹף וְיַעֲבֹר בַּמּוּעָט זְמַן מִבְּלִי שֶׁנִּשְׁאַר אַחֲרֵי' שׁוּם רֹשֶׁם כו'

The excitement was only imaginary; it would have been better to pray with the simple meaning of the words alone.

(What is preferable to the above is praying with attention to the simple meaning of the words and feeling spiritual energy in doing so. Even though this [prayer] is devoid of the excitement of love of G-d, or of the refinement of our naturally coarse character traits, still, there is a certain inner feeling there. We are able to latch on to something—namely the G-dly energy in the words of our

(וְיוֹתֵר טוֹב מִזֶּה הַמִּתְפַּלֵּל בְּכַוָּנָה בְּפִי' הַמִּלִּים וְיֵשׁ לוֹ חַיּוּת בַּתֵּבוֹת, דְּעִם הֱיוֹת שֶׁלֹּא יֵשׁ בָּזֶה הִתְפַּעֲלוּת אַהֲבָה וְגַם לֹא זִכּוּךְ חָמְרִיּוּת הַמִּדּוֹת טִבְעִיִּים מִכָּל מָקוֹם יֵשׁ בָּזֶה אֵיזֶה רֶגֶשׁ פְּנִימִי וַהֲרֵי הוּא נֶאֱחָז בְּאֵיזֶה דָּבָר הֱיִנוּ בַּחַיּוּת הָאֱלֹקִי שֶׁבַּתֵּבוֹת הַתְּפִלָּה הָאוֹחֵז אוֹתוֹ בְּמִקְצָת עַל כָּל פָּנִים גַּם בְּמֶשֶׁךְ הַיּוֹם, מַה שֶּׁאֵין כֵּן בַּהִתְפַּעֲלוּת מֵהַזִּכָּרוֹן הַכְּלָלִי

COMMENTARY

drawn upward, while the spirit of the animal is to descend"; animals are attracted by the physical world ("down"), while man is drawn to that which is above himself.

Since man is a microcosm ("small world") of the larger universe, all of the four kingdoms in the macrocosm (universe) are to be found in man himself, in a clear and revealed fashion. This is true not only of man's body, but his soul as well. As explained in Chassidic literature, letters (of the alphabet) constitute the "mineral" in man, emotions correspond to the vegetable, the intellect corresponds to the animal, and the source of speech corresponds to the human realm.

הנ"ל שֶׁאֵין כָּאן דָּבָר הָאוֹחֵז אוֹתוֹ כִּי חוֹלֵף וְעוֹבֵר מִיָּד) וּמַה לּוֹ אִם נִתְקָרֵר עַל יְדֵי הַתְחָלַת הַהִתְבּוֹנְנוּת בְּעִנְיָן פְּרָטִי (אֲשֶׁר בֶּאֱמֶת אִם יַעֲמֹד עַל דָּרְשׁוֹ וְיִתְחַזֵּק בַּהִתְבּוֹנְנוּת יָבוֹא סוֹף כָּל סוֹף לִידֵי הִתְפַּעֲלוּת אֱלֹקִי) אוֹ שֶׁנִּתְקָרֵר מִמֵּילָא מִפְּנֵי שֶׁלֹּא יֵשׁ גִּלּוּי אוֹר אֱלֹקִי בְּנַפְשׁוֹ

prayer. This grips us a little bit at least and also remains with us throughout the day. This is not the case though, in the excitement resulting from the superficial reminder of G-dliness mentioned earlier. In that case, there is nothing that holds us, since the excitement dissipates and dissolves immediately.) What difference is there whether the excitement disappears as a result of beginning a [true and] detailed meditation (although in truth if we persist in our meditation we will in the end come to G-dly excitement), or whether we cool off [and become indifferent], because there is no revelation of G-dly light in our soul?

Many beginners expect to receive G-dly illumination as soon as they begin to meditate.

(וְרַבִּים מֵהַמַּתְחִילִים בַּעֲבוֹדָה שֶׁבַּלֵּב יִכָּשְׁלוּ בָּזֶה שֶׁאֵינָם מַכִּירִים וְיוֹדְעִים עִנְיַן הָעֲבוֹדָה וְרוֹצִים שֶׁמִּיָּד יָאִיר הָאוֹר בְּנַפְשָׁם וְיִתְפַּעֲלוּ בְּהִתְפַּעֲלוּת אַהֲבָה אֲמִתִּית, וְכַאֲשֶׁר מַרְגִּישִׁים בְּנַפְשָׁם שֶׁאַדְּרַבָּא נִתְקָרְרוּ בִּתְחִלַּת הַהִתְבּוֹנְנוּת (וְסִבַּת הַדָּבָר יִתְבָּאֵר בְּסָמוּךְ) נוֹפֵל לָבָם בְּקִרְבָּם (זַיי פַאלִין בַּיי זִיךְ אַרָאפּ) וְאוֹמְרִים

Many beginners in the "service of the heart" stumble in that they don't know and recognize the nature of *avoda*. They expect to immediately receive G-dly [illumination and spiritual] light in their souls and to become truly excited with love of G-d. Then, when the excitement goes away at the very beginning of their efforts to meditate (and we will soon explain the reason), they lose heart. They then say to themselves, "Why should

---

COMMENTARY

The explanation is the following: The purpose of letters is to supply influx and revelation (the Aramaic word for letter, *ata*, indicates illumination, as in the verse, [Isaiah 21:12] *ata boker*, "the morning comes"). Letters, said to be from the soul's essence, are as deeply embedded in the soul as they are distinct from its other components. The other levels of the soul involve the person himself (emotions, for example, describe the person, whether he is a kind person or a strict person, etc.). Letters, though, are only a tool that reveals one's abilities and talents. They do not involve the person himself.

Essay on Service of the Heart - Love Like Fire and Water

we get involved in meditation? We're not suited for this!" Thus, their own false illusions lead them to give up, and it would have been better for them to pray with the simple meaning of the words alone. The positive side of this is that they do begin to pray according to the simple meaning, but what usually happens is that they eventually fall away even from that. The truth is that this is a huge error, and there is no small amount of manipulation of the *yetzer hara* ("evil inclination") involved in it. The evil inclination tries hard to entice us away from true *avoda* with all kinds of tricks, so that we won't feel love for G-d, won't come closer to Him and won't refine our naturally earthy character. It is totally incorrect to say that we are "unsuited" for *avoda* (in reality, there can be no such situation, since all souls descended into the world [in physical bodies] in order to purify and refine the animal soul, as it is written [Psalms 139:16],[xlii] "The days in which they were to be formed,

לְעַצְמָן לָמָה לָהֶן לַעֲסֹק בְּהִתְבּוֹנְנוּת שֶׁאֵינָם מְסֻגָּלִים לָזֶה לְפִי דִמְיוֹנָם וּמִתְיָאֲשִׁים מִזֶּה, וְטוֹב לָהֶם יוֹתֵר לְהִתְפַּלֵּל עַל פִּי פְּשׁוּט וְהַטּוֹב הוּא שֶׁמִּתְפַּלְלִים אַחַר כָּךְ בְּכַוָּנַת פֵּרוּשׁ הַמִּלִּים, וְעַל פִּי הָרֹב נוֹפְלִים גַּם מִזֶּה, וּבֶאֱמֶת זֶה טָעוּת גָּדוֹל וְיֵשׁ בַּזֶּה הַרְבֵּה מִתְעָרְבוֹת תַּחְבּוּלוֹת הַיֵּצֶר שֶׁמִּתְאַמֵּץ לְהַדִּיחַ חַס וְחָלִילָה מֵהָעֲבוֹדָה הָאֲמִתִּית בְּכָל מִינֵי תַּחְבּוּלוֹת שֶׁלֹּא לָבוֹא לִידֵי הִתְעוֹרְרוּת אַהֲבָה לִהְיוֹת בִּבְחִינַת קָרוֹב וְשֶׁלֹּא לְזַכֵּךְ הַחָמְרִיּוּת שֶׁלּוֹ. וּבְשׁוּם אֹפֶן אֵין הַדָּבָר כֵּן שֶׁאֵינוֹ מְסֻגָּל בֶּאֱמֶת לַעֲבוֹדָה (דְּבֶאֱמֶת אֵין זֶה בִּמְצִיאוּת כְּלָל, כִּי כָּל הַנְּשָׁמוֹת בָּאוּ וְיָרְדוּ לְמַטָּה לְבָרֵר וּלְזַכֵּךְ אֶת הַנֶּפֶשׁ הַבַּהֲמִית וּכְמוֹ שֶׁכָּתוּב יָמִים יוּצָרוּ וְלוֹ אֶחָד בָּהֶם, דְּיוּצָרוּ הוּא מִלְּשׁוֹן וַיִּצֶר בַּחֶרֶט וְהוּא עִנְיַן קִשּׁוּר הַנֶּפֶשׁ עִם הַגּוּף בִּכְדֵי לַעֲשׂוֹת הַכֹּל בִּבְחִינַת אֶחָד, וְעַל זֶה נִתְּנוּ לוֹ יָמִים וְשָׁנִים כְּפִי הַבֵּרוּרִים שֶׁצָּרִיךְ לְבָרֵר,

Their false illusions lead them to give up quickly. This is the work of the evil inclination.

xlii) See footnote of the Rebbe on page 296 ←

COMMENTARY

Since letters are a relatively superficial component of the soul, the soul-energy en-clothed in them is very contracted. It is accompanied by such great concealment that the letters themselves reveal no life force whatsoever. They don't even express the life-force corresponding to the vegetable kingdom, which is growth. That's why they are described as "mineral." In this respect, the distinction between letters and the other components of the soul is much greater than the differences between the other components themselves. Since the other powers of the soul

Everyone has their individual avoda and portion to refine in life.

וְאִם לֹא הָיָ' צָרִיךְ לְבָרֵר בְּרוּרִים לְחֶלְקוֹ לֹא הָיָה בָּא לְמַטָּה כו' וּכְמוֹ שֶׁכָּתוּב יְמֵי שְׁנוֹתֵינוּ בָּהֶם כו' וְכַנּוֹדָע, וּמִמֵּילָא הֲלֹא נִתַּן לוֹ הַכֹּחַ לַעֲבֹד עֲבוֹדָתוֹ לְבָרֵר כו' וְזֹאת וַדַּאי שֶׁהַנְּשָׁמָה יֵשׁ בָּהּ כֹּחַ הָאַהֲבָה לֶאֱלֹקוּת)

for it too was one of them..." The word for "formed" (*yutzorue*) is similar to the Biblical phrase *vayotzar bacheret*, meaning "welding," and it indicates unity of the soul with the body and making them one. For this purpose, we were given "days and years" [on earth], according to the task of purification that we must achieve in our lifetime, and if we would not need to purify our particular portion, our soul would not have descended into this world, as it is written [in Psalms 90:10], "the days [years] of his life are seventy or eighty..." as known. Thus, it is understood that we were given the potential to perform our [particular] *avoda* and purify [our portion]. [This is regarding the *avoda* of refining the animal soul. As to the *avoda* of arousing love in the divine soul], there is no doubt whatsoever that our soul has the potential for love of G-d [which only needs to be revealed].

We must persist in detailed meditation without worrying about how much time and effort it takes.

רַק שֶׁצָּרִיךְ לְהִתְגַּבֵּר וּלְהוֹסִיף אֹמֶץ בְּהִתְבּוֹנְנוּת טוֹבָה לְהָבִין וּלְהַשִּׂיג אֶת הָעִנְיָן וְלֹא יָחוּשׁ עַל הַזְּמַן וְעַל יְגִיעַת נַפְשׁוֹ בָּזֶה בְּהַעֲמָקָה טוֹבָה שֶׁיּוּנַח אֶצְלוֹ הָעִנְיָן. וּבִלְתִּי סָפֵק וּסְפֵק סְפֵיקָא. אֲשֶׁר יָבוֹא לִידֵי הִתְעוֹרְרוּת אַהֲבָה וְעַל יְדֵי שְׁקִידַת הָעֲבוֹדָה יְהִי' לוֹ בְּנָקֵל מִזְּמַן לִזְמַן עֶצֶם דְּבַר הָעֲבוֹדָה וְתִהְיֶה אֲמִתִּית יוֹתֵר).

We must persist and persevere in proper meditation in order to understand the subject without worrying about the time and the soul-effort that we are expending on this. We should delve deeply into the concept, until it becomes clear to us. There is no doubt, nor shadow of a doubt, that we will achieve love of G-d. By constant and consistent *avoda*, the process will gradually become easier and the *avoda* itself will become truer.

COMMENTARY
---

involve and express the person himself, his soul-energy resides within them in a revealed and clear fashion (and the differences between them are only in the amount and nature of the revelation, as will be explained). Letters, whose only purpose is to draw down influx and provide revelation, are a virtually separate entity from the soul. (It is the same in the macrocosm, that is, in the universe itself. The mineral kingdom expresses no

Essay on Service of the Heart - Love Like Fire and Water

The reason for our indifference at the beginning of meditation is that it feels like a burden.

The reason [we may experience indifference and] "coldness" at the beginning of meditation is mainly because we feel that the *avoda* of prayer is burdensome. We don't want to take upon ourselves the burden of meditative worship with real effort of the mind and heart. This is particularly true of those of us who have gotten somewhat used to the "easy bread" of imaginary excitement which is generated by shallow meditation. In such circumstances, the "yoke" of *avoda* [of detailed meditation] is particularly onerous. This is the main reason that when we begin to meditate—and this is the beginning of true *avoda*—we "cool off" completely; the meditation is difficult for us. (If we experience a general arousal to pray after studying Chassidut before [morning] prayers, as mentioned earlier, and experience no difficulty in the *avoda*, but, quite the opposite, are willing to put in the effort, we

וְסִבַּת הַקְּרִירוּת בְּהַתְחָלַת הַהִתְבּוֹנְנוּת הָעִקָּר הוּא מִפְּנֵי שֶׁתִּכְבַּד עָלָיו עִנְיַן הָעֲבוֹדָה שֶׁאֵינוֹ רוֹצֶה לְקַבֵּל עָלָיו עוֹל הָעֲבוֹדָה בִּיגִיעָה מַמָּשׁ בְּמֹחַ וָלֵב, וּבִפְרָט מִי שֶׁהֻרְגַּל בְּמִקְצָת בַּלֶּחֶם הַקַּל בְּהִתְפַּעֲלוּת הַדִּמְיוֹנִי מֵהַהִתְבּוֹנְנוּת בִּבְחִינַת כְּלָלוּת, כָּבֵד עָלָיו בְּיוֹתֵר עוֹל הָעֲבוֹדָה וְזֹאת הִיא הַסִּבָּה הָעִקָּרִית שֶׁכַּאֲשֶׁר מַתְחִיל לְהִתְבּוֹנֵן שֶׁזֶּהוּ הַתְחָלַת הָעֲבוֹדָה הָאֲמִתִּית מִתְקָרֵר מְאֹד מִפְּנֵי שֶׁהַדָּבָר כָּבֵד עָלָיו (וְגַם מִי שֶׁיֵּשׁ לוֹ הִתְעוֹרְרוּת כְּלָלִי לִתְפִלָּה עַל יְדֵי לִמּוּד הַדִּבְרֵי אֱלֹקִים חַיִּים קֹדֶם הַתְּפִלָּה כנ״ל הִנֵּה אִם הָעֲבוֹדָה בְּעֶצֶם אֵינָהּ כְּבֵדָה עָלָיו וְאַדְּרַבָּא חָפֵץ הוּא לַעֲבֹד עֲבוֹדָתוֹ לֹא יִתְקָרֵר כְּלָל, וְהַהִתְעוֹרְרוּת הַכְּלָלִי הַנ״ל מְסַיֵּעַ לוֹ הַרְבֵּה בַּעֲבוֹדָתוֹ לְהַרְגִּישׁ אֶת הָעִנְיָן אֱלֹקִי הֵיטֵב וּלְהִתְעוֹרֵר בֶּאֱמֶת וּלְהִתְקָרֵב בֶּאֱמֶת כוּ׳. אֲבָל

COMMENTARY

life whatsoever, it is much further removed from the other three realms than they are separate from each other. In all of them is to be found at least some life and soul-energy.)

The second category, the vegetable kingdom, corresponds to the emotions. The emotions involve and "touch" the soul, and are not considered "mineral objects," as letters are. The emotions may undergo great turmoil and excitement. Nevertheless the soul-energy invested in the emotions is unequal (and out of range) to that in the intellect. The very fact that the emotions become aroused (in Hebrew, the word for excitement is related by its root to the word for action or activity) and cause the person to

With regular meditation, we come to feel the spiritual energy of the concept immediately.

כַּאֲשֶׁר הָעֲבוֹדָה בְּעֶצֶם כְּבֵדָה עָלָיו, הִנֵּה בְּהַתְחָלַת הָעֲבוֹדָה הָאֲמִתִּית יִתְקָרֵר גַּם מֵהַהִתְעוֹרְרוּת הַקּוֹדֶמֶת) וְגַם סִבָּה לָזֶה הֶעְדֵּר הָרְגִילוּת דְּמִי שֶׁמֻּרְגָּל בַּהִתְבּוֹנְנוּת יוֹדֵעַ אֵיךְ לִתְפֹּס עִנְיָן אֱלֹקִי, וְהַיְנוּ שֶׁמִּיָּד מַגִּיעַ אֶל הָעִנְיָן עַצְמוֹ וְנִכְנָס תֵּכֶף בְּהַשָּׂגַת הָעִנְיָן, וּמַתְחִיל אֶצְלוֹ מִיָּד חַיּוּת הַהַשָּׂגָה (וְלֹא חַיּוּת הָעִנְיָן שֶׁמַּשִּׂיג, שֶׁזֶּה אִי אֶפְשָׁר לִהְיוֹת וְאֵין צָרִיךְ לִהְיוֹת בְּהַתְחָלַת הַהִתְבּוֹנְנוּת (כִּי יְהִי׳ מֻטְעֶה בְּהִתְפַּעֲלוּת מִכְּלָלוּת הָעִנְיָן לְבַד) עַד שֶׁיִּתְבּוֹנֵן וְיַשִּׂיג הָעִנְיָן הֵיטֵב) אֲבָל בְּהֶעְדֵּר הָרְגִילוּת הִנֵּה בְּהַתְחָלַת הַהִתְבּוֹנְנוּת הֲרֵי הוּא תּוֹפֵס רַק בְּזָהֳרוּרִית הָעִנְיָן לֹא בְּעִנְיָן עַצְמוֹ, וּמִמֵּילָא אֵין לוֹ עֲדַיִן חַיּוּת בָּזֶה, וְגַם נוֹדַע בְּעִנְיַן הַהִתְבּוֹנְנוּת הֲגַם שֶׁהִיא הַשָּׂגָה שִׂכְלִית הֲרֵי אֵינָהּ כְּמוֹ הַלִּמּוּד בְּאֵיזֶה עִנְיָן שֶׁהַהִתְעַסְּקוּת הִיא בְּשִׂכְלִי לְבַד, אֲבָל בְּהִתְבּוֹנְנוּת הֲרֵי צָרִיךְ לִהְיוֹת הַהֶרְגֵּשׁ שֶׁהַהִתְעַסְּקוּת שֶׁלּוֹ הוּא בְּעִנְיָן אֱלֹקִי וּכְמוֹ

won't "cool off" at all. The above general arousal [after learning] helps us immensely in our *avoda* and enables us to profoundly feel the G-dly concept and to become truly aroused and come truly close to G-d. But, when the *avoda* itself is difficult for us, then in the beginning of true detailed meditation, our previous [general] excitement will wane.) Another reason [for this coldness] is lack of consistency. When we meditate regularly, we know how to grasp a G-dly concept. We immediately go straight to the subject itself, feeling right away the [G-dly] energy inherent in the understanding. (Here, we're not referring to the energy of the concept that we grasp, because that cannot occur and also need not occur at the beginning of our meditation. If it did, the excitement would be false, being that it is based on general impressions alone. The energy comes only after we have meditated and come to solid understanding of the concept.) However, with lack of consistency, what we grasp at the begin-

---
COMMENTARY

"leave" his present status and position, indicates their distinction from intellect. However much the person thinks and uses his mind, it never brings him to change his emotional status and leave his previous (personal) position behind. He remains calm. This is an indication that the emotions fail to reach the person himself [his inner core]. They involve the person only insofar as he has to do with "another" — be it another person, idea, object, etc. Only regarding the "other" do the emotions find expression

Essay on Service of the Heart - Love Like Fire and Water

ning of our meditation is only an aura of the concept, and not the concept itself. Therefore, we feel no real energy from the subject. Also, it is known that even though meditation is a mental process, it is not similar to approaching an academic subject in which the study is strictly intellectual. During meditation, we must [also] feel that we are involved with a G-dly concept, as explained in Chapter 1. This, too, is dependent upon regularity. Those who are regular and consistent in their *avoda* acquire this awareness in their souls. They feel that along with the immense effort they put into knowledge and intellectual grasp of the depth of the concept, they also develop an awareness of, and involvement with, a G-dly concept. This awareness powerfully enlivens the meditation. Those who are just beginning their *avoda*, however, have not yet acquired this awareness in their souls, and it minimizes the energy that they experience at the beginning of their meditation.

שֶׁנִּתְבָּאֵר לְעֵיל פ"א, וְזֶה גַּם כֵּן תָּלוּי בָּרְגִילוּת שֶׁהַמַּרְגִּלִים וְשׁוֹקְדִים בַּעֲבוֹדָה נִקְנָה זֹאת בְּנַפְשָׁם, שֶׁעִם הִשְׁתַּדְּלוּתָם הָעֲצוּמָה בִּידִיעַת וְהַשָּׂגַת עֹמֶק הָעִנְיָן יֵשׁ בָּהֶם גַּם כֵּן הַרְגָּשָׁה זוֹ שֶׁכָּל הַהִתְעַסְּקוּת הִיא בְּעִנְיָן אֱלֹקִי שֶׁזֶּה נוֹתֵן חַיּוּת רַב בַּהִתְבּוֹנְנוּת, וּבַמַּתְחִילִים בַּעֲבוֹדָה לֹא יֵשׁ עֲדַיִן הַקִּנְיָן הַזֶּה בְּנַפְשָׁם, שֶׁכָּל זֶה מְמַעֵט אֶת הַחַיּוּת בְּהַתְחָלַת הַהִתְבּוֹנְנוּת.

But when we realize that the entire purpose of our descent into this world is in order to serve the One Above down here in a body with an animal soul, and to purify and refine our natural traits. **And without *avoda*, what are we doing here in the world?** Was it for this that we were created—to eat and drink like an animal? To be involved in all the matters of the world which are lower in level

אֲבָל כַּאֲשֶׁר יָשִׂים הָאָדָם אֶל לִבּוֹ שֶׁכָּל יְרִידָתוֹ בָּעוֹלָם הוּא בִּכְדֵי לַעֲבֹד אֶת ה' לְמַטָּה בְּגוּף וְנֶפֶשׁ הַבַּהֲמִית וְהָיִינוּ לְבָרֵר וּלְזַכֵּךְ אֶת הַמִּדּוֹת טִבְעִיִּים שֶׁלּוֹ. וּבִהֶעְדֵּר הָעֲבוֹדָה מַהוּ עִנְיָנוּ בָּעוֹלָם, וַהֲכִי בִּשְׁבִיל זֶה נִבְרָא לִהְיוֹת כְּמוֹ בַּעֲלֵי הַחַיִּים לַעֲסֹק בַּאֲכִילָה וּשְׁתִיָּה, וְכֵן בִּכְלָל לַעֲסֹק בְּעִנְיְנֵי הָעוֹלָם שֶׁהֵן לְמַטָּה בְּמַדְרֵגָה מִמֶּנּוּ (וּכְמוֹ שֶׁאָמְרוּ

But, if we are not involved in the avoda of meditation, then what are we doing here in the world?

COMMENTARY
---

and arousal. The matters of others, whether it be their good or bad qualities, affect our emotions. He becomes either attracted to the other with love and affection or wishes to escape and run away from them out of fear.

Kuntres Ha'Avoda - קונטרס העבודה

Man's purpose is to reach beyond the creation altogether.

xliii) See footnote of the Rebbe on page 298

הַחוֹקְרִים שֶׁכָּל דָּבָר נִבְרָא בִּשְׁבִיל אֵיזֶה תַּכְלִית דְּהַיְנוּ לְהַגִּיעַ לְמַה שֶׁלְּמַעְלָה מִמֶּנּוּ. וְתַכְלִית הַדּוֹמֵם הוּא בִּשְׁבִיל הַצּוֹמֵחַ וְתַכְלִית הַצּוֹמֵחַ לִכָּלֵל בְּמַדְרֵגַת הַחַי, וְתַכְלִית הַחַי לִכָּלֵל בְּמַדְרֵגַת הַמְדַבֵּר, וְתַכְלִית הַמְדַבֵּר הוּא לְהַגִּיעַ לְמַה שֶׁלְּמַעְלָה מֵהָעוֹלָם כו'), וּבְהֶעְדֵּר הָעֲבוֹדָה הֲרֵי הוּא נִמְשָׁךְ אַחֲרֵי תַּאֲווֹת הַיֵּצֶר הָרַע שֶׁיָּכוֹל גַּם כֵּן לְהִתְאַוּוֹת לִדְבָרִים הָאֲסוּרִים כו' שֶׁבָּזֶה הוּא גָּרוּעַ כו' גַּם מִבַּעֲלֵי חַיִּים הַטְּמֵאִים כו' וּכְמוֹ שֶׁכָּתוּב בְּסֵפֶר שֶׁל בֵּינוֹנִים פכ"ט וְגַם מִלּוּי תַּאֲווֹתָיו בְּתַאֲווֹת הֶתֵּר הֲרֵי זֶה חֵטְא וְעָוֹן, שֶׁהֲרֵי צָרִיךְ לִהְיוֹת קַדֵּשׁ עַצְמְךָ בַּמֻּתָּר לָךְ שֶׁהִיא מִצְוַת עֲשֵׂה דְאוֹ' כְּמוֹ שֶׁכָּתוּב בְּסֵפֶר שֶׁל בֵּינוֹנִים מפכ"ז וספ"ל, וּלְבַד זֹאת הֲרֵי אֵינוֹ מַשְׁלִים הַכַּוָּנָה שֶׁבִּשְׁבִיל זֶה נִבְרָא דַּאֲמִתִּית כַּוָּנַת יְרִידָתוֹ וּבְרִיאָתוֹ לְמַטָּה הוּא בִּכְדֵי לְהַעֲלוֹת אֶת הַנֶּפֶשׁ הַבַּהֲמִית וְכָל עִנְיְנֵי הָעוֹלָם וּכְמוֹ שֶׁכָּתוּב בְּתוֹרָה אוֹר דִּבּוּר הַמַּתְחִיל לְהָבִין הַטַּעַם

than we ourselves? (As the philosophers said,[xliii] everything in the universe was created for a purpose, and the purpose [of all creation] is to arrive at a level above its own. The purpose of the mineral world is to be included in the vegetable, and the purpose of the vegetable world is to be included in the animal world. The purpose of the animal world is to be included in the human, and the purpose of the human is to reach that which is over and beyond creation altogether.) Lacking in *avoda* [of meditation and prayer], we are attracted by the lusts of the *yetzer hara*, which can lead us to be attracted to forbidden matters. At that point, we become lower than even the "impure animals," as written in *Tanya*, chapter 29. Even satisfying ourselves with [the physical] lusts that are permitted by the Torah is a [sort of] transgression, since the Torah commands us to "make ourselves holy in permitted matters," which is a positive Biblical commandment, as mentioned in *Tanya*, end of chapter 27 and end of chapter 30. Aside from

───── *COMMENTARY* ─────

In this particular detail — that emotions have more to do with the aspect of the soul which relates to the "other," (unlike intellect which deals with the soul itself) — the emotions are more like letters than intellect. Neither letters nor emotions are connected with the soul itself, so inevitably they relate to the "other." (Letters are vehicles of expression of the soul, while emotions are illuminations of the soul, as it emerges into revelation).

Essay on Service of the Heart - Love Like Fire and Water

that, we are not fulfilling the intention for which we were created. For the true intention behind our creation and descent down here is in order to elevate our animal soul and all of the worldly matters, as written in *Torah Ohr* in the discourse *Lehavin ha ta'am shenishtaneh yetzirat guf ha'adam*. This is indicated [as well] in the verse, [in Isaiah 45:12], "It was I who made the earth and I created man upon it,"

שֶׁנִּשְׁתַּנָּה יְצִירַת גּוּף הָאָדָם כו', וּכְמוֹ שֶׁכָּתוּב אָנֹכִי עָשִׂיתִי אֶרֶץ וְאָדָם עָלֶי"הָ בָּרָאתִי, דְּזֶה שֶׁאָנֹכִי עָשִׂיתִי אֶרֶץ הוּא בִּשְׁבִיל הָאָדָם וְהָאָדָם עָלֶי"הָ בָּרָאתִי בְּגִימַטְרִיָּה תרי"ג לְקַיֵּם תרי"ג מִצְוֹת לְתַקֵּן בָּהֶם וְעַל יָדָם אֶת הָעוֹלָם כו'.

The true intention behind our creation is the elevation of our animal soul and our portion in worldly matters.

wherein the word for "I" in Hebrew is *Anochi*, which refers to the essence of G-d, as in "I am who I am." [See commentaries to Genesis 27:19.] He created the earth for man, and the numerical value here for "created" (*barati*) is 613, indicating the 613 *mitzvot*, which Jews are to fulfill, thereby rectifying the universe.

When we take all of this to heart, we will accept the obligation of *avoda* upon ourselves without any difficulty whatsoever. We won't feel any [indifference or] coldness whatsoever, G-d forbid. Quite the opposite, we will experience [much] stimulation and motivation in our *avoda* and will overcome our natural resistance and engage in true [and detailed] meditation. Regularity and persistence in our *avoda* will aid us as well, as

וְכַאֲשֶׁר יָשִׂים אֶל לִבּוֹ אֶת כָּל הנ"ל יְקַבֵּל עָלָיו הָעֲבוֹדָה וְלֹא תִכְבַּד עָלָיו הַדָּבָר כָּל כָּךְ, וְאָז לֹא יַרְגִּישׁ שׁוּם קְרִירוּת חַס וְחָלִילָה, אַדְּרַבָּא יְהִי' לוֹ חַיּוּת בַּעֲבוֹדָה וְיִתְגַּבֵּר לְהִתְבּוֹנֵן בְּהִתְבּוֹנְנוּת אֲמִתִּית וְגַם הָרְגִילוּת וְהַשְּׁקִידָה בַּעֲבוֹדָה יְסַיֵּעַ לוֹ כנ"ל, וְהָעוֹלֶה עַל כֻּלָּנָה הוּא הַסִּיּוּעַ מִלְמַעְלָה לְזֶה שֶׁחָפֵץ בַּעֲבוֹדָה אֲמִתִּית וּכְמַאֲמָר הַבָּא

COMMENTARY

All of this exemplifies the four fundamental categories of creation of the macrocosm, the created universe. The vegetable category is enlivened by a "body-energy," which places it closer to the mineral kingdom, while the animal kingdom is enlivened by a life-force which amounts to a "soul" energy, placing it closer to the category of the "speaking" or human world. And just as the distinction between the vegetable and animal kingdoms is that plants are limited to a particular place while animals can move about, so is the distinction between emotions and intellect

לְטַהֵר מְסַיְּעִין לוֹ בְּכָל פְּרָטֵי הָעֲבוֹדָה הֵן בְּהִתְבּוֹנְנוּת שֶׁתִּהְיֶה בְּטוֹב וְשֶׁיַּרְגֵּשׁ הָעִנְיָן בְּנַפְשׁוֹ וְשֶׁיִּתְעוֹרֵר בְּלִבּוֹ, וְהֵן בְּהִתְגַּבְּרוּת הַנֶּפֶשׁ הָאֱלֹקִית עַל הַנֶּפֶשׁ הַבַּהֲמִית כו' (וּבְקוּנְטְרֵס הַתְּפִלָּה נִתְבָּאֲרוּ כַּמָּה עִנְיְנֵי הֲכָנוֹת בִּכְדֵי שֶׁתִּהְיֶה הָעֲבוֹדָה אֲמִתִּית כִּדְבָעֵי לְמִהֱוֵי).

הָעוֹלֶה מִכָּל הַנַּ"ל דְּהַתַּכְלִית הָעֲבוֹדָה הִיא בְּהִתְבּוֹנְנוּת בְּדֶרֶךְ פְּרָט שֶׁעַל יְדֵי זֶה מִתְעוֹרֵר בְּמִדַּת הָאַהֲבָה בַּלֵּב, וְעַל יְדֵי זֶה נַעֲשֶׂה בֵּרוּר וְזִכּוּךְ הַנֶּפֶשׁ הַבַּהֲמִית, מַה שֶּׁאֵין כֵּן בְּהִתְבּוֹנְנוּת בְּדֶרֶךְ כְּלָל שֶׁהַהִתְפַּעֲלוּת הִיא בְּדֶרֶךְ דִּמְיוֹן, וְאֵינוֹ פּוֹעֵל עַל הַנֶּפֶשׁ הַבַּהֲמִית שֶׁנִּשְׁאָר בְּתָקְפּוֹ כְּמוֹ שֶׁהוּא, וְהֲגַם שֶׁאִי אֶפְשָׁר לוֹמַר שֶׁאֵינוֹ פּוֹעֵל כְּלָל עַל הַנֶּפֶשׁ הַבַּהֲמִית דְּוַדַּאי אֵינוֹ דּוֹמֶה כְּמוֹ שֶׁלֹּא הָיָ' עוֹבֵד כְּלָל,

The ultimate avoda is detailed meditation leading to love of G-d in the heart.

mentioned before. And most important of all is the assistance and support accruing from above when we desire true *avoda* of the One Above. As the Sages said, "One who comes to purify himself is assisted from above" in all aspects of *avoda*. Meditation should be done properly; be experienced in the soul and provide arousal in the heart. It should enable the divine soul to overpower the animal soul. (In *Kuntres Ha'Tefila*, it is explained that there are various preparations that can make our *avoda* true and proper.[41])

What emerges from the above treatise is that the ultimate purpose of *avoda* of the One Above is detailed meditation leading to arousal of the trait of love of G-d in our heart. This leads as well to purification and refinement of our animal soul. This is not true of cursory meditation, which leads only to an illusory excitement, and which fails to alter the animal soul. It remains at full strength. Even so, it is impossible to say that this [general meditation] has no effect whatsoever upon the animal soul,

COMMENTARY

(as they exist in the microcosm, in man himself). Emotions themselves (including the intellect leading to emotions) are subsumed in a particular category and description, from which they cannot emerge. The man of kindness is restricted by his natural tendency to perform deeds and acts of kindness toward others; however, within his emotional limitations he may grow from immaturity to full maturity. The minor fondness that he feels early in life may blossom later in life to a great love. And the same is true of the man of strength and judgment...

Essay on Service of the Heart - Love Like Fire and Water

since certainly the animal soul does not remain as if there were no *avoda* at all. Even a haphazard meditation will produce some sort of refinement. Nevertheless, the point is the following: Each and every one of us has a particular trait among our natural characteristics that we must purify and refine. It is known that the souls of our generation are not "new" souls which never came down to this world at all; they are "old" souls that were already in this world and have come down an additional time in order to refine that which they failed to purify in the previous descent. Now since the animal soul is a complete structure, it has all of its soul powers, including those that were already purified. However, those that were already purified are present in a weak form, since they've already been refined, while the trait(s) which have yet to be purified remain at full strength. Therefore, a light meditation will have an effect only on those traits that have already been refined. Any type of G-dly arousal of our [divine] soul will have an effect upon these [already purified] traits and refine them [a bit more], since they've been refined already.

דְּגַם עַל יְדֵי הָעֲבוֹדָה בָּאֹפֶן הַנַּ״ל נִרְאֶה בּוֹ אֵיזֶה זִכּוּךְ וְדַקּוּת (א אײדעלקייט), הָעִנְיָן הוּא דְּהִנֵּה כָּל אֶחָד וְאֶחָד יֵשׁ לוֹ מִדָּה פְּרָטִית מֵהַמִּדּוֹת הַטִּבְעִיּוֹת שֶׁעָלָיו לְבָרֵר וּלְזַכֵּךְ אוֹתָהּ, כִּי נוֹדָע דְּנִשְׁמוֹת דְּעַכְשָׁו אֵינָם נְשָׁמוֹת חֲדָשׁוֹת שֶׁלֹּא הָיוּ עוֹד לְעוֹלָמִים כְּלָל, כִּי אִם נְשָׁמוֹת יְשָׁנוֹת שֶׁכְּבָר הָיוּ בָּעוֹלָם וּבָאוּ עוֹד הַפַּעַם בָּעוֹלָם לְבָרֵר מַה שֶׁלֹּא בֵּרְרוּ בַּפַּעַם הַקּוֹדֵם, וְלִהְיוֹת דְּהַנֶּפֶשׁ הַבַּהֲמִית הֲרֵי בָּא בְּצִיּוּר קוֹמָה שְׁלֵמָה יֵשׁ בּוֹ הַכֹּל גַּם אוֹתָן שֶׁכְּבָר נִתְבָּרְרוּ רַק שֶׁהֵן בּוֹ בִּבְחִינַת חֲלִישׁוּת מֵאַחַר וְהִתְבָּרְרוּ כְּבָר, וְהַמִּדָּה שֶׁלֹּא נִתְבָּרְרָה הִיא בּוֹ בְּתֹקֶף וְעַל כֵּן עַל אוֹתָן הַמִּדּוֹת שֶׁנִּתְבָּרְרוּ מִכְּבָר פּוֹעֵל עֲלֵיהֶם גַּם הִתְבּוֹנְנוּת בִּבְחִינַת כְּלָלוּת, דְּהַיְנוּ שֶׁאֵיזֶה הִתְעוֹרְרוּת אֱלֹקִי שֶׁבְּנַפְשׁוֹ פּוֹעֵל עַל הַמִּדּוֹת הַנַּ״ל לְזַכּוֹתָם מֵאַחַר שֶׁכְּבָר הָיוּ זַכִּים

The souls of our generation are not "new" souls that never came down to this world before.

COMMENTARY

The intellect, though is different. Not only is the intellect not so limited by a particular tendency or description, (as we see, that one can understand even those things to which he is utterly and viscerally opposed), but pure intellect (unadulterated by emotional tendencies) can even bring about change in our natural emotional make-up. Among intellectuals, there are individuals who are insightful, analytic and deep thinkers. Emotions tend

We have "old" souls that have undergone refinement in previous generations, yet we all have character traits that remain in need of work.

(דְּוַדַּאי בְּבוֹאָם בְּהַצִּיּוּר קוֹמָה דְּהַנֶּפֶשׁ הַבַּהֲמִית מֵחָדָשׁ אֵינָם זַכִּים כָּל כָּךְ כְּמוֹ שֶׁהָיוּ כְּשֶׁנִּתְבָּרְרוּ בַּפַּעַם הַקּוֹדֵם וְאִם לֹא יְהִי' עוֹבֵד בַּפַּעַם הַזֶּה יִתְגַּבְּרוּ וְיִתְעַבּוּ בְּיוֹתֵר, וְהַיְנוּ שֶׁמְּקַלְקֵל חַס וְחָלִילָה גַּם מַה שֶּׁתִּקֵּן מִכְּבָר, אַךְ בַּעֲבוֹדָה קַלָּה כְּמוֹ בְּהִתְעוֹרְרוּת כְּלָלִי הַנַ"ל מִזְדַּכְּכִים כוּ'),

(Certainly upon entering anew the complete structure of the animal soul, these traits do not remain as refined as they were when purified the previous time around. Without *avoda* upon them now [as well], they will become much stronger and coarser. Then, even that which was previously rectified will now become damaged, G-d forbid. But, [even] with a casual *avoda* such as the general arousal [and meditation] mentioned above, they become polished and refined.)

אֲבָל בִּכְדֵי לְבָרֵר וּלְתַקֵּן אוֹתָהּ הַמִּדָּה שֶׁלֹּא נִתְבָּרְרָה עֲדַיִן שֶׁהִיא אֶצְלוֹ בְּתֹקֶף וְשָׁוֶה הָעִקָּר שֶׁמַּגִּיעַ לְחֶלְקוֹ לְבָרֵר, אִי אֶפְשָׁר לְבָרְרָהּ בַּעֲבוֹדָה קַלָּה כִּי אִם עַל יְדֵי עֲבוֹדָה וִיגִיעָה בִּיגִיעַת בָּשָׂר וִיגִיעַת נֶפֶשׁ הַמְבֹאָר בְּסֵפֶר שֶׁל בֵּינוֹנִים פמ"ב, וּבְמִדָּה זֹאת בֶּאֱמֶת הָעֲבוֹדָה בִּבְחִינַת כְּלָלִיּוּת אֵינוֹ פּוֹעֵל מְאוּמָה וַהֲרֵי הִיא בְּתָקְפָּהּ כְּמוֹ שֶׁאֵינוֹ עוֹבֵד כְּלָל.

However, in order to purify and rectify whatever character trait that did not yet become purified and that remains at full strength—and is the main component of our task to purify in the world—we must not be satisfied with casual *avoda*. We must work hard and strive with labor of the flesh and labor of the soul, as explained in *Tanya*, chapter 42. When it comes to this trait [that has fallen to us and is our specific duty to purify and rectify], a shallow *avoda* [based upon simple reminders of G-dliness] won't have any effect whatsoever. The trait will remain at full strength as if there were no *avoda* at all.

וְכַנִּרְאֶה בְּחוּשׁ בְּטֶבַע בְּנֵי אָדָם בְּאֵיזֶה מִדָּה פְּרָטִית שֶׁנִּרְאָה בָּהֶם בְּתֹקֶף הִנֵּה כַּאֲשֶׁר עוֹבֵד עֲבוֹדָתוֹ בַּעֲבוֹדָה אֲמִתִּית בְּמֹחַ וְלֵב בְּהִתְבּוֹנְנוּת פְּרָטִית בְּהַשָּׂגָה גְּמוּרָה

We see clearly in human nature that when we work on a particular personality trait that stands out and when we perform our *avoda* truly and properly in our mind and heart, [it

---
COMMENTARY
---

to be one-dimensional (either kind and outgoing, or strict and introverted, etc). (However, when our intellect gets involved with our emotions, the emotions become more varied.)

Essay on Service of the Heart - Love Like Fire and Water

has an effect]. Through detailed meditation involving full understanding and clear perception—such that we feel the concept and our heart is aroused with love of G-d ["like water"], or with "love like fire"—the personality trait gradually becomes purified and refined. It becomes weakened and, at the same time, closer [to the One Above], losing its arrogance and independence, as described in Chapter 4.

וּבַהֲנָחָה טוֹבָה וְנִרְגָּשׁ אֶצְלוֹ הָעִנְיָן וּמִתְעוֹרֵר בְּלִבּוֹ בְּאַהֲבָה בִּבְחִינַת קָרוֹב וּדְבֵקוּת אוֹ בִּבְחִינַת רִשְׁפֵּי אֵשׁ כוּ' מִתְבָּרֵר וּמִזְדַּכֵּךְ מְעַט מְעַט הַמִּדָּה הַהִיא בִּבְחִינַת חֲלִישׁוּת וּבִבְחִינַת קָרוֹב וּבִבְחִינַת כִּלְיוֹן הַיֵּשׁוּת כוּ' כְּמוֹ שֶׁנִּתְבָּאֵר לְעֵיל פ"ד

Within our *avoda*, we must identify the particular character trait that has fallen to our lot to rectify—this trait is bound to be stronger—and apply all of our powers in our *avoda* to correct this particular trait, as is known. However, when the *avoda* is only superficial [based upon "reminders of G-dliness" alone], the trait remains at full strength exactly as it was before and shows no positive change whatsoever. [For example], there are those who are lighthearted (with "white bile"), possessing a tendency toward lust and [physical] enjoyment, frivolity, scoffing, and the like. And

(וּבַעֲבוֹדָתוֹ) צָרִיךְ לֵידַע הַמִּדָּה הַפְּרָטִית שֶׁמַּגִּיעַ לְחֶלְקוֹ לְתַקֵּן הַיְנוּ אֵיזֶה מִדָּה שֶׁהִיא בּוֹ בְּתֹקֶף יוֹתֵר וְיִתֵּן כָּל כֹּחוֹתָיו בַּעֲבוֹדָתוֹ עַל הַמִּדָּה הַזּוֹ הַפְּרָטִית כַּנּוֹדָע). אֲבָל כַּאֲשֶׁר הָעֲבוֹדָה הִיא בִּבְחִי' כְּלָלוּת לְבַד נִשְׁאֲרָה הַמִּדָּה הַהִיא בְּתָקְפָּהּ מַמָּשׁ כְּמוֹ קֹדֶם הָעֲבוֹדָה וְאֵינוֹ נִרְאֶה בָּהּ שׁוּם שִׁנּוּי לְטוֹב, כְּמוֹ יֵשׁ מִי שֶׁהוּא בְּטֶבַע מָרָה לְבָנָה בְּתַאֲווֹת וְתַעֲנוּגִים וְהוֹלְלוּת וְלֵיצָנוּת וּכְהַאי גַּוְנָא וְיֵשׁ שֶׁהוּא בְּטֶבַע הַמָּרָה שְׁחֹרָה כְּמוֹ בְּכַעַס וּמִדּוֹת אַכְזָרִיּוּת וְכֵן בְּעַצְלוּת וְעַצְבוּת כוּ'

Within avoda, we must identify the traits that have fallen to our portion to rectify.

there are those with a darker nature (with "black bile"), possessing a tendency toward anger and cruelty, as well as those who tend toward laziness

---
COMMENTARY

After all is said and done, our intellect is no more than the "animal" world within his soul. The main advantage of the human species (which is completely removed from the animal world) expresses itself in the origin of the power of speech. Which is why man is called a "speaker" (*medaber*) rather than a "thinker" (*maskil*).

The explanation is the following: the spirituality and abstract refinement that accrues to man because of his intellect, which

וּבִפְרָטִיּוּת הֵן בְּהַד' יְסוֹדוֹת הַמְבֹאָרִים בְּסֵפֶר שֶׁל בֵּינוֹנִים ח"א פ"א וְכֵן יֵשׁ מָרָה אוֹכְמָא וּמָרָה יְרוֹקָא כו'.

and depression. (Specifically, these tendencies correspond to the four [physical] elements [fire, air, water, and earth] mentioned in *Tanya*, section 1, chapter 1.) There is "blue bile and green bile," etc.

In discussing the make-up of the natural soul of man, the *Tanya* (first section, end of ch. 1) says that it consists of four types of character traits, corresponding to the four physical [Aristotelian] elements: air, water, earth, and fire, which give rise to:

Fire	Anger, arrogance
Earth	Laziness, lethargy, and depression
Water	Lusts bringing physical enjoyment
Air	Scoffing, idle talk, wastefulness

COMMENTARY

gives him the power to forsake all categories and choose whatever path he wishes (including that which isn't according to his own natural tendencies, and even to transform his natural leanings), is nonetheless still associated with his own existence. Even when man chooses, by dint of his intellect, to take a path that is the opposite of his own natural character, it is because so his own existence and understanding dictates. The same is true of the other aspect of man's spirituality — that which his "spirit tends upward." Even though he is drawn to that which is beyond him, and indeed he leaves behind his own nature and character, he does so because his own intellect grasps the benefit in so doing — in achieving a spiritual level beyond his own. (With his own understanding, he comes to the conclusion that he is limited and that there are things that are beyond his intellect). It's understood then that even his striving to supersede himself is based upon his own existence.

The power of speech, though, is different: Speech allows us to transcend our own existence and communicate with another person. This implies a lack of "self." (That is, our ability to communicate with another is not based on our existence, since nothing in ourselves requires that we communicate with

Essay on Service of the Heart - Love Like Fire and Water

Light, general meditation will not produce refinement and rectification of bad character traits.

Now, when our meditation is only casual—even though we may become excited and [even] inflamed in our soul or achieve bitterness and a worried heart as mentioned earlier—no change whatsoever takes place in our natural character traits. They appear as strong as ever. That is, after prayer, we will continue with our frivolity and scoffing exactly as before prayer. Or we will indulge our lusts and hedonistic pleasures just as before. Quite the contrary, our natural character traits may be even stronger than before.

הִנֵּה בַּעֲבוֹדָה הַנַּ"ל שֶׁהַהִתְבּוֹנְנוּת הִיא רַק בִּבְחִינַת כְּלָלוּת הֲגַם שֶׁמִּתְפַּעֵל וּמִתְלַהֵב נַפְשׁוֹ מִזֶּה וְגַם בִּבְחִינַת מְרִירוּת וְלֵב דּוֹאֵג כַּנַּ"ל, אֵין שׁוּם שִׁנּוּי כְּלָל בַּמִּדּוֹת הַטִּבְעִיִּים, וְנִרְאִים בְּתָקְפָּם כְּמוֹ מִקֹּדֶם, וְהוּא שֶׁלְּאַחַר הַתְּפִלָּה יִהְיֶה בַּהוֹלְלוּת וְלֵיצָנוּת בְּשָׁוֶה מַמָּשׁ כְּמוֹ קֹדֶם הַתְּפִלָּה, אוֹ בְּתַאֲווֹת וְתַעֲנוּגִים כְּמוֹ מִקֹּדֶם, וְאַדְּרַבָּא יָכוֹל לִהְיוֹת בְּתֹקֶף יוֹתֵר

There are two reasons for this. The first reason is the joy that we feel in our soul over our excitement and agitation. (This is an experience of *yeshut*, or ego, that usually coexists with *avoda* based upon reason and logic. However, in true *avoda*, the process of meditation should coincide with *bitul*, or "self-nullification." This is similar to what was explained earlier, that *avoda* done with happiness must be accompanied by *bitul*, so that the happiness should not be selfish or egotistical. However, in the casual

מִפְּנֵי שִׂמְחַת נַפְשׁוֹ (דִּי צוּפְרִידֶענְקַייט) מֵהַהִתְפַּעֲלוּת וְהִתְלַהֲבוּת שֶׁלּוֹ (דְּהַיְנוּ הַרְגָּשַׁת הַיֵּשׁוּת, שֶׁבְּדֶרֶךְ כְּלָל יֶשְׁנָהּ בַּעֲבוֹדָה שֶׁעַל פִּי טַעַם וְדַעַת, רַק שֶׁבַּעֲבוֹדָה אֲמִתִּית יֵשׁ בָּזֶה הַבִּטּוּל, וּכְמוֹ שֶׁנִּתְבָּאֵר לְעֵיל שֶׁצָּרִיךְ לִהְיוֹת בָּטוּל בַּעֲבוֹדָה בְּשִׂמְחָה שֶׁלֹּא תִּהְיֶה בִּבְחִינַת יֵשׁוּת כוּ', מַה שֶּׁאֵין כֵּן בַּעֲבוֹדָה הַנַּ"ל לֹא יֵשׁ בָּזֶה הַבִּטּוּל כִּי אִם הַרְגָּשַׁת עַצְמוֹ) אוֹ שֶׁמְּפַקֵּחַ דַּעְתּוֹ בָּזֶה מֵהַמְּרִירוּת לֵב דּוֹאֵג (וּמוּבָן שֶׁבָּזֶה מְאַבֵּד גַּם הַמְּעַט טוֹב

COMMENTARY

someone else. Rather, the origin of speech is so high that it completely defies any description or category whatsoever, even that which "lumps" us together with another person). Therefore, the power of speech expresses the true and essential spirituality and abstract refinement of the soul.

Based upon the above explanation of the nature and distinctions between the four categories of created existence (mineral, vegetable, animal and human, in the macrocosm and in the

שֶׁיֵּשׁ בַּעֲבוֹדָה זוֹ דַּהֲלֹא מִכָּל מָקוֹם הָיָ' בּוֹ אֵיזֶה הֶרְגֵּשׁ טוֹב, וּבְהַפְקוּחַ הַנַּ"ל נֶאֱבַד הַהֶרְגֵּשׁ הַזֶּה לְגַמְרֵי)

avoda described earlier, there is no nullification of the ego, but rather experience and feeling of the self.) The second reason is that our bitterness and our worried heart lead us to [excessive] openness of mind [leaving us open to frivolity, scoffing, lust and pleasure even more then before we prayed]. (It is understood that if this happens, we lose whatever bit of good there was in our *avoda* since there was at least some positive [G-dly] feeling in it, and in this [excessive] openness [even to topics and stimuli opposed to holiness], we lose this feeling completely).

וְכֵן מִי שֶׁהוּא בְּמִדַּת הַכַּעַס וּמִדּוֹת אַכְזָרִיּוּת יְהִי' כֵּן לְאַחַר הָעֲבוֹדָה כְּמוֹ קֹדֶם הָעֲבוֹדָה לְהִתְכַּעֵס וְלִבְלִי לְרַחֵם עַל זוּלָתוֹ וּלְהִתְנַהֵג אִתּוֹ בְּמִדּוֹת תַּקִּיפוּת, וְיָכוֹל לִהְיוֹת גַּם כֵּן עוֹד הִתְגַּבְּרוּת בָּזֶה מִצַּד הַיֵּשׁוּת שֶׁלּוֹ, אוֹ מִצַּד הַמְּרִירוּת שֶׁבְּטֶבַע מֵבִיא לִידֵי כַּעַס כו' (רַק מִי שֶׁבְּטִבְעוֹ אֵינוֹ בְּהִתְפַּשְּׁטוּת כָּל כָּךְ יָכֹל לִהְיוֹת שֶׁיַּחֲזִיק הַמַּקִּיף מֵהָעֲבוֹדָה בַּדֶּרֶךְ הַנַּ"ל אֵיזֶה מֶשֶׁךְ זְמַן בְּהֶעְדֵּר הִתְפַּשְּׁטוּת הַמִּדָּה הַטִּבְעִית, וּבְיוֹתֵר הוּא בְּהִתְגַּבְּרוּת הַמְּרִירוּת (שֶׁבֶּאֱמֶת זֶהוּ עַצְבוּת) שֶׁמַּחֲזִיק אֶצְלוֹ זְמַן רַב).

Similarly, if we are hot-tempered and cruel, we will remain the same after this perfunctory *avoda*. We will become angry, have no mercy on our fellow man, and act toward others in a very hardened manner. These traits may become even stronger [than before we prayed], either because of our arrogance [as in the first reason given earlier], or as a result of our bitterness [as in the second reason], which by nature leads to anger. (Those of us who by nature are not so expansive may experience the general overall effect of this light meditation for some time, without it leading to the expansion of our natural character traits. This is especially true when the bitterness is very strong, which in truth is depression; in this case the overall effect [of the general meditation] lasts quite a bit of time.)

COMMENTARY
---

microcosm), we can gain a certain understanding of the differences between the four worlds: *Asiya, Yetzira, Bria,* and *Atzilut*.

The beginning of created existence (in which the creation has a distinct awareness of itself) is in the World of *Bria*. But, since *ayn*, or "spiritual nonexistence," still illuminates this level, it is clear in *Bria* that created existence is not true and real.

Essay on Service of the Heart - Love Like Fire and Water

Those of us who do not fool ourselves and are not too mistaken about ourselves understand well the truth of the matter. [We understand] how our principal negative character traits (those which we have not yet rectified, as mentioned earlier) remain inside of us at full strength without any change. We acknowledge that our *avoda* has not had any effect upon us. And in order to fulfill the supernal intention, for which our soul descended into this world—that being to purify our natural character traits, as described earlier regarding the imperative of doing *avoda* in this world (and all the more so, not to destroy our mission, G-d forbid, by making our natural traits even stronger)—we must agree in our heart to dedicate a fixed hour and proper amount of time to the exercise of prayer. We must resolve to do this *avoda* with effort, meditating on one of the G-dly concepts mentioned earlier or similar ones. Our meditation must be specific and detailed. (It is understood that we must

וּמִי שֶׁאֵינוֹ מַטְעֶה וּמְרַמֶּה כָּל כָּךְ יֵדַע הֵיטֵב אֲמִתִּית הַדָּבָר אֵיךְ שֶׁעִקְרֵי הַמִּדּוֹת הָרָעוֹת שֶׁלּוֹ (הַיְנוּ אוֹתָן שֶׁלֹּא נִתְבָּרְרוּ עֲדַיִן כנ"ל) הֵן אֶצְלוֹ בְּתָקְפָּם בְּלִי שׁוּם שִׁנּוּי וְלֹא פָעַל שׁוּם דָּבָר בַּעֲבוֹדָתוֹ הנ"ל, וּבִכְדֵי לְהַשְׁלִים הַכַּוָּנָה הָעֶלְיוֹנָה שֶׁבִּשְׁבִיל זֶה יָרְדָה נִשְׁמָתוֹ לְמַטָּה, דְּהַיְנוּ לְבָרֵר הַמִּדּוֹת טִבְעִיִּים הַמַּגִּיעִים לְחֶלְקוֹ, כְּמוֹ שֶׁנִּתְבָּאֵר לְעֵיל בְּעִנְיַן הֶכְרֵחַ עֲבוֹדַת הָאָדָם לְמַטָּה (וּמִכָּל שֶׁכֵּן שֶׁלֹּא לְשַׁחֲתָהּ חַס וְחָלִילָה בְּהִתְגַּבְּרוּת הַמִּדּוֹת טִבְעִיּוֹת) יְנַדְּבוֹ לִבּוֹ לִתֵּן עֵת וּזְמַן נָכוֹן לְעֵסֶק הַתְּפִלָּה, וְיִתְגַּבֵּר עַל עַצְמוֹ לַעֲבֹד בַּעֲבוֹדָה וִיגִיעָה בְּהִתְבּוֹנְנוּת בְּאֵיזֶה עִנְיָן אֱלֹקִי בְּעִנְיָנִים שֶׁנִּתְבָּאֲרוּ לְעֵיל וְכַיּוֹצֵא בָּהֶם בְּהִתְבּוֹנְנוּת פְּרָטִית דַּוְקָא (וּכְמוּבָן שֶׁצָּרִיךְ לֵידַע אֶת הָעִנְיָנִים הֵיטֵב וּבְהִתְבּוֹנְנוּת מִתְקָרְבִים אֵלָיו יוֹתֵר) וּבְכַמָּה פְּעָמִים שֶׁמִּתְבּוֹנֵן בְּאֵיזֶה עִנְיָן מִתְבָּרֵר אֶצְלוֹ הָעִנְיָן יוֹתֵר (עס ווערט אים אַלץ

In order to avoid fooling ourselves, we need to dedicate a fixed hour and appropriate amount of time to prayer and detailed meditation.

COMMENTARY

Rather, the spiritual nonexistence that creates the World of *Bria* is the true and real existence. The very awareness of this brings the creations of the world of *Briah* to nullification [as, for example, the category of animal, whose body is subjugated to its soul, to the extent that its existence is its soul, or like intellect, which strives upward toward that which is beyond it and in so doing transcends its own existence]. The creations of the World of *Bria* are comparable to simple substance, which has no form (shape, character or color). The creations of the World

As we meditate, spiritual concepts will become clearer to us and permeate us – we will become aroused with true love for G-d in our hearts.	קלערער דער עִנְיָן) וּמִתְעַצֵּם אֶצְלוֹ (עס ווערט פאראייניגט מיט איהם) וְיִתְעוֹרֵר בְּהִתְעוֹרְרוּת אַהֲבָה בֶּאֱמֶת (וּכְבָר נִתְ' בְּקֻנְטְרֵס עֵץ הַחַיִּים אֵיךְ שֶׁקָּרוֹב הַדָּבָר מְאֹד לְכָל אֶחָד וְאֶחָד) וּבָזֶה יְקַיֵּם מִצְוַת הָאַהֲבָה וְיַשְׁלִים הַכַּוָּנָה הָעֶלְיוֹנָה בְּבֵרוּר וְזִכּוּךְ הַמִּדּוֹת טִבְעַיִּים (בְּאוֹפַנִּים שֶׁנִּתְבָּאֲרוּ לְעֵיל פ"ד) וּבָזֶה יִחְיֶי חַיֵּי עוֹלָם בְּעֵסֶק הַתּוֹרָה וּמִצְווֹת כו':

know the subjects well, and then in meditation they [the subjects] will become closer to us.) Then every time we meditate on a particular topic, it will become clearer to us and permeate us. We will become aroused with a true love. (It was already explained in *Kuntres Eitz Chaim* how this *avoda* is truly close to everyone.) In so doing, we will fulfill the *mitzvah* of love of G-d and also fulfill the supreme intention of purifying and refining our own natural character traits (in the ways described in Chapter 4). At the same time, we will gain *chayei olam* ("everlasting life of the spirit") with involvement in Torah and *mitzvot*.

COMMENTARY

of *Yetzira*, possess a general [archetypal, non-specific] form, and those of *Asiya* take on a specific, particular form. [For example, in the vegetable and mineral kingdoms is felt the "bodily" character of the creation, as mentioned above. The nature of the vegetable body is not to be nullified to its bodily life-force. This is true of letters and emotions, which indicate and respond to the "other" — meaning that their existence is felt in relation to the "other"]. Even the "simple substance" of the World of *Bria* takes on "existence" and its simplicity is only that of "existence" — "simple substance." In this, it is similar to the intellect, which, as refined and abstract as it may be, remains the intellect.

Diametrically opposed to this, is the World of *Atzilut*, which is totally G-dly and spiritual, completely transcending the realm of created existence. It is the world of *ayn*, or spiritual nonexistence.

Corresponding to the four worlds of *Atzilut*, *Bria*, *Yetzira*, and *Asiya* (including the spiritual dimension of *Asiya*), which are spiritual and nevertheless bear similarities to the four categories of created existence (mineral, vegetable, animal, and human), are the four letters of the Holy Name of the One Above. The four

Essay on Service of the Heart - Love Like Fire and Water

SYNOPSIS:

Even *avoda* [of the One Above) based upon logic and reason may be superficial. This happens when we are satisfied with a general meditation [without attention to details]. Even though we may become excited and worked up (usually with bitterness and sadness), the excitement is only imaginary. It leaves no impression and does not affect our natural character traits whatsoever. They remain at full strength, [even though] our

קצור

וְהִנֵּה הָעֲבוֹדָה שֶׁעַל פִּי טַעַם וְדַעַת יֵשׁ גַּם כֵּן שֶׁהָעֲבוֹדָה הִיא בִּבְחִינַת מַקִּיף לְבַד, וְהוּא כְּשֶׁהַהִתְבּוֹנְנוּת הִיא רַק בִּכְלָלוּת הָעִנְיָן דְּעִם הֱיוֹת שֶׁמִּתְפַּעֵל וּמִתְלַהֵב (וְעַל פִּי הָרַב הוּא בִּבְחִינַת מְרִירוּת וְעַצְבוּת) הוּא רַק הִתְפַּעֲלוּת דְּמְיוֹנִי, וְאֵינוֹ מִזֶּה שׁוּם רֹשֶׁם וְאֵינוֹ פּוֹעֵל כְּלָל עַל הַמִּדּוֹת טִבְעִיִּים שֶׁהֵן אֶצְלוֹ בְּחֹזֶק שֶׁזֶּה חֶלְקוֹ וְעִנְיָנוּ בָּעוֹלָם לְבָרְרָם

COMMENTARY

letters of His Name are the transcendent source and origin of all of creation. They are comparable (on a far higher, "out of range" plane) to the four categories of creation which are indeed influenced by them after a tremendous amount of contraction and descent of His holy, infinite light. From this, it is understood that the four letters of G-d's Name (including the *yud*) do not yet constitute the highest expression of infinite abstract spirituality, because they have some relationship to the lower categories of physical creation.

Now we can begin to understand the special nature of Torah, which was given in "five voices." This tells us that with Torah there is a fifth level, beyond the four "possible" levels discussed above. It is the true abstract and spiritual infinity which is the essence of the Torah, as it is united with the infinite light of the One Above, may He be blessed. That is, as well, the explanation of the connection between a bridegroom and Torah, such that both are connected with the same number of "five voices." A bridegroom also expresses a fifth power — the power of giving birth (the commandment of "be fruitful and multiply" is the purpose of marriage) — connected with a higher and more abstract level than the "existence" of the four categories of creation mentioned above.

וּלְזַכְּכָם, וְהֶחָפֵץ בְּחַיֵּי נַפְשׁוֹ וּלְהַשְׁלִים הַכַּוָּנָה הָעֶלְיוֹנָה בְּהֶכְרֵחַ לַעֲבֹד בַּעֲבוֹדָה וְיַגִּיעָה בַּתְּפִלָּה בְּהִתְבּוֹנְנוּת בִּבְחִינַת פְּרָטִיּוּת דַּוְקָא (וְנִתְ׳ אֵיזֶה עִנְיָנֵי הִתְבּוֹנְנוּת בִּבְחִינַת פְּרָטִיּוּת) וּבְהַעֲמָקַת הַדַּעַת שֶׁעַל יְדֵי זֶה דַּוְקָא יִתְעוֹרֵר בְּאַהֲבָה בֶּאֱמֶת וְעַל יְדֵי זֶה יַשְׁלִים הַכַּוָּנָה הָעֶלְיוֹנָה בְּבֵרוּר וְזִכּוּךְ הַנֶּפֶשׁ הַבַּהֲמִית וּבְקִיּוּם הַתּוֹרָה וְהַמִּצְוֹת כוּ׳.

life's mission is to purify and refine them. If we desire life of the soul and to fulfill the supernal intention from above, we must perform *avoda* of prayer with detailed meditation, as explained in detail. The meditation must take place with deep concentration, through which we will become aroused to true love of G-d. In so doing, we will fulfill the supernal intention, which is (1) purification and refinement of the animal soul, and (2) the fulfillment of the *mitzvot* of the Torah.

COMMENTARY

Despite the tremendous elevation, essence, and abstract simplicity of Torah, which transcends the four letters of G-d's Name, it was nonetheless, given with five voices. That means that the Torah was given with the four aspects of His Divine Name, and with a fifth highest aspect that accompanied the four. That is the meaning of the Torah being given with five general levels. The reason is the following: The four levels of the Torah associated with His exalted and Holy Name correspond to and arouse the four spiritual levels in man: *Nefesh* (enlivening soul), *ruach* (emotional dimension), *neshama* (intellect), and *chaya* (will). Simultaneously, the essence of the Torah has the power to arouse the *yechida* of the soul — the level in man that is connected to the *Yachid*, the One Above. That's why all five voices of the Torah were given together; He wanted all four "lower levels" of the soul to be illuminated and permeated with the highest level, the *yechida*. He wanted the very existence of man to be permeated with the power to turn the world (which consists of mineral, vegetable, animal, and human) into a dwelling place for the One Above, in all of His holy essence.

CHAPTER 7

פרק ז

There is another phenomenon (resulting from superficial *avoda*), and it occurs when we adopt refined and elevated behavior when, in truth, we have not refined [or elevated] any detail [of our personality] at all. We demand of ourselves all that is admirable and lofty, desiring, for example, to be on high spiritual rungs of *avoda*. We want to take on new levels of carefulness and stringency and to fulfill the *mitzvot* with added elaboration. (In this particular detail, we will indeed embellish the *mitzvot* in any number of ways, because embellishment of the positive *mitzvot* is far easier than being careful not to transgress the negative *mitzvot*.) However, we are unable to control ourselves when it comes to actual situations, and in particular, when our natural character traits are involved. This is because our animal soul [still dominates, though it] does not completely hide and conceal our divine soul, and our divine soul is a little bit revealed.

וְהִנֵּה יֵשׁ עוֹד צִיּוּר בַּזֶּה (שֶׁהוּא גַּם כֵּן תּוֹלֶדֶת הָעֲבוֹדָה בִּבְחִינַת כְּלָלוּת) וְהוּא שֶׁנִּרְאֶה בּוֹ דַּקּוּת וְעִנְיָנִים נַעֲלִים. וּבֶאֱמֶת אֵינוֹ מְזֻכָּךְ בְּשׁוּם פְּרָט וְהַיְנוּ שֶׁרוֹצֶה וְתוֹבֵעַ מֵעַצְמוֹ כָּל דָּבָר טוֹב וְנַעֲלֶה וּכְמוֹ שֶׁרוֹצֶה לִהְיוֹת דַּוְקָא בְּמַדְרֵגוֹת גְּבוֹהוֹת בָּעֲבוֹדָה, וּלְדַקְדֵּק בְּכַמָּה זְהִירוּת וְחֻמְרוֹת וּלְהַדֵּר בְּכַמָּה הִדּוּרֵי מִצְוָה (וּבִפְרָט זֶה יַעֲשֶׂה כֵּן בֶּאֱמֶת וִיהַדֵּר בְּכַמָּה עִנְיָנִים, כִּי הַהִדּוּר בַּעֲשֵׂה טוֹב בְּנָקֵל בְּאֵין עֲרֹךְ מֵהַזְּהִירוּת בְּסוּר מֵרָע) וּלְהֶפֶךְ לֹא יוּכַל לַעֲמֹד עַל נַפְשׁוֹ כְּלָל בְּאֵיזֶה עִנְיָן לְפֹעַל, וּבִפְרָט בְּעִקְּרֵי הַמִּדּוֹת טִבְעִיִּים שֶׁלּוֹ, וְזֶהוּ מִפְּנֵי שֶׁהַנֶּפֶשׁ הַבַּהֲמִית אֵינוֹ מַעֲלִים וּמַסְתִּיר אֶצְלוֹ כָּל כָּךְ עַל הַנֶּפֶשׁ הָאֱלֹקִית וְעוֹמֵד הַנֶּפֶשׁ הָאֱלֹקִית בִּקְצָת הִתְגַּלּוּת

Another result of superficial meditation; we may adopt refined behavior that is out of touch with our real spiritual level.

COMMENTARY

CHAPTER 7: SPIRITUAL HONESTY

Chapter 7 of *Kuntres Ha'Avoda* describes one more phenomenon that may occur to us when we meditate in only a perfunctory, superficial fashion, contemplating G-dly topics only enough to barely awaken and reveal our divine soul. By doing so, we catch a glimpse of the highest spiritual rungs and naturally want to ascend there. But we haven't done any work on our animal soul to refine and purify it, and therefore any behavior that reflects a high spiritual level on our part isn't real. We may adopt embellishments of the *mitzvot* and stringencies in *halacha*,

This may be from birth or we may have slightly revealed our G-dly soul through loud prayer.

(אִם שֶׁזֶּהוּ אֶצְלוֹ כָּךְ מִתּוֹלַדְתּוֹ אוֹ שֶׁהֵבִיא אֶת הַנֶּפֶשׁ הָאֱלֹקִית לִידֵי הִתְגַּלּוּת עַל יְדֵי כַּמָּה פְּעָמִים בַּעֲבוֹדָה בְּהִתְגַּלּוּת נַפְשׁוֹ בְּהִתְפַּעֲלוּת וָרַעַשׁ, דְּעַם הֱיוֹת שֶׁהִיא הִתְפַּעֲלוּת חִיצוֹנִית (וְהַסִּימָן עַל זֶה שֶׁבָּאָה בִּצְעָקוֹת וְגַם בִּתְנוּעוֹת חִיצוֹנִיּוֹת כוּ') מִכָּל מָקוֹם הֲרֵי זֶה פּוֹעֵל קְצָת הִתְגַּלּוּת הַנֶּפֶשׁ הָאֱלֹקִית (רְצוֹנוֹ לוֹמַר כְּמוֹ שֶׁאָמַרְנוּ קְצָת הִתְגַּלּוּת שֶׁהִיא הִתְגַּלּוּת הֶאָרָה חִיצוֹנִית לְבַד מֵהַנֶּפֶשׁ הָאֱלֹקִית לֹא הִתְגַּלּוּת הַכֹּחוֹת פְּנִימִיִּים שֶׁלּוֹ שֶׁהֵן שֵׂכֶל וּמִדּוֹת) וְגַם בִּטּוּל כְּלָלִי בַּנֶּפֶשׁ הַבַּהֲמִית שֶׁאֵינוֹ מַעֲלִים וּמְכַסֶּה כָּל כָּךְ

This may be the case from birth or we may have caused our divine soul to be revealed on several occasions with loud praying in a state of high excitement, which brought us in touch with the divine manifestation of our soul. Although it is true that this is a superficial excitement (the proof of which is the accompaniment of shouting and exaggerated movements), nevertheless such behavior does produce some revelation of our divine soul, even if only a little. ("Some revelation" means here a lone ray of the divine soul, as opposed to full disclosure of the inner powers of the soul, [including] its intellect and emotions.) It [such behavior] also produces an overall nullification of the animal soul, such that it doesn't conceal [the divine soul] so much.

(שֶׁזֶּהוּ עַל יְדֵי הִתְגַּלּוּת הַהֶאָרָה חִיצוֹנִית דְּנֶפֶשׁ הָאֱלֹקִית וְגַם עַל יְדֵי הַבִּטּוּל חִיצוֹנִי בְּחָמְרִיּוּת הַגּוּף וְנֶפֶשׁ הַבַּהֲמִית בִּצְעָקוֹת וּתְנוּעוֹת חִיצוֹנִיּוֹת שֶׁמְּבַטֵּל עַצְמוֹ וְכָל מַה שֶּׁסְּבִיבוֹ, שֶׁכָּל זֶה פּוֹעֵל עַל הַבִּטּוּל

This is a result of the revelation of the ray of our divine soul—and also of the superficial nullification of the natural earthiness of our body and of our animal soul—which takes place with shouts and exaggerated movements, nullifying our ego and all that

---
COMMENTARY
---

but when we are tested from above, we are unable to withstand the temptations of our animal soul and our physical inclinations.

In such a situation, our problem is twofold, says the *Kuntres Ha'Avoda*. Number one: There is no connection between our barely awakened divine soul and our animal soul. The result is that, although we might find ourselves spiritually higher, there is no effect upon our animal soul, and therefore we have not changed fundamentally. Number two: We are striving for a level far beyond what is realistic and honest for ourselves, and therefore is in our environment. All of this produces an overall nullification of our animal soul, [but this] is only external. It is not comparable to the nullification of earthiness in general, which is produced by bitterness [of the soul over our distance from G-d], involving an actual shattering of the physicality that causes its complete nullification.

כְּלָלֵי דְנֶפֶשׁ הַבַּהֲמִית שֶׁזֶּהוּ גַם כֵּן רַק בִּטּוּל חִיצוֹנִי. וְאֵין זֶה כְּמוֹ בִּטּוּל הַחָמְרִיּוּת בִּכְלָל הַנַּעֲשֶׂה עַל יְדֵי הַמְּרִירוּת שֶׁהוּא עִנְיַן שְׁבִירַת הַחָמְרִיּוּת שֶׁהַחֹמֶר מִתְבַּטֵּל בַּזֶּה,

The external nullification described here does not produce a state in which the physical dimension is shattered and eradicated in and of itself. Rather, this is similar to what is described in the *Tanya*, chapter 13, regarding the level of the *beinoni* ("intermediate person") in which the animal soul is "sleeping," so to speak, but can awaken and be roused from its sleep. It is similarly possible to describe the external nullification of the animal soul, mentioned earlier. Since the divine soul is somewhat revealed, in response to it, we desire everything G-dly and demand of ourselves all that is positive and elevated. However, our animal soul has not achieved any elevation whatsoever, and when it comes to a test of our negative character traits, we are unable to control ourselves.

אֲבָל בָּעִנְיָן הַנַּ"ל אֵין זֶה שֶׁנִּשְׁבַּר וּמִתְבַּטֵּל בְּעַצְמוֹ, וַהֲרֵי זֶה בְּדֻגְמַת מַה שֶּׁכָּתוּב בְּסֵפֶר שֶׁל בֵּינוֹנִים פי"ג בְּמַדְרֵגַת הַבֵּינוֹנִים שֶׁהַנֶּפֶשׁ הַבַּהֲמִית הוּא כְּיָשֵׁן שֶׁיָּכֹל לַחֲזֹר וּלְהִתְעוֹרֵר מִשְּׁנָתוֹ כֵּן הוּא בָּעִנְיָן הַנַּ"ל בִּכְלָלוּת הַחָמְרִיּוּת דְּנֶפֶשׁ הַבַּהֲמִית) וְלִהְיוֹת דְּהַנֶּפֶשׁ הָאֱלֹקִית הוּא בְּהִתְגַּלּוּת קְצָת) לָכֵן מִצַּד הַנֶּפֶשׁ הָאֱלֹקִית הוּא רוֹצֶה הַכֹּל וְתוֹבֵעַ מֵעַצְמוֹ כָּל דָּבָר טוֹב וְנַעֲלֶה, וּמִצַּד הַנֶּפֶשׁ הַבַּהֲמִית אֵינוֹ שַׁיָּךְ עֲדַיִן לְשׁוּם דָּבָר, וּכְשֶׁבָּא לְאֵיזֶה דָּבָר מֵהַמִּדּוֹת רָעוֹת דְּנֶפֶשׁ הַבַּהֲמִית אֵינוֹ יָכֹל לַעֲמֹד עַל נַפְשׁוֹ כוּ'.

Since our divine soul is slightly revealed, we desire everything that is G-dly, positive and elevated.

COMMENTARY
---

we have no orderly personal approach to spiritual growth.

The solution is that we must look deeply and honestly within ourselves, in order to find the level of approach that is real. We must be honest about what spiritual rung we are holding onto, and where we want to — and can — go. Only then will we make our spiritual effort part of our basic behavior.

There's another crucial piece of advice for anyone who would undertake to approach the One Above in *avoda*: Find a *mashpia*.

In the state described above, there are two drawbacks. One is that there is no link between our divine soul and our animal soul. The excitement of our divine soul has no effect whatsoever upon our animal soul. The second drawback is that we want everything. We go beyond our own spiritual level, [to a level] that is not real for us and there is no order at all in our *avoda*, as will be explained soon. The reason for both of these drawbacks is that our *avoda* is only superficial. It is based solely upon a casual, overall grasp of G-dliness. (Without even the general meditation mentioned in Chapter 6, wherein we at least contemplate a concept in a passing way; here, the whole approach lacks meditation, and involves only superficial knowledge of the general concept of G-dliness.)

וְהִנֵּה בָּאֹפֶן הַזֶּה יֵשׁ ב' מִינֵי גֵּרָעוֹן, הָא' שֶׁאֵין הִתְחַבְּרוּת דְּנֶפֶשׁ הָאֱלֹקִית עִם הַנֶּפֶשׁ הַבַּהֲמִית דְּהַהִתְפַּעֲלוּת דְּנֶפֶשׁ הָאֱלֹקִית אֵינוֹ פּוֹעֵל מְאוּמָה עַל הַנֶּפֶשׁ הַבַּהֲמִית. וְהַב' מַה שֶּׁרוֹצֶה הַכֹּל וְהוֹלֵךְ לְעֵילָּא מִדַּרְגֵּי' שֶׁאֵין זֶה אֱמֶת, וְאֵין שׁוּם סֵדֶר בַּעֲבוֹדָתוֹ וּכְמוֹ שֶׁיִּתְבָּאֵר בְּסָמוּךְ, וְסִבַּת שְׁנֵיהֶם הִוא הָעֲבוֹדָה בִּבְחִינַת מַקִּיף לְבַד הַבָּאָה מִצַּד הַיְדִיעָה כְּלָלִית דֶּאֱלֹקוּת (גַּם לֹא בִּבְחִינַת הִתְבּוֹנְנוּת כְּלָלִית שֶׁנִּתְבָּאֵר לְעֵיל פ"ו דְּעַל כָּל פָּנִים הוּא חוֹשֵׁב וּמִתְבּוֹנֵן בְּאֵיזֶה עִנְיָן בִּכְלָלוּתוֹ, וְכָאן אֵינוֹ בְּדֶרֶךְ הִתְבּוֹנְנוּת כְּלָל כִּי אִם רַק בְּדֶרֶךְ יְדִיעָה בִּבְחִינַת מַקִּיף בִּכְלָלוּת עִנְיַן הָאֱלֹקוּת).

Therefore, whatever excitement is generated has no connection whatsoever with our animal soul and is unable to produce any nullification of it (as explained in Chapter 6 and even more so here, since the *avoda* is

וְעַל כֵּן אֵין לְהִתְפַּעֲלוּת שַׁיָּכוּת כְּלָל לְנֶפֶשׁ הַבַּהֲמִית לִפְעֹל בּוֹ הַבִּטּוּל (וּכְמוֹ שֶׁנִּתְבָּאֵר לְעֵיל פ"ו וְכָאן הוּא בְּיוֹתֵר לְפִי שֶׁהוּא יוֹתֵר בִּבְחִינַת מַקִּיף עַצְמוֹ. וְעִם הֱיוֹת שֶׁאֵין זֶה

However, our animal soul has not been elevated at all, and when it comes to a test, we are unable to control ourselves.

──────── **COMMENTARY** ────────

A *mashpia* is a Chassidic mentor who has already been or knows how to go to the spiritual places that we want to go. He is acquainted with the nuances and subtleties of the spiritual search, and can help others get to where they want to go. However, that means hard work: One, to take on the guidance of the *mashpia*, and two, to devote time and effort to meditation. A *mashpia* is hard to come by these days; the true *ovdim* of yesteryear were decimated by the Holocaust and our orphan generation has

Essay on Service of the Heart - Love Like Fire and Water

even more superficial; although here we are not dealing with the actual transcendent levels of the soul [that are not en-clothed in the body], nevertheless the state described above is more transcendent than that produced by a general meditation). Those of us who practice this *avoda* detach our divine soul from our animal soul and demonstrate our excitement with a lot of noise. [But] this isn't the tumult of the animal soul being nullified, as when the *ofanim* [lower angels, corresponding to the animal soul], "make a great [spiritual] noise." (See *Likutei Torah*, in the third discourse of *Parshat Ha'azinu*, and in *Ani Hashem Elokeichem* in the first discourse.) Neither is it the noise of involvement in *avoda*[xliv] according to logic and reason, which is [accompanied by] feeling of the self, as hinted at in the verse [from 1 Kings 19:11]: "...and after the wind, there was noise...", as explained elsewhere.[42] Rather, this is detachment of the divine soul, exiting [the animal soul] with superficial noise and excitement,

בִּבְחִינַת מַקִּיפִים מַמָּשׁ שֶׁבַּנֶּפֶשׁ, מִכָּל מָקוֹם הֲרֵי זֶה בִּבְחִינַת הַמַּקִּיף עַצְמוֹ יוֹתֵר מֵהַהִתְבּוֹנְנוּת בִּבְחִינַת כְּלָלִיּוֹת) וּבִפְרָט שֶׁבּאֹפֶן עֲבוֹדָה הַזֹּאת הוּא מוֹצִיא אֶת הַנֶּפֶשׁ הָאֱלֹקִית מִן הַנֶּפֶשׁ הַבַּהֲמִית (עֶר רַייסְט אוֹיס דעם נֶפֶשׁ הָאֱלֹקִית וּכְמוֹ בּוֹרֵחַ כו') וּמִתְפַּעֵל בְּרַעַשׁ גָּדוֹל (וְאֵין זֶה הָרַעַשׁ דְּבִטּוּל הַנֶּפֶשׁ הַבַּהֲמִית, וּכְמוֹ וְהָאוֹפַנִּים כו' בְּרַעַשׁ גָּדוֹל דִּבְדוּגְמָא בְּנֶפֶשׁ הָאָדָם הוּא הָרַעַשׁ דְּנֶפֶשׁ הַבַּהֲמִית כְּמוֹ שֶׁכָּתוּב בְּלִקּוּטֵי תּוֹרָה דִּבּוּר הַמַּתְחִיל הַאֲזִינוּ דְּרוּשׁ הַגָּדוֹל וּבְדִבּוּר הַמַּתְחִיל אֲנִי ה' אֱלֹקֵיכֶם דְּרוּשׁ הָרִאשׁוֹן, וְלֹא הָרַעַשׁ בְּמַרְגָּשׁ שֶׁבַּעֲבוֹדָה שֶׁעַל פִּי טַעַם וְדַעַת שֶׁהוּא עִנְיַן וְאַחֲרֵי הָרוּחַ רַעַשׁ כו. כְּמוֹ שֶׁכָּתוּב בְּמָקוֹם אַחֵר, רַק הוּא הַיְצִיאָה דְּנֶפֶשׁ הָאֱלֹקִית הַנַּ"ל שֶׁיּוֹצֵא בְּרַעַשׁ וְהִתְפַּעֲלוּת חִיצוֹנִי כו') וַהֲרֵי הוּא מִסְתַּפֵּק לְגַמְרֵי בִּיצִיאָה וְהִתְפַּעֲלוּת זֹאת, וַהֲרֵי הֵן מֵאֹפֶן הַהִתְפַּעֲלוּת מִצַּד עַצְמָהּ וְהֵן

Our divine soul is detached from our animal soul, and we demonstrate this with much noise and superficial excitement.

xliv) See footnote of the Rebbe on page 301 ←

COMMENTARY

yet to replace them with true mentors. However, like everything else in Torah, "If you search for it like silver and gold..."

Finally, the *Kuntres Ha'Avoda* tells us that the beginning of our *avoda* — our "service of the heart" — should not be focused on the highest levels of spirituality, as manifested by transcendent G-dliness. Rather, we should concentrate on G-dliness that is en-clothed in the creation enlivening it — that is, on immanent G-dliness. When we contemplate G-dliness as en-clothed in

מֵאֹפֶן הָעֲבוֹדָה, אֵין לָזֶה שׁוּם שַׁיָּכוּת אֶל הַנֶּפֶשׁ הַבַּהֲמִית, וְהַבִּטּוּל הַכְּלָלִי שֶׁנַּעֲשֶׂה עַל כָּל פָּנִים בְּנֶפֶשׁ הַבַּהֲמִית כנ"ל, הוּא מִפְּנֵי שֶׁמִּכָּל מָקוֹם הִתְגַּלּוּת הַהֶאָרָה דְנֶפֶשׁ הָאֱלֹקִית פּוֹעֵל עַל הַבִּטּוּל כְּלָלִי דְנֶפֶשׁ הַבַּהֲמִית. וְגַם הַבִּטּוּל חִיצוֹנִי פּוֹעֵל עָלָיו כנ"ל, אֲבָל הוּא בִּטּוּל כְּלָלִי לְבַד (וְגַם זֹאת לֹא בְּדֶרֶךְ שֶׁבִּירָה רַק בְּדֶרֶךְ דְּחִיָּ' לְבַד וכנ"ל) וְהַהִתְפַּעֲלוּת בִּבְחִינַת מַקִּיף עַצְמוֹ הִיא גַם כֵּן הַסִּבָּה מַה שֶּׁרוֹצֶה וְתוֹבֵעַ מֵעַצְמוֹ כָּל דָּבָר וְהוֹלֵךְ לְעֵילָא מִדַּרְגֵּי' וּבְדֶרֶךְ כְּלָל שֶׁאֵין שׁוּם סֵדֶר בַּעֲבוֹדָתוֹ.

as described earlier. And we are satisfied completely with this detachment [of the divine soul] and [its accompanying] excitement. Whether regarding the nature of the excitement itself or regarding the nature of the *avoda* [that produced it], there is no connection whatsoever with the animal soul. Whatever overall nullification of the animal soul takes place is because there is a revelation of a ray from the divine soul, which in turn produces an overall nullification of the animal soul, as mentioned earlier. Even an external nullification has an effect upon the animal soul, as mentioned, but the nullification is surface-deep (in addition, it only repels the animal soul, but doesn't shatter it). This transcendent soul excitement is what motivates us to demand everything of ourselves [that is, all that is admirable and lofty, and as a result], we go beyond our [own real] level. In general, [this means] there is no order in our *avoda* of the One Above.

We must know our true level of avoda and what to demand from ourselves.

דְּהִנֵּה לְפִי הָאֱמֶת צָרִיךְ הָאָדָם לֵידַע בְּעַצְמוֹ לְפִי מַדְרֵגָתוֹ בַּעֲבוֹדָה בַּמֶּה יִרְצֶה וּמַה יִּתְבַּע מֵעַצְמוֹ (וּמוּבָן שֶׁאֵין הַכַּוָּנָה בְּעִנְיָנִים עִקָּרִיִּים דְּסוּר מֵרַע וַעֲשֵׂה טוֹב וּכְמוֹ שֶׁכָּתוּב בְּמָקוֹם אַחֵר דְּבְקִיּוּם הַמִּצְוֹת שָׁוִים כָּל יִשְׂרָאֵל בְּלִי שׁוּם חִלּוּק וְהֶפְרֵשׁ

In truth, we must know within ourselves our level of *avoda* of the One Above; we should know what it is that we should demand of ourselves. (It is understood that here, we're not referring to the basic requirements of "doing good" [positive *mitzvot*] and "avoiding bad" [neg-

---

COMMENTARY

---

the worlds and enlivening them, we can proceed in an orderly, step-by-step fashion in understanding G-dly concepts and spiritual growth. We should apply ourselves with concentration, persistence, and diligence, and we will surely succeed in revealing the storehouse of spirituality inside ourselves that leads to love of G-d.

Essay on Service of the Heart - Love Like Fire and Water

ative *mitzvot*]. As written elsewhere, in regard to observing the commandments, all Jews are equal, without any distinction or differentiation whatsoever. Here, the intent is that those who are beginning *avoda* must be strict with themselves—this, in truth is obligatory for each and every Jew, because, as is explained in Chapter 6, the purpose of the descent to this world is to serve G-d. We must make ourselves "holy" [proceed beyond the "letter of the law"], whether in matters of "avoiding bad" or of "doing good." (Included within this are various rabbinical enactments that serve as "fences" [to prevent transgression of Biblical commandments]. Here we say "various" [and not "all"], because while many such enactments apply equally to all Jews, others are pertinent only to "servants of G-d"—to those who have chosen to be especially diligent in their *avoda* of the One Above. And among the enactments that pertain to "servants of G-d," there are variations, as stated [Psalms 50:3, regarding G-d]: "There is a mighty tempest around Him" [which suggests that the higher our level, the more precise and careful we must become]. Included within this are also admonitions regarding ethical behavior within the *Agada* of the Talmud and "Ethics of the Fathers," and various ways of "beautifying" the *mitzvot*.) This is because all of the above constitutes the main path to refinement and rectification, which is the ultimate purpose of *avoda*.

Then there is also the reason explained in *Likutei Torah*, in the discourse *V'shama aviha et nidra*. In these matters, we must know what to demand from ourselves. We shouldn't demand everything from ourselves.

כְּלָל, רַק הַכַּוָּנָה הִיא, דְּהִנֵּה כָּל מִי שֶׁמַּתְחִיל בָּעֲבוֹדָה (שֶׁזֶּהוּ גַּם כֵּן בֶּאֱמֶת חוֹבָה עַל כָּל אֶחָד וְאֶחָד וּכְמוֹ שֶׁנִּתְבָּאֵר לְעֵיל פ"ו שֶׁתַּכְלִית יְרִידָתוֹ בָּעוֹלָם הוּא לַעֲבֹד אֶת ה' כו') צָרִיךְ לְהַחֲמִיר עַל עַצְמוֹ וּלְקַדֵּשׁ עַצְמוֹ הֵן בְּעִנְיְנֵי סוּר מֵרָע וְהֵן בְּעִנְיְנֵי וַעֲשֵׂה טוֹב (וְנִכְלָל בָּזֶה כַּמָּה עִנְיָנִים מִדִּקְדּוּקֵי סוֹפְרִים בִּנְדָרִים וּסְיָגִים (וּרְצוֹנוֹ לוֹמַר בְּכַמָּה עִנְיָנִים כו' כִּי יֵשׁ בָּזֶה הַרְבֵּה דְּבָרִים הַשָּׁוִים גַּם כֵּן לְכָל נֶפֶשׁ מִיִּשְׂרָאֵל, וְיֵשׁ בָּהֶם דְּבָרִים הַשַּׁיָּכִים לְעוֹבְדֵי אֱלֹקִים, וּבָזֶה הַיְנוּ בִּדְבָרִים הַשַּׁיָּכִים לְעוֹבְדֵי אֱלֹקִי, יֵשׁ חִלּוּקֵי' עַל דֶּרֶךְ וּסְבִיבָיו נִשְׂעֲרָה כו') וְדַרְכֵי מוּסָר שֶׁבָּאַגָּדוֹת וּפִרְקֵי אָבוֹת וְהִדּוּרֵי מִצְוֹת כו') לִהְיוֹת כִּי בָּזֶה הוּא עִקַּר הַזִּכּוּךְ וְהַתִּקּוּן שֶׁזֶּהוּ תַּכְלִית הָעֲבוֹדָה,

וְגַם מֵהַטַּעַם הַמְבֹאָר בְּלִקּוּטֵי תוֹרָה דִּבּוּר הַמַּתְחִיל וְשָׁמַע אָבִי' אֶת נִדְרָהּ. וּבְעִנְיָנִים אֵלּוּ צָרִיךְ הָאָדָם לֵידַע מַה יִּתְבַּע מֵעַצְמוֹ וְלֹא שֶׁיִּתְבַּע מֵעַצְמוֹ הַכֹּל, (ניט אלץ

Those who are just beginning in avoda should be strict with themselves.

If nothing about avoda concerns us, we're in a bad spiritual state, and so if everything concerns us, it is also not good.

דְּאַרְף אָרִין,) כְּשֵׁם שֶׁגָּרוּעַ מְאֹד כַּאֲשֶׁר שׁוּם דָּבָר לֹא אִכְפַּת לוֹ (בַּוַּעֲשֵׂה טוֹב הוּא שֶׁאֵין לוֹ שׁוּם יֹקֶר וַחֲבִיבוּת בְּאֵיזֶה דָּבָר (אָז עֶס זָאל אַרִין אוּן מֶענֶען דִי זַאךְ) וְעוֹשֶׂה רַק כְּמִצְוַת אֲנָשִׁים מְלֻמָּדָה בִּקְרִירוּת בְּלִי שׁוּם חַיּוּת בַּדָּבָר וּמִכָּל שֶׁכֵּן שֶׁאֵינוֹ מְהַדֵּר בָּהּ, וּבְסוּר מֵרָע הוּא שֶׁלֹּא אִכְפַּת לוֹ לָעַיֵּן וּלְדַיֵּק בְּאֵיזֶה דָּבָר אִם הוּא בֶּאֱמֶת בְּתַכְלִית הַכַּשְׁרוּת עַל דֶּרֶךְ מָשָׁל רַק סוֹמֵךְ עַל הַסְּתָם, (עֶס רִירט אִיהֶם נִיט אָן דִי זַאךְ אוּן עֶס אַרט אִיהֶם נִיט עֶר זָאל נָאכְזוּכֶן דֶעם אֲמִתִּית הַדָּבָר) וּמִכָּל שֶׁכֵּן שֶׁאֵינוֹ מַחְמִיר עַל עַצְמוֹ בְּאֵיזֶה עִנְיָנִים כנ"ל שֶׁהָעוֹבֵד צָרִיךְ לְהַחְמִיר עַל עַצְמוֹ כו'), כְּמוֹ כֵן לֹא טוֹב כַּאֲשֶׁר כָּל דָּבָר אִכְפַּת לוֹ (אָז אַלְץ אַרט) וּכְמוֹ שֶׁיִּתְבָּאֵר.

דְּהִנֵּה בִּתְחִלָּה דְּאַרְף אָרִין דָּבָר שֶׁהוּא חָמוּר יוֹתֵר (הַכֹּל בְּחֻמְרוֹת וְדִקְדּוּקִים כנ"ל) וְכַאֲשֶׁר פּוֹעֵל בְּעַצְמוֹ הַדָּבָר הַזֶּה הֲרֵי הוּא בָּא אַחַר כָּךְ לְעוֹד עִנְיָן שֶׁהוּא דָּבָר דְּקִדּוּק וְחוּמְרָא יוֹתֵר, וְכֵן הוּא בַּעֲבוֹדָה אֲמִתִּית כַּאֲשֶׁר עוֹבֵד עֲבוֹדָתוֹ בַּעֲבוֹדָה הָרְצוּיָה וּמְכֻוֶּנֶת בְּמֹחַ וְלֵב, שֶׁהוּא עוֹמֵד בְּאֵיזֶה דַּרְגָּא (עֶר הַאלְט עֶפֶּעס בַּיי אַ עִנְיָן), אָז אִכְפַּת לוֹ בֶּאֱמֶת עִנְיְנֵי הַחֻמְרוֹת

ourselves. Those of us who care about nothing are in a very worrisome situation. (Regarding positive *mitzvot*, we evince no appreciation of the preciousness and spiritual value of any *mitzvah*, but rather we fulfill the *mitzvah* perfunctorily, "Like a man who does things by rote" [Isaiah 29:13], that is, in a cold manner. There is no energy in our performance, and we certainly don't seek to embellish and "beautify" the *mitzvah*. Regarding the negative commandments, we don't care and it doesn't concern us to look closely—for example, to see if something is definitely kosher. We prefer to rely upon assumptions. It doesn't bother us, and we don't care, so we won't trouble ourselves to get to the truth. Worse, we are not overly strict in the various matters mentioned above, with which a "servant [of G-d]"—the one who truly wants to get close to G-d—should be strict.) Likewise, it isn't good when everything matters to us, as will be explained.

In the beginning, we must be concerned about that which is especially important (within the framework of extra stringency and caution [not actual sins], as noted above). When we have accepted the new level of stringency, then we may take on other items of strictness. So it is with true *avoda*. When we pray with proper diligence and intention of the mind and heart and attain a spiritual level, then matters of strictness in fulfilling the *mitzvot* truly make a difference

Essay on Service of the Heart - Love Like Fire and Water

to us. We then strive to be very precise and to make ourselves holy. We decide what is appropriate, according to our spiritual level, such that we take on those matters that truly concern us. When our diligence in *avoda* is honest, we will not be concerned with a level of strictness or "beautification" of a *mitzvah* that is, as of now, beyond us. But what is on our level will be truly important to us, and this will empower us to go on to a yet higher spiritual level. Besides ascending in the *avoda* itself, we will advance in the level of strictness and "beautification" of *mitzvot*, and all of it will be honest. We will continue with unceasing persistence and will not discontinue at any time. The newfound level of strictness will become very important to us, and we will not deviate from it, G-d forbid, no matter the situations in which we find ourselves. With this *avoda*, we will truly rectify and refine our soul and rise to a very high spiritual level.

But, if everything is important to us, including those things that are far beyond our own spiritual level, then our approach is not honest. Although temporarily we may desire this [particular level of strictness] as a result of our superficial arousal, it isn't real; [there is no real] inner feeling. That is why the arousal is only momentary. As soon as it ends, our desire ceases as well. True *avoda* is like this: although the inner arousal doesn't last

וְהַדִּקְדּוּקִים וְרוֹצֶה לְדַקְדֵּק בְּעַצְמוֹ וּלְקַדֵּשׁ עַצְמוֹ, וְאָז הוּא מְדַקְדֵּק בְּעַצְמוֹ מַה שֶׁרָאוּי לוֹ לְפִי מַדְרֵגָתוֹ שֶׁהַדָּבָר הַזֶּה אִכְפַּת לוֹ בֶּאֱמֶת (ד"י זא"ך ארט עם טאקע מיט א אמת), וְכַאֲשֶׁר הָעִנְיָן הוּא אֶצְלוֹ בַּאֲמִתִּית לֹא אִכְפַּת לוֹ דָּבָר דִּקְדּוּק וְחֻמְרָה אוֹ הִדּוּר שֶׁלְּעֵילָא מִמַּדְרֵגָתוֹ עֲדַיִן, אֲבָל מַה שֶׁהוּא בְּמַדְרֵגָתוֹ אִכְפַּת לוֹ בֶּאֱמֶת, וַאֲמִתַּת הַדָּבָר הַזֶּה מַכְשִׁירָה אוֹתוֹ לָבוֹא לְעִנְיָן נַעֲלֶה יוֹתֵר, כִּי מִתְעַלֶּה גַּם בְּעֶצֶם עֲבוֹדָתוֹ וּמִתְעַלֶּה בְּעִנְיְנֵי הַדִּקְדּוּקִים עַל עַצְמוֹ וּבְהִדּוּרִים יוֹתֵר, וְהַכֹּל הוּא בֶּאֱמֶת בְּנַפְשׁוֹ וּבְקִיּוּם שֶׁאֵינוֹ נִפְסָק וְאֵינוֹ מִתְבַּטֵּל בִּזְמַן מֵהַזְּמַנִּים וְהֵמָּה אֶצְלוֹ כְּעִנְיָנִים עִקָּרִיִּים שֶׁלֹּא יַעֲבֹר עֲלֵיהֶם חַס וְחָלִילָה בְּאֵיזֶה מַעֲמָד וּמַצָּב שֶׁיִּהְיֶה' וּבְכָל זֶה מְתַקֵּן וּמְזַדֵּךְ נַפְשׁוֹ בֶּאֱמֶת, וּמִתְעַלֶּה עַל יְדֵי זֶה בְּמַדְרֵגָה גְּבוֹהָה וְנַעֲלֵית כו'.

אֲבָל כַּאֲשֶׁר כָּל דָּבָר אִכְפַּת לוֹ גַּם מַה שֶּׁלְּמַעְלָה מִמַּדְרֵגָתוֹ הֲרֵי זֶה אֵינוֹ אֱמֶת (הֲגַם שֶׁלְּפִי שָׁעָה הוּא רוֹצֶה בָּזֶה מִצַּד הַהִתְעוֹרְרוּת שֶׁלוֹ בִּבְחִינַת הַמַּקִּיף שֶׁלוֹ, אֲבָל אֵין זֶה בֶּאֱמֶת בִּבְחִינַת הֶרְגֵּשׁ פְּנִימִי (אז דאס ארט איהם טאקע באמת) וְעַל כֵּן הוּא רַק לְפִי שָׁעָה בִּלְבַד, דִּכְשֶׁנִּפְסָק הַהִתְעוֹרְרוּת נִפְסָק גַּם הָרָצוֹן הנ"ל, דְּלֹא כֵן הוּא בַּעֲבוֹדָה אֲמִתִּית שֶׁהֲגַם שֶׁהַהִתְעוֹרְרוּת פְּנִימִי

We must decide what is appropriate to our spiritual level, and adopt whatever is real for us.

If everything is important to us, including things far beyond our spiritual level, that our approach lacks honesty.

הֲרֵי לֹא יֵשׁ כָּל הַיּוֹם, מִכָּל מָקוֹם הַפְּעֻלָּה מִזֶּה אֵינוֹ נִפְסָק לְעוֹלָם מִפְּנֵי שֶׁאִכְפַּת לוֹ בֶּאֱמֶת (ווייל איהם אַרט טאַקע בֶּאֱמֶת). וִיסוֹד הַדָּבָר הוּא מִפְּנֵי שֶׁהוּא אֱמֶת בְּעֵת הָעֲבוֹדָה (הַיְנוּ שֶׁהַהִתְעוֹרְרוּת הִיא אֲמִתִּית) עַל כֵּן גַּם הַפְּעֻלָּה הִיא אֲמִתִּית (וְעַל כֵּן גַּם כֵּן רֹשֶׁם מֵהַהִתְעוֹרְרוּת נִשְׁאָר עַל כָּל הַיּוֹם, וְהַכֹּל עִנְיָן אֶחָד), אֲבָל כַּאֲשֶׁר הַהִתְעוֹרְרוּת אֵינָהּ אֲמִתִּית (דְּעַל כֵּן לֹא נִשְׁאָר מִמֶּנָּה שׁוּם רֹשֶׁם וּכְמוֹ שֶׁנִּתְבָּאֵר לְעֵיל פ״ו) גַּם הַפְּעֻלָּה הִיא רַק לְפִי שָׁעָה וְנִפְסֶקֶת מִיָּד,

וְזֹאת הִיא הַנִּסְבָּה מַה שֶּׁאָנוּ רוֹאִין בִּבְנֵי אָדָם שֶׁלִּפְעָמִים מְדַקְדְּקִים וּמַחְמִירִים וְלִפְעָמִים לֹא (הַיְנוּ דְּעִנְיָן אֶחָד גּוּפָא לִפְעָמִים כָּךְ וְלִפְעָמִים כָּךְ) וּמִתְחַלְּפִים וּמִשְׁתַּנִּים בְּעִנְיְנֵיהֶם מִיּוֹם לְיוֹם וּמִשָּׁעָה לְשָׁעָה, וּמִכָּל שֶׁכֵּן כַּאֲשֶׁר בָּאִים בְּאֵיזֶה מֵצַר וְדֹחַק (אָז עֶס וֶוערט איינגעפּאַר דעם אַנדערען) הֲרֵי הֵם מִתְדַּמִּים לְכָל אָדָם וּבְדֶרֶךְ כְּלָל מִשְׁתַּדְּלִים לְהַצְנִיעַ וּלְהַעֲלִים הַדְּבָרִים וְכָל זֶה הוּא מִפְּנֵי שֶׁאֵינוֹ אֱמֶת, דְּמִי שֶׁהוּא אֶצְלוֹ בַּאֲמִתִּית לֹא יִשְׁתַּנֶּה וְלֹא יֵצֶר לוֹ מֵחֲזוֹלֶת (וּלְהֵפֶךְ אֵינוֹ עוֹשֶׂה הַדָּבָר בְּדֶרֶךְ בְּלִיטָה). וְסִבַּת הַדָּבָר הוּא הֶעְדֵּר הָעֲבוֹדָה הָאֲמִתִּית דְּמִשּׁוּם זֶה לֹא אִכְפַּת לוֹ בֶּאֱמֶת שׁוּם דָּבָר, וְיָכֹל לִרְצוֹת הַכֹּל גַּם מַה שֶּׁלְּמַעְלָה מִמַּדְרֵגָתוֹ וְהוּא רַק לְפִי

the entire day, the effect it has upon us never ceases, since it truly matters to us. This is because it is real at the time of our *avoda* (the arousal itself is real), and therefore the effect is also real. (As a result, an impression of the arousal lasts the entire day, and the two things [the arousal and the impression] are one). But, when the arousal isn't honest (and therefore makes no impression upon us at all, as explained in Chapter 6), then also the effect is merely temporary and doesn't last at all.

This is the reason that we see people who are sometimes careful to take on stringencies, and at other times they are not careful (within one *mitzvah* or custom, they will only sometimes take on extra cautiousness). Such people change and vary their behavior regarding *mitzvot* from day to day and even from hour to hour. This is even more true when they are in difficult circumstances. Then, they try to appear like any other person, and generally try to hide and conceal things. This is because their conduct [in taking on extra strictness] is not real. Those of us for whom [the acceptance of stringencies and "beautifications" of the *mitzvot*] are real won't vary or be affected by anyone else. (Just the opposite — we won't act in an obvious way that stands out.) [In any case], the reason for this is lack of honest *avoda*, on account of which we are not truly concerned with anything. We may want everything, including that which is above our spiritual level, but this desire is only temporary, for as long as the arousal lasts. Being transcendent, [this desire] can occur at any time, but it soon fades and goes away (because it [results from] an easy and unreal *avoda*). Therefore, we become frequently aroused with a desire [to be extra cautious in *mitzvot*], and then [our desire] dissipates immediately. This is particularly true of the style described here, in which the *avoda* reveals a ray of our divine soul, bringing us to care about and want everything [every strictness]. However, [this desire] is not real and true. The truth comes step by step, in which each step is true and real on its own. According to the level that we achieved in our own *avoda*, we take on new stringencies and extra caution. But when we demand of ourselves to go beyond our [spiritual] level, this is not real. And then, also those behaviors that are on our spiritual level—that is, which every "servant of G-d" must be strict about—also are not honest for us. That we should truly care is still beyond us.

שָׁעָה הַיְנוּ בְּעֵת הַהִתְעוֹרְרוּת, וְלִהְיוֹת שֶׁהִתְעוֹרְרוּת הַמַּקִּיף יָכֹל לִהְיוֹת בְּכָל שָׁעָה, וּמִיָּד חוֹלֵף וְעוֹבֵר (שֶׁהִיא עֲבוֹדָה קַלָּה וּבִלְתִּי אֲמִתִּית) עַל כֵּן מִתְעוֹרֵר גַּם הָרָצוֹן הַנַּ"ל לְעִתִּים קְרוֹבוֹת וְנִפְסָק מִיָּד, וּבִפְרָט בָּאֹפֶן שֶׁמִּתְבָּאֵר כָּאן דְּהַיְנוּ שֶׁבַּעֲבוֹדָתוֹ הוֹצִיא הִתְגַּלּוּת הֶאָרָה דְנֶפֶשׁ הָאֱלֹקִית, הֲרֵי הוּא רוֹצֶה וְאִכְפַּת לוֹ הַכֹּל, אֲבָל אֵין זֶה אֱמֶת, כִּי הָאֱמֶת בָּא בְּהַדְרָגָה דַּוְקָא, וְכָל דַּרְגָּא הִיא אֲמִתִּית בְּעַצְמָהּ, דִּלְפִי עֵרֶךְ מַדְרֵגָתוֹ בַּעֲבוֹדָה הוּא מַחְמִיר וּמְדַקְדֵּק בְּעַצְמוֹ כַּנַּ"ל, אֲבָל כַּאֲשֶׁר רוֹצֶה וְתוֹבֵעַ מֵעַצְמוֹ לְמַעְלָה מִמַּדְרֵגָתוֹ אֵין זֶה אֱמֶת) הִנֵּה גַּם מַה שֶׁהוּא לְפִי מַדְרֵגָתוֹ, רְצוֹנוֹ לוֹמַר מַה שֶּׁכָּל אֶחָד וְאֶחָד מֵעוֹבְדֵי אֱלֹקִי צָרִיךְ לְהַחְמִיר עַל עַצְמוֹ גַּם זֶה אֵינוֹ בֶּאֱמֶת אֶצְלוֹ, דְּזֶה שֶׁיִּהְיֶ' דָּבָר נוֹגֵעַ לוֹ בֶּאֱמֶת (אַ אמת'ער אַרין) לֹא יֵשׁ עֲדַיִן.

The truth emerges step by step, in which each step is honest and real on its own.

This is similar to learning [Torah]. To start with, we must learn the simpler topics, and then move on to more sophisticated and elevated topics. We must progress from the "light" to the "heavy." But, when we start with the "heavy" topics, we won't come to understand them properly,

וַהֲרֵי זֶה בְּדֻגְמָא כְּמוֹ בְּלִמּוּד הֲרֵי מִתְּחִלָּה צְרִיכִים לִלְמֹד עִנְיָנִים פְּשׁוּטִים וְאַחַר כָּךְ יוּכַל לִלְמֹד עִנְיָנִים גְּבוֹהִים וְנַעֲלִים, וּמִן הַקַּל יָבוֹא אֶל הַכָּבֵד, אֲבָל כַּאֲשֶׁר יַתְחִיל מִן הַכָּבֵד הֲרֵי לֹא יֵדַע אוֹתוֹ לַאֲמִתָּתוֹ מֵאַחַר שֶׁלֹּא לָמַד אֶת

since we didn't learn the lighter topics first. Moreover, we don't know the lighter and easier subjects, and we are left "empty on both sides" [*Bava Kamma* 60:1]. Those of us who strive for a spiritual level that is beyond our own achieve an elevated level that isn't real, and even the matters that are on our level are not real.

הַקַּל תְּחִלָּה, וְגַם אֶת הַקַּל אֵינוֹ יוֹדֵעַ, וְנִשְׁאָר קֵרֵחַ מִכָּאן וְקֵרֵחַ מִכָּאן, וּכְמוֹ כֵן בְּמִי שֶׁהוֹלֵךְ לְעֵלָּא מִדַּרְגֵּי׳ הֲרֵי מַה שֶּׁלְּמַעְלָה מִמַּדְרֵגָתוֹ אֵינוֹ אֱמֶת, וְגַם מַה שֶּׁבְּמַדְרֵגָתוֹ גַּם כֵּן אֵינוֹ אֱמֶת.

In honest avoda, we stand on a definitive spiritual rung, and our behavior is appropriate to that rung. What we comprehend, we truly comprehend, with inner feeling.

(וְכֵן הוּא בַּעֲבוֹדָה בְּהָעוֹבֵד בְּהִתְבּוֹנְנוּת בִּבְחִינַת כְּלָלוּת שֶׁנִּתְבָּאֵר לְעֵיל פ״ו שֶׁהֲרֵי גַּם הוּא אֵינוֹ מַחֲזִיק בְּאֵיזֶה עִנְיָן בֶּאֱמֶת וּמִכָּל שֶׁכֵּן שֶׁאֵין סֵדֶר בַּעֲבוֹדָתוֹ דְּהַיְנוּ שֶׁנֹּאמַר שֶׁעוֹמֵד בְּדַרְגָּא זוֹ וְהוֹלֵךְ מִדַּרְגָּא לְדַרְגָּא, דְּזֶה שַׁיָּךְ רַק בַּעֲבוֹדָה אֲמִתִּית דְּמַה שֶּׁהוּא מַשִּׂיג הוּא מַשִּׂיג בֶּאֱמֶת וּבְהֶרְגֵּשׁ פְּנִימִי וּבַמֶּה שֶׁמִּתְעוֹרֵר הֲרֵי הוּא מִתְעוֹרֵר בֶּאֱמֶת וְרוֹצֶה בֶּאֱמֶת בָּעִנְיָן הַהוּא אִם בִּבְחִינַת קֵרוּב וּדְבֵיקוּת אוֹ בִּבְחִינַת רָצוֹא וְצִמָּאוֹן כו׳ וַהֲרֵי הוּא עוֹמֵד בְּאֵיזֶה דַּרְגָּא בֶּאֱמֶת, וּלְפִי עֵרֶךְ זֶה הוּא תּוֹבֵעַ מֵעַצְמוֹ בְּהַנְהָגָתוֹ בְּפֹעַל, אוֹ שֶׁבֶּאֱמֶת מִתְנַהֵג כֵּן בְּפֹעַל, וְכָל זֶה הוּא בֶּאֱמֶת שֶׁאִכְפַּת לוֹ הַדָּבָר בֶּאֱמֶת וְהוּא אֶצְלוֹ בְּתֹקֶף וָחֹזֶק וְאֵינָהּ מִשְׁתַּנָּה, וְכֵן הוּא הוֹלֵךְ מִדַּרְגָּא לְדַרְגָּא כו׳, אֲבָל זֶה שֶׁאֵינוֹ מַחֲזִיק בְּאֵיזֶה עִנְיָן (עֶר הַאלְט ניט בַּיי עֶפֶּעס אַ זאַךְ) כִּי אֵינוֹ מַשִּׂיג הָעִנְיָן כְּלָל, וּמִכָּל שֶׁכֵּן שֶׁאֵין בּוֹ הֶרְגֵּשׁ פְּנִימִי וְלֹא הִתְעוֹרְרוּת אֲמִתִּי וּכְמוֹ שֶׁנִּתְבָּאֵר לְעֵיל פ״ו, הֲרֵי אֵינוֹ עוֹמֵד בְּאֵיזֶה דַּרְגָּא, וּמִמֵּילָא אֵינוֹ

So it is for those of us who meditate in the shallow manner described in Chapter 6. We fail to truly achieve any spiritual level. There is no order in our *avoda*, so that we can hold on to one level and climb to the next. Such a description is appropriate only for those of us who perform our *avoda* honestly. We understand truly, and with inner feeling. When we experience spiritual arousal, it is genuine. We honestly desire to reach the goal of our meditation, whether it be closeness and cleaving to the One Above ["like water"], or yearning and thirst for Him ["like fire"]. We stand on a definitive spiritual rung, and what we demand of ourselves and our behavior is in proportion to that rung. We act honestly according to our level. All this is genuine, meaning that it truly matters to us, and we are firmly committed to it, without wavering. So, we progress from one level to the next. But, if we don't hold onto any particular matter [in our *avoda*]—because we don't grasp the subject at all, and have no inner feeling or true arousal, as mentioned in

Essay on Service of the Heart - Love Like Fire and Water

Chapter 6—we don't stand on any rung of spiritual ascent whatsoever. As a result, we have no real desire to hold onto any particular spiritual level. But, since we are, at least, involved with *avoda*, our soul demands that we be in the worthy situation and circumstances of "sanctifying ourselves." However, in the absence of organization and gradual ascent [in our *avoda*] and with our expectations not absolutely honest, because the matter [our spiritual level] is not really that important to us—we strive for goals that are too lofty. It is easier for us to want (and sometimes to really achieve) things that are exceedingly high, even though for us they aren't real, than to grasp and incorporate a lower level [of *avoda*] that is real. In the beginning of our *avoda*, we are likely to reach for ends that are too high, only to stop immediately thereafter and remain in a state of vacillation.

All of the above regards the divine soul. Since it is somewhat revealed, as mentioned earlier — and this is true as well of the imaginary excitement described in Chapter 6 in which there is a bit of spiritual arousal—it brings us to desire all that is [spiritually] commendable. However, this isn't a true aspiration, as mentioned earlier, and therefore we start and stop. (The arousal [for all the worthy aspects of spirituality] also starts and stops, and

But, in the absence of order and gradual ascent in our approach, we strive for lofty matters that are beyond us.

רוֹצֶה בְּאֵיזֶה דָּבָר בֶּאֱמֶת שֶׁיַּחֲזִיק בָּהּ, וּמִכָּל מָקוֹם לִהְיוֹתוֹ מִתְעַסֵּק בַּעֲבוֹדָה עַל כָּל פָּנִים, הֲרֵי נַפְשׁוֹ תּוֹבַעַת לִהְיוֹת בְּמַעֲמָד וּמַצָּב טוֹב לְקַדֵּשׁ עַצְמוֹ כוּ', אַךְ מִצַּד הֶעְדֵּר הַסֵּדֶר וְהַהַדְרָגָה וּמִצַּד שֶׁהַתְּבִיעָה בְּעֶצֶם אֵינָהּ בֶּאֱמֶת לַאֲמִתָּהּ שֶׁנּוֹגֵעַ לוֹ הַדָּבָר בֶּאֱמֶת, תּוֹפְסִים (חאפט מען זיך אָן) בִּדְבָרִים גְּבוֹהִים וְנַעֲלִים דַּוְקָא, כִּי בְּנָקֵל יוֹתֵר לִרְצוֹת (וְגַם לְקַיֵּם לְעִתִּים) דְּבָרִים גְּבוֹהִים שֶׁלֹּא בֶּאֱמֶת מִלְּהַחֲזִיק בְּדָבָר נָמוּךְ בַּמַּדְרֵגָה אֲבָל בֶּאֱמֶת וְעַל כֵּן מַתְחִילִים כַּמָּה עִנְיָנִים שֶׁהֵן טוֹבִים וְנַעֲלִים וְנִפְסָק מִיָּד וְעוֹמְדִים תָּמִיד בְּשִׁנּוּיִים כוּ').

וְכָל זֶה הוּא מִצַּד הַנֶּפֶשׁ הָאֱלֹקִית, דִּלְהֱיוֹת שֶׁהַנֶּפֶשׁ הָאֱלֹקִית אֶצְלוֹ בְּהִתְגַּלּוּת קְצָת כנ"ל (וּכְמוֹ כֵן בְּהִתְפַּעֲלוּת הַדִּמְיוֹנִי שֶׁנִּתְבָּאֵר לְעֵיל פּ"ו הֲרֵי יֵשׁ בּוֹ אֵיזֶה הִתְעוֹרְרוּת) עַל כֵּן הוּא רוֹצֶה בְּכָל הָעִנְיָנִים הַטּוֹבִים רַק שֶׁאֵינוֹ רָצוֹן אֲמִתִּי כנ"ל עַל כֵּן הוּא מַתְחִיל וּמַפְסִיק כוּ' (שֶׁכֵּן גַּם הַהִתְעוֹרְרוּת נִפְסֶקֶת וּמִתְעוֹרֶרֶת וְחוֹזֵר וְנִפְסָק וְגַם הַהֶאָרָה גּוּפָא מִתְגַּלֵּית וּמִתְעַלֶּמֶת

In the meantime, the animal soul has no aspirations, because the arousal of the divine soul has had no effect on the animal soul.

וּמִתְגַּלֶּה וְחוֹזֵר כו'), אֲבָל מִצַּד הַנֶּפֶשׁ הַבַּהֲמִית אֵינוֹ רוֹצֶה בְּשׁוּם דָּבָר עֲדַיִן כִּי לֹא פָּעַל עֲדַיִן עַל הַנֶּפֶשׁ הַבַּהֲמִית מְאוּמָה, רַק הַבִּטּוּל חִיצוֹנִי הַכְּלָלִי הַנַּ"ל, וְגַם אִם פּוֹעֵל אֵיזֶה דָּבָר עַל הַנֶּפֶשׁ הַבַּהֲמִית הוּא רַק בְּכֹחַ וָחַיִל (בִּלְשׁוֹן אַשְׁכְּנַז אפגעריסען עפעס פון איהם) לֹא בְּדֶרֶךְ בֵּרוּר, וְלָכֵן כַּאֲשֶׁר בָּא לְאֵיזֶה דָּבָר הַנּוֹגֵעַ לְנֶפֶשׁ הַבַּהֲמִית, אֵינֶנּוּ עוֹמֵד עַל נַפְשׁוֹ כִּי הַנֶּפֶשׁ הַבַּהֲמִית עוֹדֶנּוּ בְּתָקְפּוֹ (בְּיוֹתֵר בַּהֲמִדָּה הַטִּבְעִית הַמַּגִּיעַ עַתָּה לְחֶלְקוֹ כְּמוֹ שֶׁנִּתְבָּאֵר לְעֵיל פ"ו) וְלֹא נִזְדַּכֵּךְ כְּלָל בְּאֹפֶן הָעֲבוֹדָה הַנַּ"ל, וּכְמוֹ שֶׁנִּתְבָּאֵר לְעֵיל פ"ו שֶׁהַזִּכּוּךְ דְּנֶפֶשׁ הַבַּהֲמִית הוּא דַּוְקָא בַּעֲבוֹדָה הָאֲמִתִּית, שֶׁנֶּחֱלָשׁ הַטִּבְעִית שֶׁלּוֹ עַל יְדֵי קֵרוּב נַפְשׁוֹ לֶאֱלֹקוּת, וּבְיוֹתֵר שֶׁבְּאֹפֶן הָעֲבוֹדָה יוּכַל גַּם הַנֶּפֶשׁ הַבַּהֲמִית לְהָבִין אֶת הָעִנְיָן הָאֱלֹקִי (וְנִתְ' שָׁם צְרִיכִים לְהִשְׁתַּדֵּל בְּאֹפֶן הַהִתְבּוֹנְנוּת) וְעַל יְדֵי זֶה הוּא בָּא גַּם כֵּן לִידֵי אַהֲבָה לֶאֱלֹקוּת, וּבְאַהֲבָה בְּרִשְׁפֵּי אֵשׁ נַעֲשֶׂה כִּלָּיוֹן וּבִטּוּל הַיֵּשׁ דְּנֶפֶשׁ הַבַּהֲמִית כו' כְּמוֹ שֶׁנִּתְבָּאֵר לְעֵיל בַּאֲרֻכָּה:

then is aroused and once more ceases. The ray [of the divine soul] bursts into revelation and disappears, and then reveals itself and again disappears.) But, in the meantime, the animal soul aspires to nothing, because the entire arousal and revelation [of the divine soul] had no effect on the animal soul, aside from a superficial, general neutralization, as mentioned earlier. If any changes do take place in the animal soul, they are only the product of power and coercion and not of persuasion. Therefore, when it comes to something that tempts our animal soul, we are unable to control ourselves. The animal soul is still at full strength ([this is] all the more so true regarding whatever natural trait has fallen to us to purify now, as mentioned in Chapter 6). It hasn't been refined at all by the *avoda* mentioned earlier [in Chapter 6 and in Chapter 4]. As explained earlier in Chapter 4, only true *avoda* [with detailed meditation] leads to refinement of the animal soul, weakening its natural components by exposing it to G-dliness. In this way of serving G-d, the animal soul is also enabled to understand G-dly matters. (And there it is explained that this is what we must strive for within meditation.) Through this process, the animal soul comes to love G-d, and in "love like fire," the ego and natural components of the animal soul dissolve and disintegrate, as explained there at length.

Essay on Service of the Heart - Love Like Fire and Water

And therefore, in accordance with all that has been explained, those of us who are concerned about our soul should exert ourselves to serve the One Above with a proper "service of the heart"—prayer—in detailed meditation. We should not seek to go beyond our level by meditating upon lofty heights of G-dliness. Rather, we should focus upon those levels that are close to us (aside from those of us who have already gotten accustomed to *avoda* and have the ability to grasp the higher levels, each according to his own spiritual rung). In general, this refers to meditation on levels of immanent G-dliness, in which we focus upon the Divine light and energy en-clothed in the worlds.

Through honest [and detailed] meditation and deep concentration, we will achieve true familiarity with, and cleaving of, the soul to G-dliness (that is "real" according to our level). In so doing, we will fulfill the commandment to love G-d, which will bring us to learn Torah and fulfill its *mitzvot*. This love will also purify and refine our animal soul. We should strive to understand everything with our natural intellect, which is the major factor that leads to refinement of our animal soul, turning it to love G-d. As we were commanded [in Deut. 6:5], "And you should love the Lord, your G-d," which refers to love resulting from intellectual grasp and meditation. [The meditation itself] is

וְעַל כֵּן עַל כָּל הַדְּבָרִים הַנַּ"ל כָּל מִי שֶׁחָשׁ לְנַפְשׁוֹ יִתְגַּבֵּר עַל עַצְמוֹ לַעֲבֹד אֶת ה' בָּעֲבוֹדָה הָרְצוּיָה בָּעֲבוֹדָה שֶׁבַּלֵּב זוֹ תְּפִלָּה בְּהִתְבּוֹנְנוּת בְּדֶרֶךְ פְּרָט דַּוְקָא, וְלֹא יֵלֵךְ בִּגְדוֹלוֹת לְהִתְבּוֹנֵן אֶל מַדְרֵגוֹת גְּבוֹהוֹת בֶּאֱלֹקוּת רַק בְּמַדְרֵגוֹת הַקְּרוֹבִים אֵלָיו (כִּי אִם מִי שֶׁכְּבָר מֻרְגָּל בָּעֲבוֹדָה שֶׁבִּיכָלְתּוֹ לָבוֹא לְמַדְרֵגוֹת גְּבוֹהוֹת בָּעֲבוֹדָה כָּל אֶחָד וְאֶחָד לְפוּם שִׁיעוּרָא דִילֵי' כו'), וּבְדֶרֶךְ כְּלָל בִּבְחִינַת מְמַלֵּא כָּל עָלְמִין דְּהַיְינוּ בַּהֶאָרָה הָאֱלֹקִית שֶׁבָּאָה בִּבְחִינַת הִתְלַבְּשׁוּת בְּעוֹלָמוֹת,

שֶׁעַל יְדֵי הִתְבּוֹנְנוּת אֲמִתִּי וּבְהַעֲמָקַת הַדַּעַת יִהְיֶה קֵרוּב וּדְבֵיקוּת נַפְשׁוֹ לֶאֱלֹקוּת בֶּאֱמֶת (רְצוֹנוֹ לוֹמַר בֶּאֱמֶת שֶׁלּוֹ לְפִי מַדְרֵגָתוֹ) וּמְקַיֵּם בָּזֶה מִצְוַת אַהֲבַת ה' וְהִיא הַמְבִיאָה אוֹתוֹ לַעֲסֹק הַתּוֹרָה וְקִיּוּם הַמִּצְווֹת וּבָהּ וְעַל יָדָהּ מְבָרֵר וּמְמַזֵּךְ אֶת הַנֶּפֶשׁ הַבַּהֲמִית, וְיִשְׁתַּדֵּל לְהָבִיא הַדְּבָרִים לִידֵי הֲבָנַת הַשֵּׂכֶל הַטִּבְעִי, שֶׁעַל יְדֵי זֶה עִקָּר וְזִכּוּךְ הַנֶּפֶשׁ הַבַּהֲמִית שֶׁיָּשׁוּב גַּם כֵּן לְאַהֲבַת ה' כו' וְעַל זֶה נִצְטַוִּינוּ כְּמוֹ שֶׁכָּתוּב וְאָהַבְתָּ אֶת ה' אֱלֹקֶיךָ כו' שֶׁהִיא הָאַהֲבָה הַבָּאָה עַל יְדֵי הַשָּׂגָה וְהִתְבּוֹנְנוּת שֶׁזֶּהוּ עִנְיַן שְׁמַע יִשְׂרָאֵל שֶׁהוּא עִנְיַן שְׁמִיעָה וְהַשָּׂגָה כו' וּבְכָל לְבָבְךָ בִּשְׁנֵי יְצָרֶיךָ שֶׁהוּא

Those of us who are concerned about our soul should exert ourselves in detailed meditation.

Through honest meditation and deep concentration, we will achieve cleaving and devotion of our soul to G-dliness.

בְּחִינַת קֵרוּב וּדְבֵיקוּת הַנֶּפֶשׁ הָאֱלֹקִית בֶּאֱלֹקוּת וְשֶׁגַּם הַיֵּצֶר הָרָע יָשׁוּב לְאַהֲבַת ה' כו', וְזֶהוּ הָעֲבוֹדָה שֶׁבַּלֵּב לְהִתְעוֹרֵר בְּלִבּוֹ בְּאַהֲבָה לַה' וְלִהְיוֹת לִבִּי וּבְשָׂרִי יְרַנְּנוּ כו'

commanded in the verse, *Shema Yisrael...*" ("Hear O Israel..."), where "hearing" refers to intellectual understanding. [Then, we come to love] "with all of your heart" referring to both inclinations—the divine soul seeks proximity to G-d, wanting to cleave to Him, and the evil tendency changes to love G-dliness. This constitutes "service of the heart," triggering within our hearts a love of G-d such that our heart and flesh rejoice.

All of this is the product of intellectual acumen and meditation, about

שֶׁכָּל זֹאת הוּא עַל יְדֵי הַשָּׂגָה וְהִתְבּוֹנְנוּת שֶׁעַל זֶה נֶאֱמַר וְיָדַעְתָּ הַיּוֹם וַהֲשֵׁבֹתָ אֶל לְבָבֶךָ בּ' לְבָבוֹת כו'. וְזֶהוּ שֶׁלֹּא נֶאֱמַר צִוּוּי עַל אַהֲבָה כִּי אִם בְּמִשְׁנֵה תוֹרָה, דְּהִנֵּה דּוֹר הַמִּדְבָּר הָיְ' לָהֶם גִּלּוּי אֱלֹקוּת מִלְמַעְלָה בִּבְחִינַת רְאִיָּ' מַמָּשׁ מִצַּד הַחִבָּה הָעֶלְיוֹנָה וּכְמוֹ שֶׁכָּתוּב כְּבִכּוּרָה בִתְאֵנָה בְּרֵאשִׁיתָהּ רָאִיתִי אֲבוֹתֵיכֶם כו' וִיהִ' בָּהֶם הָאַהֲבָה מִמֵּילָא וּבִבְחִינַת דְּבֵיקוּת מַמָּשׁ בְּחִינַת אַהֲבָה בְּתַעֲנוּגִים כו' וּכְמוֹ שֶׁכָּתוּב וַיֶּחֱזוּ אֶת הָאֱלֹקִים וַיֹּאכְלוּ כו' וְתִרְגֵּם אוּנְקְלוּס וַהֲווּ חָדָן כו' (וְיֵשׁ לוֹמַר דְּהָעִקָּר הָיְ' בָּהֶם בְּחִינַת הַיִּרְאָה וּבִטּוּל שֶׁעַל יְדֵי רְאִיַּת הַמַּהוּת בְּחִינַת יִרְאָה עִילָאָה וּכְמוֹ שֶׁכָּתוּב וַיִּירְאוּ מִגֶּשֶׁת כו'). אֲבָל

which the verse says, "And you should know today and put in your heart..." referring to both hearts [the G-dly inclination which resides in the right ventricle and the evil tendency in the left ventricle]. This is the reason the commandment to love G-d didn't appear in the Torah until the fifth book (Deuteronomy). The generation that left Egypt and journeyed in the desert merited the revelation of G-dliness from above. They could literally "see" spirituality as a result of the great love that was expressed for them from above, as it says [in Hoshea 9:10], "Like a new fig in its beginning, so I saw your forefathers..." They spontaneously experienced *ahava b'taanugim* ("love of delights") for the One Above, cleaving to Him completely. It is written [in Exodus 24:11], "They saw G-d and they ate..." and Onkelos [the Aramaic translation there] says "and they were happy" (though it is possible to say that their main experience was one of awe of G-d and self-nullification as a result of perceiving the essence of G-dliness, *yirah ila'ah*, as it says there, "they were afraid to approach"). It was the following generation which received the command to love G-d; that

Essay on Service of the Heart - Love Like Fire and Water

is, they were commanded to undertake an *avoda* leading to love, that being meditation.

And that brings us to the ultimate purpose in the labor of "service of the heart" (prayer): it is to strive within ourselves in true meditation with depth of concentration in order to arouse love of G-d, such that it will bring us to fulfillment of the *mitzvot* of the Torah and also to purification and refinement of our animal soul. And it was already explained that it is absolutely necessary that there be acceptance of the "yoke of heaven" and the lower fear of G-d (guarding our senses), because they are indispensable and unceasing. But, the *avoda* and effort of prayer is to arrive to the love of G-d, and also in so doing to fulfill the true intention of the One Above.

SYNOPSIS:

There is another way [of serving G-d], and that is with superficial, noisy excitement, the result of general knowledge of G-liness alone, which gives rise to a revelation of a reflection of the divine soul. On account of this revelation, we desire and demand of ourselves spiritual goals beyond our [true] spiritual level. However, this isn't honest, because true "service of the heart" progresses from step to step, and each step along the way is

הַדּוֹר שֶׁאַחַר כָּךְ נִצְטַוּוּ עַל הָאַהֲבָה דְהַיְנוּ שֶׁעַל יְדֵי עֲבוֹדָתָם יָבוֹאוּ לִבְחִינַת אַהֲבָה וְהַיְנוּ עַל יְדֵי הִתְבּוֹנְנוּת כו'.

וְזֶהוּ תַּכְלִית הָעֲבוֹדָה וְהַיְגִיעָה בָּעֲבוֹדָה שֶׁבַּלֵּב זוֹ תְּפִלָּה לִיגַּע אֶת עַצְמוֹ בְּהִתְבּוֹנְנוּת הָאֲמִתִּי בְּהַעֲמָקַת הַדַעַת לְהִתְעוֹרֵר בְּאַהֲבָה לַה' שֶׁעַל יְדֵי זֶה הוּא קִיּוּם הַתּוֹרָה וּמִצְווֹת וְעַל יְדֵי זֶה הוּא בֵּרוּר וְזִכּוּךְ הַנֶּפֶשׁ הַבַּהֲמִית כו'. וּכְבָר נִתְבָּאֵר דִּבְהֶכְרַח שֶׁיִּהְיֶ' קַבָּלַת עֹל מַלְכוּת שָׁמַיִם וְיִרְאָה תַּתָּאָה שֶׁאִי אֶפְשָׁר לִהְיוֹת בִּלְעָדֶיהָ וְהוּא. עִנְיָן תְּמִידֵי אָמְנָם הָעֲבוֹדָה וִיגִיעָה דִתְפִלָּה הִיא לָבוֹא לִבְחִינַת אַהֲבָה זֹאת כנ"ל דִּבְכָל זֶה מַשְׁלִימִים אֲמִתַּת הַכַּוָּנָה הָעֶלְיוֹנָה כו':

קִצּוּר.

יֵשׁ עוֹד אֹפֶן וְהוּא עִנְיַן הִתְפַּעֲלוּת חִיצוֹנִי בְּרַעַשׁ עַל יְדֵי הַיְדִיעָה כְּלָלִית דֶּאֱלֹקוּת שֶׁעַל יְדֵי זֶה מוֹצִיא הֶאָרַת הַנֶּפֶשׁ הָאֱלֹקִית לִידֵי הִתְגַּלוּת וּמִשּׁוּם זֶה הוּא רוֹצֶה וְתוֹבֵעַ מֵעַצְמוֹ כַּמָּה עִנְיָנִים טוֹבִים וְנַעֲלִים שֶׁהֵן לְמַעְלָה מִמַדְרֵגָתוֹ אֲבָל אֵין זֶה אֱמֶת כִּי הָאֱמֶת בָּא בְּהַדְרָגָה דַּוְקָא וְכָל דַּרְגָּא הִיא אֲמִתִּית לְפִי מַדְרֵגָתוֹ וְעַל יְדֵי זֶה הוֹלֵךְ מִדַּרְגָּא לְדַרְגָּא אֲבָל בָּאֹפֶן הנ"ל אֵין זֶה

בֶּאֱמֶת. וְעַל כֵּן מִשְׁתַּנֶּה וּמִתְחַלֵּף בְּכָל עֵת, וּמִצַּד הַנֶּפֶשׁ הַבַּהֲמִית הֲגַם שֶׁפּוֹעֵל בּוֹ בִּטּוּל כְּלָלֵי חִיצוֹנִי אֲבָל בְּעֶצֶם אֵין בּוֹ בִּטּוּל כְּלָל עֲדַיִן וְאֵינוֹ רוֹצֶה בְּשׁוּם דָּבָר טוֹב וְלָכֵן כְּשֶׁבָּא לְיָדוֹ אֵיזֶה נִסָּיוֹן לֹא יוּכַל לַעֲמֹד. וְעַל כֵּן כָּל מִי שֶׁחָשׁ לְנַפְשׁוֹ יִתְגַּבֵּר עַל נַפְשׁוֹ לַעֲבֹד אֶת ה' בַּעֲבוֹדָה הָרְצוּיִ' בְּהִתְבּוֹנְנוּת פְּרָטִית כָּל אֶחָד וְאֶחָד לְפִי מַדְרֵגָתוֹ וּלְהִתְעוֹרֵר בְּאַהֲבָה שֶׁעַל יְדֵי זֶה הוּא קִיּוּם הַתּוֹרָה וּמִצְוֹת וְעַל יְדֵי זֶה הוּא בֵּרוּר הַנֶּפֶשׁ הַבַּהֲמִית וְזֶהוּ תַּכְלִית הָעֲבוֹדָה וְהַיְגִיעָה דִּתְפִלָּה (וּבְהֶכְרֵחַ שֶׁתִּהְיֶה גַּם כֵּן הַיִּרְאָה בִּתְמִידוּת כְּמוֹ שֶׁנִּתְבָּאֵר לְעֵיל פ"ב וג') וּבָזֶה מַשְׁלִים הַכַּוָּנָה הָעֶלְיוֹנָה כו':

true on its own level in such a way that we progress from one step to the next. When we reach too high, our progress is not real. Therefore it changes and vacillates all the time. And although it produces a general external nullification of the animal soul, nevertheless it produces no essential nullification whatsoever, such that the animal soul would desire anything spiritual. Therefore, when it comes to some sort of [spiritual] test [from above], we are unable to control ourselves and pass the test. So, those of us who are concerned about our soul must push ourselves to serve G-d with proper *avoda*, meaning a detailed meditation, each one of us according to our level. In so doing we will arouse a love of G-d [in himself], leading to fulfillment of *mitzvot* of the Torah, as well as purification of our animal soul. And this is the ultimate purpose of all our *avoda* of prayer (and of course there must be constant "fear of G-d" as well, as explained), and in this way we will fulfill the supernal intention from above.

NOTES

1. *Nishmata d'nishmata* is a technical term for *chaya*, the fourth level of the soul. While the *Zohar* mentions only four levels — *nefesh, ruach, neshama* and *nishmata d'nishmata* — Midrashic, later Kabbalah and Chassidic literature refers to the five levels of the soul listed in the text: *nefesh, ruach, neshama, chaya* and *yechida*.

2. *Yichuda ila'ah* literally means "higher unity." It refers to a state of mind in which our primary awareness is of G-d and His oneness in the universe, and if we have any awareness of the physical creation, it is as something very secondary. Another term for the same awareness is *da'at elyon*. Similarly, *yichuda tata'ah* means "lower unity," and refers to the state of mind in which our primary awareness is of the physical world and creation. G-d is in the background and we are not directly aware of Him. Also known as *da'at tachton*. For more explanation of both *yichuda ila'ah* and *yichuda tata'ah*, see Ch. 5 and the accompanying commentary.

3. *Hitamtut* is confirmation or corroboration of our meditative understanding. It comes as a "moment of truth" or realization from Above, hence the root word *emet*. In Chassidic literature it is usually also associated with *re'iya de eyn hasechel*, or seeing in the mind's eye. It follows a deep process of meditation on G-dly topics, wherein we penetrate to the G-dly core of the subject, stripping it of its outer layers of explanation and arriving to the very essence of the matter. Then, we may be granted a "moment of truth" in which we see the G-dly subject in our mind's eye, which accompanies *hitamtut*. For more explanation, see ch. 5 and accompanying commentary.

4. *Pnimiyut Bina* is the stage of understanding in which we strip away the external "trappings" of the G-dly concept in order to arrive to the G-dly kernel of thought. Human intellect is incapable of grasping a G-dly concept without some sort of description, example, or external "handle." However, by focus, concentration and persistence, we can break through the shrouds of intellectual "packaging" and discover the spiritual kernel. *Pnimiyut Bina*, or core understanding, is the tool to achieve this end.

5. Supernal Bride (*Kalah Ila'ah*) is a way of describing the *sephira* of *bina*, with its corresponding soul-power of analytic understanding. Since *bina* receives the raw materials of G-dly understanding from *chochma*, and then processes and analyzes them, it is on the receiving end and is therefore referred to as the *kalah*, or bride. On the other end, the analytic process of *pnimiyut bina* "consumes" the shrouds of externality and brings us to the spiritual core of the concept. Thus, it is called *kalah* for a second reason —

because it "consumes" (in Hebrew, also *kalah* from *lechalot* meaning "to consume") the external trappings of the physical world.

6. The following table should clarify the meaning of the paragraph:

Ch. 16 of *Tanya*: "and also his *nefesh* and *ruach*…"	*Ruach* combines with *nefesh* to become one (*Nehy* within *nefesh*)	In *avoda*, a slightly elevated general acknowledgment (acquiescence)
Described earlier in *Kuntres Ha'Avoda*: "our *nefesh* also rises…"	*Nefesh* rises to *ruach*	Specific acknowledgment on the level of *ruach* (natural love and fear)
Described later in this chapter: "the heart responds spontaneously…"	*Ruach* rises to *neshama* (cleaving of the emotions to intellect)	Intellectual love and fear (unity with the G-dly light)

7. Page 156-157

8. *Mochin* is the Kabbalistic term for spiritual influx. Literally meaning "brains," *mochin* is the spirituality that we bring into the world with our *avodat HaShem*. Without our service of the One Above, the universe runs according to the laws of nature. Service of the One Above insures that G-dly energy will permeate the laws of nature, elevating the universe in order to reveal the presence and oneness of G-d. *Mochin* in general has a component which is emotional, but subservient to the intellect. *P'nimiyut hamochin*, or pure intellect, though, completely transcends the emotions of the heart.

9. Inter-inclusion (described above) leads to *tikun* (rectification). It takes place in the following three steps, which are implicit in the rest of this chapter:

Ha'ara (Illumination)	The higher level illuminates the lower level	The lower becomes aware and strives for the higher level
Hamshacha (Drawing down)	The higher level interacts with the lower level	The lower level takes on characteristics of the higher but retains its own identity
Hashra'ah, or *Hitcalelut* (Permeation or Inter-inclusion)	The higher level elevates the lower level and they become one	The lower level becomes subsumed by the higher

10. *Reuta d'liba* is one of the goals of meditation. Latent in the heart are emotions of G-dly fear and love that may be awakened and fanned into flames by the active meditation described in *Kuntres Haavoda*, ch. 4 and 5. When performed properly, the heart ignites into love "like fire." The point of ignition is called *reuta d'liba*, or the "will of the heart." As described in *Sefer Ma'amorim 5670, Parshat Trumah*, "the *makif* of *chaya* is in essence *reuta d'liba*, the will that transcends reason. It is also the natural desire for G-dliness in the soul, which wants to be included in its source..." It may come either as the result of active meditation, as mentioned, or come from Above as a result of previous *avoda*.

11. *Rayayoti* — the verse in Song of Songs (4:1) reads, "Behold, you are beautiful, my love, behold, your eyes are dove's eyes..." In the Chassidic discourse (in *Likutei Torah*) on the verse, the following interpretation is offered: "Like by way of example, a pair of doves, male and female; the female receives from the male, so Above, the Blessed One is compared to a bridegroom, and the Jews to a bride. And the Jews are described as 'receiving from Him,' and just as doves peer intently at each other, so from everything, one can learn to observe intently and see that there is none other than Him, and that He is one, and to nullify ourselves completely...and just as doves peer at each other constantly and enjoy seeing each other, so the Jews are in a state of constantly "seeing the glory of the King" from everything they perceive..."

12. *Zeir Anpin* — The biggest contribution of the Ari to the study of Kabbalah was the concept of *partzufim*. A *partzuf* is a structure of *sephirot*, and while the earlier Kabbalists spoke of individual *sephirot*, it was the Ari who introduced the concept that groups of *sephirot* interact together.

Among the ten *sephirot* of *Atzilut*, there are five such major structures, or *partzufim*, and other less important groupings. The five major *partzufim* are *Arich Anpin* (in *Keter*), *Chochma, Bina, Zeir Anpin* (the seven *sephirot* from *chesed* through *malchut*), and *Nukva* (*malchut* itself). Each *partzuf* is composed of its own structure of ten *sephirot*. Since all *partzufim* posess the same set of ten *sephirot*, each on their own level, they are able to interact as groups, as opposed to individual *sephirot*.

The importance of *Zeir Anpin* (or *za'a,* as it is called for short) is its influence on the creation, through *malchut*. *Za'a* imparts the qualities of kindness, constriction, mercy, etc. in the creation. It is a "male," influence-imparting structure that is dependent upon our *avodat HaShem*. When we pray and perform mitzvot, and learn Torah, G-dly influx is drawn down from the infinite light of G-d into the *partzuf* of *za'a*, and through *malchut*, into the creation. When we do the opposite, influx is withheld, with the consequences being negative for the creation. Since *za'a* is therefore in a constant state of flux, and since like the emotions, it relates to the "other," namely, the universe, the *partzuf* of *za'a* is associated with our *"emotions."*

13. Not only *za'a*, but also the *sephirot* of *chochma* and *bina* are each blessed with full *partzufim* of ten *sephirot*. When referred to as full-fledged *partzufim*, *chochma* and *bina* are called *abba* and *imma* in Kabbalistic literature. Their importance lies in their transcendent connection with creation. Like wisdom and understanding in the person, their presence is helpful but not crucial. Just like the person can exist without being overly wise, so the universe can exist without added doses of *chochma* and *bina*. However, the universe is better off with more *chochma* and *bina*. When we serve the One Above properly, the influence of *chochma* and *bina* is revealed in the creation through increased nullification of the creation to G-d and through intellect. When we don't serve Him properly, the law of entropy predominates. Since *chochma* and *bina* transcend the creation and yet the creation is better off with them, *chochma* and *bina* are associated with intellect and understanding.

14. *Memalle kol olamim* (literally, "filling or permeating" creation). This is the term used to refer to immanent spirituality, or the level of G-dliness which is enclothed in the creation in order to create and eniven it. Its two main characteristics are that it is graspable — the person can achieve a firm intellectual understanding of this level of G-dliness — and it exists on various spiritual levels. The creation is divided into four categories — mineral, vegetable, animal and human — and the quality of G-dly energy necessary to enliven each level differs from category to category, as well as among specific species within each category. Similarly, the body is composed of different levels and systems — the head, the heart, the kidneys, etc. The soul is enlothed in each level in a different way and provides a different life-energy for each level, and yet on every level, its life-energy is evident. Therefore, "as the soul fills the body" is an apt simile to describe the phenomenon of immanent spirituality (*memalle kol olamim*) that enlivens the creation.

15. *Sovev kol olamim* (literally "transcending" creation). This is the G-dly light that transcends the creation, affecting it from afar. Unlike *memalle kol olamim*, this spiritual phenomena is not readily graspable and does not readily express itself on identifiable levels. Since it is beyond our grasp, we can only achieve a vague awareness of its presence, but we cannot grasp and understand it. Therefore, it is comparable to human will, or general knowledge. When we will or want something, we know that it won't necessarily come to fruition. And sometimes we will or know something in general, without being cognizant of all of its details, becoming aware of

them only later. So, will and general knowledge are both apt metaphors for *sovev kol olamim*, or transcendent G-dliness.

16. *Yediat Hashlila* (literally "negated, or circumscribed knowledge") is, according to the Rambam, the highest form of intellectual service of G-d. Human descriptions of G-d necessarily fall short of the mark, since He far transcends our puny ability to grasp and understand Him. But, if so, what does the Torah mean when it describes G-d with such adjectives as "almighty," "merciful," "vengeful," "wise," and the like? The Rambam suggests that these adjectives, while not precisely describing G-d in the same way as they do human beings, implies that G-d is not *not* that. That is, the adjectives of the Torah are meant to imply that G-d is not the opposite of the description. He is, of course, that which is described by the adjective, be it wise, almighty, vengeful, etc., but not in a way that is describable and graspable by human intellect. Rather, He is far Above any adjective we might apply, but He is not the opposite of it. The performance of this intellectual exercise of negating or circumscribing our knowledge of Him is, according to the Rambam, the highest form of *avodat HaShem*. But, here in the *Kuntres Ha'Avoda*, the process of stripping the intellectual concept of its external trappings and arriving to the essential spiritual core is not to be equated with *yediat hashlila*. That comes at a later stage of *avoda*, as we will soon see. For more on this subject, see commentary to Chapter 5.

17. *P'sukei D'Zimra* (literally "verses of praise"). This is the section of prayer in the morning extending from *Baruch She'amar* up to *Yistabach* (before saying *Barchu*). It is characterized by verses from *Psalms* and other parts of the *Tanach*, which praise the One Above for His wisdom and omnipotence in creating the universe. Psychologically, this section of the prayers has the effect of making an "impression from the outside" on the person who is praying. While the word *zimra* literally means "song," it also comes from the phrase, *lezamer aritzim*, or "to cut away thorns." When we approach prayer in the morning, there are many "thorns" — obstacles that could affect our mindset, distracting and disturbing us. When we give ourselves over to reciting the prayers during the stage of *P'sukei D'Zimra*, they have the effect of clearing our heads of all these "thorns" and allowing us to concentrate on getting close to the One Above.

18. See Chapter 4 and accompanying *pirush* for explanations of this level.

19. *Hakarat hahaflah* (literally, "recognition of wonderful elevation") — Chabad meditation follows a process of stripping away the external trappings of thought (the "garments" of the concept) in order to arrive at the spiritual essence of the idea. This process of *p'nimiyut bina* may be followed by an experience of *da'at*. That is, once we have arrived at the essential kernel of the concept, we may be "rewarded" with a vision of its G-dly

essence. We will experience this as a deep recognition (*hacara*, the inner dimension of *da'at*). Depending upon the subject and style of the meditation, the revelation from Above may be wonderful and astonishing (*niflah*), far transcending worldly matters. This happens when the process utilized is *yediat hashlila* (circumscribing or negation of knowledge, also known in the text as *lehavin davar mitoch davar*). Since the person is striving to penetrate matters that are beyond intellect, he is "rewarded" with revelation that is beyond intellect, with *hacarat hahafla'ah*. For more explanation, see commentary to Chapter 5.

20. *Re'iya b'eyn hasechel* (literally "seeing in the mind's eye") — Meditation undertaken on our own initiative is in the category of "hearing." That is, all that we grasp, analyze, and understand is based on our intellect, rather than upon what we directly experience of G-dliness. This happens because while we cannot directly apprehend G-d, we can be aware of Him and understand Him to some extent by studying the effect He has upon the universe in creating and maintaining it. This is called hearing. Moses, though, wanted to instill in the Jews the power to directly see G-dliness. If he would have entered the land of Israel, he would have succeeded, but G-d permitted him only to look at the land of Israel from afar, from the mountains of Moab (*M'av* — from *Av* — from *chochma*, associated with seeing). In so doing, he instilled in the Jewish soul the power to "see in the mind's eye." That is, we may meditate so deeply and accurately, that our power of imagination "sees" what our naked eye is not allowed to see (until the coming of *Meshiach*). Therefore, after the deep experience of *hacara*, we may be granted vision in our mind's eye — a visual experience in his imagination that transcends the hearing and understanding that he experienced up to now. For more on these terms see commentary to Chapter 5.

21. For more on this subject, see commentary to Chapter 4.

22. For more on this subject, see commentary to Chapter 4.

23. *Sandal* is the name of the angel who elevates the prayers of the Jewish people to the One Above. The Talmud (*Chagiga* 13) says that he "ties crowns for his Creator from the prayers of the Jews." His job is two fold; he must "shield" the Jews from excessive revelation from Above, and yet be able to capture their longing for G-d in their prayers and elevate them Above. That's why he is called *Sandal* — just as a sandal covers the foot, shielding it from dirt and ground, so the angel *Sandal* is associated with the covering — the *parsa* — that separates between the worlds of *Yetzira* and *Asiya*. He effectively cuts the illumination from *Yetzira* into *Asiya* to a minimum, and then "catches" the prayers of the Jewish people and carries them upward to their ultimate destination — our Father in Heaven (*Derech Mitzvotecha, mitzvat mila*, page 7).

24. *Ma"h* and *Ba"n*, as indicated in the chart, are numerical values of the name of G-d spelled out to its fullest in various ways, also as indicated in the chart. It remains only to elucidate what is meant by a "rectified" world as opposed to non-rectified. The world of *Atzilut* is "rectified" (and therefore also called *Tikun*) because all of its ten *sephirot* are composed of ten *sephirot* of their own. Therefore, the *sephirot* of *Tikun* are able to undergo inter-inclusion with each other, and are *butel*, or nullified, and work together for the benefit of all of them. This is called *Tikun*, or rectification, and is associated with the name *Ma"h* (*gematria* 45, or *adam* meaning "man"). The not-yet-rectified world of *Tohu* is characterized by ten *sephirot* which do not undergo inter-inclusion, do no "cooperate," and are involved only with their own individual "welfare." This situation is called *Tohu*, or chaos, and is associated with the name *Ba"n* (*gematria* 52, or *behama* meaning "animal").

25. In Chapter 1, we learn that the elevation of the lower soul-levels (*nefesh, ruach* and *neshama*) to be included in *nishmata d'nishmata* is associated with the *Shmoneh Esreh (Amida)* even though the elevation there is the result of love. And yet here in Chapter 3, it seems that the even higher level of *yirah ila'ah*, or awe, supposedly surpassing prayer, is nonetheless associated with the *Shmoneh Esreh* as well! It would seem that the elevation of the lower soul levels to be included in their source takes place during the *Shmoneh Esreh* in general, while the self-nullification and awe associated with *yirah ila'ah* take place specifically during the four occasions of bowing down during *Shmoneh Esreh*.

26. This distinction is drawn in *Likutei Torah, Parshat Bamidbar* (in the discourse *Besha'ah shehikdimu*, paragraph 3). There, *yiru mei HaShem* is equivalent to *yirah tata'ah* or lower fear of G-d, while *yiru et HaShem* is equivalent to *yirah ila'ah*, or awe.

27. As mentioned in Chapter 1, the *sephirot* go through a process of inter-inclusion, in which each of them takes on some of the qualities of all of the others. Hence, each *sephira* includes all of the other ten *sephirot*. Here, since we are interested in developing the overall quality of love of G-d (associated with the *sephira* of *chesed*), and there are two specific categories of love of G-d (like "fire," and like "water") they both are included within the overall quality. Thus, love like water is *chesed* within *chesed*, while love like fire is *gevura* within *chesed*.

28. While the influx brought down to the world by learning Torah is from the infinite, transcendent light of G-d (*ohr*), the meditation focusing upon G-dliness enclothed in the creation is transcendent light enlcothed in the immanent enlivening force of the creation (*chayut*). Thus, it is an

"intermediate" level, lower than the transcendent light of G-d, but higher than the immanent spirituality enclothed in the creation (*koach*).

29. The third paragraph of the discourse reads as follows, "And in order to bring down the fire from Above, it's a *mitzvah* to bring [fire] from below, as an arousal via meditation upon the source from whence the [animal soul] was taken in the supernal "chariot," the source of the lust of the animal soul…[the meditation consists of] how the [angels] of the "chariot" are nullified to the "image of man" [the ten *sephirot* of the world of *Atzilut*]…and are enflamed and panting with desire…to be nullified and included in the illumination of G-dliness that is shining down upon them. And automatically, this illumination of love [from Above] will illuminate as well the power of lust of the animal soul that comes from there, and arouse the person's heart to detach itself from physical pleasures…"

30. The end of the second paragraph of the discourse reads, "…like an animal sacrifice consumed by fire on the altar, so should one arouse his love in prayer with flames of fire igniting from his heart, because the source and foundation of fire is in the heart, and it will consume and burn the animal soul within him…"

31. In the discourse beginning, "*Vayigash alav*…", p. 125, "[the fire on the altar]…is the service of prayer with love, with flames and flames of fire, since this holy fire burns and consumes the foreign fire of the 'other side'…" And on page 142, in the discourse beginning, "*Vayeileich*…" is to be found a detailed explanation of the two levels of fire of the animal soul (fire from below and fire from above).

32. The summary at the end of the discourse reads, "the *seraphim* [angels which are consumed by fiery desire for G-d] are from the element of G-dly fire, and there is a corresponding element in the G-dly soul of man, but it is composed of all four physical elements [earth, wind, fire and water]. And it is written, 'G-d will illuminate my darkness' — this takes place by meditation on the subject of '*HaShem* is our *Elokim*' [essential name of G-d as He transcends the creation is our G-d within creation], through which [meditation] we come to love [Him]. This is what is meant by the 'consuming fire'…"

33. The discourse (paragraph 5) reads, "And also the G-dly soul includes and is compounded of four spiritual elements that are G-dly. The element of water is in the brain and that of fire is in the heart. And the relative composition of the four elements isn't the same in every person. There are those for whom the element of water predominates, and there are those for whom the element of fire is predominant. This is like coals, by way of example, that burst into flames, as opposed to coals that smolder quietly without burning, containing a spark of fire that remains hidden. Nonetheless, since they contain a hidden spark, when one blows hard upon the spark, it then ignites the entire coal

into flames of fire. So, also is the situation of the G-dly soul within man. It may contain an element of G-dly fire in the heart that is revealed and intense, like burning coals. Or, it may contain an element of G-dly fire that is hidden, like smoldering coals with only a spark of fire among them. But, a spark there is, inside each and every Jewish person. One has only to blow upon it hard for it to ignite and enflame and encompass the entire set of coals in a revealed way, and so the G-dly soul in man needs ignition in the heart so that it will become revealed…and this is the entire process of prayer up until *kriat she'ma*, as the person meditates on the greatness of G-d, how He uttered and the world came into existence…"

34. A discussion of this topic is to be found in the series of discourses, *Yom Tov shel Rosh Hashana* 5666, p. 142, and in the second volume of the series of discourses, *Be'sha'ah Shehikdimu*, 5672, pp. 840 and 974.

35. Here, the motivation for achieving "love like fire" is different than in footnote 3. The third paragraph of the discourse reads, "…it's a *mitzvah* to bring from [below], fire from below via meditation on the greatness of G-d, each according to his individual abilities and to excite his heart and soul to serve G-d and then his meditation gives birth to a bold love that's like flames of fire. That happens when he meditates on "something new," as when we see clearly that one who sees something new gets quite excited, and so our Sages said, 'Every day should be like new…' And this takes place when we meditate how in truth every morning brings something new [a new influx of G-dliness from Above]…"

36. See the discourses of the Rebbe Rashab of the year 5660, beginning *Samchuni b'ashishot:* "We know that there are two kinds of enjoyment, corresponding to *chesed* and *gevura*, about which it is said '*ahava beta'anugim* — love of abundant enjoyments' (plural), and they are the love of *ohr yashar* [direct illumination] and of *ohr chozer* [reflected illumination]. The enjoyment of *ohr yashar* is in the drawing down [of G-dly illumination] from Above to below, and the enjoyment of *ohr chozer* is in elevating from below to Above. The latter [is a love of] desire and yearning, as is known that such desire and yearning contains tremendous enjoyment, leading [even] to expiration of the soul…"

By way of possible explanation, *ahava beta'anugim* is composed of two elements; number one, it is aroused by meditation (*ohr chozer*, initiative of the person below), and number two, it is an essential love that is implanted in the Jewish soul from Above (*ohr yashar*). See *Besha'ah shekidimu 5672*, vol. 2, p. 754. See also vol. 3 of *Besha'ah shekidimu*, pp. 1246-7 in parentheses: "It's possible to say that this love [of desire and yearning from below] is on the same level as *ahava teta'anugim*, in terms of enjoyment…"

Alternatively, the reference may be to chapter 9 of the *Tanya*, in which it is written, "That is to say, that the person shall steadily rise to attain to the degree of 'abundant love,' a supreme affection surpassing that of 'ardent love' that is comparable to burning coals. This is what is called in Scripture 'love of delights' [*ahava beta'anugim*] which is the experience of delight in G-dliness, of the nature of the world to come. This delight is in the wisdom, in the intellectual pleasure of comprehending and knowing G-d, to the extent that one's intellect and wisdom can grasp [Him]. This is the element of 'water,' and 'seed,' i.e., light that is sown in the holiness of the divine soul that converts to good the element of 'water' in the animal soul, from which the lust for mundane pleasures had been previously derived."

It is possible that the intellectual pleasure of "abundant love" (*ahava beta'anugim*) is what is meant by "direct illumination" (*ohr yashar*) while the conversion of the element of water in the animal soul to pleasure in G-dliness is what is meant by "reflected illumination" (*ohr chozer*), as when one engages in *teshuva*, or return to the One Above.

37. The verse reads in translation, "Great is our lord, and tremendously powerful." The two words translated as 'tremendously powerful' - *verav koach* - carry the numerical value of 236. *Koach* has the numerical value of 28, which is the same as the number of letters of the first verse of Genesis, referring to the creation of the universe. *Verav*, meaning 'and tremendously' carries the numerical value of 208, which is also the *gematria*, or numerical value of *ohr* (light), with the *collel* (added value of one for the totality of letters together – a common kabalistic technique). *Ohr* is the transcendent spiritual source of *koach*, and together, they represent *orot* and *calim* (light and vessels) - the building blocks of creation and hence its spiritual "size" – 236.

38. This reference in the original is clearly a typographical mistake and should read *Sha'ar HaYichud* of the Mittler Rebbe, chapter 5, rather than chapter 4.

39. *Imrei Bina* of the Mittler Rebbe (son of the Alter Rebbe) is considered the deepest and most cerebral of Chabad Chassidic discourses. It was written for the Mittler Rebbe's chassid, Reb Yekutiel Lepleker, who through persistence and determination (and not through natural abilities alone) became an *oved HaShem*. The discourse is devoted to explaining the words of the *Shema* in Chassidic terms. In chapter 58 of the discourse, two words from the first paragraph of the *Shema* — *yoreh* and *malkosh* — are discussed. According to the Talmud (Tractate *Ta'anit 5A*), *yoreh* is the rain that falls in the fall, while *malkosh* is the rain that falls in the spring. The discourse ties the two kinds of precipitation to the two aspects of *ayn*, or spiritual nothingness, mentioned in chapter 6 of *Kuntres Ha'Avoda* and chapter 5 of *Sha'ar HaYichud*. *Yoreh*, the autumn rainfall, softens the earth and causes the seeds to rot away,

thereby causing them to germinate into plants later on. It thus corresponds to the power of nullification of creation to its spiritual source. *Malkosh*, on the other hand is the rain that causes the germinated seed to develop to its fullest. It thus corresponds to the power of creation from nothing into something. It is upon the former level (*yoreh*) that the *Kuntres Ha'Avoda* in chapter 6 recommends that we meditate. This level of *ayn shel hayesh ha'nivrah* corresponds to the *koach mah*, or power of seeing of *chochma* that descends to creative existence in order to nullify it to its source.

40. Chapter 4 of the Mittler Rebbe's *Sha'ar Hayichud* discusses the relative merits of meditation on a general topic, such as "the light of the World of *Atzilut* and how it is out of range of the infinite light of G-d," versus meditation upon particulars, such as each *sephira* in each world and how it is nullified to the particular level above it. The conclusion is that while a general meditation may lead us to quick conclusions and errors in our understanding, meditation on particulars tend to remain accurate. While the feeling of G-dly excitement and interest may be minimized in a meditation upon details, still, we ultimately arrive at a truer general picture after focusing upon the details in meditation.

41. Chapter 11 of *Kuntres Ha'Tefila* describes five preparations for prayer:
    ◦ Removing all thoughts of worldly concerns and remaining stationery.
    ◦ Meditating on G-dly concepts as presented in the Chassidic discourses of the Sages.
    ◦ Nullifying ourselves through bitterness over our distance from the One Above.
    ◦ Arousing compassion upon our souls which came from a high spiritual place to be enclothed in a physical body.
    ◦ Awareness and meditation on the fact that we are standing before G-d Himself and not just a manifestation Him.

42. See *BeSha'ah shehikdimu* 5672, vol 2, p. 822-825 (sections 399-400)

APPENDIX I
Letter from the Previous Rebbe

Translator's Note:

The following is a letter from the previous Lubavitcher Rebbe, Harav Yoseph Yitzhak Schneerson, *ztz'l* (1880-1950). He was the director of *Tomchei T'mimim*, Lubavitch Yeshiva, until he took over the helm as the Rebbe of Chabad/Lubavitch when his father, the Rebbe Rashab *(nishmato eden)* passed away in 1920. He remained in this capacity until he himself passed away in 1950. In 1927, he was briefly jailed in Bolshevik Russia for disseminating Judaism, and then expelled from Russia, whereupon he moved Poland, and subsequently (in 1940), to New York. Upon his passing, he was succeeded by his son-in-law, HaRav Menachem Mendel Schneerson, *ztz'l*. This letter was written by the previous Rebbe in Riga, in response to questions asked by the Chassidim of the city of Bilgoria, in 1931. It was added as an appendix to the original edition of *Kuntres Ha'avoda*, printed in 1963 by Kehos Publication Society. The subject matter – love of G-d – is common to both the *Kuntres Ha'avoda*, and to this letter. However, while the *Kuntres Ha'avoda* describes "love like fire" and "love like water," the letter speaks of a different (but overlapping) duality – love derived from creation *(ahavat olam)*, and "great love" *(ahava rabba)*.

4 Shvat, 5691 (1931)
Riga

TO:
Our close friends and chassidim of the city of Bilgoria
May the One Above live with you
Peace and blessings

RE:
In answer to your questions as to what is written in *Torah Ohr* (of the *Ba'al HaTanya* on *Breishit*) in the discourse entitled *Osri Legefen*, and in the *Tanya*, chapter 43, concerning the levels of *tzadikim* ("holy ones") and the service of *ba'alei teshuva* ("those who return to G-d"),

concerning the levels of [G-dliness] drawn down into the garments of the soul in *Gan Eden,* and the levels of *ahava rabba* ("great love") and *ahava beta'anugim* ("love accompanied by immense enjoyment")

There are three kinds of love [of G-d]. They are:
- *ahavat olam* ("love based in the world"),
- *ahava rabba* ("great love"), and
- *ahava beta'anugim* ("love accompanied by immense enjoyment").

Each kind of love includes myriad levels and aspects that vary one from the other and have numerous offshoots. Because of their incredible subtlety, there are inner similarities between the categories, even though overall they are quite distinct from each other.

Ahavat olam

The word *olam* [which means "world"] indicates concealment *(he'elam)* and also eternity, as is written (in Exodus 21:6), "and he will serve him forever" *(veavado leolam)*. Although in this passage the Torah is talking about a servant who will serve his master only until the Jubilee, which is the fiftieth year, nonetheless in relation to man – whose lifespan is seventy years and if he has strength eighty, and once upon a time one hundred and twenty – the number fifty is large. The word *olam* therefore connotes eternity. And also regarding the higher/supernal world, it is written (Isaiah 45:17) *l'ulmei ad,* meaning "forever and for all eternity" (from the nusach of Kaddish - *leolam u'lmay olmaya*). Now, these two definitions of *olam* – [concealment and eternity] – are diametrically opposed to each other. *Olam* in the sense of concealment implies limitation and restriction, since the very existence of concealment implies limitation and restriction. And *olam* in the sense of eternity connotes infinity. And the two – limitation and infinity – have nothing in common. They are two aspects of love, distinguished by their very essence. Yet, despite this, they are both called by one name: *ahavat olam*.

Ahavat olam [when implying concealment] means love derived from the world or from creation. Within this love are to be found many distinct sub-levels. Every level sub-divides into thousands and tens of thousands of sub-levels, since this kind of love is subordinate to the quality of our [soul levels] *neshama, ruach* and *nefesh,* our intellect, and to the composition of our personality. These sub-divisions apply not only to *ahavat olam*, but also to every category and level of love, as well as to fear of G-d. But it is especially applicable to *ahavat olam* since it is the lowest level [of love]. Overall, it is called *ahavat olam* since it derives from aspects of the world/creation, as is written (Deut. 30:20): "love G-d your Lord since He is your life." That is, just as we love the life of our soul, so we love G-d since G-d is our life. And so, it is called *ahavat olam* since the life-force of the world is G-dliness. But within it is implied another general aspect-opposite of the first – that all the life-force of the creation comes only from a ray of light and reflection [of G-dliness] that is insignificant in relation to the infinite light of the One Above, may He be blessed.

We see, then, that this one general level has two specific branches. Unique to each branch is a specific concept and a meditation associated with it. And yet, both of them are hewn from one source, and that is the limitation and restriction associated with the word *olam*, as it is describes concealment. Both are as one, even though they are distinct in their very essence, since the first level of [life-force] implies closeness and proximity, while the second level of [ray and reflection] implies tremendous distance. Nevertheless, both of these levels derive from our intellectual pursuit, meaning that they develop in proportion to our intellect and grasp.

Ahavat olam [when implying eternity] means eternal love and suggests that [the love] is natural and essential, without variation, replacement, or exchange, and it is independent of both time and place. Within it are several aspects and levels, describing its very essence. As above, in the first level [of concealment], it expresses itself differently according to our individual *neshama*, *ruach* and *nefesh* and according to our level of intellect and composition of personality. And so it is on all levels of this love, with the major difference – between the first *ahavat olam* [concealment] and the second [eternity]. In the first kind of *ahavat olam* [concealment], the essence of the love itself depends upon our level of *nefesh*, *ruach* and *neshama*. However, in the second kind, only the overall expression of love and the way it becomes revealed are determined by our *nefesh*, *ruach* and *neshama*. But the love is equally present in everyone's soul. Why this is so is simple – the first love [derived from meditation on the world] results from a reason, meaning that it is automatically derived [as a result of a specific meditation]. If so, then, love comes about as a result of a reason.

This is not true of the second kind of love – the eternal love – wherein the reason and result are one and the same. Nevertheless, there is an advantage to the first kind of love [based in concealment and limitation]: since it emerges as a result, it brings with it action that produces effects. There are consequences to this kind of love, and they magnify the love. For example, a person who loves the life of his soul will act upon it – he will eat, drink and rest. And he will engage in other activities – all of them the consequence of one factor: his love for life. The overall result of what he does will be an increased connection of the life-force with the limbs of his body, as well as elevation of the limbs of his body and their refinement in order that they receive more subtle and elevated energy of the soul (as explained elsewhere concerning the nature of connection of the life-force with the limbs).

Thus, by way of this example, we may also understand the first kind of love [associated with concealment and limitation]. Since it emerges as a result, it has consequences, and the consequences themselves bring about certain effects. And these are fulfillment of the Torah's mitzvot with desire and motivation. As the Alter Rebbe said (in the *Tanya*, chapter 4), "the one who truly fulfills the mitzvot is one who loves G-d." But, the second love [associated with eternity] is not a result of anything, and therefore doesn't have any [immediate] effects or consequences. Since it is natural and essential, it acts at all times according to its essential nature, which is not in accordance with the categories of action associated with a ray of light or reflection.

To make this clearer, we can refer to elsewhere (perhaps in *Likutei Torah* on *Shir HaShirim*, "Shishim haima malachot," p. 39A) where it is explained that the deep sources of water flowing in the core of the earth never become revealed. Those which do become revealed for some reason, or are dug up, are actually from the upper, accessible layers of the earth's surface, while the deepest waters are so subterranean that they never become revealed. However, they do exist, and even though they have no visible effect and bear no apparent relationship to anything tangible, their very existence is its own justification within the bowels of the earth. And because of them, the earth is moist. And even though there is no discernible relationship between the subterranean fountains and the moisture of the earth, nevertheless since within the earth are to be found these fountains and this water, for reasons known to the Master of All Reasons, the earth's surface is moist. And since it is precisely the land that is moist, it is land that gives rise to germination and vegetation. Even though it is water that causes the growth of vegetation, this takes place only when the water irrigates land. The proof is that as long as the water is in the clouds, it doesn't produce vegetation, and only upon its descent to the earth does it benefit humanity with vegetation. But, the very reason that growth of vegetation takes place only upon land is because the moisture is present there. And the fact that moisture is present on the land is the result of the deep fountains within the bowels of the earth. Even though there is no apparent relationship, nevertheless their presence – the presence of the deep waters within the earth – has a natural effect. Like two people who are dwelling in one apartment without any apparent connection between each other whatsoever, nevertheless the very fact that the two of them are in the same place causes them to have an effect upon one another. The effect that they have on one another takes place naturally [inadvertently]. That is, it doesn't take place as an "action and its effect." In "action and effect" the action en-clothes itself in the effect, since it takes place in proximity and can enmesh itself. But, this is not the case here, where the subterranean fountains are found deep in the bowels of the earth. Nevertheless, the very fact of their existence means that the surface of the earth will be moist.

From this example, we may understand the love of *ahavat olam*, wherein *olam* means eternal. From the very fact of its existence in the world, [this love] has an ongoing effect. Just as the very existence of the fountains deep in the bowels of the earth makes something happen, so too this love. However, this love is even more essential, since the deep waters are only essential within the framework of natural, physical elements, while this love is essential within the realm of the soul. Therefore, while we may speak of an "action" in relation to it, in this context the nature of the "action" is to be swallowed up within the nature and essence [of the love itself]. So, we discern here one level that gives rise to two aspects, divergent from each other and even opposite: 1) natural and 2) essential. Even though each exists in its own category, they come together to produce one effect.

In general, then, there is:

- *Ahavat olam* (concealment) with its two components:
  - proximity [like one's life-force] and
  - distance [as a ray and reflection from Above].
- *Ahavat olam* (eternity) with its two sub-categories:
  - natural [having an inadvertent effect on "another"] and
  - essential [existing for its own sake].

And yet they all have the same name: *ahavat olam*.

Ahava rabba

Ahava rabba ("great love") comes as a gift from Above [to the one] who has prefaced it with the first level of *ahavat olam* (concealment), in its second component [distance, based upon meditation on how entire creation is but a ray/reflection of the Creator]. It is an intellectually based love, emerging and derived from contemplation and meditation. It is certainly not necessary to explain that this love is dependent upon all of the above. That much can be deduced from the second form of *ahavat olam* (eternal). If eternal *ahavat olam* is unchanging, irreplaceable and independent of time and space, and its revelation is dependent upon all of the above, then all the more so is *ahava rabba* dependent upon all of the above factors, coming as it does after the *avoda* of *ahavat olam* (concealment).

It then becomes clear that this love has the same benefits that we mentioned earlier regarding the first level of *ahavat olam* (concealment) versus the second; that is, it produces results and has consequences, as mentioned above. The difference is that in the first *ahavat olam* (concealment), the love is in the heart alone. It has an effect and motivates us to fulfill the Torah's mitzvot, since the one who truly fulfills them is the one who loves G-d, as mentioned above.

However, this applies to the mitzvot alone. Every mitzvah that we fulfill, we fulfill with motivation and energy. *Ahava rabba*, though, is recognizable on all levels of our being and faculties, and not only in the heart, which is the seat of emotions. [For example], the person who runs to do a mitzvah; his running contains energy, enjoyment and motivation together. And at every opportunity and place, he is surrounded and motivated by this love, and he forgets about himself completely. He doesn't feel himself, because the project gets done and is completed as if it took place on its own – automatically. The aura that surrounds him from Above envelopes him from every side and angle, and enlivens him with an inner energy.

This is understood by way of learning Torah in public, to which there are two approaches. The public learning itself fulfills the commandment to learn Torah. There are those who fulfill it by rote, like learned people following a fixed routine and custom wherever Jews are found. When the learning takes place with energy – whether the learning itself occurs with desire or whether there is effort expended to gain more members to join the learning – this is an indication that there is motivation in the public learning. This is the first level.

But, when we merit an arousal of *ahava rabba*, then love permeates all of our faculties. That is, aside from the learning itself, which takes place in a completely different fashion – whether regarding the subject or in his understanding of it – we now learn in a way that we can apply to all of our actions. In addition, love surrounds us at all times. Whether we are in motion or standing, in our head and heart is always the same matter: learning Torah in public. We are so dedicated and devoted to the matter that the environment has no influence upon us whatsoever. It also makes no difference to us whether the subject is the oral or the written Torah, whether the revealed or concealed/inner dimensions of Torah, whether the participants are learned or simple folk, or whether the location is a place of Torah or not. That is, since we are so totally devoted to and overcome by this great love and concern for learning Torah in public, in every place that we find ourselves, whether in a fixed or in a temporary location, we think, consider and discuss the matter of learning Torah in public.

The truth is that Jews are not subject to "coincidence," since it is written (Psalms 37:23), "by G-d are the steps of man established." Every place that a Jew passes, even if [seemingly] by happenstance, is the result of Divine Providence that for one reason or another arose in His *machshava keduma* ("supernal thought"). When a Jew journeys and finds himself in a place where he had no plans to be and he prays there – whether the morning, afternoon or evening prayers – or recites one of the songs of David, king of Israel, or a verse of Torah, that turns out to be the very reason that he found himself in that place. For each and every movement is by Divine Providence. He may think that it was a coincidence, but in truth it was directed by the light of Torah and *avodat habirurim* – the service of elevation of the universe.

Ahava beta'anugim

This general category of love – a*hava beta'anugim* ("love accompanied by immense enjoyment") – transcends all of the others. It is associated with those whose service of G-d is on the level of *ovdei Hashem benishmatam*, "those who serve G-d with their soul." This is an overall service involving the soul [and not the purification of the body, which has already occurred on lower levels of *avoda*]. The enjoyment is of the *makifim* ("transcendent" levels of the soul) that far surpass the level of *p'nimim* ("immanent" or permeating levels of revelation of the soul). Nevertheless, there are variations and divisions to be found among these levels as well, in general and in particular.

Enjoyment, while also one of the faculties of the soul and not the soul itself, is nonetheless the highest of the soul faculties in general, and the closest to the essence of the soul. Similarly, the faculty of will is not one of the particular faculties of the soul, as [for example] the intellect is a particular soul power. Rather, the will is a general faculty consisting only of the inclination of the soul toward that which the soul wants in a particular matter. And all the more so is this true, then, of enjoyment, which is close to the soul and unites with it in total unity. Nevertheless, enjoyment also includes several aspects and levels, such as "compound" enjoyment of a particular matter versus "simple" enjoyment that is not compounded with anything else. And simple enjoyment can include "conscious" experience, or [a "subconscious" experience and] can take place devoid of any conscious feeling whatsoever. The highest of all is simple enjoyment which is not compounded with any other feeling whatsoever.

The three types of love

The three types of love described here constitute general categories, and even though each one is defined and limited by its category, nonetheless any intelligent person understands that spiritual categories are not like stone or iron dividers or like colored reflectors of red and black or green, or like taste which may be sweet or sour or sharp. All of these are merely categories of the physical and its substance. Here, though we are speaking of spiritual levels and their hierarchy, as the Rambam explained (in *Hilchot Yesodei HaTorah* 2:6-7) regarding angels. If so, then, within all three categories of love are to be found offshoots that are similar and comparable to one another. Like, for example, the first type of love [*ahavat olam*] within the first category [concealment], wherein we develop love for G-d as we love the life-force of our own body. Within this love are to be found desire and will that are also the basis and categories of *ahava rabba* and *ahava beta'anugim*. For the foundation of *ahava rabba* is will accompanied by desire (as mentioned above), and the foundation of *ahava beta'anugim* is enjoyment. This is even more true regarding the second type of *ahavat olam* [eternal], which contains elements of the first, plus an unconscious will that never ceases, that is similar in concept to *ahava rabba*, except that *ahava rabba* is conscious. And as any conscious will, [it acts] with forceful and tremendous power. But the natural will, even if essential, is unconscious. Since it is essential, it contains something of the *ahava beta'anugim* that is united with the soul, as mentioned above. And in this respect, *ahava rabba* and *ahava beta'anugim* also have something in common with each other [both are closely connected with the essence of the soul].

In this way, we can understand what [the Alter Rebbe] means in *Tanya*, chapter 43, [when he equates] *ahava rabba* with *ahava beta'anugim*. Each has within it dimensions that are similar to levels beneath them. The reason for this is that the lower levels – in *ahavat olam* – are also spiritual. And this is also true of the opposite: the highest sub-level of *ahava beta'anugim* (such as simple enjoyment that is neither experienced nor felt) is also only a power of the soul and not the soul itself. And so we see that all spiritual levels relate to one another. And therefore all of them are called by one name: love.

Servants of G-d

Now, regarding servants of G-d, there are several levels and categories. But, in general they may be divided into two: *tzadikim* and *ba'alei teshuva*. Although it's possible to sub-divide each of them into several aspects and sub-categories, the main subdivisions are also two [in each case]:

- among *tzadikim*, there are:
    - those who serve G-d with their bodies and
    - those who serve G-d with their soul
- among *ba'alei teshuva*, there are:
    - those who return to G-d upon having transgressed, and
    - those who serve G-d at all times like those who are "returning'" to Him, because they constantly feel deficient in their service of G-d

Those who are considered "servants of G-d [because they serve G-d] with their bodies" are those who do the *avoda* of the mind and of the heart. Here, the intention is *avoda* with labor: labor of the flesh and labor of the soul. The physical substance of the body conceals G-dliness and hides the light of the soul, and the entire *avoda* is for the purpose of removing the concealment and obscurity. Within this are found various levels and not all are equal.

Those who would serve G-d with their souls are those whose physical substance and body does not hide or obscure their souls at all. Even though they are en-clothed in a body, all of their limbs are holy and do not obscure any of the illumination of the soul at all. As written (in Exodus 2:2) regarding Moses, "And she [his mother] saw that he was good," meaning (according to Rashi) that the house was filled with light. This was because the physical substance of his body was itself "good," and there was no necessity for *avoda* or labor [to improve it] at all. Even though such people need some sort of real *avoda*, it does not involve the same labor as those who serve G-d with their bodies.

The *avoda* of a *ba'al teshuva* involves shattering his entire being and essence, and transforming himself from one extreme to the other. In place of the transgression, during which he turned away from the "straight and narrow path," and the fear of G-d was not "in front of his eyes," and, "he said to G-d [that] ...he doesn't desire His path" [Job 21:14], and "the wicked praises himself for the lusts of his soul" [Psalms 10:3], he now, at the time of his *teshuva* ("return"), transforms all his ways-from the inner recesses of his soul and the depths of his heart. He maintains the path of life while fulfilling the Torah's mitzvot; he develops fear of G-d and is worried and concerned over every detail, including over subtle nuances of the sages' [decrees]. His whole purpose is to eviscerate his own desires until he has no will for anything physical, and he minimizes his eating and drinking and sleeping, and [even] has enjoyment in bringing about his own suffering [for the sake of getting closer to G-d].

Now, it is known that *teshuva* does not refer merely to the simple matter of return to G-d after transgression or sin. *Teshuva* involves, as the verse (in Ecclesiastes 12:7) proclaims, "And the spirit returned to G-d who granted it." The point is: "to G-d who granted it," meaning that we elevate ourselves to a higher stage and level, about which it is said (in Morning Prayers) "the soul that You put within me." The verse (in Ecclesiastes 12:7) says, "to G-d who granted it [the soul]," because all of our *avoda* should be in order to elevate our [soul levels of] *nefesh*, *ruach* and *neshama* to a place that transcends [the level from which] "you gave." This is an *avoda* in which we are very strict with ourselves. On every level of this *avoda*, including the highest, we finds fault with ourselves, and all that we do "is considered as a sin." All we want is to raise and elevate ourselves to a higher level. This is similar in concept to the *avoda* of the High Priest in the Holy Temple on Yom Kippur, during which it was necessary for him to immerse several times in the mikveh. In general, there are two types of immersion; one that takes the person from impurity to purity, and another that takes the person from one level of purity to a yet higher level of purity. And these are the elevations of Yom Kippur.

Now, both types of servants of G-d, *tzadikim* and *ba'alei teshuva*-as distant as they may be from one another in form and essence-nevertheless bear some kind of relationship to each other. [This is because] according to the true Torah (mentioned above), that which is spiritual is not measurable within the categories and definitions of limited physical substance. [This applies] to the first type of *tzadik* and the first type of *ba'al teshuva*, as well as the second type of *tzadik* and the second type of *ba'al teshuva* in particular.

For, the first type of *tzadik*, whose every aspect is involved with cleansing and refining his physical nature, [shares a common element] with the first *ba'al teshuva*, whose entire mission is shattering his physical nature. And the second type of *tzadik*, whose entire *avoda* involves the light of his soul, [shares a common element] with the second type of *ba'al teshuva*, whose entire *avoda* surrounds the elevation of his soul.

What emerges from all this leads us to understand the two kinds of servants of G-d: *tzadikim* and *ba'alei teshuva*. Their corresponding four types of service are included in two general categories: the *avoda* of the body and the *avoda* of the soul. The first level of *tzadikim* [*ovdei HaShem* with their bodies] and the first level of *ba'alei teshuva* [those who return from sin and transgression] are considered *avoda* of the body. And the second level among *tzadikim* [*ovdei HaShem* with their souls] and the second level of *ba'alei teshuva* [those who return to elevate their souls to a higher level] are entirely involved with the *avoda* of illumination of the soul. The difference between them is only regarding the direction and path of their *avoda*. For the direction of *avoda* of the *tzadikim* involves drawing G-dliness down from above to below, while the direction of *ba'alei teshuva* is to elevate from below to above. *Tzadikim*, even of the first type [involving the refinement of the body] draw down from above to below. This is because the refinement and cleansing of their bodies takes place through the illumination of Torah, mitzvot and prayer. They have no connection with evil, whatsoever. And *ba'alei teshuva*, also of the second category [who seek to return only to approach closer to G-d, not to expiate sins], serve G-d from below to above, since all of their concern is to ascend in elevation after elevation with devotion of their soul.

The descent of the soul into the body is for the purpose of elevating it through one elevation after another by fulfilling the Torah's mitzvot down here in this world, as is known. However, how is it possible for the soul to receive such high revelation of G-dliness? This is only possible through the fulfillment of physical mitzvot in this world, as the mitzvot are garments for the *neshama* [when it ascends] to the levels of *Gan Eden*.

And in this we find the two categories of *tzadikim* and *ba'alei teshuva*. The general *avoda* of *tzadikim* is drawing down [G-dliness] from above to below and in cleansing and purifying the physical substance in order to remove the dust and dirt that has gathered there. That is what is meant by the phrase [in Genesis 49:11], "and he laundered his garments in wine." For this purpose, they draw down supernal enjoyment.

And what was suggested [in your letter] regarding *ahava beta'anugim* is inaccurate. Rather, [*ahava beta'anugim*] is a drawing down of supernal enjoyment, meaning that it is neither a drawing down of His supernal will nor of His *chochma* ("wisdom") and *bina* ("understanding"). Since here we are speaking of the *avoda* of *tzadikim* and *tzadikim* personify "fulfilling the will of G-d," therefore their path of service includes knowledge and intellectual grasp. Conceivably, they may draw down "only" His will or "only" His intellect (*chochma* and *bina*), but for this very reason, the Alter Rebbe wrote that their *avoda* draws down the element of "supernal enjoyment."

However, the *avoda* of *ba'alei teshuva* involves self-sacrifice because of the evil that is in their souls. The intention here is not to evil in the sense of transgression, but to the second kind, wherein the *ba'al teshuva* seeks to leave behind an insufficient past [and return to G-d for the purpose of elevating his soul, not for expiation of sin]. In comparison to that which exists above, however, this lower level is called "evil." Therefore, they draw down an "expensive" [refined] garment that is meant for the head. As is known, there are two categories of garments: 1) of the body, and 2) of the head. The garment of the head is called a veil and it is more refined than the garments of the body. (See the Chasidic discourse in *Torah Ohr*, starting with the words *Asri Legefen*, regarding the two aspects of white wine and red wine and two garments and the *makifim* that are over these garments.) This is the service of *ba'alei teshuva*, and it constitutes "washing his robe [*suso*-from the word *masveh*, or veil] in the blood of grapes..." [Breishit 49:11]

Now, the second kind of *ba'al teshuva* surpasses even the level of *tzadikim*. His category is explained elsewhere, regarding the *Mashiach*, who "comes to persuade the *tzadikim* to do *teshuva*".

And what [was written in your letter] regarding chapter 43 of *Tanya*, seeking to equate the *teshuva* of Rabbi Eliezer ben Durdaya and *ahavat olam*, is correct. But, in seeking to prove that this level surpasses *ahava rabba*, it is incorrect. Rabbi Eliezer ben Durdaya achieved his huge elevation because of his level of *teshuva*. The love that was revealed in his heart, the Alter Rebbe explains, was a "temporary injunction" by Divine Providence from Above for the purposes of that particular moment. As written elsewhere regarding the verse (in Shmuel 2, 14:14), "those who are repelled from you will [no longer] be repelled." [This refers to those who didn't approach G-d and the Torah before the advent of the Messianic Age for reasons that were beyond them will in the future be enabled to see the light and approach G-d.]

This can take place in one of two ways: either by G-dly proximity, [bringing about] tremendous positive influx of physical benefits, or by distance (G-d forbid) bringing about great suffering. All [physical and spiritual] paths are dangerous, and [sometimes], through various and sundry means, a soul strays off the straight path (G-d forbid) and falls into the depths of *klipot* [forces opposed to holiness]. [It then] stands ready and waiting at a crossroads and may become destroyed completely (G-d forbid), [but] G-d brings about all kinds of circumstances, [since] He-the cause of all causes and reason of all reasons-desires the *teshuva* of the wicked and not their death. Therefore, he brings about opportunities for *teshuva*. This is what occurred in the case of Rabbi Eliezer ben Durdaya; because of the simple and coarse things that were said to him, his heart was broken inside of him over his tremendous detachment [from G-d], and in his excitement and love for G-d, his soul expired. But, this took place as a private arousal at that specific moment.

In closing

According to all that is explained above, regarding the connections of the offshoots of one level [of love] to another, it shouldn't be difficult at all [to understand] how the natural love of the G-dly soul (*ahavat olam*, second type, relating to eternity) is similar to *ahava beta'anugim*, and also how "gazing at the glory of the King" on the second level is similar to the second level of *ba'alei teshuva* on the second level [those who return for purposes of elevating the soul], on which there is elevation with enjoyment.

He who desires their peace and blesses them... (R' Yoseph Yitzhak Schneerson)

Appendix II

Footnotes of the Lubavitcher Rebbe, R' Menachem Mendel Schneerson to the Kuntres Ha'avoda of the Rebbe Rashab

i) Page 4 (Page 4 in the translation as well)

Note: "Effort on all of its levels…" See *Torat Shalom, Sefer Hasichot, Sichat Simchat Torah 5666* (1905), sections 3-5. See also *Derech Chayim* (part 3 of the *Sha'ar Hatshuva* of the Mitteler Rebbe), section 12 and onward. [See also] *Kuntres Hitpa'alut* of the Mittler Rebbe, and elsewhere

From *Torah Shalom* of the Rebbe Rashab, *Sichat Simchat Torah 5666* (1905-6), Sections 3-5, Page 61 (apparently notes from the Rebbe Rayatz, *ztz'l*):

"There are four stages to prayer, corresponding to the four levels of the soul; *nefesh-ruach-neshama* and *neshama d'neshama*, which corresponds to the two *makifim* ("transcendent levels") of *chaya* and *yechida*. Our prayers begin on the level of *nefesh*, meaning "acknowledgment," as written, *Hodu L'HaShem* ("Acknowledge/give thanks to the Lord…"). Now, it is known that acknowledgment is not mere agreement (a "nod of the head"), but rather implies surrendering ourselves (while giving ourselves over). While in this state, we "relinquish ourselves" to G-dliness. For example, one who concedes to his friend, even though he may not understand why, nevertheless admits that his friend is correct. In this sense, he "relinquishes himself" to his friend. And so it is in serving G-d: We deliver ourselves to G-dliness. This means that in the beginning [when we arise in the morning] as we say *modeh ani lefanecha* ("I acknowledge/give thanks to You"), we cede ourselves to G-d in our entirety, even though we do not yet know the details that are involved in this "concession." And afterward [when we start to pray], we say *Hodu LaShem* ("Give thanks/acknowledge the Lord") and we do know the details involved, as known regarding the phrase *Hodu LaShem vekiru b'shmo* ("Give thanks/acknowledge…proclaim His name")…this is the level of *nefesh*.

And afterward, during the *pesukei dezimra* ("verses of song"), we experience the level of *ruach*, during which we recite praises of the One above; how He enlivens and creates the universe, as we say, *Baruch sheamar vehaya haolam* ("Blessed be He Who uttered and the universe came into existence…"). Or, as we also say, "He Who covers the heavens with clouds, Who prepares rain for the land, Who causes the mountains to sprout fodder, Who gives sustenance to the animals and to the offspring of ravens who call…" In this manner, we arouse within ourselves excitement that goes beyond our mere intellectual grasp. Rather, it develops in proportion to our recital of His praises, [as we consider] how He enlivens the universe and the manner in which [creations] are able to accept Him. And even though it is not understood how all of creation is able to accept Him and His energy, nevertheless they do accept Him. And about this, the psalms say, "He Who covers the heavens with clouds, Who prepares rain for the land, Who causes the mountains to germinate…" [All of these phrases] allude to the hiding and concealment [of G-dliness] that enable us to accept [His divine influx] – for from the perspective of G-dly influence it was not necessary to create the world in this manner. Yet, nevertheless He hides and conceals Himself so that we will be able to accept His [goodness]...and from this we become emotionally stimulated. And this is the level of *ruach*, which is devoid of [intellectually infused] love derived from meditation. For, [regarding meditation], the emphasis is upon what we understand of the good and the benefit of G-dliness, which is what induces us to desire and cling to G-dliness. But, this is not the case regarding the *pesukei dezmira*, which are associated with [pure] emotional stimulation.

For, there is such a thing as excitement of the emotions. While the intellect does not become excited in any more than a refined manner, the emotions are receptive to stimulation. This is what occurs during the *pesukei dezimra*, as we recite praises and our emotions are aroused. This is not the love and fear with which we "love the Lord" and fear Him, but this is rather the excitement of the very essence of the emotions themselves. This is a necessary stage of divine service, for it is impossible to achieve the characteristics of [intellectually infused] love and fear without prior stimulation of the emotions during the *peshukei dezimra*. This is a necessary pre-requisite, (which is demanded of us). Without it, it is impossible to fulfill the service of reciting the *kriat shema*, since the order of prayer requires that we first achieve the level of *ruach* during *pesukei dezimra*, only after which we recite the blessings prior to the *kriat shema*, and finally the *kriat shema* [itself], with intellectual grasp.

Now, the blessings preceding *kriat shema* require [that we activate] intellect, in order to grasp the nullification of the angels [to G-d]. [We need to understand] how they say *kadosh*, and how [they grasp] that the infinite light of G-d is holy and removed. [They grasp] that what shines down here to the worlds is a mere ray [of G-dliness], which is why the angels are nullified. The point is that this should be meaningful for us as we pray, for if not, why would the service of the angels be important to us – what have they to do with us? But, what is significant here is what [their service] means to us [which is that we as well should be nullified to G-d]. And then afterward during the phrase *baruch kavod* ["Blessed be His Honor..." – here the angels beseech G-d for divine revelation] we may attain some greater level of feeling within ourselves. That is, we may notice that we have a stronger desire for revelation of G-dliness within our soul and within the universe. For, the angels say *baruch* [indicating a desire for G-dliness that is beyond them]...because they are unable to grasp [the G-dly levels that are beyond them]. And we know that we are higher than these angels (the *ofanim*, angels of *asiya*), but nevertheless, there is still no essential divine light shining within us. And even though as we develop understanding, that is as we say the phrase *kadosh*, conscious light shines within, nevertheless this is not revelation of G-d's essential light. For, there are many different varieties of spiritual levels prior to revelation of the essential light of the Infinite One Above, as known regarding the explanation of *baruch kevod Hashem mimkomo* – "Blessed be the Lord from His place" – referring to descent of the essential infinite light below. And the difference is that with this [level of essential revelation], we become like a "*tzadik* who eats to satisfaction."

For, when the essential light does not shine [within us], extraneous aspects may remain [in our soul]. It is written that during prayer, we experience divine illumination. However, that may cause us to feel good for a short time after the prayers, but soon afterward we find ourselves attracted to the physical realm. That is why it is important to "guard" the feeling for G-dliness that we experience during our prayers, for if not, we are tempted by the physical (unless one is naturally spiritual, meaning that he prays for an extended period of time, and after many consecutive days and many prayers, he experiences the divine light and for a long duration).

That is, after much devotion during prayer, the G-dly feeling remains with us. Not that this leads us to experience anything new in our feeling for G-dliness (like one who thinks for a long time, and when he stops for a bit, new ideas arise in his mind), but just that we take much time to experience G-dliness (repeatedly, like one who is standing for awhile in the air of *gan eden*). That is why one of the explanations of the word *atzeret* [as in the festival of *Shemini Atzeret*] is that it comes from the term *atzara*, meaning "stopping," "absorbing." And so is stated in books (*Bina le'itim*), that when someone is aroused with a good trait, he must remain with it for some time and become immersed in it. But, we cannot really say "immersed," because we do not fully understand [the arousal] to such a great extent. Rather, we are "involved with it," "taken with it." And, as a result, we are less involved with the physical world.

All of this applies when our feeling for G-dliness is based upon the divine light that permeates the worlds. But, when our meditation and feeling is for the essential infinite light that transcends the worlds, then we lose our connection to anything physical whatsoever. This is the condition of a "*tzadik* who eats to the satisfaction of his soul." While meditating upon G-dliness enclothed in the worlds, it is impossible to come to a state of *bitul bemetziut* ("total nullification of the self"). Since this level of G-dliness is enclothed in the world, it is to be expected that it possesses the trait of "existence." Only from meditation upon G-dliness that transcends the worlds is it possible to attain the level of nullification of existence associated with "the *tzadik* who eats to the satisfaction of his soul."

However, it is necessary to understand that all this takes place within the "inner dimensions" of *bina* (*pnimiyut bina*), and not within the external manifestations of intellect. The external intellect is the ability to understand and grasp the concept and feel it in our soul...but [the spiritual levels described above] are associated with *pnimiyut bina*. This occurs as we meditate on G-dliness that is enclothed in the worlds and experience the G-dly illumination in our soul, and then we subsequently proceed to meditate upon the lofty and amazing nature of the essence of the infinite light which is above our grasp – for the essence of the infinite light is beyond whatever our thoughts are capable of grasping – from this, we automatically understand that whatever we do grasp is not the essence of the infinite One...

And then we meditate upon the nature of this lofty light. For this purpose, we must first return to the original meditation, but with more internal focus and with stronger concentration. And we understand that this is not yet the essence [of G-dliness], and that the essence is yet more lofty and elevated, and thus this is not the essence. And then, we focus upon the nature of that elevation, which means that [whatever we grasp in the spiritual realm] above, [we postulate that] "this is not" the essence. We must somehow develop a feeling for this – it is not enough [for us] down here to say, "this is not it" – for that goes without saying. Rather, in order to appreciate what is meant above when we say that essence is "not this" – we need to develop a sense of recognition of the nature of "lofty elevation." For example, we may recognize the nature of a great person. We may be able to pinpoint a certain characteristic of his that is lofty and elevated, because his loftiness does not mean that he is removed from all other men. It only means that he is, of his own nature, elevated and lofty. And therefore, he automatically possesses certain character traits that lend him his lofty character...[and so the person meditating] must first grasp that the essence of the infinite light is elevated and lofty. [At first], he accepts the existence of loftiness with blind faith, without any intellectual proof that this is indeed the case. And thereafter, he continues to meditate and comes to recognize the nature of the loftiness and elevation. This process is associated with *pnimiyut bina*, which is [also] the technique known as *yediat hashlila* ("negation of knowledge"). With it, one is able to shine revealed essential G-dly light below. And then, as he experiences the essential infinite light, he is becomes completely detached from anything physical whatsoever. He can "eat a bagel" without relating to it whatsoever.

And then, this is followed by meditation on the [essential] name *Havaya* in two different modes. Either everything is nullified in existence, or everything is G-dliness, and then there is no connection whatsoever to anything physical. And as is known regarding one who ate a bagel [the intention may be to the *Malach*, son of the Mezritcher Magid. He was oblivious in meditation to the extent that his soul was ready to leave his body, but the Alter Rebbe, who was his study partner, inserted a bagel into the *Malach's* mouth, thereby bringing him "back down to earth." The *Malach* later said that the Alter Rebbe "saved his life," for his soul was about to leave his body], who was on the level of, "everything is G-dly."...

And after this stage, we arrive afterward to *reiyah* – "vision" of the very essence of G-dliness, which occurs during the *shmonah esreh*. This occurs on the soul level of *yechida*, on which the *neshama* is an intermediary between the soul enclothed in the body and the very essence of the soul. And it is impossible to begin the *shemonah esreh* without first prefacing it with the order of prayer to begin with –

Except during *mincha*, when we begin our prayers with the *shemonah esreh*. For, the prayer of *mincha* is the *shemonah esreh*; one, because it follows the *shacharit* prayer, and moreover because it is an *et ratzon* – an "auspicious time." ...and therefore, we are able to begin with *shemonah esreh*, but otherwise, we are unable to begin with *shemonah resreh* without first reciting the prayers before hand...but the order of prayer is such that we must preface with the soul levels of *nefesh ruach* and *neshama* and then afterward we may arrive to the *yechida*. It comes out, then, the *neshama* is the intermediary.

From *Derech Chaim* of the Mitteler Rebbe, Ch. 12, Page 30:

"Now, the details of *tshuva* correspond to the soul levels of *nefesh-ruach-neshama-chaya*, which consist of four levels. The first is *tshuva* of the *nefesh*, as written, "The *nefesh* that sins, and it will return." The second corresponds with *ruach*, as written, "And the *ruach* will return to *Elokim*." The third level corresponds with *neshama*, as written, "If man devotes his heart, his spirit and *neshama*, to G-d he will be gathered." And the fourth level is *tshuva* corresponding to *chaya* (also called *mazla*), as written, "And man was [created as] a living (*chaya*) soul."

Now, [the level of *tshuva* associated with *chaya*] corresponds to the letters *lamed-mem* of the word *tzelem adam* ("image of man" – spelled *tzadi-lamed-mem*). The first letter *tzadi* of *tzelem* corresponds to the soul [as en-clothed in the body], including the three levels of *nefesh-ruach-neshama*. And the second letter *lamed* corresponds to *chaya* and the *mem* to the *yechida* of the soul. And the rectification of *tshuva* must affect the blemish that inflicts all of the *tzelem* [the "image" in which man was created]. For, whoever sins, blemishes the entire "image of G-d" that is within him. . . And, it is written, "But, in the image, man walks," referring to the *tzelem* ("image") of G-d alone, as known. And even if he already rectified his *nefesh-ruach-neshama* by doing *tshuva*, he will still need to rectify his *mazal*, which is blemished until he fixes the *lamed-mem* of *tzelem* (such as occurred during the *tshuva* of the *yechida* that was performed by R' Eliezer ben Durdaya and Natan Detzutzita, and the like)...

[The rest of Ch. 12 and subsequent chapters of *Derech Chayim* delve into the details of *tshuva* on the various levels of the soul].

From *Kuntres Hitpa'alut* of the Mitteler Rebbe, Page 77 (in the Kehot edition, *Maamorei Admor Haemtzai – Kuntresim*, pub. 1991)

[Here, the Mitteler Rebbe describes five levels of meditation as they occur within the natural, "intellectual" soul. Later, he goes on to describe the same five levels as they occur in the Divine soul...]

"It would appear that there are five levels, one above the other, and each one of them will be explained so that no mistake will be made. The first level, the lowest of all of them, occurs when the meditator desires only to attain some sort of excitement – from which he derives energy – and nothing more. This is just about the lowest level of them all, so low that it is near the level of external excitement of the heart explained above, in which the meditator experiences only himself. This is not G-dly excitement at all. For, he has no desire or intention regarding G-dliness at all. His goal is not that G-dliness should dwell in his soul, or that he should develop a connection to G-dliness. His only desire is to experience some of the energy of G-liness, so that he can consider himself "successful."

Nevertheless, there is some good mixed in here, concealed within his hidden love for G-d. That is, [the good] is masked as a "foreign" garment, as if he desires G-dliness. In any case, his main desire is to experience G-dly excitement, but if it weren't for G-d, he would have no desire at all for [even the excitement]. Although, this is not his conscious aim – he would never consciously entertain the notion that his real desire is to experience G-dliness in his soul (not for his own enjoyment, but out of desire for G-dliness). About this [state of consciousness], we say, "G-dliness is good for me"…

And the second level above this, is likened to "hearing from afar," wherein the meditator heard of G-dliness and meditates on G-dliness alone, understanding the concepts well until he accepts and confirms them in his mind at least, which is a true and real process. Nevertheless, the concepts remain far from him, and he asks, 'what benefit' to the soul will come from this. [He asks] because the activity of meditation on G-dliness is very important in his eyes and acceptable to him as a way of acknowledging G-d. And in his mind, the importance of G-dliness become greater and more exalted, until it occupies the ultimate pinnacle of importance in his mind and in his heart as well. But, he desires that G-dliness should become fixed in his soul and heart in a conscious and revealed manner, not quietly and "from afar." Now, this is a higher level, since it is closer to real G-dly excitement…for at least the matter of meditation on G-dliness is important to him and he greatly desires it. His main goal and will is to approach G-dliness. But, however much he labors, he fails to achieve any G-dly excitement at all in his heart and mind. He labors not for himself, but for the sake of G-dliness alone, for it is only closeness to G-d that he seeks, so that it becomes fixed in his soul. This is the main "entry level" approach to meditation for those who truly search for and demand G-dliness with integrity, with positive intention, for G-dliness alone.

Now, the third level above this is called a "positive thought that combines with action." That means, that it produces emotions of love and fear of G-d that are associated with action alone. The explanation is the following; although in the second level described above, the person has a positive attitude toward G-dliness, meaning that he desires only to be close to G-d and not far from Him. And this is because of the preciousness of G-dliness that he experiences in his mind. But, this does not mean that he becomes at all excited in his mind, for G-dly matters remain completely beyond him. He would like for these matters to be closer to him, but that has not yet happened yet. Thus, G-dliness remains a matter of acknowledgment in his mind, and nothing more. And therefore, it is not called a "good thought," but merely a "thought."

This may be understood by way of illustration regarding worldly matters. We see that there are two trains of thought. One occurs as man thinks about something [positive]; how it is good and praiseworthy until it becomes very important in his eyes. For example, a treasure of wealth that is in the possession of someone else, or upon the great honor and glory of the king or his minister or the like. This is called objective or "cold" thought, which is not at all associated with the thinker in a personal way whatsoever. He will never achieve this status - neither the wealth nor the greatness – he merely thinks about it because of its significance and importance in his eyes. He would very much like for something so positive and praiseworthy to come his direction.

And the second train of thought occurs as he considers something good for himself, such as the profit that he may gain from a good business transaction, or the honor and greatness or attainment of great wealth that he may achieve for himself. Such thoughts elicit great excitement from him, as well as interest and a bit of attraction within his soul, which is called "progress from his place." We clearly observe that upon the arrival of a good business deal that is important, he labors with all of his power of thought and becomes very attached to the proposition, with excitement that we call "cleaving" within thought…and this is what we call "hearing" within thought. The sign of this occurring is when he is so involved that it "moves him" a bit.

And so it is regarding meditation upon G-dly concepts. This type of thought, wherein he cleaves heartily to a matter that is important to him, is called a "good thought that combines with action." At the very least, from this thought will be born love and fear of G-d that spurs him to action. The "cold" and objective thought mentioned above, even when he truly desires to approach and become excited, will not stimulate him to experience "hearing" within thought. He meditates "from afar", merely acknowledging G-dliness as mentioned…and nothing emerges from this ["frigid"] thought other than a resolution to "refrain from evil." That is to say, since the meditation is real and honest, it is appropriate and [will aid him] in refraining from evil and doing good – but this is merely the lowest level…

But, the "good thought" mentioned above, also applies to reciting the *shema Yisrael* ("Hear Oh Israel…")…followed by *veahavta* ("You shall love…"), since the main point [of the *Shema*] is only the excitement of "hearing" within thought, mentioned above. And from it develops love, but nevertheless, no excitement of the heart develops as of yet, but merely excitement within thought. So, this level of love is only for the purpose of action and not for anything internal, such as excitement of the heart, at all…All this is called *dechilu verechimu* ("fear and love" in the language of the Zohar). Even though they are associated with action alone, nonetheless they lend much light and energy to his thought processes. This is similar, for example to a thought that is very personal to someone regarding worldly matters. Within this thought, he develops love and excitement at the very least, and he comes to fear the opposite, as if from damage and destruction…

The fourth level above this occurs as, upon meditating on G-dliness, we attain proper excitement as described above, and immediately experience stimulation of the heart, including illumination and great energy. This is a much more internal experience than the stimulation of the "good thought" mentioned above (and yet, it is not the real G-dly excitement of experiencing G-dliness in the heart as well, which is an experience of the G-dly soul as it expands through the body. That level is far above even the fifth level that we will presently explain). And about this fourth level, we say, "You shall love…with all your heart" – with emphasis on the heart. This is the main point of *avoda shebeleiv* – prayers – to belabor ourselves so much in meditation that our heart becomes excited…[which occurs] after much effort. For regarding matters of the world, as soon as a good idea occurs to us, and we are mentally stimulated, the excitement immediately translates into love like fire of desire or the opposite - with bitterness in response to anything negative or hateful within the thought. But, in service of G-d, it is not easy to produce excitement of the heart through stimulation of the mind, because the G-dliness that we do experience during this meditation is not drawn consciously down to the heart. Rather it remains transcendent and inspirational in the mind. Now, there are many levels to this regarding the nature of excitement of the heart; there are those who are excited in the heart more than in the mind and there are those who become excited more by joy…

The fifth level, above the previous one, is the inner intention within the heart, that transcends even excitement within the heart. The explanation of this is that, as known, even when we experience total excitement in the heart, with desire and joy or bitterness on account of our meditation, within the moment of excitement in the heart is condensed the entire "length" of the G-dly concept about which we were excited, leaving nothing but what is relevant to the excitement in the heart alone. That is, what arises from a synopsis of the intention of the meditation regarding *memalle* ("immanent spirituality") and *sovev* ("transcendent G-dliness") and the like, is the main point and origin of the intention...for everything stands before Him as naught, etc...

As a result of this concise synopsis [of the meditation], the heart becomes even more excited. However, this [experience] is actually a minor revelation compared to the essence of the intention in his heart [that develops as a result] of the full length of [meditation upon] the G-dly concept on which he focused in his mind and heart. There, [the full] length and breadth is beyond our ability to experience in the heart. By way of example from matters of the world; when man devotes attention from the very depths of his mind to the greatness of some good business deal, and his whole soul is attached to it, nevertheless he may not be able yet to direct his heart to the matter and get excited about it because he is totally involved with his whole mind and heart in the essential quality of the deal itself. This is called *mochin degadlut* ("mature mindfullness") within our intellectual faculties (*chabad*)....

...and although there are also emotions of love and fear concealed [within this level of consciousness], they are called "intellectual love and fear" alone. They are beyond natural love and fear of the heart...intellectual love and fear are inseparable from the [intellectual] essence of the meditation itself. Rather, [they emerge] spontaneously and automatically, of necessity without our choice or will at all. And within the heart, they also emerge spontaneously , just as one who spontaneously claps his hands out of happiness. And the sign of this is that the excitement is constant while he is under the influence of this meditation, and it does not interrupt at all, unlike natural love and fear [during meditation on the third and fourth levels], which dissipate only to return again. And therefore, the concept of "labor" does not apply to this intellectual love and fear so much...and beyond this there is also the simple will which far transcends any meditation whatsoever, but is rather an essential and simple will from which and because of which the intellect emerges, as known...

[Starting on page 139, the Mitteler Rebbe describes the five levels of *nefesh-ruach-neshama-chaya-yechida* in the Divine G-dly soul]:

"Above are explained five general levels of the natural soul alone, aside from the level on which there is nothing G-dly whatsoever. [That level] relates only to one who seeks excitement devoid of any conscious G-dly intention – only unconscious motivation. Now, there is a similar level as well within the Divine soul, when it is a state of ultimate lack of consciousness, or concealed awareness....When it comes to performance of mitzvoth alone, which is the lowest level of the soul, in action alone...then if it weren't for the natural essence of every Jewish spark within the soul, to refrain from evil and to do good, then their own *avoda* and fear of G-d called *frumkeit* ("religiosity"), would not suffice [to continue fulfilling Torah and mitzvoth]. But, with the motivation of *avoda* and fear within each and every one according to his abilities, the natural essential power of the G-dly soul on each and every detail of refraining from evil and doing good is strengthened and the person clings to his level without varying or becoming lenient or transgressing to err or allowing himself become permissive. And in this there are great differences from one person another, from a complete *tzadik* to one who is totally evil person in his deeds.

Now, certainly this involvement in action and avoidance of evil together with commitment to good coming from the essence of the G-dly soul is first initiated in thought. [Specifically], this is the will for G-dliness within thought, to fulfill His will in action at the very least, and not to transgress His will in deed. And this thought is devoid of any internal illumination or energy whatsoever. It is cold, like the "cold thought" of the natural soul regarding G-dly meditation.

Now, the second level, somewhat above this is more internal, for it is beyond simple positive action in merely fulfilling the mitzvoth, which is the level of *nefesh* mentioned above. It is the level of *ruach* which transcends *nefesh*, corresponding to the second level of the natural soul, called excitement of the "good thought." This is understood by way of example of the Jews who exited from Egypt, all of the nation, children and women, on account of the simple faith within their soul, since they believed in G-d. Even though to begin with, out of "lack of spirit," they did not listen to Moshe, when their spirit returned to them, they believed with a G-dly spirit that was essential and rooted in their souls from the G-dly soul, with internal light and energy. And all of them went out of Egypt, which was an act of total excitement in their thought and inner will, called "progress from their place." This is comparable to the "good thought" spoken of earlier regarding something that is close to the person. And as a result of this, even though it may not be so applicable to the person in action alone – that is, leaving Egypt - but it produces light and energy in the soul that is much more internal than the "cold thought" above, which is concealed within action of refraining from evil and doing good, without energy whatsoever…

This is further understood from the example of the ingathering of the sparks of holiness that fell through the "shattering of the vessels," whether of the idol worshippers [where the "sparks" dwelt for several hundred and thousands of years, and now they totally awaken and return], or of converts who convert, which is an amazing and wonderful phenomenon. That someone should experience a desire to convert, is due to nothing other than a G-dly spirit blowing through him, even without him being aware of it. This is comparable to the converts in the time of Abraham, such as Aner, Eshkol and Mamre, and similar [events occur] in every generation…

This is further understood by the example of *ba'alei tshuva* [Jews who strayed from the path of Torah and mitzvoth, who seek their way back]. Although formerly sunken in many kinds of evil lusts and serious transgression, nevertheless, their spirit arouses to return in *tshuva*. And there are those who return from the very depths of their heart, to the extent of crying out their soul, such as R' Elazar ben Durdaya, who expired while crying. Rebi was envious of him, saying the he "acquired his world to come in one moment."…This corresponds to what was explained above regarding the "good thought that combines with action" of love and fear in the mind, including excitement, at least…Now, from all this, we may grasp the general topic of essential excitement of the G-dly soul, in an internal manner, which is the level of *ruach*, above the level of *nefesh* which is nothing more than the action itself, as explained above.

Now, the third level above this is the essential excitement of the level of *neshama*, as written, *kol haneshama tehalel* ("the entire soul praises…"). And also as written, "If he will devote his heart and his spirit to Him, then his soul will be gathered to Him…" This level corresponds to what was previously mentioned regarding the "detached excitement" of the natural soul; as it attains the stimulation known as a "good thought" within the physical heart, with excitement that he experiences like fiery flames of desire…in the G-dly soul. This is essential excitement of the physical heart, resulting from true grasp of G-dliness within the divine soul as it is enclothed within the intellectual grasp of the natural soul. This is what is meant by, "My heart and my flesh sing to the living G-d" – the physical flesh of the heart itself sings to G-d. This is like the excitement associated with a melody that resonates in the physical heart, which emerges spontaneously, by itself and automatically, without any choice or labor whatsoever, but just because of the essential excitement of the G-dly soul...And this is the main difference between the conscious excitement within the heart coming from the natural soul – when he himself knows and is aware and feels his excitement. And therefore, without a doubt the G-dliness is distant and concealed in this state, for there is "one who is excited" and therefore he is an "entity" [implying lack of nullification to G-d] in and of himself. This is true to the extent that he turns his excitement, rather than G-dliness, into the main goal, as mentioned above regarding the excitement of the heart that is not for G-d at all but for his own enjoyment revealed in his soul. But, the essential excitement of the G-dly soul, although it is felt in the heart, is not conscious at all. And it is not a conscious experience at all, to the extent that he does not know of it at the time that it occurs and neither does it "feel" itself. This is comparable to the excitement and desire that a son has for his father in his heart. Since it is natural and essential excitement, he doesn't experience it himself as excitement and is unaware of it, for the most part, and so regarding the excitement of the father for the son....this level exists among most people who have not yet sullied their G-dly soul, nor damaged themselves with the impurity of the body and foreign lusts so much...

And the fourth level is a [concentrated point] of intention within the mind, that is above any excitement that may still be experienced within the heart. For example, this is comparable to the fourth level within the natural soul, when one is totally absorbed to the depths of his mind and heart, in the amazing nature of something positive. His soul is attracted to it, preventing him from experiencing any excitement in his heart. Now, this is called "intellectual fear and love," as when the intellect itself is excited. This is not the excitement that comes from a concise synopsis of the concept [under meditation]. Now, the essential excitement of the heart mentioned above, of which he is unconscious, emerges suddenly without any preparation. It is like, for example excitement that appears suddenly, causing one to clap his hands. So as well, this "song" within the physical heart emerges spontaneously of its own accord, just as any essential excitement, and this is the main sign of its appearance. And this level also contains a more internal element, when the meditator is drawn after a concise synopsis [of the concept] in his mind. This is the depth of essential intention within the concept...

Nevertheless, it is not within range of the essential excitement within the inner intention of the mind, when the intellectual point of the concept itself is aroused. This is called *kavana*...this *kavana* refers to the essence of the essential G-dly light in and of itself, and not as the result of his intellectual grasp and understanding. It is above the length and breadth of grasp of *bina*, although it subsequently expresses itself in intellectual grasp...and this *kavana* contains essential, unmitigated enjoyment of the essence and simplicity of the G-dly soul. It is the source of Shabbat prayers... which are above the weekday prayers... Similarly, every day of the week during the *kriat shema*, a reflection and ray shines from Shabbat...And for that reason, the excitement of the *kriat shema*, with love, is different from that of the *pesukei dezimra*. During the *pesukei dezimra*, the excitement is felt, from the mind to the heart, just as during the excitement of the angels, with a noise and commotion...and during the *kriat shema* as we say *shema Yisrael* to the soul, so that it surrenders itself as we say *echad*, up to *veahavta* – the result is that we produce love within the natural soul as well... But, during the essential excitement within the point of *kavana* in the mind, the excitement of the heart with conscious love becomes included within it...and since this is more internal and essential, it comes as something that is not felt, and does not even experience itself...in general this is the level of *chaya* – *koach mah* – of *chochma* within the G-dly soul. There is where illuminates the *mazla* and *tzelem* ("image"), which is the *makif* of *chaya*, within which dwells the *neshama yeteira* of Shabbat which is the *makif* of *yechida*, the highest of all...and it does not illuminate in a revealed manner at all, but rather shines from afar, hidden, and this is the inner fifth level to be explained...

And the fifth level is the essential *yechida* itself, which is also called the "simple song," indicating that it comes from the essence and ascends with song, and is therefore called a simple song...for the "double song" mentioned above is essential enjoyment that comes as a private revelation, particular to every person according to his grasp of G-dliness, just as souls "enjoy the ray from the *ziva ila'ah*" of *atik* within *malchut* of *Atzilut*. Each person according to the extent of his own point of grasp, enjoys G-dly intellect, and not all souls are equal in this. But, the "simple" song is accompanied by abstract enjoyment that is the source of all kinds of specific enjoyments of this [spiritual] nature. Therefore, it comes as enjoyment that is all-inclusive of all essential [kinds of] enjoyment...This is like by way of example, one who is immersed in escaping and saving himself from certain death – his entire point of will within the essence of his soul is aroused. It touches his very essence, and thus all of his other desires, such as love for money or for his wife and children, fall by the wayside. All of a sudden, they are unimportant to him, since they are included in the very essence of this will that touches his very essence. He is then fully involved and nothing remains [of his other desires], and he feels nothing whatsoever of himself. This is the love of *bekol meodecha* ("with all of your might"), without limit and above his *nefesh-ruach-neshama*, and also above the *koach mah* within his soul, that comes enclothed in the *kavana* of the mind. But, this is beyond intellect and logic completely, for there is no logic at all behind the inner, simple, abstract desire and enjoyment – not even a "concealed" will that sometimes exists in the origins of abstract intellect. And since this level is not common at all among the vast majority of people, therefore to speak of it at length is extraneous. But, nevertheless, it is present in a concealed manner in every Jewish spark [soul] on Shabbat, in their souls, and it is called the *neshama yeteira*, which is the *makif* of *yechida*...

[For more elucidation of the topic of *hitbonenut* and the soul levels of *naranchai*, see the series *Besha'ah shehikdimu 5672* (1912) of the Rebbe Rashab, vol. 2, page 803-831 (chapters 391-404)]

ii) Page 4 (Page 4 in the translation as well)

Note: "the self-nullification of acknowledgment..." See *Sha'ar lag b'omer* in the *Siddur*. See the discourse *Kol dodi* of the year *5668* (1908). And the discourse *Vayahas Caleb* of the year *5614* (1914).

From the Siddur with Chasidut of the Alter Rebbe, *Sha'ar Lag B'omer*, page 606

"...and this is why we say *modim anachnu lach sheatah Elokeinu* ("We acknowledge/thank You that You are our G-d...") – because You are our G-d. [This alludes] to the supernal thought, wherein the collective Jewish nation arose in its source, the origin from which they were hewn. And therefore, automatically, we acknowledge [Him] with this concession, without need of any sign or proof at all... but this acknowledgment takes place in the G-dly soul alone as it exists in its source and origin above in "thought." However, as the soul descends and becomes en-clad in the physical substance of the body, which obscures it, it is not capable of achieving this level of acknowledgment, of "You are Our Lord our G-d," Who constantly renews [the universe] from nothing to something, since the corporeality of the body conceals this level of acknowledgment.

For that reason, the sages established *modim derabanen* – "rabbinic acknowledgment," [the phrase that we recite during the *shemoneh esreh*, beginning with the word *modim*], which is *hoda'ah lehoda'ah* - "conceding that we must acknowledge." That is, we concede that the appropriate response to You is to acknowledge/thank You.

Now, the explanation is that there are two levels to acknowledgment. The first is acknowledgment that results from awareness and knowledge, as one who grasps [for example] and recognizes the mighty greatness and majesty of a king. And therefore, he concedes and acknowledges that so it is, since he recognizes and understands. The same is true of a sage – we concede his amazing wisdom since we recognize and grasp his greatness. However, there is a level of acknowledgment below this, which takes place when we lack knowledge. This occurs when it is not within our power to grasp or to recognize at all, any of the might, majesty or wisdom as it really exists. All that we can do is know and recognize that [the king or the sage] is lofty in his wisdom and therefore we must concede to him with admission and great praise, just as a poor person admits the greatness of the king, even though he has no concept of the king's essential greatness as it really exists. Nevertheless, he admits that he must concede and praise this greatness, even though he does not grasp it. And this takes place as a result of the great distance of the one who concedes [from the object of his praise]. For, the greater the gulf, the less he will be capable of admitting out of knowledge. Rather, we are forced to simply admit because we must do so. And this is what the sages meant when they said, "Most acknowledgments, [because] He is a G-d of acknowledgments," indicating that there are a myriad levels of acknowledgment/giving thanks.

The more that we contemplate the greatness of the infinite light above, which is exalted and beyond intellectual grasp, [the more we realize that] we do not know how to acknowledge it out of knowledge and grasp. We are only capable of admitting that we must acknowledge. And in this manner, we succeed in conceding up to the highest levels, with many acknowledgments of concession and admission, in proportion to the distance of the intellectual grasp…and this in general is the reason that the sages established *modim derabanen*, to express the general concept of admission of acknowledgment.

From the discourse *Kol dodi* of the year *5668* (1908), of the Rebbe Rashab, Page 152:

"…and the soul faculty of *hod* [is what motivates us] to bow and acknowledge G-d, Who enlivens and creates everything, as if naught before Him. And although we do not grasp this, we acknowledge, as written in Tanya, *Igeret Hakodesh, siman* 15, (entitled *lehavin mashal u'melitza*). This concept corresponds to what is written in *Likutei Torah*, in the discourse *Bayom Hashmini Atzeret*, [regarding] the distinction between prostrating oneself and bowing from the waist. We prostrate ourselves when we undersatand and grasp the truth about the greatness of G-d and His unity, and we focus our concentraion strongly upon this. Then, the concept penetrates and illuminates us in a revealed manner, and automatically we become nullfied in an internal manner. We are truly nullified within, and whatever is the opposite, meaning not nullified to G-d truly concerns us to the very inner point of our heart. [This is so] until we subdue the *sitra achra* and transform all the evil within it and it possesses no other will at all.

However, bowing (from the waist) occurs when we do not understand or grasp at all, how it is that the entire creation is as if naught before Him, and the concept does not shine in our soul, yet nevertheless we labor ourselves in prayer, meditating upon how all levels of revelation, even of the higher spiritual worlds, are nothing but a mere ray that has no significance whatsoever. And everything is before Him as truly naught, and the creations themselves are as nothing in their own estimation and experience as well. And even though we do not grasp the essence of the matter in and of itself, how and what it is, nevertheless we know that is the truth (and we also grasp how this is true, but our grasp is without true understanding that illuminates the matter, enabling us to feel and experience it inside)…

(Page 159)...Now, just as the faculty of *netzach* ("security and determination") never changes nor varies at all, so the faculty of *hod* ("acknowledgment and gratitude") does not vary or change. The faculty of *hoda'ah* is found in each and everyone, at all times, even though it may be in a state of intellectual immaturity and grasp, nevertheless *hoda'ah* still occurs. We are always capable of admitting the truth. And all the moreso that everyone possesses the attribute of admission within acknowledgment, which is permanent.

For, as known, there are two types of *hoda'ah*: One is acknowledgment that results from logic and intellect. That is, we understand, at the very least, that we must concede. For example, we concede to a friend that his perspective is correct, even though our own reasoning may not necessarily agree. Nevertheless we may grasp that the truth corresponds with the point of view of our friend, and because of that we concede to him. Or, we may acknowledge a great sage or king; even though we have no idea or grasp of his wisdom because we have no ability of intellect to plumb the depth of his wisdom. And the same may be true of the majesty and greatness of a king, of which we have no idea or grasp of even how to go about achieving knowledge of his loftiness and greatness. Nevertheless we understand that he is majestic and lofty and that he is a great king or sage.

And the second category occurs when we know nothing, meaning that we, with our intellect and grasp know nothing and totally fail to grasp that he is lofty and majestic or that the sage is very wise. All we know is the truth of the matter that he is wise, and to this we admit, and concede and acknowledge even though we in ourselves know nothing of this at all. Now, in general, the power of acknowledgment - and in particular of the second category of acknowledgment – such that even when we do not grasp anything we concede and nullify ourselves – comes from the very essence and core of the soul...

From the discourse, *Vayahas Caleb 5674* (1914), in the series *Besha'ah shehikdimu*, vol. 2, page 516:

"In general, there are three stages of development; *ibur* ("pregnancy"), *yenikah* ("nursing"), and *mochin* ("intellect," or "maturity"). *Ibur* is the ultimate immaturity, when all of the faculties are concealed and there is no indication of intellect as of yet. For example, the embryo when in the womb of its mother, is doubled over, with its head between its knees, indicating that all that is revealed of his faculties are the instinctual faculties of *nehi* (*netzach*, *hod* and *yesod*) alone. The intellectual faculties of *chabad* (*chochma*, *bina* and *da'at*) as well as the emotional faculties of *chagat* (*chesed*, *gevura* and *tiferet*) are concealed...

...Now, *nehi* within *nehi* corresponds to the attribute of *hoda'ah*, or "acknowledgment." This occurs when we do not grasp the matter at hand, for if we grasped it then it would not be appropriate to concede or admit it, for after all, we grasp the matter. Only when we do not grasp the matter does it become necessary to concede the matter. And yet there is still some amount of intellectual influence present, since we reason that we must acknowledge. That is, we reason that the matter is as stated [or described to us]. Even though the matter is not settled in our mind so that we know how and what it is, nevertheless we do know that it is so. Just as, for example regarding a very wise man, who speaks of deep and elevated concepts - even one who does not know and is not familiar with his thinking, and therefore does not grasp at all the nature of his wisdom and its loftiness, is nevertheless aware that this man possesses very lofty wisdom. He has at least that much connection to intellect, that at least he recognizes the amazing nature [of wisdom] even though he may not know the nature of [the sage's] ideas since he cannot grasp the concepts.

And so in the realm of spirituality, we say *modim anachnu lach she atah HaShem Elokeinu* – "we acknowledge You, that You are the Lord our G-d." In general, He creates the words from nothing to something, and in particular Jewish souls are aware of this, since the Jews "arose within His thought." Now, even though we may have no idea or grasp of the matter of creation from nothing to something, nor how it occurs, and in particular we have no idea of the amazing details, nevertheless we know that G-dliness creates and brings into existence from nothing to something. And when it comes to speaking of these matters, as during the *pesukei dezimra*, we experience a little bit of feeling and we become excited within, which in turn produces nullification to G-d. And although there is not a lot of intellect in this, and there is no more than a bit of knowledge alone, nevertheless we know and we have some kind of connection to the matter.

Now, this is true of most people who are not involved in attempting to grasp inner concepts of G-dliness. Still, they know of the matter of creation from nothing to something in general, and they are stimulated by it. For, acknowledgment of admission occurs as we say *modim anachnu lach, al sheanu modim lach* – "we acknowledge that we must concede to You." That is, we have no connection to this knowledge and we experience no knowledge or feeling at all, and yet we are nullified to G-dliness. Acknowledgment [alone] occurs when we have some form of knowledge and feeling…"

iii) Page 5 (Page 9 in the translation)

Note: "*Bina* – the supernal bride…" See *Likutei Torah* on "Song of Songs" at the very beginning, as well as the discourse *Beyom HaShmini, 5693* (1933), [from the Rebbe Rayatz, זצ"ל], published in *Kuntresim aleph, Kuntres* 21.

From *Likutei Torah* of the Alter Rebbe, *Shir haShirim* ("Song of songs") in the very beginning: (Page *aleph*).

"As known, G-d is called a *chatan* ("bridegroom"). And the Jewish people are called a *callah* ("bride"). And this is as a result of the descent and influence of Torah on the Jewish nation. As the sages said, the verse, "On the day of His wedding" refers to *matan Torah* – the giving of the Torah. And that is why one who makes the *chatan* happy merits to the Torah which was given with five "voices," as mentioned in the first chapter of Talmud *Berachot*. For, *chatan* is *chut darga* ("lowered level"). That is, *chatan* alludes to the descent and drawing down of the infinite light from Above, in order to enclothe in the Torah. And the Jewish nation is the source of Jewish souls, and every individual spark of the Jews is an aspect of *callah* – the bride.

Now, the word *callah* has two definitions. One, is from the Hebrew word *claiyon* ("destruction"), as in something that consumes and swallows up everything. For, the name *callah* is a noun that is indicative of action, such as *rachah* ("soft"), *zachah* ("meritorious") or *dakah* ("thin"). And here, *callah* indicates destruction and consumption…

The second meaning of *callah* comes from the phrase, *caltah naphshi* ("my soul expires"), referring to the desire of the soul to cling and be included in His G-dly illumination…And the matter is as follows; in the *kriat shema* there are found two kinds of *mesirat nefesh*, or self sacrifice. The first is when we "deliver" our souls as we say the word *echad*. And the second occurs as we say *bekol napshecha* – "with all of your soul," even if he takes your soul…

From the discourse, *Bayom Hashemini 5693* (1933) of the Rebbe Rayatz *ztz'l*, in *Kuntres Maamorim Aleph*, kuntres 21, Page 511 (*resh-nun-vov*):

"…and they are the two kinds of self-sacrifice of the *kriat shema*, to deliver the soul while reciting the words *echad*, as well as during the phrase *bekol nafshecha* ("with all of your soul") – "even if he takes away your soul." For the *avoda* required to arrive at this level of *mesirat nefesh* of *echad* takes place when we meditate on the first verse of the *kriat shema* - *Shema Yisrael Havaya* is our G-d, *Havaya* is one. For the seven heavens and the earth and the four directions of the universe are nullified and united in ultimate unity. "just as You were before the world was created, so You are after the world was created" - with total equality. And so it is concerning creation – after it was created the creatures are just as before creation, for the infinite light shines in a revealed manner after the *tzimtzum* ("contraction" of G-dly light) just as before. And if so, just like before the *tzimtzum* there was no existence whatsoever, so after the *tzimtzum* there is also no existence whatsoever. All is totally nullified in existence, as written elsewhere regarding meditation on this topic. During true meditation, delving deeply using our faculty of *da'at*, we become truly nullified and united with Him.

This is called *callah*, from the phrase *caltah she'ari* ("my self is consumed") – interpreted by Onkelos to mean "destruction of my physicality" – complete destruction of the sense of "existence." And then, not only are the lusts and foreign desires nullified, but they do not exist at all…for since the nullfication is of the nature of "all stands before Him as naught" - with a nullification and unity before Him, they are totally lacking existence."

iv) Page 7 (Page 18 in the translation)

Note: "And the heart also becomes excited…" See *Kuntres Hatefila*, chpt. 4-6

From the synopses of the chapters of *Kuntres Hatefila*, appearing on Pages 15, 17 and 18 of *Kuntres Hatefila* of the Rebbe Rashab.

Ch. 4: "True *avoda* involves labor of the mind with intense concentration, automatically producing excitement of the heart – this is what draws in the heart."

Ch. 5: "*Da'at* ("knowledge" which becomes deeply ingrained and integrated with the emotions) is an independent intellectual faculty (apart from the ability to focus and concentrate). It implies the ability to feel, and to experience the concept under consideration. The nerves (organs) responding to this feeling are mostly in the mind. And then, the excitement that develops in the heart is true and real."

Ch. 6: "Here, it is explained that there is excitement of the heart that occurs merely as the result of a *bachein* ("residual emotional impression" coming from contemplation of a topic). It is not deep and it dissipates quickly. The main goal is that the essence of G-dly light should illuminate in our mind, and this comes only as the result of laborious meditation. The advice [to aid in achieving this goal] is to accustom ourself to learning with great devotion and depth."

v) Page 9 (Page 25 in the translation)

Note: "...the world of *Briah* does not..." See the Chassidic discourse *Ain omdim lehitpalel* in the series of discourses of the year *5666* (1905-6) (*Yom-tov shel Rosh Hashana...*) of the Rebbe Rashab. See also the letter of the Rebbe R'Yoseph Yitzhak from the 15 of Mar Cheshvan, *5698* (1938) at length.

From the discourse, *Ain Omdim*, in the series *Yomtov shel Rosh Hashana 5666* (1906) of the Rebbe Rashab, page 484: "...the quality of the world of *Briah* is that it is the first entity that the G-dly void carries within itself...and therefore the world of Briah, while implying new creation, is nonetheless not a full-fledged entity... but rather possibility of creation, meaning that it 'allows room' for created existence. That is, the G-dly void [from which all creation devolves] implies lack of existence and its absence, while Briah allows room for existence."

From the letter of the Rebbe Rayatz *ztz'l*, dated 15th of Cheshvan, *5698* (1938) at length [the writer requests from the Rebbe a clarification of the concept of 'worlds,' and the Rebbe answers at length – 11 pages. Regarding the world of *Briah*, the Rebbe says], "the world of *Briah* is the second of the four worlds. It is called *Briah* since it is the first entity after *Atzilut*, and since it exists. Even though it is a spiritual world and called a "hidden world," and the spiritual light of *Atzilut* illuminates there, especially the *sphera* of *bina*, [intellectual analysis] of *Atzilut* (in the world of *Atzilut* itself the light of the *sephira* of *chochma* [spiritual insight] is dominant) – and therefore *Briah* is called the world of intellectual grasp, nevertheless, it is called *Briah* for two reasons:

Among the distinctions between the worlds of *Atzilut* and *Briah* – even though they are many – is that *Atzilut* is called *ayn* since it is not grasped by the intellect, while *Briah* is called *yesh* since it is understood. [It is graspable] since it has existence, and its existence is called *Briah*, as the Ramban said, that in the holy tongue of Hebrew, no word indicates emergence from nothing into something aside from the word *barah* (creation). That is to say, that the difference between *Briah* and *Atzilut* is that everything in *Atzilut*, whether *heichalot*, *spherot*, *orot*, or *kelim* etc. exists as well in *Briah*.' However, while *Atzilut* is a revelation of the hidden [infinite light Above] rather than an expression of anything new, *Briah* is a creation from nothing into something. And since it takes on [the qualities of] existence, even though a very refined existence, as the Ramban wrote – a refined existence devoid of substance, whose only quality is that it is prepared to take on form - nevertheless, it does exist, which is why it is called *Briah*.

The word *briah* denotes something that exists in a state of revelation, as we see in *halacha* regarding the status of an animal that has a thorn lodged in its windpipe – 'we don't suspect that [the thorn] *hivrih'* – dislodged outside of the windpipe. The Aramaic translation of *chutz* (outside in Hebrew) is *'bara.'* That is, since the object exists outwardly in a revealed manner, it is called a *briah*.

vi) Page 10 (Page 34 in the translation)

Note: "and explained elsewhere..." See *Likutei Torah* in the explanation to the discourse, *Eileh Pikudei*, section 4 and onward.

From *Likutei Torah* of the Alter Rebbe, *parshat Pekudei*, Page *zayin* (between 12 and 14), left column: "Now, just as a crown is made of precious stones, which are in essence minerals, but which have been refined so that they are translucent and shining – in this manner is created the crown of the king. Similarly, the sages said the the angel "*Sanda'l* creates crowns for his Creator from the prayers of the Jews." This is because the letters of prayers, called "stones," when refined by the self sacrifice of the Jews as they utter the word *echad* (during the *kriat shema*), become like a crown. And so regarding the fulfillment of mitzvoth, which include the mitzvoth from the Torah and the seven rabbinic commandments, are the 620 pillars of light of which comprise the *sephira* of *keter*. This occurs because when the light is forced to descend all the way to physical world of *asiya*, for example into the parchment of the *tefilin* and the wool of *tzitzit*, which is similar to mineral, the highest light becomes "wedged" in the lowest place. And that is what attracts the light from above the entire spiritual chain of creation, which is associated with the *sephira* of *keter*. And that is why the sages said that, "in the future, the righteous will sit with their crowns on their head…" For the revelation of G-dliness in *gan eden* is not merely from the "river that emerges from the *gan*" which is *chochma* and *bina* which provide revelation for the soul alone. Rather, in the future, upon the resurrection of the dead, there will occur illumination of the body as well…and this takes place via revelation of G-dly light from above the spiritual chain of creation, that is able to descend to the lowest of levels.

vii) Page 10 (Page 35 in the translation)

Note: "Even in the *amida*…" See in the *siddur* accompanied by Chassidut of the Alter Rebbe, in the discourse *Adni sfosay*… ("G-d please open my lips" - in the prayers of Rosh Hashana). See also *Torat Chaim*, parshat *Noah*, chpt. 28. See as well the end of the discourse, *VeHaish mishtaeh*, in *Torat Chaim, parshat Chayei Sarah* (chpt 17)

From the Alter Rebbe's *siddur* on Rosh Hashana, Page 474: "And this is what is meant by *Adni sfatai tiftach* ("*Adni*, open up my lips…"); as we proceed from *geula* (the end of kriat shema) to *tefila* (the *amida*), we bring the G-dly spark within our soul closer, making it into a vessel capable of receiving the light of *Z'a d'Atzilut* (the lower seven *sephirot* of Atzilut). Our G-dly soul becomes absorbed in the name *Adni*, which is also the *sephira* of *malchut* as known, and is also called *dina demalchuta* ("the law of the kingdom"). But, the *aleph* (first letter of *Adni* sweetens [the *din*]…and that is why we say *Adni sfatai tiftach*; that is to say, 'You open my lips with the five enunciators of the mouth (the "five stringencies" which break up the voice into words), which are the five divisions [of speech] in any way that You want. This is not dependent upon speech itself at all, but rather upon the *aleph*…

…the speech of prayer is silent since the person is nullified to the very essence of G-dliness. By way of example, one who is deeply involved in his own thought processes and does not consciously choose his words…rather his words are expressed and emerge spontaneously according to the nature of his intellect…so in prayer we say 'G-d please open up my lips.' There is no choice expressed in this speech, as written regarding Chana, that "her lips were moving but her voice was not heard," indicating the nullification of speech, for at that point the speech is guided only by the *aleph* that sweetens...

...and afterwards, we say *upi yagid tehilatecha* – "my mouth will tell Your praises" – as the simple voice that divides into the five enunciations of the mouth, draws G-dliness down to the lowest levels..."

From *Torat Chaim* of the Mitteler Rebbe, parshat *Noah*, chpt. 28: "...and therefore, we say *Adni sfatai tiftach*...for there are no words on my tongue at all, not even a silent word. There is only, "You open my lips," since I am totally nullified in the very essence of my soul (for silent speech in and of itself, such as one who is preoccupied and mutters words with his lips while absorbed in thought, is one who has ascended to his own source within his *koach hamaskil*, the source of intellect, called "*adam*." However, during the *amida*, all aspects of human speech are totally nullified to G-d's essence. Our silent speech emerges spontaneously without aid from ourselves. We can only say, "You open my lips," as did Chana, whose lips moved automatically because of the *makif* of *yechida* within the inner point of her heart. This is like the verse, "And they screamed from the heart," with an inner scream, since then we are like one who is completely paralyzed. As it says in the Zohar, "the still small voice – this is the silent prayer – that is where the King is found"...)

And this is a result of tremendous lowliness and bitterness of the soul, to the extent that the person cannot "go out" of himself at all, and becomes like a "point" as he exists within the essence of his soul beyond intellect and also beyond Divine will and delight, like one who prostrates himself to the ground before the king. He is totally nullified in every sense, from within and without (and that is why our prayer then has the ability to arouse the infninite light that is beyond Torah and mitzvoth, as above).

From *Torat Chaim* of the Mitteler Rebbe, *parshat Chayei Sarah* (chpt 17):

"...this is the difference between two different kinds of nullification of the self; nullification of the ego occurs during the silent *amida*. This is described by the verse, "What did you seek?" It alludes to the path of arrival to nullification of our intellect to the ultimate degree. To begin with, we grasped [to understand the concept], which is why we can now say, "What did you seek?" This is said after one has arrived to the depth of the concept, the *ayn*, or Divine void of the *yesh* of intellect grasp – this is what is expressed by the verse, "What did you seek?" This is similar to one who arrives to the depth of a concept which is above intellectual grasp, but is not (yet) concrete (in his mind). At that point, he mutters very quietly with his lips, as one who is preoccupied delving to the depths of some intellectual concept. He does not intend to speak, but his words emerge spontaneously, very silently as known (and that is why during the *amida*, since we are in such a state of nullification of the ego, that we are unable to speak with any real intention. All we can say is, "Lord, open up my lips"...and nonetheless there is some speech present.

But, the origin of *nefilat apayim* ("putting our head down" during *tachanun*, when we ask for forgiveness for transgressions) is the very essence of the Divine void (*ayn*), corresponding to the phrase, "No thought can grasp Him whatsoever." It is not appropriate to describe this state as "What did you seek..." And therefore there is no speech whatsoever, but only total silence. And that is the vessel to receive *reiya* – "vision" of G-dliness, face to face as when one prostrates himself to the ground. For, there is no vessel that is capable of accepting the very essence of His infinite light. There is no mental intention or level of nullification of the ego [that can serve as a vessel for His infinite light], but rather only this complete and total silence like a stone.

viii) Page 11 (Page 35 in the translation)

Note: "As written elsewhere regarding *avanim* (stones)" – See *Likutei Torah* in the discourse *Vesamti Cadcad...* (the second), section 3. See also the discourse, *Velakachta es shtey...* in the series of discourses of the year 5668 (1908) of the fifth Lubavitcher Rebbe, the Rebbe Rashab).

From *Likutei Torah* of the Alter Rebbe, parshat *Re'eh*, Page *Caf-zein* (27) – Section 3

"Now we may understrand the topic of precious stones: they are of the mineral category, and nevertheless they shine. And from where do they have this ability to shine? In the main, their development is from the stars – and not from the stars that we can see, for those stars are countable – there are roughly one thousand of them. Rather, it comes from the stars that are invisible to us, for they are truly unlimited in number at all. And they are not revealed and evident to us, but they have the power to illuminate within precious stones. Because they are of the mineral category, which is the lowest level, therefore they receive a ray of light from the stars, which are without number at all, which are the invisible stars that are beyond the stars that we are able to see.

Now, since there are a huge, unlimited number of stars, so there are muliple rays of light shining within precious stones, imparting multiple different appearances, and descriptions. For there are many shades of transparency – there is transparency that is completely pure, and there is transparency that is not so clear. And so are the appearances, for stones divide into a myriad different varieties, but in general there are twelve stones corresponding to the twelve tribes of Israel...

...Now, also in general, their appearance falls into two categories. There are those that shine with "direct illumination," meaning that they illuminate and with their light it is possible to see others. That is, when we bring such stones into darkness, they shine, since their light radiates from within outward. And, there are other stones that shine and throw off their light like a bolt of lightening in the eye of the observer. Their beautiful ray flashes in the eye of the observer – this is the light of "reflected illumination."

Now, these represent two kinds of *tzadikim*, the *tzadik elyon* ("upper *tzadik*"), [whose *avoda* is] from above to below, and the *tzadik tachton* ("lower *tzadik*"), [whose *avoda* is] from below to above. These are Yoseph the *tzadik* and Binyamin the *tzadik*. Binyamin shone from below to above, with "reflected illumination," representing the yearning and desire of lower creation to connect with their spiritual source...for they do not wish to remain below...

And Yoseph the *tzadik* represents "direct illumination," from above to below, to draw down influence to the lower worlds of *BY"A*...

From the discourse *Velakachta et shtey* in *Sefer Maamorim 5668* (1908) of the Rebbe Rashab), Page 109.

"In general, it is known that there are two types of precious stones. One is the kind of gem that from the beginning of its existence was essentially pure, and the light shone within it from "birth." And there is another kind of gem which was not so essentially pure, but is refined and purified during its period of development within the earth. And even after removing it from the earth, it needs some kind of action of man to draw out the light that was hidden within it.

Regarding stones and bricks in general; stones are a creation from the heavens, while bricks are made by man. And so, among precious gems, both of these categories also exist. Moreover, their illumination is also dissimilar. For the stones in which the light exists from their "birth" shine with "direct illumination," with rays of light that descent and expand. They emit rays of light of one color, according to the color of the stone. And from the stones which need polishing and refinement, the light does not descend and shine from them, but rather flashes, creating sparks of light, which are not of only one color, but of several colors.

And so we observe regarding stars as well. There are stars that shine with direct illumination such as a straight ray of light that descends from above to below, without moving. And it descends in one color. And there are stars which flash and emit sparks of light, while also moving, and appearing in several colors.

And it is known that the precious stones come from the influence of the stars, which is why we find both of these categories among precious stones as well."

ix)   Page 11 (Page 36 in the translation)

Note: "And this is what is meant by 'May it be His will…'" See *Likutei Torah*, *Shir HaShirim*, in the discourse *Ma yafo peamayich*…

From *Likutei Torah* of the Alter Rebbe, *Shir haShirim*, Page 86, in the discourse *Ma yafo peamayich*… "…all of the requests within the *shemoneh esreh*…are requests for a change in the Supernal Will that transcends the Torah, which comes from the supernal *sephira* of *chochma*. Whereas the conduct of the creation is according to Torah…similarly the long exile is according to the Torah and therefore we request that there should be a variation in His will, from above the will that is expressed in the Torah that comes from *chochma*; that is, we make our request from the *Ba'al Haratzon*, the 'Master of the Will' Himself…"

Chapter 2

x)   Page 11 (Page 39 in the translation)

Note: "And the blind person has no enjoyment…" – see *Yoma* 74B

[There the gemora discusses the nature of "affliction" on Yom Kippur, when the Jews are commanded to "afflict" themselves. The Gemora mentions a verse from the Torah, "He afflicted you and let you go hungry, He fed you the *manna*…" (*Devarim* 8:3) in order to suggest that "affliction" means "not eating" proper food. The Gemora then goes on to suggest that, "one who sees what he eats cannot be compared to one who does not see what he eats." R' Yoseph suggests that this is a reference to blind people who get no satisfaction from their food. And Abaye adds, "One who has a meal, should eat it only during the daytime."

xi) Page 12 (Page 41 in the translation)

Note: "This is similar to what is written elsewhere…" See *Likutei Torah* in the summaries of the discourse *Lo Tashbit* ("There should never cease to be salt…") that appears at the end of the section on *Vayikra*. See also the discourse beginning with the words, *Ashreinu* ("Happy are we…") in *Sefer maamorim 5696* (1936, of the Rebbe Rayatz, *ztz'l*), printed in *Kuntres 32* (found in *Sefer Maamorim Kuntresim* vol. 2).

[The reference is to the statement of R' Yochanan ben Zacai, as he lay on his sick-bed, "I do not know in which direction I am being led" - whether to Heaven or G-d forbid in the other direction (*Berachot* 28B). His students were confounded by his statement, because they knew him to be completely righteous and just, and therefore there was no reason for him to go anywhere but to "heaven." In *Likutei Torah*, it is explained, "Even though he was involved in Torah his entire life, out of tremendous modesty he found room to doubt about himself regarding the [unconscious] aspects of his soul that transcend intellect. These are faculties of the soul associated with *Keter*, and his doubt was whether he had constantly drawn down these aspects from a state of concealment to a state of revelation. This is similar to R' Akiva who said, "Whether I served G-d with all my soul, I haven't ascertained." And nevertheless by uniting the *chochma* in our soul with the *chochma* of the One above as it is manifest in the Torah, in this manner, spontaneously, the very essence of our soul becomes included in the infinite light above, the transcendent illumination of *sovev kol olamim*."

The *maamor, Ashreinu* cites the reference from *Likutei Torah* above, but gives a somewhat different explanation: (Page 732) "And now we can understand R' Yohanan ben Zakai's statement and his doubts, for although R' Yohanan was constantly involved in Torah, and was very wise sage in knowledge of G-d's Torah and also involved in serving G-d, nevertheless he was afraid of the day of judgment regarding the world to come. For, if it is necessary to rectify something in this world, then it is possible to do *tshuva*, but in the world to come, *tshuva* is not applicable. And therefore, R' Yochanan was afraid of the day of judgment. Moreover, R' Yohanan had doubts regarding "which direction he would be led," meaning that he was doubtful whether the essence of his soul had been involved in *avodat Hashem*, and whether in any case his *avoda* had been as complete as it should be when coming from the essence of the soul. And it is impossible to know the true situation regarding the essence of the soul and its level of perfection. For example, there are high souls whose intellect and emotions are stuck in the *sitra achra* ("other side," opposed to holiness) but because they are high souls residing in a high world, they can easily do *tshuva*. And there are souls of whom the intellect and emotions are involved in *avodat HaShem*, while the essence of the soul is low, coming from the *sitra achra* and they can easily be drawn back there, G-d forbid. And therefore, "I don't know my own soul," where it is, and what it is…"

All this indicates that even the spiritually "accomplished" person who peers indifferently at something indecent (as mentioned in *Kuntres Avoda*) will not remain unaffected by it. Although he may not consciously experience the effects immediately, something in the very essence of his soul may be influenced, and then the results could appear much later.

xii) Page 12 (Page 42 in the translation)

"And it will not dissipate…" See the mishna in *Zavim*, Ch.2, Mishna 2, "He saw before he thought…"

[The Mishna deals with the subject of one who experienced a seminal flow that may or may not make him impure as a *zav* (which is a particular impurity from the Torah requiring him to wait several days and then go through a purification process). With the first experience of discharge, he is not considered impure, and the mishna informs us that after the first experience, the sages would question him regarding seven factors; what he ate, what he drank, what he carried, if he jumped, if he was ill, if he saw a woman or if he thought about a woman. Certain foods, for example, such as meat and oil, or milk, cheese, eggs, wine and oil, may lead to an experience of impurity, as may drinking. Also, carrying a heavy object may strain the person to the point of experiencing a seminal flow, as may jumping or illness. Finally, if one "saw a woman, even without thinking about her" – this may lead to seminal emission, as may thinking about her without actually seeing her. If any of these events occurred, then the sages declared that the person was not a *zav* (because it was then possible to say that the experience of seminal flow was caused by one of the seven events, rather than by an unclean bodily condition). However, it was still necessary for the person to go to the *mikveh* and wait until the next evening in order to be considered 'pure.'

For the purposes of *Kuntres Avoda*, what we need to know is that "if a man saw, even without thinking about" a woman, this may also lead to an experience of seminal emission – and this proves the point that even looking upon something indecent in a "indifferent fashion" without thinking about it can lead to impurity.

xiii) Page 13 (Page 47 in the translation)

Note: "like a servant…" – See the series of discourses entitled *mikneh rav* – "Much cattle…" that begins on page 308 of *Yom Tov shel Rosh Hashana 5666* (1906) of the Rebbe Rashab

This series of *maamorim* discusses at length the difference between a *ben* ("son") and an *eved* ("servant") in service of G-d. A *ben* is of course close to his father (the corollary is a Jew in relation to G-d, our "Father in heaven"), and therefore he has some concept of what his father wants and how to achieve it. The father passes on his plans and aspirations to his son, who then sets about helping his father to put them into effect. But of course the son also has his own ideas and is affected by the moods, attitudes and level of success of his father. Therefore, the level of work and effort put out by the son may vary, depending upon whether he likes what he is doing, or thinks it is a good idea, or finds success. In other words, the *ben* is in it for his father and for himself, and he uses his mind and energy to the utmost to further his father's agenda and by extension, his own. The corollary in service of G-d is the Jew who is learned and G-d fearing, and who uses his own faculties and intelligence to "figure out" what G-d wants from him. Since he puts as much emphasis on his own understanding as upon what the Torah tells him, his service of G-d may vary, depending upon if he "agrees" or how he "feels." He will never deviate from the Torah, but he may apply its commandments in different ways, to different degrees, at different times.

The *eved* ("servant"), by contrast has no agenda of his own; his agenda is the agenda of his master. His master tells him what to do, and the effort that he pours into fulfilling his master's instructions is not dependent upon either understanding them or agreeing with the instructions. His task is to simply fulfill the will of his master, and to that he is totally dedicated. Therefore, his own intellect and emotions do not play a role in his performance of the task. He throws himself into fulfilling his master's will with all of his being because his entire purpose is to fulfill his master's will – that is why we say that his master's will is his own will. And because his entire purpose is the fulfillment of his master's will, he does not waver; he remains focused and consistent. The corollary in serving G-d is the person who fulfills the mitzvoth and learns Torah not because he wants more understanding or appreciation, but because he was told to do so. He will not look for the "why's" of the instructions that he received, but will simply set about fulfilling them to the utmost of his ability – simply because "his Master said."

Here in *Kuntres Avoda*, this approach applies to the person who "fences" and guards his senses in order to remain focused on Torah and G-dliness. Although there is a strong emotional and intellectual temptation to allow some other influences to affect him, he conducts himself like a "servant," concentrating only on the job at hand.

xiv) Page 15 (Page 53 in the translation)

Note: "In *Derech Chaim* (of the Mitteler Rebbe), Ch. 4"

[The *Derech Chaim* of the Mitteler Rebbe (son of the Alter Rebbe) was written as a book of Chassidic "*musar*" to be read during the days of Ellul, preceding Rosh Hashana, when the "King is in the field." That is, during the month of Ellul, it is relatively easy to approach G-d and to do *tshuva* and return to the ways of Torah and mitzvoth. However, when one throws off the "yoke of Heaven" in order to do whatever he wants, then he finds himself under the influence of negative forces over which he has no control.

As explained in Ch. 4 (page 14), "And the explanation is as mentioned regarding "throwing off the yoke of Heaven" – when a person conducts himself according to the dictates of his heart [evil inclination], which is the source of all his [physical] desires, the origin of his willful conduct is his own insistence upon throwing off the will of G-d. That means that he has removed his own desire to accept the will of G-d, and he lacks even the will to want [G-dliness]. From this emerges automatically the "will of his heart" which feels "good" in its "freedom," to serve "strange masters." And this is because the source of his soul, the *yechida*, which is beyond intellect and logic is cut off and excised. This condition is called *omek rah* ("the depths of evil") and it is the concealed source of the origin of all evil desires. If so, from this flows the power of the *klipot* [negative forces, which conceal G-dliness] called *kitrin demasabuta* ("crowns of impurity"), which are various stages of impurity that sully his soul with strange and foreign thoughts, without any desire or knowledge or choice on his part..."

Thus, the one who has insisted upon taking himself out of the realm of serving G-d and being subservient to Him, will find himself subservient to evil powers that are beyond him, and he rapidly finds himself out of his own control.]

xv) Page 16 (Page 59 in the translation)

Note: "The reference is to the Alter Rebbe. For the details of the story, see the *sichot* of 13th of *Tammuz 5691* (1931) in *Kuntres* 15, as well as *Kuntres Chai Ellul 5703* (1943), *sicha* 6."

[In both cases, the reference is to the well-known story of R' Shmuel Munkus, chasid of the Alter Rebbe, who while attending a *simcha* of one of the Chasidim, grabbed a plate of meat and threw it in the "garbage." The initial reaction of the Chassidim who were present at the *simcha* was to punish R' Shmuel because Jewish law does not permit Jews to waste food or other valuables. And so they did, but soon after R' Shmuel received his punishment, the local *shochet* (who was not aware that the meat had already been thrown out) entered the room with a great commotion and instructed all who were present not to eat the meat. His wife had accidentally mixed up the kosher meat with some non-kosher meat and it was the non-kosher meat that had made its way to the *simcha*. Whereupon the Chasidim grabbed R' Shmuel and asked him, "why are you getting involved in miracles and *ruach hakodesh* ("holy spirit")?" (It was considered uncouth for the Chasidim, however spiritually accomplished, to reveal knowledge of anything that they could not have known in a natural manner. That was considered to be the realm of the Rebbe, not of the chassidim). They demanded to know how R' Shmuel had known that the meat was not kosher. R' Shmuel replied, "I did not know anything. When I first met the Rebbe, I made a resolution that no physical temptations would attract me. When I brought the food, I had a tremendous desire for it, and I saw that all the others also had a strong desire for the food. I decided that this meat must be forbidden, since no permitted food causes such a strong desire. This corresponds to the Rebbe's statement, regarding the verse, "There is much grain [to be produced] from the power of the oxe" – the power of attraction of the animal soul is stronger than the power of attraction of the G-dly soul within man, and that is why I threw the meat into the 'garbage."

This is the story to which the Rebbe Rashab refers with the words, "…he succeeded in reaching a state wherein whatever desires arose from his natural, animal soul, he simply would not do."]

xvi). Page 17 (Page 60 in the translation)

Note: "From the Zohar, section 3, page 108A"

[The reference is to a verse regarding the vestments of the High Priest as he approached the Holy of Holies on Yom Kippur; "With this will Aharon approach the holy place…" (Lev. 16:3) The Zohar further explains that "this" also refers to natural, ingrained fear of G-d (that is expressed by guarding our senses, the content of Ch. 2 of *Kuntres Avoda*)– only if a person possesses this trait will he be able to approach G-d.]

xvii). Page 17 (Page 60 in the translation)

Note: From the Zohar, section 1, page 5A

Here, the Zohar calls the lower fear described in Ch. 2 of *Kuntres Avoda* the "Gate of Ascent." It is the key that unlocks all other spiritual levels, and once we possess this level, we may ascend one spiritual level after another…

Chapter 3

xviii) Page 17 (Page 63 in the translation)

Note: "In Tanya, the text reads *tamid al pnimiyutam vechiyutam* – "In this way, he will be focused **constantly on their inner core and life force**..." And perhaps it should also read that way here..."

[The text here in *Kuntres Avoda*, when quoting Tanya, Ch. 42 omits the word "on" and reads simply, "He will constantly recall their inner core and life force." This footnote corrects the omission and points out that the original text of Tanya contains the word "on."]

xix) Page 20 (Page 79 in the translation)

Note: "An amazing and wondrous process..." See the discourse beginning with the words, *Yehuda atah* (in the series, *Yom Tov shel Rosh Hashana 5666* of the Rebbe Rashab). See *Torat Shalom*, the book of *sichot* of the Rebbe Rashab, in the *sicha* of *Simchat Torah* of the year *5676* (1916), sections 5-7. See also the discourse *Veacharei uri* of the year *5702* (1942), printed in the Yiddish *maamorim* of the Fredike Rebbe (the Rebbe *Rayatz, ztz"l*).

[In the *maamor, Yehuda atah* (page 135),

"...although at first glance we might ask, what is so amazing about G-d being removed and above the worlds? The worlds in general exist on a relatively low level, so what is wonderful and amazing about Him being aloof from them? But, in truth it is known that the creation of the lower worlds is in itself an extremely amazing matter, since creation from nothing to something is in the power of the Creator and not in the realm of creation. That is, there is nothing among creatures that even hints at the process [of creation] whatsoever. He is completely removed from creation and no creature has any concept whatsoever of how it is created from nothing to something. Similarly, the [process] of creation is amazing, [since] it consists of enclothement of His creative power within creation while it [simultaneously] remains completely hidden and concealed from creation, as written elsewhere. And the general matter of creation of the worlds is a function of His greatness, as in the saying, "*Gedula* – this is the act of creation," and as written, "Great is the Lord...' That a multitude of worlds and creations and the greatness of the creations and in particular the process that takes place from nothing to something – this is a great and wonderful matter..."

From *Torat Shalom* (*Sichot* of the Rebbe Rashab), page 224-5,

"The meditation that leads to [love like fire] takes place upon the greatness of *Havaya* in the creation of the words, as written, "How great are your deeds, *Havaya*…" For, a tremendous multitude of creations without number were created, as evidenced in the four categories of mineral, vegetable, animal and man. And within each category in particular are to be found an infinite number of variations. For example, in the mineral world, there are simple stones and then there are precious stones, and so is the case throughout the four categories of creation. And each and every creation has a particular divine light and energy enclothed within it according to its level and according to the essential nature of its creation. And similarly among the supernal angels, there are a tremendous number without limit, as the sages said, "One thousand thousands serve Me, and a myriad myriads stand before Me." The quantity of angels within one "troop" is a myriad (ten thousand), and there are an unlimited myriad number of troops. And similarly regarding the meditation associated with the verse, "He Who counts the number of stars, and calls each of them by name" – try going out and counting the stars – see if you are able to count them – and yet He counts the stars and likewise calls each of them by name – it is He Himself Who calls them by name. And this is the divine providence by which He watches over each and every creation in particular, and this entire [meditation] has the affect of producing great excitement in our soul.

Nevertheless, sometimes it may occur to us that from a G-dly perspective, this is not remarkable at all. All of this is amazing from the point of view of man – the multitudinous numbers of creation and how there is a finite number of stars and how He calls each of them by name – but from a G-dly point of view, this is not remarkable at all, and if so, what is there to get excited about? Now, this is nothing more than an example of "coldness", as in the verse regarding Amalek, "who cooled you off" – this [throwing doubt into the picture] is the *klipah* associated with Amalek, as written elsewhere (in the *maamor* entitled *Zachor* of the year *5665*). For the excitement that man experiences is only regarding what is amazing to him, and this has nothing whatsoever to do with anyone else – it does not matter at all if another is not aroused that much. Only when he himself finds the matter amazing should he become quite excited. And so it is regarding the tremendous number of creations and how He counts all of them; since this to him is amazing, he should become aroused from the idea, and it need not concern him whatsoever if someone else is not excited. Since he finds the matter amazing, he should be excited, and it matters not that from a divine perspective it is not at all remarkable. For, since from his perspective, the creation is amazing, from this he should be excited. By way of example, a very wise man will become excited only by matters that arouse him – and what excites a normal person will not excite the wise person. But, it should excite the normal person, and he should not be concerned; once he himself finds the matter stimulating, he should be excited by it. And so it is regarding meditation upon G-dly matters; since all of this takes place within the person who is meditating, and from his perspective he finds it amazing, therefore he should be excited and it should not matter whatsoever that from a divine perspective the topic is unremarkable. This is nothing more than *klipat Amalek,* (a level of concealment of G-dliness that "cools us off" and throws doubt into our intellectual pursuit, without reason]) for regarding simple physical matters such an idea would not occur to him at all (that because another person is not moved, therefore he himself should not become excited). Rather, because from his perspective this is an amazing matter, he himself should be excited by it.

And so it is regarding meditation on the tremendous number of creations and how G-d counts the stars and calls all of them by name. All this should produce great excitement within the soul, as should meditation on how all is created from nothing to something, and the fact that creation from nothing to something takes place from "out of range." Now, this creation from "out of range" is associated with a command, for a command is precisely what is necessary for that which is amazing and out of range. All sovereign matters take place by way of command, since [the king and his subjects] are so out of range of one another. Regarding matters that are within range of each other, there is no need for [a king and his] subjects. How could it be any other way – but matters that are out of range necessitate a command. As, for example, the king said, "Uproot the mountain," so is the matter of creation from nothing to something. It takes place by way of command, as written, "He said and it took place, He commanded…" – this meditation, regarding how He commanded and within this [command] is felt the matter of sovereignty – implies a process that takes place precisely when the process takes place from out of range. For something that proceeds according to logic and intellect, must proceed [in a predictable fashion], and the matter of kingship does not apply. Only a process that takes place from "out of range," necessitates a command. And automatically, the meditation on this process produces a feeling for His Kingship, and therefore it elicits from within us a feeling of *bitul*, or self nullification. And so it is regarding meditation on how everything is included in its source before it is created, and how likewise after they are created they remain in their source – this is not comparable to *koach* and *poel* ("cause and effect"). For as in the case of physical movement, the movement was not "part of him" before he moved, and also after he moved there was nothing remaining of the initial power that caused the person to move. This is not true though of creation from nothing to something, for the "something" was first including in the "nothing" even before it was created, and also after it was created it remains included in its source. This is because the nature of creation is *hitchadshut* – "renewal" – just as the light and ray of the sun undergoes renewal, so the world was included in its source even before it became revealed. And also after it is "revealed" it remains included in its source. And so it is with the creations of all creatures – since they undergo the process of "renewal" from nothing to something, they are included in their source even before they are created."

From *Sefer Maamorim Yiddish* of the Fredike Rebbe, R' Yoseph Yitzhak *ztz'l*, page 71

The *maamor* is long and very nuanced, and a full translation would be difficult. Here is the summary of the second section which the Fredike Rebbe gives us on page 71: "The creation from nothing to something is not comparable to the process by which a craftsman makes a vessel. The energy [that creates and enlivens creation] is very concealed from the creation. It is not similar to "cause and effect," such as intellect and emotions or thought and speech. [In such cases], the cause is close to the effect, and the effect is aware of and grasps the cause. Creations know nothing more than the existence of existence of G-dly energy."]

xx) Page 20 (Page 79 in the translation)

Note: "As known regarding the difference between…" See *Likutei Torah* (in the discourse *Besha'ah shehikdimu*, third section). See also the discourse *Amar R' Y', Lo barah*, from the *maamorim* of the Fredike Rebbe of the year *5694* (1934) in *Kuntres 24*. See also the discourse *Amar Rabah…Kol adam* from the year *5702* (1942) in the *Sefer Maamorim Yiddish* of the Fredike Rebbe *ztz'l*.

[From *Likutei Torah, Parshat Bamidbar, Besha'ah shehikdimu*…in the third section of the discourse (page 13, column 2):

"The purpose of Torah and mitzvoth in drawing down His Will to be revealed below is in order to fulfill the verse, "And the Lord commanded us to observe all of the these laws in order to fear G-d Himself (*leyireh et HaShem*)," as it says, "All of His holy ones fear G-d Himself" (*yiru et HaShem*). Yet, we must understand – why does the verse specify, "His holy ones"? For, elsewhere there is another verse that says, "All of the earth should be afraid of G-d" (*yiru m'HaShem*)…

…The difference is that the verse, "All the earth should be afraid of G-d" refers to the lower fear of G-d, from our perspective in which the lower physical world seems to be the true existence. But in the interpretation of the verse, "All of His holy ones fear G-d Himself," there is a word (*et*) which [serves no obvious purpose, and] is nullified to His Name *Havaya*, with a true and real nullification. [From this perspective], what is above possesses true existence while what is below is truly as if nonexistent…and we facilitate this level of nullification by learning Torah, about which is said, "If there is no *chochma*, there is no fear,"…And this is what is meant by *yiru et HaShem* ("All of His holy ones fear G-d Himself") – this level of fear is brought down as we say blessings (*asher kideshanu bemitzvothav* – "He Who has sanctified us with His commandments") – for this we were commanded to fear G-d Himself]

From the discourse, *Amar R'Yehuda, Lo Bara* in *Sefer Maamorim Kuntresim Beit*, of the Rebbe Rayatz *ztz'l*, page 535 (283 in Hebrew)

"There are two types of meditation. One leads to the lower form of fear of G-d, *yirah tatah*, and the other leads to development of the higher form of fear of G-d; *yirah ilah*. For, it is written, *Kel deyot Havaya* - "*Havaya* is a G-d of Divine perspectives" – a lower perspective (*da'at tachton*) and a higher perspective (*da'at elyon*). The lower perspective is that our physical world truly exists and what is above is as if non-existent, since the creation occurs from nothing to something. And the truth is that "out of His goodness, He constantly renews the creation every day," and this takes place from nothing to something. . And when we meditate upon this, we develop fear of G-d. However, the fear that we achieve is "lower fear," as written, "All the world is afraid from G-d," and it is written, "For He said and it happened," which also refers to the meditation mentioned above. For all of creation took place from a superficial ray of His G-dliness.

More in particular, the fear of G-d associated with this verse ("All the world is afraid from G-d") stems from the fear that evolves when we delve deeply into the concept of Divine providence. But in general, both of these "fears" are in the category of "lower fear," which is why the verse employs the word "from G-d," indicating a mere reflection of something that is concealed.

But, the higher fear corresponds to the perspective that what is Above is real, and what is below is as if "nothing," since the infinite light of G-d is the most real existence, while all that is below is like nothing, since "everything stands before Him as naught." And by meditating upon this and integrating it within, that the infinite light of G-d is the true existence, we produce total nullification of the self within. And this is the *yirah ilah* ("upper fear"), to which the Torah serves as an introduction. As we say, "And G-d commanded us in all these laws to fear Him…" and it says, "All of His holy ones fear G-d Himself." The verse utilizes the word *et*, although it is extraneous and totally nullified to the name *Havaya*. This is the level called *yirah ilah*, and it occurs only among His holy ones. [He] has "sanctified us with His commandments," and it is Torah and mitzvoth that bring us to this fear of G-d."]

From the discourse *Amar Havaya Rabah*, Page 45 in *Sefer Maamorim Yiddish*

["The verse states, "*Havaya* is a G-d of Divine perspectives," implying two perspectives;

one from below and the other from above. The lower perspective is based upon the understanding of man in creation, that the lower world exists and that creation occurs from nothing to something. The explanation is that when man does not know what something is, he calls it *ayn*, or "nothing." And the fear of G-d that man attains as a result [of this perspective] corresponds to the verse, "All the world is afraid from G-d." This very same fear comes from meditation that all that is created comes from a mere reflection [of G-dliness], and this kind of fear is called "lower fear" and it serves as an introduction and entry to Torah.

The higher perspective corresponds to a higher knowledge, that what is above is the true *yesh* ("existence") and that which is below is *ayn*, or "nothing." What is above truly "exists" – it is the real existence while what is below may be described as "everything stands before Him as naught." From this meditation results an appreciation of the concept of the infinite light of G-d – how it is the true *yesh* and existence. Upon reflecting on this [perspective], the person becomes totally nullified in his own existence. This is the level called "upper fear" and Torah is the entry [and pathway] to this level of fear.

These are the two levels of fear: *yira tatah* ("lower fear") and *yirah ilah* ("higher fear"). The lower fear stems from meditation on creation in the lower world and it serves as an introduction to learning Torah. The higher fear (*yirah ilah*) comes from meditation on matters concerned with the higher perspective (*da'at elyon*), and to this level, Torah serves as an introduction and a vessel to attain this fear.

xxi) Page 20 (Page 79 in the translation)

Note: "All of this is implied in the verses, 'How many are Your works…how great…'" See *Torah Ohr* in the discourse *Vayedaber* in *parshat Vaera* (the second). See also the discourse *Se'u marom eineichem* of the *Tzemach Tzedek* (in the introduction to his *Sefer HaChakira*). See also the discourse *ein aroch lecha 5694* (1934), from the Rebbe Rayatz *ztz'l*

Torah Ohr on *parshat Vaera*, Page 111 (*nun-vov*), column 2:

"It is written, 'How many are Your works…' and it is written 'How great are Your works…' 'How many are Your works…' refers to the lower physical realms and all of the creations of this world, which are divided into various species in various different ways. There are myriad levels of creation within the mineral, vegetable, animal and human worlds – some within the mineral category and some within the vegetable category. And each and every species, such as apples, nuts and almonds, possesses its own taste. The same is true of the vegetable category; each species has its own taste, and each is distinct from the other. And so regarding different kinds of herbs; each of which has its own taste. The [origin of the] taste is spiritual, coming from the *mazal* that influences it from above. For, "There is no herb below that is without a *mazal* above [that influences it]…"

"…But the verse, 'How great are Your works…' refers to the higher worlds, including angels and souls who derive enjoyment from G-dliness. And no one form of enjoyment is similar to any other. As the sages said, 'In the future, G-d will bequeath 310 worlds to each and every *tzadik*…' And at first glance it is not understood – why does every *tzadik* need so many worlds? Does *tzadikim* have a need for property?

Rather, the matter is as follows; the reward for a mitzvah is the mitzvah itself. That is, the reward for the mitzvah is the descent of supernal enjoyment from Above, which enables souls to bask in the ray of the *shechina*. And each and every mitzvah draws down its own variety of enjoyment. Furthermore, each *tzadik* is different from his fellow in regard to his *avoda* and the quality of love and fear of G-d that he experiences. For, there are those who are aroused [with love of G-d] and there are those who are aroused [with fear…]. It is for this reason that in the future G-d will bequeath to each *tzadik* what he needs [according to his individual approach]. For, every *tzadik* resides in his own "dwelling," by himself, in regard to the reflection and the nature of intellectual grasp that he achieves, and he derives enjoyment and basks in G-dly illumination in a way that is disctinct from the enjoyment and intellectual grasp of his fellow *tzadik* – each according to his unique talents and abilities.

And this ray of the *shechina* includes an uncountable myriad number of levels and kinds of souls-enjoyment, for it stems from the infinite One above.

From Intro to *Sefer HaChakira* of the *Tzemach Tzedek*, from the discourse *Se'u Marom Eineichem*, Page 206

Similar to "He Who uttered and the universe came into existence"…the unique One of the universe, the primordial One Whose existence is obligatory – He is able to grant durability and powerful energy even to limited creatures – which is not according to the nature of such limited beings. And about this is said, "How great are Your works, Lord…"

And this is what [the Alter Rebbe] meant in his explanation of the verse, "Raise your eyes and see Who created these…" – the prophet [who uttered these words] showed us how a mere ray of the infinite light of the Unlimited One, [illuminates] even down here in this physical world of *asiya* which is certainly limited…

From *Sefer Maamorim 5694* (1934) of the Rebbe Rayatz *ztz'l* – Not found

Ch. 4

xxii) Page 22 (Page 86 in the translation)

Note: "When it comes to love of the One above, there are two general levels…" See the note in *Kuntres Eitz Hayim*, Ch. 2 (Page18)

["There are several sub-levels within these two levels. Therefore, there is no contradiction between what appears here and what appears elsewhere regarding other distinctions between kinds of love, as well as regarding the essence of meditation that is associated with them – for explanation of several of these levels of love, see further on in Ch. 16 [of *Kuntres Eitz Hayim*]. See also Ch. 4 of *Kuntres Avoda*, and the *sichot* of *Simchat Torah 5668* (1908) and *5676* (1916), both of which appear in *Torah Shalom* of the Rebbe Rashab. Furthermore regarding different kinds of love, see *Torah Ohr* (of the Alter Rebbe) and *Torat Chayim* (of the Mitteler Rebbe) in the discourses entitiled *chachlili einayim*. And see the letter that my father-in-law (the Rebbe Rayatz) wrote to the Chasidim of Bilgoria in the year *5691* (1931), which is printed at the end of *Kuntres Avoda* – etc.…]

xxiii) Page 22 (Page 86 in the translation)

Note: "with flames of fire – "An investigation is needed in order to determine why sometimes – in the handwritten text of the Rebbeim – the phrase *rishpei aish* ("flames of fire") is preceded by a *beit* (*b'rishpei aish*, meaning "with flames of fire"). While, elsewhere, including here in *Kuntres Avoda*, it sometimes appears written with a *caf* (*c'rishpei aish*, meaning "like flames of fire.")

As for example, within Tanya, in Chapters 3, 9 16, 17, 43, 50 and in *Igerot Hakodesh siman* 4, it is written in the second manner, with a *caf*. And in Ch. 44, both versions appear. However, it is possible to distinguish between the two, as anyone who examines the text will be able to discern."

xxiv) Page 26 (Page 106 in the translation)

Note: "And as written in the drosh *Yom Tov shel Rosh Hashana 5666*..."
[In the two discourses, *Yehuda atah* and *Vayeileich Ish*...

From the discourse *Yehuda atah*, in *Yom Tov shel Rosh Hashana 5666*, of the Rebbe Rashab, Page 134; "And this is the *avoda* of the Divine soul, six days of the week, to refine and rectify the animal soul, about which it is said, "Six days you shall work," referring to the service and labor of the Divine soul to refine the animal soul. And the main *avoda* takes place during prayer, as known that prayer was established in place of the sacrifices, and just as during the sacrifices an animal was offered on the altar and was subsumed in the fire from Above, [which descended] in the shape of a lion consuming the sacrifices - for, the animal itself is from the element of fire, since the animal category corresponds to fire among the [four] elements - and for that reason it is included and burnt within the fire from Above, as "fire consumes fire." And it was also necessary that fire be brought from "below," as the sages said, that "even though fire descends from above [to consume the sacrifices], it is a mitzvah to bring from the common [profane], as well. A similar process takes place now during prayer as we sacrifice our animal soul so that the two become included – fire from above and fire from below...

...(Page 136) and this [meditation on creation from nothing to something, and how all creation is constantly renewed at every instant] is the fire from below, after which must follow fire from above, associated with the animal soul in particular. This takes place during the blessings preceding the *kriat shema* and then during the *kriat shema* itself, the fire of the Divine soul descends from above in flames of fire and incinerates and consumes the animal soul completely...and yet later during the *shemoneh esreh* it receives its reward of *ahavah raba* from above, in response to the *avoda* and labor of the Divine soul working within on the mind and the heart to refine and rectify the animal soul...and then love illuminates from Above...

From the discourse *Vayeleich Ish*, from *Yom Tov shel Rosh Hashana* of the Rebbe Rashab, Page 137
[Now, the fire from above of the animal soul comes from meditation upon the nullification of the angels, and how they become ignited and excited with flames of fire to become included and nullified in the Divine light of *Havaya* that flows down upon them. For, as this occurs,

Divine light of love illuminates them, and also illuminates the power of lust and temptation that is innate within our animal soul. The light arouses our heart to become detached from the physical pleasures into which we have sunk, and to draw us after its source to be nullified and included in the light of *Havaya*. Regarding this, the sages of the Great Assembly decreed that we should say the blessings of the *kriat shema*, two of them preceding the *shema*, wherein we repeat and recite the *avoda* of the angels, and how they are nullified to *Havaya*].

xxv) Page 27 (Page 116 in the translation)

Note: "So it should be among servants of G-d"

See the discourse *Tiku* of the year *5667* (within the series, *Yom Tov shel Rosh Hashana 5666*) of the Rebbe Rashab, as well as *Torat Shalom* of the Rebbe Rashab, *sicha* of *Simchat Torah 5669*, letter *yud* and on. She also *sichot* of the year Rebbe *Rayatz 5693* (1933) in *Kuntres* 23

[From the discourse *Tiku 5667* of the Rebbe Rashab, in *Yom Tov shel Rosh Hashana 5666* page 349-50]

"...When the meditation is upon lofty concepts such as the exalted and amazing nature of the infinite light, at such times the light of the Divine soul illuminates greatly, since these are matters that are close to it. The soul grasps them and intellectualizes upon them and understand them well...And throughout this [process], much light of the Divine soul illuminates, and so occurs during the excitement and rush of the G-dly soul (as it exists on its own among those who serve G-d with their souls with *ahavah rabba* and *ahava betaanugim*) – there is a large amount of illumination and revelation of the G-dly soul as its faculties shine (and this takes place totally out of range of the animal soul...). [However], the light of the Divine soul should shine within range of the animal soul. In so doing, the G-dly soul descends to become hidden and concealed so that its illumination and power does not shine in a revealed fashion as it does on its own. But in this manner, it achieves refinement of the animal soul.

However, when the Divine soul shines with a tremendous amount of revealed light that is completely out of range of the animal soul, then although the animal soul may become rectified, this is similar to the process of *tshuva* that takes place when the Divine soul is aroused with tremendous desire just because it is tormented over its distance [from G-d]. This sort of arousal affects a transformation of the animal soul, which becomes changed in its very essence, as known and explained elsewhere. Nonetheless, this is not called "refinement" of the animal soul since the animal soul itself is not aroused to participate. Rather it becomes nullified automatically as a result of the strength of revelation and arousal of the Divine soul.

But, regarding the bitterness of those who are called *marei dechushbana* ("masters of accounting" – those who look within themselves and examine themselves closely) and also those whose arousal to do *tshuva* comes from their animal soul (this occurs because of the suffering of the animal itself), which is tormented and extremely troubled over its distance...and the scream [for freedom] emerges from the animal soul...as written [when the Jews screamed to G-d during the Egyptian slavery], "and they groaned on account of the work and they screamed" –this was the cry of the body over the difficult labor...and similarly in the spiritual realm there may occur a cry from the animal soul itself..."

Torat Shalom of the Rebbe Rashab, page 129-131

For example, regarding the *avoda* of prayer; during prayer we must also be involved with the body and the animal soul. We must meditate regarding all of our bodily matters, and we must correctly know what is the situation and status of our body regarding all of its natural matters, whether they exist as cold [temptations], or boiling [lusts], and whether we are in essence a coarse person in nature, who is focused mainly upon matters of this world, or whether our essence is not so coarse, but rather [our animal nature] is nothing more than an extension of ourselves. That is, there may be side reasons that cause us to be more coarse while eating and drinking. And so, we must also make a true accounting of our situation and the status of our animal soul, with its bad emotions that we find within, to know exactly what they are...

(page 131); And this is the explanation of what is meant by "a connection with the body and the animal soul." All kinds of intellectual meditation, whatever the meditation is from the Divine soul, which arouses all (spiritual) matters... must have a connection to the body and the animal soul as well (see what is written about this in the discourse *matzah zu* of the year 5655). And then automatically, if there is a connection with the body and the animal soul, then it will leave an impression, at least, for the entire day.

From the *sichot* of the Rebbe *Rayatz* of the year 5693 (1933)

"The proper approach, however, is that the G-dly soul should not repel its animal counterpart but refine it. This it must do by revealing its own powers, though tempered to match the receptive capacity of the animal soul; i.e., the faculties of the G-dly soul must vest themselves in the intellectual potentials (or "garments") of the animal soul's intellect. This does not mean that the G-dly soul should first understand a concept and then explain it to the animal soul, but that from the outset the G-dly soul should tackle the subject together with the animal soul — by using intellectual constructs borrowed from worldly affairs." (From the writings & talks of Rabbi Yosef Yitzchak of Lubavitch, Ch 49 (2), end of Section 16, Translated by R' Uri Kaploun, see the entire chapter there).

Ch. 5
xxvi) Page 30 (Page 126 in the translation)

Note: "This is as well the difference...See the discourse, V*ayedaber...bemidbar Sinai* (in the series *Yom Tov shel Rosh Hashana 5666*) and the discourse *Haoseh Succato 5699* (1939)

[From *Vayedaber...bemidbar Sinai*, in the series *Yom Tov shel Rosh Hashana 5666* of the Rebbe Rashab, page 235:

"Although it was explained earlier that the source of souls is higher than *Atik* which precedes the *gulgulta* of *A"K*, and although it was also explained that the source of souls is beyond the Torah, we could resolve the issue by saying that...the source of souls is the very essence of the Divine enjoyment of G-d while the source of the Torah is from *chochma* (Divine wisdom), within which is embedded the essence of *Atik*, or the very essence of Divine enjoyment (see what was explained in the discourse *Ki Yedativ* at the end). And this is the advantage that Jewish souls have even over the inner dimensions of the Torah, since Jewish souls are enrooted in the very innermost aspects [of Divine enjoyment], while the Torah comes from the inner dimension of *Atik* as it is enclothed in the *chochma* of *A"K* – see what is written in the discourse *Vayishlach Yaakov*.

In any case, the descent of illumination of the essence of *Atik* into Jewish souls takes place through [the "intermediary" of] Torah. As known, the difference between Torah and Jewish souls is that regarding Torah, it is said the Torah and G-d are entirely one, while Jewish souls were created as independent entities, with their own "self" and identity. A son, for example, although coming from the same essence and self as the father, nevertheless possesses his own self and identity, analogous to Jewish souls..."

From the discourse, *Haoseh Succato 5699* from the Rebbe Rayatz, Page 48-9

"This we do know; G-d desires a dwelling place in the lower worlds, and as is known, this means that He desires that His infinite essence should be revealed down here...Now, this desire is fulfilled by Jewish souls. For, since Jewish souls are enrooted in the very essence of the infinite light, from where they descend via the ten *sephirot*, therefore they are the only ones by whom it is possible to fulfill the Divine intention to make a dwelling place so to speak, for His very essence. Although it is true that the Torah is also enrooted in His essence, nevertheless the Torah does not by itself facilitate the fulfillment of His Divine intention. For, the unity of Torah is that it and the One above are one, since the Torah comes from the very essence, and is united with His essence. However, in order to bring that down to be revealed in the world, there needs to be one who can receive from above and draw down to "who" or "what" is below. All that is revealed in the world comes through a *mashpia-mekabel* ("benefactor and beneficiary") relationship. To begin with, we receive, and then we give, as the sages said about the Jordan river, that it "takes from here and gives to there." The matter of taking and giving exists whether in spiritual ascent or in descent. For, every ascent and descent takes place as a process of "give and take."

...Now, a descent of this nature, meaning by way of "give and take" takes place only among Jewish souls. For although Jewish souls are enrooted in His essence, nevertheless the nature of their creation from His essence is that they emerge as "independent agents," with their own identity. As for example, a son who comes from the essence of the father that is beyond anything conscious and revealed, yet the nature of his creation from the father's essence is that the son becomes an independent entity. And that is the reason that Jewish souls fulfill the Divine intention to make for Him a dwelling place in the lower worlds."

xxvii) From page 30 (Page 129 in the translation)

Note: "And as written elsewhere..." See the discourse *Vezot Haterumah* (from the series, *Tiku* of the year *5670*)

"And the explanation is as follows; the *makif* known as *chaya* is not the very essence of the soul, and for that reason it is not connected as essentially with the infinite light above as is the *makif* known as *yechida*, which is essentially included [within the infinite light above]. For, since [the *yechida*] is the very essence and self of the soul, it is near to its source and origin in the infinite light, which is experienced within. And that is why it is essentially connected without any arousal, meaning that the connection is of the essence [of the soul] with the essence [of the infinite light above]. However, the *makif* of *chaya* is not the essence of the soul, and it does not experience its own source and origin. And therefore, the arousal to become included [in the infinite light above] needs to come about via a reason and stimulus, and in that manner it is aroused. Still, the desire to be included [in the infinite light above] does not come from the intellect alone, as it does during *avoda* according to logic and reason. Rather, the desire emerges on its own, of its own nature, but nonetheless it needs a reason to arouse it.

By way of explanation; there are two types of love; one that is dependent upon something, and one that is not dependent upon anything. Regarding love that is dependent on something, its entire existence is dependent upon whatever causes the love, and when that dissipates, the love itself dissipates. But, love that is not dependent upon anything is essential love, which is not dependent upon any reason. Nevertheless, this love could weaken and disappear in the course of time, until it is re-aroused, as in two loving friends who trust each other and whose love is not dependent upon anything. Nevertheless, in the course of time, they may forget their love and it will disappear. This is unlike the love between father and son, which is never forgotten or weakened even after many years and days, since the bond between them is essential, totally within the essence of their souls. And therefore they are bound to one another with a tie that neither weakens nor disappears forever. For, even when the bond is not apparent, it is not because it has disappeared in essence. And for that reason when it is revealed, it does not occur with great excitement, since it is a bond of the very essence.

However, love between two friends does not occur with such essential bonding and for that reason there may occur some amount of weakness and concealment, whereupon something is needed to arouse it, such as a happy occasion for one of them, for the love to re-ignite. But, when it does re-ignite, it is unlimited, beyond the range of the occasion that arouses it. Moreover, the love is not limited to the reason that aroused it, such as the happy occasion that one of them experienced. Rather, the love and happiness is far greater since their love is an essential love that is not dependent upon anything – it just needs something to catalyze it."]

xxviii) From Page 31 (Page 132 in the translation)

Note: "This is the concept of *z'a b'atika talia…*" ("The G-dly emotions are united with and dependent upon His essence and enjoyment."). See *Torat Chaim* of the Mitteler Rebbe (the second discourse beginning with the word *Breishit*, in section 15 and on. See also the explanation to the discourse *Leviatan zeh* in *Likutei Torah* of the Alter Rebbe).

[From *Torat Chaim* of the Mitteler Rebbe, *parshat Bereishit*, second *drosh*, section 16]

"Although it is explained and understood from all of the above [previous sections in *Torat Chaim*] that the intellect within the mind governs and rules at the very least over the emotions of the heart [and] our natural feelings are subjugated to the intellect within the mind. Nevertheless, as they exist in their natural state, the essential power of the natural emotions is much stronger than the power of intellect. And this is because the true source of their creation as they exist in essence is far above the source of the power of intellect within the mind…And that [source] is the *yechida* within the soul itself, which is beyond the origin of intellect within the soul, which is called the "intellectual soul." And therefore the intellect has no ability to master the emotions of the heart except as the emotions "pass through the mind." And then, only their expansion and expression alone are influenced by the instructions of the intellect. But, there is no power whatsoever within the intellect to transform the very nature of the emotions. For, the nature of the emotions as they exist in the essence of the soul is very strong and powerful, far moreso than even the power of the intellect within the essence of the soul. (As will be explained, this is because as it says in kaballah, "*z'a* [the emotions] is united with *atika*," higher than *mocha stima* which is the source of intellect – which is nothing other than *chochma* within *keter* of *arich*…)

And for that reason, we see the exact opposite of what was mentioned above regarding the control of the mind over the heart. Even after the intellect within the mind instructs the natural emotions to expand and act according to the dictates of the logic of the mind alone, nevertheless when there occurs an overwhelming arousal of emotions within the heart, the excitement is far greater than the stimulation that occurs within the mind. That is, the emotions become excited without any reason or logic whatsoever. The excitement is emotional in essence, as the emotions exist in their natural state within the heart, to the extent that the intellect is unable to stop or extinguish the excitement of the heart at all. And this is because the emotions totally overwhelm the intellect in the mind because they are strong and powerful in their essence, moreso than the intellect [itself] as mentioned above."

From *Likutei Torah* of the Alter Rebbe, *parshat Shemini*, page *yud-tet* (19A, or 37), column 2

"In the *Idra Zuta*, page 292... '*Z'a* [the lower six *sephirot* corresponding to the emotions] is dependent upon *atika kadisha* [the super-conscious faculties of the soul, of which we are general unaware, but which influence us in any case] and united with it,' for *z'a*, which is the *midot* ("emotions") of *Atzilut* is, in its source, above the source of *ava* [*chochma* and *bina* – the intellect], but it descends below. Like, by way of example, the emotions of man; even though they emerge and become revealed via the intellect...nevertheless in the main, the emotions originate from above the intellect. And therefore, within the emotions, it is possible to find overwhelming energy, beyond what is present in the intellect that gives rise to them."

xxix) Page 31 (Page 135 in the translation)

Note: "Within which we find two levels, *ohr yashar* and *ohr chozer*..." See *Torat Chaim* in the discourse *Vayitain lecha*, section 2. See also the discourse *Samchuni B'ashishut* of the year *5660* (1900)

From *Torat Chaim* of the Mitteler Rebbe, in the discourse *Vayitain lecha*, section 2, Page 149, column 4:

"But, we must explain what is meant by *ahavah beta'anugim* ("love with enjoyment"), which applies to a kind of love that includes two categories of enjoyment. One is enjoyment that comes as *ohr pnimi* ("immanent G-dliness") that is clad in a vessel [illumination that shines into our mind and heart; we feel and understand it]. The second enjoyment comes down to us as *ohr makif* ("transcendent G-dliness"), which is beyond the limitations of a vessel [this enjoyment comes from awareness of something that is beyond us, but we do not feel it emotionally or grasp it intellectually].

Now, within *ohr makif* ("transcendent illumination") there are also two kinds of enjoyment. There is transcendent enjoyment that we experience as *ohr yashar* ("direct illumination"). And the second transcendent enjoyment comes to us as *ohr chozer*, or "reflected light." But, in general, they are two kinds of enjoyment, one associated with *chesed* ("kindness" which descends from above), and the other with *gevurah* ("stringency" which enables spiritual ascent), both within *taanug* ("enjoyment"). For, [the enjoyment of] "direct illumination" is associated with *chasadim* that descend and are drawn down like water, from above to below. And the illumination of "reflected light" comes from *gevurot*, which ascend from below to above, as known.

We may understand all of the above according to simple physical human enjoyments that we may observe among our fellow men. Among them are those that that we may integrate and experience with our own faculties, such as the enjoyment of taste; there is the taste of sweetness on the palate, and so forth regarding all the foods that we eat and swallow. Similarly regarding love between man and his fellow, as when the heart is attracted with interest and devotion within. And so, all of the enjoyments that attract the heart of man, such as wealth and riches and every thing positive that our heart considers – they all come from the *chasadim* that descend like water in accordance with the limitations of the vessel that contains them.

Then, there are enjoyments that come as transcendent experiences, such as the enjoyment of a journey or of a nice painting or of clothes and nice houses and the like. And similarly, there is enjoyment that accompanies honor and recognition of one's status, which provide essential enjoyment for the soul, without entering into the heart in a manner that is felt and limited. And so as well, there is the enjoyment of a pleasant aroma such as the scent of good perfume that the soul – and not the body - enjoys. And similarly, there is enjoyment associated with victory and glory, and the like.

But, the enjoyment associated with intellect and love, or with *chesed* or *gevura* – this comes to us as *ohr pnimi*, felt in a limited and conscious vessel. This is the enjoyment of one whose nature is to express kindness, etc. Like, for example the love that man experiences for his wife, is associated with the *chasadim* of "direct illumination." And there are also enjoyments that are expressed as the *gevurot* of "reflected illumination,' such as the desire of a woman for her husband, which comes with yearning and expiry of the soul…which is equivalent to "enjoyment" with flames of fire of excitement – enjoyment to the point of expiry of the soul. And so regarding any lust and desire for anything attractive, as well as the lust of the soul such as for food and for physical intimacy.

However, there is a difference between *chasadim* and *gevurot*. [The difference is] like the distinction between the flow of *chesed* and the enjoyment associated with the flow of *gevurah*, or between man and woman. Or, between mentor and student. Among all these, there are many details and fine distinctions in the way that they occur. In general, though, they are two levels; *chesed* and *gevura*, *makif* ("transcendent") and *pnimi* ("immanent").

Regarding the enjoyment associated with the *chasadim* of direct illumination (*ohr yashar*), the transcendent illumination associated with it results from the tremendous amount of enjoyment, that just does not "fit" into our mind and heart to begin with. Take, for example, the enjoyment that one might experience from a positive announcement arriving in a manner beyond comprehension. And so regarding the flow of enjoyment associated with a deep concept. Or the love that Rebbe Akiva experienced, which was so great that he could not contain himself upon hearing the deep secrets of the Torah. The illumination was so tremendous that the influx from his intellect was beyond what his faculties could contain. And so regarding a sweet taste or a journey or a very nice picture or garments of majesty and beautiful houses, about which the Torah says, "And you will multiply possession of nice houses and silver and gold and your heart will be elevated…" and as it says, "You got fat and thick…and you kicked [rebelled]." Such as occurred with the ten tribes…

Now, the enjoyment associated with the *makif* of "reflected illumination" - *gevurot* - occurs when one is unable to contain the amazing and wonderful enjoyment in his mind and heart, and [the enjoyment] then ascends as "reflected light," totally unfitted to the person's faculties ("vessel"). This is like, for example, when all of a sudden one hears a positive announcement that arrives unexpectedly. This pressures him in mind and heart, and his spirit ceases to function and may even leave his body, as when Sarah heard the announcement that her son Yitzhak was [almost] sacrificed, and as when Yakov heard that his son Yoseph was still alive. This is what happens any time that expiry of the soul is accompanied by very deep intellectual enjoyment, which is sweet to the soul, to the extent that the soul [wants to] leave the body. This was the case regarding R' Akiva, whose eyes filled with tears [as he heard secrets of the Torah]. Or in the story of the passing of the three sages of the Idra Raba. So it is regarding all kinds of enjoyment associated with "reflected illumination" – such experiences take place with great strength and power of ascent - accompanied by nullification of the "student" to his mentor and benefactor...to the point that he may become "love-sick...."

...But, the enjoyment of "direct illumination" occurs as immanent light that settles within the mind and heart, like water settling into a container. And the person then becomes sated with this kind of enjoyment...similar to [spiritual] enjoyment in the world to come. This is similar, as well, to the enjoyment of Shabbat meals, as well as to the enjoyment of souls in *gan eden*, as they bask in the rays of the *shechina*...this is the *makif* of hidden enjoyment of "direct illumination" that settles within and expands. [Finally], this is comparable to one who is capable of accepting greatness and wealth without limit.

And in general, *ahava be'taanugim* ("love with delights") is the love of a mentor for his student and the inter-inclusion of the two *makifim* ("transcendent levels") of *chesed* and *gevura*. It is the enjoyment of "direct illumination" and "reflected illumination" together. As in the word *sha'ashuim* ("delights")...and as when the *chatan* ("bridegroom") enjoys his *callah* ("bride")...

From the discourse *Samchuni B'ashishut* of the year 5660 (1900), from the Rebbe Rashab, page 77-78.

"...It is known that there are two categories of *taanug* ("enjoyment"), which correspond to *chesed* and *gevura*, about which is said, *ahava beta'anugim* – in the plural. And these are the enjoyment of *ohr yashar* ("direct illumination") and of *ohr chozer* ("reflected illumination"). The enjoyment associated with "direct illumination" comes to us from above to below, and the enjoyment of "reflected illumination" involves ascent from below to above. It involves desire and yearning, as known that desire and yearning are part of a will that includes tremendous enjoyment. And this yearning and desire produce expiry of the soul, as written, "My soul yearned and expired," as a result of this great enjoyment. Now this "expiry" transpires among the faculties of the soul that are enclothed within the limbs of the body, in a settled manner (*ohr b'cli*), as they "move" from their place to ascend and become included within the essence of the soul which is above the entire category of "faculties." This is what constitutes the expiry and ascent of the faculties of the soul, whereupon automatically the whole essence of the soul elevates and ascends above. For, the attachment of the essence of the soul to the body is only by way of the faculties. In essence, the soul is not at all within the category of the body. Although it is explained elsewhere that in general, the connection of the soul with the body occurs only on account of G-d's power "to achieve amazing accomplishments," such as uniting the spiritual with the physical, nevertheless this takes place via the faculties of the soul which are enclothed in the limbs of the body in a settled manner. For, they are contracted and limited according to the nature of the limbs, as written elsewhere. And within them is grasped the essence of the soul...

...Now, the enjoyment that is associated with "reflected illumination" is expressed as ascent from below to above. It is mainly expressed precisely as "lack of grasp" of something. That is, when one yearns for and desires something, as a result of the power of enjoyment in his soul for that particular object, and yet for the time being he is unable to attain that object, then all of his abilities and powers ascend in desire for unity with the object, to the extent that he may experience expiry of the soul. Since this enjoyment comes from the very essence of his soul, called the *yechida*, it involves every aspect of his soul. That is, all of his faculties are attracted to the object of his enjoyment. But in the absence of attaining his objective, all the faculties of his soul unite in the essence of his power of enjoyment which is the essence of his soul – the *yechida* – to the extent of expiry...But, when he does attain his goal and achieve enjoyment, then there is no ascent of the soul. Rather there occurs an amazing unity and clasping [of the soul] with the object of his enjoyment, which enlivens and "returns" his soul to him, with enjoyment from above to below.

Now, within the enjoyment of "direct illumination" as well, it is possible to find the phenomena of "expiry of the soul." This occurs when the revelation of enjoyment is so strong, that the powers of the soul are unable to contain such great "goodness." This is as explained above; enjoyment is a function of the very essence of the soul – the *yechida* of the soul. Yet, here as well, we find both "immanent light" and "transcendent light." The immanent light comes to us as limited, contracted enjoyment that is enclothed within the faculties of the soul, integrated within, such as the faculty of *chochma,* within which is clad a reflection and ray of enjoyment. We are able to observe this when, as we receive a new insight or idea, we are filled with enjoyment...The same is true with eating, when we eat a sweet food and enjoy it, the joy settles within and permeates our faculties and causing them to become stabilized. That means, that the revelation and unity of enjoyment within the limbs of the body occurs in an established and settled fashion, as it should...

...All this takes place as *ohr pnimi*, which is a contracted form of enjoyment. But, sometimes, a ray of enjoyment may illuminate from above without any contractions whatsoever. And this ray is incapable of becoming "established" within the powers of the soul and the limbs of the body. An example occurred in the Talmud when R' Akiva's eyes brimmed with tears as a result of the many secrets of the Torah that were revealed to him. And it is known that tears come as the result of the limitations of the vessel of the mind to contain illumination. The illumination of the soul is so great that the intellect and the faculties of the mind are no longer able to contain or tolerate it. And as a result, tears emerge – this is why R' Akiva's eyes teared over; his mind was incapable of accepting this level of revealed illumination. And this is as well the explanation of the three sages who passed away in the Idra, on account of the great revelation of light that was impossible for them to accept. Similar events will occur in the future, about which is written, "In tears they will come," as a result of the great level of enjoyment that will occur at that time. For, when a very high revelation of enjoyment comes down to us, it is impossible to accept it with our faculties. This may even cause total expiry of the soul, as may occur during the enjoyment of song and music.... But, all this is not because the soul and its faculties ascend above, but rather just the opposite – the soul remains below and draws down revelation from above to below, so that a strong revelation of enjoyment descends. A strong attraction of the soul occurs, [accompanied by] cleaving and unity to the pleasant melody and song. [But], since the soul-faculties are limited and contracted, when the revelation of enjoyment occurs, it completely nullifies [the faculties] and causes them to become included in the essential light of the soul that shines upon them [from above].

xxx). Page 32 (Page 138 in the translation)

Note: "the thirst of the animal soul..." See the discourse, *Vekol ha'am roim* of the year *5662* (1902) from the Rebbe Rashab. And also of the year *5678* (1918)

From *Sefer Maamorim 5662* (1902) of the Rebbe Rashab, Page 266:

"...when the animal soul hides and conceals the Divine soul and establishes obstacles and obstructions in all of its paths of worship, this causes an intense response from the Divine soul, with much ardor of *ahavah rabba* ("Great love") that is unlimited, and beyond logic and intellect.

In general, this [love] comes from beyond the source and origin of the Divine soul, for the origin [of the Divine soul] is the "form" (*tzura*) of Adam the primordial man (*A"K*). And as known, any "form" of man includes both intellect and emotions. And if so, "Great love" that is beyond logic and intellect is from beyond the source and origin of the Divine soul.

Now, true elevation of the Divine soul is a result of the thirst of the animal soul itself, meaning that when the animal soul on its own is "troubled" by its great distance and experiences a great thirst for G-dliness, this in turn creates an elevation of the Divine soul as well...

(Page 267)...regarding the thirst of the animal soul; there are times that it suffers tremendously on account of its distance from G-d, and becomes aroused with a desire [for G-dliness]. [At such times], the animal soul in essence has no connection to G-dliness so it does not feel the goodness of G-lliness. And its distance [from G-dliness] is intrinsic, meaning that it is far because of the presence of evil within it. And as it becomes tormented over the gap [between itself and G-d], it feels no additional positive element of proximity [to spirituality], but only a desire to escape from death, G-d forbid. There is no feeling of good and life within it. Rather, there is only a feeling of torment as a result of the tremendous distance, and this totally shatters the very fabric of the animal soul. And [from there], its [outward] form becomes eradicated as well.

And this then produces a tremendous desire in the Divine soul as well, as a result. That is, the soul experiences an arousal of true *tshuva* as the distance from G-d touches the soul to its very depths and inner recesses. This takes place to the extent that it forgets completely about any proximity [to G-d that it might have experienced], because of the intensity of the torment and bitterness in his soul over distance from G-d...

"And also from the year *5678* (1918)" –

This would appear to be a mistake, as there is no discourse by the name *Vekol ha'am roim* in the *Sefer maamorim 5678*. Perhaps the intention was to the year *5675* (1915 - in the series *Besha'ah shehikdimu 5672*, vol. 2, page 1007-8) in which appears a discourse entitled *Vekol ha'am roim*.

"And so it is in the spiritual realm, as in learning Torah, which necessitates great labor, as the phrase says, 'If one says, I labored and I found it, believe him.' Furthermore, the Torah remains only with the person who "kills himself" over it...and success in learning takes place only after much great labor, dedication and devotion, during which the person throws himself entirely into learning the Torah. And sometimes he will experience great sorrow and suffering, G-d forbid from his lack of knowledge. And it becomes very difficult for him, to the extent that he is ready to give up his own life and his heart and spirit are totally broken within him. And then precisely at that point, a great spiritual light shines upon him and he grasps the concept. On the contrary, it comes to him with great illumination. And so occurs regarding the labor of prayer, in which it is impossible to achieve understanding and proper meditation in order to grasp G-dly concepts in such a way that they are established and integrated in his mind and heart and he is aroused with love and fear of G-d unless he first experiences the lowliness and bitterness of a contrite mind...and the two are dependent upon one another; for according to the range that the person is broken in his heart and crushed, feeling low and heavy-headed, with a broken heart and tremendous embarrassment, over his self-induced distance from G-d, etc...to precisely that extent the divine light shines and illuminates his soul afterward with intellectual grasp and arousal of love of G-d..."

xxxi) Page 33 (Page 142 in the translation) – "the essence of the soul is defined..."

Note: See the discourse *Az yashir* of the year *5700* (1940), from the Rebbe Rayatz, ז'ל, page 62

"That the soul may become en-clothed in the body [is a phenomenon that] occurs only as a result of the power the "Infinite One," Who causes amazing events to occur. At any rate, this applies only to the *nara'n* (*nefesh-ruach-neshama*, the lower three soul-levels) of the soul, but the essence of the soul is not in the category of en-clothement within the body. In truth, the essence of the soul is also connected with the body, and that is why it is impossible for one soul to be en-clothed in two bodies. (As in the story in the *Idra Rabba*: Once Eliyahu failed to come to the *Idra*, and when R' Shimon ben Gamliel inquired as to his where-abouts, he was answered that Eliyahu had to rescue Rav Hamnuna Saba and his friends. And out of respect for R' Hamnuna Saba, Eliyahu came enclothed in a body. And if he had come to the *Idra*, he would also have had to come as a soul in a body, out of respect for R' Shimon bar Yochai. But, it is impossible for one soul to come en-clothed in two bodies. For, this is one of the distinctions between a soul and the sun; the sun is not defined by the "light" that emerges from it, [even though] the light of the sun illuminates everywhere that the sun is to be found. But, the soul, though far surpassing the spiritual level of the sun, it is not capable of entering two bodies because the essence of the soul is designated by and united with its light and illumination.

Now, as to the reason for this, we must say that it is because the [level of the] soul en-clothed in a body, although a mere ray and reflection of the soul, is also essential. That means that although it is only a ray and not the very essence of the soul, nevertheless there is a difference between the soul as it remains above and the soul as it descends to be enclothed in the body. The soul that remains above is the essence and the soul within the body is only a ray. Nevertheless since it is a ray of the essence of the soul, it contains an element of the essence of the soul itself. The light of the sun is only light – it does not reflect the essence [of the sun] at all, but the soul - although also light - is essential. And within the particular level of the soul that is enclothed in the body, is to be found the light and overall energy that enlivens the body in general. From it come the soul powers that become enclothed in the limbs..."

xxxii) Page 34 (Page 149 in the translation)

Note: "As known, including the three..." See the *sichot* of the Rebbe Rashab of *Simchat Torah 5661* (1901 – in the *sefer Torah Shalom*, *sefer hasichot*). See also the discourse *mashachni* (the second one) of the year 1940 of the Rebbe Rayatz ז'ל

"From *Torat Shalom* of the Rebbe Rashab, *5661*: *sichat Simchat Torah*, Page 10 (section 4): "One of the Chasidim asked, 'what should we do if we meditate but it has no effect on our emotions?'

Someone else who was present began to scream at the chasid who asked the question, but the Rebbe Rashab said, "Let him ask, I specifically want people to ask questions…"

And then he answered; "this is a result of the coarseness of the physical. For that reason, there must be introductions and preparations – a little bit of denying oneself – and we must ask about that, within are found three levels – the oxe, sheep and goat. The oxe is one who gores, who gores when someone bothers him – like Binyamin Shines."

The Rebbe's brother, R' M. asked him, "why do you single him out, he is here?" and the Rashab answered him, "That is what my job is, as I have several times said, I am a 'shul-klopper.' Believe me that I mean myself as well, so that if anyone thinks that I do not mean myself, they cannot say that."

And then he said a second time, "An oxe that gores is like Binyamin Shines, who asks now what do we achieve with this happiness, why are we dancing? Why are we crawling over the vent, we have not learned any Chasidut, and we understand nothing about the simcha of Torah and mitzvoth…"

From the discourse, *Mashachni* of the year 5700 (1940)…Not found

xxxiii) Page 35 (Page 153 in the translation)

"The general service at that time…" See the discourse *Shir hama'a lot mimaamakim*…" of the year 5703 (1943) of the Rebbe Rayatz ztz'l.

From the discourse, *Shir hama'alot* of the year 5703 (1943) from the Rebbe Rayatz ztz'l, page 19:

"We first begin to say the psalm *shir hama'alot* during the morning services of the first day of Rosh Hashana, which follows the introduction of worship during the night time prayers on the first night of Rosh Hashana. Now, it is known that in general the *avoda* of Rosh Hashana takes place within our concealed and unconscious soul powers, and all of the worship of Rosh Hashana and Yom Kippur invokes the essence of the soul… We know, from books and from the sages, that on the eve of Rosh Hashana as darkness falls, the inner delight and inner will [of HaShem] within the *sephira* of *malchut* ascends and departs above, far beyond to its very source, to its ultimate elevation within *malchut* of the infinite light above…this knowledge should make us quake in the essence of our soul, and should shake all of our soul faculties; not only the revealed and conscious ones, but also the unconscious faculties. And in particular, the knowledge that we, and every other Jewish individual has the power to arouse [the Divine] delight and will within *malchut*, and that this takes place when we accept upon ourselves the yoke of His reign – [should cause us to quake].

And when we meditate upon all that we experienced during the course of the year and we recall matters that were not positive, [such reflections] take away our power and strength to stand in front of G-d and request that He accept us as His servant, even before we have done any *tshuva* or expressed regret for our past deeds. Like by way of example in the physical world, a servant who has escaped from his master or rebelled out of negligence and sinned against his him, who now desires to return and to accept the yoke of his master, would not have the nerve to stand in front of him and say to him, "Now I have come and it is my will to serve my master," without first conceding his transgressions and asking for mercy from his master, that he should forgive and pardon him. And he would cry from the depths of his heart and accept upon himself the yoke of his master in anything that he says to him.

So it is regarding our *avoda*; first we must express regret from the very depths of our heart over the past, and then arouse great mercy on our soul, with requests for leniency and crying from the depths of our heart and from the inner recesses of all of our faculties. We should beg for our lives, that our Master should accept us as His servant. This, in general is the *avoda* of prayer during the nighttime of Rosh Hashana. And afterward during the morning prayers, we recite *mima'akim keraticha*, for by accepting the yoke of heaven, we call upon and draw down the delight and will of His reign upon us from the depths that exist above.

xxxiv) Page 36 (Page 154 in the translation)

Note: "Are experienced by everyone…" See *Likutei Torah* in the explanation of the discourse, *Ki Teitzei* (the second one). See also the discourse *Az yashir* in the *Sefer maamorim 5700* (1940) of the Rebbe Rayatz *ztz'l*

From *Likutei Torah* of the Alter Rebbe, *parshat Ki Teitzei*, Page 72:

"Now, similarly within the soul of man, the Torah says, "And *Elokim* created man in His image, in the image (*tzelem*, or *tzadik-lamed-memsofit*) of *Elokim*…" …The most important function of this "image" is to serve as an intermediary between G-dliness and the soul. For, the soul is a creation from nothing to something via the Divine light that is en-clad in [the *sephira* of] *malchut* of *Asiya*, in the *kelim*, or "vessels." Nevertheless, it is still G-dly, since it is created from the "image of G-d." And it is divided into two facets. One comes from the letter *tzadi* of the word *tzelem* ("image"). It is the G-dliness within the soul. And the other facet comes from the letter *lamed* (the second letter of *tzelem*, or "image"). It is the *makif* ("transcendent level"), also known as *mazla*. As the sages said, *mazleh hazi* – "their *mazal* saw." From there, the *tzadi* descends to become clad in the soul, as known regarding the saying of the Ba'al Shem Tov regarding the *bat kol* ("voice") that announces, "return, wayward children…" This is strange, for who is there to hear [the announcement]? And if so, what effect does it have? But, the *mazal* "sees" the announcement, and the result is the spiritual arousal of the soul that we experience within the body when something descends to it from above, from this *mazal*. And that is why it is called a *mazal* since it draws down flow (*nozel*) and influence. And the *mazal* is G-dliness that does not become enclothed in the soul at all, for it is above the level even of an angel. As R' Chaim Vital said in his *Shaar Hakedusha*, "And the prophecy on the highest level of them all is revelation of the soul itself, since it is above any revelation of *gilui Eliyahu*, since the soul is beyond the body which is influenced by the letters *lamed* of the *tzelem*…"

From the discourse *Az yashir* from the *Sefer Maamorim 5700* (1940) of the Rebbe Rayatz *ztz'l*, page 64 (section 5):

"…the purpose of the *cruz* ("announcement" from Above) is to awaken people so that they pay attention, return to G-d and get involved in Torah. But, since people do not hear these "announcements," what purpose do they serve? And so it is regarding *tshuva*; there occur "announcements" from above, such as the *cruz*, "Return, wayward children." Here, the word "wayward" implies wildness, or behavior that does not follow any kind of order or organized conduct. And in *avoda*, "wayward" occurs when we forget the true intention from above, which is for the soul to descend into the body…the purpose of the announcement is to arouse people to do *tshuva*, but since they do not hear the announcement, so what is the purpose in making them?…

…But the matter is as follows: People do not hear the "announcements" from above because of the opaqueness and concealment of the body and natural soul. Since they are concerned with bodily matters and heavily involved in physical lusts and enjoyment…even of permitted matters, so aside from the fact that they are "sunken" in these matters, as time goes by, things that were previously merely "permitted" become "necessary." …and then they do not even permit the person to "hear" spiritual matters…"

xxxv) Page 36 (Page 154 in the translation)

Note: "It is written elsewhere…" See the discourse *Veki tomru mah nochal* of the year 5678 (1918)

From *Sefer maamorim 5678* (1918) of the Rebbe Rashab, Page 307:

"The matter is as follows; love that is motivated by intellect and logic is limited by the intellect, and therefore it corresponds to the vessel of the heart and to the faculties that are able to contain it. And for that reason, the love includes elements of the person's own existence, since it is delineated by the powers of his soul. And that is why as much he polishes his deeds so that they are very refined, nevertheless, he remains a person unto himself, and he is not rectified to the extent of not experiencing himself at all.

But, the love that is transcendent in the soul is unlimited, and the vessel of the heart and faculties of the soul are unable to contain it. With this love, he is totally unable to remain within the [boundaries of] his own existence. And it is precisely with this [ove] that he may succeed in achieving full rectification of his deeds, so that his physical actions are also for G-d alone.

And as we see when the soul shines as a result of the transcendent levels of his soul, such as during Rosh Hashana and Yom Kippur - at such times our actions take place in a different manner altogether, in such a way that we do not experience the temptations of our soul. On a yet higher level, this is similar to what occurs on Shabbat – since according to true reality, physical enjoyment is really enjoyment of G-dliness, and it is a mitzvah to enjoy the Shabbat with eating and drinking – [therefore] the enjoyment is G-dly enjoyment…"

Ch. 6

xxxvi) Page 36 (Page 158 in the translation)

Note: "That He alone..." "*Igeret Hakodesh siman* 20"

In Tanya, fourth section (*Igerot Hakodesh*), *Igeret* 20:
"The light [of the *kav*] is similar to the Illuminator, which is the very self and essence of the Emanator, may He be blessed, Whose existence is from He Himself and is not the effect of another cause that preceded Him, G-d forbid. And therefore, He alone possesses the power and ability to create something from nothing, from absolutely zero, without any prior reason or causation..."

xxxvii) Page 37 (Page 159 in translation)

Note: "Regarding the verse *Ki Tihiyu* – see the discourse *Habaim yishrash* in *Torah Ohr*
"Now, the hundred blessings [that a Jew must say every day] occur in the mode of speech, but what brings the influx from a state of concealment into revelation? This takes place when we fulfill the mitzvoth. Take, for example, sowing seeds: Most garden variety seeds are inedible, since they are only seeds without any taste. But when the seeds are planted in the ground and the power of germination that is within the ground permeates them, the seeds produce edible food, even though the seeds themselves are totally inedible. And even though seeds of grain are edible, nevertheless when they are planted they produce much more food, similar in nature to the seeds themselves.

This is similar, then to performance of mitzvoth. Mitzvoth descend to the world and become enclothed in physical objects such as the parchment of *tefilin*, and the threads of wool that go on *tzitzit*, and the like among other mitzvoth. And when a Jew places them on his head, they produce revelation of G-dliness; first of all of *chochma* (associated with the first parchment - *kodesh*) and then of *bina* (associated with the second parsha – *vehaya ki*)...And this takes place only when a Jewish person dons them on his head, unlike if they are placed on a table, when no revelation occurs whatsoever. And although man's forehead is physical like the table, and moreover when a non-Jew places *tefilin* on his head, there is also no revelation...nevertheless the example of the power of germination within the earth is still valid. For, just as fruit will not grow just anywhere on the earth – for example, in the desert virtually nothing grows at all - similarly the Torah says about Jews, "When you will be like a desirable land for Me..."

Essay on Service of the Heart - Love Like Fire and Water

xxxviii) Page 37 (Page 161 in the translation)

Note: "This is similar to the difference…" See *Torat Chaim* in the discourse *eleh toldot Noach*, Ch. 6. *Likutei Torah* in the discourse *Alei Be'er*, first section. The discourse *VeAvraham Zaken* 5702

From *Torah Chaim* of the Mitteler Rebbe, in the discourse *Eleh Toldot Noach*, Chapter 6

"The explanation is that *chochma* is the "mentor", meaning that it is like a new flash of intellect that shines like lightening. It is called *hitchachamot* (the ability to produce *chochma*), and it [employs] the power of *havana* to bring out all kinds of new intellect. It also has the potential to develop ideas from nothing to something, from the hidden intellect called *maskil*, from which flows much new intellect, in accordance with the person's power of *chochma*, whether small or large. Now, the outer manifestation of this is a lightening flash of intellect that emerges as a new revelation of *chochma*, but it is short and concise, a hidden synopsis as in one point. And it comes to expression in the grasp and explanation of *bina*…

…but the inner manifestation of *chochma* is beyond being a source or "mentor" to *bina* as in the category of intellect mentioned above. Rather, it is as if a new idea "fell" into the mind, into the power of *chochma* within, without having yet come into revelation, even to the person himself. Rather it is like a flash of lightening that passes through the brain, "from one side to the other," without yet settling into the mind…and therefore the person is unable to express it in a conscious fashion and to bring it into manifest intellect grasp, even to himself, and all the moreso to others. This is the *ayn* ("void") of *chochma* that is concealed as if in one point, still lacking expression, although it is the very essence of the inner illumination and influx of *chochma* as it exists in its source.

From *Likutei Torah* of the Alter Rebbe, *parshat Chukat*, page *samech-beit* (or 124)

"…all the days of man's life, when his soul is enclad in his body in this world, are only in order [for the soul] to become like a 'well' that flows beneath the surface – specifically beneath the surface, since water flowing through the soil of the earth becomes purified and refined – so that the soul becomes refined by fulfillment of physical Torah and mitzvoth, as well as when the G-dly soul overwhelms and subdues the animal soul…

…however, in order to produce this "well"-like revelation, two types of digging must occur – *chafira* and *criah*. Both are needed in order to remove the soil of the earth that blocks the opening of the well. However, *chafira* involves moving the large clods of earth, while *criah* is necessary to move the smaller more refined pebbles and dirt. And we as well need to remove all of the blockages that conceal the hidden love inside of ourselves, as well as to subdue the "other side" that is opposed to holiness, whether by reinforcing ourselves by restraining from evil, or by restraining ourselves in those activities that are permitted to us [but in which we need not get overly involved]. Additionally we may need to reinforce our performance of positive mitzvoth and to learn more Torah than we were accustomed and to give more *tzedaka* than was previously our nature. All these items and similar are in the category of "digging" in order to remove the coarse physical obstacles and to nullify them, revealing our inner love…

…(next page) Now, from this 'well,' as a result of this digging, emerges "living water" that is more enduring than the "love like fire" with flames of excitement that occurs during prayers with meditation. That love dissipates after prayers and passes, but the "living waters"... are an expression of love without end..."

From the discourse, *VeAvraham Zaken*...in the *Sefer Maamorim 5702* (1942) of the Rebbe Rayatz, *ztz'l,* Page 64-65

"Now, the order of man's *avoda* as described in the *Zohar* (*Bamidbar* 120A)...must correspond to what took place on the altar, as explained in the Mishna in tractate *Zevachim*, "the priest ascended the ramp of the altar and turned, revolving to arrive at the southeast corner" – wherein south corresponds to *chesed* or love. And that is followed by the east, as is known that the east represents *chochma* ("wisdom"). The sun (which is *yesod aba* - the "foundation of *chochma*") shines from the east...and [the word] "east" (*mizrach*) is related to the word *ezrach* ("citizen") - which corresponds to *chochma* (as in the verse *maskil le'eitan ha'ezrachi* - "Instruction from Eitan the Ezrahi" – Psalm 89:1). That is, following the stimulating experience of love and cleaving to G-d, we must become nullified (self-nullification is the inner dimension of *chochma*) to G-d in a manner that surpasses our love. And this [nullification is associated with] *chochma ila'ah*. *Chochma* and *bina* are called *ayn veyesh* ("nothing and something"). *Chochma* is above intellect – it [expresses] only the essential content of intellect that flashes and shines within the mind. But, we are still unable to grasp it. And this is merely the level of *chochma* that stands in proximity to *bina*, meaning the aspect of *chochma* that is called *yesod aba*. The true nature of *chochma* transcends even the flash of inspiration. It is, rather the *hitamtut* ("confirmation" and "affirmation") that is associated with *reiyah* ("vision") of *chochma*.

Bina, however is the grasp and understanding of the intellect, as it expands and extends itself. And therefore, real excitement and arousal occur only in *bina*, where meditation takes place, rather than in *chochma*. This is because [the process] of meditation (*hitbonenut*) can only take place regarding something that has emerged from a state of intellectual grasp to become something that "exists." That is why emotional excitement, such as love and desire like fire, results from meditation, for [such love and desire] is also an "entity" that "exists," something substantial..."

xxxix) Page 38 (Page 167 in the translation)

Note: "As written elsewhere - See the previous note in Ch. 3 and in the citations there."
    From Ch. 3 See note xix on page 272

xl) Page 39 (Page 168 in the translation)

Note: "Referring to the four worlds of *Atzilut, bria, yetzira and asiya*. *Siddur* of the *Ariz'l*. For an explanation according to Chassidut, see the *siddur* (of the Alter Rebbe) regarding these verses. See also the discourse *Amar R'Y yhai chelki*... of the year *5701* (1941).

From the *Siddur* of the Alter Rebbe, on Psalm 148 in the *Psukei dezimra*, Page *Samech-Hey* (65 in the Hebrew letters):

[The first two verses say, "Praise the Lord, praise the Lord from the heavens, praise Him from the heights. All of His angels praise Him, all of His hosts praise Him." In the *siddur*, the Rebbe explains (based on the *Ariz'l*) that the four terms, "heavens," "heights," "angels," and "hosts" refer to the four worlds of *Atzilut, bria, yetzira* and *asiya*:]

"Now, the explanation of "heavens" (*shamayim*), is that it refers to *z'a* (the lower six or seven *sephirot*) of *Atzilut*....The reason is that *z'a*, which is the "emotions" of *Atzilut*, are the mainstay of the *mashpia* ("mentor" or "benefactor") to the lower separate worlds of *BY"A*, as known. And all influx must come through *chesed* ("kindness"), as it is written, *olam chesed yibaneh* ("the world is built upon kindness"...).

...Now, the explanation of *meromim* ("heights") is that it refers to *malchut* of *Atzilut* as it is concealed within *bria*. At that point, it is called *marom*, as written *se'u marom eineichem* – "Raise your eyes to the heights" – for as known, the difference between "heavens" and "heights" is that "heavens" refers to the very essence of the sky...while "heights" refers to what we are able to see. It is what is evident to the one who stands below, to whom the essence of the sky is not visible at all. He is able to detect only what descends as a ray of light, visible to the eye. And since the heavens are extremely elevated...therefore what we are able to see is called *marom*, for His [true] heights are not fathomable or graspable. But, the term *marom* indicates loftiness and elevation alone, meaning to say that He is high, above what we may see – which is why we say "raise your eyes to the heights..."

...the explanation of "His angels" is that it refers to the world of *yetzira*, as written in the *siddur* [of the *Ariz'l*] that the four worlds of *ABY"A* are hinted to in the four praises mentioned here: *shamayim, meromim*, angels and hosts...now, the reason that angels are associated with *yetzira* is because an angel – *malach* – is an emissary (*shaliach*), and the entire world of *yetzira* functions as an "emissary" to deliver something...it possesses no qualities of its own – so the world of *yetzira* merely enables revelation of what was previously concealed. And therefore, "His angels" are in *yetzira*. And in truth, there is an advantage to *yetzira* over *asiya*, in that the angels [of *yetzira*] are totally nullified within, just as a proper messenger. Similarly, the angels of are nothing more than emissaries who reveal the divine influx from its state of concealment in *bria*...unlike the angels of *asiya* who possess an existence and identity of their own....

So, "All of His angels praise Him" appears first, after which we say, "All of His hosts..." in reference to the world of *asiya*. This is because a "host" is nothing more than a foot soldier of the king. He is not one who stands before the king, ready to do his bidding, but rather one who stands ready to go out to war. And this is similar to the seventy "ministers" of *asiya* and all of the planets and constellations and the nine orbits which accept their influx from *malchut* of *malchut* of *asiya*, as known..."

From the discourse, *Amar R' Yosi*, in *Sefer Maamorim 5701* (1941) of the Rebbe Rayatz, *ztz'l*, Page 10

"...the psalm, "Praise the Lord from the heavens," alludes to all of the creations of the heavens and the earth, and the inter-inclusion of the worlds *ABY"A*, as written in the *siddur* of the *Ariz'l*, "Praise be the Lord from the heavens" refers to *Atzilut*, "Praise be the Lord from the heights" refers to *bria*, "His angels" to *yetzira* and "His hosts" to *asiya*. "Praise be the sun and the moon" refers to the inclusion of *asiya* within *yetzira*, "stars of light" to inclusion of *yetzira* in *bria*, "the heaven's heavens" of *bria* in *Atzilut* and "the waters that are over the waters" refers to the elevation of *Atzilut* to the very essence of the Emanator…

(page 12)…And thisis what is meant by "Praise the Lord from the heavens," indicating descent of illumination and revelation from the light of the world of Atzilut, from where it is drawn in order to become "Praise be He in the heights," in the "angels" and the "hosts," which are the three worlds of *BY"A*. That is, by way of meditation during the *pesukei dezimra*, we arrive to the *avoda* of *kriat shema* with nullification and unity of the worlds…"

xli) Page 39 (Page 174 in the translation)

Note: "About them, the verse (Samuel 2:2) states, 'There is no holiness like that of *Havaya*'…" – See *Likutei Torah*, in *Shir haShirim* in the discourse *Tzeana u'reana* (the first one), in the beginning.

From *Likutei Torah* of the Alter Rebbe, *Shir haShirim* ("Song of songs"), in the discourse *Tzeana u'reana* (the first one), on Page *kaf-aleph* (21 in Hebrew letters):

"…And this is what is meant by *Ayn kadosh k'Havaya* ("There is no holiness like that of the Name *Havaya*…") – the Zohar (in *parshat Tazriah* 43A) explains that there are several levels of *kadosh* ("holiness"), but none of them are holy like *Havaya*…" The matter is as follows; the name *Havaya* indicates that He creates everything, and even though He creates everything, He is nevertheless holy and removed from them. He is *sovev kol olamim* – "transcendent illumination of the worlds" – unlike the soul [that fills the body, which is *memalle kol olamim* – "immanent illumination"]. And for that reason, this category of holiness is not to be found among all the other expressions of holiness that exist above. Regarding all of the other levels of *seder hishtalshelut* ("spiritual chain of creation"), whatever is called "holy" - meaning that it is somehow "removed" - does not imply the following two opposites: On one hand, it permeates and penetrates, and on the other, it is holy and removed. Above, though, the infinite light of *sovev kol olamim*, which is holy and removed nevertheless descends to create all of the worlds. The main impetus for creation comes from the *makif* ("transcendent light"), as written in Tanya at the end of Ch. 23 and the end of Chapter 48…And that is why "there is no holiness like that of *Havaya*." And this is what is meant by "He grasps all worlds" – via *sovev kol olamim*, He creates and energizes all worlds from nothing to something - and despite all this, "there is none who grasp Him and He is holy and removed."

xlii) Page 42 (Page 185 in the translation)

"as it is written (Psalms 139:16), "The days in which they were to be formed…")

Note: "See *Likutei Torah* in the discourse, *Al ken yomru*, section 3, and in the discourse *Ki tihiyena le'ish*…"

From *Likutei Torah* of the Alter Rebbe, *parshat Chukat*, discourse *Al ken yomru*, section 3, Page 130

"And this is what is meant by *al ken yomru hamoshlim, bo'u Cheshbon* – "And therefore the poets would say, Come to [the city called] *Cheshbon...*" – here the word for "poets" (*moshlim*) also means "those who govern," and alludes to those who have control over their physical nature and temptations. And the verse is precise, referring to a city called *Cheshbon*, which also means "accounting." That is, "Come and make an accounting of the world." The word for "world" is *olam*, from the word *he'elam*, meaning concealment, and those who "govern over their natures" alludes to souls that have descended to this world. They must "make an accounting" of why they came into a physical body in this dark world. It is the ultimate descent, but it is for the purpose of ascent. That is, [they have come down] in order to subdue the "other side" that is opposed to holiness, and in the process the glory of G-d becomes publicized in the world...

And another explanation – in fact, the main one – of "accounting of the world" is that most of the hiding and concealment of this world takes place right here in the lowest of all worlds, which is why the darkness here is thick and doubled-over. And therefore, in order to illuminate this opaque darkness, we need to draw down a far greater light and illumination, so that the darkness will have no effect, and will in fact shine like light. Minimal illumination is incapable of illuminating the thick darkness. In a normal house, a conventional candle is sufficient, but deep in the cellar, where the atmosphere is thick and dark (since it is within the deepest most physical part of the earth), a huge light is necessary in order to illuminate the thick atmosphpere. A thin candle will not suffice, and may even be extinguished by the physical nature of the atmosphere.

And so it is regarding the process of illuminating the darkness of the world of physical *asiya*; it demands the highest illumination. And that is why souls descend to this world, so that by the "candle of G-d – the soul of man" [may illuminate]. Also, a candle is compared to a mitzvah and the Torah is compared to light – so that in this manner the soul is able to illuminate and subdue the darkness, [transforming it] to light. That is what is meant by "accounting of the world" – according to the amount of concealment, so we must maximize the light of Torah and mitzvoth.

From *Likutei Torah* of the Alter Rebbe, *parshat Ki Teitzei*, discourse *Ki Tihiyena le'ish...* on Page 74

"Now, the purpose of the descent of the Divine soul to this world is in order to en-clad it in the natural animal soul and do battle with it, with the goal of refining it and separating the good within it from the bad. [The purpose is to] elevate it to G-d, and in so doing transform darkness to light. That is why we are called "Yisrael," as written that "You struggled (*sarit*) with *Elokim* (in this context, "angels") and overcame," meaning that the G-dly soul will overcome the enlivening animal soul, transforming its thoughts and emotions that are not devoted to G-d, from evil to good...

...And this is what is meant by the verse, "The days of our years in them are seventy years..." The phrase "in them" is quite precise, because the verse is referring to two souls, between which there is a new war every day. And therefore, their level of energy is not equal – one has more vitality than the other. It all depends upon the level of war that is necessary to do battle with the animal soul. For, according to the portion of evil within it are the number of years that it are necessary to struggle with it until it is transformed to good.

That is what is meant by the verse, "And now, Israel, what does G-d ask from you..." where-in "now" refers to the present era, when good and evil are mixed. The soul is called "Yisrael" because it must rule over and overwhelm the animal soul, transforming it from bad to good. But, regarding the future it is said, "And I will wipe away the spirit of impurity from the land," and there will be no more evil at all. It will not be necessary to fight any more and at that time, our names will no longer be Yisrael...."

xliii) Page 43 (Page 190 in the translation)

Note: "And as the philosophers said…" – See *Sefer Ikarim, Maamor* 3, first chapter. See *Kuntres Umayan, Maamor* 1. *Sichat* 19 *Kislev* of the year 5680 (!920), section 6 (in *Torat Shalom, sefer Hasichot*). The discourse *lema'an da'at* of the year 5690 (1930) (*Kuntres vov*)

From *Sefer HaIkarim* of R' Yoseph Albo, *maamor* 3, Ch. 1 (Page 197 in the Warsaw edition, reprinted in Jerusalem in 1960)

"This that man…grasps in thought and understanding more than other animals, is because he is a higher form of creation, and more complete than them…and it is not appropriate to think that because the other animals live without need of shade from draught or of shelter from rain, and they do not need to "fix" or do anything in order to obtain their sustenance, but rather all of their sustenance is available…and even moreso, some of them have certain skills, such as predators and carnivorous birds that have the ability to hunt and thus to find their sustenance – that therefore they are a more complete form of creation than man. This was suggested by some of the earlier thinkers, who expressed this opinion, and they would said that man is incomplete in comparison to the other animals, since the other animals do not need anything to "ride" in order to travel from one place to another since they themselves travel easily, moving more than the human species. Similarly, they do not need to prepare themselves for war with their enemies, since all of the tools of war are already found with them naturally, such as the horns of an oxe and the tusks of the pig and the thorns of the porcupine and shield of the turtle…and moreover animals do not need clothes because their "garments" are created with them naturally. And they need no preparation of food since their food is ready for them at all times. But, man is missing all of this; he needs clothes for the outside of his body and buildings to live within for shelter and to protect himself from rain and water. And he needs to do much preparation of his food so that he will be able to sustain himself, and similar other activities.

But, when we look closely at this opinion, we see that it is totally lacking in basis. When we look into the creations that exist…and all of the low entities that are created, we find that all of them pursue perfection, each in its own way. That is, each creation that comes later [higher in the chain] is more admirable than the previous one, as if to say that the physical substance of creation flows always from a less perfected to a more perfected and complete form. For, first the substance of creation takes on the form of the elements [wind, water, fire and earth], and afterward it ascends to the level of the mineral world, of which the elements are the more primitive origins. And then it ascends to the vegetable category, of which the mineral world is the more primitive source, and from there it ascends to the animal kingdom, of which vegetation is a more primitive source. And then it ascends to the level of man, and the animals are the primitive form of man. And there stands the creation. It is as if each segment [of creation] prepares for the segment that follows it; so it would appear among lower creations that each one serves the purpose of the segment that follows it…ascending from one segment to the next we reach the highest segment, which is the human form – and there the creation stands because it is the ultimate purpose of all the lower creations.

As evidence that the physical substance moves always from a state of lesser being to a higher state of existence…is that we find the species known as a "sponge" as an intermediary between the mineral and the vegetable categories. And we find the sea sponge that possesses nothing more than the sense of "feeling" as an intermediary between the vegetable and the animal categories. And there is the monkey that serves as an intermediary between animals and man, and man is the pinnacle of existence.

If so, [the creation] is impossible without the existence of man, who is the ultimate goal of the lower creations; he is the most important and complete of all of them, emerging as the sum total of all of the previous forms which are more abstract than him. And therefore, he is the greatest of all of them, and conquers the animals beneath him and rules over them since his abilities are of a general nature, while the abilities of the animals are particular - they are unable to grasp general matters. And that is why they possess particular "tools" and specific skills, according to their individual abilities. There are those with particular abilities to fight in specific ways, such as the tusks of the pig and the horns of the oxe and the thorns in the skin of the porcupine and the shield on the turtle to protect it. But, since man is the ultimate being among the lower creations, he gathers together all of the perfection and particular abilities that are found among all the other animals. His abilities are general and his intellect is also general, meaning that he grasps all of the skills of the animal in general; he grasps the general drift of things, not merely particular details. And therefore, all of his skills are general, such as the hands with which he can fight any kind of war that the animals fight, and to defeat the animal bemeath him. He may grab a spear in place of horns that are on the animal, and a sword in place of the tusks on the pig, and a shield in his hand, or he may don armor to protect himself as does the turtle. And the tools of war weren't [created] as part of his form as they were among the animals, so that they shouldn't be an extra burden for him to carry constantly. And for this reason, the Creator gave him general tools and skills, whether for the purpose of war…and he gave him the power of general intellect in order to achieve the general goals and not merely particular ones and the ability to grasp the general outline of all particular ideas that all of the animals might use and use their skills when needed and to set them aside when not needed…and so regarding clothes which are separate from his body so that he need only don them when necessary during the winter and not during the summer…and gave him wisdom and understanding to build houses that are strong to fend off those who would damage him…

From *Kuntres Umayan* of the Rebbe Rashab, *Maamor* 1, Ch. 3 (page 64)

"Now, everything is the world was created for a purpose. And the purpose of everything is to ascend to a higher level than where it stands presently. The purpose of the vegetable world is to become included in the animal world, the purpose of the animal world is to become included in the human world, and the purpose of the human world is fulfilled when our spirit ascends to be included in the spiritual world above us. This takes place as we learn Torah, which is the wisdom and will of the One above, and the Torah and Holy One Blessed be He are One.

And when man is involved in Torah and delves into it carefully in order to truly understand its concepts, he becomes united with the wisdom and will of G-d, with an incredible unity (as written in the first book of Tanya, Ch. 5). And in this manner his soul ascends to become united and included in His wisdom may He be blessed, whether the person is involved in the *nigleh* ("revealed aspects" of the Torah, such as Talmud and *halacha*) of Torah, which is the essence of His wisdom and will (for thus He concluded in His wisdom that a particular object is kosher or unfit)…or whether he is involved in the inner dimensions of Torah (*nistar* – "concealed" wisdom), which are the knowledge and grasp of G-dliness. For what the rabbis revealed to us of this subject is the inner dimension of His wisdom, and when man is involved in this, it unites him with the inner wisdom of G-d, far above the outer manifestations (*nigleh*) of Torah…"

From *Torat Shalom* of the Rebbe Rashab, *sichat* 19 *Kislev, 5680* (1920), section 6, Page 243

(At the end of the meal, a rabbi came from Tshernigov and someone from Petrograd and yet another came from a general meeting, and the Rebbe Rashab said to them), "You missed the (delivery of) Chasidut, but I will say a few words: In the *Sefer Ikarim* it states that the purpose of the mineral, vegetable, animal and human worlds is to ascend to that which is above them. For, the major purpose of all creation is to ascend to what is above it: The purpose of the mineral world is to ascend to the vegetable, meaning that the vegetable world should emerge from it. The purpose of the vegetable world is to elevate to the animal world, meaning that the animals eat from it and are nourished as it becomes a part of them. The purpose of the animal world is to ascend to the human world, meaning that humans must eat [animals] and be nourished as they become part of man. And the purpose of the human is to ascend to that which is above him. Now, the advantage of the human being is that he possesses intelligence, and this is his advantage over the mineral, vegetable and animal. And the purpose of the human being is to ascend to what is beyond intellect, meaning that he must ascend to G-dliness, since that is the level of the intellect in essence.

And so it is written in the *Ikarim*. [But], we say (that is, Chasidut says) that the purpose of the human being is to become like an animal (*chai* - but also meaning "life-energy," or "vitality"). For, the animal lives without intellect. So, from what does he live – from *chai* ("life-energy"), which is G-dliness. For without G-dliness, no life exists, and *chayut* comes only from G-dliness, as written, "And *Havaya Elokim emet*, He is the living G-d." And if so, regarding the animal which has no intellect and yet lives, we come to the realization that he lives from G-dliness. Thus, the purpose of the human who is intellectual, is to arrive to this level of *chai*; that is, he should know and feel – the human who is intelligent can experience this – that he lives from G-d.

From the discourse, *Lema'an da'at* of the year *5690* (1930) from the Rebbe Rayatz *ztz'l*, in *Sefer Maamorim Kuntresim Aleph*, Page 168 (*Kuntres vov*):

"In general, the creation is divided into four categories: Mineral, vegetable, animal and human. The purpose of the mineral world is realized when it ascends beyond its level and it germinates fodder, etc. And the purpose of the vegetable world is fulfilled when it becomes included within the animal world, and the purpose of the animal world is to become included in the human. And the purpose of the human being is achieved as his spirit ascends, and becomes included in spiritual levels that are above him. [This happens] as he learns Torah, which is the wisdom and will of G-d, and the Torah and the Holy One blessed be He are one. And when man involves himself in the Torah, and delves carefully into matters in order to truly understand them, he unites with the wisdom and will of G-d with a tremendous unity, as written in the first section of Tanya, Chapter 5.

Now with this bond that unites man with Torah, he becomes connected and included in G-d's wisdom, whether he is involved in the revealed side of Torah, which is the essence of His wisdom and will, for thus He concluded in His wisdom that this particular object is kosher, and this one unfit…or whether he is involved in the inner dimensions of the Torah, which is knowledge and grasp of G-dliness. For, all matters and laws of the Torah as they appear in their physical condition, exist in their true state within the *sephirot* above and [are expressed] in spiritual matters. For example, take the *halacha* of "two who are holding on to a *talit*." Down in the physical world, this is a physical *talit* with two physical people. But, this *halacha* is learned as well in *gan eden*, where it is not appropriate to speak of anything physical at all. And the learning there takes place on the real, true level of the concept as it really exists, as our sages, such as the Rashbi and the *Ariz'l*, as well as our rabbis revealed in the inner dimensions of the soul, which is the inner aspect of His wisdom. And when man is involved in this, he becomes united with the inner wisdom of G-d, far above the unity of the revealed dimensions oft the Torah…"

xliv) Page 46 (Page 207 in the translation)

Note: "Noise of involvement in *avoda*...as written elsewhere"

See the discourse *Ve'eleh shemot* of the year 5675 (1915) of the Rebbe Rashab, Page 812 in the series *Besha'ah shehikdimu 5672* (1912), vol. 2

Page 819 (Ch. 398)

The subject is as follows; whether we are speaking of external or internal mindfulness (*chitzoniyut* or *pnimiyut hamochin*) - which in general correspond to the external and the internal elements of the heart - both are associated with the entire process of prayer, [beginning] with the *pesukei dezimra* ("songs of praise"), the blessings before the *kriat shema* and the *kriat shema* itself (which correspond to [the soul-levels of] *ruach* and *neshama*). The only difference is in their spiritual level. For it is known that the three sections of prayer mentioned above correspond to *ruach* ("wind"), *ra'ash* ("noise, commotion") and *aish* ("fire"), all of which are components of the *midot*, or spiritual emotions. *Ruach* applies to the *pesukei dezimra*, during which we arouse our emotions with great excitement through meditation upon the creation from nothing to something. In essence this is a process that goes beyond intellectual grasp, but its amazing origins arouse exhilaration in the heart. In general, this is but a transcendent excitement that does not penetrate the inner core of the soul, but remains external alone. For that reason, there is no goal ascribed to it, aside from spiritual ascent alone (just as the animal soul rises to a higher level, as explained in Ch. 382 and 392, so for the G-dly soul, there is only elevation and uplift, as the soul rises to a higher level).

And *ra'ash* applies to the blessings that we say before the *kriat shema*, as the *ofanim* (lower angels) and the holy *chayot* (higher angels) create a great tumult. This corresponds to our meditation on the subject of *kadosh* ("holiness"), as discussed in *Likutei Torah* in the second discourse beginning with the words *Ani HaShem Elokeichem* ("I am the Lord your G-d"). This tumult is the result of the amazing loftiness of the subject. It is produced as a result of the apparent newness of the concept under investigation. When a man sees something new that he never imagined, he becomes greatly excited, with a lot of commotion. Something to which he is already accustomed or which is already within his normal range of experience does not stimulate him at all. Only that which is outside of his ordinary experience and is new to him is capable of greatly exciting him. Like [*istarei belegina*], which is the result of the novelty of the situation. And similarly in the realm of spirituality, intellectual grasp of anything holy is novel regarding the creation, since the inner vitality and experience of any created being comes from a mere ray and reflection of G-dliness, while the infinite essence of G-d, may he be blessed, is holy and beyond. And therefore, [intellectual grasp] among created beings is a rarity, and causes much excitement and commotion. Part of the wonder of it is that it doesn't come into full intellectual grasp, since no thought can truly grasp Him. And this is further cause for excitement, since that which a person grasps, he internalizes and accepts in a settled manner, while that which he does not totally grasp, meaning that he may understand it, but not in totality, produces "noise" and tumult (and this as well is new and novel, since that which is not entirely understood is novel).

And therefore, the noise and commotion of the *ofanim* is greater than that of the *seraphim*, since their grasp is on a lesser level. They know of holiness, but they do not know what it is, and this is what produces a great amount of commotion. And nonetheless, this is a more internal feeling than is *ruach*, since at least they grasp how the infinite light is holy and removed from the worlds. And in particular, as they grasp the nature of the loftiness of G-d's infinite light, the resulting excitement, while noisy, nevertheless contains an element of inner vitality since it arrives via the intellect. And therefore the excitement includes a goal and endpoint – the desire to becomes subsumed and included in G-d's infinite light – all this because the excitement is internalized within...

Ch. 399 ...Now, regarding the three levels of *ruach* ("spirit" or "wind"), *ra'ash* ("noise" or "commotion") and *aish* ("fire"), the scripture says that they are not the *ruach* of *Havaya*, nor the *ra'ash* of *Havaya*, etc... The topic is as follows; *ruach* ("spirit" or "wind") is associated with the *pesukei dezimra*, and involves meditation upon the creation of the worlds, which came into being from the *ruach* or breath of His mouth, may He be blessed. Now, this is not the *ruach* of *Havaya*, but the *ruach* of *Elokim*, as known that from the name *Havaya* it was not possible to create. The creation took place using the name *Elokim*, as we see in the first verse of the Torah, "In the beginning, *Elokim* created." Only the final '*hey*' of the name *Havaya* was associated with creation, as we see from the word, *behibaram* ("when they were creation," Gen 2:4) – which may be re-written, *be Hey baram* ("with the *hey* they were created"). The final *hey*, described in the Zohar as a "light letter that has no substance," is nothing more than a breath of external *ruach*.

And the *ruach* is followed by *ra'ash* ("noise" or "commotion") corresponding to the *yotzar ohr* – [the blessings preceding the *kriat shema*], which involves nullification of the angels and souls in the higher spiritual worlds. [This occurs] as we meditate upon the concept of *kadosh* ("holy"). This word *kadosh* (Hebrew letters *kuf-dalet-vav-shin*) contains the letter *vav*, indicating descent of a ray of spirituality from a higher transcendent level called *kodesh elyon* ("supernal holiness"), in order to bring together both immanent (*memalle*) spirituality and transcendent (*sovev*) G-dliness. The meditation is upon the holiness of the infinite light of G-d may He be blessed, how there is nothing as holy as *Havaya*, (as written in *Likutei Torah*, in the second discourse entitled *Tze'ena Ure'ena*). And yet, this [meditation] is does not lead to the *ra'ash* of *Havaya*, since it involves only the *vov-hey*, or final two letters of His name, and not the first two (*yud-hey*). And also, the G-dliness that descends with the *vov* remains *makif* [beyond us, not internalized], which is what is meant by *kadosh vov* – transcendent holiness that descends.

Appendix III
Shiurei HaRav Chaim Shalom Deitsch on *K' Ha'avoda*

Introduction

The following is a series of *shiurim*, or "classes," given by Rav Chaim Shalom Deitsch שי' (Rosh Collel of the Tzemach Tzedek in the old city of Jerusalem) on the text of *Kuntres Ha'avoda*, during the years 2011-2012 and then again, 2018-2019. Together, the *shiurim* cover most of the text of *Kuntres Ha'avoda*, with the exception of the first and final chapters. The *shiurim* are available in audio and video on the website, http://video.chasidut.net/category/ The *shiurim* are available online in Hebrew and Yiddish, and the following transcriptions/translations are in abbreviated and concise form. In order to appreciate the importance of these *shiurim*, it is important to appreciate the role of a *mashpia* or "mentor" in general, in the Chassidic context:

In the early days of the Chasidic movement, during the era of the Baal Shem Tov (1698-1760) until the late 1790's, the written word played a minor role in the transmission of the movement. For the first seventy-eighty years at least, the movement initiated by the Baal Shem Tov (R' Yisrael Ba'al Shem) was transmitted only by the personality and teachings of its leaders, rather than by written principles that could be passed on from generation to generation. The Baal Shem Tov cultivated tens of *talmidim* ("students") and his successor, R' Dov Ber (the "Mezritcher Magid") attracted hundreds of *talmidim*, but their mode of teaching and transmission was via direct contact and verbal instruction with their disciples, rather than via written doctrine. Both leaders left behind *seforim* ("books" – in the case of the Baal Shem Tov they were written down by his followers), but nevertheless, their preferred method of transmission was via word of mouth and example.

This began to change toward the end of the 1700's, when the youngest *talmid* of the Magid, R' Shneur Zalman of Liadi (the "Alter Rebbe" or "Baal HaTanya"), committed the principles of the Chasidic movement to writing, with his famous masterpiece, <u>Likutei Amarim Tanya</u>. In the introduction to *Tanya*, R' Shneur Zalman writes that because of the number of Chasidim approaching him for spiritual advice, he could no longer receive all of them individually. Therefore, he sought to commit the principles of Chasidism to writing so that everyone who needs spiritual advice would be able to find it in his writings. Even so, he conceded that not everyone would be able to find the advice that they seek within Tanya, even though the advice is undoubtedly present. And therefore, the Alter Rebbe requested (in the introduction), that noone should "withhold sustenance" by failing to help another Jew looking for spiritual advice within Tanya. Quite the opposite, one who is in a position of knowledge and experience should assist those of less experience, and help them find their needed advice.

This injunction of the Alter Rebbe, not to "withhold sustenance" is probably the first official mention of what came to be called the *mashpia-mekabel*, or "mentor-student" relationship that is vital to the transmission of the Chasidic message. From this time on, the leaders of the movement acknowledged that they could not transmit the message alone, and yet the written word alone was also insufficient to convey the message to subsequent generations. What was needed was a combination of the written word to convey the concept, together with personal assistance of a mentor who had himself received the Chasidic tradition from a previous mentor or Rebbe, and who therefore knew how to translate the "book" concept into concrete behavior and conduct. Thus was born the *mashpia-mekabel* relationship, and with it the mode by which the Chasidic movement propagated itself from generation to generation.

During the first three generations of Chabad, as the Alter Rebbe's intellectual branch of the Chassidic movement came to be named, the *mashpia-mekabel* relationship took on the form of an accomplished Chasid, usually himself very close to the Rebbe, who accepted small groups of *bachurim*, or young unmarried men, to mentor. The famous early *mashpi'im* of Chabad – R' Hillel Paritcher, R' Pesach Molostofsky, R' Isaac Hummiler, R' Michele Potsker, among others – were all in this category of accomplished older Chasidim who accepted small groups of *bachurim* for introduction into the Chasidic way of life and *avodat Hashem*.

However, with the establishment of *Tomchei T'mimim* (the Chabad yeshiva) in 1897, under the tutelage of the fifth Lubavitcher Rebbe (the Rebbe Rashab, who not coincidentally wrote *Kuntres Ha'avoda*), a new concept of the *mashpia* emerged. The *mashpia* became an "in-house" mentor who was available and gave direction to all of the *bachurim* of the yeshiva. Rather than going to one of the well-known older Chasidim of the congregation, the young yeshiva students would go to the older Chasid who was the *mashpia* of the Yeshiva for guidance and direction in learning and in *avodat Hashem*. Thus was born the modern concept of the "in house" yeshiva *mashpia* that survives until this day. The "grandfather" of all these *mashpi'im* was R' Shmuel Gruenem Esterman, known simply as "Gruenem," who was a Chasid of the Rebbe Maharash (the fourth generation of Chabad) as well as of his son, the Rebbe Rashab. Other famous *mashpi'im* of the early days of *Tomchei Tmimim* included R' Shilam (R' Meshulam Yedidia Koratin, who was also the Rebbe Rashab's *chozer*),

Rav Chanoch Hendel Kugel, Rav Shmuel Betzalel Sheftel (the Rashbatz), R' Michael Beliner, R' Ze'ev Wolf Levitin, and R' Yaakov Baruch Karasik. The Previous Rebbe, R' Yoseph Yitzhak Schneerson, was the director of the Yeshiva.

In the days of the Bolshevik Revolution (1917-1923), Yeshivat *Tomchei Tmimim* was forced to move from Lubavitch and became headquartered in Rostov. As the situation in Russia worsened, the yeshiva was forced underground, and even before the Previous Rebbe (who took over upon his father's passing in 1920) emigrated to Poland in 1929, *Tomchei Tmimim* was re-established, first in Warsaw in 1921, and then later in 1935, in the suburb of Warsaw called Otvotsk. From the memoirs of R' Avraham Dov Hecht (*A"H*), we know that some 400 yeshiva students were studying in the Chabad yeshiva in Otvotsk in 1939, most of whom were lost in the holocaust. Some 100-150 students survived, 36 of them by making their way to Shanghai.

After the war, though, it was not the remnants of *Tomchei Tmimim* in Poland who led the next generation of teachers and *mashpi'im* in Chabad. Most of the notable Chassidic mentors, whether in the US after the war, or in Europe (France), or in Israel, came from among the Russian Chasidim, who had somehow managed to survive not only the Bolshevik Revolution and Stalinist regime, but also the onslaught of the Nazis into Russia and Ukriane during WWII. Not only did the Russian Chasidim keep Chabad alive in the Soviet Union but they also kept the candle of Judaism burning in that vale of tears. The following passage (translated from HaMashpia, R' Shlomo Chaim Kesselman, written by R' Yisrael Elfenbein, Page 48) describes the circumstances in which the Russian Chasidim found themselves during and after the war, and also happens to name those who became notable *mashpi'im* after the war:

> "The detectives of the NKVD arrived in Malhovka and came to the house of R' Zalman Kornitzer and asked him: "Are you Zalman Kornitzer?" And he answered, "No, I am Zalman Alpert." Nevertheless, they arrested him and took him to the jail of Malhovka. As he sat in jail, he heard someone reading a list, giving instructions to the police to arrest R' Shmuel Leib Paretischer, R' Shlomo Chaim Polotzker, R' Avraham Meier, and others. R' Zalman understood that they intended to arrest many of the Chabad community of Malchovka. He stood up and began to scream, "What do you want from me? I am not Zalman Kornitzer, I am Zalman Alpert! Leave me alone!" They allowed him to return to his house.

However, he ran immediately to the house of one of those who name was mentioned, and informed them they need to run away immediately, thus saving the lives of many of the Chasidim in the town. What had transpired was the following: The police arrested two young lads from among the Chasidim, and by using manipulative tactics, succeeded in getting them to mention the names of many of the Chassidim. But they mentioned them according to the manner in which they called themselves at the time – according to the city from which they came; "Kornitzer, Polotzker, Meirer, Particher."

The officers of the NKVD also sought R' Nisan Nemenov around the same time. R' Nisan immediately wrote a letter to the Previous Rebbe, in a secret manner (he utilized the letter of the alphabet after each letter that he intended to write, which for some reason was called the 'mezuzah script'). And this was its content: "The 'other side' caused much distress today, which is that yesterday from the location known as the GPO, they took two lads from off the street, held them overnight, and asked them about R' Shmuel ben Teme (Levitin), and about R' Avraham Drizen, and about R' Nisan Neminov, and about R' Shlomo Chaim Kesselman..."

As matters would turn out, R' Nisan Nemenov later became the *mashpia* of the *Tomchei Tmimim* in Brunoy (near Paris) after the war, R' Shmuel Levitin became the *mashpia* of *Tomchei Tmimim* in Crown Heights (New York) after the war, and R' Shlomo Chaim Kesselman became the *mashpia* of *Tomchei Tmimim* in Lod and Kfar Chabad after the war. These were the three largest and most important Chabad yeshivot after the war, and in each case, the *mashpia*, charged with transmitting the Chabad lifestyle to Chabad *talmidim*, came from the ranks of Russian Chasidim. (Major figures such as R' Mentlick A"H, Rosh Yeshiva of *Tomchei Tmimim* in Crown Hts, and R' Yoseph Wineberg A"H were products of the Chabad yeshivot in Poland, but by and large it was the Russian Chasidim who took on the role of *mashpia*).

R' Chaim Shalom Deitsch (שיחיה לשנים טובים וארוכים) was born in 1944 to an illustrious family in Jerusalem. His mother (Marat Miriam, OBM) was among the descendants of R' Moshe, third son of the Alter Rebbe. After R' Moshe went into hiding in Russia in order to avoid the authorities who sought to incarcerate him, his wife immigrated to Israel with their children in the early 1800's, and settled in Hebron. Rav Deitsch's mother A"H was a descendant of one of those children. His great grandfather on his father's side was descended from the R' Yoel Sirkus (author of the *Bach*, an important

17th century commentary on the *Tur Shulhan Aruch*). Originally from Chechoslavakia/Hungary, he arrived in Israel in the early 1900's, together with his unmarried children (two daughters and three sons). He was a wealthy man in Chechoslavakia/Hungary, but he foresaw a downturn in business, sold everything that he possessed and gave it to *tzedaka* ("so that it would remain of value"), and brought his family to Israel (the married children remained behind in Europe; some of them managed to escape the holocaust and relocate to America).

Rav Deitsch was born in Jerusalem and educated in the Eitz Chaim school in the old city (then located in the Hurva Shul just opposite the Tzemach Tzedek shul). Excelling in learning from an early age, he was sent to Ponevitz Yeshiva in Bnei Brak at age 14 and rapidly rose among the ranks of yeshiva students and became close to the Rosh Yeshiva at the time, R' Elazar Menachem Shach (A"H). While in Bnei Brak (where yeshivat Ponevitz is located), Rav Deitsch also came into contact with R' Shlomo Chaim Kesselman A'H (the mashpia at Kfar Chabad) and was attracted to his path of Chasidic *avodat Hashem* ("service of God"), in *hitbonenut* and Chasidic prayer. From his own home, R' Deitsch had always prayed *Nusach Ari,* which is the version of prayers utilized by Chasidim, and the Chasidic style, with its deep meditation and prayers as well as R' Shlomo Chaim's farbrengens, appealed to him. With the passage of time, R' Deitsch's heart became set on a Chasidic path, and at age 18, he decided to make the move to become a yeshiva student at Kfar Chabad. There he learned Torah and basked under the influence of R' Shlomo Chaim, who was the *mashpia* at the time. The move was traumatic for his fellow *talmidim* at Ponevitz as well as for the Rosh Yeshiva there (when asked about their response, R' Deitsch responded, "Don't ask"). Rav Deitsch learned in Kfar Chabad for only two years, from 1963 until 1965, when he married. But, even after his marriage he continued to travel from Jerusalem to Kfar Chabad for farbrengens and in order to maintain his connection with R' Shlomo Chaim.

After marriage, R' Deitsch was determined to learn Torah in the foremost Collel (house of study for married men who receive a small monthly stipend) of the time, located at Mossad HaRav Kook in Jerusalem. However, he was not immediately accepted there, and in the interim he was invited to join the newly formed Collel of R' Zalman Nehemiah Goldberg A"H [who passed away as these words were being written], son in law of R' Shlomo Zalman Auerback *ztz'l* (R' Deitsch himself is related to R' Auerbach through marriage – his sister married a son of R' Shlomo Zalman, A"H). R' Goldberg's collel was located in Har Zvi, in the neighborhood of Geula in Jerusalem, where the first chief Rabbi, R' Unterman *A"H* had also made his synagogue. R' Deitsch soon found that R' Goldberg's approach to learning Torah, which combined

Gemora with poskim and Shulhan Aruch, in an organic "whole," suited him well. It was this approach that he later took with him to become the Rosh Collel of the newly opened Tzemach Tzedek Collel in the old city, which was refurbished and opened to the public after the six day war in 1967.

In 1971, the Lubavitcher Rebbe let it be known that he wanted a Collel established in the Tzemach Tzedek Shul in Jerusalem's old city. At the time, the Tzemach Tzedek Shul was under the auspices of Collel Chabad, one of the largest welfare and charity organizations in the Jewish world. A committee of three men was established for the purpose of organizing the Collel: Rav Shlomo Yoseph Zevin (A"H), R' Shmuel Schneerson (A"H) and Rav Lazar Nanis (A"H). This committee also consulted with R' Deitsch (who at the time was both learning with R' Goldberg (A"H) and also teaching gemora to young bachurim in the yeshiva of Karlin), and the committee came up with the names of several candidates to appoint as Rosh Collel of the Tzemach Tzedek. For various reasons, none of the people suggested for the role could accept it, and the committee turned to R' Deitsch himself (who as an *avreich* still in his twenty's was not even thinking of the role for himself). When he pointed out that in his own opinion he was too young for the job, R' Zevin replied that his age was a *mum ovair* – a "passing blemish" and "deficiency" that would disappear with time. Thus in roughly 1971-1972 was born the Collel of the Tzemach Tzedek synagogue in the old city, with Rav Deitsch as the Rosh Collel.

At the time, R' Deitsch was also teaching gemora to young Karliner Chasidim, and he asked the Rebbe if he should relinquish his role with Karlin. The Karliner Chasidim were very pleased with R' Deitsch and did not want to see him leave; on the contrary they moved his gemora class from the morning to the afternoon so that R' Deitsch could continue with both jobs. The Rebbe cited a gemora about Gideon (Judges 6:13) who was appointed "even on the grain floor," and instructed R' Deitsch that, "Since you were appointed..." as Rosh Collel of the Tzemach Tzedek, he certainly should not give up that role, but that neither should he relinquish his role in the Karliner yeshiva. Rav Deitsch's connection with the Karliner Chasidim continues until this day, with at least once or twice a year that the Rav delivers a shiur or words of inspiration to the Karliner Chasidim, based upon their *sefer*, the *Beit Aharon* and from the *Shaloh* and other authorities.

Not long after the Tzemach Tzedek Collel was formed, it became difficult to find young married men to commit themselves to learning in the Collel. Even though the monthly stipend was relatively generous for the times ($400/month, higher than the average $250/month at other Collel's), nevertheless, housing was more expensive in Yerushalyim than elsewhere in the country, and not many Chabad *avreichim* could afford to live in Jerusalem. The administration of the Collel wrote to the Rebbe about this situation, and the Rebbe instructed the Collel to accept *avreichim* from other streams, outside of Chabad, and to teach them Chabad Chasidut as well. In this manner, quite a few Chasidic *avreichim* from outside of the Chabad educational system found their way into Chabad. In order to instruct them in the study and application of Chasidut, R' Deitsch sought to bring in other teachers (among them, R' Fitchie Ofen and R' Zelig Feldman *A"H*), while simultaneously searching for someone to take on the role on a permanent basis. As happened previously, it was difficult to find someone to take on the role in a fixed manner. Again, the administration wrote into the Rebbe, who answered (with an express letter, not at all common in those days, in the 1970's) that the administration should not bring anyone else in to teach in the Collel. Once more, it was R' Shlomo Yoseph Zevin *A"H* who interpreted for Rav Deitsch: "You are to be the teacher and *mashpia* in the Tzemach Tzedek." Since then, there has been a daily Tanya and Chasidut shiur in the Kolel, taught by Rav Chaim Shalom Deitsch יש״נ. Rav Deitsch teaches Tanya with the *pirushim* and commentary that he heard from R' Shlomo Chaim *A"H*, whom himself taught with the *pirushim* that he heard from R' Gruenum in the original Tomchei Tmimim in Lubavitch, so the tradition continues on…

[Note from the Translator/Commentator: I arrived in Jerusalem in late 1982 after two years of yeshiva study in in New York, another two years in Hebrew in Kfar Chabad and a year by the Rebbe in "770." I was immediately taken under wing by R' Chaim Shalom Deitsch, who made me feel at home not only in the Tzemach Tzedek shul but also in his home, where I regularly joined him and his family for Shabbes and Yomtov meals and occasionally even slept there. My initial goal in learning was to complete the Israeli Rabanut smicha program (*Rav Shechuna*), which I did over the next several years. But, R' Deitsch made it clear that the true goal of learning *lishmah* – "for the sake of the Torah" and for Hashem – lies not in the study of *halacha* alone, but in *iyun* ("learning in depth") to plumb the depths of the sayings of the sages of the Talmud and how they develop into the halachic decisions with which we run our Torah lives. Ultimately, R' Deitsch adopted the "holistic" approach of R' Zalman Nehemiah Goldberg *A"H*, which he applies to the studies of the *avreichim* in the Tzemach Tzedek Collel, with an emphasis on the *Shulhan Aruch Harav*, the "Alter Rebbe's Shulhan Aruch." At the same time, he is an original *chadshan*, who after exhaustive investigation of the material at hand, offers creative and enlightening solutions that enable the Collel students to understand the basic elements underlying Torah discussions. After a twenty-five year "detour" during which I acted as a voluntary *shaliach*, or "emissary" of the Rebbe in the old city, bringing in *olim chadashim* ("new immigrants") and introducing them to a life of Torah and mitzvoth (holy work which continues), I "circled back" to the Tzemach Tzedek Collel and R' Deitsch and now have the pleasure of learning with the *avreichim* in the Tzemach Tzedek shul under the leadership of R' Deitsch].

Note: All comments in brackets [ ] are from the translator/commentator Rav Deitsch on *Kuntres Ha'avoda*

Shiur 1), October 30, 2011

Ch 1 - One of four *Kuntresim* by the Rebbe Rashab, it contains very difficult matters (the four are *Kuntres U'Mayon, Kuntres Eitz Chaim, Kuntres Ha Tefila* and *Kuntes Ha'avoda*). The Rav said that just last night, R' Zalman Gopin farbrenged (made a Chassidic "get together") and said there are 3 types of *nisyonut* ("tests"): 1) Tests involving matters that are not possible, 2) Tests involving matters that are unwanted, and 3) Tests regarding matters that are not needed (in Yiddish: *Ir ken nisht, Ir vil nisht, Ir darf nisht*).

In Russia, the tests that Jews faced were regarding matters considered "impossible" (fulfillment of Torah and mitzvoth). Today, all is possible, but there are tests regarding whether or not we "want" (to fulfill Torah and mitzvoth to their fullest). But the most difficult tests are regarding matters that we think we "don't need." This is an issue in the head (psychological), for example, "Today we need *hitbonenut*?" ("Do we really need to practice meditation")? Some people think that it is not necessary to "meditate", but that's not the case (In *Kuntres Eitz Chaim* the Rashab writes at length about how much we need *p'nimiyut* and *Chasidut*).

Here in *Kuntres Ha'avoda*, there are sections that are very difficult; for example, the first chapter includes a lot of parentheses and discusses very subtle topics. If we begin our study of *K'Avoda* with these high spiritual levels (*madreigot*), we might very quickly give up ("come to *yiush*"), so it is better to save the material contained in the parentheses until after finishing the whole *Kuntres*. And throughout the *K' Avoda* there are a lot of *sograyim* ("parentheses"), each describing another detail, etc...Theoretically then, it is better to study the parentheses the second time around, not the first time. So, we'll begin by skipping the large parentheses, that are three pages long...

There are two goals of prayer and meditation: 1) To cleave our soul to God, and 2) To refine and transform the character traits of our animal soul. Both occur via *avoda* ("work" on ourselves). The textual sources for Chassidic *avoda* are explained in *Kuntres Eitz Chaim* (which cites and explains the sources of *avoda* as they appear in Kaballah and Zohar). *Kuntres Ha'avoda* is about how to undertake the path and process of *avoda*, according to Chasidut. *Ahava* ("Love of God") is for the purpose of cleaving our soul to HIm. *Nishmeta d'nishmeta* (the highest expression of the soul) is the peak of *avoda*. It occurs during the highest point of prayer, during the *Shemonah Esreh*, but there is much effort necessary to achieve it prior to the *shemonah esreh*. The effort occurs during *psukei de'zimra* ("songs" and verses that we recite at the beginning of our prayers), *birchot Kriat Shema* ("Blessings preceding" the *Kriat Shema*), and the *Kriat Shema* ("recital" of the *Shema*) itself. The attitude of a Jew during *Shemonah esreh* should be as an *avdei kamei marei* ("a servant standing before his Master") – a servant before his King. The connection to God that we create during payer is a conscious connection – if we don't feel it, then our prayer is not considered *tefila*. Torah and mitzvoth may be fulfilled even without conscious awareness (the halachic principle of *mitzvoth tzrichot kavana* ("commandments demand conscious awareness") comes down to a *machloket* (a "matter of contention" among halachic decisors), but *tefila* ("prayer") without *kavana* ("awareness, intention") is not *tefila*. The parentheses goes into details about how this awareness "works" on the various soul levels of *nefesh, ruach, neshama* and each *olam* ("world") to which the soul levels correspond. There is *pninut* ("inner dimensions of awareness") and *chitzoniyut hamochin* ("standard, external awareness"). This part of the explanation in parentheses concludes on page 10 of the Hebrew *K'Avoda*, Page 32 of the translation). Look on page 7 (Page 17 in the translation) for the level of *neshama*, "(The sign of this occurring is that we completely lose awareness…")…

Page 10 (Page 32 of the translation) – this is what *tefila* is, "pouring out the soul," *shfichut hanefesh*. *Teshuka*, "desire" to be included like flames of fire. Without *teshuka*, there is no *tefila*. "Mitzvoth need *kavana*, and that's *tefila*."

Page 33 in the translation: "The second aspect of prayer is *birur* ("purification") and *zichuch* ("refinement") of the *nefesh habahema* ("animal soul"). The source for this aspect of prayer is the comparison to a *korban* ("offering" or "sacrifice"), and the *korban* is burned. *Raza d'kurbana olah ad raza d'ain sof* – ("The secret of the *korban* is the secret of His infinite light Above" – Zohar). *Kavana* applies mostly to the first goal, of cleaving the soul to Hashem, whereas the words of *tefila* ("speech") are for the purpose of refining the animal soul, *zichuch*. And it works on the animal soul *davka* ("only") if there is *ahavah* ("love") within the *otiot* ("letters," as we pray).

Shiur 2, October 31, 2011,

Ch 2 - There is no *ahava* ("love of God") without *yirah* ("fear of God"). The Rebbe explains that there can be *ahava* alone, but then it is without *kedusha* ("holiness"). The "world" knows that love of God is important, but they are unaware of the benefit of fear of God. Maharal of Prague brings from a Gemora (Talmud, second chapter of Berachot): *Vehaya emunatecha hoshen yeshuot…chochma v'da'at* – six words corresponding to the six orders of *Mishnayot*. The Gemora concludes that *yirah* ("fear") is necessary and Maharal explains as does Chasidut, that with *yirah* is associated more *bitul* ("self nullification")…and *yirah* is the *ikar* (main "pillar") of *avoda* ("Godly service") and it's the beginning of *avoda*. Bottom line is that what is necessary for everyone is to develop *yirat chait* ("fear of sin").

- Once R' Deitsch heard from his father that Chasidim wouldn't look out the window or the *mirpeset stam* ("would not look from the balcony without reason") because "who knows what you might see"? If I look out the window, I open myself to whatever "they" might want to show me. It is permissible to open up to see "whose there," but it is not permissible to "wait for something/someone" to just pitch up. The very fact that a Jew is "open" (to stimulus) is not a good thing, there has to be an *ohl* ("yoke") on him. Has to be *mugdar* ("fenced") because eyesight is our main source of enjoyment.

- This was the *ikar* ("main") claim against the *mahn* that descended in the desert: That there was no *taiva* ("temptation, lust") in looking at it.

- In the old city (where the *Tzemach Tzedek* synagogue and Collel is located and where the Rav is the Rosh Collel), it's impossible to raise your eyes at all, *rachmana l'tzlan…ayom v'norah* ("God forbid..it's awful and terrible") here in the old city this summer, *lo aleinu* to raise the eyes [this was in 2011 but it is true of every year].

- R' Shlomo Chaim (the Rav's *mashpial*/"mentor" in Kfar Chabad when he learned there as a yeshiva student from 1963-5 and afterward as well) once said, "Chasidut is an *atzmusdik inyan* ("essential matter"), if you don't use it properly it will "break out in not good places, if we're not careful…"

- *Maaseh sh'hay*a ("story that once occurred")… There was a Jew who learned Chasidut but had a *nefila ruhani* (suffered a spiritual descent), and he went to the Belzer Rav to complain about his *matzav ruhani* ("spiritual status")…the Belzer Rav, who it seems already knew of this man's situation, told him to stop learning Chasidut, and rebuked him. R' Shlomo Chaim said about this that since Chasidut is an *atzmiyus inyan* ("essential matter"), one who learns it and doesn't use it properly for *avodat Hashem* ("serving God), "It comes out from bad places" [meaning it causes *chatat neurim*, "noctournal emission"]... also one who just starts to *daven b'avodah* ("pray at length") may find that his *yetzer harah* ("evil inclination") is stronger, but if so, he should ignore it, just keep doing what he's doing...and that's the *diyuk* here in the word "*adaraba...*" – "quite the opposite."

- Good story – the Sadigura Rav would go on a walk, and he went with a *mesharet* ("assistant") on the Ruzhnier Rebbe's *yahrtzeit* (the Sadigura dynasty was descended from the Ruzhiner Rebbe), who as they were walking, bumped into a pillar, and said, "Oy, I thought that was a woman." The Sadigura Rav said to him, "I try to train you to think that a woman is a pillar ("of the house" – *ikar habayit*), and you think that the pillar is a woman?!"

- *Teshuva* ("response") from the *Tzemach Tzedek*, brought by R' Shlomo Chaim...an event occurred to someone on erev Yom Kippur about which it is written that, "If such an event occurs, one should worry about it for the entire year." What the event was is unknown, but the *Tzemach Tzedek* answered him (based on the Alter Rebbe and on *ziknei* Chasidim ("older Chasidim") that this event is a matter of concern only for those who are on a high spiritual level, who do not suffer from *machshavot zarot* ("foreign thoughts"), but if you have *machshavot zarot* then it doesn't apply to you. One might argue though, that since Erev Yom Kippur is so holy, most people don't suffer from "foreign thoughts" in any case. Even so, though, he certainly experienced tensions that could cause him to make mistakes and transgress, and it's actually possible that those fears that he experienced could causes one to sin, as written by the *tevi'im* ("scientists") that *pachad* ("fear, nervousness") can give rise to the same result as the sin itself.

- A Hungarian Rav ("Yomtov" something) wrote *seforim* ("books") about *mikvaot*, and the Rebbe wrote to him that once there were things [possibly a reference to single women going to the mikveh] going on in certain places that "you just didn't talk about it." But now since those things are going on everywhere and it's totally open, so now it is obligatory to talk about it. Comes out that these are matters that demand *zehirut* ("extra care, discretion") whether to talk or not to talk about it...Someone suggested that's the meaning of *gesher tzar me'od* – the "very narrow bridge."

- R' Deitsch once saw R' Mendel Futerfas speak with an elderly woman, with whom it was not *shayach* ("it was highly unlikely") at all that anyone would have *machshavot* ("thoughts") or *hirhurim* ("stray ideas")…on the corner of Kingston and Union – all the time his eyes were down. It's not easy to speak to someone without looking, but that was the *minhag* ("custom") by Chasidim.

- R' Deitsch once heard someone say that in the car his eyes were always down not because he's a *tzaddik* but because just wants "rest."

Shiur 3, Nov 1, 2011 (Perek 2, part 2)

One has to be "closed" to surrounding impulses, not like a car that is *panui l'hovala* ("available for taking on" passengers or baggage), but like a vehicle that is *tafus* ("occupied"). That's *kabalat ohl* ("accepting the yoke"), he's not "open to everything" – *hagadara b'chushim* ("fenced-in senses"). Must always and constantly check and examine whether or not to be open. That's *yirat chet* ("fear of sin"). In *reiah* – "vision" – there is a lot of *ta'anug* ("enjoyment"), so looking at the wrong things is very much *pogeah b'nafsho* ("hurts his soul"). Some people are not aroused, but that's because the person is attached to the object *b'etzem*, "in essence," it's the man himself. So in his *etzem* ("essence"), he could be *kashur* ("connected") with *klipah* ("negative forces"), even if it doesn't not affect him in action, still it affects him deeply in his soul. And it's bound to come out in the end, because the essence has to emerge at some point.

- *Sippur Hasidim* ("Chassidic story") about a wealthy man who used to eat some duck every morning that was very tasty. One morning he invited in a poor man, who was so excited over the food that he started drooling. The Chasidim began to think, who is the greater *ba'al taiva* ("lustful person")? The wealthy man sat relaxed so it seemed that the poor man was the *ba'al taiva* (was "coarser") but in truth the wealthy man ate this food every day, so perhaps he's the bigger *ba'al taiva* (even tho he acted "relaxed")? The Chasidim decided the wealthy man is the bigger *ba'al taiva* since he himself was one big "piece of duck." How prove this? Try taking the duck away and see who gets more excited. (Obviously the poor man wouldn't get nervous cause he never ate it anyway, it was the wealthy man who would get excited over his lack of duck). Thus, R' Shlomo Chaim said that the test is in the "negative" (*shlilah*) when you take the *taiva* ("lustful object") away from him…the test whether it comes from the *etzem* ("essence" of the person) is what happens with the *shlilah* (when you negate, take the lust away)…support from this comes from R' Zelig Feldman (*alov hashalom*) who used to review what the Rashab said, "what is the difference between *mesirash nefesh* ("self sacrifice") of a Jew and that of a non-Jew?" Non-Jews are also ready to die for a cause (those blowing themselves up as "suicide bombers" are not going on *mesiras nefesh*, they are promised something, they are fooled, thinking they'll get all kinds of *taivot* in gan eden, so they blow themselves up over the *taivot* not because of a cause). The Rebbe Rashab mentioned three distinctions, but R' Deitsch remembered only two of them 1) by a non-Jew it's only the more distinguished kinds of people who are ready to die for an ideal, 2) a non-Jew approaches it from a positive perspective – he is ready to die for an idea, but a Jew from a negative perspective – he is in no way able to do the "opposite" of what Hashem wants, such as to serve *avoda zarah*. He has to die in order to avoid idol woship? Okay, but it's not because he wants to die…so the test of whether or not *etzem* ("essence" of the person) is involved is in the *shlila*, the negative. With our conscious abilities, we think, "Why do I want"? With the *etzem*, the *heshbon* is, "This, I don't want, this I cannot do *b'shum ofen*."

- Story from R' Shlomo Chaim that he told R' Deitsch after his *hatuna* ("wedding") and young married men need to know…once someone went to the Rebbe Rashab and complained that his wife is not the way he wants her to be. The Rashab answered him, the *ba'al* ("the husband") is *chochma*, the wife is *bina*. *Chochma* is the *yud*, the first letter of God's name, which has the form of a *nekuda* ("point"), while the *hey* represents its *hitpashtut* –its expansion in all directions. In the *yud* we cannot detect a problem, but if it is present, it comes into expression in the *hey*. So what you say is a problem by the wife is really a problem in the husband, the *yud*, but there it isn't visible.

- Another story with the Mitteler Rebbe (he didn't usually travel, like the Magid of Mezritsch, but sometimes the Mitteler Rebbe did travel). While on the *derech* ("road"), he received Chasidim and said *maamorim* (Chassidic discourses)…in the middle of one *yechidut* ("private audience"), he suddenly removed himself, closed himself in a room, and there the Chasidim could hear him saying psalms while crying. Only after several days, during which he fasted and prayed, and he took no one in *yechidut,* and travelled back to Lubavitch, did it become known what happened: Someone went into the Rebbe and asked for a *tikun* ("rectification") for a certain sin. What sin is not known, but it's known that the Rebbeim, in order to find a *tikun* for someone, had to find the sin within themselves, even if in the most refined manner possible. Yet this sin he couldn't find within himself…*yesh lomar* ("some say") that maybe this is the reason… when one searches and can't find it within, perhaps it's in the *etzem*, in the very essence of the person. That's what brought the Mitteler Rebbe such *agmut nefesh* ("agony"), but in the end he was okay, but he did actually find the sin in himself (*b'dakut shb'dakut*, in the most refined possible manner). The sin was that if he said Chasidut and it had no effect on the Chasidim, this was the sin that he found within himself that could be a *tikun* for that Chasid who came to him.

- Rav Deitsch spoke about someone who went off the *derech*, and they spoke about a *hidduch* ("marriage match") for him, but of course the father of the girl did not want his daughter to meet him. They took the person to someone to test him, and found that he had *emunah* ("faith"). An expert examined him and found that in essence he was good, had *emunah* and that he was outwardly off the *derech* was not his *etzem* and that ultimately, "it will be good." In fact, someone said that in the end, "he will be better (more *yirat shamayim*) than her." And that's what happened. So you see that one can be negative on the outside but really fine on the inside, and the expert checked that out by examining his *emunah*.

"What *tzaddikim* see elevates them…" (Esther Rabba 7:10) "to gaze on the glory of the King." Clinging of the soul to the essence of *taanug, ohr ein sof*… the opposite of the *klipah* which pulls the person down.

Shiur 4, Nov 2, 2011 - K' Avoda Ch 2

1) *Yirat H'* ("fear of God") is necessary 2). It's the basis of *Ahava* ("divine love") as well. First, like in *parnassa* ("income," making a living) you have to convince the person that it's necessary, and then only afterward do we consider HOW. Next chapter (3) we'll consider how…at a minimum, *yirah* is *yirat chet* ("fear of sin," not because of fear of punishment, but because it's against God and we don't want to do anything against His will). So, at a minimum, we don't want to act against Hashem. Now this doesn't mean only that we won't do anything *neged* ("against") but also that we are prepared and ready, *mugdar* ("fenced off") to avoid coming into contact with any negative stimulus. This is most important in *re'iyah*, "vision." Even

before we come to the questionable situation, we must think – this is called *hagdara* – "fencing ourself off." For example, there are people whom, if informed, will not eat foods that are unhealthy. But you have people who don't wait until they are told, they investigate ahead of time by themselves. They are "careful" even before entering the situation, and so it should be regarding *yirat Hashem* ("fear of God"). A person must ask, "Is this good to do? Do I need to do it, do I need not avoid it?"

- R' Shlomo Chaim used to employ a comparison of someone knocking on the door. The custom is to ask, "Who is it"? If the guest outside said, "Open and I'll tell you,"

  of course you're not going to open until you know. That's called that the "house is *mugdar*," fenced, guarded. Something like this must take place in *avodat Hashem* – you don't let in the *yetzer harah* and then try to push him out. It has to request permission to come in – this is called *mugdar b'chushim*.

- Something like this happened in Hevron, R' Deitsch said his grandmother was from Hebron and pointed to someone else [R' Dovid Boaz, or perhaps R' Shalom David Segal?] and said – "his father was born in Hebron" – the Arabs knew the Jews very well, worked with them up close in their houses. They would knock on the doors as if "friends." Very disturbing story about a doctor, gynecologist, went to examine an Arab woman who was complaining she didn't feel well – they immediately killed him (this must have been 1929). Also here in Jerusalem, there were *hafraot* ("disturbances") at the same time. Back to *yirah* – the "fence, the *sayag*," is the *yirah*. If one says, "Let's see," it means he has no *pachad*. *Pachad* – "fear" – means that he has a thought or suspicion about the matter. If someone is afraid of poison for example, he tries to be aware of it before it can damage him. This is because the whole *taanug* is in *reiya*, in "vision." The difficulty is only at the beginning and then once a person is used to it, it's not difficult to avoid such situations.

- Once upon a time, Chasidim used to be careful not to look out the window...why? R' Deitsch said his father used to say about his grandfather that he would avoid looking, because they didn't know what they might see. Do you know for sure who will pass by the window? You should look only in places that you know what you will see. Before you go do something, make sure it's okay. The Rav also mentioned the sefer, *Derech Haim* of the Mitteler Rebbe – if a person is in a status and *matzav* ("situation") of true *yirah* (the soul situation of *hagdarat hachushim*), the *klipot* (negative forces opposed to holiness) do not approach him. The Rav mentioned how he saw R' Mendel Futerfas, as much as he was involved in the world, when he spoke with a woman, his eyes were down.

- R' Deitsch told a story about a *Baal Teshuva* who went out on many *shidduchim*, was looking for all the best qualities, finally found one and decided she was the right one, wanted to get R' Deitsh's opinion, Rav Deitsch was thinking, "Who am I, I'm supposed to look at someone else's *callah* ("potential wife")?" So he decided he would go downstairs, keeping his eyes on the ground and not look. He thought to himself, "This won't be good for the *chatan* (the *Baal Teshuva*), the woman will think, what a fanatical rabbi he is, he won't look at her." So he goes down, eyes looking at the ground, says 'Hello,' and goes back upstairs. Next day the *chatan* comes to R' Deitsch and says, "Listen, my *callah* says that she wants only you to be *mesader*

  Kiddushin ("to officiate at the wedding"). Rav Deitsch says, "I went nuts."

- In the end, everyone knows the truth...one of the guys asked, "When I get on the plane in Rio De Janeiro, how am I supposed to get on the plane with eyes closed?" R" Deitsch said that when Chasidim were in the world they were very *makpid* ("careful") not to go with *blitut* – not to "stand out," to avoid making the world notice that they were *mugdar*...he told a story of a *Baal Teshuva* who worked in the same place with women that he worked in before he did *teshuva* and he asked the Rav he very much wanted to control his urges but found it difficult. The Rav told him, exactly as it says here in the *sefer*, you have to control your eyes...no choice.

- R' Eliyahu Hadad mentioned the Rav's brother, R' Moshe, who told him that he was going to buy glasses (he was already an older man), but he was going to buy glasses that were five or six times less powerful than what he needed. "The main thing I'll be able to walk." One of the guys suggesting getting sunglasses, the Rav agreed and said if someone comments, tell them, "It's for health reasons. Everyone accepts that as a good reason. You mean 'health of the soul,' they'll understand bodily health..."

- One rabbi who used to teach women asked R' Yoel Kahan if the role was appropriate for him. R' Yoel told him to take off his glasses. It was quite recognizable when he did that…and even though before the shiur he was supposed to read off a list of the girls in the class, he gave it to one of the girls to do, and his entire career, he did not get to know even one of the girls in the class. The feedback from the class was that actually all of the girls respected him because of that. It is written in Chasidut that also the *klippot* ("negative forces") know who is weak in this matter, and who is strong. Also, the Rebbe would walk with a newspaper in front of his eyes when in Paris before he became the Rebbe…it turned out the paper was from several months previously. There's a witness [R' Soloveitchik?] that under the textbook in class, the Rebbe would be learning Gemora. There's a witness that every day the Rebbe would walk on the beach and not raise his eyes. There are different kinds of people, some with more lust some with less but the *eitzah* ("advice") is to guard the eyes, and people do respect that.

Regarding hearing as well, we have to be *mugdar* ("fenced in"). Need to mention here that so far we spoke only about men who don't look. But the wife of one who does not look, once she knows how he looks at nobody but her, sees this is very okay and *beseder*…a *shaliach* (Chabad emissary) once arrived to Jerusalem from Russia together with the governer of his area; Lev Leviov brought them with a very distinguished committee of people to Israel, and the *shaliach* and his wife came along. There was a get-together and the governor also went to shake hands with the *shaliach's* wife. Sounds "dangerous"? Afterward the governor was heard saying to his wife, "She (the *shaliach's* wife) won't touch anybody."

Shiur 5, Nov 3, 2011 K' Avoda, page 13 (Ch 2)

Mugdar ("fenced in" senses) is the opposite of "open," *mugdar* means that you have to knock in order to "come in" (and so a person shouldn't be open to visual or audio stimuli from the outside, the stimuli should need "permission" in order to "enter"). The Mitteler Rebbe in *Derech Chaim* mentions the Gemora (also mentioned later in *K'Avoda*), that tells us that in *hurvas* ("ruins" of buildings) there are evil spirits. At that time, the "spirits" could even do physical damage to a person, now it seems only spiritual, but a *hurva* is defined by that fact that that they (the "evil spirits") are in charge. Spiritually, same thing applies… if one acts as if there is no one in charge, "come in, go out, come and go as you wish, house without a door or lock"…this situation "invites" all the *klipot* to enter. The Mitteler Rebbe says that the opposite situation is *kaballat ohl malchut shamayim* ("acceptance of the yoke of Heaven"). Someone wrote into the *shiur* via internet in the name of R' Shlomo Zarchi (not known in whose name) that the main intention of the Rebbe Rashab in writing the *K'Avoda* was to establish *hagdara* in the sense of sight, that was his main intention. R" Deitsch already heard that from R' Fitchie Ofen...like in Tanya, *K'Avoda* first establishes the goal – *ahavat Hashem* ("love of God") and *yirat Hashem* ("fear of God") – and then tells us how to get there.

- Once in a Rosh Hashana discourse in *Likutei Torah*, we learned that *teshvua* means return "to your house," and therefore you must know where your house is, where is the "house of a Jew" – it's in the verse *Shema Yisrael* – the discourse establishes that *Shema* is the "house" – once you know where your house is, so go back to it. Also here in *K'Avoda*, you must know where your house is – it's *yirat Hashem* ("fear of God")...The opposite of *kabbalat ohl* ("accepting the yoke") is *prikat ohl* ("throwing of the yoke") – which is what happens when the person goes with *shrirut libo* ("follows the inclination of his heart") – see *Targum* (Aramaic translation) of the verse (Deut 29:18) in parshat *Nitzavim*. The Targum is *hirhur libi* ("thoughts of the heart") – but Rashi explains *b'marit libi* – "visions of the heart" - something that the heart "sees," having to do with vision.

- The Mitteler Rebbe says that *ta'avot* ("lusts") are one matter, but even worse is "wanting" or "searching" for *taavot*. The Mitteler Rebbe calls this *omek rah* ("depth of evil"), and it is *prikat ohl* ("throwing off the yoke"). And *lav davka* ("not necessarily") doing the *taava b'poel* ("actually doing the deed") but *etzem inyan* ("the very fact") that he is "open" to it. Once R' Deitsch saw in *Yaarot Dvash* (R' Yonasan Eybeshitz) on the verse, *V'haElokim asah sh'yiru m'lefanav...* – "God created the world in a manner that man should fear Him" – *Ya'arot Dvash* says that God established fear of God as an integral part of nature, that fear of God is built into nature. *Yirat Shamayim*, "Fear of Hashem," is embedded into the creation itself. A proof is that, for example, man has much more fear of God than he has of for example, a *mishpat*, a "court case." Someone afraid of a court case can become sick from that...and why? One who has *yirat shamayim* has much more fear...but the reason is that one afraid of a *mishpat* is not natural, it's a sickness, while *yirat Shamayim* is a natural phenomena. *Yirat Shamayim* was instilled in creation by God, it is natural.

- Rav Deitsch once saw in Dr. Spock about raising a child that a parent who gives a child too many choices, destroys the child, the child is waiting to be told – instead of "what do you want to eat," and offering five or six options, the child wants to be told – he may oppose, but that's part of the game, he wants to be told and then to oppose it. The point is that fear and the desire to be told is part of the natural makeup of the child. By Bar Mitzvah, the child accepts *ohl mitzvoth* (the "yoke of mitzvoth"), but the *ohl* is *besimcha,* with happiness. With children, the parents sometimes expect something from one child that they don't demand from another, and then the child complains, "Why don't you criticize him, why only me." The mature response is that each child is different, and the demands from one child don't have to be the same as the demands from another child.

- R' Deitsch once heard, not from R' Shlomo Chaim, but nonetheless it came from him, that the Rebbe Rashab said, "I invest much more time in bringing those who are *marei levana* (loosely translated, "naturally happy and positive people") to *avodat Hashem* ("divine service")... even though there was much more success to be had by investing in the *marei shechora* (those who are naturally inclined to discipline and asceticism), since they are anyway more inclined to *avodat Hashem* (they are more inclined to discipline and being strict with themselves)...because if he is able to bring a *morah levana* into *avoda*, the result is *gevaldig* ("very special")...[*marei levana* are those who are more naturally happy, positive, outgoing, so to rope them into *avodat Hashem* which involves *hagdara* of the *chushim*, is more difficult, but the results are greater. *Marei shechora* are more introverted, less positive, easier to draw them into *hagdarat hachushim*...]. A *Marei levana* is a "*vilder*" – ("wild") – mischievous, they are the ones with more talents and abilities. R' Deitsch didn't hear any explanation of this statement of the Rashab.

- The phrase *pogem b'nafsho* (one who "makes a blemish on his soul") occurs in *Derech Chaim* of the Mittler Rebbe as well...the two phrases, *neged ratzon Hashem*, and *pogem b'nafsho* – are in both *seforim* (*Derech Chaim* and in *K'Avoda*). At first glance, *shpitz Chabad* (those who come from Chabad families and consider themselves "close" to the Rebbe) will tell you, *kabalat ohl* ("acceptance of the yoke") means only to think "about *HaKadosh Baruch Hu*." The fact that with an *aveirah* ("sin, transgression"), you are *pogem b'nefesh* (you "make a blemish on your soul") isn't associated with *kabalat ohl*; rather, it is associated with *avoda* according to reason and logic (the reasoning being that a person doesn't need *kabalat ohl* to figure that he shouldn't do an *aveirah* – it's logical that the transgression has a negative effect on him...). Nevertheless, these are concepts that are repeated in both *Derech Chaim* and in *K'Avoda*. In *Derech Chaim*, one who has *kabalat ohl*, has a better developed *chush hahargasha* – his ability to "feel" – is more developed, he can "feel" and "sense matters" better than one who has no *kabalat ohl*. For example, a good wine expert has well developed sense of taste. The spiritual sense of "feeling" – *chush hahergesh* – is associated with *kabalat ohl*. The opposite, says the Mitteler Rebbe, is *afeila* – darkness, and of *afeila* there are two types: one who does not know into what *aveira* he fell, and one who does not even know that he fell into an *aveira*… this is something that we see clearly…the biggest *tzaddikim* were all very sensitive, even down to the smallest matters…

Shiur 7, Nov 6, 2011

There has to be *hagdara* ("limiting, fencing in") regarding our thoughts as well, in order to avoid *machshavot zarot* ("foreign," or "stray" thoughts). There are two stages to this: 1) that one may have *m"z*, and 2) that one may lead himself to *m"z*…when one gazes and looks at things that lead to *m"z*, this is the 2nd stage. Ultimately the "cure" is to change the *ratzon* and the *midot*, which is what gets to the *shoresh* ("root") of the problem. The proof is that when we work on ourselves, we won't experience *m"z* at all, and when we let up and fail to work on ourselves, the *midot* that bother us return. It emerges that the *m"z* are symptoms…and the only way to change the *midot* ("character traits") that are the basis of the *m"z*, is via *ahava* ("love"); via *yirah* ("fear") won't help. Thought is a consequence of our *midot*, so unlike speech during which we can just close our mouths, how can we change the *midot* that provide the impetus for *m"z*?

- R' Shlomo Chaim once said to a certain *bachur* (yeshiva student) who today is one of the most important Chabad personalities: At the time, this *bachur* didn't so much hold from *avoda*, he was more into *kabalat ohl* ("acceptance of the yoke") and not so much into *avoda* (prayer and meditation) and *hitbonenut* (now he thinks differently), but then, he wasn't so *mekabel* ("accepting") from R' Shlomo Chaim. So, in farbrengen, R' Shlomo Chaim told him, "Anyway you have have a war…but why fight against *hirhurim ra'im* ("negative thoughts") when you can do *avoda* ("divine service") with *hitbonenut* ("meditation") and automatically you won't have *m"z*…" R' Shlomo Chaim wrote to the Rebbe…he spoke not only this with the *bachur*, but spoke with him like one on one in the midst of the farbrengen. R' Deitsch said that R' Shlomo Chaim was *mesugal* ("able") to work on one person in a farbrengen *yechidani* ("individually") and sometimes one farbrengen would be enough to transform the *bachur* from one extreme to another. So in this case he was anyway an *ehrliche bachur* ("refined student"), he just wasn't into *avodat hatefila* and *hitbonenut*, but he did push away *m"z*, so R" Shlomo Chaim's message was "why fight with the *yetzer harah* on his field? Drag him to another field and there you'll be able to defeat him." Stop fighting with the *m"z* themselves and shine some light via *avodat hitbonenut* and *tefila*. *Avodat Hatefila* "softens" the *midot* so that they no longer produce *m"z*. (Which doesn't guarantee that afterward the person won't have *m"z*, if he wants, after *tefila* he can be a *ba'al taiva*, etc…). So basically R' Shlomo Chaim said, "Anyway you'll have to fight, so fight now, and save yourself all the later fights…"

- R' Deitsch told story of someone suffering from high blood pressure, R' Deitsch told him, "There are things you can do, eat differently, etc…the guy said, "I have no patience for that, I eat what I want and take a pill…" Same idea, whether or not you like, there's a war… pills are also a problem, they have side effects that can come into expression sometimes only thirty years later, so why not just change your nutrition? Eat healthy things…"Want to tell you something… statistically, many *Baalei Teshuvas*, their first stage of *teshuva* was when they ate better and more healthy…became healthy, they weren't *hefker*, were *mugdar* in nutrition. Also, nutrition orientation means that you're thinking about the future, not merely about the present that something is "tasty" at this moment, but you're thinking about how it will affect you in the future. Comparable to Yiddishkeit in which you sacrifice something of the present in order to be good with the future. If one gives up something tasty of the present in order to be healthy in the future, that is giving up the present and living in the future. This is a *yesod* ("foundation") of Yiddishkeit, which is not to look at the present [alone]. This is *nogeah b'gashmiyut* ("has influence on our physical life") as well, not only in *ruchniyut* ("spiritual life").

- Story of someone who is alive now, but nevertheless the story is *l'ilui nafsho*…R' Deitsch knows someone who wanted to contribute to Ponevitz yeshiva so that the entire physical structure will be made out of marble, both above and below, both above and also the dining room. The Rebetzin of the Ponevitzer Rav (Rav Kahanamen) was a special lady, she asked him, "Why not give the money now, you'll be able to see the results of your donation? You'll see the marble…" (he had wanted to leave it as a contribution in his will). He was persuaded…and gave the money and saw the marble…

- Rav Deitsch now knows someone who his wife "threw him out of the house." Why? Because he's was looking for others...one wasn't enough...he remarried and in the end, he threw her out because she said, "Why is one enough for you but for me, two is forbidden?" [R' Deitsch didn't want to say outright what her claim was but apparently he wanted another wife and she complained about it so he divorced her]. Once he came to the shiur, thought maybe he would find a solution, but nothing developed, meantime he sat in jail, he had children from both marriages...). Rav Deitsch sat with him in his store, they spoke, and it came out that he would "surf the web" [meaning he would find pornography], and when R' Deitsch heard that, he said, "oy, oy, oy" and that's what brought the problems cause he couldn't control himself... when that happens it drags all the problems with it. He's now around 80 years old...and R' Deitsch's point was that in the end, we have to tolerate difficulty (also in *gashmiyut*) in any case, so why not encounter it now, in the beginning? Why wait til later? If one doesn't control himself, in the end, he suffers *b'gasmiyut* as well as *ruhniyut*. You do have people for whom the present is more influential and they suffer later...and this is a constant battle, is doesn't stop ("the only reason that older men don't sleep in is because they have to get up for the *sherutim*, so anyway they just stay up...").

- Wrap-up: In order to avoid *m"z*, it's necessary to get involved in polishing the *midot*. So if so, how does *hagdarat hachushim* lead to *yirah*? It's true that *m"z* are dependent upon *midot*, and by the *beinoni*, we never completely transform the *midot*...

Shiur 8, Nov 7, 2011

Still on the topic of *yirat haShem, yirat Cheit* (not fear of punishment but fear of *aveira* ("sin"), of going against the *ratzon Hashem* ("will of God"), which mainly results in *hagdarat hachushim*. Not enough to be opposed to going against *ratzon Hashem*, we have to actively guard against it. Some people when you ask them to do something, will immediately get on board and do it, others will say, "Let me think about it." So we have to actively monitor our *chushim* ("senses"), not to remain in a status of, "Let me think about it," but rather, "Let's do it." We cannot lose our *yishuv hada'at*...("calm settled thinking").

- R' Deitsch heard a story from the Amshinover, whose hours of davening are entirely different and at odd hours, that he never loses his *yishuv hadaat*...when we're under pressure, we lose it, but not him. His wife had to give birth and doctors said she may need an operation and they need his permission. He asked how much time is there before a decision is necessary, they told him, "half an hour." He started to walk around, they started nudging him, he replied, "You said half an hour." He did not allow them make him crazy and at the end of a half hour he made a decision (not known what it was, the *hemshech* is unknown)...that's *hagdara*...R' Farkash said about R' Motel Kozliner that whenever he met him he requested to hear the vort of R' Shlomo Karliner – what was that vort? R' Deitsch didn't know exactly the content but the message is that everything must be done with *yishuv hada'at* – and that drives the *yetzer harah* ("evil inclination") crazy. This *yishuv hada'at* is called *mugdar*...Yaakov Avinu's claim against his oldest son Reuven was not on his content but that he was "*pachaz k'mayim*" – impulsive, acting before fully considering the results of his actions. We have to think before seeing, before listening – and also about the content of our thoughts.

But then, the question comes up, *machshava* arises automatically from the *midot* (the "emotions"), so how can we work on our thoughts in order to make them *mugdar*? To truly change our thoughts, we need to change our *midot*, but this is not associated with *yirah*...to this the Rashab explains that for the *beinoni* ("intermediate" person who struggles to maintain his thought, speech and action focused on God), *hithafchut* ("transformation" of his character traits) is not applicable. But, *itkafia* (subduing, "bending" his *yetzer harah*) is applicable. There are two elements, the *etzem* ("essence") of the soul, and its *hitpashtut* (emanation or "extension" of the *etzem*), and the *beinoni* is only *poel* ("only has an effect") on the *hitpashtut*, not on the *etzem* (he has power to affect only the "extensions" of his soul, not its essence). Only *tzadikim* are able to achieve total transformation, but the *beinoni* nonetheless manages complete transformation of something...when he davens properly, the effect remains for a long time, the *yetzer harah* goes to sleep, and especially when a person davens properly every day (not only on Shabbat). Nevertheless the impression from davening helps so that at least when a negative thought arises, he repels it. In Tanya, the Alter Rebbe explains that even the initial negative thought was not an *aveirah* since "it wasn't him, it wasn't his fault, it arose from his heart."

- Someone once told R' Deitsch that the *Beit Yisrael* (previous Gerer Rebbe), who worked a lot with the youth, helped them to work against negative thoughts, etc, would say, "the first thought is not an *aveirah*" – the first thought comes from *teva* ("nature"), not from the person, but he pushes it away, "with both hands" (language of Tanya). R' Shlomo Chaim explained that "both hands" means that there shouldn't be *yamin mekarevet v'smol docheh* ("while the right hand draws near, the left hand repels"). Meaning that he shouldn't arrive to a situation wherein he has to discuss within himself whether or not the thought is a "good thought" – before the thought is fully formed in his mind, he must push it away. As soon as he starts to argue within himself, there's already proximity to the negative thought; therefore, he must "push it away with both hands," before he even begins to entertain the notion.

- The Chafetz Chaim said to his son that Hashem created the Chasidim as "guardians of the generation." At the time, there were all kinds of groups such as the *maskilim* ("enlightened"), Communists and others trying to lead the Jews astray (the Chasidim were more resistant than any other group), and about them the Chafetz Chaim said to his son, "they provide *shmira* ("protection") for the *dor*." The Chafetz Chaim told his sons that the Chasidim have *chutzpa d'kedusha*, they throw out negative thoughts like they are "nothing." "We are 'R' Shlomo Zalnikers' – from *Sefer michtavei haChafetz Chaim*' – by us every thought has a place, by them (the Chasidim), they throw it out." *Azut d'kedusha*...like the Rebbe said about giving up land, "Don't even get into an argument about it, it's completely not up for discussion."

This is where *yirah* comes in, one who possesses the trait of *yirah* won't continue to think about it after it arises in his thought. When he continues to think about it, this is *prikat ohl,* lack of *yirah*. And then if one entertains these negative thoughts, they return exactly when he doesn't want them, and to a much greater extent, such that he can't get rid of them. And they torment and bother him and he can't get rid of them – *memshelet zeidim* ("government of the criminals"). For this we need *hagdara b'machshava*. When learning the section about when the *klipot* "smell" the aroma of *ohl malchut shamayim,* they "run away" – R' Shlomo Chaim would read over and repeat these lines. *Ha'arat malchut shamayim*...see Ch 27 in Tanya. A little effort from below brings a lot of response from Above.

- R' Deitsch once heard about R' Zalman Nehemiah Goldberg *A"H* (son in law of R' Shlomo Zalman Auerbach *ztz'l, dayan* on *Beit Din Gavoa,* was R' Deitsch's Rosh Collel for *dayanut* after he married)...Someone in the US said about him that, "He is the R' Moshe Feinstein of our day." Questions that aren't in Gemora, he builds a *teshuva* from Gemora and Rishonim, etc... so this fellow from the US said that there was a gynecologist, an expert who said he does not believe that Jews keep *taharat hamishpacha*. How can they hold themselves back ("how can the couple refrain from intimate relations?"). R' Zalman Nehemia answered that *b'kol zot* ("nevertheless") we do hold ourselves back, even though here was this doctor who said it's not possible. How do we hold ourselves back? R' Zalman Nehemiah said the answer is that the doctor is not aware of the *sayagim* ("limitations, fences") that the oral Torah places on the whole commandment of *taharat hamishpacha*. He's only aware of the *issur* itself, but not the "fences": "Not to pass from hand to hand, not to sit to eat together..." All these things the doctor didn't know, and it is in the merit of all these *sayagim* that we keep the mitzvah...and don't come to tests... this explanation is "*balabatish*" ("standard, does not require much wisdom"), but according to Chassidut, a *sayag* is *kaballat ohl*...when a person is afraid he might fall, so he makes a *sayag*...this comes from fear. Like in Chumash regarding Avraham Avinu; *ki yadativ* ("because I know")– this is first time that God mentions His love for Avraham, and His love for Avraham is because of Avraham's fear of God, since Avraham kept all these *mishmerot* ("fences").

- Rav Deitsch mentioned that once they would drop off the newspapers (*Maariv* and *Yediot* in the courtyard of the *Tzemach Tzedel* Shul until the store across the street opened up and took them in – R' Deitsch said *Aizeh niseyonot hayu li lo l'histakel* – "How difficult was it for me not to look into the newspaper..." He just wanted to see the headlines...but the headlines these days are followed up by photos and they are awful...once R' Deitsch complained to the Rebbe that, "I take on myself *kabalot* (*hachlatot*, "resolutions" – seemingly things to guard himself) – and they don't remain." The Rebbe answered that it's because he takes too much on himself, he should take on less, and for shorter periods of time. Take on for shorter times and see if it "sticks," then you can take on more and continue. Rav Deitsch took on himself that for a few months he wouldn't look at the paper...in the shiur, R' Eliyahu Haddad mentioned *eitzah* to "trick the *yetzer harah*" – just like the *yetzer* says, 'try a little bit now, be a *tzadik* tomorrow,' so also we have to say, 'today I'll be a *tzadik*, tomorrow who knows..." – Rav Deitsch said this trick comes from R' Nachman of Breslav. *M'oivei t'chakmeini* – "From my enemies, I grow wiser." Also R' Shlomo Chaim would say this...(Rav Deitsch it appears turned toward R' Shalom Dovid Segal at this point and asked him if he remembers that at the shiur, since R' Segal used to also be a part of the yeshiva with R' Shlomo Chaim...).

Shiur 9, November 8, 2011

As explained here in *K'Avoda, hagdarat hachushim* ("guarding the senses") is comparable to the function of the "immune system" – it protects us from all kinds of illnesses; in this case, illness of vision, of hearing, of thought. At the moment that the immune system fails to function, it's like the bone marrow isn't present (God forbid). And then, only after destroying all the white cells that protect the body, is it possible to give him a new portion of blood (otherwise the white blood cells see the new blood as foreign object and attack it. So, first even before the infusion, they have to give a lot of chemotherapy to kill the white blood vessels, and the chemo weakens the person tremendously). *Kabalat ohl* ("acceptance of the yoke") is the spiritual "immune system." If there's no *kabalat ohl*, we can go very wrong, so it's very necessary to maintain the "acceptance of the yoke." The Gemora in tractate Shabbat (*Perek Bameh Madlikin*...daf 31) brings the verse ("*Vehaya Emunat Itecha...Choshen yeshuot... yirat Hashem otzro*") and says that it alludes to all six sections of Shas (Mishna) and then says that if the *otzar yirat shamayaim* ("storehouse of fear of God") is present, then all will be fine. But, if not, then no, and then the Gemora compares it to a store of wheat – if you put a certain amount of dirt in with the wheat, the grain retains its quality, but otherwise it rots. The Maharal of Prague (In the book, *Tiferet Yisrael*) explains; Why would anyone learn Torah if he has no *yirat Hashem*? And he answers, "Because of love of God," but if there was no fear also "mixed in" – nothing will help. This is because love of God means there is someone there who loves, there is some *yeshut* ("ego")...so without some fear "mixed in," it doesn't work to attach him to God. And therefore, the beginning of Yiddishkeit and serving God, is *yirah*.

Once, Chasidim used to make the *brit milah* late in the day, but now they do so early. Acc to the Rebbe, it is correct, it is the right thing to make the *brit milah* early...according to halacha, there is room to discuss which principle takes precedence, whether *zrizim makdimim* ("those who are "on top of matters" do the mitvah with alacrity") takes precedence or *rov am hadrat melech* ("better to beautify the mitzvah by doing it later when more people can attend") takes precedence. If *zrizim*, then better early but if *rov am*, then it is preferable to do it later in the day when more people can attend. The Rebbe says that once upon a time if the *brit* was late, the attendees would stay, wash, and make a farbrengen. They would not merely eat and drink, but sit down together and talk over matters of Torah and *avodah* (farbrengen). Since the farbrengen could add to *yirat Hashem* ("fear of Hashem"), *v'tziveinu Hashem la'asot et hachukim ha'eleh l'yirah et Hashem* ("God commanded us to fulfill these laws, to fear Him"), so it was okay to delay the mitzvah of *milah* until later in the day. Even tho *yirah* ("fear," that should motivate us to fulfill the mitzvah early) is the basis and foundation and therefore the *brit mila* should come first but since in the final analysis as long as it took place, all was fine. So therefore, the *brit* would take place at the end of they day, followed by a farbrengen.

- Again, the Rav mentioned from R' Shlomo Zarchi and from R' Fitchie Ofen that these two Chapters [most likely the second and third chapters of K' Avoda, which discuss fear of God] were the *ikar kavana* ("main intention") of the Rashab in writing the *K'Avoda*. R' Zarchi heard it from R' Shlomo Friedman, R' Deitsch himself heard from R' Fitchie Ofen. "Strange to hear from others, I myself thought so."

- Once there was a *bachur* looking for a shidduch and when a prospective match asked about him, they replied that "he learns, he prays..." When they asked, "what about his level of *yirat Hashem*," the answer was, "I don't know, how can I know." *Yirat Hashem* is in the heart...

- *Yirat Chet* ("fear of sin") is *hergesh hane'elam* – a concealed feeling, not conscious. Other levels of fear – *yirat Elokim* ("fear of *Elokim*") or *yirat Havaya* ("fear of *Havaya*") – are conscious.

- *Ohl* ("yoke") is what you put on a *behama* ("animal") so it doesn't go off the path. Same with man, *Tov sh'yisah alav ohl m'neurav* – "good he should have a yoke from his youth" – which the sages interpret to mean that it is, "good to get married early." As R' Deitsch said, "It's good if there is someone to tell you, 'this we don't do." R' Deitsch said after his *hatuna* he went to borrow money cause he didn't have any. His wife said to him, "From where will you have money to return to them?" He hadn't thought of that, it was new for him, as a *bachur* he never was in this situation. So he started to spend less (margarine instead of butter until he couldn't deal with it anymore).

K' Avoda there goes on to speak of *ahavat Hashem* ("love of God") and says that without *ahavat Hashem* there is no proper *kiyum* ("fulfillment") of the mitzvoth. Quotes Tanya perek 4 which mentions but does not explain *kiyum amiti* – "true fulfillment" of the commandments. Explains that when the fulfillment is without *chayut* ("life, vitality"), then it's not *kiyum amiti*. That's how *K'Avoda* here explains Tanya Ch 4. From the Yekkes ("German Jews"), "If one lost money, he lost nothing. If he lost his will, he lost everything."

- R' Deitsch heard a *pirush* ("explanation") of *masbiah l'kol chai ratzon* (from *Ashrei*, Psalm 145) – "He satisfies the will of every creature."

Why "the will"? Man has several different wills and desires? Hashem gives everyone a will, and without this will, man is nothing. There was someone in the Holocaust, a Rav Godel (Gerer Chosid), whose job it was to go around and encourage and support people. He himself lost everything, his wife and only daughter and he was left bereft and alone for the rest of his life. But he would go around and encourage people to keep going. As long as man had a will to continue living during the Shoah, he could continue, but without that *ratzon*, without that will, he couldn't keep going. The book described how he would persuade people: "Soon we'll arrive to the Shtiebel in Tel Aviv, we'll have herring and schnapps…until he elicited a smile from him, then he would ask, 'do you want to live?" <u>B'mechitzat R' Godel</u> was the name of the sefer.

Shiur 10, Nov 9, 2011 (Page 15, seven lines before the end of page)

If we want to achieve a state of *avoda* ("service") of the heart, we first of all need *yirah* ("fear"), it is the *yesod* ("basis, foundation"). Man is born with physical needs and *ratzonot* ("desires"). Here, we are not speaking of sins, but of natural needs. For example, as soon as a baby is born, it opens its mouth and requests food – how is this possible? Its mouth was closed during pregnancy and immediately it's born, it screams for food – so these are physical needs that demand attention way before we get involved with *ruchanyut* ("spirituality") at all. So, man is used to physical things, and being rooted in these things, and accustomed to them, he becomes almost "addicted" to them. (This is one of the problems in marriage, each brings his/her "habits" to the marriage which the other may not go along with, but to him/her, it is natural). And these natural, unthinking habits hide and conceal the Godly soul. This is our *teveyut*, our "natural tendencies" that we know we can change but it's difficult, we don't want to change. Here in *K'Avoda* he does not explain why, but Tanya explains that all habitual needs are based on ego, they are based on the "I-ness" or "*Anochyut*" of the person. In the language of Chasidut, *hargashat atzmo* ("self feeling")… all natural habits such as these are called *akum* ("crooked") – things that bend and make the Godly soul go "crooked." Tanya explains that the animal soul, in whatever situation it might be, thinks only about itself. This is *Eitz Hada'at* ("tree of knowledge")…written in Rambam (*Moreh Nevuchim*), "What's wrong with *da'at?*" Rambam clarifies that before the sin of *Eitz hada't*, the goal of the world was to discern between truth and falsity, and people understood the difference. The sin of *Eitz Hada'at* though led people to think about "good and bad": What's "good" in it for me, and "What is in it for me?" That's the ego…

- Once someone got news that they had a certain sickness and they became distraught, the doctor tried to explain that it wasn't so serious, can do this, can try that, etc…saw nothing calmed him down so tried another tact: "It could be worse." He asked the doctor, "How could it be worse?" The doctor answered – it would be worse if I (the doctor) got this sickness." No joke, if something happens to us, it's much "heavier" than if to another person. *Hargashat atzmo – yesod hayesodot* ("feeling ourselves") is the source of all *klipat nogah* ("negative forces" that are mixed good and bad). And it's the opposite of *bitul l'elokut* ("nullification to Godliness").

From this, we see that it's not necessary to do an *aveira* ("transgression") in order to distance ourself from Hashem. [The existence of ego and *hargashat atzmo* already creates separation].

- Sometimes in cases of *shalom bayit* ("peace between husband and wife"), one side charges that the other side is an "egoist" – *pirush hadavar* ("explanation") that he/she "ate a bite from *Eitz Hada't.*"

Da'at is *hitkashrut* ("connection" – from Tanya), and somewhere in Rebbe Rashab's *Kuntresim*, he writes that *da'at* is not well enough explained, but *da'at* is *hargashat atzmo* ("experience of 'self,' ego")…There is *havana* ("understanding," based on intellect) and there is *hargasha* ("feeling, emotion"). For example if someone hears about a matter and understands that something is going to happen or will happen…"another war, or etc…" and then the event happens and he says, "Wow I didn't know it was going to be like this." "But you were warned"…"Yes I was told all the details, yet I didn't know it was going to be like this." This is called *da'at*. From the perspective of *Chochma* (pure intellectual insight) and *Bina* (pure intellectual analysis), the question of the gemora applies: "Who says my blood is redder than yours? Maybe your blood is redder than mine"? [This is a paraphrase from a section of Gemora that investigates what to do when two are walking in the desert and there is only enough water for one of them; The Gemora indicates that the one with the water should drink it himself, for "Who said the other person's blood is 'redder than his'?]. That's without *da'at,* without the feeling of "self." But when *da'at* is involved, the feeling of "self" comes into play. There's *da'at* of *kedusha* ("knowledge associated with holiness") – when one "feels" Hashem: there is "belief" in God, "understanding God," and "feeling God."

- When one of the students of the Metzritcher Magid returned to his former town where he was born and lived, they asked him, "What do you get there by the Magid"? He answered, "I found out that there is God in the world." His host laughed and called over the non-Jewish woman working there, and asked her if there is God in the world, to which of course answered, "Yes." The student of the Magid replied, "She believes, but I feel…" That's what he received from the Magid – visceral knowledge of God's existence, that he could "feel," not just "believe in." Someone in the *shiur* said the story applies to the Alter Rebbe, and his answer was that, "She says, but I know." And this visceral knowledge of course is *da'at*.

Ego is not found in the intellectual attributes of *Chochma* and *Bina*, but it is found in *Da'at*. Moreover, there is *da'at* of *kedusha* ("holiness") and *da'at* of *klipah* – *hargashat atzmo* ("feeling oneself, ego").

- Example: There are right wingers in Israel who can explain their position and left wingers who can also explain their position, of course in the opposite manner from one another. Yet, we see clearly that the *smolanim* ("left wingers") totally failed – but they show no regret and continue espousing the same policies. Why do they demonstrate no regret? Because their policies are not emerging from clean pure *sechel* ("intellect") – they come from ego, from which they are unable to detach themselves. In this world, there is no "clean *sechel*" ("objective intellect"). Also among judges, we find that if they were left wing before they studied law, they remain *smolanim* afterward as well, and if right, the same. All this is coming from *hargashat atzmo*, from *rigushim*, from "fellings" and ego. Those with a right wing perspective can also be egotistical, but if he/she is coming from Torah perspective then not.

Explains what is meant by "weakness" of the Godly soul. The *inyanim tevi'im* that we are regular about, we need to remove, and then we can begin to experience love of God (but first of all need basis of *yirah* because otherwise the ego is there).

Shiur 11, Nov 10, 2011 (Page 16)

First of all, in order to enter into *avodat Hashem* ("divine service"), we have to make an exit from whatever we were "regularly habitual" in. Why? Because in natural fashion, man becomes accustomed to those matters that are habitual for him, and that already weakens the divine Godly soul. This occurs (3 bottom lines of the text on page 16), either because the habitual conduct completely hides the Godly soul, or because (after the parentheses) the minimal revelation of the Godly soul does not have enough power to overwhelm the animal soul and its *humriyut* ("coarse physicality"). Here, R'

Deitsch points out that in the first case (no revelation of the Godly soul), the *K'Avoda* does not mention *humriyut*, but *gufniyut* (experience of the body and its physical needs).

- The uncle of R' Dovid Boaz (sitting at end of table), spoke of his uncle, R' Yoel, his mother's brother…R' Deitsch heard from him – his ability to save himself and part of his family was in the *zchut* ("merit") of the yearning that he had for his Rebbe, the Rebbe of Slonim. He was from Lodz, even tho Slonim were Russian Chasidim and Lodz were mostly Polisher Chasidim, when the talk about war began, his father was in Branowitz, also in Russia (white Russia), with the *Beit Avraham* (Slonimer Rebbe?). The father came to Lodz, and after a short time time, the son wanted to go back home to Branowitz, but the father told him, "It's dangerous." The son said, "But also here (Lodz) it's dangerous." The father told him, "With money, it's possible to get thru everything." In Lodz, they were wealthy, but the father told him, "If you go back to Branowitz you won't have money and how will you get by?" But after some time, the son's yearning for the Slonimer Rebbe (who it seems was in Branowitz) was too much and after davening in the morning, the son didn't return home (in Lodz). He went to the train station in his tefilin, and told someone to inform his father. The info arrived to the father and he took off (perhaps with his mother as well) to the train station to stop him from going. The son said he can't hold back, had to go to Rebbe, and he went. Everyone in Lodz, the father etc, were murdered, since Poland was the first in the Holocaust to go…but there by the Slonimer Rebbe he was saved and even managed to save part of his family. R' Dovid Boaz in the shiur told more details (roughly 8 minutes into the video), but inaudible. The point? The ability of the Godly divine soul to overwhelm the animal soul and its *humriyut* (that is, the son's yearning for the Rebbe was a divine manifestation that brought the son out of Lodz), but if there is only a small *hitgalut* ("revelation"), it's not enough to pull the animal soul out of its *humriyut* (the father who remained in Lodz).

Back to the text…the parentheses contain details that sometimes you have to skip because they contain too much explanation, miss the forest for the trees…but here (Page 57 in the English translation), it's possible to go into the details…*hesech hada'at* in our instance means "totally unaware of any divine matter or feeling," when the Godly soul completely feels nothing… not that he will do an *aveirah* ("sin"), but just that he's not feeling anything divine, no *hergesh eloki* ("divine feeling")…no "taste," as if no taste on the palate…the Godly soul does have taste but when it's in a state of *hit'almut* ("concealment"), it feels nothing, *keseph* ("money") it grasps, nothing else – this is *hesech hada'at*.

- After his first son was born, Rav Deitsch, it was the *minhag* in those days that the mother would hang out with her parents for awhile until she "returned to herself." In this case, Rav Deitsch's mother in law lived in Tiberius, they went to T'veria in Shvat when he was born and didn't return to Ylm and home until Pesach, she was by her mother, and R' Deitsch would travel every week to Tiveria for Shabbat, 4 hour trip. There were a few other regular travelers, including a Kibbutznik, with whom he became friendly and they shared thoughts, exchanged opinions, etc. R' Deitsch told him about how one who lives only for *olam hazeh* is like a "horse," who only eats straw, "you're eating *basar* and other things but in essence it's the same thing as a horse." He argued fiercely with him but at the time R' Deitsch was young and wasn't about to back down, until the guy said, "Okay, so what, I'm like a horse…but that's the way I enjoy." At first he didn't agree and he argued but in the end he agreed (that he is like a horse)…this is one level but there are those who know there is something higher, more elevated but don't go for it cause they are unable to let go of their *humriyut*, their attachment to the physical.

- Another story: Rav Deitsch would learn exactly a half hour with an accountant…there weren't so many telephones but the accountant had one in his office (afterward he became independent but at the time he was an employee) and as they learned together many employees and bosses used to come in and out…in a large printing establishment. At one point, the accountant's son spoke with him and R' Deitsch couldn't help but hear an unpleasant conversation with the son of the accountant. Afterward, he apologized and said he couldn't help but hear, but that if the accountant had given the son a religious education, this would not have occurred…the accountant replied that, "I know but if I go in that religious direction, then I'll have to eat cholent on Shabbat, how can I do that, I eat fresh cooked food every day, how can I eat cholent on Shabbat, can't do that…" Exact words…his devotion to habit was so great that even tho he knew there was a better way, he couldn't take himself out of his habits.

From the text, the Godly soul is like a polished gem, it shines with the *ohr* that comes its way. But, we won't feel that if we are too *chumri*, too physical. When we start to feel something from the *nefesh Eloki*, that's a sign that some of the blockage began to come off. Otherwise, it's like any "dirt," it blocks the illumination. If so, though how does one begin *avodat Hashem*, he's starting off from a position of blockage and lack of illumination? Therefore, *K'Avoda* says first thing to do is begin beyond logic, accept *ohl malchut shamayaim* ("yoke of heaven"), leave behind our habitual behavior, and give ourself over to *Elokut* ("Godliness").

- Napoleon had to get up for a drink of water, he really didn't want to but was *mitgaver* ("pushed himself"), and then thought, "what am I, like a horse? This is what I am, I give in to my needs like this?" When he got to the water, he was upset with himself for being so driven by habitual needs, and he ended up not drinking any water. He got up from his bed only in order to avoid being "lazy," and similarly decided not to drink water in order to maintain control over his natural tendencies. Also, Aristotle he had a wife who made problems for him, when they asked him why he doesn't divorce her, he said that "he needs her to refine his character."

Here the question is asked, if this is only a matter of overwhelming our habitual nature, perhaps it's sufficient to do so without *kabalat ohl*? (that is, without accepting a "yoke" on ourselves)? But *K'Avoda* concludes that in truth, leaving behind one's habitual nature has to be, "Because his habitual nature is opposed to the the will of God." We do not seek to change our nature merely in order to be "more human." Either way, transformation of our habitual traits is most effective when combined with an experience of Godly illumination.

- There are roles that require a lot of training and preparation, such as preparing to be a soldier in the army. But what if war breaks out before a soldier finishes his training? He can't stop the war until his training is finished. The soldier has to make do with a shortened abbreviated course, and that's our situation today as well. To hold off learning Chasidut until such and such, and "then I'm ready"? That's not our status now. Our situation is "grab and eat, grab and drink" – do what we can.

- R' Eli Hadad, sitting across from the Rav, asked, "There are all kinds of people in all kinds of situations, who remain in their habitual status, "addicted" to their regular habits, yet they also "feel" spiritual events…maybe this is only delusion? On the other hand there are people who sit all day and learn but if you ask them, 'What are you feeling,' they'll answer, "I don't feel anything." Someone sitting next to Eli said something with which the Rav agreed, but wasn't audible.

The Rav wanted to expand upon it and say that every *Baal Teshuva* who makes a decision to join the group that is called *Ba'alei Teshuva* is performing an act about which, "There is no *aziva* ("leaving behind"), no forsaking of his previous situation, greater than that." At that moment, the B"T effectively says to all of his habits, etc, "Wait in the corner for me…" Although there are other matters that the B'T has to work on at all times because he has *yetzerim* (temptations and seductive factors) that others may not have, but the *etzem aziva* (the very act of forsaking his past) of his previous situation…[This reminds me of an episode I experienced with R' Adin Steinzaltz A"H…upon reading a very esoteric section in *"eyn-beis"* of the Rebbe Rashab, I approached Rav Steinzaltz and asked him if the spiritual state of mind described in the *maamer* was still applicable in our day and age. R' Steinzaltz looked at me and replied that 'if a Jew can come from Los Angeles and put on tefilin, then anything is possible.']

Shiur 12, November 11, 2011, end of Ch 2. Page 16, middle of the parentheses

The *avoda* ("divine service") of *tefila* is *ahavat Hashem* ("love of God") which brings *d'vekut* ("cleaving to God") and also *tikun hamidot* ("rectification of our character traits"). But the portion that we learned previously is that first of all, we have to have *yirat Hashem* ("fear of God"). Without *yirat Hashem*, we are limited to our natural tendencies. How do we escape our natural tendencies? By forsaking our habitual and regular behavior. In the parentheses, the Rebbe Rashab refers to a certain Chasid – this is R' Shmuel Munkis…who worked on himself so that whatever he wanted *mitzad* his own nature – he wouldn't do. That was the effect of the first *yechidut* ("private audience") that he had with the Alter Rebbe. Power of the Rebbe…many stories about R' Shmuel Munkis, he was a *chasid shovev* ("mischievous Chasid").

- R' Shmuel was present when the Alter Rebbe was informed that he would be taken to prison. The Alter Rebbe could have prevented that from happening via super natural powers. Instead, he "consulted" with R' Shmuel before allowing himself to be taken. R' Shmuel answered him with a story from R' Mendel (R' Mendel Horodoker/Vitebsker, who took over leadership of the Chasidim when the Magid passed away) when he traveled with his own wagon and wagon driver and stopped at a house on the way, at the palace of a local *paritz* ("landowner") and entered through the stone fence, knocking part of it down. The *paritz* emerged from his house with a pistol, and the wagon driver motioned to the back of the wagon where R' Mendel sat. The pistol didn't work, but R' Mendel asked him afterward, "What did you do, why did you motion to me?" The wagon driver answered him, "If you're a Rebbe, the pistol wouldn't hurt you. If you're not a Rebbe, why do you deceive the entire world"? R' Shmuel said this *ma'aseh* to the Alter Rebbe and told him, "If you're a Rebbe, prison won't hurt you. If you're not a Rebbe, why did you take away enjoyment of this world (*olam hazeh*) from all the *avrechim* ("young Torah scholars")?

- Another R' Shmuel story; when he first came to the Alter Rebbe, R' Shmuel didn't know where the Rebbe lived in the city. But according to his estimation, at night there would be light in the Alter Rebbe's house. So, he looked for a house with the light on, knocked on the door and "Yes," it was the house of the Alter Rebbe. The Alter Rebbe got up and answered the door, and R' Shmuel said he wants to stay there in the house of the Alter Rebbe, who answered him, "Why here, is there a lack of houses in this town?" R' Shmuel said, "Yes, I want to stay here." The Alter Rebbe told him, "I"ll bring the goy to kick you out." (The Rebbe himself told this story, with a complete explanation). R' Shmuel answered, "My goy (inside) is stronger than your goy." When the Alter Rebbe heard this, he allowed him in (because the Alter Rebbe saw he was a "serious" person).

- But, R' Shmuel didn't *stam* tell a story…there was background to it: Where he lived, there was a *shochet* ("ritual slaughterer") who brought a certain tray of roasted lung to a farbrengen (A "farbrengen" is a Chasidic get together in which the participants speak words of Torah and *avoda* and sing Chasidic melodies and say *lechaim*). This was a dish that had a strong savory aroma. R' Shmuel said, "I'm in charge of this *farbeisen* ("food")." So, they sat together and spoke and said *lechaim*, and everytime one of the young *avreichim* who were present asked for a bit of the roast lung, R' Shmuel gave a "jump." The *avrechim* saw that R' Shmuel did not intend to give it to them, so they decided together to "rush him" and take it away from him. In the shul were two barrels, one of clean water and the other of dirty water. R' Shmuel grabbed the whole roast and quickly ran to the dirty water and dumped the roast lung into the dirty water. The *avrechim* were upset with him and decided he deserves a *mashkante* – a "solid beating." As they were about to give it to him, the town *shochet* came running in the door and announced that the cow from which the lung came, was *treif* (ritually unfit for eating)! All of a sudden the *avreichim* realized that R' Shmuel had done a *mofet*, a "miracle," and according to Chasidic custom, this was just as bad (almost) as doing an *aveirah* (because the role of a Chasid is to be nullified to his Rebbe, and not to do anything that would demonstrate his own spiritual level)…so (instead of administering a *mashkante* for throwing away the meat), they decided he deserves a *mashkanta* for performing a "miracle" (of guessing that the meat was treif). When the previous Rebbe told this story, he added that the younger scholars did not take part in this *mashkante*, only the older ones. The younger ones saw that they had *esek* with someone serious, and after the older ones were finished with R' Shmuel, they asked him, "From where did you powers to do such a *mofet*?" He answered, "The first time I went into the Alter Rebbe for *yechidut*, I worked on myself so that anything that I want to do that comes from my own nature, I won't do. When that roast lung came in the door, I saw that the *ta'ava* ("lust") for it (not clear if the *taa've* was his own or of the *tzibur*) was totally unusual. From this he realized that there was a "problem" here. He didn't do a *mofet*, just understood that the level of *taavah* was too great and there must be a problem.

Kabalat ohl has two components: 1) Not to invest oneself in physical matters – this weakens his *chumriyut* ("physical tendencies") and 2) To devote himself to God (*Noten et atzmo*) – *hacarah* ("recognition") that he's a servant." *Mesirah v'netina*. Both of these factors are part of *kabalat ohl*. *Ahavah* comes later.

- R' Deitsch asked a question of the Rebbe, in *yechidut*, "How can man decide about *kabalat ohl*, and resolve to accept upon himself to serve God as an *eved* ("servant")? The Rebbe answered, "You must learn the benefit of *kabalat ohl* in *sifrei Musar* [books about 'ethics' that were written prior to the Chasidic movement, mostly from the medieval Jewish authorities from 1000-1400, known as *rishonim*], better in *sifrei Chasidut* [volumes of Chasidut], repeat it to yourself verbally, *b'al peh*, during your free time and as you are walking on the way (*uvelechtecha baderech*)." And then the Rebbe added, "*vet zeyn kabalat ohl*" – "there will be *kabalat ohl*." The Rebbe also said, "You don't have to ask the question overseas [apparently to the Rebbe], ask a *mashpia*." So R'Deitsch asked R' Mendel Futerfas (*mashpia* in Kfar Chabad), where does one learn the *ma'alah* of *kabalat ohl*? R' Deitsch himself knew of the *Derech Chaim* of the Mitteler Rebbe and of the *hemshech mikneh rav* in *samech-vov* of the Rebbe Rashab, and R' Mendel revealed to him that the *makor* and source of the series on *eved ne'eman* and *eved pashut* (in the Rebbe Rashab's *Yom Tov shel R"H 5666*) was from the Mitteler Rebbe, in his sefer, *Torat*

Chaim, end of *Shemot* (Not sure). R' Deitsch also found in other places, such as in *Likutei Torah*, that compared *kabalat ohl* to "bones." Without the skeleton, the body has no foundation, no framework. That comes only from the bones, upon which the flesh, muscles, etc are bound. The same applies to *kabalat ohl*, it forms the foundation, the framework upon which everything else is built. Israeli slang says "it's *bli etzem*," without stiffness, without "backbone." In regard to what the Rebbe told R' Deitsch, the question is, "If learning about *kabalat ohl* from *sifrei Chasidut* is "better," then why learn about it at all from *sifrei Mussar*? R' Deitsch answers that it seems that both are necessary. We must learn *Mussar* from *sifrei Mussar* and also from *sifri Chasidut*, but to know that from *sifrei Chasidut* is "better." (*Sifrei Mussar* includes also the *shemonah perakim* of the Rambam, not only what the Litivish yeshivot permit (which was only 3 *seforim* in Litvish yeshivas)…in the Intro to the Mitteler Rebbe (*Torat Chaim*), it is written that was accepted by the Chasidim to learn two "Mussar" volumes: *Shaloh* (*Shnei luchot habrit*) and *Reishit Chochma*. The three permitted in Litvish yeshivas are *Mesilat Yesharim*, *Chovot Halevavot*, and *Sha'arei Teshuva* (of Rabeinu Yonah), also another one that they also learned, but "not so much" – couldn't catch what it was (perhaps *Orchot Tzadikim*). But the Previous Rebbe said that with his father, he learned the *Ohrchot Tzadikim*. Moreover, once Rav Hadikov (secretary of the Rebbe, but really his role was greater than that of "secretary"…) called in Rav Rosenfeld of Machon Alta (seminar for B"T women in Tzefat) and asked him what he is learning with the girls…"Are you learning *sifrei Mussar*?" It was known that when Rav Hadikov called in someone it was according to instructions from the Rebbe, it was not his own initiative. He was a good example of an *eved ne'eman* – a "faithful servant." First, he was an *eved* of the Rebbe and only later became a Chabadnik. R' Rosenfeld replied that he learns Chasidut with the girls. R' Hadikov said (as per instructions from the Rebbe), "that's not enough, you must learn *mussar* with them as well." R' Rosenfeld himself told R'Deitsch about this. And R' Deitsch has an explanation for this: Chasidut contains the *shoreshim* ("roots") of mussar, Chasidut speaks all the time about *bitul, bitul, bitul* ("nullification" on oneself), but what if someone comes and insults you publicly? What do you do? *L'maaseh*, you close your mouth and you don't answer. And that – exactly how to respond – you find only in *Sifrei Mussar*. (There were *maamorim*, discourses from the Previous Rebbe that the Chasidim said, "These are *maamorim* of *mussar*, not *Chasidut*"). *Sifrei Mussar* are more *lema'aseh*- contain more actual instruction, than do *sifrei Chasidut*.

- In conclusion of the *shiur*, R' Deitsch cited from Ch 7 of the *Shemonah Perakim* of Rambam (which appear at the end of Gemora tractate *Sanhedrin*), "In Midrash, Agadeta and Gemora, you find quotations from the prophets, some of whom perceived *Hashem* behind a few *mechitzot* ("separations") and some of whom behind many *mechitzot*." It depends on their proximity to Him. If we ask, "What are the *mechitzot?*"…The answer is that some come from *sechel*, others from *midot*…Yet, what the sages said was that "nothing comes between ourselves and Hashem aside from our sins." And what are the "sins"? Rambam mentions a few, but some are the lust for money, being stuck in our various individual lusts…And who is *zoche* ("merits") to *nevuah* ("prophecy") – Those who are *chacham, gibur* and *ashir* ("wise, strong/disciplined, and wealthy") – One who is "wealthy," is he who is happy with what he has. "Anyone who is angry, prophecy abandons him." For example, all the time that Yaakov mourned over Yoseph, *nevuah* left him. And then when he found Yoseph alive, "And he lived" – the *targum* says his *ruach nevuah* ("spirit of prophecy") returned. And all of these high spiritual levels are based on *kabalat ohl*…

Shiur 13, November 13, 2011

Summary end of Ch 2, moving on to Ch 3…

Ch. 3 is about how to achieve *yirah* ("fear of God"). The previous chapter described why *yirah* is necessary. However, *yirah* is not the *avoda* ("divine service") of *tefila* ("prayer"). Instead, *yirah* is the *avoda* of the entire day, not specifically of *tefila*. But *ahava* ("love of God") is associated with *tefila*. We cannot meditate all day long but we should meditate before and during tefila. *Yirah* is a matter that must be associated with *zicharon* ("memory"), with "reminders." *Ahava* is *regesh* ("emotion") that occurs during *tefila*.

- Some ask about marriage, "Why couldn't the entire marriage be like the love of the first day?" But that's the thing, "love" is good for the first day, but after that we have to get used to the daily grind. Likewise, *ahava* is associated with *tefila*, but less so after *tefila*, because after *tefila*, only an impression of the daily prayers is left with us.

How do we achieve *yirah*? The *K'Avoda* (Page 63 in the translation) quotes from Tanya…Ch 42 (Page *samech-aleph*) – "Furthermore, one also must remember…" When one thinks about the creation, we see that it "lives." There is energy, the entire world is full of energy.

- R' Deitsch did tests to determine what food was good for him. Once upon a time, there were tests that took months to determine what foods one should eat. Now they have a machine that helps tell you on the spot. This machine sets up a connection between the person and the machine which shows either positive or negative. With this test, R' Deitsch saw *hatzalat nefashot* ("lives saved"). A grandson was obviously allergic to something, was "red," and they brought him to the doctor (Henlich), "Mendele" 7 years old – the test indicated that two things are not good for him; tuna and bamba, both of which the boy liked a lot. They removed it from his diet and within days he looked better. R' Deitsch asked someone what was the principle behind it ("What is it, *kishuf, mah zeh*?"). The answer was that every product has an "energy" associated with it, as does the person. By comparing the energies (several hundred products), one can know if they are compatible or not…by R' Deitsch he knew already that milk products weren't good for him, and the machine also confirmed that [perhaps bio-feedback machine?] – but after checking several basic foods, he also checked various candies and found that milk chocolate was bad for him – even though only a minute amount of milk present, still it was enough to indicate negative. The previous portable machine (*metultelet*) worked even over the telephone, the machine could even discern the energy over the telephone.

So in the world, one finds "energies" – *chayut*. Why davka this word, *chayut*? Because it's found in *Derech Mitzvotecha* of the Tzemach Tzedek. "When man meditates on the nature of the world, he sees that everything has energy. Everything "lives." The *pnimiyus* of the *chayut* is *Elokut*, Godliness. The *Chayut* comes enclothed in a garment – and no difference between if you hug the King in one garment or many (from Ch 42 of Tanya). It requires *hergel* – constant, regular reminders – that everything we see in the world are the outer garments of the King, and in that manner one arrives to the *pnimiyut*, to the "inner intention." Now, *hergel* – constant reminders – is not *hitbonenut*, it's not meditation. This is also tied in with *emunah* ("faith," which requires "practice" from the word *lehitamen*), because it's a skill – not just "faith" but a craft – something that requires practice. Also, one has to recall what the sages said, that God is "interested" in us, in uniting His presence *davka* ("only") with us.

- Imagine that twenty people are brought before the King and he picks one and says, "I want to be the king just for him." What about the rest of them? "Never mind, *azov otam*..." So Jews have to think and believe that He wants a connection, a special connection with us. This is something to maintain in *zicharon* ("memory"), to always remember...this *hergel* is in thought, in *machshava*...not *in maaseh* ("action").

Some of the students in the *shiur* seemed to want to claim that Tanya Ch 42 ("does not matter how many garments when hugging the King") is speaking about *hitbonenut*, about meditation, but R' Deitsch emphasized that "No," it's referring to *zicharon*, "reminders."

Returning to beginning of *K'Avoda*, Ch 3...there are matters that lead us to *ohl malchut shamayim* (see beginning of Tanya Ch 41), and other topics that lead us to *yirat Elokim*. The former is associated with *malchut*, with Hashem's reign, the latter is something else, more emotional. If someone meditates how Hashem places His reign upon us, he will achieve *kabalat ohl*. In that case he will be like an *eved*, a "servant." But if he wants to be an *eved* who also has conscious fear of his master, of Hashem, then he has to meditate also on how Hashem is *bochen clayot v'lev* ("checking his kidneys and heart"), standing over him at all times.

- There is an *eved* who is told by the King, "I'm going out, clean up the house." The *eved* knows he has a task to do, but he can do it in a relaxed manner. But if the same *eved* is told by the king, "Here, use this soap and that brush, and I'll be sitting here watching you," so obviously the *eved* has to be more concerned about what kind of job he's doing, and how. He isn't a mere *eved*, he's an *eved* who also has fear. That's *regesh*, emotion. If all that is necessary is for the job should be done properly, then the *eved ne'eman* ("faithful servant") can be relied upon, he'll do his job. But there's an additional factor beside the job being done properly – that the job should be done with *yirah*, with fear. That's the beginning of Ch 42 of Tanya.

Previously in *K'Avoda* on page 13 – we read that *ohl Malchut Shamayim* ("yoke of the reign of Heaven") is concealed and unconscious, but that *yirat cheit* ("fear of sin") and *yirat Elokim* ("fear of *Elokim*") are conscious and aware states of mind. For the latter two, *hitbonenut*, meditation is necessary, while the former (*ohl malchut Shamayim*) is automatic and spontaneous, and does not require meditation. On page 19, *K'Avoda* continues to discuss the *shiluv* ("meshing") of *hitbonenut* and *zicharon*...not only Nebuchednazar (wicked king of Babylonia, who destroyed the first Temple) was rewarded for the 3 steps of *yirat Shamayim* that he took, but also we ourselves, Hashem counts every step...

- *Sippur* ("story"): About two women in Jerusalem, who were *Tzedaka* collectors (the Rav's grandmother also did this, collecting old clothes, etc…for the poor). They promised each other that whoever left the world first would tell the other what they experienced above. The Rav didn't remember all the details, but while one remained downstairs, the other actually went upstairs to collect. The one who went upstairs was the first to leave this world, and she reported to her friend that for her extra steps she also received extra reward…

Shiur 14, Nov 14, 2011

Beginning of Ch 3: It is necessary to begin the journey with *yirah* (which requires "reminders") which must apply to the entire day, but it is not the *avoda* of love, which requires *hitbonenut*…

Page 64 in the translation: "In addition, this [lower level of] fear is only that which is required to prevent us from rebelling…" *Yirah* is to ensure that we don't "rebel against the King," but it is not sufficient to gain for us the description of *eved Hashem*, a "servant of God." What the Rashab is describing here is *avoda pnimiyut*, "inner *avoda*." R' Deitsch says that here, the word *avoda* is an abbreviated expression. The goal of *avoda pnimi* though, is to connect and unite our souls with Godliness and to polish the *chumriyut* ("coarse physicality") of the animal soul (Page 65). Fulfillment of mitzvoth does not require *avoda pnimi* ("internal work"). *Yirah* does not require *avoda* "in various ways." It is simple and straightforward, but *ahava* does require internal work on many levels. Moreover (Page 65), there are those who accept the need for *hagdarat hachushim* naturally (without work and effort), as if to say, "How can it be any other way?"

- It is told that once the Rebbe Rashab had a *havruta* ("study partner") in Chasidut…and the Previous Rebbe (son of the Rashab) happened to be there sleeping as they studied together. The Rebbe Rashab watched over him as they were learning and said to his *havruta*, "He deserves a kiss." The Rashab said that his son demonstrates *taharat hamachshava* – "purity of thought." Many years later, the Previous Rebbe said that his father told him that from the time he was a child, his father "owed him a Chasidishe kiss," and invited him in to hear a *maamar* (Chasidic discourse). This was his Chassidishe *neshika* ("kiss"). The point? R' Deitsch said that there are those who when they sleep, exude "purity of thought," people for whom looking or hearing or thinking the wrong things, are just naturally "off limits." As the *K' Avoda* says in Yiddish, "We're not allowed…"

The point is that you don't find people who naturally love God. It demands *avoda*. There is such a thing as natural love innate within us, but it is unconscious, concealed within, and only emerges in situations when a Jew is faced with *mesirat nefesh*, forcing him to give up his life for YIddishkeit. Otherwise, love only comes to conscious expression via *avoda*, and several chapters of Tanya are devoted to such *avoda*. It's not automatic…the only place *ahavah* comes naturally into revelation are in *emunah* ("faith") which isn't in the category of *avoda*, and in *mesirat nefesh*. The only way it comes into expression in mitzvoth is with the *derech ketzara* ("short path" described in Tanya, ch 18-25 – wherein we use mentally apply the principle of *mesirat nefesh* to every mitzvah that we do); without *avoda* it doesn't happen. So, it seems that *yirah* is "easy" in comparison to *ahava* that demands *avoda*. But on the other hand, there are times that *ahavah* arrives as a "gift" from Above even without an arousal from below…can happen suddenly. But *Yirah* doesn't come suddenly from Above. See the siddur in *ha'arah* to *tikun chatzot*.

- There was a Jew in Tiveria, a big *oved Hashem* (one dedicated to prayer and study) a Slonimer Chasid whom R' Deitsch knew, and the *mashgiach* ("principal") of Slobodka (an important non-Chasidic yeshiva) came to do *Hamei Tiveria* ("Tiberius hot springs"). The important *mussar* rabbis spoke all the time about the *avot* ("forefathers"), and this *mashgiach* of Slobodka Yeshiva, on his return trip said that, "You can meet all of the *avot* in Tiveria at the *hamei Tiveria* – Avraham Avinu is Rav Werner (Rav Deitsch's father in law), Yitzhak Avinu is the Slonimer Chasid mentioned above (R' Deitsch doesn't remember his name, but he would farbreng every Purim. He would say, 'the main thing is that it – the *hitorrerut* ("spiritual arousal of Purim") - should remain after Purim'). Another time when he was lying on his bed, not well, he told R' Deitsch a story of someone with a very high *avoda* – then afterward he told R' Deitsch – "this *avoda* is not relevant to us, but we should know that there is such a thing"). So, once this Slonimer Chasid sat at a farbrengen with other Slonimers (this was the way of Chasidim in general, not just Chabad, to sit with schnapps and farbeisen ("nosh") and speak words of inspiration and encouragement. In Slonim they called it a *zitz* – a sitting together, even tho Chabad calls it a "farbrengen" or *hitva'adut*, in Viznitz they call it a *bahdey*). So he was sitting in his Slonimer *zitz*, and some youngsters were sitting not far away and speaking about their own matters while he was speaking words of *hitorerut* ("inspiration")…he was convinced that they were disagreeing with him (not likely they were talking about his *inyanim* at all), and he said to them, "Don't argue with me on theory, I'm speaking from practical experience..."

- The Rav read from what looks like the siddur, from *ha'arah l'tikun chatzot*. There it says that frequently love will "descend" to the person, *ahavah* as a gift from above, and it's a *milta d'skicha hee* – a "frequent occurrence." However, almost never will a person experience fear from Above without *hitore'rut* – fear is associated with the *Shechina* ("God's presence") and now that we're in *galut* ("exile"), there is little or no *gilui Shechina* ("revelation of the *Shechina*"), and therefore no sudden revelation of fear that occurs to us. Instead of Yerushalyaim – *yirah shalem* – we now have *chum Y'lm* (no *yirah*) - instead of *kabalat ohl malchut shamayim* ("acceptance of the yoke of Heaven"), we have *prikat ohl* ("rejecting the yoke"), expressed by failure to fulfill positive mitzvoth, and most of all, failure to learn Torah. Also, when one is afraid that he won't have *parnasa* ("livelihood") and therefore he accepts upon himself *ohl derech eretz* ("yoke of trying to make a living") – this is a *yirah chitzoni* ("superficial fear") that takes a person away from *yirat shamayim*. There are all kinds of such external fears that cause one to forsake *avodat Hashem*. (Rav Deitsch spoke of someone in the *shiur* who was marrying off his first son – everyone is very worried after the wedding of the first child, but already by the second child, they're not so worried, they see things are *mistader* (things "work out"), but between the first and second, needs a lot of *bitachon*). At any rate, though, we don't find people who are born naturally with conscious revealed love of God, but we do find so by fear.

(Page 66 in the translation) – We don't find spontaneous, automatic love of God, but there is such a thing as an "inclination" to *avodat Hashem*...one who has a talent for Godly matters...

- After the Magid passed away, there were three matters about which there was argument involving the Alter Rebbe: 1) Division of the physical territory: Within the Alter Rebbe's area there were also Chasidim of R' Shlomo Karlin and he asked permission from the Alter Rebbe to visit them one Shabbat a month: The Alter Rebbe agreed on 3 conditions: a) that he won't *mevatel* ("make light of") their *yirat shamayim tivi* ("natural fear of God"), b) that he won't *mevatel Talmidei Chachamim* (that he wouldn't speak badly of non-Chasidic Torah scholars - R' Shlomo used to say that "they don't have any *avodat Hashem*"), and c) that R' Shlomo would demand from his Chasidim that they do their own *avoda* without being dependent upon their Rebbe. R' Shlomo agreed to the first two conditions but not to the final condition. (The concepts have changed since then, Karliner Chasidim themselves are no longer so dependent upon their Rebbe, but back then, it was a major pillar of their *avoda*. Now, such matters as dependence upon the Rebbe you find more in Chabad than in Karlin, and Chabad is also *mevatel natural yirat shamayim* and also *talmidei chachamim*, claiming they aren't *ovdei Hashem* – regarding all 3 conditions one finds more in Chabad now than in Karlin.

- A lot of things changed, also Sfardim changed…once they were those who learned with straightforward logic and it was the Ashkenazim were the *ba'alei pilpul* and *halacha* (who made complicated intellectual calculations in Torah), now it's different. Once Rav Deitsch met someone from Yeshivat *Porat Yoseph* (a Sfardi yeshiva) who told him that in Yeshivat *Porat Yoseph* in the old city (there is more than one branch), they now learn like Ashkenazim, with *havana* and *iyun*. R' Deitsch told him that's mistaken, that originally it was the Sfardim who learned with straightforward logic, and it's the Ashkenazim who adapted that approach from the Sfardim. The entire approach of *iyun* (but not *pilpul*) came from the Sfardim; the Rambam told his son not to learn by *chachomei Tzarfat* (the "French sages," – [this must have been the school of Rashi and later the Tosafot] because they are *m'palpalim*), all the early sages of the "modern period" – the *aharonim* - were Sfardim (*Sha'ar Hamelech, Mishneh LeMelech, Maharit, Machanei Efraim*)…The Rosh took from both "schools" of thought, Sfardi and Ashkenazi.

Shiur 15, November 15, 2011

(Page 66 in the translation) – One isn't born with awareness of *Elokut* ("Godliness"). It comes with meditation and *hitbonenut*, but one may be born with more or less potential to achieve it. That may occur if, 1) If one has "positive talent," with what's called a "high *neshama*" (just like one who has a talent for music), or, 2) the animal soul doesn't hide and conceal so much.

- The Previous Rebbe used to say that the Berdichever (R' Levi Yitzhak) had a grandson. The Berdichever himself had a talent for music, but he had a grandson who was also a grandson of the Alter Rebbe (the Alter Rebbe's daughter married a son of the Berdichever, that's why the name Levi Yitzhak is not uncommon in Chabad). Once the family was together on some kind of journey (France?), and they rented a few rooms in a hotel. One of the family members entered the room and found the grandson of R' Levi Yitzhak flat on the floor, almost fainted. What happened? He overheard someone in the next room singing or playing music, and it touched him so much that he almost fainted. The Alter Rebbe said about him that it was the *chush*, or "talent" of the grandfather who passed on the talent to his grandson.

- Previous Rebbe said that *chushim* ("talents") sometimes pass on to grandchildren, not to children. The Tzemach Tzedek had a talent for engineering that was passed on to grandchildren, and some say that his *kavana* was to the Rebbe. [This must have been passed on to his son the Maharash, who could take apart and put together a complicated watch. But the Rashab, who was a grandson of the Tzemach Tzedek, had no *chush* in physical matters; there is a story from the Rav in which after the Maharash passed away and the family had to figure out the finances, the Rashab asked for the figures and accounting. When they explained it to him, he "didn't get it." He asked twice for an explanation, and still didn't comprehend]. There's a Chassidic explanation for this: There are *kishronot* ("talents"), *cochot* ("abilities") and *chushim* ("sensibilities")…some have a *chush* for *Elokut*.

- R' Shlomo Chaim said that R' Hillel Paritcher spoke of Yoseph who was punished because he requested help from the *Sar Hamashkeh* – Pharoah's "butler" who had been in prison with him. Instead, he should have relied on the One above Himself (Rashi). But Yaakov Avinu relied on the *maklot* ("shepherd's staff") and other means for making *parnassa* (a "living"), why didn't he just have *bitachon* and wait for the riches to come from Above? Chasidut explains that Yoseph had such a high soul, even higher than Yaakov in its root, that he did not have to put in such efforts. How did Yoseph's higher soul become evident? By the fact that even in Egypt he remained on his high spiritual level (which is why his brothers didn't recognize him; they didn't think he could remain "Yoseph" even while involved in everyday life). This is a very high level, to be able to remain on a spiritual level even when involved in the physical world – even Yaakov needed some "removal" from the world in order to maintain his spiritual level – so written in Chassidut. Acc to R' Shlomo Chaim, R' Hillel Paritcher would ask, 'How is it possible to come with claims against Yoseph that he didn't hold himself higher than his father?' Why would anyone expect a son to think that he is "higher" than his father (and therefore should not have asked the *Sar Hamashkeh* ("butler") if that's what his father Yaakov was likely to have done if in the same situation). R' Shlomo Chaim answered that Yoseph had a *chush* – a talent and potential – in this matter of Godliness, and it was *assur* ("forbidden") for him not to utilize it. The various *cheshbonot* ("investigations"), etc, whether he was more or less than Yaakov his father, were not the point. The point is if you have a *chush* (and Yoseph did), don't waste it. In the case of Yoseph, the *chush* was associated with the high level of his soul.

- But, what are *chushim tovim* ("good sensibilities")? What does it mean to have a positive potential? In general, there are various *chushim* – one of them is for example, a winemaker – someone who knows how to identify and make good wines, that's a *chush*. It's possible to develop and cultivate such a talent, but there's a huge difference between one who is born with such a talent and one who is not born with it but cultivates the talent. There is also a *chush* in drawing and "art." Also in music. These days, we call it a "talent" (*kisharon*), but the truth is that according to Chasidut, a *chush* and a *kisharon* are two different things, acc to Chasidut. *Kisharon* (talent) is more associated with *sechel* (Intellect), but R' Deitsch doesn't remember exactly the differences. (R' Eliyahu Hadad told story how he and a friend pursued mathematics together but a teacher told him, "Don't look at what the friend is doing, he has a *chush* and you don't. It will be very hard for you to get to the same place where he can get easily").

- Rav Deitsch has a cousin who learned *graphologia* – "handwriting analysis." He came once a week from the south to Jerusalem in order to learn the subject. He would come and visit R' Deitsch at home after going to two different *graphologim* (who taught him the topic). R' Deitsch asked him why two? He answered, "One of them has a *chush* [that was R' Lifshiptz, a well known handwriting expert in French Hill], the other only learned the subject." R' Deitsch asked the cousin, "who is more accurate," and the cousin answered that the one who only "learned the subject" is more accurate in his handwriting analysis. If so, why go to both? He answered (in the words of R' Deitsch), "The one who has a *chush*, his *neshama* is in it." The other one only knows the principles and he's more accurate, but the first one with the *chush*, "his soul is in it." That's what it means, a *chush*. The other one knows "according to the book," according to the principles and the *clalim* ("general rules"). Like one who knows *Shulhan Aruch* well, for each situation he knows the principles and the details, so he knows what to do according "to the book." On the other hand, there is one with a *chush tevi*, a "natural flair" for *halacha*, he may not know the principles or details of the Shulhan Aruch. The one who knows *Shulhan Aruch* is more precise, more correct halachically, he's called a *tzaddik*. He goes by the book, he gets close to Hashem via the *Shulhan Aruch*. But there's more *neshama* to the *ba'al teshuva*...he has a *chush tevi*...the B"T's maybe miss a little of the *Shulhan Aruch* here and there, but they put more *chayut* into the matter...more *neshama*. There's an advantage here, and an advantage there. At any rate, there's such a thing called a *chush b'Elokut* ("talent for Godliness") – what they do is with *chayut* ("vitality")...every Jew has a *chush* for *Elokut*, and that is the *hagdara* ("what classifies") a soul, but still just like by music there are some with more of a talent, so it is by some Jews who have more of a natural inclination for divine matters. And so by winemakers as well, everyone can taste, but some have more ability than others. Regarding their sensitivity, Rav Deitsch's brother in law, R' Auerbach, told R' Deitsch that the winemaker for Yarden wines, where he gives the *hechser*, told him that he cannot drink the wine, he can only taste and spit it out. If he drinks it, he will ruin his sense of taste. (The wine taster meantime hasn't done *teshuva*, so there is a problem of *yayin nesach*...)

There are some who have a *chush*, but are *ba'alei teshuvah* and because of that they don't make progress, since they often lack the confidence to capitalize on their abilities.

- Long story that the Previous Rebbe told about the Rebbe Maharash... regarding the Maharash's chasid, R' Munyeh Monsour, who was an accomplished Chasid, *oved Hashem*, who used to accompany the Maharash on his trips *b'inyanei tzibur* ("public matters") and *askanut* ("public involvement"). They went to France for some reason, and there the Maharash wanted to rent a room in a very expensive hotel. There was a third person with the Maharash and he said that he could stay at a less expensive hotel, but they were one group. The Maharash wanted a room on the same floor as the gambling/gaming room. R' Monyeh narrated that he saw the Maharash enter the room and sit near the gaming table, as the people there were playing and drinking wine. The Maharash approached and tapped one of them on the shoulder and said to him, *Yungerman, yayin nesach m'tamtem es halev* – "Young man, non-Jewish wine blocks the heart." R' Monyeh said he never saw the Maharash in such a state of emotional agitation as he saw him at that moment after saying those words to the young player. After a short period, the young man (he was Jewish of course, the others may not have been Jewish) looked for the Rebbe and asked, "Where is the man who spoke with me?" He went and knocked on the Rebbe's door and sat with him for several hours, and became a complete *baal teshuva* ("one who did total *teshuva* and from then on kept the Torah"), the Rebbe said that a certain French family (beginning with "Resh") comes from that individual. Some French Jews know of the hotel and of the family. The Maharash said that for many years such a high soul had not come down, but that it had fallen into the *Klipot* ("forces of negativity") and that's why it was necessary for him to travel to France to pull it out of the *klipot*. This is an example of a high *neshama*, but you see that nonetheless, the *yayin nesach* ("non-Jewish wine") and *klipah* could conceal his spiritual greatness. There are also souls that possess both advantages; the soul is high (he has the *chush*) and the *nefesh behamit* doesn't conceal. Another example is *Resh Lakish* who made a transformation being from the chief of a band of robbers to a total *B"T*.

Page 66-67: – *Yirah* does not demand that we contemplate *pratim* ("details"), but *ahava* does demand that we meditate on the details. *Yirah* truly touches on *atzmut* ("essence") that is beyond details, but this is the kind of *yirah* that is not conscious, it's concealed, like one who likes himself, even tho he doesn't feel himself. It's not "feeling," emotion, it's something so essentially a part of him that it can only come into expression in a negative manner. The Mitteler Rebbe explains in *Derech Chaim* that this level of *yirah* can come to expression in a certain part of the person, while in another part it is not expressed. *Yediah* – "knowledge," for example – either you know or you don't. But something essential – a person can be aware of it on one level, but unaware of it on another level, this can happen. Not *makif* ("transcendent") but also not specific *yediah pratit*. (Skip parentheses, hopefully in a second reading, we'll come back to it). The *yirah* that we need does not necessitate *tefila*.

- The Rav said to R' Eliyahu Hadad, sitting across from him, that sometimes reading the writing of the Rebbeim, you get the feeling that they are speaking of matters that are occurring so to speak, within their own house, "heimish" - feeling "at home." Once R' Deitsch spoke to someone (a student of the *Hazon Ish*, who became very upset with him in response) – about a letter in which the *Hazon Ish* wrote that, "We don't have clear guidelines how to achieve fear and love of God in *tefila*" – to which R' Deitsch replied, "In Chasidut we do have." (The Rav mentioned that the *Hazon Ish* respected Chasidim, even though he was opposed to the *derech* of Chasidut. It was the *Hazon Ish* who brought Rav Landau to be the Rav in Bnei Brak [according to Rav Landau's grandson, the *Hazon Ish* merely did not oppose his appointment]).

Shiur 16, November 16, 2011

Page 68 (in the translation), "In Tanya, Ch 42…" there it is written that in order to achieve *yirah* ("fear" of God), it is necessary for us to labor in thought"… at first glance this seems to be in contradiction to what was stated previously, that there are some who are born with a tendency toward natural fear of God. However, here is stated that it is necessary to medidate at length for an hour. In Tanya (also as quoted here in *K'Avoda*), it states there are those who attain *yirah* immediately, as soon as they start meditating. But *ahavah* ("love" of God) is not like that, no one achieves *ahavah* immediately. The main topic of *K'Avoda* is *ahavah*. Nevertheless, without *yirah*, *ahavah* will not develop. The Rebbe Rashab writes that at any rate one must understand that nothing is concealed from God. See Ch 42, (*nun-tet amud beit* in Tanya) – Here, the Rav asks if the *Shulhan Aruch* (Ramah in *Orech Chaim* 1:1, based on language from Rambam's *Moreh Nevuchim*), which says, "When we consider that the King… is standing over us…we immediately become fearful" - is referring specifically to the *nefesh zachah* ("pure soul") that the Tanya mentions here ("immediately as he meditates, *yirah* falls upon him")? The Rav's question - for which he has no answer meantime: Is the *Shulhan Aruch* written for the *nefesh zacha* ["pure soul," which needs no lengthy meditation]?"

- R' Avraham ben HaRambam wrote about his father that when he would don tefillin, he would shake uncontrollably and when he grasped the table to steady himself, the table also shook.

- R' Zusia of Anipol prayed to achieve the *yirat Hashem* of the Rambam, but as it came down to him, it was too much for him. He then requested the *yirah* of R' Avraham Ibn Ezra, and also for this he couldn't handle it. (R' Deitsch didn't see this written anywhere, but "heard it").

(Continuation in Tanya Ch 42): Another level, a lower level are those who can achieve *yirat Hashem* only with great difficulty, particularly if they are sullied with *Chatat Neurim* ("sin of youth" - spilling seed)…as written in *Sefer Chasidim siman* 35. So, we know that there are at least two levels: *nefesh zacha be'tivah* ("naturally pure soul") and *nefesh shfeila* ("low soul"), both of which may be affected by sins. Tanya continues and tells us that even so, one who works hard on himself can attain *yirah tata'ah*. It's a "treasure" that we can reveal with hard work, like looking for a buried treasure.

- A common question arises: "How is it possible to instruct/command love and fear of God?" Several answers are given, but one of them, given by Chassidut, is that love and fear are natural and intrinsic within a Jew, and the challenge is to reveal and activate them. It's as if someone might ask, "Why should I love my children?" or "Why should I love myself?" The soul contains natural *ahavah* and *yirat Hashem*, but in order to reveal it from within, one must think about it and contemplate the topic until it emerges, becomes revealed. If it were a matter of time, it would mean that the love and fear are limited. But since we say that it's within us, that means it has no limitations. If something is beyond time, then it's without limitations, and therefore we say that the *ahavah* and *yirah* within are "unlimited." And therefore, "time" does not apply to these reservoirs of love and fear of God within us. But, if we want to "utilize" these storehouses of love and fear, we have to find our own words and concepts to access them. "To bring it down into accessible concepts you have to bring it into "time." Just to say, "I have that in potential, or even, "I have that inside" – will not lead to anything. So how do we "bring it down" to access it in our own life? By way of *hitbonenut*, "meditation." And that enters into the realm of time, because it depends on how much time we dedicate to meditation. If we meditated in the morning, we could already face "problems" at night…even though the love inside remains unlimited. This is because the love inside is far beyond the limitations of time. So, it emerges that our job is to reveal what's inside of ourselves. If one says to himself, "I have this," and he reviews to himself over and over again, he will reveal it. If he says, "I have to run after other things and look for them," he will lose the desire to find it. It is similar to telling someone, "You have *kishronot*, you have talent" – which encourages him. As we see in Tanya, beginning of Ch 42, everyone has a bit of Moshe Rabeinu within him…and at the end of the chapter, we find out that the "piece of Moshe" within us is the attribute of *da'at* within us. It's Moshe Rabeinu who elicits *da'at* from us. A good *mashpiah* ("mentor") or *magid shiur* ("teacher") can do the same.

- Here, we find two components, 1) *hitbonenut* and 2) *segula*. Fulfillment of mitzvoth is *seguli*, meaning that it's something supernatural that we can't even analyze or grasp; we don't know what's in it. But *hitbonenut* focuses on matters that we do know how to understand and explain. So the message of Tanya here is, "You should know that what you seek to reveal is beyond the limitations of time. But in order to reveal it, depends on how much time you put into thinking about in *hitbonenut*." Which *hitbonenut*? It is necessary to think into how He is "*mabit* (observes) and *makshiv* ("listens") and *mavin* ("understands") and *tzofeh* ("watches") all of our deeds, and examines *clayot* ("kidneys") and *lev* ("heart")." God "observes and listens and understands and watches all of our deeds, and examines our *kishkes* and heart." And when we work on this and meditate for a "long time," it becomes fixed in our awareness, and all we will need to to is review it from time to time.

Now back to *K'Avoda*, page 68, "Here, the *K'Avoda* is saying that one has to be aware that God "sees him." Is that enough, that God "sees him"? Or does he need to explain to himself and bring it closer to himself and understand how it is that nothing conceals him from God? Doesn't he also need that? *K'Avoda* says "yes," he needs to know and understand that nothing is hidden from Him. In other words, we need to inject it with some understanding…"He who formed the eye, can He not see? He who made the ear, can He not hear?"

- Rav Deitsch heard in the name of the Chafetz Chaim, but others also said, that the purpose of all electronic gadgets, such as telephone, radio, telegraph, etc…is in order to understand and feel the presence of Hashem…so we know that it is possible to be aware from afar. Sound waves, radio waves, etc, coming at us at the speed of light or more…so we know there is something that "exists," the antennae detect it.

So all of this is in order to bring us to *hasaga* ("grasp") of the matter. And the *hasaga* helps us to achieve *yirah tata'ah*. In parentheses, *K'Avoda* says even one with a *nefesh zacha* ("pure soul") needs this *hitbonenut*, all the more so one who is not *zacha*…who is tainted with "sin of youth" (spilling seed), etc, needs this *hitbonenut* even moreso. Quite the opposite, one who is on a lower, more coarse level, needs more *hitbonenut*. (Page 71) The best time for this is *zman hatefila*, the "time of prayer." If so though, it emerges that *tefila* is also a good time for *hitbonenut* on *yirah*? And that would be opposite to what was established earlier (that meditation to attain fear is not at the time of *tefila*, because *tefila* is the time for meditation to attain love of God)? On this, *K'Avoda* answers that it "doesn't have to be *b'zman tefila* – can be any other time as well." The time of *tefila* is better, more auspicious, but this thought process can take place at other times as well. This feeling is "easy" for every Jew to achieve.

- In answer to a question from R' Eliyahu Hadad, R' Deitsch said that the question appears in *Sifri*: "One who fears does not love, and one who loves does not fear." This is human nature: One cannot both love and fear – one either loves or fears another person – and there is only one situation in which we can feel both love and fear, and that's love and fear of God.

- Rambam in *Hilchot Yediat Hashem* Perek 2, same meditation brings to both fear and to love.

Summary: From time to time one needs meditation to achieve fear, but not necessarily *b'zman hatefila,* at the time of morning prayers.

Shiur 17, November 22, 2011

In summary, now that we're in Ch 3: Even though the main goal is to achieve *ahavat Hashem* ("love of God"), one of course needs *Yirat Hashem* ("fear of God") as well, but *Yirah* ("fear") is not associated with *hitbonenut* ("meditation") but with *zicharon* ("memory and recall") and is not necessarily associated with *tefila* ("prayer"). Then, *K'Avoda* on page 19 (page 68 in the translation) quotes from Tanya Ch 42, which among other things states that the time most *mesugal* ("appropriate") and auspicious even for *yirat Hashem* is during *tefila* – but it doesn't have to be during *tefila,* it can be anytime. Page 71 in the translation…"It is understood that the most propitious time…" that man can feel that God is everywhere and therefore all is known to Him – can be a meditation anytime and anywhere. If this seems "far" from us, it's possible that's because we simply haven't tried it…but if we would try it, it would not be difficult.

- Once R' Deitsch sat with R' Shmeryl Sassonkin, who was *shaliach* ("emissary") of the Rebbe Rashab in Batun in Buchara or Georgia. R' Deitsch arrived with *bachurim* (young yeshiva students) from Kfar Chabad and they organized to go in to see R' Sassonkin…he agreed to farbreng with the guys, they sang *"Essen, essen, trinken trinken… but what can we do that the tefila does not flow as it should?"* The *bachurim* sang it seriously, but R' Sassonkin stopped them suddenly in the middle and asked, "How do you know that your *tefila* doesn't flow *(fun vannen veist ir…probirt?)*, did you try? Maybe it does flow…" Same here, we don't try it, maybe if we try, it would "go"? We learn all about our sins and it makes us afraid, maybe if we would be less afraid of our own sins we would be more willing to try…the Rebbe says that man doesn't put in *yagiah* ("effort") for *sur ma'rah* (to turn away from bad), but rather for *aseh tov* (in order to do something constructive).

- Rav Deitsch was once in a Sfardi shul where they say *Shir Hashirim* ("Song of songs" - the Rebbe also wanted to institute that we should say *Shir Hashirim*) before Shabbat. The Rav looked into Rashi to get the *pshat* ("textual meaning" of the words) in the words, and there Rashi says that the entire *Shir Hashirim* is about accepting *ohl malchut Shamayim* ("yoke of Heaven"). Look in *Shay leMorah, Vayikra*…"All the writings are holy, and Shir haShirim is holy of holies, full of *yirat shamayim* and *kabalat ohl.*" Similar question as regarding *tefila: Ohl malchut shamayim* is associated with fear, not love, yet we find *ohl malchut shamayim* in *kriat shema*, which is dedicated to love of God, so what's the connection (between *Shir Hashirim* and *ohl malchut shamayim*?) R' Deitsch wanted to suggest a very conventional (*balabatish*) answer; "The *yetzer harah* "positions itself" to get involved in of all kinds of "foreign" love, so therefore for the *yetzer harah* to accept divine love upon itself requires *ohl malchut shamayim*..."

The main point is that this *yirah* comes from knowing that the One above is watching, observing, etc, sees us at every point and every time (Page 72).

- Like someone who brings a cleaner into the house and tells her to clean it. But sometimes the employer stands over her and says, "Hey, over there you didn't clean..." so she feels someone is watching at all times. In our case, the *Baal habayit* ("Master of the house") not only watches but sends us messages, as it says in verses from the Torah..."All these sorrowful events and problems...and we say, 'Because Hashem is not among us...'" (Deut 31:17). It hurts a lot when He sends signals and we don't get it. The sages said that our generation is not able to accept signals of *yisurim* ("suffering"), only of *simcha* ("joy"). Signs of *yisurim* will only bring *nefilat ruach* ("depression")...once upon a time, the generations could even deal with *macot* ("striking") and the teachers could give a potch. The Rebbe wrote about it: "In this generation, if the father strikes, the child will run away or they'll put the father in jail."

The Rav emphasizes from page 72, "This feeling is easy to generate in the soul, even at times that are not appropriate for prayer." And this is because that's the way God created a Jew, so that it's "easy" for him to feel this *yirah*. So, we're back to the original point...*yirah* demands *hitbonenut*, which occurs best during *tefila*, but is not necessary to be at time of *tefila*. The Rebbe said that all the negative things that happen to us are because we no longer have the feeling that "someone is watching over us and observing our actions." If that were ever to be re-established then crime would go down...so the Rebbe wanted to institute a "moment of silence" [this was after a period that the Rebbe wanted prayer in the public school, since anyway the US currency says on it, "In God we trust"] but this was instituted in only a few locations. The concept of, "The eye sees and the ear hears," is very basic, "it's not even a *madreiga* ("spiritual level")." Now, we need to arouse this during *tefila* a few times, and then it will be easier to attain after that. It is also possibly aroused via *shkeida* (constant, regular repetition of behavior, being consistent about it)... so either during *tefila* or spending a significant amount of time on it outside of *tefila* – as in Tanya, "If He is *mitbonen sha'ah gedolah b'kol yom* ("if he takes a substantial amount of time to meditate every day"). But this amount of time required to meditate is not "equal for everyone," it's very individual. (In response to a question from R' Eliyahu Hadad, R' Deitsch answered that apparently the experience of *yirah* is different during tefila than during "off-prayer" hours, or perhaps the *hitbonenut* is different).

- Rav Deitsch says he doesn't know how to explain it spiritually (in *ruchniyut*), but physically, we all know for example that we can eat the cholent and then one day, it strikes us that, "Today it was really special." So in *tefila* we might find it different...difficult to nail it down...but we know it's different.

Page 73-74, "The general point..." – no *ahava* without *hitbonenut*.

- When the *yetzer* ("evil inclination") attacks, the Gemora says, "Mention *kriat shema* and if that doesn't work, remind yourself of the day of *petira* (of the day you will pass away)." R' Deitsch once heard that "*kriat shema*" applies to Chasidim (that it's Chasidim who should remind themselves of *kriat shema*) and "*Yom hamita*" applies to Litvaks (that it's Litvaks who should remind themselves of the day they will die). On the other hand, from this expression, the Litvaks have a "proof" that *mussar* is more effective than Chasidut. Since the expression, "*yizkor lo yom hamita*" follows the expression, "If *kriat shema* doesn't work," that is evidence that recalling *kriat shema* by the Chasidim is not sufficient to calm down the evil inclination, and therefore one must (like the Litvaks) recall the "day of passing away." But the Rebbe explained that the words mean, *yizkor lo* – mean "remind him," the *yetzer harah* – "you (the *yetzer harah*) are going to die," implying that, "I will remain alive." So, the advice of the Gemora is to start with *ahava*, with *kriat shema*, and only if "love" doesn't work, do we try something more shocking like visiting a jail or a hospital (to remind the *yetzer harah* of *yom hamita* – the "day of passing away").

Shiur 18, November 23, 2011

Page 73-74 in the translation, in the parentheses: "The meditation that brings it [love] about...that is integrated and absorbed...is possible only at the appropriate time of prayer." The two cardinal points are "integrated" and "absorbed." Like a smell that gets into an object, becomes indelibly attached to it, the only way it dissipates is by just leaving it over time. Same thing with spirituality; the minute it's absorbed, it's integrated. But if you don't deal with it, cultivate it, slowly slowly it dissipates.

- The Rebbe Rashab (in the midst of other matters) describes how he would not say a *maamer* ("Chasidic discourse") until he had absolutely integrated it within himself. If he felt that a particular *maamar* that he wanted to say, based on a *maamar* from his father, the Rebbe Maharash, was not sufficiently absorbed and integrated in his mind, so he would go to the *kever* ("burial site") of the Maharash. And he would return there (not known what he did there), until as his son the Previous Rebbe put it, the Maharash gave his "okay" on it, learned something with him…but the point is that until the Rashab completely absorbed the *maamar* that he wanted to say, it was an *avoda gedola* – a "major effort."

- R' Deitsch wants to emphasize that there is a difference between the "Intellect" of a concept, and the *Elokut* ("Godliness") of that same concept. If one grasps and understands a concept, his understanding can stay with him for years. But to grasp the *pnimiyut* within the concept, the *Elokut* at the core of the concept, demands much *avoda, avoda gedolah beyotar* ("a huge amount of effort and work"), *nefesh zachah* ("pure soul"). It requires more than intellectual effort and understanding in order to grasp the *Elokut* behind a concept, because the intellectual grasp is only a *keli*, a "vessel" for the *Elokut*. For example, the Previous Rebbe explained – we know that most *hitbonenut* in Chabad is based on *achdut Hashem*, the knowledge that He is one and united. Much explanation and understanding is required in order to enable us to grasp it:

- One story is about a Chassid who spent hours davening with great *hitorerut* ("arousal") and devotion, and he was asked, "What are you meditating about with such devotion during davening?" He answered that someone went into *yechidut* ("private audience") with the Alter Rebbe (the Rebbe was recorded telling this story) and the Alter Rebbe said, "*Shamor v'zachor b'dibur echad…*" ("Keep and guard in one utterance" – this refers to the Ten Commandments – the Alter Rebbe said it means that we must "remember and 'preserve' the *echad* in every thing." In everything there is *echad* ("oneness, unity"), since there is *Elokut* ("Godliness") in every thing. We do not know whether the Alter Rebbe meant every "word" or every "thing," that's not clear (because the Hebrew for "word" is the same as "thing" – *davar*), but the *ikar* is to find the *achdut Havaya* (the "unity of God" in everything). So, the Chasid answered that he davens with this vort from the Alter Rebbe, to find and to live with the *echad* within everything. In the recording, the Rebbe says that this Chassid would daven with this thought every day, "every Sunday, every Monday… mentioning every day." So this Chasid davened every single day with the vort from the Alter Rebbe.

- The *maskilim* ("intellectuals" among the Chasidim) explored and investigated the concept of *achdut Hashem*, there are *maamorim* ("Chassidic discourses") from the Rebbeim involved with this topic and all the notable chasidim and *maskilim* were involved in the topic. Yet, here you have this one Chasid who heard from the Alter Rebbe that everything is *achdut Havaya*, and he felt such *hitrerut* that he meditated upon it until it became absorbed and integrated within him – not only the *haskala* ("grasp") and *hesber* ("explanation"), but the concept itself. This requires a tremendous amount of *avoda pnimi* ("inner work"), not only intellect. To uncover this feeling of *Elokut*, it is written in both *K'Avoda* and *K'Tefila* that we need to do *itkafia* ("bending, subduing" our natural physical inclinations). *Klitah* of this sort is more than just *ruchniyut* ("spirituality"). *Klitah* of *Elokut* relative to *ruchiniyut* is akin to *ruchniyut* relative to *gashmiyut*. For example, a good taste in the mouth compared to hearing a nice piece of music – the music is *ruchani* ("spiritual") compared to the taste, and so is *Elokut* in comparison to *ruchniyut*. Regarding one who does a favor for another Jew, it is written about him that his mind and heart become *zachin* ("purified") a thousand times over. *Zachut* ("pureness") is *adinut* ("refinement") that comes as a *segula* from Above.

Back to page 73-74, after mentioning "integrated and absorbed," the *K'Avoda* mentions another stage: *yurgash* – the concept must become "felt," and it is written in Chassidut that this is associated with the attribute of *da'at*, or "visceral knowledge." Sometimes we may feel that something is about to occur and we are nervous or experience some other emotional apprehension; for example if we suspect that war is approaching. Yet, when the situation itself arrives, we experience something else entirely. And if we are asked, did you all of a sudden absorb new knowledge about the situation, the answer is, "No, I knew all of this already." The difference between what we knew and understood before it happened and what we now feel, lies not in our knowledge and understanding of the situation, but in our experience of it and feelings about it. What brings this *hergesh*, this "feeling," is *re'iyha*, or vision. When we are faced with the situation in front of our eyes, the feeling is different. The Rebbe Maharash writes that when King David said to his son, Shlomo (in his final testament), *Da et Elokei Avicha* – "Know the God of your fathers" - why command him to "know" something, "tell him" and he'll know it!? But King David meant to convey to his son Shlomo – "the things that you know, bring them into *daat*, into *hergesh* ("emotion"), so that you feel it." This is *hitkashrut* ("cleaving, connection to," as in a father to a son, or a mentor to a student) as well. Why *regesh*? Why does *regesh* or "feeling," when associated with *Havana* ("understanding"), lead to *ahavah*, "love of God"? *Regesh* and *havana* mesh the mind and heart together. *Regesh* is associated with the heart, and *havana* with the mind, but *da'at* is the intermediary that leads from the mind to the heart, that's why it serves as a passage way from mind to emotions.

- When a boy becomes Bar Mitzvah, we say that he becomes a *bar-da'at* (a person whose opinion we can respect). Not that he becomes a *bar chacham* ("wise person") or *bar havana* ("understanding person"), but a *bar da'at*. There is such a thing as a young kid (under 13) who is a *chacham* or a *baal havana*, but not who is a *bar da'at*.

- The Rebbe Maharash asks, why do we say *chonen hada'at* ("Who grants us *da'at*") as the conclusion of the first of the twelve middle blessings of the *shemonah esreh*? We do mention *chochma* and *bina* in the blessing, but why do we conclude specifically with *da'at*? The answer is that *chochma* and the *bina* are only a bridge and passageway that lead us to *da'at*. The main goal and the conclusion is *da'at*, which is also the ability to distinguish between matters. A *shochet* ("ritual slaughterer") needs the ability to feel a *pegima*, to feel a blemish on the blade of his knife, and that feeling is called a *hargasha*. It is written in *Shulhan Aruch*, that one who is more *yirat shamayim* will be able to feel the blemish easier. Also one who goes to the mikveh will be able to feel the blemish more readily. And there in the Shulhan Aruch, the ability to "feel" this blemish in the knife is called a *hargasha*.

And these are special qualities that specifically require the time of *tefila*. But *yirah* does not necessarily require the time of *tefila*. The reason for this is that *yirah* is associated with *atzmut* ("essence"), the very essence of Godliness, while *ahava* is associated with *giluim* ("specific revealed levels") and *ohr ein sof* ("infinite light of Hashem"). So, we should not think that *yirah* is somehow "lower" than *ahavah* just because it doesn't require *tefila*. In its inception, it is just the opposite; what "emerges" from *atzmut* does not require specific times and circumstances, but *ahava* associated with *giluim* does require specific time and avoda.

To bring this down to a more understandable level: If someone were to ask, "When is one "alive" and at his best?" You might answer that man is at his best when he is happy, perhaps about getting married…But if you think about it, you realize that the happiness that we attain thru music, etc, is only external and superficial. It is happiness of a certain kind and category (*giluim* – specific levels, so to speak), it's not the "real thing." Real happiness is associated with "regular" life; it is what comes through when things are just "normal," grey so to speak. What we feels at such times is more expressive of our *etzem*, of who we are in essence. In *kedusha* (the realm of "holiness"), the same dichotomy exists: the *atzmi* ("essence") and *giluim* ("specific levels"). What we "feel" is not "us" as we are, it is not the person, but what we feel. By way of further example, what attracts us to food is the spices, the taste and smell of the spices…but the spices are only an intermediary that draws us to the food itself, the meat. Or music; we don't listen at all times, we cannot sing all day long. There are specific times for music, such as during *tefila* (there were claims against K. David that he called *tefila zemirot*).

- Once R' Deitsch read an article from a *ba'alat teshuva*, within a *choveret* that included stories of many *B'T's*…she wrote about herself that one of the things that bothered her was *shidduchim*…what is this business of meeting someone just a few times before tying the knot? Until she looked into it and saw the statistics and found just the opposite, those who hung out longer before marriage got divorced at a higher rate, and she investigated why…she concluded that those who hang out more just like doing things together such as restaurants, plays, whatever, but that does not mean they are at all compatible with one another. But those who meet a few times and get married are not checking into all the items that are part of personal connection, they are looking into his *midot* ("character traits") and what kind of a person is he *yom-yom*, on a daily basis. And the decision whether or not to get married is made on how the person lives and interracts on a daily basis. Afterward they can check out the personal connection.

- One who is unable to get up in the morning to go to work to support his family – this is a trait that a person either possesses or does not. The need to support the family is an essential trait, coming from within, and very difficult to instill if it is not there to begin with.

Shiur 19, November 24, 2011

There has to be *klita* ("absorption, integration") and *hargasha* ("feeling") of the concept during *hitbonenut* in order to achieve *ahava*, and that happens during *tefila*, unlike *yirah* which is dependent upon *zicharon* ("reminders") and can take place any time (even though the best time is during *tefila*).

In the Hebrew text, end of second line page 20 (page 76 in the translation), "Furthermore…" *Ahava* ("love") cannot remain conscious and revealed all day long. Generally speaking, only an impression of *ahavah* is left after our *tefila*. There are specific times for love, can't be constant. (Question then arises, how can *ahavat Hashem* be called one of the "constant mitzvoth"? And the answer seems to be that either the leftover impression or the actions that result from the *ahava* maintain its constancy). *Roshem* – "impression" – is not as strong as *zicharon* ("reminder, memory"). *Yirah* is a situation; for example – one remembers all day long not to eat certain things that damage his health. But to eat rogaloch (not so healthy), for example – we only do so certain times during the day [the Rav said this as he and the hevra were eating rogaloch on the table].

Regarding the constant mitzvah of love of God, the verse itself commands us to love Him "with all your heart, with all your soul, with all your might" and these are all expressions of love. So the commandment is not to arouse love to become an active emotion throughout the day, but that the emotion should have results, should have extensions that carry through the day. So, if all day long we give *tzedaka* and we do that as an expression of *ahavat Hashem*, it's logical that also constitutes fulfillment of *ahavat Hashem*, the mitzvah of loving God. It's not possible for the emotion to extend throughout the day, it's just not natural, and it's not the way Hashem created the world.

In the text, page 76, "In the Zohar…" Here the Zohar emphasizes a different *yirah*, a different "fear" that comes from awareness of God's essential existence – and this occurs only during *tefila* – "as servants of God can testify." The previous *yirah* was a result of awareness of Hashem standing over us, watching and "checking out" our kidneys and heart, etc – this fear need not occur during *zman hatefila,* the "time of prayer." Just like people have "fear" of a *tzaddik* (righteous person) because *man malchei, Rabonen* – "who is the king? The rabbis." Even so, the *hergesh* ("feeling") once you entered the office for *yechidut* ("private audience" with the Rebbe, who was of course a *tzaddik*) was something else entirely, *pachad v'aima* ("fear and trembling"), and not because the Rebbe was going to do something to you. This is *yirah boshet* ("fear with self effacement, awe"), *yirah ila'ah* ("supernal fear"). Awe. And this may occur during *tefila*. (R' Yoseph Halbfinger *olav hashalom* – a Chabad psychologist who attended R' Deitsch's *shiurim*, mentioned that in this situation one is afraid to move, afraid to approach). As R' Deitsch said, "he can't find room for himself." This *yirah* is mentioned in perek 43 and 41 of Tanya. Clearly not a *madreiga* ("spiritual level") that is possible to maintain all day long. And it's beyond *tefila* and beyond the *ahava* that we attempt to attain during *tefila*. It's beyond any attempt to cleave and cling to the One above, it is the feeling of "*kulo kamei k'lo chashiv*" – "all is as if non-existent" – and it's associated with *shemonah esreh*. We are completely *butel* ("nullified"), lose our own identity. The *shemonah esreh* is not a time for *hitbonenut*, for meditation; we even ask Hashem to "open our mouths" for us so that we can pray. Since we are "standing in front of the King," we cannot open our own mouth. This is a halachic category.

- R' Eliyahu Hadad asked, "How is it at this moment we ask for our needs, if we're "standing *butel* before the King"? Maharal of Prague asks, is this *avoda sh'belev*? We're asking for our physical needs in front of the King? (Maharal in *Netivot Olam, netiv ha'avoda*). Maharal emphasizes that the whole purpose is to be, "Like a servant before his master, like a maidservant before her mistress, so we are in front of the King, until He answers us." *Sefat Emet* also mentions, what about someone who has *parnasa* ("income"), yet he also says the *bracha* ("blessing") requesting *parnasa* – the *Sefat Emet* answers that the request is that we should "recognize that our *parnasa* comes from God." And that's actually more difficult than asking for *parnasa* when we don't have.

R' Deitsch himself asks about the *nusach* ("liturgy") in *shemonah esreh* during the *bracha, Hasheiva Shofteinu* ("Return our judges…"); later in the *bracha* we request, *haser me'imanu yagon v'anacha* – "remove from us misery and sighing" – what is this doing here in the middle of the blessing about bringing back our judges and rabbis? R' Deitsch answers that the presence of misery and sighing mentioned here is because our courts and judges are not what they should be. For years and years, one hires a lawyer and goes to court until *sof-sof* he gets his money, *Hashem yerachem aleinu*…commentaries say that this *inui din* ("suffering from the time it takes to receive a legal decision") and *ivut hadin* ("receiving a 'wrong' and distorted legal decision") is what leads to *yagon v'anacha*, "sighing and misery." And what if in the end, he gets his money and there is no sighing and misery? Will he then stop talking to *Hashem*? About that there is the conclusion of the blessing, wherein we ask for *chesed v'rachimim*, "mercy and kindness" – grant us the kind of *melucha* ("reign") and nation in which the judgment comes with "mercy and kindness," not with sighing and misery. We request that there will be a situation in which He will remind us to serve Him and ask Him not only when there is not "sighing and misery," but also when there is "kindness and mercy." This is not a simple *bracha*…

- Rav Deitsch mentioned that he heard from R' Dovid Boaz about the *Chozeh* ("Seer" so named because of his ability to spiritually "see" the future and other matters) of Lublin, who said he thanked Hashem everyday that he had the *sechel* ("intellect") to ask God to be able to serve Him from a position of *harchava*, of "wealth" and comfort, and not from *yisurim*, "troubles and suffering." Because if from *yisurim*, he was afraid he would have been *meva'et* ("kick"), meaning he was afraid he would have "rebelled." Where do we mention this everyday in *tefila*? When we ask Him to give us what we need with *chesed v'rachamim*, with "kindness and mercy." This is a different *malchut* and a different approach in general.

- An important doctor discerned a big difference between religious Jews and Arabs. By the Arabs, if the operation is successful, they come and kiss his hands and thank him. If it's not successful, they say, "This is from Hashem." By Jews, it's just the opposite: if the surgery is not successful, they blame the doctor and curse him, and if it is successful, they praise Hashem and tell the doctor, "You're a good *shaliach* ("emissary" of God)." What's the explanation of this? The natural connection of a Jew to the One above is positive, "with kindness and mercy." So, when the operation is successful, the Jews bless, and if not, they look for reasons, and come down on the head of the doctor. But the Arabs do not have high expectations from Hashem for positive results, so if the operation is not successful, they bless the One above and if it is successful they look for a reason: It must be the doctor. [translator's note: A Lubavitcher doctor who works in Sha'arei Tzedek hospital and prays in the Tzemach Tzedek shul informed me there is much more sickness among the Arabs than among Jews]. The Jew expects good, and is surprised if it doesn't happen, "How could something negative come from Hashem"? So the Jew expects good things from Hashem but he does have an animal soul, *Hagoy sh'bekirbecha* – "the goy within you." So in this prayer we request that the *nefesh Eloki* ("Godly soul") will be more successful and all will occur *b'chen b'chesed ub'rachamim* ("harmony, kindness and mercy").

- R' Deitsch heard in *yud Shvat* farbrengen with the Rebbe, *arichut gedola* ("at great length"), *Basi legani…gani* ("Come to My garden" - words from *Shir haShirim* to begin a Chasidic discourse) is a *gan*, a "garden" – *olam hazeh* ("this world is a garden"). The *Shechina* ("God's presence") left and then returned to *olam hazeh* ("our world"), to the *gan* ("garden"), to the *pardess* ("orchard"), this world that we live in is a good place, full of fruits, the best place. You see a lot of *tzarot* and problems? That's not the essence of the place, it's merely "tacked on," the essence of this world is good. That's what it means, *Basi le'gani*. And therefore, according to the *Sefat Emet*, this is what a person must request in the midst of *harchava* ("plentifulness, abundance"), that he will be able to remember *Hashem* and to thank Him. One has health, *parnassa*…

Page 78 in the translation: this *yirah* (the higher form, *yirah ilaah*, that is "awe") arrives during *shemonah esreh* and especially during the bowing of the *shemonah esreh*. In Sfardi Siddurim before *Baruch She'amar*, it says *B'dhilu verehimu* and *b'rehimu u'dehilu*, "in fear and love, in love and fear" – why reverse the order? Because of the four letters of Hashem's name. Starting from below, "fear" from below, associated with *malchut* and lower "*hey*." Followed by love associated with the *vov*, followed by higher love associated with the higher *hey*, and then again fear associated with the letter *yud*, the highest level, also associated with *shemonah esreh*, the highest level of *bitul*.

Shiur 20, November 25, 2011

We're going to learn *iyun shalem* regarding *yirah* – "fear of God."

Page 20, page 79 in the translation. Now that we know that *yirah* in general is not necessarily associated with *tefila*, but that nonetheless specific levels of *yirah* are associated with *tefila*, we can divide *yirah* into three categories: *Yirat cheit* ("fear of sinning"), *Yirat Elokim* ("Fear of God") and *Yirat Havaya* ("Awe of God" – called by the Zohar *Yirah Ila'ah*). Each divides into sub-divisions, but these are the three mentioned by the Mittler Rebbe in his introduction to *Derech Chaim*, and he brings *posukim*.

1) את האלקים אני ירא (יוסף אמר)
2) סוף דבר הכל נשמע את האלקים ירא ואת מצוותיו ישמרו
3) הן יראת הוי' היא חכמה

Yirat Cheit (verse #1) is mainly fear of doing something "against" God's will, and therefore it is expressed mainly by *sur marah* – "avoiding evil." Fear of rebelling against the good.

Yirat Elokim (verse #2) is mainly fear but includes *aseh tov* – "doing good" which is why the verse mentions doing mitzvoth

Yirat Havaya (verse #3) – not only about listening and fulfilling mitzvoth but about awe of Hashem Himself. Like walking in to meet a great man that you're just in awe of him.

There are also two verses, *Yiru et Hashem kedoshav* ("His holy ones fear God")

and *Yiru m'Hashem kol haaretz* ("The entire land has fear from God") that apply to *yirah ila'ah* and *yirah tata'ah* respectively. The implication of the former verse is that *yirah ila'ah* is not applicable to everyone, but only to "His holy ones," meaning only those who fear Him. [Chasidut explains that the second verse, "The entire land has fear from God" implies distance between man and God which explains the use of the word "from," implying distance, or the lower level, *yirah tata'ah*. But, the first verse, "His holy ones fear God" does not utilize the word "from" but rather it utilizes wording that emphasizes closeness and proximity to God; therefore, *yirah ila'ah*].

Each of the three is associated with its own *hitbonenut*, its own meditation. (About *ahava*, there are high levels such as *ahava rabba* and *ahava b'taanugim* that are not for everyone).

Page 20, fifth line…(page 76 in translation, even though we learned it already, going back to this to pick up the continuity) – "In Zohar part 1…" this refers to the higher fear, characterized by consciousness that *kulo kamei k'lo chashiv* ("everything is before Him as naught"). This fear only occurs at the time of *tefila*. How do we know? Ask those who are involved in *avodat Hashem*…like saying, "Check it out in the laboratory." What's mentioned in the Zohar and also in Tanya Ch 4 – are both the same thing, they refer to *yirah boshet*. Also called *yirah ila'ah*, from *pnimiyut Elokut* within the *olamot* ("worlds"), also called *Yirah boshet*. Explanation – that he is *mamash butel* ("totally nullified"). All forms of fear of God involve *bitul* ("self nullification") – but lower *bitul* is not real nullification of the self. We just don't want to rebel against the King – but what kind of fear is that? He just "won't steal the *beigel*"? Real fear is not merely fear that prevents us from rebelling against the "King"; real fear is the feeling that we are "nothing" in front of the King. Relative to other people, we're not a *shmata,* but here in front of someone great, we are immobile…

- Once R' Deitsch walked from Bnei Brak to Yafo in Tel Aviv, for an *ufruf* (pre-wedding celebration) on Shabbat. Walking together with someone to the *ufruf* of one R' Shia Kornblitt, R' Deitsch said to someone on the way, "we're *shomrei Shabbat*, otherwise we would go via car or bus…" But the fact that they didn't even think of going by car or other transport is a form of *bitul*…there was a discussion about whether they walked because they were just used to walking… but here the point is that they walked because they did not want to do anything "against the will of Hashem."

But this category of *bitul* that is not the essential *bitul* of *yirah ila'ah*, which is *butel* in the presence of Hashem…

- R' Zelig Feldman *alav hashalom* once spoke of the difference between one who serves Hashem with Chasidut and one who does not: There's a principle in the Talmud that whoever wants to recover an object from someone else must bring a proof – *hamotzi m'chavero alav haraiya*... but the question is which party is *muchzak* ("which party is granted a presumption of ownership")...in the non-Chasidic perspective (without Chasidut), the person, the human is the *muchzak*, he is the player with presumption of ownership and to change that requires proof (that man is not the "owner"). But in the Chasidic world (with Chasidut), the assumption is that Hashem is the *muchzak* and the burden of proof is upon man...The *nafka minah* ("difference") in *halacha* occurs when one has *sfekut*, or "doubts" in his faith and belief system – in that case, on whom is the burden of proof? Without Chasidut, the Jew feels that God has to bring the proofs, because he, the man, is *muchzak*. With Chasidut, he realizes that the burden of proof is upon him, because it is beyond doubt that God exists, is omnipotent and created the world, and He created the world for man to serve Him. Therefore, if man is not sure whether something is permitted or not, the burden is on him to provide proofs, otherwise he is not permitted. Without Chasidut, it's the opposite, man is *muchzak*, the burden of proof is on God (so to speak) and man "deserves" proofs that God exists, etc...(but there is such a thing as mitzvoth that he is commanded to fulfill)...afterward someone showed R' Deitsch that this is in *sichot* of the Rebbe...

And this level of fear is even higher than the love described above as, "To draw his soul closer and cleave to Hashem." Because to cleave to God is also about him, it's "he" who loves, which is not the case with higher fear ("awe") in which he is completely *butel*. "Because He said and the world was created" – if so, He can make the whole thing reverse and go back to *ayn v'efes* – to being nonexistent. And *Reishit Chochma* says something similar, so it becomes a personal worry – not only might everything return to nothing but, "Maybe he'll cause a sin" – this becomes his fear...

- R' Deitsch heard from *chochmei haMussar*, who reiterate this theme constantly: Before *R'H*, when there is *din* ("judgment") and *mishpat* ("trial"), man should connect himself with the *tzibur* – with the "public" body of Jews – because there is a promse that the *tzibur* will always remain. Any particular person or individual may not be covered in that way, something could God forbid happen to him/her, so the advice is to make sure one is part of the *tzibur*. All the *havtachot* ("promises") were made to the public but regarding one acting as a *yachid* ("individual"), *din* and *mishpat* applies and that's why *chochmei haMussar* advise to be part of the *clal*. Rambam asks, "Why, if Egypt was meant to punish the Jews, were the Egyptians were punished for doing so?" Rambam answers that they were supposed to punish the Jews as a public matter, but that didn't apply to any particular Egyptian, who could therefore still be punished for his behavior.

- God created man with such a nature – and not without reason – that he is afraid to move from his "place." Even if you explain to him that his move will be an improvement, or that he'll return to his place, nevertheless he has natural fear of change. So need to use that in service of developing our fear of God.

But continues on page 78 in the translation: "However the inner dimension of this fear…" is reverence over God's ability to create from nothing to something, *m'ayin l'yesh*. *Otzem G'dulato* ("the incredible greatness") – because man cannot perform this creation from nothing to something – "He said and it came into existence." Nevertheless, fear of His awesome ability to create is *hitzoni* ("external, superficial") – the proof being that it is *yirah tata'ah* ("lower fear") – *yiru m'Havaya* – fear "from" *Havaya*. And the end of the verse is *kol haaretz*…"everyone." But, the other verse, *Yiru et Havaya* ("fear Hashem" without mentioning "from") means that whomever is in fear of God is *tafel*, he is "nothing" before God – and that applies to *kedoshav* – "His holy ones." So why is the first verse – *yiru m'Havaya kol haaretz* – described as an "external," *hitzoni* fear? After all, it's God's essential name *Havaya* that we are afraid of in this verse? Because the meditation leading to this fear is based on the *olamot*, on the world and creation, which are the *levushim* ("garments" of Hashem) – not because of Hashem Himself, but because of His results, His creation (which are *levushim,* or "garments" of the King). Like you can be very impressed with a computer program and figure out that whoever designed it must be a genius. But you don't know him, the programmer, you only know his program…

- One of the first Hebrew-English word processors that came out, "Einstein" was the product of a Chabadnik in LA and Rav Deitsch was very curious to meet him, saw him in the *mikveh* a few times…but R' Deitsch didn't get to know him, just heard from him that "in Israel they're stealing his program." But still, R' Deitsch didn't get to know him, only his program…

So, this fear is *hitzoni*, "external" because it's not getting close to Hashem Himself. How do we do that? How does one get close to the One above, that "no thought can grasp Him"? Not via intellect, only via Torah and mitzvoth. It's something *Eloki*, associated with the *neshama*…*hacara Eloki*, *koach Eloki*… (it's a "soul thing, demanding Godly recognizition and Godly talents").

- R' Shlomo Chaim told a story: He said there was a Chassid who would go to the Rebbe Rashab, but before he arrived, he went to the "fair" – to the place where they buy and sell merchandise – and there someone was selling *kelim* ("items") of tzadikim, and he claimed that one of them was the Kiddush cup of the Baal Shem Tov, another was a *keli* for *bsamim* ("spice holder")... from the Maggid. So he was a man of means and he thought how nice it would be to bring these *kelim* ("items") as *matanot* ("gifts") to the Rebbe...he bought them and before he went in to the Rashab's room, his son the Previous Rebbe was also there, in another room. He showed the *kelim* to the Previous Rebbe sitting in a different room, and the Previous Rebbe went thru each item and told him, "this is genuine, this is not, they fooled you," going thru each one and "selecting" those which were genuine and which not. So when Chasid went into the Rebbe Rashab, he showed the items to him as well, and the Rashab looked at each one and came to exactly they same conclusions as his son – telling the Chassid which was genuine and which not. When he left his audience with the Rashab, the Chasid said to the Previous Rebbe, "What is this, are you a *Chasid* doing *moftim* ("signs and miracles")? Okay, your father, he's the Rebbe, but you? A Chasid who does signs and wonders, deserves a *mashkanta*, a "potch"...the Previous Rebbe answered him that, "This wasn't a *mofet* or "sign." Any article that a tzaddik used, contains revealed Godliness. And when there is *gilui neshama* ("revelation of the soul"), the *neshama* feels the revelation of Godliness in the article. Those were the words of the Previous Rebbe. R' Shlomo Chaim explained; it is written in *kadmonim* (early sages such as Rambam), every *chush tofes m'chusho* – "every sense grasps its own stimulus." The eye grasps light rays, the ear detects sound waves, the nose grasps smells, etc...and there is also a *chush* ("sense") that is able to grasp *Elokut* - what is it? The *neshama*... since the soul is Godly, so it picks up Godly "vibes." But in order for this to occur, the *neshama* has to be "awake" and "alert"; if not, it grasps nothing. Sometimes, our sense of taste or hearing, etc doesn't work, but here the Previous Rebbe said that when the *neshama* is revealed, it detects *Elokut*. And that's why about this *yirah*, *yirah m'Havaya*, Tanya tells us that "not everyone merits to it." It's a high level. To arrive to *yirah* not via the *olam* and not via *hitbonenut*, but via Torah and mitzvoth, is a very high level.

- R' Deitsch heard from his *mechutan* (R' Shimon Rabinowitz, but doesn't remember about which *tzaddik* the story was told), that in Ruzhin the Rebbe would give a coin for *shmira* ("guarding, protection") (by us in Chabad the Rebbe would give a dollar to *tzedaka*, ppl would "redeem" it by holding on to the dollar that the Rebbe gave, and giving another dollar to *tzedaka* in its place). In Ruzhin, the Rebbe would give a coin *lechatchila* ("initially") for *shmira*. Like a *k'meah* (special parchment that some people keep for "protection"). One of the chasidim received a coin from the Rebbe but mixed it up with another coin exactly similar, and didn't know which was which. So, he held on to both of them. Still, he wanted to know which one was which. So, he went to one of the other branches of Ruzhiner Chasidut (there's Boiyon, and Siatner, Sadigura, etc) and asked their Rebbe which coin was which. The Rebbe told him, "Give them to me." And he told him, "This is from the the Rebbe, the other is not." This is called *Chush Elokut*. These are examples, but not that we understand what it is.

- Shabbat story about one Viznitzer, Admor Meir was very "into" Shabbat, three days before Shabbat, would already sanctify himself for Shabbes: one day for thought, one for speech and one for action. "Shabbes Yid" – When he was old and weak, couldn't speak or daven, he was in a state of *sacanat nefashot* ("danger of losing his life"). Doctors told him not to be active, just to rest, and his Rabanit (wife) got a *bachur* ("young man") to watch over him. The *bachur* covered him with a blanket, etc. But the Admor wanted ppl around him and when got to *Mizmor leDavid* in Kaballat Shabbat, the bachur tells about how he threw off the blanket and it wasn't possible to stop him at all. At any rate as he got older, they stopped telling him at all that it was Shabbes, because it wasn't healthy for him at all to get so excited. But when it came to Shabbat, he would ask the *bachur* or attendant, "Tell me, is today a normal regular day?" (In other words, he felt that something was different). This is *regesh Eloki* ("Godly feeling"), not intellectual. It doesn't come from *"beigelach"*

Page 79 in the translation (still page 20 in the Hebrew text): This is a *hitbonenut hitzoni* ("superficial meditation") since it is based on the world and creation but it also includes deeper dimensions such as "how many" and "how great" are the creations. What's unique and special about this? That each creation has its own *chayut* ("vitality") and each is different from any other. Nevertheless, even though the *yirah* that results from this *hitbonenut is higher than yirat chait, nevertheless it is still within the category of Yirat Elokim* ("fear of *Elokim*") that leads to proper conduct and fulfillment of mitzvoth alone. It's not *hitbatlut legamri* ("complete *bitul*") as we see in *Yirah Ila'ah* and *Yirat Boshet*.

Shiur 21, November 27, 2011

Page 80 in the translation…As above, that even the *yirah* that we derive from meditation on "how many are Your creations," and "how great…" is a form of *Yirat Elokim* that leads to *maaseh* ("action") alone, as fulfillment of mitzvoth. *Yirat cheit* places emphasis on *sur merah* – "avoid the bad." But *yirat Elokim* places emphasis on the positive – *aseh tov*. The *yirah* is conscious, and we feel the *Elokut* in our performance of the mitzvoth, that they are Hashem's commandments. This is a *yirah* of *gadlut* ("maturity").

Page 81: There are different levels of *hitgalut* ("revelation") among the categories of divine fear; and during *Yirat Chait,* one is afraid of the sin and transgression, while during *Yirat Elokim,* what one feels is fear of God. And *Yirat Cheit* is conscious in comparison to *ohl malchut shamayim*, which is a totally subconscious attitude. Even though *kabalat ohl* leads to fulfillment of mitzvoth, nevertheless it is a concealed power within the soul, not consciously emotional.

Page 82: "The spiritual element in our fear of God…" Regarding *Yirat Elokim,* there is *katnut* ("immature," lower level) and *gadlut* (minor and major, or immature vs mature) forms…the immature *katnut* is explained end of Tanya Perek 42…reminders that all of creation are the *livushim* or "garments" of the One above. And the *gadlut* is a detailed meditation on the details of creation, *Mah gadlu maasecha Havaya*…explained in Tanya Ch 43.

Bottom of page 82 – *yirah ila'ah* – not based on *livushim* or creations or leading to fulfillment of mitzvoth, but *b'etzem* the very essence of nullification, we are nothing before the One above.

Shiur 22, November 28, 2011

In general, we're dealing with categories of *yirat Hashem*, "fear of God." Here they divide into *yirah tata'ah* and *yirah ila'ah*. *Yirah tata'ah* includes 1) *kabalat ohl* 2) *yirat cheit* 3) *yirat Elokim*. The difference between the latter two categories is that *yirat cheit* places emphasis on *sur marah* ("avoiding the negative") while *yirat Elokim* emphasizes *aseh tov* ("doing good"). The question then arises: Is not failure to fulfill a positive mitzvah also a sin, a transgression? And if so, *yirat cheit* should apply to positive mitzvoth as well, not only to *sur marah*? In a broad sense, one could answer that there are those who don tefilin, for example, not because they want to do the mitzvah of *hanachat tefilin* ("donning tefilin"), but because they do not want the inverse – they do not want to refrain from putting on tefilin. They do not want to "rebel against."

But, the Rebbe Rashab wants to draw a more refined distinction: In *Yirat Elokim*, one feels the *Elokut*, the Godliness of the matter. During *Yirat Cheit*, we do not feel the *Elokut*, and neither are we so consciously aware much that the mitzvah is a commandment of God. We experience ourself and have little or no *hergesh* ("feeling") about the matter, but during *Yirat Elokim*, we feel the Godliness and the *romemut* ("uplifiting nature" of the mitzvah). But if so, why is this not considered *Yirah Ila'ah*? Because the *romemut* and *hergesh Eloki* ("Godly feeling") is only regarding the mitzvah and not regarding ourself. This is the *hagdara*…our entire *kesher* ("connection") with Hashem is due to Torah and mitzvoth, but not because we are personally affected. [It hasn't come "home" to us personally, to affect our personality; rather we know that we are doing something spiritual and divine, but what we are doing is one matter, while we ourselves are another matter].

- R' Deitsch had a grandfather named R' Aharon Luria, who wrote a sefer, *Avodat Pnim*, he was a Slonimer Chasid, and they once wanted to make him an *Admor* ("Chassidic Rebbe"). He was an *adam gadol* ("great man"), and he said, "Without Chasidut, all *avodat Hashem* is *avoda sh'aina tzricha legufa*." That is, without Chasidut, any attempt to do *avodat Hashem* is as if you're trying to do one thing and you do something else. [For example (From tractate Shabbat 73B), if he needed some dirt for some reason on Shabbat and dug a hole in the ground for that purpose, he performed the forbidden labor of "plowing." But, since the purpose of digging was not in order to plow, but rather to obtain the dirt, this is called *melacha sh'aina tzricha legufa* – "labor that is not needed for its own purpose" – and there is a difference of opinion as to whether such an action is permitted]. There are some who do *avodat Hashem* for *olam haba'ah* (in order to merit to the "world to come"), some who serve God in order to be "part of the group," but those who do *Avodat Hashem* because they want to get close to God – for that Chasidut is necessary. Chasidut turns *avodat Hashem* into *melacha sh'tzricha legufa* ("labor that is performed for its own sake"). (R' Mendel Vechter sat in farbrengen and heard this vort from R' Deitsch, and mentioned it to him several times later).

Once one experiences *HaKadosh Baruch Hu* and the *Elokut* ("Godliness") of the mitzvah, he will achieve not only *yirah*, but also *ahavat Hashem* and *simcha*. This, the Rebbe said (and also the Brisker Rav), that this is regular Chasidut, without anyone arguing (*leit man d'palig*).

- Once someone asked the Rebbe, "For what do we need Chasidut?" And the Rebbe answered, for *simcha shel mitzvah* (to experience the "joy of a mitzvah"). And the questioner continued, citing someone who wasn't a Chasid and asked the Rebbe – "and this [specific person] (who was great and a *lamdan*, etc) did not experience *simcha shel mitzvah*"? The Rebbe thought and answered – "This he did not have."

- There is *eidut brurah* ("clear testimony") from the Brisker Rav, who was a *mitnagid* himself (not politically, but not a Chasid by any stretch of the imagination), that he said it's certainly true that the Chasidim brought *simcha shel mitzvah*. And he told a story about himself: During the holocaust, he had an *etrog* in the ghetto. The Previous Rebbe got out of the ghetto (Warsaw) earlier, but made sure that the Brisker had an *etrog* (was very important to him). Both the Previous and the Rebbe himself greatly held by the Brisker Rav. All day long, there was a line at his house to bless on the *etrog*, because no one else in the ghetto had one. One Jew in particular approached and blessed on the *etrog* with great happiness, and the Brisker Rav asked "who is this man." He was a Chassid whom, the day before, lost all of his children to the Nazis (*yemach sh'mam*), yet he blessed with great happiness. The Brisker said, "Only Chassidut could produce such a person." The Brisker Rav himself told the story: "That the day before he could lose his children and the next day bless with joy, only Chassidut could do that."

When one feels the *yoker*, the "preciousness" of the mitzvah, that's when it produces not only *Yirat Elokim* but also love and happiness. Like for example one who wants to eat, and another who does not want to eat, but says to himself, "but I can't be hungry, so I'll have to eat." What kind of enjoyment will he get from his food? He's eating not because he likes the food, but in order to avoid hunger. What flavor will it have? This exemplifies *yirat cheit* – not that the mitzvah interests him, but that he wants to avoid the opposite.

Page 82 – *Yirah ila'ah* is "awe," he feels he is *clum* – "nothing" – before Hashem. The *hitbonenut* leading to this state is that *kulo kamei k'lo chashiv* ("everything is before Him as naught"). [Skip the parentheses]...another *hitbonenut* leading to this abject *bitul*, written in several places...is that *yirah* arrives after one first experiences a desire to ascend to *Hakadosh Baruch Hu*. This is *ahava*. It is followed by *shov*, or "return," with the *cheshbon* ("reasoning, accounting") that, "Why ascend above, Hashem is here as much as He is above." It is written that this *yirah*, is *yirah pnimi*, "inner *yirah*." This is also accompanied by *bitul b'metziut* ("nullified from existence"). When one feels His presence down here just as above, this is *bitul b'meitziut*, just like *omed lifnei haMelech* ("standing before the King"). But in summary if we want to summarize all of the *madreigot* ("levels") of *yirah* – they all come down to *bitul*, to self nullification. *Ahava* ("love") leads to *d'veikut* ("clinging and cleaving"), *yirah* leads to *bitul* ("nullification"). Regarding their effect on the animal soul, *ahavah* produces *zichuch* – "polishing and refining." But *yirah* produces *bitul*. In the order of things, *yirah* has to precede *ahavah*. *Yirah* is *hanachat atzmuto*…putting our "self" aside. Page 83 at the bottom.

- Question from R' Eliyahu Hadad: "What is the *taanug*, the enjoyment in this *avoda* of setting aside your ego, *bitul*? To this, R' Deitsch responded with a quote from R' Shlomo Chaim *A"H*; "The *neshama* has *taanug* from *bitul*." "The soul delights in nullification." The soul is *b'etzem* ("essentially") nullified to *Elokut*, that's its nature, so when it happens *b'poel* ("actually"), it derives enjoyment. By angels, that's not the case. It's not the essence of an angel to be *butel*, but the essence of a *neshama* is to be *butel*. (Speaking of someone who was perhaps at that farbrengen with R' Shlomo Chaim, R' Deitsch mentioned that he could not accept this answer at all, since "how could there be *taanug* in *bitul*?" But this is the difference between one who "hears" Chasidut, because this person was "into" Chasidut, and one who is steeped and educated in Chassidut).

- A story to bring the idea home…a certain Chasid of the Rebbe Rashab, was a "friend" of the Previous Rebbe (the Rashab's son), so when the Previous became the Rebbe, it was doubly hard on this Chasid (R' Deitsch thinks it was R' Choni Marazov), both to lose a "friend" (because as Rebbe, he couldn't be a regular "friend" any longer) and also to nullify himself to the Previous Rebbe, but he worked on himself to be *butel*. He had been very close to the Rashab, like a son, the Rashab had even taught him some things that passed only via *masorah* ("tradition") in the Rebbe's family, such as the ten *niggunim* of the Alter Rebbe. On Purim, R' Marazov drank a lot of *mashkeh*, and laid himself down under the table where the Previous Rebbe was sitting. The Previous Rebbe (who had been his "friend") told him, "Choni, stand up!" And he answered, "No, you lift me up." The Previous Rebbe again told him, "Choni, stand up!" And he again answered, "No, you lift me up!" This back and forth went on, and how it concluded is not known, but the idea is that R' Choni wanted that his elevation ("stand up") should come *mamash* from the Rebbe. This is the *taanug* of *bitul*, the enjoyment of nullifying oneself. The Rebbe uplifting the Chassid is like a father and son, especially you see when the son is young, he enjoys being with his father, like he's not his own being at all. The son enjoys being "under the wing" of his father, this is the *taanug* of *bitul*. "*Yismach Moshe…ki eved neeman hu.*"

- The Rebbe speaks of two *dargot* ("levels") in servants: 1) One who sold himself into servitude 2) One who was sold by the *Beit Din* into servitude. According to Jewish law (*halacha*), the *eved* sold by a B"D is deeper into servitude, there are more laws involving him, than the *eved* who sold himself into servitude. There is a "one" (a person) who sold himself, while if sold by the B"D, even that tiny amount of ego was taken away from him, since it was the B"D who made the decision, and not him. At *Matan Torah* ("giving of the Torah"), why did Hashem hold the mountain over the Jews and threaten to drop it on them? They had already said *naasseh v'nishma*, "we will first accept and then we'll understand," so why was any kind of coercion necessary? The Rebbe answers, because it was they who said "we will do and then understand," it was their response and decision. But, by holding the mountain over the Jews, Hashem indicated that it was not their decision to make, just as one sold into servitude by the B"D did not make the decision himself. "You don't get to decide, the decision is made for you." This is called *hanachat atzmuto* ("giving oneself up") and it comes as a result of *kabalat ohl malchut shamayim* ("accepting the yoke of Heaven"). It is written in Chasidut that "Moshe was the most humble of all men" because he was jealous of those who had *kabalat ohl*, because he himself could not achieve that *madreiga* (He was associated with *chochma* and understood what was going on, and for this a person needs no thought, no feeling…just *bitul*).

Page 84 in the translation: All of the *dargot* in *yirah tata'ah* are lower (in terms of conscious spiritual level) than the love of God that we attain thru *tefila*, but *yirah ila'ah* is a higher level than the *ahava* of *tefila* [*yirah ila'ah* is associated with *shemonah esreh*, which is the pinnacle of tefila]. And the two *inyanim* of *zichuch* and *d'veikut nafsho* – "refining his animal soul and clinging to the One above" – arrive only as a result of *ahava*.

Shiur 23, November 29, 2011

Page 84-85 in the translation, page 22 in the Hebrew text, end of Ch 3 (Summary of previous chapter in order to provide intro to the next chapter):

It's certainly true that everyone must develop the trait of *yirah*, but *yirah* is not the *avoda* of *tefila*. *Yirah* requires constant ongoing reminders that need not occur during *tefila*, but nevertheless, the best time for these reminders is during *tefila*. The main thing is to recall that Hashem is standing over us, watching all that is going on, including within us, and this awareness requires brief concise meditation. There is *yirah tata'h* ("lower fear") that includes *kabalat ohl* ("acceptance of the yoke"), *yirat chet* ("fear of sin") and two levels of *yirat Elokim*, none of which must occur during *tefila*. However, to bring down *shem Havaya* (the transcendant four letter name of God) to *shem Elokim*, requires *ahava* and occurs only during *tefila*.

- R' Deitsch saw in the *Tzemach Tzedek* that when the soul inside of the body undergoes *aliya*, it is considered "reception of reward." R' Shlomo Chaim, while in the hospital, pinched the skin on the back of his hand, and said, "All is for this, all the world was created in order to refine the body and the animal soul, that is why it was created." He showed and emphasized how he grabbed the skin on his hand.

There must be labor and effort during *tefila*, and that purpose of the labor and effort is to achieve the attribute of *ahava*. And now we'll start now with Ch 4 to learn about *ahava*. Once upon a time it was thought that the difference between Chasidim and non-Chasidim was that Chasidim put the emphasis on *ahava* and the others on *yirah*. R' Yitzhak Ginsburg explained that's why we're called Chasidim, from *chesed* or "love."

- The son of the Chafetz Chaim told about how his father very much praised the Chasidim, and particularly their boldness (*azut*), brushing off all the nonsense that was influencing the others (communism, socialism, haskala, etc) – the Chasidim just threw it off like nothing, and the Chafetz Chaim praised that greatly, calling it *azut d'kedusha* ("holy boldness"). He described the Chasidim, saying that they stand like a "wall of iron." And the end of the verse, *al kol pisha'eihem* ("… all of their sins" – because there were various and sundry accusations from the non-Chasidic Jews, such as praying late or whatever against the Chasidim), *yechaseh ahavatam* – "…are covered by their love…" Words of the Chafetz Chaim. The *pshat* ("textual meaning") of the verse [as applied to the Chasidim] is that their love of one another "covers over" their failings, but the Chafetz Chaim meant to say that their *ahavat Hashem* ("love of God") covered for their "failings."

- Story, unknown origin, but there are many stories about the local non-Jewish landowners in Poland/Russia – the *paritz* – who would occasionally leave his palace and go out to visit his surrounding lands and small towns, etc. In one instance, a *paritz* came to a Jewish shtetl and listened to the Jews praying in the shtiebel. He said to his wife who was with him, "You know what, they love Hashem more than

I love you." Rambam in *Hilchot Teshuva* writes that love of Hashem can reach a level of craziness…wherein a person can go crazy from *ahavat haTorah*.

- R' Dovid Boaz's father was a Slonimer Chasid in Lodz, Poland. At that time, the procedure was that the ruler would come and visit the Jewish community and see how they were living (there was a certain amount of *haginut,* or "propriety" in those days even from the king). The King would meet the Jews in the central location, in the shul. But the Chasidim usually didn't daven in the central shuls but in various *shtiebelach* (smaller local houses of prayer) throughout the city. Efforts were made to distract the king's attention away from these *shtiebelach*, because there might have been some dirty towels or leftover pieces of herring, etc…but on one of the visits, the royal retinue heard cries of *tefila* from another shul and asked what it was… the "leaders" of the community were afraid and didn't want the king to know about the Chassidishe *shtiebelach* so they told the king, "That's the shul of the crazies." After awhile, the response of the royal retinue came in, "We were in general very impressed with our visit and the activities of the Jews. We were especially impressed that the Jews establish *batie Knesset* for the crazies." That was the *shtieble* of Slonim. R' Deitsch also had a connection with Slonim via his wife, who was from Slonimer descendants. So that's the way it is among Chasidim, since they express love, so there is "craziness" there as well, while from *yirah*, all is *mesudar* ("organized") and in place.

- *Lev Nishbar* – a "broken heart" - is an introduction to *yirah* – This the Rav said in response to R' Eliyahu Hadad. The Introduction to *Imrei Bina* of the MIttler Rebbe, which the Rebbe Maharash said is a *sefer* in itself, and also the *hakdama* to *Sha'arei Teshuva* of the Mitteler Rebbe, is the third of four *seforim* that the Mittler Rebbe wrote about *teshuva*. The Miteller Rebbe wrote the introduction to *Shaarei Teshuva* because he saw there was confusion among the Chasidim about how to balance the two approaches of *avoda*; whether from *simcha* ("joy") or from bitterness and a *lev nishbar* ("broken heart"). There, he writes that the *lev nishbar* is the foundation, but the *simcha* is the building. On the one hand, you don't have a building without a foundation, but on the other hand, the foundation without the building is nothing. Another way of describing it: *Lev Nishbar* is like a medicine, and *simcha* is the food. One must always eat (that's the *simcha*) but occasionally take medicine (*lev nishbar*), and if you try to reverse it, taking the medicine more than you need, then it's not good for you). The Mitteler Rebbe explained what is *teshuva shleima*... (from the blessing during *Shemonah Esreh*, "and return us in *teshuva shleima*")...which seems to imply that there is such a thing as *teshuva* that's not *shleima* ("not complete")? And if so, what could that be, and what does *teshuva shleima* mean? He answers *teshuva shleima* is the *simcha* that occurs after *lev nishbar*. ("Complete *teshuva* is the joy that we experience after a broken heart"). *Teshuva* without *simcha* afterward is *teshuva* but not *teshuva shleima*, says the Mitteler Rebbe.

- R' Eliyahu Hadad mentioned that he needed to "re-program" himself, because up to this point he learned with Litvaks who taught him that *avoda* is only about *lev nishbar*, and to be *b'lev nishbar* all the time is difficult. In humor, R' Deitsch responded that now that he came to learn Chasidut, it's in order to "acquire *shleimut*" – ("perfection"). But that was only in humor because he went on to say that Chassidim actually "hate" that word *shleimut*. *Shleimut* is in the purview of the Creator, and even wanting it is *posul* ("invalid"). One could even say that this is a basic difference in lexicon between the path of *Mussar* and the path of Chasidut – *Mussar* does estabish a goal of attaining *shleimut*, Chassidut rejects the notion. Anyone using the language of *shleimut* among Chasidim was detested.

- R' Mendel Futerfas (*z'l*) told a story of a *Baal Teshuva* in the early stages of *chazara b'teshuva* (early stages of returning to a path of Torah and mitzvoth) but not there yet...the B"T approached the Rebbe and told him that he is a *chasid shalem* – a "full and perfect Chosid" (meaning that he not only began putting on tefilin, etc but praying, etc...). The Rebbe answered him that a "full and perfect" and a "Chassid" are two things that stand in contradiction. R' Mendel repeated this story over and over. R' Eliyahu Hadad mentioned how one who feels himself incomplete, the *yetzer harah* is not present while one who feels himself "complete," the *yetzer harah* attacks. The embryo when first born does not have a *yetzer harah*...someone else asked, before Chasidut, people didn't work on themselves? Didn't try to improve their *midot* ("character traits") etc? R' Deitsch answered that it's all in the most basic *seforim*, but as he heard in the name of the Previous Rebbe, Chassidut comes not to originate something new, but to place emphasis and make certain themes stand out. So, what did they do before Chasidut? There are the *seforim*, the *Sheloh*, etc... but the emphasis on *simcha* came from the Chasidim, not that it wasn't present previously but that Chasidut placed emphasis...

Beginning Ch 4, Page 86 in the translation.

Two kinds of love: Like water, and like fire. Both associated with *Chesed* ("kindness"), but water is *chesed within chesed*, fire is *gevura within chesed*. This is *hitkalalut*, "inter inclusion" of the *sephirot*. In Chasidut, this subject is usually mentioned in conjunction with the phrase, *oseh shalom bimromav*, ("Make peace on the heights"). Regarding this phrase, Chasidut explains that the angel Michael ("minister of water") and the angel Gavriel ("minister of fire"), usually work in opposition to one another, but in the presence of the King, they make *shalom*, and the result is *hitkalalut*.

"Love like water" "flows," it brings us closer to God. "Love like fire" is explained later in the sefer (page 104 in the translation)…"love like fire" is based on "thirst for God." The nature of water is *kiruv* ("closeness" and "proximity") and *devekut* ("clinging and cleaving"), while the nature of fire is to disintegrate. So, there can be love of *devekut* ("clinging") or love of *tzimaon* ("thirst")…for example, you can see children in gan, in kindergarden, who are drawn to one another. It's a natural thing, they gravitate together. They don't run after each other, but *tov lahem* ("they like to be") together.

- Once R' Deitsch brought a *bachur* to R' Shlomo Zalman Auerbach (*ztz'l*) regarding a *zivvug*, and the question was regarding *meshichat halev*…"attraction." R' Shlomo Zalman replied, "Yes, I know about this, there's a gemora regarding *meshicha* as a *kinyan*, and the question is whether there is *meshicha* of only the front legs or also the back legs…" [There is a play on words here, *meshicha* is both the method of "drawing an animal" closer to the buyer to indicate an acquisition, and *meshicha* is also "attraction of the heart" between *hatan* and *kalah*. So, R' Shlomo Zalman was poking fun at the concept]. The Rebbe relates to *meshicha* ("attraction") in his letters, saying that it's not "fiery love" and that's not necessary in order to decide to marry, but there should be the potential for that to develop. *Mashpi'im* in this day and age ask, "When you sit and talk together, do you feel good? That's enough already in order to marry." Rav Deitsch then turned to R' Yoseph Halbfinger (who was a psychologist) sitting across from him and asked him, "What is *meshicha*"? He answered, it means a *kesher* ("connection"). So Rav Deitsch asked him, "But must it be like fire?" and he answered, "Could be." That brought some laughs, so R' Deitsch said, "The Rebbe says it's not so, it doesn't have to be like fire." The Rebbe said it's not possible to marry without any *meshicha* but it doesn't have to be a huge fiery attraction; quite the opposite, if they are waiting for that, they're in for a great disappointment. In the world of *kedusha* ("holiness"), *tzimaon* – "yearning" – is without limits, but the *tzimaon* ("thirst, yearning") of this world is limited. It sometimes fizzles out, it comes and goes…as will be explained here, these are two types of *hitbonenut*, the meditation that brings to "love like fire" is not the meditation that leads to "love like water"…and vice versa.

- Tanya, Chapter 18 or 19, also speaks of natural love, but there it is in order to know *inyano* ("to illustrate something") which turns out to be inclusion in the object of love, like a candle flame to its source, even though with its inclusion in its source, the candle will no longer exist. Here though, there is someone who loves, a separate entity even when he feels the attraction, and achieves his goal, he is there with someone whom he loves, and he maintains his own independent existence. Thus it is different than *ahavah* of *tzimaon*.

Shiur 24, November 30, 2011

Page 22 in the Hebrew text, page 86 in the translation. *Ahava* like water is *Kiruv* and *d'veikut* – "proximity" and "cleaving." It is characterized by desire to become close to God. *Tzimaon* ("thirst") though is fire. "Love like water" is defined by *meshicha*, "attraction" and being drawn closer to something. Now, the *hitbonenut* that is necessary in order to attain this love is meditation on the *ohr* ("light") and *chayut* ("energy") that enlivens the worlds. Within each and every creation there is an *ohr* and *chayut* that enlivens it. Just as man feels the life that maintains him, so he may experience the light that permeates creation, and this leads to experience of the Godly light that enlivens the world. So, the advice in order to gain this awareness is that man should first feel that *chayut* within himself that energizes and enlivens him. We don't see or detect this energy, but when we think about it, it's clear that there is "energy" in the world, every creation has its "energy." Even in stones and dust, we see that there is a *chayut pnimi*, an "internal energy" there. We don't know what it is but we are aware that it exists. As it says in *Derech Mitzvotecha* of the Tzemach Tzedek (third Lubavitcher Rebbe), "the *chayut* that you feel in the world, is *Elokut*." We may call it by other names, such as "energy" or "vitality" but in truth it is Godliness.

Rav Deitsch recalled seeing somewhere but can't remember where – that it is much easier to attain this *hacara* or "recognition" of *Elokut* from the *chayut* or "energy" enlivening specific creatures, than from the creation itself. The more one is *mitbonen* ("meditates") on this *chayut* – *hitbonenut* that includes *bina* ("understanding") and *da'at* ("visceral knowledge") – the more it leads to *hergesh* ("feeling") of the *chayut Eloki*. We begin to feel that there is a Godly divine power in the creation – and the result is that we become more and more aware of the elevated and precious nature of *Elokut* in the world. Here in *K'Avoda* is explained something that's not often explained in Chasidut – and that is, "what is the process" in the soul that occurs when one thinks about *Gadlut Hashem* ("the greatness of God") in order to attain *ahava* ("love" - that's the way it's mentioned in Rambam as well, that in order to attain divine love of God, we must meditate on *Gadlut Hashem* - but how does this take place?). The language of *K'Avoda* is that as we meditate, we experience *yoker* ("preciousness") and *ilui* ("elevation"). We experience that *Elokut* is something very precious and elevated. Here, the *K'Avoda* is speaking not in relation to the person (which it will do later on) who is meditating, but about the *etzem*, the "essence" of the matter, of divine love of God.

Consider what would happen, for example if a wealthy or famous person entered the room. People would turn to him and look at him. Why? Are they getting something from him, does he gives them anything? They respect him, they feel the "specialness" of what he is capable of doing. Or, even more coarse…those who allow their children to watch movies (*lo aleinu*) and then when the children meet the actual "hero" of the movie…this is the worst. Because the child respects the actor/actress, of course he wants to be close to him/her. But, generally the reasoning in these cases is because the protagonist, the actor/actress makes the child or person feel good about their performance – it does the observer "good" inside. And therefore, he respects the actor/actress and assumes that he or she is a "winner," a successful person. [The implication of the Rav's words are that if the actor/actress does not make any kind of special impression on the child, he is left with "nothing," and the meeting is a major disappointment, which is not the case] regarding the wealthy man, people still respect him even if they have nothing from him, even if they know that he is a *kamtzan* ("tight fisted").

- Someone once entered the *Tzemach Tzedek* collel and appeared like a total *batlan* ("inconsequential person"). But someone who was present told R' Deitsch that he was very wealthy. R' Deitsch looked at him and his tallit was torn, etc…but people are interested in such a person because they respect money, because they think it's possible to do whatever you want if you have money, as if the money is the source of creation. And this is even if they have nothing from the wealthy person. They just want to be "close" to it.

But once someone tastes *Elokut*, then his entire will and desire is for that, he wants nothing else. Everything else is *bupkes*…and this desire becomes amplified and increased when he considers that the same *chayut* that enlivens the world is the *chayut* of his soul in particular. Skip the parentheses… on page 87 continues, "as written, *nafshi aviticha b'layla*…" when does a person experience the "life of his soul"? Either when he is sick (or "weak" as mentioned in Tanya) or when he goes to sleep and he feels the absence of *chayut* and vitality…then he realizes that there is a *chayut* that enlivens his soul…like by way of example one who respects his "boss," from whom he receives his check…but after some time he realizes that his boss has a superior or supervisor and it's not his immediate boss whose running the show, but the one above him. Similarly, since *Elokut* is the *chayut* of the soul, so it is *chayei amiti*, or "true life." And the way to bring this down is by learning Torah, as in Tanya Perek 44. (In contrast to "love like fire," in which Torah learning is not an immediate follow-up to achieving the love). Regarding "love like water," learning Torah is a natural *hemshech* ("continuation," as is fulfillment of mitzvoth). But, regarding "love like fire," the learning of Torah that follows expresses the opposite dynamic, it is *shov* – "return" – unlike the fire which is *ratzoh*. After we experience "love like water", Torah learning follows naturally, just as one who is hungry sits down to eat. But the whole dynamic of "love like fire" is to leave the world, so the Torah learning that follows is "return" to the world. We overwhelm our desire to abandon *gashmiyut* and we utilize our spiritual attainments to learn Torah. About this "love like fire," the Alter Rebbe wrote that it is impossible to describe it and explain, and that only one who has tasted it knows what it is (Ch 49 or 50).

- In general, one who wants to be healthy, eats healthy. During the holocaust, sometimes they would give the prisoners something to eat that was known to be bad for their health. They gave them for example, fish that had gone bad. They knew they shouldn't eat it, but some were so hungry they couldn't hold back, and they ate it. On the 'death march' near the end of the war, the Klausenberger Rav was on the march and he watched over and supported the hevra to keep going. They got to some water and it wasn't good water, it was dangerous and he told them not to drink it but not everyone could hold back from drinking it. So also regarding this love like fire, it's almost like a desire of the soul to leave the body, but it's necessary to overwhelm this urge and remain alive. But when it's normal times, unlike the war or the *shoah*, then drinking and eating are a normal *hemshech* ("continuation") of the daily events, there is no *nigud* ("opposition").

There is a benefit/advantage to "love like water", and that is that it's 1) more *pnimi* ("internal") and 2) it leads to Torah learning. This is one form of *hitbonenut*, and next *K'Avoda* explains other forms of love that are found in Tanya.

Shiur 25, December 1, 2011

Summary of previous material: We learned about *yirah* but began to learn about *ahava*. Within *ahava*, we discussed two levels: Like water and like fire. Yesterday (previous shiur), we learned about which *hitbonenut* leads to "love like water". To meditate on how Hashem creates everything and there is *chayut Eloki* within each and every creation. There are quite a few paths of meditation on the greatness of God in such a way that leads to love. We will soon get into some of those paths. But the meditation upon how He creates the world at every instant, leads to greater love of God. That He creates, is a meditation on *richuk* ("distance"), that He creates from "distance," so to speak. But meditating on how He is found in each particular creation brings the concept closer to the person meditating. Such meditation provides a "reason" for the person to approach and become closer to Hashem.

- Note from R' Eliyahu Hadad, confirmed by the Rav: "Love like water" leads to *kiruv* and *dveikut* because water leads to clinging; only something that is moist or wet can lead to cleaving and clinging. *Aish*, fire, causes disintegration. Man knows about his own soul that there is something there, enlivening the body – it's a simple *cheshbon* ("calculation") because without the life force and vitality, all that is left is the body. And so if one meditates on the world, he comes to the realization that there is something, an energy that is present in the creation.

- There is a *kibbutz* where they created small melons. They very successfully grew them, marketed them and it took off in the world and they became very wealthy from the small melons. However, they used the ground so much that it went "dry," couldn't produce the melons anymore. Destroyed the land. This again proves that there is a *pnimiyut*, an "internal energy" – this energy itself is called Godliness in *Derech Mitzvotecha* of the Tzemach Tzedek. And these days there is a machine that detects the energy…it checks whether the food is good for you or not. Rav Deitsch himself experienced this machine…On Sundays (after Shabbat), he was "*lo ben adam*" – he couldn't speak, he was weak, couldn't give shiur…he thought maybe the cholent was not good for him, then the wine…nothing that he removed from his diet helped. The person with the machine checked him and found it was the milk he was drinking that caused the weakness. Also white bread and wheat. And he started eating rye bread which at that time wasn't available in bakeries, as soon as he started with rye bread, he "gained another day" in his week. The doctor told him he could eat cholent as well, but not beans. Also not potatoes. "Grape juice isn't good, wine you should drink." R' Deitsch asked him what's the deal with these foods and the doctor replied that each food has its energy and when you hook up with the machine, it tells you which energies interact with you and your body, and how. So, there is energy in everything, and it is the *pnimiyut* of each and every creation. To know how refined this can get, Rav Deitsch said he knew that milk was not good for him…the doctor put a bunch of candies on the machine and it went negative. Then he just picked out the milk chocolate, and the whole thing went positive. And that piece of chocolate was not merely one in sixty, it was one of a thousand pieces of candy…but even such a miniscule amount had influence. It is this energy that *Derech Mitzvotecha* says, is "*Elokut*." And, it is written in Chassidut that, "Also in the mineral world, there is *Chayut Eloki*." The entire world is filled with energy, *chayut*, and "this is *Elokut*." That is a *hitbonenut* based on *m'basri echzeh Elokut* – "from my own flesh I grasp Godliness."

Now, this *hitbonenut* leads to love of God. Why? Because in this manner, the meditator experiences, feels, the preciousness and elevation of *Elokut*.

See page 22 in the Hebrew text, third line…and back to page 86 in the translation…our simple awareness of this leads to love. Back to the *mashal* ("illustration") of money, which people love because it offers them possibilities to do all kinds of things. The money itself is not attractive, it has no taste or smell, etc…on Shabbat it's *muktza*, and it's *muktza machmat gufo* ("intrinsically unnecessary") – because it has no value of its own. Yet it is the source of all *ta'avot* ("lusts and temptations") because some people think that if they had money, they would have everything. If one thinks into Hashem and how He is truly the source of everything, and He enlivens everything, then the true preciousness of God and creation would come through.

- Note from R' Dovid Shalom Segal: As one becomes aware of the preciousness of the *chayut* of the world, he then becomes more committed to learning Torah (and keeping mitzvoth) because they bring down the *chayut* of the creation. And this is written in a *maamar* ("Chassidic discourse") that R' Shlomo Chaim would advise the *bachurim* ("yeshiva students") to learn, from *Eter* (*5670*/1910) of the Rebbe Rashab...there were *maamorim* that they learned and *maamorim* that they learned in order to practice meditation (*hitbonenut*) with them – *Achat Sha'alti* – there it states R' Segal's point above; the *maamar* quotes the verse from parshat *Re'eh:* "I have put before you the good and the alive, as well as the bad and the dead; choose life." Here, the *Baal Shem Tov* says that "alive" refers to the *chayut* that is in every creation [the simple explanation is that "if one does good he will live and the opposite if he does evil," but the *Besht* (*Baal Shem Tov*) adds that "live" here does not mean simple life, but the *chayut,* or "Godly energy" within every creation. In other words, he says that the spiritual energy is what enlivens]. The physical body goes to waste but the "energy" remains – this the Rebbe would tell many scientists in *yechidut* ("personal audience"); it's one of the laws of thermodynamics that energy does not go to waste. It's the eternal portion, and in every object there is this "good and bad."

The *maamar* continues on to say that the "good" is the source of life, while the "bad" is the source of death. Meaning that if you lend importance to the *chai* ("life"), then by extension it means you lend importance to the *chayei ha-*, the "life of the living," which is Torah and mitzvoth. Doctors will tell you that a *haredi* Jew respects life more than one who does not lead of life of Torah and mitzvoth. Who requests the private doctors for surgery and important procedures? It's the *haredim* who do so. Others say, *kupat cholim* will do the procedure for free, for what do I need to go to a private doctor? Why do the frum *macherim* [there are *haredim* who make a point of having access to the top doctors and experts in the medical field in order to advise other Jews to whom to go for each medical procedure that they have to undergo] have access to the best doctors? Beause the doctors know that the *haredim* will pay for private care, so they don't mind getting closer to the *macherim.* These *macherim* evaluate the doctors and what they say because they have access to them since it brings more money to the doctors.

- Rav Deitsch heard from the Ponevitzer Rav [most likely R' Kahaneman A"H] before Rosh Hashana, that man must love life and this is acc to Torah. And who is it that cares about life – the Jew. Some like only the *ta'avot* ("lust and temptation") of life, but not the "life of life." And what is the point of this distinction? What happens when life becomes difficult? Some decide to die, they have pills of poison that they take when life gets difficult. Because according to them, if no *ta'avot,* what is life worth? But a religious Jew isn't ready to give up on life so easily, he values life, he values the *chayei haChaim* ("life of life") which is Torah and mitzvoth. And that *chayei hachaim* leads to Torah and mitzvoth.

- R' Deitsch was very impressed, recently someone told him that statistics show that often the first stage of *teshuva* was eating healthy. If you're not mindful of health, then you eat for *ta'avot* but if you eat for health, then you put *ta'avot* aside. There are other things correlating to *teshuva*, but this is one of them.

And the extension of that is to love the *chayut* because it is the *chayut* of his own soul as well, as discussed in the previous *shiur*.

Page 88 in the translation: ("The advantage of this level…") is that it is more *pnimi* – R' Deitsch says that the meaning of this is that the meditation leading to "love like water" (on the *chayut* within every object) is "more *pnimi* than love like fire," because it leads to Torah learning (which like in the previous shiur, is not the case with "love like fire"…learning Torah is not a natural result of "love like fire"). After "love like fire," one wants to escape from the world and live a very abstract life, doesn't even want to learn Torah (and the prophet says, "All your thirst should be for water" – Torah). This, Tanya tells us is *ratzoh v'shuv* – "running and returning."

Skip to page 91: "There is, though a certain advantage…" - The advantage of "love like water" (over "love like fire," which lifts the person up out of the world) is precisely that it relates to the world, and applies to the physical objects of creation. When our *hitbonenut* is about *gadlut Hashem* ("the greatness of God" – in the transcendant sense of *kulo kamei k'lo chashiv* that leads to "love like fire"), then we do not apply our meditation to each and every object as if Hashem is found in every object of creation. When we're thinking about the greatness of God during *tefila*, we think about Hashem, but the minute we consider the world…we forget about (lose consciousness of) the world. But if the *hitbonenut* takes the physical world into account, then we look for Godliness in everything, and this is a high level. All this is from the discourse, *Achat Sha'alti* in *Eter* (*Sefer Maamorim 5670*/1910), where the Rebbe Rashab writes that the more the person is more interested in the *gashmiyut* ("physical nature") of the item, the more he separates the item from its Godly *chayut*. And once we separate the *chayut* from the object, that's called "death." And that which is "dead" actually stinks…

In an office situation, there are those who care where their check comes from and kiss up to the person who brings it. And there are those who really don't care, as long as the check arrives. There is a third character who *davka* looks for the boss of the business because he realizes the importance of the boss and wants to get to know him, because he's the one who connects the whole business together and makes it work. The Mittler Rebbe writes that there are two kinds of *prikat ohl malchut shamayim* ("removing the yoke of Heaven"):

One kind is not to give *chashivut* (not to "lend importance") – not to attach any importance to the *baal habayit* (the "One in charge"). Like Mordecai in regard to Haman…this disturbs the "boss" more than one who goes against him and rebels (the second kind of *prikat ohl*). Like a cat compared to a dog, the cat doesn't care at all, it just gets its food, but the dog is tied to the *baal habayit*. Also one who eats for the *ruchniyut* (the "spiritual energy") of the food, this is a high level, but since it is a topic that appears in Chassidut, it must be applicable to us as well.

Conclusion is: We must do *hitbonenut*.

- Rav Deitsch's wife's grandfather, R' Aharon Luria was a Slonimer chasid, very involved in *avoda*, almost made him a Rebbe, but he used to ask R' Deitsch, "what is this *hitbonenut*, what is this"? In Slonim, there was something similar – *chazrim* – they used to *chozer* over ("repeat") phrases and sayings and verses…repeating over and over again…in Tiveria it was so hot they couldn't sleep in the house, they slept on the roof, but on the roofs, everyone could see what the other was doing, and hear. With that heat, it was difficult to sleep even on the roof and they could hear one man repeating over and over again, "The moon and stars that You created…" from Psalms 104 (*Barchi Nafshi*). He repeated this all night long… So one of the differences between Chabad and Slonim is that Chabad was with the head and intellect, while Slonim with the mouth, repeating things over and over again.

- In the writings of the Previous Rebbe, he says that those who think there is no *hitbonenut* outside of Chabad, are mistaken. There is *hitbonenut* outside of Chabad, but by other Chasidim, it is considered sufficient to meditate on *hanoten koach lasechvi lehavchin*… ("He who grants power to the rooster to discern…") while in Chabad one must meditate on [difficult concepts] such as *memalle* ("immanent Godliness") and *sovev* ("transcendant Godliness")…on the way to their Rebbe, Slonimer chasidim would repeat, "I believe that I believe…" because there is a belief that as Chasidim travel to their Rebbe, they begin to experience *sefeikot* ("doubts") in their *emunah* ("faith"). R' Nachman spoke about this, and R' Deitsch also experienced it…after all the *hachanot* ("preparations") and the travels, one asks himself, "Why did I come?" So Slonim would deal with this by repeating, "I believe that I believe." But by Chabad, we practice *hitbonenut*…

- R' Matis Luria (one of the brothers, there was R' Aharon, R' Matis, R' Mordecai (Rosh Collel), each with a different *signon*, or "style"…)

who were notable Slonimer chasidim, related thru marriage to R' Deitsch, and when he was still a *bachur* ("yeshiva student") in Bnei Brak, they pointed out R' Matis to R' Deitsch and told him that, "This is R' Matis," the Beit Yisrael (Gerer Rebbe) would stand up in front of him (and they also considered him to make him Rebbe)… anyway they pointed him out to R' Deitsch and he saw a man with a *talit gadol* on his shoulder, preparing to daven, clearly in *hitbonenut*… this was a pose struck by many chasidim, also Chabad, to meditate with the *talit* on the shoulder (in Tanya Ch 41 discusses *hitbonenut* before morning prayers while wearing *talit* and tefilin). His mouth was closed, he said nothing but he was apparently deep in meditation. The nature of *hitbonenut* is described in some places in the Mittler Rebbe, to repeat things over and over (this instills it inside), this is called *shkeida* ("constant practice"), to go into detail, and finally to bring *mashalim* ("illustrations, parallels")…there is *hitbonenut* in order to understand and then there is *hitbonenut* in order to bring the concept "closer" to you. The Previous Rebbe said, "When you learn in order to understand, you bring yourself closer to the *sefer*. When you learn for *hitorerut*, for "arousal" during tefila, you bring the *sefer* closer to you." The Previous Rebbe mentioned this in a *maamar*.

- R' Segal mentioned that it emerges that there is more ego in *tefila* [cause you feel "yourself" being aroused by divine love] than in learning Torah, during which you are *mevatel* yourself…but no big deal cause there obviously is a benefit in *tefila* as well. But in *tefila*, it is important to bring the point – the *b'chen* – close to "me," so that "I understand it." While in Torah it is important for "me" to understand but what I have to understand is the *sechel* of the Torah…

Shiur 26, December 2, 2011

Page 23 in the Hebrew text, page 88 in the translation (parentheses): "The advantage of this level…" here speaking of *nafshi aviticha* ("my soul desires You"), which is the love born of meditation on how God enlivens not only the creation, but "my own" body and self, is more *pnimi* ("internal"), leads to recognition of the preciousness and closeness to God. The divine love derived from meditation on Godliness in the world (that enlivens everything and creates it) does not take into account the "me," the affect that meditation can have on the soul. Perhaps this is better, not to think of "myself," but rather on the matter itself – the greatness of God enclothed creation? (Either way, here we are speaking of "love like water", but there is a difference whether we consider the Creator of the world in general, or if we meditate on how this energy is the vitality of "my soul" as well). The feeling that it is "my soul" is more *pnimi,* more "internal," more associated with me. It leads to more learning Torah, that is, although it is more "about me," nevertheless the advantage is that it encourages us to learn more Torah.

- Once, R' Deitsch saw in a *maamar* from the Rebbe Rashab that the sin of the tree of knowledge is that it led to *hargashat atzmo* – "feeling myself" – what we know of as "egoism." Rambam wrote that before the sin of tree of knowledge, man knew the difference truth and *sheker* ("dishonesty"). The sin brought to knowledge of "good and bad," which boils down to, "What is in it for me?" Once man begins to relate the objective facts to himself, this is the influence of the "tree of knowledge." Once, R' Deitsch said in jest that one who is an egotist, "Took a bigger bite from the Tree of Knowledge." Rambam explains why; he says that there are 24 items that prevent *teshuva*. One of them is peering at forbidden images (originally, Adam and Hava did not even look at the forbidden fruit, but the snake convinced them to look; once they did so, they were "caught" in the snare of the *klippot* ("negative forces"). The Ariz'l said that the snake seduced them into looking, and that was a fatal mistake, just like looking at the internet …). Rambam categorizes them into 1) matters that are forgiven 2) matters that don't seem to be such a big *aveirah* ("transgression"), and for that reason people don't do *teshuva* over it. Looking at forbidden pictures is one of those things. So is "building yourself up" at the expense of your fellow. Rambam explains that this is because we excuse ourself by saying, "I did nothing, I just demonstrated how I'm more important than he is."

- R' Eliyahu Hadad mentioned someone who came to his house and asked, "What *hechsher* is this," he answered him *Beit Yoseph* and the guest did not want to eat, saying, "For you it's fine but I keep this or that *hechsher*…" and asked if this is in the category of building yourself up at the expense of your fellow – R' Deitsch answered it depends on his intention. If he wanted to "put someone down," then it was problematical, but if not, then it was permitted).

- R' Deitsch mentioned that the *Hafetz Haim* did not want to speak at events where there were other speakers so that they wouldn't compare him to the other speakers who were present, and someone would lose out or be embarrassed.

Returning to the *maamar* of the *Rashab*, it emerges that any feeling of *zich* (Yiddish for "self") or *Ani* (Hebrew for "I") is *posul* ("invalid"), since it comes from the sin of the tree of knowledge. And the *tikun* ("rectification") is to use that feeling for matters of *kedusha* ("holiness"). So, the *ahava* and love in which there is some feeling of *zich*, and *Ani*, is the rectification of the sin of the tree of knowledge. As the Rebbe once said to Rav Deitsch in *yechidut* ("personal audience"), "you must utilize the *yetzer harah* itself" in order to fix it. Yet, this isn't *hithafcha* ("transformation") of the *yetzer harah*, because all you did was "utilize it," you didn't turn over its *etzem mahut* (you didn't transform its "essential nature").

Getting back to the love of *nafshi aviticha* – Page 89 in the translation - here also we utilize the love developed by thinking how the Godly energy is the vitality that enlivens us as well, in order to learn Torah. That is, the love developed by meditation on how He is the force enlivening "me" results in a desire to learn Torah in order to draw Him into us. And because the force drawing Him to us is coming from *ohr ein sof* ("infinite light") that is beyond the creation, so this love is higher than the love based on *hitbonenut* on the Godliness within creation. That is, the Godly *chayut* ("energy") that we bring down with *hitbonenut* on the Godliness within the world is on a lower *madreiga* ("spiritual level") than the *chayut* that permeates a Jew. Because the *chayut* of the entire world is the *chayut* of creation, of *nivraim* ("creations, creatures"), while the *chayut* of a Jew is that of the soul, *neshama*. So, when we meditate on how He is my life force and vitality, the focus is on a higher level than the *chayut* that enlivens the creation in general. For two reasons: 1) because it is more *pnimi*, more "internal," and 2) because the spiritual level itself is higher. There is the "life of the body," and the "life of the soul." When we meditate on how He is the "life of my soul," this in its source is a higher spiritual level. This is a general principle in Chasidut: Whenever the meditation is on a higher level, the resulting feeling inside is also higher. They go together.

So we have described two levels of ""love like water"," but in essence they are one level: one focused on Godliness in the world, and the other focused on the Godly *chayut* that enlivens us. Now, the *K'Avoda* describes several other kinds of divine love mentioned in Tanya, without going into detail, but classifying them according to their relative levels. Page 90 in the translation: Beginning with a love mentioned in Perek 44 that's actually difficult to understand, but it's mentioned in the Zohar as the love of Moshe Rabeinu for Hashem, described as, "Like a son drawn after his father." When we meditate not only that he is "our life," but that we are a "son" and He is our father, then what is the difference between the two meditations? In both cases, whether because He is the source of my *chayut hanefesh* ("vitality of my soul") or whether because He is "my Father," either way He is my source. In Tanya this is difficult to grasp but here in *K'Avoda* it is explained that love like a son for his father is higher than the love of *nafshi aviticha*.

• A Jew named R' Shmaya Zilberberg, a big *oved Hashem*, like a Rebbe even tho he's not a Rebbe, has his own *kvutza* ("group") of people around him whom he encourages them in *avodat Hashem*, and he all the time is involved in *avodat Hashem*, he has someone who wakes him up every morning. He's so accomplished in matters that are "between man and his fellow" that he found a way to be awoken without waking up his wife. Someone else might have said, "So she wakes up, she'll go back to sleep," but he ties a rope to his hand and threads it out the door so that the person coming to wake him up can just pull the rope and that will pull his hand and wake him up (and on Shabbat night, how much does he sleep, maybe 50 minutes…). Someone said about him that he's a Jew that thinks to himself twenty-four hours a day, "What does Hashem want from me at this instant." He always says, *Tati in Himmel*, "Father in Heaven"…what does He want from me right now? Every Jew needs to think of Him as "father," this love comes from Moshe Rabeinu, from the *Raya Mehemna* (Aramaic for "faithful shepherd"). Tanya asks, "Who is it that has the *chutzpa* to approach the level of Moshe Rabeinu?" How can we presume to reach such a level? Tanya answers that "something like that," a very minor amount, can be attained by every Jew, and it especially helps if he does so by constantly repeating about Hashem, that he is "Abba," He is our father. As Tanya (Ch 44) says, this level of love is concealed within us, and yet it is "not far and not overseas" to reveal it, "by being regular in speech and *kavana* of his heart…" and being accustomed to think about it, and even if it seems imaginary to him, not to worry…" This is another form of *kiyum hamitzvoth* ("fulfilling the mitzvoth"). One may be like an *eved* ("servant"), one may cling to Him, or one may do mitzvoth because he is "like a son" and therefore wants to fulfill the will of his father. There are some who want only to receive from their father, and there are others who are willing and able to give as well.

So, back to the question, both kind of love – *nafshi aviticha* ("My soul desires You") – and the "Son who strives after his father," are based on the same concept – that He (God) is my source. And if so, what is the difference between them? In answer: 1) *nafshi aviticha* is only for him, for the meditator, but the *ben d'ishtadel acher aviv* ("son who strives for his father") is willing to give up his life for his father. 2) *nafshi aviticha* is *sichli*, it's "intellectual," it's the meditator thinking to himself, while *ben d'ishtadel* is also *regesh* of the heart, it's "feeling"..

In the translation, page 90: "…which in reality is far beyond the level of "You, God are my soul…" – but the Rebbe Rashab doesn't explain here…other than it is *pnimi* and *atzmi* – "internal and essential." The love of *nafshi* is associated with the name *Elokim* and that of *ben d'ishtadel* is associated with the four letter name *Havaya*, much higher. Not well explained, but the Rebbe does provide the *geder*, or classification, for us.

Even so, there is an advantage to meditation on Godliness that enlivens the world over the meditation of *nafshi*. Meditation on Godliness enlivening the world means that, "When we encounter a piece of cake, we think about the Godliness in the cake," but when meditating on *nafshi*, we do not think of the Godliness enlivening creation but rather upon the Godly energy enlivening ourselves. If we meditate on how God enlivens every creation, then when we enounter the cake or other physical item, we think about the *Elokut* within it. But that does not lead us in the direction of learning Torah, and that's the advantage of *ahava* of *nafshi* – it leads to learning Torah. When thinking about *Elokut* in the world, it does not lead to learning Torah, but when we think that it is associated with "My soul," this leads to Torah learning.

- R' Deitsch tells that when the holy Ruzhiner Rebbe was young, he would wander in the forest and wilderness. His older brother R' Avraham asked him, "Why aren't you more in the *Beit Midrash* ("study hall")"? He answered, "Our father, before he passed away, told me to 'try to go wherever God is.' I find God in the forest as much as here in the *Beit Midrash*." But the aveirage man finds God more in the shul or B"M than in the forest.

Since the *tachlit* ("ultimate goal") is learning Torah and fulfilling mitzvoth out of love, therefore the love of *nafshi* ("He is the vitality of my soul") is more important in the end. The idea that the *regesh* and the emotion of love is sufficient, is true but it is more true that they are a means to another end – that there should be *avoda* ("service") motivated by love; fulfilling Torah and mitzvoth out of love. Tanya brings proof from the Zohar, which calls the mitzvoth, "wings." The body of the bird is the Torah and mitzvoth, and the wings are love and fear. Without the "wings," the bird can't fly. So, the purpose of love is to learn Torah out of love for God.

- There's an even greater divine love that high souls such as *Tzaddikim* who have great love of God, "insert" into physical items. Story about the Alter Rebbe and R' Avraham, son of the Magid (nicknamed the *malach* – "angel"), who decided between the two of them, to "leave this world in *calot hanefesh* ('expiry of the soul')." So, they made circles, did *hitbonenut* and approached the level of "leaving this world." As the Alter Rebbe saw that it was about to occur, he grabbed the *malach* (literally means "angel," but in reality he was the son of the Magid of

Mezritch) and took both of them out of the circle – apparently he did not want the *calot hanefesh* to really occur. (Originally, upon arrival in Mezritch, the Alter Rebbe met the *malach* and made a *heskem* ("agreement") with him – the *malach* would teach him *kabala* and he would teach the *malach, nigleh* (the "revealed side" of the Torah; Shas and poskim). After "dancing" outside of the circle they had made, the Alter Rebbe declared – "*chachmati amda li*" – even though I made this agreement on *calot hanefesh*, "the *chochma* ("wisdom") that I learned, that *shov* ("return") – the dynamic of finding *Elokut* in *gashmiyut* is more important – stuck with me." And he was happy that he ended the episode in that manner, preventing *calot hanefesh*.

- Afterward, the *malach* went to visit the Alter Rebbe and saw him eating a beigel with butter, and asked him, "after such high *madreigot* ("spiritual levels" close to *calot hanefesh*), how can you eat this?" It is explained that the Alter Rebbe, *davka* after such a high encounter, wanted to bring it down into a physical act. This kind of behavior is for *tzaddikim*, but for us "common folk," after attaining love of God, we must bring it down into a mitzvah. It's the Ramban who said on *Shir haShirim* on the verse, "If you arouse the love…until you desire" – the word for desire is *hefetz*, and it also means "physical item." When there is *hefetz*, you have to put it into physical action…R' Eliyahu Hadad added that perhaps that's why Avraham Avinu wanted to take a little bit of *dam* ("blood") from Yitzhak at the *akeida*, but Hashem wouldn't allow it; instead, He showed him the ram and that became the article on which to fulfill his love of God.

Shiur 27, Dec 4, 2011

Page 23 in the Hebrew text, page 91 in the translation, "…therefore we must develop…" Here the *K'Avoda* refers to Perek 46 of Tanya, speaking of love of *chibuk* and *nishuk* – "embracing and kissing" – the King descending to join the common Jew in his home or room…and relating to him personally. When man does a mitzvah, Hashem so to speak embraces him. Torah is like *neshikin*, "kissing." And this *ahava* also leads to learning Torah. Here, the reason is simple, because the entire *hitbonenut* is about how Hashem gave us the Torah. Where do we see the closeness of Hashem? By *Matan Torah*, the giving of the Torah.

- There's a "problem" in the yeshiva where R' Deitsch delivers a shiur, that there are *bochurim* ("yeshiva students") who get up in the middle of the shiur and leave. R' Deitsch is very disturbed by this. There are all kinds of *bochurim*, including those who are diligent and stay in the shiur. Upon reflection, R' Deitsch concluded that the *bochurim* think that the *shiur* is a general *shiur* for all of them, so what's the problem if one of them leaves? But by R' Deitsch, he goes into detail in the subject and if someone gets up and leaves, it's as if he's speaking personally to someone and they turn their back, get up and leave. The same *bochur* who wouldn't do that personally, might do it in a *shiur*, because he thinks the *shiur* is for the *clal*, not for him specifically. Some *magidei shiur* ("teachers") can deliver the *shiur* regardless of whether they have the attention of the students, but others are plainly incapable of doing so. R' Deitsch needs the feedback and personal reaction of the students. Once a group of Gruzini men asked him to give a *shiur* from the middle of the shul, from the *bima* – and it was more of a "lecture" situation and afterward he says he almost walked out of there feeling "sick" because of the lack of interaction. From there he went to a second yeshiva and delivered the same *shiur* – but there, the students responded, gave feedback, etc – and it was a pleasure. All this is a *mashal* ("illustration") so that we understand what it means that when God creates each and every object in the world, it doesn't mean that he created as a *clal* – it means that He is *mashgiach* ("watches closely over") each and every detail. When we say, "For me, the world was created," the intention is not "for me as part of the *clal*," but "For me He created the world and I have His complete and total attention as a detail of His creation." [Thus, the *hitbonenut* on *Gadlut Hashem* in creation is on each and every individual creation]. There are only a few people who can deliver a *shiur* regardless of who is listening and taking it in. Most very much need the attention and feedback of the listeners. So, when we consider Matan Torah, we have to consider that God "thought about me." (But the only meditation that does not lead to Torah and mitzvoth is the initial one, *Gadlut Hashem* creating and enlivening each and every creation).

Further on page 91 in the translation: "So, we also must practice and become constant in the love of the 'son who exerts himself...'" which also leads to Torah and mitzvah fulfillment. Page 92-93: "The meditation and closeness based on the ray of Godliness invested in the worlds..." is easier...[that is, the entry level meditation on how Godliness enlivens the world] is easier, closer to the *nefesh*...R' Shalom Dovid Segal added by way of explanation that, "When you look at yourself, what do you see? But all you have to do with this [initial] meditation is look out the window and think about what you see." "Just as the soul enlivens the body, so *HKB"H* enlivens the world." We knows what our soul is, "and from my soul I grasp Godliness" and so we knows there is an energy enlivening the world – and that energy is Hashem. But in our soul, we first feel the *chayut* and only afterward do we realize it comes from somewhere – from God, from *Chayei HaChaim* ("enlivener of life"). So, this [second meditation] is not so easy. There is an extra step (first to identify the divine energy, then to realize it is Godly). But the *hitbonenut* on *chayut* in the world is easier.

R' Deitsch thinks there's another reason why the meditation on the creation is "easier" to achieve: Because there is no ego, no self involved. The minute a person has to "take responsibility" because it applies to him, ego comes into the picture and makes it harder. This is confirmed in Tanya, where after speaking about *achdut Hashem*, Tanya says (Ch 41), "And he should not remove himself from the *clal*," meaning that he (the meditator) is a part of the unity of God upon which he is meditating.

Furthermore, the *K'Avoda* on page 93 says that the entry level *hitbonenut* on *Gadlut Hashem* in the the creation, has a salutary effect on the *nefesh behamit* to weaken it, so that the animal soul finds itself included in "unity of God." Here, *K'Avoda* doesn't explain, just informs us of these benefits of the initial meditation. Page 93: "Therefore, *avoda* of the One above begins with this love and closeness…" And here, unlike previously, *K'Avoda* says that this entry level meditation of, "You enliven and create everything…" leads to Torah learning. Earlier, *K'Avoda* said that learning Torah was more associated with the second level of love, *nafshi aviticha*… In general, we desire *Elokut* ("Godliness"), and the result is that we desire Torah and mitzvoth. And since the commandments are God's "emissaries," he respects them. And then this "entry level" love will help him attain the higher levels as well.

- We see this physically as well: Sometimes when we are weak, we have no appetite, but once we gain strength, our appetite returns and we can eat more. With some meditation, we develop a sense of the preciousness of *Elokut* and we work on achieving it. This is how Onkelos became a convert – he asked his uncle what he is buying and he replied, "Something that will become very precious."

Page 93-94 in the translation (page 24 in the Hebrew text) – "This is especially true when we meditate on levels of Godliness above those invested in the lower worlds…" That is, when we raise our meditation to levels that are beyond this world, meaning that we access higher revelation of Godliness. Similar to different levels of intellect, the higher the intellect, the more revelation and illumination is present. Like psychology and philosophy. R' Yitzhak Ginsburg שי' is a genius in abstract math, and those who are drawn to abstract math are also often drawn to kabbalah (as R' Ginsburg is), but that is not the usual nature of our generation. In regards to math, our generation is much more associated with applied math, etc…the Rav says that in our generation if he teaches an abstract concept, a *svarah*, the students don't get it unless he brings a *nafka minah l'maaseh* (a "difference in application"), then they get it. It wasn't always that way, it used to be possible to introduce a *svarah* without bringing a *nafka mina*. On the other hand, the world knows how to respect someone who is a craftsman, or a person with refined *sechel* ("intellect"), with more abstraction, because there are fewer of such people around. And similarly, the higher world offers more abstraction, more revelation and more illumination. And all the moreso within the ten *sephirot* in each world. This of course leads to higher levels of love of God, as well.

Shiur 28, Dec 9, 2011

Here, *K'Avoda* speaks of the *yesodot* ("basics") of *Yahadut* ("Judaism"), *ahavat Hashem*, etc. which to our sorrow are not as well known as they should be.

- R' Zusia wasn't known as a *lamdan* or *Talmud Chacham*, and yet once he found the Alter Rebbe referring to him with all the descriptions of one who is learned and wise in *nigleh d'Torah* (*Shas* and *poskim*). They asked him "Why?" and the Alter Rebbe replied that there are mitzvoth with which a lot of people are not fully familiar, such as *ahavat Hashem*, and R' Zusia is a *gaon* ("genius") in these mitzvoth. These (the six "constant mitzvoth") are mitzvoth of the Torah with which people are not sufficiently familiar. In *Hovot Halevavot* ("Duties of the Heart"), it is mentioned that there are important mitzvoth that although some people are knowledgable in general in Torah, yet they are not knowledgeable enough about these mitzvoth, and they are *ahavat Hashem* and *yirat Hashem* ("love of God" and "fear of God").

Here, we are learning about how to attain *ahavat Hashem*. There are two kinds: "Love like water" and "Love like flames of fire." Like water – with *meshichat halev* ("attraction of the heart"), while like fire is with a *bren*, excitement. Entry level "love like water" occurs when we meditate on the *chayut Eloki* ("Godly energy") that is within everything, and that everything was created by God. This becomes stronger as we consider that this *chayut* also enlivens us – then we come to recognition of the preciousness and elevation of Godliness, after which we want to get closer to Him, and the path to approach God is via Torah and mitzvoth.

Page 23 – (page 94 in the translation): "This is especially true when we meditate on levels of Godliness above those invested in the lower worlds…"

At first glance we might think it would be more effective to meditate on matters that are part of "my world," part of events and items and people that populate the world with which "I" am familiar. Most people would say that what happens in the higher worlds "doesn't speak to me that much." "Doesn't hold much interest for me." But here, the Rebbe Rashab says, "Not so"...he says the higher worlds hold much interest for us. He does not explain here but in the continuation it becomes clearer. The light of *sovev* ("transcendant Godliness") is not contracted, so it illuminates equally in all worlds...it is not enclothed in the worlds and therefore we don't experience or feel it at all. Then there is also the *ohr* ("light") of *memalle kol olamim* – (immanent spirituality, "filling all worlds") – which is contracted light, within which there are several levels. At the higher levels, the light illuminates with less contraction and therefore more revelation. Skip the parentheses...page 95, "There are as well variations in each level..." *Bina* ("intellectual analysis") is associated with the world of *Bria*, the six *midot* with *Yetzira*...in each world a different level of revelation.

Also within man, *nefesh* is associated with action, *ruach* with *midot* ("emotional attributes"), and *neshama* with intellect. There's a *Maharsha* (18th century Talmudic commentary) in gemora *Berachot* on the topic: "Three *mishmarot* at night, during the first one, the donkey breys..." *Maharsha* says that for sure these statements are to be taken at face value but also they have symbolic meaning: He quotes from the *shemonah perakim* of the Rambam that there are three powers in the soul of man: *tevit* ("natural"), *chiyunit* ("evlivening" or "vital") and *sichlit* ("intellectual"). And acc to Kaballah, they are "*nefesh, ruach* and *neshama*." Man feels that he possesses these abilities. At times he feels physical strength but not mental, and the opposite. As *K' Avoda* says, "We all know the advantage of our *ruach* over our *nefesh*, and of our *neshama* over our *ruach*..." And by using ourselves as examples, we can understand what's going on Above...

Page 96-97: In order to achieve *ahava* – divine love of God – we must first experience the preciousness of *Elokut*. And the more we consider that Godly illumination is found in the higher worlds, the more we appreciate the preciousness...by way of example, I might know a wealthy man in the neighborhood, who I consider to be wealthy but only in the limited circles of my neighborhood. Then, I hear that he is wealthy even in comparison to "this person" or "that person," etc...then in my eyes he takes on more value, more "preciousness." Same thing here – that which I know up close and personal, I accept for what it is, but then I find out that it's far more than that and I ask myself, "Why do I need what's 'over there,' on the other side, in the higher worlds, for what do I need that when I have something so precious right here…and that is why R' Vital wrote in the intro to *Eitz Chaim* that kabbalah was revealed in the world in order to increase *ahavat Hashem* ("love of God"). Kabalah speaks of many different spiritual levels, and the whole point is to increase our love of God. "You cannot love someone who you do not know at all."

Ahavah works like this: At the moment that you respect or like something/someone, you want to be close to it/him. If for example, someone wealthy or important enters the room, then people want to stand by him, speak with him, even get his signature. If someone is crazy about soccer for example, a good soccer player is someone who people want to approach. The minute that you revere someone, you want to be close, that's love. So if you have some grasp what's going on in *olamot elyonim* – "higher worlds" – you also develop more love for Godliness on those higher levels.

- Chasidut stories mention several personalities who experienced *regesh*, feelings for Hashem, even though their intellectual grasp was weak. They didn't grasp the greatness of *Hashem*, there are several personalities like that…

Page 98, "By approaching God and cleaving to Godliness…" The moment that we love God, we distance ourself from physicality. Because *ahava* transfers us from one place to another – like Avraham who was *haloch v'noseah hanegba* – "going and traveling to the south" – and the south is the "right side," or *chesed* and love of God. And this is not understood: What does the Torah want to tell us, it does not mention a place or a goal to where Avraham travelled, but only that he "travelled to the south," to the "right." This is the spiritual level of Avraham who went from one level to the next in love of God. One spiritual level to the next. From this we understand that "love" means moving from one place to another. He arrives (in soul) to a more spiritual place, so naturally he becomes more distant from physical temptations. And in Rambam's *shemonah perakim*, it's understood that the more we love God, the more we attain a status of wanting nothing from the world but Him – this is love of God *b'kol nafshecha* ("with all of your soul"). *Bekol levacha* means, "with all your heart," but what is "with all your soul"? The sages say, "even if He takes your soul," but Rambam explains it more *k'pshuto* – more simply; "with all parts of your body." Meaning, whatever we do, whether eating, or any other activity, it should be for the purpose of approaching God, so that the food then becomes a part of the process. This is also, *Kol ma'asecha leshem Shamayim* – "all your deeds for the sake of Heaven." It's not easy. R' Levi Yitzhak of Berditchov said, "To refrain from eating – a non-Jew can do that. But to eat, and eat properly (for the sake of God), only a Jew can do that."

(A newly wed guy entered the room), and R' Deitsch quoted from Rebbe Rashab, "a *bochur* doesn't believe," he doesn't know what it means to belive in God. Let him get married, then if he remains Chasidish, that's *koach*. Sages said *tov l'adam lisa ohl b'neurav* – "It is good for man to accept a yoke when he is still young" – and they interpreted it to mean that it is "good for man to get married young." Because both physically (his needs are taken care of before he marries) and spiritually (he has to take on himself the responsibility of being involved in the physical world but finding the spirituality within it), he has to accept responsibility. It's easier when one doesn't have responsibility.

- Alter Rebbe asks about the saying of the sages, *Noach l'adam sh'lo nivra* – "It would have been easier on man if he weren't created." The Alter Rebbe asks, "What do this mean? After everything was created, God 'looked' at creation and saw that it was "good," so what does it mean, "easier if man were not created"? But the text does not say it would have been "better" if man weren't created, but rather "easier." – The creation of man is "good" but that doesn't mean it's "easy."

Shiur 29, December 11, 2011

Page 24 in the Hebrew text, page 98 in the translation, at the top, reviewing material from previous lesson. The more we develop *ahavah*, the more we distance ourselves from the physical world and its temptations. From *Hovot Halevavot*: "Just as fire and water don't exist together, so love of God and love of this world don't dwell together in the heart of one who believes."

- Once R' Deitsch heard from his mother (doesn't remember regarding whom though) that before they would accept a *bachur* as a *chatan* (potential son in law for one of their daughters) they would test him in *limudim* ("learning" and Torah knowledge; R' Deitsch himself underwent this). Without talking in *limud*, they wouldn't take a *chatan*. This was a time honored tradition, even though today the *chatanim* are more sensitive…some don't even want the prospective family to meet him. But in the case that R' Deitsch's mother mentioned, someone said, "I'm going to test him how he eats."

- They would test how he learns at night…there was a story right here not far away (seemingly in the old city), R' Sonenfeld (lived 1848-1932, so the story probably took place ~1868) who later became the Rav of Jerusalem, they checked him out to accept him as *chatan* and of course the learning was fine…and the *minhag* then was that from the *vort* ("engagement") to the *chatuna* ("wedding") was one year. In his case, they noticed that he doesn't come to yeshiva. One person said, "He goes to help an elderly man," but they couldn't verify that and they were very broken over it. And the *calah* ("bride") was also broken cause she thought she was going to marry a *Talmud chacham* ("Torah scholar") and here they don't know what's going on with this *bachur*. So they went to a Rav to ask what to do…they told him that the *bachur* had ceased learning and they want to call off the *shidduch*. They went to the Rav during the day and he told them to come back tomorrow, because he has to ask Hashem what to do (during *maariv* – *ten eitzah tov m'lefanecha*…"give good advice from before You"). Not like today that a Rav answers off the top of his head or "shoots from the hip" with an answer – this Rav needed to pray on this to give him advice from Above. So they came back the next day and the Rav told her to dress up as an Arab girl and go to such and such a place, and hire herself out as someone who would clean their *kelim*, but cheap, so they would take her on. In that way she would be able to see if the *chatan* came there to learn Torah, or to help the elderly man…so that's what she did, dressed up as Arab woman covering eyes so she couldn't even be recognized…so they brought her in to rinse the *kelim* and sure enough she heard the *chatan* learning for hours with the old man…according to the story, she "rinsed the *kelim* with her tears." Tears over the fact that she had suspicions, and tears of happiness that such a person was her *chatan*. The story took place not far away, in *Batei Machsa*…in the old city. The more we tell such stories, the more we are able to "identify" and "join" with what once was, because, "Who are we…"

Continuation in parentheses on page 98 – When we serve God…[a more literal translation here is "as experienced by those who are *ovdei Hashem*, who serve God…"]. If he does so properly, he feels like a "different person" for several hours during the day, or even a whole day. Here the Rav turned to R' David Boaz and said, "You see, it says the same thing in *eyn-beis* (the famous long *hemshech*, "series of discourses") from the Rashab that apparently R' David Boaz was learning at the time. The only way to make this happen on a daily basis is by *hitbonenut*, taking time to do it every day.

- Rav Deitsch said that he "married early," and before he married, he was under the *hashpa'ah* ("mentoring") of R' Shlomo Chaim Kesselman (*z'l*) who educated the *bachurim* to pray at length. There were people who didn't hold from this *avoda*, claiming it was *dimyonos* ("delusions") and not real. R' Deitsch got married early but his friend (he didn't want to say his name but he was an *adam mucar* – a "known person"

– most likely R' Zelig Feldman *alav hashalom*) remained single and came to visit him. R' Deitsch told him what these "others" were saying, and his friend told him, "Listen, perhaps they're right, it's "delusions." But this that it says here in *K'Avoda* about distancing oneself from the physical world – that's not delusions, it really happens. So, the *poel mamash* ("what actually happens"), the fact that one feels further away from *olam hazeh*, that happens…it's real. Regarding our emotions during prayers, it's possible that one goes through delusions about his spiritual level, but in action, he distances himself from physicality, and that's real.

- R' Nissenov, the famous *mashpia* ("mentor") in Brunoy (Paris) married off a son in the US. As they prepared for the *chatuna*, he sat with them to know what the menu will be…first course, entrée, etc…when they got to dessert they suggested ice cream. He asked what is "ice cream" and they told him in Russian (*marizinov*) and his reaction was *Zos lo* – "this, NOT!" with a big movement of his hand. He eliminated it with a lot of certitude as if he didn't want to hear about it at all.

- R' Deitsch heard about the Admor of Boyan (grandsons of Ruzin), an American Chassidic Rebbe who speaks perfect English, very very *adin*, very refined and special. He sat together with one of the *gedolei haLitaim* (a Litvish *gadol* – an important non-Chassidic Rav) at a *chatuna*, the Litvish *gadol* ate the ice cream but the Boyaner Rebbe did not. So, the Litvak asked him, "Why don't you eat, something about the *hechsher*"? He answered, "By us, everything that we do must be with *yishuv hada'at* – with a "settled mind," in a "settled manner." And when you eat ice cream, you can't eat it with *yishuv hada'at* because it melts. That's a sign that it shouldn't be eaten.

- Also the Machlifger Rebbe, from Russia, went thru the darkest days there, but was said about him that he had no fear whatsoever of the Communists at all, conducted himself as if they didn't exist at all. He was in the US but visited Israel in the early *cuffim* (1960's), and he was also at a *chatuna* where they served ice cream. But, they understood that it wouldn't be appropriate to serve the Rebbe ice cream, and they didn't give him. He was an open kind of person, and he asked why they don't give him some. So they served him some ice cream, he tasted it and said, "It's not bad. But why don't they serve it warmer?"

- Also regarding the Machlifger, he was responsible for all that arrived in Israel after the holocaust. Whatever arrived via the big organizations, the Joint, for example…everything went thru him. Also what went to the yeshiva came thru him. But he asked the *bachurim*, "I know you have to eat butter, butter is healthy. But why do you have to have it on the bread? You can eat bread and afterward eat butter…"

The point is that those who are *ovdei Hashem* are not involved, they distance themselves from the physical world. And the way to turn this *avoda* into something real, where no one is fooling themselves, is by constant daily *avoda*. And then, the weakening of the animal soul that occurs is that it doesn't spread into the "garments" and expressions of the person. The soul remains an animal soul, but it doesn't come into expression. When it comes time to eat, the animal soul leaves him alone, what the *yetzer harah* really wants to do is disturb him during *tefila*, but during eating it leaves him alone. (Here, the Rav said something about the Ruzhiner, even the shortest *tefila* is a mitzvah *d'orayta*, even wishing someone good tidings or requesting a bracha for yourself, is a mitzvah *d'orayta*, yet the *yetzer harah* doesn't get involved, because it seems like "small change").

- To "confuse the Satan" during *tekiat shofar* is yet another matter, about which halachic questions are raised and much is written. *Sefer Toda'ah* ("Book of our Heritage" by R' Eliyahu Kitov) brings, without *mekorot* but known that all that he mentions has a *makor*; "Why does the *tekiat shofar* confound the accuser? Because he's afraid it might be the shofar of *meshiach*, and that will spell his end, he won't exist anymore." And in truth, the *kol* of the shofar can arouse Jews to *teshuva* and bring *meshiach*, so the "accuser" has what to be afraid of. There is also a *sicha* of the Rebbe on the topic.

The concept that by lack of usage, the body gets used to it, is exemplified by one whose arm or leg is in a cast for an extended period. He may forget how to use it, and have to do physiotherapy to recover full usage. Rabeinu Yona says that a *ba'al teshuva* ("returnee" to Judaism) must be careful even of things that are *mutar*, permitted. Since his senses are very developed, so there's a danger that he can fall into matters that are forbidden as well. This concept, that by increasing or decreasing involvement, we can control the urge for physical temptations, is not something that the "world" is aware of, but it's in Chasidut. The *K'Avoda* comes to tell us that via *ahavat Hashem*, we can minimize the temptation for physical matters.

K'Avoda goes on to tell us that *tikun hamidot* ("rectifying our character traits") is most effective during *tefila*. Our task is to determine which of our character traits is most in need of *tikun* ("rectification"), and then focus on that during *tefila*. And that helps. The question is, why? Why, as we're meditating on the greatness of God, should we all of a sudden focus on some negative character trait such as anger? This character trait, this anger or whatever, is not the explanation of the words of prayer that we are reciting, so why is prayer the time to work on the trait? *K' Avoda* explains the reason: During *tefila*, the Godly soul illuminates and the animal soul slips into concealment, and then, during prayers, it is easier to have influence over the negative trait and eliminate it. It's simply easier to be effective at that time, and if we make a resolution at that moment "not to become angry," for example, we'll stick with it. Another example; one who looks at newspapers or has a temptation to look at bad stuff on electronic media; when does he decide not to do so? At the moment he's thinking, "How great are Your works..." that's the time to resolve not to do that anymore.

- Story of an *avreich* who worked by someone who was a tough employer. As Ellul approached, he realized that he was transgressing certain *aveirot* by "hating him in his heart." He was careful about all kinds of things, but he realized he was carrying this hatred in his heart and therefore he decided that during the bowing down of the *Aleinu* prayer on Yom Kippur, he would decide to no longer hate his employer. Rambam: "Anyone who hates another Jew in his heart transgresses the mitzvah of *lo tisna et achicha b'levavecha* – 'Do not despise your brother in your heart' (*Vayikrah* 19:17). This applies only to one who hates in his heart, but one who hits and wounds another Jews, transgresses other commandments, but does not transgress this negative command." Rather, one should tell his friend why he hates him and ask him why he is doing such and such to him, as it says, *hocheach tochiach et achicha*..."Your should certainly rebuke your fellow man" (*Vayikrah* 19:17). At any rate, this *avreich* decided he would bow down to the ground (during *Aleinu* on Yom Kippur) and would not get up until he resolved not to hate him. And so it was, and he stuck with his decision and did not hate him any longer. *Davka* when one is at the highest point of *tefila* is the best time to make a resolution about such private matters as *tikun hamidot*.

- R' Deitsch told a story where he asked the previous rosh yeshiva of *Tshebin* (right next to his house), R' Shneerson, what if "everyone knows" that so and so did something wrong? What if both necessary factors are present: He tormented or hurt someone, and he did so in public? If his victim then hates him, the hatred is not merely in his heart, the public knows that he hates him – is it perhaps then permitted to hate him? You put someone in jail and then you want him to come out and smile at you? *Mutar lo*, he is permitted to hate him in this case, because it's not *b'levavecha* ("in your heart")...If for example someone beat you, then do you have to ask him, "Why did you beat me"? No, this is not a case of *b'levavecha*, it was revealed and obvious. What if he beats others as well? Do we have to put up with that and tolerate him in our heart?

Page 100-101: The other reason why *tikun hamidot* works during *tefila* is because that is precisely the time that we see and feel the *grubkeit* and coarseness of the physical. Moreover, the physical becomes "a bit disgusting" to us, and we become a *keli* ("vessel") for the *ohr* ("spiritual illumination"). At first, this is expressed merely as acquiescence of the animal soul not to get in the way and interfere with Godliness, and the second stage is that the animal soul itself wants Godliness.

- Aristotle had an evil wife and his students suggested that he divorce her. He responded that she enables him to change and improve his character traits. Now, did he want to get closer to Hashem? Aristotle's belief was that God is far away and has no interest in the creation. He wanted to improve his character because of himself. (He wrote a *sefer hamidot*). He sought self perfection. They once caught him with certain *ta'avos* ("lusts") and he just responded that, "I wasn't Aristotle then." (Story in the gemora as well, one of the Amoraim had an evil wife who whenever he asked for something to eat, she would prepare it the opposite. One of his students took it on himself to tell her to provide the opposite of what the Amora wanted, but as it happens, the Amora himself was already doing that, so in the end it was reversed twice and back to the original).

Shiur 30, December 30, 2011

B'hashgacha Prati (by "divine providence"), one of the participants in the shiur, R' Yoseph Halbfinger *A"H* took out a copy of *Torah Ohr*, and in it he found a section on the exact topic that we are learning in *K'Avoda*. Look on *daf Lamed-Tet, amud beit* (39B): In the middle of the column: "There are two kinds of *ahavah* and *yirah*. One is *ahavah* and *yirah* that are limited in proportion to our intellectual grasp. And the second is the *ahavah rabba* ("great love") and mighty fear that are beyond what the limited mind is capable of apprehending. The unlimited is a result of *hitbonenut* on *sovev* ("transcendant Godliness"); from this perspective, all *olamot* ("worlds") relative to Hashem are "equal." The first love ("limited') is *b'kol nafshecha*... the second love ("unlimited") is *b'kol meodecha*... And that is the purpose of the *neshama*, to achieve *b'kol meodecha*. *Teshuva* without limitations. This love of *b'kol meodecha* is *teshuva* and via this love, the soul draws down the infinite light from Above that is beyond the original contraction...and this *ahava rabbah* of *bekol meodecha* is also called *ohr chozer* ("reflected light"). The reason it is described as *ohr* ("illumination") is related to the difference between *ohr* and *aish* ("fire"), as opposed to *mayim* ("water"). From *aish* it is possible to ignite other fires without limit. But water is limited, once it is gone, there is no more. The flame itself is limited, but within it is something unlimited; it can light up other objects without limit, which is not true of water."

Now of course it is not absolutely "unlimited," because what person can tolerate something unlimited. However, it is unlimited in relation to the person, which is why we call it "unlimited" because it is beyond our own capabilities, and therefore it draws down from the infinite light of the One above, and we call it *ohr*, or "light." And we call this "unlimited love," "love like flames of fire" – just as in *K'Avoda*. The *Ohr Chozer* ("reflected light") is from the *neshama* being enclothed in the body (where it meets *hitnagshut* or "opposition"), and where it performs a *birur* ("refinement, purification") on the body. See the *maamar* there in *Torah Ohr* (page 39B). So it is only *ahava* like fire that does a *birur* on the animal soul, and the animal soul is called a *petila*, or "wick" in regard to that.

And now on to what it says in *K'Avoda*...On page 25 in the Hebrew text and page 104 in the translation, we will now learn about (previously we learned about "love like water"). The main effect of cleaning up and nullifying the animal soul though, comes from "love like fire." R' Eliyahu Hadad suggested that Avraham Avinu was the source of love like fire, and R' Deitsch answered that, "No he was the source of "love like water". And moreover that "*Kiddush yedid m'beten*" that we say after the *brit milah*, applies to Avraham Avinu. This is acc to Rashi, but Tosafot says it applies to Yitzhak (because when he was conceived, Avraham was circumcised already).

- Nice vort from Rav Huntner *z'l*: Avraham Avinu was the first *gevorner* (the first person "to become Jewish"), Yitzhak the first *geborner* ("who was born" Jewish) and Yaakov the first *farfallener* ("too late, can't do anything about it, you're Jewish"). By Yaakov, no exit. Avraham had Yishmael, Yitzhak had Esau, but Yaakov was *mitato shleima* ("his bed was perfect" – all of Yaakov's offspring were *tzaddikim*, no *reshaim*).

- Told story of Tuvia, the Italian *ger tzedek* ("convert") who came to *Tzemach Tzedek* shul a few years ago, how difficult it was for him to convert, the *Beit Din* wouldn't cooperate, but in the end, he did *ma'amatzim* ("struggled") and converted. He used to do '*mivtzoim*' (the Rebbe's mitzvah campaigns, such as donning tefilin, giving *tzedaka,* house full of *seforim,* etc…) as a non-Jew, saying to Jews, "I'm not a Jew but I'm telling you to put on tefillin," and "I'm a Lubavitcher even before I'm Jewish…" When he finally converted, they danced with him in the Collel, and R' Deitsch told him, "You're a *ger* because *Hashem* decided you would be born a *goy* and decide to convert. We here are all Jewish because we were born that way – "farfallen" – we had no choice."

At any rate, even though Rambam writes that Avraham found his way to Hashem on his own, this saying of the sages (*Kiddesh yedid mibeten* – "Avraham was sanctified from the womb") implies that Avraham's great spiritual level was not merely a result of his own labor and *avoda*. In any case, Avraham Avinu is the "symbol" of "love like water". (A discussion ensued in which one person claimed that Avraham was the source of *mesirat nefesh* ("devotion and dedication") as we learn from the *Akeida,* and *le'chora* ("at first glance"), *mesirat nefesh* takes place without limitations and is therefore more associated with "love like fire," while someone else claimed that the *Akeida* achieved something else; it revealed a level of holiness in Avraham Avinu that was not previously revealed. And that's why Hashem said to Avraham, "Now I know that you are God fearing" – you are not doing this merely from love but out of fear – this explanation is from the Tzemach Tzedek, though someone else thought it was from Tanya (but there it mentions *zrizut* – "alacrity" – not *mesirat nefesh*). It is correct that the act of following God's command was motivated by *ahavah,* but of course *gevurah* was needed in order to carry out the *akeida,* with its blood, *shechita, mila*…likewise, all people are *murcav* ("composed of") different mixtures of *midot* and attributes, and no one should say, "That's me, take me as I am, that's who I am…" Every Jew needs to be multi-talented in *avoda* ("serving God"). It does not suffice to be ONLY a learner who has no good deeds to his name. Quite the opposite…the greatest *gedolei Yisrael* used to collect *tzedaka* for everyone…The Tzemach Tzedek had a *g'mach* ("fund") for which he would collect, and the Netivot (*Gaon m'Lisa*) collected…according to Torah, there must be *hitcalalut* ("inclusion")… quoted from Tanya regarding Avraham (*Ohavi* – "who loves me") and Yitzhak (*Pachad* - "fear") how each was included with the opposite as well.

Back to *K' Avo*da on page 104: Why does only "love like fire" affect the animal soul? Because fire corresponds to the category of creation called *chai,* or "animal." "Heat of lust" - the search for excitement in animal temptations is what characterizes the animal soul, but "love like fire" consumes the heat of the lust. Elsewhere, it is mentioned that fire causes matter to dis-integrate and that's one more reason that "love like fire" devours the animal soul. There's no laboratory [dedicated to analysis of the composition of materials] without fire – and there's no glue without water. One of the differences between mussar and Chasidut: Mussar wants to destroy for the sake of destruction, to crush, wipe out the *yetzer harah*. Chasidut wants to destroy for the purpose of transformation, to utilize the *yetzer harah* and the animal soul.

Now, the *hitbonenut* of "love like fire" is different than the *hitbonenut* of "love like water." "Love like water" emphasizes the presence and the *chayut* of creation – "consider the creation and the force that enlivens it." Such meditation brings us to "love like water" and *dveikut* ("cleaving" to the One above). But "love like fire" demands that we meditate on *Kulo Kamei k'lo chashiv* – "All is as if it does not exist" – "all is like naught." We feel as if the entire world is nothing, it doesn't "exist." This is a very high *hitbonenut*. (*Hitbonenut* on Shabbat is different, it is not like "flames of fire," because on Shabbat, there's no "war." Meditation on Shabbat is meditation without any opposing force, it is *beshalom*, it takes place peacefully).

Two paths to this "love like fire": 1) Either it's via the *hitbonenut* above *kulo kamei*... or it's "love like water" *betziruf* ("combined") with *teshuva*. Important note here:

- The first time that the Alter Rebbe mentions *Ahavat Hashem* ("love of God") in Tanya is in the third chapter, and there it mentions *davka* "love like fire." R' Shlomo Chaim would ask, "The Alter Rebbe is only in Ch. 3 of Tanya and he already mentions the highest level of love? The explanation and *biur* is found in the final chapters of Tanya...in the three chapters that speak of *hashrat haShechina* (the "dwelling of God's Presence" in the holy Temple)...But R' Shlomo Chaim answered, "First of all you have to know who you are – you must know that you have the *koach* and potential to reach this level of "love like fire." Tanya also explains that in essence, everyone wants to be a *tzaddik* – not that he wants the "title" or "name" of *tzaddik* – but that he wants the content (like for example, there are those who want to be "wealthy," not because they want money but because they seek the "title" and the description, and there are those who want the opposite, just the content but not the title). Also similar to a *shiur* the Rav teaches in which the *bachurim* are a bit "older" (22-24) and they all want to be *chatanim* ("bridegrooms"). The Rav asks them, "Do you want to marry or do you want the title/description of "being married"? Here, we need to know that the love we're learning about – "love like fire" - is very high, associated with very accomplished *ovdei Hashem*, but nevertheless we have the *zechut* ("merit") and the potential to learn about it, but "don't rush," there are many levels and *madreigot* of love ahead of us...

Shiur 31, January 1, 2012

Now on the theme of "love like fire" – the task of eradication of the *nefesh habehamit* takes place with love like "flames of fire." In Hebrew, four lines before end of the page (page 25), end of page 104 and onward in the translation… "Now the true love like flames of fire…" – This is unlike "love like water" which is the result of meditation on the energy that creates and enlivens the world, and how there is Godly *chayut* in every single creation, by which the person meditating brings Hashem "closer to him." Godliness takes on "importance" in his eyes, and he wants to get closer to Him. But in order to achieve true "love like fire" (and not some kind of "imitation") we must meditate not only about the "greatness of God," but moreover to meditate on how everything is essentially "nothing" in comparison to Him. Everything is *klum*, nothing has any standing before Him. So, the *hitbonenut* in order to arrive to "love like fire" is how everything is *k'ayin v'efes* – "like nought and nothing" - before Hashem. As a result, the meditator experiences no desire or temptation for anything else, other than Hashem. Everything in the world loses its meaning and temptation completely, like at the end of Ch 43 and beginning of 44 in Tanya.

- R' Yosef Halbfinger (*A"H*) claimed that one cannot really eradicate his desire for all physical things, but R' Deitsch replied that "Yes, you can and I'll give you an example." If you're in a restaurant and the food looks good and smells good, and you ask yourself 'why should I have such a lust for this food?' All you have to go is go into the kitchen where they're making and preparing the food, and you won't have the *ta'ava* anymore. (But R' Yosef replied that even if so, the *ta'ava* returns…). In *ruchniyut* ("spirituality"), it's certainly the case [that you can lose your desire]. *Ruchniyut* is based on intellectual grasp, so when the person "gets it" intellectually, he feels [the spirituality]. The rest of the time, he's like a pile of "wood and stones" [he does not feel or have a desire for spirituality] – to which R' Yosef replied that if so, the person is always in a state of "up and down." R' Deitsch replied, "Yes, all the time in a state of *avoda*, all the time…" Rav Deitsch added, "There are two things here; the *ta'ava* ("lust") and the "love of the *ta'ava*." That a person enjoys the *ta'ava* is natural, he was born that way. That he is drawn to it? That depends on whether there are other things on his mind…if he is pre-occupied with other matters, the level of *ta'ava* goes down. In one of the *Kuntresim*, the Rashab says that a person's *ta'anug* or "enjoyment" is dependent on how much he "wants" to enjoy. He who has a desire to enjoy, does so, while he who does not, will not enjoy. This applies as well to eating and physical desires…

- One of the characteristics of a Tzaddik is *siluk hata'anug* ("removal of enjoyment"), [*tzadikim* are able to stop deriving enjoyment from any physical act, at will] - they don't experience any enjoyment in food. For example, when R' Aharon Karliner arrived as the Shabbat guest of the Alter Rebbe, everyone wanted to have the honor of preparing his Shabbat food for him, so each one chose something to prepare. However, they forgot to put some salt into the food. When they figured that out, each one put in some salt and left...at the table, R' Shlomo Karliner wasn't able to eat it. The Alter Rebbe had no problem eating it, and he asked R' Shlomo Karliner why he wasn't eating..."Is it missing salt?" – The Alter Rebbe got some more salt and added it to R' Shlomo Karliner's food...Afterward, the Alter Rebbe said that from the time that he was by the Maggid, he no longer tasted food. In one of the Rashab's *Kuntresim*, he explains this: Was the Alter Rebbe a *Baal mum* ("defective") *has veshalom*? He couldn't taste anything? The Rashab explained that the Alter Rebbe had *siluk haratzon*, he had no desire to taste the food. There are levels in this...there are many who "don't want to taste, but *nu*..." So it depends on how MUCH the person doesn't want.

- Once, the Rebbe Rashab complained that he wasn't hearing well from one of his ears, went to the doctor...who could not find anything wrong. So, the doctor needed the Rashab to participate, so to speak in the check-up to figure out what was wrong, and the Rashab recalled that once as he was praying, someone was standing nearby and talking, and it disturbed him so much that he "removed his hearing" which then went back "to its source" in his soul...not known if afterward he brought it back or not...there are several categories of this kind of phenomena; 1) when one is sick, he naturally has no apetite and isn't attracted to food 2) then you have one who is just "broken and depressed," not sick and such a person may even throw up when eating cause the whole concept of food is foreign to him at that point. He's simply not interested in eating. 3) But here we're speaking of high *madreigot* ("high spiritual levels"), he simply isn't interested in physical things, and in fact is interested in nothing but Hashem alone.

- In order to bring that idea a little closer to home, consider someone who is working in a place and he likes his boss, he has a good rapport with him. He has a natural desire to be close to the boss. And then he discovers that his boss is not the "real" boss – there is someone above him, his boss's supervisor or even the owner, and he sees how his immediate boss stands up for him, and shows him respect, etc…if the higher boss or owner sticks around, then the employees are going to lose their respectful connection with their immediate boss, cause they'll be more connected to his boss. This is true of many things, when one discovers the *makor* ("source"), he transfers his loyalty and connection to that *makor*. So, the moment when one "discovers" that Hashem is truly the *makor* of all *ta'avot* and *ta'anugim*, he's not interested anymore and becomes interested only in the source, in Hashem Himself…

This level of *tefila* is called *tefila b'makom korban*, or "prayer in lieu of sacrifices." The sages said that the *tefilot* were in place of the *tmidim* (the specific sacrifice that was offered every morning and every evening in the Temple, that maintained the *chayut* or "vitality" of the creation), which were *korbanot*. So what is the connection? Answer: The purpose of the *korban* is to "sacrifice" the animal soul, to transform and elevate it so that it becomes included in its source. Skip the parentheses, move on to page 108 in the translation: "Where" does this occur? *K' Avoda* answers: It occurs during *hitbonenut* in *psukei d'zimra* and *kriat shema*. R' Yonatan Glass asked something, R' Deitsch answered three times, "You have to *mitbonen, bein hashurot, toch hashurot* – "You must meditate between the lines, within the lines…"

Shiur 32, January 2, 2012

How do we achieve "love like fire"? Via *hitbonenut* on *memalle, sovev* and *kulo kamei k'lo chashiv* ("imminent spirituality, transcendent Godliness, and 'all stands before Him as naught'). *Davka* this *madreiga* ("level") that everything is "nothing" before Him – this is what leads to "love like fire." Brings from Tanya to prove that all desires and lusts associated with *olam hazeh*, all of it must be transcended in order to achieve *ahavat Hashem*, because there is nothing but Him.

- Story that R' Deitsch heard in his youth…about when R' Levi Yitzhak of Berdichev wanted to travel to R' Baruch Mezibuz, grandson of the *Baal Shem Tov*. R' Baruch's *avoda* was "still and quiet," it wasn't with a lot of movement, and noise, etc…while R' Levi Yitzhak was expressive, including "running here and there," with lots of action…(the Alter Rebbe was also like R' Levi Yitzhak, rolling on the floor…). So, R' Baruch asked him, "Are you going to get excited here? That's not my thing…" R' Levi Yitzhak promised that he wouldn't get too excited in his *avoda*...R' Deitsch said he heard this story in his youth, he thinks from R' Shmuel Lazar Halperin...so during *tefila*, R' Levi Yitzhak was reserved, quiet (*eingehalten*), also during the Shabbat meal...then at a certain stage of the meal, R' Baruch asked him, "Berditchever Rav, *vas hast er lieb, zaltz oder pfeffer*" – "What do you prefer, salt or pepper"? R' L"Y answered him, *pfeffer zeh basheffer*, "pepper is the Creator! You're asking me what I love? I love the Creator," and he gave a smack on the table and things fell off the table and got on R' Baruch's clothes...and R' Deitsch said that he knew a Jew in Beit Yisrael – R' Yitzhak Isak Eizen – (an elevated person) who had in his possession a cloak of R' Baruch that was soiled with Shabbat food...R' Yosef Halbfinger in the *shiur* then asked (tongue in cheek), "Why didn't they clean the cloak?" to which R' Deitsch responded, "*Mah itcha*" – "what's with you"? Someone who has such a cloak, shame to clean it..."

- In other words, the *mussar haskel* ("lesson") – one who is on such a level that only God matters, to such a person when you ply him with a question about *olam hazeh* ("salt or pepper"), then he just extrapolates that to *kedusha*..."Pfeffer that's the Basheffer." Nothing but God. Expression of "love like fire."

- It is known that R' Levy Yitzhak *ztzl* was loud and expressive during prayers, and someone wanted to come and imitate his *avoda*. So he entered the shul where R' Levy Yitzhak *ztzl* was praying, and started also walking around and shouting. R' Levy Yitzhak *ztz'l* turned to him and made a motion with his hand across his throat (as if someone is slaughtering a chicken), which isn't a positive gesture. This happened a few times until after davening, R' Levy Yitzhak explained to him that roosters crow in the morning, and the gemora explains that what causes a rooster to crow is the change in weather that occurs around that time of the morning, making it necessary for the rooster to "clear its throat." In general, it's only the male that crows, not the female. Once a female got jealous and decided that she also wants to "crow" and make noises. The owner grabbed her and took her away to slaughter her and she asked, "Why do you want to slaughter me?" He answered, "Because you're crowing, that's a sign that you're sick. If I wait longer, you'll become inedible, it's therefore better for me to slaughter you now rather than waiting until you are too sick to eat." So she asked, "So why don't you slaughter the male chicken as well?" He answered, "The male crows because his throat needs clearing and he feels a need, he's not sick. But you crow even though there's no problem in your throat, that's a sign that you're sick, so the time has come to slaughter you." This was R' Levy Yitzhak's explanation to the guy who wanted to imitate him...as if to say, "The one who is screaming during prayers has a reason why he screams. He is in a state of "love like fire," so he makes noise...but you who scream without reason..." It was known that R' Levy Yitzhak had a lot of "bren," a lot of fire in his *avodat Hashem*.

- Once, R' Levy Yitzhak *ztz'l* found himself in the shul of the *Shvut Yaakov* (a famous Torah scholar) for Yom Kippur. He grabbed the *amud* ("prayer lectern") and started to pray *Kol Nidre* (the introductory Yom Kippur prayers), even though there was a *hazan* ("cantor" or prayer leader) there. He remained at the *amud*, prayed there the entire Y"K, and nobody bothered or disturbed him. The son in law of the *Shvut Yaakov* said afterward he thought he was a *malach*, an angel, not a person at all. Immediately after Y"K, R' Levy Yitzhak *ztz'l* said he was hungry, and they brought him food, but he wouldn't eat even tho they kept bringing him more food. Finally he said, "I'm hungry, I haven't learned all day long, please bring me Gemora Succah." So they brought him the gemora, he put his leg up on the bench and propped up the Gemora on his knee, and learned the entire night.

Page 26 in the Hebrew, page 110 in the translation (skip the parentheses): "But this "fire from Above"...Here the *K'Avoda* is speaking of high *madreigot*, *hitgalut haneshama* ("revelation of the soul") which not every person achieves. However, for lower souls such as ours, there is another path to "love like fire," and that is by meditating on the path of "love like water," but adding "another component" to the meditation. We should add consideration of our distance from Hashem. With the addition of this factor of "distance" to the meditation on "love like water," in this manner we may achieve "love like fire." "Love like water" is about how God is found in everything...add to that consideration of our distance from Him, and the result will be "love like fire"...

Shiur 33, January 3, 2012

How does a Chasid achieve high levels of divine love, including "love like fire"? He does so via *hitbonenut* on *Gadlut Hashem*, including *kulo kamei k'lo chashiv*..."all is like naught before Him." Because with this meditation, he is able to eliminate his *ta'avot*, and he wants only to cleave to God in excitement. But, this is not a simple matter for the average person...

Starting again on page 110 in the translation, "But this 'fire from Above..."

In Yiddish, a man on a high level of spirituality is called a *geheibener Yid*...an "exalted Jew"...What is a "high *madreiga*"? When there is revelation of the Godly soul, when the Godly soul is active...

- Story of the chasid of the Rashab who bought *kelim* at a fair, objects that the seller claimed were previously owned by various *tzaddikim*, the chasid brought them to the Rashab as gifts, showed them to the Previous Rebbe on the way into *yechidut*, who told him that "this yes, this no..." ("this object was in the possession of a *tzaddik*, this one not..."). When he went into the Rashab and showed the items to him, the Rashab said the same as his son...when he left his *yechidut* he again encountered the Previous Rebbe (who wasn't yet the Rebbe at that time) and asked him, "Are you doing *moftim*? Are you doing miracles? You have a *mashkanta* (punishment) coming..." [It is an *issur* for a Chassid to display spiritual abilities such as discerning holiness in a physical object; that is a task for the Rebbe, not for the Chassid, even if the Chasid has such powers]. The Previous Rebbe answered him, "No, that wasn't a *mofet* ("miracle"). "When there is *gilui neshama* ("revelation of the soul"), then you know what was used by a *tzaddik* and what was not used..." This is revelation of the *ohr* ("light") of the soul.

- Someone in the *shiur* asked, why didn't R' Shmuel Munkus (a Chasid of the Alter Rebbe) give the same response in the known story of the fried lungs that he wouldn't allow people to eat, and instead threw it into the garbage, after which the *shochet* ran in to tell everyone not to eat it, "It's *treif*"...upon which everyone turned to R'Shmuel and said "You deserve a *mashkanta*," and indeed they gave it to him...why didn't R' Shmuel tell them "It's not a miracle, it's *gilui neshama*"? 1) Perhaps simply that R' Shmuel allowed himself to be beaten but the Previous Rebbe did not, or 2) that by R' Shmuel it was the *shlila*, the "negation" of something *treif*, but here it was something positive, to reveal the *Elokut* in the *kelim*...

- Rav Deitsch heard from R' Shlomo Chaim *A"H* (perhaps in the name of R' Hillel Paricher) that "to be aware of someone else's *machshavot zarot* ("foreign thoughts") is not a high *madreiga*, not a high level." R' Deitsch was by a farbrengen with R' Shlomo Chaim and there were such farbrengens at the time that he would latch on to a certain *bachur*, and "do an operation on him." These were very special farbrengens. R' Shlomo Chaim latched on to a certain *bachur* who was known to have *s'feikot b'emuna* – "serious doubts regarding his faith in Hashem."

R' Shlomo Chaim jumped on him, comparing him to another *bachur* who was well known for his *emunah*, and asked the first one, "Why do you think that you have *sfeikot* and this other *bachur* does not? Is it because you are brighter, smarter, etc? Why does he have no doubts, but you do? It's because he has no *machshavot zarot* ("foreign thoughts") and you do have *machshavot zarot*, and that's why you have *sfeikot b'emunah*. And then, R' Shlomo Chaim told a story of a *bachur* who went to R' Grunem, the *mashpia* in Lubavitch and told him that he has *sfeikot b'emuna*...Grunem told him *betach pagamta balaila, lech l'mikvah*. "You must have had a nocturnal emission last night, go to the mikveh." So the *bachur* went to the mikveh and returned. In those days, it wasn't so simple to go to the mikveh, it wasn't clean and nice as it is now, but the *bachur* came back to Grunem and said, "it all went away, it's all gone." So R' Shlomo Chaim said to the *bachur* with *sfeikot*, "So it seems that if something happens, you have to go to the mikveh. Have you gone to the mikveh?" It turned out that the *bachur* had not gone to the mikveh. R' Shlomo Chaim told him, "All the *sfeikot* and everything starts from not going to the mikveh." Then he turned to the other *bachurim* and checked out if there are others who didn't go to the mikveh. He started a public investigation who goes to the mikveh and who not, one *bachur* spoke up and said sometimes he doesn't go...R' Shlomo Chaim asked, "who sleeps with you in the same room," as if to ask if this one goes or doesn't go to the mikveh...they found his roommate and asked him, "Does your roommate go to the mikveh?" He answered that he doesn't know. R' Shlomo Chaim said to him, "you can't tell, you can't "smell" whether someone went to the mikveh or not?" The next day, the initial bachur who R' Shlomo Chaim latched onto walked about in a very serious manner...went to the mikveh...the other *bachurim* thought that after such a farbrengen and a *hashpala* ("put down") that maybe he wouldn't go, but he did go to the *mikveh* at least the next morning. Point is, it doesn't require *ruach hakodesh* ("holy spirit") to determine if someone went to mikveh or not. And also one who went to mikveh himself feels the difference...he understands the words of *kriat shema* better after the mikveh than before...once Rav Deitsch told this to a *bachur* in Ponevitz who responded, "That's just because it 'refreshes you'" – R' Deitsch laughed at that. ("Perhaps that also the case, I don't deny, but I think it's also because...")

- As a child, R' Deitsch knew a Breslaver by the name of R' Velvel Cheshin, who made a lot of *baalei teshuva*...R" Deitsch passed by as he was teaching *Likutei Maharan*, told of someone in a certain city who was involved in witchcraft…this "witch" saw the Jews going to the mikveh and wanted to know to where they are going and coming back, "When they go, I see on them a lot of 'evil spirits' which I know, when they return, those *ruchot ra'ot* ("evil spirits") are gone, where do they leave them?"

Back to *K'Avoda*…and revelation of the soul…here the *K'Avoda* cites *Likutei Torah* of the Alter Rebbe, where it brings a different *hitbonenut* that also leads to "love like fire," and that's not *hitbonenut* on *Gadlut Hashem*, but rather on the newness of creation at every instant, how it is new…every day he sees the re-creation of the universe. At first glance, this should not be only for someone on a high level, but upon further investigation, this meditation is also for one who experiences revelation of the Godly soul. For, why does one experience the *chiddush* ("re-creation") of the creation – because he is close to the One above! And how do people on our level nonetheless arrive to such a level? By meditating on how we are far from Him, distant from Hashem. That's the added ingredient…when we meditate on the Godliness in the world (the same meditation that brought us to "love like water"). This seems to be a low bar, it does not require us to think about Godliness above the world but about Godliness within the world…this is identical to "love like water" that draws and attracts him…but to this we add the following thought process: "Where am I? I am so far from Him in thought speech and action and in general in his soul." This bitterness over our distance is the key.

R' Deitsch added, "I don't know if you'll find this *hitbonenut* anywhere else besides here in *K'Avoda* – certainly not in Tanya, there it mentions only the *hitbonenut* on *gadlut Hashem*. But *K'Avoda* adds the factor of "distance" – and together they lead to "fire." (Post *shiur* comments from the Rav…"When one thinks and wants to become closer to Hashem, and then feels how far away he is from God. From the perspective of God, I'm close, but from my own perspective, I distance myself…like for example, someone who worries for you, helps you, etc…for him you develop a chemistry, a rapport…*k'mayim hapanim l'mayim* ("like the reflection of a face in the water"), but then you respond by ridiculing and distancing yourself from him…this *hitbonenut* can totally knock you off your rocker so that you lose your equilibrium – that's "love like fire," it's a "loss of mental equilibrium" – going out of limitations. In general when speaking of love, we speak of drawing closer to the object of our affection. But, when we add the ingredient of feeling our distance ["Where am I, who am I"], that brings the *bren*, the "burn…")

Shiur 34, January 4, 2012

To achieve "love like fire," the only path is through *hitbonenut*, meditation on *gadlut Hashem* ("greatness of God"). But even the *hitbonenut* itself is not sufficient, and it is necessary to descend a *madreiga* and consider our distance from Him. Only the combination of both of these factors together leads us to love like flames of fire. Without the added factor of our perceived "distance" from Hashem, the love that we achieve via *hitbonenut* on *Gadlut Hashem* remains "love like water". The component that we should consider in order to achieve "love like fire," is that He, Hashem is close to me, but I distance myself from Him, with my thought speech and action. He (Hashem) is close to everyone, but in our own estimation we feel distance. This is very frequent between father and son. The father feels close to the son, but the son is distant from the father. The opposite perspective, that the son feels close to the father but the father does not feel close, is almost not to be found. The sages said, "Your sins separate between you and your Father above." We do not say that our sins separate "from" Him, or "between you and Him," but rather "between you and your Father…" That means that from God's perspective there is no separation, and the separation is only from our perspective. From our point of view, there is separation, in as much as He is our father. But if we consider that the father from his point of view wants to get close to the son, and the son distances himself, this brings to a strong arousal of emotion, an arousal of fire. The problem is that in general the son doesn't want to think about it, because it bothers him.

- The Maharal of Prague wrote a *sefer* about *galut* entitled *Netzach Yisrael*, in which the main point is that it's not like people think, that God forsook the Jews, but the opposite, Hashem is with us more than in the times of the Temple. For example, a father sent his son from the house, "expelled him," but nonetheless he sent messengers to make sure that his son is taken care of, has food, etc…the father was angry but nonetheless he worries for the son…therefore the verses say that even though, "He loathes us," nevertheless He worries, so the same relationship that exists between an earthly father and son exists as well between Hashem and the Jewish people. It's said that the time when a friendship is tested is when there are differences in opinions. That's also the problem with *shidduchim*; when the couple is going out, "everything goes well." But after the marriage, then the problems start. Because sometimes, one side is "not in the mood," etc…and one who claims that he doesn't have such problems, probably does not have a good connection even when he is "in the mood"…it says that when Mashiach arrives, we will long for the days of exile. The

Rebbe said that in the time of *geula* ("redemption"), we will see the benefit and true level of our current exile, that we don't see right now. Why don't we see it right now? Because Hashem wants us to request the *geula*, the redemption.

In any case, this conflict, that He is close to us but we distance ourselves...is what arouses "love like fire." And then we seek to be close to Him, we seek to erase the obstacles between ourselves and Him. That occurs as we meditate in general on how Hashem is close to us and then we add in the factor how we separate and distance ourselves from God.

Now, if we think further and add, how *Atah Havaya Nafshi* – "You are *Havaya*, my soul"...(Page 112 in the translation)...Previously our discussion of "love like water" was divided into two categories; regular meditation into how He enlivens and creates every creature and object in the world, followed by how He is our own *chayut* and vitality (*Nafshi aviticha balaila*...). Now, when this level of "love like water" is combined with consideration of our distance from Hashem – this especially leads to "love like fire." As the *K' Avoda* says, "we will become even more inflamed..." And then, in conclusion, the *K' Avoda* says that this level of "love like fire" incinerates and destroys the animal soul. "Love like water" does not achieve eradication of the animal soul, it only weakens the animal soul. The person meditating focuses on the Godly concept and feels the Godliness, but that only weakens the animal soul, it doesn't eradicate it. However, the distance experienced by the Godly soul causes the animal soul to become nullified. As much as we amplify the Godly soul, we weaken and eradicate the animal soul.

The secret here is that the animal soul corresponds to "fire," since among the four categories of creation, "animal" (*chai*) correspond to "fire" (*aish*) among the four elements. So, the *aish* of the Godly soul consumes the *aish* of the animal soul.

- There is a *sefer*, the *Chovot HaTalmidim* ("Obligations of the Students") by the Piazetzner Rav, *Hashem yinkom damo* (he was killed in the Holocaust). He was a great figure, a great man. We have only a small number of his works, which were found after the Shoah, and perhaps more will be found. He wrote in a very special style, and there he writes that there are some people who pray well when they are young but as they grow older, their level of *tefila* goes down. He writes the reason for this is that when they were young, the fire in their animal soul helped them to pray. But when the fire of the animal soul subsides, the ability to pray also subsides. We are no longer so tempted by physical lusts, and when we relate to them with "coldness," our *tefila* also goes down.

- Incredible piece from the *Bnai Yisaschar* in his sefer, *Igra d'Pirka*: He writes that there were some people with whom he was afraid to daven in their vicinity when they were young, since their *avoda* was so holy. When he visited them later in life, they were not at all on the same spiritual level. Upon investigation, he concluded that it was desire for money that ruined their *avoda* and took them down spiritual levels.

- R' Elyahu Hadad mentioned how money issues can get in the way of *avoda*…R' Deitsch said that the Rebbe Rashab said, *Ich gleib nish kein bachur* – "I don't believe any single man" who isn't married – meaning that until he is married with responsibilities, he does not know if his *avoda* is authentic or not. So even if some of the *bachurim* in his time were *ba'alei madreiga* ("on a genuine spiritual level"), the Rashab did not believe in them…and the Rogachover would not give *smicha* ("rabbinical ordination") to one who was not married.

End of page 113, "Furthermore, the power of the natural element of fire…" There is a verse (*Kohelet* 9:8) that says, "At all times your clothes should be white, and there should be no lack of oil on your head." The *Baalei Mussar* ("sages of the Mussar movement") say, "You must think of yourself as wearing white clothes and having oil on your head and if you move your head the wrong way, the oil will drop on your white clothes and soil them." (R' Deitsch poked fun at this interpretation, saying, "Happy is the man who is always afraid"). Another verse from Chumash (Deut 20:12), "Do not lay siege to them, and do not wage war against them" – Chasidish interpretation is not to "make a *tzura* (grant a 'form' –a play on *tetzureim* – "lay siege") out of the *yetzer harah*, and do not "wage war" – do not transform the *yetzer harah* into such a "big deal" that it becomes necessary to wage war against it. Another story of the *yetzer harah*: There were some Jews were sitting in Beit Midrash and talking, someone walked in and asked them what they are talking about. They answered, "the *yetzer harah*." He replied, the *yetzer harah* says, "Spit on me, embarrass me, etc…" the main thing is to pay attention to me." The point being that the *yetzer harah* only gets worse when we give it attention. Same thing with Adam Harishon (Adam the first man) – the *klipot* only said, "Look at us," nothing more, just "don't ignore us."

Shiur 35, January 5, 2012

Final line on page 113 of the translation: "Furthermore, the power of the natural element of fire becomes elevated…" That is, not only is the natural soul weakened, but it is actually transformed and elevated to holiness.

On page 114, Regarding "love like fire" that is associated with people who are not on the high *madreiga* ("spiritual level") associated with the meditation of *kulo kamei* ("All is as naught…"), such as most of us who meditate on Godliness in the world and then combine that with our awareness of distance from Hashem – if so, the resulting "love like fire" should be similar to the process of *teshuva*. *Teshuva* is also associated with a feeling of *merirut* ("bitterness") over our situation, bitterness over our distance. It emerges that if we seek elevation of the *nefesh habehamit* ("animal soul") without *pe'ilut* (action or "results," such as "love like fire"), then the bitterness of *teshuva* is enough. But one who is looking for the *pe'ilut*, the "results" (in this case, the "love like fire" that should result from meditation), for that you need love rather than *teshuva*. During the process of *teshuva*, all of our involvement is focused on the theme of *richuk* – of "distance." This is not the case during "love like fire," during which we love God but there is also a mixture of distance – during the process of *teshuva* we are involved only in the distance.

Within the thought processes of *teshuva* there are two matters to consider: The details of our mis-behavior that we want to correct, and also the overall picture that emerges of our relationship with Hashem. Either way, both of these factors (our personal need for rectification and our overall relationship with the One above) are what occupy us now during the process of *teshuva*. By doing proper *teshuva*, we break the *klipah* of the *nefesh habehamit*, but we don't elevate it as we would during "love like fire." Only *teshuva ila'ah* (the "higher form of *teshuva*" that is about becoming "one" with God, returning to Him) transforms the animal soul. The lower for of *teshuva* (which is about correcting our sins) is equal to "love like fire" in terms of "breaking" the *klipa*. Where they are not equal is in transforming and elevating the *klipa*: That's something that "love like fire" (as well as *teshuva ila'ah*) can achieve, but *teshuva tata'ah* cannot accomplish.

- Rav Deitsch turned to R' Eliyahu Haddad and asked him, "Is it possible to read all about this and not put it into practice?" Then he told a story about R' Mendel Veg in Tiberius, the Rav saw him perhaps twice, he was an old man. R' Isaac Sher who was *mashgiach* of Slobodka Yeshiva, saw R' Mendel in Tiberia when he was there for *Chamei Tiberia* ("Tiberius hot springs"), and on the way back, he told his students, who were speaking matters of *avodat Hashem* and the *avot* ("forefathers"), "If you want to see *avodat Hashem*, look at R' Mendel." Not simple at all for a Mussar *mashgiach* (a mentor and teacher from the Mussar movement) to say such a thing about a Chasid to his students, but everyone agreed about R' Mendel…R' Deitsch didn't know him when he was young but once sat next to him at a Purim farbrengen in Tiveria (on Purim they would farbreng during the day). He heard him say, "The main thing is that something should remain afterward, something should remain…" (he was speaking of after Purim, after the farbrengen, "something should remain" after the Purim farbrengen…). Another time, R' Deitsch saw him at home, in bed and he told R' Deitsch a story that he doesn't remember, but then he said to him, "This story isn't about us, but the main thing is we should know that such a level exists…" Yet another time, R' Deitsch saw him in shul and at the end of the table was another man who was speaking of other matters with his friend, and R' Mendel Veg turned to him and said, "Don't argue with me, I'm speaking from practical experience…" (apparently he had a word with him earlier about *avodat Hashem*, and then when he saw the guy stam talking with his friend, R' Mendel Veg assumed they were talking about the same subject, about *avodat Hashem*).

At any rate, the *ikar* in "love like fire" is the *hitlahavut*, the "excitement," which is not present in the process of *teshuva*. During *teshuva*, the *ikar* is the *merirut*, the "bitterness." Elsewhere, the Rebbe Rashab explains that with *teshuva*, the *ikar* is that the person is running away from something, running away from the "not good." But with love, he is running to Hashem, what hurts him is his *richuk*, his "distance" from Hashem, and *adaraba* ("just the opposite"), he wants to get closer and approach Godliness. And this is the theme of *korbanot* ("sacrifices"). All *korbanot* require that we offer the *chelev v'dam* – "fat" of the animal (enjoyment) and its "blood" (*aish*). You see two kinds of people when they're eating: One who is totally still and the other who makes a lot of slurping noise as he eats and smacks his lips, etc: One has *retichot hadamim* ("lust" and "hot blood" for the food) and the other simply enjoys his food. The one making noise is *retichot hadamim* (the slurper), he's into his food, and the other simply gets enjoyment (*chelev*).

- One *tzaddik* had nothing for Succot, his wife sold something so they would have something to eat. Came the *chag*, he ate with great excitement. Suddenly he stopped and said, "I'm sitting in the plate, not in the succah."

So, the *korban* mainly is about *dam* ("blood") and *chelev* ("fat"), and those are two necessary ingredients of *tefila*. They symbolize the enjoyment and the lust of the animal soul. More in detail, *chelev* in *kedusha* is "love like water," while *dam* is "love like fire." In *avoda*, both require that the Godly soul has influence on the animal soul rather than leaving it to its own vices. There is such a thing as the Godly soul understands a Godly concept, but that its intellectual grasp has no effect on the animal soul. Indeed, to have an effect on the animal soul is not simple. There is a collection of letters from the Rebbe in which he explains to Jews who were either in early stages of *hitkarevut* ("approach") to Judaism or even prior to that, about how to "get" Jewish themes and understand them on their level. The Rebbe's secretary at the time for English matters – R' Simpson – helped the Rebbe put the letters together and saved copies of them, and the magazine Kfar Chabad began printing excerpts, from the book "*Moreh l'nevuchim*" or something like that, explaining the basics of Judaism. Such explanations demand a lot of expertise. If you want to include the animal soul in the process, you have to "explain it to him." Otherwise he remains "out" of the picture.

In Jewish history, this was a problem for Jewish women before the establishment of Beit Yaakov. Women did not learn how to read or write, R' Deitsch said that one of his grandmothers could write, the other could write only with difficulty and wrote once a month to the Rebbe. Only with establishment of the girls' school, Beit Yaakov did women begin to learn something. They had *emunah* and good *midot*…R' Deitsch told about how when his grandmother would clean the floor, do "sponje" (cleaning tile floors with a wet rag) so if a grandchild came in she would tell him, "Move, I'm doing sponje" and they would respect her. That's what we have to do within ourselves, to have a dialogue with the animal soul within us. This makes a big difference.

Skip the parentheses on page 116 and go to 117: "love like water" alone without "explanation" will not convert the animal soul, for that purpose, explanation is needed, to find the right *otiot* ("letters") in order to explain. But "love like fire" itself influences and converts the animal soul. It does not need to "enclothe" itself and explain itself to the animal soul, its very presence has that effect.

Shiur 36, January 6, 2012

Kitzur ("summary") from previous *shiurim:* Two kinds of love, "love like water" based on "attraction." "Love like fire," with "excitement." Two different kinds of meditation: both on *Gadlut Hashem*, but "love like water" is based on how God is found in the world, enlivens the world, and this kind of meditation does not lead to excitement, but to "attraction" (*meshichat halev*). "Love like fire" – *aish* – implies by definition that the meditator wants to "go out of himself," wants to forsake his own existence. Such *teshukah* ("desire") requires a very high *hitbonenut* of which not everyone is capable. And therefore the *K'Avoda* suggests a "lower" *hitbonenut* on how Hashem enlivens the world, how a contracted ray of light enlivens the world (which leads to attraction and "love like water") and to combine that with consideration of how our own thoughts, speech and deeds have placed distance between ourselves and Hashem. This is similar to the *teshuka* of a *Baal Teshuva* (as we learned yesterday), in that both require a perception of distance. In general, love is based on attraction and proximity, but "love like fire" requires an additional factor: experiencing our distance from God.

So, it emerges that there are two ways to achieve love like fire: 1) for higher *neshamot*, it is enough to meditate on *Gadlut Havaya* (the "Greatness of the Creator" – in the sense of *kulo kamei*... "all is nought before Him"), but for lower *neshamot* it is necessary 2) to add the element of "distance.": First, regular meditation on contracted Godly illumination that enlivens the world, and then to combine with that consideration of our distance from Hashem. And this *hitbonenut* completely consumes the animal soul. (In response to question from R' Eliyahu Hadad, Rav Deitsch mentioned the *ahavah b'ta'anugim* mentioned in Tanya, that is also "love like water," but associated with *tzadikim*, not with us...).

Today we'll learn why this happens...bottom of page 117 in the translation: Why does the *richuk* ("distance") provide the additional ingredient necessary to trigger "love like fire"? Because that makes it *nogeah li* – it converts the meditation into a topic that "relates to me." The meditation on "distance" delivers the message that, "I am the one who is far, and you, the *nefesh habehamit*, are the one who causes my distance." But the reason that "love like fire" of the higher variety (involving direct meditation on *Gadlut Hashem*, that doesn't require the "distance" factor because it's appropriate for higher souls) works, is because of *aish achla aish* – "fire consumes fire." Not because the meditator is "speaking to" his animal soul (at this point in the meditation he is actually absorbed in the very high recognition that *kulo kamei k'lo chashiv* – "all is like naught" before Him - and he is in a state of high spiritual communion with God). But because the fire itself (generated by his meditation) consumes the animal soul. When speaking of the lower meditation in which we must combine the "distance factor," it's understood why it works – our meditation is "speaking" to the animal soul which is the very factor causing the distance. But the higher meditation in which we simply meditate on *kulo kamei*...there it is more difficult to fathom how "love like fire" consumes and eradicates the animal soul.

- Here, R' Deitsch brought an illustration from the Rebbe Rashab... the Rashab asks why is it that precisely in the middle of *tefila* is when we experience *machshavot zarot* ("foreign thoughts")? Before *tefila* we didn't experience such thoughts but now in the middle of prayers, we do so? One explanation is that the animal soul feels it is going out of existence so it fights back [The Rashab mentions this in *K'Avoda*]. But the Rashab gives a *mashal*: One practical joke that we play on people is to sometimes tie their shoes or pants to the chair when they are sitting down. As long as the person remains seated, he is not aware that he has been tied down. But, as soon as he wants to get up, he is unable to do so, his garments holds him fastened to the bench or chair. The same occurs regarding *machshavot zarot*...before and after *tefila* when we are not interested in "ascending," we do not feel the hindrance of the animal soul and *yetzer harah* who want to hold us back. Only when we want to pray and ascend above, then we feel something holding us back...The *machshavot zarot* tell us, "Hey, where do you think you're going, you're one of us"!

Something like this applies even to the highest *tzadikim* focused on *gadlut Hashem*. The excitement of "love like fire" means that they want only to cling and cleave to Hashem, "There is nothing but Him." But, *tachlis*, something holds back the person back, each person according to his level – and that is the animal soul. It emerges then that even those who attain "love like fire" after direct *hitbonenut* on *Gadlut Hashem* (even without the added element of "distance") – they as well experience something holding them back. The lower level *hitbonenut* that includes consideration of our *richuk* ("distance") is plain and obvious, we know that our animal soul is holding us back. But even for those capable of meditating on the higher level, they naturally feel that something is "holding them back." Within the meditation, there is something concealed (the animal soul) and it is holding them back even if they don't have to consciously think about their *richuk* from Hashem in order to achieve "love like fire" – the obstacle is there nonetheless. Those who need to consider their "distance" feel it before achieving "love like fire," but those for whom "love like fire" comes naturally thru *hitbonenut* on *Gadlut Hashem*, feel their distance after they achieve "love like fire," as a result of their love, not before it. See page 118.

R' Deitsch wanted to do the parentheses on page 28 (page 116 in the translation)..."It is true that all of our understanding..." In this parentheses [which in the translation are not in parentheses], the Rashab differentiates between how different people grasp deep topics; some with more *hitlabshut* (needing more explanations and illustration) and some with less...R' Deitsch asks, "Why do we need this differentiation (that also applies to two people meditating, one who achieves "love like fire" via consciously thinking about his *richuk*, and the other who does not have to consciously bring it up)...

what is the *neshama* that does grasp, and what is the *neshama* that does not grasp? All of these matters come up in Chasidut and are explained, everyone has *sechel,* so why differentiate in this manner? It was already mentioned that we need to bring the meditation down into examples and parables that the animal soul will grasp. On the other hand, who works without these examples and parables to illustrate matters? Can the Godly soul work by itself? Everthing that we understand comes via the filter of the animal soul as well, are there matters that the Godly soul understands alone? This is the question leading to the parenthetical statement on page 116, "It is true that all our understanding…" All such matters must come thru the intellect, which is associated with the natural (animal) soul – so is there such thing as the Godly soul alone "understands"?

In many places in Chasidut it states that only the Godly soul understands the command, *Shema Yisrael*… but how can this be? Is it possible to "understand" without the intellect of the natural soul? And there are times that a person prays with his Godly divine soul alone, while the animal soul "sleeps." And when he finishes davening, the animal soul wakes up and says, "My turn, you can go to sleep and I'll take over." The solution is that during the davening, we must also utilize our animal soul, and persuade it to get involved. So, how exactly does that work? Here (third line page 28, page 116 in the translation), he explains…that the question is "what is the Rebbe coming to tell us, all matters have to come to the attention [and through the filter] of the natural intellect." So the Rebbe explains here that there's a big difference: If our preparation is to understand the matter with our Godly soul alone, we will not be able to apply our understanding to the animal soul, and our *hitbonenut* will have no strong effect on the animal soul except to weaken it. But if the preparation is that our natural/animal soul should also be involved, then in the end it will have influence on the intellect of the animal soul as well.

Here, R' Deitsch explained that the question of the participation of the animal soul is not a question of whether it "understands or not." It's a question of whether it "gets it." In Hebrew, *hanacha*, in Yiddish, *leits zich up*. There are things that we understand, there are things that we just "get," even though it may not be based on intellect. It could come from the person's upbringing, or *minhag*…

- Story of a couple who got divorced because he did not go to her parent's house on the night of Rosh Hashana to wish them a *shana tova*! There were problems between the couple, but what broke the back was his failure to keep this custom of going to say *shana tova* to the parents on the night of *R"H*. (On night of *R"H* the entire haredi street of full of people going to their parents for *R"H* wishes. By Chabad it's different, *R"H* is about *kabalat ohl Malchut shamayim*…R' Soloveitchik had a Chabad *cheder* teacher who taught him that, and later he said that anyone who doesn't read *Likutei Torah* about *R"H*, doesn't understand what *R"H* is).

So, what's necessary for the animal soul is not to understand, but to "get it," and in order for that to occur, it must "give itself over" (devote itself) to the matter. For example, there are people who are ready to listen and understand you, but not to change their own opinion. For the animal soul to "get it" and work with it, it must "give itself over" [devote itself, abandon the ego] and then the Godly matter will have an effect on it.

Shiur #37, January 8, 2012

Rav Deitsch read the Hebrew text from top of page 119 in the translation to 120, saying this was a summary and synopsis of the entire chapter. Arriving to, "A further development…" on page 120, R' Deitsch said this is a summary of "love like water", the purpose of which is to approach and cleave his soul to *Elokut,* to Godliness. This love does not destroy the negative aspects of the animal soul, but weakens it. The meditation is focused on the ray of Godly illumination that enlivens the world.

- He brought as an example the cup of coffee in front of him, that has a good smell. While we might say it has a good smell "because it's Elite coffee," but in truth one should say, "It has a good smell because Hashem infused it with a greater level of *chayut Eloki.*" At any rate, that's what we should think. Once we do so, we approach Godliness and feel the preciousness of it. (All during *galut,* Hashem enlivens not only kosher but also treif items, and the goal is to present a test that Jews have to withstand and overcome. He doesn't really want to enliven such creations, but "throws them their *chayut* as if "over the shoulder." Rav Deitsch is in touch with a nutritionist who is very strict, who does not become either *halavi* nor *basari* the whole year long, is over 80 but walks like a young child in the street…and he says that one cup of coffee a day does not do any damage and in fact he himself drinks a cup of coffee a day…but here we're focused on the good and preciousness of Godliness…).

Ultimately the *kiruv* and cleaving to Godliness as a result of "love like water" results in greater fulfillment of Torah and Mitzvoth…why? Because with mitzvoth there is direct revelation of Godliness…not like in the coffee for example, wherein the Godliness is "enclothed" in the smell, etc, and remains concealed. Therefore the great revelation of Godliness that we experience during *hitbonenut* leading to "love like water" influences us to learn more Torah and fulfill more mitzvoth. As in parshat *Re'eh*, and acc to the Besht, there is *v'tov* ("and good" – the verse there says, "Behold I have placed before you life and good...") in everything, as well as evil and death...the part that is *kayam*, that has lasting power, is the Godly *chayut* while the "evil and death" is the physical aspect. Everything physical has a "date of expiry," even wine. Interesting factoid; they found wheat in the pyramids, that was still intact; however when planted, it could not germinate. "The source remains, but the 'results' dissipate, and that's the explanation of "*Re'eh* I put before you life and good..." and choose the "life," the source...

Shiur 38, January 9, 2012

Page 120 in the translation (page 29 above, in the original Hebrew), "A further development..." mentions *nafshi aviticha* ("I desire you," because "I recognize that You Yourself are my *chayut*, and *bra d'ishtadel* ("son who puts out effort for his Father") – these *dargot* ("levels") of "love like water" also may lead to love like fire – at any rate, even if we are not on these levels, we should get used to the concept. Even if the *dargot* are not truly revealed to us, we should be aware of them and get used to the idea. And an even higher level is *k'mayim hapanim el hapanim*...how He loves and draws me closer, like a high and majestic King who descends to unite with a low person...this is Hashem taking us out of Egypt. And in return, we love Him...this is a higher and more *pnimi* love of God. Rav Deitsch once heard that this chapter in Tanya (46) that deals with this level of divine love, is "obligatory learning" for Chasidei Ger. All of this is within the category of "love like water".

Page 29, five lines from the top, continues "bridging" into "love like fire," and here the Rebbe adds that even though "love like fire" is a high level, "we must of necessity come to this level, because only it strongly reveals the light of the divine soul..." and the *ratzo*, or "rush" to Godliness also takes place with fire. And on all of these levels, we reach "love like fire" by taking into account our distance. On the level of true *hitbonenut*, even one who does not need to take "distance" into account, nevertheless he must meditate on *Gadlut Hashem* (*kulo kamei*...). The entire *avoda* is to bring this awareness into *hitgalut* – into our conscious awareness. The *d'veikut* ("cleaving of the soul") on this level in its purest form is not possible for the animal soul to attain, but nevertheless this level will *mezachech*, "purify" and "refine" the animal soul and make it more refined.

The Rav says there's an even higher level than "love like fire," that's not mentioned here, and that's *ahava beta'anugim*...Two *dargot* or characteristics to *mayim* – one is that it attracts us (*nimshach k'mayim* – "drawn like water") and the other is "enjoyment of water" (*ta'anugim b'mayim*). There's water that is the source of all pleasure, and water that imparts *ta'anug* (ultimate enjoyment). There's water as it descends to land, and there's water that's already giving rise to all kinds of fruits and delectibles, which is similar to *olam haba'ah*.

Shiur #39, January 10, 2012 – page 29 in the Hebrew text. Page 122 in the translation, the summary...the *ikar* in "love like water" is to find Hashem in everything. And that leads us to greater performance of Torah and mitzvoth. It weakens the animal soul but does not destroy it. "Love like fire" incinerates the animal soul, or uplifts it to holiness.

- R' Deitsch recalled a Russian author (couldn't remember his name) who gathered the sayings and statements of Chasidim who were *ba'alei mesorah* (who were good at maintaining and recalling tradition): One such tradition was the phrase uttered by some Chasidim of the Mitteler Rebbe, who used to say before reading the opinion of Abaye (an *amora* who appears frequently in the Gemora), for example, "The *Ratzon Ha'elyon* says..." – "The supernal will says..." meaning that at every *daf* or every *amud* of the Gemora, we should remember that it is the divine will within the Torah. This is what Hashem wants.

- R' Eliyahu Hadad asked, "How can I find the *Elokut* in everything? This is difficult..." and R' Deitsch answered, "In Avraham Avinu's search for God, he tried this, he tried that, he theorized maybe like this, "No it must be like that," until as Rambam says "God appeared to him." *Hitzitz alov Ba'al Habira* – "The 'Master' of the place appeared to him" (to Avraham Avinu). We have to say that the sages told us this for a reason...it must mean that it's up to everyone to look for Him until Hashem appears to him. If this search were only for Avraham Avinu, the sages would not have told us about it.

- There were several stories of people who were sent by the Rebbe to various places. One story in particular Rav Deitsch told; one whom the Rebbe told to go to a certain village and when he arrived at village, he did not know what to do. So, he asked if there was a Jewish person in the area? Someone directed him to a house and he knocked on the door. The people were very surprised when they opened for him. It turned out that the local priest had pressured them into converting out, and they had no connection with anything Jewish because their village was so isolated. One of the guys in the crowd said it was R' Gutnik in India…another in Australia, story with a *sofer* (HaSofer)… bottom line is that those who cry to Hashem that they need Him, He finds ways to send emissaries to help them.

Ch 5 (Page 123 in the translation) – *Ahavah* ("love") from the word *ava*, or "will." The *ratzon* ("will") is the master over the *midot* ("emotions"). The *ratzon* is also the *pnimiyut*, or inner core, of the *midot*. This works in both directions; a person can decide they want something or the opposite; that they don't want it. Even if one has benefit or enjoyment from something, if the one imparting the enjoyment to him is someone whom he doesn't like or hates, he will not accept that benefit or enjoyment. He's not interested, he won't want: This shows that *ratzon* is greater than the enjoyment itself. And the opposite; if he has *yisurim* ("torment") from something but he knows that it's good for him, he will accept it with pleasure.

- R' Deitsch's mother (*a"h*) had a heart attack, and the doctor interrogated her to find out why…she explained, it took place on erev Pesach and she was on the street walking, felt pains and sat down to rest. Afterward she went to her son, and there in the middle of the night she got the heart attack. The doctor told her, the pains that you felt were *min hashamayim*, sort of a "warning" for you. If you would have heeded the "warning," you could have avoided the heart attack. (Because she could have gone straight to emergency room and received care at the time. R' Eliyahu Hadad mentioned that there are people who do not or cannot feel those pains, and that is a big problem). Now, if she had known that the pains were a warning sign, would she have "enjoyed" them? She would have said "Thank you" for the warning! When you get benefit from the pain and *yisurim*, it's not *yisurim* at all.

Thus the *K' Avoda* brings example of *Ta'anit chalom* ("fast over a dream" – when someone is disturbed by a dream, they may choose to fast over it) even on Shabbat (during which we are not supposed to torment ourselves), because even tho in general one is not allowed to fast on Shabbat since normally fasting is the opposite of enjoyment, nevertheless for one who wants to fast in order to ameliorate a dream, the fast is pleasurable for him and it's permitted. From this we know that the *ratzon*, or "will" is the internal driving force behind the *midot*, or "emotions." The *K' Avoda* cites *Likutei Torah* of the Alter Rebbe, where it asks the standard question regarding *kriat shema* – "How can there be a commandment to "love"? How can we be commanded to have an emotion? And the answer is that a Jew loves anyway, he naturally loves God, but the commandment is to meditate and contemplate until his latent love becomes conscious and aware. Again, it is the *ratzon*, the "will" that is activated and then the emotion emerges.

- We have a palate, with which we taste and enjoy food and drink. But, in general, we may not be particularly conscious or aware of what we taste, because our interest may be in other matters; for example, making money. We do not attach much importance to the taste of our food. There are many men for whom food and sleep are not that important; what matters to them is money. Once on Rehov Yirmiyahu, R' Deitsch pointed out lights in a building on a higher floor and mentioned, "That is 'so and so,'" at 2 or 3 AM he is still awake, because his desire for money won't let him sleep. Now, if the doctor would explain to him the importance of sleep, he might start sleeping better. Again, this demonstrates the importance and the role of the will in determining how we feel and approach various matters.

- The Alter Rebbe says that a Jew is born with a talent for *taanug ruchni*, "spiritual enjoyment." The question is whether we develop a will for that *ratzon*, whether we want to actualize it or not, and that is where we have a choice.

- Australian fellow told story of Prof HaSofer in Australia, who went out to Tasmania for a job and he and his wife felt something was missing, and they began keeping mitzvoth as well as they could, but it was difficult. So he prayed to God to illuminate his path because otherwise he did not know how he could continue. It was then that R' Gutnick (R' Yosel Gutnick's father) was there in Tasmania and they ran into each other on the street, met, and that was how Prof HaSofer learned about Yiddishkeit. It was also at that time that he presented a paper demonstrating that there is no way that the necessary number of mutations could have occurred in a given time period to produce a species as we know them, thus casting a lot of doubt on the theory of evolution. To be continued…

Shiur 40, January 11, 2012

Still on page 29 in the Hebrew text, page 123-4 in the translation. This process, by which the *ratzon* ("will") guides and determines the *midot*, is called (in Kaballistic terminology), "*Tiferet d'imma na'aseh Keter l'za'a*" ("The *sephira* of *tiferet* within *bina* becomes the 'crown' of the emotions"). In other words, the "attribute of harmony and mercy (*tiferet*) within intellect (*bina*) becomes the supra-conscious guiding principle (*Keter*) of the emotions (*z'a*)." We must invest in this process, nothing is for free. To persuade the intellect to act as it should, guiding our emotions (and not the opposite), requires discipline and effort, it is not automatic. But when we do invest in it, there are un-ending *madreigot*, endless spiritual levels, one higher than the next. Until now, we explained that the *ratzon* is the *ba'al habayit* (the "boss"). But, (two lines from the bottom of page 29): "There is *ratzon*, and there is *ratzon*" – there are two kinds of will, one will that follows the intellect and the other that guides the intellect (it is called *makif* ("transcendent"), since it is beyond intellect. The entire remainder of the chapter (Ch 5) speaks of the two different levels of "will," or *ratzon*.

Within the *ratzon* that is beyond intellect, there are two levels: *ratzon atzmi* ("essential ratzon") and "*hitpashtut haratzon*" or "extension of the will." For example, that a person loves himself, is this the *etzem haratzon*, or *hitpashtut*? Is that his own essential will or is it only an extension of his will? The answer is that his love for himself is *ratzon atzmi*, "essential will." Every living creature desires its own *kiyum*, or "maintenance" (continuity). For example, R' Deitsch knew someone who was ill, and who wanted to do himself in, but he went to a psychologist who re-instilled in him the desire to live. He later met someone in the street who asked him, "Do you want to live?" When he answered, "Yes," the other person asked him, "Why?" He went on to explain to him, "I know why you want to live; it's more important to you." But in truth, is that a "reason" to live? If you need a "reason," that's a problem…and the truth is that even the person who wants to do himself in, does not want to do so because he no longer has a desire to live, but because he imagines to himself that his "life" will be better if he is no longer alive. At any rate, that a person loves himself, or loves his children and his children love him – is a *ratzon atzmi*, an essential will. This will is usually concealed and unconscious, but it emerges at specific times, such as when we must give ourselves up *b'Kiddush Hashem*, in order to establish and maintain the "honor of God." For example, if a Jew is presented with a choice to either "bow down to this idol or be killed," the Jew (in the majority of cases) will give up his life. If the person needs to meditate and contemplate in order to attain a certain level of will, then the will can change (and will change), because it is dependent on intellect, and as the Mishnah says and we'll learn, it's a will or *ratzon* that is "dependent" on something else. Now, the love that is essential, associated with the highest level of the soul, the *yechida* – [is hidden but] can be aroused and revealed from time to time – this is what Chapters 18-25 in Tanya is all about. But the love associated with *chaya* (the next lower level of the soul) of the *nefesh* is on one hand *makif* ("transcendent"), but on the other hand, it is subject to *hitorerut*, "arousal" at any time that we choose to work on it. And there are specific meditations associated with both levels of *makifim*.

Shiur 41: January 12, 2012

Page 30 in the Hebrew text, Page 126-7 in the translation:

There are two levels of *ratzon*, both of which serve as sources of love of God, and both of which are above intellect. There is the *yechida*, which is an essential *ratzon* without any reason. No meditation is necessary; spontaneously we our drawn to our soul-source and origin, since we are a *chelek Eloka min'aal* ("an integral part of Godliness") and everything is drawn to its source. This *koach* ("power") becomes revealed during *mesirat nefesh* ("self devotion," "self sacrifice") on *Kiddush Hashem* ("for the honor of God"). That we don't see it prior to *mesirat nefesh* is because the *ruach shtut* – the "spirit of folly" (associated with the body and the *yetzer harah*) – conceals it. This "spirit of folly" works in various ways: 1) It conceals 2) It convinces the person that he remains a Jew even if he does something he shouldn't do. Tanya mentions it, as does the discourse from the previous Rebbe, *Bati Legani*…but in itself the *yechida* of the soul is one with God, and therefore when it comes to a test that would disconnect us from Hashem, we're ready to die. (There are some who are not ready to die, but they are the minority, as Tanya says, *al harov* – "the majority" are willing to give up their lives).

- R' Deitsch once said something to R' Yoel Kahan, the famous *chozer* of the Rebbe, to which R' Yoel heartily agreed…two people bring two chairs to sit on. Sometimes each one brings a chair for him to sit on, sometimes each brings for the other. If he brings for himself, then he brings a "chair." If for the other person, then he is not bringing a chair, he brings *Elokut*. Same applies to the coffee that R' Eliyahu Hadad just brought the Rav as well…

- R' Deitsch mentioned the Crusades as example of *mesirat nefesh* [the Rav mentioned *shin-chet, shin-tet* or 1648-9, but those were the years of the Chelmnitzi uprising in Poland and Ukraine; the Crusades were long before that, in the 1000's in Europe]; the father *shechted* the sons after reciting a blessing. Also by the *Anusim* (Jews forced to convert during the inquisition, or who converted out but kept maintaining Jewish customs secretly), there was a lot of *mesirat nefesh*, at first the *ruach shtut* ("spirit of folly") could tell them that their *shmad* ("conversion out of Judaism") was only external but internally they remained Jews, but ultimately when they came to take them away, they gave up their lives on *mesirat nefesh*. And those who acted like non-Jews instead of allowing themselves to be killed with *mesirat nefesh*, when they wanted to return to Yiddishkeit had to do *teshuva* like a *Yisrael Mumar* (like one who had "converted out" and sought to return to Judaism), see *Teshuvat Rivash* on the subject. *B'poel* they worshipped *avoda zara* ("idol worship"), so they had the status of a *Yisrael Mumar*.

The *mesirat nefesh*, the revelation of the *yechida*, is always there, but comes to expression only in tests of *mesirat nefesh*, or if one knows how to utilize the potential as described in Tanya in the appropriate chapters (18-25). There, the point is not *hitbonenut*, but just reminders of who we are, in order to jolt us into acting as we should as a Jew. Nothing to do with meditation, just revelation of who we are and what is our connection with the One above. Since the hidden love (*ahava mesuteret*) is there anyway, present in our soul, the matters mentioned in Tanya simply reveal it, bring out the latent love, but not via meditation, rather by reminding us who we are, this brings out the *mesirat nefesh*.

The *K'Avoda* goes on to provide examples of how this works with more simple actions, not only *mesirat nefesh*. Page 127 in the middle, in the parentheses, "This is also expressed in our sincerity…" Our *temimut*, that we know what we have to do, and we do it…this is also *mesirat nefesh* and an expression of the *yechida*. One who maintains his position steadfastly during a test and does what he has to do, expresses *mesirat nefesh* as well as the *yechida* of the soul. And this is what is meant by *masbi'im oto* – we make him "take an oath" – *masbi'im* ("swear") from *sova* ("satiation") and also "oath" because that oath is coming from the *yechida* of the soul, which is what gives us the power later to fulfill mitzvoth under all circumstanes. Once R' Deitsch heard from R' Zalman Nehemiah Goldberg (*A"H*) that this is a positive mitzvah – in Gemora Nedarim there are some who say that it's a mitzvah to take an oath to fulfill the mitzvoth. One is *metzuva v'omed…*"ongoing commanded"…the Gemora discusses it. Why an oath? Prior to the oath, we were also commanded, so what's the difference? The answer is that the oath arouses *kochot* ("talents" and abilities) that are beyond intellect, from the *yechida* of the soul.

The second level of essential will is the *Chaya* of the soul. It is also essential (*Atzmi*) but not on the same level as the *yechida*. To reveal the *Chaya*, it is necessary to meditate on the *romemut* ("heights, majesty") of the infinite light of Hashem. This is the difference between the previous soul level [*ruach* and *neshama*, "love like water"] that also required *hitbonenut* on *Gadlut Hashem*. Here as well, meditation on *Gadlut Hashem* is necessary, but [rather than contemplate on the Godliness within creation and of our soul, here the contemplation is] on the level of *romemut ha'Einsof*, the "majesty of the infinite light." This is a meditation on the *hafla'ah* ("wondrous aspect") of the matter. Important to note that regarding the regular level of love, too much focus on the *hafla'ah* of the matter will prevent us from achieving love. (R' Deitsch saw elsewhere in a *maamar* that *malachim* – "angels" – possess fear of God but not love. So it is asked, how could this be? The Zohar replies that "Who am I, am I then a "friend" of God that I can love Him?" And therefore speaks only of fear of God by the *malachim*, and not love…). Now, *neshamot* ("souls") do possess and develop love of God…*neshamot* are called *achim* ("brothers") and *banim* ("sons") to Hashem which is not the case regarding angels…"love like water" is closeness to Him, "love like fire" also requires *hafla'ah*, but this love of the *chaya* is even moreso, based on *makif*…it is essential…this is a *ratzon* that requires arousal but when it is aroused it is essential and above intellect. And therefore it is without limit (page 129). [Apparently, meditation on the *hafla'ah* of creation is higher than the meditation of *kulo kamei*… while *kulo kamei* focuses upon how creation is "naught before God," *hafla'ah* focuses upon Godliness that is beyond creation. And therefore, *kulo kamei* is still associated with the soul level of *neshama*, while *hafla'ah* is associated with the higher soul level of *chaya*].

R' Deitsch read on to page 130, regarding love dependant on something as opposed to love that is not dependent. Love that dissipates after some time (because of distance or time or both, such as two fast friends who parted ways, as mentioned in *K'Avoda*, is subject to what the Rav mentioned his mother would sometimes say, "Far from the eyes, far from the heart") is associated with the *chaya*, but love that never dissipates, such as between father and son, is associated with the *yechida*.

Shiur 42, January 13, 2012

We have learned that the *midot* (emotions) are dependent upon the *ratzon* ("will"), and that even though we may harbor latent natural emotions, they may change because they are dependent upon our *ratzon*. If we remove our *ratzon* ("change our mind") by deciding that we do not value something, that will also transform our emotions as well. So it is regarding Godliness as well; all depends on *ratzon*. When we want to love God, we find a way to do so. We delved into various levels of *ratzon*, of will. Acc to the Zohar, *Eit ratzon v'eit ratzon*, "there is will and there is will." There is *ratzon* that varies in accordance with our intellect; this *ratzon* changes depending on the nature of our meditation on the *Gadlut Hashem* ("greatness of God"), but it always results in a desire to get closer to Hashem. And there is *ratzon* that is beyond our intellect, because a Jew possesses a natural desire to get closer to God, regardless of intellect. Regarding the *ratzon* that is beyond intellect, there are two levels; one is the *chaya* and the other the *yechida*. The *yechida* is natural and spontaneous, an essential connection with Hashem that cannot change. It becomes revealed in situations of *mesirat nefesh*, but also in actions that a Jew takes *b'temimut* – in "earnestness." As in *Derech Chaim* of the Mitteler Rebbe, we see that even a Jew on a relatively low spiritual level, will (usually) surrender his life if called upon to do an action or transgression that disconnects him from Hashem. One thing is for sure; the *neshama* has the nature of a candle, and *ner Havaya nishmat Adam*, "The candle of Hashem is the soul of man," and it always strives to ascend. Just as the flame of the candle ascends, so every Jew strives to return to his source. There is another essential love of the soul, but it's not the *yechida* – these names come from the Midrash that says, "The soul is called by five names, *nefesh, ruach, neshama, chaya* and *yechida*…" and the reference is to well defined levels of the soul, not merely to "names." The level of *chaya* is also essential, as is *yechida*. But unlike the *yechida*, to which we cannot connect via meditation, the *chaya* may be awakened and aroused via *hitbonenut*. And when awakened, it is unlimited. Then it's called "love that is not dependent upon anything."

It emerges then that there are three categories of love of God: Love that is "dependent upon something" – such love is the result of *hitbonenut* and without *hitbonenut*, it will not develop and will eventually dissipate [this is love of God on the soul level of *neshama*]. There is love that is "not dependent on anything," but without *hitbonenut*, it is not possible to access and arouse it [this is the *chaya*]. And then there is pure love that is "not dependent on anything" – and is not accessible or attainable by any *hitbonenut*. It is totally essential [the *yechida*]. Now there are physical examples associated with each of these categories of love. For the third category, love not dependent on anything (*yechida*), the example is the love between father and son. It's not possible for the father to "not be there" - he may be hidden but he is present and when the fatherly love is aroused, it's with all of its essential power.

- Story with a son who was kicked out or left yeshiva, claimed his father doesn't like him and the son was so angry that he "wanted to kill" the father. The psychologist wanted to convince the boy that it's not true, and he told the boy that the father loves him, etc, but the boy wasn't having any of it…So the psychologist told the son that his father was in the hospital, was close to end of his life, and then the son perked up and said, "Okay have to go see him." But the psychologist said, "No, I don't know if it's appropriate, it's near the end already," but the son insisted on going to see his father. Then the psychologist pointed out to the boy, "But a few minutes ago, you wanted to kill your father. Now you want to go visit him?" In other words, this is a demonstration of the essential love between father and son. The love was present all the time. [At this point in the *shiur*, R' Deitsch hesitated, pointing out that the parable of father and son was appropriate for the *chaya*, in which the love may be hidden, but not for the *yechida* in which the love is always there...at any rate this needs more clarification...].

Page 31 in the Hebrew text, page 131 in the translation,

"And so it is with the soul..." there it speaks of "love dependent on something," that is dependent on logic and intellect. Skip the parenthese, and move on to page 133. "Now, the love in the soul..." There is also love of the essence of the soul that is catalyzed by *hitbonenut*, but the *hibonenut* does not create the love, it's merely the catalyst, like lighting a match that ignites the fire (this is the *chaya* of the soul, as mentioned above).

- There was a *shadchan* ("matchmaker") who used to come and ask for more *d'mei shadchanut* ("payment" for putting the couple together) every time a new baby was born to a couple for whom he made the *shidduch*. But the couple said, "Sure you put us together, but now to make the baby, we're on our own."

- Another time Rav Deitsch met someone who was *mesader Kiddushin* (presided at a wedding), who said, "I am the one who made the *Kiddushin*, אני קדשתי אותה..." [everything in jest, he was a *mesader Kiddushin*, not the one who says "*Hari at mekudeshet li...*"] R' 'Deitsch was at the *hatuna* ("wedding") of the son of R' Adin Steinzaltz and R' Steinzaltz was *mesader Kiddushin*, and he described himself as the *shamash*, not as anyone doing anything special, just the facilitator to make the *Kiddushin* happen – and that's the truth, the *mesader Kiddushin* is just a "*shamash*"].

- R' Deitsch mentioned that many *Ba'alei Teshuva* ("returnees to Torah Judaism") come to Yiddishkeit via Shabbat, they see a Shabbat table and that's what initially attracts them. They see the pleasure and relaxation of Shabbat, and that's what brings them in, but *oy vey* if they think that's all there is to Yiddishkeit. R' Deitsch asked a B"T if all *Ba'alei Teshuva* think that Shabbat is all of Yiddishkeit, and one answered that at least some B"T's think so. If so, this is a good example of "love dependent on something."

Page 134 in the translation: Here we have a definition (*hagdara*) of the *yechida*: "Although not expressed, it never disappears..." [reminiscent of the Rashab's *hagdara*: *nimtza, bilti metziut nimtza,* or "Existing without being found, but existing nonetheless"] - (like love between father and son). R' Deitsch says, "I don't know, but here there are words..." But perhaps like in Tanya, as soon as we feel our distance from Hashem, we are ready to surrender our life on *mesirat nefesh*. Like for example, we may do some transgressions because we are not aware of how they distance us from Hashem. Nevertheless, our love does not disappear...we just aren't aware that we are distancing himself by doing *averot*. So, the essential closeness never disappears (as described in the *hagdara* above), but its expression (really being close) does disappear (we think that we remain close to Hashem even while doing *aveirot*, but it really isn't so). It emerges then, that the essential love never disappears, but we think we are close to God when we really are not. Only if we encounter a test that involves *mesirat nefesh* in which we can not hide from the fact that THIS *aveira* (whatever it is) distances us, and to that we cannot acquiesce and therefore we surrender our life.

- Similar to what was discussed on another occasion; the *yechida* is expressed by *temimut b'maaseh*; "earnestness in deed or action." Story of "Yankele" (one of the guys who comes regularly to learn in the Tzemach Tzedek but because his *shvigger* is not well, so not happening right now), that whenever he flies (which is a lot), he is careful to carry his *tallit* and *tefilin b'yad*, in his hands, not to pack it away, at any cost. Once he had to take a small plane from one city to another, and there wasn't room and they told him he has to check it. He didn't want, and he argued with them. They told him, "it's only one hour travel," so he had to give up his *tallit* and *tefillin*. In short, the plane was damaged and he got to his destination only a short time before sunset, without having put on *tefilin* that day. He did wild stuff to get ahold of the local *shaliach* to bring him *tefillin*...R' Deitsch asked him afterward, "Did you know that you have such a strong connection to *tefillin* that you would go to such lengths to put them on?" We put on *tefillin* every day, do we think about it that much? Yet, here R' Yankele was ready to turn over worlds to don *tefillin* before sundown. This is the *yechida sh'benefesh*: It's not revealed and conscious, but it is always present and functional. The fact that it comes to awareness when there is something that prevents him from doing a mitzvah, is proof that the awareness (love) was there all the time. Like the will to live. One is not aware of that will until he is faced with a life threatening illness or injury. In this way we can explain the *yechida* that is "Not expressed but never disappears."

- This is the *pirush* of "*Lech Lecha*" – for what is the *lecha* in this case? Zohar and Chasidut say, "to your *etzem*, to your essence." This was the beginning of Avraham Avinu's revelation to the world: "Start with yourself, start by going to your essence." Go to yourself, "join up" with yourself.

In summary, Three levels: 1) love dependent on something; proportionate to our *hitbonenut*, based upon logic and intellect [*neshama*]. 2) Love above intellect and not dependent, but in need of an intellectual catalyst to ignite it, and when that catalyst is present, it triggers essential and unlimited love [*chaya*], 3) Love not dependent whatsoever on any *hitbonenut* [*yechida*]. As far as which level is "best," of course the higher level is most sought after, but in terms of what effect does the love have on our physical nature and animal soul? There's room to suggest that the lowest level, love based on logic and intellect, has the most effect on us.

- Edited *maamar* from the Rebbe in which he mentions the tremendous *mesirat nefesh* of the Jews in Russia for Yiddishkeit, but when some of them arrived to the US, where matters are much easier, their *mesirat nefesh* was no longer evident. In the US, *avoda* according to logic and intellect also applies [has more effect on the animal soul].

- *Maaseh* with R' Mendel Horodok, R' Mendel of Vitebsk, buried in Tiveria...On the verse)Gen. 2:18), "*Ezer k'negdo* (regarding the creation of woman, that she is intended to be a "helpful assistant")... The sages comment (about the woman): Either she's *ezer* (either she is a "your helpmate"), or *k'negdo* ("she opposes you"), depending on your deeds. But what right do the sages have to break up the verse and analyze it? The straightforward understanding is that "your wife is also your helpmate." R' Mendel answers that there are two kind of help (and therefore it is permissible to break up the verse and interpret it...). One is direct, as when your wife offers support and encouragement. The other is when she helps by opposing you; she goes "around and against you" by questioning your deeds and intentions, and that is meant to increase your commitment to Torah and mitzvoth even more than before. So two kinds of assistance: If you are meritorious, you receive direct assistance; if not, then the other reaction of "indirect assistance."

- R' Deitsch gave his own *pirush* on the blessing from the *shemonah-esreh*, *Hoshiva shofteinu*...("Return our judges...You alone Lord reign over us"): There are two kinds of judges and we request that God return our judges who once served us properly, without *shochad* ("bribery") or *ivut hadin* ("misunderstanding or misinterpreting the law")…But what is the word *levadcha* ("alone") doing here in this blessing? R' Deitsch suggests that we want to avoid serving Him out of negative incentives, and seek to serve Him for positive reasons. If for negative incentives, then our service is not because of God alone; but because we want to escape negative consequences. Therefore we request that He alone should judge us, *levadcha*… the Chozeh of Lublin thanked Hashem every day for allowing him to serve God *bechesed* (easily without physical struggle or suffering). Here as well, the reason for serving God in *chesed* is so we will serve Him "alone," not as the result of negative incentives to escape *yisurim*. And also to avoid risking the possibility that we might *me'vaet b'yisurim* ("kick" and rebel against the suffering).

Shiur 43, June 4, 2012 (Review of Ch. 4)

There were a number of subjects (*Purim, Pesach, Sefirat ha'omer, Shavuot*) in the preceding four months, so now the *shiur* will return to *K'Avoda*, and specifically to a review of Ch 4. Ch 3 discussed *yirat Hashem*, Ch. 4 discusses *ahava*.

Page 22 – two general categories of love. Like water, and like fire is found on page 25 (beginning with *Amnom*…). "Love like water" is the lower level, Tanya describes the advantage of "love like fire" over "love like water" as, "like the advantage of gold over silver." "Love like water" is *chesed* within *chesed*, "love like fire" is *gevurah* within *chesed*. The *hagdara*, the "defining characteristic" of "love like water" is *kiruv u'devekut*, or "proximity and cleaving" to Godliness. The *hagdarah* of "love like fire" is *tzima'on*, or "thirst, yearning" for God.

In general, we need to know that Chasidut follows the approach of the Rambam, that the path to love and fear of God flows through meditation on *Gadlut Hashem* – the "greatness of God." Although Tanya discusses some levels of love (like a son to a father, or like "gazing into the water…") that are not associated with *Gadlut Hashem* and are indeed a completely different category, nevertheless most of the matters that Chasidut discusses regarding love of God are associated with *Gadlut Hashem*. In any case, meditation on the greatness of God can lead to either love or fear of God. The particular meditation that leads to love is meditation on the Godly illumination that is enclothed in the worlds, as written, "You enliven them all." That is, within each and every creation there is a specific energy that vitalizes it. Our goal should be to feel that the world "lives" from the vitality of Godliness that is invested in it.

Someone asked, "What does it mean that the world 'lives' from Godliness?" Answer: One thing that becomes clear from the writings of the *Tzemach Tzedek*, is that we are not speaking of the energy that creates, but the energy that 'maintains' creation. *Sha'ar Hayichud v'haemunah* (second section of Tanya) speaks of the energy that creates, but the simple *pirush* is the energy that "maintains" and enlivens the creation.

R' Eliyahu Hadad asked if it is possible that the energy to create is *sovev* while that of "enlivening" is *memale*, and the Rav agreed, saying, "It's possible that it is even written that way." The *Ikar hithavut* ("main component of the creation process") of the universe is from *sovev*, while the details, the *tzura* ("form") are from *memalle*. Here in any case is written *chayut* ("energy, vitality") so it is clear that the text is speaking of the energy that enlivens (not that creates). When we delve into the *mashal* ("example, illustration") dictated by *m'basri echzeh Elokah* ("from my own flesh I grasp Godliness"), we see that the vitality of the world is divided into the categories of mineral, vegetable, animal and human, and the Tzemach Tzedek says that, "The *chayut* is *Elokut*." (This *lashon* is in *Derech Mitzvotecha*, mitzvath *He'emanut Elokut*, page *mem-hey*, middle of *amud aleph*). That is, what Torah calls *chayut*, the world today calls "energy." The "energy" is *Elokut*. That there is a created object at all, is because it is "created," the *mamashut* (*chomer*, or "substance") of it comes from *sovev*. The creation comes "<u>from</u> Godly *koach* (power)." But about the *chayut* that continually enlivens, it is written, "This (it) is *Elokut*."

- When the Rambam (*Hilchot Avoda Zarah* 1:8) tells of the spiritual journey of Avraham Avinu it also becomes apparent that Avraham Avinu meditated upon the *chayut* that enlivens the world. He writes that Avraham began by considering all the orbits of the planets and stars and concluded that there must be a force that causes them to orbit. Rambam uses the terminology of *mitgalgal* (which is reflexive, implying that there is a force operating on it, either the orbit itself or something external) for "orbit," but if we meditate on what that means, it means the *chayut* of the orbit, the energy that enlivens the object. That the sun shines, is because that's how it was created. But that everything moves in an orbit, implies there must be an entity that moves it. The same principle applies to every creation; there is a force behind it enlivening it, but it is most clear by the sun and moon and various heavenly bodies since they change from day to day, and therefore acc to Rambam, Avraham Avinu concluded there must be something there that "operates" on it, a force that causes it to orbit.

- Rav Deitsch theorizes that it's not *chayut* alone that makes it a subject of meditation. There are created objects and there is energy. What's interesting as a subject of meditation is the *chibur* or "connection" between the orbit and the energy. It's the *tium*, the "partnership" and "coordination" between the created object and its associated energy, that cannot be independent, that requires a force to put them together. For every *tium* (between energy and creation) there is a *metaem* (a "coordinating factor"). For every "partnership" between energy and creation, there is a "supervisor" that governs and 'supervises' that connection and "partnership." When you see for example an object that fits into an opening, and there is *tium* between the object and the opening, they are *matim* (they "fit together"). Take for example the limbs of the body (moving his upper arm), there is the arm, there is the shoulder, and they work together, implying that there must be a force that puts them together. Who puts them together? There must be a force putting them together, and in this way, R' Deitsch possibly understands the *chiddush* of *mitgalgal* that appears in Rambam regarding Avraham Avinu. The best argument for this comes from the body itself. If you extend your arm and see five fingers, you have to conclude there is someone who made the arm and the fingers. But if there is someone without a hand, just an arm that extends without dividing into a hand and fingers, who said he is not "normal"? Perhaps he is "normal" and the guy with a hand is not normal? But we're forced to conclude that a man needs hands and fingers in order to grasp an object and hold it, so obviously, that's the "normal" situation. But who "spoke" to the hand and "explained" to it that there has to be a hand and fingers? Obviously, there is an Organizer and Planner behind the whole thing. Moreover, there is a component in the hand between the joints and the muscles that ensures there won't be friction – all of this "screams" out that there is a Creator and Planner. For Avraham Avinu the vehicle for him to come to this recognition was the planets and orbits, for us it's the body.

Shiur 44, June 5, 2012 (review of Ch 4)

Via meditation, we can experience the *chayut* that enlivens the creation… *mibsari echzeh Elokut.* We can feel and see how the world is alive with this energy, but it demands *hitkashrut* ("focus, concentration") and *ha'amakat daato* ("delving in depth"). That is, it demands focus and concentration, not to merely glance over the topic and then move on to something else. But, how does this lead to *ahavat Hashem*, to love of God? Rambam writes that it is meditation on *Gadlut Hashem* that leads to love of God. And then the question becomes according to Rambam, how does *hitbonenut* on *Gadlut Hashem* lead to *ahava*? How does the meditation affect our emotions? Rambam tells us that the meditation leads to a *ta'ava leidah* – "a thirst to know" – and that thirst to know Hashem is *ahava*, love of God. (see Rambam *Hilchot Yesodei haTorah*, Ch 3). The desire to "know Him" is the definition of love. In man, the definition of *ahava* is the desire to be close. (Someone asked if the desire that "it should be good" for someone is also "love." R' Deitsch answered that it is a special category of *ahava*, that the Tanya says is associated with *bnei aliya*, higher souls, not concerned with themselves but with Him and with others. It is rare, and the regular love is the desire to "be close").

But, what is being close to Hashem? Love of God is possible even before mitzvoth, and if it weren't for God's love for us, He would not have given us mitzvoth. Rambam defines this love as, "To know the great Name of God." That's Rambam. In *K'Avoda,* the Rashab writes that *hitbonenut* leads to "feeling the preciousness and importance of Godliness." In parentheses on page 87 in the translation: "That is, that Godliness in itself is very desirable and uplifting" – which seems to negate the concept that the creation itself [as opposed to the Godliness embedded in creation] generates love and desire to get closer to it. Just like people love money not because it is an end to itself, but because it is the means to many other things. So here, love of Godliness is an end to itself, not because the creation is so "beautiful" or "harmonious," etc…the logic is that "if Godliness enlivens everything, then Godliness (that is, the Godly energy that vitalizes creation) is itself dear and precious." Like one in a work situation gets to know the boss, wants to be close to him since he's really the one who is paying his salary, etc…here as well once we know that He is the true Boss who vitalizes everything, we want to be close to Him. And therefore we come to desire only *Elokut* and nothing else. Everything else loses value in our eyes.

At this point on Page 87, the *K' Avoda* switches to love like *nafshi aviticha* which is a yet higher form of love where we find this closeness because we conclude that the force out there enlivening the world is also the force that enlivens us. When the love "increases and grows," and we know that it applies to us, it expands our emotions. (There ensued a conversation reg the *Eitz hada'at tov v'rah* ("tree of knowledge of good or bad")…the question arises, why *da'at*? There was no *da'at* before they ate from the tree? Hashem wanted his human creations to be dumb, un-intelligent? Rather, before they ate, man used his *da'at* to distinguish between truth and lies, but after he ate, he used his *da'at* to distinguish between "what is good for me and what is not." That is a whole different "ball game," equivalent to egoism.

According to Chasidut, there are two kinds of love: *Kirvat Elokim zeh tov* ("Proximity to God is good") and *Kirvat Elokim li tov* ("Proximity to God is good for me"). The Rebbe Rashab writes (R' Deitsch doesn't recall where) that the *tikun* of *eitz hada'at* is to use *hargashat atzmi* (experience of "myself") for *kedusha*. That's *lilah* ("night") as in *nafshi aviticaha balilah*, "I want you at night," and the *tikunim* ("rectifications") take place at night. Also in *Aishet Chayil, vatakam balilah vatiten teref l'beita...*("She arises at night and provides food for her house...") - also at night. Learning Torah is *siyuah* ("support") and assistance to this process. But *hitbonenut* takes place only at daytime during prayers. The *yetzer harah* doesn't want to allow man to meditate because it knows that once he begins meditation (*hitbonenut*), the *yetzer* has nothing to do. As R' Zalman Moshe (who knew *samech-vov* by heart) said, "The *yetzer* allows me to learn Chasidut for four hours but won't let me meditate for five minutes."

Shiur 45, June 6, 2012, Page 23 in the Hebrew text, Page 87 in the translation (continued review of Ch 4)

The purpose of "love like water" is to achieve *kiruv* and *dveikut* ("proximity and cleaving") to Godliness, like water, which clings and cleaves. How do we achieve this state? We start with *hitbonenut* on the *ohr* and *chayut Eloki* (the "illumination and Godly energy") that enlivens the worlds. By thinking of the individual level of *ohr* and *chayut* that enlivens each and every creature, we gain recognition of the value and preciousness and the elevation of *Elokut*. You see how nice this thing looks? That's from Godly illumination. You see how tasty this food is? That's from *ohr Eloki*. It's like a credit card with which you can buy everywhere, and therefore you place value on the company of the card. Similarly, since it is Godly energy and illumination that enlivens everything, it takes on value and elevation in our eyes, and you want to cling to it. Money and a credit card only have value because all of us agree to give them value, but Godly energy is essential – every creation requires it and without it nothing is alive. The recognition of the preciousness and elevation of Godliness leads to desire to cleave to Him. Then, *K'Avoda* adds, when I apply the factor of "myself," meaning that the precious and elevated Godliness is not only the *chayut* of the universe, but it's also my own personal *chayut* and energy, from this develops an added love; it's not only "out there," but it's also "in me," it's "mine."

In the parentheses, Page 88 in the translation, "The advantage of this level of love..."

Here, R' Eliyahu Hadad noted yesterday's *shiur* in which we learned that the sin of the tree of knowledge led to general awareness about "what is good or not good 'for me" (as opposed to prior to the sin, when the general awareness was about "whether this is true or not true") – to this, the Rav added that the point of this parentheses is that whatever is more internal and leads to more "Godliness is good for me," is a *tikun* for the sin of *Eitz hada'at*. Although in truth there are those who say that even from this, a *nefila* (a spiritual "fall") can occur, [perhaps the Rav is referring to what the Rashab called the *klipah* of *Re'u Mah*, "See me, I'm getting close to Hashem"]. The parentheses then tells us that even though the *hitbonenut* of *nafshi aviticha* (that the *chayut* is also what enlivens "me") is more internal, on the other hand, there is an advantage to the original *hitbonenut* based on, "He is the *chayut* of the universe," because it leads us to emphasize the inner dimension of all that exists in the world, outside of ourselves. This is, in essence the Torah of the Baal Shem Tov – *U'vacharta ba* – "choose the life (the *Elokut*) and the good within in every creature." For example, within this cup of coffee (that the Rav was drinking), choose the Godliness and not the pure physicality.

On the other hand, the result of this ability to see Godliness in everything, will not lead to learning Torah. The appreciation of Godliness in the entire universe precedes Torah. But the minute we recognize that the same vitality and energy is what enlivens us as well, then we turn to the Torah as the source of that vitality. The Torah is the *chayei ha-*, the "source of life," and automatically we come to desire Torah as well.

Here, R' Eliyahu Hadad asked, "Why do I need the cup of coffee in order to tell me that there is Godliness in everything? Do away with the coffee and give me the *Elokut*." To this, the Rav answered (paraphrase), there is special nature of Godliness in each object. For what do I need this coffee? It arouses and stimulates me when I drink it. So instead of drinking it for the coffee itself, drink it for the God given power that it has to stimulate and arouse me. In other words, instead of the "negative" (do away with the coffee), choose the positive ("I want the power of stimulation within the coffee"), which is a "thing" in my own estimation, it is not "nothing." So, we drink it because of the Godly power within it.

- There were *tzadikim* who were always in touch with *Elokut* at every instant. This is not the regular person, we are not on that level. But, the Rav was by Baba Sali, observing his conduct and saw that he would sit at a *seuda* for hours, leaning against a post, and it would appear as if he were sleeping. But then you would see him moving his hands in a purposeful manner and you realized that he was awake. Other times he would be sitting and learning for hours. Hours! What was he doing?! I don't know…But there is such a thing as *devekut*…

Page 91 in the translation: "And since the ultimate purpose of love of God is to serve Him with love..."

Hashem gave us the mitzvah of divine love in a manner that is different than other mitzvoth. Tanya (based on Zohar) describes love as *gadfin* ("wings") to uplift the other mitzvoth. The Alter Rebbe says based on this that the *ikar* is the mitzvoth, not the *ahava*. Just like the bird can live without its wings, so you can fulfill a mitzvah without love and fear. On the other hand, without the body, the wings are nothing. The Alter Rebbe then asks, "But love and fear are also mitzvoth, so why are they different? Why are they only "wings"?" He answers that God gave these mitzvoth for the purpose that there should be an *avoda* of *ahava* – not merely *ahava* as an entity of its own, but that it should be the subject and vehicle of our *avoda*. One who focusses on *ahava* for its own sake is on the level of *tzadikim* who already "taste the world to come" in this world. For the rest of us, who are still on a path of *avoda* (effort and labor to reach this level), so *Hayom la'asoto* – "Now is the time for action" – for fulfilling mitzvoth that we do while imbued with love. We say this every day, second paragraph of *Kriat Shema*: "And if you will fulfill the mitzvoth that I command you this day, to love Hashem and to serve Him..." wherein "service" means fulfilling the mitzvoth with love. And the love of *nafshi aviticha* (wherein we meditate how the energy enlivening the universe is also the energy that enlivens us), leads us to more learning Torah and *kiyum hamitzvoth*. And therefore, says *K'Avoda*, even though *hitbonenut* on the energy in the world in general may lead to higher levels, nevertheless with meditation of *nafshi aviticha* comes more *kiyum hamitzvoth* and *limud haTorah*.

In response to a question, the Rav responded that, "The world is used to viewing love of God as the ultimate goal, and the world also calls divine love, *d'vekut* ("clinging to God"), but that's not what Tanya says." The argument whether the mitzvah itself is the *ikar* or love of God is the *ikar* is an argument without end, but the difference is like between one who eats with an appetite as opposed to one who eats without any enjoyment or appetite. One who has an appetite is a "live man." One without an appetite is semi-alive.

- Even those who put the emphasis on "appetite" (love of God) say that the important thing is the fulfillment of the mitzvah. Do you know how much Chasidim would invest in achieving love of God? Story: There was once a Chasid who so practiced *hitbonenut* and *avoda* that he became very weakened. In fact, he fainted. That very day he failed to don *tefilin* (out of weakness or lack of consciousness), and he declared that all the years that he was involved in *avoda* were not worth it because of that one day that he failed to put on tefilin. A Rebbe or another Chasid responded to him, "That's true, but in order to achieve such a grasp and understanding (of the importance of the mitzvah), you needed all the *avoda* of the previous thirty years."

- Known story in and out of Chabad regarding R' Michele Zlotchover, who had his father's *tefilin* (his father was R' Yitzhak of Drovitz, Chasid of the Besht, about whom the Besht said that he had a very small *neshama* that he elevated to the level of the soul of Rashbi). There were many who wanted to buy his *tefilin* after his father passed away, but R' Michele refused. Finally, one year before Succot, there was no food in the house and they were very poor, (R' Shlomke' Zviller was also a grandson of R' Michele and told stories about the R' Michele's poverty, and his *bitachon* in a difficult situation). There were no local *etrogim* for Succot and someone brought a very nice one for sale at a large price. R' Michele sold his father's *tefilin* and bought the *etrog*. He and his five sons (each was a very special and high neshama about whom they said they were "the five Chumashim") made a dance of *simcha* before Succot because they now had an *etrog*. But there was no food in the house, and when his wife saw them dancing and asked, "Why are you so happy, there's no food in the house," they told her about the new *etrog*. She was so upset that she bit the *pitom* off the *etrog* and invalidated it. R' Michele responded, "I have no *tefilin*, I have no *etrog*, I should have anger?" So he did not get angry. Was said that Above, they had more pleasure from his lack of anger, than they would have had from his *tefilin* and his *etrog*. Chabad tacks on an additional line here, "But R' Michele had no etrog." All the heavenly pleasure and lack of anger were fine…but still, he didn't have an *etrog*, so he could not fulfill the mitzvah.

- Story from the Gemora about the *yenuka* ("young child") whose mother told him to go ask for a blessing from the students of the Rashbi. He returned to his mother without a blessing, because he claimed about the students that, "I smell from your garments that you did not fulfill the mitzvah of *kriat shema* today." They replied, "Yes, we were busy with the mitzvah of redeeming the captured (*pidyon shvuyim*), and one who is busy with one mitzvah is not obligated in another." So, according to the letter of the law, the *halacha*, they were not required to fulfill the mitzvah of *kriat shema*, yet nonetheless, there was something missing (no "smell" of *kriat shema*). A simple man has an *etrog* and does the mitzvah, and R' Michele does not have an *etrog*, cannot do the mitzvah (but the simple man remains simple and R' Michele remains R' Michele). And "*oy voy voy*" to anyone who says that because the simple man had an *etrog*, so he's more important than R' Michele…

- There was once someone in *Shikun Chabad* (the Chabad neighborhood in Jerusalem) who was very *makpid* and precise in his fulfillment of mitzvoth. He once did not want to have the Amshinover Rebbe as *sandek* for his son because the Amshinover did things on his own time in all that he did, whether davening, eating matzah, etc…and therefore he was apparently not precise and exact in his fulfillment of mitzvoth. R' Deitsch told him, "there is a *gan eden* for this one and a *gan eden* for that one. So which *gan eden* do you want, the *gan eden* of one who is precise and exact in fulfillment of mitzvoth, or the *gan eden* of the Amshinover? Everyone said they prefer the *gan eden* of the Amshinover." Bottom line, there's room to say like this or like that, but best to try for both – precision in *halacha* together with love of Hashem.

Shiur 46, June 7, 2012 (continued review of Ch 4)

One of the benefits of the love called *nafshi aviticha* is that it leads to more *kiyum mitzvoth* ("fulfillment of mitzvoth") as well as *limud haTorah* ("learning Torah"), which is the *tafkid* ("purpose") for which we are found here. Since we seek the *chayut* (energy) that enlivens us, automatically that leads us to increased performance of Torah and mitzvoth. The purpose of love is *avoda* leading to love – to merely enjoy Godliness similar to *olam haba'ah* ("the world to come") is in the realm of *tzadikim*, they are the ones who sit and enjoy the ray of the *Shechina*, but the rest of us need to use love of God as motivation to do mitzvoth and learn Torah.

Page 23 in the Hebrew text, page 91 in the English translation,

"And since the ultimate purpose of love of God is to serve Him with love…" – and the love described by, "As in water, face answers to face," discussed in Ch 46 in Tanya is a development that leads to more love of Torah and mitzvoth. *Musar seforim* (books on the topic of Torah "ethics") also discuss this level of love, but in a more simplistic manner: "He supplies me with what I need, so I express gratitude to Him." And there is no gratitude without love ("gratitude comes from either love or respect"). But Rav Deitsch is not at all sure that this level of love as expressed in *mussar seforim* will lead to *kiyum hamitzvoth* ("fulfillment of mitzvoth") and *limmud haTorah* ("learning of Torah"). Those who receive but express no gratitude, are either lacking love or they think that they deserve everything [and therefore, love in return for "receiving" is not likely to lead to increased level of Torah and mitzvoth observance].

R' Eliyahu Hadad mentioned that such love (based either on *hitbonenut* on creation or upon *nafshi aviticha*...) did not occur at Matan Torah [when God "held the mountain over the Jews," implying that their love for God was compelled or coereced from Above], but only later during Purim [when the Jews willingly accepted the Torah], when because of their love of the miracle (*ahavat haness*), the Jews developed love of God. R' Deitsch responded that this is true according to *pshat*, but that according to *sod*, in *Torah Ohr* it is written that *kafah aleihem har k'Gigit* – "He held the mountain over them like a board" – is a reflection of the great love of God for the Jewish people, which in turn generated love of God by the Jews. So, according to *sod*, there was love of God at Matan Torah, the Jews did love God. In this case, the love was "compelled": It's one thing when we Jews meditate in *hitbonenut* and generate love of God, but when He reveals Himself from Above in a public manner, then love of God is "compelled" from Above. R' Eliyahu mentioned that this is a contradiction between the *pshat* and the *sod*, and R' Deitsch agreed, saying that it needs explanation. The Tzemach Tzedek said that *sod* to *pshat* is like *neshama* to *guf*...they need to "match" and have to "work together." So, it needs explanation.

Then, we come to the love of the "son who loves his parents and has mercy on them and is ready to die for them." He has more mercy for God than he has for himself. This is the love of the *Raya Mehemna* (Moshe Rabeinu in the Zohar) and it is the love between son and father. How is such love associated with Torah and mitzvoth? How does the son take the parents "out of the prison" (part of the *mashal* regarding love like a "son loves his parents")? Tanya states openly that it takes place by way of Torah and mitzvoth, as in the phrase)Berachot 18A), "Whoever prays with the *tzibur*...is as if they redeemed Me from among the nations of the world."...or as Rav David Shalom Segal said, "Hashem brings man into the world as a 'son,' but it's up to us to direct and arouse that aspect of ourselves [and that we do via Torah and mitzvoth]." All of us are born with this inclination but it can get lost with time...

- Here the Rav told the story of the son who decided that his father doesn't love him. Until they convinced him that his father is on his deathbed...and all of a sudden he realized he wants to see his father... the moral of the story is that deep within we have a great love but different things can happen to cover it over and conceal the love.

- Story from the *shoah*, one survivor said to his friend, "I want no more Torah, no more mitzvoth..." Then his friend found him in another *shtetl* where he was praying *mincha*, asked him, *Mai hai* ("what's going on")? His friend explained, "Listen what happened to us was a *rachmanus*, a terrible thing. But if nobody talks with Him, it's also a *rachmanus* on Him, on Hashem. So I came to daven *mincha* and have *rachmanus* on Him." So, we can also *k'bayachol* ("so to speak") have mercy on Hashem, and that was the conduct of *tzaddikim*, when they were suffering, they said that Hashem is with them, and He was suffering as well. And inside each and every one of us Jews we have love for God like a son. When it's revealed, it is called the love of the *Raya Mehemna*, as also stated in Zohar.

If so, that there is a benefit and advantage to the two kind of love, *nafshi aviticha* and *k'ben d'ishtadel*, and their benefit is that they result in *kiyum mitzvoth* and *limud haTorah*, then what is the benefit of the initial kind of love based on meditation on *Gadlut Hashem* in the entire universe? *K'Avoda* answers (P. 92) that this initial meditation is easier and closer to us to achieve, and moreover it has a greater effect on the animal soul, weakening it. [To a certain extent, this is against our intuition because it would seem that meditation on the *chayut* within us, that Godliness is our *chayut*, would be closer to us and therefore also have more of an effect on the animal soul. But the Rebbe Rashab says that practically speaking, the *hitbonenut* on Godly energy in the world is easier and closer]. Interesting then, the *hitbonenut* on *nafshi aviticha* perhaps leads to more Torah and mitzvoth but does not have as strong an effect on the animal soul as the initial meditation on the *Gadlut Hashem* in the world. When one meditates on the *chayut* that enlivens the world, and that the *ikar* is the *chayut*, this leads to weakness of the various lusts of the animal soul.

Here the *K'Avoda* (regarding the initial "entry level" love of God, "love like water") is not speaking of love born of meditation on *Gadlut Hashem* [in the sense of *kulo kamei k'lo chashiv*], but rather of the awareness that there is Godliness in everything and that Hashem enlivens everything, every creation. R' Deitsch once asked himself on what are we meditating here that brings to recognition of the *yoker* and *ilui* ("preciousness and elevation") of *Gadlut Hashem*? There are many possibilities in this meditation, *mah gadlo Hashem, mah rabu ma'asecha*...what *davka* here is associated with developing love? Rav Deitsch once concluded that *Gadlut Hashem* is close to us only in the sense that the same *hitbonenut* on *romemut* ('greatness, elevation' of God) can lead to either *ahava* or *yirah* (see Rambam), even though *romemut* is transcendant above us. But meditation on the *chayut* in creation implies that He is with us, He is together with us, He is "one with us."

- One of R' Deitsch's grandson's was told by his mother, "We have to be afraid of Hashem." He said in *t'mimut*, "Afraid of Hashem? I have to be afraid of Arabs, Hashem is my friend."

Thus the feeling of closeness to Hashem brings love, but the minute we consider *romemut*, elevation, it leads to fear of Him. So, when we think of the *chayut* in everything and that the *chayut* is present out of His *chesed*, this leads to something we can feel and sense closeness. (All this in more detail in *maamar*, *Matzah Zo*). *Hitbonenut* on *romemut* leads to fear; *hitbonenut* on His proximity in every creation leads to love.

- Once somebody asked, "Why do I have to be afraid of *ta'avot* ("lusts")? Hashem is in everything, His *chayut* enlivens everything, including the object of my desires. Someone clever (perhaps a Rebbe) answered, "It says הוא אמר ויהי – "He said and it came into existence," הוא צוה ויעמוד – "He commanded to stop (lit: "and it stood"). That is, "He created the lust, and He commanded not to touch it."

- The Rav referred to someone at the *shiur* whose grandfather and great grandfather came to the US when it was doubtful whether the meat was kosher or not, and there was no *chalav Yisrael*, so for years he was neither *basari* nor *halavi*.

In the end, though, the Rashab concludes on page 93 that also this initial love based on meditation on the *kiruv* and preciousness of Godliness, also leads to Torah and mitzvoth, which are "His emissaries."

Shiur 47, June 8, 2012 (Review of Ch. 4, continued)

During *Avodat Hatefila*, the "service of prayer," the main objective is to achieve *ahavat Hashem*. We're now in the middle of Ch 4 of *K'Avoda* that speaks of love of Hashem and in general we know that there are two levels: "love like water" and "love like fire." The main meditation leading to "love like water" is that for every creation and every world, there is Godly illumination that enlivens it. Additionally, the *ahava* ("love") is strengthened when we consider that the same Godly illumination also enlivens us, each and every one of us. There is additional love that results from this and leads to learning Torah and keeping mitzvoth. This brings us to the *kiruv* ("closeness") and *dveikut* ("cleaving") to *Elokut* that is characteristic of "love like water". As we'll learn later, "love like fire" is with thirst and desire for *Elokut*.

- Someone asked a child, "What is the most important thing in your house"? He answered, *kesef* (money). It turned out that was always the reason why they couldn't buy anything; there was "no money," and "money" was mentioned so frequently in his house that he understood that money is "important." Another child was asked, "What is most important on Shabbes?" and he answered "cholent." The class laughed thinking that he was kidding but the teacher saw he was serious and asked him. He said in his house they are always speaking words of Torah but when the cholent arrives, the *divrei Torah* ("words of Torah") stop and "Abba is into the cholent."

- These stories and other advice emerges from a book of investigations on the subject put out by Yeshivat *Sha'arei Yoshar*, that deals with young *bachurim* who "fell thru the cracks" (who did not fit well into the educational system). Among the things the research found is that it's important for the father to tell his kids, "I love you." Not enough to demonstrate love, the parent must say so.

By ongoing and constant meditation, the meditator arrives to the same level of love for the creation as the family mentioned above regarding money. From this we can conclude that it is not only the *chayut* of creation that is lovable, but also its source is worthy of love. It's as if someone asked for money and the responder said to him, "Here, I'll give you not only money but I'll reveal to you the source of money." Similarly here, the love of God that we develop leads to Torah learning and fulfillment of mitzvoth, and they are the source of the *chayut* of all creation. It is as if the One above grants us not only love but also the source of love from Above. (See translation, Page 93, the mitzvoth are His "emissaries").

The difference between the *chayut* in His mitzvoth and the *chayut* in creation is the difference between concealment and revelation. Godliness is revealed in His mitzvoth (that we don't see it is because our personal situation does not permit it, but the *chayut* of His mitzvoth is present in a revealed manner). However, divine *chayut* is not revealed in His creation; even though it is present, we must labor and work in order to reveal it. In general, the Godly *chayut* is not revealed. Reg Torah and mitzvoth, the concealment is only because of our own limitations; if we "had eyes to see," it would be evident. But regarding the creation, the concealment is not only a result of our limitations, it is also a result of the nature of creation. The creation itself is a product of concealment. One of the distinctions between these two different kinds of divine concealment is that if a *tzaddik* sees us after we do a mitzvah, we look like a different person to him:

- Story of R' Meir Schechter, whose father who was an important man, and he was close with R' Shlomke Zvelier. R' Shlomke often learned with him and one day he looked at him and asked, "What did you do today"? He replied, "That's between me and God, I don't have have to tell anyone." "If so," R' Shlomke told him, "We don't have to learn together today." So R' Schecter's father saw he had no choice and told him: He was on the way to the Kotel and behind him was a man who let out a big sigh. He paid no attention but the man groaned a second time and he turned and asked him, "What are you groaning about"? The man replied, "Nothing that you can help me with." But R' Schechter's father persisted and got him to tell what was bothering him; 'I have to marry off a daughter soon and I don't have money.' He asked him how much does he need? "Fifty lira" (a big sum in those days). So R' Schechter's father answered him, "I also have to marry off a daughter in a couple months but meantime take my fifty lira." So the fellow asked him, "Why would I take your money"? But R' Meir's father persisted and eventually ended up giving the man all the money he had set aside for his own daughter's *hatuna*. That's what R' Shlomke saw – the mitzvah that he had done and he told him, "You should know that you fixed and rectified 'all the *gilgulim*' (all the previous transmigrations of his soul)." As they were speaking, in walked a man who wanted to give a *kvitel* (a "note" with information) to R' Shlomke to pray for him, and R' Shlomke turned to the father of R' Schechter and said, "Give it to him." R' Schechter's father said, "What am I, a Rebbe?" [It is usually Rebbe's and tzaddikim who accept such notes with requests to pray for someone]. R' Shlomke said, "Yes at this point after this story you can be *mashpia*" ("You can have influence like a Rebbe"). In the *kvitel* were five lira. He told him, "go give this to your *mechutan* (future in-laws)," but he said, "I owe him 50." "So give him 5…" He gave him the five and reported back that he never again had to ask him for anything for the *chatuna* [probably, the *mechutan* saw how difficult it was for R' Schechter's father to get the money together and didn't ask him for it]. For our purposes, the point is that in any case, R' Shlomke could see on R' Schechter's father that he had done this good deed and mitzvah. He could see it on his face and being. R' Schechter's father himself wasn't aware, he knew he had done something significant, didn't want to tell anyone, but R' Shlomke could see…

- Many such stories of *tzaddikim* who could see, one was the story of R' Hershel Tzieg ("goat"): Not only the Besht but also his *talmidim* could see that with him there was illumination all the way up to the heavens. They did a lot of research to know from where this light was coming, and asked R' Hershl himself and he explained about all the orphans and others whom he was assisting. But, R' Hershel Tzieg himself was not aware of the light.

All this is particularly true regarding *hitbonenut* on higher worlds (Page 94 in the translation). There the text speaks of *sechel amok* ("deep intellect") – R' Deitsch says this is about more abstract intellect (more *chochma* than *bina*). *Chochma* is more abstract...R' Pinchas Menachem Alter, the Gerer Rebbe said that if one is deficient in *havana* he will be deficient in *hasbara* ("one who is deficient in understanding will also be deficient in his ability to explain") but that regarding *chochma*, there may be matters that are impossible to explain (that is, one may possess the attribute of *chochma*, but still be unable to explain certain matters). That is, the trait of *chochma* can be present without the ability to explain it. In *bina*, the *otiot* ("letters" with which the concept can be explained) are "felt," which is not the case in *chochma*, wherein *otiot* are unconscious. But in any case, all the concepts and matters that are mentioned and discussed in Chasidut are presented in a manner that enables us to *mitbonen* and meditate upon them.

- The first thing, when meditating, according to R' Shlomo Chaim, is to focus our thoughts. To start slowly, bit by bit, getting accustomed to having the thought remain without drifting off the topic. For purposes of *hitbonenut*, we should not learn new matters that we have not yet learned already, but rather meditate on matters that we already know. At the time in yeshiva, R' Deitsch was learning *Tof-Shin Gimel* (1943) of the Previous Rebbe, which is a series (*hemshech*) of Rosh Hashana discourses speaking of several *madreigot* ("levels") of *ratzon* – "several levels of the will of God." On *Adon Olam asher malach beterem kol yetzir nivra* ("Master of the universe, Who reigned before anything was formed or created..."), it is asked, "If there was nothing yet created or formed, why was "King" needed?" And the answer given in the discourse was that even if the universe was not yet created, nevertheless, it already existed in the will of Hashem. And therefore, there were *gaonim* ("geniuses") and *gedolei nigleh* ("giants" in the halachic portion of Torah), way prior to Chasidut, who said that one who meditates on the opening lines of *Adon Olam* at the time of *tekiat shofar* ("blowing of the Shofar") will not and cannot be attacked by all the *mekatragim* ("accusers" – bad angels). [That is, his meditation is so high that it is beyond the reach of such spiritual creations as "accusing angels].

- Here R' Deitsch remarked on an amazing fact; It is not recognizable, within Chasidut, that the Shoah was happening. [The year 5703/1943 in which the *maamor* was said, was during the Shoah, yet there was nothing within the content of the discourse that revealed anything whatsoever about the shoah]. If you saw the Previous Rebbe before or after saying Chasidut, you could see that the Rebbe was extremely distraught and disturbed, he would cry without stop. They had to bring a psychologist just to relax the Previous Rebbe. And yet within his Chasidut, it was not at all recognizable that the Shoah was happening at all. [I have noticed the same regarding the Torah of other *Gedolei Yisrael*; the events of the day are not noted at all, or if noted, they have no discernible effect. Somewhere in the *Shach* on *Choshen Mishpat*, he mentions that he is quoting a specific *sefer* by memory because "we are running away from the Cossacks right now and I don't have the *sefer* at hand"]. During *sichot* (when the Rebbe spoke less formally) on the other hand, the Shoah was discussed and felt. The same true regarding the Rebbe Rashab (the previous Rebbe's father); he would say Chasidut even as shells were flying around him (in Rostov as the Bolsheviks defeated the white Russians). After the Bosheviks won, the Rebbe said, "Myself and them cannot exist in the same world. I cannot live with them." He said this in a *maamar*, and at the end of the revolution a few months later he passed away.

- Someone in the *shiur* gave the sefer *Tof-shin-gimmel* (of the Previous Rebbe) to R' Deitsch and he recalled learning the *maamorim* with R' Shlomo Chaim …at the time he had an infected toe and there was no doctor in Kfar Chabad, R' Deitsch had to travel to Jerusalem. He asked his *mashpia*, R' Shlomo Chaim, "What will be with the Chasidut *shiur*"? At any rate, the *maamorim* that he learned at that time, were the discourses with which R' Shlomo Chaim told them to start meditating, first with the text in front of them, and then with his own *otiot*, his own understanding. By way of example, R' Shlomo Chaim told them about the Previous Rebbe going into his father, the Rebbe Rashab and reviewing a *maamar*, after which the Rashab told him, "Nu and in your words"? Therefore, first of all one should meditate for five minutes, then slowly increase to ten minutes, and it's a *segula* ("helpful aid") to meditate before prayer davka in *tefilin*. Then he gave R' Deitsch private attention, asking, "What are these *ratzonot* (various levels of "will") spoken of here in *tof-shin-gimmel*"? What is this all about? All this has to arrive to a *b'chen* (a "result," a "goal"), it is not sufficient to remain abstract. "What is all this talk about wanting to be the King? Ultimately it boils down to that I am a servant," and my service is so so important that it touches the very essence [of whom we are]. For there are presents you can give someone that indicate friendship and connection, but sometimes you give something so precious and personal that it awakens the very depth of the soul – *omek hanefesh* (the "depth of the soul"). That is the meaning of *m'mamakim keraticha*... ("From the depths I called to You" – Psalms 130), in which the purpose is to arouse His *ratzon*. And ultimately, the meaning is that, "I have to be His servant," but that desire reaches to the very highest level of *ratzon* as portrayed in the *sefer* there...this is how R' Shlomo Chaim guided R' Chaim Shalom שי' in Chasidut and *hitbonenut*. And so it is written in many places in Chasidut, that one must take out the *b'chen*, the realization of "what does this mean for me," how do I relate to it?

Back to our text, applying the same idea, we must start with *hitbonenut* on our own world, and to repeat and *lehargel* ("accustom ourselves") to regularly undertake *hitbonenut*. We have to constantly and consistently remind ourselves that all that we see are the "outer garments" of Hashem (end of Tanya, Ch 42). The Hebrew word for "faith" is *emunah*, which is also the root of the word *lehitamen*, which means "to practice." One of the *avreichim* asked, "Why not *yirah*? It seems as if the same *hitbonenut* could lead to *yirah*?" But R' Deitsch explained that *ahava* has two components: 1) Desire to get close to someone and 2) The enjoyment and delight that we have in being close to someone. And in order to arouse the desire and *ratzon* for closeness, for this purpose we practice meditation. As far as the *taanug* and enjoyment in being close, that's something that if you weren't born with it, nothing will help. If you don't have a sense of *ta'ava* for proximity to God, you can't develop it....what is common to all the levels of love is the desire for proximity. The closeness itself occurs when we learn Torah and fulfill mitzvoth, but for that we need desire, and that is what the *hitbonenut* comes to arouse. Once, someone who missed one day of *tefillin*, said that all his previous *avoda* was not worth anything since he missed that one day of *tefillin*. But he was answered that in order to arrive to such a realization, he needed thirty years of *avoda*.

- R' Eliyahu Hadad spoke of Rashi end of parshat *Vayeishev* where Yaakov Avinu went down to Egypt and settled in Goshen. There, Rashi quoted the same Midrash Tanhuma that the mitzvoth are "My emissaries..."

Shiur 48, June 10, 2012 (ongoing review of Ch 4)

Kuntres Avoda: The purpose of the book is as stated in the beginning, *avodat hatefila* has two facets; 1) clinging and cleaving our soul to Hashem and 2) refining and developing our *midot*. Page 98 in the translation: What more that we "move" toward proximity to Hashem we simultaneously distance ourselves from forces that are opposed to Godliness.

- R' Deitsch told a story of a son who fell off the path of Torah and mitzvoth, and met a non-Jewish woman and wanted to marry her. The father went to Rav Grossman of Migdal Haemek who tried to speak with the son but didn't succeed. Instead, he sent him to the Lelov Rebbe. The son agreed to go to the Lelover Rebbe alone by himself. The Lelover removed his outer "rebbeishe" clothes, went out on the balcony and offered him a cigarette…but didn't say a word about the upcoming "wedding." His father asked the son about his meeting with the Lelover, and he replied, "It was nice, we spoke but he didn't say anything about the woman." "So what did he say?" "At the end," the son said, "I told him that I like him." So the father wasn't happy and went to R' Grossman, who went to the Lelover to find out what happened. And the Rebbe (R' Mordecai Moshe, grandfather of the later Lelover Rebbe) said, "If he likes me, he'll stop liking her." Given this story, why was it necessary for the boy to go to a Rebbe? He could have liked any Jew and gotten the same result…but the definition of an elevated person such as a Rebbe is that when he is involved with someone, he is "involved" with all of his personality and engages the other as well with all his personality.

- In Slonim there was a Chosid by the name of R' Mordechai Lieder who was one of several students of the *Yesod Ha'avoda* (a Chasidishe Rebbe) who came to Tiveria after the war, and together they became the basis and foundation of Chassidut Slonim in Eretz Yisrael (the Chabad "Lieders" are also from him), and probably most of today's current Slonimer Chasidim are his grandchildren. The *Yesod Ha'avoda* said about him, "He is through and through a Jew." One who is elevated, means that the elements that elevate him permeate every level of his being, even when, for example he is smoking a cigarette. And therefore,"If he likes me, he'll stop liking her."

Here as well, when we love Hashem, we automatically distance ourselves from matters of the animal soul. How can we discern when there is some *chalishut* ("weakness") of the animal soul? When the person can "do without" the particular lust or temptation that he previously experienced for the physical item. For example, he may no longer need his coffee in the morning. At other times, a person may want something but doesn't put it into action. *B'ruchniyut* this is certainly the case. Ask a person if he wants, why didn't he do it? "He wants, but…" If the *ratzon* is weak, then it doesn't permeate his thought speech and action. This applies to any of our traits and abilities – if we don't use them, we lose them. "A sharp knife that you don't use, ceases to be sharp."

Shiur 49, June 11, 2012 (ongoing review of Ch. 4)

Page 24 last two lines in the Hebrew, Page 99 in the translation: "In addition [involvement in spirituality...]" – One who draws closer to spiritual matters begins to feel the coarse physicality of worldly matters. We're not speaking here of sins, but of matters of the world. One who is attracted by such matters doesn't feel their spiritual "danger," because he is "within it." One who is coarse and low doesn't experience his own coarseness and lowliness. There is *gasut* ("coarseness") in *kedusha* as well.

- After his first son was born, R' Deitsch spent much of the next year in Tiveria, since the custom was for the wife to be with the parents first year. Since his wife was there, R' Deitsch would be most of the week in Jerusalem and travel to Tiveria for Shabbat. In those days it was a long bus through Shechem (Nablus) to Tiveria, 4.5 hours and there was time to talk with another person who rode regularly at that time between Tiveria and Jerusalem...R' Deitsch spoke regularly with one passenger and told him that one who works but who is not involved in anything higher than his work is like an "animal" that just pursues its own physical interests. The one with whom he was discussing matters argued back, saying he's not an animal, he's a man...but R' Deitsch kept after him, pressured him til he said, "So, what? So I'm an animal...but the main thing is that I enjoy." And that's as low as can be, if man doesn't care if he's an "animal." The goal of every level of creation is to ascend to the next higher level...so that if one level declares that it doesn't need to ascend, then what was the purpose of creating it?

- The biggest foolishness, if we think and meditate a bit, is to claim that He who created the world, created it with no goal or idea. That's ultimate foolishness. The diameter of the world is 42,000 kilometers. If we stretch out all the veins, vessels and limbs, etc of the body, it is twice that much – 84,000 kilometers. All that, God put into one man. To declare that such an achievement was for no reason whatsoever, makes no sense. And therefore we say that the purpose of every level of creation, including man, is to rise beyond his own level of creation. It certainly isn't just to "become what you are," cause what goal is there to that? Might as well be created, each of us, "as we are."

- Once R' Deitsch travelled on *Purim Meshulash* to army camps to read the Megilah. On *Purim Meshulash* (*Shushan Purim* that falls on *erev Shabbat*), there are the same times for reading the *megilah* in

Jerusalem and out of Jerusalem, so it works out to travel from Jlm to IDF camps that are outside Jlm. They sat around with an impromptu "farbrengen" afterward with a few *hevra*, and decided that there must be a purpose to the creation because everytime that we arrive to any particular level (of any physical or intellectual endeavor), we ask, "Now what"? And there is disappointment with this state of affairs. But within *ruchniyut* ("spirituality"), this is not the case, there are no limits. One soldier, apparently previously religious, admitted, "How correct you are," with great emotion.

- One Purim in Tiveria, the Rav heard someone ask, "What's the difference between *gashmiyut* ("physicality") and *ruchniyut* ("spirituality")"? When *gashmiyut* is missing, we search for it. But, when we possess it, it means little to us. When *ruchniyut* is absent, we do not look for it. But when we have it, there is no end to our desire for more of it.

- Shia (not clear if R' Shia Yuzevitz or R' Shia Werner or someone else) told a nice story of ending up among a group of retirees, people of all stripes and kinds. Someone remarked on how if he had more money, he would be better off, and they all broke up in laughter. Money does not make us happier. Another wealthy man spoke of how when he had money, people came to him for advice. After he lost his money, people stopped coming to him. He asked, "The money I understand, they won't come for money because I don't have any. But when did I lose my *sechel*?"

Shiur #50, June 12, 2012 (ongoing review of Ch 4)

Page 25 in the Hebrew text, Page 100 in the translation. Looking at the parentheses in the middle of the page: ("In order to achieve the maximum effect...")

When is the time for us to focus on our particular character traits that are in need of rectification? During a period of *romemut hanefesh* ("when the soul is in an exalted state")? No, the Rashab tell us *davka* during *tefila* – precisely during prayers - at the moment when we are clinging and cleaving to Him, that's when we say, "This thing I won't do today, that thing I won't ever do at all." Why during prayers? Because that's when the divine soul is shining and the animal soul is in the background and since it is weak, it is easier for the divine soul to have an effect. Moreover, at that time we feel the *grubkeit* and coarseness more, and we are more aware of what our animal soul seeks to achieve. Not during

Shemonah Esreh but during *pesukei dezimra*. *Davka* during his state of elevated awareness during *pesukei dezimra*, is when we become aware of the lowliness of our desires and we can make a decision and a resolution to improve. This is the time of the *milchama*, the "war," and the *yetzer harah* raises its head, but because of the high illumination of the divine soul, it cannot maintain its "presence." Because of the proximity to Hashem and to *ruchniyut*, the animal soul "loses it" and becomes weakened. This is the difference between prayer and Torah: *Tefila* is revelation of Godliness, while Torah is cleaving to Godliness without necessarily being aware that we are doing so. We may not feel it. Torah is from Above to below, while *tefila* is from below to Above. The difference is that in order to daven ("pray") properly, the person has to change himself. Via *da'at* and *hitbonenut*, he becomes "another person." But, Torah comes to him, in whatever situation he may find himself. He may not feel God's presence but He is there...*behamot hayiti imach*...("I was an animal with You..." – this is what King David in Psalms said, describing his status in relation to Hashem). *B'etzem*, Torah is with us in a revealed manner, we just don't know how to detect it. The difference is that ultimately, our eyes will be opened and we will see how He is with us through Torah.

- For example: If you give a small child a package of $100 bills, he looks at them and says, "This is boring, they're all the same." But if someone comes and offers to exchange them for one dollars or ten dollar bills, he will be interested. Then, you have another boy, a, *tamim* who simply accepts what was given him and even tho someone might make an offer to exchange, he holds on to his $100 bills. Later, when he matures, he will realize that he became rich simply because he held onto what was given to him. Moreover, he realizes that he was rich back then as well. And the one who traded and exchanged for smaller bills is the one who lost out in the end, because previously he was wealthy and now he is less so. The greatest *rachmanut* ("pity") on us is that we are wealthy and don't know it. Tanya tells us that we are wealthy in that manner precisely because we lack awareness. If we had such awareness, we would be "bursting" from the high level of revealed Godliness. We're not *mesugal* ("able") to feel Torah. So, when do we feel revealed Godliness? During *tefila*, during prayers. If we don't feel at that time, then it's a big question whether we fulfilled our obligation to pray at that time. So, more *devekut* ("cleaving") while learning Torah, but more *hargasha* ("feeling") during *tefila*, is necessary. In Karlin, they say that, "In order to learn Torah properly, we need *tefila*, we need prayer." And then it's possible that even during Torah we'll experience Godliness.

- There was a Kotzker Chassid who walked back and forth, debating whether to don his pair of *tefilin*. He picked them up and put them down, walking back and forth. Finally near the end of the day he picked up the tefillin and put them on. They asked him, "What happened?" and he said that every time he reached to put on the tefilin, he reminded himself that they were a commandment of Hashem, and that made him very afraid and he walked away. Finally, at the end of the day he realized that if he doesn't put them on, he wouldn't fulfill the command of God that day, so he said to himself, "Forget about the Commander and just consider the commandment. I have to put on *tefilin*." This is similar to the story of Rambam who would shake whenever he was about to put on tefilin…he needed someone to hold on to him in order to put on the *tefilin*. (His son wrote about this).

- How does *ta'anug* ("enjoyment, delight") *mistader* ("go together") with *bitul* ("self effacement, self nullification")? There are many levels of *taanug*, there is *ta'anug murgash* ("enjoyment that we feel and experience"), there is *ta'anug* that is "good for him," *ta'anug* that is "good in general"…but in general *ta'anug* is the highest of our senses.

- There is a story of an *avrech* (young newlywed man, usually learning with a stipend for the first year or two of marriage, but can also apply to a working man) with a difficult employer, and since he grew to dislike his boss, he realized that he was transgressing on the *issur* ("injunction") of, "Do not hate your fellow in your heart." He worked on himself in various ways to overcome his hatred, but he wasn't successful. As the ten days of *teshuva* approached, he was very concerned and when it came to *nafal korim* (prostrating on the ground while saying, "*v'anachnu korim u'mishtachavim…*"), he decided that would be the best time to work on himself. The first time he prostrated himself, it didn't work. The second time, he decided that he won't get up until he achieves his aim. And that's what happened, in that manner he managed to uproot the hatred from his heart. That's what *K'Avoda* discusses here, the ability to work on ourselves *davka* during prayers. 1) Because then the Godly soul is strong and able to work on the animal soul (but he must be careful not to do a 'reverse' later on, like for example after the six day war, when a white flag hung from every Arab apartment in surrender, but like idiots the Jews allowed them to lift their heads instead of behaving toward them as the Rebbe recommended. We offered them university, etc…). 2) It is precisely during prayers that we experience our own lowliness, and because of that it's easier to rectify ourselves.

- *Kadkod shimshotayich* – Gemora says that the *shoham* stone and the *yashpeh* stone were the two stones in the shoulder straps of the High Priest. Why two? Because one applies to Yoseph, the "higher *tzaddik*" who was focused on the highest spiritual matters even while fully involved with the physical world, and the other applied to Benjamin, who was the "lower *tzadik*" who could only maintain his spiritual status by avoiding worldly matters. The Gemora asks, "Why two?" And Hashem answered, "Use both." The Alter Rebbe explains that one (Yoseph) represents *avoda* (divine service, in this case Torah) from Above to below, and the other (Binyamin) represents *avoda* from below to Above (prayer).

- The Ruzhiner Rebbe says that now what preserves and protects the Jews is *v'asfu* – gathering together. Jews getting together, not in large groups but in *shteibelach* (small shuls). These days, everyone (even the *Litvaks*, or non Chasidic Jews) are praying in *shteibelach*. The point is that Jews getting together to learn Torah and demonstrate concern for one another is what protects and preserves the Jewish people as a whole. [A shteibel allows the congregants to get to know each other, unlike a typical large shul in which one may have some friends but the overall atmosphere is too large to allow the congregants to become like a "family."]

Shiur 51, June 13, 2012 (ongoing review of Ch 4)

Page 25 in the Hebrew text, page 100 in the translation, "In particular, when we meditate on the concept…" We already mentioned that the *etzem* ("essence") of every creation is the *chayut Eloki*, the Godly vitality of the object, while the physical component of the object is the opposite of life…the Godly vitality is eternal, but the physical is the opposite. Once we appreciate the Godliness, that leads us to *ahava*. Simultaneously, it distances us from physical matters, and the reason is that this *hitbonenut*, this meditation, separates the Godly vitality from its opposite. R' Shlomo Chaim mentioned on multiple occasions where this topic is the subject of *hitbonenut*. That is, besides teaching the content, he pointed out several examples of content for meditation.

- *Ma'aseh* ("story") from R' Chaim Shmuelevitz: The gemora (*Nazir* 23B and *Horiyot* 10B) says, *Gedola aveira lishmah, m'mitzvah sh'lo lishmah* – "A transgression performed for the sake of heaven is greater than a mitzvah that is not performed for the sake of Heaven." Regarding what was this said? It was stated regarding *Yael eishet hekeini* ("Yael, the wife of the *Keini*"), who slept with Cicera in order to kill him. The Gemora "objects" that she had *hana'ah*, she enjoyed the act. But even if she enjoyed it, that should not have been a problem, because a mitzvah that one enjoys, is still a mitzvah. Even if one derived enjoyment from fulfilling a mitzvah, it was still a mitzvah. Yael's act though was not a mitzvah, it was an *aveirah*, even though it was performed *lishmah* – "for the sake of heaven." The fact that the gemora objects proves that her act was an *aveirah*, if one gains any kind of enjoyment from the *aveira*, that's a problem, even if the act is *lishmah*, for ultimately positive reasons (from R' Chaim Shmuelevitz).

- The Rebbe Rashab had a very talented brother by the name of R' Mendel, and the Rashab had claims against him (in *Torat Shalom*), because their father the Maharash wanted them to learn together, but R' Mendel wanted to do business. "It's easier to learn Torah *lishmah* than to do business *lishmah*," according to their father, the Rebbe Maharash. Even the mussar of the Rashab didn't help, and he wasn't successful. And therefore whenever we have the opportunity to learn Torah, with a little or a lot of *kavana*, we should do so.

- There are a lot of *Litvish mashgichim* (non Chassidic rabbis) who point at the results of families in which the husband learns Torah full time, in order to tell their yeshiva students that a Torah life is more relaxed, more successful, etc…but here in the *K' Avoda* the point is much deeper; that Godliness is *b'etzem* better, is intrinsically the right choice, and not merely because it yields "better results."

Shiur 52, June 14, 2012 (Ongoing review of Ch 4)

The "distance" from physical desires that results from meditation can be described as "weakness" – as if to say regarding *ta'avot* (our "physical lusts"), "this (my situation) can be different, I can do without this." Not speaking of *tzadikim* but of "normal" people in relation to their animal soul.

- For example, the first time the Previous Rebbe travelled to the US (in 1927), he travelled alone, no family with him. R' Yisrael Jacobson had been there for some time already, and he received and accompanied the Rebbe in the US, and kept a diary of the Previous Rebbe's movements and customs. He did not eat much, but he ate *kichelach* (the light, airy *mezonos*) in the morning. On several occasions, R' Jacobson brought *kicheloch* but the Fredker Rebbe wouldn't eat it. Being it was after the Russian revolution, the Previous Rebbe had a name and reputation and wherever he went, people wanted to meet him. In one place there were so many people who came to see him that he wasn't able to get away, and the police had to bring a crane in order to extract him from the crowd. The next day was one of the days that the Rebbe refused to eat, and R' Jacobson commented that the Rebbe wasn't eating. He answered, "One has to starve *kavod*." ("One has to starve his sense of pride"). On another occasion, he brought the Rebbe food and he didn't eat, saying, "It isn't necessary to eat every day. It's also possible not to eat." The *kavana* ("intention") was that eating is not something that's "necessary," and this is an expression of the "weakness" of the animal soul.

- There is something that is very dangerous, and in fact some say it was the downfall of Shabtai Zvi – "trying on" a *ta'avah* in order to elevate it. Sometimes a tzaddik or Torah scholar will be very careful in matters of eyesight and vision, yet a common man might suggest, "Why be so sensitive about this matter, I pay no attention to it." To which the sages replied; "On a white shirt, the smallest speck appears dirty. On a discolored garment (such as worn by an *am haaretz*, one who is not versant in Torah), the stain is not so noticeable." It's written that, "One should always be clever regarding *yirat Hashem*." And because of that, there are chasidim who make sure not to go hungry (so they won't be tempted to partake of something not kosher). One of the *avrechim* in the Tzemach Tzedek Collel used to always bring a sandwich with him to shul, wrapped up in his Talit and tefilin, he called it his "*shalom bayit* bread." In order not to be unpleasant when he returned home and to avoid saying anything he might later regret [such as, "why isn't dinner ready"], he used to eat the sandwich before returning home so he wouldn't be hungry. If one is not hungry, then all the lusts and *ta'avot* are anyway weakened.

- One of the students asked about the Torah commandment, "Make yourself holy in permitted matters," and R' Deitsch responded that it is a very individual matter. For some it means like the *Ra'avad* suggests that he eat but leave over a bit (he fails to finish his food in order to show that he eats only what he needs for his bodily maintenance and not more). For someone else it means simply delaying and postponing his eating (Tanya). And the Rebbe told R' Deitsch in *yechidut* ("personal audience") that one must go very slowly in such matters. "Take on a little bit of something, if it works that's fine then take on more…but not to jump in and take on too much too quickly." Chasidim also were careful to marry early. R' Deitsch spoke of one who at age 50 wrote to the Rebbe and said that he wants to be a *porush* (to act with *prishut*, apparently to separate from his wife, not to have relations), and the Rebbe wrote to him against such conduct. The Berdichever Rav said, "Not to eat at all, a non-Jew can also do. To eat like you should – this only a Jew can do." That was the Chasidishe conduct – "to eat like you should." At any rate, it is closeness to Godliness that results in this "weakness."

- One of the explanations is that after one experiences this proximity to *Elokut*, the natural *sechel* begins to grasp how it should act as well.

Page 25 in the text, 101 in the translation:

"Another effect of weakening…" That the divine soul graps these matters is not a *chiddush* (is "nothing new"). But in order for the animal soul to grasp such matters, it must first undergo *chalishut*, "weakening." Otherwise, it grasps only animal matters. You find some people who daven well and properly, but immediately afterward the person falls into matters of the *nefesh habehamit*, the "animal soul." The explanation, according to the Previous Rebbe, is that at the time of prayers, the animal soul was not involved, it was "absent." And then after davening, the animal soul gets down to its own business as if nothing changed because in truth, the animal soul did not participate in the davening, and therefore it wasn't affected at all. In Chasidut, it is explained that *mi'krav li* ("from within me," wherein the word *krav* means both "battle" (war) and also "close" – Psalms 55). In order to do battle with the animal soul, we have to face it, face to face, up close. In fact, the Mittler Rebbe says that's the reason for *machshavot zarot* at the time of *tefila*. The animal soul is also "speaking," so it presents strange thoughts for us to battle with. This was the impetus in Poland to set up the girls' school, Beit Yaakov. The man of the house was a Chasidishe mench, but his wife and daughters "were at the theatre." They weren't taking part in the Chasidish way of life. They didn't even know how to pray. So it was necessary to relate to them, "come down" to their level, and this also is part of the *chalishut* ("weakness") that takes place via proximity to Hashem.

- The Midrash says, "Hashem made a condition with the sea, if it agrees to split when the Jews are ready to pass thru, fine. If not, Hashem will not create the world." The sages, especially the Rambam ask, "Why was it necessary to make this a 'condition' from the beginning of creation?" And the *Ohr HaChaim* asks, "When was the condition fulfilled? Not when the waters were created, but later when the sea split." The Rebbe explains: *Kriat Yam Suf* (the "splitting of the sea") was accompanied by revelation of Godliness. The sea itself is natural, but the splitting of the sea was accompanied by miraculous Godly revelation. The question is, was this revelation additional to the creation, or is it built into the creation? That Hashem "conditioned" the creation on this splitting of the sea proves that it was not an "additional" element but that it was built into creation, part of it. Hashem created the universe with built in capacity to reveal Godliness. The Godly revelation is built right into the sea. Meaning that when the waters fulfilled their "*tanai* (original 'contition') – they returned *l'eitano* – to their "real strength" (their original strength from the day of creation). It means that they returned to their original condition that He made with the sea – that it should reveal *Elokut*. That the creation itself will express and reveal Godliness.

- There is a similar idea regarding eating with a *bracha*, a "blessing." The sages say if we eat without a uttering a blessing, it's as if we are "robbing the world" – *gozel et habriot*. Because what right do we have to eat of all the foods that Hashem created? "All that He created, He created only to reveal His *kavod* ("honor")." He created on condition that we reveal His *kavod*, His honor in the creation, and this we do by reciting a blessing. Without a blessing, we do not reveal His *kavod*, His honor, and therefore we are *gozel* (we are "robbing"). (*Maharsha* in *Berachot*). The animal soul was also created "in His honor," but it's very concealed and it's up to us reveal it.

At the beginning, this process of persuading the animal soul to "allow" Godly revelation, is only "acquiescence," it is not full participation. It is only "agreement" that the animal soul "won't disturb." (page 103 in the translation). But, by regular and constant *avoda*, the animal soul comes around as well, so that it as well wants and participates in the desire for Godliness.

- Once upon a time in Jerusalem, there were *talmidei chachamim* ("Torah scholars") around, who knew Shas (the entire Talmud), and one in particular from among *Radzin* chasidim – who said, "What you have now, you never had before. A woman arrives to the Collel in a taxi to take her husband with her"? That didn't exist then. Americans who either can't get along without a car, or Israelis married to American women and she drives but not him – "She brings him to the Collel"? That never happened…with all the *gadlut HaTorah*…that there is so much *cheshek* ("desire") for Torah even expressed in simple *gashmiyut* ("physical") matters, this didn't exist! And that exists within each of us as well, the desire to learn can be so strong that it drags the natural soul along with it as well.

Until this point, we learned about "love like water," soon we'll begin with "love like fire"…Here there were comments from R' Deitsch about how with kids, one must teach them in a manner that "hits them in the stomach," that bears a relation to the gut level. Otherwise they think you are only teaching them spiritual things that YOU want them to know, but it's not for them. Truth is that it's ALSO for them, and the things you are teaching them will lead them on the best path, ALSO *b'gashmiyut* ("physically"), but they don't understand that. People (R" Deitsch) have seen what works, and the path of Torah works better also in *gashmiyut k'pashuto*…

Shiur 53, June 15, 2012, Page 25 in the Hebrew text, P 104 in the translation (Chapter 4 in review)

"Love like water" weakens the soul…but "love like fire" nullifies the animal soul. The reason is that the animal soul in the human corresponds to fire in the four elements of creation. Broadly speaking, the four categories of creation (mineral, vegetable, animal and human) correspond to the four elements; earth, water, fire and air. Here, the Rav read from *Likutei Torah* regarding parshat Nesachim on *Kriat Shema*.

- The *Avnei Nezer* (R' Avraham Borenstein, 1838-1910, son-in-law of the Kotzker Rav and founder of the Sochachov dynasty of Chassidim), was not well as a young man. His *shver* ("father in law"), was the Kotzker Rav. His father, the Bialeh Rav, went to see the Kotzker, and spoke highly in praise of his son. The Kotzker listened but said, "Nu, that's not such a huge *ma'alah* ("good character trait")…" As the father was mentioning his praises, the Kotzker was speaking of his deficiencies, and the father was wondering, "Why is this the time to mention deficiencies? This is the time to speak his praises…" After the *Avnei Nezer* recovered, his father asked the Kotzker, what was this all about, speaking his *chesronot* ("deficiencies")? The Kotzker answered, "According to you, he was perfect, he was *shalem*, and if so he had nothing more to achieve in this world, and no more reason to live. Therefore I spoke of his deficiencies so that indicates he still has what to do in this world [in order to rectify and fix his character traits]."

Page 105 in the translation: "Now, the true love like flames of fire…arises from deep understanding of the heart and recognition of the greatness of God…" During "love like water," *Gadlut Hashem* is not emphasized and is not the main focus of *hitbonenut*. Rather, the topic of how Hashem enlivens the creation is the focus of meditation. During "love like fire" though, the person wants nothing else but Hashem, and nothing compares to His importance. This "fiery desire" consumes all other lusts and desires. With this, the person ascends and elevates (in *Likutei Torah*, it is explained that's why tefilin are necessary, in order to bring the person back "down" again afterward).

Shiur 54, June 17, 2012 (ongoing review of Ch 4)

Page 26 in the Hebrew text, Page 110 in the translation. "But this fire from Above takes place on most elevated levels…" That is, in order to achieve such a spiritual level, intense revelation and illumination of the soul is required. When the divine soul is in a state of revelation, then the effect is to "ignite" the soul like flames of fire.

Another path to "love like fire" is by meditating on the *chiddush* ("novelty") and *hitchadshut* ("renewal") of the creation. If we can be aware of the renewal of creation every day, we can become aware that it occurs at every instant as well. Nevertheless, this level of illumination is also associated with revelation of the soul, it is not merely a result of *hitbonenut* on creation.

The Rav comments here, almost as an aside, that "what is says here is a *yeshua*, a 'saving grace,' or "salvation." All over Chasidut, the Rebbeim speak of "love like fire," and if it didn't mention here in *K' Avoda* that it's a high *madreiga* (high "spiritual level"), then we might become afraid that we are *m'tumtamim* ("stuffed up, clogged") or something of the sort, because of our inablility to attain this level. R' Deitsch says that the meditations on "renewal of the creation at every instant, etc…" are fine, but that in truth he suspects that without revelation of the soul, this level of love itself doesn't occur [at all].

- As young yeshiva students, R'Deitsch and friends landed in NY, took a taxi to Crown Heights. They asked the Israeli taxi driver how he is, what he does, does he put on tefilin, etc…until he burst out, "What do you guys want from me? I came here for the *yerokot*, for the "greenbacks," the US dollars, not for anything else…" In other words, for the taxi driver, there was no revelation of the Godly soul… the same applies here; in order for the meditation to have an effect, the soul needs to be *b'hitgalut* ("revealed").

Page 111 – But the aveirage man who wants to achieve "love like fire," needs 1) meditation on the level of "love like water" (*Elokut* enlivening the worlds), plus an additional factor; he must add the element of 2) his *richuk*, his "distance" from Hashem. In addition to his meditation on Godliness in the world, he must add in the fact that he is *b'tachlit harichuk* (at "ultimate distance") from Hashem. A person who makes a proper *cheshbon* ("self accounting") realizes that he is far from God. It works like this: "love like fire" is based on desire, and a fiery will to get close to Him. (In the very next section, it compares this *tenuah* ("dynamic") of meditation in order to attain "love like fire," with the *tenuah* of *teshuva*. During *teshuva*, the emphasis is only on distance. But during the meditation to achieve "love like fire," the emphasis is also on desire and love as well. It's a *shiluv* ("meshing") of two meditations). Here, we are looking for the *yoker* (preciousness) and *ilui* (elevation), not merely on our distance as during *teshuva*. We'll learn this more in depth...

Shiur 55, June 18, 2012 (review of Ch 4)

The *K'Avoda* tells us that achievement of "love like fire" via meditation alone requires *madreigot gavohot* – "high spiritual levels." By "high spiritual levels" is meant revelation of the soul. Not that it requies a high *neshama*, but that whatever level the *neshama* is on, it must be in a state of "revelation."

- A merchant went to the Rebbe Rashab straight from the "fair," where he bought several articles of *kedusha*, that were claimed to come from the Besht or the Magid, etc…and since he was a Chasid he wanted to bring them to the Rebbe Rashab as gifts. The previous Rebbe sat outside the Rebbe's office and he had a look at the items. The Previous Rebbe told him which were truly items that used to belong to *tzadikim* and which items were not from *tzadikim*. Since he wasn't yet the Rebbe so the merchant didn't accept his word 100%, and went into the Rebbe Rashab with the articles in hand. The Rashab lifted up each one and said exactly as his son the Previous Rebbe had said; "This one is truly from a *tzadik,* this one not…" etc. On his way out of the office, the merchant said to the Previous Rebbe, "You deserve a '*mashkanta*' – a 'chasidishe potch' for doing *moftim* (demonstrating *ruach hakodesh*, "holy spirit"), since a chasid is not supposed to demonstrate such spiritual abilities…

- To understand this idea of *mashkanta* a bit better, there was another story reg R' Itzy *HaMatmid*, a Chasid of the Previous Rebbe who was *b'clal* in a class and a world of his own, davening all day long, later a *shadar* ("emissary") of the Previous Rebbe in the US, would fast all day long. His was completely removed from the world…for example he was known to complain about those in the US who would, "take a shower before they go to sleep." In short, the Previous Rebbe called him to come while the Rebbe was at a *tish* or farbrengen, and R' Itzhy was davening. He was absolutely *butel* ("nullified") to the Previous Rebbe, but in the middle of davening he was unable to come immediately, he motioned with his hand that he would come soon, and then returned immediately to his deep meditation and prayers. The Previous sent another messenger and another and each time the same thing happened; R' Itzhy motioned that he would come but returned to his davening. Finally, R' Itzhy came to the Previous Rebbe, who said to him, "Itzhy, Itzhy you deserve a *mashkanta*, but there is nobody here to administer it…" That's the *mashkanta* that a Chasid deserves – if he is so uplifted that he forgets that he is nullified to the Rebbe, for that he deserves a '*mashkanta.*"

- The *mashkanta* was something that actually occurred, but the younger chasidim would distance themselves out of respect for the older chasidim who gave or received the *mashkanta*. The story of R' Shmuel Munkus and the lung that he threw away was of a similar nature. When a chasid does a *mofet* ("performs a sign"), he could come to think that he is a Rebbe…therefore, to "remind" him who he is, he gets a *mashkanta*. Chasidim were very afraid of "high *madreigot*" – "exalted spiritual levels." There was a statement from the Baal Shem Tov: "I know a Jew who hears Torah from Hashem Himself but stands in great fear that he might have a *hirhur ga'ava*, a "hint of arrogance" that could God forbid hurl him down into the deepest klipa (*'nukva d'thom raba'*)." There were *tzadikim* who said that the Besht was referring to himself…

- At any rate, back to the merchant and the Previous Rebbe…the Previous Rebbe answered him, "This event [identifying which items were from a tzadik and which not] was not a *mofet* ("miracle"). In an item that was used by a *tzadik*, there is revealed Godliness. One who experiences revelation of the *neshama* can 'see' the revealed Godliness. (something about a *biur* from R' Shlomo Chaim)…the previous Rebbe's point is that this was not a *mofet*, which is a "Rebbeishe maaseh" (behavior that is appropriate only for a Rebbe). *Hitgalut haneshama* ('revelation of the soul') is appropriate for a chasid, who can certainly experience such levels, and therefore he does not deserve a *mashkanta* for such a story. R' Shlomo Chaim explained according to a general principle found in the early sages: *Kol chush tofes m'chusho* - "every sense or ability grasps its own stimulus." For example, we can touch and lift up a cup. Why can't we touch or lift up intellect though? Because it requires intellect to "get" an intellectual concept. Every sense grasps its own *chush*, but those matters that are outside of its own boundaries, it cannot "grasp," it has no bearing on it. So R' Shlomo Chaim explained that every object used by a tzadik contains *gilui Elokut* – "revealed Godliness." But who is able to grasp this? A "regular" person grasps only the *gashmiyut* ("physical nature") of the article, the physical manifestation. But there is the *ruchniyut* ("spiritual side") as well, which only the intellect can grasp, and who can grasp the revelation of *Elokut* in the item? That, only the *neshama* can grasp. The *neshama* grasps Godliness, and therefore it also grasps the Godliness in the item that was used by a tzaddik. The problem of a "regular" person is that his soul is not "revealed," is not *b'hitgalut*, even though he has the potential. But, when there is *gilui haneshama* it does grasp the Godliness…this is not a *mofet* at all. Neither is it associated with a Rebbe necessarily. (Someone asked, "How is this *chush*, how does it work?" and R' Deitsch answered, "I know there are things that I don't understand. When I was in a Litvish yeshiva I didn't get that, but Chabad successfully inculcated in me that there are things I don't understand." And we have the potential to develop that *chush*, it only depends to what extent we want to develop it).

- Rav Deitsch had a teacher in *cheder* by the name of R' Feivel Aidelman who was a *baal chush*, should have been a Rosh Yeshiva but he taught young men. He used to say, "Everyone wants to know *Shas*, and they want to learn it overnight. The problem is that the very same night, it's good to sleep." The same applies regarding *hitgalut haneshama*; it depends on how much we want it. All that stands in the way is the body. We must refine and do away with the desire for *gashmiyut* (for the "physical world"). There are different levels of abilities and some *neshamot* are more or less revealed than others.

- Story about R' Avraham from Europe who is a *ger tzedek*; groups of secular Israelis from *Beit Beryl* (home of the Labor movement, Mapai) in Tel Aviv somehow met Avraham and they used to come and visit and they wanted to know why he converted. He tried to explain and they didn't understand. Finally, Avraham said to them, "You are educators, you know that some students are attracted to math, others to philosophy, etc?" They answered, "Yes of course." He told them, "I was attracted to *Yahadut*, to Judaism." Like we say, "It's in the genes," meaning that it's part of his individual makeup. Then Rav Deitsch said (about himself) that he learned in a Litivish yeshiva and "found himself" there [he was successful in Ponevitz, eventually learning with the Rosh Yeshiva]. He was "successful," but the entire time, he "looked for Chasidut." R' Shlomo Chaim told him, "You have a *chush* ("talent, sense") for Chasidut, shame to let it go to waste." That is, just like R' Avraham had a *chush* for *Yahadut*, so

> R' Deitsch has a *chush* for *Chasidut*. His *mashpia*, R' Shlomo Chaim told all kinds of stories from R' Hillel..etc...

All this is fine if one has a revealed *neshama* that is drawn to Godly matters, in which case "love like fire" becomes "easier," but if not, what do we do? In that case, the advice is as we learned yesterday: First, meditate on matters that we can understand, utilizing the lower meditation on Godliness within the world, that does not require a revealed *neshama* to grasp. And then, we must ask ourselves, "Am I *karov* ("close") to Godliness? (We can make a real accounting, based on our thoughts speech and action as well as emotions, and if we do so, we will recognize we are not close even to this "entry level" meditation level). Then, with the realization that we are not close even to the "low" level of Godliness upon which we are capable of meditation and grasp, then that gives birth to a love that is "similar to love like flames of fire." At least, this meditation imparts a will for *hitlahavut* ("fiery excitement")... One of the students then asked, "Why doesn't that cause the person to feel hurt and disappointed?" to which R Deitsch answered, "We were supposed to learn that today but the intro has been so long..."

One of the students then asked, "It's one thing if the Rav or my wife nags me to work on something, to make a *cheshbon* inside, but to expect that of myself, every day to make a *cheshbon* on my own, that's not likely." R' Deitsch replied that he is correct, for that we have a verse (Num 21:27), *Al Ken yomru hamoshlim bo'u cheshbon...* "About this, those who speak in parables said, "Come to the city of *Cheshbon*..." The Gemora (Baba Batra 78B) embellishes the meaning of the verse: "R' Shmuel bar Nachman said in the name of R' Yochanan, 'the *moshlim* are those who govern (from the word *moshel*, meaning "governor") over their evil inclination and say to it, "Come let's make a *cheshbon* (accounting)..." [That is, those who are serious about controlling and elevating their evil inclination do not hesitate to take the initiative and make an "accounting" with themselves]. The *Chafetz Chaim* made a verbal *cheshbon hanefesh* ("accounting of the soul") everyday. He was asked, "Why?" They could hear him talking to himself as if someone were right next to him and they are having a conversation, and they wanted to hear what he was saying. Once they got close enough to hear him, they heard that his main internal "accounting" was about *simcha shel mitzvah* ("happiness in fulfillment of mitzvoth"), why wasn't he happy enough while doing a mitzvah?

Once, R' Deitsch sat next to the brother in law of R' Shlomo Zalman (*ztz'l*) at a simcha, and the brother in law remarked on how the Chafetz Chaim wrote and claimed about himself that he never fulfilled a mitzvah the way he should have, and the brother in law wondered how that could be, did the

Chafetz Chaim not follow the *Mishneh Brura* (which he himself wrote)? So R' Deitsch told him about the issue of *simcha shel mitzvah* ("happiness of the mitzvah"), and that it was because he felt he never did the mitzvah with enough *simcha*…

Shiur 56, June 19, 2012 (ongoing review of Ch 4)

Page 26 in the Hebrew text, Page 111 in the translation.

Others (those – most of us – whose souls are not in a state of "revelation"), require meditation on the nature of Godliness in the world, enlivening creation, which leads us to recognition of the preciousness and elevation of Godliness. Then, we must think to ourselves, "how far away am I from this preciousness and elevation?" And then, recognizing our distance, we think to ourselves, "How can I approach and experience this preciousness and elevation?" In each detail of our meditation, we must consider the wonder of *Hashem* in the created object. As a consequence of this recognition, we want to approach Godliness, to get closer. The only place where there is *Elokut netto* – "nothing but Godliness" - is in Torah and mitzvoth. Yet here in the creation, every detail of the object expresses the Godliness that creates and enlivens it. Regarding other fruits, we say, "This is a fruit that contains (is enlivened by) *Elokut*." But, about the *etrog* we say that, "It is *Elokut*." If we exit the meditation at this point, it is after having reached the conclusion that, "It is appropriate to grow closer to this." But if we reach this point and then add consideration of how far away we are from grasping that the etrog is *Elokut*, then that imparts a fiery desire for *Elokut*. It's similar to *hitnagshut* ("conflict") – lots of things are borne of *hitnagshut* ("opposition") of one thing against another. In our case the *hitnagshut* leads to desire for that from which we feel far away and removed, "love like fire." On one hand, we seek the preciousness and elevation, yet on the other hand, we find ourselves performing actions that push it further away. This gives rise to *hitlahavut*, to "excitement," and releases (pent-up) energy. There is one chapter in Tehilim (45) that Rashi explains applies to *talmidei chachamim* who are arguing over Torah matters. It's called *Milchamta de Torah* – "wars of Torah." What emerges from the psalm is that, "There has to be war in the world," the question is "where." If we are involved in the "war of Torah," then our enemies fall before us.

There's a theory that says that "sports" is a substitute for war. The media expands upon it and makes sports into something huge, otherwise who would care about a few men out to "kill each other" or play a game against one another? But by inflating sports into a major topic, it prevents war in the world. Man must fight, the question is just with whom. In *Likutei Torah* (parshat *Eikev* or *Ve'etchanan*, regarding first and second paragraph of the *Kriat Shema*), it seems to imply that if a person does battle with his *yetzer harah*, then he won't have to do battle elsewhere. We find that those who have no battle, come out "wounded." For example, R' Deitsch knows people in S.America who provide servants for their children, and yet each and every child turned out emotionally "wounded" because they didn't know how to deal with the world when they went out of the house.

As a general rule: There is no trait or potential in man, that is found naturally, that is from *gimmel klippot t'meot* (the "three impure 'shells' that conceal Godliness irredeemably). All such natural traits and talents come from *Klipat Noga* (the one level of concealment that is "neutral," and can be transformed and elevated to a state of holiness). That includes anger as well, and the proof is that one can use it for *avodat Hashem*, by getting angry at his *yetzer harah*. The same regarding arrogance. There is a verse, "Lift up his heart in the ways of Hashem" (Chronicles 2, 17:6) that mentions personal pride. As long as anger or pride do not come into expression, they remain *klipat noga*. But if either trait comes into expression, it can come in the wrong way [or the correct way]. "Either you'll fight with your wife or with yourself." The idea is that war and anger are traits we have within and if we suppress them, they will emerge in a destructive manner. In previous generations, if someone would have said, "I'm not a frier" ("I'm not a sucker") they would have received a fist in the face as if that's the lowest thing he could say. Once, someone gave a talk at *sheva brachot* to the effect that one must respect and honor their wife, but "not to be a frier." Someone else arose to speak and said, "You say not to be a frier, but let's see what the Torah says." And he quoted from Eliezer and Rivka when she said, "Not only will I provide water for you but also for your camels." "Super-frier," no? But Rav Deitsch says that according to Torah, our behavior has to be with *chesed*, with kindness. When the world says, "Don't be a frier," that's in accordance with *gevura*, not according to Torah.

Page 112 – The flames of fire of this love destroy all the fire of the animal soul. Via the initial meditation, we develop love and grow closer to Hashem. But when we combine this love with our perceived distance from God, including regret for our past mis-deeds (which separate between ourselves and God), we develop "love like fire." R' Eliyahu Hadad suggested that means we could be a *tzaddik* already because we incinerated our *yetzer harah*? But the Rav responded that this meditation requires work that must recur over and over again, and that there is nothing in the Torah that fails to have an effect on us.

- Story of an *avreich* (young newly married) who came in one day after learning in Collel for fourteen fifteen years and thought to himself to give up because the Torah wasn't having any effect on him. R' Deitsch suggested that he go home and think about things, and whether or not it was true that the Torah had "no effect on him." When he returned the next day he realized what a mistake he had made and how different he is now from what he was many years earlier.

- The holy *Chidushei HaRim* (R' Yitzhak Meir Alter, 1799-1866, founding Rebbe of Chasidut Ger and author of novella on the Torah) said, "What was the lesson from R' Akiva who saw the water dripping on the rock?...The simple *pshat* ("surface meaning") is that if water could have an effect over time on the rock, so certainly Torah could have an effect on him. So what is the deeper meaning, that perhaps the ten thousandth drop is the one that would finally have an effect? Rather, we have to say that the first drop already had an effect, but that R' Akiva at forty years old, probably already went thru a few ups and downs in life, so he realized it would take time. We don't see the progress as it's happening, but in truth the first drop mattered, the second mattered...etc. It works, we just don't see it until the ten thousandth time...in the meantime though, we must just be careful not to fall into depression.

Shiur 57, June 20, 2012 (Review of Ch 4)

Page 27 in the Hebrew text, Page 113 in the English translation,

"Furthermore, the power of the natural element of fire…" In general, "love like fire" leads to the incineration of the animal soul. "Love like Fire" results from a combination of two factors: 1) proper *hitbonenut* on the *yoker* ("preciousness") and *ilui* ("elevation") of Godliness embedded in and enlivening the world, combined with 2) realization that in all kinds of ways we are far from properly recognizing and experiencing that love – together these factors lead to "love like fire."

- R' Shlomo Chaim spoke of *bachurim* (young yeshiva students) who complained about the *ta'avot* ("lusts, temptations") that get in the way of their *avodat Hashem*. *Bachurishe inyanim* ("students' issues"). They complained they had been advised to learn *Reishit Chochma* (a kaballah based *mussar* sefer) but that didn't help. R' Shlomo Chaim told them that the only thing will help them is *davening b'arichut* ("praying at length," with meditation). Here, we see the content of his advice. *Davening b'avoda* ("praying at length with devotion and application") amplifies our "love like fire," which in turn burns and eradicates the fire of the "other side." This leads to the weakening and eventual destruction of the *ta'ava* ("lust").

- Those seeking *eitza* ("advice") will receive it – this is what R' Shlomo Chaim said to Rav Deitsch himself. After taking some *mashkeh* ("liquor," usually vodka), R' Deitsch told R' Shlomo Chaim that he wants to learn how to *daven b'avoda* ("pray at length with devotion"). R' Shlomo Chaim told him, "Come when the *mashkeh* is finished." That's what R' Deitsch did, though it was very difficult for him to approach the *mashpia* (R' Shlomo Chaim) without *mashkeh*. R' Shlomo Chaim told him, "It's very difficult to begin with *machshava* ("thought")," with thought processes. "First, go through a process of *hitkafia* (disciplined withdrawal from physical temptations), weaning yourself away from all physical matters that you don't need" (R' Deitsch thought the instruction was to do that for three weeks). Even the smallest matter of *itkafia* makes a difference, just like if you go to someone and even the slightest word from you, if he thinks it's in order to "put him down," he will be insulted at the slightest hint. But if he doesn't think that is your intention, then it doesn't matter so much. That's the nature of the *sitra achra* ("other side," the side of negativity) as well, you can tell it that you "want to subdue it."

- Two Chassidim would sit and farbreng every Thursday night, two cups of *mashkeh* and they spoke all night. Came the morning, they would pour the *mashkeh* back into the bottle, and they did this week after week. The *mashkeh* need not be drunk, but it must be there [this in reference to a bottle of Johnny Walker Black that someone just placed on the table in front of R' Deitsch].

Until this point, the *K'Avoda* told us that "love like fire" destroys and incinerates the fire of the animal soul, of the "other side." Now (bottom of page 113 in the translation), it tells us more, that "love like fire" elevates the natural element of fire that is in our soul. And that elevation is the advantage of "love like fire" over *teshuva*. For at first glance, if the motivating factor is our perceived distance from God, and that is what triggers "love like fire," then how is it different from *teshuva*? (Page 114) – During *teshuva*, we "break" the power of the animal soul and its *ta'avot* but we don't elevate it. But during "love like fire," we also elevate the elemental desire of the animal soul. Even though there is a tinge (and more than a tinge) of *merrirut* ("bitterness") over our situation and our distance, nevertheless the *ikar* is the elevation that occurs. When the *merirut* over our distance is combined with love, the result is "love like fire" that elevates the fire of the animal soul. The animal soul then uses its natural fire for *kedusha*. This is also how *korbanot* ("sacrifices") work: We offer up the *chelev* ("fat," corresponding to physical enjoyment) and *dam* ("blood," which houses the *aish*, or "fire" within us). Our experience with "love like fire" enables us to derive "enjoyment" from matters of *Elokut*.

Shiur 58, June 21, 2012 (Ongoing review of Ch 4)

Page 27 in the Hebrew text, Page 116 in the English translation;

"The sacrifice of hot blood…" Generally speaking, "love like fire" elevates the animal soul. But getting down more into details, there is the offering of the *chelev* ("fat"), also associated with "love like water" [as in Ch 1 of Tanya which states that water is the source of all physical pleasures, and *chelev* is also symbolic of pleasure], which weakens the animal soul and prepares it for elevation. And the offering of the blood is associated with "love like fire" in which the element of fire in the soul is elevated. The emphasis is more on the offering of the "fat," representing enjoyment and "love like water". When we sacrifice this element of enjoyment, it removes the enjoyment that we experience in physical matters (*inyanei hachumriyut*). But this does not occur spontaneously, it demands a special effort to bring *sechel* down to an intellectual level that the animal soul can also recognize. The animal soul has to devote itself to this effort, and be involved.

Now on page 117, "But on its own without effort…" "Love like water" is associated with the Godly soul, it does not automatically have influence on the animal soul. Enjoyment of Godliness requires special effort for the animal soul to understand. This demonstrates that if the love does not have a direct effect on the animal soul, then it is not associated with the natural animal soul at all. That's the meaning of "offering the animal;" it means that effort is needed in order to get the animal soul involved. This is not true of "love like fire" – as soon as we experience "love like fire," it eliminates and incinerates the fire of the animal soul, automatically. Just like fire in general, it does not require any special action or effort for it to burn something; the innate nature of fire is to burn, as long as the item is combustible, such as the animal soul.

One of the students then asked, "So is 'love like fire' without *hitbonenut*, without meditation?" To which the Rav answered, "All of this is with meditation, with *hitbonenut*…without *hitbonenut*, nothing happens." It's just that the true meditation to bring about "love like fire" is meditation upon *Gadlut Hashem* itself, on *romemut*…and few of us are on a level to perform this meditation. So, *K'Avoda* recommends meditation on Godliness IN the world (and within us, etc), *memalle kol olamim*, in combination with contemplation of our distance from Him…

- It's like regarding a *tzadik*, we sometimes want to speak of his own *tzidkut*, his own special qualities of piety or knowledge. At other times though, we want to speak of the effect and influence that he has on others, on his own "Chasidim." It's one thing to get excited about the *tzadik* himself, about his level, matters from which we are far. It's something else to consider how he goes out and helps others, activities that attract us. *Aish* ("fire") acts from distance, while water is about attraction, desire to be close, it feels good to us.

Shiur 59, June 22, 2012 (ongoing review of Ch 4)

We learned that although love like fire automatically "burns" the animal soul and its lusts, "love like water" only "weakens" the animal soul. It requires additional special effort to influence and have an effect on the animal soul; it is not influenced "automatically" by "love like water." We mentioned already that there are two paths to 'love like fire': 1) For those on *madreigot gavohot*, "higher spiritual levels" who can meditate directly on *Gadlut Hashem*, it is possible to meditate directly on the infinite light of God [*kulo kamei*…] in order to attain 'love like fire' 2) Those on a lower, more simple level (*madreigot pashutot*) require meditation on a combination of Godliness in the world leading to "love like water", together with consideration of our distance from Him.

Now, we want to understand why 'love like fire' has this power to incinerate the lusts of the animal soul…Page 28 in the Hebrew, 117 in the translation: "Now, when love is combined with meditation upon our distance from Him, it becomes apparent how it has an effect on the animal soul." But think about it, why does it "become apparent"? What is easily understood about this process? "If we combine the element of 'distance,' it certainly influences the animal soul." Why? The answer is because it's the animal soul that creates the distance…it's the animal soul that creates all the problems…so when it recognizes that it is causing the distance, the result is that it struggles to overcome the distance! [

- In politics there are coalitions…here a totally unique coalition is formed, between man (the meditator) and animal. The difference is that in a political coalition, each party is concerned about itself. In this coalition, the Godly soul has a *shlichut*, a "mission." Its task to have an effect on the animal soul. Therefore, it has to deal with the animal soul in an entirely different manner. It won't "work" for the Godly soul to merely "scream and yell" at the animal soul, it must "work with" it.

Still on page 117 near the bottom…"And so it is when the true 'love like fire'… then as well, it is understood how "fire consumes fire." Why? Here [regarding one who is on a high enough spiritual level to meditate directly on *romemut HaShem* – on God's infinite light], it is not the distance from Hashem that "dawns" on the animal soul and makes it understood that it is the cause of the distance. Here, that cannot be the case, because here the animal soul is not far (subjectively); in fact, the animal soul has been uplifted and its relationship to Godliness is characterized by *romemut*, "elevation," rather than distance. Instead, the meditation works to ignite 'love like fire' because both the Godly soul and the animal soul come from the element of "fire," and "fire consumes fire." [Perhaps this may be explained by the simple illustration of a spark near a camp fire. When the spark is close enough to the larger fire, it "jumps in" and is subsumed by the larger fire. Thus, "fire consumes fire." The same may apply to the fire of the animal soul, that is already uplifted and "ready" for Godliness…when the fire of the Godly soul is ignited, it simply overwhelms and subsumes the fire of the animal soul as well].

Even so, even in this love resulting from meditation on *romemut Hashem* (page 117-118), there is a "hidden tinge of bitterness." This is because, as much as the meditator desires to "ascend," he is reminded that he is unable to do so…and who prevents him? It is still the animal soul, and from this he has sorrow. So, even when meditating directly upon *madreigot g'vohot* ("high spiritual levels") that lead directly to "love like fire," he also experiences bitterness over his distance. If so, then what is the difference between the two paths (both of which lead to "love like fire"), one meditating directly on *Gadlut Hashem* and the other meditating on "love like water" but combining it with "distance"?

Page 118 – The difference is in the order: When focused on *madreigot gavohot*, the "love like fire" arrives first, and only later does the feeling of distance arrive. But regarding *madreigot namuchot* (the "lower levels" associated with "love like water") - the lower meditation - the two experiences arrive together. As soon as his animal soul confronts its distance from God, the meditator experiences "love like fire" (following the introduction of "love like water"). [For him], there is no "love like fire" without a combination of "love like water" and distance together. Ultimately then, there are some high *neshamot* who can go straight to "love like fire" and only later does the emotion of distance come into play. But most others (*madreigot namuchot*), require recognition of their distance before they can experience "love like fire." The love doesn't even begin until there is recognition of distance.

Shiur 60, June 24, 2012 (Ongoing review of Ch 4)

Intro to *K'Avoda*, which is about *tefila*…unlike those who think that *tefila* is mainly about *bakashot* ("requests"), *tefila* is about *hacara*, "recognition" of *HaKadosh Baruch Hu* - this is the main point of *tefila*. *Hacara* has to come to expression through meditation, and in feeling (emotion). So, *K'Avoda* teaches several different paths of meditation leading to *hacara* of *Hashem* – that is the main goal.

- Rav Deitsch learned from, spoke with and sat near R' Hatzkel Levinstein (a Litvish Rav and *mashgiach ruchani*, in Shanghai, and later in yeshivat Mir in Jerusalem and Yeshivat Ponevitz in Bnei Brak, d. 1974) during *tefila* so he saw how he davened. And R' Deitsch testifies that the prayer that R' Hatzkel Levinstein said with the most excitement, was *Shir Hayichud* that he would say on Yom Kippur night. He would pound on the table as he sang this song. There were rabbis who said that R' Hatzkel Levinstein actually veered off the path of *mussar*. Generally, *shiurim* in *mussar* speak of improving the *midot*, but Rav Hatzkel spoke of the *shefa* ("abundance, influence") of Hashem. Those most attached to him were, in fact Chasidim (R' Deitsch was one of a group of Chasidim who were attached to him, as opposed to the mussar advocates, who were not as attached). R' Chatzkel spoke mostly about *emunah* and about Hashem, in fact the entire *Shir Hayichud* of *Y"K* is about *Hashem*, not about *midot*. It is obvious that he was exceptional among the *mussar* rabonim. He prayed with a lot of *hitlahavut* ("excitement") and once he gave R' Deitsch *mussar* – "Why don't you pray in yeshiva, why in the *shteiblach*?" Rav Deitsch replied that in the *shteiblach* they pray faster, so he said to R' Deitsch, "But you're a Chasid, you have to pray, what is this about "praying fast"?

So, here in *K'Avoda*, we have discussion of what do we have to meditate upon and think about during *tefila*, and what is the purpose of *tefila*. Here at the end of *Perek dalet* (fourth chapter), we have a summary of all that was said until now. Page 28, Page 119 in the translation – "Thus, the main focus of our effort in the "service of the heart," which is prayer, should be to approach and unite our soul with Godliness through meditation on the Godly light enclothed in the worlds." *Tefila* is from the word *tofel*, meaning to "join things together," to cleave our soul to *Elokut*, to Godliness. Whether Godliness in the higher worlds, or whether in each and every creation in particular…this meditation itself is enough to enable us to focus on and experience the preciousness and closeness of Godliness, to feel good about it and appreciate that proximity to God is a precious matter.

- Already mentioned last week, why are people interested in money? Because it is the *shoresh* and root of things, with money you can do this, you can do that… plus we naturally want to be closer to wealthy people, why? Because they have money. But what's the big deal, you can't eat money, can't consume it…but since it is the root of many things, we value it. If we would understand that Godliness is the source and foundation of everything, then it would be valuable and precious to us.

- In response to a question, R' Deitsch answered, 'What does it mean to love"? First of all it means to desire to be close to that person or object…if you would be invited somewhere that could provide you with everything, except for electricity, would you agree to go? No, of course not, because electricity is everything, how can man exist without electricity? That you don't want to detach from it, indicates that you love it, it's called "love." Aside from that, feelings of love are only for something that is alive. "Love" for an inanimate object is very different than love for another person. From another person or something that is alive, you want "feedback." If Reuven likes Shimon but Shimon doesn't respond, this is the greatest distance. Of course though if you love food, you don't expect response from the food. So, it's two different kinds of love.

- There's a poem from the ibn Ezra, *tzama nafshi*, the entire poem repeats itself around the word *chai* ("alive")…some say it on Shabbat, and it is a different kind of love. If your friend comes in and you don't give him any recognition because you're eating, this is the biggest disgrace you can do to him [it is the opposite of *chai*, of "life"]. This *hitbonenut* on something "alive," something *chai*, is the kind of *hitbonenut* that we can adapt to *tefila*.

- In the future, "all precious things will be as common as the dust of the earth" (Rambam, *Hilchot Melachim*) but if so, what is the preciousness of it? If it will be so common that it no longer has any value, so what's the point? In the sefer *Beis Aharon* of Chasidei Karlin, is a principle: "Every love that exists today is based on deficiency." That is, if you love the daytime, it is in relation to night that you don't like, if you love your food it's because previously you were hungry...there's no "love" that is intrinsic. But in the future, the enjoyment that we receive will be entirely based on intrinsic value, not on some kind of deficiency. Now, from where does the entire concept of jealousy come? You have a nice car but the other guy has a nicer car? So obviously your entire "love" for your car is not based on a positive concept but on a negative concept. But in the future it will not be that way, we will be happy with what we have for its intrinsic value.

Shiur 61, June 25, 2012 (Ongoing review of Ch 4)

Here on page 119 (in the translation) is a *sicum* and summary of the entire chapter. The *hitbonenut* on Godliness in the world and in every creation of the world is sufficient to bring us to awareness of the preciousness and elevation of Godliness. Additionally, we must consider that the *Elokut* within each creation is the *ikar* ("main component") of the creation. Superficially, it may appear to us *b'chitzoniut* ("externally") that the form, taste and color etc are the most important aspects of creation, but in reality, the Godliness embedded within creation is the true reality. In any case, our *hitbonenut* has to take a form that leads us to recognize the preciousness and elevation of Godliness.

- The Rav told a story about a family that he tried to help out financially from time to time. All of a sudden, the family received a large electricity bill. Until then, the bill had only been estimated but now it was measured truly with a meter...and then it turned out that the one who had come in to take the reading quietly paid it for them, asked for nothing and told nobody, just paid it. So *Hakadosh Baruch Hu* looks out for us as well, quietly without asking for anything... and when we discover that He is behind it, we respond with more gratitude and love for Him.

K'Avoda continues and tells us of the additional meditation of, "Choose good and life, not evil and death..." (Deut 30:19) and then on *olamot elyonot* ("higher worlds"), which are also higher *madreigot* ("spiritual levels"), about which R' Chaim Vital writes in his introduction to *Eitz Chaim* (of the Ari z'l) that all of it is "for the purpose of adding to our *ahavat Hashem*, our love of God."

R' Yosef Halbfinger (*A"H*) asked, "It is known that many foods are not so good for us, is it simply a matter of free choice not to eat them?" The Rav answered that is certainly the case, we have free choice and Rambam says not only in *Shemonah Perakim* but also in the *Mishneh Torah*, that man should choose to eat healthy foods in order to serve Hashem well, because otherwise it is just a *ta'ava*, a "lust" to eat healthy foods.

- Statistics shows that many *ba'alei teshuva*, before becoming religious, practiced some form of healthy eating. This meant that 1) they were thinking not only about the present but about the future. When thinking of the future, we are more likely to recognize the truth, and ultimately to recognize the truth of Torah and Judaism. And 2) The fact that they were prepared to sacrifice, to be overlook a specific kind of food in order to eat better food, indicates commitment to a higher ideal. This also paves the path for a Torah lifestyle. It's true without question that what we eat makes the difference between good health and not good health for many people. This may not be true of all people; in general there is a difference between younger and older people. Younger get over things, older not so easily.

All of this greatly weakens the animal soul; yet does not destroy it (that occurs only during "love like fire"). We are no longer attracted by physical matters, nor do we lend them any importance. After the animal soul is weakened somewhat, the road is paved for it to accept and receive Godliness (for example, the story the Rav told of the Israeli driver in the US who said, "What do you want from me, I came here for the green" – meaning the US Dollars – this is a story about one who wasn't yet ready to hear about *Hashem*). The result, after the *chalishut* ("weakness") of the animal soul, is that the person then becomes stronger in Torah and mitzvoth. After we find Godliness in creation, we begin to seek Godliness itself; this is found in Torah and mitzvoth. (Here the Rav remarked that in *K'Avoda*, "every few lines is a complete topic")…

Shiur 62, June 26, 2012 (Ongoing review of Ch 4)

We are still in the midst of the *sicum* of Ch 4…after achieving "love like water" via *hitbonenut* on Godliness in the world, we may further increase our love for God by considering that He is also, "My *chayut* ("vitality") and the energy that enlivens me." *Nafshi aviticha balaila*. And we now seek *gilui Elokut* ("Godly revelation") in our *nefesh*, as it says in Zohar that this is the love that motivates man to get up in the middle of the night and learn Torah.

- Story of the *Chozeh* ("Seer") of Lublin, he was a *chozeh*, he could "see." He was once receiving people and stopped in the middle, learned a chapter of Mishna and then went back to receiving people. He said that he needed to "renew his ability to 'see," and then he went back to receiving people. The truth is that this is *gilui Elokut*, this revelation of Godliness, the fact that we don't see it is a *rachmanut* ("pity") on us, as the Alter Rebbe says "even tho I'm like a *behama* ("animal") when I'm like You and I don't see You, nevertheless I'm always with You."

- R' Shlomo Chaim told a story: The Tzemach Tzedek (before he was Rebbe), during the period of the Mittler Rebbe, would answer questions, deliver *piskei dinim* ("halachic decisions"). People would send in questions to the Mitteler Rebbe, who would pass them on to his *edim* ("son in law," the Tzemach Zedek) to answer, from which we have the *Teshuvot Tzemach Tzedek*. There was one question that was difficult for the Tzemach Tzedek to answer and he came to the Mittler Rebbe to complain about it. The MIttler Rebbe took down a *sefer*, and told him, "I'll tell you the *maskana* ("conclusion," or *psak din*) and then it will be easier for you to arrive to the *maskana*." And so he did. Later, the Tzemach Tzedek came into the Mittler Rebbe's room when the MIttler Rebbe wasn't there, and saw that the *sefer* the Mitteler Rebbe had chosen was a book of Kaballah. That is, from the book of Kaballah, the MIttler Rebbe knew the *psak* ("halachic conclusion"). But, how to arrive at the *psak* via *nigleh* (the "revealed," legal dimension of the Torah), he left to the Tzemach Tzedek. This is called *gilui Elokut* ("revelation of Godliness")…he saw the *psak* as what it was in the higher spiritual realms (according to Kaballah), and he left it up to the Tzemach Tzedek to arrive at the appropriate conclusion according to the revealed sections of the Torah. So, what is preferable, to know the *pnimiyut* (Kaballah) and from there to reason our way to what must be the *hitzoniyut* (the *halacha*)? Or is it the opposite, to know the *hitzoniyut* and from there to arrive to the *pnimiyut*? For example, is it better to be the guy who programs the computer (*pnimiyut*), or the technician who inputs the data and allows the computer program to crunch the numbers (*chitzoniyut*)? If computer technician had known from the "inside" what's going on, perhaps he could have saved himself the busy work of inputting the data [that is, if the technician had known ahead of time how the data was to be handled, perhaps it would not have been necessary to input it to the computer]. Let us suppose that the technician met the programmer and described to him what's going on from his point of view, would the programmer just laugh? Some say that's the difference between today's doctors, and the doctors of the past. Today's doctors look at the results of tests and they know from the results what the status of the patient is. They fail to get down to the root of the problem. Whereas the doctors of the past used the basis and root of the illness in order to understand that patient's health (or lack thereof). The same occurs *b'ruchniyut* ("spiritually"), people ask questions of rabbis, and the rabbis try to answer according to the information that they have at hand, but once upon a time the rabbis knew better how to get to the bottom of matters. With the *ohr* ("illumination") and *gilui Elokut* of Torah, they could give much better answers.

The *sicum* adds another level of "love like water": The love of a son who wants to do well for his father. And then, "There must be love like fire because it strongly reveals the light of the soul, and it is the "main expression of the desire of the divine soul for *Elokut*."

*Here the Rav read from the Rebbe Maharash, from the series of discourses entitled *Mayim Rabim 5636/1876*, Ch. 28 regarding the necessity of *hitbonenut* in *pratiyut*... [This was intended as continuation of the Rav's morning shiur in Tanya/*Sha'ar Hayichud* regarding *otiot* – "letters" – but is also appropriate for this section of *K'Avoda*, because the more we are *mitbonen* on details, the more illumination shines in the words of *tefila*...but an hour or two of *hitbonenut* is necessary]: "Since every letter of the twenty-two letters represents a specific descent of divine vitality and influx that is distinct and separate from every other letter, therefore each letter possesses its own unique form. The shape of each written letter therefore also has its own particular form in writing that indicates the nature of the descent of Godliness that is associated with that letter. The shape of the letter reveals how the Godly influx is drawn down through that letter, from His holy attributes, His will and His wisdom, all of which exist in total unity with Him, as explained above at length. And when we delve into this topic in depth, with great focus for an hour or two, a true impression of His unity and expansiveness becomes engraved upon our mind and heart. It becomes clear that in the heavens and on the earth, there is none other than He, even in space. [This meditation] is associated with the letter *hey* of His name (*Havaya*) and within the soul of man, it corresponds to meditation on the infinite light of God and His unity. It is especially associated with recital of the *shema*, including the two blessings that precede the *kriat shema* which refer to this topic. In each and every word of these prayers, we should feel the Godly illumination and vitality that is present, and in this manner we will be vitalized with a spiritual energy while experiencing the infinite light that enlivens us and creates us. And in this manner we will merit to become included in the infinite light above, which is the source of all life."

Shiur 63, June 27, 2012 (Ch 5)

New topic: We'll see that within *ahava* ("love") there is also *ratzon* ("will"). Associated with every category of divine love, there is also *ratzon* and *ta'anug*, "will and delight." Although most people put more emphasis on the "delight" within love, there is also a lot of "will" (*ratzon*) within love.

Page 29 in the Hebrew text, Page 123 in the English translation.

Just as the word *ahava* ("love") contains *avah* ("will"), so the *pnimiyut* ("internal core") of the *midot* ("emotions") is associated with *ratzon,* or "will." From where does our will originate? The intellect has the power to arouse the will. We know this because the will has the power to govern over and even change the nature of our *midot* ("emotions"). For example, a person might like a certain food, but if the wrong person gave it to him, he won't be interested. Or he might sit and enjoy a certain restaurant until he goes into the kitchen and sees how they prepare the food. So he still likes the food but he no longer has any will to eat it. Who removed his will? It was his *sechel* – utilizing his intellect, he realized that the food is 'dirty,' so he no longer wants to eat it. The *sechel* though must always work against someone or something (in this case, against our desire to taste the food) and it is not always successful. If a person wants to stop smoking, he needs to bring his *sechel* onboard, because otherwise he won't succeed. There are always *shinuim* ("variations"), and therefore the intellect as well goes through changes. This is true of the field of medicines, for example; one day aspirin is "okay," then tylenol is okay, but not aspirin, then back to aspirin, and similarly, since there are changes in *sechel*, there are also changes in our will. So, here we're speaking of the kind of will that results from *sechel,* intellect. This *sechel* is *sholet* ("controlling"), it controls the *midot*. The proof is that the Torah commands us not to be afraid before going out to battle – this is proof that man has control over all of his *midot*. (There is no doubt that if man conducts himself according to *sechel*, he will achieve a state of *kedusha*, a state of holiness. See the book, *Chovot Halevavot* ("Duties of the Heart") regarding *nefesh* vs *sechel* (*regesh* vs *sechel*). The "catch" though, is that without *kedusha,* what is the end point? Without the intellect, the endpoint is merely to "enjoy"…whereas in *kedusha* the endpoint is truth. This is *ratzon* acc to logic; *tiferet d'aima naaseh keter d'z'a* – "the heart of intellect becomes the crown of emotions." But there is *ratzon* that is beyond logic as well…

R' Eliyahu Hadad asked, "All of the *dargot* in *ahavat Hashem* and all that we have discussed is still based on matters that are beyond logic, beyond understanding…" To which R' Deitsch answered, "Yes, that is true but He (God) was *mitzamtzem*, He "contracted" His infinite holy light in order to bring it down to our level. He, so to speak "contracted His illumination into a small ray of a ray" in order to enable our feeble intellect to grasp something Godly…because ultimately the goal is to elevate our *sechel* as well. If we don't "give something" to the intellect to enable it to grasp Godliness, then the intellect will remain opposed, or at least won't be "for" *Elokut*. The goal is for every part of creation is to ascend, to elevate. Where do we see this? In the prayer *Nishmat*, in the siddur for Shabbat. First, the *nusach* tells us how we cannot understand, and then it goes on to say, "Therefore, the limbs with which You created us praise, and sing…" But wait, the same prayer just said it's "impossible" to grasp and understand Him, so how can we praise Him?

- Once there was a plumber in the Rebbe's house…his kids were *yeshiva bochurim* (students in yeshiva). They requested him to ask the Rebbe the question above ("How can we grasp God if He is infinite and beyond understanding"). The Rebbe replied, "It's true, I cannot grasp, understand, follow Hashem – but the limbs that He gave me, the *sechel* that He gave me, the breath that He put into me – they can grasp and praise, etc…" Rav Deitsch adds that you see the word *Ki* in the answers, "Because every part of me, because every limb…" in order to tell us that each limb and each breath and every part of us was created with its specific purpose, "in order" to praise and exalt Him, that's why the *nusach* of the following prayer, *Yishtabach* says *Ki* ("because") for each limb. I.e. There is a saying of the sages that says, "Why was a mouth created?" In order to praise Him. The same is true of *sechel*…it was created in order to understand Him, even if ultimately it can not do so. See also Tanya (one of the early chapters, Ch 5 regarding the connection between intellect and Torah). Even if we consider the *Chumash*, does a five year old truly understand? And do we comprehend? We comprehend nothing, He gave it to us so that our heads would be busy with *Chumash*, that's all. And so the entire Torah was given so that each of our limbs could come to their full *tachlis* or "purpose." As the Berdichever Rav said about Tanya, "How did the Alter Rebbe fit such a big God into such a small *sefer*."

Shiur 64, June 28, 2012, Ch 5

Page 124 in the translation – in the Alter Rebbe's Chasidut, it is understood that there is a *ratzon* that is beyond logic and reason, and it is the *ratzon tivi* – "natural will" of every Jew. This chapter (5) in *K' Avoda* will go into this level of *ratzon* at length. The basis for this is in Tanya, where it describes how every Jew possesses "hidden love" - *ahava mesuteret*. *Likutei Torah* of the Alter Rebbe goes more into *arichut*, and explains at length how within this hidden love are the two soul levels of *chaya* and *yechida*…and here (in *K'Avoda*), the Rashab goes even more into detail. At the end, he uses this concept to explain why what happens to us during *R"H* and *Y"K* does not always continue into the year, or at least not through the entire year. This *ratzon hapnimi*, "inner will," is also called *makifim*, "transcendant love." We must employ *ratzon al pi sechel* – "will based on intellect" - all year long, for if not, the higher *makifim* of *R"H* and *Y"K* will not remain with us. We need to know how to approach, grasp and utilize each and every *et ratzon* ("auspicious time" such as a Jewish festival) for our *avoda*. This is similar to a doctor, who needs to know first and foremost the nature of the human body and how it functions normally in a healthy manner, and only afterward can he answer questions about sicknesses and malfunctions.

Within *makifim,* are two *madreigot*: *Chaya* and *Yechida*. While the three lower levels of the soul, the *nefesh, ruach* and *neshama* (*NRN*) are *pnimim* ("enclothed in the body"), *chaya* and *yechida* (*CHAY*) transcend the body, which is why they are *makifim*. The definition ("category") of *yechida* is that it "exists" without any reason and requires no arousal whatsoever. No *hitbonenut* is needed whatsoever to "trigger" the *yechida*, since it is from the very essence of the soul. Therefore, it is always united with the *ohr eyn sof* ("infinite light")…which is what comes into revelation *b'msirat nefesh al Kiddush Hashem* (during "self sacrifice for the sake of God"). Because the *yechida* cannot be disconnected from its source, it has no option to express itself other than as a manifestation of the essence of the soul. (From Tanya, we understand that a Jew is willing to sacrifice his life for the honor of God in "most" instances that demand it. There are individuals for whom this won't be true, they won't give up their lives, but this principle of revelation of the *yechida* when under existential threat, describes the majority of Jews). For example, there are some people with confused heads – about them do we want to say that they adequately represent logic and reason? Of course not. The same applies here. The *Anusim* ("forcibly converted") in Spain, for example reasoned that, "We can be like the Xtians outwardly but live like Jews inwardly." Who fell for this *pitui* ("seduction")? For the most part, it was the wealthy and educated Spanish Jews. This we know from a *sefer* written by somebody with the name, Chasid Yaavetz, who lived slightly before the Beit Yoseph (that is, in the mid 1500's), who was himself from *m'gurshei Sfarad* ("those who were expelled from Spain" - the Beit Yoseph – R' Yoseph Karo - was from a family that was expelled from Spain in 1492). The *B'nei Yissaschar* wrote a commentary on the *sefer,* called *Mayan Ganim*, or perhaps the *sefer* itself was called that. R' Deitsch saw it by his father. He writes there that the Jews who stood up to the *gezera* ("decree") were the "simple" Jews whose connection to Judaism was not via philosophy, while the ones who fell to temptation were the ones with "philosophy" – as written in Chasidut that *ta'am v'daat* ("logic and knowledge") is a *hester* ("concealment"), hiding whatever is above *ta'am vda'at*. But the *anusim* who were later caught by the Inquisition [the Inquisition was not interested in Jews who refused to convert, but in those who "converted" outwardly while attempting to maintain a Jewish life inwardly] suffered greatly but many stood up to the Inquisition. *Teshuvat Rivash* (very beginning of *aharonim*) issued a halachic ruling that those who escaped the inquisition later had to do *tevila* – mikveh immersion' - like a *ger*, or "proselyte" to Judaism.). Tanya expresses this concept in general while here in *K' Avoda*, the Rebbe Rashab goes more into detail, regarding the *chaya* and the *yechida* of the soul…Tanya so to speak is the "written Torah" and this (*K' Avoda*) greater *arichut* is the "oral Torah."

Shiur 65, June 29, 2012 (Ch 5)

Two *makifim*: One of the *yechida*, which is part of the makeup of every Jew, becomes revealed in situation of *mesirat nefesh* ("utter devotion and dedication" to God for His sake). In the Maharal of Prage we find a *pshat* ("interpretation") of the Gemora in which Hashem says to Avraham (in the future), "You're sons sinned." Avraham answers Him, "Erase their sins for Your own Honor." God says the same thing to Yaakov, who answers Him in the same vein. He then went to Yitzhak, and said, "Your sons sinned," whereupon Yitzhak replied, "My sons and not Yours? At *Matan Torah* (the giving of the Torah), You said, *Bni, b'chori Yisrael, banim atem l'Hashem Elokecha*: "My son, the firstborn of the Jews, you are sons of the Lord your God." How much could they have sinned? Prior to age 20 doesn't count, that leaves only 50 years. Of that fifty, for 25 years it was nighttime and they were sleeping, so no sins. Of that 25, half the time they are praying, eating and taking care of their needs. All that is left is 12.5 years…half on me and half on You…and if You don't want to take this half, I offered myself up before You, and I am willing to take all their sins on me."

The question here is; what did Yitzhak achieve in the end? Only because Yitzhak had *mesirat nefesh* was he able to take anything on himself…but why did Hashem go to Yitzhak at all? Yitzhak is *din*, "judgment," so if God sought amelioration for his "children," the Jews, why did he ask Yitzhak? The Maharal (*Netzach Yisrael* Ch 12 or 13) says that among the forefathers, only Yitzhak could get to the bottom of *Omek Hadin* – the "depth of judgment." It's *Omek Hadin* that brings out the deep truth that, "They are also Your children" – for how could they be mine and not Yours? It is Yitzhak who reveals the depth of the Jew on which the sin is not *tofes makom* (has no effect, does not touch them). Yitzhak is ready to take the sins of all the Jews on himself, just as he did by the *akeida*.

This concept is also the Chasidic concept of *Y"K*, that reveals the depth of the connection between Hashem and the Jews and vice versa, in which there is no room whatsoever for transgressions. That's what Yitzhak revealed…one of the students of the *Baal Shem Tov* said, "A small *tzaddik* can love a small sinner, a big *tzaddik* can love even a big sinner," since he can see the depth of the good in him. The Belzer Rav of our days, was not ready *b'shum ofen* ("in any way, shape or matter") to hear anything negative about another Jew.

- An older Chasidishe *bachur* who worked in diamonds wanted to move to Netanya, where the wages were better. His father did not agree since Netanya was a secular city, and since they disagreed they went to the Belzer Rav to help them decide. The father explained to the Belzer Rav, "Since there are *freier Yidden* there" – there are secular Jews living there – for that reason he did not want his son to move there. No sooner did he say the words "secular Jews" than the Belzer Rav told to wash his hands three times and say *chalila v'chas, chalila v'chas*…("God forbid, God forbid…"), three times. After he washed his hands and did *teshuva*, the Belzer Rav said to him, "We're all Jews, but some of us are *batlanim*." "We're all Jews but some of us are a bit lazy…" [meaning, there are a few Jews who are too "lazy" to fulfill Torah and mitzvoth]. The big *tzaddikim* such as the Belzer Rav are like Yitzhak, in that it requires a "big" tzaddik to see the *omek* of every Jew.

Page 127 discusses *tmimut b'maaseh* (straightforward honest approach in action), about which the MIttler Rebbe asks, "From where does this trait come? From the *yechida sh'bnefesh*."

- Someone went to the Tzemach Tzedek and complained that he is facing a "test" (*nisayon*) that he is afraid he cannot stand up to. The Tzemach Tzedek told him, "You are a Jew, and you have the talent and ability to withstand this test." He said this three times and that gave the person the power to stand up to the test.

Shiur 66, July 1, 2012 (Ch 5)

It is not only tests of *mesirat nefesh* on *Kiddush Hashem* that bring out the *yechida* of the soul. It is also the simple conduct of a Jew, termed *tmimut b'maaseh* ("straightforward integrity in action") that expresses the *yechida sh'bnefesh*, each Jew in his or her own way. This we see from *Derech Chaim* of the Mittler Rebbe. There are no two ways in this conduct; *tmimut b'maaseh* is the approach of one who has decided on a path and undertaken that path and once having set on the path, he does not ask questions or deviate.

The second level of *makifim* is the *chaya* of the soul (Page 30 in the Hebrew text, Page 128 in the translation): "The second transcendant level of the soul…" is also from the essence of the soul, but not *mamash* the essence. The *chaya* is triggered via *hitbonenut* on *atzmut ohr eyn sof* – the "essential infinite light" – this is the path to arouse something that is beyond logic and reason. *Hitbonenut* on the *hafla'ah*, the "wondrous nature" of *bli g'vul* ("unlimited"). When such love becomes revealed, it is *bli gvul* and out of range of the meditation that we utilized in order to reveal it. This is because in truth, the meditation and the unlimited love uncovered by the meditation are not dependent upon one another. The meditation is only a "catalyst" that triggers the reaction. The meditation is not within range of the love that it reveals. Even so, the love is without limit, "love not dependent upon anything," such as the love between two good friends or parents and children…such love can become concealed for a period of time, but never disappears, always ready to come forward and "light up" again.

It happens that sometimes two people are out of contact with one another for a long time, and then someone gets involved and tries to bring them back together again. It wouldn't be a good situation if that person in the middle would have to be there all the time in order to keep them together. But if there is a true love between the two people, then it "catches on" between them and the intermediary does not need to be present, except on the odd occasion.

- The love that a person has for himself is a form of *ahavah atzmit*, "essential love." Even one who is ready to commit suicide falls into this category. R' Deitsch says he heard that the reason one commits suicide is because he so loves himself that he cannot accept how bad things have gotten for him, how difficult. And some have illusions that after suicide, "things will be better" for them (this we know because they often leave a letter behind). So even though it appears the opposite, even this situation can be one of essential love.

Shiur 67 July 12, 2012

Page 31 in the Hebrew text, Page 131 in the translation.

Love that is "dependent on something" is love based upon logic and intellect.

Shiurim on K'Avoda from the Mashpia R' Deitsch שיח׳

The entire basis and foundation of this love is built on grasp and understanding of Godliness. Why does the meditator love Godliness? Because he meditates on it and therefore achieves love of God. The "essential love" discussed above (regarding the "second level of *makifim*") does not come into illumination on this level – it is of course present, but it is not conscious within this level of love according to logic and intellect, which is "dependent on something." The "logical" love is associated with emotions of the heart, and is limited by the amount of meditation and the style of meditation, and it "disappears" when the understanding itself disappears. Yet, the "love that is dependent on something" (on reason and logic), is a *keli* or "vessel" for the inner essential love…(although there are things that man does as preparation, that ultimately get no further than preparation…)

- Story of the Dubnover Maggid who once spent Shabbat with the Maggid of Mezritch. The Maggid of Mezritch requested him to say words of Torah at all three meals, which he did. The Magid of Dubnow was known for his preaching in a style of creating *mashalim*, "parables" to explain matters, but not for his depth. One of the students of the Mezritcher Maggid said to him in jest, "From the time the Dubnover Maggid arrived, we haven't heard any words of Torah on Shabbat" (they were peeved that the Mezritcher said nothing, allowing the Dubnover to speak the entire Shabbat). The Mezritcher understood and replied, "When you arrive at the palace of the King, there are beautiful articles, and as you enter further and further you see more and more beautiful objects. But, your desire must be to enter into the room of King himself, not merely into the external rooms, as nice as they are. (R' Deitsch once saw the palace of Napoleon in France, said it was grandiose and beautiful…*malchut*). The Dubnover Magid described the appearance of the outer external room, and I (the Magid of Mezritch) wanted to bring him into the inner rooms, so I waited until the Dubnover would request me (the Mezritcher Maggid) to say words of Torah, and then I would have brought him in. But he never requested…*pirush hadavar* ("the explanation being") that "in order to enter the inner chambers, you have to want to enter." The Dubnover was so pleased with his own *mashalim* of the "outer rooms" that he never requested to enter the "inner chambers." So, while it's true that the external meditation on the "external chambers" is a *keli*, a vessel for the inner, nonetheless there must be a desire to enter the inner chambers…

- R' Deitsch saw in a *sefer* (he can't recall where), that the explanation of *mitoch sh'lo l'shma ba l'shma* ("One who learns Torah with impure intention will eventually come around to pure intention") – is only on condition that he wants to learn *lishmah*, that he wants to achieve pure intention. If he has no desire to do so, it won't help him even if he learns not *lishmah*. Preparations are important, but there must be a desire to arrive to the goal of the preparations. There was someone who used to learn Chasidut before prayers, who became so engrossed in his preparations that he forgot to pray…tomorrow we'll learn about love that is "not dependent on anything."

Shiur 68, July 13, 2012

Page 133 – Love that is not dependent on anything is *atzmi* ("essential"), and it is natural and innate, independent of any logic and intellect. Within this "essential" love, there are two levels. One level requires *hitbonenut* and meditation in order to achieve it. But if so, how is it different from love that is "dependent on something" (on meditation)? First of all, it is different regarding the content and nature of the meditation; the meditation to achieve essential love that is independent of the intellect, takes place with concentration on the *hafla'ah* ("wondrousness") of the greatness (*gadlut*) of God. Not merely on the *gadlut* itself (which is what occurs during meditation that leads to love that is "dependent on something," even the high level of *kulei kamei*…), but on the *hafla'ah* of the *Gadlut*. In practice, this means that we do not simply focus on His greatness, but on how His greatness is not understood or grasped whatsoever [*avodat hashlila*].

There is a *sicha* from the Rebbe (Vol 33 of *Likutei Sichot*, page 164) on the nature of *peleh* – the Gemora tells us that, "One who sees Pinchas in a dream will experience *peleh*" – something "wondrous" – since several miracles occurred to Pinchas. So the Rebbe asks, "But the gemora says *peleh* – one miracle, not several." The Rebbe explains there are *nisim* ("miracles"), and there are *pela'im* – which is greater? From one side, we can say that *nisim* are greater (because they change nature, even if only temporarily, while *pela'im* could be surprising merely to man, without any corresponding change in nature), but on the other hand, *niflotecha* ("Your *pela'im*," "Your wondrous signs") are greater, because they bear no connection to nature whatsoever, and therefore *niflotecha* are greater. From the *sicha*: We are told that in the future redemption, God will show us *niflaot* that will be even greater than the miracles that occurred when the Jews were freed from Egypt.

Rashi mentions that several miracles happened to PInchas but they were all in the *geder* ("category of, defined by") of *hafla'ah*. From the sicha, "All the miracles that happened to Pinchas were completely beyond, they were in the category of *peleh*. The number of miracles was not important at all – what was important was the fact that they were all *peleh*. Miracles are defined as a transformation of nature, indicating that nature has a "place," exists, so to speak. Therefore, each time there is another *nes*, another "miracle," it requires another change another transformation of nature. But, when discussing occurrences described as *peleh*, they are from inception not included in nature. When a *peleh* occurs, it is not a *shinui* or "change" in nature, it is not in the *geder* or category of nature at all. And therefore one becomes used to something occurring that has nothing whatsoever to do with nature. Not only that it is not a transformation, but it is not in the category of "nature" to begin with. Such are the *niflaot* that occurred to Pinchas and will occur in the future redemption.

- To *mishpachat* Abuchatzeira (the Rav doesn't remember to which one of them, perhaps R' Yaakov, the scion of the family), the title of of *melumed b'nissim*, "steeped in miracles," was applied. Meaning that he was *l'chatchila* in the category of miracles. It was not something that he had to strive for it. So therefore, all miracles that occur to such a person or from him, are all one. He does not need to work to change nature each time. Rather, nature changes for him at all times. Nature is *nikveh*, or "fixed" around him, in a wondrous manner. Here, the Rebbe adds an amazing (*peladik*) matter; why was Pinchas rewarded with *Cahuna* ("priesthood"), why did he become a Cohen? The priesthood became "fixed" to him – not only he but also his descendants after him were Cohanim ("priests"). What was beyond nature ("miraculous") became "his" in a fixed manner – this is *peleh* – a step beyond "miraculous." Such a matter and its reward does not fit into our intellect and understanding, and therefore it is *niflah*. The Rav mentions that regarding a man, we don't say "he's a miraculous person (*ish nisi*)." Rather, we might say that he's a "wondrous person"- an *ish muflah*. A man cannot exist constantly in a status of miracles, since each miracle is new. But, one who lives constantly in a state of wondrous matters is called *muflah*.

Someone asked, "How do we meditate on *hafla'at ha Ein Sof*? (on the "wondrous nature of the infinite"?) How are we to *mitbonen* on the *hafla'ah* of the infinite light? R' Deitsch answered, with *hasagat hashlilah*..."negative *hasagah*." A lot is said about this, but those are the words; *hasagat hashlilah*. Take for example, the words of *Petach Eliyahu* (from Zohar, we say it *Erev Shabbes*) – "You are One without *cheshbon*, You are above all that is above… You are the most hidden of the hidden." The phrase begins with a *hagdara*, with a definition – "One without *cheshbon*," and continues with "You are above" – but concludes with "hidden," meaning beyond definition. And then, *leit machshava t'fisa bey clal* – "no thought can grasp Him whatsoever." So we have three levels before we reach "no thought…" R' Deitsch says there are *maamorim* about these three levels.

Someone once asked R' Deitsch, if the main thing is to be a *peti* ("fool" in a positive sense of nullified to Hashem), to de-emphasize intellect while emphasizing faith, then why do we need Chabad at all? In answer to this question, R' Shlomo Chaim quoted Shlomo HaMelech, "I said I will gain wisdom, but it is far from me." That Shlomo understood everything previous to this point, was based on his *havana* ("understanding," intellect). That here he reached a point of no understanding – this is *hafla'ah*. And the love associated with this level of not understanding is – it's a feeling of "running, running, running" – for sure toward a goal [toward the goal of understanding or whatever is beyond it]…it is written that angels – *malachim* – do not achieve love of God, but only fear of Him. And the reason is precisely because they cannot imagine being "close" to Him. They experience their distance so strongly that they cannot achieve love of God (which is associated with closeness and proximity). But Jews, *neshamot Yisrael* are like "children of God," so we are less afraid of proximity to Him, and we are commanded to love Him, because as far away as we are, we are still "children of God." A son has a desire to be close to his father – but what kind of desire? A son feels that his father is very very high, wants very very much to be close to his father.

Back to the text on page 133 in translation; "But once ultimately aroused, this love expresses the very essence of the soul." The desire is there, it just needs arousal (unlike love that is "dependent on something" – the entire basis of the love is from the *hasaga* of his *hitbonenut)*. Here, the *hasaga* does not "develop" into love, since the love is there anyway. All the *hasaga* achieves is to reveal and "trigger" the essential love. As the text continues, "This is because in truth, it is not the meditation that gives rise to this love. Rather, within the essence of the soul…" there is love that needs arousal. But upon arousal, it is "essential." It is *atzmi*. This is the *chaya*, but the *yechida* needs no arousal whatsoever. We may not feel and experience the *yechida* – but it is hidden but present nonetheless.

It is written in Chasidut that *mesirat nefesh* ("utter devotion and dedication") is from the *yechida*, but *emunah* - that all Jews are *ma'aminim* and *b'nei ma'aminim*, comes from the *chaya* of the *nefesh*. Perhaps that is the difference; from time to time we need to think about and refresh our *emunah* via *hasaga*, etc…not because the *emuna* isn't present (it's there at all times), but because it requires occasional "reinforcement." But *yechida* and *mesirat nefesh* need no *hitbonenut* – "not able to do *Avodah Zara*" – no explanation.

Once R' Deitsch heard that all the *madreigot* in Tanya are found in a minor way with all of us. *tzadik, beinoni…*

Shiur 69, July 15, 2012

Now that we know that there are two levels of love – one that is "dependent on something" (on logic and intellect) and the other "not dependent on anything," and that within love that is "not dependent on anything," there are two levels: *Chaya* that needs meditation in order to "ignite" love but not in order to "develop" it (because the divine love is present in any case and all that the meditation achieves is to reveal the essential love), and *Yechida* that requires no meditation whatsoever to awaken it; it is always present if not revealed…

So now we want to know which of these levels has more of an effect on our animal soul.

Page 31 in the Hebrew text, 134 in the translation:

"Now the will for connection mentioned earlier…" *K'Avoda* says that the *ratzon* here and the resulting divine love that is above reason and logic is too high to have an effect on the animal soul, because the animal soul relates only to reason, not to that which is above reason. There is an aspect of the animal soul that is above reason and logic, but that aspect does not apply to divine Godly matters. There are many things that the animal soul "wants" that it cannot explain – these matters may be either "above" intellect or "below" it, but they are not Godly. If you explain Godly matters to the animal soul, it "gets it," but if you try to explain Godliness that is beyond reason and intellect to the animal soul, it does not "get it." (That the animal soul has a lust and *ta'aveh* for something, and that the animal soul has a *geshmak* (Yiddish for "enjoyment") in something, is not connected to the *ratzon*. The animal soul is born with lust and *ta'avah*. As the Alter Rebbe said, "about a *ta'aveh*, we cannot ask questions" – yet it is not clear whether the Alter Rebbe said this regarding matters that are above the intellect, or below it. Because the fact that we have various lusts and temptations is connected to our nature, it's not something that we "develop." "Excitement" over the *ta'aveh* is not necessary, but nevertheless it's built on the fact that the animal soul finds it attractive, that's its nature to find it attractive. There is such a thing as sadism, wherein one has a *geshmak* in making things bad for another person. This is egoism.

- R' Deitsch heard from R' Zelig Feldman *alov hashalom* that man is compounded of "*elyonim* and *tachtonim*." *Elyonim* is the *neshama*, *tachtonim* is the body. It's written in Chasidut (in *Torah Ohr* of the Alter Rebbe) that the *Elyonim* in man is far higher than by animals, while the *tachtonim* is much lower. How does this come into expression? R' Deitsch said he heard from R' Zelig that it comes from sadism, and if you want to see sadism, watch children. We try to hide the trait among ourselves, knowing that it's "not nice," but nonetheless, it exists. Another place we see it? When a person falls, everyone laughs. We don't see this by animals, that they enjoy the sorrow of another animal, but we see it by humans. The whole concept of "sweet revenge" exists by man, not by animals.

Why do we mention this? Because the fact that one has enjoyment over giving sorrow and pain to another human being, may be an example of a *ta'aveh* that is "below" reason and logic. At any rate, love according to reason and logic has more of an effect on the animal soul than does love that is above reason and logic. And this is one of the answers to the question that is asked regarding Tanya, "If it is possible to get there with meditation in the shorter path (*derech katzara*), so why does the Alter Rebbe suggest the longer path (*derech arucha*)?" R' Shlomo Chaim answered that it's for this very reason: Love according to reason (*derech arucha*) will have a lasting influence on the animal soul, while love above reason (*derech katzarah*) does not effect the animal soul. *Itkafia* ("bending" and subduing the animal soul) also works... there are steps and levels on this path.

- As known, there was a differentiation between "Galicianers" (Jews who lived in the European countries south and east of Poland, such as Hungary and Romania) and Polish Chasidism...the Galicianers put more emphasis on *minhagim* ("customs"), davening with a *chazzan* ("cantor"), on lots of heart-felt *niggunim*...("melodies" such as found in Jikov, Bnei Yissachar, Dinover...). While the Polishers, especially Kotzk, nullified all the outer trappings such as the *chazzan,* and emphasize only the main point, which is not to forget that the point of prayer is to petition God...another difference existed regarding reciting psalms. The Galicianers (as well as Chabad and Chernobyl), put great emphasis on saying Tehilim but in Kotzk (Polish Chasidim), they used to say, "Dovid Hamelech said Tehilim for seventy years, you want to say them in two hours?" So there was one Galicianer Chasid who got involved in Kotzk and became a Kotzker but nonetheless kept his Galicianer customs, and the the Kotzker Chasidim nudged him about that until the Kotzker Rav told them to leave him alone.

Nevertheless, the Kotzker chasidim kept asking him why don't you change your *minhagim* to Kotzk? He answered that there are two types of businessmen: Those who do big business but not always do they have a free cash flow at hand from which they can buy something small (all their money is tied up in the business). On the other hand there are small businessmen who don't have huge turnover but they always have coinage at hand (they always have some spare change that's not tied up in the business). "I'm like a small business man doing big business in Kotzk." One should remain small while doing big business. And the same is true *b'ruchniyus*…In Kotzk you did "big business" but not always was there "money" available. R' Deitsch said you could walk around for hours in preparation for *tefila* before actually praying in Kotzk. That's "big business." But if you have a Sefer Tehilim you can say it at any time you want…

- Important story from R' Deitsch. R' Shlomo Zalman Auerback (*ztz'l*) had a son in law who was a Rosh Yeshiva (Yeshivat Eitz Chaim) in Antwerp. By the name of R' Yehuda Treger. R' Treger told R' Auerbach (son of R' Shlomo Zalman *ztz'l*) that after the war, there were two cities in Belgium to which haredi Jews came to live: Antwerp and Brussels. After the war the spiritual situation in Brussels was every bit as good as in Antwerp. Polisher Hasidim settled in Brussels and Galicianers in Antwerp. These days, Brussels is weak, not much of a spiritual life, even tho after the war there was a lot of Torah there, but the Polishers (Kotzkers) stopped keeping *minhagim*. But in Antwerp where the Galicianers kept their *minhagim*, Torah thrived. Their life was dependent on *minhagim*, for example it was unthinkable not to make two kugels on Shabbat Rosh Hodesh…

Skip the parentheses to page 32 in Hebrew, page 137 in the translation… "But, one cannot say about the *yechida*…" and then to page 140…the *chaya* does not have an effect on the animal soul, but the *yechida* does…

Shiur 70, July 16, 2012

Same intro (more or less) as previous *shiur*.

Achia Hashiloni ("Achia from Shiloh," who was a prophet in the days of King Solomon and also reputed to be the teacher of the Baal Shem Tov) was called *Ba'al Hachaya* ("master of the soul level of *Chaya*") in Kaballah…There are many things that initially require our thought and intellectual justification, but after we have made up our mind and are ready to get involved, it's becomes clear why we are doing it. Such as eating healthy...at first we need proofs and evidence, but once we start eating healthy, we already understand why. The same applies in *ruchniyut,* in "spiritual matters. In the beginning of consideration of matters that are beyond our intellect, the *chaya* requires some thought and logic but once we apply ourselves, we no longer need that.

R' Eliyahu Hadad mentioned Avraham Avinu in this regard, who began his journey with reason and logic and then later achieved love that is beyond reason. Avraham allowed himself to be thrown in the furnace *al Kiddush Hashem* and was saved, his brother Nahor reasoned that since Avraham was saved, so he would also be saved, but he was not saved. Why? He who transcends reason and logic with *mesirat nefesh* in order to fulfill God's will is saved, but he who approaches the same topic using reason is burned? This seems to be the opposite of the way things should be...but here, since Avraham conducted himself in a manner that was beyond nature, so the response from Above was supernatural. When his brother approached the same matter but with an intellectual approach, he was answered with a "natural" response – he was burned alive according to nature.

- Here the Rav told a long story, the gist of which is that if a person conducts himself as if beyond nature, then nature itself transcends nature. "The entire universe was placed in the hands of man" – if man conducts himself beyond nature, the universe "responds in kind." And if he conducts himself within the bounds of nature, so will the world. This is the simple reason that *tzadikim* deal with the world in a supernatural manner and the world also responds to *tzadikim* in a manner that is beyond nature. The small amount that a *tzaddik* eats becomes "blessed" in his innards, the small of amount of sleep is sufficient...story with the Rav that he once went in to see a *gvir* ("rich man") in the US (together with Harav Cohen from Monsey) and the *shamash* ("assistant") asked the *gvir* to "tell his story." The wealthy man (who himself was a Chasid) told them that he once experienced dizziness and felt faint, so he went to the doctors, who found a *gidul* ("growth") in his head. The doctors figured it out by something in his eyes, and from there they found the tumor (*lo aleynu*) in his brain. He was a Gerer Chosid, of the *Beis Yisrael* (the Gerer Rebbe after the war, who came to Israel). Before Purim, he wrote in to his Rebbe and during the Purim tish, the crowd heard the Gerer Rebbe say, "What does the *Aibishter* want from my *yungeleit*" What does God want from my young married men?" After Purim, the *Beis Yisrael* asked a neighbor who lived nearby him (by the young Chasid), "How is this *avreich*"? He answered, "I don't know" – and the *Beis Yisrael* said,

"He's in the hospital and you don't know"? Afterward, the neighbor returned to the US, and the *Beis Yisrael* instructed him, "Ask him, did he perhaps fall recently? Maybe the growth was a result of a fall? Ask the doctors to do another exam." The *Beis YIsrael* was very *zariz* ("quick") and definitive, there was no "playing around" with his words. The neighbor returned to the US and even from the airport he called up his friend in the hospital and told him what the Rebbe, the *Beis Yisrael* had said. The patient recalled that "Yes, there was snow and he fell." So the patient tried to convince the doctors to do another exam, but they wouldn't listen, they said that they "saw the growth in the microscope, so there was no point in doing another exam." Until one low ranked doctor agreed and did another exam and – there was no growth. He showed the rest of the doctors and they also had to agree, there was no growth there. And this was the man himself, to whom this happened, telling R' Deitsch the story. To that very day, an "impression" of the fall stayed with him, making it hard for him to walk sometimes. Now, the doctor at that particular hospital, was the personal physician of the Satmar Rav. And when he saw the Satmar Rav, he asked him, "What is the deal here? A Jew sits in Israel, tells the doctors in NY to re-examine the patient? We saw the growth, we knew it was there and now all of a sudden it's gone? What's going on here?" To this, the Satmar answered him, "When a Jew acts above nature, then he has the *zechut* to also change nature."

- Same thing in the Shoah, those Jews who had a strong investment in "nature," a certain amount of food, a certain amount of rest, etc… were the first to collapse and lose it in the Shoah, while those whose conduct was anyway beyond nature, were much greater survivors – the Klausenberger Rav, for example. On the Death march, they had to walk a long way, those who collapsed were killed. It was the Klausenberger who convinced them to keep going…at one point on a hot day they stopped and there was water but it was bad water, unhealthy and he convinced them not to drink it. There were *edim* and witnesses to all this. And on a cold day, he gave a woman his socks, she herself told the story. And after the war, when he lost his wife and 11 children and his entire congregation, he went from one DP ("Displaced Person") camp to the next and worried for their needs and went to the US to raise money for them…he "never had any *sefekot* ("doubts") in *emunah*," in his own words…"*Shem Havaya* was before him in all of the situations." This is according to nature? And just as he was beyond nature in the Shoah, so his conduct after the Shoah…

At any rate, this conduct that is beyond nature, is from the *yechida* of the soul. So what is preferable, *avoda* that is according to nature or that is beyond nature? At first glance whatever is higher, is better…but here the *K' Avoda* comes to tell us that there is a certain benefit to *avoda* according to our intellect (which works within the bonds of nature)…When we utilize logic and intellect, the animal soul grasps, but if our *avoda* is beyond logic and intellect, the animal soul does not understand. Nevertheless, it is dragged along anyway, against its will. That is what takes place when the *chaya* is operative, but the *yechida* does change the person, even though it is far above and beyond the animal soul and body.

Page 137: "But, one cannot say about the *yechida*…that it has no effect…" That is, logically there is room to think that the *yechida* has no effect on the animal soul, but *K'Avoda* tells us the opposite; the *yechida* of the soul transforms the animal soul from one extreme to the other. Not that the *yechida* "explains" to the animal soul, but that the *yechida* is such an overpowering experience that the animal soul cannot stand against it, and is transformed automatically.

- The Rav told a story about a young boy who was not taken away by the Nazis *yemach shemam* ("may their names be erased"), even though there was a transport of older men who knew they were going…this reminded R' Deitsch of another story that he heard from R' Chatzkel Levinstein (the *menahel ruchani* at Ponevitz yeshiva), "People ask, 'why didn't the victims resist?' R' Chatzkel responded, "What is the question? This was all decreed from Above, was there anything "natural" about the Holocaust? This that they failed to resist was part of the decree! They knew they were going to die anyway, why not go down with resistance? Why did they go like sheep? Because that was a part of the decree…R' Deitsch heard R' Chatzkel eulogize one of the young students, R' Leib Zallen (?) who had been saved from the shoah by a miracle and survived together with others in Shanghai (there were Lubavitchers who were a part of the group together with Mir students), and when R' Chatzkel eulogized him, he said that he should have gone to *Eretz Yisrael* after the war, but he went to America instead and died young. "After such miracles that we saw in the Shoah and Shanghai, you went to the US?" That was R' Chatzkel eulogizing his student, and sometimes *ba'alei mussar* (of whom R' Chatzkel was one) can be sharp…Anyway getting back to R' Chatzkel and his story of the elders being taken away, he saw one of them throw a package in the direction of the young man. He opened the package and found tefilin, and realized the old man had known what was about to happen, and wanted to give his tefilin to him. So he took them, hid them under his bed with intention to put them on very early in the morning. But when he got up early and donned the tefilin, that's precisely when a Gestapo officer came in and found him. And as known, the greatest hatred and violence was reserved for the religious Jews – not as some people think for the nation in general (though that is also true), but especially against the religious Jews. There are witnesses to this; their greatest hatred was against Judaism, it's just that Jews of course are the symbol of Judaism. So when this Gestapo officer saw the young guy with the tefilin, he brought him to the central "square" of the city (or camp?) and decreed that he would be hanged. He was brought up to the platform and asked, "What's your last wish?" He said, "I want to put on the tefilin and you will kill me with the tefilin on." They agreed, "Everyone should see the reason for why you are to be killed." He went on top of the table and the rope was tied around his neck, he began to say *kriat shema*, and they started to move the table away so that he would be left hanging…when all of a sudden a big major commander walked in and said, "Such a punishment for such a deed? For such a thing, he deserves a much worse punishment!" The removed the rope and started beating him, murderous blows. And all the while they made him hold two heavy stones, one in each hand, while they beat him with blows that should have taken down a normal person. But he remained standing and holding the stones; the Gestapo told him, drop the stones (with the idea that then they would shoot him and be finished)…he collapsed and looked as if dead, so they put him somewhere with other corpses. After a number of hours, he awakened, remained alive and came to Israel and created a family. His son told the story and mentioned that his whole life he had aches and pain at the back of his head where he was struck.

- That was the story – but what is the lesson? R' Deitsch told it as a story of one who was saved, and that's what *K' Avoda* discusses on page 137, one who was saved from certain death.

Acc to R' Deitschs's calculations, he remained alive even though the intention was to kill him with *yisurim* ("suffering")…hanging was not sure to kill him, but the beating was sure to kill him, yet he lived. And all on the *zechut* of his *mesirat nefesh* putting on tefilin. As *K' Avoda* writes, it is without doubt that such a person is transformed completely by the event, because the Godly soul has such a powerful influence on him that nothing prevents him from surrendering his life, even though the natural/animal soul wants nothing other than to live. And yet at such times of *mesirat nefesh*, the Godly soul overwhelms the animal soul so that it surrenders...That the natural soul surrenders and is ready to "go," means that its nature was changed by the divine soul so that it puts up no resistance, even though it is about to expire. And not only does it not resist, it actually cooperates, and this means that not only the animal soul but the very physical existence of the person changes. The gist of it is that the *yechida* of the soul does influence and have a powerful effect on the animal soul [but it seems only in a situation of *pikuach nefesh* and *mesirat nefesh*, not under normal circumstances, when the *yechida* is not revealed, even tho it is present].

R' Deitsch mentioned here the story of R' Eliezer ben Durdaya...skip til after parentheses on page 141.

Shiur 71, July 17, 2012

We learned that the *yechida* of the soul has the ability to influence the animal soul to such an extent that it is willing to give itself up to die in situations of *mesirat nefesh*.

R' Eliyahu Hadad asked, "If a person had *mesirat nefesh* at the last minute, does that mean that afterward he is a different person, that the Godly soul changed him from one kind of person to another?" R' Deitsch replied that, "Yes, that's what the *K'Avoda says*." R' Eliyahu Haddad continued, "Do we see the difference? Do we see how they are different before and after the incident"? R' Deitsch answered (humorously), "We'd have to check them out all day long at every moment..." No doubt about and no question of a doubt about it...

R' Deitsch says that a true professor knows the results of his investigations even before he performs them. For example, Einstein's theory preceded his experiments [apparently the Rav was referring to Einstein formulating the theory of relativity it was tested]. All of a sudden someone came in and there was a lot of dancing and singing in the middle of the *shiur*...someone recovered from being sick.

Page 33 in the Hebrew text...Page 143 in the translation.

The hidden love in every Jew though – the *chaya* – does not affect the person's nature or his *humriyut*. It is a *makif* ("transcendent illumination") that remains beyond the person's physical nature. (Or, when the *chaya* comes into revelation, it comes into revelation as *ratzon* ("will"). But the *ahava mesuteret* that is discussed in Tanya, during the *derech arucha* (Ch 1-17), is not *makif*. It's impossible to call what the Alter Rebbe discusses over there in those chapters of Tanya, as *makif*). Here in *K'Avoda*, the *makif* is like the thief who prays for success, without recognizing that his behavior is contrary to belief in God...

- Like the vort from the *Beit Aharon*, R' Aharon Karlin regarding the animal soul…"when he davens with me, he is with me step by step. But when it comes to the kugel after *tefila*, he is focused on the kugel."

Shiur 72, July 18, 2012

The *ratzon* ("will") that is associated with the *chaya* of the soul, does not produce any change in the animal soul. Because this *ratzon* of the *chaya* is "above enclothement in the animal soul, therefore it does not have an effect on the animal soul."

Two paths in *avodat Hashem*: 1) There is the path of logic and reason, in which the animal soul is persuaded by reason, and that produces change in the animal soul. 2) There is the path of *avoda* that is beyond reason, but which does not affect the animal soul. The Godly soul is like a *ben* – a "son" that is drawn naturally toward its father. But the animal soul is not called a "son" of Hashem, and it does not grasp Godly matters. (An *eved*, or "servant" can reach Godly levels – in response to a question).

Page 34 in the Hebrew, page 146 in the translation…we see that during Rosh Hashana and Y"K, that some people are not affected.

- Rav Deitsch says he used to collect *tzedaka* in Manhattan [I remember those days, in the mid-80's…] and someone pointed out to him that nobody is walking, everyone is running somewhere…all day long in Manhattan everyone is walking fast, not in a normal manner. This is called *tirdot haparnasah* – the "worries of parnassa" - and about this the Alter Rebbe says, "they [the 'worries'] have to be burnt."

- Story from the Ruziner, "There was a *chasid* who had a business in wool furs. He bought them in the summer and then sewed and sold them, and this business brought him a decent income. Someone else entered the picture and started competing with him, and his income declined. He had invested a lot of money and was unable to sell. He went to shul to pray, and on the way he met two representatives of the Russian army (or Polish?) who said to him, "Do you have furs to sell? We want to buy." The Chasid answered, "Right now I'm before prayers, I don't do business before *tefila*." That was the story as it was heard from the Ruziner. At this point, one of his chasidim asked him, "And what happened afterward"? The Ruziner asked him, "He didn't ask what would be afterward. You're asking?" Rav Deitsch though heard the complete story. The Chasid went to pray and the Russian Army reps went to someone else. However, they didn't manage to cut a deal, and instead returned to the original guy after his prayers. And they bought all of his furs, for even more than what a private citizen would have bought them, since it was a cold winter and the army needed them for the soldiers. Now, comes along yet another guy who was sitting in farbrengen and adds, "I heard the story, and the Ruziner stopped in the middle; he only told the story up until the point where the Chasid is going to shul."

Putting together all of the perspectives, the Rav wants to do an interpretation of the story: The Jew going to pray made a decision: "I don't do business before *tefila*." Such conduct and such a *din* exists in *halacha* as well, but under some circumstances (for example, even during *hol hamoed*), if it's a deal that if missed will result in financial loss, it is permitted. Nevertheless, this Chasid went beyond reason and logic and said, "I'm not doing business before *tefila*" (even though it would have caused him a serious financial loss). Now, the *yetzer harah* was probably claiming, "If you don't do this business deal, your *tefila* itself will be confused and will not be received Above." Or, the *yetzer harah* might have said to him, "You want to be a *tzadik* and pray at the expense of those to whom you owe money"? Or, "Part of *tefila* is to give thanks and praise Hashem, how great the praise and thanks you will give if you now do the business deal before prayers!" These are all claims that the *yetzer harah* could have made to try to "convince" him to make a deal with them even before he prayed. It emerges that the *yetzer harah* knows "everything," it even knows the Torah that you learn and it knows how to make claims, etc. It comes dressed as a *Talmud Chacham* (a "Torah scholar" in order to claim that the deed is not *l'shmah* – not for the sake of the mitzvah). It even knows Chasidut (seems that some people learn Chasidut not *lishmah*).

(R' Mendel Futerfas used to say, "If you learn *nigleh sh'lo lishmah*, that's not good. But learning Chasidut *sh'lo lishmah*? That's the worst… There are women who are pregnant, with a protruding stomach, that's normal. But a man who is pregnant"? A man who has *ga'va* from learning Chasidut is like a man who is pregnant).

We don't know how the Jew who said that the Russian army reps first went to someone else and then came back to him after *tefila,* knew that part of the story. What we do know is that the Ruziner told this story, and stopped short of telling any other details. And there are not a lot of stories at all of *tzadikim* who speak with excitement about their Chasidim. So the takeaway must be that the Ruziner wanted us to know about the "above logic and reason" approach of this Chasid. This was truthfully a high form of behavior, not a "standard" approach. It's a matter that is above *ta'am v'daat*. This story is the true opposite of *tirdot haparnassah*.

Shiur 73, July 19, 2012

Page 34 in the Hebrew text, page 146 in the translation:

Here, the text discusses people who pray seriously, and sometimes with devotion on *R"H* and *Y"K*, but the love and fear that they develop does not have any lasting effect upon them. There are a number of variations of this phenomena, such as: 1) One who prays about his physical status but not his spiritual status 2) Even those who are *ovdim*, who pray properly regarding their spiritual status and at that time really do feel close and take on themselves to be close to Hashem, and their *avoda* is *emet*, but nevertheless after *R"H* and *Y"K* they return to their previous status.

Here, R' Eliyahu Hadad asked about *Kabalat HaTorah* at Har Sinai: Is it possible that the reason the Jews later built the calf after the giving of the Torah was also because they did not pay sufficient attention to their spiritual status?...Rav Deitsch answered that, "No," because 1) it was the *erev rav* ("mixed multitude" of converts from Egypt), not the Jews who instigated the calf, and 2) They did not decide not to serve God; rather, their decision was to look for a "replacement" for Moshe Rabeinu. So, the calf after *Matan Torah* is not similar to the situation discussed here in *K'Avoda*.

The *yetzer harah* comes in a number of different costumes and guises…

- There's was a *talmid* ("student") of the *Chozeh* of Lublin who was very careful not to speak *lashon harah*, but he was the one who created *pirud* ("separation") between the *Chozeh* and the *Yehudi HaKodesh* [The *Chozeh* and the *Yehudi Hakodesh* were two *tzaddikim* who later had a falling out and argument, apparently instigated by this *talmid* that the Rav refers to]. He did this by saying *lashon harah* about him, and the students said, "The *yetzer harah* guarded him for thirty years against speaking *lashon harah* so that when the time came, the *lashon harah* he spoke against the *Yehudi HaKodesh* would be accepted."

The reason though for all these failures to change our nature is due to lack of *avoda* to change our nature the entire year (as opposed to working on it only on *R"H* and *Y"K*). It is necessary to work on these matters *b'ofen pnimi* (in an "internal manner") the entire year. The one who takes things *b'pnimiyut* ("internally," absorbing the lessons) makes a schedule for everything; "At this hour, I do *hitbonenut*, at this hour, I pray, at this time I learn…" This is the proper approach to *Rosh Hashana*…(there is such a thing that if a *tzibur* ("public body") does not learn and pray properly as an organized group, but one of them does so as an individual, he receives the reward of all of them).

- R' Deitsch once heard two young married men speaking, they were learning *halacha b'iyun* (learning *halacha* "in depth") in *yeshivat Torat Emet* (the Chabad yeshiva in Jerusalem), and he overheard one of them say, "*Teshuva* is not for me." R' Deitsch was very taken aback and asked him, "What do you mean, '*teshuva* is not for you'?" He answered, "I did *teshuva* once or twice, and afterward, I just returned to the way I was previously, it didn't 'stick." R' Deitsch answered, "I also went thru that, but the difference is that I didn't decide that I'm okay and *teshuva* is not for me. Hashem gave us the mitzvah of *teshuva*, you cannot decide that it's not for you." R' Deitsch thought to himself, "True, I don't maintain the same level as when I first did *teshuva*, I do fall back spiritually. But, if I take small steps, such as learning a half hour Chasidut every day, then I do maintain, and the whole day is different. And this is not difficult. It's more than just a reminder, it's an "facilitator" (a *netinat koach*) that enables us to get thru the day." When R' Deitsch mentioned this to the *avrecih* who had said that, "*Teshuva* is not for me," the *avreich* replied that, "Yes, there are such things that I can maintain and can keep doing." So R' Deitsch told him to keep doing those things, not to do *teshuva* on the past results alone over which you don't have control, and that didn't "stick," but to pick the small, effective activites that he can maintain. About those activites and that *teshuva*, Rambam says, "*Yodeah ta'alumot* – the "One who knows 'concealed matters' knows that you will do *teshuva*." In other words, pick the matters on which you can work, and do them, and it will stick. It's like vitamins, you take some and you stick with it and that influences other aspects of your *avoda* as well. After a few months, R' Deitsch saw the *avreich* again on the street, and he told R' Deitsch, "You made [me into] a *Ba'al Teshuva*." The *avreich* regained confidence in himself.

- There's a *sefer* called *Erech Apayim* written by a Chasidic Jew from a couple generations ago, he advises to keep his *sefer* around to look at in order to maintain our composure when we start to get angry. Regarding *lashon harah*, R' Deitsch says the main thing is to recall the saying of the sages, *Gadol Torah hamavi l'yadei maaseh* – "Great is the Torah that leads to action" – so that the best way to avoid *lashon harah* is to learn *hilchot lashon harah* and in that way we are always reminded not to speak *lashon harah*. One who learns the *halachot* of *ma'avir sedra* ("reviewing the Torah portion every week") will be *ma'avir* the *sedra* ("will review the Torah portion"). Once, a yeshiva student said about himself that he is not *ma'avir* the *sedra* (he does not read the weekly Torah sections, repeating each verse in Hebrew twice with one recital of the Targum of each verse) but R" Deitsch happened to mention to him that it's a *siman* in *Shulhan Aruch* (section appearing in the Jewish code of law) and then all of a sudden, it became important in his eyes and he began to review the *sedra*...that's what it means, *Gadol Talmud...l'maaseh* ("Great is learning, because it leads to action").

- Try going out on the street, and telling someone that it's not good to express anger. The one thing everyone agrees is that one who gets angry, suffers. But if they were to know what the Torah says, that "The soul of one who gets angry runs away," and that according to the Zohar, anger causes negative things to happen that are not caused by anything else, then these kinds of statements go into his "safe" (his memory), he remembers them. That's number one. After that, he knows that a meeting or conversation with one person or another is likely to anger him...and he decides before meeting or speaking with him that he won't get angry – this will guarantee that he doesn't get angry. One must make this decision at a quiet moment, just before he gets to the situation that can trigger the anger. The sefer was originally called *Erech Apayim* but now changed it to *Orech Apayim*.

- Rav Deitsch told R' Eliyahu Haddad that they would learn matters of *Rosh Hashana* during the upcoming month of *Ellul* (of 5772/2012), rather than *Derech Chaim* (of the Mitteler Rebbe, which is the Rav's preferred learning for Ellul). They would learn either *Tzadik-Dalet Tzadik Hey* (5694-5/1934-5) or *Tuf-Shin-Gimmel* (5703/1943) of the Previous Rebbe on *R"H*, which are the two *maamorim* that R' Deitsch learned together with R' Shalom David Segel as taught by R' Shlomo Chaim Kesselman (in Kfar Chabad). The *ikar avoda* of *R"H* is not *teshuva* over *aveirot* ["sins" - that's *chodesh Ellul*], but judgement over whether we accepted *ohl malchut shamayim* on ourselves.

Shiur 74, July 20, 2012

Parentheses, page 146-147…

One who engages in *avoda pnimi* ("internal work on himself") during the course of the entire year will ascend spiritually, both in terms of his *neshama* and also the *zichuch*, or "refinement" of his animal soul. As known, the animal soul also contains levels, such as the *shor* ("oxe"), *keves* ("sheep") and *eiz* ("goat"). The oxe gores, the sheep is merciful ("passive") and the goat is bold ("insolent"). So, there are levels to the animal soul, and one who is engaged in *avoda pnimi* the entire year will experience an *aliya* ("ascent") on *R"H* and *Y"K* as well. Part of this *avoda pnimi* is guarding our senses, including our eyes, which is difficult only in the beginning (as stated in Ch 2 as well).

- The story mentioned in the previous *shiur*, of the student of the *Chozeh* for whom the *yetzer* waited 30 years to snare him with the sin of *lashon harah*, refers to *anashim gedolim*, "great men of spiritual stature," for whom the *yetzer* is willing to wait around. But, for small people like us, the *yetzer* doesn't play such long term games. It hopes to "scalp" a few *aveirot* or a lot, here and there. By way of example in *ruchniyut*, when the Cardo first opened as a shopping strip under the Tzemach Tzedek Shul (roughly in 1985), everyone rushed in to buy or rent a stall or store, because it was thought that it would be very profitable, given the foot traffic and number of tourists to the old city. However in the course of time, it did not turn out that way, and who were the first stores to go out of business? The small business owners. There was one such man who used to maintain a small store in the Cardo and also had a connection with the Tzemach Tzedek Shul, but one day he came in and announced that he is closing. There's a big difference between the way big business does business and the way small fry do business. A small guy can't continue to absorb losses, he has to close. But a big business can keep a store open for years while losing money, until it becomes profitable. The same applies in our case; the *yetzer harah* of a great person is not concerned about small people like us, with our ups and downs. It wants to snare people with large potential, for good or for bad. So it can hang around for a long time before it becomes "profitable" by causing the person to sin, God forbid.

Shiur 75, July 22, 2012

Page 34 in the Hebrew text, Page 148-151 in the translation.

We learned that many people serve Hashem well and with sincere devotion during *R"H* and *Y"K*, only to fall back to their previous spiritual level after the *Yamim Noraim* (after the holidays of Tishrei). The reason for this is their failure to work continuously and constantly on *avodat Hashem* before *R"H*. Since there was no proper *avoda* before *R"H*, so the *avoda* of Tishrei has little or no effect on the *humriyut* ("physicality") of the animal soul. Here, we're talking about Chasidic Jews, "Shpitz Chabad," who maybe daven a little longer on Shabbat, but who don't put any effort into davening *b'avoda* during the week. If you ask them about "love like water" or "love like fire," they'll ask you, "Sorry, what are you talking about, where did you see that, in what *sefer*?"

- A poor person, who has nothing, will have what he needs if you give him bread. But is that all he needs? Certainly not, he needs much more and it's a *rachmanut* ("pity on him") if he doesn't have a house, etc.... The same applies to us in *ruchniyut*, one who learns some Chasidut, is *mitbonen* a little…etc…, and that's all that he does, when in truth he is capable of "love like water," and "love like fire…." This is a *rachmanut* on him.

What is true *avodah p'nimi*? *K' Avoda* states clearly (page 148), "But there are those who continue to serve the One Above all year long by subjugating their physical natures in general, but mainly by subduing specific traits through internal service of the mind and heart, whether with "love like water" or "love like fire." This transforms our *midot*, our anger, our lusts…But without this, the arousal of *R"H* and *Y"K* remains *makif* ("transcendent") alone (page 150), even on *R"H* and *Y"K* themselves.

- There was a Chasid, R' Zalman Moshe Yitzhaki, who was very *charif*, very "sharp." There were Chasidim who would go to the Rebbe for *R"H*, but one year the Rebbe wasn't there and the Chasidim were upset about it. There was another Chasid, R' Shmuel, who was more calm, and he wanted to create an atmosphere similar to what it was like by the Rebbe, so he said, "Do you remember how the *tekiat shofar* was this year, or that year…" – he wanted to arouse memories of how it was by the Rebbe. So a wise guy answered him, "Do you remember the *latkas* that we ate afterward at the hotel?"

- Stated by Chasidim that they uprooted all the natural *ta'avot* ("lusts, temptations") that a person has, aside from the natural mercy that a father has for his son. Why? Because that is the mercy that Hashem has on His "children," the Jews.

- R' Eliyahu Haddad asked at a certain point, "What is *shayach* ("applicable") the 'elevations' that a Jew can undergo, what are these *aliyot*?" [In other words, "Are these elevations of the soul applicable to us?"]. In answer, R' Deitsch told the story of R' Lazar the Limper, who was a Jew who had trouble walking, and used to limp. He lived originally in Tzfat, but when a *shadar* (emissary of the Alter Rebbe) arrived, the *shadar* would recite Chasidut for the Jews. The job of the *shadar* was, "To sow spirituality and to reap *gashmiyut*." That is, his task was to present spirituality in the form of the Chasidut that he heard from the Rebbe, and the Chassidim would give him *tzedaka* for the needs of the public. At any rate, when R' Lazar the Limper heard the *maamar* (Chassidic discourse) of the *shadar*, he asked him, "From where are these words that you just recited"? The answer was, "From Liozna" (where the Alter Rebbe lived). Without hesitation, R' Lazar the Limper left his house and took off on foot for Liozna. But meantime at home, the *kapeida* ("anger") of his wife was great, and it is said that because of her *kapeida*, he broke his leg on the way. (R' Deitsch heard the story from R' Shlomo Chaim). He never completely healed from the broken leg, which is why he was called "the Limper." Nevertheless it didn't stop him from continuing all the way to Liozna, where he found what he was looking for. Meantime, the *shadar* continued on his path and made a full circle and returned to Tzfat. There, they told him about R' Lazar who had left his house behind and his *bnei bayit* ("wife and children") didn't know at all what happened to him, perhaps he had gone on 'galut' ('exile' – a common form of *avodat Hashem* in those days, in which the men walked from one city to the next), and detached himself from his home and family? So, they told the *shadar* R' Lazar's details so that he would know and be able to identify him, since he was one who went all over the world (the *shadar* at that point had no idea that he had anything to do with the whole story). The *shadar* made another *sivuv* ("trip" around to the various cities) and found himself back in Liozna, where he saw and identified R' Lazar, and asked him who he is and what is he doing, and he replied "Yes, I'm from Tzfat, and yes I left behind my family and children." The *shadar* brought R' Lazar into *yechidut* ("private audience") with the Alter Rebbe, who persuaded him to send a *get* ("bill of divorce"), while R' Lazar remained in Liozna…after a period of time, his friend from Tzfat also arrived to the Alter Rebbe, and this friend was a *baal madreiga*, as was R' Lazar, clearly a *baal madreiga* even before he left Tzfat for Liozna. The friend who arrived from

Tzfat asked him, "What was all the noise? We were friends and served God together in Tzfat, what did you see here in Liozna that made you prepared to leave your family and Tzfat and come here?" (Rav Deitsch added that this R' Lazar was "strange," because to leave a wife and family was not normal even for a *baal madreiga*, perhaps in our days a *baal teshuva* might do such a thing but it wasn't considered "normal" even in R' Lazar's day). At any rate, to his friend, R' Lazar replied, "When we were in Tzfat, we wondered if Hashem has a great enough *Gan Eden* to reward us. Now that I'm here, I'm amazed that He doesn't drop the ceiling on me in response to my low level of *tefila*. It's a *rachmanut* ("mercy") from Hashem that He accepts my *tefila*."

- So, in answer to R' Eliyahu Hadad's question regarding the relevance of spiritual levels, "You see what's possible to add." You can add the awareness that, "All that you think you have achieved is 'nothing' compared to the greatness of Hashem." This is a completely different *hasaga* ("grasp, perspective"). In conclusion, R' Deitsch said that one of the greater Chasidim of the Alter Rebbe (R' Zalman Zesmer) told R' Lazar, "To give you a *bat Yisrael* to marry would be cruel. But take my daughter and marry her." [He wanted R' Lazar as a son-in-law, and it seems that this was a way of "forewarning" him not to be cruel to his daughter]. It appears this R' Lazar was a very high *neshama* but *orot* ("illumination") without *kelim* ("vessels" to contain the illumination), because to do such a thing, leaving a wife and children behind, was "cruel." But after hearing the Alter Rebbe's Torah, he felt he had no choice. (This is a "dangerous story," because if someone learns from this God forbid not to treat the wife properly…however the positive lesson to learn from this is that these are two different kinds of *avodat Hashem*, opposite from one another from one extreme to the other). The *ein-sof* ("infinity") that the Alter Rebbe put into everything, is what R' Lazar received. [R' Deitsch is very careful not to tell this story, lest someone conclude that it's okay to abandon the house…]

- Questions arose regarding the Alter Rebbe's path: Why did he put Chabad – *chochma bina* and *da'at* – into Chasidut, acc to R' Avraham Kalisker and others, it would have been better not to inject intellect into *emunah*, it would have been better to leave it as *emunah pshutah* ("simple faith")? But, the Alter Rebbe claimed that he had received otherwise from the Magid – that Chabad enhances *emunah*, that "intellect enhances faith." And so we see, anything that Chabad touches is permeated "through and through" with *emunah*. All the concepts of *ein sof* and *leit atar panui minei* ("there is nothing void of His presence"), etc...all of these are concepts that are beyond intellect, but the Alter Rebbe succeeded in putting *ein sof* into matters that are *mugbal* ("limited"), the "infinite" into the "limited." What is demanded of us in *avoda*, to do matters that are limited, or unlimited? Since we feel the *ein sof* in all that we do, that means that we have to be involved in matters *bli gvul*, "without limitation." Like a *baal teshuva* who needs *shmira* ("guarding"), we have to watch over and "guard" whoever seeks to live "beyond limitations, without *gvul*." Which is why the Torah commands us (and the Rebbe encouraged), *asei lecha Rav* ("Appoint someone as your Rav") - this applied to R' Lazar; if he had had a Rav or Rebbe, he would have had to ask him if he is doing the right thing by taking off out of the blue to Liozna). Somewhere it is written that *malachim* – "angels" – have no free choice, but "a little bit of free choice they do have." What would that "little bit" be? Their "choice" is not to go out of their *kelim*, not to abandon their own personal boundaries, but to do what is demanded of them according to their *shlichut*.

- Rav Shaul Bruck was a Chabad mashpia in Tel Aviv, these were years (1945-1970?) in which the "city" was Yaffo, and Tel Aviv was still rural and agrarian, chickens and goats around the house. There was one yeshiva student who would daven *b'avoda* (meaning "pray at length" with devotion)...at that time, the dining hall was not together with the yeshiva and it was necessary to walk from the yeshiva to the place where they ate...R' Shaul asked the yeshiva student, "After such a nice davening, and then you walked to eat, 'what were you thinking' as you heard the goats and animals...you don't think that even the goat knew that you davened well and therefore it said, "*meh, meh*"? We don't know what the student thought, but it's entirely possible that the world responds to a Jew who davens the way he should (even tho on the other hand we shouldn't think that the world revolves around us)...there was a great man who once said, "Chabad is *chochma, bina and da'at*...but a little *sechel* doesn't hurt..."

- There's a long Purim sicha from the Rebbe on "*Kam Rabba v'shachta*" (a famous Talmudic passage in which after drinking wine on Purim, one rabbi got up and "shected" the other and later brought him back to life again) that the Rebbe said on Shabbat after Purim, not on Purim itself (this was *mem-vov*/1986 or *mem-zein*/1987), and there was someone present at the time who suggested this was because on Purim itself there was a simultaneous broadcast on radio or TV, and the Rebbe didn't want the *sicha* to get out to people on the street. That's what it means, "One needs a little bit of *sechel*." There was a young man among the Ger Chasidim who didn't have the greatest *shalom bayit*, and the reason it turned out was because "everything he heard in *shtiebel* (in shul), he repeated to his wife." Again, the idea is that "a little *sechel* won't hurt." On the other hand, this is not *sheker*; each person, man and woman must approach the Torah according to their unique abilities.

- R' Baruch Halberstam, who was a *mesharet* in the home of the Rebbe, is a first cousin of R' Deitsch's wife. The Rabbanit (the Rebbe's wife) would sometimes call him to assist in the Rebbe's house. Once, he called in and heard the Rebbe's voice on the telephone answering machine, and wondered what was going on. What happened was that R' Baruch had told a joke and the Rebbetzin liked the joke, and she called the Rebbe to tell him the joke that she heard from R' Baruch. So, the Rebbe lifted the phone to hear the joke, and then he himself responded to the joke, and the Rebbe's response was recorded on the answering machine. That the Rebbe would "lower himself" to hear the joke that the Rebbetzin liked, was a huge huge *tzimtzum* and lowering, but that's what the Rebbe did… to know how and when to do this is part of what it means to "put a bit of *sechel* into Chabad."

Shiur 76, July 23, 2012

Back to the previous point; without *avoda pnimi* ("internal work" on ourselves) all year long, the *avoda* of R"H and Y"K, even if undertaken with real arousal and devotion, will not have an effect on the person's physical nature.

Final two lines of the Hebrew text on page 34, and middle of Page 150 in the English translation: "The arousal itself, even though honest within our soul…" is not experienced in our inner soul powers because it is transcendent. Meaning that it will not change our behavior after R"H and Y"K. What this means is that the person will not become aware of his own specific lackings and deficiencies. Instead, he will experience only a general deficiency over his situation, but not in a manner that gets down to details. There are those who can point out that in "this matter" or "that detail" they are not okay, and there are others who can only say that they aren't okay "overall." What's the difference? The one who only feels a general "distance" will do nothing to rectify any of his deficiencies. While the one who feels the details will get to work on them. That's the difference between *makif* and *pnimi*.

- One of the biggest problems these days is that people do not *mefargen* ("praise, encourage"). Once the situation in Israel was that basically nobody had much of anything and life was a struggle for existence. Now, *Baruch Hashem* things are better and everyone has basic needs. What is the best way to cure *tzarut ein* ("jealousy")? [the Rav didn't answer but apparently the answer is to "encourage" and be happy for the other person rather than to be jealous]. Why should it bother you if someone else has something? This is nothing more than ego... The Rav asked, "Why do we say חטאתי לפניך בבלי דעת – "I have sinned before You without knowing" – on *Yom Kippur*? What does it mean, "without knowing"? You would think it would be better to sin without knowing, without being aware of it...but R' Deitsch suggests that the sin itself comes from lack of *da'at*...when we lack *da'at* ("knowledge, awareness") in the sense of ingrained knowledge and awareness, that itself is a sin (*Da et Elokiei Avicha*..."Know the God of your father")

- Story of the rabbi in the US who was asked to speak before the congregation on Shabbat, so he spoke about keeping Shabbat. The president of the congregation told him, "You can't speak about that, too many people are driving to shul." So he spoke the following week about *taharat hamishpacha* ("family purity" regarding women going to the *mikvah*) and again the president told him he can't speak on that subject because most of the congregation doesn't go to *mikvah*. So he asked, "Okay, so what should I speak about?" The president of the congregation answered: "About Judaism, about *YIddishkeit*." This is the problem regarding grasp of matters in general, without getting down to details.

Page 152 – there must be appropriate *kavana* and effort regarding "both matters" – meaning about specific details and about the appropriate action to take in order to rectify them. And then, after all is said and done, the *tikun* ("rectification") must be undertaken with *pninimiyut*, with inner intention of the heart. Not like an "accountant," but like a *balabayit* (owner of the business). The "accountant" makes a cold reckoning because that is his job, the *balabayit* is personally involved and concerned about the matters that he is calculating...

Shiur 77, July 24, 2012

Yesterday we focused on why, without *avoda* the entire year, our *avoda* on *R"H* and *Y"K* falls short. Now, the *K'Avoda* explains how it works when we do proper *avoda* the entire year...

Shiurim on K'Avoda from the Mashpia R' Deitsch שיח׳

Page 35 in the Hebrew, and Page 152 in the English translation, bottom half of the page…we were given a set of *midot* (our own personal character traits) that need *tikun*, that is a gift that we were granted – like the boss who gives his employees diamonds and tells them to polish them. Similarly, Hashem gave us *midot* that were ugly and dirty and tells us to fix and refine them.

- Story that the Rashab educated his son the Previous Rebbe, saw him once playing with friends who requested some watermelon from him and he did not share with them willingly. The Rebbe Rashab instructed the Previous Rebbe to share with pleasure and R" Deitsch thinks the story has it that he even gave the Previous Rebbe some more watermelon to share. At any rate there is such an advice, that when it is difficult for someone to do something, to tell himself and repeat it over and over again how he needs to do it.

- R' Deitsch recalled a gemora (*Baba Metzia*): When one encounters a choice between loading a fallen donkey or unloading another friend's fallen donkey, halacha gives preference to unloading the donkey because of *tzar ba'al chaim* ("suffering of the animal"). However, if one encounters a friend whose donkey needs unloading and an enemy whose donkey needs loading, then the Gemora says to load the enemy's donkey, "in order to subdue the *yetzer*." R' Deitsch heard a fantastic *pshat* from R' Shmuel Rozovsky on this gemora; what does it mean to "subdue or subjugate the *yetzer*"? R' Shmuel says that we are permitted to ignore the principle of *tzar ba'al chaim* (which would have dictated that we unload our friend's suffering donkey) because we are allowed to use the animal for our own purposes, and here the purpose is to subdue our own *yetzer harah* (so that we don't hate the Jew who is not our friend). If instead of unloading the friend's donkey, we load the enemy's donkey, this is using the animal for our purposes; we subdue our *yetzer* [by helping the Jew whom we don't like]. *Tosafot* there asks, "How did a *soneh*, a "hater" or 'hated one' come into the picture here? There are *dinim* that it's forbidden to hate someone unless they are *apicursim* or something similar. We're discussing Torah, not *stam* hatred. *Tosafot* gives two answers, the second one is that Reuven who had to choose whom to help, hated Shimon according to the Torah (meaning over something Shimon wasn't doing properly acc to Torah) and in return, Shimon hated Reuven not according to Torah. Finally when he saw that Shimon hated him, Reuven also hated him, not *al pi Torah*. It is about this that the Gemora says that Reuven must overcome his hatred, subdue his *yetzer* and uplift Shimon's donkey.

If, after all he worked *b'ofen pnimi* (with a serious "internal" approach) the entire year and then he comes to *R"H*, then his avoda on *R"H* and *Y"K* will uplift all of the previous year's *avoda* as well. A "bonus," so to speak…but only if we worked *b'atzmut hanefesh* (from the "essence of our soul") the entire year. If we worked, for example the entire year on anger, then *R"H* will help. But if not, then *R"H* will not help.

R' Eliyahu Hadad mentioned something about all of *tefila* being preparation for *kriat shema* and if you davened well before that, then your *kriat shema* will be better as well…R' Deitsch agreed that *kriat shema* is like *R"H* because both are *kaballat ohl malchut shamayim*…and proved it from *Likutei Torah*, parshat *Shelach*.

Shiur 78, July 25, 2012

Those who are relying on *R"H* to change will be disappointed if they haven't preceded it with *avodat Hashem* for the entire previous year. The arousal of the day will happen, but they won't be able to use it to produce any lasting change within themselves.

What about a person who knows that he needs to fix and rectify certain matters, but just does not commit himself to doing so? "I know I need to fix this, so what?" The answer to this is that one who fails to work on himself even though he needs to do so, doesn't really know that he is in need of a *tikun*. At that point, the person needs to think overall, "What am I doing here in the world." Hashem presents us – from the beginning and intentionally – with a situation that we have to fix and rectify.

- Two years ago (would have been in 2010), R' Deitsch said that he gave a good *hagdara* ("definition") of this situation. The story was that someone was pushing hard and pressuring to destroy something. After he did so, he regretted it, went into a crisis over what he had done. And he started once more to do negative things (self-destructive?). It was at that point that he came to R' Deitsch to sort out what was going on there. Here is what the Rav concluded: Hashem created man in order "to do." How do we know? Because one who does nothing, simply goes nuts. He goes crazy. Even a child has to be doing something. That's what it says in the Torah, *Barah Elokim laasot* – "God created the world in order to do." That's the written Torah. The *chazal* (oral Torah) came along and said that *la'asot* ("to do") means *letaken* – "to rectify." What does this mean? A young child will play lego or whatever game, and once he has built or made something, he will break it down and destroy it. In essence, what has he done? He fulfilled the written Torah (*la'asot*, "to do") without the oral Torah (*letaken*, "to fix"). He "did," but did not "fix." An older child will build and invest time and effort into his "project." He won't let anyone destroy it. He feels a *tikun* in his efforts. Sure, he has to continue to "do," but for that purpose he finds other lego to build, he won't destroy his previous project. That's analogous to man's existence in the world, it is totally natural for him "to do," as written in the Torah. The urge "to do" is written in the Torah, and does not necessitate any *avoda*. The very nature of creation is "to do." But "to fix" – *letaken* as written in the oral Torah – for this a certain *ramah*, a certain level is required. The Rav arrived at this analysis after watching this person destroy what he had built, and then go back to trying to make something again. One who "does" in this manner, without "fixing," is involved with written Torah without the oral Torah. This differentiation between "fixing" and "doing" is one of the most basic differences between *kedusha* ("holiness") and *klipa* (forces opposed to holiness). *Klipa* is about "spending the time," wiling away the time, this is the essence of *klipa*, and what is common to all matters of *olam hazeh*.

- It emerges then, that one who does not get involved in his own *tikun hamidot* ("personality traits") even though he knows that he has what to rectify, is missing something very basic in life. "Menachem" once gave R' Deitsch a newspaper clip of an interview with one of the "founders" of Zionism that it's possible to say about her that she is a "spokeswoman for the *klipa*." The slang that one hears on Israeli media is attributed to her, they say she is the one who introduced Israeli slang on the radio and TV. She stated quite openly in the interview that the purpose of Zionism was to uproot people from Judaism. At the end of the interview, the interviewer asked her, "So what are we doing here in the world, what is our purpose?" She actually got angry, "Don't ask me such questions, what do I care what my purpose is, I found myself in this world and I do what I want." So the question is, "Why the anger?" And the answer is that the question pushed her into such a corner that if she would have answered it, it would have undermined her entire reason for existence. She would have had no basis for continuing, because the *klipa* has no "reason." She couldn't relate to the idea of having a goal for her life cause that would have meant she is here for a purpose, and that's a position that the *klipa* rejects. The interview was from fifteen to twenty years earlier, so mid-90's, in either *ma'ariv* or *yediot*. The *klipa* admits that it cannot tolerate the concept of "goals."

- The Rav spoke of someone (perhaps this same "Menachem") who as a journalist offended and insulted a lot of people, then discovered Chasidut and did *teshuva*, called up all those whom he had insulted and asked for *mechila*, for "forgiveness." They all forgave him except for one person, who didn't take him seriously, and closed the phone on him. Rav Deitsch told of someone famous who showed up (to a *shiur* or perhaps to a farbrengen), and they all wondered, "What is he doing here?" and the Rav started to tell him that he must be looking for someone else, another Rav. The journalist ("Menachem") was there at the farbrengen and told him, "Stop doing what you're doing, or you'll get in trouble and sit in jail." He knew even then...[I suspect this was Olmert when he was mayor of Jerusalem] – this Menachem already knew what he was up to. Anyway, someone who has nothing going on, no goal, needs to know that he should put oral Torah in his head, so he becomes aware that he has a purpose, *letaken*, "to fix."

- One of the students there mentioned that, "All that the Rabonim were *metaken*, *k'eyn d'orayta metaken* – meaning, "All that the rabbis decreed, they decreed in a manner (with details) similar to the Torah." And the Rav added that we refer to rabbinic decrees as *takanot*, again from the word "fix." Bottom line; anyone who takes the time to think about it a little bit must come to the conclusion that we have a task, a *tafkid* here on earth. It is not, "for no reason" that man is divided into one part that goes to the bathroom, another that feels, another that thinks...etc...there's a complete system here – without a goal? There must be a goal, and only in Torah is there a goal that is suggested, which is *letaken*, to "fix," to "rectify." Aside from YIddishkeit, the question does not even get asked.

- One of the *talmidim* asked, "Why does man think about himself all the time when he knows that in the end he goes to ashes and dust"? The Rav said the *Maharal* of Prague asks this question, and the answer is that if man thought about his "end," he would go nuts. It's written that one whose *yetzer* is getting the better of him, should recite *shema*. If that doesn't work, he should learn Torah and if that doesn't work, "Mention to him the day of his death." What does it mean, "mention to 'him'? "Him" is the *yetzer harah* – mention to "him" that he is going to die. "Me," the Godly soul, will live on because the Godly soul is holy, and holiness is eternal. And that's why, according to the *Maharal*, man feels he will live on and doesn't think about his end, God forbid. Because what's working in his mind – his conscious awareness - is his eternal divine soul. Even though the effect is on his animal soul, nevertheless it is his Godly soul at work. How do we know?

The Rav referred to a *maamar* from the Previous Rebbe regarding one who tries to pray well *b'avoda* but fails, then tries again and succeeds. After he succeeds, what happens? He becomes full of pride because he prayed well. What's going on here, it was not his animal soul that prayed well, it was his Godly soul. So, why is the animal soul now full of *ga'ava* ("pride")? Why is the animal soul proud? Because it's proud of the great high level of the divine Godly soul!

- In conclusion, R' Deitsch says that man must think, "For what am I here?" The main problem is that we don't contemplate about this, but rather we think, "I'm here and this is where I belong." If we would think about our *tafkid* and purpose, this is where *k'fiah*, "subduing" and "forcing" ourself, comes into play. Which *kfiah*, which forceful subduing of himself? That someone comes along and tells him, "Think about it, don't be an animal, why are you doing things that only destroy you?" Here is where one's deepest *ratzon* and sense of purpose must rise to his awareness – he must want to "fix" and "rectify." Once he thinks about it, he must come to the realization that he is here to "fix" and not to tear down, God forbid.

- R' Deitsch knew an *avreich* from the US who had gone off the *derech*, someone persuaded him to come to *Eretz Yisrael* and started learning Chasidut in the collel. It didn't "stick" at first, but then he started asking specific questions about *simcha*. He said about himself that he had everything but that still, he wasn't happy. R' Deitsch told him, "I have advice for you, but I know it won't help." Until the *avreich* begged from him to tell him, and R' Deitsch told him to go to the mikvah. The mikvah is a *segula* for happiness (R' Deitsch doesn't know where this is said, but got it from somewhere). *Taka*, the *avreich* started going to the mikvah and it changed his life, he now goes to the mikvah everyday and he's a *B"T gamur* who also brings in others (he was an *istanis*, had to go to the mikvah first with no one else around, it was the Rav's brother Shlomi who (*A"H*) persuaded him to go). The Rav knows two *B"T*'s for whom mikvah was the turning point, almost like *gerut* for them.

Shiur 79, July 26, 2012

Page 35 in the Hebrew text, 152 in the English translation.

"The reason for this…" Everyone received their set of *midot* ("character traits") to fix and rectify, and each of us has to work with labor of the soul and of the flesh. The idea is not merely that we should put "extra" arousal and devotion into our prayers on *R"H* and *Y"K*, but that the arousal and devotion from the essence of the soul, is the very essence of how the soul operates. (This is the theme of *tekiat shofar*, a *kol* ("voice") without speech, coming from the very essence of the soul).

- R' Eliyahu Hadad asked, the Gemora differentiates between our prayers during the ten days of *teshuva* ("Call Him when He is close") and our prayers during the rest of the year, as well as between whether we are davening alone or with a minyan. If so, is our prayer *b'tzibur* (with a minyan) during the rest of the year comparable to our prayers on *R"H*? If 'when He is close' is when we daven *b'tzibur* (during ten days of *teshuva*) wouldn't that apply to the entire year? [To strengthen the question; Our emphasis here in *K'Avoda* in Ch 5 is that if the entire year we are involved in *avoda pnimi* as it should be, then our prayers on *R"H* will be even more elevated. So if so, perhaps our prayer with *avoda pnim*i with the *tzibur* the entire year might be comparable to *R"H*].

- Without the *avoda* as it should be, though, then *R"H* davening is no more than *davar b'ito* – the "energy of the day" – and of course later he will go back to where he was previously.

- Story from the Rav, who heard of a certain statement, which, it emerged later had been a topic alluded to by King David: In Tiveria, the Rav heard an explanation of why we say *viduy* ("confession"): Because if the *mekatragim* ("accusers") say something Above about a certain person, the angels tell them, "Shah, he himself is already confessing, go away…" And in Tehilim, we find a verse in Tehilim 32, the commentaries explain, "When I was quiet and refrained from confessing, I had *tzarot* and problems all day long." All because he failed to confess *al chait* ("over his sins"). The halacha is that *Modeh b'kanas patur* ("One who admits to a mis-deed for which he is liable to pay a fine, is absolved of the fine"– since he himself has regret, he is absolved of the fine). Similarly above, the accusers do not bother him, once they see that he himself is confessing. Perhaps the explanation of *modeh b'kanas patur* is that since the person admits wrongdoing, the *knas* no longer has a purpose. The Mitteler Rebbe explains that *viduy* works because of *hachna'ah* – "self crushing." The Rav went on to appease R' Yosef Halbfinger (*A"H*) that we learn *Derech Chaim* of the Mittler Rebbe during Ellul because of *teshuva*, as preparation for *R"H*, preparation for accepting the yoke of heaven – *kabalat ohl malchut shamayim* – on Rosh Hashana. The *hachna'ah* is preparation for *R"H*.

- R' Deitsch used to hear from R' Zelig Slonim how the Rebbe Rashab would approach his mother, the Rebbetzin Rivka (wife of the Maharash) and request *mechila* with great *hachna'ah* before *Y"K*. She would respond, "I am *mochelet* (forgive) and the *Aibishter* ("One above") should forgive all of us."

Shiur 80, July 27, 2012

After the long parentheses from page 146-154 in the translation, we return to the original concept of Ch 5, which is that there are two kinds of *avoda* that are beyond logic and intellect: the *chaya* and the *yechida*. While these two levels of *avoda* do not have a direct effect on our *humriyut* ("physical nature") and that of the animal soul (only the *yechida* does so under certain circumstances), the *ratzon* that functions according to logic and intellect, does have an effect on the animal soul. From there we segued into the long parentheses that tell us that during *R"H* and *Y"K*, there is an arousal with which we daven seriously, but if we weren't involved in *avoda pnimi* the entire year, the arousal of *R"H* and *Y"K* won't last.

Page 36 in the Hebrew text: Only *Ahavah Rabba* transforms the animal soul – but only after *avoda* according to logic and intellect. First, we must do *avoda* with *moach v'lev*…"mind and heart." However, this *avoda* leads only to *bitul hayesh* ("ego nullification"), and in order to achieve the higher level nullification of *bitul b'metziut* ("utter self nullification"), *avoda* that is beyond logic and intellect – *ahavah rabba* – is required. *Bitul hayesh* means, "I exist, I do what I'm told, but not beyond that." But, the *bitul* of *ahava rabah* utterly transforms the animal soul and turns it into "good." There are *madreigot* within this level – but all of them occur only if preceded by a proper *avoda* of the mnd and heart. For this, we must meditate on *Gadlut Hashem* ("Greatness of God" – in the creation of the universe), while simultaneously directing and intending the meditation to have an effect on the *midot* – on our personal attributes. The meditation has to take a direction – not to be aimless – in order to affect the *midot*.

[Here, I asked the Rav if *hitbonenut* on the level of *Chaya* is too high to affect the animal soul, yet "love like fire" is also *Ahavah Rabba*, which at first glance is on the level of *Chaya* and *K'Avoda* tells us that "love like fire" incinerates and transforms the animal soul, so is this not a contradiction? The Rav answered that, "The *clal* – the "general rule" – is that *hitbonenut* is *avoda pnimi* on the *mochin* and *midot*," the explanation being that it is not on the level of *makifim* such as *Chaya*. And therefore, "love like fire" which emerges from *hitbonenut* "can be" on the soul level of *neshama*. And if *Ahava Rabba* is equivalent to "love like fire," then it must be that it is *pnimi*, and *shayach* to the soul level of *neshama*…I then asked the Rav if *avodat hashlilah* is *avoda pnimi*, and he replied that he "has to think about that" – here tho it seems that *avodat Hashlilah* is associated with the *chaya* of the soul, which is *makif*, and also the reason why it has little or no effect on the animal soul].

In response to a question, R' Deitsch answered that it seems that only *ahavat Hashem* – "love of God" - can have this effect of transforming the *midot*. But it does require us to give *kivun*, to incline the *hitbonenut* in the direction of the *midot*.

- Parable: a blacksmith needs fire in order to do his job, but he has to direct the fire in a specific direction. R' Deitsch recalls that once they did that with their mouth (apparently blowing on the fire). They put a straw in their mouth and blow the fire in the direction that was needed. So, here also the love that we develop should be directed to each *midah*, each particular attribute.

- Story of the worker who prostrated himself on *Y"K* and did not stand up again in order to ask Hashem to help him not to hate his employer, who was giving him a hard time. He worked on himself hard but he couldn't overcome the hatred that he felt toward his employer, so he did *korei noflim* – protrating himself to call out to Hashem. He declared that he would fall to the ground (on *Y"K*) and not get up until he achieved a resolution that he doesn't hate his employer. In our case as well, the person must direct his prayers so that they affect his *midot*. One must consider the effect that his prayers will have after he prays. "One must pray with his heart directed above and his eyes below." The simple explanation is that physically he should look down, while in his heart he should think about God. But if at that time he does not consider what's going to be after prayers, and how his prayers will affect him, then it is as if he closed his eyes and said, "*Hashem echad*" during *Kriat Shema* but then opened his eyes to find a world of division and plurality – and then he falls completely. The solution is that during his *tefila*, he should consider how he will conduct himself after the *tefila* – how he will commit himself to conducting himself acc to Torah. He can't be *butel b'metziut* after *tefila*, so he must decide to apply whatever spiritual attainments he achieved during prayers, to after his prayers.

- Look on page 44 in parentheses, Page 194-5 in the translation at the bottom, "We see clearly in human nature…" and then (page 195), "Within our *avoda*, we must identify the particular character trait that has fallen to our lot to rectify…" The explanation is that we must focus all of our attention on what we need to rectify. The goal of *tefila* is *bitul* – utter self nullification - but that may be expressed in many things. It could be in proper conduct, in emotion, in whatever the person concludes that is necessary in his status and situation.

- In our situation, spiritual and physical, everything is demanded of us. Rav Deitsch's wife went to lectures on the subject of nutrition and heard a lecture from a woman who was a true expert in the field of nutrition. This expert said that we should eat from everything. We keep finding more items in Hashem's creation from which we derive something that we need, so it is necessary to eat everything for good nutrition. There are vitamins in one thing, minerals in another, proteins elsewhere…this is a good *mashal* for spiritual matters as well: If someone thinks they can focus on one thing at the expense of another, it doesn't work that way. Focusing only on *gmilut chasadim* is not enough, and only on one kind of *gmilut chasadim* also not enough, etc…there has to be also *limud haTorah* and *tefila*. Everything is demanded of us. If someone does something *lifnim m'shurat hadin* – "within the letter of the law" – this is also a necessary component of our *avoda*.

Page 36 in the Hebrew text, 154-5 in the translation.

In the *maamorim* cited, *Vayakhel* and *Levaer* in *Torah Ohr* and *Likutei Torah* respectively, it states that the "*avoda* of *Erev Shabbat*" (during the six thousand years prior to the arrival of Meshiach) is according to reason and logic, while the *avoda* of Shabbat (after arrival of Meshiach, in the 7th millenium) is beyond reason and logic. The duality applies to the entire week, as well; there is a time of *erev Shabbat* and of *Shabbat* within the week itself. These are also the two *madreigot* of Yaakov (during the week) and Yisrael (on Shabbat). That's why on Motzai Shabbat, we say *Al tira avdi Yaakov* ("don't be afraid, Yaakov My servant"), lest we be afraid of entering the week. That's what is meant by, "Whoever works on *erev Shabbat*, rests on *Shabbat*." There has to be preparation of *avoda* according to logic and reason and only then can we attain the *avoda* that is beyond logic and reason.

Even though Tanya says that *ithafcha* ("transformation" of our animal soul to *kedusha*) applies to *tzadikim*, nevertheless something similar to *ithafacha* is also applicable to us as well. If, for example we change a *midah*, change a natural emotion, this is our own personal *ithafcha*. Rav Deitsch knew a Jew who was angry, but changed this attribute completely and became a calm person, relaxed. This *tikun*, rectification takes place slowly, bit by bit. Like finishing furniture, first it is necessary to sand it down, etc…only afterward can we apply the finish. R' Akiva also started slowly, not knowing when the Torah would have an effect on him…bit by bit…regarding jealousy, someone asked a question and the Rav replied that the Alter Rebbe says the first step to restrain jealousy is *hesech hada'at* ("distracting, removing our thoughts" from the emotion) – see Tanya Ch. 12 at the end. That may be followed by actions taken to counter our jealousy; for example to be kind and to act positively toward the person who is the object of our jealousy. This could be a good example of what is written in *Sefer Hachinuch*: *Halevavot nimshachim acharei hapeulot* – "The heart follows the actions." When we act nicely toward someone, it actually helps us change our minds about them as well. So here, it's not working directly on the *midot* (the emotions themselves) that brings success, but working on the action itself – *hesech hadaat*. This is the beginning of *hithafcha*…not complete and total *hithafcha* like by *tzadikim*, but successfully transforming one of our own *midot*…

Shiur 81, July 30, 2012

Beginning of Ch. 6 of *K' Avoda*, Page 36 in the Hebrew, Page 157 in the English translation. Here, the subject is that it is impossible to undertake proper *avoda* without attention to details during meditation. A mere general approach without delving deeply into details will not suffice.

- The Rav once brought support from this from King David's psalm 104, *Barchi Nafshi*. First the psalm discusses the greatness of Hashem, then of man, then of animals, followed by *Mah rabu ma'asecha Hashem* ("How many are Your works, *Hashem*"…) and then he continues with more details. More evidence can be brought from Job, which is a very difficult *sefer*. There are five friends who came to Job with their ideas about why Job is going thru all his difficulties, and Job rejects all of their explanations. And then, Hashem Himself comes to speak with Job. Finally, there is a section in which Hashem describes the greatness of creation…the Leviatan, its scales, etc…from Ch. 38 onward. Commentaries explain that it's appropriate for a great King to have great creations. And therefore the book of Job does not merely speak of *Gadlut Hashem* (the "Greatness of Hashem"), but goes into detail. With details, the person can change, not only details of the creation but of the *inyan*.

Shiur 82, July 31, 2012

Starting again from beginning of Ch. 6.

When one meditates without going into detail, his meditation remains *makif* ("transcendant") and has no effect on the physical nature of his body. In order to change and transform the physical, it is necessary to be *pnimi* (to "go internal"), which requires us to delve into details, in order to know the matter well and grasp it with *hasaga* and *da'at* – then and only then can our meditation have any effect on our body. For example, "creation from nothing to something." If one merely grasps that all Hashem created is from nothing to something, he is missing details in his meditation; mainly he is missing the *hafla'ah*, the "amazing" aspect, the awareness of "beyond." He is missing how amazing it is that God created ex nihilo.

Here we'll do the parentheses in the text, Page 157, second paragraph:

("We may also sense the general wonder of the subject, but we don't direct our attention toward becoming aware of the Godly power…") That is, we may meditate in general about the *hafla'ah* but miss the fact that it's a Godly force and energy behind it that makes it happen. We may completely miss the level of Godliness behind this creation and the details of just how amazing that is. The nature of all of creation is that there is a *mashpia* ("mentor") and a *mekabel* ("recipient"), a teacher and a student, a giver and a receiver, etc…either among people or within the person himself, since *sechel* ("intellect") to *midot* ("emotion") is "cause and effect." Everything in creation is based on *siba-mesubav* ("cause and effect"). Yet, there is not distance between *siba* ("reason," or "cause") and the *mesubav* ("effect"), and therefore the *mesubav* is "aware" of the *siba*. For example regarding a teacher (*Rav*) and student (*talmid*): When does the student begin to change? When he feels and understands what the Rav tells him. But if the Rav speaks "above him," not according to his level, then the student won't understand and will not continue to be his student. Here though, the explanation of creation from nothing to something is that the distance between Creator and created is infinite, without end. There is a Godly force that enlivens and creates the world, and yet the distance between the Godly force and the creation is infinite. This is *yesh m'ayin* ("something from nothing"). As if there is *clum* – "nothing" – and then all of a sudden there is "something." The gulf between them is infinite. From *yesh* ("something") to *yesh* between two comparable or even incomparable objects, there is a known or measurable distance. But from *ayn* ("nothing") to *yesh*, is a gulf that is unlimited. Man is not capable of bridging this gap, thus creation from nothing to something is only "within the purview of the Creator." And since this is not within human reach, we get "excited" over it. And it brings us an arousal of *ahava* and *yirah*.

But one whose meditation remains superficial, on an external level, may receive only a momentary "wow" from his meditation, and fail to develop siginificant appreciation of the creation process. For that, it is necessary to "know the details of creation from nothing to something." He needs to become acquainted with the power to create from nothing to something, on what level it operates; that is, what is this power, and how does it work on each spiritual level…so that in addition to awareness of the *hafla'ah*, we also gain knowledge of the manner in which Hashem applied this *hafla'ah* to His creation. The *shoresh* and root of creation nothing to something is from the very essence, the *atzmut ohr ayn sof*, which is enclothed in a ray of His inifinite light, imparting to it the ability to create from nothing to something. Within this process, there are details. At the moment that the meditator goes into the details, the whole meditation becomes *pnimi* – becomes "internal" in a manner that can change the person.

- By way of example, there was a known story of a kid from Musrara, a very poor neighborhood of Jerusalem, who became fabulously wealthy all of a sudden. Anyone who heard this would say, "Wow," but the newspaper went into the details of how he became wealthy. And as soon as we hear the details, the matter becomes "close" to us. What is the difference between "close" or not? The minute that we hear the details, we begin to feel, "Hey I also want that to happen to me." That's called *kirva*, or "closeness." Or the person may say, "If I can't be like him, I want to be his friend." That is, the more we think of the person as "far" from us, the less the whole narrative will affect us. But if we think either that it could happen to us, or that at least I'm in the same league and therefore we can be "friends," then the story begins to motivate me and urge me to perform in a similar manner.

- There is a Baal Shem Tov story that the Rav heard in Mezibuzh once from one of the Rebbe's there, either R' Shimon the Leilover or the Rachmastrivker, the Rav doesn't recall. The story goes like this: During the first year after the passing of the Besht, R' Zvi the son of the Besht, was the *memalle makom* ("substitute") for the Besht. But the following year on Shavuot, he transferred the task to the Mezritcher Maggid, saying he had heard from his father that "the Magid won't be opposed." And indeed the Magid took the Rebbishe clothes of the Besht and donned them. This R' Tzvi, son of the Besht, was a refined and high level person but was not at all in the world of *parnassa* ("making a living"), so the other students arranged for him to have a store from which to maintain himself. But, with the passage of time, people bought on credit and he didn't ask them to pay, and so he ended up without money. From this they understood that he just wasn't cut out for this kind of work. So it ended up that the *talmidei haBesht* ("students of the Besht") had to support him, and this kind of support is called *maamad gelt* ("maintenance money"). But the students were scattered all throughout the *yishuv* ("area of settlement" in Ukraine and elsewhere), so how could they get the money together to support R' Zvi, son of the Besht? Most did not live in Mezubozh, most lived far away. So, one or two of the *talmidim* took R' Zvi with them to make the rounds and gather money for him. They arrived to R' Michel of Zlotochov, one of the *talmidei haBesht* ("students of the Baal Shem Tov"), and when R' Michel saw him, he burst into tears. Why? Because seeing R' Zvi reminded him of a previous instance when he had cried…once the Besht sat in a very elevated state and when the students saw him in this state, the decided, "This is not a human being." That is, the state of the Besht was so elevated that his students thought he was a *malach* ("angel") or other supernal creature, not a person. And then, R' Zvi who was then a small child, bumped up against his father the Besht, and nudged him. Then the child R' Zvi fell and started crying, and the Besht was aroused from his state of *devekut* ("clinging, cleaving") and picked up his son and said, "Hershele, what happened to you?" So then, R' Michele said that he and the students realized the Besht is a person: One, he came out of his *devekut* and two, he had a son and related to him as a son. So, clearly he was a human, not an angel. At the point, the students burst into tears…why? Because if this was a human being, then his spiritual level obligated them to strive for such a level. Previously, thinking that he was an angel, or spiritual being of some sort, then his spiritual level did not obligate them to think about themselves. But once they understood that a human being could reach this level, they realized that they too had to strive for it. And that's why R' Michele cried upon seeing the son of the Besht, because he recalled the story of the son falling and crying and how that awakened the Besht and they realized he was a human being and cried.

So what we can glean from this is that if the *hafla'ah* (component of "wonder") is too high, too great, without any "handle" on it, then there is no possibility to approach that level. It should be known that it is written somewhere: Why did Hashem create the world with *seder hishtalshelut*, with a hierarchy of spiritual levels, from one level to another? God is *bli g'vul*, without limitation, so He could have created *bli g'vul* without *tzimtzumim* ("contractions") and without all the *madreigot* that man needs in order to grasp Godliness…but the answer is that He created in this manner in order to enable man to grasp and understand and progress and grow in our understanding of God and creation.

- Once the Rav heard in the name of the *Magid* (he thinks), that if God had created from His state of *eyn-sof*, from "nothing to something," then we also would not be able to ascend spiritual *madreigot*. We would not have the *kelim* ("tools") to ascend above. So, He created *histalshelut* in order to enable us to ascend like a ladder or to descend. [See *Sefer Maamorim 5680-5681*/1920-1921 of the Frierdiker Rebbe, page 288-289]

It emerges then that the *hafla'ah* can lead to excitement, but understanding and desire and closeness and *avoda pnimi*, will not result from this; to achieve such results demands attention to and meditation on details. About the *Shaar Hayichud* of the Mittler Rebbe, the previous Rebbe said either that it is the *Aleph-beit* of Chasidut or it's the *mafteichot* ("keys") to Chasidut (the other *sefer* is the *Sha'arei Orah*) – and when we look into *Sha'ar Hayichud* of the Mitteler Rebbe, we see that it's full of details on the *seder hishtalshelut*. Why? Why is it not sufficient to learn about the unity of Hashem, what more do we need? In fact, all that is written here in *K' Avoda* and also in *K' Tefila* about *hitbonenut* in detail, is found originally in the Mitteler Rebbe. Although it's easier to dwell on generalities, the results come quickly and go quickly. But if one gets used to meditation on generalities alone, then it becomes more difficult to focus on details. On the contrary, though, if we focus on the details, then the *avoda* is *pnimi* and remains *pnimi*.

Shiur 83, August 1, 2012

Page 37 in the Hebrew text, Page 158 in the English translation.

"Or, we may briefly…" this refers to the kind of meditation that is more like a short consideration of matters: "Yes, the creation is amazing! That's *nechmad*!" He may also consider matters that are more *pnimi* – such as *sovev* and *memalle* ("transcendant and immanent light") for example – but everything in general alone. The problem with this approach is that since he considers everything in "general," it is not enough in order to arouse true *ahava* within him.

Page 159 – this "general" meditation is similar to "memory." Memory and "reminders" are sufficient in order to attain *yirah*, but not in order to achieve love, which requires deep comprehension. Why is it that *ahava* requires more *b'hasaga* and *pnimi*?

- The Rav recalled a question from the Maharal of Prague, "Why do we use the phrase *yirat shamayim*, but there is no equivalent phrase for love, such as *ahavat shamayim*? (We do say *Ahavat Hashem*, but not *Ahavat shamayim*). In truth the question applies to *yirat shamayim* as well, since we are not afraid of *shamayim*, we're afraid of Hashem. But regarding love, it is more understood because *shamayim* is revealed, we're afraid of the revealed presence of Hashem, so we say, *yirat shamayim*. The Maharal though answers that *yirah* is a result of perceived distance, that the phrase *shamayim v'aretz* is indicative of distance and that's why we use the phrase, '*yirat shamayim*.' For example, when we want to say something is close (such as the mitzvah of *teshuva*), the Torah says, *Lo bashamayim*...meaning "it's not far." The Rav suggests that the same is true here...when we want to consider distance, then *zicharon* ("memory") is sufficient. Since it's far from us and anyway we cannot integrate and internalize it, therefore it is as if far, and recall/memory is sufficient. *Ahava* on the other hand is about *kiruv* and proximity, and that requires *hasaga*, understanding. Later in the sefer, the Rashab gives another explanation, but this is good for now.

The sefer continues (159-160 in the translation) to tell us that Jews are naturally blessed with *bitul* within the soul, and that's what is meant by, "You are the smallest of all nations")Devarim 7:7). The Rav in Chasidut of the Previous Rebbe said that "smallest" in this case does not mean the least numbers, the least in quantity, but the "least" in ego, being the most *butel* ("nullified") of all nations. If so, though what is the *pirush* of the beginning of the verse, "Not because you are such a large nation..." The simple meaning of "large" is numbers, the greatest population...but that cannot work here. The Previous Rebbe explains (the Rav thinks he recalls) that "large" in this context means "with the most qualities." Positive *ma'alot; chachamim, gomlei chasadim*...etc. But not for this were we "chosen," but rather because we are the most *butel*. Now, it's true that all Jews contain natural love as well, but not in the same manner as *yirah*, which is an essential part of the genetic makeup of a Jew. Since *yirah* is more naturally engrained in the Jew, it is easier to arouse, but *ahavah* requires *hitbonenut*.

- There is a *klipah* now that many Jews cannot tolerate that the Jews are the "chosen nation." Once it was the non-Jews who couldn't handle it, but now it's the Jews who don't want to hear that. It sounds "chauvinist and egoist." H-tler *yemach shemo* was bothered by this point; that the Jews claimed to be the "chosen nation." The Mufti asked him, 'What do you have against the Jews,' and he answered,

"There cannot be two chosen nations in the world." But when the world understands that the concept of "chosen" is to be *ovdei Hashem*, then their response, is; "Okay, then if you want to be *frierim* ("naïve and gullible"), then go ahead. We weren't chosen for that."

Another reason that loves requires intellectual meditation is that love is from "*hitgalut davar*," from revelation of that which was hidden, and that requires *hitbonenut* and meditation. Fear is more internal, concealed, from *kivutz* and contraction, not from revelation…

- The Rav said, "We've been speaking about this, we have to do something to make it happen. Need *hitbonenut*. R' Shia Lipkin (*A"H* – a Chasid who lived in Meah Shearim and reviewed a *maamar* from the Rebbeim every Shabbat during *Seudat Shlishit* in the *Baal Ha Tanya* Shul) used to say, "We have to take our head into our hands." *Nafsho b'capo* – have to take our heads in our hands and meditate."

Shiur 84, Aug 2, 2012

General meditation, likened to "recall" and memory, is not sufficient to produce *avoda pnimi* that affects the animal soul. For that, *hitbonenut pnimi* is necessary. General meditation is sufficient to produce *yirah* but not to produce *ahava*, which requires detailed meditation.

Page 37 in the Hebrew text, Page 161 in the English translation.

"As a general rule, light meditation…" General meditation leads to "contraction of the mind," which is part of the same family as *merirut* or "bitterness." When the *keli* ("receptical" or "vessel") is receptive to *ohr*, it expands. When the brain is not receptive, the mind contracts – that's what occurs with "general" meditation that fails to delve into the details. "Contraction in the heart and the mind, which leads spontaneously to a worried heart." Also, during "general" (light) meditation, we experience the *hafla'ah*, the "amazing elevation" of Godliness in comparison to ourselves and our own spiritual level. Among the topics that we can grasp during meditation, we find *gadlut* ("greatness") of God (in creation) and also His *romemut* ("majesty," beyond creation). But, all that "general meditation" allows us to experience is fleeting awareness of the *hafla'ah*, the "elevation" of Godliness. Since that fleeting experience only emphasizes our distance from Hashem, it leads us to a state of *merirut*, or "bitterness" over our distance. In order to be happy, we have to feel that we can get closer to Hashem. For this, we need *hasaga* [grasp of the details of *seder hishtalshelut*]. Without that *hasaga*, we naturally experience only our distance and hence, *merirut*.

- For example, one who learns kabbalah, may feel good about it. But one who does not learn Kabalah and hears about it, may be taken aback and surprised, "Kabbalah?! Who learns Kabalah?" Aside from feeling the *gadlut* ("greatness") of God, we need to feel the closeness as well. That's what leads to *simcha*.

Here we find a long parenthesis with several sections. Some are easier sections. We'll start on page 162, "…When our meditation is shallow and based on simple reminders of God alone, we will [find ourselves] praying with a feeling of tremendous bitterness and crying, accompanied by a very worried heart." So, the question is whether this bitterness and crying is positive or not? On page 63 in parentheses, the text tells us that bitterness of the heart is a *keli* ("vessel") to receive the secrets of the Torah. (There is a gemora, "We don't teach secrets of the Torah except to those who have worried hearts" – and based on that, R' Hillel Paricher would teach Chasidut on Tisha b'Av. And they asked him, "but this is learning Torah and it leads to *simcha*?" He replied with the saying, "We don't teach secrets…except to those who have worried hearts," and what more auspicious time for a "worried heart" than Tisha b'Av?"). So, at first glance it would seem to be a positive development, to have a worried heart, since the worried heart is a vessel for the secrets of the Torah! But, what is meant by "secrets of the Torah"? If Kabalah, then we don't need a "worried heart" because learning Kabalah does not require the heart. Rather, a "worried heart" means "to experience Godliness in the inner recesses of our soul…" (Page 163). "To feel Godliness."

Accordingly, this experience of Godliness within us ("worried heart") has to occur before *tefila*, before prayers in the morning, and especially during *Tikun Hatzot* ("midnite prayers," during which we mourn over the destruction of the Temple). The preparations before *tefila* (beginning with *Tikun Hatzot*) create the *keli*, and the *tefila* itself brings down the *ohr*. However, all of this occurs only if our meditation took place with attention to details. If the meditation remained "general," we may experience a *lev doeg* ("worried heart") and we may have created the *keli*, but the *keli* will remain bereft of *ohr*. It is necessary to put something into the *keli*, and when we do so, the result is *simcha*, happiness. From all of this, there emerges a new *hagdara* of *simcha* and *merirut*. This gives rise to a new understanding of joy versus bitterness. Both are needed, but one who suffices with *merirut* is like one who prepares "clean" *kelim*. He becomes a *keli* for the *ohr* of *tefila*, but the preparation is *merirut*, that is the *keli* for *tefila*. When one meditates only superficially, he prepares the *keli*, it is a "clean *keli*," but with nothing to put in it. Like cleaning all the kitchen utensils but when you want to eat, there is nothing to eat.

- In Jerusalem, it used to be an *inyan* to have "clean *kelim*," but there wasn't any *parnassa*, people had no money. The *kelim* would be shiny – but nothing to eat. So what's better, the *kelim* should be clean and ready but no *ohr*, or *kelim* that are not clean (no *merirut*) but there is *ohr* (*simcha*)? Obviously, both are necessary: *merirut* as preparation and then *simcha* as the *ohr* from above.

Another piece of advice to ensure that our prayers are meaningful, has to do with goals. None of us fulfill all of the demands that we place on ourselves, whether physically or spiritually. It is written that we do not even fulfill "half of our desires." But the question becomes, "half of what?" For one with a lot of desires, "half" is a lot, but for one with much less, half isn't much. The Rav heard in the name of the *Kotzker* that he said to his *avreichim*…"We wanted to be like the *Baal Shem Tov*, so whatever we achieved, we achieved. You *avreichim lechatchila* ("to begin with") don't want to be like the Baal Shem Tov…" [Meaning that the higher we set our sights, the more we will achieve].

- The Slonimer Rebbe (R' Avraham) spoke of one who was nicknamed the "Istanbuler." Many jokes originated from the "Istanbuler," but he was a great man, and he was either the *gabbai* or Chasid of R' Baruch of Mezibush. They found his *kever* ("burial place") by the Baal Shem Tov, in Mezibush. R' Baruch was known as a man of *gevura* ("discipline" and "sharpness"), and the "Istanbuler's" task was to "sweeten the *gevurot*" ("lighten the atmosphere") around R' Baruch. So the story is that guests arrived, and he served them water. These days, clean fresh water is "something," since so much water is contaminated, but in those days it was not *kavod* at all to serve water, since anyone who wanted could draw their own water from a lake or river. So, he told the guests that he had gone to look for meat for them, but the butcher told him that the meat was so good and fat that it was like *shemen* ("fat" or "oil"). He reasoned that if so, *shemen* – "oil" - is the standard by which to measure meat, so *shemen* itself (oil) must be better than meat. He then went to the merchant to buy oil, and the man selling the oil told him, "My *shemen* is so clear that it is like water." So, he reasoned that water must be better than either oil or meat, and therefore he brought them water. This story is printed at the end of the book, *Beit Avraham* (from Slonim), and the Slonimer Rebbe supposedly remarked, "One who seeks too much for the truth, who tries to be overly *amiti*, ends up in the end with simple water." The "moral" (acc to R' Deitsch): If one attempts to meditate in "general" and in "particular," and works on it, but sees that he isn't achieving anything (or at least feels that way), then at least he'll come to davening with *pirush hamilot* – "praying with the simple meaning of the prayers." But if to begin with, he does not even strive for anything beyond himself, in the end, he won't even pray with the simple meaning of the words in mind.

Shiur 85, June 26, 2018 (A second time through *K'Avoda*)

The Rav read from the first page of *K'Avoda*…up to bottom of page 4 in the translation. The purpose of the *aliya* of the soul during *tefila* is *hitkashrut*, connecting with the essence of the soul. This (on page 32 of the translation, after skipping all the parentheses), is *shfichut hanefesh*, "pouring out the soul." And the second goal of *tefila* is refinement of the animal soul, and it is in this second matter that *tefila* was established in place of the *korbanot*. "From you" (Lev 1:2) – from the animal soul. And these two matters – connecting to the source of the soul, and refining the animal soul – correspond to *kavana* during *tefila*, and speech during *tefila*. If man only thinks, without reciting the words, then the soul ascends but the body remains behind. It is necessary to "speak" (say the words of prayers) in order to assist in refining the animal soul.

The letters of prayer correspond to *levanim* (bricks, which are man-made), and the letters of Torah correspond to *avanim* (stones, which are natural creations). *Levanim* and *avanim* in turn correspond to the name *ba'hn* (the four letter name *Havaya* spelt with the letter *hey* in the *milui*, that carries the gematria of 52 – *behama* – "animal") and *ma'h* (the four letter name *Havaya* spelt with the letter *aleph* in the *milui* that carries the gematria of 45 – *adam* – "man"). The name *ba'hn* is associated with the elements of creation that are in need of spiritual elevation, and the name *ma'h* is associated with man who has the ability to sanctify and rectify the creation. *Tefila* is associated with *ba'hn*, and Torah is associated with *ma'h*. When we learn Torah, and say the words, we are "calling to God."

- Once someone said (in farbrengen), "If that's the explanation of קריאה בתורה ("reading or calling in the Torah" - "calling God's names"), and Hashem "arrives," and says to us, "Nu, where are you, you called me?" and all we can say is, "I didn't even know that I called you…" The same applies during prayer between *Kriat Shema* and *Shemonah Esreh* – Rashi in Gemora Berachot (4B) brings a Yerushalmi that when a person mentions *geula* ("redemption"), Hashem stands at the doorway and waits for him, [but if he doesn't sufficiently want *geula*] as he goes into *Shemonah Esreh*, then it is as if he has failed to respond to Hashem's presence. "Like one who came to the door of the King and knocked, and the king responded and came out to meet him, and found that he had left, he was no longer at the door. So Hashem leaves. Rather one should draw near to God by mentioning all the praises of *yetziat Mitzrayim* (which we do during *Kriat Shema*) and while he is still near to Him, he should make his requests" (Rashi there).

The Rav does go into the parentheses on page 35: "(Even in the *Amida a*bout which it says…)" – this is a request from Above (even tho it is *tefila*) – to this the *K'Avoda* answers that it's still the man from below who is uttering the request. The letters of *tefila* in this request are coming from the man. In fact, the Rav adds that at the end of each *bracha* of the *Shemonah Esreh*, it is permitted to add requests that are related to that particular *bracha*. (There's a letter from the Rebbe in which he mentions that our *minhag* is to add such requests only at the end of the blessing *shomeah tefila*, not during the other blessings).

In any case, both goals of *tefila* – elevation of the soul and refinement of the animal soul – are the result of divine love of God, and therefore the entire goal of *tefila* is to arouse love of God. Chapter 2 and 3 deal with *yirah* – "fear" – and afterward the *K'Avoda* goes into *ahava*.

Shiur 86, June 28, 2018

Summary of the first chapter: Two *inyanim* regarding *tefila*. Connecting our soul to Godliness, so it achieves *ratzoh* ("will or desire" for God). Second, to refine and elevate the animal soul.

Ch 2 – there must also be fear. Fear of God is necessary, it is the foundation and the beginning of *avoda*, even tho it is not the *avoda* of *tefila* ("fear of God is not the path of prayer"). The Rav read from page 38 onward. Regarding guarding our eyesight, there are two matters: 1) Any *peula* (action) that we might take in order to shield our vision, and 2) to "fence" our vision so that even before something comes into our line of sight, we are "fenced in" and guarded. And in order to "open" up to something that comes into line of sight, we have to consider if we want to "give permission" to open up to it or not – this is called *hagdara* – "fenced off." There are people who walk in the street and see something that they don't want to see so they block it off – this is not called *hagdara*, it is called fulfillment of the mitzvah of *Lo taturu* – "do not be led astray after your heart or after your eyes." *Hagdara* though occurs when the person blocks the visual stimulus even before it reaches his eyes: He guards himself and closes himself off; he does not see unless he opens his eyes. His vision is not "open" and all the moreso regarding items that are forbidden to see.

Here, the Rav does go into the parentheses, bottom of page 38, "The truth is that seeing…" Seeing (passive) is one matter, gazing and observing (active) is another matter, and *K'Avoda* says that peering and gazing is the source of all evil. There are such people who are completely removed from what they see, but this is not the norm; even among *ovdei Hashem* their vision affects them at least somewhat. But since they are *ovdei Hashem*, it "bounces off them." But on those who are not *ovdei Hashem*, their eyesight can bring them down.

- A coarse *mashal* to illustrate…a virgin by whom it was possible to see that she was "a little bit pregnant." "Just a little bit"…[similarly, we cannot guard our eyesight "just a little bit." Once we allow even a "small" negative stimulus to enter, it cannot be "unseen"].

- Someone in the US, a Litvish rosh yeshiva, wrote a *kuntres* regarding *re'iya* ("vision") and quoted a lot from Tanya and Chasidishe sources…he wrote that until now, it was thought that only Chasidim protected and guarded their eyesight. But now it is clear that the issue of vision involves *issurim d'oraita* ("Torah prohibitions"). And this Rosh Yeshiva in Lakewood who wrote his *kuntres* speaks of those who "saw" and "watched" things that they should not have seen, and then they justify looking at more of the same with the excuse that, "I already lowered myself, I'm already in the garbage, might as well look at more." The Litvish Rosh Yeshiva quotes from Tanya that "*b'kol dechiya v'dechiya*" – every time you push away the *yetzer harah*, the "glory of God permeates all worlds." In other words, the appropriate response is not to continue looking, but to repel the urge.

- After *tefila* with Rav Shteineman in Bnei Brak, the *minhag* was to approach him and shake his hand. One person who prayed there, approached the Rav who extended his hand, and the person said, "If you knew how many *aveirot* ("transgressions") I committed, you would not extend your hand to me." Rav Shteineman asked, him, "Did you ever overwhelm your *yetzer harah*?" The man answered, "Several times." R' Shteineman once more extended his hand and told him, "Do you know what you achieved [by repelling the urge to look], you know what kind of effect you had on the world?" – and he praised him, like a Chassidishe Rebbe (many of the stories from him are in that direction). This is the way to influence people; rather than criticizing them for negative behavior, praise them for their positive behavior. R' Yoel (Kahn?) says that the explanation of *kol dechiya v'dechiya* ("each and every time that you repel your *yetzer harah*") is that even if you think you have achieved nothing because you keep pushing away the same *yetzer harah* every time – the explanation is that "you" may not feel that each *dechiya* has an effect, because it is Hashem who makes it have an effect, not you. You push it away, and the effect that repelling has Above is from God. This is the *dagesh* ("emphasis") that the Litvish rosh yeshiva in Lakewood writes in his *kuntres*. (The *sefer* itself mentions Tanya, and the *rosh yeshiva* gave his *haskama*).

- This shiur was on 15 Tammuz so was the yahrtzeit of the Ohr HaChaim…the Rav read from the Ohr Hachaim on parshat Balak on the verse, *Mah tovu ohalecha Yaakov* – four kinds of tzadikim: 1) like Shmuel Hanavi who would travel all over *Eretz Yisrael* to teach Jews 2) tzaddikim who sat in *Lishkat Hagazit*, and people came to them 3) those who learn for themselves 4) those who don't learn but support learners.

Shiur 87, July 2, 2018

Summary: The purpose of the *avoda* of *tefila* is to achieve love of God, and via divine love to effect a transformation of our *midot* ("character traits"). In fact, the only way to change the *midot* is via *ahavat Hashem* ("love of God"), otherwise it is impossible. To "break" the *midot* is possible without love, but to change the *midot* necessitates *ahava*. The Rav read again from beginning of Ch 2, page 38. "Fear of sin" is the basis, and we must guard our eyes so that from the beginning they don't look and therefore they don't see, and they are only open if we take an active decision to see. Not that the eyes are open – rather, that they are "not available for use."

- R' Eliyahu Hadad pointed out that Chabad is internet friendly only to those sites that are worthy, not open to every site in the world. If you want to allow the site you have to give special permission (don't know if he is speaking of a certain browser or a policy or what).

Page 40 in the translation: To "fence oneself in" is difficult only at the beginning of the process, but with time it becomes natural and quite the opposite, it brings peace and calm because we are not faced with temptations and tests.

- The Rav heard once from a Chashidishe *bachur* who learned in a Litvish yeshiva, and the Rav heard from both the *bachur* and his Rosh

Yeshiva – the Chasidishe *bachur* spoke about a Litvak whom he saw sitting in the bus with his eyes down. The Rav thought about this and said, "That's not because he wants to guard his eyes. Quite simply he has no *koach* for tests (*nesionot*) and therefore he guards his eyes."

From the text: There are those who are far from any *aveira b'poel* ("far from any actual sin") who allow themselves to look "coldly" at something because they feel nothing, but the Rebbe Rashab says that they have *taanug b'etzem* (a subconscious but "essential enjoyment") from this gazing, and that is not good.

- Previous Rebbe told a story about the Mitteler Rebbe, at length… the Mitteler Rebbe would travel from time to time, in the area where his Chassidim lived, in order to reinforce and support his Chasidim. When he arrived to a Chasidishe village or settlement, he would recite a Chassidic discourse (a *maamar*)…and he granted *yechidut* ("private audiences") with the locals. Once in the middle of one such *yechidut*, he all of a sudden stopped, closed the door and was alone in the room. From outside, the house members could hear a lot of crying and were very worried, "What happened"? This occurred in the middle of the *yechidut*. And the Mitteler Rebbe returned home and fasted… nobody knew what happened until much later it became clear. A certain Jew had gone into the MItteler Rebbe for *yechidut* and requested a *tikun* ("fixing, rectification") for a particular *aveira* (R' Shlomo Chaim used to tell his students, "when you go in for *yechidut*, don't be too shy to ask for a *tikun* for what you did in your youth"). So this Jew asked for a *tikun* for a certain *aveira* and as known, in order to find a *tikun*, the Rebbe has to look inside of himself (so to speak) and find that matter within himself, at least *b'dakut* (in a much more "refined manner"). When the Rebbe couldn't find this *aveira* within himself, he could not find a *tikun* for the *aveira*, and he became very distraught that perhaps the evil was so hidden within him that it was an essential part of his makeup, *b'etzem* ("essential," like mentioned here in *K'Avoda*) and that's why he couldn't find it. And that was what bothered the Mitteler Rebbe so much. And he only relaxed when he found the *aveira* "within himself" – and it turned out to be when he says Chasidut and the Chasidim fail to find any way in which they can apply it to their *avoda*. That was the "sin" that he found within himself. Someone asked, "What was the *aveira* that the person did, the one who requested a *tikun*?" In the *sicha*, it is not written, and R' Shlomo Chaim would not answer, but in quiet he would say. (Was necrophilia, apparently).

Shiur #88, July 5, 2018

The Rav: "There's a similar *nusach* in Chabad, the Rebbe mentioned it and I wrote about it to R' Zevin. R' Hillel Paritcher was a big *machmir*. He said that all of his *chumrot* (personal stringencies that he adopted) were for the purpose of integrating (*upleigin zich*) a Chasidishe vort by davening." That is, the point of all of his *chumrot* were to enable him to integrate a Chassidishe vort while davening. "Chasidut is *Havaya Elokim*, that's Chasidut…"

- R' Chaim Brisker would frequently come to see the Rebbe Rashab, they had a close relationship because of public matters (*inyanei hatzibur*) that they worked on together. R' Chaim saw the Rashab's *k'tavim* ("writings") and told the Rashab, "I see that all of Chasidut speaks of two or three different themes." The Rashab told him, "That's not correct, all of Chassidut speaks of only one matter; *Havaya* is *Elokim*." (In the background, R' Zalman Springer can be heard giving a different version involving two answers of the Rashab…) In any case, the Rav says that "all that you learn is in order to achieve recognition that *Havaya is Elokim*…" *Hagadarat hachushim* ("fencing in the senses") is for the same purpose…

- Once the Rav heard in a farbrengen, "How would you know if you are holding in a good place, how can you discern whether or not you fell into some kind of *taiva* ("lust, temptation") or not?" There is someone in the gemora (Shmuel?) who used to regularly bring *korbanot* to the Temple. The way to know if you're in a good place or not is by your *tefila*. Does it go, does it flow? If so, that is a sign that you did not stumble. If your *tefila* does not flow, it's a *siman* that you stumbled…

On page 43 in the translation: "The same holds true for the sense of hearing…" Once an older person sat opposite R' Deitsch and started to tell him about the things that he wished he could do as when he was a younger man. R' Deitsch told him, "Stop, why are you telling me this"? He said, "It's good to know," and then the Rav put his hands over his ears so he wouldn't hear him. There's a gemora that says, 'Why did Hashem create the fingers as they are? So that you can insert them in your ears if necessary.'

- Among Chasidim, there was a great emphasis on not speaking before davening. This is somewhat forgotten these days, but there was a sharp letter from the Alter Rebbe (in addition to the one that appears at the end of the siddur not to speak *leitzanus* – "nonsense and scoffing"), instructing not to speak at all. It is preferable not to speak

Shiurim on K'Avoda from the Mashpia R' Deitsch שיח׳   537

any *d'varim b'teilim* ("empty speech") before *shacharit* ("morning prayers") and also for a full hour before mincha/maariv. This was actually a *takana* ("decree") from the Alter Rebbe, that appears in his *Igerot Kodesh* (the Rav couldn't find it tho). R' Benyamin Landau found it for him in the Mitteler Rebbe, not the Alter Rebbe.

The Rav read from the *K'Avoda* until page 47 (in the translation), and then quoted from the MItteler Rebbe that "one who takes upon himself *ohl malchut shamayim*, the *klipot* run away from him."

As the Rav read the *YomYom*, he mentioned that it was the yahrtzeit of R' Shlomo Karliner *ztz'l*, about whom the Alter Rebbe said that he was "a *tefach* higher than the velt" (he was a handsbreadth higher than the world). The Rav couldn't find it but said that the Tzemach Tzedek in Derech Mitzvotecha explained that "*tefach* above the velt" meant that he was a *bechina* of *yesod*; the world is *malchut* and the *tzadik* is *yesod*.

Shiur 89, July 9, 2018

Back to the section on hearing: Page 43 (13 in the original Hebrew): The explanation of "ears" in the verse (Deut 23:14) is "clothes" so that it means, "make a peg on your clothes." The gemora says the word means "ears," and the peg is a digging instrument. But here we are saying that the word means "finger" that you can stick into your ears…Chasidish translation – "ears" *k'pshuto*, and the peg becomes "finger"…and this is the twist on it given by the gemora (Ketubot 5).

- R' Moshe Alperovitz was a *shochet* ("ritual slaughterer"), a student in Tomchei Tmimim, and he was a *tzadik*. Erev Yom Kippur everyone went to him to slaughter their *kaparot* chickens. Since there was a long line, he went to check on the other *shochet* in the city and found that no one was there. He understood that he was taking away his livelihood from the other *shochet* and he decreed on himself that he would not be a *shochet* at all. Not only in this place but not at all. In order to make a living, he took a job at the Dead Sea works, part of which was part of Israel at the time, before the six day war. His son told R' Deitsch that he took only bread with him for the entire week, and ate only bread and water. There at work, were simple folks who spoke matters that he didn't want or need to hear (*nivul peh*), so what could he do? He couldn't put fingers in his ears since he was at work, so he asked from Hashem to make him deaf. Hashem listened to his prayers, and a stone or something fell near him and from the echo or the blowback he became deaf. If you wanted to speak with him, you had to raise your voice. Yet, if it was holy matters, he would hear even from far away – the Rav himself saw this happen, since R' Moshe would spend every Shabbes with his daughter in Bnei Brak (where the Rav was learning in yeshiva at the time), he would stand far away and yet hear *Kriat HaTorah*.

- During the war of Independence (the Rav would have been only four or five years old then), there were pockets of Chabadniks in Ramat Yitzhak (?), in Ramat Gan and in Tel Aviv, but everyone scattered, each one looking for shelter, some people even sought shelter under the *Aron Kodesh*. There were no shelters as we know them today, etc… but during the war they gathered together (the Rav thinks in Ramat Yitzhak) and among them was R' Nahum Goldschmidt, a big *maskil* in Chasidut. Also the GurAryeh family, who were there from even before the war. And they sold *maftir Yona* (it's accepted that *maftir Yona* is a *segula* for *parnassa*, but in Chabad it is said to be something special spiritually, very high). R' Nahum Goldschmidt bought it, but he gave it to R' Moshe. Everyone applauded because R' Moshe was a simple man in relation to a *maskil* such as R' Nahum. He was a *baal avoda*, a *tamim*, but not a *maskil*. R' Zelig Feldman was there at the time and he described how R' Nahum got agitated and asked everyone, "What's going on with us? Why all the excitement? As if the 'big *maskil*' gives up his right to *Maftir* Yona?' Have we gotten the true hierarchy?" That is, to R' Nahum it was quite obvious that the *maftir* should go to Moshe, the *baal avoda*. R' Nahum had money but still it was only appropriate that Moshe should get the *maftir* (and R' Moshe would also say amazing things about R' Nahum, as well…).

- R' Zelig Feldman (*A"H*) also told about an experience of a gathering of people at *Tzach* (*Tzeirei Agudat Chabad* – the outreach arm of Chabad) in the US when R' Moshe was a guest there during *chol hamoed* Succot. They called him up to to speak, and he said that in "*Torat Shalom* it speaks of two pieces of advice for *timtum hamoach*…" (*Timtum hamoach* is "clogged intellect," or "stupidity"). That is, to a bunch of *askanim* (Chasidim working in the public sphere for the good of the public, who were not especially interested in meditation or the other Chassidic practices involving *avodat Hashem*), he spoke of real *avoda* in a way that totally put them in their place, "like taking of pail of cold water and throwing it on their heads."

- Yet another story of R' Moshe: At work at the Dead Sea Works, the director wanted to promote him to a better job, realizing that he was very kosher and *yosher*, very "straight and honest," he wanted him to not work so hard and yet get better pay. R' Moshe declined and when they finally got out of him why, he said that in his current job he could work with his hands and think *divrei Torah*, but in the suggested job, he would have to use his brain for work and wouldn't be able to think Torah. The Rav says that just by looking at him, you would get thoughts of *teshuva*.

The Rav continued on page 44, and defined *devarim beteilim* as "things that you don't need to speak about." Even asking someone, "What's happening" is in that category... Discussing *ohl malchut shamayim* (the "yoke of the kingdom of Heaven"), the Rav said it is a "condition," not an arousal or a feeling. Therefore, it is spontaneous, "Cannot be any other way." But the maint thing is that the *oved Hashem* doesn't even open his eyes, he's not "available for work." He is *mugdar b'chushim*. And the Rav emphasized the *inyan* of "doesn't get angry." Why? Because he is like an *eved pashut* ("simple servant") with *ohl malchut shamayim*...

Shiur 90, July 10, 2018

We learned about *kabalat ohl* ("acceptance of the yoke"), whether conscious or unconscious, and the explanation of *kabalat ohl* is that the person is *mugdar*, is "fenced in." He is not "available for work." He has to give permission to any of the senses; whether eyesight, whether hearing, whether speaking...

Now on Page 49 in the translation: Here, it seems that the "location" where *tikun* must take place is in the *midot* ("emotions, character traits"), since that is where the *chumriyut* ("coarse physicality") of the person is concentrated. Since "foreign thoughts" occur to us as the products of our coarse character traits and emotions, it follows that if they are refined, the coarse physical thoughts won't arise at all.

- R' Shlomo Chaim said that *bachurim* (yeshiva students) would come to him complaining that they had lusts and "foreign thoughts" (*ta'avot* and *machshavot zarot*). They would say that they already looked into the book *Reishit Chochma* (which is supposed to offer a "cure") and the other *seforim* and it didn't help. He would tell them that, "The only thing that helps is *avodat hatefila*" – the only thing that helps is proper prayer with *avoda*.

The Rav read from the text until page 51, then explained: "True, the main problem begins with the *midot*, with the natural emotions that are built into us, and arises spontaneously to the heart. Which is why the *avoda* has to be on the *midot*, and then the strange thoughts won't arise. Nevertheless, since we're speaking of the *beinoni* (the "intermediate" person who is still struggling with his *yetzer harah*) and it's only a *tzadik* (a truly righteous person, devoid of a *yetzer harah*) who can change the nature of his *midot* – therefore we are forced to arrive to the concept of *hagdara*, "fencing in" the senses. What is *hagadara*? When a negative thought occurs to us, we repel it. That's *hagdara* when it comes to our thought processes.

- The Rav already pointed out on other occasions that the original thought, as it arises in our mind that and we are required to repel it, is not called an *aveirah* – it is not a sin. That it arose to our consciousness is inevitable and unavoidable, since we possess a *yetzer harah*. Since it's not possible to "erase" the thought, but only only to suppress it, it's not called a "transgression." The Alter Rebbe writes in Tanya that a *beinoni* who does this (suppressing the thought) is not guilty of any sin.

- The Rav already spoke of R' Hirsh, an *avrech* who told him about the *Beit Yisrael*, the previous Gerer Rebbe, who was very careful about anything having to do with *kedusha* ("holiness")... He went around to every *avrech* in the *Beit Midrash* and informed each and every one, "In Tanya it is written that the first thought is not an *aveirah*, In Tanya it is written..." [It's written in Tanya that a *beinoni* never transgressed a sin during his entire life, and yet at the same time Tanya tells us that if a foreign thought arises in the mind of the *beinoni* – which itself seems to be a sin - he should "repel it with both hands." From this we deduce that the "first thought," when it arises, is not an *aveira*]. The *nefesh habehamit* ("animal soul") provides the suggestion (it sends the foreign thought, the "snare"), and he rejects it. Then the *yetzer harah* comes along and says, "Listen you already fell into the garbage by thinking of this, so think of it again..." And in order to "push it away," we need *kabalat ohl* ("acceptance of the yoke," acceptance of the need to fight...)

- [Another story from the Beit Yisrael: The brother of R' Shlomo Zalman Auerbach *ztz'l* was Rosh Yeshiva of *Yeshivat Hamekubalim*, *Sha'ar Hashamayim* (I asked the Rav if this brother was a Kaballist himself, and the Rav replied that he doesn't know and in truth he would like to know). The Rosh Yeshiva's son had a friend who was a Gerer Chasid, who told him that he met up with the Beit Yisrael on one of his early morning *shpatziren* ("walks"), who "accosted him," saying "...הירא את דבר ה׳...הניס את עבדיו" "He who fears God...should hide his servants..." (Ex 9:2). "How does a Jew achieve fear of God?" The Beit Yisrael asked this question to the *avrech* as a challenge, but since the Beit Yisrael was a Rebbe, the *avrech* remained silent, did not answer. The Beit Yisrael asked him again, and then answered, "Through *hitbonenut* ("meditation") – that's what it says in Tanya"!]

- *B'derech agav* ("By the way"), here the Rav mentions that this is what constitutes a *Talmud Chacham* – a "real Torah scholar" - he knows well "how to *magdir.*" [This is a double entendre...*lehagdir* ("to fence in") our senses is one meaning, and the other is *lehagdir* the concept – to place a Torah concept in proper perspective and in its appropriate category, which is a mark of a genuine Torah scholar].

- There is a tradition among us that it is impossible to "erase" a thought and eliminate it, but what we can do is to "pass it on to another thought." R' Shlomo Chaim used to say, "What is this language [of Tanya in Ch 12] to "repel it 'with both hands'?" In the name of R' Hillel, there are times when we repel the thought in a manner of *yamin mekarevet v'smol docheh* ("The right hand brings closer while the left hand repels"). What does that mean in our case? It means we might think that it's acceptable to (briefly) consider the enticing thought of the *yetzer harah*, in order to "examine it" to know if we should push it away. And our purpose in doing so would be in order to repel the negative thought. If we do so, we ultimately we both bring it closer to us and also repel it. R' Hillel explained that, "push it away with both hands" means "don't bring it closer to even think about it." Rather, push it away with both hands without considering it at all. Like one person argueing with another, and the second person doesn't want to hear it. He says, "I don't even want to hear from you." - That's what Tanya means with "repel it with both hands."

- Here, R' Eliyahu Hadad pointed out that the *yetzer harah* does not make its approach as an objective observer. It mentions "mitzvoth" such as *limud, tefila, midot*, etc in order to fool us into thinking that its suggestion is good for our *avodat Hashem*, our path of service to approach God. About this, the *Baal Shem Tov* says that in the future, the *yetzer harah* won't be judged on what its own task was – after all, it was created in order to try to entice man off the path and seduce him. However, it will be judged for "trying to turn an *aveirah* ("sin") into a mitzvah," for using mitzvoth as a way to try to entice a person into sinning...

On page 154, "the *klipot* run away." – R' Shlomo Chaim would repeat this frequently, that the advice to save onself from *machshavot zarot* ("foreign thoughts") and negative ideas that rise to mind spontaneously, is via *yirat shamayim* ("fear of God"), since as he would frequently say and as written, "Because of *malchut shamayim* ("Kingdom of God"), the *klipot* run away." That is, in general the *klipot* (forces opposed to *kedusha*) demand a war, but if one adapts *ohl malchut shamayim*, they just run away and melt away. Like in the Zohar, when the *eishet znunim* ("wandering wife") "smells" the *eishet chayil* ("woman of valor"), she runs away. The Rav mentioned that this is the smell of the *korban omer*…in general, the Rav says that there are many sections of the Zohar that truly "illuminate the eyes," that are very enlightening but they are long. Someone wrote a book, *Matok m'devash* which quoted these long sections and then someone else (his son?) took out short lines from the Zohar and put them in the *siddur*. In any case R' Shlomo Chaim frequently quoted the sentence about "The *klipot* run away," and also another pithy statement: *Ribui dabat* leads to *Ribui Machaz* – "a lot of *d'varim b'teilim* leads to a lot of *machshavot zarot*." This is the language of the Mitteler Rebbe's *Derech Chaim*. R' Shlomo Chaim would speak of the *Heilige Ruzhener* ("the holy Ruziner Rebbe"), who illustrated this point with a *mashal* of a pipe going into the water: When you want to block the flow of water…you can either put your hand over the part of the pipe that is immersed in the water, or you can block off the flow of water from its origin, from the top from the source of the water. So the holy *Ruzhner* says that the *brit milah* is connected with one "pipe" to the *lashon* ("tongue"), so if you close the upper end (the mouth, that is your mouth, you don't speak *devarim beteilim*), spontaneously you won't suffer *zerah l'vatalh* either).

- R' Shlomo Chaim would often speak about *itkafia b'dibur* – "controlling your tongue" so you don't speak negative matters. And once (he didn't speak about this often) – he revealed that it was something that the Rebbe Rashab told him during his first *yechidut* with him (R' Shlomo Chaim was born in 1894, the Rashab was the Rebbe from 1883 until 1920). The language of the Rashab was that he should "do *itkafia b'dibur*, and that aside from guarding him for the future, it would also be a *tikun* for the past."

Shiur 91, July 12, 2018

Page 54 in the translation, "Therefore, fear of God…" *Kabalat Ohl* must be present, *Ahavat Hashem* alone is not enough. It's impossible to continue serving God without *kabalat ohl*. One can continue to fulfill Torah and mitzvoth without *kabalat ohl*, but if he is lacking *ahavat Hashem*, he will be lacking *dveikut* ("clinging") to God and therefore he will also become more physical and coarse. And he will become involved in permitted *ta'avot* ("lusts"), and lacking warmth and life in his *avodat Hashem*. That is, his *yirah* will protect him from forbidden matters, but not from permitted temptations. [Here was a discussion between Eliyahu Hadad, R' Dovid Boaz, R' Shalom Dovid Segal…]. The minute he has *ahavah* though, he wants to do the mitzvah and when he does so, he feels *dveikut*.

- The Rav wanted to say something that he heard or perhaps saw: "Any *hamshacha* ("drawdown" or "influx") of Godliness – one must want it, must desire it. The moment one loves God, he desires *dveikut* with Hashem, and the minute he does a mitzvah, he feels the *dveikut*, it is conscious. But one who has no love, who doesn't look for *dvekut* with Hashem, merely wants to "avoid friction." He wants only to avoid the feeling that he is "not doing what Hashem wants." So, when the mitzvah comes his way, it provides no support for him, and he feels nothing. He is simply satisfied not to be "in a state of friction."

- Here, R' Eliyahu Hadad argued that we learned in Tanya that we do not feel the mitzvah when we do it, we do not get a feeling of Godliness when we fulfill a mitzvah. To this the Rav replied, "There are *dargot*, there are different levels." And he answered with a *mashal*: When the doctor tells you, "This food gives you this vitamins, this food supplies this nutrients," do you feel it? Do you tell the doctor, "But I don't feel that"? You don't feel it because you don't have the 'tools' (*kelim*) to feel it, and neither do the doctors. The doctors themselves only know through a process of experimentation and numbers that one thing or another "works." They don't "feel it," they don't have the tools to feel it. At a certain point, the Rav didn't feel well, he went to a doctor who examined him to see if the Rav digests what he is eating. They check what "comes out" after eating and they found all the vitamins and good things weren't being digested, they also "came out." Something similar occurs with mitzvoth: one can do a mitzvah and it has an effect on him while another does not feel the effect, but the "doctor" can tell that even if he didn't feel it, nevertheless it had an effect on him.

- R' Aharon Tchernobler had a *gabbai*, whom the Chassidim would bother and irritate all the time, asking him, "When can I go into see the Rebbe?" And they would bother him when he was davening as well, until one day he just decided it's not worth it to pray anymore.

That day, he didn't pray and went into the Rebbe, who immediately asked him, "Why didn't you pray today"? The *gabbai* told him the story and explained that his *tefila* didn't achieve anything because the Chassidim were bothering him all the time. So the Rebbe asked him, "If your *tefila* makes no difference, then how can I see the today you did not pray while yesterday you did pray? That proves that the *tefila* does have an effect on you." The Rebbe is like the doctor; the difference being that the doctor doesn't really know what's going on with the patient, he can only make educated guesses using statistics and his trained observations, but the Rebbe knows by just looking.

- And in truth the great doctors in Jewish history – Rambam for example, examined their patients just by looking at them. There is a story about the ibn Ezra, who very much wanted to meet the Rambam. At one stage, the Rambam saw him and wrote, "We must be sure that he has money." That is, he saw that Ibn Ezra was healthy but that he needed money – that also he could see. The mitzvah works, everything works, but the question is how much of all that becomes revealed? If someone stopped eating because he wasn't getting what needed from his food, obviously that would not be the correct approach. He may need to change his lifestyle so that he eats better or eats different foods or exercises, etc…but to stop eating completely is not the answer. The same is true regarding mitzvoth. One who isn't deriving the most love and *dveikut* from the mitzvoth, does this mean he should stop doing them? Of couse not, he should develop the *kelim*, the "tools" such as *kabalat ohl* and *ahava* in order to bring the effect of the mitzvah into revelation by him and make the effects conscious. The mitzvoth do have an effect anyway, but it may require a Rebbe to see the effect.

- There is a story about R' Aharon Tchernobler with the Tzmemach Tzedek. There were accusations against a certain woman that, if true, would cause her to become forbidden to her husband. She herself claimed that, "nothing happened" and some *rabonim* said she was permitted to her husband and others said she was forbidden…when she came to R' Aharon Tchernobler he said that she is "clean," and permitted to her husband. There was disagreement among the *rabonim*, and they went to the Tzemach Tzedek who was both a Rav and a Rebbe, and he said she is "forbidden." They told the Tzemach Tzedek that R' Aharon Tchernobler had said she is "clean" and "permitted." The Tzemach Tzedek replied that "She did *teshuva*, and that erased the sin, so that R' Aharon could not see the sin." But, acc to Jewish law (*halacha*), she remained forbidden even if she erased the sin. So we see an amazing situation; *teshuva* wipes out the sin, but according to *halacha*, the sin remains. And so it is with mitzvoth: It's possible that one feels no *chayut*, no vitality in doing the mitzvah, but it nevertheless remains a mitzvah.

- R' Eliyahu Hadad asked, "Just like when eating sometimes you may not receive the full value of the food, if you do a mitzvah not *lishmah* (not "entirely for the sake of God"), you do not receive the full qualities of love and *dveikut*. But if you do the mitzvah *lishmah* (for its own sake), you get it. So, there must be something in the mitzvah that enables you to turn it around from not *lishmah* to *lishmah*. So, how do we achieve that transformation? The Rav answered, "It is found within, you have to find it. The minute it's *lishmah*, you reveal it, it emerges." Nevertheless, R' Eliyahu insisted, "there must be something, a *levush* ("garment"), that allows us to make this switch…

- Here, the Rav told another story…one of the Ruzhiner Rebbeim, perhaps the Sadigora, had a son who wanted to learn in Yeshiva. In those days, there weren't Chasidishe yeshivas (when the Rashab set up *Tomchei Tmimim*, it was a *chiddush*), there were only Litvish yeshivas. So the father didn't know whether to allow him to learn in a Litvish yeshiva, since he was Chasidishe. He went to ask the Rebbe, who told him, "No." He said that there, in the Litvish yeshiva, there is no *chayut* ("energy, vitality") in *kedusha*, and when there is no *chayut* in *kedusha*, there is *chayut* in *klipah*. The father went and asked several times and the answer was always, "No," but the son went and learned there anyway. The Rav heard this story many many years ago, and then R' Shmuel Hefer in Kfar Chabad told the Rav that he met the Jew who was that son of the Chassid, to whom the Sadigora Rebbe said that his son should not to learn there and that there is no "holy energy" there, and if no holy energy, then there is energy of *klipa*… and the son was without a *kippa* and without anything… And in fact, the son told R' Hefer, "I am the one who they said not to send." That tells you that if there is no *chayut*, there is a problem… At any rate, R' Eliyahu Hadad continued his search for the key inside that flips the person from not *lishmah* to *lishmah*, and the Rav said that it's there inside of the person at all times, it never left him, it's always there.

Shiur #92, July 13, 2018

We began Ch 4 yesterday, learned a little bit of it. Here we have parentheses, and the Rav says that he has a *kabala* ("received tradition") that the parentheses in both *K'Tefila* and *K'Avoda* are *pilpulim* ("complicated and deep intellectual investigations") that we save for the second or third time that we learn the *Kuntresim*. "There's Rashi and there's Tosfos." First of all, we learn Gemora and Rashi…here (in *K'Avoda*), the parentheses are *dakot shb'dakot*…("very refined")…we learned that in general there are two categirues of love, "like water" and "like fire." The definition of "love like water" is that it's *kiruv u'dvekus b'Elokus* ("proximity and cleaving to Godliness"). It's not fire and desire, rather it arrives via meditation on the Godly *chayut* ("energy") in the world ("And You enliven everything…"). His love is twofold: Because of how God enlivens the world in general and also how He enlivens our own soul in particular. When we begin to experience the elevation and preciousness of God, that's what brings us closer. Man is attracted to what he feels is important and in this case of experiencing Him as our "vitality and energy," it leads to us to place more emphasis on *limud haTorah* – "learning Torah." This experience of preciousness is from the Godly soul but meditation is required in order to draw it out. What is present naturally in the Godly soul is the feeling that we don't want to be separate from God. But the feeling that we want to be close demands *hitbonenut*, and that is the *derech ha'arucha* ("long path") at the beginning of Tanya (Ch 1-17). (The *cheshbon hanefesh* or "accounting" of Ellul is that we have potential, we have abilities, why aren't we using them?).

- Regarding potential, R' Shlomo Chaim spoke of a Chasid who would read the first lines of Perek 2 of Tanya, "The second soul among Jews is a a true portion of Godliness," and would sit for ten or fifteen minutes just thinking about this. Then he would go back once more and say the words, and then meditate on it…he would repeat this process a few times, then blurt out, "If so, where is it?" Would break into tears and then fall asleep…Rav Deitsch says this is a huge lesson: The "mussar" aspect ("Where is it"?) was only momentary, but the entire *hitbonenut* on the positive constructive aspect ("The second soul…") took sustained time.

- R' Eliyahu Haddad asked, "I have trouble grasping this…the Godly soul on its own will sprout and grow, but the animal soul holds it back? I have trouble understanding this." The Rav said, "Let's illustrate the matter. Let's say you know someone who is very talented but he is lazy. If he finds a way to separate the laziness and neutralize it, automatically he'll use his talents. Now if the person works on the negative, trying to neutralize his laziness, he won't succeed as well as if he focuses on motivating and enabling his positive abilities and talents. So the focus has to be on putting his talents into effect."

Shiurim on K'Avoda from the Mashpia R' Deitsch שיח׳ 547

The Rav moved on to page 23 in the original Hebrew, skipping the parentheses (Page 94 in the translation), *ohr memalle* bring *chayut* to each creation according to its level, and the same in the *nefesh/neshama*. There is also *nefesh ruach neshama* in the *sephirot*. (See Ch 18, P 46 in Tanya) – in connection with these divisions of the souls and the worlds, the Rav mentions that in his intro to *Eitz Chaim* , R' Chaim Vital writes that the entire purpose of all these levels is to arrive to *ahavat Hashem* – love of God. Point is, we must use out our potential (there are some who say that this was the purpose of the *Baal Shemtov*).

Shiur #93, August 12, 2018

The Rav quotes from the *Bach* (R' Yoel Sirkus, the *Beit Chadash*, a commentary on the *Tur Shulhan Aruch* from the early 1600,'s from whom the Rav is descended) who mentioned that "Ellul" is *Ani leDodi*… indicating since we call Hashem, "*Dodi*," "My beloved," that the *avoda* of Ellul is "love of God." Some think that it's only about fear, but here we see that the *avoda* of Ellul is about love.

Kitzur from Page 22, end of Ch 3, before going into the topic of love, in Ch 4. The takeaway is that *Yirah* – fear – is also necessary, but *Yirah* does not derive from *hitbonenut* before or during *tefila*. Rather, the *ikar* is *shkida* ("persistence" and consistency, "perseverance"), reminding ourselves of His presence at all times. This need not occur during *tefila*, but such contemplation and reminders that bring to *yirah* may occur anytime during the day (including during *tefila*); but it does not require *tefila*. *Yirah* does not require the same long *hitbonenut* that *ahava* requires. *YIrah* is certainly associated with *tefila* but the question is, how do we achieve *yirah*? It requires "reminders" that there is a King, that He is watching, that He knows exactly, etc…not the long *hitbonenut* of *ahava*. This is possible during the day as well (even though *tefila* is a more auspicious time to develop *yirah*). But the *avoda* of *tefila* is to achieve *ahava* – love of God.

Two kinds of love, one like water that is characterized by *kiruv u'dvekut l'elokut* ("proximity and clinging to Godliness"), and the other (also mentioned later on p 25) is like fire, with a *Koch* (Yiddish for "cook," "burn"). And the text goes straight into the meditation leading to these kinds of love. In general, "love like water" requires meditation on how God enlivens the world, and every creation, as well as how He enlivens us (*m'basari echzeh Elokut* – "from my flesh I grasp Godliness"). From the Zohar, we begin to feel and yearn for the *chayut* that enlivens us *davka* when we are weak. What is this *chayut*? It is the vitality that Hashem grants to us. It demands that we delve into the topic of meditation and grasp it thoroughly so that we know that He enlivens the world, causing us to feel the dearness and preciousness of Godliness. We thus arrive to a condition in which we want nothing other than Godliness. And then, the love becomes even greater as we grasp that the vitality is also what enlivens us…

R' Eliyahu Hadad asked, "When I learned biology and got a good idea how every part of the body works, the nose, the mouth, how the eyes see, this brings love of God…but here from *K' Avoda,* on what are we supposed to meditate?" The Rav answered that there is the description of each of the parts of the body ("this is what the biologists know"), and then there is the investigation of, "From where did this come, how did it arrive here?" And this you must learn from the *Sifrei Hasod,* the "books that are in the category of *sod,* or secrets of the Torah." [This can mean Kaballah, or Chassidut or any number of other *seforim* that are pre Chassidut but employ the secrets of the Torah to explain matters, such as the *Sifrei Maharal* of Prague, the *Sheloh Hakodesh,* and *Reishit Chochma,* for example]. And here it comes down to the difference between the "love" itself, and where the love is coming from (its source): Do you love your eye? Or do you love the "source" of your eye? The Rav said, "Look, if you know a good person, a calm person whom it's nice to hang out with, and you ask him, "How did you get this way? How did you establish this calm personality?" Even if he tells you, you will not necessarily achieve the same results that he attained, by using his methods. That won't necessarily help you. As R' Eliyahu Hadad points out, he might be a big *vatran* (a "soft" person who is willing to overlook others' traits), one who is willing to overlook all kinds of things, but you may be an entirely different kind of person…

But in any case, our goal is to achieve love of God, so we need to look at everything in terms of, "What is the process from Hashem (source of the eye) to the 'eye' (that we observe as a biologist)? What is the [creative] process?

- On the radio, someone once interviewed the scientist who discovered DNA, and he described the process that led to the discovery. The interviewer, who was not religious (or at least it wasn't a religious station) asked, "Did it seem to you that there is a hand guiding the process and guiding the creation?" To which the interviewee answered, "That's not my area of expertise, it doesn't interest me." The wisdom and craft behind it interested him, but not the "how" or the "why." But that is exactly what interests the student of Chasidut: "What He brought about, How He brought it about, why, etc…" *Chazal* ask about the command to love Him, "How do I love Him?" And they answer, "You shall speak about them, *divrei Torah*." Our goal is to get to the One who made it happen, as in R Hanina ben Dosa who said, "He who told the oil to light, can tell the vinegar to light." Why can't we do the same? The difference is that R' Hanina was *davuk b'mi sheamar* ("clinging to his source") – R' Hanina ben Dosa was cleaving to the Creator! We are less interested in the *poel* (the "effect" – what we see in front of us), and more interested in, "How did it get there." If we're stuck in the material itself, in the oil, in the vinegar, it won't help – our goal thru *hitbonenut* is to arrive to *Mi she'amar* – "He who said," and thereby created it.

- So, our effort has to be in finding Him as the source of our life vitality and that we do by learning Torah.

Shiur 94, August 14, 2018

Page 24 in the Hebrew, Page 98 in the translation: As we approach Godliness, we also distance ourselves from negativity. This process is exemplified by Avraham Avinu, about whom the Torah tells us that he was *haloch v'nasoah henegba* ("He progressed and travelled to the south…" – the "south" is the direction of *chesed* and kindness, positivity). The participants in the shiur pointed out that we need to do *itkafia* ("bending," subduing the *yetzer harah*) in order to progress in *avodat Hashem*…the Rav said that's correct and that it helps both in the beginning in order to initiate *hitbonenut* and also in essence after we've already begun. The parentheses (page 98-99) state that after *itkafia*, the *nefesh behama* is weakened, although that seems to be different than the normal status of *itkafia*, which takes place only when the person experiences a desire or *taiva* and not when the animal soul is weak. The Rav says that you can't insert holiness unless you prepare the *keli*, the "vessel," and *itkafia* means to prepare the *keli*.

- R' Shlomo Chaim would make a *diyuk* ("implication") in Tanya… we are *mitkaven l'kifayeh lesitra achra* ("we have intention to subdue the *sitra achra*"). Ch 27 in Tanya, "…Not only that but in whatever manner man is able to control himself regarding permitted matters… and **intends** in this manner to subdue the *sitra achra*…" - from this, R' Shlomo Chaim deduced that if a person was just busy or otherwise unable to eat or drink, is not called *itkafia* – there has to be intention. On the other hand, *itkafia* alone will not help, if the person isn't doing *avoda* and *hitbonenut*. *Itkafia* is only preparation for the beginning [of *avoda*].

- R' Eliyahu Hadad asked, "*Itkafya* though is *nekudati* ("local, specific"), it applies only to particular items [for example, "I am tempted by this ice cream, so I deny myself the ice cream" or "I am tempted to watch this movie, so I postpone it for the time being" – these are examples of specific items to which we apply *itkafiya*]. Love of God though is general...yet, nevertheless the *itkafiya* on particular matters has influence in general?" To which the Rav answered, "Yes, correct, it is written that *itkafiya* brings *syua d'kedusha* – "aid and support from the side of holiness."

- R' Hillel Paritcher observed a lot of *chumrot* ("stringencies"), all of them for the purpse of understanding Chassidut better, the Rebbe quoted this. Though from the Besht we understand that we should not to take on too many *chumrot*, since it's possible they come from the "other side," nevertheless R' Hillel adopted a lot of them and when the Chassidim challenged him, R' Hillel told them that he had no particular interest in the *chumrot* themselves, he only adapted them in order to "understand Chassidut better." (In general, one who takes on *chumrot* does so for the sake of the *chumrot* themselves, he has satisfaction in being extra-strict). R' Hillel used to raise money for the Jewish *cantonistim* (youngsters who were forcefully drafted into the Russian Czarist army) as a Chassid of the Tzemach Tzedek. He had assistants, he would pray at length while they went out to the cities and gathered money. Once they came with money and a sizeable *shtar* ("contract" – an "IOU"). He gathered the money and left the *shtar*. So they took that with them and the next day after gathering the money they tried to combine the *shtar* with the rest and again, he accepted the money but left the *shtar* behind. After two or three attempts, they asked him why he did not accept the *shtar*. He replied, "It's my expertise to know what to accept and what not." So, they went to clarify what was the story with this *shtar*. It turned out that it was a *shtar shel aveira* (an *etnan* – meaning that someone had paid for a forbidden act with this "IOU," and now the person in possession sought to give it as *tzedaka*, which R' Hillel could not accept). He discerned that's what it was, that was R' Hillel...

- Page 100 in the translations – the time to do *itkafia* on oneself regarding a specific matter is during *tefila*, because that is when the Godly soul is revealed and conscious. At that time, the animal soul is weakened, and we can have more of an influence and impact on ourself with proper resolutions.

- R' Eliyahu Hadad interjected; "What difference does it make to decide during *tefila*, the time to decide is when the sin or temptation is in front of you." To this, the Rav answered with a quote from Tanya explained by R' Shlomo Chaim: There are *midot* ("character traits") and there are *anafim* ("branches") of the *midot*. The *midot* are the emotions that we experience during *tefila*, such as fear and love. The *anafim* are *netzach hod yesod*, perhaps *malchut* as well. The *midot* provide the "juice" and vitality, the *anafim* bear the fruits. The time of *tefila* is like the *midot* with their "juice" and conscious love and fear. But if there is no energy and vitality, the *midot* cannot nurture the branches. The same applies to us when we pray: Only if we are inspired and devoted during *tefila* will it later have an effect on our behavior after *tefila*. If we fail to make a decision during *tefila*, then he won't have the power to enact and behave the way we want during the course of the day. (It is written that while doing *cheshbon hanefesh* (personal accounting of our conduct during the day), we should not spend a lot of time thinking of our bad behavior, because that can bring us to *machshavot zarot* ("foreign thoughts"). Some people when coming for advice launch into detail about exactly what happened; but this is not necessary and they should be told not to go into details but rather to emphasize how it's possible to avoid repeating the same situation, and how we can extract ourself from the situation.

- Moreover, since during *tefila*, we feel our *grubkeit* and "coarseness," that gives us more power to make resolutions.

- Here is an important principle from the *Baal Shem Tov*...(page 100-101 in the translation): "And choose life..." Generally we think the *pshat* ("explanation") is that there are two objects among which we should choose; one side is "good and life," the other is the opposite. But the *Besht* says that every object is actually composed of both "good" and "bad." Regarding the physical aspect, you see that it fades away. ("Man doesn't pass away all at once, he slowly disintegrates..."). So, to choose "life" means to choose the Godly element, the part that enlivens the object. And in so doing, *K'Avoda* tells us that at least in part we will begin to detest the physical and the negative.

- (Here after the Rav closed *K'Avoda* and *YomYom*, someone showed him a quote from the Rebbe where he writes that if we refuse to hear something bad about our friend, then also when we go "upstairs," if there are accusations against us, they will also refuse to hear about it).

Shiur 95, August 15, 2018

Page 25 in the Hebrew, 101-102 in the English…

Again, the further we progress in our approach to Hashem, the further we distance ourselves from the animal soul and from physical temptations. There are a number of explanations for this, but the basic idea is that the more we weaken the animal soul, the more "room" there is for the Godly light to enter. That is, the natural intellect (of the animal soul) also becomes capable of absorbing Godliness, and appreciating how Godliness is the "main thing" and there is nothing especially "good" about *gashmiyut* at all. Another result of weakness of the animal soul is that the person gains more desire for Torah and mitzvoth, as long as the animal soul is involved and also desires Godliness. In the beginning, the animal soul merely acquiesces to Torah, and does not interfere. At later stages, it actively seeks Godliness and *Elokut*.

But the main transformation of the animal soul occurs through "love like fire"…love like fire is what incinerates the animal soul. This is because the category of *chai* (animal) corresponds to fire among the four elements, and "fire consumes fire." The time for arousing this "love like fire" is during *kriat shema*, and in a *maamar* (parshat *Shelach*, in *Likutei Torah* of the Alter Rebbe), it says that we receive the same number of opportunities to change our lives as the number of times that we are granted to recite *kriat shema* (and that is also the number of opportunities we are given in order to achieve "love like fire"). The *hitbonenut* that brings to this love is *kulo kamei k'lo chashiv* – "all is before Him as nought." *K'Avoda* (on page 106 in the translation) mentions Chapters 43 and 44 of Tanya speaking of "love like fire," and the Rav asks, "why not Ch 50, which is the main place where Tanya discusses love like fire…"

Next we'll learn that it is possible to achieve "love like fire" not only through the *hitbonenut* of *kulo kamei*…but by joining together the two items: "love like water" and *cheshbon hanefesh*…this can bring us to "love like fire" as well…tomorrow…

Shiur 96, August 16, 2018

The first five minutes, the Rav spoke about *Hilchot Talmud Torah* of the Alter Rebbe, how someone (not Chabad) found an original printing (without the Alter Rebbe's name on it) in the library of the Tzemach Tzedek Shul, and was very excited about it, and wanted to know who wrote it. *Hilchot Talmud Torah* was the first set of *halachot* that the Alter Rebbe produced.

We're learning about "love like fire" in *K'Avoda*. It comes from a very high *hitbonenut*, on *gadlut Hashem*, based on the meditation that *Kulo kamei k'lo chashiv*…("All is like naught before Him"). Page 26 in Hebrew, Page 110 in the English translation. "But this…takes place on the most elevated levels…" - "vision of renewal of creation."

But for most of us, we can achieve "love like fire" only by considering our distance from Hashem. Our *hitbonenut* must be a combination of two meditations: "love like water," combined with realization that we are far from God, in thought, speech and deed, and that in general we are far from Godliness. We want to abandon all matters that disturb us and devote ourselves exclusively to Hashem.

In response to a question from one of the *hevra*, the Rav said that the Rebbe emphasized that in this kind of meditation where we are thinking of our distance, we must be very careful to stay within the bounds of *merirut* ("bitterness") and not to fall into *atzvut* ("depression").

R' Shlomo Chaim heard from the Rebbe Rashab: *Cheshbon Hanefesh* ("self accounting") is composed of thee elements: "How things should be, how they could be, and how they are now…" and the Rav demonstrated with hand movements and voice how R' Shlomo Chaim said this…and in order not to fall into *yiush* ("giving up"), we require what Tanya (in *Igeret Hateshuva*) says, "The heart should be *batuach b'Hashem* ("confident in God"), Who is all forgiving…" and one who thinks to himself that he has less chance to do *teshuva* because of his distance…it's really the opposite, this is from the *yetzer harah*…

Shiur 97, August 19, 2018

On Page 27 in the Hebrew…the Rav began with a summary of "love like water" and "love like fire," and mentioned that "love like fire" is with a "burn" (*Koch*) that likely they have in their own personalities anyway. Then he recalled that the Bnei Yissachar writes that there were some people in his youth whom he was afraid to stand near because of their great "burn" and energy during *avodat Hashem*, but that in later years those people calmed down…the Rav clarified that these people were true *baaeli madreiga* (people who were truly on a high spiritual level), but their high level was motivated their youthful energy and that later in life when that energy had waned, their *avoda* also took a nosedive…

At any rate, the main transformation of our *midot* takes place via "love like fire." How do we achieve "love like fire?" For this, one needs meditation on a very high level. More than *hitbonenut* on *Gadlut Hashem* ("Greatness of God" within creation, which is the basic meditation of "love like water"), "love like fire" requires *hitbonenut* that *Kulo kamei k'lo chashiv* ("All is nought, as if non-existent"). The meditator desires nothing other than Hashem Himself. Since this is such a high meditation, and out of reach of most people, *K'Avoda* gives another bit of advice…"love like water" combined with consideration of our distance from Him (see page 110 at the top in the translation). The Rav explained here that sometimes fire emerges as the result of *stira* ("contradiction"), friction between objects [such as when striking two stones, a fire may emerge]. The implication is that here also, the perceived closeness and clinging to God that we achieve via "love like water" competes with the meditation on our distance from Him, and this generates "love like fire."

One must be very careful utilizing this meditation not to fall into depression. The Rav mentioned a *maamor* from the Rebbe Rashab that explains the difference between "bitterness" (*merirut*) and "depression" (*atzvut*). During *merirut*, we think about our distance from Hashem (and we're bitter about it). During *atzvut*, we think about ourselves, how "bad off" I am.

R' Eliyahu Hadad asked, "Why develop this? Why not remain with "love like water"? R' Deitsch answered from the text: "Because the main love that transforms the *midot* is love like fire." Fighting fire with fire…

Once upon a time, this was, externally the difference between "Polish" Chassidim and Chabad: On the surface of it, the "Poilishers" expressed more *hitlahavut* ("excitement") [that is how it appeared externally], with more "excitement." Story from R' Meilich…

- A certain Chasidishe Rebbe knew of a simple wagon driver who once met R' Meilich (R' Elimelech of Lizensk, otherwise known as the *Noam Elimelech* in honor of the book that he wrote), so he travelled to the wagon driver to ask him about the great *tzaddik*. The wagon driver told him, "I used to bring the Chassidim to R' Meilich for Shabbat and then return them home after Shabbat, and I would sleep the entire Shabbat in order to have the strength to bring them back home. But once I decided to also go in to see R' Melich like they did." So the Chasidishe Rebbe asked him, "And what did you see?" He answered, they were all drunk, all of them, and R' Meilich more than the rest." (What he meant was "they were all red from excitement, and R' Meilich was even more red than the rest of them.") The "moral of the story"? They were all red from their emotional excitement, the wagon driver was too simple to understand that and he thought that they were all red from drinking.

- The Rebbe said that the Baal Shem Tov would place a bottle of red wine by him as he said words of Torah so that people would think he is red because of the wine. The Rebbe asked in a sicha, why didn't the Besht put the bottle next to him while he was praying, as well? Why only while he said *divrei Torah*? But the Rav doesn't recall the Rebbe's answer to that, it is in a *sicha*…

Here the Rav pointed out that just as "love like water" becomes becomes amplified when we consider it in relation to ourselves (*nafshi aviticha*…the Godly force creating and enlivening the world is also my *chayut*, the energy that enlivens my soul), so when we meditate on our distance from Hashem, that's what amplifies our "love like water" and transforms it into "love like fire." And then the "love like fire" incinerates the animal soul, unlike "love like water" that only weakens it.

- Some ask, from where do we learn that we need "fire" and excitement in our *avodat Hashem* and *limud HaTorah*? The Besht replied that's something we are supposed to figure out ourselves, the Torah won't tell us. And the Rav mentioned a *mashal* of someone who bought a new machine, and didn't know how to use it, brought it back to the seller and said it doesn't work…the seller asked him what's going on and it emerged that he didn't know that you have to "apply fire" [perhaps "plug it in" to the electricity], to get the machine to work…the buyer said "why didn't you tell me," and he answered, "you should be able to figure it out yourself."

Shiur #98, August 21, 2018

The straightforward approach to "love like fire" is via meditation on "the Greatness of God" (*Gadlut Hashem - kulo kamei k'lo chashivei* – "all if like nought before Him") but for most of us, this is too high of a meditation. The alternative is to meditate with "love like water" and combine that with meditation on our distance from the One above, and the combination of the two brings us to "love like fire."

- A coarse illustration; One who has no appetite, may be approached in two ways: Either we can explain and persuade him that food is good or at least "good for him," or we can tell him that if he doesn't eat, he will be fasting for several hours…the combination of both approaches will cause him to develop an appetite. The appeal of food combined with the "threat" of fasting will cause him to develop a real thirst and fire for food, and at that point it will require watching over him to make sure he doesn't eat too much.

Back to the text, we can ask, we seem to be combining love with *teshuva* (because consideration of our "distance" from God is similar to *teshuva*), so what is the nature of this meditation? And the text (page 114-115 in the English translation) tells us that the advantage of "love like fire" over *teshuva* is that during *teshuva*, our entire involvement is only with *richuk*, the "distance" that we feels from Hashem and our bitterness over our distance [unlike during "love like fire," during which our focus is on our *kiruv*, "proximity" to God].

- R' Eliyahu Haddad asked, "According to the Rav, there are two components to "love like fire": The positive meditation how this is good for me, and the negative on how I am far from the goal. But in practice, the person trying to achieve "love like fire" has already achieved "love like water", and knows how far away he is. So, in practice the two occur simultaneously, why does he need a second *hitbonenut* on how he is "far"? To this, the Rav answered that the meditation on our distance only triggers "love like fire" for those who are [not yet] on a high level. One who meditates and simultaneously realizes that he is far from God is already holding at an advanced stage and high level of meditation. See Page 110 where *K'Avoda* mentions, "But this 'fire from Above'…" there it says this takes place on "most elevated levels." The difference is that "love like water" is "attraction of the heart" (*meshichat halev*), while "love like fire" is "excitement" (*hitlahavut*). These are two different dynamics; as it says in Tanya that one ("love like fire") comes from *gevurah* (within *chesed -hitlahvut*) and the other ("love like water") from *chesed* (within *chesed - meshichat halev*). "Love like fire" is a very strong mixture of *gevurah* and fire. For those of us on a lower level, we need to add our own "fire on the side" – and what is that? *Merirut* – "bitterness" over our distance.

So here (page 114) the question becomes, why deal with two components. If our goal is to achieve "love like fire," why not go straight for the feeling of distance. To which the text answers us: With bitterness [over our perceived distance] alone, in essence we are thinking only of ourselves, not about Hashem (and the parentheses emphasizes that the feeling of distance and need for *teshuva* nonetheless must be "mixed" with awareness of Hashem). While contemplating our distance, the emphasis is on our own personal situation and the gulf between us and God, which is what causes the shattering and breaking of our animal soul. That's the benefit of *teshuva*; it shatters the animal soul and the *yetzer harah*. [Nevertheless, the meditation is about "me," how "I" am far from God]. However [unlike love of God], that does not mean that *teshuva* leads to elevation of the animal soul and its inclusion within *kedusha*. *Merirut* does not help to elevate the animal soul (only *teshuva* on very high levels achieves that; only *teshuva ila'ah*), it only breaks the animal soul.

- The Rav heard R' Shlomo Chaim say the following on several occasions: In Tanya, it appears that *ithafcha* ("transformation" of the animal soul, as opposed to *itkafia,* which is "suppression" of the animal soul) is associated with *tzaddikim* (only the righteous and not with *beinonim*). But in *Likutei Torah* (also from the Alter Rebbe), *ithafcha* (*shinui hateva,* "changing our nature") appears many times (which implies that it applies to us as well and not only to *tzaddikim*). How does that fit with what is written in Tanya? The *maamorim* (Chassidic discourses) in *Likutei Torah* were said for us, not for *tzaddikim*…In answer, R' Shlomo Chaim said on a number of occasions that "there are *madreigot* to *ithafcha*": There are levels. In Tanya, there is the *ithafcha* of *tzaddikim* in which he totally transforms his *midot* and in *Likutei Torah* there is *ithafcha* that is more "surface" and "external."

- R' Eliyahu Haddad continued to ask though; "*Ithafcha* is like a switch, it's either on or off, there's nothing in between" (so how can there be *madreigot* – "different levels" of *ithafcha*?) To which the Rav answered with an example of one who easily gets angry. He works on himself though and everytime that an opportunity comes up, he holds himself back and does not become angry. After awhile, people come to him and tell him, "I don't recognize you, you're not the same person." And he truly is not the same person. From time to time he may burst out in anger, which reminds him of whom he previously was. He has suppressed who he previously was, but the anger remains…but on a certain level this is also *ithafcha* even though he hasn't totally eradicated the anger. He has eliminated enough of it to seem like a "different person."

- Another example: One who can't stop himself from looking at certain images and *posul* pictures. He knows they are not good but upon seeing them, he is *nidbak,* he cannot tear himself away. *Ta'avot* ("lusts"), etc…by some it develops into a condition that they have to "see everything," by others, they have to "read everything." Once upon a time in Lubavitch (here the Rav mentions R' Lazer Nanis *A"H*), they would make sure that one does not even have a possibility of reading…by not accepting anyone who was a Russian speaker (R' Lazer was an exception since he came from outside the area and needed someone to care for him). There are some who work on themselves to change that and in truth they are not the same but still from time to time they can have a *yerida* and look at things that

- they shouldn't see. Like returning alcoholics, they have to go through *gemila*, "weaning" themselves away from addiction until they are rehabilitated. As Eliyahu Hadad points out, this isn't "for the whole life." They still have to work on it. So, the Rav says that nevertheless this is still *ithafcha* – transformation. To whatever extent they have trained themselves, it is *ithafcha* on that level.

- And the Rav gave another example of that: At a farbrengen, the Rav wanted to give a *Lechaim* to someone, who said, "No, I can't accept that because if I do, I could slip back into my previous ways." So the Rav asked him for how many years he hadn't said *lechaim*, he replied, "for forty years." The Rav said, "that is *ithafcha*." "Can you call that only *itkafiya*," asked the Rav? Eliyahu say, "Yes" but the Rav says, "No." The Rav says this is *ithafcha* in "borrowed terminology," the problem has not been uprooted from its source, but it's nevertheless *ithafcha*. That's what R' Shlomo Chaim said, "The *ithafacha* in *Likutei Torah* is not the same *ithafcha* that we find mentioned in Tanya. The same applies to smokers, the minute they try a cigarette again, they are back into the old habit, but if they go for years without smoking, they can't stand even the smoke from cigarettes. R' Eliyahu claims tho that the addiction, the need for cigarette or whatever is merely "sleeping," like the *yetzer harah* of the *beinoni*…to which the Rav replied that the *yetzer harah* is only sleeping during *tefila*, the rest of the day it is at war with the Godly soul.

Back to the text (Page 115) and highlighting the differences between "love like fire" and *teshuva*: While *teshuva* emphasizes our distance plus our failure to consider Hashem (because we are focused on ourselves and our perceived distance from God), nevertheless when it is combined with "love like water," it then becomes elevated to *kedusha*. And this is because "love like water" itself attracts him to Godliness and he derives *taanug* ("pleasure") from that alone (Godliness), while rejecting and repelling all other varieties of *ta'anug*. What "love like fire" adds, is the element of "*reticha*," the *Koch* or fire (*bren*) in our *avodat Hashem*. Now, "love like water" weakens the animal soul, but to transform it, requires *hitbonenut* [on our distance], plus it must involve the animal soul. Regarding "love like water," the person does *hitbonenut*, but who takes part in the *hitbonenut*? There is meditation in which the Godly soul participates and natural soul does not interfere, doesn't get in the way, but in order to achieve more than that, the natural soul has to actively participate. It is *ovdei Havaya* – those who serve Hashem on a high level – who succeed in bringing their natural soul into the *avoda*.

These are matters that are not so clear to us. We have *sechel* from the Godly soul, which grasps Godly concepts very quickly and thoroughly, and we have the natural soul that does not grasp so quickly, and even when it does, it doesn't "get" exactly from where this concept arrived. (In Tanya, the "natural soul" and the "animal soul" are one and the same).

Question from one of the *avreichim*: The Godly soul doesn't grasp things except through the natural soul, it's the natural soul that possesses intellectual grasp, so how can we "understand" or "grasp" a concept with the Godly soul? There ensued a lively discussion in which the Rav pointed out that according to Tanya, both the Godly soul and the animal soul include ten *sephirot*. Then, this: In *Torah Ohr* (of the Alter Rebbe), it is written that we have *mesirat nefesh* twice: Once when we say *Shema Yisrael…echad* – this is the *mesirat nefesh* of the Godly soul. And then a second time when we say, *bekol levavcha bekol nafshecha*…this is the *mesirat nefesh* of the animal soul. We may find it difficult to discern between them, but clearly according to Chassidut, they are two different "loves." They are "mixed" in our understanding, the Rav calls it a *mishmash* and said that he doesn't know where this *mishmash* comes from. The Rav says there are times when there is *gilui haneshama* – "revelation of the soul" – he sees it clearly when he goes to Shabbat davening in Kiryat Sanz (the neighborhood in which he lives) and the young children there are reviewing what they learned during the week and the Rav says he hears and sees in this *gilui haneshama* – "revelation of the soul." Eight year old children reviewing what they learned the previous week. They are there early, like 7 am, and without prizes, etc…

Back to the text; there are times that the Godly soul grasps, but the animal soul does not. Page 116, and in answer to the *avreich* who claimed that there is no intellectual grasp without the natural soul – so here we see that in truth there is participation of the animal soul but in such a way that it does not properly understand the concept. It depends on preparation, and on the labor that we put into it. We see this as well in the *mashal* during the month of Ellul of the "King in the field." The Rebbe asks, it isn't the *derech* of the Alter Rebbe to bring *mashalim* ("examples, illustrations") as "solutions" for the questions that he asks…yet here we have the well known *mashal* of the "King in the field." The Rav summarizes the gist of the Rebbe's answer: When the Godly concept is so high that it is difficult to understand, then the Alter Rebbe brings it "down" in a manner that appeals to the animal soul, with a physical *mashal* that supports our understanding even though it does not (in the strict sense) provide an intellectual solution to the question. For example, here in *Likutei Torah*, the question is, "Why isn't Ellul a *yomtov* an 'official' festival? And we don't find that the Alter Rebbe gives a clear answer there. And the Rebbe also elaborates and asks, "Okay not a *yomtov*, but why not a time of special *simcha*…" The matters that the Rebbe uncovered and discussed regarding the month of Ellul, are impossible to describe, according to the Rav. In any case, the question of the Rebbe here was, since when does the Alter Rebbe ask a question and then answer it with a *mashal*? That was the accepted custom of some *tzaddikim*, such as the Magid of Dubnow, but it was rare for the Alter Rebbe to resolve a question with a *mashal*.

Regarding "love like water," it changes the animal soul only if we work at it, but "love like fire" automatically incinerates the *nefesh behamit* (the "animal soul"). In *Kuntres Hatefilah*, there are very difficult parentheses, and among the matters there that one needs to understand are not only the intellect, but "the Godliness within the intellect." The Rav asks, what does it mean, "The Godliness within the intellect"? In Tanya (Ch 42), we are told that it is difficult to achieve fear of God because of our sins and transgressions… "There are some souls that are naturally *zach* ("pure") and *bahir* ("bright"), that grasp the concept…and there are lowly souls that grasp the Godliness of the concept only with difficulty, in particular those souls who were trapped by *chatat neurim* ("sins of our youth") because our sins block us off (as written in *Sefer Chasidim*)." In this manner we can resolve the question: Why would our sins disturb our intellectual grasp, what is the connection? But, the answer is that our sins and transgressions can disturb our grasp of the "Godliness" of the matter…"to feel the Godliness" of the matter. What is that? He who knows, understands what it means. There was one by the name of R' Dovid Horodoker who had much understanding and ability to explain (spoken of in *Ken shel Tomchei T'mimim*). But when it came to matters of *avoda*, he told his students, "When you're holding by this, then you'll understand it."

Shiur 99, August 22, 2018

Two levels of "love like fire"…the higher level that higher souls are capable of approaching directly (via *hitbonenut* on *Gadlut Hashem/ Kulo kamei*…) is beyond most of us, who need to meditate to achieve "love like water," and to add to that *hitbonenut* on how we are "far" from Hashem in order to achieve "love like fire" (written in Ch. 50 of Tanya that "love like fire" is the highest, *oleh al culanu*).

- R' Eliyahu Hadad asked a great question: We learned earlier in Tanya (Ch 45) that focusing on our distance from Hashem is a way of arousing mercy from Above – not "love like fire" as we see here in *K'Avoda*…to this the Rav said that's a different *hitbonenut* altogether because there in Ch 45, the goal is to arouse *rachmanut* on the soul that comes from a very high place and descended to a low place. But here, the goal is to arouse desire (*teshuka*), not *rachmanut*…here the meditation is to achieve love (*chesed*) and if "love like fire," then combine the love with *gevurah*, which is why it is described as "like gold" (in Ch 50). *Rachmanut* is something else, it's the *midah* of Yaakov…[On July 15, 2020, a similar question was asked in Tanya shiur: "Is the *rachamim rabim* that we arouse during *teshuva* (Ch 7-8 of *Igeret HaTeshuva* in Tanya) the same as the meditation on our "distance" that we are discussing here in relation to "love like fire"? The Rav answered that most likely not, since here we are not discussing sins and *aveirot*, but only "distance." The goal here is to feel our distance, our *merchak*, but there in *Igeret Hateshuva* the goal is to achieve a "broken heart" – *lev nishbar*].

In both approaches to "love like fire," the advantage is that it incinerates and eradicates the animal soul. When using the second approach of combining meditation on our distance from Hashem with "love like water," it is understood that awareness of our distance produces fiery desire to approach Him. But also in the first instance of "higher souls" who are able to achieve "love like fire" directly via *hitbonenut* on *Gadlut Hashem*/ *Kulo kamei*, it is also understood, because "fire consumes fire." That is, the animal soul is from the element of fire, and therefore fire easily consumes it…as soon as there is fire of *kedusha* ("holiness"), it either overwhelms the animal soul or transforms it, in any case it changes it. [Perhaps this is understood from the *mashal* of the spark that "jumps" into the fire when the fire is close enough to subsume the spark].

- Story mentioned by Ze'ev from Russia regarding "fire on fire"; the Rav told the story – on Succot the Chasidim were sitting by the Alter Rebbe and it became very cold, dangerously cold in the Succah to the extent that they became sick with fever. They came and told the Alter Rebbe and he said that the Chasidim should come to the *hakafot* of Simchat Torah and there, the heat of the *hakafot* will heal the fever of the Succah, because "heat consumes heat." But some of those who caught the fever simply found it impossible to come to the *hakafot*…in particular there was one person who stayed with his uncle, and the uncle was dead set against allowing his nephew out of the house, claiming, "This is murder." But the youngsters of the town said, "The Rebbe said," and "this will be his *refuah* his cure," and dragged him and all the sick people to shul for *hakafot*. There, the Rebbe made Kiddush, and gave some of the Kiddush wine to all the sick people. But even before he distributed the wine from the Kiddush, somebody got up and announced, "It is known that this kind of healing works only for those who have *emunah*, who have "faith." They then distributed the *kos shel bracha*, everyone was healed and returned home healthy. And the uncle who had been so opposed, became a Chasid of the Alter Rebbe. As the Maggid said ten times (corresponding to the ten powers of the soul) to the Alter Rebbe, "The fire on the altar will never be extinguished," wherein the Hebrew of "never extinguished" is *lo tichbeh* – can be turned around to "it will be extinguished," referring to the animal soul.

- It was known that the Alter Rebbe himself was "fire" – during *tefila* he was so *b'hitlahavut* ("on fire") that he would throw himself against the walls, to the extent that they had to add cushions and pillow to the walls to prevent him from hurting himself. From this stemmed the difference of opinion between R' Aharon Strashele who was a *talmid* of the Alter Rebbe and the Mitteler Rebbe, who was his son. R' Aharon, who was older, held that the *ikar* was the *hitlahavut*, the "excitement," while the Mitteler Rebbe pivoted to a quieter form of *avodat hatefila*, virtually without movement or noise.

- R' Eliyahu Hadad told of his experience on Simcaht Torah in Crown Heights, after morning *hakafot* he returned home, wife in the kitchen, and there was a knock on the Torah, R' Kievman (?) asked him what he is doing, "Come to 770." Okay, so R' Eliyahu went to 770, as soon as he opened the door, a huge "wave" of heat hit him, with smell of herring and *mashkeh*, etc…he wanted to faint…about this, the Rav said, "Yes, have to know that the Rebbe totally held from the concept of *hitlahvut* and excitement, for example, the phrase, *kochen zich in lernen* – "burning for learning" – the Rav didn't hear that phrase anywhere else, only from the Rebbe. Others say *lign in lernen* – "located or placed in learning," but not *koch*, which means "cooking or burning." Also the *shluchim* whom the Rebbe most loved were those who had a *bren*, or *koch*, in the Rebbe's *inyanim*. Also the Rebbe's movements, during farbrengens with his hands, etc…But his *tefila* was still and quiet and the Rav said it seems that was *derech avoda*, meaning that the during *avodat hatefila* the Rebbe was *makpid* to be still.

- R' Shneur Zalman Ofner mentioned that some say the Rebbe was *marah shachora* (was by nature introverted and reticent) but that he worked on himself to be *b'simcha*…the Rav said there is a *sicha* from

Shiurim on K'Avoda from the Mashpia R' Deitsch שיח׳

the Rebbe about the Baal Shem Tov who kept a bottle of red wine by him as he learned, so that people would think the reason he was red was because of the wine. Why didn't he need it as well during *tefila*, during prayers? (the Rav doesn't remember the answer though…).

- Similar story with the Rebbe R' Meilich (the *Noam Elimelech*), once a Rebbe wanted to know why so many chassidim went to him, so he went to ask a certain wagon driver, a simple Jew, who used to take Chassidim to R' Meilich. The wagon driver told him that once he went in to see R' Meilich and saw that, "all of the Chasidim were big drinkers, and the Rebbe was the biggest drinker of all." He said that because they were all so red with *hitlahavut* and "excitement" over Hashem, he thought they were drunk.

- Similarly there were differences in the Rebbe's *hanhaga* when he learned Torah from when he prayed. When he prayed he was very still and no movements. But during Torah, those who knew how to discern could see that under the table, the Rebbe was moving his hands and was apparently in a state of excitement over the flow of intellect. Sometimes he would put his hands under the table cloth and then you could see that he was moving.

(Page 118 in the translation): Regarding the two different approaches to love like fire, there is a difference. Even during the "first" approach that is direct with *hitbonenut* on the greatness of Hashem, there is also a feeling of *richuk*, "distance" – but it arrives after the attainment of "love like fire." As a result of "love like fire," the meditator feels forelorn, 'Why am I so distant?' Whereas in the "second" approach that combines "love like water" together with contemplation of our "distance," the experience of distance is something that we cultivate and occurs before we achieve "love like fire."

- R' Shlomo Chaim used to speak of the uncle of the Tzemach Tzedek, who had a sore at the end of his thumb, something serious, that prevented him from meditating and praying. He began hitting the table, "Why do you prevent me from davening?" Until the sore burst open and the pus went out and he recovered (he didn't hit the table in order to cure himself, he hit it out of frustration).

Here the Rav points out that when the text mentions a *maamor* as a source without saying where, it means it comes from *Likutei Torah* of the Alter Rebbe. In this case, the *maamor* he references (*parshat nesachim* in *Shelach*), it states that the main purpose of the soul in this world is to refine and uplift the "fire of the animal soul" (see the end of first *perek* of parshat *Nesachim*, Page 40A and beginning of second perek, 40B (80) in *Likutei Torah*). And there also it says that according to the number of years we have to live, we have that many "*kriat shema's*" (see first column on 40B). The Rav said once someone came out of *yechidut* with the Rebbe and said that the Rebbe blessed him with *arichut shanim*. When asked more about it, he said that in truth the Rebbe blessed him to become *yirat shamayim*, and he understood that would require *arichut yamim*. The Rav read the relevant passage from *Likutei Torah*.

Shiur 100, August 22, 2018

This is the same as the *shiur* above, but with a few more minutes to it at the end...

- R' Eliyahu Hadad asked, what is *hitlahavut* ("excitement," "arousal")? He thought that *hitlahavut* comes from *taanug* ("enjoyment"), yet here regarding "love like fire," the text tells us that the person has no *taanug* in either physical or spiritual matters. If so, what is this *hitlahavut*? Is it something intellectual? The Rav says that it's certainly emotion, it's love, but emotion that emerges from *hitbonenut* [which is intellectual]. Regarding someone who is "cold" by nature, we are told that it is more difficult for him to achieve this love, but that also he can achieve it, "as explained later," and the Rav says that "later" refers to Perek 50 in Tanya.
- The relevant passage in *parshat nesachim* is in *Shelach*, *perekim aleph and beit* at the end (the Rav read from the beginning of *perek beit*), Page 40A and 40B in *Likutei Torah*.

Shiur 101, August 26, 2018

Here, we begin Ch 5 (Page 29 in the Hebrew, Page 123 in the translation):

First of all, the summary on page 122. Then, *ahavah* from *lashon ratzon*, "will." *Ratzon* ("will") with *taanug* ("enjoyment") is love. The will is the *pnimiyut* ("internal core") of the *midot, a*nd is capable of causing the person to withdraw himself from any particular enjoyment, such as food or a person. If, for example a person goes to the back of the restaurant and sees how they prepare the food, he may very well decide that he doesn't want to eat it, since the *ratzon* has control over what events will provide us with *taanug*. The Rav either heard or read somewhere that love is compounded of will and delight (*ratzon* and *taanug*). Within the *midot,* they (*ratzon* and *taanug*) function together, while in *Keter* they are two different entities.

- R' Eliyahu Hadad returned to what we learned in a previous chapter that one who experiences "love like fire" loses all enjoyment of anything "physical or spiritual." The Rav said though, that refers to matters of *olam hazeh*, "this world" that we live in. Looking at the top of page 26, he wants "nothing but Hashem Himself," but abandons all spiritual and physical pleasure of this world – here, the Rav says, "spiritual enjoyment" means enjoyment of something intellectual. (Later we'll see in the learning that there are two kinds of *ratzon* – a higher *ratzon* and a lower, and *davka* it's the lower *ratzon* that is more "active on the *shetach*").

Shiur 102, August 27, 2018

There is such a thing as a *ratzon* ("will, desire") that is beyond intellect, that is associated with the *makifim* ("transcendent") levels of the soul. It is called *makif* for two reasons: 1) Because it is high, above and beyond the intellect, and 2) because we don't have the *kelim* ("vessels") to contain it, for these reasons it is called *makif*. There are two levels of *makifim*; *chaya* and *yechida*. The *yechida* is *atzmi* ("essential"), needs no arousal or *hitbonenut* because in any case it is *havuka v'devuka bach* – it is "embracing and cleaving to You." But if so, why is it *nimshach* ("drawn down")? If it is always clinging to God, then it isn't appropriate to describe it as a *makif* that is "drawn down." But rather the *neshama* is like a *ben*, a "son" to Hashem – it has a different *mahut* ("quality of self") because it is a *metziut* ("existence") of its own in a body, but *b'etzem* (in essence") the *neshama* is a "piece of Godliness." Unlike the Torah which even when it descends to us, it remains connected to the One above ("And God said to Moshe…").

- The Rav has a story to demonstrate the essential nature of the *yechida* of the soul…in the US people travel from a large city to a small one even by small jet. A Jew wanted to carry his tefilin on the plane but they wouldn't let him, but then, the plane had mechanical failure and couldn't go, so he wanted his tefilin back and they wouldn't give it to him. So he went on the new plane that came along as a replacement, but they didn't put his belongings on the new plane so he ended up in the smaller city without his tefilin. He told the Rav that he turned circles and somersaults to find tefilin, because the local *shaliach* was nowhere near the airport, and he ended up putting on tefilin near the end of that day. The Rav wondered and perhaps even asked him if he had known how important the tefilin were to him. That's the *yechida* of the *nefesh*…the expression of the *yechida* comes through in the *shelila* – the "negation" of the mitzvah (in this case, he could not go without putting on tefilin and "turned over worlds" in order to find and put on a pair of tefiln, so the "negation" lay in being denied the mitzvah – that's what triggered his *yechida* to find a pair at any price) – such as *mesirat nefesh* (or in this case, inablitiy to don tefilin). *Tmimut b'maaseh*.

- R' Zelig Feldman said in the name of the R' Rashab that there are 3 differences between the *mesirat nefesh* of a non-Jew versus a Jew: 1) A non-Jew is willing to give up his life for a positive idea or value [i.e. – Plato drinking the poison is one example that comes to mind], but a Jew gives up his soul "because it can't be otherwise." He is not willing to serve idols or do anything that will separate him from his *Yahadut*. 2) He himself (R' Zelig?) was in year of *aveilut* for his father, and he said that his *aveilut* is expressed in the sense that he can't stand any music or songs.

- R' Eliyahu Hadad asks what's difference between this and *ahava mesuteret*. It also "sleeps" but is awakened under certain circumstances. The Rav responded that *ahavah mesuteret* (like *mesirat nefesh*) also comes from the *yechida* of the *nefesh*. R' Eliyahu said though that according to Tanya, we have to "arouse" the *ahava mesuteret* so if so, how is it a *davar atzmi*? The Rav said that according to Tanya, the *derech ketzara* (Chapter 19-25) described in Tanya is that since it comes to expression in *mesirat nefesh*, our *avoda* is to see that it comes to expression in everything else as well – we "don't want to be *nifrad* ("separated") from Godliness. So, R' Eliyahu says that if so, it seems contradictory cause we shouldn't have to "arouse" it since it is essential. To this the Rav responded that the point is that the essence of soul as well as *ahava mesuteret*, is "there," it's not so much we have to arouse it as we have to remove whatever is concealing it.

Shiur 103, October 8, 2018

Back to the concept at the beginning of Ch 5, that *ahava* – "love" – is at root from the word *ava*, meaning "will" (*ratzon*). People think that "love" means something that is "tasty," as when we say, "I love that candy" – I find it tasty. But really at the root of the concept is our will, or "desire." Some people think that *ahavat Hashem*, "love of God" is associated with "a *geshmake* davening" (a pleasurable davening, or learning). But in truth, such "tastiness" or enjoyable davening, etc, is *taanug*, "enjoyment." But what *ahavat Hashem* really is, "I want to get close to God." The difference is that while eating or davening, we enjoy it, but there is little or no enjoyment after the fact. But with true *ahavat Hashem* ("love of God"), there is a lasting positive result, such as we want to do mitzvoth or learn Torah, etc, in order to approach closer to Hashem.

- Here the Rav opened up Rambam's *Hilchot Yesodei HaTorah*, Ch 2: "What is the *derech* ("path") to achieve love of God? Via meditation on His works, His creation…" Here we see that Rambam speaks not of *taanug* ("enjoyment") but of *ratzon* ("will" – will to create). The underlying question that Rambam asks is, "What leads to love" – is it "values" or "enjoyment"? If you respect something a lot, does that lead to love? In the words of Rambam, you see that *hitbonenut* and meditation on creation leads to respect and love of God, but you don't see anything about "enjoyment" (*taanug*). So, really everything depends on what we respect and value, not on what we enjoy. So, the root of love is "value." We may have gotten used to thinking these days that "love" is what gives us enjoyment, but that perspective comes from *Eitz Hada'at* ("Tree of Knowledge"), which places emphasis on, "What is good for me"?

- R' Eliyahu Hadad here asked, what about the love of *nafshi aviticha balaila* [during which we apply to energy of creation to "ourselves" – we reason that the *chayut* that energizes the creation is the energy that enlivens "me" as well], in which it seems that our main concern is, "What I want for myself and my enjoyment" – so the Rav answered that there is such a thing as love motivated by *yesh*, by "what's good for me," but here Rambam speaks not of my *yeshut* but of the amazing nature of creation, "His great deeds and creations…"

- The Rav recently spoke with someone who needed support and encouragement, explained to him the difference between *Eitz Hadaat* which is "what I need," "my pleasure," and *Eitz HaChaim*, which is "values." Even in the secular world, people look down on someone who does things merely because it is good for him, good for that person, but in truth where there is the most emphasis placed on "values," is in regard to *kedusha* ("holiness") – that is where values play the largest role, because the highest value is placed on *kedusha*. The Rebbe Rashab says in the name of the Rambam that the source of *Eitz Hadaat* is what is good "for me." If what is important to us is "values," that's associated with *Eitz HaChaim*. If what's important is "what is there for me in this?" then that's associated with *Eitz Hadaat*.

- R' Eliyahu Hadad mentioned that the entire approach of *kiruv rechokim*, drawing people closer to Yiddishkeit, is based on *Eitz Hadaat*. The rabbis tell the prospective *baal teshuva* about how good it is to enjoy Shabbat, the *chagim*, etc...it's about the enjoyment... and it's about *yeshut*, "what do I get out of YIddishkeit" – [not the approach of Chabad], to which the Rav mentions that also appears in Rambam, Ch 10 of *Hilchot Teshuva* (last *perek* in *Sefer Hamadah*), where Rambam says that one should not do mitzvoth because of the reasons listed there (enjoyment), but because it is the truth – this is the path of *Ahavah*. But not everyone gets to this level, only those such as Avraham Avinu, who was called, *Avraham ohavi* – "Avraham who loves Me." So you see that true love of Hashem is associated with doing mitzvoth and learning Torah because it is truth. But regarding children and others, *mitoch sh'lo lishmah, ba lishma...*"they start by loving God for the wrong reaons, and end up loving Him for the right reasons."

- Based on this, R' Eliyahu asked, "So its' impossible to start with the truth and *mekarev chevra* with the truth, that the Torah is true and therefore one should value it enough to become *shomer 613*?" To which the Rav answered, "That's what it says. It is not possible to start with the truth but what happens is we start with *klipah* and then eventually transform the *klipah* into an elevated status."

So, how do we arrive to this *ratzon*, this core of love? End of Page 29, final lines, page 124 in the translation..."Nevertheless, there is an old Chasidic discourse..." In any case, *yechida sh'bnefesh* is revealed either in *mesirat nefesh* (when one is faced with the opposing force), or with *temimut shb'maaseh* (page 127).

- Here the Rav tells the "tefilin" story: Story of the fellow who travelled with tefilin...but put them on the plane and then had to transfer to another plane. Ended up in the new location without his tefilin, and turned over worlds until he managed to put on tefilin just before *shkiya* ("sunset") that day...to which the Rav asked him, "Did you know that you are so connected to your tefilin?" So we see that the essential *kesher* ("connection") is more expressed in the *shlilah* ("negation") than in the *chiyuv* ("positive" response). That is, the essence becomes revealed not in how you feel as you do the mitzvah, but in how you feel when when something prevents you from doing it. And what kind of connection is this? It's not based on logic, but on *mesirat nefesh* ("self sacrifice, devotion"). And it's not based on avoidance of *avoda zarah* ("idol worship" - the other instance in which the *yechida shb'nefesh* comes into play), but on *tmimut hama'aseh* ("straightforward dedication to necessary action). The *Derech HaChaim* (from the Mitteler Rebbe) speaks of *temimut hama'aseh* that comes from the essence of the soul. The expression is not to die *b'Kiddush Hashem* but in action. (The Russian Chasidim practiced this when they resisted the Communist regime).

- There was an older Russian Jew, Dr Mazal, *niftar* not long ago, who was son after son from R' Zusia *ztz'l*, his son in law learned in the Collel, and he told of how the Jews in his town resisted Communism even though the Rav of the town felt that it was okay to compromise here and there...he himself (the Doctor) kept everything down to the details, in accordance with the instructions that he received from his father or grandfather, went to college to become a doctor...and after many years he met up with the former Rav of the city who had been willing to compromise...The former Rav's children didn't hold by much, one of them even married out, and when they saw each other, the former Rav told Dr. Mazal, "Your father was right." That is, the father or grandfather who guided him not to compromise at all, was correct. Again, this is *tmimut b'maaseh*. Not for nothing was the Chabad yeshiva called *Tomchei T'mimim*...

- Once, R' Shlomo Chaim made a farbrengen on a *Beit Nissan*, second day of Nissan, which is the *yahrtzeit* of the Rebbe Rashab, and he said that the Rashab, "put *timimut* into *Tomchei Tmimim*." Yes, he introduced *Chassidut* and *hitbonenut*, etc...being precise and *mehudar* in performance of mitzvoth, such as being willing to pay a lot for "special kosher" matzot. And this *tmimut bema'aseh* comes from the *yechida hanefesh*. Every Jew should read the book אלו שלא נכנעו, "Those who did not surrender" – stories of the Holocaust. Written down by a Gerer Chasid according to the witness of survivors...Gerer Chassidim themselves were divided into groups, each of which had its own "commandant." In one case, the "commandant" was from Germany but became a Gerer chassid. The Belzer Rav met up with the Gerer Rebbe, the *Imrei Emet* and asked him to give regards to his *tmimim*, those who survived the Holocaust...everyone who survived any of the "isms," whether *haskala*, communism, the holocaust – they all survived it on account of their *t'mimut*.

- The Rav heard this story first hand from one who was "not suspected of being Chassidic." R' Shlomo Zalman Auerbach *ztz'l* had a *chatan*, who passed away not long ago...by the name of Rav Treger – he was rosh yeshiva of yeshivat *Eitz Haim* in Antwerp, and R' Deitsch knew him, because he had a brother who was also R' Deitsch's bro in law. He told R' Deitsch that after the war, Jews came to Antwerp from all over Europe, from Poland, from Hungary and from Galicia. Those from Hungary and Galicia settled in Antwerp, the Polish Jews settled in Brussels, the capital city. Antwerp is a Jewish city *l'tiferet*, with all the *mosdot* and all the Jewish life one could ask for, but Brussels is the opposite; *shluchim* are needed there for the grandchildren of those who arrived after the war. So this non-Chassidic Jew in Antwerp told R' Deitsch, "The difference between the Galicianer Jews in Antwerp and the Polish in Brussels is that the Galicianers were very careful about maintaining *minhagim*, Jewish customs. The Polish were not, they even made fun of *minhagim*. And he gave as an example, heard from someone else: Once as the artillery shells were falling during the war, a Jew went out to find an egg…why? Because the Belzer Rav said that for Jewish customs, we must have *mesirat nefesh* ("dedication and devotion" to the extent of putting our lives in danger if necessary") and one of their *minhagim* was to have egg and onion on Shabbat…so he went out to find an egg even as the shells were falling. The descendants of such Jews remained, but from the Polish Jews, not so much. This is *tmimut* in action. There is no reason for *minhagim*, but still Jewish survival can be dependant upon *minhagim* – that's why the *Ramah* (R' Moshe Isserles) put *minhagim* in the Shulhan Aruch ("Code of Jewish Law"). The *shoresh* of *tmimut b'maaseh* is very high…

- R' Eliyahu Hadad asked though, there are those who are *makpid* in Torah and mitzvoth not because of *tmimut*, but because of arrogance and *stam akshanut* ("stubbornness"), we cannot say about them that they are acting out of *tmimut*…he mentioned a story in which they investigated a certain Jew by asking if he kept this and kept that, and in each case he answered "Yes" because that's what a Jew does…finally they asked him if he kept *gebraks* [refraining from eating matzah on Pesach with water and liquids, even though after the matza is fully baked, it is permitted to eat it with liquids], and he said he did but that in this case he felt "special" about it, not just because "that's what a Jew does."

Shiur 104, October 9, 2018

Page 30 in Hebrew, Page 128 in the English translation:

Until now, the *K'Avoda* (in this chapter) has discussed the *yechida* of the soul. But there is a second level of the soul, also above logic and intellect, the *chaya*. From the *yechida* emerge two traits: *mesirat nefesh* and *temimut* ("self sacrifice" and "pure integrity"). The *yechida* may become revealed, but it does not require or "respond" to arousal. The *chaya* on the other hand does require arousal. It is essential, but requires arousal. Like for example if one wanted to hurt himself. This goes against the natural tendency and basis of man, who wants to live (does not want the opposite of that).

- The Rav once saw in R' Yonatan Eibeshitz…there are people who are afraid of a trial, afraid of the law to the extent that it could give them a heart attack, make them actually sick. But true *tzaddikim*, who have real *yirat Shamayim*, are more "afraid" of Hashem than those who fear a court trial. Why don't they "die" or otherwise become sick from this fear? R' Yonatan Eibeshitz answered that there is a verse, "והאלקים עשה שיהיה יראו מלפניו" – (Eccl/Kohelet 3:14) "Hashem arranged that we should have fear of Him." That is, He instilled into the nature of creation that man should be afraid of God. However, that is not true of a human court case, which is not part of the natural course of things. (Don't do wrong things and you won't be called before a court). On the other hand, "*Yirat Hashem le'chai*" – "One who has fear of God, lives," since his fear induces him to cleave to the One above. He is our source, so the more we cling to Him, the more *chayut* we have. Like we say in *Modim* (during *Shemonah Esreh*), "on our lives that are dependent on You." There is a love called *Cholat Ahava* – "love sickness" for Hashem – but we don't see that *Tzaddikim* are affected negatively either by their tremendous love or fear of God – quite the opposite, they need less sleep and rest because they have additional vitality from this love and fear.

But this level of *chaya* needs arousal – and the arousal comes not from meditation on *Gadlut Hashem* (the "greatness of God") but on His *romemut* ("highness," "majesty"), which the Rav defined as "what we don't know about Him." The text says, *Atzmut ohr eyn sof* – His "essential infinite light," and on His *haflah* ("amazing highness"). Here, the meditation is on "what we don't know, and the fact that we don't know." There are times that we understand, and there are times when we are forced to conclude that, "We don't know." Although this conclusion and the love that accompanies it require arousal via meditation, nevertheless once aroused, it is essential and beyond logic and intellect. The manner in which the essential aspect of this love arrives is that it is *bli gvul* – without limit. [Previously, we said that it is *avodat hashlilah* – "negation of our concepts of Godliness" – that triggers this level of love of the *chaya*]. Our *sechel* only triggers the love, but once triggered it is unlimited.

The love of the *yechida* does not require arousal, in fact it is aroused precisely when we enounter a situation that is *keneged* – "against" ("I won't do this, I won't serve *A"Z* or *gilui arayot*"), that's what arouses the *yechida,* but here the arousal is from *hitbonenut.* The meditation arouses it, and then it flows on its own.

- R' Eliyahu Hadad asked, "If this is unlimited love, so it is Godly and infinite, and should not need renewal, should proceed on its own with out meditation, more like a *davar atzmi*, "essential love."

In the translation Page 130, the love proceeds on its own after it's triggered, and without bearing any relation to the meditation that triggered it, because the meditation is not really the reason for the love. In other words, the meditation was the "trigger" or the "catalyst," but not the reason for the love, and the love itself is essential, unlimited. The text also speaks of a much higher love that is "similar" to the *yechida*, and it is also aroused by the *keneged,* but there are forces that may impinge in a negative fashion upon it.

- Here, the Rav told the story of the son who ran away from anything religious or anything to do with his family, and claimed that if he could, he would "shoot" his father. The psychologist told him that his father was in a car accident and in the hospital, near death and then all of a sudden the son wanted to see the father, was willing to do everything he could to see him…and in this way, the psychologist proved to him that really underneath, he didn't hate his father, he loved him.

Shiur 105, October 10, 2018

Page 131 in the English translation, "And so it is with the soul…" Love that is "dependent upon something" is love that requires logic and reasoning in order to achieve it. So, as soon as the logic is absent, so is the love. This level of divine love requires that there be no *hesech hadaat* – "interruption of the thought process." In this case, the *hesech hadaat* would be after davening, after *tefila*. Furthermore, the text (page 131-2) differentiates between *pninimyut hasaga* and *chitzoniyut,* but says that in *pnimiyut hasaga*, interruption of the thought process is not so common [because at that point one is quite fixated and focused on the meditation, which causes him to be in a state of unawareness of his surroundings – this is the level of *neshama* described there in Ch 1].

In parentheses on page 132, "It is known that love can grow to surpass even the intellect that gave rise to it." If so, then the question becomes, from where does this increased and amplified emotion come from? And the Rebbe answers acc to the Zohar: the *midot* (emotions) have a source that is higher than intellect: *Z'a b'atik achid v'talia – Z'a* is united with and dependent upon *Atik*. And that is why in *Keter*, the source of emotions is called *arich* (the "long countenances") while in Atzilut it is called *zeir* ("small countenances"). The *shoresh* ("root") of *midot* is higher than the *shoresh* of *mochin*. That's why people value emotions more than they value intellect. People understand that the emotions are important, but *sechel* – meh. There are people who begin to pray and immediately experience emotions, and the question becomes, from where do they experience this emotion, and the Rav says that some explain that it comes from this source (the higher emotions in *Keter*).

The *sechel* in general gives more *kiyum*, more basis and foundation to our endeavors. Even though we go thru ups and downs and sometimes we feel stronger or weaker intellectually, nevertheless in general, the intellect provides a solid foundation for whatever we want to do, at least the most solid that we can hope for. Which is not true of the emotions, which ascend and descend.

Page 133: There is a *ratzon* associated with the *chaya* and a *ratzon* associated with *yechida*: Both are beyond reason and logic. Regarding the *Chaya*, the meditation "triggers" the *ratzon* (and then, the response is "out of range" of the arousal), but regarding the *yechida*, even that arousal is not necessary.

Shiur 106, October 11, 2018

Page 31 in the Hebrew, Page 134 in the English translation:

"Now the will for connection…" But this level (*chaya*) cannot influence the animal soul, it is too high…even though "love like fire" does transform the animal soul, but this love on the level of *chaya* does not have that much of an effect. It depends on the type of *hitbonenut* involved: If it is a *hitbonenut* of *shlilah* (wherein his distance from *Elokut* bothers him), then it does influence the animal soul. But if the *hitbonenut* is about *kiruv* (*chiyuvi*), this kind of very high meditation does not influence the animal soul. It's like someone who has no concept of Torah looking at Torah scholars who learn all day long and asking them, "Well, what do you do for rest and relaxation?" That's why meditation based on logic and reason is necessary.

[This *shiur* needs more explanation, and the explanations appear later in Shiur #108 in which the Rav explained that there are two kinds of meditation that arouse the soul level of *chaya* – and it would appear, "love like fire" and *ahava rabba*. Those are the two levels discussed above; first of all the direct but very high meditation on *kulo kamei k'lo chashiv* which is beyond the ability of most people to achieve. This is the *hitbonenut* of *kiruv* (*chiyuvi*) that the Rav mentioned, that will not have much influence on the animal soul. However, the second path, in which we perfect our *hitbonenut* on "love like water" and then add to that a contemplation on our distance from Hashem (which the Rav described as *shlilah*, apparently in the sense of "distance"), then such *hitbonenut* will have an effect on the animal soul. What needs further explanation here is which, if either of these meditations, is based on *avodat Hashlilah* – is it the higher meditation of *kulo kamei*...or the lower meditation in which we combine our "distance"...Either way though, this differentiation provides an answer to how "love like fire" can incinerate the lusts of the *yetzer harah*, and yet *K'Avoda* tells us that meditation on the level of *chaya* (with which "love like fire" is associated) is too high to have an effect on the animal soul. The first, direct *hitbonenut* on *kulo kamei* is too high, but the second *hitbonenut* involving our *merchak* – our "distance" - is not too high to have an effect on the animal soul. However, all of this is true only if the meditation to achieve "love like fire" is associated with the *chaya* of the soul. In other discussions with the Rav, I understood that it is still associated with *neshama*, not with *chaya*].

[In further personal discussion with the Rav, I asked, "If *avodat hashlilah* has an effect on the animal soul, then what aspect of the *chaya* does NOT affect the animal soul? *K'Avoda* tells us that *avodat hashlilah* affects the animal soul and is on the level of *chaya*, and yet *K'Avoda* also tells us that *hitbonenut* on the level of *makifim*, of which *chaya* is an example, do NOT affect the animal soul. The Rav answered that *makifim* may or may not affect the animal soul. Sometimes it will, sometimes it won't: For example, the thief praying for success at the mouth of the tunnel, is an example of how *makifim* fail to influence the animal soul. And yet a Jew who is put in a position of *mesirat nefesh*, such as one who is threatened with death unless he bows down to an idol and then the threat dissipates, will undoubtedly be affected by his experience, even though that as well is an example of *makifim* (he does not consciously think whether or not to bow down to the idol; he knows spontaneously and automatically that he cannot do so. That is the influence of *makifim* as well.

I then asked the Rav, can we possibly say regarding meditation leading to "love like fire," that the more common path of first attaining "love like water" and then combining it with contemplation on our "distance" from God, operates on the level of *neshama*, while the less common but more direct path of meditation on *kulo kamei k'lo chashiv*, which is meditation on *romemut Hashem* leading to "love like fire," is on the level of *chaya*? The Rav replied that we would have to see that written in order to claim it, we cannot assume so].

Shiur 107, October 15, 2018

Chaya, after arousal, is beyond reason and logic. However, it does not have much influence over the animal soul. Since it's very high, the animal soul doesn't connect with it so much. Page 32, Page 137 in the English translation…But the *yechida* of the soul certainly has an effect on the animal soul and transforms it from one extreme to the other (even though you would think since it's even higher than the *Chaya* therefore it would have no effect on the animal soul – but this is not the case). Here, the Rashab introduces an investigation as whether, at the time of *mesirat nefesh*, the animal soul "agrees" to its own expiration or not, and he tends to the side that the animal soul does not agree, but just bends to the will of the Godly soul that requires it. At any rate, even if the animal soul itself is not aroused to die *b'kiddush Hashem*, there is no doubt that the Godly soul does influence it to change.

- Story that the Rav heard from R' Shlomo Chaim, in those days, the *paritz* (local non Jewish landowner) was the boss over the forest area with all the villages within it. The *paritz* would pass thru the area once a year or so, to remind the villagers that "he's the boss." He would meet the villagers in the "square" of the village and then as part of the ceremony, they would provide a wagon and driver to accompany him to the next village. In our story, the driver this time around was a Jew, and the *paritz* wanted to make fun of him. He pulled out a cross and demanded that the Jew should kiss it. Of course the Jew refused to do so. So, the paritz pulled out his sword threatened to kill the Jew. The Jew agreed and extended his neck for that purpose. This so surprised the *paritz*, who had only intended the whole thing as a joke, that he was utterly taken aback. He called the local priest over and told him to do something disgusting, like urinate on the cross, which he argued about until the *paritz* threatened him and he did what he was told. The completely confounded the *paritz*. (The Rav says that as far as he remembers, R' Shlomo Chaim told this story in his daily Tanya shiur). He was so confused that instead of continuing on to the next village, he went home. But in the meantime, the reputation of the "simple" wagon driver made the rounds. They happened to be in the area of the Admor of Kodinov (Bylerus), (R' Shlomo Chaim's father was a Kodinov chasid, but R' Shlomo Chaim himself lived more in Zhitomer. Kodinov was in that area of Slonim and Karlin). The Kodinover said that either this Jew would go crazy or he would not live out his year, and R' Shlomo Chaim said that one of those things is what happened, but he couldn't remember which. But the story, with the statement of the Kodinover, reached Lubavitch, where they "explained it." For such a revelation of Godliness, it would have been too much for this simple Jew to integrate, so he would have either gone crazy or died.

- R' Eliyahu asked, "What about the simple non Jews at *Kriat Yam Suf* that the Midrash says could see what the prophet Yehezkel saw, and yet they were not nullified and went back to being "normal"? –to which the Rav replied, "*Kasheh*" – "you have a question…"

Shiur 108, October 16, 2018

Page 31 in K'Avoda, Page 134 in the translation:

"Now the will for connection…" *Ahava* from *Ava*, meaning *ratzon*, or "will." So if someone says, "I love Hashem," they mean, "I want Him…" Enjoyment contains an element of love, but love itself means, "I want." So there are two levels; *ratzon* based upon reason and logic, and *ratzon* that is beyond intellect. Regarding *ratzon* that is above reason and logic, there are also two levels: the *chaya* and the *yechida*. *Yechida* is the essence of the person, completely beyond logic and reason. It becomes evealed either when there is a test that demands the Jew to go counter to his essential nature (like to serve *A"Z*), or in simple action, like the Jew knows he has to do one thing or another – put on *tefilin* or even a *minhag* such as finding an egg for Shabbat – and then nothing gets in his way. That is called *tmimut b'maaseh* ("integrity in action") and it comes from the *yechida* of the *nefesh*.

- The Rav told a story to illustrate *tmimut*; there was a Jew who needed to learn *pirush hamilot* (the "meaning of the words" of prayers), so he found someone to teach him. But after learning, he said, "They are so good, the words themselves, why do I need the explanations?" This is very deep…he doesn't even know what he's saying but he feels very good with it. This is *tmimut* from the essence of the soul. R' Shlomo Chaim said in farbrengen that the Rebbe Rashab founded the yeshiva, *Tomchei Tmimim*, in order to insert *tmimut*…prior to *Tomchei Tmimim*, the Chassidim would start learning Chassidut later in life, when they were already well based and solid in their Torah and their outlook…but the Rashab initiated learning Chassidut when they were still *yeladim*, still "children," even when they were in *yeshiva k'tana*. The reason for this was that there should be *tmimut*…

- The Rav heard from R' Zelig Feldman (*A"H*) in the name of the Previous Rebbe, who told a story from the Rebbe Rashab, about

Kaiser Wilhelm of Germany, who was clever and Czar Nikolai of Russian, who was not clever. The two were related, via their wives, and Wilhelm prepared for war against Nikolai for years, managed to pull all kinds of information out of him. He said to Nikolai, "All that you have, I also have, but I don't know how you produce Cossacks." The Cossacks were very bold and nothing stopped them. Nikolai for all his dim wittedness answered a clever answer, "Cossacks aren't 'made,' they are born." They would take the Cossack from a young age, put him on a horse and tell him, "You and the horse are one," and train them in all kinds of maneuvers and challenges, so that from a very early age, he was already trained as a "Cossack." That was the aim of the Rebbe Rashab, to insert *tmimut* into the *talmidim* of *Tomchei Tmimim* from a young age. The Rebbe Rashab praised the manner in which the Cossacks were trained from an early age, and the Previous Rebbe said, "And that is *tmimim*" – that's what it means to educate someone in the manner of *tmimut*. The Rav says that's what happens on *shlichut* (Chabad emissaries going to foreign countries) when either the *shaliach* doesn't know the language of the place, or the person he is reaching out to also does not know…under those circumstances it takes a certain boldness of the soul to accept the mitzvah or the Jewish act upon himself. That's *tmimut* from the *yechida* of the soul.

Then there is the *chaya* of the soul, also above reason and logic, but it is aroused via logic and reason. And then once aroused, it takes on a life of its own. It's an expression of the essence of the soul. That's where we are right now, on Page 31 (134 in the translation, "Now the will…"). Even though it's a high level, nevertheless is does not have much influence on the animal soul because it's too high to engage the animal soul. Even though love on this level is usually "love like fire," which does subdue if not eradicate the animal soul, here (love on the level of *chaya*) does not have such influence since it is not enclothed within the animal soul. Even though the animal soul does hide and conceal the *chaya* (see Ch 19 of Tanya and also *Igeret Hakodesh* #4), when the arousal of the Godly soul comes from meditation on the amazing wondrous level (*hafla'ah*) of *Ohr Eyn Sof*, then it does not have much effect on the animal soul.

The Rav explains: The love of God associated with *Chaya* is essential (like the *yechida*), but (unlike *yechida*), it is possible to arouse such love via two different meditations: 1) on *Gadlut Hashem*, on a very high level – *kulo kamei k'lo chashiv* – that itself arouses the essential love. Arouses *teshuka* that is very high but has no influence on the animal soul. 2) Or, one can bring the love of the level of *Chaya* to revelation via meditation on how "far" he is from *Elokut*, and this is a meditation that does have an effect on the animal soul.

- Once upon a time, the situation in religious education was that the boys would get a solid yeshiva education and ascend to high levels, but the girls did not receive such an education and as a result they descended spiritually. "The husband in the *shteibel* (the shul) and the wife in the theatre." Because no attempt was made to bring the education of women to a level that the woman could relate to (until a certain woman, the Rebbe when referring to her just called her a *tzedeket* without mentioning her name, Sarah Schneurer, founded the women's seminary, Beit Yaakov) – same thing here; if no attempt is made to bring the level of *hitbonenut* down to the animal soul, it simply doesn't relate to it).

Shiur 109, October 17, 2018

Now on page 32 (page 137 in the translation):

What is clear though is that the *yechida* of the soul does influence the animal soul, even though it is very high, nevertheless it is capable of eradicating the animal soul. And that requires the cooperation of the animal soul, otherwise it would certainly choose to live. Like one who is ready to die on *Kiddush Hashem* but saved from it at the last minute, he certainly won't be the same person as he was before the event (so says the text). So also one who does allow himself to die by *Kiddush Hashem*, is because his Godly soul has managed to persuade his animal soul…otherwise why would he submit to his own death? Like two partners in business, if one does not want to move forward, the other cannot do so either, each side has "veto power." Same thing with fifty partners, one can veto the whole plan.

- R' Yehezkel Finkel asked from the opposite direction – "If a Jew does a sin, does that mean that the Godly soul "agrees" with it? If it's a partner, the Godly soul should have had "veto power"…but to this the Rav replied as does Tanya and Chassidut – the Godly soul was in galut, "exile" at the time of the sin. Like the Nazis (*yemach shemam*) forcing Jews to manufacture arms for them… the Rav cites Ch 24 in Tanya…or, according to R' S.Z. Ofner, although to get the person to do a sin, the *nefesh Eloki* has to be in galut, but in order to work the other way, to get the animal soul to listen to the Godly soul, it (the Godly soul) has to "be there" to convince and persuade the animal soul to go along with it…and therefore we cannot say that in order to agree to die, the Godly soul puts the animal soul "in galut." Rather, the Godly soul has to convince and persuade the animal soul to agree...

- This formulation works well with what is written in the *Chovot Halevavot* ("Duties of the Heart"), which discusses *sechel* and *regesh* ("intellect and emotion") in the same way that Tanya discusses "Godly soul" vs 'Animal soul." And here as well we see that the intellect can persuade and convince the emotions, but we do not see the opposite dynamic: The emotions cannot persuade, they can only overwhelm the intellect so that it's as if in *galut*, in "exile."

- The emotions spoken of here, that must acquiesce to the Godly soul, are not emotions detached from the intellect. They must be emotions within intellect. R' Eliyahu Hadad suggested that this isn't a fair comparison, because the animal soul is far more in control, far "wealthier" than the Godly soul and in fact it's the animal soul that holds all the keys...the "electricity, the water, the food..." And if the Godly soul wants to coerce the animal soul, all the animal soul has to say is, "Okay I'm turning off the electricity..." (meaning, okay you might want to die but I'm 'out of here'). To which R' Yehezkel Finkel answered, "The Godly soul has to use *tachbulot* – "tricks" – to convince the animal soul. The Godly soul has to be clever...to this the Rav agreed (and brought a *posuk*...seems the Godly soul has to "seduce" the animal soul, so that at least it will be ready to listen).

Shiur 110, October 18, 2018

When the *yechida* becomes revealed, there is no doubt whatsoever that it has an effect on the animal soul. And if the animal soul is willing to die for Hashem, then certainly the person's nature has changed. Page 32 in Hebrew, Page 140 in the translation.

- R' Eliyahu Hadad asked, "According to what we learned about the *derech ketzara* ("short path" utilizing *mesirat nefesh*) in Tanya (Chapters 19-25), it applies only to unique one time circumstances for which we need *mesirat nefesh*, but it doesn't have a lasting effect on us. If so, then here too, even if our animal soul agrees to *mesirat nefesh*, it should not have a lasting effect on us. And yet, we see that *K'Avoda* says that it does have a powerful effect on us?! To which the Rav answered, what Tanya means by "not lasting" is that our *mesirat nefesh* to do a mitzvah does not last forever. However, it does apply to more than a particular event or one time circumstance; in fact, it applies for that entire day. All positive mitzvoth are based on *emunah*, and all negative mitzvoth are based on the injunction against *avoda zarah*, and the "short path" demands that we take our response to A"Z ("I would never do that, would rather die") and apply it to every one of the mitzvoth. This level of application of the "short path" of *mesirat nefesh* cannot remain with us "forever," but it can remain with us for that day. The phenomena of "real" *mesirat nefesh* and its application to the entire Torah can remain with us for the day. The person to whom it physically occurred, who experienced a demand to give up his life and his animal soul acquiesced, remains with that his entire life, or at least in the immediate aftermath. But even if it was not a real, physical event in his life, he can still apply the principle to his daily fulfillment of Torah and mitzvoth in order to remind himself to stick with it.

In general when we do *teshuva*, it's the Godly soul that screams to return to its Creator and wants to do *teshuva*. But there is such a situation that the animal soul is the one that screams to "return." The animal soul can't find itself at all, it feels "lost" and then it screams to Hashem. (This is because the animal soul itself has gotten a taste of spirituality since the Godly soul worked on it). This is the kind of situation in which the animal soul needs the Godly soul like a *talmid* needs his Rav, and indeed can really "lose it" and descend spiritually without his Rav.

- Vort from the Alexander Rebbe regarding, "the *nefesh* (souls) that they 'made' in Haran…" Rashi explains that Avraham was *mekarev* the men and Sarah the women…the Alexander Rebbe says, "They were the students of Avraham Avinu, whose *derech* was love of God. But when he passed on and another Rebbe took his place (Yitzhak) who had a different path of *avodat Hashem* (*yirah*), so they didn't connect with his path, and that's why they were lost. (Rav Zevin brought this story from the Alexander Rebbe).

- The Rav saw in the Mitteler Rebbe something interesting: He asks, why in *kedusha* do we see that the son often has a different path in *avodat Hashem* from the father (i.e. Avraham *chesed*, Yitzhak *gevurah*…)? But his other son, Yishmael, was on the side of *klipah* and he remained with the approach of love like his father. The same applied to Yitzhak and his son: Yaakov on the side of *kedusha* took on a different path than his father, he took on *rachamim* as opposed to *gevura*. But, his brother Esau remained with Yitzhak's *gevura* (but in *klipah* of course)…this is what the Mitteler Rebbe asked…but the Rav doesn't remember what the Mitteler Rebbe answered, but in any case we see this interesting phenomenon that in *klipah* the *avoda* of the father continues, but not in *kedusha*.

- By the Rebbeim this is very clear, to the extent that if someone coming from outside of Chabad were to ask, why doesn't the Rebbe continue in the path of the Previous Rebbe, R' Deitsch suggested (half in jest) that if he continued in the path of *avoda* of the Previous Rebbe, that would be *klipah* (*chas veshalom*).

- The Chassidim of the Mitteler Rebbe had trouble transferring their allegiance to the Tzemach Tzedek, especially to his Chasidut, which was a very different style. About that, the Tzemach Tzedek said, "They'll get used to me." By R' Hillel Paretcher it was especially evident, he was very attached to the Mitteler Rebbe, and later he became very attached to the Tzemach Tzedek. In the beginning, he would come and visit the Tzemach Tzedek and request from him to say a *maamor* for him (despite the fact that there was plenty of Chasidut from the Mitteler Rebbe available to him - the history is interesting here, the *Torat Chaim* of the Mitteler Rebbe was printed before the *Torah Ohr* of the Alter Rebbe was printed). Generally, the Tzemach Tzedek would say a *maamor* for him but on one occasion he didn't do so, and R' Hillel became very sick. His Rebbetzin went and told the Tzemach Tzedek who then agreed to say a *maamor* for him, but R' Hillel was so weak that he could not walk, so they took him to the Tzemach Tzedek in his bed. No sooner had the Tzemach Tzedek said the *maamor* than R' Hillel recovered his strength and was able to walk back. This is the same R' Hillel who was so attached to the Mitteler Rebbe that it was impossible to describe. Also R' Nisan Neminov (*mashpia* in Brunwah, Paris) was very attached to the Previous Rebbe (used to begin every farbrengen with the *maamor* of the Rebbe that he had for that week), but managed to become attached to the Rebbe. Somebody asked (might have been me) if R' Shlomo Chaim also was attached in that manner, but the Rav answered, "not to the extent that R' Nissin was attached."

Shiur #111, October 21, 2018

Here (starting page 34 in Hebrew, page 143 in the translation), the content of the *shiur* is about how *ahava,* on the level of *chaya,* does not have an effect on the animal soul, because it is *makif* ("transcendent"). However, from the soul level of *yechida*, even though it is higher, it does have an effect on the animal soul. And that leads to a discussion of our spiritual status after Tishrei, after Rosh Hashana and Yom Kippur (P 146 in parentheses): This *shiur* was delivered in October after Tishrei, during the period of "Yaakov went on his way." And here the *K'Avoda* speaks of the effects on our soul from the *avoda* of Tishrei…and if we didn't "take away" *ruchniyut* from Tishrei, it is because it was *romemut* ("exalted spirituality") that did not have any effect/influence on our *pnimiyut*. So, the question is, what's the advice to ensure that the spirituality of Tishrei remains with us?

The Rebbe Rashab says there are several ways in which we fail to absorb and integrate all of the high spirituality of Tishrei (p 146). But the reason for all of them is: Lack of *avoda* during the entire previous year. One who successfully serves Hashem the entire year, knows how to bring down Rosh Hashana properly for the next year.

Shiur 112, October 22, 2018

Page 34 in the Hebrew at the bottom, page 143 in the English. Many *dargot* in inability to absorb the *orot* of Tishrei.

- The Rav went to be *menachem avel* ("comfort the mourner") by his relative, R' Shalom Dovid Segal, who lost his wife…and there he met up with one of R' Segal's sons, who has a Beit Chabad. Some 12 or 13 of his hevra came with him to share in the mitzvah. This son had once requested the Rav to come down to the Kotel and say a few words to some hevra who had arrived with him from his Beit Chabad. The Rav told them a story, and there was one older Jew there who changed his whole life from this one story. What was the story? Once a couple of Jews came to a Rav to settle some friction between them. The Rav decided in a certain way that was not acceptable to one of them and he kept arguing. Even after the Rav explained several times, he kept arguing. Finally, the Rav said to him, "If you keep arguing, I'm going to have to bring down my 'black box.'" So he asked him what is the "black box"…and he explained that, "I accepted on myself to put this black box up on the top shelf, and if I feel myself getting angry, I tell myself that I can't get angry until I bring down the black box. In the meantime, I consider to myself whether it is really appropriate to get angry or not. So, the older man who heard this story was a wealthy man, but had a tendency toward anger, and he adopted this story and every time he would start to get angry, he would say, "I didn't yet take down the black box." From this, the Rav concluded that you can't know how one word or *vort* will affect someone – it can have a life saving change.

- R' Eliyahu Hadad said that this is just like those rabbis who get up and say, "I invested so much in so and so, in *m'kareving* this person or that person…" when in truth, the rabbi may have said or done something, and just happened to be the right person in the right place at the right time – but not that his "investment" made the person frum. To this, the Rav agreed.

- The Rav told another story about someone who came to him and said, "I can't take it at home, my wife doesn't clean up the place and it angers me." So the Rav advised him, before you enter the house, as you're opening the door, take upon yourself not to get angry. You're just not going to get angry about this. So after a few weeks the fellow comes back to the Rav and tells him that there are still problems. The Rav asks him, "What about the advice that I gave you"? And he answered, "It works, but sometimes I forget." From this the Rav said an important *musar haskel* – a decision made ahead of time – before entering the situation – holds.

Back to the text, which gives three examples of how a person returns to previous negative behavior after Tishrei: 1) returns to *ta'avot* and lusts 2) returns to *ga'ava* ("pride") and arrogance, 3) returns to anger.

- The Amshinover Rebbe tells *hatanim* ("bridgegrooms," and not all of them, some of them) that he has a *kabbalah b'yadav* (a "received tradition") from the first Anshinover ("R Yitzhak of Vorke" who was a student by R" Bunim and by the Yid, from that "group" of *tzaddikim*) that what is the reason that man gets married? If the reason is "to have children," so Adam Harishon was born without parents, and that could have continued…the only reason to get married is because that is the only way that man is enabled to "change his *midot*." (R' Eliyahu Hadad murmured something about, "What if he doesn't want" to change his *midot*? The Rav answered, "If he has *sechel* he'll change. If not, it will happen *bk'fiya*, "under duress").

Back to the text, the Rashab marvels, "How is man able, after such high revelations of the *chagim* of Tishrei, to return to his negative character traits?"

- The Rav heard in the name of the Sanzer/Klausenberger Rebbe, "Why is it called "*mar cheshvan*"? "Mar" is *merirut*, "bitterness" over our situation, that we fall back to our bad *midot* and bad ways after Tishrei.

But the reason for all these '*nefilot*' ("falls") is a lack of *avoda d*uring the entire year. And according to Chassidut, the way to change our *midot* is via *ahavat Hashem* – "love of God." The *clal* ("general rule") in Chasidut Chabad is that only divine love can enable us to change our *midot*. Not fear. Must sit in *hitbonenut* and arrive to love of God. Without Torah and mitzvoth, there is no such thing as changing our *midot*. And that doesn't exist outside of *Yahadut*.

- R' Yehezkel Finkel mentioned that at Matan Torah, Hashem went around to the *umot* and by each of them they had a *midah* that wasn't compatible with Torah so it wasn't given to them. But what happened by the Jews? They said *naaseh v'nishmah*. Without that, they also possessed a *midah* that they couldn't change: "Don't be envious" – *al tahmod*. But after we received the Torah we had the ability to work on this *midah* as well… the Rav was very *mit'poel*, had never heard this before.

In any case, when we are involved in *avoda* the entire year, it raises the level of the animal soul and enables us to refine ourselves.

Shiur 113, October 23, 2018

Page 34 in the Hebrew, 150 in the English translation: "But, lacking the service…" – that is, when one is not involved in *avodat Hashem* the entire year, then the arousal of Tishrei remains *makif*, while with daily *avodah*, the arousal greatly enhances our *avoda*. *Makif* means that we don't apply it to particular details, we may feel "broken" in general, but we don't apply our spiritual attainments to the specific needs of our *avoda*.

- Once upon a time when the Chasidim would sit and farbreng together, they would volunteer or request blessings for one another. If someone asked for a blessing about something specific, it was a sign that he was involved in *avoda*. If not, and he asked for something general, it was a sign he was not so much involved in *avoda*. One can make this clearer with an example of a businessman or merchant; when he has a specific trade in mind, he will ask for a blessing for that trade to succeed. If though he is a poor person, he'll just ask for a blessing to become wealthy. How wealthy? "Multi-millionaire," why not? So it is *b'ruchniyut* as well.

- R' Eliyahu Hadad asked here regarding, "Having an effect on our *humriyut*" (our "physicality"). He said, "What has an influence on our *chumriyut* is *itkafiya*, etc...what person entering a *shul* on *R"H* or *Y"K* is thinking about being "*poel* on his *humriyut*"? What kind of person is thinking about how to refine his character traits and be less "physical"? To which the Rav answered that it's a general rule in *K'Avoda* that the way to change the nature of our *midot* is via *ahavat Hashem*. What does that mean? If a man has a feeling for and feeling of *kedusha*, that automatically changes or reduces his attachment to *gashmiyut*. Thus, his *itkafiya* leads to love of God.

- The foundation of every *midah* is the importance that man lends to it. If it bothers someone that he lost money, it bothers him because he likes money. If someone caused him financial loss, and he's angry, it's because money is important to him. One who likes a good meal and is willing to pay a lot for it at a restaurant, will be welcome but they won't let him into the kitchen while it is being prepared, because that will take away all of his desire for the food. So we see that the basis for the *midah* is that he lends it importance. And that happens in two elements; first he respects himself, and second, he likes and wants the object of his desire. But the minute that he varies his stance and changes his level of respect, everything else changes.

- The Rav was involved in a *shalom bayit* case that resulted in the following conclusions: "Man is composed of two elements: Values and emotions. Both need reinforcement. Values need support; to begin with, one needs to know and grasp what is a *bayit Yehudi* that deserves respect, for which we get married? This requires learning and education and then when we understand what marriage is and is supposed to be, the result is that we can develop value around that matter, and we begin to value it. Without this, our emotions, without values, are associated with *humriyut* and *taavot*...and these two matters are *eitz hada'at* and *eitz haChaim*. What is *da'at*, is it not good? According to Rambam, *eitz hada'at* is all about "what is good for me, what is bad for me." Prior to *Eitz hada'at* there was truth vs lies...*Eitz haChaim* is values, *Eitz hada'at* is egoism, "what do I get from this?" – which is emotions.

- Here, R' Eliyahu Hadad asked, "If your project is to change the values of the husband in order to persuade him to value his wife and marriage, isn't it too late? He already took the wife and got married for the wrong reasons, how can he now change that? And the Rav's answer was, "Yes, it's never too late to change it." By a *Baal Teshuva* (acc to Rambam, because he has tasted sin), it's more difficult but it's never too late. Gemora tells story of one of the *Amoraim* (sages of the Talmud) who had problems with his wife. He would ask her to cook one thing, she would cook something else…and the other *talmidim* saw what was happening. So he would purposely change what he told her so that she would cook what he wanted…the *talmidim* asked him, "Why don't you divorce her? He answered, "It's enough that she saves me from sin and raises my kids with Torah." In other words, the *talmidim* were saying, "She has no *midot*." But he replied that he has values – and his values were that, "She saves me from sin and raises my children in Torah!" Therefore, he valued her and had emotions for her as well. And with this, older couples can also live together, even without the "thunder" for which he initially married her. Thus when the person develops proper values, it transforms his *humriyut* as well…

Shiur 114, October 24, 2018

Page 152 in the English translation: "The reason for this…" One who works on *tikun hamidot* the entire year, is then able to use the extra illumination to work on himself *b'poel mamash* when it comes to *Rosh Hashana* and *Y"K*. It is a strong added shot of divine revelation that enables us to work on ourselves in a concrete manner.

- R' Eliyahu Hadad asked, "If we did not work on ourselves all year long, is that a sign that we did not daven properly all year long? R' Deitsch did not answer directly ("yes or no"), just said that there is illumination all year long as well and if we concentrate on our specific problems using that illumination…Then the Rav gave a *mashal*: Once farmers thought it was best to water the whole field, now they direct the water to each specific plant using thin water pipes that arrive to each individual plant. The moment that we identify a particular problem we have that is in need of rectification, then we can use that special revelation of that time of the year to focus on it. "If at this moment they say something to me that has the potential to anger me, I'll maintain my quiet." Or, "I will now walk in the street and I won't look." And then he must maintain that approach for the entire year. And then when Tishrei comes around with its extra energy and focus, he will be able to use it. But if he failed to work on these specific problems during his *avoda* the entire year, then the extra illumination of Tishrei won't help him. That *ohr* is *atzmi*, "essential," very powerful for use working on our *midot*.

- The Rav heard from a *Lelover* chasid about his own great grandfather: He told the Rav something about his great grandfather (who was a *Lelover* and a *tzaddik*) that wasn't known in the Rav's family...R' Moshe...he arrived as a single man to Israel, left behind his family, when someone in the US passed away they wanted to send him part of the *yerusha* ("inheritance"), but he said, "That will just confuse me, send me just what I need to live on a monthly basis." In spite of his righteousness though, he had a tendency to anger, and his wife complained to the *Lelover Rebbe*, R' Dovid'l of Lelov, who said that he would take care of the matter. The *minhag* was that on Purim, every Chasid would give *mishloach manot* ("gifts") to the Rebbe. When this R' Moshe brought his *mishloach manot*, the Rebbe told him, "I will only accept your *mishloach manot* if you promise not to get angry anymore." R' Moshe said, "How can I promise? How can I promise that I won't get angry?" The Rebbe told him, "If you don't promise, I won't accept your *mishloach manot*." So, R' Moshe went on his way, because he didn't feel he could keep such a resolution. But he kept coming back to try to give his *mishloach manot* and each time, the Rebbe told him, "Only if you promise..." This went on a few times. Finally he came and saw that the Rebbe isn't changing his mind, and he said, "Okay I accept on myself not to get angry," and then the Lelover Rebbe accepted his *mishloach manot*. R' Deitsch said that when he heard the story, it was if someone would come and tell him at 12 noon that it's "nightime now." Because R' Deitsch knew this great grandfather and he was always pleasant and good with the grandkids and very pleasant, so very difficult to believe that he had once been someone with a tendency to be angry. Apparently he changed from one kind of person into another. And since he was unable to make the decision himself (he kept going in and out from the Rebbe), it is apparent that it happened with the *koach* and power of the Rebbe and his connection with his Rebbe.

- Here, R' Eliyahu Hadad said, "It's one thing if you have a Rebbe who can *mamchish* – bring the *midah* into reality for you since he although is a tzaddik is also a *basar v'dam* (a "'physical being") – but what if you don't have a Rebbe, then how can you just rely on Hashem to help you change and transform a *midah*? In response, the Rav said that if one fails to follow the instructions of the Torah, he has transgressed, and the transgressions can be on the level of *malkut*, or *caret* or a *lav*. But if you fail to follow the King's command, you are obligated in the death penalty, no matter what. The Rebbe asks, how could this be? And he answers that because you see the King in front of you, and fail to follow his commands, therefore from the angle of human psychology, it's more serious than failing to follow the Torah. Just like Eliyahu claimed, that you need someone human like a Rebbe in order to help make things happen.

Shiur 115, Oct 28, 2018

We are now in Ch 6 (Page 36), page 157 in the English translation…

Previous chapters dealt with soul levels such as *chaya, yechida*, etc…even *hitbonenut* acc to logic and *sechel* (which should be *pnimi* and internal…) can be *makif* if we don't go into the details of the *hitbonenut* but merely contemplate in general terms. It was the Mitteler Rebbe (in *K'Hitbonenut* within his *Sha'are Hayichud*) who wrote against the whole idea of *hitbonenut b'clalut* (a "general meditation") and the *K' Avoda* is based on that. "General" meditation means that we don't go into details; for example in contemplating creation from nothing to something, there are many details but we don't think about them, except to note that the process is "amazing." By way of example, if we know a great person, we might just think that he is "great," without being able to describe how. Or, we know for example that the Amshinover Rebbe is "amazing" because he keeps unusual hours, but we have no idea about the real essence of the *tzaddik* and how he works.

- Story about someone whom the Amshinover sent to see a particular doctor, went to his door late at night, ten PM, the doctor opened the door and the person said, "The Amshinover Rebbe sent me to you." The doctor replied, "I'm not the Amshinover Rebbe, I have to sleep at night." From this you see the doctor knew that the Amshinover was special, but you don't see in what exactly and how he was "great." A Chabadnik would go into *kabalat ohl* or some other detail to try to grasp who the Amshinover is. Some people don't know how to look for the details of how great Hashem is, and therefore they meditate only in a general manner, without going into detail. But without the details, there is no *pnimiyut*…

- R' Eliyahu Hadad wanted to claim that any kind of *hitpa'alut* is *makif*, but the Rav said, "No, there are various kinds of *hitpa'alut* and they don't all have to be "wow." There is such a thing as "sudden" understanding but there are other kinds of understanding as well. *Hitpa'alut* is from *lashon liph'ol*, to "have an effect"…not necessarily a sudden "wow."

Shiur 116, Oct 30, 2018

Three stages: *mochin* (*limud*), *midot* (*tefila*) and *maaseh* ("action" - farbrengen, how to bring things down)...

Page 37 in Ch 6, Page 161 in the translation ("As a general rule...").

The foundation of *yirah* is *bitul*, and therefore it is easier to achieve *yirah* utilizing reminders alone without *hitbonenut*. But love of God requires meditation...*ahava* is in addition to *bitul*, and therefore requires meditation. But, if this meditation is only general (without getting into details), so then it leads to *merirut* ("bitterness") and not to *simcha*. The reason for this is that the topic on which we are meditating remains "beyond" us, way beyond, and therefore we fail to internalize it in a settled manner. We fail to focus on the details, and therefore it remains beyond us. The *clal* ("general principle") upon which we meditate remains a *nekuda nifla'ah* ("amazing point"), way above us, and only the details can bring it closer to us. Until we concentrate and meditate on the details, all we feel is the *peleh*, the *makif* (the "wondrous nature") and as a result we experience only our own distance from Godliness, which leads to *merirut*...

Shiur 117, October 31, 2018

Again page 37 (page 161 in the English translation), the Rav went through this material quickly because we went over it yesterday. During minute 7:00 of the video, the Rav gives examples how to meditate properly with details... this is also found in the *Kuntres Hahitbonenut* of the Mitteler Rebbe, which is found in his *Shaar Hayichud*.

- The Rav told a story about one who had trouble getting up in the morning, he had a profession but didn't want to use it, he was very interested in giving his kids a good and proper education, but when they would ask for something he would always say, "I don't have." The Rav said that saying, "I don't have" cuts off the connection with the kids and if you do have and you give them, it helps build the connection. He helped persuade the man to get up in the morning and go to work, by walking him through the details of the process of how he needs *parnassa* ("livelihood, income") and that in turn leads to better relations in the family and better education as well. The Rav added that there are all kinds of people who don't want to work or support their family, using all kinds of *tirutzim*, but this is not good for the family.

- *Kiruv* to *Elokut* brings *simcha*, which is why the verse says *Ivdu et Hashem Besimcha...* ("Serve Hashem in joy") - the Godly soul gets enjoyment from general meditation, but not the animal soul, which needs details.

- At the end of the *shiur*, R' Eliyahu Hadad asked the Rav, "How can anyone feel 'far' from Hashem, we know He is everywhere, so isn't that an *eitza* of the *yetzer*?" The Rav answered with an illustration from Likutei Torah: It's as if both are standing close to each other, the Chasid and Hashem, but when the Chasid is doing Torah and mitzvoth, he is turning his face away from Hashem. That is, they may be close to each other, but acting like two who are far from each other.

Shiur 118, November 1, 2018

Page 38, Page 166 in the translation...

"Therefore, the main *avoda*..." (I hear my own voice in the *shiur*, saying "*K'Avoda* gives us the general meditation, and each individual has to supply the details," to which the Rav says, "Yes this is correct. Each one has to identify his own details on which to focus, no one individual is similar to the other." Then I commented that not everyone merits to identify the details that are appropriate for him to focus on during meditation, to which the Rav said, for that we need *siyata d'shmaya*, and a Rebbe, that's what's written in the intro to Tanya, everyone needs to find their our own *avoda*).

The Rav said that he knew of two people who had *yechidut* with the Rebbe on the same night, each asked if they should continue in their task or not. One was involved in learning (successfully) and the Rebbe told him to go into education. The other was involved in *shlichut* and *kiruv*, yet the Rebbe told him to go back to learning. Both were successful in their respective fields, both spoke with the Rebbe on the same night, and both were told by the Rebbe to go into another field of endeavor.

Detailed meditation is *yegiat hanefesh*.

- R' Eliyahu Hadad told the Rav that he was at the beach and looked at the ocean and was just overwhelmed by the sight because the ocean was always there and never changed, etc...and asked whether this was the kind of *hitbonenut* that the *K'Avoda* meant? The Rav replied that that was a "head" *hitbonenut* (apparently meaning that it was an intellectual *hitbonenut* of the kind that may not descend to the emotions). And the Rav heard from R' Baruch Shufrin about one Chassid who would get up in the morning and before prayers, say to the sun, "*Kum, kum* ("come, come")...whose pushing you from behind?" (Allusion to Avraham Avinu who "discovered" Hashem by reasoning that if the sun moved, it didn't move itself, there must be a "Cause" behind it, moving it...). And the Chasid did this as a form of *hitbonenut* – the Rav doesn't remember who this Chasid was, or if R' Baruch Shufrin mentioned his name.

Shiur 119, November 7, 2018

Page 38 (page 166 in the translation) – brings several examples of meditations focused on details...("Therefore, the main avoda...").

It's possible to recognize the greatness of creation without actually acknowledging God in the situation, and therefore it's necessary to focus on the Godly *chayut* of each and every detail. Like for example a good teacher even with as many as thirty kids in the class, will try to give special attention to each and every one of them. Hashem has so many creations and yet each one receives the appropriate *chayut* and *tsumat lev* ("personal attention") from Above that is appropriate for it. And of course, that is different for each individual creation just as it is for every individual person.

- Here I interjected (in the *shiur*) that apparently it isn't enough to focus on the physical details, it's necessary to think more *pnimi,* to go into depth more, and the Rav agreed, saying, "That's the *ikar*," telling a story how he heard on the radio when they interviewed the person who discovered DNA, and he told the story...the interviewer, not a religious Jew, said to the person who discovered DNA, "If nature is so *mesudar* and so precise, there must be an intelligent force behind it..." and the interviewee replied, "That's not our area, I have no expertise in that."

- The Rebbe Rashab asked, why do *chochmot chitzoniyut* repel man from *kedusha* (that is, what is it about the sciences and philosophy, etc, that makes it foreign to holiness?) Why are these *chochmot "chitzoniyut"* at all (That is, "what is superficial and external" about these areas of study?). If one learns, for example medicine, this is *chochma chitzoni*... why does this push people away from *kedusha*...it's *klipat nogah*...the Rashab answered, "The more you learn about the creation, it becomes in your eyes something 'bigger,' a "bigger creation," more significant. The more you think into the nature of the creation, for example, how does man work, with a brain, a heart, etc…the more you think of it as *yesh* (something that "exists") and the further it pushes you away from *kedusha* (even more than *taavot* repel you). The Rav said that doctors in general have more pride than regular people. But he heard something more interesting; that's in regard to regular doctors, they are the ones who perhaps have more pride, *ga'ava*. But the "biggest" (most important) doctors are not *ba'aeli gaava*, or so the Rav heard (but among them are also those who are…).

- The Rav says there are many who speak in the name of "science," and it's questionable who is authorized and who not…once the Rebbe wrote a letter about the age of the world [I think it was the one that said dinosaur fossils could have been created "as is," not that they are millions of years old, and that the most advanced science declares that it's possible to see the sun as going around the earth…but at any rate it's completely erroneous to call it "science" when in truth it's not even deductive reasoning but inductive reasoning, essentially no more than "guesses" about the past and therefore not truly scientific]. At the time, there was someone who was in the process of doing *teshuva* and this letter bothered him. His response was, "The Rebbe is a man of Torah, why does he get involved in the world of science, we scientists don't mix in the Torah world?" Afterward, he saw the Rebbe was correct. How did he see it? R' Nahum Zevin, a grandson of R' Zevin in Kfar Chabad, spoke to this *baal teshuva*, who told him he was at the Nobel prizes when someone making a *cheshbon* about the age of the world got a Nobel prize…he asked him, "You're confusing us and driving us nuts with all these *cheshbonot* of millions of years, etc…" whereupon the guy said to him, "And you think I believe this? It's my profession, I don't believe in it." So from that event, the person who previously had been irritated by the Rebbe's letter, saw that the Rebbe was correct.

- At the beginning of the 1970's, new immigrants began arriving also to Jerusalem, and the Rav was involved in helping them, kashering kitchens and the like. There was a Russian speaking family who asked, "This world that is so big, how was it possible to create it in six days"? That is, they tried to apply raw intellect to a topic that isn't intellectual, it's *ruchani*, "spiritual." At any rate, the problem with science and in general with *chochmat chitzoni* is that it can end up portraying the creation as a *yesh* in and of itself, which repels people from Hashem. But if contemplation on the world brings Hashem into the equation…that's the kind of meditation necessary to develop *ahavat Hashem*. There's a saying of the sages, "If you want to know how strong someone is, observe what kind of rock he can move…" In similar fasion, by becoming acquainted with the nature of the creation, we "get to know He who created it."

- Another time, there was a group of scientists who arrived to the US and wanted to meet the Rebbe, they came in and had a personal audience with the Rebbe, who explained *emunah* ("faith") to them in simple words…afterwards one of them wrote to the Rebbe and asked, "The Rebbe explained the topic so well, how is it possible that there are *kofrim*, people who don't believe, among the scientists?" The Rebbe answered that it is the nature of man to be *mechadesh*, to come up with something "new" and original, so therefore they would come up with theories like the theory of evolution for example, that are "new" and "original" because that is their nature (these were Jews from Israel and the letter is published).

Shiur 120, November 12, 2018

Page 39 in Hebrew, page 169 in the translation:

On page 173, One should not meditate only on the fact that He creates and enlivens, but to go into detail, *V'atah mechayeh et kulam* ("You enliven them all"), wherein *atah* is the letters from *aleph* to *tof*, so clearly the implication is to focus on the letters…and the Rav mentions that in *Shaar Hayichud* the text also mentions the *hey gevurot* ("five stringencies") as well [they are represented by the five final letters [מנצפך]. Then, the text goes at length into the nature of that meditation…

Page 175 in the translation: "Therefore, the beginning of our detailed meditation…" Here the text comes to tell us that meditation on the details includes knowing the source of our vitality, from the spiritual *mazalot* above, including the *ofanim* (lowest of angels, associated with the world of *asiya*) and *shemori ofanim* ("remainders" of the *ofanim*). And the *ofanim* from the *chayut* (world of *yetzira*), and the *chayut* from *seraphim* (world of *bria*) all the way up to *malchut* of *Atzilut* – this is what it means to meditate on the details. In this manner, the meditation becomes *nechkak* ("engraved") within us because we know the process. Within the process there is the *chayut* that itself divides into two categories of *koach* (more *pnimi*) and *ohr* [here I can hear my own voice in the background asking the Rav if there aren't three categories here, of *koach*, *chayut* and *ohr* (based on a maamar from R' Hillel), but the Rav responds that here the text divides the *chayut* into two catgegories; *koach* and *ohr*]. And the meditation continues until we reach the *kav* itself [it seems the intention is the source of the *kav*, after the *tzimtzum*], the source of all *ohr pnimi*…and within the *kav* illuminate the *orot* and more *pnimi* is the essence of the infinite light Above (*orot*, and *atzmut ohr eyn sof*), the *kav* concludes in Atzilut, but "breaks" through the *parsa* to shine into *olamat BY"A* as well. The Rav says that all this is in the writings of R' Chaim Vital, (student of the Ariz'l, who wrote down the Ari's teachings) who himself says the knowledge of all these details leads to and adds to our *ahavat Hashem*, or "love of God."

R' Shalom David Segal commented that in this meditation, we begin with what is close to us, and the higher we go in the meditation we reach levels that are in truth beyond us, *makif*. To which the Rav answered that nevertheless, the meditation connects us with the higher levels because each of the lower levels that we begin with is connected with and in fact comes from the higher level. Like as if you see a Chasid doing what he is supposed to do and you praise him and he says, "All this is because I am connected to the Rebbe who gives me guidance." Then of course you want to get to the source of what the Chasid has, and you go to the Rebbe…if you 'get' one part of the meditation, though the rest may be *makif*, but because you know where it's coming from in its source, it takes on a different nature. (R' Eliyahu Hadad asked if this was the same meditation in detail that they studied in *Shaar Hayichud* of the Mitteler Rebbe and the Rav replied that "yes" it is, but that there they found the *limud* so difficult (on the higher levels) that they stopped, R' Eliyahu remarked that, "It was like Chinese").

- Here the Rav told the story of the group in the concentration camps who lived longer and held out longer than the others, the Nazis (*yemach shemam*) suspected they were stealing food and planted someone among them to find out…he revealed that they weren't steaing but that they had a doctor who told them how to eat…not just how much and when, but how to get the most out of each part of the food, to think, "this gives me protein, this gives me carbs…etc" and thus they held out longer than the other prisoners who generally died of starvation and exhaustion even before they got to the gas chambers. So the Nazis (*yemach shemam*) killed the doctor and then the whole group disintegrated…but here the *mussar haskel* ("moral of the story") is the opposite, "take each *prat*, each detail, and connect it to its source…"

Shiur 121, November 14, 2018

The Rav began with a passage from the Maharal of Prague, discussing Avraham, Yitzhak and Yaakov and how they corresponded to the three Temples. The third Temple will be permanent because the association with Yaakov is *atzmi*, it is "essential"… the *rachamim* ("mercy") associated with Yaakov is also the love associated with Avraham Avinu, which we know because the Aramaic translation of *ahava* is *rachmuhi* (*rachamim*), and this ties in with the current text in *K'Avoda* (page 169 in the translation) that speaks of the internal connection with Hashem that is *nechkak* ("engraved") within us.

But the Rav jumped to page 172, where we see that the *hitbonenut* focuses on the lower levels and the contracted *ohr* that is enclothed in lower worlds to enliven it, yet this meditation leads us to *chakika*, and to *hitchavrut* ("joining"). [And here it becomes clear that the meditation must focus on *otiot* ("letters") because here the Rav says that if we think merely about how Hashem enlivens the world, that is called "general meditation," but if we go into the details of how He creates and enlivens via the letters, that is called "going into the details" and meditating in a more *pnimi* manner…until it is *nechkak* within ("engraved within")].

- The Rav heard once from R' Fitchie Ofen that sometimes the Alter Rebbe, the Mitteler Rebbe and the Tzemach Tzedek (perhaps the Maharash as well) would send *talmidim* to elder Chassidim or *mashpi'im* to get their *chinuch* (perhaps to get their "finishing"), and one of the younger Chassidim of the Alter Rebbe was R' Pesach Molostovsky. R' Hillel Paritcher was also around at that time, and both he and R Pesach had some *talmidim* under their tutelage. (The Rashbatz, who mentored the Previous Rebbe, was sent by the people of his city to R' Michele Potsker). The arrangement was for the younger chasidim to be mentored by the elders; it was said that every Chasid needs a Rebbe, an elder Chassid and a "friend." On one occasion, the *talmidim* of R' Hillel met up with either the *talmidim* of R' Pesach, or perhaps with R' Pesach Molostovsky himself, and he asked them, "What are you studying with R' Hillel?" They answered by mentioning the high concepts that they were learning at the time (it was known that R' Hillel tended to focus on high and abstract matters, while R' Pesach focused on more basic matters). R' Pesach then asked them, "How do you pray"? They answered, "With *pirush hamilot* – the simple meaning of the words." "If so," he asked them, "Why learn all the high and abstract matters?" And they answered, "Because [after learning lofty matters with R' Hillel], our *Baruch*

Atah ("Blessed be You") is a very different *Baruch Atah*." That is, the "Blessed be You" at the beginning of every blessing, is a very different "Blessed be You" if they first studied the lofty concepts, than if they had not studied them before prayers. Same *pirush hamilot*, but a different "You" (in reference to God).

- R' Eliyahu Hadad asked the Rav about *hitbonenut* on the *clal* ("general meditation") and pointed out that there's no *yeshut* ("ego") involved since the person isn't going deeply into the matter, but if he meditates at length on the details, he is likely to experience "himself" and develop *yeshut*...to which the Rav answered that he's correct, "There's an advantage and disadvantage to each, to meditation in general and to detailed meditation in particular." And the Rav said that they would say about the *ovdim* (those who prayed at length, with attention to details), that they had *yeshut*, they had pride. The Rav himself heard them described as "a *gantse getschke*" – an "entire idol" (humorously of course). And the *maskilim* would say about the *ovdim*, that the *ovdim* have more *yeshut*.

Back to the text, here in any case, the point is that by meditation on *tzimtzum* and *dargot*, etc, the matter becomes "engraved" on our minds. (The Rav paused to think, and said, 'What do you think, there were those who accused...' – probably referring to students in the yeshiva or *balabatim* who assumed that the *avodat Hashem* of the *ovdim* was not for real). Now on page 175, "Therefore, the beginning..."

- Here, the Rav got into *koach* and *ohr*, and suggested that electricity is also compounded of these two elements [perhaps particles vs waves?].

Now on page 40 in Hebrew, page 177 in the English...on page 178 regarding the difficulty of performing the labor (*yegiat hanefesh*) of *hitbonenut*, the Rav stopped and said, "But this applies to our generation, once upon a time, it was not like this."

- The Rav brought a solid proof from a book called *Beit Rebbe*, that recorded the history of the early Chassidic Rebbeim and perhaps even the Baal Shem Tov, but certainly from the Alter Rebbe. And there he mentions the *cherem* on the Chassidim (from the Gra) and asked, "Who removed this *cherem*"? The intro to this sefer is very interesting and good to read; there, the author points out that one who learns Chasidut can easily fulfill the obligation to talk and think about Torah all day long, but it's much harder to do so if one learns only *nigleh*.

Shiurim on K'Avoda from the Mashpia R' Deitsch שיח׳

But the Rav says that in our *dor*, our generation, it's just the opposite: It's very easy to think about *nigleh* because it has *cheshbonot* and facts, and solid topics to consider, whereas Chasidut is abstract and harder to think about. Aside from certain very high people, such as R' Avrumke Zhebinov, who was the *mashpia* ("mentor") of Gruenim (the *mashpia* in Tomchei Tmimim, who was a Chassid of the Rebbe Maharash and became a chasid of the Rashab. R' Avrumke would sit and think Chassidut (before Shacharit) from 2 AM until the morning.

- Today (28 Tammuz 5780, July 20, 2020), the Rav mentioned a story in *Torat Shalom*: the main *avoda* in the days of the Maharash was *kriat shema al hamitah*, and it wasn't until the Rashab that the main *avoda* became *hitbonenut* before *Shacharit* and *tefilat Shacharit*. When the Rashab first introduced the change, R' Gruenum argued against it – see *Torat Shalom*. The Rav also said that R' Gruenum asked the Rebbe Maharash for a *tikun*, and the Maharash asked him if he "finished *chan*" – if he finished his *tikun* for *chatas neurim*. When Gruenum told him "yes," he asked him if he finished the easier one or the more difficult one, and he answered the "easier one." So he asked the Maharash for a blessing/tikun and the Maharash told him, "By us, it's not so easy, you have to do *teshuva*." So for two years, as he was working as a porter at the local train station, while waiting for the train to arrive, Gruenum would have a sefer Tehilim with him and would cry a lot – the other porters, who weren't Jewish, would say that "they don't know what's with him." Anyway after two years, Gruenum completed his *teshuva* and went again to the Rebbe for a Bracha/Tikun, and received it). [Slightly different version heard on 25 Ellul, 5780 during Chasidus shiur: R' Gruenem asked the Maharash for a *tikun* for *timtum halev vhamoach* – a "clogged heart and mind" – and the Maharash asked him if he had finished *chan*...]

- Another story: In those days (now seems the days of the Alter Rebbe), there was one Rav in the city (didn't really need more than that) and you didn't have yeshivas, each individual would learn by himself and try to make a living for himself...R Binyamin Kletzker (and you knew he had a profession because his name, "Kletzker" meant "wood chopper"), others got involved in trading, and since they didn't have telephones so they would go from city to city to trade and once one trader couldn't find his colleague and therefore sat down to wait for him to arrive and meantime started thinking Chasidut, until the hours passed and he realized he needs to daven mincha and asked, "where is the *sefel*" – where is the handwasher for washing hands – he thought he was still in his own house, didn't realize he was elsewhere…

- Another story about a chassid who could think at length, sat down after Shacharit in the garden, started to think Chassidut until all of a sudden he realized the entire day had gone by…he missed mincha and it so bothered him having missed mincha that he asked himself, "What do I need this power of concentration if I'm going to miss mincha," and he consciously "rid himself" of this power of concentration to meditate on Chassidut. He was a Chassid of the Tzemach Zedek or the Mitteler Rebbe but lived so long that he even became a chassid of the Rashab (the Rav heard this from R' Avraham Hirsh Hacohen), and when he went into *Yechidut* he cried asking for a *tikun* over that he missed mincha [I believe this story is in *Zichronot* of the Frierdiker Rebbe).

- In the time of the Rav, when he was in yeshiva or afterward, there were *bachurim* who were *mitbonen*…the Rav heard from R' Meir Gruzman A"H – that R' Shlomo Chaim (who was both a Rosh Yeshiva and *mashpia*, would daven at home and then arrive to yeshiva for *shemonah esreh*) achieved his highest with *bachurim* who were *mitbonen* for an hour and a half and then prayed for an hour and a half – that was the maximum that he managed to instill and educate his *bachurim*.

The Rav concluded with the words on page 179, that although it is difficult, we should enter into *hitbonenut* with *kaballat ohl* and then we will be successful!

- Here R' Eliyahu Hadad asked about R' Shlomo Chaim, "He didn't just tell the guys what to do – go do *hitbonenut?*" And the Rav answered, "No he would totally educate the *bachurim* on a personal level, very personal…"

- [From Tanya Shiur 28 Tammuz 5780/July 20, 2020 – It was not R' Gruenem who educated the bachurim in davening *b'avoda* and *b'arichut*, it was R' Shilem, the *chozer* (who had been a *yatom* from a young age and he was taken care of by his sisters, he left "gymnasia" for yeshiva and became the Rashab's *chozer*). I asked the Rav, "What about the Frierdiker Rebbe, wasn't he the main *mechanech* and *mashpia* of the yeshiva *Tomchei T'mimim?*" The Rav was surprised at the question and said, "First of all you have to know that the Frierdiker Rebbe was very hidden, made himself as if he was not an address for understanding his father's Torah. Once, one of the *bachurim* asked him to explain and he said, "You think I know? Am I an address for 'lost items' that maybe someone will 'find' them by me?" Yet, the *bachurim* happened to pass him by at a certain stage, look over his shoulder, and saw that he was writing, "In answer to the question asked by so and so…" so they understood that the Frierdiker was in fact the address to ask… but he still made himself as if he didn't know…next time he saw the *bachurim* approaching, he made sure he was playing chess with one of his daughters." Much later, when the Frierdiker Rebbe was in the US, he said about his son in law, the Rebbe, "People think that I was hidden, I am nothing compared to him…" referring to the Rebbe… In any case though, R' Deitsch sad that the Frierdiker's role in the yeshiva was administrative, bringing in new *bachurim* and running the yeshiva, not as a *mechanech* or *mashpia*, that was R' Shilem's role.

- During Tanya Shiur erev Rosh Hodesh Av (July 21 2020), I asked the Rav, "If the emphasis during the Rebbe Maharash's *nesiut* was on *kriat Shema al hamitah*, then where was the emphasis during the period of the Tzemach Tzedek? The Rav said, "On Shacharit." Meaning that really that's where the emphasis should be, but during the *tekufa* of the Maharash it shifted temporarily to *kriat shem al hamitah*.

- Tanya Shiur 7 Av (7/28/2020), the Rav mentioned his own *yichus*: from his mother's side, from R' Moshe the 3rd son of the Alter Rebbe (who had to run away from the Russians). On his father's side, from Czchech or Hungary, he wasn't sure, it was his great grandfather who came to Israel. (But prior to that on his father's side, the Rav came from the Bach, R' Yoel Sircus, in Crakow). The land was *shemam*, barren, impossible to make a living…his own father used to buy "scripts" from people and then go to Tel Aviv/Yafo to pick up the food, come back and sell it to make a living. There was a young man who learned a profession as a *zagag*, or worker in glass, thinking, "for sure there will be *parnassa* in that." When he arrived in Israel during the summer, he saw broken windows but no one requested his services, so he thought, "for sure in the winter they'll need me." But in the winter he found the same windows stuffed up with rags and cardboard to protect from the elements.

- From *Chai Ellul 5780* frabrengen in the Collel Tzemach Tzedek: The order of learning *hitbonenut* was that first, R' Shlomo Chaim told R' Deitsch to do a few weeks of *hitkafia*, couldn't approach *hitbonenut* directly without doing *hitkafia* first. Second, learn the *maamar* of the Rebbe well. Third, repeat it (*leshanen*) in *otiot haRav* – be able to say it over as written. Then, be able to say it in your own *otiot* (this learned from the Frediker Rebbe by the Rashab, the Rashab told him to say it over in *eigener otiot* – "his own words"). Then think over the *maamar* and internalize it, emotions witin the mind, *midot sh'bemochin*. Finally, daven with it.

Jerusalem Connection is a non-profit organization
dedicated to Jewish outreach and education.
It was created with the blessing of the Lubavitcher Rebbe ztz'l in 1991,
and has since flourished in the Old City of Jerusalem.
It is frequented by Jewish university students, tourists and
new immigrants to Israel who seek spiritual guidance
and connection with the One Above,
and also instruction in the inner dimensions of Torah
(Chassidic and Kabbalistic literature).
It is located at Rechov HaMekubalim 3/5 in the Old City of Jerusalem.
For more information, visit the Jerusalem Connection website at
www.jerusalemconnection.org
or email jerconn1@gmail.com

www.ingramcontent.com/pod-product-compliance
Lightning Source LLC
Chambersburg PA
CBHW080537230426
43663CB00015B/2621